THIRD CANADIAN EDITION

CHILD
PSYCHOLOGY
A CONTEMPORARY VIEWPOINT

Ross D. Parke
University of California, Riverside

Mary Gauvain
University of California, Riverside

Mark A. Schmuckler
University of Toronto
Scarborough

McGraw-Hill
Ryerson
Connect. Learn. Succeed.

**McGraw-Hill
Ryerson**
Connect. Learn. Succeed.

Child Psychology: A Contemporary Viewpoint
Third Canadian Edition

ISBN-13: 978-0-07-078238-9
ISBN-10: 0-07-078238-5

1 2 3 4 5 6 7 8 9 10 TCP 1 9 8 7 6 5 4 3 2 1 0

Printed and bound in Canada.

Vice-President and Editor-in-Chief: Joanna Cotton
Publisher: Cara Yarzab
Marketing Manager: Michele Peach
Developmental Editor: Liz Radojkovic
Editorial Associate: Marina Seguin
Supervising Editor: Jessica Barnoski
Photo/Permissions Research: Alison Lloyd Baker
Copy Editor: Joe Zingrone
Team Lead, Production: Jennifer Hall
Cover Design: Greg Devitt Design
Cover Image: © The Estate of William Kurelek; painting owned by a private collection;
  photo taken by Paul Birnie.
Interior Design: Greg Devitt Design
Page Layout: Brian Lehen Graphic Design Ltd.
Printer: Transcontinental Printing Group

Library and Archives Canada Cataloguing in Publication

Parke, Ross D.
    Child psychology : a contemporary viewpoint / Ross D. Parke,
Mary Gauvain, Mark Schmuckler. -- 3rd Canadian ed.

Includes bibliographical references and indexes.
ISBN 978-0-07-078238-9

    1. Child psychology--Textbooks. I. Gauvain, Mary
II. Schmuckler, Mark A. III. Title.

BF721.P279 2010   155.4   C2009-907189-4

To the most important people in my life;
my wife, Katalin, and my daughter, Madeleine

Mark A. Schmuckler

About the Authors

ROSS D. PARKE is Distinguished Professor of Psychology and director of the Center for Family Studies at the University of California, Riverside. He is past president of the Society for Research in Child Development and of Division 7, the Development Psychology Division, of the American Psychological Association, and in 1995, he received the G. Stanley Hall award from this APA division. Parke was elected a fellow of the American Association for the Advancement of Science in 1997. He has served as editor of both the *Journal of Family Psychology* and *Developmental Psychology* and as associate editor of *Child Development*. Parke is the author of *Fatherhood*, co-author of *Throwaway Dads* (with Armin Brott), and co-editor of *Family-Peer Relationships: In Search of the Linkages* (with Gary Ladd), *Children in Time and Place* (with Glen Elder and John Modell), and *Exploring Family Relationships With Other Social Contexts* (with Sheppard Kellam). Parke's research has focused on early social relationships in infancy and childhood. He obtained his Ph.D. from the University of Waterloo, Ontario, Canada, and is well known for his early work on the effects of punishment, aggression, and child abuse and for his work on the father's role in infancy and early childhood. Parke's current work focuses on the links between family and peer social systems, ethnic variations in families, and the effects of the new reproductive technologies on families.

MARY GAUVAIN is a Professor of Psychology at the University of California, Riverside. She is a fellow of the American Psychological Association and past secretary/treasurer of Division 7 (Developmental Psychology) of the APA. She is also a fellow of the American Association for the Advancement of Science and a member of the Society for Research in Child Development. Gauvain is currently an associate editor of *Child Development* and on the editorial board of the journals *Child Development Perspectives* and *Cognitive Development*. She is the author of *The Social Context of Cognitive Development* and co-author of *Readings on the Development of Children* (with Michael Cole). She is well known for her research on cognitive development, in particular, for her research on social and cultural contributions to the development of planning skills and spatial thinking. Gauvain obtained her M.A. in sociology of education from Stanford University and her Ph.D. in psychology from the University of Utah. She has held post-doctoral positions in developmental psychology at the Graduate Center of the City University of New York and the Oregon Social Learning Center. Her current research focuses on the ecology of children's everyday lives, including how experiences in the family and cultural community provide opportunities for the development of cognitive skills.

MARK A. SCHMUCKLER received his Ph.D. from Cornell University, working with Eleanor J. Gibson and Carol L. Krumhansl. After a two-year post-doctoral fellowship at the University of Virginia, he moved to the University of Toronto Scarborough, where he is a Professor of Psychology. Schmuckler is currently an associate editor for the journal *Music Perception*, and also serves on the editorial board of journals such as *Infancy* and *Psychomusicology*. Schmuckler's research efforts have been divided into two streams of research. The first focuses on the processes involved in perceptual and motor development, as well as perceptual-motor integration, looking specifically at the role of perceptual information during motor-skill acquisition and motor performance. In his second line of work, Schmuckler explores the perceptual and cognitive processes involved in adults' apprehension of musical structure, focusing specifically on the perception and production of pitch structures.

Brief Contents

Contents

Chapter 6

Emotional Development and Attachment 194

Chapter 7

Language and Communication 250

Chapter 8

Cognitive Development: Piaget and Vygotsky 296

Chapter 9

Cognitive Development: The Information-Processing Approach   338

Chapter 10

Intelligence and Achievement   382

Chapter 13

Gender Roles and Gender Differences   502

Chapter 14

Morality, Altruism, and Aggression   536

Preface

For many years, students in my developmental psychology course at the University of Toronto Scarborough used to comment that based on the research discussed in class, as well as the statistical data presented in the accompanying textbook, one would think that developmental psychology was a uniquely American undertaking. This, of course, is not true, and as an author, a researcher, and an instructor, I am proud to be able to provide students with a textbook that corrects this misperception.

Though Canada and the United States share a common culture, with similar influences, there are striking differences that potentially have an important impact on a child's development. For instance, what impact does Canada's universal health-care system have on children's health in terms of both their prenatal and postnatal development? What impact does multiculturalism have on a child's social relationships, friendship choices, and prejudices? What impact does bilingualism and, as is the case in many urban centres, multilingualism have on a child's development? These are, in many ways, distinctly Canadian issues and Canadian students should have course materials that explore these issues in a Canadian context.

Finally, I am pleased to be able to produce a resource that highlights the significant contribution Canada's scholars and researchers are making in this field. Canadian researchers are among the best in the world. Whenever possible and appropriate, I have showcased our scientists and the work in which they are involved. Before discussing the specifics of what has been added and updated to this third Canadian edition, I want to briefly discuss the founding principles that make this book a tremendous resource for anyone taking an introductory course in developmental psychology.

DISTINGUISHING CHARACTERISTICS OF THIS BOOK

Current Research and Canadian Content

The third Canadian edition of *Child Psychology: A Contemporary Viewpoint* continues to offer seamlessly integrated coverage of both Canadian researchers and research and data about Canadians. As the subtitle of the text promises, we continue to provide the most up-to-date and current perspectives on the field, while retaining important research classics.

This new edition adds over **900 new references, almost 600 of which have been published since 2004**. Publications by Canadian researchers have been flagged with an asterisk (*) in the References section at the end of the book.

Balanced Theoretical Perspectives

The topical approach lends itself to a sophisticated presentation of theories that guide research in the many areas of child development. As the research continues to accumulate, however, the limitations of such theories become evident. For example, developmentalists have found that some of Piaget's classic studies are open to new and intriguing interpretations. Thus, rather than focus on a few grand theories that attempt to account for many aspects of development, we now recognize the value of additional theories that guide research in specific topic areas, such as language acquisition, motor development, and emotional understanding. Thus, throughout this edition, to supplement the grand theories, we explore newer approaches, such as dynamic systems theory, sociocultural perspectives, and evolutionary theory.

Child Psychology: A Contemporary Viewpoint strives to be both theoretically eclectic and to emphasize the multi-layered nature of development. In each discussion of a topic, one or two causative factors predominate, but others are influential as well. For example, in our discussion of genetics and early development, the predominant factors are biological, but the role of environmental factors in shaping the way genetic predisposition is expressed is emphasized. When we discuss language and gender typing, we emphasize cognitive learning, information processing, and social interaction, but inherited factors take the stage when we explore the biology of gender and the nativist view of language learning. Although cognitive theories such as information-processing and Piagetian approaches dominate our discussion of intellectual development, we also consider sociocultural processes as contributors to cognitive growth. Similarly, social and affective factors predominate in our coverage of family and peers, but we explore cognitive, behavioural, and biological issues. This approach underscores the contemporary recognition that child development evolves out of the interplay among biological, cognitive, social, and emotional factors.

PROCESS ORIENTATION   Our emphasis is on the *processes* of development, a hallmark of contemporary child psychology. Focusing on the processes that generate changes in the child's development enables students to learn what development comprises and what specific changes take place across time. By examining what changes and how, students come to understand why these changes occur. And in this way, they gain insight into why two children with seemingly similar capabilities may develop very different ways of understanding and interacting with the world.

Some of our readers have been curious as to why some sections of our book cover adolescence more fully than others. This approach arises out of our process orientation. When the completion of a developmental process or a milestone in that process occurs in the teenage years, we follow the process from childhood through adolescence. Thus, for example, we discuss physical development through puberty, cognitive development into adolescence, and, as part of our exploration of changes in the nature of friendships across time, we follow beginning romantic relationships into adolescence. Because our book focuses, however, on the period of childhood, we do not cover adolescence for all developmental processes.

THEMES OF DEVELOPMENT   This edition of the book continues to characterize theoretical perspectives by focusing on several cross-cutting themes of development. We have trimmed the number of these themes to three: biological versus environmental influences, continuity versus discontinuity of development, and individual characteristics versus contextual and cultural influences. Throughout the book, we illustrate these themes, and in our Epilogue, we link the themes with broad principles that summarize our views about the research and theory-building needs of the field of child development.

Basic and Applied Research: A Reciprocal Relationship

In this book, we present child psychology as a scientific discipline, illustrating and discussing the techniques used by psychologists in the field. It is important for students to become familiar with the methodological approaches unique to child psychology so that they can understand, interpret, and use the results of research intelligently. We present findings in sufficient detail to enable the student not only to understand the steps in the research process, but also to appreciate the complex nature of drawing valid conclusions about development.

Although some instructors express a preference for a basic research focus and others favour an applied approach, we emphasize the interactive nature of basic research and its applications. Basic information about the processes of development can help us understand a wide range of real-life problems and, conversely, insights we gain from applications of research can help improve research and sharpen our theoretical understanding. In Chapter 10, for example, we consider what the scientific community has learned about the fundamental processes of development from early educational intervention programs like Head Start and Canadian equivalents such as Better Beginnings, Better Futures and Staying on Track. In Chapter 6, we discuss research on homesickness that demonstrates the relevance of attachment theory for real-life problems. Throughout the book, teachers and students will find fascinating examples of the dynamic interplay between basic and applied research.

Sociocultural Diversity in Child Development

In this edition, we have intensified our focus on the ethnic, racial, and cultural diversity of heterogeneous societies like Canada, as well as on differences between cultures around the world. Our expanded discussions of Vygotskian theory, with its strong emphasis on the role of culture, provide a framework for understanding how culture and development interact. We introduce the theme of cultural pluralism and have integrated it into every chapter; in each topical discussion, we explore research with the many ethnic groups that make up North American culture as well as with people in nations around the world. In addition, one of our box series in each chapter highlights cross-cultural and intra-cultural studies of particular interest.

ORGANIZATION

Several organizational decisions and changes were made in this third Canadian edition to distinguish our book from other texts in child development. We have trimmed and combined Chapters 1 and 2 from the previous edition into a single introductory chapter that presents fundamental theoretical and methodological issues in heightened focus. This presentation enables students to move more rapidly into content chapters. We have removed the chapter on schools, computers, and the media; instead, we include this material in other chapters where we tie it more closely to related concepts and issues. For example, the topic of achievement is part of Chapter 10 on intelligence, and the effects of mass media on children are now discussed in Chapters 1, 13, and 14. By integrating our presentation of these issues into our discussions of specific developmental outcomes, we are able to explore these matters in more meaningful ways and at the same time reduce the overall length of the book.

WHAT'S NEW IN THE THIRD CANADIAN EDITION?

We have rewritten *Child Psychology: A Contemporary Viewpoint* to feature the most recent developments in theory and research. Every chapter has new information, some of which is highlighted below. Beginning with this edition, Mavis Hetherington, a co-author who has guided the development of this book from its first edition in 1975, has decided to move on to other interests in her retirement. We recognize her wonderful and thoughtful contributions to this book and to the field of child psychology over many decades. *Child Psychology* is now under the authorship of Ross Parke, Mary Gauvain, and Mark Schmuckler. Mary Gauvain, who joined the writing team for the US sixth edition, is a respected cognitive developmental psychologist. She continues to bring new depth to our treatments of cognition, information processing, and language learning. Her expertise balances Ross Parke's widely respected coverage of emotional and social development, and Mark Schmuckler's knowledge of physical, perceptual, and motor development.

In this edition, we have introduced Learning Objectives and Making the Connections graphics for each chapter, and have added a new chapter on developmental psychopathology Chapter 15. We have also expanded our program of illustrations and have revised many graphics and tables to achieve better clarity.

Multiple instructors provided us with in-depth evaluations of the third Canadian edition, and the text in your hands offers many improvements to meet the needs of faculty and students in today's learning environment. Revisions for this edition have focused on clarifying and updating key content areas, enhancing the already extensive Canadian content, expanding the contribution of culture on children's development, and condensing and streamlining coverage to offer a more accessible and inviting text.

The following are some highlights of the new coverage in the third Canadian edition:

CHAPTER 1: CHILD DEVELOPMENT: THEMES, THEORIES, AND METHODS

- New historical research on developmental psychology in Canada
- Clear, concise presentation of three major themes of development: biology versus environment, continuity of development versus discontinuity, individual characteristics versus contextual and cultural influences
- Emphasis on research methods that are unique and central to developmental inquiry
- Streamlined overview table of developmental themes and theoretical perspectives

CHAPTER 2: HEREDITY AND THE ENVIRONMENT

- New work on effects and/or prevention of genetic diseases such as Huntington's disease, Turner syndrome, and fragile X syndrome
- Role of father's age in the development of Down syndrome
- Updated information on the Human Genome Project
- Updated discussions of new reproductive technology, including the ethical dilemmas
- Updated information on the uses of genetic counselling, including Canadian programs that offer degrees in this area
- New illustrations of the way expression of genes varies with the child's environment
- New research on temperament and later developmental problems for "difficult" babies

CHAPTER 3: PRENATAL DEVELOPMENT AND BIRTH

- New studies of the effects on the fetus of maternal stress, fear, and anxiety
- Recent work on the impact of moderate maternal prenatal nicotine exposure and alcohol consumption and long-term effects of nicotine and alcohol on later development
- Updated coverage pertaining to the effects of exposure to marijuana on prenatal development

- Recent work on environmental toxins and their effects on prenatal development
- Updated international data on infant mortality rates
- New information on low birthweight and its consequences for preterm infants' development
- New coverage of recent intervention programs for preterm babies
- Updated information on the international incidence of AIDS in babies and on interventions for these infants
- Recent data on the continuing rise in Caesarean deliveries and effects on mothers and subsequent births

CHAPTER 4: INFANCY: SENSATION, PERCEPTION, AND LEARNING

- Updated information on risk factors for SIDS
- Updated material on the rapidly expanding areas of infant perception and memory
- Increased coverage of neurodevelopmental approaches to research on infant cognition
- More "big picture" or "why" information in multiple sections such as face perception, depth perception, and intermodal perception
- New research on early object knowledge and processes of infant learning, including imitation
- Recent studies of haptic sensitivity in newborns

CHAPTER 5: THE CHILD'S GROWTH: BRAIN, BODY, MOTOR SKILLS, AND SEXUAL MATURATION

- Cross-cultural studies show how specific ways of caring for infants can alter their motor development
- New research on the association between brain development and musical study and performance
- More focus on latest brain-assessment techniques, such as SPECT, fMRI, and TMS, and new evidence of brain plasticity
- Expanded discussion of the growing problem of obesity in childhood, and updated discussion on the genetic and environmental origins of obesity and anorexia nervosa
- New research on the benefits of breast-feeding
- New data on the determinants and impact of early timed puberty

CHAPTER 6: EMOTIONAL DEVELOPMENT AND ATTACHMENT

- New focus on primary and secondary emotions
- New work on the recognition of emotions and the impact of abuse on a child's ability to recognize emotions
- Updated material on jealousy in young children; change over time in children's jealousy reactions
- New work on cross-cultural differences in children's recognition of emotions
- Expanded coverage of research on attachment in international adoptees
- Updated research on attachment relationships between fathers and their children, including hormonal correlates of fathering as well as cross-cultural variations in fathering
- Latest studies on the effects of child care on children, including research on increased aggression among children in child-care facilities

CHAPTER 7: LANGUAGE AND COMMUNICATION

- New research on challenges to the nativist view of language learning

- Expanded discussion of infant speech perception and challenges to categorical perception in infancy
- Expanded coverage of social contributions to language learning, including the contributions of communication to cognitive development
- New research on whether to explain language by a unique cognitive processing system or a general learning system
- Expanded section on young children's queries, especially their "why" and "how" questions
- New research on the role of early communication
- Expanded discussion of bilingualism
- Additional coverage of metalinguistic awareness, including monitoring of speech

CHAPTER 8: COGNITIVE DEVELOPMENT: PIAGET AND VYGOTSKY

- Recent research examining the predictions of Piagetian theory, especially in the sensorimotor and preoperational stages
- New research on infant categorization abilities
- Greater coverage of social cognition, including theory of mind and understanding of intentions
- Expanded and updated section on research stemming from Vygotsky's approach, including classroom designs based on a sociocultural approach to cognitive development
- Updated section on cultural contributions to cognitive development, including the role of tools in intellectual development

CHAPTER 9: COGNITIVE DEVELOPMENT: THE INFORMATION-PROCESSING APPROACH

- Updated discussion of basic assumptions and models of information-processing theory
- Greater discussion of how changes in knowledge contribute to cognitive development
- Expanded coverage of cognitive tools, including symbolic and material supports for thinking
- Updated discussion of attention, including the role of attention in planning
- Recent research on memory, including organization and strategy development

CHAPTER 10: INTELLIGENCE AND ACHIEVEMENT

- Updated and expanded discussion of intelligence testing, including recent developments in testing infant intelligence
- New information regarding the availability of Canadian norms for the Wechsler scale
- Updated and expanded discussion of how ethnicity, cultural experience, and social class relate to IQ testing
- New material on changes in IQ over time, including recent research on the Flynn Effect
- New research on the long-term stability of intelligence, based on the Scottish Mental Surveys
- Updated section on achievement motivation and creativity in children
- Expanded discussion of intellectual development among exceptional children

CHAPTER 11: THE FAMILY

- New work on co-parenting and alliances among family members

- New data on ethnic variations in child-rearing and the role of neighbourhood risk
- Updates on incidence of pregnancy and STDs among teenagers
- New data on the effects of parental age and parenting knowledge and practices
- New information on child abuse and neglect and the long-term effects of sexual abuse on children

CHAPTER 12: EXPANDING THE SOCIAL WORLD: PEERS AND FRIENDS

- New evidence of toddler social skills and their abilities to function in triadic situations
- Fresh perspectives on types of popular children
- New information on peer rejection and victimization
- New research on how close, same-gender friendships differ between boys and girls
- New evidence on romantic relationships among teenagers
- New data on whether parents or peers have more influence on children's behaviour and cross-cultural variations in peer relationships

CHAPTER 13: GENDER ROLES AND GENDER DIFFERENCES

- Integration of recent evolutionary perspectives on the basis of gender differentiation
- New focus on Hyde's similarity hypothesis to provide a balanced portrait of gender similarities and differences
- Discussion of why girls continue to drop out of math courses internationally
- New research on the effects of fetal androgen effects
- New research on gender and computer use
- Updated discussion of the outcome of Money's most famous case of sexual reassignment
- New data on siblings as shapers of gender identity
- New material on the effects of a father's absence or unavailability
- New section on development of same-sex orientation and identity during childhood and adolescence

CHAPTER 14: MORALITY, ALTRUISM, AND AGGRESSION

- More focus on morality in individualistic and collectivistic cultures
- New work on the neuroimaging correlates of Gilligan's care versus justice approach to moral development
- New work on the affective side of morality and the development of guilt in children
- New material on children's understanding of freedom of speech, civil rights, and religion
- More work on the biological basis of prosocial behaviour, including recent neuroimaging studies
- New material on closing the gender gap in victims of violence
- New work on the effects of violent video games on aggression and new neuroimaging correlations of exposure to film violence

CHAPTER 15: DEVELOPMENTAL PSYCHOPATHOLOGY

- New data on children's age and substance abuse in Canadian society
- Update on suicide rates among various ethnic groups, especially First Nations youth

- Updates on the genetic and biological roots of autism, such as chromosomal abnormalities and brain chemistry differences
- New research on the cognitive effects of ADHD
- Cross-time prevalence rates for autism and reasons for the increase
- Updates regarding the rates of mental health problems among affluent adolescents

SUPERIOR SERVICE

Service takes on a whole new meaning with McGraw-Hill Ryerson and *Child Psychology: A Contemporary Viewpoint*. More than just bringing you the textbook, we have consistently raised the bar in terms of innovation and educational research. These investments in learning and the educational community have helped us to understand the needs of students and educators across the country, and allowed us to foster the growth of truly innovative, integrated learning.

Integrated Learning

Your Integrated Learning Sales Specialist is a McGraw-Hill Ryerson representative who has the experience, product knowledge, training, and support to help you assess and integrate any of our products, technology, and services into your course for optimum teaching and learning performance.

Whether it's using our test bank software, helping your students improve their grades, or putting your entire course online, your *i*Learning Sales Specialist is there to help you do it. Contact your local *i*Learning Sales Specialist today to learn how to maximize all of McGraw-Hill Ryerson's resources!

*i*Learning Services Program

McGraw-Hill Ryerson offers a unique *i*Services package designed for Canadian faculty. Our mission is to equip providers of higher education with superior tools and resources required for excellence in teaching. For additional information, visit www.mcgrawhill.ca/highereducation/iservices.

McGraw-Hill Ryerson National Teaching and Learning Conference Series

The educational environment has changed tremendously in recent years, and McGraw-Hill Ryerson continues to be committed to helping you acquire the skills you need to succeed in this new milieu. Our innovative Teaching, Technology, & Learning Conference Series brings faculty together from across Canada with 3M Teaching Excellence award winners to share teaching and learning best practices in a collaborative and stimulating environment. Pre-conference workshops on general topics, such as teaching large classes and technology integration, are also offered. We will also work with you at your own institution to customize workshops that best suit the needs of your faculty.

SUPPLEMENTS

A complete, integrated supplements package supports students and instructors to help them meet their learning and teaching challenges.

For Instructors

McGraw-Hill Connect™ assessment activities don't stop with students! There is material for instructors to leverage as well, including a personalized teaching plan where instructors can choose from a variety of quizzes to use in class, assign as homework, or add to exams. They can edit existing questions and add new ones; track individual student performance—by question, assignment, or in relation to the class overall—with detailed grade reports; integrate grade reports easily with Learning Management Systems such as WebCT and Blackboard; and much more. Instructors can also browse or search teaching resources and text-specific supplements and organize them into customizable categories. All the teaching resources are now located in one convenient place.

INSTRUCTOR'S MANUAL   The instructor's manual provides ideas for lectures, class discussions, and in-class activities. Available online within CONNECT™ or from your *i*Learning Sales Specialist.

TESTBANK   The testbank includes over 1500 multiple choice, short answer, and essay questions. Multiple choice questions are tagged to include type (factual, conceptual, or applied), difficulty level, learning objective, and page number for the appropriate reference in the text. Available in Word or EZTest (McGraw-Hill's computerized testbank software) within CONNECT™ or from your *i*Learning Sales Specialist.

MICROSOFT® POWERPOINT® SLIDES   Lecture preparation is easier with slides designed for every chapter of the book. Instructors can access these slides within CONNECT™ or from your *i*Learning sales specialist.

VISUAL ASSETS DATABASE

The Visual Assets Database (VAD) provides hundreds of easily accessible media resources for use with lifespan and developmental psychology courses. These resources include video demonstrations and interviews, photographs, audio clips, weblinks, figures and graphs, and suggested in-class activities. For more information, visit vad.mhhe.com.

MULTIMEDIA COURSEWARE FOR CHILD DEVELOPMENT

This video-based two CD-ROM set covers classic and contemporary experiments in child development. Respected researcher Charlotte J. Patterson selected the video and wrote modules that can be assigned to students. The modules also include suggestions for additional projects as well as a testing component.

For Students

Developed in partnership with Youthography, a Canadian youth research company, and hundreds of students from across Canada, McGraw-Hill Connect™ embraces diverse study behaviours and preferences to maximize active learning and engagement.

With McGraw-Hill Connect™, students complete pre- and post-diagnostic assessments that identify knowledge gaps and point them to concepts they need to learn. McGraw-Hill Connect™ provides students with the option to work through recommended learning exercises and create their own personalized study plan using multiple sources of content, including a searchable e-book, multiple-choice and true/false quizzes, chapter-by-chapter learning goals, interactivities, personal notes, videos, and more. Using the copy, paste, highlight, and sticky note features, students collect, organize, and customize their study plan content to optimize learning outcomes.

Acknowledgments

I would like first of all to express my respect and gratitude to Ross Parke and Mary Gauvain, the authors of the most recent edition of *Child Psychology*. The third Canadian edition is deeply indebted to their outstanding scholarship, insightful writing, and lively sense of students' interests and needs.

Next, I wish to thank Katalin Dzinas for her support and help in tackling this endeavour, and for her hard work in helping to untangle the confusing web of history of Canadian psychology and developmental psychology.

The third Canadian edition has benefited from a number of people who teach the child development course and offered their insights and suggestions for the manuscript of this book. For this invaluable assistance I thank,

Julie Bélanger, University of British Columbia
Wendy L. Bourque, St. Thomas University
Dr. Elizabeth Bowering, Mount Saint Vincent University
Jeremy Carpendale, Simon Fraser University
Susan Chuang, University of Guelph
Susannah Cole, Fleming College
Mary L. Courage, Memorial University
Jason Daniels, University of Alberta
Fatma Fisharah, University of Winnipeg
Patricia Franke, Trent University
Grace Iarocci, Simon Fraser University
Nancie Im-Bolter, Trent University
Bina John, University of Toronto
Cheryl Kier, Athabasca University
Tobias Krettenauer, Wilfrid Laurier University
Laura Melnyk, University of Western Ontario
Scott Miller, University of Windsor
Colleen Orrick, Loyalist College
Jason Ramsay, Ryerson University
Dr. Danielle Renaud, Fanshawe College
Heather Sago, Trent University
Susan Thompson, Kwantlen Polytechnic University
John Vervaeke, University of Toronto
Anthony Volk, Brock University

Other important members of the team include everyone at McGraw-Hill Ryerson who contributed to the development of the book: Cara Yarzab, publisher, Humanities, Social Sciences, and Languages; Kelly Dickson, managing editor, Development; Liz Radojkovic, developmental editor; Margaret Henderson, manager, Editorial Services; Jessica Barnoski, supervising editor; Joe Zingrone, freelance copy editor; Jennifer Hall, team lead, Production; Marina Seguin, editorial associate.

Finally, I thank my closest friend, collaborator, and colleague, and my beloved wife, Katalin Dzinas. She provided invaluable help and feedback throughout the entire process of producing this book. Without her love and support, this work truly would never have been accomplished.

Mark A. Schmuckler

Walkthrough

In this edition, we have expanded and refined our special features.

CHAPTER OUTLINES, LEARNING OBJECTIVES, AND SUMMARIES Our chapter outlines facilitate students' survey of a chapter's contents; our learning objectives inform students of the chapter's objectives and expectations; and our comprehensive, bulleted summaries reiterate the chapter's main ideas.

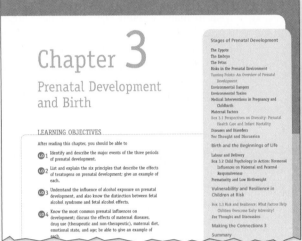

Chapter **3**
Prenatal Development and Birth

LEARNING OBJECTIVES

After reading this chapter, you should be able to

LO 1 Identify and describe the major events of the three periods of prenatal development.

LO 2 List and explain the six principles that describe the effects of teratogens on prenatal development; give an example of each.

LO 3 Understand the influence of alcohol exposure on prenatal development, and also know the distinction between fetal alcohol syndrome and fetal alcohol effects.

LO 4 Know the most common prenatal influences on development; discuss the effects of maternal diseases, drug use (therapeutic and non-therapeutic), maternal diet, emotional state, and age; be able to give an example of each.

Stages of Prenatal Development
The Zygote
The Embryo
The Fetus
Risks in the Prenatal Environment
Turning Points: An Overview of Prenatal Development
Environmental Dangers
Environmental Toxins
Medical Interventions in Pregnancy and Childbirth
Maternal Factors
Box 3.1 Perspectives on Diversity: Prenatal Health Care and Infant Mortality
Diseases and Disorders
For Thought and Discussion
Birth and the Beginnings of Life
Labour and Delivery
Box 3.2 Child Psychology in Action: Hormonal Influences on Maternal and Paternal Responsiveness
Prematurity and Low Birthweight
Vulnerability and Resilience in Children at Risk
Box 3.3 Risk and Resilience: What Factors Help Children Overcome Early Adversity?
For Thought and Discussion
Making the Connections 3
Summary

SUMMARY

Stages of Prenatal Development

- Prenatal development is divided into three distinct periods (zygote, embryo, fetus). These periods represent phases of development during which the organism, protected and sustained by the **amniotic sac**, the **placenta**, the **umbilical cord**, and, after the fifth month, the **lanugo**, undergoes a systematic series of sequential changes to become increasingly complex and differentiated.
- The period of the **zygote**, which lasts about two weeks, extends from fertilization to implantation, when the zygote becomes implanted in the wall of the uterus. The period of the **embryo** begins at that point and lasts until the end of the eighth week.

For Thought and Discussion

1. Are the various developmental themes we have discussed independent of one another or are they interrelated in some fashion? For example, if you assume that the environment plays a fundamental role in his or her development, does this assumption have implications for continuity–discontinuity or the importance of situational–individual characteristics, and so on?

2. Are the different themes of development of equal significance? If not, why might some themes be more important than others?

3. What is the best characterization of these themes—as opposing positions (i.e., one versus the other), or as end points on a continuum? To put it differently, is it possible to come up with positions between the strong statements of either view, and if so, what might be some of the implications of these middle-ground positions?

FOR THOUGHT AND DISCUSSION questions follow each major section of text, prompting students to apply the material, generate new insights, and draw new connections between ideas.

CHILD PSYCHOLOGY IN ACTION boxes pick up the thread of our research-application theme, focusing on how the results of basic research can be and are being applied daily to the solution of significant problems in children's development.

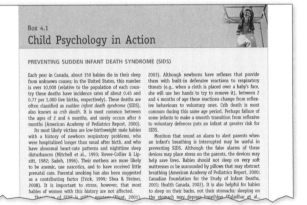

Box 4.1
Child Psychology in Action

PREVENTING SUDDEN INFANT DEATH SYNDROME (SIDS)

Each year in Canada, about 150 babies die in their sleep from unknown causes; in the United States, this number is over 10,000 (relative to the population of each country these deaths have incidence rates of about 0.45 and 0.77 per 1,000 live births, respectively). These deaths are often classified as *sudden infant death syndrome* (SIDS), also known as *crib death*. It is most common between the ages of 2 and 4 months, and rarely occurs after 6 months (American Academy of Pediatrics Report, 2000). Its most likely victims are low-birthweight male babies with a history of newborn respiratory problems, who were hospitalized longer than usual after birth, and who have abnormal heart-rate patterns and nighttime sleep disturbances (Mitchell et al., 1993; Rovee-Collier & Lipsitt, 1982; Sadeh, 1996). Their mothers are more likely to be anemic, use narcotics, and to have received little prenatal care. Parental smoking has also been suggested as a contributing factor (Frick, 1999; Shea & Steiner, 2008). It is important to stress, however, that most babies of women with this history are not affected. The cause of SIDS is still mysterious (Hunt, 2001;

2003). Although newborns have reflexes that provide them with built-in defensive reactions to respiratory threats (e.g., when a cloth is placed over a baby's face, she will use her hands to try to remove it), between 2 and 4 months of age these reactions change from reflexive behaviours to voluntary ones. Crib death is most common during this same age period. Perhaps failure of some infants to make a smooth transition from reflexive to voluntary defences puts an infant at greater risk for SIDS.

Monitors that sound an alarm to alert parents when an infant's breathing is interrupted may be useful in preventing SIDS. Although the false alarms of these devices may place stress on the parents, the devices may help save lives. Babies should not sleep on very soft mattresses or be surrounded by pillows that may obstruct breathing (American Academy of Pediatrics Report, 2000; Canadian Foundation for the Study of Infant Deaths, 2001; Health Canada, 2002). It is also helpful for babies to sleep on their backs, not their stomachs; sleeping on the stomach may depress breathing (Skadhar et al.,

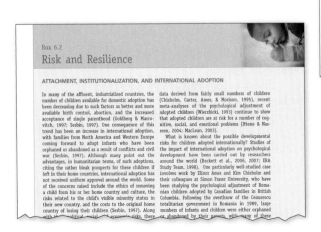

Box 6.2
Risk and Resilience

ATTACHMENT, INSTITUTIONALIZATION, AND INTERNATIONAL ADOPTION

In many of the affluent, industrialized countries, the number of children available for domestic adoption has been decreasing due to such factors as better and more available birth control, abortion, and the increased acceptance of single parenthood (Goldberg & Marcovitch, 1997; Serbin, 1997). One consequence of this trend has been an increase in international adoption, with families from North America and Western Europe coming forward to adopt internationally. Studies of the impact of international adoption on psychological development have been carried out by researchers around the world (Beckett et al., 2006, 2007; ERA Study Team, 1998). One particularly well-studied case involves work by Elinor Ames and Kim Chisholm and their colleagues at Simon Fraser University, who have been studying the psychological adjustment of Romanian children adopted by Canadian families in British Columbia. Following the overthrow of the Ceaușescu totalitarian government in Romania in 1989, large numbers of infants and children were either orphaned or abandoned by their parents, with many of these

data derived from fairly small numbers of children (Chisholm, Carter, Ames, & Morison, 1995), recent meta-analyses of the psychological adjustment of adopted children (Wierzbicki, 1993) continue to show that adopted children are at risk for a number of cognitive, social, and emotional problems (Iftene & Nasreen, 2004; MacLean, 2003).

What is known about the possible developmental risks for children adopted internationally? Studies of

RISK AND RESILIENCE boxes focus on how we can support and encourage the resilience that children often display in the face of a wide variety of risks, as well as on how we can work to alleviate or eliminate the risk factors.

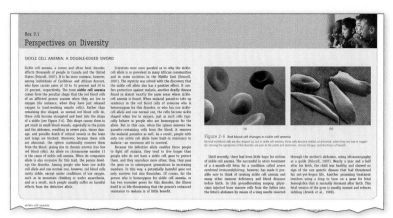

PERSPECTIVES ON DIVERSITY boxes examine child development research that not only spans nations and continents, but explores differences among children of the many different cultural groups who make up the North American population.

WEB ICONS in the margins signal that students can find additional resources about the topic within CONNECT. (www.mcgrawhillconnect.ca)

KEY TERMS AND MARGINAL GLOSSARY are set in boldface type and are repeated, with their definitions, on the same page in a margin glossary; the terms and their definitions also appear in the alphabetized Glossary at the back of the book.

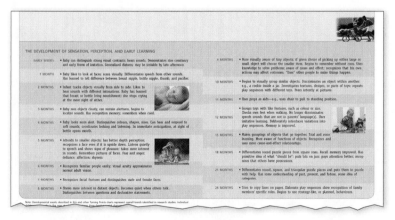

TURNING POINTS IN CHILD DEVELOPMENT charts appear in Chapters 3–9 and 12–14, providing a chronological overview of a child's evolving skills and abilities. These charts help students synthesize the topically presented material from a chronological viewpoint.

MAKING THE CONNECTIONS GRAPHICS enable the student to relate discussions in one chapter to topics explored in other chapters. These graphics underline the interrelatedness of issues across different domains of development.

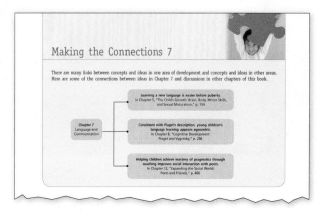

Pablo Picasso (1881–1973). *Claude With Horse*, 1949.

Chapter 1

Child Development: Themes, Theories, and Methods

LEARNING OBJECTIVES

After reading this chapter, you should be able to

LO 1 Define development and state why the study of child development is important.

LO 2 Summarize each of the "themes" of child development and describe the controversies underlying each theme.

LO 3 Describe each of the theoretical perspectives presented in Chapter 1; understand relevant terminology associated with each theory; comment on the unique contributions that each theory makes to the study of child development.

LO 4 Integrate the themes and theories by understanding the perspective of each theory on issues such as biology versus environment, continuity versus discontinuity, and situational influences versus individual differences.

LO 5 Describe each of the research methods outlined in this chapter, and discuss the strengths and weaknesses of each.

LO 6 Compare correlational and experimental methods; discuss when each method is appropriate to use and provide examples.

LO 7 Discuss the reasons for choosing either a field or a laboratory setting and new designs that incorporate both.

LO 8 Describe different procedures for investigating change over time, and list the pros and cons of each.

LO 9 Explain why it is important to protect children's rights when conducting research; discuss special ethical issues that should be considered (e.g., informed consent) and what precautions are taken to ensure that children are protected.

LO 1

Two-year-old Madeleine has a pile of blocks in front of her of all shapes, sizes, and colours. She can put all her red blocks in one group and all the blue ones in another, but she does not sort the blocks by their shape. By the time she is 5, however, Madeleine can now sort her red and blue blocks into different groups, and then within each group she can divide them into small, medium, and big blocks. And when Madeleine is 7 years old or so, she can use this strategy of categorization in learning new information; for example, if her teacher gives her a list of words, including *shirt*, *eyes*, *carrot*, *apple, nose, shoes*, *pants*, *cereal*, and *mouth*, she can learn the words more efficiently by classifying them into groups: clothing, parts of the body, and foods.

Justin, who is a year and a half, plays with his toys next to another child but does not talk to the other child or interact with him except, perhaps, to grab one of his companion's toys. At this age, Justin has difficulty taking into account the other child's perspective. When Justin is 6 or 7 years old, he will now engage in group play with other children. As well, he now understands that people have different points of view about the world, and that not everyone sees things the way he does. By the time he is in his mid-teens, Justin will understand social life in complex ways, including the need for positive human relationships, and the concept of societal law and order.

What accounts for this gradual but steady change in the child's ability to understand and create complex relations, to learn new information, and to interact with and feel responsibility toward other people? The field of **child development**, a sub-area of the discipline of developmental psychology (which could, for instance, include lifespan development), seeks to answer this complex question in two major ways: First, it identifies and describes *changes* in the child's cognitive, emotional, motor, and social capacities and behaviours from the moment of conception through the period of adolescence. Second, the field attempts to uncover the *processes* that underlie these changes to help explain how and why they occur. In other words, developmental psychologists are interested in *what* things change as children get older, and *how* these changes come about. To understand the changes and processes that underlie child development, researchers devise theories, design and carry out empirical studies to test these theories, and suggest practical applications based on their research. In this chapter, we introduce the field of child development by describing the main theories and methods used by developmental scientists to uncover the fascinating process of human psychological growth.

Although research in child development plays a significant role in the general field of psychology, this subdiscipline is a relatively young enterprise. It got its start barely a century ago, when the topic drew the attention of scholars from various regions of the world. One of the most notable was Charles Darwin, who conducted research on infants' sensory capacities and young children's emotions (Cairns & Cairns, 2006). In his research on infants' early sensory and perceptual capacities and children's emotions, Darwin (1872) clearly demonstrated that scientists could study infants and children. Later, in the United States, John B. Watson continued the formal analysis of children's learning capacities. And in Europe, Sigmund Freud and Jean Piaget, who you will read about in this chapter, were two other important early contributors to our understanding of children.

The scientific study of child psychology in Canada (see Wright, 2002) has about as long a history as it does in the United States, despite the fact that the Canadian Psychological Association—a national organization of Canadian psychologists—was not formed until 1938 (Dzinas, 2000), some 46 years after the American Psychological Association (Sokal, 1992).

Child Development

child development

A field of study that seeks to account for the gradual evolution of the child's cognitive, social, and other capacities first by describing changes in the child's observed behaviours and then by uncovering the processes and strategies that underlie these changes.

Psychological Associations

One of the earliest and most significant events in Canadian developmental psychology was the appointment of James Mark Baldwin to the University of Toronto in 1889 (Green, 2002, 2004; Hoff, 1992). Although often remembered for establishing the first laboratory of psychology on British soil (Baldwin, 1930; Wright & Myers, 1982), Baldwin is also an important figure in the history of research on child development through his work on mental development. Using his own daughter as a subject, Baldwin examined, and published papers on, such topics as handedness (Baldwin, 1890), suggestion and will in infancy (Baldwin, 1891, 1892), and imitation (Baldwin, 1894).

As for other notable events in the history of developmental psychology in Canada, one important landmark was the opening of St. George's School for Child Study in Toronto in 1926 (Northway, 1973; Pols, 2002), which still operates today as the Institute for Child Study. St. George's school was initially headed by developmental psychologist William Emet Blatz (Wright, 1996), who later became known for his three-year study of the Dionne quintuplets (Blatz et al., 1937; Blatz, 1938). The Dionne quintuplets were a group of five sisters, born in 1934, who were raised from 2 months to 8 years of age in a special compound that was "on display" to the general public (Prochner & Doyon, 1997).

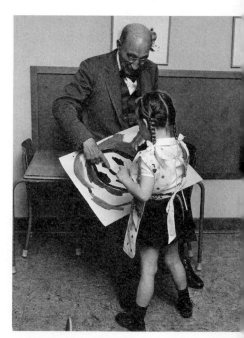

Dr. William Blatz at the Institute for Child Study in Toronto.

Although some have argued that these detailed observations of the Dionnes failed to produce any dramatic insights into child development (Prochner & Doyon, 1997), others have suggested otherwise (Winestock, 1994). Regardless of the ultimate status of this work, the study of the Dionne quintuplets did a lot for promoting the study of child development generally and the work of developmental psychologists in Canada in particular.

Why should we be concerned with the study of children, and learning about child development? Simply put, better information about child development can help society protect and advance the well-being of children (Renninger & Sigel, 2006), and can also be used to shape social policy on behalf of children (Jutras, 2003; Parke & Clarke-Stewart, 2002). To understand the scientific study of child development, it is important to appreciate the central themes of development that underlie current theory and research. It is also important to be familiar with the main theoretical views that guide this research, and the methods that are used in it. Throughout our exploration of contemporary child psychology, we will discuss how we can use what we learn to improve children's functioning and opportunities for development in important areas of their lives, especially relationships with family, friends, and peers; academic pursuits; and personal development. ●

THEMES OF DEVELOPMENT   LO 2

As scientists have studied children's development, they have examined and debated three key issues of themes pertaining to psychological growth. These themes concern the origins of human behaviour, the pattern of developmental change over time, and the individual and contextual factors that define and direct child development. We will encounter these three themes repeatedly throughout the book as we discuss the many aspects of development—*biological*, *cognitive*, *linguistic*, emotional, and social. In this chapter, we describe each of these themes and we use them to discuss the main theories of child development that underlie contemporary research.

Origins of Behaviour: Biological versus Environmental Influences

Most contemporary theories recognize that both biological and environmental factors influence human development, but they disagree about the relative importance of each of these factors for development, or the balance between the influences. In the early years of the field, some psychologists held strictly biological or environmental views. Psychologists such as Arnold Gesell (1928) believed that the course of development was largely predetermined by biological factors. In his research, Gesell concentrated on **maturation** or the natural unfolding of development over the course of growth. Other early theorists, such as the behaviourist John B. Watson, placed their emphasis strictly on the environment. Watson (1928) assumed that biological factors placed no restrictions on the ways that the environment can shape the course of a child's development. In fact, he claimed that by properly organizing the environment, he could produce a genius or a criminal.

Today, there are no theories that support either of these extreme positions. Instead, modern developmentalists explore how biological and environmental factors, or nature and nurture, interact to produce developmental variations in different children. Research on child maltreatment, for example, finds that children with certain genetic characteristics are more likely to exhibit behaviour problems than are children who do not have these characteristics (Plomin, DeFries, McClearn, & McGuffin, 2001). When children with these genetic dispositions live in abusive environments, they are more likely to be maltreated than other children. Thus, the *combination* of the child's biological characteristics, the way he or she expresses these characteristics behaviourally, and the abusive environment itself puts a particular child at risk.

Children intentionally try to understand and explore the world about them. The active nature of the human organism supports interaction between biological propensities and the environment over the course of development (Kuczynski, 2003). Also, socializing agents such as parents, peers, or teachers do not simply mold the child; instead, children actively influence and modify the actions of their parents and other people with whom they interact. Thus, the interaction between biology and environment is an active, dynamic process in which the child also contributes to the process.

Pattern of Developmental Change: Continuity versus Discontinuity

Another major question that confronts developmental psychologists is how to describe the pattern of developmental change. Two basic patterns are debated. Some psychologists view development as a continuous process whereby each new event builds on earlier experiences (Figure 1-1a). In this view, development is a smooth and gradual accumulation of abilities. Developmental changes add to, or build on, earlier abilities in a cumulative or quantitative way without any abrupt shifts from one change to the next. For many behaviours, this seems like an apt explanation. For example, as we learn a new skill—let's say how to swim—we usually observe gradual improvement from day to day. However, we sometimes notice an abrupt change in our ability. Whereas yesterday we were swimming competently, today it seems as if some big improvement has occurred—all our practice seems to have finally paid off. Compared with the earlier, more incremental changes, our more recent changes seem more qualitative in nature, and our smoother or more rapid swimming stroke now bears little resemblance to the choppy, halting strokes we had when we first began to swim. This latter type of change is of interest to developmental psychologists who view development as discontinuous. This view likens development to a series of discrete steps or stages in which behaviours get reorganized into a qualitatively new set of behaviours (Figure 1-1b).

---

maturation

A genetically determined process of growth that unfolds naturally over a period of time.

Most contemporary child researchers see development as basically continuous or quantitative, but sometimes interspersed with periods of change that are discontinuous or more qualitative (Figure 1-1c). Some recent research aims to understand how behavioural continuities are sustained or disrupted by an individual's experiences. Although a disruption to behavioural continuity may sound problematic, it may not be so. For example, Rutter, Kreppner, and O'Connor (2001) have investigated how children who were reared early in life in deprived institutional settings experienced positive change after they were adopted into healthy families.

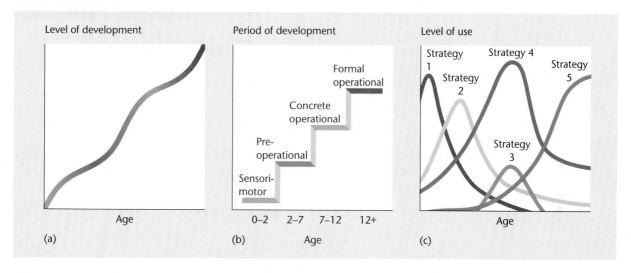

Figure 1-1

Continuity and discontinuity in the child's development

The continuous view (a) sees development as a gradual series of shifts in capacities, skills, and behaviour without any abrupt changes. Those who hold the opposite perspective (b), in which development is discontinuous, propose just such abrupt, step-like changes, each qualitatively different from the one that precedes it. Most contemporary developmentalists believe a third view, which holds that development is fundamentally continuous but interspersed with transitions that may appear sudden, most accurately represents the progress of child development over time. Robert Siegler's "overlapping waves" model (c) suggests that children use a variety of strategies in thinking and learning and that cognition involves constant competition among different strategies rather than the use of a single strategy at a given age. Although each strategy may take a qualitative step forward in effectiveness, at any given point in time, the child uses several strategies of varying levels of sophistication. The use of each strategy ebbs and flows with increasing age and expertise, and it is only gradually that the most successful strategies predominate. As a result, from a macroscopic perspective, development appears generally continuous, but at a microscopic level, we can observe specific qualitative changes.

Source: Parts (a), (b), and (c) from Siegler, Robert S., Alibali, Martha W., *Children's Thinking*, 4th Edition, Prentice Hall, copyright © 2005. Adapted and reprinted by permission of Pearson Education, Inc., Upper Saddle River, NJ.

Forces That Affect Developmental Change: Individual Characteristics versus Contextual and Cultural Influences

Child development occurs in a variety of settings. Do children behave similarly across a broad range of situations, or do the contexts in which children live affect how children behave and even how development occurs? Developmental psychologists differ in their emphasis on individual characteristics versus situational or contextual influences. Many resolve the controversy by adopting an *interactionist* viewpoint, stressing the dual role of individual and contextual factors (Magnusson & Stattin, 2006). For example, children with aggressive personality traits may often seek out contexts in which they can display these characteristics; thus, they're more likely to join a gang or enroll in a karate class than to opt for the church choir or a chess club (Bullock & Merrill,

In the world's many varied cultures, children begin, often at an early age, to develop specialized skills. In Somalia, a son learns the care and management of camels from his father.

And some behaviours are the same the world over. This mother is clearly quite attached to, and cares for, her child.

1980; Magnusson & Stattin, 2006). But these same children, in settings that do not allow or promote aggressive behaviour, such as a choir or book club, may be less likely to behave aggressively and perhaps even be friendly and co-operative.

RISKS TO HEALTHY DEVELOPMENT AND INDIVIDUAL RESILIENCE One very important way in which individual characteristics have been studied is by examining how different children respond when they are confronted with *situational challenges or risks to healthy development*. Risk can come in many forms. Some risks are biological or psychological: for example, a serious illness, or living with a psychotic parent. Other risks are environmental, such as family income, the child's experience at school, or marital conflict in the home (Davies & Cummings, 2006). Individual children respond to such risks in different ways. Many seem to suffer permanent developmental disruptions. Others show "sleeper" effects; they seem to cope well initially, but exhibit problems later in development. Still others exhibit resilience and are able to deal with the challenge. And some children, when they confront new risks later in life, seem better able to adapt to challenges than children who have experienced little or no risk (Cummings, Davies, & Campbell, 2000; Luthar, Cicchetti, & Becker, 2000). Finally, a recent trend in resilience research has been to identify factors that promote resilience under normal conditions (Davey, Eaker, & Waters, 2003).

RESEARCHING ACROSS CULTURES Researchers who emphasize contextual influences on development have studied a range of settings including the home, the neighbourhood, and the school. Examination of the contribution that context makes to child development has also led to increased interest in how culture relates to development. We know that children who grow up on a farm in China, in a kibbutz in Israel, in a village in Peru, or on the prairies in Canada have very different kinds of experiences that influence their development. For example, in some cultures, children are encouraged to walk very early and are given opportunities to exercise their new motor skills. In other cultures, infants are carried or swaddled for long periods of time, which reduces their chance to walk until they are older. Examining child development across cultures provides information about variation in the range of human potential and expression that may emerge in different circumstances of growth (Rogoff, 2003). Moreover, cultures differ not only across national boundaries but also within single countries. Canada, Australia, and Russia, for example, all contain a wide range of subcultural groups representing very diverse racial and ethnic traditions (Demo, Allen, & Fine, 2000). And, of course, in Canada, another fundamental source of cultural variation arises from differences in the linguistic environments of anglophone and francophone classrooms.

The three themes we've been discussing—biological versus environmental origins, continuous versus discontinuous patterns of growth, and individual versus contextual influences on development—have inspired several different theories about child development. In the next section, as we discuss the main theoretical perspectives on child development, we will describe how each of these theories takes these three themes into account.

For Thought and Discussion

1. Are the various developmental themes we have discussed independent of one another or are they interrelated in some fashion? For example, if you assume that the the environment plays a fundamental role in his or her development, does this assumption have implications for continuity–discontinuity or the importance of situational–individual characteristics, and so on?

2. Are the different themes of development of equal significance? If not, why might some themes be more important than others?

3. What is the best characterization of these themes—as opposing positions (i.e., one versus the other), or as end points on a continuum? To put it differently, is it possible to come up with positions between the strong statements of either view, and if so, what might be some of the implications of these middle-ground positions?

THEORETICAL PERSPECTIVES ON DEVELOPMENT

(LO)3

It is not sufficient that a developmental theory focus on children. What is critical is that a theory describes psychological change or development over time (Miller, 2002). Theories serve two main functions that are critical to scientific understanding in general, and to the study of developmental psychology in particular. First, they help organize and integrate existing information into coherent and interesting accounts of how children develop. Second, they generate testable hypotheses or predictions about children's behaviour. As such, a good scientific theory allows one to make sense of a great number of observations, usually based on the fewest number of premises, and can then be subsequently used to formulate settings for the collection of new observations.

In the field of child psychology, no one of several theories dominates the field, and no theory is complete on its own. In fact, most developmental psychologists today might be considered theoretically eclectic, in that they mix and match concepts from different theories to enable them to explain different types of observations. Also, as you will see, each theory is framed by specific questions about development, and, therefore, it focuses on particular aspects of development that are relevant to these questions. In addition, different theories favour particular methods or ways of studying development.

In the following sections, we group the main theories of child development in relation to five general approaches in the field. These are 1) structural-organismic, 2) learning, 3) dynamic systems, 4) contextual, and 5) ethological and evolutionary views. Our aim is to provide an overarching perspective that presents the commonalities and differences across these various theories. However, we recognize that there are other ways to group the theories. We also aim to give you a sense of the breadth and diversity of different theoretical approaches to child development. We begin this section by discussing two of the earliest theoretical attempts to focus specifically on psychological development: Freud's psychodynamic theory and Piaget's theory of cognitive development.

Structural-Organismic Perspectives

Both Freud and Piaget developed their theories in the early twentieth century when scholars from a number of disciplines wanted to understand how complex systems,

structural-organismic perspective

Theoretical approaches that describe psychological structures and processes that undergo qualitative or stage-like changes over the course of development.

psychodynamic theory

Freud's theory that development, which proceeds in discrete stages, is determined largely by biologically based drives shaped by encounters with the environment and through the interaction of three components of personality—the *id*, *ego*, and *superego*.

id

The person's instinctual drives; the first component of the personality to evolve, the id operates on the basis of the *pleasure principle*.

ego

The rational, controlling component of the personality, which tries to satisfy needs through appropriate, socially acceptable behaviours.

superego

The personality component that is the repository of the child's internalization of parental or societal values, morals, and roles.

Freud

Erik Erikson (1902–1990) left his native Germany after finishing school and wandered through Europe, sketching and writing about what he saw, in search of his own identity. This journey led him eventually to the practice of psychoanalysis and to one of his best-known concepts, that of the child-adolescent's identity crisis. Erikson's psychosocial theory of development, spanning the entire life course, continues to inform the thinking of many psychologists and other social scientists.

such as societies and kin systems, work. To tackle this issue, many of these scholars tried to describe the formal structure, or organization, of the system in which they were interested in the hope that this description could provide insight into how the system worked. Freud and Piaget, who were interested in psychological development, adopted this approach, called *structuralism*. The theories that Freud and Piaget introduced focused on different aspects of development—Freud was interested in emotions and personality, whereas Piaget was interested in thinking. Yet, both devised theories that incorporated their mutual interest in biology, especially evolutionary theory, which was prominent at the time. Both Freud and Piaget used what has come to be known as the **structural-organismic perspective** in their theories. They shared the view that the organism goes through an organized or structured series of stages, or discontinuous changes, over the course of development. Both also saw the stages they proposed as universal—that is, all members of the human species were thought to experience these stages, regardless of when and where a child develops. Despite these common features, Freud's and Piaget's theories are markedly different from each other.

PSYCHODYNAMIC THEORY   In the early twentieth century, Sigmund Freud introduced **psychodynamic theory**, which emphasizes how the experiences of early childhood shape the development of adult personality. This theory is very complex and covers many aspects of psychological functioning. Here, we concentrate on the parts of this theory that have influenced developmental psychology.

For Freud, the developing personality consists of three interrelated parts: the id, the ego, and the superego. The roles of these three components of personality change across development as the infant, who is largely under the control of the **id**, or instinctual drives, gradually becomes more controlled by the ego. The **ego** is the rational and reality bound aspect and attempts to gratify needs through socially appropriate behaviour. With further development, the third component of personality, the **superego**, emerges when the child *internalizes*—that is, accepts and absorbs—parental or societal morals, values, and roles and develops a *conscience*, or the ability to apply moral values to her own acts.

To Freud, personality development—that is, changes in the organization and interaction of the id, ego, and superego—involves five stages (see Table 1-1). In the first, *oral* stage, the young infant is preoccupied with pleasurable activities such as eating, sucking, and biting. In the second to third year, the child enters the *anal* stage and learns to postpone personal gratification, such as the pleasure of expelling feces, as he is trained to use the toilet. Following the anal stage, the *phallic* stage begins, and curiosity about sexual anatomy and sexuality appears. Freud saw this stage as critical to the formation of gender identity. During the *latency* period, from about 6 years of age to puberty, sexual drives are temporarily submerged and children avoid relationships with peers of the other gender. In the last stage, the *genital* period, sexual desires emerge and are directed toward peers, a topic we return to in Chapter 12.

One of Freud's primary contributions to developmental psychology is his emphasis on how early experiences, especially in the first six years of life, influence later development. For him, the way in which the child negotiates the oral, anal, and phallic stages has a profound impact on emotional development and the adult personality. For example, infants who have unsatisfied needs for oral stimulation may be more likely to smoke as adults. Although current developmental theory does not adopt Freud's exact views about early experience, the idea that Freud introduced, namely, that events in infancy and childhood have a formative impact on later development, remains central in the study of child development. Another

Table 1-1 Freud's and Erikson's developmental stages

Age Period (Years)	Stage of Development	
	Freudian	**Eriksonian**
0–1	**Oral.** Focus on eating and taking things into the mouth	**Infancy.** Task: To develop *basic trust* in oneself and others. Risk: *Mistrust* of others and lack of self-confidence
1–3	**Anal.** Emphasis on toilet training; first experience with discipline and authority	**Early Childhood.** Task: To learn self-control and establish *autonomy*. Risk: *Shame* and *doubt* about one's own capabilities
3–6	**Phallic.** Increase in sexual urges arouses curiosity and alerts children to gender differences; period is critical to formation of gender identity	**Play Age.** Task: To develop *initiative* in mastering environment. Risk: Feelings of *guilt* over aggressiveness and daring
6–12	**Latency.** Sexual urges repressed; emphasis on education and the beginnings of concern for others	**School Age.** Task: To develop *industry*. Risk: Feelings of *inferiority* over real or imagined failure to master tasks
12–20		**Adolescence.** Task: To achieve a sense of *identity*. Risk: *Role confusion* over who and what individual wants to be
20–30	**Genital.** Altruistic love joins selfish love;	**Young Adulthood.** Task: To achieve *intimacy* with others. Risk: Shaky identity may lead to avoidance of others and *isolation*
30–65	need for reproduction of species underlies adoption of adult responsibilities*	**Adulthood.** Task: To express oneself through *generativity*. Risk: Inability to create children, ideas, or products may lead to *stagnation*
65+		**Mature Age.** Task: To achieve a sense of *integrity*. Risk: Doubts and unfulfilled desires may lead to *despair*

*Freud's genital stage encompassed both adolescence and adulthood.

contribution that Freud's thinking makes to contemporary developmental psychology is the vital role that emotional attachment early in life, especially to the mother, has in socio-emotional development, as you will read in Chapter 6. Psychodynamic theory has also been influential in certain areas of applied and clinical psychology, as we discuss in Chapter 15.

Freud had many followers who went on to devise their own theories of development, many of which contain concepts that stem from Freud's ideas. Erik Erikson devised the most prominent of these theories in his **psychosocial theory** of human development. In Erikson's theory, development is seen as proceeding through a series of eight stages that unfold across the lifespan. Each stage is characterized by the personal and social tasks that the individual must accomplish as well as the risks the individual confronts if she fails to proceed through the stages successfully (see Table 1-1). Of these ideas, the most influential for current research in child development is the stage of adolescence, in which the child focuses on identity development and seeks to establish a clear and stable sense of self.

PIAGETIAN THEORY The Swiss psychologist Jean Piaget introduced a structural-organismic theory to describe intellectual development. The **Piagetian theory** of intellectual development uses two basic principles of biology and biological change: organization and adaptation. For Piaget, the principle of *organization* reflects the view

psychosocial theory

Erikson's theory of development that sees children developing through a series of stages largely through accomplishing tasks that involve them in interaction with their social environment.

Piagetian theory

A theory of cognitive development that sees the child as actively seeking new information and incorporating it into his knowledge base through the processes of assimilation and accommodation.

A child psychologist at the universities of Geneva and Lausanne, Switzerland, Jean Piaget (1896–1980) framed a theory of the child's cognitive development that has had a great impact on developmentalists, educators, and others concerned with the course and determinants of children's development. The literature on child development today continues to examine Piagetian concepts and techniques as it also refines and expands his work.

that human intellectual development is a biologically organized process. Thus, the child's understanding of the world changes in an organized way over the course of development. Piaget used the principle of *adaptation* to describe the process by which intellectual change occurs as the human mind becomes increasingly adapted to the world.

Piaget proposed that all children go through four stages of cognitive development, each characterized by qualitatively different ways of thinking. Whereas infants rely on their sensory and motor abilities to learn about the world, preschool children rely more on mental structures and symbols, especially language. In the school years, children begin to rely more on logic, and in adolescence children can reason about abstract ideas. According to Piaget, cognitive development is a process in which the child shifts from a focus on the self, immediate sensory experiences, and simple problems to a more complex, multi-faceted, and abstract understanding of the world. In Chapter 8, we discuss Piaget's theory in greater detail including some of the important contributions and main criticisms of this theory.

The theories introduced by Freud and Piaget offer descriptions of development that focus on the structure of the developing system. We now turn to theoretical perspectives that emphasize learning; these approaches highlight process more than structure.

Learning Perspectives

The process of learning is one of the oldest areas of study in psychology. In this section, we explore some of the learning theories that have been applied to developmental issues. We begin with the work of the behaviourists, consider the approaches of the cognitive social learning theorists next, and then explore the information-processing perspective on cognitive development.

BEHAVIOURISM   The behaviourist approach to development is exemplified in the work of John B. Watson, Ivan Pavlov, and B. F. Skinner. **Behaviourism** focuses, quite simply, on the learning of behaviours. This approach emphasizes the role of experience, and it is a gradual, continuous view. The same principles of learning shape development throughout childhood and across the entire lifespan.

In the early twentieth century, the US psychologist John B. Watson used Pavlov's notion of **classical conditioning**—a type of learning in which two stimuli are repeatedly presented together until individuals learn to respond to the unfamiliar stimulus in the same way they respond to the familiar stimulus—to explain many aspects of children's behaviour, such as fear. For example, Watson conditioned an 11-month-old infant to fear furry animals by showing the baby, who was easily frightened by noises, a white rat and simultaneously making a loud noise. B. F. Skinner's notion of **operant conditioning**, in which learning depends on the consequences of behaviour, was also applied to children's behaviour. Positive reinforcement of a particular behaviour in the form of praise or a special treat was shown to increase the likelihood that a child would exhibit that behaviour again. On the other hand, punishment in the form of criticism or the withdrawal of privileges, such as watching television, can decrease the chance that a child will repeat the same behaviour. Gerald Patterson and colleagues (Patterson, 1982; Patterson & Capaldi, 1991), for example, have shown how children's anti-social behaviour is the result of how parents and children's mutually train each other to behave in ways that reinforce and

behaviourism

A school of psychology that holds that theories of behaviour must be based on direct observations of actual behaviour and not on speculations about such unobservable things as human motives.

classical conditioning

A type of learning in which individuals learn to respond to unfamiliar stimuli in the same way they are accustomed to respond to familiar stimuli if the two stimuli are repeatedly presented together.

operant conditioning

A type of learning in which learning depends on the consequences of behaviour; rewards increase the likelihood that a behaviour will recur, whereas punishment decreases that likelihood.

increase the probability that children will develop aggressive behaviours problems, and that parents will then have decreasing control over these problem behaviours. Operant conditioning has been incorporated into many applied programs to help teachers and parents change children's behaviour, including hyperactivity (restlessness, inattention, impulsivity) and aggression.

COGNITIVE SOCIAL LEARNING THEORY   According to **cognitive social learning theory**, children learn not only through classical and operant conditioning but also by observing and imitating others (Bandura, 1989, 1997, 2001). In his classic studies, Albert Bandura showed that children exposed to the aggressive behaviour of another person would imitate that behaviour. For example, after a group of nursery school children watched an adult punch, kick, and pummel a large Bobo doll (a clown-like, inflated rubber doll that pops back up after each attack), the children were more likely to attack and play aggressively with the doll than were a group of children who had not seen the model. Neither the adult model nor the children had received any apparent reinforcement, yet quite clearly, the children had learned some specific behaviours.

Further research on how the process of imitation aids learning has revealed the important contribution of cognition to observational learning. Children do not imitate blindly or automatically; rather, they select specific behaviours to imitate, and their imitation relies on how they process this information. Four cognitive processes govern how well a child will learn by observing another person (see Figure 1-2). First, the child must *attend* to a model's behaviour. Second, the child must *retain* the observed behaviours in memory. Third, the child must have the capacity, physically and intellectually, to *reproduce* the observed behaviours. Fourth, the child must be *motivated*, or have a reason to reproduce the behaviour.

INFORMATION-PROCESSING APPROACHES   **Information-processing approaches** to development focus on the flow of information through the cognitive system, beginning with an input or stimulus and ending with an output or response, much like the way computers process information (Klahr & MacWhinney, 1998). In human information processing, output may be in the form of an action, a decision, or simply a memory that is stored for later use. Information-processing theorists are especially interested in the cognitive processes that a child uses to operate on knowledge and the gradual changes over the course of development in children's ability to use these processes. What cognitive processes does the child use? He attends to information, changes it into a mental or cognitive representation, stores it in memory, compares it with other memories, generates various

cognitive social learning theory

A learning theory that stresses learning by observation and imitation mediated by cognitive processes and skills.

Albert Bandura

information-processing approaches

Theories of development that focus on the flow of information through the child's cognitive system and particularly on the specific operations the child performs between input and stimulus phases.

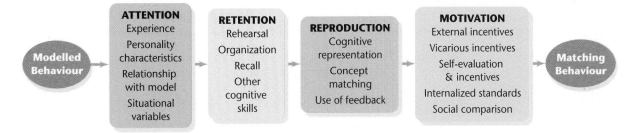

Figure 1-2

Bandura's model of observational learning

To produce a behaviour that matches that of a model, a child goes through four sets of processes. Her ability to attend to the modelled behaviour is influenced by factors in her own experience as well as in the situation; her skill in retaining what she has observed reflects a collection of cognitive skills; her reproduction of the behaviour depends on other cognitive skills, including the use of feedback from others; and she will be motivated to produce the behaviour by various incentives, her own standards, and her tendency to compare herself to others.

Source: Based on Bandura, 1989.

responses, makes a decision about the most appropriate response, and, finally, takes some specific action. This approach has been applied to a wide range of problems of cognitive development, including attention, memory, problem solving, and planning. Information-processing theory is also proving valuable in studying how children develop an understanding of reading, mathematics, and science (Siegler, 2000; Siegler & Alibali, 2005) as well as social behaviours, such as social problem solving and aggression (Kupersmidt & Dodge, 2004; Lemerise & Arsenio, 2000). In Chapter 9, we examine this approach more closely in relation to the development of individual thinking and problem solving; in Chapters 11 and 12, we discuss this approach in relation to social behaviour.

Dynamic Systems Perspectives

dynamic systems theory

A theory that proposes that individuals develop and function within systems; it studies the relationships among individuals and systems and the processes by which these relationships operate.

Another approach to child development concentrates on changes over time and considers these changes the result of the coordination of elements of a complex, integrated system. Systems theory has been applied to a variety of developmental issues, including motor development, perception, language, cognition, and social behaviour. We will encounter many different applications of systems theory throughout the book. *Dynamism* is what makes a system more than just a collection of parts. In **dynamic systems theory**, individuals and their achievements can be understood and interpreted within the framework of the interacting components of the system (Lewis, 2000; Sameroff, 1989; Spencer, Clearfield, Corbetta, Ulrich, Buchanan, & Schöner, 2006; Thelen & Smith, 2006). The term *dynamic* underscores the constant interaction and mutual influence of the elements of the system. (Table 1-2 summarizes some of the principles of the theory.)

Dynamic systems theories are a diverse group that covers a wide range of topics in child development. In some theories, the focus is on the child herself and how the child, as a biological and psychological system, functions and grows in a physical world that both supports and challenges her development. For example, in learning to walk, infants must coordinate many physical abilities, including muscle strength, balance, and momentum, with the features of the physical world such as gravity and the properties of the walking

Table 1-2 Some principles of dynamic systems theory

Complexity   Each part of a system is unique but also related to one or more of the system's other parts. For example, a family comprises individual members (mother, brother, niece) and subsystems (a married couple; their daughter and her husband and children), and extended members (cousins, other more distant relatives, and sometime even long-time family friends).

Wholeness and Organization   The whole system is organized and more than just the sum of its parts. For example, to understand a family system's functioning, we must study not only the characteristics of individual family members and the relationships among them but the organization of all family relationships and the whole family as an interacting unit.

Identity and Stabilization   No matter how a system may change, the identity of the system remains intact. For example, the family unit continues even when new members join it and older members die. The system's tendency toward stability is maintained over time by the ongoing interactions among individual members and their relationships with one another. The continuing care parents give their children and the relations among group members help to maintain the family as a system.

Morphogenesis   This principle refers to changes in the system. A system must be able to grow and adapt to internal and external changes. Children go to school, leave home, and marry. Parents raise children, change jobs, and retire. Catastrophic change, such as a divorce, may force a family system to reorganize itself, perhaps by adapting to a step-parent or to single parenthood. The family must also adapt to changes in social values and institutions such as economic cycles and social ills like crime, substance abuse, and discrimination.

Equifinality   This principle holds that most individuals reach essentially the same developmental milestones, even though, in the process, each one experiences varying combinations of genetic and environmental influences.

Sources: Based on Fogel, 1993; Holt, Fogel, & Wood, 1998; Lewis, 2000; Novak, 1996; Sameroff, 1989, 1994; and Thelen, 1995.

surface. Only when the entire system of forces is coordinated and mastered does the child succeed at walking. In other systems theories, the focus is on the child within the nexus of a social system, such as the family or school. Many therapists who adopt a family systems approach contend that they cannot help a child unless the entire family is involved in the therapeutic process. Despite variation in the specifics of different systems theories, all attempt to describe how child development arises from the system as a whole, not from any single factor. A child who has muscle strength but lacks balance will not walk, or a child who needs to learn to co-operate more with others at home cannot succeed without the support of other members of his family.

A recent study by Spencer, Vereijken, Diedrich, and Thelen (Spencer et al., 2000) provides a nice example of the dynamic systems approach in action. In this study, the authors wanted to examine the interrelation between infants' manual skills, such as reaching, and their skill in controlling their body more globally, or their postural abilities. According to these authors, successful reaching actually requires multiple components, or systems, including eye–hand coordination (the ability most typically assumed to be important for reaching), muscular control and postural ability, and aspects of visual development. In terms of dynamic systems theory, ". . . behaviours such as reaching arise from the interaction of multiple, interdependent components under particular task and environmental constraints" (p. 216), with all these components contributing to behaviour at any time, and with one or more elements particularly important in determining the nature and form of this behaviour. In support of this theoretical idea, these authors found that the transition to reaching in a group of infants was systematically preceded by the acquisition of such behaviours as head and body control, the ability to extend the arm towards a target, and the ability to touch and grasp nearby objects. And the transition from reaching to stable reaching (consistent motor actions in how infants reached for toys) was found to be preceded by infants' acquiring the ability to sit independently. Moreover, there were important individual differences among their subjects when these different components were "in place," highlighting the idea that it is the ensemble of components that is important, not the particular order of their development.

Contextual Perspectives

Developmentalists and other psychologists know that children as well as adults function in many different settings—such as the home, school, and workplace—as well as in broader contexts, such as communities and societies. In response to this view, some theorists have concentrated on the role of contextual factors in human development. We consider three theoretical perspectives that illustrate contextual approaches to development: 1) sociocultural theory, 2) Bronfenbrenner's ecological theory, and 3) the lifespan perspective.

SOCIOCULTURAL THEORY **Sociocultural theory** places particular emphasis on the impact of social and cultural experience on child development. This approach traces much of its roots to the writings of Lev S. Vygotsky, a Russian psychologist who worked in the early part of the twentieth century. Vygotsky's theory proposes that the child's development is best understood in relation to social and cultural experience. Social interaction, in particular, is seen as a critical force in development. Through the assistance provided by more experienced people in the social environment, the child gradually learns to function intellectually on her own. Thus, the social world mediates individual cognitive development.

By emphasizing the socially mediated nature of cognitive processes, this approach offers new ways of assessing children's cognitive potential and of teaching reading, mathematics, and writing (Brown & Campione, 1990; Hyson, Copple, & Jones, 2006). A vivid example in the classroom is peer tutoring, in which an older child helps a younger pupil learn to read, write, add, subtract, and so on.

sociocultural theory

A theory of development, proposed by Lev Vygotsky, that sees development as evolving out of children's interactions with more skilled others in their social environment.

Sociocultural theory has also increased our appreciation of the profound importance of cultural variation in development. The ways in which adults support and direct child development are influenced by culture, especially the values and practices that organize what and how adults and children think and work together and use cultural tools to understand the world and solve cognitive problems. These tools are devised by cultures and they take a variety of forms including language, mathematical symbols, literacy, and technology. As children develop, different tools help children to function more effectively in solving problems and understanding the world. Thus, tools of thinking, which are products of culture, become incorporated into the ways in which individuals think about and act in the world. We discuss this theory at greater length in Chapter 8. Throughout this text, many culturally based examples will touch back to this theory.

ecological theory

A theory of development that stresses the importance of understanding not only the relationships between the organism and various environmental systems but also the relations among such systems themselves.

BRONFENBRENNER'S ECOLOGICAL THEORY   **Ecological theory** stresses the importance of understanding not only the relationships between the organism—such as the child—and various environmental systems—such as the family and the community—but the relations among the environmental systems themselves.

Urie Bronfenbrenner (1979; Bronfenbrenner & Morris, 2006), a major advocate of ecological theory, provides a framework that describes the layers or environmental or contextual systems that influence child development. As Figure 1-3 illustrates, these environmental systems range from the most direct or immediate settings in the child's experience, such as the family or peer group, to more remote contexts of the child's life, such as

Figure 1-3

Bronfenbrenner's ecological model of development

Bronfenbrenner emphasizes the importance of the developing child's interactions with the people and institutions closest to her within the microsystem and mesosystem, as well as the effects on her life of a widening array of social and cultural institutions, attitudes, and beliefs within the exosystem and the macrosystem. The fact that all these systems change over time is represented by the chronosystem.

Source: From *Child Development in a Social Context* (C. Kopp and J. Krakow, Eds.). Gararino, J., "Sociocultural risk: Dangers to competence," p. 648. Copyright © 1982 Addison Wesley Publishing Company, Inc. Reprinted by permission of Pearson Education, Inc., Glenview, IL.

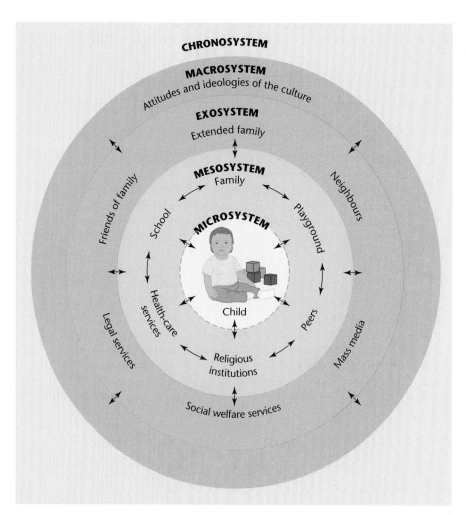

the society's value and legal systems. The **microsystem** is the setting in which the child lives and interacts with the people and institutions closest to him. The **mesosystem** comprises the interrelations among the components of the microsystem. Thus, parents interact with teachers and the school system; both family members and peers may maintain relations with a religious institution; and so forth. The **exosystem** is composed of settings that impinge on a child's development but with which the child has largely indirect contact. For example, a parent's work may affect the child's life if it requires that the parent travel a great deal or work late into the night. The **macrosystem** represents the ideological and institutional patterns of a particular culture or subculture.

Finally, these four systems change over time, a process that Bronfenbrenner refers to as the **chronosystem**. Over time, both the child and her environment undergo change, and change can originate within the individual (e.g., puberty, severe illness) or in the external world (e.g., the birth of a sibling, parental divorce, or even war). For Bronfenbrenner, development involves the interaction of a changing child with the changing ecological context in all of its complexity.

THE LIFESPAN PERSPECTIVE The **lifespan perspective** incorporates historical factors that may influence psychological development (Baltes, Lindenberger, & Staudinger, 2006; Craik & Salthouse, 2000). This phenomenon is generally referred to as an *age cohort effect*; the term **age cohort** means a group of individuals who were born in the same year or during the same general historical period of time. As cohorts develop, they share the same historical experiences. For instance, children born in the United States in the 1950s were teenagers during the turbulent 1960s, and their adolescence occurred against a backdrop of considerable social upheaval.

A striking example of cohort effects has been provided in research by Elder and colleagues (Elder & Shanahan, 2006); they studied children who lived through the Great Depression in the 1930s. Dramatic changes in family roles and relationships occurred in more economically deprived families. Due to the disappearance of fathers' jobs, mothers entered the workforce in larger numbers, resulting in mothers' increasing power in the family. Children's roles changed as well, with girls doing more housework and older boys taking jobs outside the home. Finally, parent–child relationships also changed, with fathers becoming more punitive and less supportive of their children. Moreover, these effects were long-lasting. Boys who had taken jobs as teenagers preferred secure but more modest positions, and girls married men who were lacking in ambition, and raised children who were prone to angry outbursts due to ill-tempered

microsystem

In Bronfenbrenner's ecological theory, the context in which children live and interact with the people and institutions closest to them, such as parents, peers, and school.

mesosystem

The interrelations that occur among the components of the microsystem with which the child interacts.

exosystem

The collection of settings that impinge on a child's development but in which the child does not play a direct role.

macrosystem

The system that surrounds the microsystem, mesosystem, and exosystem, and that represents the values, ideologies, and laws of the society or culture.

chronosystem

The time-based dimension that can alter the operation of all other levels, from microsystem through macrosystem.

lifespan perspective

A theory that sees development as a process that continues throughout the life cycle, from infancy through adulthood and old age.

age cohort

People born within the same generation.

These children, from the early 1940s, are helping to keep their family going in the post-Depression era. Although the Great Depression is often thought to be a tragedy that exclusively afflicted the United States, Canada also suffered a severe economic depression in the 1930s, with similar types of effects on families, and hence, on child development.

Proposing one of the first theories of children's emotional development, Charles Darwin (1809–1882) based much of his theorizing on his infant son's earliest emotional expressions. Although Darwin is more widely known for his theory of organic evolution, his work on children's emotional behaviour continues to have considerable influence on the field of child development.

ethological theory

A theory that holds that behaviour must be viewed and understood as occurring in a particular context and as having adaptive or survival value.

evolutionary psychology

An approach which holds that critical components of psychological functioning reflect evolutionary changes and are critical to the survival of the species.

parents (Elder & Shanahan, 2006). Thus, economic hardship left its imprint on three generations of these families, demonstrating the important influence of historical context on the developing child.

Ethological and Evolutionary Approaches

The final type of approach to studying development has come from the fields of ethology and evolutionary psychology. Since Charles Darwin introduced evolutionary theory, other scientists have sought to understand both the evolution of behaviour and its adaptive, or survival, value to the species exhibiting it (Bjorklund & Pelligrini, 2002; Hinde, 1994). Central to this line of thought is the necessity to view and understand behaviour in relation to the biology of the organism and the ecosystem in which the organism functions. For example, in attempting to understand children's cognitive skills and behaviour, it is important to understand the child's biological nature and needs and the nature of the setting in which behaviour takes place, such as a classroom, playground, or library.

ETHOLOGICAL THEORY **Ethological theory**, which was developed by biologists, contends that behaviour must be viewed and understood as occurring in a particular context and as having adaptive or survival value. This view has generated interest in the behaviours in human infants and children that are "species-specific" (unique to the human species) and that may play an important role in ensuring that others meet children's basic needs, which are critical to survival. Studies have found, for example, that emotional expressions of joy, sadness, disgust, and anger are similar across a wide range of cultures (Ekman et al., 1987; La Freniere, 2000).

Ethologists' basic method of study is the observation of children in their natural surroundings, and their goals are to develop detailed descriptions and classifications of behaviour. For developmental psychologists, ethological theory is useful for understanding that many behaviours seen across a range of cultures, such as smiling and crying, may have a biological basis and play an important role in ensuring that caregivers meet children's needs. For example, crying can be viewed as an "elicitor" of parental behaviour; it serves to communicate that a child is distressed or hungry. It, thus, has clear survival value, for it ensures that parents give the young infant the kind of attention she needs for adequate development.

Although human ethologists view many elicitors, such as crying, as biologically based, they also assume that these types of behaviours are modified by environmentally based experiences. For example, children may learn to mask their emotions by smiling even when they are unhappy (La Freniere, 2000; McDowell, O'Neil, & Parke, 2000; Saarni, Campos, & Camras, 2006). Thus modern ethologists view children as open to learning and using input from the environment; they are not solely captives of their biological roots. One of the areas of developmental psychology that has been greatly influenced by ethology is the study of early relationships. In particular, John Bowlby's research on infant–mother attachment, discussed in Chapter 6, stems directly from the perspective offered by ethological theory. And, as we will see in Chapter 12, ethologists have also made important contributions to our understanding of how children's groups are organized.

EVOLUTIONARY DEVELOPMENTAL PSYCHOLOGY **Evolutionary psychology** has influenced the study of child development in a somewhat different way from that of ethology. Although ethologists and evolutionary psychologists share many of the same basic assumptions about the origins and social organization of behaviour, evolutionary psychologists have had a major impact on the study of cognition and cognitive development. This perspective holds that the critical components of human evolutionary change are in the areas of brain changes and cognitive functioning (Cosmides & Tooby, 1987). This approach is influential in child development in that it directs attention to the types of capabilities and constraints of the cognitive system that enable humans to understand and act in the world in the ways that support their survival. In developmental terms, the main questions stemming from this view hover around when and how these cognitive capabilities emerge (Bjorklund & Pelligrini, 2002).

Although the focus in evolutionary perspectives is largely on cognitive processes and their development, these processes are seen as instrumental to human functioning more broadly (Bugental & Grusec, 2006). Different contexts of development present humans with different problems to solve. For example, a child who lives on a remote island has many different types of experiences and problems to solve in his everyday activities compared to a child who lives in an urban, industrial centre. One feature of human cognition, which is a product of evolution, is the adaptation of our intelligence to the types of problems that are important to solve in the environment we inhabit. Also of interest are the capabilities that human children develop that enable them to learn from their interactions with other people. For instance, Tomasello (1999) considers the development of the ability to understand others' intentions to be a central feature of human cognitive functions. Through understanding that other people have mental states and intentions behind actions, children are able to learn meaningful, goal-directed behaviours by watching and interacting with others. Therefore, the behaviours children observe and learn are not just mindlessly imitated—they contain the meaning or intention of the human action.

THEMES AND THEORIES: A FINAL COMMENT

LO 4

As we will stress throughout this book, the understanding of children's development can be approached from many perspectives. Table 1-3 on the next page summarizes the theories we have discussed in relation to the themes of development, specifically their views on the biological versus environmental influences on development, the continuous versus discontinuous nature of developmental change, and their emphasis on individual versus contextual characteristics. You can see from even the brief descriptions that these theories have some differing positions vis-à-vis the three themes. Although the presence of many different theories adds a layer of complexity to studying child development, many questions about development benefit from these different theoretical perspectives. Different theories can often point to different aspects of a developmental process. Also, it is increasingly clear that different aspects of development, such as language and emotional and social behaviour, are interlinked. For example, children's learning takes place in social contexts and the experiences and relationships children have with other people will affect what and how they learn from them. To understand such complex processes, several theoretical points of view are needed. In addition, interest in explaining complex processes of development leads to a greater acceptance of systems and contextual approaches to development. Ethological and evolutionary approaches add species-specific capabilities and needs to these views. Many developmental psychologists today draw on some of the assumptions of these approaches. In addition, it seems that several theories can tell us a great deal more about the causes and course of children's development than any single one alone can. Now, we turn to research methods, that is, how developmental psychologists test the ideas that stem from these various theories of child development. Although the theoretical perspectives we have discussed are not wedded to particular methods, theories do tend to favour some methods over others. We will point out these theory–method links in our discussion.

Table 1-3 Overview of developmental themes and theoretical perspectives

Perspectives	THEMES		
	Biology vs. Environment	Continuity vs. Discontinuity	Individual Characteristics vs. Contextual and Cultural Characteristics
Structural-Organismic Perspectives			
Freudian theory	Interaction between biology and environment	Discontinuity (stages of development)	High on individual traits
Erikson's theory	Interaction between biology and environment	Discontinuity (stages of development)	High on individual traits
Piagetian theory	Interaction between biology and environment	Discontinuity (stages of development)	High on individual traits
Learning Perspectives			
Behaviourism	Environment	Continuity (no stages)	High on situational influences
Cognitive social learning theory	Environment	Continuity (no stages)	High on situational influences
Information-processing approaches	Focus on environment but recognition of biology	Continuity (no stages)	High on situational influences although individual characteristics important
Dynamic Systems Perspectives			
	Interactions among all systems—biological, psychosocial, environmental	Continuity (no stages)	High on situational influences
Contextual Perspectives			
Vygotsky's sociocultural theory	Interaction between biology and environment	Discontinuous for some aspects of development	Situation and context are important
Bronfenbrenner's ecological theory	Focus on environment but recognition of biology	Continuity (no stages)	High on situational influences
Ethological and evolutionary approaches	Emphasis on biology, but environment plays role in eliciting and modifying behaviour patterns	Varies among individual theories (e.g., depends upon theory's view of critical periods)	High on situational influences
Historical and lifespan	Focus on environment but recognition of biology perspectives	Continuity (no stages)	High on situational influences

1. Often, theoretical perspectives are characterized as endorsing or assuming a particular expression of a given theme (e.g., the socio-cultural approach assumes the importance of culture). Is it the case that these theories will (a) be committed to a particular theme (e.g., the child is always active in the socio-cultural approach) and (b) always have an opinion or position regarding all themes?

2. Do all these theories generate testable hypotheses? What might be some of the criteria for determining the "correctness," or validity, of a theory? Just because a theory is elegant, does that make it true?

3. What advantages and disadvantages are there to subscribing to one particular theory, as opposed to being eclectic and borrowing parts of different theories that you feel "work?" In fact, if no one theory is always correct, why does one want a theory at all?

Making the Connections 1.1

There are many links between concepts and ideas in one area of development and concepts and ideas in other areas. Here are some of the connections between ideas in Chapter 1's discussion of developmental themes and theories and discussions in other chapters of this book.

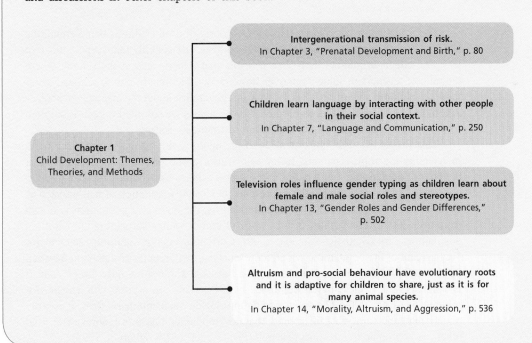

Chapter 1
Child Development: Themes, Theories, and Methods

Intergenerational transmission of risk.
In Chapter 3, "Prenatal Development and Birth," p. 80

Children learn language by interacting with other people in their social context.
In Chapter 7, "Language and Communication," p. 250

Television roles influence gender typing as children learn about female and male social roles and stereotypes.
In Chapter 13, "Gender Roles and Gender Differences," p. 502

Altruism and pro-social behaviour have evolutionary roots and it is adaptive for children to share, just as it is for many animal species.
In Chapter 14, "Morality, Altruism, and Aggression," p. 536

RESEARCH METHODS IN CHILD PSYCHOLOGY

Like other scientists, child psychologists use the **scientific method** in their research; that is, they formulate hypotheses on the basis of a theory and use measurable and replicable techniques to collect, study, and analyze data in an effort to test the theory's usefulness.

scientific method

The use of measurable and replicable techniques in framing hypotheses and collecting and analyzing data to test a theory's usefulness.

The main issues in a scientific approach to psychological development include selecting a sample, designing a study that taps development in some way, and ensuring that all ethical protections are in place.

Selecting a Sample

If you wanted to study the typical play activities of grade 1 children, how would you go about collecting your data? How many children do you suppose there are at a given time in Canada? Rather a lot. You couldn't possibly study all of them, but you could select a **sample**, or a group of manageable size made up of individuals who, you hope, are representative of the entire population of preschoolers that you want to describe.

REPRESENTATIVENESS OF A SAMPLE   If we want our research conclusions to be applicable to the population our sample is designed to reflect, we must ensure the **representativeness** of that sample. That is, the persons we choose to study must possess nearly the same characteristics evidenced by the larger population in which we are interested. Also, depending on that population, we may need a very broad sample in which many cultures, social classes, or ethnic backgrounds are represented. Consider the following example:

> A researcher wants to study the way children's vocabularies change over time. Living near a private nursery school in an affluent suburban community, she selects thirty 3-year-olds and thirty 5-year-olds from the school population and tests their vocabulary levels. Based on the performance of these children the investigator reports that she has a set of norms or guidelines for what may be expected of preschoolers' vocabulary knowledge. What's wrong with the researcher's conclusion?

The investigator has chosen her sample poorly, for, other things being equal, the children of affluent professionals are likely to have verbal skills that surpass those of less well-educated parents. It is also possible that experiences at the school, where the ratio of teachers to students may be more favourable than in public schools, better facilitate children's learning. Clearly, we can't generalize about the average vocabulary accomplishment of all children of ages 3 and 5 unless we sample a range of children from different backgrounds and in different instructional settings.

This simple example illustrates one of the major problems that a researcher faces in selecting a sample—namely, to try to recruit a group of people representative of the larger population about which the researcher wishes to hypothesize. Of particular concern is obtaining a sample that represents the diverse population of nations such as Canada. According to the 2006 Canadian Census, the country's population is drawn from over 200 different ethnic groups, with 11 ethnic origins surpassing the 1 million population mark (Statistics Canada, 2008). Currently, visible minorities account for 16.2 percent of the population, which represents a growth rate of 27.2 percent between 2001 and 2006; for comparison, the population as a whole grew only 5.4 percent. It is estimated that if these trends continue, by 2017, visible minorities will account for roughly one-fifth of the Canadian population. Given such numbers, then, it is truly remarkable, and somewhat disturbing, that developmental research ignores these (and other) demographic trends in its research (Fisher, Jackson, & Villaruel, 1998).

ANOTHER APPROACH: THE NATIONAL SURVEY   In an innovative approach to sampling called the **national survey**, researchers interested in a particular issue or issues select a very large, nationally representative group of people. For example, in Canada, the National Longitudinal Survey of Children and Youth (NLSCY), begun in 1994, was launched to monitor children from birth to 25 years of age, collecting data for analysis of biological, social, and economic factors affecting children. In the NLSCY's first round of data collection, almost 23,000 children were surveyed,

---

sample

A group of individuals who are representative of a larger population.

representativeness

The degree to which a sample actually possesses the characteristics of the larger population it represents.

national survey

A method of sampling, in which a very large, nationally representative group of people are selected for a particular study.

with participants drawn from different subpopulations across Canada. A similar project in the United States, the National Longitudinal Survey of Youth (NLSY), was begun in 1979 with a sample of young men and women who then ranged in age from 14 to 24.

Source: PEANUTS reprinted by permission of United Feature Syndicate, Inc.

Both projects have been used to investigate a range of topics (e.g., Brooks-Gunn, Smith, Berlin, & Lee, 2001; Ho, Bluestein, & Jenkins, 2008). For example, data from the NLSCY has been used to examine developmental trajectories in the smoking behaviour of Canadian youth from childhood to adolescence (Maggi, Hertzman, & Vaillancourt, 2007; Maggi, 2008). This work has uncovered at least five separate developmental pathways of smoking behaviour in young children, two of which ultimately lead to daily smoking by 16 to 17 years of age.

Although the NLSCY, NLSY, and other similar large-scale studies can reveal overarching patterns in people's behaviour and relationships among particular factors, these studies are less suited to answering specific questions about the processes that may account for particular aspects of development. For this reason, a national survey is sometimes used in combination with a more intensive look at a smaller sample of people.

Canadian National Surveys

Methods of Gathering Data About Children

Once researchers have decided what group or groups they want to study, they must decide how they will study these youngsters. Essentially, there are three methods of gathering such data: We can ask children about themselves; we can ask people who are close to these children about them; or we can observe the children directly. Each approach has its advantages and limitations, and the researchers' choices depend on the kinds of questions they want to answer.

CHILDREN'S SELF-REPORTS   A **self-report** is information that a person provides about himself, typically by answering a set of questions devised by a researcher. Soliciting such information from a child, as you may imagine, presents special problems. Compared with adults, children—especially younger ones—are apt to be less attentive, slower to respond, and will likely also have more trouble understanding the questions that researchers ask. Despite these limitations on children's self-reports, some kinds of information, such as how a child feels about an experience or another person, are difficult to obtain in any other way (Cummings et al., 2000).

self-report

Information that people provide about themselves, either in a direct interview or in some written form, such as a questionnaire.

REPORTS BY FAMILY MEMBERS, TEACHERS, AND PEERS
A second way of collecting data on child development is to solicit information from people who know a child or children well. Most commonly, child-development researchers seek this information from family members, teachers, and peers.

A strength of interviews with parents and other family members is that these reports are generally based on many observations made over time in a variety of situations. Another advantage of reports by family members is that even if parents and siblings are not totally accurate in their reporting, their perceptions, expectations, beliefs, and interpretations of events and behaviour may be just as important as what we can only assume is objective reality (Bugental & Grusec, 2006; Collins & Repinski, 2001). For example, whether or not a child's parents explicitly insist on exceptionally good academic performance, a child's belief that her parents want her to do very well in school may greatly influence her behaviour. There are some clear disadvantages in soliciting parental and other family reports about a child's growth and development. Human memory is not completely reliable. Also, because people are motivated to remember themselves in the best light possible, parents often remember themselves as more consistent, patient, and even-tempered with their children than more objective assessments might have revealed them to be.

In an effort to increase the accuracy of parents' reports about their children, investigators have devised a number of new interview strategies. For example, they may have parents report only very recent events so as to ensure more reliable memories; or they may phone parents every evening and ask which of a list of specific behaviours (such as crying or refusing to comply) their children have exhibited in the past 24 hours (Patterson, 1996; Patterson & Bank, 1989); or they may ask parents to keep a structured diary in which they record the child's behaviours at regular intervals (e.g., every hour; Hetherington, 1991a). Child development researchers have even asked parents to carry pagers, which experimenters then beep randomly, asking the parents to record their activities or feelings or those of their children (Larson & Richards, 1994). This approach allows for a random sampling not only of behaviours but also of the situations in which these behaviours occur.

To learn about a child's behaviour in school and other settings when parents are not present, researchers can ask other people, such as teachers and peers. Investigators may ask teachers to rate children on a specific series of dimensions such as attentiveness, dependability, and sociability, in the classroom or on the playground. One technique researchers often use is to ask children, such as classmates, to rate how well a particular child's peers accept him. For example, investigators might ask all the youngsters in a classroom to rate each of their peers in terms of "how much I like to play with" a particular classmate. The researchers then combine all the ratings to yield a picture of each child's social status in the classroom (Ladd, 2005; Rubin, Bukowski, & Parker, 1998).

Although children's self-reports, parental reports, and reports by others have their limitations, researchers have found that these reports offer them the best understanding of many issues. In addition, as we will see next, these kinds of reports are often used in conjunction with other data-gathering strategies.

DIRECT OBSERVATION   There is often no substitute for researchers' own **direct observation** of people, and students of child development may make such observations in naturalistic settings, such as participants' own homes, or in laboratories where they give children and sometimes parents a structured task to perform. Observational data are valuable resources in examining human behaviour. However, such data are valid only to the extent that the presence of an observer or other demands of the situation do not distort the participants' behaviour and responses.

These distorting factors are sometimes hard to avoid because children and parents often behave differently in various kinds of settings or when they know they are being watched. Both adults and children tend to express less negative emotion and to exhibit more socially desirable behaviour when observations are conducted in unfamiliar settings, such as a laboratory, compared with at home (Lamb, Suomi, & Stephenson, 1979). Even in home observations, customary behaviour can be distorted by the presence of an outside observer. Parents, for instance, tend to inhibit negative behaviour when they

direct observation

A method of observation in which researchers go into settings in the natural world or bring participants into the laboratory to observe behaviours of interest.

Research with very young children, like this 6-month-old infant, is becoming increasingly common as psychologists seek to expand our knowledge about early development. A video or digital recording will permit closer study of this child's behaviour after the observation session is over.

are being watched (Russell, Russell, & Midwinter, 1992). Attempts to minimize such distortions in studies in people's homes include the use of less obtrusive observational methods, such as camera or sound recordings without the observer present, and by conducting many regular visits from an observer—for example, an observer being at a family's home each dinner hour over a period of several weeks (Feiring & Lewis, 1987). As surprising as it may seem, people can get used to such observational techniques; as observations proceed, one sees gradual increases in less socially accepted behaviours, such as quarreling, criticizing, and punishing (Boyum & Parke, 1995).

Debra Pepler of York University and Wendy Craig of Queen's University (Craig, Pepler, & Atlas, 2000; Hawkins, Pepler, & Craig, 2001; Smith, Pepler, & Craig, 2004) provide an interesting example of naturalistic observation methods in their work on aggression and peer interaction. To overcome some of the problems inherent in observing children in the laboratory, these researchers employed remote audiovisual observations of children on the playground in which the researcher sets up a video camera away from the children who were being observed and attached a wireless microphone to a previously selected target child. With this set-up, the researcher is able to remain remote from the target child while still recording the child's behaviour at close range.

When researchers observe children and their families directly, they must decide what kinds of behaviours to record (Bakeman & Gottman, 1997), such as how detailed the observations will be or how frequently they will be recorded. When a child development specialist is interested in a specific behaviour, she may arrange a situation to observe the behaviour using a method called **structured observation**. Suppose a researcher is interested in the way mothers instruct their children about how to solve problems. The researcher may invite mothers and children to the laboratory to participate in a joint problem-solving session, perhaps one that involves putting together different types of puzzles, and observe how their interaction changes as the child attains skill and understanding of the task.

The strengths of using such a set-up are obvious—these authors are able to observe interactions that typically occur outside the researcher's view, and because children are completely free to move around when and where they wish, the method has a great deal of **external validity**, which means that the results can be easily generalized outside the immediate context of the study. On the other hand, there are ethical issues to consider with the use of such a method (we discuss ethics in research at the end of this chapter), as well as several limitations inherent in this methodology, including a lack of experimental control over the subjects, the inability to observe different children over time (which has implications for the issue of time sampling, discussed below), and the

structured observation

A form of observation, in which researchers structure a situation so that behaviours they wish to study are more likely to occur.

external validity

The degree to which the results of an experiment can be easily generalized outside the immediate context of the study.

possibility that children will actually be somewhat conscious of the fact that they are wearing such equipment. In fact, Pepler and Craig found that the oldest children in their study, about 11 to 12 years old, seemed aware of the equipment, with some a bit reticent about being observed in this fashion. Nevertheless, this study, and the technique in general, provides an excellent example of the strengths and the weaknesses of direct observational techniques.

Research with very young infants has become increasingly possible through the use of a number of very clever and imaginative techniques. In these photos from Darwin Muir's laboratory, you see an example of a technique that has been used to investigate the social and emotional development of infants. In this "still-face" procedure, infants see a video image of another person's face, with the face either being highly interactive with the infant, or showing no responsiveness to the infant. By assessing the infants' reactions to these variations, researchers have been able to explore the nature of infants' interpersonal interactions with a range of people, including parents, siblings, and strangers.

converging operations

A research strategy in which a variety of research techniques are used to investigate or converge upon a particular experimental or research result.

The potential usefulness of child self-reports, reports by others, and observational methods to provide insights into many aspects of child development is great. However, because of the limitations inherent in all these methods of gathering data, many investigators use several methods in the same study; for example, they combine observations with parent surveys or interviews. If the findings of a variety of methods converge, researchers can reasonably conclude that the findings are valid. The idea behind this approach is that of **converging operations** (Proffitt & Bertenthal, 1990), or the idea that if a variety of assessment techniques produce the same result, researchers can reasonably conclude that the findings are valid.

For Thought and Discussion

1. A researcher is interested in conducting a study on the impact of socio-economic factors on parent–child interaction. To recruit subjects for this study, she obtains a list of families in three different suburbs of a large metropolitan city and randomly selects people from these lists. What potential problems are inherent in this procedure with respect to sampling issues? What might this researcher do to try and overcome some of these problems?

2. What are the advantages of direct observation relative to (self- or parental) report measures? If you could choose between the two methods, what factors would lead you to select one over the other?

3. What sense might you make of a study in which parental self-report techniques and direct observational techniques produce different results? What implications does such a finding have for the idea of converging operations?

Research Design: Establishing Patterns and Causes   **LO** 6

Selecting a sample and a method of gathering information enables us to describe some aspect of human development, but what will this information do for us? To make use of it, we need to design a study to determine how the various factors of development that we have described are related to, and interact with, each other, with the goal of identifying the reasons why development occurs as it does. In this section, we offer a brief discussion of the most common research designs—the correlational method, the experimental method, and the case study—that are used by psychologists to study the nature and process of child development. In describing these methods, we have chosen illustrations that pertain to a single topic: the effect on children's development of television viewing. Our aim is to show how different designs yield different approaches and answers to this question.

THE CORRELATIONAL METHOD   Many questions in child development reflect an interest in whether some experiences of childhood are related to other experiences of childhood in a regular or systematic way. For example, how do educational television programs such as *Sesame Street* relate to better performance when children enter school? To illustrate the **correlational method** of research, a design that enables researchers to establish that certain experiences or factors are related to each other and to assess the strength of the relations, let's examine a study that addressed this question. John Wright and Aletha Huston (1995) studied the television-viewing behaviour of preschool children in more than 250 families, all from low-income areas. The children were either 2 or 4 years old at the start of the study, and either 5 or 7 at its conclusion. The parents were asked to make detailed reports on how their preschoolers spent their time, including which TV shows they watched and for how long each day. Every year, the children were given a variety of cognitive achievement tests, such as measures of mathematical skill and word knowledge. The researchers found that the more educational programs the children watched, the higher they scored on the tests (see Figure 1-4).

   Thus, these factors were positively correlated with each other in that scores for both measures increased. Children who viewed more educational TV shows did better on the academic tests. However, the researchers also found that the more time children spent watching cartoons or adult programs, the lower they scored on these tests, which is a negative correlation; that is, as one score increased the other score decreased.

correlational method

A research design that permits investigators to establish relations among variables as well as the strength of those relations.

Test score gains

Rarely | 2 to 3 times per week | 4 to 5 times per week | More than 5 times per week

Frequency with which children watched *Sesame Street*

Figure 1-4

Watching *Sesame Street* makes test scores rise

In one of the first studies of the effects on children from watching *Sesame Street*, researchers found that on such tests as identification of body parts, recognition of letters, numbers, and geometric forms, and classifying and sorting, preschoolers who watched the show frequently performed significantly better than those who watched little.

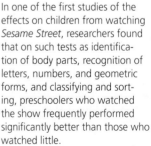

To make things even more complicated, however, research on the educational impact of media materials made explicitly for infants, such as the Baby Einstein videos, or television shows such as *Blue's Clues* and *Barney & Friends*, have recently found that such materials actually have a negative impact on children's development (Zimmerman, Christakis, & Meltzoff, 2007). Using questionnaire data, Zimmerman et al. (2007) related 8- to 16-month-old infants' language development with the number of hours they spent each day watching infant videos. The results of this analysis revealed that the number of hours spent watching such material was actually negatively related to language development. Additionally, these researchers also found no relation between such watching such programs and language for older toddlers between 17 and 24 months, a pattern that also contradicts the earlier positive correlations found between educational television and academic performance.

Although it is difficult to fully interpret these shifting patterns of results, the critical point to remember is that in correlational research, a correlation does not indicate causal relations between factors—it simply tells us that two factors are related to each other and indicates the strength or magnitude of that relation. Thus, the correlations found by Wright and Huston do not indicate that watching educational programs caused higher test scores. Any number of factors other than watching educational shows could have improved the children's test scores. For example, suppose that children whose parents give them a great deal of encouragement and guidance in academic subjects are the same ones who watch the educational programs.

If correlational research does not allow us to determine causation, why do we use it? For one thing, many questions are difficult to study in a controlled laboratory design. For example, the effect of viewing educational programs on cognitive development is cumulative, meaning it happens over a long period of time. An experiment would be difficult to design to study such long-term exposure. Also, understanding causal processes is not the goal of all developmental research. Many investigators are primarily interested in describing the patterns and paths of development as they naturally occur, which are what the correlational method describes.

EXPERIMENTAL DESIGNS   The primary way researchers investigate causal connections among factors is by experiment. An experiment can be carried out in a laboratory, in the field, or in natural situations. In a **laboratory experiment**, researchers are able to control factors that may influence the variable they are interested in, and, therefore, their results allow them to draw conclusions about cause and effect. Researchers will control or hold constant—or equate—every possible influence except the one factor they have hypothesized to be the cause of the variable they want to study. They then create two groups of participants. One group, called the **experimental group**, is exposed to the proposed causative factor; the second group, the **control group**, does not experience this factor. Researchers put people in these two groups by using **random assignment**, which will rule out the possibility that the people in each of the groups differ from one another in some systematic way that could distort the results of the experiment (more skilled people in the experimental group, for instance). Thus, the principal advantage of experimental studies is that they allow one to make stronger causal statements than correlational studies because we can rule our many possible confounding variables (although, admittedly, one can never rule out *all* possible confounds).

To understand how these various controls enable the laboratory experimenter to determine causality, let's look at a classic study of the relation between watching violent television programs and aggressive behaviour. Liebert and Baron (1972) randomly assigned 136 boys and girls ranging in age from 5 to 9 to either an experimental group or a control group. The children in both groups first saw two brief commercials selected for their humour and attention-getting value. Then, half the children—those in the experimental group—saw three and a half minutes of a TV program about crime that contained a chase, two fistfights, two shootings, and a knifing. In contrast, the children in the control group

laboratory experiment

A research design that allows investigators, through controlling variables and treatments and assigning participants randomly to treatments, to determine cause and effect.

experimental group

In a formal experiment, the group that is exposed to the treatment, that is, the independent variable.

control group

In a formal experiment, the group that is not exposed to the treatment, that is, the independent variable.

random assignment

The technique by which researchers assign individuals randomly to either an experimental or a control group.

watched a highly active but non-violent sports sequence of the same time length. Finally, the children in both groups watched another 60 seconds of a tire commercial. The only difference between the two groups was the three-and-a-half-minute video they watched; that is, exposure or no exposure to violent TV episodes. This is the **independent variable**, or the factor the researchers deliberately manipulate. The researchers thus hypothesized that if the children in the experimental group later behaved differently from those in the control group, it would be reasonable to conclude that exposure to TV violence was the cause.

In the second phase of the study, the experimenters told each of the children that they were to play a game with another child in an adjoining room (whom they could not see and who, in fact, was purely imaginary). The researchers seated each child before a panel that had two buttons labelled "Hurt" and "Help" and told the child that the buttons were connected to a handle in the other room that their "play partner" would use. The experimenter explained that if the child wanted to make it easier for her play partner to turn the handle she could press the "Help" button; but if the child wanted to hinder her play partner, she could press the "Hurt" button, which would turn the handle burning hot. Of course, this entire scenario was a deception, and nothing a child did hurt anyone else. (The issue of deception raises ethical questions that we discuss shortly.) The amount of aggressiveness the children display is the **dependent variable**, or the factor that researchers expect to change due to the independent variable. The researchers believed that by measuring how long and how often children depressed the "Hurt" button, they could find out how aggressively children in the experimental and the control groups would behave toward another child. Liebert and Baron discovered the causal relation they predicted. Children who had seen the violent TV segment were more willing to harm or behave aggressively toward their play partner than were children who had watched the non-violent sports program.

Although this study was carefully designed, it has limitations that may prevent generalization from the experimental situation to the natural world. Ensuring a study's **ecological validity**, or its accurate representation of events and processes that occur in the natural environment, is often difficult (Lewkowicz, 2001; Schmuckler, 2001). For example, Liebert and Baron edited their violent TV program to include more acts of violence in three and a half minutes than would normally occur in a randomly chosen TV segment of the same length, even in a show that has a lot of violence. Despite these limitations, experimenters can gain important insights about human behaviour from laboratory experiments. For instance, finding out what are the softest ranges of sound a child can hear requires controlling all outside noise, which is rare if not impossible in everyday experience. When scientists want to use an experiment yet study behaviour in a more ecologically valid way, they conduct experiments in the field.

In a **field experiment**, investigators deliberately introduce a change, called a manipulation, in a person's normal environment and then measure the outcome of their manipulation. To illustrate, let's consider a field experiment about the impact of viewing TV violence on aggressive behaviour in children (Friedrich & Stein, 1973). Preschoolers enrolled in a summer program were the participants in this study. During the first three weeks of the study, the researchers observed the children during their usual play sessions to determine how much aggressive behaviour each child displayed under normal circumstances. This is called a *baseline measure*. Then, for the next four weeks, they showed the children, who were randomly assigned to one of three groups, a half-hour TV program each day. Some children always saw programs depicting interpersonal aggression, such as Batman and Superman cartoons; others saw programs with a message of caring and kindness toward others, such as *Mister Rogers' Neighborhood*; and others watched neutral shows, such as nature programs.

The researchers found that children who had been rated high in aggressive behaviour before the TV-watching manipulation behaved even more aggressively after repeated exposure to aggressive cartoons, but not after exposure to the other two kinds of shows. For children who were rated low in aggression during the initial assessment period, watching

independent variable

The variable, or factor, that researchers deliberately manipulate in a formal experiment.

dependent variable

The variable, or factor, that researchers expect to change as a function of change in the independent variable.

ecological validity

The degree to which a research study accurately represents events and processes that occur in the natural world.

 7

field experiment

An experiment in which researchers deliberately create a change in a real-world setting and then measure the outcome of their manipulation.

aggressive TV shows had no effect; they were still less likely to behave aggressively. Children who watched neutral shows did not change either. The researchers concluded that exposure to TV violence can increase aggression in children, but only among children already likely to behave aggressively. These findings were especially interesting in that the researchers took care to minimize **observer bias**, that is, the tendency of observers who are knowledgeable about a hypothesis to be influenced in their observations by that knowledge. The observers who assessed the children's behaviour after the TV viewings did not know which types of programs the different children had seen.

One advantage of the field experiment over the laboratory experiment is that the results can be generalized more readily to real-life experiences. Friedrich and Stein did not edit the TV programs the children saw in any way, and these programs were among those that many of the children watched in their homes. Moreover, the children's aggressive behaviour was measured in an everyday setting, not in a situation that allowed or encouraged them to behave aggressively. At the same time, the field experiment retains some important features of a laboratory experiment. Because the independent variable—the type of TV program—was under the control of the researchers, and the participants were randomly assigned to the various groups, Friedrich and Stein could be reasonably confident that they had demonstrated a causal connection—namely, that exposure to TV violence may encourage aggressive children to behave even more aggressively.

There is yet another type of experiment that developmental psychologists use that is discussed in this text. For ethical or practical reasons, researchers may not be able to introduce changes into the natural world. In these instances, they may conduct a **natural experiment**, in which they measure the effects of events or changes that occur naturally in the real world. Unlike a laboratory or field experiment, the research participants are not randomly assigned to experimental conditions. Instead, the researchers select the children they study because the children are already exposed to a set of conditions that are of interest to the researcher, such as enrolment in daycare or a nutritional-supplement program.

One example of a natural experiment is a study conducted by researchers at the University of British Columbia that investigated the way the introduction of television into a community affected aggressive behaviour among children (MacBeth, 1996). By monitoring the level of aggressiveness in children's play both before and after the debut of television in a small Canadian town, the investigator was able to show that aggressive behaviour did, in fact, increase after TV arrived in the community. As our example suggests, a great deal of research has been devoted to children's television viewing and, more recently, Internet use. In Box 1.1, we discuss this research and its impact on legislation.

THE CASE STUDY APPROACH   Can we learn anything about development by studying a single child or perhaps a single group, such as a particular classroom? The study of individual persons or a group, called the **case study method** is sometimes used in developmental research. The case study allows investigators to explore phenomena that they do not often encounter, such as an unusual talent, a rare developmental disorder, or a model classroom. In the nineteenth century, in one of the first recorded case studies, Charles Darwin (1872) kept a highly detailed diary of his infant son's emotional expressions, a record that became the basis for his theory of emotional development in infants and children.

Sometimes, a case study provides insights or hypotheses that later investigations pursue in a more systematic fashion. For example, careful observation of one child who experiences a new treatment for child conduct problems may shed light on how the treatment works for children with certain behavioural patterns. However, the chief limitation of the single-case approach is that without further study or a larger sample, it is difficult to know if the results of the case study generalize from one individual to other people or situations.

observer bias

The tendency of researchers/observers to be influenced in their judgments by their knowledge of the hypotheses guiding the research.

natural experiment

An experiment in which researchers measure the results of events that occur naturally in the real world.

case study method

A form of research in which investigators study individual persons.

Box 1.1

Child Psychology in Action

HOW CAN WE MAKE BETTER USE OF RESEARCH ON CHILDREN'S TELEVISION AND INTERNET USE?

The impact on children of the amazing growth of communications media in the twentieth and twenty-first centuries cannot be denied. From early radio, movies, and comic books to television and its electronic cousins—DVDs, video games, CD-ROMs, and the Internet—children have been bombarded with new information and experiences via the media.

What has the wealth of research on children and television revealed? It has shown that some television programs do help young children learn, but it has also shown a negative effect on children who watch programs filled with violence and sex, as well as commercials that prey on the young child's limited understanding (Comstock & Scharrer, 2006). Research on children's and adolescents' use of the Internet has also revealed some positive effects, such as improved reading scores (Jackson et al., 2006), and some negative effects, such as increasing adolescents' awareness of dangerous behaviours (e.g., various forms of self-injury) (Whitlock, Powers, & Eckenrode, 2006).

Given such possible influences, are there existing regulations that protect children from negative programming or that require the media to provide educational and informational programming?

The Canadian Radio-television and Telecommunications Commission (CRTC), responding to public concerns following Montréal's 1989 l'École Polytechnique mass shootings, commissioned two studies on the issue of violence in television. On the basis of a report by Florian Sauvageau of the Institut Québécois de Recherche sur la Culture and Laval University (Atkinson, Gourdeau, & Sauvageau, 1991) and an internal CRTC report (Martinez, 1992), the commission decided that there was a link, although not necessarily causal, between television violence and violence in society.

Coincidentally, at about the same time, 13-year-old Virginie LaRivière presented a petition to the federal government containing over 1.5 million signatures calling for a ban on television violence.

What was Canada's response to these concerns? One striking feature of the Canadian approach has been its insistence on minimizing direct governmental regulation, trying to balance the rights of free speech with a concern for children's mental health, without passing laws. In attempting to achieve this aim, the CRTC, in 1993, adopted five guidelines on media violence and has put its efforts into three areas—implementing strong, self-regulatory industry codes, changing public attitudes through public awareness and media literacy programs, and providing parents with the tools to make informed programming choices for their families (CRTC, 1996).

The primary tool involved in giving parents more control over their children's television viewing is the "v-chip" technology, developed at Simon Fraser University's School of Engineering. When installed in a TV set, and combined with a national classification system for all television programming, the v-chip allows parents to block programs that have ratings indicating a high violence level or offensive language. Thus, parents can determine what they think is appropriate viewing for their family. Research has shown that parents can also help their children understand the content and utility of such information sources, as well as help them cope with fears aroused by specific content (Wilson & Weiss, 1993). Clearly, media exposure is a family affair, and families as well as the government and those who produce content for media outlets need to share responsibility for this increasingly important aspect of children's lives.

Canadian Media Resources

COMBINATION DESIGNS IN DEVELOPMENTAL RESEARCH The research method that a developmental scientist uses depends on the question being asked and the ages of the children studied. Table 1-4 on the next page summarizes the differences among the research designs we've examined so far. Researchers may also

Table 1-4   Research designs: Advantages and limitations

Design	Control over Independent Variable	Control over Dependent Variable	Generalizability of Findings
Correlational method	Low	Low	Medium
Laboratory experiment	High	High	Low
Field experiment	Medium	Low	High
Natural experiment	Low	Low	High

combine designs over a series of studies on the same topic. For example, a researcher may start off in an unexplored area by using a correlational approach to establish some possible relations among the factors studied. Then she may use an experimental approach to achieve a clearer view of the causal links among these factors. Finally, she may examine closely a single-case study, either of an individual or a group, to provide more details about the process under study. In the field of child development, the use of multiple methods is becoming increasingly common.

For Thought and Discussion

1. Can you think of a situation that highlights the distinction between correlation and causation? Why is this distinction important?

2. What are some factors that might influence a study's ecological validity? What is the relation between ecological validity and experimental control?

3. You are speaking with some friends and telling them all about the problems that can arise with the choice of one or another of the various research methods discussed in this chapter. After listening to you talk for a while, they ask you the question, "Given all these problems, why do research at all?" How would you answer your friends?

LO 8 Studying Change over Time

Recall that the main focus of research in child development is change over time. To study developmental change, the field makes use of certain methods intended to measure this type of change. The main research methods used to study time are the cross-sectional, longitudinal, and sequential methods.

cross-sectional method

A research method in which researchers compare groups of individuals of different age levels at approximately the same point in time.

THE CROSS-SECTIONAL METHOD   The most common strategy for investigating age-related differences in development is the **cross-sectional method**, in which researchers compare different individuals of different ages at the same point in time. Cross-sectional research compares different age groups of children on a topic, such as a behaviour or cognitive performance, to determine how changes associated with age may unfold over the course of development.

Consider the cross-sectional research done by Rheingold and Eckerman (1970) on developmental changes in children's independence from their mothers. These researchers observed mothers and their children, with the children representing nine different ages between 12 and 60 months. There were six children (three boys and three girls) at each of the six-month intervals between 12 and 60 months of age; for example, there were six children who were 12 months old, six children who were 18 months old, and so on. The researchers observed the children's behaviours in a controlled outdoor setting. They positioned the mothers and children at one end of a large lawn; the mothers sat in chairs, and the children were free to roam. Observers were stationed nearby and they recorded the paths the children took. A positive correlation between child age and distance travelled from the mother was found. The average farthest distance from mothers for 1-year-olds, the youngest age group was roughly 23 feet (6.9 metres); by 2 years of age, children ventured about 50 feet (15.1 metres); 3-year-olds went 57 feet (17.3 metres); and 4-year-olds went 68 feet (20.6 metres).

Using the cross-sectional method, the researchers were able to determine how independence differs across age levels. However, this approach yields no information about the causes that lie behind these age-related changes because we cannot know what the children in the study were like at younger ages. For example, we do not know if the child who is very independent at 1 year old is likely to be more independent at age 5 than a peer who exhibited little independence when he was 1 year old. Another research design, the *longitudinal method*, is better suited to tackling the issue of individual change over time.

THE LONGITUDINAL METHOD   The Fels Longitudinal Study began in 1929 and continued until the 1970s. It followed the same groups of children from birth to age 18. Parents who enrolled their newborns in this study agreed to have the child weighed, measured, observed, and tested until the child was old enough to graduate from high school. One conclusion of this study, which could be obtained only by studying the same children over time, was that certain behaviours are stable over time and that in some cases, the stability of a behaviour was affected by the child's gender. For instance, boys were more likely to show stable patterns of aggressive behaviour from childhood to adulthood (Kagan & Moss, 1962; see also Chapter 13, "Gender Roles and Gender Differences").

This type of research uses the **longitudinal method**, in which researchers study the same individuals repeatedly at various points in their lives in order to assess patterns of stability and change over time. A longitudinal design allows researchers to follow the development of individuals and, as a result, it can explore possible causes of any observed pattern. It is a powerful method for evaluating the impact of earlier events on later behaviour. Box 1.2 on the next page provides you with an example of longitudinal research and what it can say concerning the factors and processes of child development.

But the longitudinal method also has disadvantages. It takes years to collect longitudinal data, and researchers often want to obtain information more quickly. In addition, there is the problem of losing participants. Over time, people move, become ill, or simply lose interest, and no longer participate in the study. In addition, the questions and concerns that inspired the research may not be of interest later on in the study. Another problem arises from what we call *practice effects*, or the effects of repeated testing. Since the same measures may be used in several successive years, participants' answers may be the result of their familiarity with the items or questions.

A way to avoid some of these problems is to conduct a short-term longitudinal study. Here, researchers track study the same group of people but for a limited time period, usually a few months or a few years. Their focus is usually limited to a few key questions, often questions that this relatively brief time period can address adequately. For example, Joanna Blake (Blake & Dolgoy, 1993) of York University examined the relation between infants' communicative gestures and more general cognitive skills, looking at four infants biweekly from 9 or 10 months of age until they were about 14 months old. These researchers found that the appearance of specific gestures (described in Chapter 8) were actually preceded by gains in certain forms of cognitive processing, suggesting a role for cognition in the transition to language. Others using short-term longitudinal projects, such as John Abela and his colleagues at McGill University (Abela & Taylor, 2003; Abela & McGirr, 2007; Auerbach, Abela, & Ho, 2007), have

longitudinal method

A method in which investigators study the same people repeatedly at various times in the participants' lives.

Box 1.2
Risk and Resilience

LONGITUDINAL STUDIES AND THE TRANSFER OF PSYCHOSOCIAL RISK

One of the advantages of longitudinal research is that it allows one to study "intergenerational continuity and the transfer of psychosocial risk" (Serbin & Stack, 1998, p. 1159), or how the events experienced by one generation affect the lives of both that generation and its offspring. Psychologists, for example, have long recognized that children who grow up poor and who are at risk for psychosocial problems will likely become parents of a future generation also raised in poverty (Chase-Lansdale & Brooks-Gunn, 1995; Furstenberg, Levine, & Brooks-Gunn, 1990). Longitudinal research provides an opportunity to describe the lives of these successive generations, as well as a way to study how such risk is transferred across generations (Granger et al., 1998; Serbin et al., 2002; Stack & Serbin, 1998). Moreover, such studies provide a means for designing and assessing interventions that may prevent the transfer of such unwanted outcomes (Serbin & Stack, 1998).

Unfortunately, longitudinal projects like these are notoriously difficult to conduct, particularly when they span several generations. Nevertheless, one notable example of such a study is the Concordia Longitudinal Risk Project. Begun in 1976 by Jane Ledingham and Alex Schwartzman from Concordia University, this project examined almost 1,800 francophone schoolchildren living in the lower socio-economic, inner-city sections of Montréal (Schwartzman, Ledingham, & Serbin, 1985). The goal of this project was to identify childhood behaviours that might predict serious psychosocial problems later in life. These researchers were primarily interested in two aspects of children's behaviour: aggression and social withdrawal. On the basis of initial screenings, the researchers identified children who were classified as aggressive, socially withdrawn, or both aggressive and withdrawn.

What did the Concordia Longitudinal Risk Project reveal about intergenerational risk in these children? One finding from the study (Serbin, Peters, McAffer, & Schwartzman, 1991) is that childhood aggression predicts high-risk sexual behaviour and medical fallouts (e.g., gynecological problems, sexually transmitted diseases, pregnancy) in girls during adolescence, a pattern since confirmed by other researchers (Cairn & Cairns, 1994). In fact, children with high childhood aggression and social withdrawal scores actually experienced many problematic outcomes later in life, including a higher rate of teen pregnancy, more complications during delivery, and having multiple children before 24 years of age (Serbin, Cooperman, Peters, Stack, & Schwartzman, 1998). In a subsequent project (Saltaris, Serbin, Stack, Karp, Schwartzman, & Ledingham, 2004), mothers who had behavioural problems as children, and particularly those with a history of aggression, were less likely to provide cognitive stimulation to their preschool children when they themselves were mothers. Moreover, evaluation of the children's actual cognitive competence revealed that parental stimulation did indeed influence the intellectual performance of these children. As such, these findings outline a pathway for the intergenerational transfer of risk through the process of cognitive stimulation.

Thus, not only can longitudinal designs highlight factors that are important for the transfer of risk across generations, they also can identify characteristics that might help prevent such intergenerational transfer. Clearly, despite the inherent difficulties and drawbacks of conducting longitudinal research, such designs play a critical role in understanding the processes of child development.

found that depressive symptoms in school-aged children are linked, over the short term, to response styles or self-esteem. Such research has the advantage of shortening the period of data collection and thereby avoiding dropouts in the sample.

A different kind of drawback to lengthy longitudinal studies is the problem of generalizing to generations other than the one being studied. Children today grow up with many experiences unknown to children growing up in their parents' or grandparents' generations: for example, think of the differences computers and the widespread use of daycare create in today's world. Findings from a longitudinal study may lose relevance as society changes and be descriptive of only a particular age cohort, that is, members of the same generation.

THE SEQUENTIAL METHOD   A creative way around the problem of separating age-related changes from changes caused by the unique experiences of a particular age cohort is to use the **sequential method**, which combines features of both cross-sectional and longitudinal studies. In this method, researchers begin by selecting samples of children of different ages as they would in cross-sectional research. Suppose, for example, that we wanted to study the change in the development of children's reading skills throughout their early years. We might begin by recruiting and testing three samples of children: 2-year-olds, 4-year-olds, and 6-year-olds. We would then test these same children again at periodic intervals, let's say every two years. Then, at each of the two-year measuring points, we would add a new sample of 2-year-olds to the study, which would enable us to compare a larger number of age cohorts. Figure 1-5 displays the design of this study.

There are several advantages of the sequential method. First, the longitudinal aspect of the study allows researchers to examine age-related changes in children. Second, the cross-sectional aspect allows researchers to examine the impact of the year of evaluation and testing or practice effects. Third, in following each age cohort, the design can explore generational effects, or effects of the particular time period in which each group of children was born and raised. For example, perhaps the 6-year-olds originally recruited for this study entered kindergarten at a time when mathematics curricula in the primary grades underwent much change. By comparing these and other age cohorts, we might be able to assess changes in children's mathematics abilities as instructional techniques changed. And, finally, the design has a time-saving advantage. Six years after the start of the study, in 2006, the study would include data on changes in mathematics ability that span a period of 10 years (look again at Figure 1-5). This is a four-year saving over a traditional longitudinal study.

sequential method

A research method that combines features of both the cross-sectional and the longitudinal methods.

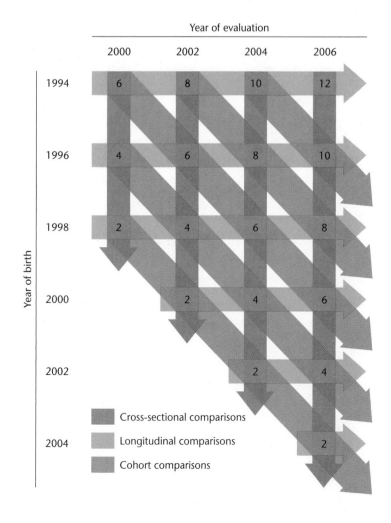

Figure 1-5

Design for a sequential study

This combination of the cross-sectional and longitudinal designs yields a third dimension of measurement that compares cohorts, or people of the same age, at different points in time. The numbers within the arrows are the ages of the groups of children to be studied. For example, in the year 2000, we would do a cross-sectional study of three groups of children, ages 2, 4, and 6. In 2002, we would add a new group of 2-year-olds and we would again measure the earlier groups of children, who would now be 4, 6, and 8. A number of different types of comparisons are possible from such a design. Can you describe some other comparisons that might be made?

When studying change over time, developmental researchers clearly have a number of design and methodological options. What they choose depends on the particular kinds of data they want to gather, on the availability of participants, and on the time and money they have to carry out the project (see Table 1-5 for a comparison of the pluses and minuses of all three approaches). No single strategy is best in all situations. This is why different researchers use different methods, and the same researchers use different methods at different times.

LO9 The Ethics of Research with Children

Concerns with the ethics of psychological experimentation became an issue in the late 1960s, when some began to question the ethics of deceiving subjects in research (Kelman, 1967). In response to such concerns, the American Psychological Association (APA) proposed a code of ethics in 1972, which was then followed in 1974 by US federal government regulations concerning human research. Within Canada, government regulations have slowly emerged, beginning first within the social sciences and humanities (Adair, 2001) and resulting in a document, in the late 1970s, by the Canada Council on the ethical principles that should be observed by researchers when experimenting with human subjects (Canada Council, 1977). Most recently, the Canadian Institutes of Health Research, the Natural Sciences and Engineering Research Council, and the Social Sciences and Humanities Research Council (1998) issued a tri-council policy statement regarding ethical conduct in research with human subjects. According to Adair (2001), the objectives of this new joint policy were to increase awareness of ethical considerations in research with humans, to provide public accountability for the use of funds in research, to provide greater protection for both the human subjects and the researchers and institutions involved in research, and to encourage the development of uniform standards of ethical conduct across disciplines, universities, and research ethics boards.

There are important ethical issues involved in doing research with children as well. As such, the same governmental agencies, along with professional organizations such

Table 1-5 Comparison of methods of studying developmental change over time

	Cross-sectional	Longitudinal	Sequential
Time required	Short	Long	Moderate
Ability to control costs	High	Low	Moderate
Ability to maintain potential pool of participants	Excellent	Very problematic	Moderate to good
Continuity of staff	High	Medium to low	Moderate to high
Flexibility in adapting to new tests and measures	High	Low	Moderate
Likelihood of practice effects	Low	High	Medium
Ability to assess research issues:			
Normative development data at different ages	Excellent	Excellent	Excellent
Impact of early events on later behaviour	Poor	Excellent	Good
Stability vs. instability of behaviour	Poor	Excellent	Good
Developmental paths of individuals	Poor	Excellent	Good
Historical or cohort issues	Excellent	Poor	Good

as the APA and the Society for Research in Child Development, have also suggested guidelines for the participation of children in research, in an attempt to protect children from danger and harm (see Table 1-6). All legitimate research projects involving children (and adults) are scrutinized and approved by review boards at the institutions where the research is carried out, including colleges and universities. This scrutiny ensures that researchers follow ethical guidelines.

Among these ethical guidelines, one critical aspect is **informed consent**, an agreement to participate in research based on a clear understanding of the purposes and procedures to be employed in the study. All research with human subjects requires that researchers obtain informed consent from all participants before being included in a study. When participants are young children, parents or legal guardians must provide informed consent on their behalf (Institute of Medicine, 2004). Participants also have the right not to be harmed. This includes protection not only from physical harm, but also from psychological and emotional harm, such as feeling uncomfortable or embarrassed. Such experiences are of particular concern in research that involves deception. Recall the experiment by Liebert and Baron (1972), discussed earlier, on the effects of viewing violent TV programs on children's later aggressive behaviour toward other children in a mock game situation. Even though no child was actually harmed, how might the children have viewed themselves after they participated in the study? Might they have felt ashamed of themselves? Laboratory research involving deception is becoming less common. However, such questions remain important, and careful scrutiny of all ethical issues in research with children is critical.

Are children, even older children, able to understand these rights? Researchers at the University of Toronto (Abramovitch, Freedman, Henry, & Van Brunschot, 1995) have investigated whether children between 5 and 24 years of age understand what

informed consent

Agreement to participate in a research study that is based on a clear and full understanding of the purposes and procedures of that study.

Canadian Ethics Guidelines

Table 1-6　A Bill of Child Participants' Rights in child-development research

1. **The right to be fully informed.** Every child has the right to full and truthful information about the purposes of a study in which he or she is to participate and about the procedures to be used.

2. **The right to give informed and voluntary consent.** Every child has the right to agree, either orally or in writing, to participate in a research project. If a child is too young to understand the aims and procedures of the study and to make an informed decision, researchers must request the informed consent of the child's parents.

3. **The right not to be harmed in any way.** Every child has the right to know that he or she will not experience any physical or psychological harm or damage as a result of the research procedures.

4. **The right to withdraw voluntarily from research.** Every child has the right to withdraw at any time from continued participation in any research project.

5. **The right to be informed of the results of research.** Every child has the right to information about the results of the research project. If the child is too young to fully understand this information, it must be provided to the child's parents. It is understood that sometimes information is in the form of group measures or scores on a task rather than individual scores.

6. **The right to confidentiality.** Every child has the right to know that personal information gathered as part of the research project will remain private and confidential and that it will not be shared with any other individuals or agencies.

7. **The right to full compensation.** Every child has the right to be fully compensated for her or his time and effort as a research participant, even if the child withdraws and does not complete her or his participation.

8. **The right to beneficial treatments.** Every child has the right to profit from any beneficial treatments provided to other participants in the research project. When experimental treatments are deemed beneficial—for example, participation in a program designed to enhance reading or math skills—participants in control groups, who do not receive this treatment during the research study proper, have the right to the same participation in the beneficial treatment after the project is completed.

Sources: American Psychological Association, 1992; Society for Research on Child Development Committee on Ethical Conduct in Child Development Research, 1993.

it means to give free and informed consent for participation. These researchers found that even though children understood the purpose of the study, they did not seem to understand the risks or benefits of participating and were much more likely to stop participating if the experimenter made it clear that she would not be upset if they stopped. These researchers suggest that experimenters should pay more attention to describing the risks and benefits of research to children and to making it much clearer to children that they can stop participating if they wish.

Developmental research is a tool for increasing our knowledge about children, and it is hoped that the lives of children will benefit from this knowledge. Recently, some investigators and child advocates have called for more stringent criteria regulating the participation of children in psychological research. Others worry that too many additional restrictions will seriously impede the ability of psychologists to learn more about issues that may ultimately lead to benefits for children. The ethics of research in child psychology continue to comprise a topic of much debate.

For Thought and Discussion

1. Throughout the text, studies are presented as having clean, all-or-nothing findings, with the results often simply presented as "x is related to y," or "group x was significantly greater than group y." Unfortunately, in practice, research is not nearly as clear-cut, with large individual differences often occurring among children. And sometimes differences between groups, or relations between measures, although statistically significant, are small in an absolute sense. How might such intersubject variability, or the fact that differences or relations might be at best modest, influence your interpretations or conclusions concerning a given experimental result?

2. Now that you know something about the ethics of doing research, what are some of the ethical considerations raised by Pepler and Craig's (1995) method of using remote audiovisual monitoring to observe children in the playground?

Making the Connections 1.2

There are many links between concepts and ideas in one area of development and concepts and ideas in other areas. Here are some of the connections between ideas in Chapter 1's discussion of research methods in child development and discussions in other chapters of this book.

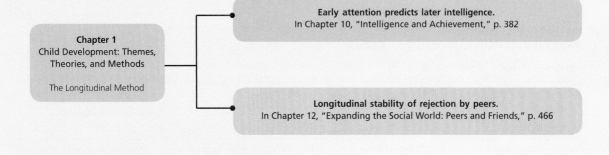

Chapter 1
Child Development: Themes, Theories, and Methods

The Longitudinal Method

Early attention predicts later intelligence.
In Chapter 10, "Intelligence and Achievement," p. 382

Longitudinal stability of rejection by peers.
In Chapter 12, "Expanding the Social World: Peers and Friends," p. 466

SUMMARY

- **Child development** attempts to account for changes in children's abilities and behaviours as they develop by uncovering the processes that underlie these changes.
- Scientists also study children to develop practical information that can help those who care for children, such as parents, teachers, health professionals, and legislators.

Themes of Development

- Although in the past, development was held by many to be the result of **maturation**, most modern developmentalists recognize the importance of both biological and environmental influences. Many psychologists are concerned with discovering the ways in which biological and environmental factors interact to produce developmental differences.
- Most contemporary developmentalists believe that children actively shape, control, and direct the course of their own development. A number of theorists view development as a continuous process, whereby change takes place smoothly and gradually over time, but others see development as a series of qualitatively different steps or stages. The more closely and more frequently we examine the child's development, the more gradual or continuous the process appears.
- Some developmentalists continue to debate the question of whether individual or contextual influences are more important in determining development. Most developmentalists agree, however, that cultural contexts must be considered in any account of development.

Theoretical Perspectives on Development

- Theories serve two functions. First, they help organize and integrate existing knowledge into a coherent account of how children develop. Second, they foster research by providing testable predictions about behaviour. Different theories take different positions on the issues or themes of development, and they also account for different aspects of development. In this sense they can be seen as complementary rather than as competing with each other.
- **Structural-organismic perspectives** focus on the organized components of the developing organism and how these change in a qualitative way over the course of human development. Two examples of structural-organismic theories are Freud's **psychodynamic theory**, in which the child is motivated by a set of basic biological drives that direct behaviour, and Erikson's psychosocial theory. The concepts of **id**, **ego**, and **superego** are integral to Freud's notion of the development of personality, and Freud considered early experiences to be determining influences for later development. According to Freudian theory, later adult personality is a direct result of whether the child's drives were deprived or satisfied at each earlier stage.
- Erikson expanded Freud's theory to include social and cultural factors as influences on the child's development as well as to extend the theory into a lifespan perspective. Erikson's **psychosocial theory** is organized around a series of fundamental personal and social tasks that the individual must accomplish at each stage.
- **Piagetian theory**, also a structural-organismic approach, focuses on intellectual development. In this theory, the child is seen as actively seeking information and new experiences. Children adapt to their environment by assimilating new information or by accommodating their existing frameworks to new information. Development results from increasingly complex reorganizations of understanding as the child moves to more advanced levels of cognitive functioning.
- Learning perspectives emphasize how new behaviours are acquired and see development as a gradual and continuous process. The early learning theories, conceived within the traditional school of **behaviourism**, proposed that learning is regulated by environmental factors that modify behaviour by either **classical** or **operant conditioning**.
- **Cognitive social learning theory** has extended the behavioural perspective to include imitation as another form of learning. According to this theory, children are selective about who and what behaviours they imitate.
- **Information-processing approaches** are derived from a learning perspective and focus on how children process information and use this knowledge to guide behaviour. This approach has been applied to a wide range of problems in studies of cognitive development and social behaviour.
- **Dynamic systems theories** view development from the system level in which individual behaviours are influenced by the other elements or members of the system. The continuing interactions among system members make development a highly dynamic process.
- Contextual perspectives focus on the contributions of social and cultural factors to psychological development. In his **sociocultural theory** of cognitive development, Vygotsky emphasized the interaction

between the active child and his social environment. According to Vygotsky, the child grows and changes as a function of his own efforts and by the guidance of more skilled others.

- **Ecological theory** stresses the importance of understanding the relationship between the organism and various environmental systems, such as the family, school, community, and culture. Development involves the interplay between children and their changing relationships with these different ecological systems—the **microsystem**, **mesosystem**, **exosystem**, **macrosystem**, and **chronosystem**. The child's subjective experience of, or understanding of, the environment and the child's active role in modifying the environment are important aspects of this perspective.

- Historical approaches examine the contribution of **cohort** events to development. Psychologists who view development from a **lifespan perspective** are particularly interested in the effects of historical events on human development.

- **Ethological theory** takes a biological-evolutionary approach to describing development. Ethologists, whose primary mode of study is direct observation of behaviour in natural settings, study patterns of behaviours across human and infrahuman species and across human societies and cultures.

- **Evolutionary psychology** has influenced developmental research especially in areas related to cognitive development. The focus in this work is on how the cognitive capabilities and constraints of the organism may reflect survival needs and processes of human evolution.

Themes and Theories: A Final Comment

- Some theoretical perspectives on child development are particularly useful in explaining certain aspects of children's growth and change, whereas other perspectives illuminate other aspects of development. Because every aspect of development is related to several others, it is often useful to apply several different theoretical perspectives to the analysis and study of a particular problem or issue. The interrelatedness of different domains of development makes a systems approach increasingly attractive.

Research Methods in Child Psychology

- Child psychologists use the **scientific method** in their research. They formulate hypotheses on the basis of theories, and they use measurable and replicable techniques to collect, study, and analyze data to test the usefulness of these theories.

- Selecting a **sample** is an important first step in any research because it determines the extent to which the researcher's conclusions can be applied, or generalized, to people other than those who were studied. To ensure the **representativeness** of a sample, or the degree to which it accurately reflects some larger population, it must include individuals who represent the diversity of the larger population. Conducting a **national survey** is one way to ensure that a sample is representative of a broad range of people.

- Soliciting **self-reports** from children, usually by means of interviews, is one way to gather information about child development. Getting self-reports from children can be more difficult than getting them from adults, for children tend to be less attentive, slower to respond, and less likely to understand the questions put to them. Self-reports, however, are the only way to obtain information about such things as children's feelings and their unique perspectives on their lives.

- Another data-gathering method is to solicit information about a child from other people who know that child well, such as parents, siblings, teachers, and peers. Attempts to increase the accuracy of parents' reports about their children include focusing on specific current issues in the child's life and using structured procedures such as daily diaries or phone calls. Often, of course, there is no substitute for researchers' **direct observation** of children. Such observations can occur in natural settings, such as a child's home, or in a laboratory; in the latter case, a **structured observation** allows researchers to observe the child as he performs some highly structured task. One limitation of direct observation is that, when children and parents know they are being watched, they act in more socially acceptable ways than they ordinarily would. To minimize such distortions, researchers try to observe unobtrusively for relatively long periods to enable subjects to adapt to the situation.

- When researchers use direct observations, they must decide what kinds of behaviours to record. They can record everything the participant does (a *specimen record*), record only particular events (*event sampling*), or identify which behaviours of a predetermined set occurred during a particular time period (*time sampling*). Because of the limitations of all data-gathering methods, researchers often use multiple measures of the same behaviours.

- The **correlational method** involves examining the relationship between two variables, such as children's aggressive behaviour and the amount of aggression they watch on TV. If two factors are correlated, they are systematically related to each other, but a correlation does not tell us whether one factor causes the other.

- A **laboratory experiment** permits researchers to establish cause-and-effect relationships by assessing a specific behaviour (such as aggression toward another person) in a controlled setting. A certain factor of interest (such as viewing TV violence) is introduced to an **experimental group** of participants, while a **control group** is exposed to some neutral factor. Researchers use **random assignment** to assign participants to either of these groups. The **dependent variable** is the behaviour affected by the manipulation of the **independent variable**.

- Laboratory experiments cannot easily be generalized to real-world settings. A **field experiment**, in which a researcher deliberately produces a change in a real-life setting and measures the outcome there, has more **ecological validity**. However, researchers have to guard against **observer bias** when working in the field.

- Another way to increase the generalizability of findings is to conduct a **natural experiment**. In this case, the investigator measures the impact on children's behaviour of some naturally occurring change. But because of lack of control over the independent variable and other factors that could affect behaviour, it is often difficult to interpret the results of a natural experiment.

- The **case study method** takes an in-depth look at a single child or group (like a classroom), often (but not always) one with some uncommon feature that makes the child or group of special interest to developmentalists.

Studying Change over Time

- The most common strategy for investigating developmental change over time is the **cross-sectional method**, in which researchers compare groups of children of different ages at a given point in time. This approach is economical in terms of both time and money, but it yields no information about change nor about the causes of any observed age-related differences in the child participants.

- The **longitudinal method** overcomes these two drawbacks of cross-sectional research because the researcher examines the same children at different points in their lives. But longitudinal research has its own disadvantages, including high cost, gradual loss of subjects, limited flexibility in using new insights or methods once the study has begun, and the question of the applicability of findings to other age cohorts.

- To overcome some of these limitations, researchers can use the **sequential method**, which combines features of both cross-sectional and longitudinal studies. This design enables researchers to compare not only groups of children of different ages at one point in time, and to track individual children over a period of years, but also to track age cohorts over a number of years.

- A major consideration when deciding on a research strategy is the effects the procedures will have on participants. Various governmental and institutional review boards, in addition to professional organizations, are involved in setting and maintaining guidelines for the proper treatment of human subjects in research. These guidelines include the right to **informed consent** before participating and the right not to be harmed. To determine if certain research procedures are ethical or not, the costs to participants must be carefully weighed against the potential benefits of increased knowledge about children's development.

Frida Kahlo (1907–1954). *My Grandparents, My Parents, and I (Family Tree)*, 1936.
Museum of Modern Art, New York.

Chapter 2
Heredity and the Environment

LEARNING OBJECTIVES

After reading this chapter, you should be able to

LO 1 Describe the processes that lead to the transmission of genetic information, including conception, chromosomes, genes, and DNA; define relevant terminology associated with each process.

LO 2 Describe the process of inheritance for Mendelian characteristics, including sex-linked characteristics; compare these "simple" patterns with complex gene interactions; give examples of each type of genetic transmission.

LO 3 Describe the effect of chromosomal abnormalities, and give examples; indicate how abnormalities contribute to evolution.

LO 4 Describe and discuss the roles of genetic counselling and methods of genetic engineering; discuss the ethical issues related to genetic engineering and the new reproductive technologies.

LO 5 Describe the methods used for prenatal diagnosis and what can be learned from each one.

LO 6 Discuss the findings of adoption and twin studies and how that data has influenced understanding of the nature–nurture issue.

LO 7 Understand both the positive and negative aspects of the theory of behaviour genetics.

LO 8 Discuss the principles and processes that describe the influences of heredity and environment on intelligence, temperament, and personality.

LO 1

One of the most striking things about newborns in a hospital nursery is their diversity. From the moment they are born, babies differ from one another not only in physical appearance but also in behaviour. One baby may sleep most of the time; another may be quite alert, visually scanning the surroundings, as if exploring them; a third baby may often be irritable and cry a lot. What contributes to these individual differences at such a young age? Transactions among a vast array of hereditary and environmental factors begin before birth. Such transactions between genes and the environment make each newborn unique, and they continue to shape the individual's characteristics throughout his or her lifespan.

The concepts of genotype and phenotype provide a framework for exploring the interactions of genes and environment. A **genotype** is the particular set of genes that a person inherits from her parents. With the exception of identical twins, no two people have exactly the same genotype. During the course of development, the genotype interacts with the environment in complex ways to produce the **phenotype**, which is the observable and measurable expression of an individual's physical and behavioural characteristics. Psychologists study these kinds of characteristics—for example, motor abilities, intellectual skills, social behaviour, and personality traits—to increase our understanding of how genetic and environmental factors interact to produce each unique human being.

We begin this chapter by exploring what genes are and how they are transmitted from generation to generation. Next, we examine how genes guide development, from determining a child's sex to countless other characteristics. We go on to examine genetic testing and counselling for would-be parents who face the prospect of having a child with a troubling disorder, and we explore the growing field of genetic engineering. Then, we consider heredity–environment interactions. We discuss both the ways environmental factors influence the actual expression of an individual child's genetic makeup and, conversely, the way that genetic makeup can shape the environment. Finally, to further our understanding of how genes and the environment interact, we explore the relative contributions of these two forces to intellectual development and to aspects of socio-emotional development such as temperament, personality, and emotional reactivity. ●

genotype

The particular set of genes that a person inherits from her parents.

phenotype

Created by the interaction of a person's genotype, or genetic makeup, with the environment; the visible expression of the person's particular physical and behavioural characteristics.

LO 1 THE PROCESS OF GENETIC TRANSMISSION

In the moist environment of a woman's *oviduct*, the sperm and the egg unite to create a new living organism that has the potential to develop into a human being. This new organism, called a *zygote* (which we discuss in detail in Chapter 3), results from the union of the male and female gametes, or reproductive cells, each of which carries genetic information. The egg, or **ovum**, the largest human cell, is about 90,000 times as heavy as the sperm that penetrates it; nevertheless, it is still quite small—smaller even than the period at the end of this sentence. The **sperm**, the smallest of all human cells, is the shape of a head, where the hereditary information is, with a whip-like tail, which it uses to propel itself through the woman's reproductive system in search of the ovum. This beginning is the start of a 9-month period that normally ends with a full-term baby, 7 or 8 pounds and roughly 50 centimetres long, ready to enter the world.

ovum

The female germ cell, or egg.

sperm

The male germ cell.

Chromosomes and Genes

Chromosomes and genes are located inside the nucleus, or centre, of the cell. At the moment of human conception, when the sperm and the egg unite, 23 chromosomes from each of these cells join together to create 23 chromosome *pairs*, or 46 chromosomes in all. The thread-like **chromosomes** carry genetic information that helps direct

chromosomes

Thread-like structures, located in the central portion, or nucleus, of a cell, that carry genetic information to help direct development.

development. An individual's 46 chromosomes are said to come in 23 pairs, with half of each pair from the father and half from the mother. This pairing is possible because each chromosome is *homologous* (similar in shape and function) to one of the chromosomes contributed by the mother's egg. Copies of these original 23 homologous pairs of chromosomes are passed on to every cell in a person's body with one exception: the reproductive cells. Each reproductive cell contains only 23 single chromosomes instead of the usual 46 because during its development, it undergoes a special form of cell division, called **meiosis**, in which its 23 chromosome pairs are halved (see Figure 2-1). The reason for this halving becomes clear when the sperm and the egg unite. Now, 23 chromosomes from the sperm combine with 23 chromosomes from the egg to produce the correct number of 46 chromosomes for a new human being.

meiosis

The process by which a germ cell divides to produce new germ cells with only half the normal complement of chromosomes; thus, male and female germ cells (sperm and ovum) each contain only 23 chromosomes so that when they unite, the new organism they form will have 46 chromosomes, half from each parent.

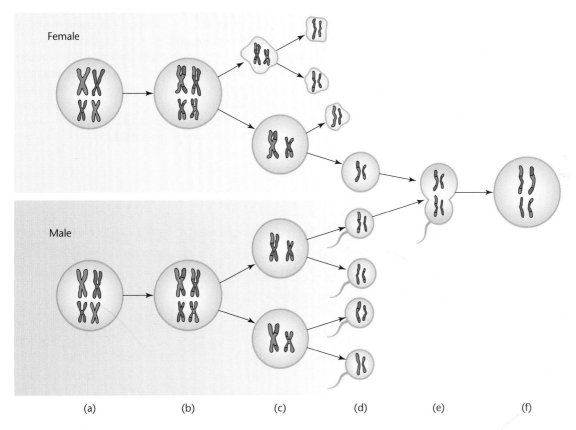

(a)   (b)   (c)   (d)   (e)   (f)

Figure 2-1

Meiosis: The reproductive cells divide to produce new germ cells with half the normal complement of chromosomes

As meiosis, a type of cell division that produces male and female reproductive cells, begins in both sexes, all the chromosomes in the cell replicate themselves as if they were about to undergo *mitosis*, or normal cell division (see Figure 2-2 on page 46). In (a), we see the results of this replication (we show cells with only four chromosomes, or two pairs, rather than the full complement of 46 chromosomes, or 23 pairs). In (b), crossing over between chromosomes ensures the zygote's unique genetic inheritance. In (c), the male chromosome pairs separate to form two cells, each with 23 chromosomes. In the female, two cells are also formed, but one is non-functional and may or may not produce two more non-functional cells. In (d), the chromosomes separate once again, in the male, forming four sperm cells and in the female, a single ovum and a fourth non-functional cell. (The genetic material in the female's four non-functional cells degenerates.) When a sperm cell fertilizes an ovum (e), a zygote is formed (f) with 23 chromosome pairs, or 46 in all.

Both meiosis and sexual reproduction are crucial to the process of genetic transmission because each facilitates the production of a tremendous diversity of genetic combinations. During meiosis, when a male's or a female's set of chromosomes is halved to produce a germ cell—sperm or egg—that halving process mixes the chromosomes that originated from the individual's father with the chromosomes that originated from the individual's mother. Moreover, this mixing process is totally random. The only requirement is that one of each pair of homologous chromosomes ends up in the new reproductive cell. This random assortment of homologous chromosomes makes possible the production of about 8 million different chromosome combinations in both the female's eggs and the male's sperms. Further genetic variability is added during meiosis by a process called **crossing over**, in which equivalent sections of homologous chromosomes randomly switch places (see Figure 2-1) so that genetic information is shuffled even more. No wonder that the chance of any given man and woman producing two genetically identical children is one in many trillions (except, of course, when a single fertilized egg splits to form identical twins).

In Chapter 3, we will follow the progress of the fertilized egg, or zygote, as it develops within the mother's body, becoming an embryo, then a fetus, and finally, at birth, a living human infant. Here, we may ask, however, how the single cell created by the union of the egg and the sperm becomes that complex, living being. By a process called **mitosis**, which occurs in all **autosomes** (chromosomes that contain matching pairs) and sex chromosomes (which we discuss later), a cell duplicates its chromosomes and then divides into daughter cells that have the exact same number of chromosomes as their parent cell (see Figure 2-2). Thus, the zygote divides and continues to divide, each time producing new cells that have the full complement of 46 chromosomes, and gradually becomes a multi-cellular organism.

crossing over

The process by which equivalent sections of homologous chromosomes switch places randomly, shuffling the genetic information each carries.

mitosis

The process in which a body cell divides in two, first duplicating its chromosomes so that the new, daughter cells contain the usual 46 chromosomes.

autosomes

The 22 paired non-sex chromosomes.

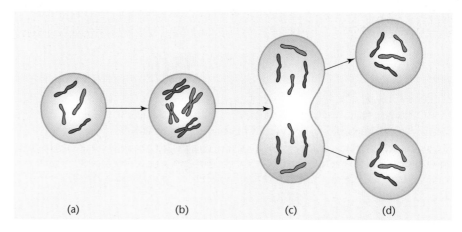

(a)   (b)   (c)   (d)

Figure 2-2

Mitosis: The zygote divides and keeps dividing to produce a multi-cellular organism

In (a), we show a zygote with only four chromosomes, rather than the 46 each cell normally contains. In (b), each chromosome splits in half (length-wise) to produce a duplicate of itself. Next, in (c), the duplicates move away from each other as the cell begins to divide. Finally, in (d), the cell has divided in two, and each new cell has the same set of chromosomes as the other and as the original parent cell (a).

Genes, DNA, and Proteins

deoxyribonucleic acid (DNA)

A ladder-like molecule that stores genetic information in cells and transmits it during reproduction.

Scientists know that the binding element of a chromosome is a long, thin molecule of **deoxyribonucleic acid**, or **DNA** for short. This molecule, which stores genetic information and transmits it during reproduction, is made up of building blocks called nucleotides that are held together by two long, twisted parallel strands that resemble the two side rails of a spiral staircase (see Figure 2-3). From each **nucleotide**, which is a compound consistent of a nitrogen base, a simple sugar, and a phosphate group, one of four different nitrogen-containing bases projects out toward the base on its opposite side to form one of the staircase's "risers." Only bases that are compatible with each other will bond together. As Figure 2-3 shows, adenine and thymine form a bond, as do cytosine and guanine, but no other combination of these four is possible.

How do chromosomes carry the units of hereditary information? Portions of the chromosome's DNA molecule, called **genes**, are located at particular sites on the chromosome where they code for the production of certain kinds of **proteins**. The genetic code is "written" in the order in which the four bases are included in the gene, much as the code for the meaning of a word is written in the order of its letters. At some point, the gene, or DNA segment, splits down the middle so that its pairs of bases are no longer joined, and the bases bond with other, "free" nucleotides to form new pairs. The resulting copy of the gene then acts as a template for building protein molecules.

Each of the many different types of proteins serves a different function. Some proteins give cells their characteristic physical properties. For example, bone cells get their hardness, skin cells their elasticity, and nerve cells their capacity to conduct electrical impulses from the different kinds of proteins they possess. Other proteins do many other jobs, such as triggering chemical reactions, carrying chemical messages, fighting foreign invaders, and regulating genes. It is the combined action of all the proteins in a human body, each of whose specialized cells and organ systems has distinctive characteristics, that composes a living organism.

GENETIC INFLUENCES ON DEVELOPMENT LO2

Scientists are learning more and more about how genes exert their influences on development. The central message they have gleaned is that, at least with respect to behaviour, *genes never work in isolation, but always in combination with environmental influences* (Rutter, 2006a; Turkheimer, 2000). A gene alone is useless. Its coded message cannot be "read" unless it is embedded in an environment that signals when and how it should respond. But because the topic of gene–environment interactions is so complex, we will focus, in this and the next major section, on genetic influences apart from environmental ones. We will return to the critical determining process of gene–environment interaction in the last two sections of the chapter.

The Transmission of Traits: A Basic Model

Much of the original work that is the basis of modern genetics was done in the nineteenth century by Gregor Mendel, an Austrian monk, who, from his observation of pea plants, worked out the basic principles that govern the inheritance of characteristics from one generation to the next. Mendel spent years cross-breeding pea plants and then cataloguing the results of these hybridizations. What he found was that many of the characteristics of the pea plants, such aspects as flower colour, the height of the stalks, and so on, varied from one generation to the next, with a trait that had been present in one generation disappearing in the next generation but, then, reappearing again in a following generation.

From these observations, Mendel worked out the mechanisms, or laws, of inheritance of characteristics. These two principles are known as the *principle of segregation* and the *principle of independent assortment*. The first principle states that each inherited trait comes from one's parent as a separate unit (e.g., flower colour, stem height). The second principle states that the inheritance of various traits occurs independently of one another (e.g., inheritance of flower colour has nothing to do with inheritance of stem height).

nucleotide

A compound containing a nitrogen base, a simple sugar, and a phosphate group

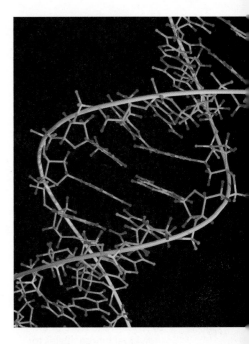

Figure 2-3

The structure of DNA

The two twisted strands of DNA form a kind of spiral staircase whose risers are composed of the complementary base pairs of nucleotides: adenine–thymine or guanine–cytosine.

gene

A portion of DNA that is located at a particular site on a chromosome and that codes for the production of certain kinds of proteins.

proteins

Proteins are fundamental components of all living cells, and are any of a group of complex organic molecules containing carbon, hydrogen, oxygen, nitrogen, and usually sulphur, and that are composed of one or more chains of amino acids.

In order to understand these principles, it is helpful to look at an example. Say Mendel (or any researcher for that matter) crossed a tall pea plant with a short pea plant. When looking at the offspring produced from such a mating, Mendel found that the next generation of plants was tall. In fact, this result went against the prevailing wisdom in Mendel's day, which was that what one should see is a combination of the two traits, or a medium height plant. Now, what happens when you mate two of these second generation plants—are their offspring also tall? Here, Mendel had another surprise. Although most of this generation were tall, some turned out short! Thus, the characteristic of a short stem had reappeared in a subsequent generation.

What do Mendel's principles have to say about the disappearance and reappearance of short and tall stems? Two basic concepts are crucial to understanding genetic influences on development. First, at any given gene's position on two homologous chromosomes, there can be more than one form of that gene. These alternative forms are called the gene's **alleles**, with one allele coming from the organism's (a person, plant, or animal) mother and the other from the father. Second, if the alleles from the two parents are the same, the organism is **homozygous** for that gene and the trait that goes with it. If the alleles are different, then the organism is **heterozygous** for that characteristic. If *A* represents one allele and *a* another, then there are clearly three possible combinations of alleles: *AA*, *aa*, or *Aa* (*aA*).

Given this formulation, why do certain characteristics disappear and then reappear in a later generation? To understand this, let us think about how alleles can combine. When an organism is homozygous for a trait (*AA* or *aa*), then that organism will simply inherit the coded-for characteristic. Thus, to use our earlier example, if *A* codes for tall plants and *a* for short plants, an offspring that is *AA* will be tall, and the one that is *aa* will be short. However, what happens when the organism is heterozygous for this trait?

Sometimes, the combination of two dissimilar alleles will produce an outcome intermediate between the traits, for which each single allele codes. An example here is skin colour, with light-skinned and dark-skinned parents producing a child of intermediate skin colour. A second possibility is that both alleles will express their traits simultaneously; that is, the two traits will combine but will not blend. This pattern, called **co-dominance**, is exemplified by blood type. If a person inherits the allele for blood type A from one parent and blood type B from the other parent, they will be of blood type AB, with both A and B blood antigens. A third possibility is that in a heterozygous combination the characteristic associated with only one of the alleles is expressed. The more powerful allele is said to be **dominant** over the weaker, **recessive**, allele. In our earlier plant example, the tall allele is dominant over the short allele, meaning that heterozygous plants (*Aa* or *aA*) will be tall. In fact, many inherited characteristics follow this dominant–recessive type of relation, such as curly (dominant) and straight (recessive) hair, and dark (dominant) and light or blond (recessive) hair. Table 2-1 lists a number of different examples of dominant and recessive characteristics. Fortunately, many harmful alleles are recessive, which greatly reduces the incidence of genetic abnormalities. One of the reasons why many societies prohibit marriage among close blood relations is that a harmful recessive allele possessed by one relative is more likely to be possessed by other relatives as well, thus increasing the chances that children of their intermarriage will by homozygous for the harmful trait.

Genes on the Sex Chromosomes: Exceptions to the Rule

The genes on the sex chromosomes provide an exception to the rule we have just discussed, for not all of these genes have two alleles. But before we examine this special situation, we must back up a bit in our story. In every human being, one of the 23 pairs, or two of the 46 human chromosomes we have discussed, are called **sex chromosomes**;

allele

An alternative form of a gene; typically, a gene has two alleles, one inherited from the individual's mother and one from the father.

homozygous

Describing the state of an individual whose alleles for a particular trait from each parent are the same.

heterozygous

Describing the state of an individual whose alleles for a particular trait from each parent are different.

co-dominance

A genetic pattern in which heterozygous alleles express the variants of the trait for which they code simultaneously and with equal force.

dominant

Describing the more powerful of two alleles in a heterozygous combination.

recessive

Describing the weaker of two alleles in a heterozygous combination.

sex chromosomes

In both males and females, the 23rd pair of chromosomes, which determine the individual's gender and are responsible for sex-related characteristics; in females, this pair normally comprises two X chromosomes, in males an X and a Y chromosome.

Table 2-1

Some common dominant
and recessive traits

Dominant	Recessive
Curly hair	Straight hair
Normal amount of hair	Baldness
Dark hair	Light or blond hair
Blond or brunette hair	Red hair
Normal skin colouring	Albinism (lack of skin pigmentation)
Roman nose	Straight nose
Thick lips	Thin lips
Cheek dimples	No dimples
Double-jointedness	Normal joints
Normal colour vision	Colour "blindness" (red and green not distinguished)
Farsightedness	Nearsightedness (myopia)
Immunity to poison ivy	Susceptibility to poison ivy
Normal hearing	Congenital deafness
Normal blood clotting	Failure of blood to clot (hemophilia)
Normal protein metabolism	Phenylketonuria
Normal red blood cells	Sickle cell anemia

these chromosomes have the important function of determining the individual's gender, and they differ in males and females (see Figure 2-4 on the next page). A female has two large, homologous sex chromosomes, the so-called XX chromosomes—one from her mother; the other from her father. A male, on the other hand, has one X chromosome from his mother and a smaller, Y chromosome from his father; this pattern is referred to as XY. Because an X chromosome is about five times longer than a Y chromosome, it carries more genes. This means that some genes on a male's X chromosome will have no equivalent genes on his Y chromosome, and as a result, any recessive **X-linked genes** will automatically be expressed; the male's Y chromosome has no counteracting dominant genes. In females, X-linked recessive genes are expressed much less frequently because females, who have two X chromosomes, have a chance of inheriting a dominant and counteracting allele on the other X chromosome.

Hemophilia, a disorder in which the blood fails to clot, is an example of an X-linked recessive characteristic. Because the allele for hemophilia is recessive, a female who inherits it will have normally clotting blood as long as her second allele, inherited from her other parent, does not code for hemophilia. Only if she is homozygous for the recessive allele will her blood clotting be impaired. If a male receives the hemophilia allele on his X chromosome, he is in greater danger of developing hemophilia. Like the female, he will develop the disorder if he receives another hemophilia allele on his Y chromosome; however, he will also develop hemophilia if he receives no counteracting gene on his Y chromosome. Only if the small collection of alleles on his Y chromosome happens to include one for normal blood clotting will he escape the disorder.

Many other X-linked recessive disorders are more common in men than in women, including colour blindness, certain forms of night blindness, atrophy of the optic nerve, and so on. Even resistance to certain childhood diseases appears to be X-linked. Thus,

X-linked genes

Genes that are carried on the X chromosome and that may have no analogous genes on the Y chromosome in males.

hemophilia

A disorder caused by an X-linked recessive gene, in which the blood fails to clot; found more often in males than in females.

Hemophilia

Figure 2-4

Normal chromosome arrangements

These karyotypes, or photographs, show the normal lineup of chromosomes in a female (a) and a male (b). As you can see, the 22 pairs are similar in both sexes, but the 23rd pair is different. In the female, this pair shows an XX pattern, and in the male, an XY pattern.

(a)

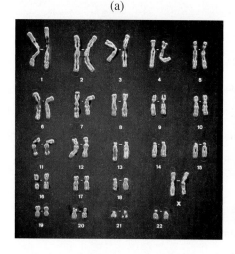

(b)

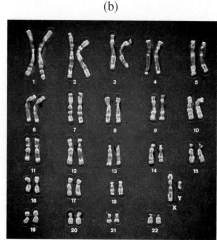

although 120 males are conceived for every 100 females and 106 males are born for every 100 females, this numerical imbalance between the genders is rapidly eliminated over the course of development.

Interactions among Genes

So far, we have presented a relatively simple genetic model, in which a single allele or a single pair of alleles determines a particular characteristic. Although this model applies to certain human traits, many other characteristics are determined not by one pair of alleles but by many pairs acting together. In fact, most of the characteristics that are of the greatest interest to psychologists, such as intelligence, creativity, sociability, and style of emotional expression, are probably influenced by the interaction of multiple genes.

This interaction may help explain why some traits that are influenced by genes do not tend to run in families. Development of such traits usually depends on a certain configuration of many genes, and that particular configuration is not likely to be passed on from parent to child. A likely example is genius. Why are geniuses sometimes born to parents of quite ordinary intelligence, and why do geniuses go on to produce children of their own who are not unusually talented? Such cases make sense if you consider genius to be a trait that emerges from a particular configuration of many genes, all interacting with each other (Lykken, McGue, Tellegen, & Bouchard, 1992; Turkheimer, 2000).

To further complicate the nature of genetic inheritance, we now know that a single pair of alleles may influence more than one trait. Moreover, they may do this not directly, but indirectly through their effects on the expression of still other genes. Genes that act in this manner are called **modifier genes**. One example is the modifier gene that affects the early development of *cataract*, a condition in which the lens of the eye becomes clouded, obscuring vision. Although the occurrence of early cataract is determined by a dominant gene, the nature of cataract formation is influenced by modifier genes. It is these kinds of genes that determine, for example, whether the cloudiness forms along the periphery of the lens or in its centre.

modifier genes

Genes that exert their influence indirectly, by affecting the expression of still other genes.

LO3 Genetic Disorders

Genes can have both positive and negative effects on development. As we have seen, people can inherit harmful alleles of certain genes, such as the ones that cause hemophilia or early cataract. It is also possible for a person to receive whole sets of genes that are not only harmful but also fatal. In this section, we will look at some of the genetic abnormalities that can interfere with normal development. Table 2-2 summarizes the chief characteristics of some of the disorders that these abnormalities cause.

Table 2-2 Some disorders that are caused by genetic defects

Disorder and Its Nature	Incidence	Cause	Method of Diagnosis	Current Methods of Treatment and Prevention
Hemophilia Blood disease characterized by poor clotting ability	1/10,000 (80–90% males)	Heredity: X-linked recessive trait	Blood tests	Hemophilia is treated at present by transfusions of clotting factors. New gene-splicing techniques may make it possible to provide these factors without running the risk of the transmission of blood-borne infections from donated blood products. Genetic counselling can help determine whether a couple risk bearing a child with this disorder.
Diabetes mellitus Body's inability to metabolize carbohydrates and maintain proper glucose levels	Type I: 1/200 Type II: 1/50	Heredity: multi-gene, exaggerated by environmental factors	Blood and urine tests	Sufferers can often control this disorder by special diet alone. In other cases, oral medication and/or insulin injections are required to maintain the body's equilibrium.
Phenylketonuria (PKU) Inability to convert phenylalanine to tyrosine; untreated, leads to mental retardation	1/10,000	Heredity: recessive allele	Blood tests prenatally or at birth	Genetic counselling can indicate the risk that a couple will have a PKU child. Modern genetic techniques can detect recessive alleles before such a child's birth, and immediately after birth a special diet can be instituted that will prevent the disorder's toxic effects.
Sickle cell anemia Blood disease characterized by malformation of red blood cells that are low in oxygen	1/600 North American infants of African descent affected; 1/13 North Americans of African descent are carriers	Heredity: two recessive alleles in combination	Blood tests	Blood transfusions have until recently been the only treatment. However, the recent in utero treatment of a fetus for an autoimmune disorder has brought hope that sickle cell anemia and other similar diseases may be treated successfully before birth.
Down syndrome (trisomy 21) Physically and mentally retarded development; sometimes cardiovascular and respiratory abnormalities	1/1,000	Heredity: extra full or partial chromosome 21	Amniocentesis, alphafetoprotein assay, chorionic villi sampling, chromosome analysis	Special physical training; special education, including speech therapy. Surgical corrections of problems with the heart and with hearing are sometimes necessary.

Table 2-2 continued Some disorders that are caused by genetic defects

Disorder and Its Nature	Incidence	Cause	Method of Diagnosis	Current Methods of Treatment and Prevention
Turner (XO) syndrome Underdeveloped secondary sex characteristics; infertility; short stature; social immaturity; webbed neck; cardiovascular and renal abnormalities	1/1,200–4,000 (females)	Chromosomal abnormality: only one X chromosome instead of two	Blood tests	Hormone therapy can promote development of secondary sex characteristics. Counselling; special education to lessen deficits in spatial understanding.
Triple X (XXX) syndrome Some physical abnormalities, including menstrual irregularities and premature menopause; some limitations on cognitive abilities	1/1,000 females	Chromosomal abnormality: extra X chromosome	Blood tests	Special education to improve cognitive skills.
Klinefelter's (XXY) syndrome Some female physical characteristics; sterility; mild to severe cognitive difficulties	1/1,000 males	Chromosomal abnormality: extra X chromosome	Blood tests	Testosterone treatments can enhance development of male secondary sex characteristics as well as sexual interest and assertiveness. Special education to improve cognitive skills.
XYY syndrome Unusual height; some cognitive impairment; attention deficit	1/1,000 males	Chromosomal abnormality: extra Y chromosome	Blood tests	Special education.
Fragile X syndrome Physical abnormalities; mental retardation that deepens with time; psychological and social problems	1/1,200–4,000 males 1/5,000 females	Heredity: breaking of an X chromosome near its tip	Blood test	No known treatment.

Sources: Lambert & Drack, 1996; Lin et al., 1993; Martini, 1995; Money, 1993; Nightingale & Meister, 1987; Postlethwait & Hopson, 1995.

WHY HARMFUL ALLELES SURVIVE   A major reason why potentially harmful alleles survive is that they are not harmful in the heterozygous state—that is, when a person inherits both a normal allele and a recessive one. A good example is the allele that causes **phenylketonuria**, or **PKU**. The cause of PKU is a recessive allele that fails to produce an enzyme necessary to metabolize the protein phenylalanine in milk, the basic diet of infants. As long as a person also possesses a normal allele, the PKU allele has no ill effects. In fact, roughly 1 out of every 20 people of European ancestry carries the recessive PKU allele and does not even know it. Problems arise only in infants who are homozygous for the recessive gene. After birth, when they start ingesting milk, their bodies cannot break down phenylalanine. If infants are not treated, these toxic substances accumulate in their bodies, damaging the nervous system and causing mental retardation. Figure 2-5 shows that two heterozygous parents have a one-in-four chance of producing an infant who is homozygous for PKU. Most people who carry the PKU allele also have a normal allele, so they do not succumb to the disorder. Because these individuals survive and reproduce, however, the defective allele also survives from generation to generation, even though it is activated only 25 percent of the time.

phenylketonuria (PKU)

A disease caused by a recessive allele that fails to produce an enzyme necessary to metabolize the protein phenylalanine; if untreated immediately at birth, it damages the nervous system and causes mental retardation.

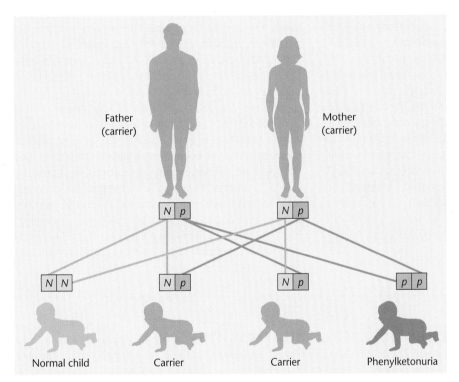

Father
(carrier)

Mother
(carrier)

| N | p |

| N | p |

| N | N | | N | p | | N | p | | p | p |

Normal child   Carrier   Carrier   Phenylketonuria

Figure 2-5

Genetic transmission of phenylketonuria

When both parents carry the recessive allele for phenylketonuria, they have a one-in-four chance of producing a child with the disorder. If their dominant genes for normality (*N*) are passed to their offspring, the child will be normal. If the child receives one dominant and one recessive gene (*p*), he will be a "carrier"—that is, he will not have the disorder himself, but he may pass the recessive allele to his own children. And, of course, if the child receives recessive genes from both parents, he will have phenylketonuria.

Some potentially harmful alleles may survive because they are actually beneficial in combination with a normal allele. Sickle cell anemia, a disease to which some individuals of African descent, as well as people in some African countries, are subject—provides an example. Box 2.1 on the following pages describes this disorder and how its allele actually helps some people survive another life-threatening disease: malaria.

Perspectives on Diversity

SICKLE CELL ANEMIA: A DOUBLE-EDGED SWORD

Sickle cell anemia, a severe and often fatal disorder, affects thousands of people in Canada and the United States (Driscoll, 2007). It is far more common, however, among individuals of Caribbean and African descent, who have carrier rates of 10 to 14 percent and 20 to 25 percent, respectively. The term **sickle cell anemia** comes from the peculiar shape that the red blood cells of an afflicted person assume when they are low in oxygen (for instance, when they have just released oxygen to hard-working muscle cells). Rather than remaining disc shaped, as normal red blood cells do, these cells become elongated and bent into the shape of a sickle (see Figure 2-6). This shape causes them to get stuck in small blood vessels, especially in the joints and the abdomen, resulting in severe pain, tissue damage, and possible death if critical vessels in the brain and lungs are blocked. Moreover, because these cells are abnormal, the spleen continually removes them from the blood, giving rise to chronic *anemia* (too few red blood cells). An allele on chromosome number 11 is the cause of sickle cell anemia. When its companion allele is also recessive for this trait, the person develops the disorder. Among people who have one sickle cell allele and one normal one, however, red blood cells rarely sickle, except under conditions of low oxygen, such as in mountain climbing or under anaesthesia, and as a result, such people usually suffer no harmful effects from the defective allele.

Scientists were once puzzled as to why the sickle-cell allele is so prevalent in many African communities and in some societies in the Middle East (Driscoll, 2007). The mystery was solved with the discovery that the sickle cell allele also has a positive effect. It confers protection against malaria, another deadly disease found in almost exactly the same areas where sickle-cell anemia is found. When malarial parasites take up residence in the red blood cells of someone who is heterozygous for this disorder, or who has one sickle-cell allele and one normal one, the cells become sickle shaped when low in oxygen, just as such cells typically behave in people who are homozygous for the allele. But in this case, when the spleen removes the parasite-containing cells from the blood, it removes the malarial parasites as well. As a result, people with only one sickle cell allele have built-in resistance to malaria—an enormous aid to survival.

Because the defective allele enables these people to fight off malaria, they tend to live longer than people who do not have a sickle cell gene to protect them, and they reproduce more often; thus, they pass the gene on to subsequent generations in increasing numbers. In this way, a potentially harmful gene not only survives but also flourishes. Of course, for the person who is homozygous for sickle cell anemia, or has two recessive genes for this disorder, the illness itself is so life-threatening that the person's enhanced resistance to malaria is of little benefit.

sickle cell anemia

A disorder, caused by a recessive gene, in which the red blood cells become distorted when low in oxygen, causing fatigue, shortness of breath, and severe pain, and posing a threat to life from blockage of crucial blood vessels.

Down syndrome

A form of chromosome abnormality, in which the person suffers disabling physical and mental development and is highly susceptible to such illnesses as leukemia, heart disorders, and respiratory infections.

CHROMOSOMAL ABNORMALITIES Developmental disorders can be caused not only by single genes or gene groups but also by defects in entire chromosomes. Almost 1 percent of all newborns have diagnosable chromosome abnormalities, and it has been estimated that 60 percent of early spontaneous abortions and 5 percent of later miscarriages are attributable to aberrations in chromosomes. Normally, such chromosomal defects are not present in a child's parents. Instead, they generally arise during the process of meiosis, when the eggs or the sperms are formed. In a great many instances, the aberration proves lethal and the zygote produced by the union of the sperm and the egg spontaneously aborts. But sometimes, particularly when certain chromosomes are involved, a zygote is able to survive the abnormal condition, and a baby with a chromosomal defect is born.

DOWN SYNDROME **Down syndrome** is characterized by physical and mental retardation and a distinctive physical appearance. People with this syndrome are typically of short stature, usually have almond-shaped eyes with a fold in the eyelid, and one or more other unusual physical characteristics. More troublesome is their

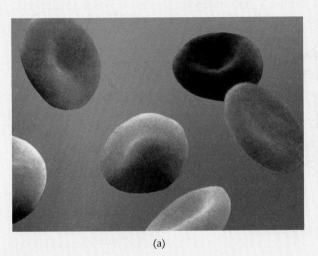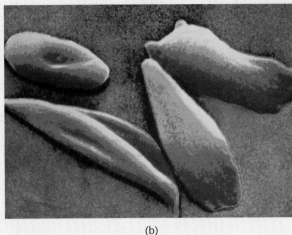

(a)   (b)

Figure 2-6   Red blood cell changes in sickle cell anemia

Normal red blood cells are disc shaped (a), but in sickle cell anemia, these cells become sickled, or distorted, when they are low in oxygen (b). Among the symptoms of this disorder are pain in the joints and abdomen, chronic fatigue, and shortness of breath.

Until recently, there had been little hope for victims of sickle cell anemia. The successful in utero treatment of a 4-month-old fetus for a condition called *severe combined immunodeficiency*, however, has made it possible now to think of treating sickle cell anemia and many other immune deficiency and blood diseases before birth. In this groundbreaking surgery, physicians injected bone marrow cells from the father into the fetus's abdomen by means of a long needle inserted through the mother's abdomen, using ultrasonography as a guide (Driscoll, 2007). Nearly a year and a half after his birth, the child was healthy and showed no sign of the rare genetic disease that had threatened his not-yet-begun life. Another promising treatment involves using a drug to turn on a gene for fetal hemoglobin that is normally dormant after birth. This fetal version of the gene is usually normal and reduces sickling (Atweh et al., 1999).

heightened susceptibility to such illnesses as leukemia, heart disorders, and respiratory infections and their moderate to severe mental retardation. However, with advances in the treatment of these physical disorders (such as the use of antibiotics for pneumonia), the lifespans of people with Down syndrome have greatly increased; currently, about 70 percent of individuals with Down syndrome live into their sixties. Unfortunately, they are at greater risk for developing Alzheimer's disease in later life than the average person (Nelson, Scheibel, Ringman, & Sayre, 2007; Zigman & Lott, 2007).

Probably the most well-known chromosomal disorder, Down syndrome is caused by a deviation in the set of chromosomes labelled number 21. Instead of a pair of these chromosomes, the person with Down syndrome has three chromosomes, which is why the disorder is also called *trisomy 21*. The extra 21st chromosome most often comes from the mother's egg, when her homologous pair of 21st chromosomes fail to separate during meiosis. The male sperm carries the extra chromosome in only about 5 percent of cases (Antonarakis & Down Syndrome Collaborative Group, 1991). And for reasons that are not yet fully understood, this error occurs more often when older women become pregnant (Sherman, Allen, Bean, & Freeman, 2007) (see Table 2-3 fol-

Down Syndrome

With some special help, the child with Down syndrome in this affectionate family may complete school, get a job, and have loving friends and a satisfying life, much like anyone else.

lowing). The father's age matters, too; Down syndrome births are higher for men over 40, especially if the mother is over 35. It is the combination of two older parents that increases the risk since in younger women who are not at risk for producing a Down syndrome child, there was no paternal effect (Lewis, Legato, & Fisch, 2006). Scientists have recently identified a gene that may play a role in the mental retardation associated with Down syndrome, but it is likely that other genes play a role as well (Smith et al., 1997; Patterson, 2007).

Table 2-3

Risk of giving birth to a Down syndrome infant, by maternal age

Maternal Age	Down Syndrome Detected at 9 to 11 Weeks by CVS	Down Syndrome Detected at 16 Weeks by Amniocentesis	Frequency of Down Syndrome among Births
20–24			1/1,400
25–29			1/1,100
30			1/900
35	1/250	1/250	1/385
40	1/80	1/70	1/100
45	1/25	1/25	1/40
50	1/20	1/15	1/25

Sources: Adapted from Gaulden, 1992; Hook, 1982.

Infants with Down syndrome may develop fairly normally in their first six months, but unless they receive special therapy, their rate of intellectual growth begins to decline after about a year. These children are generally slow to learn to speak (Abbeduto, Warren, & Connors, 2007) and often have difficulty articulating words and even producing complex sentences in adolescence (Price et al., 2008). They also have trouble attending to, discriminating, and interpreting complex or subtle information in their environments (e.g., Burack & Enns, 1997; Zelazo & Stack, 1997). These difficulties are reflected in problems in communication between children with Down syndrome and their caregivers (Legerstee, Bowman, & Fels, 1992; Legerstee, Varghese, & van Beek, 2002); often, parents of children with Down syndrome are encouraged to talk more and be more directive than the parents of normal children (Hodapp, 2002; Tannock, 1988). Children with Down syndrome develop more competence when their caregivers provide them with stimulation and encourage them to be more attentive to and involved in their environments. Although these efforts are more apt to enhance emotional, social, and motor development than cognitive development, training can help children with Down syndrome to learn to read and write (Fidler & Nadel, 2007; Hodapp, 2002), and children with Down syndrome can become competent adults who hold jobs and live independently in group homes.

SEX-CHROMOSOMAL ANOMALIES Abnormalities may also arise in the sex chromosomes. For example, some females are born with only one X chromosome, rather than the normal XX pattern. Usually, this occurs because the father's sperm contained neither an X nor a Y chromosome. Girls with this XO pattern, called **Turner syndrome**, remain short, with stubby fingers, webbed necks, and unusually shaped mouths and ears. They usually have normal intelligence, although there is some evidence of deficits in visual and spatial processing (Hepworth & Rovet, 2000; Murphy & Mazzocco, 2008; Rovet, 2004; Rovet & Buchanan, 1999), as well as in arithmetic reasoning (Mazzocco, Murphy, & McCloskey, 2007; Murphy & Mazzocco, 2008; Rovet, 2004). As teenagers, they do not develop secondary sex characteristics, such as breasts and pubic hair, unless given female hormones. Because their internal reproductive organs do not develop normally, they remain sterile throughout their lives. Women with Turner syndrome tend to be docile and pleasant but do have problems in social relationships because they are immature and lacking in assertiveness (Kesler, 2007; Rovet & Ireland, 1994). These problems are related, in part, to others' responses to these women's physical appearance. More importantly, women with Turner syndrome have difficulty discriminating and interpreting emotional cues and facial expressions in others—skills essential for maintaining appropriate social interactions (Kesler, 2007).

Another sex-chromosomal abnormality found in females is the XXX pattern, in which a girl inherits three X sex chromosomes instead of the normal two. These *triple-X* girls appear normal physically and have normal secondary sexual development, but their cognitive abilities are affected, especially their short-term memory and verbal skills (Rovet et al., 1996; Rovet & Netley, 1983). When a male inherits an extra X chromosome, producing an XXY pattern known as **Klinefelter's syndrome**, he is sterile and has many female characteristics, such as breast development and a rounded, broad-hipped figure. Like the triple-X female, he tends to have verbal language deficits and reading problems (Rovet et al., 1996), memory and reasoning problems (Fales et al., 2003), inhibitory skills (Temple & Sanfilippo, 2003), and is sometimes retarded. Also likely to suffer some cognitive impairment is the male who inherits an extra Y chromosome, the XYY pattern once thought to be accompanied by excessive aggressiveness. Although XYY men are generally taller than normal men, they have not been shown to be any more aggressive or violent than others (Burns & Bottino, 1989).

Finally, some people carry an X chromosome that appears to be pinched or narrowed in some areas, causing it to be quite fragile. This **fragile X syndrome** is more frequent in males than in females. It accounts for roughly 5 percent of retarded males whose IQ scores range between 30 and 55, although not all males with the syndrome are retarded (Reiss & Hall, 2007). In addition, people with fragile X syndrome often have physical abnormalities and psychological and social problems (Methot, Berthiaume, Aunos, & Pidgeon, 2001). Cleft palate, seizures, abnormal electroencephalograms (or EEGs), and disorders of the eye are some of the more common physical symptoms. Psychological and social problems include anxiety, hyperactivity, attention deficits, and abnormal communication patterns (Garrett et al., 2004). Males may have deficits in social interaction, and females may be more likely to suffer from depression and also to show cognitive and linguistic deficits (Reiss & Hall, 2007).

In considering these chromosomal anomalies, it is important to remember the influence of the environment on the way genes are expressed. The severity of the symptoms that arise with hereditary disorders is often related to the degree to which the person has a supportive environment (Evans & Gray, 2000; Hodapp, 2002). We will return to the topic of how environmental conditions can lessen the effects of genetic abnormalities a little later in this chapter. It is also important to remember that with special therapeutic and educational methods, some manifestations of these abnormalities may be modified. Recent studies with animals show promise of developing enzyme-inhibiting therapies that may be able to lessen or even reverse the symptoms of fragile X syndrome (Hayashi et al., 2007).

Turner syndrome

A form of abnormality of the sex chromosomes found in females, in which secondary sex characteristics develop only if female hormones are administered and in which abnormal formation of internal reproductive organs leads to permanent sterility.

Turner Syndrome
Klinefelter's Syndrome
Fragile X Syndrome

Klinefelter's syndrome

A form of chromosome abnormality, in which a male inherits an extra X sex chromosome, resulting in the XXY pattern, and has many feminine physical characteristics as well as language deficits and, sometimes, mental retardation.

fragile X syndrome

A form of chromosome abnormality, more common in males than in females, in which an X chromosome is narrowed in some areas, causing it to be fragile and leading to a variety of physical, psychological, and social problems.

For Thought and Discussion

1. Assume that the trait of left-handedness versus right-handedness is genetically coded, with right-handedness being dominant over left-handedness. A heterozygous right-handed woman marries a heterozygous right-handed male. What are the odds that their children will be right- versus left-handed? (*Note:* You may want to study Figure 2-5 on page 53 to figure this one out!)

2. In the previous question, what happens if the woman is now homozygous right-handed? What if she is homozygous left-handed? Can either the woman or the man be heterozygous left-handed? Why, or why not?

3. One aspect inherent to the study of genotypes and phenotypes is that we often infer genotype from observations of phenotype (e.g., inferring that twins are identical because they look alike). What limitations are there to such inferences, and what are the implications of such limitations? How might you get around such limitations?

LO4 GENETIC COUNSELLING AND GENETIC ENGINEERING

Advances in biology and genetics have opened new opportunities for shaping and controlling some aspects of development. For some time now, it has been possible to sample cells from a developing fetus to determine whether the fetus carries genes for any of the disorders we have discussed, as well as for many others. With this knowledge, it is now possible to get *genetic counselling*, which is a health-care service that provides medical information about genetic disorders and risks to couples, and that can help people to make personal, and often difficult, decisions regarding their health, their pregnancies, and their child's health. Such genetic counselling is available for people who are concerned about their own risks for a genetic problem or the risks to a child because of family history or ethnic background, or who have a child with a genetic or medical condition, as well as for discussing the implications of various prenatal diagnostic techniques, which we will discuss in the next section.

Currently, there are over two dozen masters-level genetic-counselling programs in North America, with three of them in Canada, located at McGill University, the University of British Columbia, and the University of Toronto. These programs are accredited by the American Board of Genetic Counseling, and enable graduates to then apply for certification by the Canadian Association of Genetic Counsellors. These programs provide genetic counsellors with the knowledge they need to be able to answer questions for couples facing difficult, and often ethically problematic, decisions regarding the implications of genetic testing.

More recent advances in the study of genes and their influence have made it possible to offer what we might call preventive genetic counselling. In this type of counselling, couples wanting to have a child can themselves be tested for various defective genes. If they find that they carry defective alleles, they may elect to adopt a child or to conceive a child through one of various *assisted reproductive techniques* in which a donor's egg or sperm may be substituted for one of their own germ cells. These techniques were originally developed to make parenting possible for couples who could not conceive and bear a child of their own. Box 2.2 describes some of the most common of these techniques, along with the implications of such work.

Box 2.2

Child Psychology in Action

THE NEW REPRODUCTIVE AND GENETIC TECHNOLOGIES

The technique of *in vitro fertilization*—literally, fertilization "in glass" or in a glass dish—is most often used to make child-bearing possible for a woman whose fallopian tubes are blocked. Physicians administer hormones to the woman to stimulate ovulation and then remove mature eggs from her ovary. They then place the eggs in a nourishing solution in a glass petri dish, where they are mixed with the husband's sperms. If fertilization is successful, the zygote begins to divide, and when it is at the eight-cell stage, approximately two to four days later, it is inserted into the woman's uterus. For the pregnancy to be successful, the embryo must implant itself in the lining of the uterus. If the woman's uterus is not at the optimum stage to facilitate implantation, the embryo may be frozen and stored until the uterus reaches the proper stage.

In vitro fertilization was a remarkable breakthrough when Louise Joy Brown, the first baby conceived outside of her mother's body, was born in England in 1978. Since then, the techniques have become common, with 200,000 babies born each year, and, to date, nearly 3 million babies have been born worldwide using some form of new reproductive technology (de Mouzon, June, 2006). This technique is used in a variety of situations (for example, when a male spouse has an insufficient supply of sperm to fertilize the female's egg; or if the woman cannot produce an egg, the man's sperm may be used to fertilize a female donor's egg, which is then implanted in the wife's uterus). The zygote produced by a man's sperm and a woman's egg may be implanted in the uterus of a surrogate mother who carries the child to term. Using this technique, in 1991, a woman carried her own grandchild for her daughter who had been born without a uterus. This feat of becoming a mother and a grandmother at the same time has since been repeated by other women. But the costs of in vitro fertilization are high whether the procedure involves using a woman's own eggs (US$12,500 to $25,000) or donor eggs (US$20,000 to $35,000). In the United States, insurance will cover only part of these costs (or none at all); in Canada and Britain, these procedures are treated as part of medical coverage, and are, thus, available to individuals regardless of income level (Golombok, 2006).

Like many other medical breakthroughs, these new reproductive and genetic techniques present numerous social, ethical, and legal dilemmas (Health Canada, 1999a;

Parke, Gailey, Coltrane, DiMatteo, 2008; Schwartz, 2003). These issues are serious enough that the Canadian Institutes of Health Research, the Natural Sciences and Engineering Research Council of Canada, and the Social Sciences and Humanities Research Council of Canada said in a joint statement (Tri-council policy statement, 1998), in no uncertain terms, that some of these new reproductive procedures are not only disturbing, they are clearly problematic and unethical as well.

The Canadian government has responded to the ethical issues as well. In 1996, Bill C-47, the Human Reproductive and Genetic Technologies Act, which legislated the prohibition of certain reproductive and genetic technologies, was tabled in Parliament (although the bill subsequently died in 1997). On October 28, 2003, Bill C-13 was passed. This new bill on reproductive technology addresses issues related to assisted human reproduction and related research practices such as cloning, the sale and purchase of human embryos, commercial surrogacy, gender selection for babies, genetic-code alteration (so-called "designer-babies"), the creation of embryos solely for research purposes, and the transplanting of reproductive material from animals to humans. And in March 2004, Bill C-6, the Act Respecting Assisted Human Reproduction and Related Research, became law. The

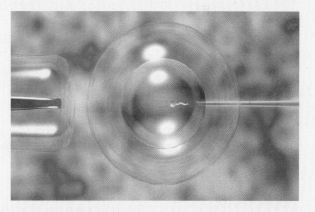

In this computerized rendering of the microscopic in vitro fertilization procedure, we can see that the egg (rounded, greenish) lying in a petri dish has just been penetrated by a micro-needle (green, at right), allowing one tiny sperm cell (pinkish head, with yellow tail) to enter and fertilize the egg. The device at the left, called a pipette (green and white), holds the egg steady as the needle is inserted.

Box 2.2 continued

Child Psychology in Action

bill addresses the creation of stem cells from human embryos, providing guidelines governing stem-cell research.

What are some of the ethical issues involved? For one thing, although these techniques can enhance the life of people, they have the potential to treat both women and children, and reproduction itself, as commodities. Also, Health Canada (1999a) has asked, What about the children born from such procedures, who will be exposed to physical, emotional, and legal risks? Finally, the legal issues are considerable. What legal rights does a donor or the woman acting as a surrogate

have over the zygote of another couple? What legal rights does a male donor have? What should be done if one or both parents die while the zygote is in storage, as happened in a recent Australian case?

Despite these serious issues, many people feel that the hope, joy, and prospect of parenthood provided by these technologies outweigh the other more problematic considerations. That said, whether, how, and when to use such procedures are questions that will have to be decided by individuals and couples, as well as governments and society as a whole.

LO 5 Prenatal Diagnostic Techniques

It is possible that someday, we may be able to replace defective genes in a fetus through gene therapy, thus preventing a genetically determined disorder before it even happens. Already, physicians have been successful in injecting healthy bone marrow into a fetus to counteract an autoimmune disorder (Anderson, 1995). Before we discuss the exciting new work in this area, however, let us look at the major existing methods for testing the viability and health of a fetus.

amniocentesis

A technique for sampling and assessing fetal cells for indications of abnormalities in the developing fetus; performed by inserting a needle through the abdominal wall and into the amniotic sac and withdrawing a small amount of the amniotic fluid.

chorionic villi sampling

A technique for sampling and assessing cells withdrawn from the chorionic villi, which are projections from the chorion that surrounds the amniotic sac; cells are withdrawn either through a tube inserted into the uterus through the vagina or through a needle inserted through the abdominal wall.

COMMONLY USED TESTS The risk of disorder, as in the case of an older expectant mother, may prompt testing of a fetus. In **amniocentesis**, the most widely used technique for sampling fetal cells, a physician inserts a needle into the amniotic sac, or the fluid-filled membranous cover that surrounds and protects the fetus, and withdraws a little of the amniotic fluid. This fluid contains cells sloughed off from the fetus (such as skin cells), which pathologists can then analyze for their chromosomal and genetic makeup. The 16th week of pregnancy seems optimal for performing amniocentesis. By this time, there are enough cells in the amniotic fluid to draw an adequate sample, yet the fetus is still small enough not to be injured by the insertion of the needle. Nevertheless, this technique does carry a small risk of miscarriage; about 1 woman in 200 or 300 miscarries after this procedure.

Slightly more risky is **chorionic villi sampling**, which can be done as early as the ninth or tenth week of pregnancy. Physicians draw cells from the chorionic villi, the finger-like projections from the chorion, which is the outermost membrane that surrounds the amniotic sac. The villi help the zygote to embed itself in the uterine lining and then multiply to form the placenta. Although the villi are not part of the embryo itself, the chromosomes and genes in them are identical to the embryo's because they all arise from the same fertilized egg.

With a prenatal sample of cells in hand, it is possible to examine the fetus's chromosomes and genes for any signs of chromosomal disorder. The critical abnormalities (such as missing or extra chromosomes) are clearly visible under a high-powered microscope. In addition, scientists have identified particular pieces of DNA, called *genetic markers*, that can serve as indicators of many disorders caused by one or more defective genes. For example, the gene for cystic fibrosis has been located on the midsection of chromosome 7, and a gene for familial Alzheimer's disease is found on the long arm of chromosome 21 (Lander, 1996). The latter discovery may, in part, account for the fact that children with Down syndrome, as we have already noted, face a greater chance of developing Alzheimer's disease, as they have an extra chromosome 21 (although we cannot be certain that this is so without further research).

One of the more personal hunts for a genetic marker was led by neuropsychologist Nancy Wexler whose mother had died of **Huntington disease**, a fatal deterioration of the nervous system that begins in mid-adulthood. Wexler had a 50 percent chance of inheriting Huntington. She charted patterns of the disease in 5,000 Venezuelans who were all descendants of a woman who had died of Huntington more than 100 years ago. By using DNA samples from living relatives who had the disorder, Wexler and geneticist James Gusella (Gusella et al., 1983) were able to identify a Huntington marker that was located near one end of chromosome 4. This discovery made it possible to develop a test for the Huntington gene. Recent work with animals suggests that new drugs may prevent the deterioration of cells associated with this disease (Tang, Chen, Liu, & Bezprozvanny, 2007).

Two other prenatal tests are now routinely done for most pregnancies, not just in cases of suspected risk based on family history. The **alphafetoprotein assay (AFP)** is a maternal blood test that can reveal fetal problems, such as Down syndrome or defects of the central nervous system, as well as the presence of multiple embryos. **Ultrasound**, or ultrasonography, a method of visualizing deep body structures, is now commonly used to detect gross physical abnormalities in a fetus. The technique, which scans the uterus by means of sound waves, produces a sonogram, or film, that shows the size and structure of the developing fetus and that has the added feature of determining the baby's gender, if parents want to know this information. Ultrasonography has other benefits as well. The opportunity to observe that the developing fetus is healthy and normal probably reduces parents' anxieties.

ETHICAL AND POLICY ISSUES   When prenatal genetic testing reveals some major chromosomal or genetic abnormality in an unborn child, parents have the option of aborting the pregnancy. But this raises the ethical dilemma of deciding when an abnormality is severe enough to warrant an abortion. If a fetus has a lethal genetic disorder that will lead to a painful death in a few months or years, the choice is often easier than if the disorder is one that is not so devastating. What about a female fetus with Turner syndrome or the XO chromosome pattern or a male with the XXY pattern that gives rise to Klinefelter's syndrome? Although these children have both physical abnormalities and some cognitive impairments, they are capable of leading very productive lives. Confronting prospective parents with such difficult ethical choices is one result of developing the new technology to analyze chromosomes and genes (Murray, 1996). Even non-genetic testing, such as ultrasound, is associated with ethical problems. For example, in some cultures where male children are preferred over females, this kind of prenatal assessment could lead to an increase in the rate of abortions of female fetuses (Murray, 1996; Shanley, 2001).

The new availability of genetic information also raises troubling issues of ethics and policy in such areas as employment and personal insurance, as well as among people who oppose abortion (Plomin & Rutter, 1998). For example, it is conceivable that employers might decide to require in-depth genetic screening for potential employees and to reject individuals who have a gene that may someday put them at risk for cancer, heart trouble, or other diseases. Equally disturbing is the possibility that insurance companies might decide to use information about the genetic risks people may have for certain diseases to exclude such individuals from insurance protection or to adjust rates for insurance coverage (Kass, 2002; Murray, 1996). Finally, religious and social groups are concerned about the rising rate of abortion owing to increased use of genetic screening. The best route to developing guidelines for addressing such dilemmas may be to heighten public awareness of these issues (Bentley, 1996).

Huntington disease

A genetically caused, fatal disorder of the nervous system that begins in mid-adulthood and is manifested chiefly in uncontrollable, spasmodic movements of the body and limbs and eventual mental deterioration.

alphafetoprotein assay (AFP)

A blood test performed prenatally to detect such problems as Down syndrome, the presence of multiple embryos, and defects of the central nervous system.

ultrasound

A technique that uses sound waves to visualize deep body structures; commonly used to reveal the size and structure of a developing fetus.

Gene Therapy

Scientists hope not only to locate the genes responsible for inherited disorders but also to use gene therapy to alleviate or even cure these problems. Gene therapy involves inserting normal alleles into patients' cells to compensate for defective alleles. The most effective current technique uses modified viruses (viruses from which harmful properties have been removed) to carry the new genes into patients' cells. Scientists have adopted this strategy because viruses are, by nature, adapted to penetrate another organism's cells. Most often, target cells in the patient are first removed from the person's body, infused with the new gene by way of the virus, and then returned to the body. This procedure was first used in the United States in 1990 in treating a 4-year-old girl who had a deadly genetic disorder that shut down her immune system, leaving her defenceless against infections. Doctors inserted the gene needed to produce a critical enzyme that her immune system lacked into some of the child's blood. Ten years later, she continued to do well with some additional medication (Thompson, 2000). Not all the news about gene therapy has been good, however. Few effective treatments have been found despite more than 400 clinical trials. More ominously, patients in some trials have died.

It may be some time before gene therapy is perfected, but much information has been gathered to assist in this work. Box 2.3 on pages 64 and 65 describes the work of the Human Genome Project, whose aim was to map the identities and locations of all human genes in the hope of ultimately being able to prevent or treat the more than 4,000 diseases to which our genes make us susceptible.

But again, as science enters this new age of genetic engineering, we confront significant ethical issues (Kass, 2002; Murray, 1996). As greater genetic manipulation becomes possible, how should we use it? It is one thing to replace a defective allele in a person who is seriously ill, and quite another to attempt to create a race of superhumans. Even more troublesome to many is our newfound ability to clone living creatures. The potential benefits of many of our new technologies are great, but the dangers of using them unwisely may be even greater.

LO6 HEREDITY–ENVIRONMENT INTERACTIONS

In the past, many scientists took up opposing positions on what was referred to familiarly as the nature–nurture issue. Scholars who were more biologically oriented emphasized the role of heredity and maturational factors in human development, whereas those who were more environmentally oriented emphasized the role of learning and experience. In societies in which political and social philosophies stressed the importance of opportunity, education, and initiative, theories of biological determinism fell on rocky ground. In contrast, the environmentalist position of John B. Watson and the behaviourists flourished. In 1926, in the heat of the nature–nurture debate, Watson boasted,

> *Give me a dozen healthy infants, well-formed, and my own specific world to bring them up in and I'll guarantee to take any one at random and train him to become any type of specialist I might select—a doctor, lawyer, artist, merchant-chief and, yes, even into beggar-man and thief, regardless of his talents, penchants, tendencies, abilities, vocations, and race of his ancestors.* (Watson, 1926, p. 10)

Today, psychologists see neither nature nor nurture as wholly responsible for the development of a human being. Instead, scholars focus today on how heredity and environment interact to shape the developing person. Although they see genetic endowment as to some extent limiting what a person can become, most believe that social and environmental experience exert a tremendous influence on the developing child. Moreover, gene–environment interactions are highly complex, with environments influencing how genes are expressed, and genes helping to shape the environments to which people are exposed. We will explore both sides of this complex story.

How the Environment Influences the Expression of Genes

The concept of **range of reaction** exemplifies how environments influence genes (Gottesman, 1963; Plomin, 1995). According to this concept, heredity establishes a range of possible developmental outcomes that may occur in response to different environments. As you might expect, individuals with different genetic makeups also have different ranges of reaction; their particular sets of genes set boundaries on their range of developmental possibilities. But within those boundaries, it is largely the environment that determines how the person will develop.

A good example of the interaction between range of reaction and the environment is provided by the hypothetical example illustrated in Figure 2-7. Each of the three children represented by curves A, B, and C has a different range of possible scores on an achievement test. If all three children experience exactly the same level of environmental stimulation, child C will always outperform the other two. However, child B could achieve a substantially higher score than C, if B experiences a more enriched environment than C does. (An enriched environment may have a high level of physical stimulation, such as a wide array of toys and books; social-emotional stimulation, such as the presence of highly responsive and attentive caregivers; or cognitive-linguistic stimulation, such as caregivers who talk and read a lot to a child.) Note, too, that child C has the widest range of reaction, that is, the difference between child C's potential performance in either restricted or enriched environments is much greater than the analogous difference for child B and child A. Child A has both the lowest and the most limited range of reaction. This child not only scores below average (50), whether raised in a stimulating or unstimulating setting, but also shows less ability to respond to environmental enrichment.

range of reaction

The notion that the human being's genetic makeup establishes a range of possible developmental outcomes, within which environmental forces largely determine how the person actually develops.

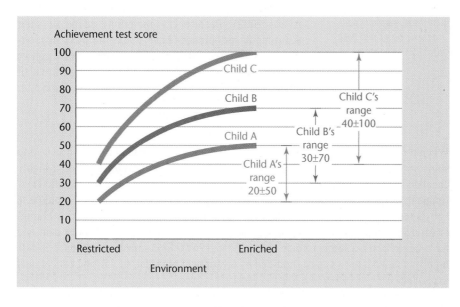

Figure 2-7

Interaction between environment and genotype

Providing any child with an enriched, stimulating environment can substantially improve the child's performance on various measures of achievement. However, each child's genotype—in this hypothetical illustration, these are represented by the labels "child A," "child B," and "child C"—will determine the limits within which his or her performance may vary.

Source: Adapted from Gottesman, 1963.

Child Psychology in Action

THE HUMAN GENOME PROJECT

The Human Genome Project (HGP) is an international co-operative scientific endeavour, funded by both private and public dollars, the aim of which is to locate all the genes of the human genome and then to sequence all human chromosomes (list the actual base pairs) accurately. The US Congress authorized funding in 1988, and mapping and sequencing were completed in 2003 (International Human Genome Sequencing Consortium, 2004). Due to public and private lab co-operation and improved technology, the work was completed ahead of schedule. The final version of the human genome contains an estimated 20,000–25,000 human protein-coding genes, about 15,000 genes fewer than previously predicted (Venter et al., 2001). Recently, Craig Venter published his complete DNA sequence, the first time that the full 6-billion-letter genome of a single individual has been available (Levy et al., 2007). It is likely that similar information about others will be available soon, and in the future, as costs go down, many of us will know our own genomic information.

Consider this description of the cataloguing of the human genome:

> Some geneticists compare these segments (of genes) to books on a library shelf and for chromosomes 21 and Y, all the books now shelved are in the correct order. Researchers still can't decipher the locations or meanings of most phrases (genes) and letters (nucleotide sequences) within these volumes. At least, though, once an experimenter does discover which large segment contains a gene or base sequence of interest, he or she gets it straight off the "library shelf." (Postlethwait & Hopson, 1995, p. 281)

Work is also being done on animal genomes to increase our basic knowledge and to help provide more accurate models for the study and treatment of human diseases and conditions (US Department of Energy, 2002; NIH, 2002). Work that compares the human genome sequences with animal genome sequences has given scientists some insights into the birth and death of genes in the human genome. Over 1,000 new genes arose in the human genome after our divergence from rodents some 75 million years ago. For example, there are two families of new genes in the human genome that encode sets of proteins that may be involved in the extended period of pregnancy in humans. Similarly, other genes have died or stopped functioning, such as those involved in olfactory or smell reception. This may account for humans having a poorer sense of smell than rodents.

The implications of the HGP are sweeping. Not only will it give us insight into the basic workings of the human body, but it will provide us with important insights into genetic diseases, such as sickle cell anemia, Huntington disease, Turner syndrome, and Williams syndrome. These and several hundred other diseases are carried on single genes, but most illnesses, such as cancer or heart disease, are determined by interactions among multiple genes; figuring out the origins of most genetically caused illnesses will be a truly daunting task (Benson, 2004; Plomin et al., 2002). Despite the incredible scope of their assignment, researchers have made progress in identifying genes that may, in part, account for diseases such as Lou Gehrig's disease (ALS), some forms of Alzheimer's disease, epilepsy, and even cardiovascular

canalization

The genetic restriction of a phenotype to a small number of developmental outcomes, permitting environmental influences to play only a small role in these outcomes.

When a reaction range is extremely narrow, even narrower than child A's, it is said to show strong **canalization** (Waddington, 1962, 1966). The development of a highly canalized trait is restricted to just a few pathways, and intense or more specific environmental pushes are required to deflect the course of development. For example, a baby's tendency to repetitively utter consonant–vowel combinations (called babbling) is strongly canalized because babbling occurs even in babies who are born deaf and have never heard a human voice (Lenneberg, 1967). In contrast, intelligence is less highly canalized, for it can be modified by a variety of physical, social, and educational experiences.

Gilbert Gottlieb (1991, 1992; Gottlieb & Lickliter, 2004), from the University of North Carolina at Greensboro, has offered a view of gene–environment interaction in which genes play a less determining role in shaping development. Gottlieb argues that individual development is organized into multiple levels—genetic activity, neural

disease and resistance to HIV (Lander, 1996). New insights into the genetic origin of disease may lead to new therapeutic procedures.

Finally this information is shedding new light on the interplay between genes and the environment as well. Caspi and his colleagues (Caspi et al., 2003; Moffitt & Caspi, 2006) have studied a gene identified through HGP that affects the breakdown and uptake of neurotransmitters in the brain. Interestingly, these pioneering researchers discovered that although this gene has effects on anti-social behaviour, these effects are seen only in people exposed to child abuse during childhood. Once again, we are reminded that genes do not act alone; their impact on human behaviour depends on the particular environmental factors that also affect the individual.

As with genetic testing, there are ethical concerns about how doctors, employers, and insurance companies will use the data and about possible abuses of the new genetic information (Lowrance & Collins, 2007). For example, even if scientists determine that a person is genetically prone to develop a disease, she may never do so; as a result, caution in the use of this information is critical.

Not all are as wary as others. As Nobel laureate James Watson argued, "When finally interpreted, the genetic message encoded within our DNA molecules will provide the ultimate answers to the chemical underpinnings of human existence" (Postlethwait & Hopson, 1995, p. 281).

A geneticist examines a computer display of a DNA sequencing pattern. These patterns are used to write the human genetic codes for protein production and for various structural and functional characteristics that are transmitted from generation to generation.

Human Genome Project

activity (activity of the nervous system), behaviour, and environment—all of which influence each other. As Figure 2-8 on the next page shows, this influence is bidirectional—that is, both from bottom to top and from top to bottom. Consequently, genes and the environment mutually influence each other; for example, the prenatal environment could alter the expression of the genes, and the postnatal environment, in part, will determine whether a genetic predisposition finds full expression in behaviour. Thus, although each of the figure's levels generally influences the level directly above or below it, other interactions across non-adjacent levels are possible as well. In his work on mallard ducklings, Gottlieb found that the ducklings' usual preference for the sounds of other ducks—a genetically governed preference—could be modified if the ducklings were exposed before birth to sounds made by chickens. The ducklings exposed to "chicken sounds" preferred these sounds over duck sounds.

Figure 2-8

Bidirectional influence in gene–environment interactions

In the developmental systems view, the influence wielded by each of the four levels of individual development is bidirectional, that is, each level influences both the one above and the one below it. Any level may also influence non-adjacent levels.

Source: Gottlieb, 1992.

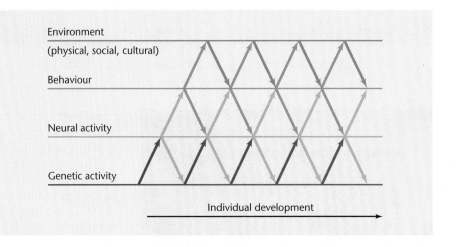

The most important point of this view is the recognition that genes are part of an overall system and that their activity—that is, the expression of the characteristics they carry—is affected by events at other levels of the system, including the organism's environment.

Another factor in gene–environment interaction is the stage of the child's development. Both developmental stage and the environment determine the likelihood that a genetically based trait or characteristic will be influenced by environmental forces. For example, as we discuss further in Chapter 3, if a fetus is exposed early in its development to the virus that causes German measles, the child is very likely to have some damage to its hearing. After the third month of pregnancy, however, fetal exposure to this virus generally does not affect the child's hearing. The window of opportunity for this particular environmental influence has largely closed because the fetus has reached a more mature stage of development.

Another example of the importance of critical periods can be seen in the treatment for PKU, the genetic disorder we discussed earlier. Babies today are routinely tested for PKU, and if they are found to be homozygous for the trait, they are placed on a special diet low in phenylalanine to prevent the buildup of toxins that results in mental retardation. In Figure 2-9, we see once again that in the interaction between genotype and the environment, there is a window of opportunity. The special PKU diet must begin immediately after birth, for delays of even a few months can have devastating effects on a child's intellectual development. On the other hand, if this diet is begun at once and continued until the nervous system is mature, a PKU child can develop intellectual abilities that are close to normal. Whether a child must stay on this diet indefinitely is subject to controversy; at present, most experts recommend that females, at least, remain on it for life if they plan to bear children. If they do not do this, they may have to go back on the diet in pregnancy; if they fail to do this early enough in a pregnancy, they may miscarry or the fetus may develop mental retardation (Verp, 1993). This example illustrates not only the importance of the timing of environmental influences but the complex way in which developmental outcomes—even those involving a genetically based predisposition—arise from the interaction between genes and the environment.

How Genetic Makeup Helps Shape the Environment

It is now widely accepted that the environment influences gene expression. However, the idea that the environment can be shaped by genes is relatively new and is less commonly acknowledged. Scientists have proposed several ways in which people's genetic makeup

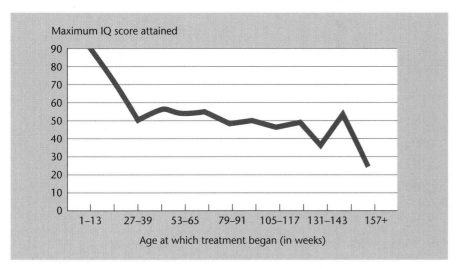

Figure 2-9

Diet and intelligence in PKU children

Clearly, delaying the age at which a special diet for the child born with phenylketonuria is begun can have seriously negative effects on the child's intellectual functioning. If the diet is begun at birth, however, the child can eventually achieve an IQ score close to average (which would be 100; see Chapter 10).

Source: Adapted from Baumeister, 1967.

passive genetic–environmental interaction

The interactive environment created by parents with particular genetic predispositions who encourage the expression of these tendencies in their children.

evocative genetic–environmental interaction

The expression of the gene's influence on the environment through an individual's inherited tendencies to evoke certain environmental responses.

active genetic–environmental interaction

A kind of interaction in which people's genes encourage them to seek out experience compatible with their inherited tendencies.

niche picking

Seeking out or creating environments that are compatible with one's own (genetically based) predispositions.

can influence their environments (Moffitt & Caspi, 2006; Scarr, 1996; Rutter, 2006a). In one of these pathways, known as the **passive genetic–environmental interaction**, parents with certain genetic predispositions may create a home environment that suits those predispositions and that may also suit and encourage the inherited predispositions of their children. Intelligent, well-educated parents may provide a home with books and stimulating conversation, enhancing their children's inherited tendencies to be bright and encouraging them to learn. In another pathway, known as **evocative gene–environmental interaction**, genes can influence the environment through people's inherited tendencies to evoke certain responses from others—that is, from their social environment. For instance, babies with an inborn tendency to smile often will probably elicit more positive stimulation from others than will very serious-looking, unresponsive infants (La Freniere, 2000; Plomin, 1995). The evoked stimulation reinforces the babies' smiling and ultimately, by a circular process, tends to magnify the babies' genetic predisposition.

Finally, genes can influence environment in a third way, namely through an **active genetic–environmental interaction**. People's genetic makeups may encourage them to actually seek out experiences that are compatible with their inherited tendencies (Scarr, 1996; Scarr & McCartney, 1983). In a process called **niche picking**, people search for, select, or build environments that are compatible with their predispositions. Thus, people genetically predisposed to be extroverted or gregarious actively seek the company of other people and become involved in a wide range of social activities. The importance of niche picking probably increases from childhood to adolescence and adulthood, as people gain more freedom to choose their own activities and companions.

As children develop and have more freedom to choose companions and contexts, they may, in what is called niche picking, select activities compatible with their genetic predispositions. They give expression to these predispositions by choosing endeavours that support them.

These influences of genes on environment underscore the difficulty of determining the relative contributions of heredity and the environment to individual differences in development. If genes influence environmental experiences, which, in turn, influence genes, it is difficult to separate the factors involved in these complex feedback loops. In fact, most view the issue as a search for how genes and environment operate together in shaping development rather than assignment responsibility to one or the other source (Rutter, 2006a). As we will see in the next section, researchers have attempted to demonstrate the importance of both heredity and the environment on individual differences for a large number of characteristics.

For Thought and Discussion

1. With the relatively new technological success of cloning, many have become worried that people will actually want to clone themselves in order to attain immortality. Given what you have learned about gene–environment interactions, how likely is it that a clone would actually be a copy or an imitation of the individual from whom she was created? Do you think a clone would be any more similar to the parent than, say, a typical son or daughter?

2. All the advances in genetic and reproductive techniques have induced governments to start being concerned with regulating and controlling such advances. Clearly, the nature and use of these different technologies can be placed on a continuum. At one end, one can see procedures that most would consider either harmless or beneficial to parents, such as knowing the gender of one's child or testing for Down syndrome, for example. At the other end, there are procedures that raise much more serious ethical, moral, and legal concerns, such as cloning babies for their organs or creating "designer babies." At what point would you draw the line and begin to legislate in such technologies? Why?

ⓛ⑦ HEREDITY, ENVIRONMENT, AND INDIVIDUAL DIFFERENCES

An important issue is why people develop in such widely different ways. Why, for example, does one child achieve an IQ score of 105, whereas his sister has a score of 150? Why is one child so outgoing and sociable and another more introverted and shy? For years, psychologists interested in human personality struggled with questions such as these. The field of **human behaviour genetics** arose in the 1960s when some scientists began to focus their attention particularly on the relative contributions that heredity and environment make to the array of individual differences observed in human behaviour (Plomin, DeFries, McClearn, & McGuffin, 2001; Rutter, 2006a).

Unlike biologists who study heredity, behaviour geneticists can conduct their research without ever directly measuring chromosomes, DNA, or genes. Instead, using sophisticated statistical techniques, they calculate what are called **heritability factors**, or percentage estimates of the contribution that heredity makes to a particular ability or type of behaviour. When discussing heritability factors, a caution is in order. These percentage contributions should not be viewed as applicable to all groups of children or adults at all points in their development. The relative contribution of heredity to an observed difference in human behaviour depends on how wide a range of environmental influences the subjects of the studies have been exposed to. For example, when children experience virtually the same environment, we may assume that heredity plays the greater role in any individual differences in their behaviours. When environments are extremely different, however, things get more complex. Whereas environmental factors may exert greater influence on people's behaviour, their very abundance may sometimes obscure the genetic influences that are at work.

human behaviour genetics

The study of the relative influences of heredity and environmental forces on the evolution of individual differences in traits and abilities.

heritability factor

A statistical estimate of the contribution made by heredity to a particular trait or ability.

British psychiatrist Sir Michael Rutter (1992, 2006a) believes that people have many misconceptions about what the study of genetics contributes to our knowledge of human development (see Table 2-4). According to Rutter, the field of behaviour genetics has as much to say about environmental influences as about genetic effects on the human being. With the right research strategies, Rutter claims, it is possible not only to reveal the interaction between these two forces but also to distinguish them and to estimate the extent to which each contributes to any given trait or ability.

- **Genes limit potential.** Wrong. Genetic factors do affect potential, but that potential is affected in turn by a child's environment. Change the environment, and the potential changes, too.

- **Strong genetic effects mean that environmental influences are not important.** Wrong. Although genetic effects account for individual variability, the environment may affect changes in the average expression of a characteristic. For example, the range of individual differences in IQ of children from disadvantaged families who are adopted into more advantaged families is more closely related to the IQ range of the children's biological parents. Nevertheless, these children show a general rise in IQ levels, demonstrating the effect of a stimulating environment.

- **Nature and nurture are separate.** Wrong. Both genes and environment are necessary for an individual to develop: "No genes, no organism; no environment, no organism." (Scarr & Weinberg, 1983)

- **Genetic influences diminish with age.** Wrong. The relation between genes and aging is highly complex. Some hereditary characteristics are most evident in the early stages of development; some are more evident in later stages. For example, the age at which puberty occurs is largely under genetic control, whereas the contribution of genetic factors to individual differences in intelligence is more evident in older than in younger children.

- **Genes regulate only static characteristics.** Wrong. Genes affect developmental change as well. Deviations in the normally expected environment can upset the timetable for the child's physical and psychological development, producing gross delay. However, the time at which particular characteristics emerge and the sequence in which they appear are determined primarily by the child's genetic makeup.

Table 2-4

Some misconceptions about the study of behaviour genetics

Sources: Rutter, 1992, 2006a; Shaffer, 1996.

Methods of Studying Individual Differences

The method used most often to investigate the contributions of heredity and environment to individual differences is the study of family members whose degrees of biological relatedness are known. Studies of this type generally compare adopted children with their biological and adoptive parents, examine similarities and differences between fraternal and identical twins, or explore the effects of similar and different environments on twins and ordinary siblings (Plomin et al., 2001; Rutter, 2006a).

ADOPTION STUDIES   In adoption studies, researchers usually compare characteristics of adopted children with those of both their adoptive and biological parents. Although the adoptive parents exert environmental influences on their adopted children, investigators can assume that there is no genetically determined similarity between these adoptive parents and children. Adopted children, of course, have genes in common with their biological parents, but the latter exert no postnatal environmental influences on the children. (These kinds of studies include only adopted children who have no contact with their biological parents.) Based on these assumptions and conditions, researchers reason that any similarity between adopted children and their adoptive parents must be due to their social environment, whereas any similarity between these children and their biological parents must be the result of similar genetic makeup (Moffitt & Caspi, 2006; Rutter, 2006a).

TWIN STUDIES   Twin studies take a different approach to uncovering the contributions of heredity and environment to human differences. Often, these studies involve comparing the similarities of identical and fraternal twins raised together in the same home. Identical, or **monozygotic**, twins are created when a single zygote splits in half and each half becomes a distinct embryo with exactly the same genes; both embryos come from one zygote (*mono* means "one"). In contrast, fraternal, or **dizygotic**, twins develop from two different eggs that have been fertilized by two different sperms, producing two different zygotes (*di* means "two").

Because they are conceived independently of each other, fraternal twins are no more similar genetically than any other pair of siblings; on average, they have half their genes in common. When comparing sets of identical and fraternal twins, researchers assume that each set has been raised in essentially the same type of environment. Thus, if identical twins show more resemblance on a particular trait than do fraternal twins, we can assume that the resemblance is strongly influenced by genes. On the other hand, if on a given trait the two kinds of twins resemble each other almost equally, we can assume that the resemblance is strongly influenced by the environment.

One of the most significant problems with conducting twin research is finding these participants in the first place. One way of facilitating such comparisons is through the creation of twin registries, with such databases now existing in up to 52 different countries around the world, including North America, Europe, Asia, the Middle East, and Australia (Busjahn & Hur, 2006). In Canada, the largest twin registry was begun in 1991 at the University of British Columbia (Jang, Livesley, & Vernon, 2000; Jang, Taylor, & Livesley, 2006). The goal of research making use of this registry has been to examine personality and its disorders from a behavioural genetics perspective (Jang, 2005). Because of the very existence of this registry, and the breadth of the measures taken from its participants, this device allows for detailed assessments of the genetic contributions to personality and a range of anxiety disorders, and it also enables comparisons of these constructs cross-culturally, in both Western (e.g., German; Riemann et al., 1997) and non-Western (e.g., Japanese; Ando et al., 2004) societies.

SHARED AND NON-SHARED ENVIRONMENTS   One concern with twin studies involves whether it is indeed legitimate to assume that each member of a twin pair truly experiences the same environmental conditions, with some investigators questioning this proposition. These investigators argue that the experiences of identical twins, when reared together, are more similar than those of fraternal twins (Wahlsten & Gottlieb, 1997) because their inherited predispositions evoke more similar responses from people outside the family. Similarly, identical twins select more similar settings, companions, and activities for themselves than do fraternal twins (Scarr, 1996; Scarr & McCartney, 1983). Thus, these critics claim, identical twins have more **shared environments** than fraternal twins, and so, any similarities in their traits must be attributed to both the environment and their genetic makeup (Rutter, 2006a). Fraternal twins and siblings, they suggest, have more **non-shared environments**, or experiences and activities of varied sorts.

Those with this viewpoint stress that people are active creators of their own environments, not just passive recipients of environmental influences, both deliberately and unintentionally shaping the many experiences to which they are exposed. This perspective helps explain why adoptive siblings, and even biologically related ones, often show only a modest similarity on behavioural traits. Moreover, the initially modest similarity caused by a shared childhood home tends to decline with age, as personal niche picking exerts more and more influence on people's behaviour (Reiss et al., 2000; Towers, Spotts, & Reiss, 2003).

---

monozygotic

Characterizing identical twins, who have developed from a single fertilized egg.

dizygotic

Characterizing fraternal twins, who have developed from two separate fertilized eggs.

shared environment

A set of conditions or experiences that is shared by children raised in the same family with each other; a parameter commonly examined in studies of individual differences.

non-shared environment

A set of conditions or activities that is experienced by one child in a family and not shared with another child in the same family.

Children raised in the same family, then, have both shared and non-shared experiences. Shared conditions would include such factors as being poor or well off, living in a good or a bad neighbourhood, and having parents who are employed or unemployed, in good health or physically or mentally ill (Reiss et al., 2000; Towers et al., 2003). Experiences not shared would include factors or events related to the individual characteristics of a particular child, such as the specific activities in which the child engages, or how she is treated because of age, gender, temperament, illness, or physical and cognitive abilities. Even small differences in non-shared experiences may cause differences in how twins and siblings develop. Furthermore, siblings' perceptions that their experiences—for example, the way their parents treat them—are different can affect their behaviour whether or not these perceptions are accurate. Clearly, researchers in individual differences can no longer assume a homogeneous home environment for all siblings, and you must be alert to this fact when you read the reports and conclusions of such studies.

Behaviour Genetics: An Alternative View   LO 8

In recent years, some have argued that the attempt to separate the relative contributions of heredity and environment in individual differences research is misleading, and ultimately doomed to failure. Douglas Wahlsten (Wahlsten, 1979, 1990, 1994a, 1994b, 2000; Wahlsten & Gottlieb, 1997) of the University of Alberta has pointed out that the mathematical calculations central to behaviour genetics hold only if one assumes that genetic and environmental factors are independent, such that an individual's phenotype is a strict additive sum of the genetic and environmental components. The problem, according to Wahlsten, is that this simply is not true. Researchers have recognized for decades that there is compelling evidence for the importance of gene–environment interactions. A classic example of this type of interaction is seen in the work on the McGill maze-bright and maze-dull rats (Cooper & Zubek, 1958; Hughes & Zubek, 1956), who were selectively bred for fast or slow learning of a maze. However, when Cooper and Zubek (1958) reared these lines of rats in either enriched or restricted environments and then tested them on the same mazes, the difference between the two lines disappeared in both restricted and enriched environments. According to Wahlsten and Gottlieb (1997), such findings provide convincing evidence of gene–environment interactions, although others have debated this point (Surbey, 1994) and remain convinced of the usefulness of heritability factors for individual differences in behaviour (Scarr, 1987).

Some Individual Differences and Their Contributors

In this section, we examine the effects of heredity and environment in three important areas. We begin by looking at differences in intellectual abilities; we then explore differences in temperament and personality; and we conclude with a look at differences in the tendency to develop behavioural disorders.

INTELLECTUAL CHARACTERISTICS   Interestingly, studies comparing the intelligence quotient, or IQ, scores of twins have been remarkably consistent in their findings (we discuss intelligence at length in Chapter 10). This research indicates that genes heavily influence similarities and differences in individual performance on intelligence tests. Generally, the closer the genetic links between two people, the more similar their IQ scores. As you can see from Table 2-5 on the next page, which summarizes more than 100 family-resemblance studies of twins, siblings, and other relatives, identical twins reared in the same household are most similar in IQ scores (+.86 is a very high positive correlation). The least similar in IQ scores are cousins, who have relatively few genes in common and are not raised in the same home (only +.15). Even identical twins raised apart have IQ scores that are more similar than are those of fraternal twins raised in the same home.

Table 2-5

Resemblance in intelligence scores among family members*

Source: Adapted from Bouchard & McGue (1981).

Relationship of Family Members	Correlation between IQ Scores
Identical twins reared together	.86
Identical twins reared apart	.79
Fraternal twins reared together	.60
Siblings reared together	.47
Parent and child	.40
Foster parent and child	.31
Siblings reared apart	.24
Cousins	.15

*Correlations are compiled from 111 different studies from all parts of the world. In general, the closer the genetic relationship of two people, the higher is the correlation between their IQ scores.

Genes contribute not only to differences in general intellectual performance but also to differences in specific mental abilities. Differences in spatial and verbal abilities, for instance, are more influenced by genetic factors than are differences in memory and perceptual speed (Plomin, 1990). In a surprising finding, however, differences in creativity, that aspect of cognitive behaviour that includes scientific and artistic innovation, show less genetic influence than differences in any other specific cognitive ability. It looks as if geniuses are largely made, not born.

Heredity affects not just differences in the level of mental development but also differences in the timing and rate of development. Just as children show spurts and plateaus in their physical growth, they also show variations in the rate and timing of their mental growth. Heredity apparently contributes substantially to these individual differences, as suggested by the fact that identical twins are more similar in this regard than fraternal twins (Wilson, 1983). For example, Figure 2-10 shows how the scores achieved by two sets of identical twins on infant intelligence tests rose and fell in very much the same patterns over their first two years. Tests of infants typically show wide fluctuations like these over time; what is remarkable here is how similar the patterns of the fluctuations were for each pair of twins.

Figure 2-10

Twins' intelligence test scores over the first two years

These two sets of identical twins paralleled each other closely in intelligence test scores as they developed over a period of about two years.

Source: Adapted from Wilson & Harpring, 1972.

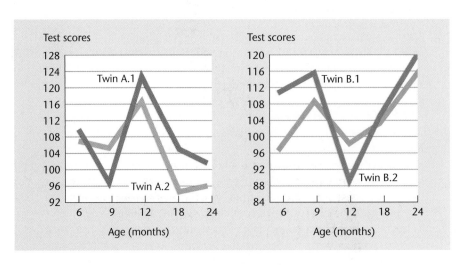

Adoption studies also reveal significant genetic contributions to individual differences in intellectual development (Plomin et al., 2001; Rutter, 2006a). Even if children have been adopted in their first year of life, their intellectual performance at school age correlates more closely with their biological parents' intelligence ratings or scores than it does with those of their adoptive parents; moreover, the correlation with foster or adoptive parents declines with age (Scarr & Weinberg, 1983).

Bear in mind that the results of adoption studies do not mean that adoptive parents fail to influence their adopted children's intellectual performance (Turkheimer, 2000). In one classic study, adopted children often averaged 20 or more IQ points higher than their biological mothers (Skodak & Skeels, 1949). In this study, because the adoptive parents tended to be more highly educated and more socially and economically advantaged than the biological parents, this result was probably due to the more stimulating home environments that the adoptive parents provided. But note also that despite this environmental influence on development, individual differences still seemed to be substantially influenced by genetic inheritance. The rank ordering of the children's IQ scores more closely resembled that of their biological mothers than that of their adoptive parents. The children whose biological mothers had the lowest IQ scores were likely to have lower IQ scores than the children whose biological mothers scored higher. Thus, although the absolute level of intellectual development was apparently boosted by the environmental influences provided by the adoptive parents, individual differences among the adopted children in intellectual performance appeared to stem more from their biological inheritance than from the increased intellectual stimulation provided in their adoptive homes.

Another qualification of the findings of this research is that because it studied primarily children who were adopted into middle-class families, it may have limited the expression of environmental influences. Among children adopted into families from a wider range of socio-economic backgrounds, environment probably makes a greater contribution to individual differences in intellectual performance. For example, studies have shown that adopted children in economically disadvantaged homes have lower IQ scores and are more likely to drop out of school than those placed with more well-to-do families (Capron & Duyme, 1989; Duyme, 1988).

Finally, some have argued (Wahlstein, 2002) that even though genetic influences, as exemplified by brain structure, correlate with test IQ scores, it is not clear that these variations in IQ are actually the result of genetic variation. Instead, there is evidence that differences in the environment may be exerting a strong influence on both brain structure and the environment. Accordingly, it is simply not possible to answer the question of intelligence by referring solely to the brain or genes.

Thus, although twin studies and adoptive studies agree in showing that genetic factors make an important contribution to individual differences in IQ, environmental factors can also be important contributors to these differences, especially when there are wide disparities in the contexts in which individuals live. As you will see in Chapter 10, very poor or stressful environments can dramatically lower IQ scores, and cognitively stimulating environments or intervention programs can raise them.

TEMPERAMENT AND PERSONALITY Even in infants' earliest days of life, we can see marked differences in what we call **temperament**, or the individual's typical mode of response to the environment, including such things as activity level, adaptability to new situations, and intensity of emotional expression. We use the term *temperament* to describe these kinds of individual differences in infants and children. In adolescence and adulthood, these styles of responding to the world are often discussed as different aspects of *personality*, such as emotionality, activity, and sociability.

Thomas and Chess (1986) have proposed a typology of temperament that has been widely accepted. This framework classifies infants as *difficult*, *easy*, or *slow to warm up*, and each of these types is associated with a distinctive pattern of behavioural responses (Rothbart & Bates, 2006; Thomas & Chess, 1986). Difficult infants (about

temperament

The individual's typical mode of response to the environment, including such things as activity level, emotional intensity, and attention span; used particularly to describe infants' and children's behaviours.

10 percent of all babies) sleep and eat irregularly, become easily upset by new situations, and experience extremes of fussiness and crying. In contrast, easy babies (about 40 percent) are friendly, happy, and adaptable. Even in the same family, babies may exhibit both these dramatically different temperaments:

> *Nothing was easy with Chris. Mealtimes, bedtimes, toilet training were all hell. It would take me an hour and a half to get part of a bottle into him and he'd be hungry two hours later. I can't remember once in the first two years when he didn't go to bed crying. I'd try to rock him to sleep, but as soon as I'd tiptoe over to put him in his crib his head would lurch up and he'd start bellowing again. He didn't like any kind of changes in his routine. New people and places upset him, so it was hard to take him anywhere.*

> *John was my touchy-feely baby. From the first day in the hospital, he cuddled and seemed so contented to be held I could hardly bear to put him down. He didn't cry unless something was wrong—when he was wet, or hungry, or tired. We took him everywhere because he seemed to enjoy new things. You could always sit him in a corner and he'd entertain himself. Sometimes I'd forget he was there until he'd start laughing or prattling.* (Thomas & Chess, 1986, pp. 19–20)

The slow-to-warm-up child is low in activity level and tends to respond negatively to new stimuli at first but adapts slowly to new objects or novel experiences after repeated contact with them. Essentially, these children fall somewhere between difficult and easy children; on first exposure to something strange, they may look like difficult children, but they gradually show quiet interest, much like an easy child.

Rothbart and colleagues (Putnam, Sanson, & Rothbart, 2002; Rothbart, 1981) have developed one measure of temperament known as the Infant Behaviour Questionnaire. The six scales of this instrument are (1) positive affect, (2) irritable distress, (3) fearful distress, (4) activity level, (5) attention span/persistence, and (6) rhythmicity (see Table 2-6). They have also developed a similar temperament measure for toddlers, children, early adolescents, and adults (Goldsmith et al., 2001; Putnam et al., 2002). Temperament, of course, is expressed in different ways as the individual grows older. For example, in infancy, we may index persistence by the length of time a baby looks at an object, whereas in childhood, we may measure this component by the length of time a child continues to work on a puzzle or problem.

Table 2-6

Components of infant temperament

Source: Rothbart & Bates, 2006.

Component	Description
Positive affect	Measured by a child's smiling, laughter, co-operativeness, and manageability
Irritable distress	Indexed by a child's irritability, fussiness, anger, frustration, and distress at limitations on her behaviour
Fearful distress	Assessed by the length of time a child requires to adjust to a new situation, or his adaptability, and by the child's tendency to withdraw and show distress in new situations
Activity level	Indexed by the child's tendency to be more or less active
Attention span/ persistence	Measured by a child's ability to concentrate, focus on a task, and continue to work at a problem
Rhythmicity	Assessed by the predictability or regularity of a child's behaviour patterns

Researchers have also compiled evidence for differences in temperament among newborns of different ethnicities and races. For instance, Pomerleau, Sabatier, and Malcuit (1998) compared Québécois, Haitian, and Vietnamese infants living in Montréal and found that the latter two groups reported more difficult temperamental characteristics in their infants, with these variations in infant temperament reports likely due to differences in values and caregiving practices specific to the various cultural contexts. And looking at somewhat older children, de Boo & Kolk (2007) found temperament differences between Dutch 9- to 13-year-old children, and similarly aged Turkish and Moroccan schoolchildren.

A variety of cultural differences in infant temperament have been found among different East African societies. The Digo, for example, view the infant as active and able to learn within a few months after birth, whereas the Kikuyu view their infants as passive, keep them swaddled for the first year, and believe that serious education is not possible until the second year (DeVries & Sameroff, 1984). Culture shapes temperament, just as temperament shapes the ways in which caregivers behave (Kerr, 2001; Rothbart & Bates, 2006; Sameroff, 1994).

A higher rate of developmental problems is found in later life among children described by their mothers as difficult babies (Goldsmith et al., 2001; Halverson & Deal, 2001; Rothbart & Bates, 2006). Two factors may contribute to this relation. First, a less malleable child is likely to find it harder to adapt to environmental demands and so is more prone to stress and the toll it takes on emotional well-being. Second, and demonstrated in research studies, is that a child with a difficult temperament is more apt to elicit adverse reactions from other people and, thus, to suffer the psychological damage caused by social rejection. Children with difficult temperaments have been found to serve as targets for parental irritability, especially when the parents are under stress. Stressed mothers are especially likely to withdraw affection from temperamentally difficult boys and to show irritation with them (Rothbart & Bates, 2006).

On the other hand, the finding that a difficult baby is not likely to suffer any long-term negative effects if his parents are calm and supportive (Rothbart & Bates, 2006) suggests that the match between the child's temperament and the environment is important. Thomas and Chess (1986) have termed this match between the child's temperament and the child-rearing environment **goodness of fit**. This model reminds us that the effects of temperamental predispositions will depend on how well parents and other agents of socialization are able to accept and adapt to each child's particular temperament. As we will see in our later discussion of moral development in Chapter 14, fearful children have been found to develop greater self-control, or conscience, when their parents use gentle discipline; in contrast, however, parental strategies that focused on positive motivation were seen to promote more self-control in fearless children (Kagan & Snidman, 2004; Kochanska, 1997). As the goodness of fit model suggests, development progresses more smoothly when parents adjust their approach to suit the child's unique temperament.

How do heredity and environment affect temperament and personality? Recent studies have suggested that the prenatal environment and environmental factors at birth may make larger contributions than heredity to infant temperament (Riese, 1990). At the same time, genetic influences on temperament seem to become increasingly prominent throughout early childhood (Dunn & Plomin, 1991; Schmidt & Fox, 2002; Wachs & Kohnstamm, 2001). Personality traits show some stability over time, which might suggest a genetic influence, but most psychologists today consider that both heredity and environmental factors contribute to personality (Jang et al., 2002).

Studies have shown that heredity contributes to individual differences for a number of temperament characteristics and personality traits, including affect, or emotionality; fears and anxieties; activity level; attention span and persistence; and the tendency to maintain high moral standards and to obey authority (Kagan & Fox, 2006; Kochanska & Thompson, 1997; Stein, Jang, & Livesley, 2002). According to Plomin (1995), inheritance apparently contributes most to emotionality, activity level, and sociability.

goodness of fit

A measure of the degree to which a child's temperament is matched by her environment. The more effectively parents and other agents of socialization accept and adapt to the child's unique temperament, the better this "fit."

Temperament and personality show a declining link with genetic factors as people age, however, and among older people, differing life experiences seem more significant (Plomin, McClearn, Pedersen, Nesselroade, & Bergeman, 1988).

This couple could conduct their own individual differences study by comparing interactive abilities, or personality traits, among their different children.

For Thought and Discussion

1. Can you think of abilities or developmental achievements other than babbling (which we discuss in the text) that might be highly canalized? Under what conditions might environmental effects influence abilities?

2. Given what you have now read about the influences of genes and environment, as well as about all the possible ways in which gene–environment interactions may occur, what do you think the status is of heritability studies? Do you feel confident that one can portion out certain parts of the variance due to true "environment" or "genetic" influences?

3. The assumption underlying twin studies is that because identical and fraternal twins typically live in the same home, these siblings share the same environment. Is this a reasonable assumption? Do you feel that your sibling (or siblings) experience the same environment as you do? What implications does this have for interpreting the results of twin studies?

Making the Connections 2

There are many links between concepts and ideas in one area of development and concepts and ideas in other areas. Here are some of the connections between ideas in Chapter 2 and discussions in other chapters of this book.

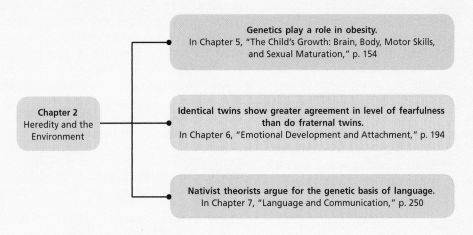

Chapter 2
Heredity and the Environment

Genetics play a role in obesity.
In Chapter 5, "The Child's Growth: Brain, Body, Motor Skills, and Sexual Maturation," p. 154

Identical twins show greater agreement in level of fearfulness than do fraternal twins.
In Chapter 6, "Emotional Development and Attachment," p. 194

Nativist theorists argue for the genetic basis of language.
In Chapter 7, "Language and Communication," p. 250

SUMMARY

- During the course of development, the **genotype** interacts with the environment in complex ways to produce the **phenotype**. It is the phenotypic expression of individual physical and behavioural characteristics that scientists study in an effort to understand how genes and the environment interact to produce each unique human being.

The Process of Genetic Transmission

- Within each cell nucleus are threadlike structures called **chromosomes**, on which **genes** containing the genetic code are located. Genetic variability is the result of the huge number of chromosome combinations that are possible during the formation of sperm and egg cells. Sexual reproduction, or the union of the **ovum** with the **sperm**, also contributes to genetic variability, as 23 chromosomes from a woman unite with 23 chromosomes from a man to form the zygote.

- Chromosomes are bound by molecules of **deoxyribonucleic acid (DNA)**, which, in turn, are made up of **nucleotides**. Genes—portions of the DNA molecule— are located at particular sites on the chromosome where they code for the production of certain kinds of protein. Each of the many different kinds of proteins in the human body serves a different function.

Genetic Influences on Development

- At any given gene's position on two homologous chromosomes there can be more than one form of that gene, called the gene's **alleles**. If the alleles are the same, the person is **homozygous** for that particular characteristic; if the alleles are different, the person is **heterozygous**.

- The 23rd pair of human chromosomes are the **sex chromosomes**, differing in males and females. Females have two large homologous sex chromosomes, forming an XX pattern; males have one X and a smaller Y chromosome, an XY pattern. Because an X chromosome is about five times longer than a Y chromosome, it carries more genes. This means that in males, some genes on the X chromosome have no equivalent genes on the Y chromosome; the person inherits only one each of these **X-linked genes**. If the inherited gene happens to be a harmful allele, the associated genetic disorder will automatically be expressed.

- Many human characteristics are influenced by complex interactions among multiple genes acting together. This interaction of multiple genes may help explain why some traits that are influenced by genes do not tend to run in families. Further adding to the complexity of genetic influences on development, a single pair of alleles may influence more than one trait, and, if they are **modifier genes**, they may do so not directly but indirectly through the effects they have on how other genes are expressed.

- Harmful alleles survive generally because they are not harmful in the heterozygous state. They may also survive, as they do in people who carry the allele for **sickle cell anemia**, when, in addition to threatening people with that disease, they also protect people who carry them from malaria.
- **Down syndrome** is one example of the many identifiable human chromosome disorders. It is caused by inheriting three 21st chromosomes instead of the normal two and is characterized by both physical and mental retardation and a distinctive physical appearance. Abnormalities can also arise in the sex chromosomes. The physical, psychological, and emotional characteristics of people with these chromosome aberrations vary widely depending upon the specific chromosome pattern and environmental factors.

Genetic Counselling and Genetic Engineering

- Advances in biology and genetics have opened new opportunities for diagnosing genetic disorders before birth. The two methods most commonly used to collect samples of fetal cells for genetic analysis are **amniocentesis** and **chorionic villi sampling**. Other diagnostic techniques include the **alphafetoprotein** assay and **ultrasound**.
- Scientists hope to eventually locate the genes responsible for all inherited disorders. With the aim of treating or curing genetic disorders, scientists are exploring gene therapy, which involves inserting normal alleles into patients' cells to compensate for defective alleles. Theoretically, normal genes could even replace defective ones in sperm or egg cells, or they could be inserted into a newly created zygote.

Heredity–Environment Interactions

- According to the concept of the **range of reaction**, heredity does not rigidly fix behaviour but, instead, establishes a range of possible developmental outcomes that may occur in response to different environments. When a reaction range is extremely narrow, it is said to exhibit **canalization**. With a highly canalized trait, there are few pathways that development can take.
- Not only does environment influence genes, but genes also influence the environments to which people are exposed. One way this can happen is for parents with certain genetic predispositions to create a home environment that suits those predispositions and also the inherited predispositions of their children. Another way is for people's inherited tendencies to evoke certain environmental influences from others. A third way is for genes to encourage people to seek out experiences that are compatible with their inherited tendencies.

Heredity, Environment, and Individual Differences

- *Human behaviour genetics* seeks to explain why significant differences exist in the ways that people develop by calculating **heritability factors**—percentage estimates of the contribution that genes make to some observed individual difference. Commonly, researchers study family members with known degrees of biological relatedness, such as **monozygotic** and **dizygotic** twins and adopted children.
- Family resemblance studies consistently show that individual differences in IQ scores, as concerns more specific cognitive abilities, are substantially influenced by genetic factors. Nevertheless, an enriched environment can boost a child's level of intellectual development considerably.
- Heredity contributes to many individual differences in **temperament** and personality, especially differences in emotionality, activity level, and sociability. However, the contribution of heredity to differences in these traits appears to decline with age, as people's personalities become increasingly influenced by their life experiences.

House door panel with an X-ray drawing of a pregnant woman. Collected in 1887 at Sieby Village, Geelvink Bay, Irian Jaya.

Rijksmuseum voor Volkenkunde, Leiden, The Netherlands.

Chapter 3

Prenatal Development and Birth

LEARNING OBJECTIVES

After reading this chapter, you should be able to

LO1 Identify and describe the major events of the three periods of prenatal development.

LO2 List and explain the six principles that describe the effects of teratogens on prenatal development; give an example of each.

LO3 Understand the influence of alcohol exposure on prenatal development, and also know the distinction between fetal alcohol syndrome and fetal alcohol effects.

LO4 Know the most common prenatal influences on development; discuss the effects of maternal diseases, drug use (therapeutic and non-therapeutic), maternal diet, emotional state, and age; be able to give an example of each.

LO5 Know the stages of birth and various methods of childbirth, including complications that may arise.

LO6 Describe methods of assessing the newborn.

LO7 Describe short-term and long-term effects of prematurity and low birthweight; identify interventions that have been used to assist these infants.

LO8 Describe how the effects of adverse perinatal influences are either compounded or compensated for by subsequent conditions throughout development.

Waiting for the birth of a child can be one of the most joyous times in peoples' lives. Couples look forward to becoming parents and enjoy preparing for their baby's arrival. They may even try to influence the new family member by playing favourite music or reading to their unborn child.

Whether it is possible to influence a baby in such positive ways during pregnancy is not entirely certain, although, as we will see, there is some evidence of babies learning in utero. Unfortunately, however, clear evidence indicates that the developing organism is vulnerable to a variety of negative influences. Some of these influences are genetic, as we saw in the last chapter, and others result from variations in the prenatal environment caused by factors and events that affect the mother during her pregnancy. A large number of negative influences—including medication and diagnostic procedures; prescription, non-prescription, and other legal and illegal drugs; maternal age and *parity* (whether a woman has had a child before); illness, dietary deficiencies, and emotional distress; and environmental toxins—can effect the normal development of a child from its first weeks of gestation. In addition, events occurring during childbirth may threaten the viability or the good health of a newborn.

We begin this chapter by exploring the normal development of the human being from conception to delivery and then discuss the many factors that can threaten this normal development throughout a pregnancy. We look at normal childbirth and at some of the complications of labour and delivery, including the problems of prematurity and low birthweight. We conclude the chapter with a review of research that has explored the long-term effects of pregnancy and birth complications as well as the resilience some children show in the face of such difficulties. Throughout these discussions, we will ask several questions: What are the most significant of these negative influences? How does the timing of their appearance in the *prenatal* environment affect their impact on the developing infant? And, perhaps most importantly, how do *perinatal* factors (those occurring shortly before and/or after birth) affect the child's later development, and can any *postnatal* experiences alter the effects of these negative influences? ●

LO1 STAGES OF PRENATAL DEVELOPMENT

Conception usually takes place during a woman's ovulation or within a few days of it; the ovum, or egg, once released from the mother's ovaries, lives only about three to five days. Prenatal development, then, encompasses the 38 weeks, or approximately 9 months, between conception and birth. Over these months the new organism changes in many ways. The kinds, numbers, positions, sizes, and shapes of cells, tissues, and bodily systems change, and these systems usually increase in size and complexity.

The nine months of prenatal development are characterized in two ways. Traditionally, pregnancy has been described as occurring in three *trimesters*, or three periods of three months each, and we often speak of a particular event as occurring in one or another trimester. Increasingly, however, we talk about the three periods of (1) the zygote, (2) the embryo, and (3) the fetus. Although they are distinct in many ways, these periods comprise continuous phases of development during which the organism becomes increasingly complex and differentiated. Figure 3-1 illustrates these changes, from ovulation, when the ovum embarks on its journey to the uterus, to the end of the second trimester, when the fetus appears fully human.

The Zygote

zygote

The developing organism from the time of the union of the sperm and the egg to about the second week of gestation; the period of the zygote is comprised of the implantation of the fertilized egg in the wall of the uterus.

The period of the zygote is approximately the first two weeks of life. During this time a sperm fertilizes the ovum, now referred to as **zygote** or fertilized egg, which then proceeds down the mother's fallopian tube and implants in the wall of the uterus. When this occurs, about seven days after conception, the zygote is very small: 100 to 200 zygotes placed side by side would measure only an inch and some five million would weigh only an ounce. Gradually, tendrils from the zygote penetrate the blood vessels in the wall of the uterus. At this point the zygote forms the physiological dependence with the mother that will continue throughout the course of prenatal development.

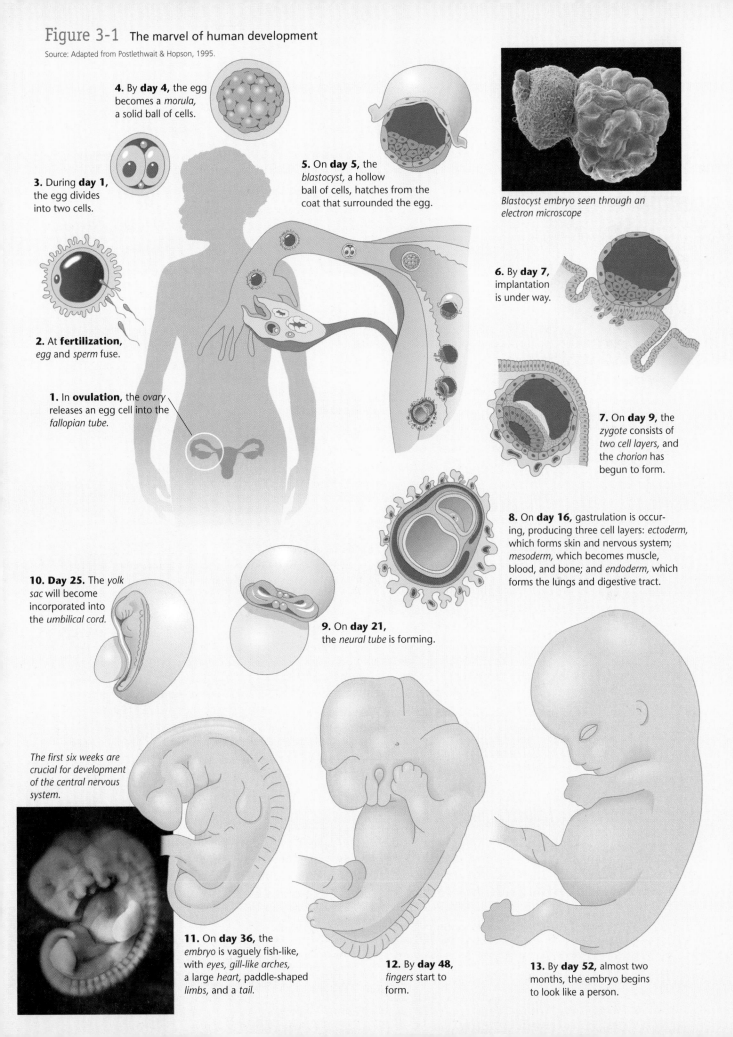

Figure 3-1 The marvel of human development

Source: Adapted from Postlethwait & Hopson, 1995.

4. By **day 4**, the egg becomes a *morula*, a solid ball of cells.

3. During **day 1**, the egg divides into two cells.

5. On **day 5**, the *blastocyst*, a hollow ball of cells, hatches from the coat that surrounded the egg.

Blastocyst embryo seen through an electron microscope

2. At **fertilization**, *egg* and *sperm* fuse.

6. By **day 7**, implantation is under way.

1. In **ovulation**, the *ovary* releases an egg cell into the *fallopian tube*.

7. On **day 9**, the *zygote* consists of *two cell layers*, and the *chorion* has begun to form.

8. On **day 16**, gastrulation is occurring, producing three cell layers: *ectoderm*, which forms skin and nervous system; *mesoderm*, which becomes muscle, blood, and bone; and *endoderm*, which forms the lungs and digestive tract.

10. Day 25. The *yolk sac* will become incorporated into the *umbilical cord*.

9. On **day 21**, the *neural tube* is forming.

The first six weeks are crucial for development of the central nervous system.

11. On **day 36**, the *embryo* is vaguely fish-like, with *eyes, gill-like arches*, a large *heart*, paddle-shaped *limbs*, and a *tail*.

12. By **day 48**, *fingers* start to form.

13. By **day 52**, almost two months, the embryo begins to look like a person.

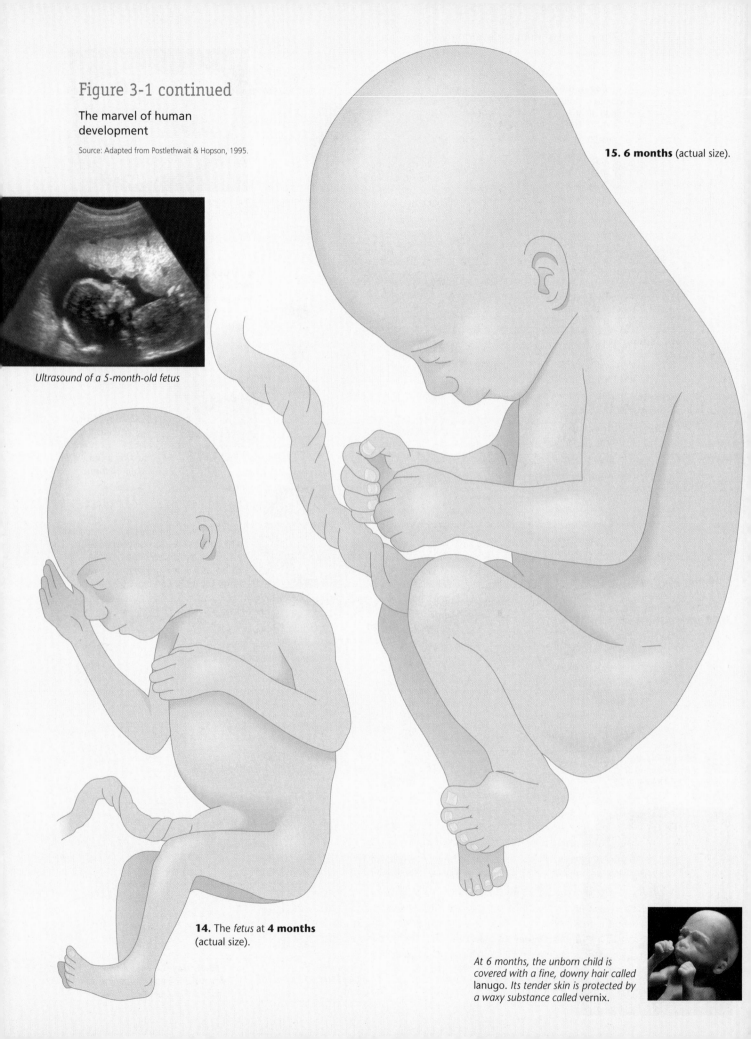

Figure 3-1 continued

The marvel of human development

Source: Adapted from Postlethwait & Hopson, 1995.

Ultrasound of a 5-month-old fetus

15. 6 months (actual size).

14. The *fetus* at **4 months** (actual size).

At 6 months, the unborn child is covered with a fine, downy hair called lanugo. *Its tender skin is protected by a waxy substance called* vernix.

The Embryo

Once the zygote is firmly implanted in the mother's uterus, the second prenatal period, the period of the **embryo**, begins. This is a period of rapid growth that lasts from the beginning of the third week of **gestation** until the end of the eighth week. During this embryonic period, the organism's most important physiological structures and systems become differentiated, and the embryo also becomes recognizable as a tiny human being. From the time of fertilization until the end of this period, the infant increases 2 million percent in size!

During this period, three crucial structures develop to protect and support the growing life within the mother's uterus: the amniotic sac, the placenta, and the umbilical cord. The **amniotic sac** is a thin membrane around the developing organism that contains the *amniotic fluid*, a watery liquid in which the developing embryo floats and which serves as a protective buffer against physical shocks and temperature changes. The tendrils that attach the embryo to the uterine wall increase in size and complexity to form a fleshy disc-like structure, called the **placenta**. The embryo is joined to the placenta at the abdomen by the **umbilical cord**, a tube that contains the blood vessels that carry blood back and forth between the infant and placenta. (The umbilical cord attains a final length slightly greater than that of the growing organism, permitting it considerable mobility within the uterine environment.) Because semi-permeable membranes within the placenta separate the bloodstreams of the mother and child, some substances pass from mother to infant. The placenta and umbilical cord transmit oxygen and nutrients to the infant and remove carbon dioxide and waste products from it, but they do not permit direct exchange of blood. Unfortunately, certain potentially destructive substances, such as drugs, hormones, viruses, and antibodies from the mother, do pass through the placenta to the embryo.

During the embryonic period, the inner mass of the developing organism differentiates into three layers: the ectoderm, the mesoderm, and the endoderm. From the *ectoderm*, the hair, nails, and parts of the teeth, the outer layer of the skin and skin glands, and the sensory cells and the nervous system develop. The *mesoderm* forms into the muscles, skeleton, circulatory and excretory systems, and inner skin layer. From the *endoderm* comes the gastrointestinal tract, trachea, bronchia, Eustachian tubes, glands, and vital organs, such as the lungs, pancreas, and liver. The especially rapid development and differentiation that occur at this time make the embryo more susceptible during this period than any other to environmental assault. For example, at about the fourth or fifth week of gestation, the *neural folds* (formations that evolve ultimately into the central nervous system) begin to close. If something occurs to prevent them from closing completely, the child will have *spina bifida*, a disorder in which the spinal cord and the membranes that protect it may protrude from the spinal column.

Prenatal development is guided by two principles: cephalocaudal and proximal-distal. **Cephalocaudal** (the term *cephalocaudal* derives from the Latin words for "head" and "tail") means that development proceeds from the head downward to the trunk and legs. **Proximal-distal** (again, from Latin words for "toward the centre" and "away from the centre") means that growth occurs first in central areas, such as internal organs, and then in more distant areas, such as arms and legs. (We return to these principles when we discuss postnatal physical growth.)

By the end of the period of the embryo, the growing organism's face and features are delineated, and fingers, toes, and external genitalia are present. Even at six weeks, the embryo is recognizable as a human being, although a rather strangely proportioned one, the head being almost as large as the rest of the body.

Most **miscarriages**, or spontaneous abortions, occur during this period; for one reason or another, the embryo becomes detached from the wall of the uterus and is expelled through the vaginal canal. The rate of miscarriage has been estimated to be as high as one in four pregnancies, but many such miscarriages remain undetected because they occur in the first few weeks of pregnancy, when women may not even realize they are pregnant. This high rate of natural abortion may be advantageous to the mother, in terms of the cost of carrying a child who ultimately has little chance of survival, as well

embryo

The developing organism between the second and eighth weeks of gestation; the period of the embryo comprises the differentiation of the major physiological structures and systems.

gestation

The carrying of an embryo or fetus during pregnancy, usually for nine months in humans.

amniotic sac

A membrane containing a watery fluid that encloses the developing organism, protecting it from physical shocks and temperature changes.

placenta

A fleshy, disc-like structure formed by cells from the lining of the uterus and from the zygote, and that, together with the umbilical cord, serves to protect and sustain the life of the growing organism.

umbilical cord

A tube that contains blood vessels that carry blood back and forth between the growing organism and its mother by way of the placenta; it carries oxygen and nutrients to the growing infant and removes carbon dioxide and waste products.

cephalocaudal

The pattern of human physical growth in which development begins in the area of the brain and proceeds downward, to the trunk and legs.

proximal-distal

The pattern of human physical growth wherein development starts in central areas, such as the internal organs, and proceeds to more distant areas, such as arms and legs.

miscarriage

The natural or spontaneous end of a pregnancy before the infant is capable of survival outside the womb and generally defined in humans as prior to 20 weeks gestation.

as to the species, for the great majority of embryos aborted in this manner have gross chromosomal and genetic disorders.

The Fetus

fetus

The developing organism from the third month of gestation through delivery; during the fetal period, development of bodily structures and systems becomes complete.

lanugo

A fine, soft hair that covers the fetus's body from about the fifth month of gestation on; may be shed before birth or after.

respiratory distress syndrome

A condition of the newborn marked by laboured breathing and a bluish discolouration of the skin or mucous membranes, and which often leads to death.

age of viability

The age of 22–26 weeks, by which point the fetus's physical systems are well enough advanced that it has a chance at survival if born prematurely.

During the third and final period of prenatal development, the **fetus**—the term for the developing organism from the beginning of the third month of gestation to delivery—experiences rapid growth in muscular development and the central nervous system. At the end of the third month, the fetus has all of its body parts, including external genital organs. By the end of the fourth month, mothers usually report movement of the fetus. At around five months, reflexes such as sucking, swallowing, and hiccupping, usually appear. After the fifth month, the fetus develops nails and sweat glands, coarser, more adult-like skin, and soft hair, called **lanugo**, which covers the body. Most fetuses shed this hair in utero, but some continue to shed it after birth. By six months, the eyes can open and close. If an infant is born prematurely at six months, the regulatory processes and nervous and respiratory systems are usually not mature enough for survival without intensive intervention. At this time, the fetus cannot produce and maintain an adequate amount of *surfactant*, a liquid that allows the lungs to transmit oxygen from the air to the blood. Without surfactant, infants are often unable to breathe adequately, and they may develop **respiratory distress syndrome**, a condition of the newborn marked by laboured breathing and a bluish discolouration of the skin or mucous membranes. This syndrome, which is often heralded by such symptoms as flaring nostrils and a grunt-like sound on expiration, can result in death.

The age of 22 to 26 weeks, sometimes referred to as the **age of viability**, is an important point in fetal development. By this time the fetus's physical systems are sufficiently advanced such that the child, if born prematurely, has a reasonable probability of surviving. With the exceptional resources available in modern intensive-care nurseries, infants as immature as 22 weeks can sometimes live. Note in this chapter's Turning Points chart (pages 88 and 89), however, that many systems are still developing; the respiratory system, in particular, continues to evolve into the ninth month of gestation. Thus, babies born before 28 weeks can have many difficulties, especially if they encounter other, adverse environmental conditions (Moore & Persaud, 1998).

teratogen

An environmental agent, such as a drug, medication, dietary imbalance, or polluting substance, that may cause developmental deviations in a growing human organism; most threatening in the embryonic stage but capable of causing abnormalities in the fetal stage as well.

LO2 RISKS IN THE PRENATAL ENVIRONMENT

During the course of prenatal development, many agents may cause developmental deviations in the fetus. These agents are called **teratogens**, a term that derives from the Greek word *teras*, meaning "monster" or "marvel." Teratogens encompass a wide variety of agents, including prescription and non-prescription drugs taken by the mother and environmental toxins, such as pollution. Although teratogens are environmental factors, other factors like the mother's age, her diet, and her emotional state affect the response of mother and child to any given teratogen. In this section, we will consider first the prenatal hazards in the environment, along with the risks these pose to the developing child.

In considering the effects of teratogens on prenatal development, we discuss physical defects or mental impairments that may occur. We also discuss how these factors change the life experiences of the child. How is the emotional bond between parent and child affected by an infant's longer stay in the hospital? Is the parent more anxious or more protective? Or does the parent reject the child? Experiential factors such as these may ultimately be the most important in sustaining or minimizing the long-term effects of early difficulties.

Teratogens exert their effects on prenatal development in specific ways (Friedman & Polifka, 1996; Moore & Persaud, 1998).

1. *A teratogen exerts its effects largely during critical periods.* As Figure 3-2 shows, the organism is most vulnerable to teratogens during the embryonic

stage. However, each organ system has a different critical period. For example, the most vulnerable period for the heart is between 20 and 40 days of life.

2. *Each teratogen exerts certain specific effects.* Different teratogens influence different developmental processes. For example, *rubella*, or German measles, in the mother affects mainly the fetus's heart, eyes, and brain. The drug thalidomide causes primarily malformations of the limbs.

3. *Either maternal or fetal genotypes may counteract a teratogen's effects.* Maternal and fetal genotypes affect the developing infant's response to teratogenic agents and play a role in determining whether the infant displays abnormalities. For example, not all pregnant women who have German measles have defective infants. Infants who do develop defects do so because of their own genetic vulnerability to that teratogen.

4. *The effects of one teratogen may intensify the effects of another.* The mother's physiological status, nutrition, and hormonal balance modify the impact of a teratogen. For example, nutritional deficiencies, which interfere with healthy prenatal development, also intensify adverse effects of drugs that the mother has ingested.

5. *Different teratogens may produce the same defect.* For example, deafness may result if the mother contracts rubella or if she ingests quinine or streptomycin.

6. *The longer a fetus is exposed to a particular teratogen and the greater the intensity of the teratogen's effects, the more likely it is that the fetus will be seriously harmed.* This is the *dose–response* principle at work: In general, the higher the does, the more severe the damage to the developing fetus.

Figure 3-2

The child's prenatal susceptibility to teratogenic agents

Sensitivity of the growing embryo to teratogens is greatest in the first four to eight weeks of gestation, peaking around the fifth week. Normally, the zygote is not susceptible to specific teratogens, but if it does succumb to a teratogenic agent, its tiny mass is usually so defenceless that it dies. The defects that occur early in development, when critical organs are being formed, are generally structural; teratogenic agents that impinge on the fetus in later weeks are more likely to stunt its growth or cause functional problems.

Source: Adapted from Moore, 1989.

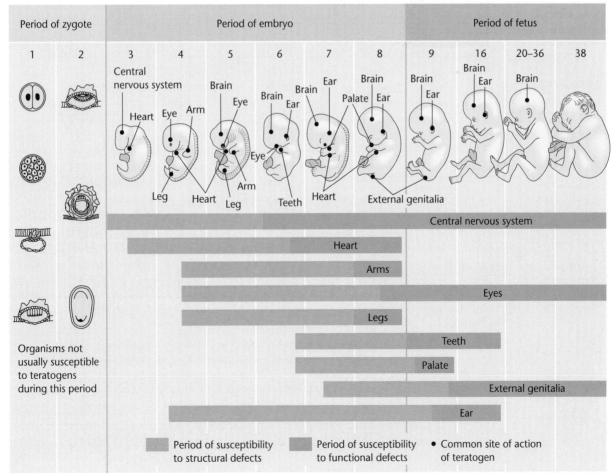

Turning Points

AN OVERVIEW OF PRENATAL DEVELOPMENT

Month	Size & Weight	Nervous & Sensory Systems	Cardiovascular & Respiratory Systems	Musculoskeletal & Dermal Systems	Digestive & Urinary Systems	Endocrine & Reproductive Systems	Other Events
1	0.2 in. .007 oz	Neural tube (B) Eyes, ears (B)	Heartbeat (B) Trachea & lungs (B)		Intestinal tract, liver, pancreas (B)		
2	1.1 in. .09 oz	Nervous system organization, growth of cerebrum (B) Taste buds, olfactory system (B)	Heart structure, major blood vessels, lymph nodes (B) Blood formation in liver (B) Bronchial branching (B) Diaphragm (C)	Cartilage formation (B) Muscles that support central portion of body formed (C)	Intestinal subdivisions including salivary glands (B) Kidney formation (B)	Thyroid, pituitary, adrenal glands (B) Mammary glands (B)	
3	3.2 in. 1.6 oz	Basic spinal cord & brain structure (C)	Tonsils; blood formation in bone marrow (B)	Cartilage replaced with bone (B) Muscles that support appendages (e.g., legs, arms) formed (C) Skeleton visible in X-rays by 14 weeks	Gallbladder, pancreas (C)	Genitalia (B) Differentiation of gonads into ovaries & testes	Fetus responds to stimulation Form is recognizably human Mother's abdomen visibly distended Mother can feel baby's movements
4	5.3 in. 5 oz	Rapid expansion of cerebrum (B) Eye & ear structure complete (C)	Blood formation in spleen (B) Lymphocytes migrate to lymphatic organs (B)	Lanugo & head hair form (B) Skin thin, wrinkled, translucent Sweat glands (C)		Genitalia distinct by 16 weeks	
5	8 in. 17 oz	Myelination of spinal cord (B)	Nostrils open (C)	Adult-like skin Eyelashes & eyebrows Nail production (B)	Intestinal subdivisions (C)		Fetus sucks, swallows, & hiccoughs Evidence of Babinski & grasping reflexes

Zygote ← → Embryo ← →

First trimester — Second trimester

Third trimester	Fetus 6	11.2 in. 1 lb, 10 oz	CNS tract formation; layering of cerebral cortex (B)	Spleen, liver, & bone marrow (C) Formation of lung alveoli (B)	Perineal (sphincter) muscles (C)		Adrenal glands (C)	Survival outside womb relatively rare
	7	14–15 in. 2 lb, 11 oz	Eyelids open; retina sensitive to light		Nail & hair formation (B)		Pituitary gland (C) Descent of testes into scrotum (B)	Survival outside womb not uncommon Rapid weight gain begins Sensitivity to sounds
	8	15–17 in. 4 lb, 6 oz	Taste receptors become functional	Pulmonary branching & alveolar formation (C)			Descent of testes complete at or near time of delivery	
	9	19–21 in. 6 lb, 10 oz to 7 lb, 10 oz				Kidney structure (C)		Normal birth 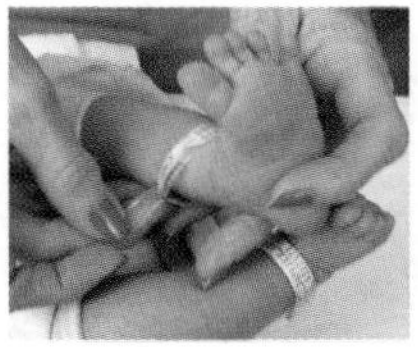
	Postnatal develop-ment		CNS tract formation continues	Immune system becomes operative	Hair changes in consistency & distribution Skeletal growth continues Muscle mass & control increase		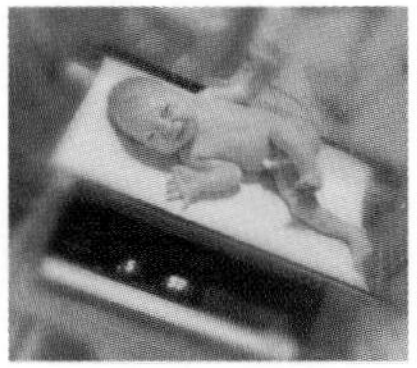	

Key: B = Begins to form C = Completes formation
Sources: Based on Fischer & Lazarson, 1984; Martini, 1995; Moore & Persaud, 1998.

(LO)3 Environmental Dangers

We know that illegal drugs, such as heroin, and other drugs in common use, such as alcohol and nicotine, are often harmful to human beings. Thus, it should come as no surprise that these substances can be extremely harmful—even life-threatening—to the prenatal infant.

LEGAL AND ILLEGAL DRUGS Although most physicians agree that pregnant women should not take too many drugs, according to one estimate, nearly 90 percent of women take some sort of drug during pregnancy (Cunningham, MacDonald, and Grant, 1993). In many of these cases, these women do not yet realize they are pregnant. Even so, some over-the-counter (non-prescription) drugs, such as Aspirin and diet pills, may have adverse effects on the fetus.

For example, heavy use of Aspirin has been associated with low birthweight, lower IQ, and poor motor control (Barr, Streissguth, Darby, & Sampson, 1990). Too much caffeine, too, can adversely affect a developing fetus. Studies have found that women who drank three or more cups of coffee a day were at higher risk for miscarriage or for low-birthweight infants (Klebanoff, Levine, Der Simonian, Clemens, & Wilkins, 1999).

NICOTINE AND ALCOHOL The effects of nicotine and alcohol are particularly concerning. In Canada and the United States, over 30 percent of women smoke while pregnant (Health Canada, 1999a); the United States has a high rate of women who drink during pregnancy (over 80 percent), whereas in Canada, only 17 to 25 percent of women report drinking at some time during their pregnancy (Dzakpasu, Mery, & Trouton, 1998). Smoking and drinking are associated with disturbances in placental functioning and with changes in maternal physiology that lead to oxygen deprivation and, thus, to changes in the fetus's brain (Chomitz et al., 2000). The rate of miscarriages, prematurity, and low-birthweight babies is higher in mothers who smoke or drink than in those who do neither (Gilliland, Li, & Peters, 2001; Mills, 1999). In addition, *sudden infant death syndrome* (SIDS), in which infants under the age of 6 months stop breathing and die without apparent cause, is more common in the offspring of mothers who smoke, drink, or take narcotic drugs (Hunt, 2001). Smokers' babies are also at greater risk for nicotine addiction in adolescence and adulthood (Law et al., 2003).

Some have suggested that prenatal nicotine exposure has significant cognitive effects as well. In the Ottawa prenatal prospective study, researchers from Carleton University have found that maternal smoking has effects ranging from poorer performance on measures of verbal comprehension and fine motor skill at 13 months (Gusella & Fried, 1984); to poorer language development at 3 and 4 years (Fried & Watkinson, 1990); to problems in visual and auditory attention between 4 and 7 years (Kristjansson, Fried, & Watkinson, 1989); to visuoperceptual functioning problems between 9 and 12 years (Fried & Watkinson, 2000); to intellectual, attentional, and memory problems in adolescents (Fried, Watkinson, & Gray, 2003, 2006).

Even passive smoking—that is, smoke breathed in by non-smokers—can contribute to low birthweight, even in babies of mothers who do not smoke. One study found that if fathers smoked during pregnancy, their babies were 3 ounces (88 grams) lighter at birth than babies of non-smoking fathers (Martinez, Wright, & Taussig, 1994). Other studies have shown that passive smoke can cause delays in intellectual and behavioural development (Friedman & Polifka, 1996) and that babies exposed in utero to passive smoke are at increased risk for a variety of illnesses, such as pneumonia, bronchitis, laryngitis, and otitis media, an inner-ear infection (Charlton, 1994).

As early as 1800, abnormalities in children of alcoholic mothers were reported in England. Concerns were expressed that the high consumption of gin, euphemistically known as "mother's ruin," was leading to increased rates of dwarfism in these women's offspring. Today, we know that **fetal alcohol syndrome (FAS)** characterizes 6 percent of infants of alcoholic mothers (Day & Richardson, 1994). Infants with this disorder have a high incidence of facial, heart, and limb defects; they are 20 percent shorter than the average child of their age and are often mentally retarded (Streissguth, 1997, 2007). Recently, researchers have introduced the term **fetal alcohol spectrum disorder (FASD)**, as an umbrella used to describe any number of effects associated with prenatal exposure to alcohol (Nulman, Ickowicz, Koren, & Knittel-Keren, 2007). Unfortunately, it is currently not known how much or how little alcohol consumption leads to problems in infants.

The mental retardation observed in these cases may be related to the loss of oxygen to the fetal brain when the fetus's breathing movements cease temporarily. The fetal damage from alcohol appears to be greatest in the last trimester. If women can cease drinking in this period, their babies tend to be taller, weigh more, and have a larger head circumference than those babies of women who continue heavy drinking (Streissguth, 1997). Children with FASD exhibit a wide range of abnormal behaviours. They may be excessively irritable, distractible, and hyperactive and may engage in such behaviours as repeatedly banging their heads or rhythmically rocking their bodies. They may also exhibit failure to become accustomed to repeated stimuli, and they may be slow or unable to learn to perform such actions as turning their heads or even sucking (Jacobson & Jacobson, 1996; Streissguth, 1997). Although the worst cases of FASD are seen in babies of alcoholic mothers, even moderate drinking by a pregnant woman—say a glass of beer or wine per day—can cause abnormal behaviour patterns in her baby (Abel, 1998; Willford, Leech, & Day, 2006). Studies of older children indicate that many children whose mothers drink during pregnancy have problems paying attention. They also do more poorly in school, and get lower IQ test scores than other children (Burden, Jacobson, & Jacobson, 2005; Connor et al., 2001; Streissguth, 1997), and in young adulthood (age 25) are at higher risk for alcohol problems and psychiatric disorders (Streissguth, 2007). Those who engage in bouts of heavy drinking are three times more likely to have a child with alcohol-related problems by age 21 (Baer et al., 2003). It is also important to note that the negative effects of alcohol on prenatal development may not be solely due to maternal drinking since men who drink heavily may sustain genetic damage that leads to birth defects in their offspring (Cicero, 1994).

Given the potential risks of FASD, health workers in numerous countries have given attention to the prevention of these effects. One primary method of prevention adopted by health agencies has been to increase public awareness of the potential risks of drinking during pregnancy. Such initiatives have taken a variety of approaches. One example is the publication of joint guidelines by the Canadian Centre on Substance Abuse and the (former) Addiction Research Foundation in 1993 (Anderson et al., 1993) and the more recent joint statement on fetal alcohol syndrome and fetal alcohol effects led by the Canadian Pediatric Society and signed by 19 national and provincial/territorial organizations (Health Canada, 1996). Other initiatives include televised public awareness campaigns, such as one that occurred in Manitoba (Casiro et al., 1994), and the inclusion of warning labels on containers of alcoholic beverages (as mandated in the United States since 1989, and, more recently, in the Yukon) or warning signs put up in places selling alcohol.

How have such initiatives fared in terms of raising public awareness of FAS and in changing drinking during pregnancy? In general, knowledge about the potentially dangerous effects of drinking while pregnant has increased. According to a recent survey commissioned by Health Canada (Environics Research Group, 2006), since 1999 and 2002 (when similar surveys were conducted), there have been clear increases in the awareness of both men and women that even small amounts of alcohol consumed during pregnancy can be harmful for the developing child.

Other research, however, suggests a more mixed response to these initiatives. For instance, studies conducted in Manitoba suggest that knowledge about FASD among

fetal alcohol syndrome (FAS)

A disorder exhibited by infants of alcoholic mothers and characterized by stunted growth, a number of physical and physiological abnormalities and, often, mental retardation.

fetal alcohol spectrum disorder (FASD)

An umbrella term used to describe the range of effects associated with prenatal exposure to alcohol.

Native populations is still below that of the general public (Williams & Gloster, 1999). Another study (Graves, 1993) compared US (where labels were mandatory) and Ontario samples (where there were no labels) and found slightly greater awareness of the possible dangers of drinking during pregnancy in the United States, compared with Canada. Other researchers (MacKinnon & Fenaughty, 1993; May, 1995) have proposed that even though public awareness programs might show limited short-term effects, there may well be long-term behavioural effects on women; for example, some women may be prevented from falling into high-risk drinking patterns in the first place.

One issue for such public awareness programs is that unless research can delineate a threshold for the safe consumption of alcohol during pregnancy, these campaigns must walk a very fine line between creating undue anxiety in women who may have unknowingly consumed small amounts of alcohol while pregnant and raising awareness of the risks of dangerous behaviour patterns, such as frequent or binge drinking. In a literature review on FAS prepared for Health Canada, Roberts and Nanson (2000) reiterate the recommendations of Reynolds, Raftis, and Michel (1994) when they suggest that promotional materials for pregnant women need to be developed with specific focus groups in mind, to avoid fear-arousing messages, and to impart a sense of hierarchy to the risk that might exist.

 HEROIN, COCAINE, AND OTHER DRUGS The prenatal effects of such drugs as heroin, morphine, methadone, cocaine, and lysergic acid diethylamide (LSD) are of increasing concern. Mothers who are addicted to heroin, which is a form of morphine, or to morphine itself or who use cocaine have offspring who are also addicted or who sustain toxic effects from these drugs. Babies addicted to one of these drugs go through withdrawal symptoms, some of which are similar to those we described in infants born to alcoholics: irritability, minimal ability to regulate their state of arousal, trembling, shrill crying, rapid respiration, and hyperactivity. Moreover, because these infants are often premature and of low birthweight, it is even more difficult for them to cope with the trauma of withdrawal symptoms (Lester, Boukydis, & Twomey, 2000; Messinger & Lester, 2006). In some cases, symptoms can be severe enough to result in an infant's death in the first few days of life (Lester et al., 2000). In general, the severity of the newborn's symptoms is related to the length, continuity, and intensity of the mother's addiction. If the mother stops taking drugs in the third trimester, the infant is less likely to be affected (Messinger & Lester, 2006).

Substance Abuse Information

At a time when an infant needs special attention and loving care, the behaviour of infants exposed to these drugs may elicit the opposite kind of behaviour from drug-using parents (an interesting example of an evocative gene–environment interaction). Although addicted babies' symptoms are likely to get the attention of a caregiver, these infants do not readily cuddle or cling. When their parents physically stimulate them or place them on their shoulders, these infants do not become alert like normal babies. Clinging, acting alert, and maintaining eye contact are the main behaviours by which infants initiate and sustain social interactions with their caregivers (Lester et al., 2000), and the lack of these behaviours in addicted newborns may disrupt parenting and produce long-term adverse outcomes in parent–child relationships (Phillips et al., 1996). In fact, observations of interactions between mothers and addicted babies reveal their interactions tend to be out of synch with one another and negative (Tronick et al., 2005).

Although not all mothers who take cocaine have babies with developmental anomalies, cocaine use is related to a series of physical defects in infants, including bone, genital, urinary tract, kidney, eye and heart deformities, and brain hemorrhages. Some long-term studies of the effects of maternal cocaine use have reported that children have problems with sustained attention, and are impulsive, highly distractible, and difficult to control (Bandstra et al., 2001). Recent research also suggest that maternal cocaine use effects children's school performance, with this effect dependent on how supportive the child's environment turns out to be (Messinger & Lester, 2006).

The question of how severely maternal cocaine use affects the developing fetus remains controversial. Some researchers have concluded that maternal cocaine use does indeed have negative effects (Phillips et al., 1996); others, however, have questioned this impact (Frank et al., 2001). For example, Koren and colleagues (Koren, 1993; Koren et al., 1998; Loebstein & Koren, 1997), at the Hospital for Sick Children in Toronto, found no differences in global IQ between children who were exposed to cocaine prenatally and a group of control children, although the cocaine-exposed children did show lower scores on a language test (Loebstein & Koren, 1997). Koren suggests that most fetuses exposed to prenatal cocaine, in fact, develop normally (Koren, 1993), and that the negative outcomes sometimes observed in children exposed to cocaine prenatally are instead due to factors such as socio-economic status, low maternal education, and other forms of maternal addiction (Koren et al., 1998).

Finally, researchers, such as Peter Fried from Carlton University, have been looking at the impact of exposure to marijuana, starting prenatally and up to adolescence, in a longitudinal project entitled the Ottawa Prenatal Prospective study. Research such as this has found admittedly a mixed pattern of results. For example, most (but not all) studies have found few effects of prenatal marijuana exposure on fetal growth (Fried et al., 1999), or on other physical growth parameters throughout the toddler and early-childhood years (Day et al., 1992; Fried et al., 1999) and even up to the onset of puberty (Fried, James, & Watkinson, 2001). In contrast, there have been some reports of cognitive impairment associated with heavy marijuana use by mothers, although this impairment is not evident until about four years (Fried & Watkinson, 1988, 1990). Continuing this trend, these researchers have noted continued effects on attention and visual memory beyond the toddler stage, up through adolescence (Fried, 2002; Fried et al., 1998, 2003; Fried & Watkinson, 2000, 2001; Fried & Smith, 2001). Most recently, Smith, Fried, Hogan, and Cameron (2006) found long-lasting neurophysiological effects of prenatal marijuana exposure in 18- to 22-year-olds using brain-imaging (fMRI) techniques during a visuo-spatial memory task, although there did not appear to be any actual differences in cognitive performance.

Environmental Toxins

Dangerous substances in the everyday environment are also harmful to children. Some of these substances are radiation, lead, mercury, herbicides, pesticides, pesticides, household cleaners, and even food additives and cosmetics. Although there is still much to be learned about prenatal neurotoxicity, we have known for many years that radiation can harm the developing fetus; it is for this reason that health personnel routinely advise pregnant women to avoid X-rays.

Lead is a well-documented source of harm for both pregnant women and children. Women and babies may be exposed to lead by inadvertently inhaling automobile exhaust, drinking water contaminated by industrial waste, or living in an environment painted with lead-based paint. Exposure to lead during pregnancy has been associated with a variety of problems in newborns, including prematurity and low birthweight, brain damage, and physical defects, as well as with long-term problems in cognitive and intellectual functioning (Dietrich, Berger, Succop, Hammond, & Bornschein, 1993; Evans, 2004).

Another environmental hazard is polychlorinated biphenyls (PCBs), which were used routinely in electrical transformers and capacitators. The use of these substances has been banned since the mid-1970s, when it was discovered that pregnant women who ate PCB-contaminated fish gave birth to infants with various deficits. These babies were smaller, less responsive, and less neurologically advanced than infants who had not been exposed to PCBs (Jacobson & Jacobson, 1996; Sagiv, Tolbert, Altshul, & Korrick, 2007). Long-term effects of prenatal exposure include lower IQ, poorer memory, lower reading ability and higher levels of impulsivity in 4- and 11-year-old

Over the past decades, researchers have become increasingly aware of the potential dangers posed by environmental toxins such as PCBs, or even industrial air pollution. How would you (and your young infant) like to live next door to this plant?

children (Jacobson & Jacobson, 2004). Even though PCBs have been banned, they are still a considerable health concern. Inuit infants in Nunavut, for example, currently have much higher levels of PCBs in their umbilical cord blood than other children, presumably due to the large amounts of fish and marine mammals eaten by their mothers (Muckle, Dewailly, & Ayotte, 1998). Even postnatal exposure to breast-feeding mothers with high levels of PCBs in their breast milk is linked with lower mental and motor development at 30 months (Walkowiak et al., 2001).

Fathers' exposure to environmental toxins can affect men's sperm, and thus ultimately have harmful effects on the developing fetus also. Men who work in occupations that expose them to toxic substances, such as radiation, mercury, or lead, may develop chromosomal abnormalities that may affect their fertility or may increase the risk of their pregnant wives miscarrying or bearing infants with birth defects (Bentur & Koren, 1991; Merewood, 2000). Wives and husbands planning to have a child should both monitor their exposure to environmental toxins.

Medical Interventions in Pregnancy and Childbirth

Because even many normal pregnancies and deliveries are not without discomfort, physicians may prescribe drugs or diagnostic procedures to alleviate such problems. Sometimes, these, too, have proven dangerous.

SOME THERAPEUTIC DISASTERS   Between 1947 and 1964, the synthetic hormone **diethylstilbestrol (DES)** was often prescribed to help prevent pregnant women from miscarrying. Tragically, this drug turned out to be anything but therapeutic, for, in the late 1960s, scientists discovered its delayed effects. Many female offspring of the millions of women who had taken DES during pregnancy developed vaginal abnormalities and cancer of the cervix in adolescence (Nevin, 1988). In addition, these young women also experienced high rates of problems in pregnancy, including spontaneous abortions, premature deliveries, and babies with low birthweight (Linn et al., 1988). Moreover, the sons of women who ingested DES during pregnancy also sustained damage to the reproductive tract, such as seminal fluid abnormalities (Giusti, Iwamoto, & Hatch, 1995; Wilcox, Baird, & Weinberg, 1995).

Another therapeutic tragedy of the early 1960s made the public keenly aware of the potentially devastating effects of drug use by pregnant women. **Thalidomide**, an anti-anxiety and anti-nausea drug, was prescribed by many physicians to relieve the symptoms of morning sickness. The children of these women were sometimes born with abnormalities that included deformations of the eyes, nose, and ears; cleft palate; facial palsy; fusing of fingers and toes; and dislocations of the hip joint and malformations of the heart and the digestive and genito-urinary tracts. The most characteristic and most horrible deformity was something called *phocomelia*, in which limbs are missing and the feet and hands are attached directly to the torso in such a way that, to many, they look like flippers (Moore & Persaud, 1998).

It was extremely difficult at the time when these types of abnormalities appeared for doctors and scientists to figure out that these drugs were causing birth defects. This is because the pregnant women themselves showed no adverse effects from the drugs, and in the case of thalidomide, only a small percentage had children with deficits, And the animal studies that led up to the production of these drugs did not always produce adverse effects in offspring. Today, diethylstilbestrol is still on the market in Canada (and the United States), but it is recommended only for the alleviation of symptoms in advanced breast and prostate cancers, and thalidomide is available only for the treatment of cancer and of other illnesses such as AIDS and Hansen's disease (leprosy).

diethylstilbestrol (DES)

A synthetic hormone once prescribed to pregnant women to prevent miscarriages but discontinued when cancer and precancerous conditions were detected in the children of such women.

thalidomide

A drug once prescribed to relieve morning sickness in pregnant women but discontinued when found to cause serious malformations of the fetus. Current controversy surrounds possible use in treating symptoms of such diseases as AIDS, cancer, and leprosy.

Other drugs that are common administered to pregnant women for therapeutic reasons may have deleterious effects as well. Maternal ingestion of reserpine, a tranquilizer, may lead to respiratory problems in an infant. Tetracyclines may depress infant skeletal growth. Anti-convulsant drugs may result in the development of cleft lip and palate as well as heart and skeletal defects (Meador et al., 2006). Even Aspirin, if taken in high doses by pregnant women, may produce blood disorders in their offspring (Vorhees & Mollnow, 1987). Clearly physicians must use great caution in prescribing drugs for women during pregnancy.

MEDICATIONS USED IN LABOUR AND DELIVERY   In recent years, researchers have focused attention on the effects of local anaesthetics, such as the epidural or spinal block, and general anaesthetics used to ease pain and to sedate women during labour. Babies of mothers who received large amounts of obstetrical medication during labour showed less responsiveness, less smiling, and more irritability for several days after birth, as well as depression, motoric disorganization, and disruptions in feeding responses (Brackbill, McManus, & Woodward, 1985). The also have impaired attention and motor abilities at 1 month of age, but not usually longer (Emory, Schlackman, & Fiano, 1996). The extent to which obstetrical medications affect infants is determined by genetic factors, the mother's general health, the length of labour, the size of the baby, and even the mother's attitude (Lester, Als, & Brazelton, 1982).

Maternal Factors

Some factors affecting the fetus are directly related to characteristics of the mother herself. In this section, we discuss how a mother's age, choice of diet, emotional state, and health may affect her unborn child. Table 3-1 on the next page gives an overview of this material.

AGE AND PARITY   A woman's age and *parity*, or the number of children she has already borne, may interact in influencing the development of her fetus. Women who have their first child when they are under 15 or over 35 years are likely to experience more problems during pregnancy and complications during delivery than other women. Older women have more difficulty conceiving a child. Indeed, the chance of becoming pregnant declines steadily after age 27, and by age 40, it is less than 5 percent (among women who are trying to become pregnant). In addition, as Figure 3-3 on page 97 shows, the incidence of both miscarriage and chromosomal abnormality increase with the age of the mother and her reproductive system. Among older mothers, emerging health risks—such as increases in hypertension and diabetes—rather than age per se contribute to difficulties in these pregnancy and birth. Despite the increased incidence of miscarriage, due in part to the greater likelihood of conceiving a child with chromosomal abnormalities, the vast majority of older women have normal pregnancies and healthy babies (Brockington, 1996). Recent evidence suggests that older fathers may also contribute to poor birth outcomes. Men not only become less fertile as they age but tend to have more infants with birth defects due to the deteriorating quality of sperm in older men (Lowe et al., 2001; Wyrobek et al., 2006). Clearly, both men and women have biological clocks.

Teenage mothers may have problems with their pregnancies because their reproductive systems are immature, they are more likely to have unhealthy personal habits, such as the use or abuse of drugs, they are more often of low socio-economic status and, thus, lack good nutrition and prenatal care, and they tend to live in environments characterized by high rates of disease and environmental pollutants. Sometimes, the failure of teenagers to seek formal prenatal care contributes to the relatively high rate of infant mortality (see Box 3.1 on pages 98 and 99). Studies of young mothers show that they are also more likely to have pregnancy complications like *toxemia* (a condition that re-

The tragedy of the thalidomide disaster is written on the face of this young Brazilian mother. Her love and her sadness are apparent as she kisses and cradles her newborn son in her arms.

Table 3-1 Maternal characteristics, diseases, and disorders that can have a negative impact on prenatal development

Potential Negative Effects	
Characteristics of the Mother	
Age	Teenage mothers tend to live in risky environments, to neglect their health and diets, and to use drugs, thus risking premature and low-birthweight babies; older mothers risk bearing a Down syndrome child as well as problems posed by illnesses that are more common as people age.
Diet	Malnourishment can lead to miscarriage, stillbirths, prematurity, low birthweight, physical and neural defects, smaller size in newborns, and sometimes cognitive difficulties.
Emotional state	Mothers who are stressed may have more troubled pregnancies, miscarriages, long labour and delivery complications, and more need for childbirth anaesthesia; their infants may be hyperactive and irritable and have feeding and sleep problems.
Diseases and Disorders	
Mumps	Infant may suffer malformation of some kind.
Rubella (German measles)	Infant may be born deaf or mentally retarded or have cardiac disorders or cataract formation.
Rh factor incompatibility	If mother's and infant's blood types are incompatible (mother's negative, infant's positive), on second and subsequent pregnancies antibodies produced by mother's blood can kill the fetus.
Hypertension (high blood pressure)	Fetal abnormalities, miscarriage, fetal death.
Diabetes	Pre-eclampsia or eclampsia, associated with hypertension; possible stillbirth or death of newborn.
Gonorrhea	Infant may be infected in the birth canal.
Syphilis	Miscarriage; if infant survives it may be born blind, mentally retarded, or have other physical abnormalities.
Chlamydia	Miscarriage or stillbirth; surviving infant may acquire disease in birth process, or develop pneumonia or a form of conjunctivitis.
Genital herpes	Infected infant may be blind, mentally retarded, or have motor abnormalities or a wide range of neurological disorders. Half the surviving infants are seriously disabled.
Acquired immune deficiency syndrome (AIDS)	Infants infected often suffer neurological impairments, defects in mental and physical development, microcephaly (small head), and other physical abnormalities. More than half survive beyond 6 years of age, but most eventually die from this disorder.
Toxoplasmosis	Eye and brain damage in the developing baby.

sults from the spread of bacterial products in the bloodstream) and to bear infants with lower birthweights (Smith, 1994), and their children are at risk for delays in developing intellectual, language, and social skills (Moore & Brooks-Gunn, 2002). When teenage mothers have adequate diets and prenatal care, however, they do not show any higher rates of complications in birth or pregnancy than do mothers in their twenties (Moore & Brooks-Gunn, 2002; Smith, 1994). Also, when they live in supportive environments, their infants do not suffer any higher rates of developmental delays. (See Chapter 11 for more discussion of teen parenthood.)

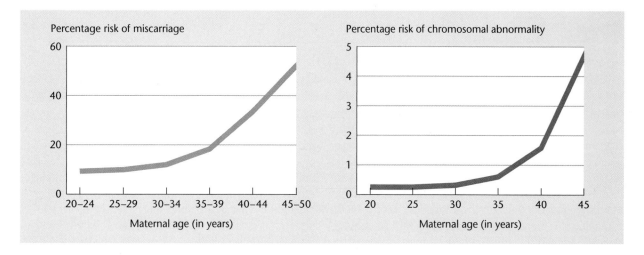

Figure 3-3

Maternal age and reproductive risk

As women age, the risks of miscarriage and of chromosomal abnormalities increase.

Source: From *Time*, April 15, 2002, p. 53. Copyright © 2002 Time Inc.

CHOICE OF DIET   It is difficult to separate the effects of maternal malnourishment from those of other harmful factors. The malnourished mother often lives in an environment of poverty and disadvantage, characterized by poor education, inferior sanitation and shelter, and inadequate medical care (Evans, 2004). In North America, malnutrition and high maternal and infant mortality rates are also associated with ethnicity. Families of African and Latino descent are often poorer than European and Asian families, and the women in these former groups are more likely to be exposed to these harmful environmental factors and to experience more of their destructive effects.

Studies have shown that gross dietary deficiencies in the diets of pregnant women, especially of some vitamins, minerals, and proteins, are related to increased rates of miscarriage, stillbirth, and infant mortality. Moreover, these same studies have concluded that such deficiencies are likely to lead to prematurity, physical and neural defects, and smaller size in neonates (Shonkoff & Phillips, 2000). The specific form the damage takes depends on the age at which the malnutrition occurs. For example, if the mother takes a supplement of folic acid daily in the last two months of her pregnancy she can reduce her risk of having a premature birth (Scholl et al., 1996). Impairment of a child's intellectual development due to prenatal malnutrition is most likely when the mother's malnutrition has been severe and long lasting and when dietary deprivation continues after childbirth (Lozoff et al, 2006; Sigman, 1995). Researchers have found that prenatal malnutrition is detrimental for children's social and motor development and cognitive abilities (Lozoff et al., 2006; Ricciuti, 1993; Sigman, 1995). Cognitive difficulties may not only be the result of biological changes in the brain but may be linked with behavioural aspects of malnutrition—lowered energy, inattention, and lack of motivation and responsiveness. Nutrition supplement studies in Jamaica, Indonesia, and Colombia found that both motor and cognitive abilities improved when infants were given enriched diets (Grantham-McGregor, Powell, Walker, & Hines, 1991).

Finally, the effects on an infant of prenatal malnutrition may be worse if tired, malnourished parents respond to their malnourished and irritable or non-responsive malnourished infants with lack of support or rejection (Lozoff et al., 2006). For this reason, many successful intervention programs have focused on training economically deprived parents, who are often working frequently and have inadequate child care, to interact with their children in a more sensitive, involved, and stimulating manner (Campbell et al., 2001).

Box 3.1

Perspectives on Diversity

PRENATAL HEALTH CARE AND INFANT MORTALITY

International Health Data

One of the most important indicators of the health of a country and its children is its rate of infant mortality, or the number of infants who die within their first year of life. In 1996, Canada's infant mortality rate dropped to just under 6 deaths per 1,000 live births (Statistics Canada, 1998) and, as of 2005, was reported to be at about 5.4 deaths per 1,000 live births (Statistics Canada, 2008). Although this figure sounds quite low, on an international level, it is disturbingly high. Figure 3-4 shows the rates of infant mortality for a sampling of countries throughout the world. Japan, for instance, has the lowest infant mortality rate (3.8 deaths per 1,000 births; Iceland is in a virtual tie with Japan), and there are at least 11 additional countries with lower mortality rates. The comparison for the United States is even more shocking, with 9 of the 14 countries shown having lower levels of infant mortality (OECD, 1998).

Interpreting these differences in mortality rates must be done cautiously, however, because of the differences in clinical practices and the methods used to record live births across the world (Howell & Blondell, 1994; Health Canada, 1999a; Sachs et al., 1995). But the rates of infant mortality in North America are perplexing. Why are mortality rates so high, given the advanced degree of medical technology available?

In the United States, the answer is at least partly tied to the type of prenatal care provided to pregnant women (Wegman, 1994). In any one of 10 Western European countries—Belgium, Denmark, England, France, Germany, Ireland, Netherlands, Norway, Spain, and Switzerland—pregnant women automatically receive prenatal and postnatal care at very little cost because it is subsidized by their governments. They also get from 8 to 40 weeks of paid maternity leave from work. Many pregnant women in the United States, however, face a much more difficult, situation. There are no uniform national standards to guarantee pregnant women either consistent high-quality maternity care or, of equal importance, financial coverage. In the United States, at least 1.3 million women receive insufficient prenatal care. Moreover, many of these women are the ones who need it the most (Healy, 1995). The groups least likely to receive care are teens, unmarried, poor, less educated, recent immigrants, and minorities. These women are at greatest risk of bearing babies with complications such as prematurity and low birthweight.

Unfortunately, universal access to health care does not ensure uniform rates of either prenatal care or infant mortality. The Canada Health Act, passed by Parliament in 1984, ensures that all residents of Canada have access to a comprehensive health-care system regardless of income. Despite such universal access, however, research on the use of the health-care system for prenatal care indicates that utilization varies as a function of socio-economic levels. Mustard and Roos (1994), for example, have found that in a Winnipeg sample, there was a lower rate of utilization of prenatal care by poorer women. Moreover, universal access does not negate the differences in infant mortality as a function of socio-economic and ethnic factors. As Figure 3-5 shows, infant mortality drops with greater income, with mortality rates for upper-, upper-middle-, and middle-income groups being lower than the Canadian average, whereas lower-middle- and lower-income groups have above-average mortality rates. Moreover, infant mortality among First Nations children is twice as high as in the Canadian population as a whole (Health Canada, 1999a).

Is the difference in prenatal care and infant mortality solely a result of differences in socio-economic class and ethnic identity? According to Young and her colleagues (Young, McMahon, Bowman, & Thompson, 1989), there are also motivational and social reasons that might explain why women do not seek prenatal care. For example, in one study, African-American women, in particular, reported problems with scheduling and keeping appointments for prenatal care as a reason for delaying such care, whereas Caucasian Americans often noted that they did not feel they needed prenatal care. Scheduling difficulties were more often cited by women under 20 years than older women. Among social problems, those most often cited were unemployment, being a single parent, psychological stress, interpersonal conflicts with the father of the baby, and family crises.

Thus, despite the fact that both Canadian and US rates of infant mortality have declined steadily since 1960, there is still much room for improvement, both among different socio-economic and racial groups within a country and in comparison with other countries throughout the world. What can be done about this situation? In the United States, the resistance to a national health-care system has been monumental. As a result of this resistance, a large proportion of mothers have had no access to prenatal care. Even with universal access, such as in Canada, it is important that all segments of the population take advantage of the opportunities they do have, particularly given the emotional and financial costs of infant mortality, infant prematurity, and handicapped infants.

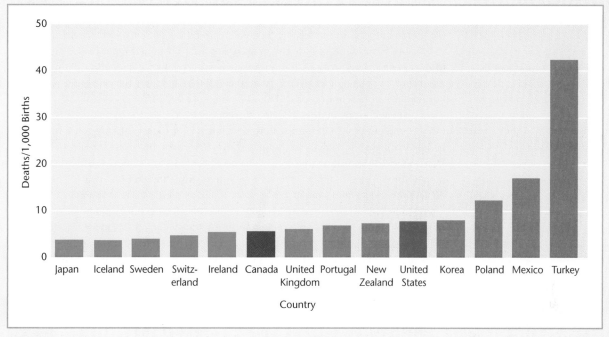

Figure 3-4

Infant mortality rates in selected countries throughout the world

Source: OECD, 1998; Statistics Canada, 1998.

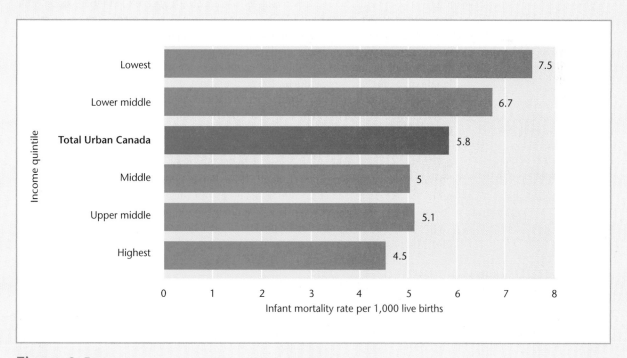

Figure 3-5

Infant mortality rate, by income quintile, urban Canada, 1999

Source: *Toward a Healthy Future: Second Report on the Health of Canadians,* Health Canada, 1999a. Adapted and reproduced with the permission of Minister of Public Works and Government Services Canada, 2009.

EMOTIONAL STATE Stresses during pregnancy can come from a wide array of problems, such as marital discord, disagreement about whether to continue the pregnancy, relocation to a new city, or illness and death of relatives—these stresses can affect the mothers' emotional state and, in turn, her baby. A pregnant woman's emotionality can lead to metabolic or biochemical changes that affect the fetus. In fact, fetal stress hormones reflect those of the mother (DiPietro, 2004; DiPietro et al., 2006). Studies have found that women who suffer sustained emotional distress tend to experience complications during pregnancy and delivery, including nausea during pregnancy, spontaneous abortion, prolonged labour, and a greater need for anaesthesia during childbirth (Monk et al., 2000; O'Conner et al., 2005).

Women who are anxious and under emotional stress during pregnancy tend to have infants who are physically more active in utero. After their birth, these infants tend to be hyperactive and irritable, to cry more, and to have feeding and sleep problems (Van Den Bergh, 1992); these children are also more likely to develop a difficult temperament (Huizink et al., 2002). At the age of 7, they are more likely to exhibit behavioural difficulties, depression, and anxiety (O'Conner et al., 2005). And in an extremely interesting natural experiment, Laplante and colleagues (2008) examined the impact of stress on mothers who were pregnant during the January 1998 ice storm in Quebec that left almost 3 million people without electricity for up to 40 days. In June of 1998, Laplante and colleagues had mothers complete questionnaires about the extent of their stress during the ice storm. Subsequently, when the children of these mothers reached 5½ years of age, the children were given a variety of cognitive and linguistic tests. The results of comparisons between these two sets of measures revealed that mothers who experienced high levels of stress in utero had children with lower levels of cognitive and linguistic ability.

Interestingly, the effects of stress may be moderated by the support available to a pregnant woman (Brockington, 1996; DiMatteo & Kahn, 1997). One study demonstrated the effects on labour and delivery of the actual presence of a supportive companion (Sosa, Kennell, Klaus, Robertson, & Urrutia, 1980). These researchers studied the childbirth experiences of healthy Guatemalan women. The women in the experimental group were assigned a *doula*, a supportive female companion who talked to them, reassured them, rubbed their backs, and held their hands until delivery. The control group went through the normal hospital routine with no supportive person present. The mean length of labour was 19.3 hours for the control group and 8.7 hours for the women who had supportive companions. Similar beneficial effects of having a trained, supportive companion have been found in women having their babies delivered in North American hospitals (Kennell, Klaus, McGrath, Robertson, & Hinckley, 1991).

Fathers' presence during labour and delivery also has a beneficial effect on mothers, reducing their pain and their need for medication and making their view of the birth experience more positive (Lindell, 1988; Parke, 2002). And currently, it is not just fathers who are present. According to a survey of Canadian hospitals (Levitt, Hanvey, Avard, Chance, & Kaczorowski, 1995), another support person, in addition to the woman's partner, was encouraged to be present in the labour and birth room over 80 percent of the time.

Diseases and Disorders

A wide range of maternal diseases and disorders can affect an infant's development either prenatally or during birth. Like the effects of other teratogenic agents, the effects of these disorders depend on their timing. For example, if the pregnant woman contracts the viral disease *mumps* during her first trimester, her infant is more likely to suffer some kind of malformation than if the disease is contracted later in pregnancy. Similarly, if a woman contracts *rubella* during the first month of her pregnancy, her fetus risks cardiac disorders, cataract formation, deafness, and mental retardation; if

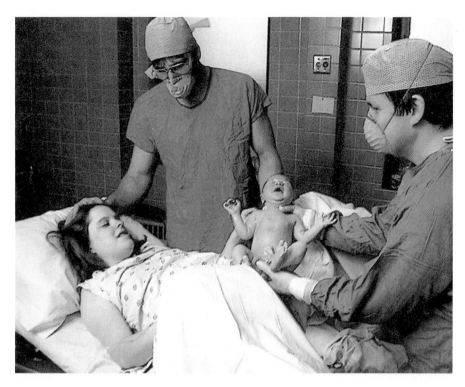

More and more fathers are electing to be in the delivery room these days, and many couples report their shared experience of the birth of a child as one of great joy and happiness.

she contracts this illness in her third month, however, the likelihood that her infant will suffer disability declines substantially (Cochi et al., 1989).

Timing is also an issue in the potentially life-threatening condition of **Rh factor incompatibility**, in which an infant's blood is Rh positive (Rh+), and the mother's blood is Rh negative (Rh–). (Rh factors are antigens, or substances in the blood that can induce specific immune responses.) Because positive and negative blood types are incompatible, if fetal and maternal blood should commingle, the mother's blood could produce antibodies that would attack the fetal blood cells, causing the death of the fetus. Because such antibodies are scarce in a woman who is pregnant for the first time, Rh incompatibility is not an issue during a first birth. To prevent it from ever becoming an issue, Rh immune globulin can be administered to the mother after the birth of each child to prevent antibody formation and to ensure the birth of other healthy children (Turner & Rubinson, 1993).

Other maternal conditions that may increase rates of fetal abnormalities, miscarriage, and death include *hypertension*, also known as high blood pressure, and *diabetes*.

Rh factor incompatibility

A condition in which an infant's Rh positive blood opposes its mother's Rh negative blood, and threatens fetuses in second and third trimesters and later births when the mother's body has had time to produce antibodies that will attack fetal blood cells.

PARASITIC AND BACTERIAL INFECTIONS Parasitic infections, such as **toxoplasmosis**, which is acquired by eating undercooked meat or by contact with feces (e.g., in handling cat litter) can affect the infant. Transmitted through the *placenta*, toxoplasmosis can cause eye and brain damage in a developing baby.

Bacterial infections can also cause problems for the infant. **Gonorrhea**, which is spread, for the most part by direct sexual contact with an infected person, can cause *pelvic inflammatory disease* in the woman, and this can cause an *ectopic*, or tubal, pregnancy. In an ectopic pregnancy, the zygote implants in the woman's fallopian tube instead of in her uterus, and to save the mother's life, the pregnancy must be terminated (Turner & Rubinson, 1993). Gonorrhea in the mother can also infect an infant as it passes through the birth canal. If not treated, the disease can cause blindness; for this reason, in most hospitals, a few drops of silver nitrate or penicillin are placed in the eyes of newborns to prevent infection.

toxoplasmosis

A parasitic disease acquired by eating undercooked meat or by making contact with feces in handling cat litter.

gonorrhea

A sexually transmitted bacterial infection, which, in a pregnant woman, can cause blindness in her infant; normally treatable with antibiotics.

AIDS Information

Some chronic infections invade the developing embryo and remain active but do not exert their worst effects until later stages of development. For example, the harmful effects on the fetus of maternal **syphilis** do not occur before 18 weeks of gestation, and, therefore, early treatment of a syphilitic mother may avert abnormalities in the child. If the mother is untreated, however, invasion of the fetus by bacteria from the mother may result in spontaneous abortion, blindness, mental retardation, or other physical abnormalities. Moreover, the negative effects of syphilis are sometimes not apparent even at birth but emerge gradually during the early years of development, and take the form of deterioration in thought processes, judgment, speech, a decline in motor and mental abilities, and, eventually, death. Although years ago, syphilis was virtually a death sentence, today, if it is detected and treated early with antibiotics, it can be cured.

Chlamydia is probably the most widespread bacterial infection among sexually transmitted diseases. Babies born to women with this infection often acquire it during the birth process and may develop pneumonia or a form of conjunctivitis. Mothers with chlamydia also run the risk of spontaneous abortion and stillbirth. In addition, like gonorrhea, chlamydia can lead to pelvic inflammatory disease.

VIRAL INFECTIONS   One of the most common sexually transmitted diseases is **genital herpes**. Currently, the rate of neonatal herpes ranges from about 1 to 6 per 20,000 live births (Gesundheit et al., 2004). The risk is especially great if the mother is having an active outbreak of herpes and the infant is exposed to the virus in the birth canal. If a herpes infection is detected in a pregnant woman before labour, a Cesarean delivery will usually succeed in preventing the infant from coming into contact with the disease and, thus, protecting it from contagion. Herpes can also be transmitted by exposure to the virus after birth, although this occurs less frequently. Because an infant does not have a fully developed immune system before 5 weeks of age, if it is infected with herpes, the disease can cause blindness, motor abnormalities, mental retardation, and a wide range of neurological disorders. Sixty percent of these babies will die; roughly 90 percent of the babies who survive are left with serious problems, including skin and mouth ulcers and eye and brain infections. Nearly half have major developmental disorders (Healy, 1995).

Of course, the viral infection that has caused the greatest alarm in recent years is the *human immunodeficiency virus* (HIV) infection and its expression in **acquired immune deficiency syndrome (AIDS)**. In the absence of treatment, an infected pregnant woman has about a 25 percent chance of transmitting the AIDS virus to her child. Most are infected prenatally—through passage of the virus via the placenta during gestation or the birth process—but drinking the mother's milk after birth can also infect them. However, through the use of anti-retroviral drug therapy and a Caesarean delivery, the rate of transmission is reduced to 1 percent (Coovadia, 2004). In Canada, by the end of 1999, of the over 45,000 positive HIV tests reported, 664 involved children of 15 years of age or younger, and another 597 HIV-positive tests were reported among 15- to 19-year-olds (Health Canada, 2000d). Worldwide, in 2005, around 700,000 children under age 15 contracted HIV, mainly through mother-to-child transmission; the majority of the infected children reside in sub-Saharan Africa (UNAIDS, 2006).

The incidence of AIDS, both among children and adults, varies with race. In the United States, over half the children under 5 years of age with AIDS are African American, whereas Caucasian Americans account for 18 percent (Centers for Disease Control, 1996). In Canada, although there is no information on the incidence of AIDS in children as a function of race, in adults, the percentage of AIDS among ethnic minorities, primarily African Canadians and First Nations people, has been increasing since 1989. In contrast, AIDS infections have been decreasing in Caucasian Canadians during this same period (Health Canada, May, 1999).

Children with AIDS often suffer neurological impairments, delays in mental and physical development, and such structural deformities as *microcephaly*, or an unusually small head, a square forehead, and widely spaced, slanted eyes. Of greater significance, is the fact that AIDS is an autoimmune disease, or one in which the body's immunological forces are disabled and/or attack the body's healthy cells. Thus, these children are vulnerable to disease and infections of all sorts that may cause their early deaths (Centers for Disease Control and Prevention, 2007). Children with HIV and/or AIDS and their families are desperately in need of specialized care and support systems and without external assistance, remain highly vulnerable.

Camp Moomba is a summer camp for children who are living with or affected by HIV and/or AIDS. The camp is a charitable organization run by the Western Canadian Pediatric AIDS Society.

For Thought and Discussion

1. Your cousin has just become pregnant and asks you all about the course of prenatal development. What are some of the important developmental milestones in the growth of her child that you are going to point out?

2. After describing these developmental trends, your cousin, who is a regular smoker, asks you about the effects of tobacco and alcohol on her fetus. What will you tell her about the sensitivity of her child to these substances? At what points in her pregnancy is she most susceptible to such influences?

3. One very important concern with the observed relation between AIDS and race is that in both Canada and the United States, race is correlated with poverty. As such, it is quite likely that it is poverty, and not race itself, that leads to these relations. Given this possibility, what implications does this have for public education, and for the prevention of diseases such as AIDS?

BIRTH AND THE BEGINNINGS OF LIFE   LO 5

Birth is one of the most dramatic and significant events in the lives of parents and children. For parents, the last few weeks of pregnancy are typically characterized by joyous anticipation and, especially in first births, by apprehension about labour and childbirth, anxiety about whether the child will be normal, and concern about whether the mother will be permanently altered physically by pregnancy and delivery. Although both parents are exhausted by the end of the process of birth, most are exhilarated, even awestruck, by seeing and holding their newborn for the first time.

Labour and Delivery

Birth is also a momentous physical and social transition for the infant. The baby moves from the warm, wet, dark environment of the uterus to the colder, dry, bright environment of an external world full of changing lights, objects, movements, touches, voices, and faces. Even before birth, during pregnancy, the parents and the child have established a relationship, and following birth, the construction of this relationship becomes more intense and accelerated.

THE THREE STAGES OF CHILDBIRTH   Birth involves a series of changes in the mother that permit the child to move from the womb out into the external world. Figure 3-6 shows the way the fetus appears and is positioned in the uterus just before labour begins, as well as the three stages in the birth process that we describe next.

The first stage of labour begins as the mother experiences regular uterine contractions that are usually spaced at 10- to 15-minute intervals; these contractions become more intense and frequent as labour progresses. This first stage, which generally lasts between 8 and 14 hours for first-born children and half that for later-born children, concludes when the cervix is dilated sufficiently to permit the infant's head to pass through it and into the vaginal canal.

In the second stage of labour, which usually lasts less than an hour, the infant descends through the birth canal and is delivered through the vaginal opening.

The third and final stage of birth takes only a few minutes, as the uterus expels the placenta.

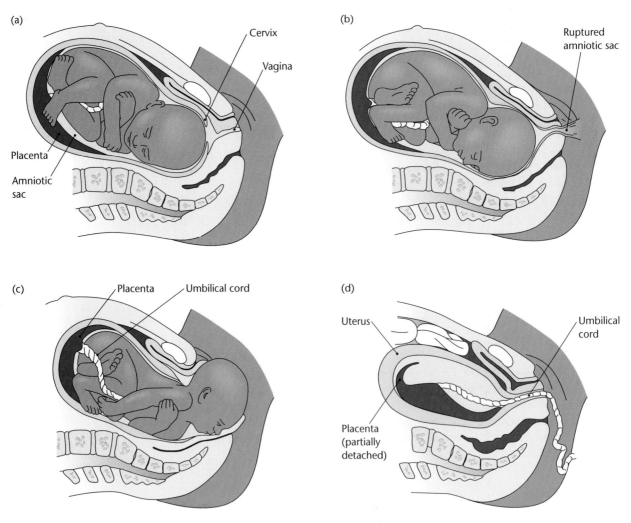

Figure 3-6

The stages of the birth process

With arms and legs folded and head pointed toward the birth canal, the fetus is ready to be born (a). In stage 1, the fetus moves toward the cervix, as it gradually dilates (b). In stage 2, the fetus moves through the vaginal opening (c). In stage 3, the nourishing placenta detaches from the uterine wall preparatory to expulsion (d).

Source: Adapted from Vander, Sherman, & Luciano, 1994.

NATURAL CHILDBIRTH: NOT SUCH A NEW IDEA Having a baby in the relatively isolated and unfamiliar setting of a hospital, separated from one's relatives and often from one's husband, was a practice that began in the nineteenth century as a response to a rise in health problems and in infant and maternal mortality rates associated with rapid urbanization and industrialization. Before that time, and still in many regions of the world, women gave birth in their homes, attended by relatives or a midwife.

Currently, the vast majority of North American women are still assisted in childbirth by a physician. However, birth is more and more becoming a shared family experience, and occurring in the home or in home-like birthing centres. A common preparation for childbirth is the Lamaze method. The Lamaze childbirth technique uses breathing and muscle relaxation exercises to teach women how to manage the pain of labour and delivery. Many couples take classes during pregnancy to learn these techniques. Fathers are taught to help their partners with the relaxation procedures and to be a relaxation and breathing coach during the labour/delivery process.

The presence of a supportive partner, in combination with the Lamaze breathing techniques, does, in fact, lead to an easier labour and delivery. Mothers who choose to take Lamaze classes experience shorter labour, require less medication, and are less stressed and more positive about the birth experience (Mackey, 1995; Wilcox, Kobayashi, & Murray, 1997). Midwife-assisted births have increased nearly 800 percent since the early 1970s (Carmichael, 2004). Although Canada has only recently begun to treat midwifery as a recognized profession (McIntyre, Officer, & Simpson, 1996), midwives are now registered in many provinces across the country, and there is growing support for the idea that women have a right to choose their place of delivery, including the home (Health Canada, 2000b). Home deliveries by trained personnel or delivery in a birthing centre are suitable for normal births; however, between 15 and 25 percent of women who begin labour in such settings are subsequently moved to a hospital because of birth complications (Olsen, 1997). Many of the recent trends in home birthing go back to ancient times. The kneeling position, which some modern women prefer, was favoured by native Hawaiian women up to the twentieth century, and the birthing stools that are gaining in popularity are modelled after stools designed 4,000 years ago in Egypt (Carmichael, 2004).

CAESAREAN DELIVERY The **Caesarean delivery** (also known as *Caesarean section*), in which a baby is removed from the mother's uterus through an incision in her abdomen, is performed in a variety of situations. Labour may be unusually slow or prolonged, the baby may be in difficulty or be exceptionally large, there may be vaginal bleeding, or the baby's position may be such that a normal vaginal delivery is impossible (e.g., the baby's feet may be in position to deliver first, or the baby may lie horizontally in the uterus). From the 1960s to 2005, the rate at which Caesarean deliveries were performed increased from 5 to 30 percent of all births in the United States (National Center for Health Statistics, 2006), although the rate is lower in Canada, at around 20 percent (Health Canada, 2003; Liu et al., 2007). There are several reasons for this increase, including the convenience of physicians, convenience of patients, and an effort to minimize physician liability associated with the potential complications of vaginal delivery. Concerns have been raised that the rate of Caesarean sections is unnecessarily high and that these procedures themselves may have unforeseen long-term adverse consequences.

Caesarean births place mothers at greater risk of infection and involve longer hospital stays (Liu et al., 2007); such deliveries also increase the risk of mothers having preterm and low-birthweight infants in a subsequent birth (Kennare, 2007). In addition, Caesarean babies are exposed to more maternal medication during delivery; as a result, they tend to have more trouble breathing and are less responsive and wakeful than other newborns, and, in turn, breastfeeding may be more difficult (Emory et al.,

Caesarean delivery

The surgical delivery of a baby, whereby the baby is removed from the mother's uterus through an incision made in her abdomen and uterus; also known as *Caesarean section*.

Box 3.2

Child Psychology in Action

HORMONAL INFLUENCES ON MATERNAL AND PATERNAL RESPONSIVENESS

In humans, an important factor for infant survival is adequate parental care. In popular culture, as well as the scientific community, it is taken for granted that a mother is prepared by nature to be responsive toward her child. Similarly, infant survival in humans, as well as in other species, is enhanced by paternal care as well (Gubernick, Wright, & Brown, 1993; Hurtado & Hill, 1992; Wynne-Edwards & Lisk, 1989).

Although social and situational factors play a hugely important role in driving parental care, another critical underlying factor in parenting is biological and involves hormonal influences. As you might expect, many researchers have suggested that hormonal changes in females, both human and animal, are related to maternal responsiveness. Various primate species, such as marmosets and New World monkeys, show hormonal changes that are associated with mothering (Pryce, 1993; Pryce, Abbott, Hodges, & Martin, 1988; Pryce, Doebli, & Martin, 1993; Pryce, Martin, & Skuse, 1995). Although it is not known exactly which hormones control this maternal responsiveness, the general pattern of hormonal changes includes high levels of progesterone during pregnancy, followed by a decline in progesterone and a rise in other hormones, such as estrogen and prolactin (Fleming, Ruble, Krieger, & Wong, 1997; Pryce et al., 1995).

In humans, the story is a bit more complicated. For one, only a few studies have explored the role of hormones in parenting, and for those that have, the picture is mixed. Some researchers have actually observed that it is the adrenal hormones, as opposed to the ovarian or placental hormones as found in the animal work, that vary (Corter & Fleming, 1995; Fleming et al., 1997; Fleming, Steiner, & Anderson, 1987). And there are even some studies (Fleming et al., 1997) that have failed to find correlations between the levels of hormones in the blood and mothers' ratings of their

attachment toward their infants (although this study did observe that changes in the relative levels of two different hormones, estradiol and progesterone, were related to mothers' feelings toward their infants both during and after pregnancy). Probably the best way of characterizing these mixed, and somewhat complicated results, is that there may, in fact, be a hormonal role in relation to maternal responsiveness, with this relation both strongly influenced and constrained by social and situational factors.

And how about hormonal changes in fathers as a function of the mothers' pregnancy and in subsequent caregiving? Work with animals suggests that not only does the amount and type of paternal care vary with different species but that there are hormonal changes in male animals as well. For example, some researchers have found that the males of rodent, primate, and canid species who display paternal care also have increased prolactin levels after the birth (Brown, Murdoch, Murphy, & Moger, 1995; Gubernick & Nelson, 1989; Reburn & Wynne-Edwards, 1999), and prolactin has been found to increase prior to the beginning of parenting behaviour by male and female mammals (Brown et al., 1995; Fleming & Corter, 1988).

Given that hormonal changes do seem to occur in the females and males of animal species, and in human females as well, it becomes an interesting question as to whether or not human males also show hormonal changes with parenting (Berg & Wynne-Edwards, 2002; Delahunty, McKay, Noseworthy, & Storey, 2007; Wynne-Edwards, 2001).

To look at this question, Anne Storey of Memorial University and Katherine Wynne-Edwards of Queen's University and their colleagues (Storey, Walsh, Quinton, & Wynne-Edwards, 2000) measured hormone levels in new fathers, and in men whose wives were pregnant, in response to infant stimuli. These research-

1996). However, short-term studies of Caesarean births suggest that this method of delivery has few effects on infants' cognitive or neurological development (Entwisle & Alexander, 1987). Moreover, recent longer-term evidence indicates that babies delivered by Caesarean did not have higher rates of hospitalization or outpatient visits during their first 18 months of life (Leung et al., 2007). Although early mother–child interactions can be adversely affected, by the time Caesarean children are 1 year old, these relationships are positive (Reilly, Entwisle, & Doering, 1987). One advantage of Caesarean births is that because mothers have a longer recovery period after delivery,

ers gathered two blood samples from couples (both men and women) at four different times: early in the pregnancy (between 16 and 35 weeks of a 40-week pregnancy), late in the pregnancy (within the last three weeks), just after birth of the child (when babies were 0 to 3 weeks old), and late after birth (when babies were 4 to 7 weeks old). After providing an initial blood sample, the couples received visual, auditory, and olfactory stimuli of newborn infants. A short time after receiving such stimulation, a second blood sample was taken from the couples.

Using these blood samples, Storey and her colleagues compared hormonal levels in new and expectant mothers and fathers both before infant stimulation and after receiving the stimuli. In keeping with the earlier work in humans, the women had higher concentrations of prolactin and cortisol just before birth and lower amounts of sex hormones (estradiol) just after birth. But the surprising result found by these researchers was that the men showed a similar pattern to the women, with higher prolactin and cortisol just before birth and lower sex hormones (in this case, testosterone) just after birth. Moreover, men who exhibited two or more pregnancy symptoms, such as weight gain, nausea, fatigue, emotional changes, and so on, during their partner's pregnancy (this is called couvades syndrome; Masoni, Maio, Trimarchi, de Punzio, & Fioretti, 1994), as well as men who were most affected by the infant stimulation, had higher levels of prolactin than did men with either one or no pregnancy symptoms. Finally, these authors observed that hormonal levels were actually correlated between partners, with men's cortisol levels correlated with womens' hormonal levels before birth. Interestingly, for this result, the women's hormone levels were strongly related to the number of days remaining before they were to give birth, suggesting that hormonal changes in women were being driven

by the physiological processes of pregnancy. For men, however, there was no relation between hormonal levels and the number of days before the birth; this finding suggests that hormonal changes in the men were actually being influenced by their partners.

Taken together, these results do indicate that some men actually undergo hormonal changes that are similar to what their pregnant partners go through. One interpretation of these findings is that it might be these hormonal changes that actually provide the basis for paternal behaviour in fathers. Unfortunately, of course, such a sweeping conclusion is not yet justifiable on the basis of merely one study.

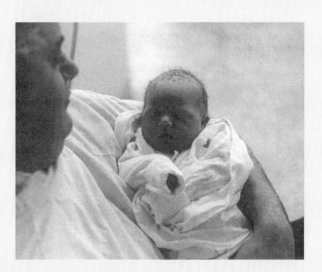

What role do hormones play in the positive emotions this father is displaying for his child? Recently, researchers have suggested that men undergo significant hormonal variation as a result of their partners' pregnancies.

during which time it is often difficult for them to handle all the caretaking of their infants, fathers may become more involved in looking after their babies in the first few months than is usually the case (Parke, 1996). Also, as described in Box 3.2, the parenting process can actually have an effect on hormone production in fathers.

BIRTH COMPLICATIONS Although labour and childbirth are normal processes in human development and, in the majority of cases, go smoothly, there sometimes are complications. We have already seen that sexually transmitted diseases can be passed to the infant as it moves through the birth canal. In addition, it has been found that more males than females are born with physical anomalies. This has been attributed, in part, to the role of the sex chromosomes (see Chapter 2) and, in part, to the larger size of, and hence greater pressure on, a male's head during birth. The majority of infants do not suffer serious impairment at birth, however. Fewer than 10 percent have any type of abnormality, and many of these difficulties disappear during subsequent development.

To assess the condition of the newborn after birth and check for any problems, doctors often use the Apgar scoring system, named for its developer, anaesthesiologist Dr. Virginia Apgar (see Table 3-2). At one minute and five minutes after birth, the doctor or nurse measures the heart rate, respiratory effort, reflex irritability, muscle tone, and body colour of the infant. Each of the five signs is given a score of 0, 1, or 2; the higher the score attained, the more favourable the baby's condition. A total score of 7 to 10 indicates that the newborn is in good condition, a score below 5 indicates that there may be possible developmental difficulties, and a score of 4 or lower alerts medical staff to possibly life-threatening conditions and the need for immediate emergency procedures.

Table 3-2

Apgar's evaluation of the newborn infant

Source: Adapted from Apgar, 1953.

| Sign | Score | | |
	0	1	2
Heart rate	Absent	Less than 100 beats per minute	100 to 140 beats per minute
Respiratory effort	No breathing for more than one minute	Slow and irregular	Good respiration with normal crying
Muscle tone	Limp and flaccid	Some flexion of the extremities	Good flexion, active motion
Reflex irritability	No response	Some motion	Vigorous response to stimulation
Colour	Blue or pale body and extremities	Body pink with blue extremities	Pink all over

preterm

Descriptor for a premature baby born before its due date and whose weight, although less than that of a full-term infant, may be appropriate to its gestational age.

small for date

A term describing a premature baby that may be born close to its due date but who weighs significantly less than would be appropriate to its gestational age.

Prematurity and Low Birthweight

Premature or **preterm** babies are those born before they have completed the normal or full-term gestational period, at 37 weeks after conception or less. About 9 percent of infants are born prematurely. On average, they weigh less than 5.0 pounds (2,273 g), which is low compared with the 7.7 pound (3,500 g) weight of a normal full-term baby. Infants whose weight is *less* than appropriate for their time in utero are called **small-for-date** babies. Although babies who weigh much less than three pounds, because they are preterm or because they are small-for-date, have many odds against them, modern technology is becoming increasingly successful in enabling very small babies to survive (Goldberg & DiVitto, 2002; McIntire, Bloom, Casey, & Leveno, 1999). (See Table 3-3 for a summary of types of preterm babies).

The likelihood of having a premature baby varies according to race as well as the age of the mother. In Canada, low-birthweight babies are most common in mothers

Description	Timing of Delivery	Average Weight at Delivery
Full term	Average of 38 weeks from conception	7.7 lb (3,500 g)
Premature Preterm	Several weeks before due date	Less than 5.5 lb (2,500 g), but weight is often appropriate to time spent in utero
Small for date	Either at about due date or several weeks before	Less than 5.5 lb (2,500 g) and less weight than would be expected for time spent in utero; survival of babies who weigh less than 3.3 lb (about 1,500 g) is severely compromised

Table 3-3

Preterm and small-for-date babies

younger than 15 years of age and older than 40 years (Health Canada, 1999b). In the United States, African Americans are almost twice as likely as Caucasian Americans to have babies of low birthweight (McLaughlin, Rusen, & Liu, 1999). Mexican-American women's chances of having such babies are about halfway between these two groups (Goldberg & DiVitto, 2002). Several factors account for the higher risk of prematurity among minority women; among these are poor diet, inadequate prenatal care, and drug and/or alcohol use. However, premature and low-birthweight babies are also more common in multiple births, which often result from reproductive technologies that are used more often by affluent women of European background.

Being born premature sometimes results in developmental delays, but it does not necessarily mean that the child will have long-term problems. Having a very low birthweight is more often associated with intellectual impairment. Although most low-birthweight babies catch up in motor and intellectual development by the time they are 4 years old, about 15 percent of those who weigh less than 3.3 pounds and about 30 percent of those weighing less than 2 pounds at birth continue to show some cognitive deficits (Goldberg & DiVitto, 2002).

Problems in academic achievement, hyperactivity, motor skills, and speech and hearing disorders occur more often in very-low-birthweight babies than in normal infants (Anderson et al., 2003; Goldberg & DiVitto, 2002). However, it is not clear to what extent these problems are the consequence of low birthweight and to what extent they are the outcome of a number of other, possibly related, factors, such as delivery complications, experiences in the NICU (newborn intensive care unit), neonatal anomalies other than prematurity, and the way parents respond to their infant's apparent frailty and small size (Field, 1990; Korner, 1989). When these high medical risks are compounded by adverse environmental circumstances, long-term developmental difficulties are most likely (Goldberg & DiVitto, 2002).

STIMULATION PROGRAMS FOR PREMATURE BABIES   Researchers have experimented to improve the environments of premature and low-birthweight babies by administering extra stimulation. Some have provided stimulation that approximates the conditions the baby would have experienced in utero; for example, tape-recorded heartbeats (Barnard & Bee, 1983), rocking hammocks (Neal, 1968), and waterbed mattresses (Burns, Deddish, Burns, & Hatcher, 1983), which presumably simulate the rotation, movement, and rhythmic activity experienced by the fetus within the amniotic sac. Other investigators have used stimulation characteristic of the experiences of full-term infants, such as mobiles, tape recordings of the mother's voice, manual rocking, talking and singing, and cuddling and stroking (Diego, Field, &

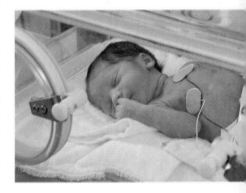

Premature infants are at risk for many complications after birth. Here, you see a premature baby in an incubator, which provides continuous monitoring of the infant and a means for keeping the baby as healthy and as germ-free as possible.

Hernandez-Reif, 2008; Field, 2001; Field, Diego, & Hernandez-Reif, 2007; Goldberg & DiVitto, 2002). Both approaches have shown positive results.

As Figure 3-7 shows, stimulated premature infants are more advanced than unstimulated premature infants in physical development (Field et al., 2007). They are also more advanced in neurological development as measured by reflexes, in sensorimotor and motor skills, in muscle tone, in weight gain, and in exploratory behaviour (Field et al., 2007; Goldberg & DiVitto, 2002). In addition, fewer incidents of *apnea* (temporary cessation of breathing, associated with later crib deaths) occur in stimulated infants (Korner, 1989). Stimulation clearly has at least a short-term salutary effect on the development of premature infants, although long-term gains are rarely found (Field et al., 2007; Korner, 1989).

However, programs must be sensitive to individual differences (Als et al., 2003); not all premature babies benefit from additional stimulation. Children who are ill, who have intensive medical care routines that disrupt their sleep, or who are being weaned from breathing assistance or other physical support systems may not respond positively or may actually be distressed by added stimulation (Oehler, Eckerman, & Wilson, 1988).

PREMATURE BABIES AND PARENTAL CONTACT   Another type of intervention to help premature and low-birthweight infants is to facilitate parents' contact with the infants. Some mothers of premature babies report feelings of guilt, failure, and alienation from their infants and loss of self-esteem, and they appear apprehensive about handling and caring for their fragile-appearing infants. When mothers of preemies are eventually able to take their babies home from the hospital, they tend to show less emotional involvement with them than do mothers of full-term babies (Goldberg & DiVitto, 2002). Their infants sometimes fail to gain normal weight and height and they are at risk of becoming battered or failure-to-thrive children (Bugental & Happaney, 2004). Premature babies' typical physical appearance, small size, high-pitched cry, feeding difficulties, and low responsiveness may make them unappealing and increase their parents' frustration. In addition, most premature infants are born to mothers who are poor, young, and uneducated (Brooks-Gunn et al., 2000), although there has been an increase in premature and multiple births among middle-class women associated with new reproductive technologies that are used to boost fertility.

Figure 3-7

Everyone, including premature babies, likes a massage

A group of premature infants were given three 15-minute, daily massages for 10 days, while another group received no massage. The infants given extra stimulation averaged 47 percent more weight gain per day, were awake and active for more of the time, showed more mature behaviours on the Brazelton Neonatal Scale, and were in hospital for six days fewer than the other infants. Moreover, six to eight months later, the first group weighed more and performed better on the Bayley mental and motor scales than the second group.

Source: Adapted from Field, 1990.

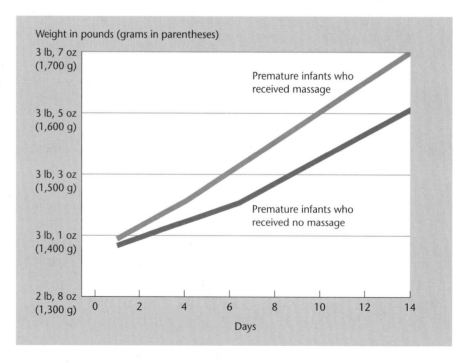

Recent work on early skin-to-skin contact with premature infants, or what has been called "kangaroo care" (Anderson, 1995; Dombrowski et al., 2000; Feldman, 2007), suggests that this form of close parental contact has a number of positive effects on premature infants. Some positive effects include the growth of regulatory state processes, such as more mature startle responses and more organized sleep–wake cycles (Feldman & Eidelman, 2003; Feldman, Weller, Sirota, & Eidelman, 2002), increases in body temperature (Diego et al., 2008), more tolerance to pain (Castral et al., 2008), and even higher IQs (Tessier et al., 2003) than infants receiving more traditional care. Kangaroo care also seems to have a positive effect on parents' social interactions with their child (Feldman et al., 2003), with parents who used kangaroo care more sensitive and less intrusive toward their infant, and showing more affectionate touching of the infant.

LONG-TERM EFFECTS OF PREMATURITY Long-term effects of prematurity are more marked and enduring in economically deprived families than in middle-income families (Bradley et al., 1994; Klebonov et al., 2001). When effects on parent–child relations or on the child's cognitive development do endure, they seem to be due to a host of factors in addition to prematurity: the child's responsiveness, the mother's competence, the family's environmental stresses, and the kind of support available to the parents from other family members, nursing staff, and self-help groups (Gross, Spiker, & Haynes, 1997).

The stress of raising a premature baby may have a negative impact on relations between the parents. Some research has reported a high incidence of marital discord in the first two years following the birth of a premature infant (Leiderman, 1983); however, if a couple views their coping strategies as complementary and if they can share the task of caring for a child with special needs, the challenge may draw them closer together (Affleck, Tennen, & Rowe, 1990). Intervention programs for low-birthweight children involving parental training and child preschool classes have improved parenting and child outcomes (Klebonov et al., 2001).

VULNERABILITY AND RESILIENCE IN CHILDREN AT RISK

LO8

In this chapter, we have discussed a number of events and conditions that can cause things to go wrong in pregnancy and childbirth. At this point, you may be wondering if things ever go right! Indeed, they do; most pregnancies proceed without major disruptions, and many couples find the period of waiting and preparing for the arrival of a child one of the happiest times of their lives.

Things do go wrong often enough, however, that scholars have attempted to determine how the effects of adverse perinatal influences are either compounded or compensated for by subsequent conditions. They have tried to uncover the reasons why some children with early problems develop *resilience*, or the capacity to achieve competence and satisfaction in life despite initially challenging circumstances.

In trying to understand resilience, researchers have found that both features of the environment and biological characteristics of the child can play roles in determining how successfully a child develops. The kinds of prenatal and perinatal biological factors that can affect the child negatively range from relatively minor perceptual, attentional, intellectual, motor, and behavioural disabilities to gross abnormalities. The environmental situation the infant enters can range from a healthy intact family with good caregiving skills and adequate financial support to a family or parent struggling with highly adverse conditions including poverty, drug abuse, divorce, and violence (Sameroff & Chandler, 1975; Sameroff, 2007). For most researchers, resilience— the ability to overcome difficulties—results from the interaction between risk and

Risk and Resilience

WHAT FACTORS HELP CHILDREN OVERCOME EARLY ADVERSITY?

At the time that Emmy Werner and her colleagues began their longitudinal study of children born on the Hawaiian island of Kauai, there was considerable literature on children born with serious defects or disorders and the course their lives were expected to take. However, research on those factors that protect children and enable at-risk children to develop a remarkable degree of resilience was still in its infancy (Aldwin & Werner, 2007; Werner, 1995). Werner's study, which followed nearly 700 participants for more than 40 years, was one of the first to focus on such questions as, What is *right* with the children who develop this sort of resilience? How can we help other children to acquire this same near-invincibility in the face of severe adversity?

When the participants in the Kauai Longitudinal Study were born, 47 percent suffered birth complications, and of these, one-third were classified as specifically "at risk." In addition to experiencing moderate to severe birth complications, these children were born into poverty, their mothers had little formal education, and their family environments were characterized by discord, desertion, divorce, alcoholism, and/or mental illness. Despite these early stresses, fully a third of this at-risk group developed into confident, competent, and caring young adults.

As toddlers, the children who matured into resilient young adults were alert, autonomous, and more advanced in communication, self-help, and motor skills. They tended to seek out novel stimuli and had a positive social orientation.

The main effects of deviations caused by perinatal complications occurred early in a child's development; after that, development was increasingly influenced by environmental circumstances, such as chronic poverty, family instability, and mental health problems. By the age of 10, the effects of environmental variables had almost obliterated those of perinatal damage. No relation was found between measures of birth complications and a child's IQ score.

When they were 18, resilient children in families of low socio-economic status seemed to share four personality characteristics: an active, resourceful approach towards solving life's problems; a tendency to perceive even their painful experiences constructively; the ability, from infancy on, to gain other people's positive attention; and a strong ability to use faith to maintain a positive vision of a meaningful life (Werner, 1984). Evidencing cognitive abilities, such as effective reading skills by grade 4, served as an additional protective factor (Werner, 1995). Finally, certain features of these children's social environment served as protective buffers: small family size, favourable parental attitudes, a continuous relationship with a caring adult (not necessarily the parent), low levels of family conflict, a smaller load of stressful life experiences, and the availability of counselling and remedial assistance. In addition, in middle childhood or adolescence, high-risk resilient children often assumed responsibility for the care of another person—a sibling, aging grandparent, or ill or incompetent parent. Both such "required helpfulness" and being cared for oneself were critical in

protective factors (i.e., those that help minimize the effects of adversity such as strong family and community support) in the child and the environment (Luthar, 2007; Selman & Dray, 2006).

In a longitudinal study of the development of the entire population of 698 children born in 1955 on the Hawaiian island of Kauai, Werner and her colleagues (Werner, 1995; Werner, Bierman, & French, 1971; Werner & Smith, 2001) assessed the long-term consequences of birth complications and adverse early-rearing conditions. An update is given in Box 3.3. The researchers discovered that the effects of adverse perinatal complications often lessen in intensity or disappear with age. This is in large part a function of the caregiving environment in which children mature. The Kauai study offered "a more hopeful perspective," according to Werner (1984), than did the previous literature on children with problems, and it has been followed by other similarly

buffering these high-risk children from adversity (Werner, 1984, 1995).

At age 30 years, among the resilient adults who were parents, the primary goals for their children were the acquisition of personal competencies and skills. About three-quarters considered themselves happy and satisfied; a few had divorced, had experienced psychological problems requiring them to seek professional help, or had drug problems (Werner, 1995; Werner & Smith, 2001). Ten times more of the study participants had problems related to the effects of poor environment rather than to the effects of perinatal stress. Indeed, birth complications, unless they involved serious damage to the central nervous system, were consistently related to impaired physical or psychological development only if they were combined with chronic poverty, parental psychopathology, or persistently poor rearing conditions (Aldwin & Werner, 2007; Luthar, 2007; Selman & Dray, 2006). Clearly, the environment plays a critical role in helping children overcome a poor beginning.

Thanks both to their own resilience and to environmental supports such as healthy child-rearing practices, fully a third of the at-risk children studied by Emily Werner and her colleagues developed into self-confident, successful adults. These children had a positive and active approach to problem solving, the ability to see some useful aspects of painful experiences and to attract positive responses from other people, as well as a strong tendency to use faith in maintaining an optimistic vision of a fulfilling life.

Thanks to their own resilience, one-third of the at-risk children studied by Emmy Werner and her colleagues developed into self-confident, successful adults. These children had a positive and active approach to problem solving, the ability to see some useful aspects in painful experiences and to attract positive responses from other people, as well as a strong tendency to use faith in maintaining an optimistic vision of a fulfilling life.

designed studies that tend to support its findings. More than one of these studies showed that a close and continuing relationship with another caring person is a significant factor in the development of resilience. Often, the caring person is not a parent but a grandparent, an older sibling, a neighbour, a daycare provider, a teacher, a minister, a youth worker, or an elder mentor who can help tilt the balance from negativity to resiliency. These people accept children's problems and allow them experiences that challenge but do not overwhelm their coping abilities. They guide the children in developing a sense of responsibility and caring and reward them for helpfulness and co-operation; they model for a child the conviction that life makes sense despite its adversities (Masten & Obradovic, 2007). Thus, even in what may look like the darkest situations, there may be opportunities for children to thrive.

For Thought and Discussion

1. Traditionally, it used to be that fathers and the rest of the family and relatives waited elsewhere while mothers were delivering their babies. Today, family members and sometimes even friends are present in the delivery room during delivery. What do you think are the effects of having these people in the room during the birth process?

2. As the authors describe, another recent trend in North America is the growing presence of midwives, either alongside, or sometimes in place of, doctors during delivery. What are some of the advantages and disadvantages of having a midwife?

3. Recent advances in medical science have made it possible for very preterm infants to survive, although these infants are host to a wide assortment of potential physical and mental problems. What do you think about the ethics of such measures to assist these premature infants?

Making the Connections 3

There are many links between concepts and ideas presented in one area of development and concepts and ideas in other areas. Here are some of the connections between ideas in Chapter 3 and discussions in other chapters of this book.

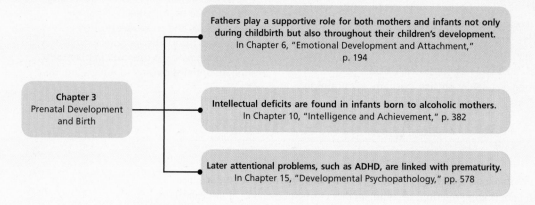

Chapter 3
Prenatal Development and Birth

Fathers play a supportive role for both mothers and infants not only during childbirth but also throughout their children's development.
In Chapter 6, "Emotional Development and Attachment,"
p. 194

Intellectual deficits are found in infants born to alcoholic mothers.
In Chapter 10, "Intelligence and Achievement," p. 382

Later attentional problems, such as ADHD, are linked with prematurity.
In Chapter 15, "Developmental Psychopathology," pp. 578

SUMMARY

Stages of Prenatal Development

- Prenatal development is divided into three distinct periods (zygote, embryo, fetus). These periods represent phases of development during which the organism, protected and sustained by the **amniotic sac**, the **placenta**, the **umbilical cord**, and, after the fifth month, the **lanugo**, undergoes a systematic series of sequential changes to become increasingly complex and differentiated.

- The period of the **zygote**, which lasts about two weeks, extends from fertilization to implantation, when the zygote becomes implanted in the wall of the uterus. The period of the **embryo** begins at that point and lasts until the end of the eighth week.

During this period, most of the important organs and physiological systems develop.

- The period of the **fetus** extends from the beginning of the third month until birth, during which the central nervous system continues to develop at a rapid pace, reflexes develop, and regulatory processes and the respiratory system continue to mature. If the child is born before the **age of viability**, it may not have developed enough to survive.

Risks in the Prenatal Environment

- During prenatal development, **teratogens**, agents that produce developmental abnormalities, may affect the growing organism. Seven general principles summarize the effects of teratogens on prenatal development, indicating that the type, timing, and duration of the teratogen play a role in the outcome as well as the genotypes of the mother and child.
- Mothers who smoke cigarettes or drink alcohol are more likely to bear premature or low-birthweight babies than women who do not smoke or drink. In addition, maternal drinking is related to **fetal alcohol syndrome**, which results in facial abnormalities, short stature, and mental retardation. Even modest amounts of alcohol and passive smoking have been related to negative effects in the offspring.
- In the case of illegal drugs, such as cocaine or heroin, drug-addicted infants may exhibit symptoms that disrupt parenting and result in long-term adverse outcomes for both child and parent.
- Drugs taken by the mother during pregnancy, whether legal or illegal, may have a negative impact on the developing fetus. Sometimes, the effects of the prescription drug on the infant are not known until much later.
- Some obstetrical medications used to ease pain and sedate women during labour and delivery may affect the newborn's behaviour for several days after birth.
- Mothers who have their first child when they are over 35 or under 15 years of age are likely to experience more problems during pregnancy and difficulties during delivery than women between these ages. In both groups, the risks are related to maternal health, although for different reasons.

- Deficiencies in maternal diet are related to increased rates of prematurity, stillbirths, infant mortality, physical and neural defects, and small size. Dietary supplements provided during pregnancy and after birth have been successful at reducing some of these effects. Continued ill effects seem to be related to the mother's history of dietary deprivation; the length and severity of the malnutrition; and continuing adverse nutritional, social, and economic factors following birth.
- Maternal emotional disturbance has been related to complications during pregnancy and delivery and to hyperactivity and irritability in infants after birth. It is difficult to discover the causes underlying these relationships because women who are emotionally upset during pregnancy may be poorly adjusted in a variety of ways that affect their caregiving and their infant's adjustment after birth.
- A wide range of maternal diseases and disorders can affect prenatal development, including **Rh factor incompatibility**; high blood pressure; diabetes; rubella; and sexually transmitted diseases. The effects of maternal diseases are related to the stage of fetal development during which they are contracted and the length of time that they last.

Birth and the Beginnings of Life

- Birth involves a series of changes in the mother that permit the child to move from the womb to the outside world. These include uterine contractions during the first stage of labour that allow the cervix to become large enough for the child's head; the child's descent into the birth canal and emergence out of the canal during the second stage; and the expulsion of the placenta during the third stage. If problems arise before or during the delivery, a **Caesarean delivery** may be performed by removing the baby through an incision in the mother's abdomen.
- Birth complications occur in only about 10 percent of deliveries. Some important birth factors that are related to developmental deviations are prematurity and low birthweight, which have been associated with physical, neurological, cognitive, and emotional deficits. Most of these negative effects diminish with age, except in extreme cases.

Boris Kustodiev (1878–1927). *The Morning Bath. (The Wife and Son of the Artist.)*
Russian State Museum, St. Petersburg, Russia.

Chapter 4

Infancy: Sensation, Perception, and Learning

LEARNING OBJECTIVES

After reading this chapter, you should be able to

LO1 Describe several reflexes found in the neonate; discuss the usefulness of the reflexes for the infant's interactions with the world and for assessing the infant's neurological capabilities.

LO2 Explain the concept of infant states and be able to describe the various infant states, ranging from sleep to crying; describe developmental changes in states and techniques used to soothe infants.

LO3 Describe the problems with assessing infants' sensory capacities and ways in which these problems have been overcome by innovative assessment methods.

LO4 Discuss research on face perception, focusing on the question of whether or not the perception of faces is truly special; if it is, why is this important?

LO5 Give a brief description of the infant's perceptual capabilities in the areas of hearing, vision, taste, and smell; give one research example that demonstrates each area.

LO6 Describe bimodal perception and how it develops; raise the issue of the divergent results between Maurer et al. and Meltzoff and Moore, and discuss possible reasons for this difference.

LO7 Discuss basic learning processes that are present early in life (classical conditioning, operant conditioning); include how each develops and give an example of each process.

LO8 Explain some of the findings related to infants' abilities to imitate.

LO9 Describe the infant's memory capabilities and limitations.

Anabel's mother just purchased a new baby DVD series to show her 1-month-old infant. Carlos's dad plays classical music for his 3-day-old son while rocking him in his cradle; Michael's grandmother bought him a brightly coloured mobile for his crib so on the day the newborn arrives home from the hospital, he can see it. Each of these adults has different ideas about what a baby is able to do early in life. Researchers are very interested in this question and much of their work focuses on the sensory and perceptual world of infants. They have discovered that babies can hear, see, and respond to various types of sights and sounds at a much earlier age than was once believed. Even in the first few minutes after birth, infants show remarkable capabilities.

We begin this chapter with a look at the newborn's earliest behaviours, including the baby's normal reflexes. We also examine ways of assessing the newborn's health, maturity, and capabilities. We then look at the growth and development of the infant's sensory and perceptual abilities—auditory, visual, taste, and touch. We conclude with a discussion of the early learning processes, including what is known about an infant's memory abilities. ●

THE NEWBORN

neonate

A newborn baby.

Parents are sometimes quite surprised at the appearance of their newborns. At the moment of birth, and for a little while afterward, most newborns, or **neonates**, are pretty homely little beings. Their noses, ears, and entire heads often bear the marks of the pressures exerted on them as they passed through the birth canal, and their skin is often red, wrinkled, and blotchy, partly as a result of floating for nine months in the amniotic fluid. Their heads are oversized in proportion to their bodies (in fact, from childhood to adulthood, the head goes from a quarter to an eighth of total body size), and their little legs appear weak, even useless. But despite these characteristics—most of which disappear even before the neonate period of three to four weeks is over—most parents welcome their newborns with joy and love.

A New Baby's Reflexes

reflex

A human's involuntary response to external stimulation.

Newborns have many capabilities. They have well-developed reflexes and sensory responses, and they can respond and adapt to the environment from the first moments after birth. Moreover, these early behaviours are not random and disorganized; rather, human behaviour appears organized from very early in life. Some of the first behaviours to appear are **reflexes**, or involuntary responses to external stimuli. Table 4-1 describes the newborn's major reflexes, some of which are permanent (e.g., eye blink). Other reflexes disappear during the first year of life, and in some cases these are replaced by voluntary behaviours that the baby learns early in life (e.g., rooting and sucking reflexes). Many of these reflexes help ensure the newborn's survival. For example, the eye blink helps shield the eyes from strong light, and the rooting and sucking reflexes help the newborn to locate and obtain food. The functions of other newborn reflexes are less obvious. Researchers speculate that some of them may have bestowed as-yet-unknown survival benefits on the infants of our evolutionary ancestors.

Abnormalities in a baby's reflexes during the first days or weeks after birth can be useful indicators for identifying visual and hearing problems, and they can even help predict abnormal functions that do not appear until months or years later (Dubowitz & Dubowitz, 1981; Francis, Self, & Horowitz, 1987). Reflexes that are either weak, absent, unusually strong, or that fail to disappear when expected can be a sign of neurological problems. At birth, physicians often test the newborn for certain reflexes to evaluate the baby's central nervous system. As we saw in Chapter 3, infants exposed

Table 4-1 The newborn's major reflexes

Reflex	Testing the Reflex		Significance of Response	Developmental Course of Reflex
	Method	Baby's Response		
Permanent				
Biceps reflex	Tap on the tendon of the biceps muscle	Baby displays short contraction of muscle	Absent in depressed babies or those with congenital muscular disease	Brisker in first few days
Eye blink	Flash bright light in baby's eyes	Baby blinks or closes eyes	Protects baby from strong stimuli	Relatively unchanging
Patellar tendon reflex ("knee jerk")	Tap on the tendon below the knee cap, or patella	Baby quickly extends or kicks leg	Weak or absent in depressed babies or those with muscular disease; exaggerated in hyperexcitable babies	More pronounced in first two days than later
Withdrawal reflex	Prick sole of baby's foot gently with a pin	Baby withdraws foot and pulls leg up, bending knee and hip	Absent when there is damage to the sciatic nerve, the largest nerve of the body	Constantly present during first 10 days; less intense later
Temporary				
Babinski reflex	Stroke bottom of foot from heel to toes	Baby's big toe curves up and other toes fan and curl	Absent in defects of the lower spine	Usually disappears near end of first year; replaced in normal adult by plantar flexion of big toe
Babkin or palmar reflex	With baby lying on his back, apply pressure to both of baby's palms	Baby opens mouth, closes eyes, and moves head to midline position	Inhibited in general depression of the central nervous system	Disappears at 3–4 months
Moro reflex	Suddenly allow baby's head to drop back a few inches; lower baby's overall position about 6 inches or make sudden, loud noise	Baby throws arms outwards and extends legs; then brings both arms back toward centre of her body, clenching fists	Absent or consistently weak reflex indicates serious problem in central nervous system	Disappears at 6–7 months
Palmar grasp	Press a finger or cylindrical object against baby's palm	Baby grasps finger or object	Weak or absent in depressed babies	Initially strong; disappears by 3–4 months; replaced by voluntary grasp within a month or so
Plantar or toe grasp	Press on the ball of the baby's foot	Baby curls all toes, as if grasping	Absent in defects of the lower spinal cord	Disappears between 8 and 12 months
Rooting response	Stroke baby's cheek lightly	Baby turns head toward finger, opens his mouth, and tries to suck	Absent in depressed babies	Disappears at about 3–4 months and becomes voluntary
Stepping reflex	Support baby in upright position and move her forwards, tilting her slightly to one side	Baby makes rhythmic stepping movements	Absent in depressed infants	Disappears at 3–4 months
Sucking response	Insert finger 1–1.5 inches into baby's mouth	Baby sucks finger rhythmically	Weak, slow, interrupted sucking found in apathetic babies; maternal medication during childbirth may depress sucking	Often less intensive and regular in first 3–4 days; disappears by 6 months

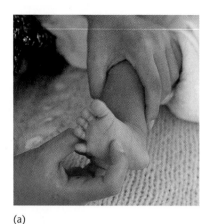
(a)

(b)

(c)

Newborns have lots of reflexes (many are described in Table 4-1 on page 119), some of which they maintain throughout life and others that, though temporary, are important indicators of physical well-being. The 6-week-old's Babinski reflex (a) tells the examiner that the child's lower spine is fully functional; the infant's palmar grasp (b) and rooting response at 4 weeks of age (c) both confirm the absence of harmful depression. A healthy rooting response may also rule out pre-natal exposure to cocaine, and is very useful in helping the newborn to locate and obtain food.

in utero to harmful substances often suffer neurological defects that can be assessed by observing the infants' reflexes (Phillips et al., 1996). For example, babies exposed to cocaine show abnormal patterns in the intensity of the sucking and rooting reflexes.

LO2 Infant States

infant state

A recurring pattern of arousal in the newborn, ranging from alert, vigorous, wakeful activity to quiet, regular sleep.

Just like adults, babies have alternative patterns of sleep and wakefulness. These patterns are referred to as the **infant state**, which is defined as the recurring pattern of arousal that ranges from alert, vigorous, wakeful activity to quiet, regular sleep.

Infant states tell us some important characteristics of human behaviour (see Table 4-2). First, they indicate that from early in life, human behaviour is *organized* and *predictable*. Infant states do not occur in a random, haphazard manner. Rather, they recur in a regular fashion. Second, human beings are not passive creatures that merely react to the environment. Internal forces regulate much of our behaviour and explain many of the changes in our activity levels (Schaffer, 1996). This is not to say a baby's states cannot be affected by outside forces; our later discussion of soothing techniques shows that they can be. Our point here is simply that internal forces play a central role in infant states and their changes.

Studies of fetal activity and premature infants tell us that arousal patterns begin to form before birth (Sontag, 1944). In one study, babies born two months prematurely exhibited regular changes in state that developed and became more organized as the infants grew older (Holditch-Davis, 1990). Also, as we discussed in Chapter 2, individual differences in state of arousal and the ability to regulate states of arousal are important components of temperament.

There are two basic infant states—waking and sleeping. Each of these states includes several variations. When infants are in the waking state they may be quite, active, or distressed, as in fussing and crying. The state of sleeping also includes variations. Here, we will focus on sleeping, and one variation of the waking state: crying behaviour.

SLEEP The newborn, on average, sleeps about 70 percent of the time in a series of long and short naps during the day and night. By the time an infant is 4 weeks old, her periods of sleep tend to be fewer but longer, and by the time she is 8 weeks old she is

Table 4-2 Newborn infant states

State	Typical Duration	Characteristics
Regular sleep	8–9 hours	Infant's eyes are closed, and body is completely still. Respiration is slow and regular. Baby's face is relaxed, with no grimacing, and eyelids are still.
Irregular sleep	8–9 hours	Baby's eyes are closed, but baby engages in gentle limb movements of various sorts, writhing, and general stirring. Grimaces and other facial expressions are frequent.
Drowsiness	½ to 3 hours	Baby's eyes open and close intermittently and display recurrent rapid eye movements. Baby is relatively inactive. Respiration is regular, though faster than in regular sleep.
Alert inactivity	2–3 hours	Infant's eyes are open, have a bright and shining quality, and can pursue moving objects. Baby is relatively inactive; face is relaxed and does not grimace
Waking activity	2–3 hours	Baby's eyes are open but not alert, and respiration is grossly irregular. Baby frequently engages in diffuse motor activity involving the whole body.
Crying	1–3 hours	Baby makes crying vocalizations and engages in diffuse motor activity.

Sources: Wolff, 1966, 1987.

sleeping more during the night and less during the day (Ingersoll & Thoman, 1999). As Figure 4-1 shows, the infant also becomes less fussy as she gains better control over her states of arousal. By the end of the first year, most infants sleep through the night, much to the relief of their parents. This shift illustrates how the infant's internal biorhythms adapt to the demands of the external world (Ikonomov, Stoynev, & Shisheva, 1998).

Not all cultures organize sleep patterns in the same way that North American parents do (Harkness & Super, 1995). Among the Kipsigis tribe of rural Kenya, infants are

Figure 4-1

Infants' sleep patterns

At 2 weeks of age, infants tend to maintain roughly the same ratio of total sleep, active sleep, and fussy crying in the morning, afternoon, and at night; by the time they are 8 weeks old, they begin to spend appreciably more time in quiet sleep during the nighttime hours.
Source: Sostek & Anders, 1981.

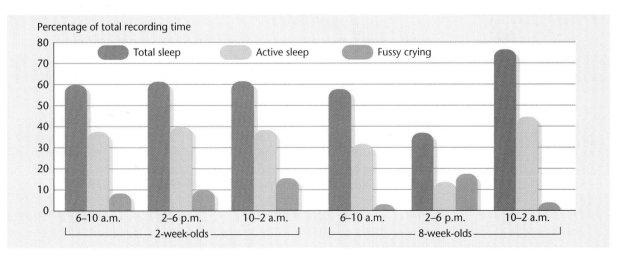

constantly with their mothers and regularly take naps throughout the day. In contrast to North American babies, who gradually begin to sleep longer at night and less during the day, Kipsigis babies continue to take shorter and more frequent naps. Although these Kenyan babies eventually sleep through the night, they show this pattern much later than North American babies (Super & Harkness, 1981).

Sleeping arrangements differ across cultures as well (Milan, Snow, & Belay, 2007). In contrast to the North American custom of putting babies to sleep alone in their own rooms, many cultures encourage co-sleeping arrangements, with parent(s) and infant in the same bed (Rogoff, 2003). Kipsigis babies sleep with their mothers, but when a new child is born, the older sibling sleeps at the mother's back, indicating that breastfeeding and constant carrying are over for the older infant (Harkness & Super, 1995). Some mothers, like Mayan mothers in Guatemala, view the North American custom of separate beds for babies as "tantamount to child neglect" (Morelli et al., 1992, p. 608). Even within a nation, norms for co-sleeping can vary depending on culture. Abel et al. (2001), for instance, found that infant sleeping practices among different ethnic groups in New Zealand varied, with caregivers from the Pacific Islands (e.g., Tonga, Samoa, and the Cook Islands) encouraging bed sharing, whereas Pakeha caregivers (the Pakehaka population constitutes the majority group in New Zealand) encouraged infant sleeping in a cribot. And recently, middle-class families in North America have shown more interest in closer arrangements with infants, as evidenced by sales of bedside cribs for parents who want to have their infants nearby at night. Clearly, the sleeping arrangements of parents and children "represent central ideas about family relationships and the proper course of human development." (Harkness & Super, 1995, p. 228) Moreover, as Box 4.1 suggests, co-sleeping arrangements may also have specific health benefits for the developing infant (McKenna & Mosko, 1993), such as the risk factors of **sudden infant death syndrome (SIDS)**.

Researchers have used brain recording techniques when infants sleep and they have distinguished different phases of the infant sleep cycle. One distinction that has been identified is between **REM sleep** and **non-REM sleep**. Rapid-eye-movement (REM) sleep, is often identified with dreaming because, in adults, it is during dreaming that the eyes, under closed eyelids, have been observed to dart around in rapid, jerky movements. Although infants also have REM sleep, there is no real way of knowing if infants dream.

In addition to rapid-eye movement, REM sleep is characterized also by fluctuating heart rate and blood pressure. The full purpose of REM sleep is unknown, but we do know that if has functional value: If people are awakened repeatedly as they begin REM sleep, and thus prevented from obtaining sleep of this type, they tend to be irritable and disorganized during their later waking hours.

Compared to adults and older children, newborns have a lot of REM sleep. In newborns, 50 percent of sleep is REM sleep. As children age, REM sleep declines to about 20 percent by the time they reach adulthood (Ingersoll & Thoman, 1999). By the age of 18 and onward through adulthood, most people sleep about eight hours a day, and of that amount, only about an hour and a half is REM sleep. An explanation, referred to as the **autostimulation theory**, has been proposed to account for the high level of REM sleep in newborns. Researchers have suggested that this type of sleep is self-stimulating, that is, it stimulates the infant's brain, and thereby, helps in the development of the central nervous system (Roffwarg, Muzio, & Dement, 1966). As the infant develops and becomes more alert and capable of processing external stimulation, this type of built-in stimulation may become less necessary. If this theory is right, the speed with which infants reduce their percentage of REM sleep could depend on how much external stimulation they receive. In one study, infants who were encouraged to stay awake and were exposed to visual stimuli spent less time in REM sleep than infants in a control condition who were not provided with these opportunities (Boismier, 1977).

CRYING   Crying is one of the infant's earliest means of communicating needs to caregivers. Three different patterns of crying, reflective of the infant's varying needs, have been identified:

SIDS

sudden infant death syndrome (SIDS)

SIDS refers to the sudden and unexpected death of an otherwise apparently healthy infant under 1 year of age. The death usually remains unexplained after all known and possible causes of death have been ruled out.

REM and non-REM sleep

Rapid-eye movement (REM) sleep is characterized by rapid, jerky movements of the eyes and, in adults, is often associated with dreaming; infants spend 50 percent of their sleep in REM activity, whereas adults spend only about 20 percent. This activity is absent in the remaining, non-REM sleep.

autostimulation theory

The theory that during REM sleep the infant's brain stimulates itself and that this, in turn, stimulates early development of the central nervous system.

Box 4.1
Child Psychology in Action

SUDDEN INFANT DEATH SYNDROME (SIDS)

Each year in Canada, about 150 babies die in their sleep from unknown causes; in the United States, this number is over 10,000 (relative to the population of each country these deaths have incidence rates of about 0.45 and 0.77 per 1,000 live births, respectively). These deaths are often classified as *sudden infant death syndrome* (SIDS), also known as *crib death*. It is most common between the ages of 2 and 4 months, and rarely occurs after 6 months (American Academy of Pediatrics Report, 2000).

Its most likely victims are low-birthweight male babies with a history of newborn respiratory problems, who were hospitalized longer than usual after birth, and who have abnormal heart-rate patterns and nighttime sleep disturbances (Mitchell et al., 1993; Rovee-Collier & Lipsitt, 1982; Sadeh, 1996). Their mothers are more likely to be anemic, use narcotics, and to have received little prenatal care. Parental smoking has also been suggested as a contributing factor (Frick, 1999; Shea & Steiner, 2008). It is important to stress, however, that most babies of women with this history are not affected.

The cause of SIDS is still a mystery (Hunt, 2001). It is not due to accidental suffocation, to mucus or fluid in the lungs, or to choking on regurgitated food. Nor has there been any success in isolating a virus associated with it, although this is still a possibility. Another possibility is that *apnea*, the spontaneous interruption of breathing that sometimes occurs during sleep, especially REM sleep, may be a factor in SIDS (Kelmanson, Groswasser, Franco, & Kahn, 2003; Steinschneider, 1975). The brain stem, which controls breathing, may not be well-enough developed in some infants to overcome brief cessations in breathing.

One hypothesis about the cause of SIDS is that its victims may have failed to develop adequate response to nasal blockage and other threats to breathing (Lipsitt, 2003). Although newborns have reflexes that provide them with built-in defensive reactions to respiratory threats (e.g., when a cloth is placed over a baby's face, she will use her hands to try to remove it), between 2 and 4 months of age these reactions change from reflexive behaviours to voluntary ones. Crib death is most common during this same age period. Perhaps failure of some infants to make a smooth transition from reflexive to voluntary defences puts an infant at greater risk for SIDS.

Monitors that sound an alarm to alert parents when an infant's breathing is interrupted may be useful in preventing SIDS. Although the false alarms of these devices may place stress on the parents, the devices may help save lives. Babies should not sleep on very soft mattresses or be surrounded by pillows that may obstruct breathing (American Academy of Pediatrics Report, 2000; Canadian Foundation for the Study of Infant Deaths, 2001; Health Canada, 2002). It is also helpful for babies to sleep on their backs, not their stomachs; sleeping on the stomach may depress breathing (Tuladhar et al., 2003; Willinger, Hoffman, & Hartford, 1994). In the years since organizations have been promoting that babies sleep on their backs, there has been a 50 percent decline in infant deaths attributable to SIDS.

Finally, some researchers have suggested that in Eastern cultures, such as Japan and China, in which parent–infant co-sleeping is common, rates of SIDS are lower (McKenna & Mosko, 1990). The co-sleeping arrangements may aid the baby in breathing regulation, and it does put parents close at hand (McKenna & Mosko, 1993). It is worth noting, however, that the Canadian Paediatric Society does not recommend co-sleeping in the same bed with infants, although sleeping in the same room is a possibility.

Pattern	Characteristics
Basic	Linked to hunger, among other factors. Starts arrhythmically and at low intensity; gradually becomes louder and more rhythmic; sequence is cry–rest–inhale–rest.
Angry	Same as basic pattern except that segments of crying, resting, and inhaling vary in length, and crying segments are longer. Causes include removal of a pacifier or toy.
Pain	Sudden in onset, loud from the start, and made up of a long cry followed by a long silence that includes holding of the breath, and then followed by a series of short, gasping inhalations. Causes include discomfort from soiled diaper, a pin prick, or stomach pain.

Source: Schaffer, 1971, p. 61.

The Canadian Foundation for the
Study of Infant Deaths

Most mothers can distinguish among these different types of crying but only when listening to the cries of their own babies (Wiesenfeld, Malatesta, & DeLoach, 1981). In general, fathers are less skilled than mothers at distinguishing among types of cries, men are less skilled than women, and non-parents are less skilled than parents (Holden, 1988). These differences are probably related to varying amounts of experience with babies and differences in the amount of time spent caring for them (Kamiya, 2002).

In the early months of life, crying is related to the infant's physiology. By 3 or 4 months, however, crying is less associated with physiological distress and increasingly related to psychological needs, such as wanting to be picked up or played with. Also, by this age, most infants spend less of their days crying and are easier to read and soothe (Kopp, 1994; Shonkoff & Phillips, 2000).

Crying often leads to a response from the caregiver. In one study, 77 percent of 2,461 episodes of crying that were observed were followed by some intervention by the mother (Moss, 1967). This intervention becomes an opportunity for social interaction, so the caregiver is rewarded in two ways: The crying stops, and the caregiver and child engage in a mutually enjoyable exchange (Lester, 1988).

For years, people have debated the wisdom of *always* responding promptly to a baby's cries. In the earliest part of the twentieth century, many people believed that rushing to soothe a crying infant would "spoil" the baby and encourage the infant to cry at the least little thing. Then, in the 1970s, research suggested that the opposite might be true. When mothers respond promptly to their crying infants, the frequency and duration of crying may actually *decrease*, as the baby develops the expectation that the mother can be counted on to help (Bell & Ainsworth, 1972).

To test this latter hypothesis, Hubbard and van IJzendoorn (1991), from Leiden University in the Netherlands, observed infants in their homes over the first nine months of life. Crying declined greatly after the first three months, perhaps because the babies were adjusting to life in their new environments, or because of changes in neurological organization at about three months (Nelson, 1999a). Individual differences in the duration of crying could not be explained by differences in how promptly mothers responded to their babies. However, the researchers did find that delays in responding seemed to cause a decrease in the number of crying bouts. This result makes sense if we differentiate two situations in which parents respond to infant crying. In some instances, parents respond to severe infant distress. In other cases, they respond to mild fussing by the infant over a minor matter (such as an uncomfortable body position). Parents are generally able to distinguish between these levels of distress without difficulty. Delaying a response to this second kind of crying may help to make the baby more self-sufficient in dealing with minor irritations, and so the child fusses less often and, with time, has fewer crying bouts overall. The parent, however, must be a good judge of the causes of the baby's cries, as ignoring the cries of a severely distressed infant could have serious consequences.

Crying patterns can also be a helpful diagnostic tool that alerts paediatricians to possible abnormalities in early development (Barr, Hopkins, & Green, 2000; Worchell & Allen, 1997). Sometimes, in a condition called **colic**, babies cry a great deal for no apparent reason. In this state (the word *colic* means "pain"), there is a prolonged period of unexplained crying in infants that sometimes lasts several hours at a time. Infantile colic, which occurs in roughly 20 percent of infants, usually begins between 2 and 4 weeks of age, and its causes are not known (Lester, 2005). This loud, continual crying can be frustrating, even frightening, for parents. In most cases, it stops by the time the baby is 3 or 4 months of age. Although colic is usually harmless, in some cases, it may indicate an illness, such as a hernia or an ear infection. A high-pitched, urgent, and "piercing" cry can help to differentiate babies with colic from those who simply cry a great deal or are ill (Lester, Boukydis, Garcia-Coll, Hole, & Peucker, 1992). The infant cry is not only an important communicative signal but also an early warning sign of developmental problems and illness.

This infant is probably crying because of some form of physiological distress, like hunger, need for a diaper change, or digestive problems. By the time this baby is 3 or 4 months old, its crying—which is a clear form of communication—will often be related to psychological needs, such as the desire to be picked up and loved or played with.

colic

A prolonged period of unexplained crying in an infant.

How to Soothe an Infant

As infants grow and mature, they are less likely to cry as a way of communicating their distress. Because not all forms of distress go away, ways of dealing with distress appear to be an increasingly important part of the baby's life. To understand how infants relieve their distress, researchers have studied what infants do to soothe themselves.

INFANTS' ABILITIES TO SOOTHE THEMSELVES   Even very young infants have some techniques available to relieve their own distress. One way is by sucking, which the baby routinely engages in, even while still in utero. After birth, sucking on things, including the baby's own thumb and hand, may comfort very young infants. Although it was long assumed that sucking was effective because of its association with feeding, researchers have found that, immediately after birth and before the baby's first oral feeding, simply sucking on a pacifier reduces a baby's distress (Smith, Fillion, & Blass, 1990). It may be that sucking has a soothing effect because when the baby sucks, its overall body movements are lessened. Recent studies indicate that sucking on certain substances calms infants more effectively than sucking on other substances. For example, Barr and his colleagues have found that sucking on substances with a sweet taste is more effective in calming young infants than sucking on plain water (Barr et al., 1999; Barr & Young, 1999; Gormally et al., 2001). The soothing techniques that work will change as the infant develops. While sucking on a sweet liquid appeared to be effective in calming a 2-week-old baby, it was less effective in soothing a 4-week-old unless accompanied by eye contact with an adult (Zeifman, Delaney, & Blass, 1996). It seems that as early as 4 weeks of age, the infant begins to rely on social contact with caregivers to soothe him and help regulate his states.

HOW PARENTS SOOTHE THEIR BABIES   Infants pay more attention to events in their environment, and therefore can learn more, when they are in a calm but alert state. This suggests that soothing babies in order to help them reach a state in which they are neither too drowsy nor upset is one of the critical tasks of parenting. Because sucking can soothe infants, parents may use a pacifier with very young infants. This technique can comfort infants rapidly and effectively (Campos, 1989). A variety of other techniques are effective in soothing, including rocking, swaddling, and massaging (Cathey, 2006; Elliot, Reilly, Drummond, & Letourneau, 2002; Evanoo, 2007; Field, 2001; Rock, Trainor, & Addison, 1999). In swaddling, a baby is wrapped tightly in a blanket or cloth, thus keeping her arms and legs immobile. Swaddling has been used successfully in hospital nurseries throughout North America and in many cultures around the world to soothe infants (Valsiner, 1989). For some cultural differences in babies' soothability, see Box 4.2 on the next pages.

Brazelton Institute

Evaluating the Newborn's Health and Capabilities

To find out about the health, maturity, and the capabilities of the newborn, tests of the baby's reflexes (see Table 4-1 on page 119) may be combined with other assessment techniques. One of the most widely used tests for newborns is the **Brazelton Neonatal Assessment Scale** (Brazelton, Nugent, & Lester, 1987). As you can see from Table 4-3 on page 128, this test measures many of the capacities of the infant that we discuss in this chapter: sensory and perceptual capacities (including orientation to sights and sounds); early learning capabilities (such as familiarity or habituation to sensory stimuli); motor development (such as muscle tone); infant states and the ability to regulate them (such as soothability); and signs that the brain is properly controlling involuntary responses (such as the startle reflex).

Brazelton Neonatal Assessment Scale

A scale used to measure an infant's sensory and perceptual capabilities, motor development, range of states, and ability to regulate these states. The scale also indicates whether the brain and the central nervous system are properly regulating autonomic responsivity.

Box 4.2

Perspectives on Diversity

HOW CULTURE AFFECTS CRYING AND SOOTHABILITY

Although no one would argue with the idea that all infants cry at some time or another, many people have wondered whether infants around the world, from different cultures and nations, all cry in the same way. In fact, psychologists have, for a number of years, explored this question of how infants from different cultures cry and the related aspect of how people in different cultures will then soothe a distressed infant.

Take crying, for instance. Over the past decade or so, researchers have examined whether there are cross-cultural differences in the circumstances under which infants cry, as well as in the development of how infants cry. It has been widely accepted that there is a "normal" crying curve that regulates the amount of infant crying, with infants' crying gradually increasing over the first two months of life and then subsequently decreasing until roughly the fourth month of life (e.g., Bell & Ainsworth, 1972; Brazelton, 1962). A number of researchers, however, have noted that the studies demonstrating this pattern have focused virtually exclusively on infants in the Western World. Ronald Barr, from the University of British Columbia, and his associates in the United States (Barr, Konner, Bakeman, & Adamson, 1991), have suggested that because of different caregiving practices around the world, it is possible that this early crying pattern may be more specific to Western, rather than non-Western, cultures.

To examine this idea, these researchers compared crying in the !Kung San infants of northwestern Botswana with Western infants (Barr, 1990; Barr et al., 1991). By looking at the frequency of crying and fretting in these infants, the researchers found that the patterns of these behaviours were very similar for the !Kung San infants and for samples of both Dutch and North American infants, with the !Kung San infants showing a peak in crying/fretting at about 3 months, which then declined to a steady level at roughly 6 months of age.

These authors did, however, observe cross-cultural differences in infants' duration of crying, with !Kung San infants crying for about half the time of the Western babies. Thus, the variation in caregiving in the !Kung San, which differs from Western care in that it includes holding and carrying for more than 80 percent of the time during the day (Konner, 1976, 1977), does seem to have an impact on at least some aspects of crying behaviour. Other differences in crying patterns have been reported in regard to Korean infants reared at home and in institutions (Lee, 1994, 2000), with no definite peak in crying occurring in the first few months.

The flip side to crying, of course, is soothability. Are there cross-cultural differences in the ease with which babies in distress can be soothed? As we saw earlier, some babies are easily calmed, while others are much more difficult to console. In fact, just as with crying, there are differences across cultures in the ease with which babies in distress can be soothed (Kagan & Fox, 2006). For example, studying infants in the United States, Freedman (1974) found that European-American babies shifted more frequently between states of contentment and distress than did Chinese-American babies. Additionally, Chinese-American babies tended to calm themselves more readily when they were upset and were also more easily consoled by their caregivers. Soothability also varies among babies in other cultural groups., Japanese babies, for example,

---

The Brazelton scale has been used for a variety of purposes. It is used to identify infants at risk for developmental problems, and it can aid in diagnosing neurological impairment (Black et al., 1993; Eldredge & Salamy, 1988). The scale is also useful in predicting later development. For instance, newborns who score high on it tend to score higher on later measures of cognitive, motor, or social development (Keefer, Dixon, Tronick, & Brazelton, 1991). Finally, the Brazelton scale has been used as an intervention technique, teaching parents about their newborn's capacities either by having them watch a health-care professional administer this test to their baby or by having them try the same test with their baby themselves (Wendland-Carro, Piccinini, & Millar, 1999).

and babies of the Zinacanteco Indian tribe of southern Mexico are more easily quieted than other infants (Nugent et al., 1989).

Navajo babies in the American Southwest who, for about the first year of their lives, spend most of the day encased in a cradleboard are also easier to soothe than many other babies. The cradleboard, which is used in the Navajo and other Native North American tribes as well as in other parts of the world, is made up of a wooden back, a hinged footboard, and a hoop that arches over and shields the baby's head and face. Newborns and sleeping infants are swaddled from the neck down with a blanket, but after about three months of life, babies' arms may be left free (Chisholm, 1963).

Experts disagree on whether to attribute the Navajo infant's greater soothability to the motoric restrictions experienced on the cradleboard over the first year. It may be that Navajo newborns are calmer at birth and that this is the reason why Navajo babies are comfortable on the cradleboard (Chisholm, 1963). However, some researchers suggest that swaddling has a calming influence on most newborns (see, for example, Tronick, Thomas, & Daltabuit, 1994).

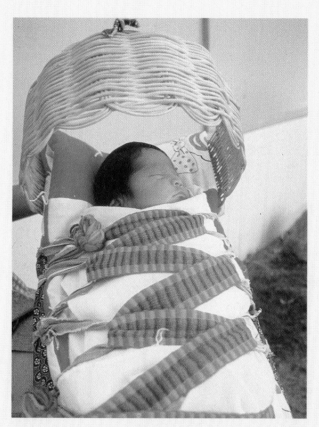

Tight swaddling of this Havasupai infant provides the baby with a feeling of comfort and security. Like many choices in child-rearing, the First Nations cradleboard has clear tradeoffs. Although it restricts a child's movements (until the infant's arms are freed, at about 3 months of age), because the mother carries the infant with her and can set her offspring up against a firm backing, it also allows the baby to see and experience many things that the infant who spends most of its time in a crib may miss.

Cross-cultural research on infant motor development has shown that a baby's behaviour during the Brazelton assessment may predict later parent–infant interaction. Using the Brazelton scale, researchers identified superior motor performance by infants in the Gusii community of West Africa in comparison with North American babies (Nugent, Lester, & Brazelton, 1991). This superior ability was found to be related to more vigorous handling by caregivers early in the child's life, including carrying the child on the mother's body in a sling, which has the effect of strengthening various muscles in the infant's body as she grips the mother (Keefer et al., 1991). The infants' motor abilities influence the way caregivers treat them, which, in turn, is influenced by cultural practices and behavioural routines. Together, these forces give infants opportunities to improve their motor control.

Table 4-3 Brazelton Neonatal Assessment Scale

Capacity for Habituation

Habituation, a form of learning in which repeated exposure to a particular stimulus leads to reduced response to that stimulus. The infant's ability to habituate is also a measure of her capacity for attention to new things in her environment:

1. Light
2. Rattle
3. Bell
4. Pinprick

Orientation to Sights and Sounds

The baby's ability to focus on and track various stimuli is measured as an indication of his capacity to see, hear, and orient to things in his physical and social environment:

5. Visual focusing and following an inanimate object
6. Reacting to an inanimate auditory stimulus
7. Visual focusing and following a human face
8. Reacting to the sound of a human voice
9. Reacting to both the sight of a human face and the sound of the person's voice

Motor Development

These tests measure the infant's motor skills:

10. Baby's ability to pull to a sitting position
11. Defensive ability: baby's ability to free herself of light cloth placed over eyes
12. Degree of alertness
13. General tonus
14. Motor maturity
15. Activity

State: Range in Degree of Arousal

Tests measure the variability and intensity of the infant's periods of arousal:

16. Peak excitement
17. Rapidity with which excitement builds
18. Irritability: number of times the baby fusses and things that appear to irritate him are recorded
19. Lability, or variability, of state: frequency and intensity of changes in state are noted

State: Regulation and Self-Regulation

These tests measure the infant's responsiveness to efforts to quiet or soothe her as well as her ability to quiet herself:

20. Cuddliness: A measure of the baby's willingness to be held and to conform to the examiner's body
21. Consolability with intervention: A measure of how long it takes an examiner to quiet a baby who is upset
22. Self-quieting: The baby's own efforts to soothe herself, as by thumb sucking, are measured
23. Whole hand to mouth

Autonomic Stability

Tests measure the infant's autonomic (uncontrolled) reactivity to various stimuli:

24. Tremors: Severe tremulousness may indicate problems in the central nervous system
25. Startles: The baby's tendency to react to sudden movement, loud sounds, and other strong stimuli with a startle response is measured
26. Skin: Reactivity is assessed by measuring electrical activity on the surface of the skin

Source: Adapted from Brazelton et al., 1987.

For Thought and Discussion

1. Given that infant reflexes typically disappear during the first few months of life, why do you think that they actually exist in the first place? What purpose(s) might they serve?

2. You have two cousins who both had babies a few months ago. One day, your cousins get into an argument about whether parents should respond immediately to their babies when they cry or whether parents should wait and let the baby "cry himself/herself out." Given what you know about developmental theory and research, what would you tell your cousins about these two positions?

3. On the basis of the discussion in the text, it is clear that infants spend a lot more (relative) time in REM sleep than do older children or adults. The text suggests that such sleep encourages nervous system development. Can you think of other possibilities? Given that REM sleep has been associated with dreaming, do you think this might mean that infants dream more?

THE INFANT'S SENSORY AND PERCEPTUAL CAPACITIES

Infants have limited knowledge of the world. They learn a lot about the world very quickly and much of this learning occurs by using their sensory and perceptual capabilities. The infant's sensory receptors, such as their eyes and ears, teach them about the world through their **sensations**—the stimuli their sensory receptors detect—and their **perceptions**—their interpretations of the stimuli they detect. Researches have discovered that babies' sensory and perceptual capabilities are quite well developed even at birth, allowing infants to begin adapting immediately to the environment.

As the Turning Points chart on the next two pages shows, the infant's sensory and perceptual abilities are especially sensitive to the social environment. This suggests that babies' sensory and perceptual systems may be biologically prepared to process and respond to social stimuli. Such preparation is clearly adaptive: a baby's responsiveness to other human beings increases caregivers' interest in the child and, thereby, enhances the child's well-being and survival. The infant's inborn sensitivity to social stimuli is one of the issues we will examine more closely in this section.

A second issue we will explore is the connection or interdependence among various sensory and perceptual systems—vision, hearing, taste, smell, and touch. To present the different systems in an orderly way, we discuss each one separately. However, it is important to remember that these systems develop together, and that advances in one may trigger changes in another. For example, improvements in vision that come with age may help the infant identify the location of a new sound. Later in this section, we will discuss how these systems influence each other and how, by working together, they help the infant understand the world. Our discussion of the interplay of developing systems continues in Chapter 5, where we examine how changes in an infant's motor capabilities, such as the emergence of crawling or walking, can have a profound effect on how a child perceives the world.

sensation

The detection of stimuli by the sensory receptors.

perception

The interpretation of sensations in order to make them meaningful.

Unlocking the Secrets of Babies' Sensory Capabilities

Studying infants' sensations and perceptions is not easy. Without language skills, babies cannot respond to direct questions as to whether one tone is louder than another or whether two colours appear different. Very young babies even have trouble reaching or pointing toward something that interests them, and crawling in the direction of an

THE DEVELOPMENT OF SENSATION, PERCEPTION, AND EARLY LEARNING

EARLY WEEKS
- Baby can distinguish strong visual contrasts; hears sounds. Demonstrates size constancy and early forms of imitation. Generalized distress; may be irritable by late afternoon

1 MONTH
- Baby likes to look at faces; scans visually. Differentiates speech from other sounds. Has learned to tell difference between breast nipple, bottle nipple, thumb, and pacifier.

2 MONTHS
- Infant tracks objects visually from side to side. Likes to hear sounds with different intonations. Baby has learned that breast or bottle bring nourishment; she stops crying at the mere sight of either.

3 MONTHS
- Baby sees objects clearly, can sustain alertness, begins to localize sounds. Has recognition memory; remembers when cued.

4 MONTHS
- Baby looks more alert. Distinguishes colours, shapes, sizes. Can hear and respond to soft sounds; coordinates looking and listening. In immediate anticipation, at sight of bottle opens mouth.

5 MONTHS
- Attends to smaller objects; has better depth perception; recognizes a face even if it is upside down. Listens quietly to speech and shows signs of pleasure; takes more interest in sounds. Remembers pictures of faces. Fear and anger; defiance; affection; shyness

6 MONTHS
- Recognizes familiar people easily; visual acuity approximates normal adult vision.

7 MONTHS
- Recognizes facial features and distinguishes male and female faces.

8 MONTHS
- Shows more interest in distant objects. Becomes quiet when others talk. Distinguishes between questions and declarative statements.

Note: Developmental events described in this and other Turning Points charts represent overall trends identified in research studies. Individual children vary greatly in the ages at which they achieve these developmental changes..

Sources: Haith & Benson, 1998; Kellman & Arterberry, 2006; Kopp, 1994; Saffran, Werker, & Werner, 2006.

interesting stimulus is far beyond their skills. Thus, many of the research methods we use to study sensation and perception in older children and adults are not available for studying infants. What's more, even if we determine that infants possess a certain sensory capability (e.g., distinguishing between the tastes of sweet and sour), we cannot be sure they experience the same sensations as older children and adults. Sensations may mature or change with age.

In their efforts to solve these problems, psychologists have used techniques that measure whatever responses young babies are able to make. In particular, to study an infant's sensory capabilities researchers have relied on information from the autonomic nervous system, which controls involuntary bodily functions as heart rate and breathing. For instance, a change in a baby's breathing following a change in the pitch of a sound suggests that the infant heard the pitch change. A newborn's motor responses,

9 MONTHS	• More visually aware of tiny objects; if given choice of picking up either large or small object will choose the smaller item. Begins to remember without cues. Uses knowledge to solve problems; aware of cause and effect; recognizes that his own actions may affect outcomes. "Uses" other people to make things happen.
10 MONTHS	• Begins to visually group similar objects. Discriminates an object within another: e.g., a cookie inside a jar. Investigates textures, designs, or parts of toys; repeats play sequences with different toys. Peers intently at pictures.
11 MONTHS	• Uses props as aids—e.g., uses chair to pull to standing position.
12 MONTHS	• Groups toys with like features, such as colour or size. Checks own feet when walking. No longer discriminates speech sounds that are not in parents' language(s). Uses imitative learning. Deliberately introduces variations into play sequences. Memory is improved. 
15 MONTHS	• Makes groupings of objects that go together. Trial and error learning. More aware of functions of objects. Recognizes and uses more cause-and-effect relationships.
18 MONTHS	• Differentiates round puzzle pieces from square ones. Recall memory improved. Has primitive idea of what "should be": puts lids on jars; pays attention better; recognizes that others have possessions.
21 MONTHS	• Differentiates round, square, and triangular puzzle pieces and puts them in puzzle with help. Has some understanding of past, present, and future, some idea of categories.
24 MONTHS	• Tries to copy lines on paper. Elaborate play sequences show recognition of family members' specific roles. Begins to use strategy-like, or planned, behaviours.

although limited, can also give clues to sensory abilities. For instance, a slight turn of the head or kicking of the legs may be used to assess an early ability. Researchers have also used infants' well-developed sucking pattern to measure sensory abilities. Infants' sucking patterns can change in intensity or duration in response to input from the environment. For instance, one technique used to study infants called the *violation-of-expectation method* introduces an unusual or impossible sight, such as an object floating in space or suspended without adequate support (Baillargeon, 1994). If, upon seeing this information, the baby responds by altering his behaviour (e.g., by slowing down or stopping his rate of sucking), it suggests that the baby knows something about how objects normally work and that this expectation of the normal course of events has been violated. By noting changes in the types of behaviours babies are able to produce on their own at the moment that stimuli are presented to an infant, researchers can determine that the baby has discriminated or detected a difference among the different stimuli presented or whether he expected certain patterns to occur.

visual preference method

A method of studying infants' abilities to distinguish one stimulus from another by measuring the length of time they spend attending to different stimuli.

Another commonly used technique for examining infants' abilities to distinguish visual stimuli is the **visual preference method**, which was pioneered by Robert Fantz (1963). In this technique, the researcher presents an infant with two stimuli and measures the amount of time that she spends looking at each. If the infant looks longer at one stimulus than at the other, we can assume that she can distinguish between the two stimuli. Looking longer at one stimulus may also indicate that the infant finds one stimulus either new or unfamiliar, more interesting, more complex, or more pleasurable than the other one. Such interpretations are speculative, however. We cannot know for sure why the infant looks longer at one stimulus than another.

habituation

The process by which an individual reacts with less and less intensity to a repeatedly presented stimulus, eventually responding only faintly or not at all.

In many of the methods used to study early sensory and perceptual capabilities, the assessment of the baby's abilities depends on infants' tendency to **habituate** to a stimulus when it is presented repeatedly. When researchers repeat experience with a stimulus, infants gradually lessen the intensity of their initial reaction until, eventually, they respond only faintly or not at all. This pattern, or behaviour, is used to assess learning in the Brazelton Neonatal Assessment Scale (see also Table 4-3 on page 128). To illustrate, imagine if you were to shake a rattle near a baby's head. The first time you shake the rattle the child may display a *startle* response, thrashing her arms and legs and moving her body. However, if you repeated the noise a second time, this behaviour would diminish: The infant might give only a brief kick. And after a few more times, the infant appears to ignore the sound completely and shows no response at all. Now, if you presented a different sound, such as with a bell, the baby will once again show a reaction. Notice that this reaction to the new sound tells you that the baby has distinguished between the sounds of the rattle and the bell. Habituation can also be used to study the baby's ability to distinguish stimuli presented to the other senses—sights, smells, tastes, and tactile sensations. Therefore, habituation is widely used to explore infants' sensory and perceptual capabilities. You will see that this research technique was used to obtain much of the information that we discuss in the next few sections on the infant's senses of hearing, vision, smell, taste, and touch.

Hearing: Babies Are Good Listeners

An infant's hearing can be tested shortly after birth and these tests show that the newborn's hearing is extremely well developed (Saffran, Werker, & Werner, 2006). This is not surprising when you recall that the development of the fetus's auditory system is completed well before birth (see the Turning Points chart on pages 88 and 89 in Chapter 3). In one study, researchers monitored changes in fetal body movements and heart rates and showed that even before birth, fetuses may hear complex sounds presented outside the mother's body (Kisilevsky & Muir, 1991; Kisilevsky, Fearon, & Muir, 1998), musical passages (Kisilevsky, Hains, Granier-Deferre, Jacquet, & Lecanuet, 2004; Lecanuet, Granier-Deferre, Jacquet, & DeCasper, 2000), as well as be able to recognize their own mother's voice (Kisilevsky et al., 2003). Such sounds are carried through the amniotic fluid to the fetus as a series of vibrations. Even more interesting is the evidence that infants may learn and remember what was read to them before they were born. As you can see in Box 4.3, fetuses can apparently learn to distinguish not only their mother's voices but the sounds and rhythms of the material their mothers are reading.

It is important to remember, however, that a newborn's hearing is not as well developed as an adult's. For a newborn, a sound must be louder—about 10 to 17 decibels louder—than the sound that an adult can detect (Hecox & Deegan, 1985). (A decibel is a measure of sound-pressure level, which we perceive as loudness.) Normal conversational speech is generally measured at about 60 decibels, a whisper at around 20 decibels, and the sound of a train at approximately 100 decibels. In addition, compared with adults, babies are less sensitive to low-pitched sounds; they are more likely to hear a sound that is high in pitch (Saffran et al., 2006). This may help explain why adults so often raise the pitch of their voices during infant-directed speech, also called *motherese* (Hoff, 2005). They know instinctively that a high-pitched voice is more likely to capture

Box 4.3

Child Psychology in Action

CAN INFANTS LEARN EVEN BEFORE THEY ARE BORN?

Speculating as to why newborn human babies perceive sound so well, Anthony DeCasper asked himself if, perhaps, they had already learned to listen in the womb. How could he test such a proposition? With a colleague, DeCasper designed a clever procedure in which babies could suck to control what they heard on a tape recorder: either their mother or a strange woman speaking to them (DeCasper & Fifer, 1980). As you will learn elsewhere in this chapter, newborns can learn to vary their patterns of sucking. In this study, when infants sucked in a pattern of longer and shorter bursts, they activated their mother's voice on the tape recorder; a different sucking pattern activated the stranger's voice. The researchers found that infants sucked to hear their own mother's voice in preference to the voice of the stranger.

It could be argued, of course, that the infants probably heard their mother's voice from the time of birth and, thus, could have learned to prefer it in their first hours of life. To rule out this familiarity hypothesis, DeCasper and Spence (1986) designed another study in which 16 pregnant women were asked to read Dr. Seuss's famous children's book *The Cat in the Hat* to their fetuses twice a day for the last six and a half weeks of pregnancy. Some remarkable results occurred. After birth, when these women's infants could suck in one distinctive pattern to hear their mother's recorded voice read *The Cat in the Hat*, or in another pattern to hear them read *The King, the Mice, and the Cheese*, they sucked to hear *The Cat in the Hat*! Because in this test condition the mothers read not just one of the stories but both of them, it seems pretty clear that what the babies preferred was not their mothers' voices per se but their mothers' voices reading the poem to which the infants had been exposed prenatally.

Although these studies give us evidence that prenatal auditory experiences influence postnatal auditory preferences, we do not have a clear understanding of the exact mechanisms involved in prenatal learning. The sounds babies hear in utero filtered through the mother's body and the amniotic fluid, must be different from the sounds of their mothers' voices as they hear them after birth. It may be that the component of maternal speech to which the fetus responds is *prosody*. Prosody

This mother, reading *The Cat in the Hat* to her unborn baby, may well know that the fetus is sensitive to its mother's voice as heard in the womb. Whether this woman believes that her baby will get a head start on learning language, we can't know; however, research has also shown that newborn babies prefer to hear not only their own mothers' voices but also the specific pieces of poetry or prose their mothers read to them before they were born!

includes the rhythm, intonation, and stress of speech and is carried by the sound frequencies that are least altered in the prenatal environment. Because both the books the mothers in DeCasper and Spence's study read to their babies are stories but of very different poetic meters, the infants may also have been expressing a preference for the familiar prosody.

Since this original work, researchers have continued to explore various aspects of fetal perception. For instance, there is evidence that newborns may exhibit a postnatal preference for a specific passage or melody experienced prenatally (DeCasper & Spence, 1986, 1991; Fifer & Moon, 1989). Moreover, fetuses can discriminate in utero between male and female strangers' voices (Lecanuet et al., 1993), and between a recording of their mother's voice and that of a female stranger (Kisilevsky et al., 2003). Finally, newborns have been found to prefer the sound of their mother's language (Moon, Cooper, & Fifer, 1993), suggesting that language learning may begin prior to birth! Clearly, there is more going on in utero than one used to think.

the child's attention. Over their first two years, however, babies rapidly improve in their ability to discriminate sounds of different pitches, until they eventually reach adult levels of discrimination (Saffran & Griepentrog, 2001).

Babies can also locate where a sound comes from and judge how far way it is, which is called **auditory localization**. Newborns, for example, will turn their heads toward the sound of a rattle, suggesting that they know what direction the sound came from (Clifton, 1992). Morrongiello and colleagues (Morrongiello, Fenwick, Hillier, & Chance, 1994) found that newborns can not only detect which side (left versus right) a sound is coming from, but they can also actually determine the (approximate) location of the sound. Young infants are also very good at gauging a sound's distance, particularly when it is getting closer (Morrongiello, Hewitt, & Gotowiec, 1991). In one study, for instance, infants not only moved backwards when hearing a sound that sounded like it was approaching, they also discriminated between fast and slow approaching sounds, showing a bigger response to faster-approaching sounds (Freiberg, Tually, & Crassini, 2001).

Babies hear more than the qualities (loudness and pitch) and location of sounds, however; there is now very good evidence that infants perceive many different aspects of musical structure as well. Sandra Trehub and her colleagues at the University of Toronto, for instance, have revealed a number of interesting musical-processing abilities in infants in the first year of life (Ilari, 2002; Trehub, 2006; Trehub & Hannon, 2006). For example, infants more easily detect changes to tone combinations in which the pitch frequencies are in simple ratios (e.g., 2 to 1, or 3 to 2) as opposed to more complex ratios (e.g., 45 to 32; Schellenberg & Trehub, 1996). Infants of this age are also sensitive to changes in melodies that alter the overall pattern of rises and falls in pitch (Chang & Trehub, 1977; Trainor, McDonald, & Alain, 2002) and distinguish unnaturally segmented musical passages from naturally segmented ones (Jusczyk & Krumhansl, 1993; Krumhansl & Jusczyk, 1990). Others have investigated infants' perceptions of musical rhythm and meter, and have found that infants can categorize melodies based on their underlying metric structure (Hannon & Johnson, 2005). Even more surprisingly, some researchers have found that infants of this age are sensitive to Western musical scale structure (Trehub, Schellenberg, & Kamenetsky, 1999; Trehub, Thorpe, & Trainor, 1990) as well as Western versus non-Western rhythmic and metrical structure (Hannon & Trehub, 2005), and can even distinguish melodies based on both Western and Javanese scales, whereas adults did better with Western scales (Lynch, Eillers, Oller, & Urbano, 1990). "This suggests that in the early stages of development, infants are equally adept at processing either scale type but that culture specific experience enhances their ability to process one type of scale over the other" (Aslin et al., 1998, p. 177). As we will see in Chapter 7, research has revealed a similar shift in the infant's response to speech sounds.

These early abilities have led some to speculate that human beings are biologically prepared for processing music (Winner, 2006). And some have even suggested that listening to music early in life has particular developmental benefits. For example, the idea known as the Mozart Effect suggests that listening to classical music can stimulate brain development and increase intelligence (Rauscher, Shaw, & Ky, 1993, 1995). As intriguing as this idea sounds, current research does not support the claim that listening to classical music or any kind of music increases intelligence (Crnĉec, Wilson, & Prior, 2006; Thompson, Schellenberg, & Husain, 2001).

The human auditory system may also be programmed for special sensitivity to the sound of human voices (Saffran et al., 2006; Trainor & Desjardins, 2002). Babies as young as 2 days old prefer to hear the human voice over other sounds, particularly a voice that is high in pitch with exaggerated pitch contours—the exact type of sound that makes up much of infant-directed speech (Fernald, 1992). Adults and even older children appear to be aware of these preferences, for when they are with an infant, they speak in a high-pitched voice and sing in a high-pitched and melodic fashion (Trehub, Unyk, & Trainor, 1993). Perhaps this accounts, in part, for the fact that lullabies are sung throughout the world to soothe infants (Trehub & Trainor, 1993). And infants notice. Babies ranging in age from 4 to 7 months prefer infant-directed playsongs and

auditory localization

The ability to determine from where in space a sound is originating.

Canadian Researchers, Hearing

lullabies over non-infant-directed singing (Trainor, 1996), and they turn their attention toward themselves during lullabies (Rock, Trainor, & Addison, 1999). Moreover, maternal singing has been found to modulate infant arousal, with infants showing increased arousal in response to hearing their mothers' singing (Shenfield, Trehub, & Nakuta, 2003).

Babies also learn to discriminate among voices very quickly. Even newborns can distinguish their mothers' voices from those of other female's voices (DeCasper & Fifer, 1980). This ability facilitates the development of an emotional bond between parent and child. Even before babies can understand the words their parents say, the familiar tones and speech patterns of their mothers or other primary caregivers help form the foundation of the early parent–child relationship. Thus, early auditory skills, preferences, and experiences have significance for social development.

Vision: How Babies See Their Worlds

Some baby animals, such as kittens, cannot see at all for days after birth, but the eyes of a newborn human being are physiologically ready to begin responding to visual stimuli. Newborn humans can detect changes in brightness, distinguish movement in the visual field, and follow or track a moving object with their eyes (Kellman & Arterberry, 2006). In this section, we look at several important aspects of visual development.

THE CLARITY OF INFANTS' VISION **Visual acuity** is sharpness of vision, or the clarity with which a person can discern fine details. Because it is harder to see the details of a small object than those of a big one, acuity and viewing distance are related. If you can read from 20 feet away a letter of the alphabet that people with perfect vision can read from 40 feet, you have 20/40 vision, a relatively small deviation from the optimum of 20/20. The vision of infants under 1 month of age ranges from 20/200 to 20/800 (Cavallini et al., 2002; Courage & Adams, 1990). Visual acuity improves rapidly over the next few months, however, and seems to be within the normal adult range by the time a child is between 6 months and a year old (Banks & Shannon, 1993). One way visual acuity is assessed in infants is by testing how sensitive a baby is to visual details such as the width or density of a set of stripes in a pictorial image. Figure 4-2 displays the finest black stripes that most 1-week-old infants can discriminate

visual acuity

Sharpness of vision; the clarity with which fine details can be discerned.

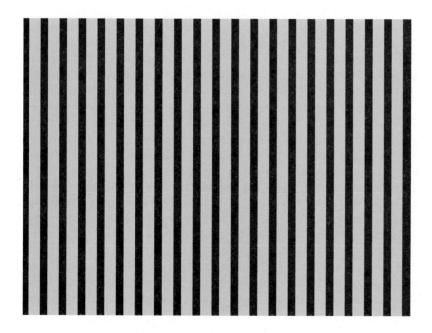

Figure 4-2

Visual discrimination in infants

At 1 week of age, infants can discriminate black stripes of this size from a grey field when they are a foot away from the target. This is only about one-thirtieth as fine a discrimination as an adult with normal vision can make, but by the time infants are 8 months old, they see about one-fourth as well as adults, and they achieve adult levels by the time they are about 5 years old.

Source: Maurer & Maurer, 1988.

from a grey field when the target is 1 foot away. Gradually, babies develop the ability to detect more detailed patterns; thus, little by little they are able to detect stripes that are closer together (Kellman & Banks, 1998). To appreciate this ability to see details more clearly, examine Figure 4-3, which shows how well an infant can see at birth and at 1, 2, 3, and 6 months of age, in comparison with what an adult sees.

Figure 4-3

How well can infants see?

Newborn infants can perceive motion of large, high-contrast objects, but they probably have no depth perception or colour vision and very little, if any, ability to detect low contrast or fine spatial details (a). At 1 month, babies still show little response to colour (b), but 2-month-old babies can begin to see colour (c). At 3 months, babies' colour vision is good, although their depth perception is still poor (d). By 6 months of age, infants see quite well (e), and scientists presume that children's vision continues to improve until it reaches the clarity of the normal adult's sight (f).

Source: Teller, 1997.

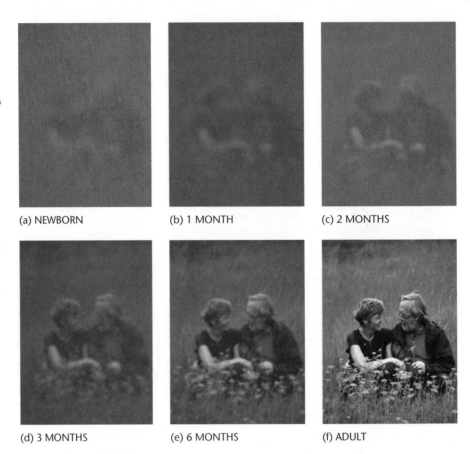

(a) NEWBORN   (b) 1 MONTH   (c) 2 MONTHS

(d) 3 MONTHS   (e) 6 MONTHS   (f) ADULT

Canadian Researchers, Vision

HOW BABIES PERCEIVE COLOURS   Although newborns clearly have limited colour vision, there is some evidence that babies can perceive some aspects of colour early in life. Adams, Courage, and their colleagues, for example, using a habituation procedure, have found that newborn infants of only one day can discriminate coloured, or *chromatic*, stimuli from non-coloured, or *achromatic*, ones (Adams, 1989, 1996; Adams, Courage, & Mercer, 1994; Adams & Courage, 1998), with the ability to distinguish among reds, greens, and yellows developing gradually over the first three months of life. By 3 to 4 months of age, infants can clearly distinguish among most colours (Thomasson & Teller, 2000) and can group colours into basic categories, such as reds, blues, and greens (Teller, 1997; Teller & Bornstein, 1987), with further development occurring over the course of the first year (Adams & Courage, 2002). Moreover, by 3 months of age, infants show spontaneous colour preferences (Zemach, Chang, & Teller, 2007; Zemach & Teller, 2007), with a strong preference for stimuli that adults see as blue, purple and red, and a marked non-preference for white. By 4 months of age, infant colour vision is similar to that of adults (Kellman & Arterberry, 2006).

The brain structures and neural pathways important in colour discrimination are quite immature during the first weeks of life, which may account in part for the limited ability to discriminate colour in very young infants. Research with infant monkeys indicates that early visual experience may be essential for normal colour perception to develop (Sugita, 2004). In this study, the monkeys were raised, from 1 month of age, in a room where the lighting was monochromatic and they could not see the normal spectrum of colours. When their colour vision was tested at 1 year of age, their ability to distinguish colours was much poorer than that of normally reared monkeys. With training in colour perception, the monkeys reared in monochromatic illumination were able to develop some but not all of these abilities. Although these results pertain to monkeys and not humans, they suggest that early visual experience with colour may be essential for normal colour perception to develop.

HOW BABIES PERCEIVE PATTERNS   Psychologists have long debated whether the visual world of a young infant, like that of an adult, is organized into patterns, forms, and unified wholes or whether a baby sees merely unrelated lines, angles, and edges, only gradually learning through experience to perceive larger patterns. The nativist, or biological position supports the first of these two viewpoints, arguing that pattern perception is innate. The empiricist, or environmental, position supports the second viewpoint and argues that experience is needed to piece the elements together into meaningful patterns. Most research findings suggest that both learning and experience are generally required to see patterns in an adult manner.

In one classic study, Salapatek and Kessen (1966) used an infrared camera to determine precisely where on a triangle newborns directed their eyes. They found that a newborn's gaze was not distributed over the whole triangle, as an adult's would be. The typical newborn centred his attention on one of the triangle's angles, sometimes, in a limited way, also scanning part of an edge. This suggests that, although certain elements of a complex pattern attract a newborn's attention (angles, edges, boundaries), we should not conclude that babies this young perceive whole forms. If they did, they would scan entire forms more completely. The scanning of forms improves quite quickly with age, however (Hunius & Geuze, 2004). By the age of 2 months, babies visually trace both the edges of a pattern and the internal areas (Aslin, 1987; Kellman & Arterberry, 2006). This suggests that they have made some advances in seeing the various parts of a pattern in a unified way.

By 3 months of age, babies are also almost as good as adults at picking unified patterns out of generalized movement (Bertenthal & Clifton, 1998; Booth, Pinto, & Bertenthal, 2002; Pinto, 2006). For example, researchers use the technique of a point-light display to determine how infants interpret visual information from a moving form. If 10 or 12 points of light are attached to a walking person's head and major joints, adults quickly recognize this moving display as depicting a person (see Figure 4-4 on the next page). By testing 3- to 5-month-old babies with this same kind of stimulus, researchers have found that even infants this young can extract the same kind of form information from motion (Bertenthal, Proffitt, & Cutting, 1984; Pinto, 2006). However, although infants from 3 to 5 months old can extract a human figure's structure from information about its motion, they do not seem to recognize the form as a person until they are somewhat older—around 9 months of age (Bertenthal, Proffitt, & Kramer, 1987). And other studies have found that young infants can use the motion information contained in point-light displays to discriminate and categorize animate versus inanimate objects, such as animals and vehicles (Arterberry & Bornstein, 2001, 2002). Finally, there is now evidence that even 2-day-olds prefer to look at biological motion (the motion produced by a human point-light walker) over non-biological, randomly moving point lights (Simion, Regolin, & Bulf, 2008); such a preference is suggestive of an innate predisposition to biological motion.

A PREFERENCE FOR FACES   Faces are complex patterns. Although all humans' faces are arranged similarly, there are many differences across individual faces. In addition, any single face can be experienced from various angles and with

This little girl appears fascinated by the patterns displayed in the mobile over her crib. Perhaps this is because, at 3 months of age, she may be perceiving the patterns in their entirety rather than just the portions of them—such as a corner or periphery—that she perceived at an earlier age.

Figure 4-4

Extracting information about form from movement

Three- to 5-month-old infants are able to detect a form from a moving array of lights (panel a) but not from a static display. Interestingly, when the display is flipped upside-down (panel b), or the actual components are moved to random locations (panel c), infants (and adults) experience much more difficulty in perceiving coherent motion.

Source: Bertenthal, Proffitt, & Kramer, 1987.

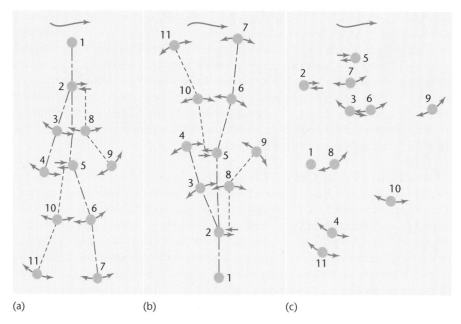

(a)　　　　　(b)　　　　　(c)

different expressions. Despite this visual complexity, research indicates that the infant's ability to perceive faces develops rapidly in the first year. This development is aided by what appears to be an innate preference for human faces. Newborns as young as 30 minutes old show a preference for images that are face-like as compared to images that are not face-like (Johnson et al., 1991; Mondloch et al., 1999). This early bias toward faces is then combined with a neural system that supports the rapid learning of faces and a human environment that provides extensive, and often close-up, experience with faces (Kellman & Arterberry, 2006). Together, these factors result in a developmental course in this particular type of pattern perception that is truly remarkable.

Early and rapid changes in face perception are evident in how babies scan faces. As you can see in Figure 4-5, infants 1 month old tend to scan the outer contours of the face, just as they would any other visual pattern (Simion et al., 2002). However, by 2 months of age, infants concentrate on internal features (Hunius & Geuze, 2004; Maurer & Salapatek, 1976), and seem to focus a lot on the eyes (see Figure 4-5). Other researchers, using real adult faces, have found these same developmental changes in infants' scanning (Haith, Bergman, & Moore, 1977). These investigators highlighted a

Figure 4-5

How infants scan the human face

A 1-month-old baby sticks pretty much to the outer perimeter of the face (a), although she shows some interest in the eyes. An infant who is 2 months old focuses particularly on the features of the face (b), paying a lot of attention to the eyes and mouth.

Source: Maurer & Salapatek, 1976.

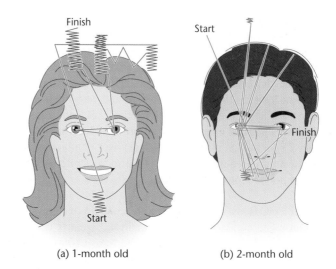

(a) 1-month old　　　　　(b) 2-month old

finding that can also be seen in Figure 4-5. Not only did 7-week-old infants spend less time on the contours of real faces, they looked at the eyes more than the younger infants did. But the fact that internal facial features, especially the eyes, strongly draw the attention of infants by 7 weeks of age does not mean that babies this young are seeing faces as unified wholes. Facial features may simply have an abundance of perceptual qualities, such as contour, contrast, and movement that are intrinsically appealing to the infant. Even the discovery that newborns prefer their mothers' faces over the faces of strangers does not necessarily mean that newborns are seeing faces as adults do (Walton, Bower, & Bower, 1992). Instead, the newborn's recognition of and preference for the mother's face may simply reflect the baby's focus on one particular feature of her face. In fact, Pascalis and his colleagues (1995) found that 4-day-old newborns looked longer at their mothers' faces than at those of strangers only when the mother was not wearing a head scarf. This may suggest that the hairline and the outer contour of the face play an integral part in the newborn's face recognition.

Some research suggests that the pattern of information present in faces—for example, the great number of high-contrast areas seen in the upper portion of the face pattern—is preferred by newborns (Turati et al., 2002). This suggests that rather than being born with sensitivity to human faces per se, babies may be biased toward particular types of patterns that happen to coincide with the type of information presented in faces. In one experiment, researchers showed 1½- and 3-month-old infants the computer-generated stimuli displayed in Figure 4-6 (Dannemiller & Stephens, 1988). Although stimulus (a) looks much more face-like than stimulus (b), the two are identical except that the shading is reversed. At 1½ months, babies showed no preference between these two stimuli, but at 3 months, they looked longer at (a), which is more easily seen as a face. Note that this was not simply because they had a preference for pictures with black borders and white interiors, given that there was no preference for control stimuli with these features. These findings suggest that by 3 months of age, babies identify a face as a unique pattern. The shift from perceiving parts to perceiving whole patterns appears to occur at about the same time for both objects and faces. However, infants continue to look longer at, and show more brain activity in response to, faces as compared with objects (Johnson, 2000; Nelson, 1999a).

Over the first year, infants also come to process facial information more quickly. A study of facial recognition found that, whereas 7-month-olds needed 14 trials to know a face well enough to recognize it reliably, 12-month-olds needed only about 9 trials (Rose, Jankowski, & Feldman, 2002). As we will see in Chapter 9, greater speed of processing is one consistent characteristic of cognitive change associated with age. Being able to extract information from stimuli quickly and reliably is a keystone of developing intellectual ability.

Beyond a general interest in faces, babies seem to prefer faces that are attractive. Judy Langlois and her colleagues (1987) showed colour slides of women's faces to two groups of infants who were 2 to 3 months old and 6 to 8 months old. The researchers presented these slides in pairs. One of each pair had been rated attractive by adult judges; the other had been rated unattractive. Both the younger and the older babies looked longer at the "attractive" faces; babies as young as 2 months of age showed a preference for attractiveness. And this effect holds not only for adult faces, but for infant faces as well.

Using a preferential looking paradigm, Van Duuran, Kendall-Scott, and Stark (2003) found that young infants preferred to look at infant faces that adults had judged to be attractive, with this preference disappearing when the faces were turned upside-down (see also Rubenstein, Kalakanis, & Langlois, 1999; and Rubenstein, Langlois, & Roggman, 2002). And quite recently, Quinn and colleagues (2008) found that 3- to 4-month-old infants preferred attractive domestic and wild cats (i.e., tigers) over unattractive cats. These studies clearly challenge the idea that standards of attractiveness are learned through experience.

Why do infants prefer attractive faces? Some argue that such faces contain more of the features that the infant's visual system is organized to react to: Infants prefer high

Figure 4-6

Evaluating infants' preferences for faces over other patterns

By the time they were 3 months old, infants looked longer at the face in (a) than its reverse (b). The finding that infants had no preference between patterns (c) and (d) established that it was the pattern of the face in (a) that they liked rather than its borders.

Source: Dannemiller & Stephens, 1988.

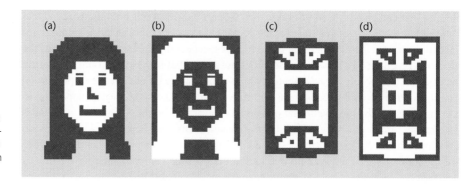

contrast, contours, curves, and vertical symmetry, and attractive faces may have more of these characteristics than unattractive faces (de Heering et al., 2008; Turati, Valenza, Leo, & Simion, 2005). However, some research has shown that when attractiveness and symmetry are varied independently—for example, an attractive face that lacks symmetry or an unattractive yet symmetrical face is presented—babies, like adults, prefer attractiveness to symmetry (Samuels et al., 1994). Thus, rather than symmetry explaining attractiveness, some suggest that there might be something about an attractive face that is interesting to babies. When faces identified as attractive have been examined more closely, what seems common across them is the averageness or prototypical aspects of these faces. It may be that their averageness is what makes attractive faces interesting to babies and adults alike (Slater, 2000). Attractive faces may simply be more average or face-like than unattractive faces. They are seen as better examples of faces because they contain many of the familiar features of other faces and are, therefore, more readily classified as a face. Or, alternatively, it may be that average faces are interesting because they are more difficult and time-consuming to process, especially to determine what makes such faces distinctive from other faces. We need a better understanding of why both infants and adults are interested in faces that judges have identified as attractive.

Exactly how babies develop these impressive face-processing abilities is a subject of much debate. The evidence that newborns are predisposed toward faces suggests that there is some innate human ability that is important to this development (Johnson, 2005). However experience clearly plays a vital role because this bias needs to be elaborated and fine-tuned over the first year of life. Some researchers argue that pattern-based learning of this type is not specific to faces but that because faces are particularly important for infants to learn about, they do it quickly (Nelson, 2001).

According to this view, over the first year of life, infants use their powerful general-learning capability to process their many experiences with human faces. Gradually, this face-processing system learns to focus on the types of faces most important for infants—namely human faces—with importance determined by frequency of exposure (Turati, 2004). Evidence by Pascalis, de Haan, and Nelson (2002) supports this claim. They found that both 9-month-olds and adults could discriminate between pictures of human faces. However, neither these infants nor adults were able to distinguish between different faces of monkeys. In contrast, 6-month-olds are able to discriminate facial information for both human and monkey faces. Essentially, face processing by human infants becomes specialized to human faces over the first year of life. This pattern is similar to the specialization that occurs in the development of speech perception (Werker & Vouloumanos, 2001), which we discuss in Chapter 7. The idea that learning in infancy is regulated by a general, rather than a specific, set of processing systems brings these two similar and important learning patterns together and suggests that infants have the ability to learn—and to learn rather rapidly—the many types of complex information that are important to their survival.

 DEPTH PERCEPTION   Newborns' eyes do not work together in the way that the eyes of older children and adults do. The eyes of newborns move in the same direction only about half the time (Maurer & Maurer, 1988; Kellman & Arterberry, 2006), so, young infants must rely on depth and distance cues that are available to each eye independently. Some of these cues involve motion. As objects approach us, they fill more of the visual field (Schmuckler & Li, 1998), and when we move our heads, the images of close objects move more than the images of distant objects. These kinds of changes associated with movement help babies judge depth. The ability to perceive depth improves with age, as eye coordination develops and more cues to depth and distance become available to the infant (Johnson, Bremner, Slater, Mason, Foster, & Cheshire, 2003).

By 3 to 5 months of age, babies can coordinate their two eyes and so can begin to see depth as adults do, using stereoscopic vision (Birch, 1993; Mohn & van Hof-van Duin, 1986). **Stereoscopic vision** is the sense of a third spatial dimension produced by the combination of the images perceived by both eyes, each of which reflects the stimulus from a slightly different angle. The brain's fusion of these two images creates the perception of depth. Proper use of the two eyes together at an early age is necessary for normal stereoscopic vision to develop. Babies born with crossed eyes (a condition called *convergent strabismus*) usually do not develop normal stereoscopic vision, unless the eyes are surgically corrected before the age of 2 years (Banks, Aslin, & Letson, 1975; Banks & Salapatek, 1983).

The ability to perceive depth has much practical value. For example, it helps keep us safe by preventing us from walking off cliffs and other high places. Researchers have wondered how soon a baby becomes cautious of high places as a result of depth perception. To investigate this issue, Gibson and Walk (1960) developed an apparatus called the **visual cliff** (see Figure 4-7). The visual cliff consists of an elevated glass platform with a checkerboard pattern directly beneath the glass on one side (the "shallow" side) and the same pattern several feet below the glass on the other side (the "deep" side). Gibson and Walk found that babies 6 to 14 months old would not cross the "deep" side to get to their mothers even when the mother encouraged the child to do so. Thus, babies this age were fearful enough of heights to avoid them.

This fear apparently does not exist in very young infants. When Campos and his associates (Campos, Langer, & Krowitz, 1970) placed 1-and-a-half-month-old babies first on the shallow side of a visual cliff and then on the deep side, the infants' heart rates *decreased*, which generally indicates interest rather than fear (fear is normally accompanied by an *increase* in heart rate). In contrast, when researchers placed older infants who could crawl on the deep side, these babies showed heart-rate accelerations, suggesting

stereoscopic vision

The sense of a third spatial dimension produced by the brain's fusion of the separate images contributed by both eyes, each of which reflects the stimulus from a slightly different angle.

visual cliff

An apparatus that tests an infant's depth perception by using patterned materials and an elevated, clear glass platform to make it appear that one side of the platform is several feet lower than the other.

Figure 4-7

Babies don't take chances

This baby is hesitant to venture beyond the safety of the visual cliff's "shallow" side, despite mom's coaxing. Clearly, the child perceives the "deep" side as threatening.

that they had learned to be afraid of cliffs (Campos, Bertenthal, & Kermonian, 1992; Campos, Hiatt, Ramsey, Henderson, & Svejda, 1978).

Apparently, locomotion is involved in the development of a fear of heights (Witherington et al., 2005). Baby animals that are able to walk shortly after birth avoid the deep side of the visual cliff when they are only a day old. And when human infants who are unable to crawl are provided with 30 to 40 hours of experience in wheeled walkers, they begin to show fear of high places (Bertenthal, Campos, & Kermonian, 1994; Campos, Bertenthal, & Kermonian, 1992). (An interesting side note: wheeled walker devices are quite dangerous. They have been associated with nearly 30,000 accidents involving infants, (American Medical Association, 1992; Marcella & McDonald, 1990). In fact, recently, Canada banned the sale of such devices.)

What is it about locomotion that triggers a fear of heights? Perhaps, motion itself in some way helps a baby to judge distances more accurately. Or, perhaps, locomotion gives the baby an opportunity to fall more often so that she begins to recognize heights as potentially dangerous. Even when an infant nearly falls, frightening a caregiver, the strong emotional reaction she evidences may prompt the baby to learn vicariously to fear heights (Campos et al., 1992; Lamb & Campos, 1982). Whatever the link, a fear of heights involves an interplay of biology and experience.

SIZE AND SHAPE CONSTANCY Regardless of how distant an object is, you can judge its size and shape. For example, even though a truck looks toylike from far away, you still perceive it as a normal-sized vehicle. This ability relies on **size constancy**, the tendency to perceive an object as constant in size, regardless of changes in the distance from which you view it and regardless of the corollary changes in the size of the object's image on the retinas of your eyes (see Figure 4-8). Research with newborns suggests that this ability may be present from birth, suggesting again how well prepared newborns are to interact with their perceptual world (Slater, Mattock, & Brown, 1990). Demonstrating that a newborn displays this or any other ability does not mean, of course, that the ability is at its full power. As the child's binocular vision develops, between 4 and 5 months of age, recognition of size constancy improves (Granrud, 2006; Kellman & Arterberry, 2006).

If older babies are able to perceive that a receding object really stays the same size despite the fact that its image grows smaller, they should also be able to perceive that an image that grows larger is of an approaching object. It is not surprising, therefore, that by 3 months of age, and perhaps even by 1 month, babies show that they relate image growth to decreasing distance by blinking when the "moving" object seems to be on a collision course with them (Kayed & van der Meer, 2000, 2007; Yonas, Arterberry, & Granrud, 1987). Moreover, infants appear to distinguish obstacles approaching on a collision versus a non-collision course (Ball & Tronick, 1971; Schmuckler, Collimore, & Dannemiller, 2007), and show a stronger looming to an approaching obstacle, which

size constancy

The tendency to perceive an object as constant in size regardless of changes in its distance from the viewer and in the image it casts on the retinas of the eyes.

Figure 4-8

Size constancy

The two blocks pictured here are exactly the same size and the viewer perceives them as the same size. However, because they are placed at different distances from the viewer, they cast retinal images of different sizes. Four-month old infants will see the blocks as different sizes, but by 6 months of age, babies have grasped the concept of size constancy and see the blocks as the same size.

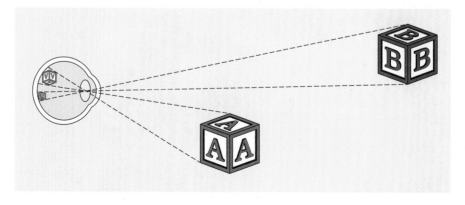

indicates a subsequent collision, compared with an approaching aperture, which indicates a possible passage through the aperture's centre (Schmuckler & Li, 1998). The fact that this ability appears earlier than size constancy may reflect the fact that the avoidance of impending collisions has survival value. Alternatively, it may simply be that the perception of an approaching object on the basis of the increasing size of its image is easier to measure than size constancy in very young babies (we simply have to record a blinking response).

Analogous to size constancy, **shape constancy** is the ability to perceive an object's shape as remaining constant despite changes in its orientation and, hence, the angle from which one views it. Shape constancy, and the related ability of form constancy, has been demonstrated quite early in infancy (Kellman, 1984; Quinn, Slater, Brown, & Hayes, 2001; Schmuckler & Proffitt, 1994), with some even suggesting that this ability may be present at birth (Slater & Morison, 1985). Perhaps, as researchers further improve their techniques for probing infants' visual capacities, we will find evidence of even earlier competence in some other areas as well.

shape constancy

The ability to perceive an object's shape as remaining constant despite changes in its orientation and the angle from which one views it.

VISUAL EXPECTATIONS Not only do babies begin to perceive colours, forms, depth, and perceptual constancies at quite an early age, they also soon start to develop expectations about events in their visual worlds (Haith & Benson, 1998). To demonstrate this remarkable ability, Haith and his co-workers (Canfield & Haith, 1991; Haith, Hazen, & Goodman, 1988) presented pictures to babies in either a regular alternating sequence (left, right, left, right) or an unpredictable sequence (left, left, right, left, and so on). When the sequence was predictable, 3-month-olds began to anticipate the location of the next picture by looking to the side on which it was going to appear. And they developed this pattern of expectations in less than a minute! Younger infants did not show this ability to anticipate a picture's location based on a regular sequence. It may be that more cognitive or perhaps biological development is needed for this ability to emerge (Tamis-LeMonda & McLure, 1995).

More recent work in this vein has shown that infants develop visual expectations based on the content of the event, such as particular colour combinations, as well as being sensitive to the temporal characteristics of when an event should occur (Adler & Haith, 2003; Adler, Haith, Arehart, & Lanthier, 2008; Wentworth, Haith, & Hood, 2002). For example, research by Scott Adler at York University (Adler et al., 2008) manipulated the temporal predictability of when particular events should occur, and found that 3-month-old infants produced more anticipation when the events were predictable in time than when the events were temporally unpredictable. These findings suggest that infants are also representing time in their event representations, and form definite expectations about what and when things should occur in the future.

Experience seems to contribute to the ability to perceive the trajectory or continuity of an object when part of the object or array of objects is obscured from view. Johnson and his colleagues (2003) showed 2- to 6-month-old infants a line or row of objects partly occluded by a screen; for example, a line of balls with several of the balls in the centre of the image covered up by a screen. Two-month-olds showed little awareness of the continuity of the line of balls; 6-month-olds were aware of it, and 4-month-olds showed such awareness only when the occlusion period was of short duration (67 milliseconds). It seems that the understanding of perceptual continuity emerges over the first six months of life. This type of understanding helps set the stage for more complex understanding of objects, discussed at greater length in Chapter 8.

This study, like others we have discussed, shows that the infant's overall level of visual ability is much greater than had been presumed only a few decades ago. It also indicates that even though the development of vision is greatly influenced by biology and its progress is rapid in the first year, visual experience plays a crucial role in this process (Johnson, 2004).

Smell, Taste, and Touch

Like vision and hearing, smell, taste, and touch are well developed at an early age. For instance, even newborns can discriminate among a variety of odours, and they show "appropriate" facial expressions in response to odours that adults rate as either pleasant or aversive. In one study, infants less than 12 hours old reacted to the odours of strawberry and banana with a look of satisfaction, whereas a whiff of fish or rotten eggs elicited a rejecting look (Steiner, 1979).

Young infants' well-developed sense of smell seems to provide another early guide to the people and things in their world. In a study in the United Kingdom, Macfarlane (1975) showed that 1-week-olds could distinguish the odour of their own mother's breast pad from the odour of the breast pad of another nursing woman. When the two pads were positioned above the infant's head, the baby turned to look at the mother's pad more than at the pad of the stranger. This preference was not evident in the first few days of life and seems to depend on babies learning to recognize their mother's special smell. Subsequent studies have shown that it is not just the odour of a mother's breast secretions that is attractive to a breast-fed baby. Breast-fed babies come to learn and prefer the overall scent of their own mothers (Porter, Makin, Davis, & Christensen, 1992). Infants also prefer the odour of milk to the odour of amniotic fluid (Marlier, Schaal, & Soussignan, 1998).

Newborns also respond selectively to different tastes. In one study, 2-hour-old infants produced facial expressions in response to sweet, sour, bitter, and salty substances, similar to the faces adults make when given these tastes (Rosenstein & Oster, 1988). Because these infants had never been fed anything but milk or formula, it appears that at least some taste preferences may be innate. Research has also shown that infant taste preferences can develop in early infancy (Liem & Mennella, 2002; Mennella & Beauchamp, 1999). Mennella and Beauchamp (1996) found that infants exposed to vanilla-flavoured milk were more accepting of the flavour of vanilla later on. Babies will accept garlic-flavoured milk if exposed to garlic during breastfeeding. Animal studies indicate that the more varied the mother's diet, the more likely it is that offspring will consume novel foods after weaning (Mennella & Beauchamp, 1993). Perhaps one benefit of breastfeeding is that "it provides an opportunity for the infant to become familiar with the flavours of the foods of her or his mother, family, and culture" (Mennella & Beauchamp, 1996, p. 19).

The sense of touch is activated long before birth (Field, 2001); indeed, it may be one of the first senses to evolve. As Klaus and colleagues (1995, p. 52) point out, "the skin is the largest sense organ of the body . . . [and] babies are surrounded and caressed by warm fluid and tissues from the beginning of fetal life. . . . [Moreover,] the lips and hands have the most touch receptors; this may explain why newborns enjoy sucking their fingers." Babies are clearly responsive to different types of touch. They show positive reactions to gentle stroking and usually negative reactions to sudden changes in temperature or texture and to uncomfortable pressure on the body, for example, when blood is drawn for testing.

Although it was once assumed that newborns were indifferent to pain, this is untrue. In fact, newborns are more sensitive to pain than older infants (Axia, Bonichini, & Benini, 1999). Evidence of the infant's sensitivity to painful procedures comes from studies of infant stress reactions; for example, male infants have shown higher levels of plasma cortisol (a stress marker) after a circumcision than before the surgery (Gunnar, Malone, Vance, & Fisch, 1985). Research has also demonstrated gender differences in pain: females show stronger behavioural reactions to pain than males do (Fuller, 2002). Finally, there are some reports of cross-cultural differences in pain response. Rosmus, Johnson, Chan, & Yang (2000), for instance, observed that 2-month-old Canadian-born Chinese infants showed a greater response to a routine immunization than did non-Chinese Canadian babies.

Not only do babies respond to touch—recall the positive impact that massage had on preterm babies (Field, 2001)—but before the end of their first year, they can learn to discriminate among objects using only their sense of touch (Streri & Pêcheux, 1986a). Researchers found that 2-day-old infants showed habituation to an object placed in their hands, suggesting that tactile or haptic information can be learned at this early age (Streri, Lhote, & Dutilleul, 2000). After the infants habituated to the first object, the researchers placed a new object in the baby's hands—and holding time increased. Videotape analysis showed that the infants were not just grasping the object rigidly; small movements of the baby's fingers were observed. And even more recently, Sann and Streri (2008) demonstrated that newborns could even transfer information about an object's shape and texture between their two hands, without any visual experience of the object. Studies like these, and others, suggest that neonates have tactile sensitivity to object shape and that they use touch to explore the environment and encode this information.

Intermodal Perception: How Infants Coordinate Sensory Information

When an infant sees a ball bounce or when her father speaks to her, does she perceive separate visual and auditory events in each case? Or does she match the sight of the moving ball with the sound the ball makes as it hits the floor, and the sight of her father's lip and mouth movements with the sound of the voice she hears? **Intermodal perception** is the use of sensory information from more than one modality—in these examples, both vision and hearing—to identify a stimulus and make sense of it.

Researchers have explored babies' ability to perceive intermodally by pairing two different sensory systems, such as vision and touch, or vision and hearing. Exploring the first of these pairs, Meltzoff and Borton (1979) designed two different pacifiers, one smooth and one knobby (see Figure 4-9), and gave 4-week-old infants a chance to suck one or the other of them. Later, when the researchers let their small participants look at both pacifiers—but not suck on them—the infants looked longer at the pacifier that they had sucked on earlier than at the unfamiliar one. Given that infants this age have had little opportunity to simultaneously touch and look at objects, the researchers concluded that human beings are able to recognize and coordinate information obtained from different sensory modalities (Meltzoff, 1981). More recently, Sann and Streri (2007, 2008) studied the visual–tactile intermodal perception of object shape and object texture in newborns. These researchers found that texture was bidirectionally intermodally perceived (e.g., there was transfer from vision to touch and from touch to vision), but that shape failed to be bidirectional, with infants visually recognizing a shape they hand previously held (e.g., tactile to visual intermodal transfer), but failing to tactually recognize a shape they had previous seen (e.g., visual-to-tactile intermodal transfer).

Others, however, have questioned whether such young infants truly do have these intermodal sensitivities. Maurer, Stager, and Mondloch (1999), for example, attempted

intermodal perception

The use of sensory information from more than one modality to identify a stimulus; also, the apprehension of a stimulus already identified by one modality by means of another.

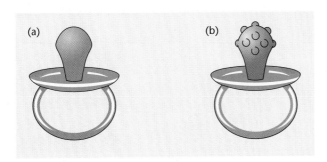

Figure 4-9

Testing a baby's intermodal perceptual abilities

Just by looking at these pacifiers, 4-week-old babies knew which one they had sucked earlier, no matter whether it was the smooth (a) or the knobby (b) one.

Source: Meltzoff & Borton, 1979.

to replicate Meltzoff and Borton's original finding, as well as to provide some important controls for infants' preferences to simply look at one side over the other (a side bias), or to watch one stimulus over the other (a stimulus bias). In this more controlled situation, and across three separate studies, these authors were unable to find any reliable evidence of intermodal perception of shape by 1-month-old infants.

Despite the skepticism engendered by Maurer et al.'s study of the intermodal abilities of 1-month-olds, there does seem to be reliable evidence of intermodal perception of vision and touch by about 3 to 4 months of age, although there are still limitations in this ability up to at least 6 months (Rose, Gottfried, & Bridger, 1981; Streri, Lemoine, & Devouche, 2008). Streri and colleagues (2008), for instance, found that although both 2- and 6-month-olds demonstrated intermodal perception of object shape, only the 6-month-olds were able to transfer information about object shape between the two hands. Finally, there has also been the suggestion that recognizing the equivalence between vision and touch is easier when touch is the basis of the initial information; thus, touch to vision is easier than vision to touch (Streri & Molina, 1993). One explanation given for this asymmetry is that these two modalities may be sensitive to different stimulus properties, rather than to common aspects across the two modalities (Rose, 1990, 1994).

Studying when infants can coordinate vision and hearing, Elizabeth Spelke (1987) used two animated films and accompanying soundtracks of a kangaroo and a donkey, each bouncing at a different rate and producing sounds in keeping with its bouncing. Spelke then showed these two films, side by side, to 4-month-old babies as she played only one of the soundtracks from a speaker positioned between the two screens. The infants looked at the animal whose bouncing "matched" the sounds they were hearing. Because the infants had never seen or heard kangaroos or bouncing before, their reactions were clearly not the result of prior learning. Other studies have shown that babies this age can also "match" the sounds of particular words being spoken with the sight of a face whose lips are synchronized with those sounds (Rosenblum, Schmuckler, & Johnson, 1997), and can even form arbitrary visual and auditory associations early in life (Brookes et al., 2001; Slater, Quinn, Brown, & Hayes, 1999).

Intermodal matching can also help infants determine whether an object is approaching or retreating. Pickens (1994) showed 5-month-old infants films of a toy train either approaching the viewers or moving away from them (see Figure 4-10). Infants looked more at the approaching film when the decibel level of the soundtrack increased and more at the retreating train when the sound of the train diminished. Infants did not show evidence of matching in other conditions in which the soundtracks were paired with videos depicting changes in the brightness of the train's image or showing the train moving horizontally with no change in its size. This experiment suggests that infants may be aware of the rules that guide the integration of visual and sound information and that they can use this information to help them judge distance.

The findings we've discussed in this section challenge the commonly held view that babies begin life experiencing unrelated sensations in each sensory system and

Figure 4-10

Combining vision and hearing to detect distance and direction

Babies can match an engine sound that is becoming louder with the toy train in photo a, which is approaching the watching infant, and an engine sound that is growing fainter with the train shown in photo b, which is moving away from the infant.

Source: Pickens, 1994.

(a)   (b)

only gradually learn to put the separate pieces together. At 1 month old, infants can integrate vision and touch, and babies as young as 4 months of age appear to experience a world of integrated visual and auditory sensations.

For Thought and Discussion

1. Infant study methodologies, such as habituation and preferential looking, are based on the assumptions that infants respond to novelty over familiarity and prefer complex to simple stimuli. What do you think of such assumptions? Given these assumptions, what are the limitations of these procedures?

2. Why do you think infants might treat human faces as special? Is this a result of simple perceptual preference, or is there a social component as well?

3. You and your partner have just had a baby girl last week. Your mother hovers over your new child, picks her up, coos in her face, and smiles and talks gibberish to her. After a week of this, your mother announces that your new daughter definitely recognizes and loves her new "nana." What would you tell your mother about your 3-week-old's visual perception abilities and, thus, the likelihood that she actually recognizes her grandmother?

EARLY LEARNING AND MEMORY   LO7

Our discussions so far have concentrated on a particular kind of infant learning—that is, what babies know about the world's objects and their properties. Much of the research we've described has assumed that as babies develop and have experience interacting with people and things, they learn more about the world. How babies learn—in fact, how all humans learn—is a topic of long-standing interest to psychologists. As you will recall from Chapter 1, psychologists have been particularly interested in the process of learning through imitation and learning through association, as in classical and operant conditioning. In this section, we not only explore these kinds of learning in infants, we also consider what these and other kinds of learning abilities tell us about a baby's memory capabilities. As you will see, basic learning processes appear to be present very early in life. What changes over the course of development seems to be the nature of the information that babies are capable of learning and the speed and efficiency with which they learn.

Classical and Operant Conditioning

For years, psychologists have debated the issue of how early babies can be classically conditioned, and the controversy is not over yet (Rovee-Collier, 1997). For a refresher on the mechanisms of classical conditioning, look at Figure 4-11 on the next page, in which we diagram the way a child might become conditioned to fear his doctor. There is some evidence that newborns can learn by association or conditioning, especially in biologically meaningful contexts such as feeding. In one study, babies as young as 2 hours old learned to associate a stroke on the head with delivery of a sugar solution to their mouths, and, eventually, the stroke alone elicited puckering and sucking responses (Blass, Ganchrow, & Steiner, 1984). However, newborns have more difficulty learning associations that involve unpleasant stimuli, such as loud noises or things that are painful (Rovee-Collier, 1987). Perhaps because human infants have parents to protect them, it may be less critical at an early age to learn the stimuli associated with unpleasant events. And, interestingly, there is evidence that neurological mechanisms aiding the formation of negative associations develop later than neurological mechanisms aiding positive associations (Rovee-Collier, 1987; Rovee-Collier & Shyi, 1992).

Figure 4-11

How a baby may be conditioned to fear a doctor

At their first meeting (stage 1), the baby may show no particular reaction to the doctor, but when the doctor gives the baby a painful injection that causes the baby to cry (stage 2), the baby may expect the same pain at the next meeting with the doctor (stage 3) and cry even if the child does not see a needle in her hand.

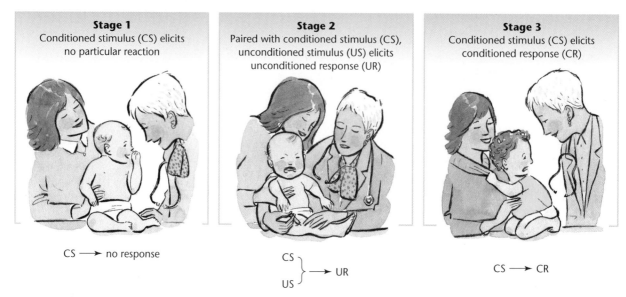

Stage 1
Conditioned stimulus (CS) elicits no particular reaction

CS ⟶ no response

Stage 2
Paired with conditioned stimulus (CS), unconditioned stimulus (US) elicits unconditioned response (UR)

CS ⎱
       ⎰ ⟶ UR
US ⎰

Stage 3
Conditioned stimulus (CS) elicits conditioned response (CR)

CS ⟶ CR

Operant conditioning involves learning to exhibit (or inhibit) some behaviour because of the rewarding (or punishing) consequences it brings. Just as babies can be classically conditioned, they can also learn by operant conditioning (Gewirtz & Peláez-Nogueras, 1992). Sandra Trehub and her colleagues, for example, have developed an operant conditioning head-turn procedure for the study of infant auditory and musical relations (as described earlier in this chapter). In this procedure, the infant is trained to turn her head to the side whenever she hears a change in an auditory sequence and is rewarded for correct turns by seeing a little motorized monkey light up and clap its hands. This procedure—and the propensity to learn through operant conditioning in general—provides a powerful technique for testing basic capacities in infancy.

As in the case of classical conditioning, successful operant conditioning in newborns typically involves behaviours such as sucking and head turning (related to the rooting reflex), behaviours that are components of feeding and thus of considerable importance to the baby's survival. Researchers take advantage of these early behaviours to investigate how infants learn specific behaviours.

LO8 Learning through Imitation

Acquiring behaviours through classical or operant conditioning (displaying a behaviour, being rewarded, repeating the behaviour, being reinforced again, and so on) is uneconomical in terms of time and energy because to be learned, the behaviour has to be experienced directly by the infant. Fortunately, infants are able to learn a great deal without any overt reward or punishment simply by observing the behaviour of parents, siblings, peers, teachers, and other people. As you learned in Chapter 1, this is observational learning, or learning through imitation.

Imitation begins early in life; it may even be possible in the first few days after birth. Meltzoff and Moore (1983), for example, found that babies between 7 and 72 hours old imitated adults who opened their mouths wide or stuck their tongues out—these movements that are components of the sucking response. These findings are somewhat controversial. Many developmental theories, such as Piaget's, argue that imitation requires the capacity for symbolic representation, which is generally not achieved until the end of the second year of life (see Chapters 1 and 8). Others argue that the infant who sticks his tongue out at the sight of an adult doing the same thing may not be truly imitating another's behaviour (Anisfeld, 1991). There is evidence that the sight of any protruding object may cause newborns to stick out their tongues, not in imitation but because they see these objects as suckable.

This woman and her child are playing a lively game of "stick-out-your tongue," with the baby trying to imitate mom. Although the game might be silly, for infants, imitation provides a powerful means for learning all sorts of different behaviours.

Babies, however, soon become capable of genuine imitation. Nine-month-olds, for example, can imitate a series of modelled behaviours (such as shaking plastic eggs filled with pebbles) immediately after seeing the behaviours and 9-month-olds can also carry out these imitations both immediately and after an interval of 24 hours, with no opportunity to practise the behaviours in between (Herbert, Gross, & Hayne, 2006). At 14 months of age, infants can delay (or defer) imitation over a period of one week (Meltzoff, 1988b). And between 14 and 18 months, they cannot only defer imitation, they can generalize it to new settings. For example, children this age who saw a peer model a new behaviour at a daycare could imitate that behaviour two days later in their own homes (Hanna & Meltzoff, 1993). By 2 years of age, children can reproduce behaviours later, even when the materials they use to carry out the behaviours have changed (Herbert & Hayne, 2000).

Canadian Researchers, Imitation

What mechanisms underlie the ability of babies, especially young ones, to imitate behaviours that they see others perform? Legerstee (1991), for example, has suggested that such early imitation is a social response. Supporting this argument is her finding that infants will more likely imitate an adult who is modelling gestures (tongue protrusions and mouth openings), compared with two objects simulating these gestures. Others, however, have suggested that imitation actually involves some form of intermodal matching (Meltzoff, 1990; Nelson, Thomas, & De Haan, 2006). For instance, newborns might form cognitive representations of the behaviour they saw a model perform; they would then have to translate these initially visual perceptions into movements and actions that they themselves could perform. This interpretation suggests that babies may be ready for some form of representational thought at an earlier age than had been proposed, and that imitative learning relies on transforming these representations into action.

Memory in Babies

Even very young infants can remember what they see and hear over relatively long time spans. Two researchers found that newborns could remember a previously seen visual event over a 24-hour period (Werner & Siqueland, 1978). The babies in this study altered their sucking patterns when the colour and pattern of a visual stimulus changed, even though they had not seen that stimulus for nearly a day. Other studies show that newborns can also remember speech sounds over a similar time period (Bauer, 2007; Swain, Zelazo, & Clifton, 1993; Ungerer, Brody, & Zelazo, 1978). In one study of mothers and their 14-day-old infants, the mothers repeated the words *tinder* and *beagle* to their babies 60 times a day for 13 days (780 exposures); as you may imagine, 2-week-olds rarely hear these particular words. At 14 and 28 hours after this marathon training ended, the researchers tested the babies' memory for the words. The infants showed not only that they remembered the words but that they recognized them better than their own names.

Older babies have even more impressive memory capabilities. In one study, using a variant of the preferential looking procedure, Courage and Howe (1998) tested 3-month-olds' recognition for moving stimuli after retention intervals ranging from one minute up to three months. These researchers found evidence of recognition memory after one minute and one day (indicated by a preference for a novel item) and after one and three months (as shown by a preference for a familiar stimulus). Thus, it appears that with a short time period, infants prefer a new stimulus, and after a longer interval, they actually prefer a familiar one.

Others have found similarly impressive memory in 3-month-old infants using a somewhat different procedure. In this work, 3-month-old infants first learned to make a mobile move by kicking one of their legs, to which the researcher had attached a long ribbon that was also attached to the mobile suspension bar (see Figure 4-12) (Rovee-Collier & Gerhardstein, 1997). Usually, babies this age will forget the connection between a kick and a bobbing mobile after about eight days. However, with a brief reminder before being tested, these little individuals could remember the connection for as long as four weeks. The reminder, provided roughly 24 hours before a memory test was given, consisted simply of letting the babies see the mobile bobbing about for three minutes. During the reminder session, the babies' legs were not attached to the mobile, so they could not relearn the connection. The visual reminder was enough, however.

Babies who had experienced the reminder kicked their legs more often in the testing session (when the ankle ribbon was again attached) than babies who had learned the leg-mobile connection but who had been given no reminder of it in the interim. And this memory can even be quite long term. In one study, Hartshorn (2003) has shown that, for 6-month-old infants, brief reminders at monthly intervals (7, 8, 9, 12, and 18 months) allowed these infants to remember the behaviour when tested again at 24 months, 1 and a half years later than the original learning. Another cue that helps babies remember is the context or setting in which the original learning took place (Rovee-Collier, 1999). Babies were able to remember better when tested in the same setting in which they originally learned, such as the daycare centre, rather than in a novel context, such as the laboratory (Hayne, McDonald, & Barr, 1997).

Figure 4-12

Memory lessons for babies

Rovee-Collier found that when she taught 3-month-old infants to make a mobile move by attaching the mobile to one of their legs with a ribbon (photo a), the babies forgot the association between kicking and moving the mobile after about a week. When this researcher gave these infants a "reminder" session, however, during which she removed the ribbon so that they could look at the mobile but could not make it move (photo b), and then reattached the ribbon (as in photo a), she found that most babies were able to remember the association for as long as four weeks.

Source: Rovee-Collier, 1986.

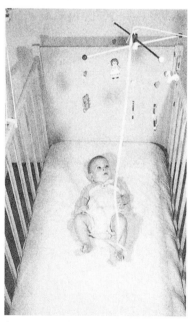

(a)

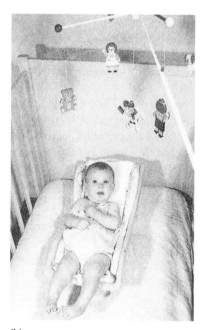

(b)

From the age of 3 months, babies' memory powers improve even further. Consider a study in which infants who were about 10 months old saw pictures (e.g., a whale), touched objects (e.g., a clothespin), or heard sounds (e.g., a bell, a rattle). Upon returning to the laboratory when they were 3 years old—two years later—these children were more likely to touch the objects and recognize the sounds that they had been exposed to on their earlier visit than were the children in a control group who had not had the earlier experience in the laboratory (Myers, Clifton, & Clarkson, 1987). This study suggests that children have some memory of events that happened to them before they could even walk or talk. Similar evidence comes from the work of Bauer (1996, 2002), who found that 13-month-old infants were able to remember a simple sequence (e.g., putting teddy bear to bed) after an eight-month delay (see Figure 4-13). These memory studies with infants and young children have led developmental psychologists to re-evaluate the widely held belief that infants and children younger than age 3 cannot recall the events of their lives. And recent research in neuroscience is providing new ways of studying and understanding what is developing in the infant brain that supports these early memory abilities (Bauer, 2007). It is increasingly apparent that babies and young children can recall much more of their early lives than we thought possible. In Chapter 9, we will revisit the topic of memory and examine in more detail the kinds of strategies that children develop to help them remember.

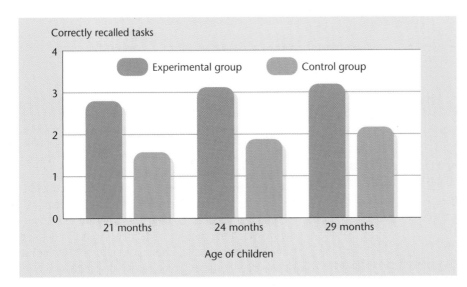

Figure 4-13

Young children have surprisingly good memories

Bauer and her colleagues tested young children, ranging in age from 21 to 29 months, on their memory for events in which they had participated eight months earlier, such as setting up an inclined track and letting a car roll down the track, and found that the youngest group did very nearly as well as the oldest. All three groups recalled significantly more of the tasks than control groups in which children had had no experience with the tasks.

Source: Adapted from Bauer, 1996.

For Thought and Discussion

1. How might you explain intermodal perception on the basis of learning or associationist theory? Are there any problems with this explanation?

2. What are the implications of habituation procedures for the existence of infant memory? In what way does habituation rely on memory?

3. What are some of the limitations inherent in the research by Andrew Meltzoff and his colleagues on infant imitation? Put differently, do you think this is evidence that infants are truly imitating adult behaviour? If not, what would make it more convincing?

Making the Connections 4

There are many links between concepts and ideas in one area of development and concepts and ideas in other areas. Here are some of the connections between ideas in Chapter 4 and discussions in other chapters of this book.

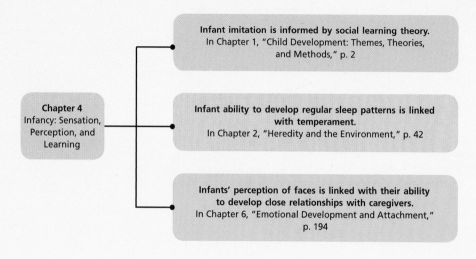

Chapter 4
Infancy: Sensation, Perception, and Learning

Infant imitation is informed by social learning theory.
In Chapter 1, "Child Development: Themes, Theories, and Methods," p. 2

Infant ability to develop regular sleep patterns is linked with temperament.
In Chapter 2, "Heredity and the Environment," p. 42

Infants' perception of faces is linked with their ability to develop close relationships with caregivers.
In Chapter 6, "Emotional Development and Attachment," p. 194

SUMMARY

- Babies can see, hear, and respond to interesting sights, sounds, and other sensory stimuli at a much earlier age than was originally believed.

The Newborn

- The newborn, or **neonate**, has a repertoire of **reflexes**, or involuntary responses to external stimuli. Many of these reflexes disappear during the first year of life.
- Babies experience predictable changes in state, or recurring patterns of alertness and activity level, ranging from vigorous, wakeful activity to quiet, regular sleep.
- Between the ages of 2 and 4 months, babies may succumb to **sudden infant death syndrome (SIDS)**. Preventive measures include the cessation of parental smoking, preventing infants from sleeping on their stomachs, and parent and infant co-sleeping.
- The **autostimulation theory** proposes that infants spend more than twice as much time as adults in **REM sleep** because such sleep stimulates higher brain centres that, in turn, promote development of the central nervous system.

- Crying, which is an effective means of early communication, follows distinct patterns that also change with development.
- Although there are wide differences among individuals, genders, and races in soothability, certain caregiver techniques, such as holding the baby on the shoulder or swaddling her, are widely successful in helping calm a distressed baby. Infants can also help to soothe themselves by sucking on a thumb or pacifier.
- Tests of reflexes may be combined with other assessments to gauge the health, maturity, and capacities of a newborn. The **Brazelton Neonatal Assessment Scale** is one widely used assessment tool.

The Infant's Sensory and Perceptual Capacities

- To study infants' sensations and perceptions, investigators often make use of the infant's tendency to **habituate**, or become used to, a given stimulus. Another technique is to use the **visual preference method**, in which researchers pinpoint a baby's preference for looking at one of two alternative stimuli.
- At birth, a newborn's hearing is very well developed. Newborns can distinguish among different kinds of sounds and tell what direction a sound

comes from. They are also predisposed to respond to human voices.

- Although visual capacities continue to develop throughout the first year of life, newborns are sensitive to brightness and can track moving objects, although they have poor **visual acuity** at distances beyond close range. During the first three months, acuity improves and babies improve their ability to perceive patterns, including the patterning of human faces.
- Accurate distance perception improves with age, too, as babies begin to coordinate their two eyes and use **stereoscopic vision**. Experiments with the **visual cliff** demonstrate that by the time babies are between 6 and 14 months old, they are capable of depth perception.
- Newborns can discriminate among a variety of odours, and by 1 week of age, they have learned to distinguish their mother's smells from those of other people. Newborns are also able to discriminate different tastes.
- The sense of touch is activated long before birth, and newborns are clearly responsive to both positive and negative types of touch. Contrary to past beliefs, they are highly sensitive to pain. Infants also quickly learn to discriminate among objects only on the basis of their sense of touch.
- From a very early age, babies display **intermodal perception**, integrating information from two different senses, such as the sounds that go with a certain sight.

Early Learning and Memory

- Even newborns can be classically conditioned when a previously neutral stimulus is repeatedly paired with a pleasant stimulus that naturally elicits some involuntary response. Young babies do not seem to be biologically prepared to learn such associations easily.
- Newborns can also learn to emit a certain behaviour when that behaviour is repeatedly rewarded. Successful *operant conditioning* in newborns typically involves a behaviour like sucking, which is a component of feeding and of considerable importance to the baby's survival.
- Although newborns may be capable of some imitation, the basis of the ability to imitate others and the amount of such behaviour the child displays changes significant with age.
- When given adequate retrieval cues, babies can remember information over substantial periods of time.

Jacob Lawrence (1917–2000). *The Life of Harriet Tubman*, #4: On a hot summer day about 1820, a group of slave children were tumbling in the sandy soil, and among them was one Harriet Tubman. Dorchester County, Maryland.
1940, Hampton University Museum.

Chapter 5

The Child's Growth: Brain, Body, Motor Skills, and Sexual Maturation

LEARNING OBJECTIVES

After reading this chapter, you should be able to

LO1 Describe the growth of the brain during infancy; include the concepts of hemispheric specialization and laterality; learn about aspects of musical and speech processing and lateralization.

LO2 Cite and discuss the evidence for the effects of the environment on brain plasticity.

LO3 Describe the course of motor development in the area of hand skills; discuss the concept of "visually guided" reaching.

LO4 Describe the course of motor development in the area of locomotion; compare the different theoretical approaches to the development of walking.

LO5 Discuss the roles of experience and culture in the development of motor skills; give examples and relate these to the psychological implications of locomotion; discuss the idea of perception-action coupling and some experimental examples of this concept.

LO6 Explain the principles that guide physical growth, and discuss the general trends in rates of maturation.

LO7 Look at the differences in growth and the possible explanations for these differences.

LO8 Discuss the factors that influence obesity and other eating disorders; know the causes for these problems and strategies for helping children who experience them.

LO9 Describe the course of puberty for boys and girls; include social and emotional changes as well as physical.

LO10 Discuss some of the factors that determine early versus late maturation, and identify possible outcomes of this variation.

Canadian Researchers

Laboratory Web Sites

Tina's development was rapid from the start. She crawled and walked early, and by her first birthday, she was forcing her parents to put their favourite vases on a high shelf out of her reach. When she was 11 years old and in the sixth grade, she reached sexual maturity, well ahead of her classmates. Jason, in contrast, grew at a more leisurely pace. Breakable objects were safe in Jason's house until he was 14 months old, and Jason was nearly 16 years old when he experienced his pubescent growth spurt.

The differences between these two children illustrate two common findings. First, there is enormous variation in the rates at which children develop, and second, girls usually develop more rapidly than boys. In this chapter, we examine children's growth and motor development. First, we explore the development of the brain and the way genetic and environmental forces work together to determine brain growth and function? Next, we explore the motor and growth patterns that infants and children follow and the factors that speed up or slow down these patterns. We answer questions such as, "Are children growing taller and if so, why?" "What are the causes and consequences of being too thin or too fat?" "What role does nutrition play in growth?" "Can children who are deprived early of such things as proper nutrition "catch up" in growth?" Finally, we explore puberty, its characteristics, and the factors that influence its course. ●

1 BRAIN DEVELOPMENT IN INFANCY

Before we look at the growth of the brain, it is reasonable to consider what role the development of the brain plays in our theories of child development. Looking at this question historically, Segalowitz (1994) has argued that up to now there is really very little in our theories of development that rely on some specific aspect of the developmental pattern of brain growth. However, with the advent of new technology for assessing brain growth, developmental neuropsychology is now in a position to usefully relate brain development to behavioural development. Thus, understanding the course of brain development can now help refine, and even drive, developmental theory. It is within this context, then, that we look more specifically at how the brain develops, and the implications of such growth on children's behaviour.

In the prenatal period, as Figure 5-1 dramatically illustrates, the brain grows very rapidly, and it continues to grow at an amazing pace. Although at birth an infant's brain weighs only about one-fourth as much as a mature brain, by the time the baby is about 6 months old, his brain weighs half of what an adult brain weighs, and the brain of the 2-year-old child weighs 75 percent as much as an adult brain (see Figure 5-2; Shonkoff & Phillips, 2000).

The largest portion of the human brain consists of the two connected hemispheres that make up the **cerebrum**, a mass of tissue that embodies not only attributes particular to humans—such as speech and self-awareness—attributes shared with other vertebrate animals—such as sensory perception, motor abilities, and memory. The covering layer of the human cerebrum, the **cerebral cortex** (see Figure 5-3 on page 158), is highly convoluted and contains about 90 percent of the brain's cell bodies. Although we do not yet know how these cells control complicated traits, we do know that specific functions, such as seeing, hearing, moving, feeling emotions, thinking, and speaking, can be traced to specific regions of the cerebral cortex.

The Turning Points chart on pages 160 and 161 highlights some significant milestones in the development of the brain as well as important steps in the child's motor and physical growth; you may find it useful to refer to this chart as you read through this chapter.

cerebrum

The two connected hemispheres of the brain.

cerebral cortex

The covering layer of the cerebrum that contains the cells that control specific functions, such as seeing, hearing, moving, and thinking.

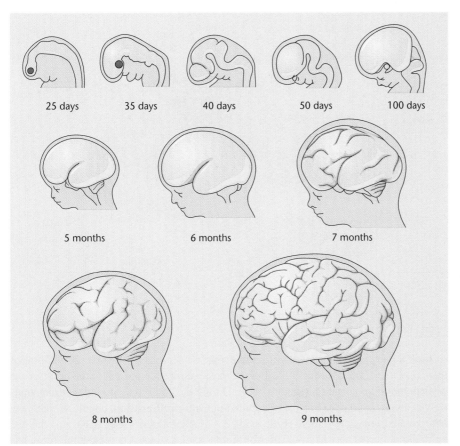

Figure 5-1

Fetal brain development

As the brain develops, the front part expands to form the cerebrum—the large, convoluted upper mass that in the adult dominates the upper and side portions of the brain. The cerebrum is covered by the cerebral cortex (see Figure 5-3 on the next page), specific areas of which are devoted to particular functions, such as motor, visual, and auditory activities. (The first five of the drawings in this figure have been enlarged to show details.)

Source: From *A Child's World*, 7th ed. by Restak, p. 172. Copyright © 1996 The McGraw-Hill Companies. Reprinted with permission.

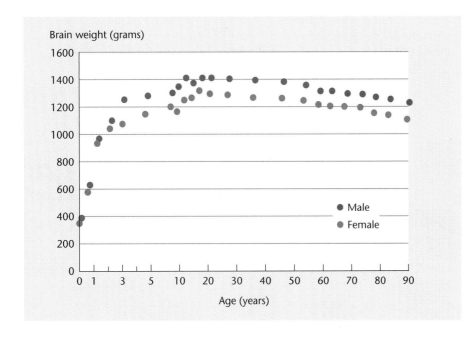

Figure 5-2

How brain weight increases with age

In this figure, the age scale for the early years has been expanded to show this period of rapid growth more clearly. As human beings mature, male brains tend to be heavier than female brains because of men's larger body size. Although scientists are discovering other differences between the brains of women and men, none of these differences have differential effects on either gender's intellectual abilities.

Source: Rosenzweig, Leiman, & Breedlove, 1996.

Figure 5-3

The brain's cortex

The cortex is divided into four *lobes*—frontal, temporal, occipital, and parietal—and specific areas within the lobes tend to specialize in particular functions. The left hemisphere, shown here, is generally associated with the processing of language, whereas the right hemisphere plays a greater role in visual and spatial processing. Because of the brain's plasticity, however, functions lost because of damage to a hemisphere, lobe, or area may be compensated for by another brain region.

Source: Postlethwait & Hopson, 1995.

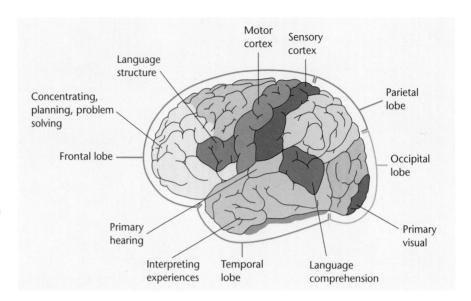

neuron

A cell in the body's nervous system, consisting of a cell body, a long projection called an axon, and several shorter projections called dendrites; neurons send and receive neural impulses, or messages, throughout the brain and nervous system.

neuron proliferation

The rapid proliferation of neurons in the developing organism's brain.

glial cell

A nerve cell that supports and protects neurons and serves to encase them in sheaths of *myelin.*

Neurons and Synapses

At birth a baby's brain has most of its **neurons**, or nerve cells—100 to 200 billion of them (LeDoux, 2002; Nash, 1997). In fact, most neurons are present in the brain by the seventh month of gestation (Rakic, 1995). During the embryonic period, neurons multiply at a very rapid pace in a process called **neuron proliferation**; about 250,000 new neurons are born every minute (Kolb et al., 2003). Neurologists used to assume that the brain did not grow new neurons after birth, but studies suggest that the adult brain has the capacity to regenerate nerve cells (Gould et al., 1999; Rosenzweig et al., 1996).

Whether or not we grow new neurons, after birth, the brain increases in size. It gets bigger because existing neurons grow and the connections between them proliferate. **Glial cells**, which surround and protect neurons, also grow. These cells also provide neurons with structural support, regulate their nutrient, and repair neural tissue. Some glial cells are responsible for the important task of **myelination**, in which parts of neurons are covered with layers of a fatty, membranous wrapping called *myelin* (see Figure 5-4). This insulation makes the neuron more efficient in transmitting information (Johnson, 1998). Most myelination occurs during the first two years of life but some continues into adulthood, a reminder that change in the brain is a lifelong process (Sampaio & Truwit, 2001).

Figure 5-4

A myelinated neuron

The neuron's axon terminates in synaptic knobs, which, in synaptic connection with the dendrites of another neuron (see Figure 5-5) or with other types of cells, transmit messages through the nervous system. The myelin sheaths that encase much of the axon facilitate the transmission of signals rapidly and efficiently. Neurons are the longest cells in the human body and may reach more than 3 feet in length.

Source: From *Fundamentals of Anatomy & Physiology*, 3rd ed., by Martini, figure 12-7b, p. 389. Copyright © 1995 Prentice Hall, Inc., Upper Saddle River, NJ. Reprinted with permission.

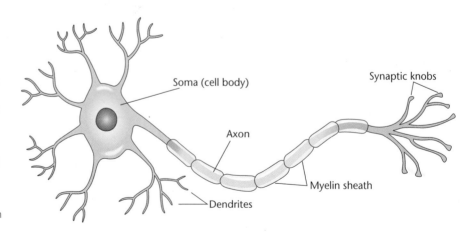

Neurons are "always on the move" (Rosenzweig et al., 1996, p. 105) in the process of migrating to their final location. Guided by neurochemical processes, this **neural migration** ensures that all parts of the brain are served by a sufficient number of neurons. The absence of sufficient neurons in their proper locations is associated with various forms of mental disability and with disorders such as dyslexia and schizophrenia (Johnson, 1998, 2005; Kolb et al., 2003).

Perhaps as essential as the neurons themselves are the connections between neurons, known as **synapses**. At these specialized junctions the extended *axon* of one neuron transmits a message to the projected *dendrites* of another neuron, usually by means of chemicals that cross the small space between the neurons (see Figure 5-5). This activity is crucial to survival and learning, for as the brain's neurons receive input from the environment they create new synapses, allowing for increasingly complex communications. **Synaptogenesis**, or the forming of synapses, begins early in prenatal life, as soon as neurons begin to evolve. The brain forms many more synapses than neurons; for example, at birth, in the brain's visual cortex alone, there are 2,500 synapses for every neuron; when the child is about 2 years old, when there are about 15,000 synapses for every neuron (Huttenlocher, 1999, 2002; Huttenlocher & Dabholkar, 1997).

Are all these neurons and synapses necessary? Do they continue to function throughout life? The answer to both questions is no. The brain is programmed to create more nerve cells and more connections between these cells than are needed. With development, two processes reduce the number of neurons and connecting fibres (Sowell et al., 2003). When new synapses are formed, some surrounding neurons die in what is called **neuronal death** (Webb, Monk, & Nelson, 2001) or *programmed cell death* (Kandel, Schwartz, & Jessel, 2000), apparently to provide more space for these crucial loci of information transmission. In **synaptic pruning**, the brain disposes of a neuron's axons and dendrites if that particular neuron is not often stimulated (Abitz et al., 2007; see Figure 5-6 on page 162). This frees up space for new synaptic connections (Webb et al., 2001). The goals of both neuronal death and synaptic pruning are to increase the speed, efficiency, and complexity of transmissions between neurons and to allow room for new connections that develop as the child encounters new experiences (Huttenlocher, 1994; Kolb et al., 2003). Loss in this case leads to a gain for the developing organism.

myelination

The process by which glial cells encase neurons in sheaths of the fatty substance *myelin*.

neural migration

The movement of neurons within the brain that ensures that all brain areas have a sufficient number of neural connections.

synapse

A specialized site of intercellular communication where information is exchanged between nerve cells, usually by means of a chemical *neurotransmitter*.

synaptogenesis

The forming of synapses.

neuronal death

The death of some neurons that surround newly formed synaptic connections among other neurons.

synaptic pruning

The brain's disposal of the axon and dendrites of a neuron that is not often stimulated.

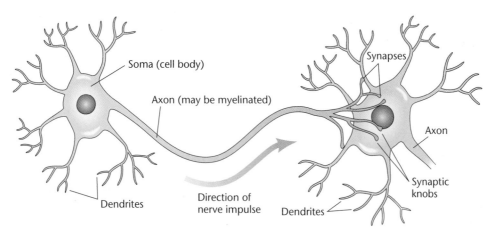

Figure 5-5

Synaptic connection between two neurons

Across the small space between one neuron's synaptic knobs and the dendrites or soma of another neuron, a chemical substance effects the transfer of information.

Source: From *Fundamentals of Anatomy & Physiology*, 3rd ed., by Martini, figure 12-7d, p. 389. Copyright © 1995 Prentice Hall, Inc., Upper Saddle River, NJ. Reprinted with permission.

Turning Points

GROWTH OF THE CHILD'S BRAIN, BODY, AND MOTOR SKILLS

AT BIRTH
- Infant's brain weighs one-quarter of adult brain weight; it has 100 to 200 billion neurons and 2,500 synapses for every neuron. Baby generally assumes fetal position.

EARLY INFANCY
- Baby shows some evidence of hemispheric specialization. Most infants show right-hand dominance. When baby is held with feet touching flat surface, she makes stepping motions that resemble walking; this response disappears at about 2 months.

ABOUT 2 MONTHS
- Motor cortex of infant's brain begins to control voluntary movement. Baby lifts head and shoulders off mattress.

3 MONTHS
- Within first 3 months, baby doubles his weight.

3–4 MONTHS
- Baby looks at and swipes at objects, retains toys put into her hand, but makes no contact with objects on a table. She holds her head up for extended time, plays with her fingers, and kicks actively.

4 MONTHS
- Baby sustains head control and rolls from his tummy onto his back; sits with support.

4–5 MONTHS
- Baby contacts toys on table; grasps block precariously.

5 MONTHS
- Baby sits on adult's lap and grasps object; rolls from back to tummy, makes incipient crawling movements.

5–6 MONTHS
- There may be some indication of an inherited tendency to be overweight.

6–7 MONTHS
- Baby bangs, shakes, and transfers toys from hand to hand; uses palmar grasp with a block; tries to grasp a raisin with whole hand.

7 MONTHS
- Baby sits alone.

Note: Developmental events described in this and other Turning Points charts represent overall trends identified in research studies. Individual children vary greatly in the ages at which they achieve these developmental changes. Milestones in sexual maturation are covered in Table 5-3 on page 187.

Sources: Adolph & Berger, 2006; Bertenthal & Clifton, 1998; Kopp, 1994; Shirley, 1931.

ABOUT 8 MONTHS	• Baby uses finger grasp with block, scissors grasp with raisin. Begins creeping; pulls up into unsteady stand but can't get back down; overall body control is better, with fewer unintended movements.
ABOUT 8 OR 9 MONTHS	• The brain's hippocampus, which aids in memory processes, becomes fully functional.
ABOUT 9 MONTHS	• Baby holds one block in each hand; approaches a raisin with index finger. Easily moves between sitting and lying; sitting is balanced and steady; stands holding furniture.
10 MONTHS	• Baby begins cruising (creeping); stands on toes while holding on to something but stands alone unsteadily; begins to use some implements, such as spoons.
11 MONTHS	• Baby is obsessed with learning to walk—walks when led; cruises till exhausted; feeds self with thumb and forefinger.
11–12 MONTHS	• Uses forefinger grasp of block and pincer grasp of raisin.
12–15 MONTHS	• Child's brain has about half as many synapses as adult brain; synaptic pruning gradually reduces this number. Child stands alone and walks without assistance.
18 MONTHS	• Child runs and gallops.
2 YEARS	• In most children, right-handedness is usually fully established.
3 YEARS	• Roughly 90% of children show left-hemisphere bias for language. Children can hop.
4 YEARS	• Children who will be obese later in life begin to gain weight at a faster rate than other children.
9 YEARS	• Boys catch up with girls in height, but then slow down again until about 14 years.
10 YEARS	• Some young girls succumb to anorexia or bulimia between this time and the early twenties.
14 YEARS	• Girls' height gain slows down considerably while boys' gain takes off; boys' weight gain also shoots up.
16–17 YEARS	• Most young people have attained their full height.

Figure 5-6

Developmental changes in neurons of cerebral cortex

During childhood, the brain overproduces neural connections, establishes the usefulness of certain ones of these, and then "fine-tunes" the extra connections. Especially in the frontal cortex, overproduction of synapses may be essential for infants to develop certain intellectual abilities. According to some scientists, the connections that are used will survive, and those that are not will die.

Source: Reprinted by permission of the publisher from *The Postnatal Development of the Human Cerebral Cortex*, Vols. I–VIII by Jesse LeRoy Conel, Cambridge, MA, Harvard University Press. Copyright © 1939, 1967 by the President and Fellows of Harvard College.

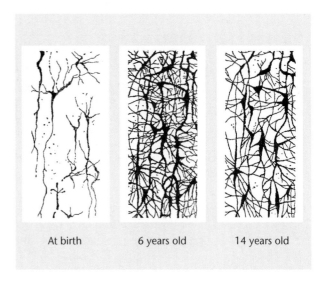

At birth   6 years old   14 years old

By adulthood, each of the brain's approximately 1 trillion neurons makes 100 to 1,000 connections with other neurons. That adds up to about 1 quadrillion synapses in the adult human brain (Huttenlocher & Dabholkar, 1997).

Sequential Development of the Brain

There is an orderly sequence to brain development during infancy. As the baby moves from mostly reflexive behaviour in the early months of life to voluntary control over movements, the motor area of the brain develops most rapidly. When the infant is about 2 months old, motor reflexes, such as rooting and the startle response (see Chapter 4), drop out, and the motor cortex begins to oversee voluntary movement, such as reaching, crawling, and walking. As we have already noted, in the visual cortex the number of synapses per neuron is multiplied some six times within the first two years of life. As a result, infants' visual capacities are greatly enhanced; for example, they become more skilled at focusing on objects at different distances (Nelson, 1999a; Nelson et al., 2006). A similar sequence of synaptic and behavioural development characterizes the evolution of the auditory cortex as well as other areas of the brain (Nelson, 1999b; Nelson et al., 2006).

Hemispheric Specialization

hemispheres

The two, left and right, halves of the brain's cerebrum.

corpus callosum

The band of nerve fibres that connects the two hemispheres of the brain.

hemispheric specialization

Differential functioning of the two cerebral hemispheres; for example, the control of speech and language by the left hemisphere and of visual-spatial processing by the right.

lateralization

The process by which each half of the brain becomes specialized for the performance of certain functions.

One of the most important organizing features of the brain is its left–right division into two halves or **hemispheres**. The left and right hemispheres, which are connected by a set of nerve fibres called the **corpus callosum**, are anatomically different and, in general, control different functions (Kandel et al., 2000). However, because a great deal of cross-wiring occurs between the hemispheres, the separation is by no means complete. Not only do both hemispheres play some role in most functions, but when one side of the brain suffers damage, the other half may take over some functions.

LEFT- AND RIGHT-BRAIN FUNCTIONS **Hemispheric specialization** begins early in life (Stephan et al., 2003). The left hemisphere of the motor cortex controls simple movement in the right side of the body, and the right hemisphere controls the body's left side. **Lateralization** describes the specialization of each hemisphere in specific perceptual and cognitive tasks. The right hemisphere processes visual-spatial information, non–speech sounds like music, and the perception of faces (Nelson & Bosquet, 2000; Nelson et al., 2006). When damage occurs to the right side of the brain, people may have difficulty attending to a task requiring visual-spatial perception, their drawing skills may deteriorate, they may have trouble following a map or recognizing friends, or they may become spatially disoriented (Bryden, 1982; Carter, Freeman, & Stanton, 1995; McManus & Bryden, 1991). The right hemisphere is also involved in processing emotional information (Stuss & Alexander, 2000; Voyer, Russell, & McKenna, 2002), as shown by the fact that people with right-brain damage can have difficulty interpreting facial expressions (Bryden & MacRae, 1989; Dawson, 1994; Nelson et al., 2006). Marc Pell of McGill University has investigated the ability of individuals who have damage to either their right or left brain hemispheres to understand the emotional prosody and content of speech (e.g., Pell, 2006). Pell (1998), for instance, found that individuals with both right-brain and left-brain damage have trouble interpreting the emotional meaning of utterances (although left-brain-damaged subjects have additional problems with the linguistic content of the sentences; Baum, Pell, Leonard, & Gordon, 2001) and that right-brain-damaged subjects have difficulties in producing emotional tone in their utterances (Pell, 1999a, 1999b) and in understanding the emotional attitudes of a speaker based on her speech (Pell, 2007). Although the role of the hemispheres in detecting and producing emotional information is complicated, one current model suggests that the left hemisphere is activated in the expression of emotions associated with approach to the external environment, such as joy, interest, and anger, whereas the right region is activated in emotional expressions that cause the person to turn away or withdraw from that environment, such as distress, disgust, and fear (see Figure 5-7, as well as Fox, 1991; and Davidson, 1994).

The left hemisphere of the brain is associated with language processing. Although people with left hemisphere damage can recognize a familiar song and tell a stranger's face from an old friend's, they may have trouble understanding what is being said to them or in speaking clearly themselves (Springer & Deutsch, 1993). Evidence of the genetic basis of lateralization is seen in the positive association of the degree of language lateralization between parents and children (Anneken et al., 2004). Interestingly, however, in persons who are deaf and use sign language to communicate—a language that involves motor movements of the hands—the right side of the brain takes over language functions (Neville & Bruer, 2001; Sanders, Weber-Fox, & Neville, 2007). Music has also traditionally been associated with processing in the right hemisphere (Peretz, 2001), although arguments have been made for music accessing both hemispheres,

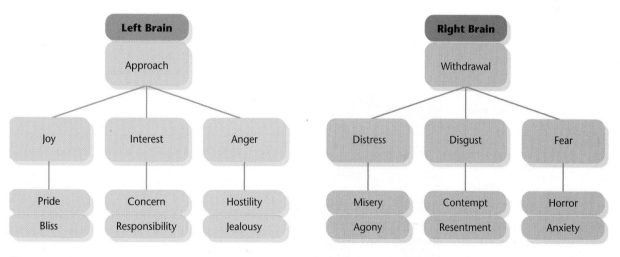

Figure 5-7

Emotions associated with left- and right-brain hemisphere activity

According to one theory, both hemispheres are involved in emotional expression, but the left focuses on feelings that trigger approach to the environment, the right on feelings that cause a person to turn away from the environment.

Source: Dawson, 1994.

albeit for varying reasons (Peretz, 2006). Nevertheless, there is evidence that individuals with right-hemisphere damage have more difficulty in processing auditory and musical pitches than do people with left-hemisphere lesions (Zatorre & Halpern, 1993; Lassonde, Mottron, Peretz, Schiavetto, Hébert, & Décarie, 1999).

These and other findings demonstrate that the brain is capable of adapting to external change. If brain injury occurs in the early years of life, because the young brain is not fully developed and hemispheric specialization is not yet complete, infants and young children often recover their losses (Fox, Calkins, & Bell, 1994; Stiles, 2000). For instance, in a longitudinal case study of a traumatic brain injury to a 17-month-old girl, although this child showed initial decreases in vocabulary and other language functions, there was no long-lasting impairment on any aspect of lexical or grammatical development (Trudeau, Poulin-Dubois, & Joanette, 2000). Even in adults, there is still a great deal of modifiability, and lost function can often be partially recovered through treatment (Black, Jones, Nelson, & Greenough, 1998; Briones, Klintsova, & Greenough, 2004).

CONSEQUENCES OF BRAIN LATERALIZATION   The degree to which a newborn's brain is lateralized in processing speech sounds—that is, prone to use one hemisphere rather than the other—has consequences for the child's language ability three years later (Molfese & Molfese, 1985). Infants whose left hemisphere differentiates among speech sounds and whose right hemisphere differentiates among non–speech sounds exhibit better language skills at age three than infants who do not show such strong lateralization. However, infants' brain responses to hearing speech and matching it with concrete objects are multidimensional and involve a variety of processes, some of which are lateralized and some of which are not (Molfese, Morse, and Peters, 1990). Clearly, brain functioning between the hemispheres is highly complex and requires continued study.

One reason we need to know more about this issue is that theories about lateralization underlie current explanations of **dyslexia**—the difficulties some children (and adults) experience in learning to read. As many as 5 to 10 percent of North American children experience such problems. Typically, they have difficulty integrating visual and auditory information, for example, in matching written letters or words to the sounds of those letters and words. Some children confuse letters, for example, calling a "d" a "b"; others have difficulty breaking up the letters and syllables of a word and, treating the word as a whole, have no clues with which to figure it out (Liberman, Shankweiler, Liberman, Fowler, & Fischer, 1976; Veuillet et al., 2007). Some researchers have suggested that children with dyslexia do not show the normal lateralization pattern—that is, they process spatial information on both sides of the brain rather than primarily on

dyslexia

A term for the difficulties experienced by some people in reading or learning to read.

Over the past few decades, researchers have found that music may be processed in the brain's right hemisphere, unlike speech and language, which are processed on the left side of the brain. And as the text suggests, the right hemisphere is also associated with emotional information. The implications of this concurrence are, to say the least, intriguing.

the right and, thus, their left hemispheres may become overloaded, leading to deficits in language skills such as reading (Baringa, 1996; Witelson, 1983). The view that reading difficulties are caused by faulty lateralization patterns continues to receive support (Banish, 1998; Bryden, 1988; Veuillet et al., 2007).

Handedness is another function that is lateralized. About 90 percent of adults are right handed, and a majority of young infants even show right-hand dominance: they use the right hand more than the left for reaching, touching, pointing, grasping, and manual exploration (Butterworth et al., 2002; Dean & Anderson, 1997; Streri, 2002). Even 90 percent of fetuses prefer to suck their right thumbs, which suggests that handedness develops in the womb (Hepper, 2004). Recently, a gene for left-handedness has been identified

(Francks et al., 2007), a finding consistent with the genetic basis of handedness. An illustration of the genetics of handedness comes from the British royal family, which has a large number of left-handers, including Prince Charles and Prince William. However, some left-handed people are ambidextrous, able to use both hands for some tasks. This suggests that their brains may be less clearly lateralized than the brains of right-handed people (Coren, 1992).

The Brain's Plasticity: Experience and Brain Development

The brain continues to develop so rapidly after birth that it is clear that stimulation from the environment plays a role in brain development. The human brain's **plasticity**, or the responsiveness of its neural structures and functions to input from the environment, is one of its most remarkable features.

Two types of experience influence brain development (Greenough & Black, 1999). One type is those experiences such as touch, patterned visual input, sounds of language, affectionate expressions from caregivers, and nutrition, which are all expected in normal environments. They trigger synaptic development and pruning and are critical for normal brain development. When there is interference with this normal stimulation, basic abilities are impaired. For example, when children have congenital cataracts, their visual system is deprived of stimulation and fails to develop properly, so that even when the cataracts are removed, the adult is blind.

The second kind of experience that influences brain development are experiences that are unique to individuals—experiences encountered in particular families, communities, and cultures. Brains respond to different environments by developing synaptic connections that encode specific and unique experiences. For example, children in Mozambique develop aspects of the motor cortex that correspond to the skills associated with hunting and fishing, whereas North American children develop parts of the brain that reflect the fine-motor and eye–hand coordination needed for success at video games.

Animal research shows that the size, structure, and even the biochemistry of the brain can be modified by experience. Rosenzweig and his colleagues (Benloucif, Bennett, & Rosenzweig, 1995; Rosenzweig, 2003) placed young rats in two very different environments. The "enriched" environment consisted of large, brightly lit, communal cages with wheels, ladders, platforms, and other toys that were changed daily to ensure that the rats had a steady stream of new learning experiences. In the "impoverished" environment, each rat was alone in a bare, isolated cage located in a quiet, dimly lit room. When the researchers compared the brains of the young rats after nearly three months, they discovered that the weight of the cerebral cortex, which controls higher-order processes, was about 4 percent heavier for rats in the enriched environment and the weight of the occipital region, which controls vision, was 6 percent heavier.

One reason that the enriched rats had bigger brains was that enriched environments tend to increase the complexity of neurons as measured by the number of dendrites they develop (Black et al., 1998; Jones & Greenough, 1996). More dendrites means more synapses formed with other neurons, which in turns means that more information can be sent via these synaptic connections. At the same time, the activity of key chemicals in the brain, especially in the cerebral cortex, increases significantly as a result of an enriched rearing environment.

It may not be only the young who can benefit from enriched experiences. Adult rats exposed to impoverished or enriched environments after being reared in normal laboratory conditions show changes like those seen in young rats (Black & Greenough, 1998; Briones et al., 2004). Still, the effects of differential experience may be greater during the earlier periods of life.

Research on human infants also demonstrates the brain's plasticity. For example, although infants respond to the sounds of all languages, over the first year of life they

plasticity

The capacity of the brain, particularly in its developmental stages, to respond and adapt to input from the external environment.

become more selective, responding increasingly to sounds in their own language (Kuhl, 2004; Kuhl et al., 1997). Apparently, different sets of neuronal connections become programmed to respond to particular aspects of speech so that infants' brains develop "auditory maps," or templates to respond to certain auditory features and not others. These maps then guide infants in recognizing their native language.

Exposure to music can also enrich brain development. The natural harmonics of music may help the brain develop a wiring diagram that promotes spatial-temporal reasoning. In one study, after six months of weekly piano lessons, 3- and 4-year-olds improved markedly in this kind of reasoning as demonstrated by their ability to look at a disassembled picture of an elephant and to tell the researcher how to put the pieces together (Sarnthein et al., 1997). In contrast, children who received computer training or no stimulation showed little improvement. Although recent years have seen a great deal of debate over whether or not listening to music by adults and musical training in children truly cause differences in spatial abilities (Chabris, 1999; Nantais & Schellenberg, 1999; Schellenberg, 2006a; Schellenberg & Peretz, 2008; Steele, Bass, & Crook, 1999), the idea that stimulation of the brain in some form or another (as would, for example, be provided by musical training) can cause differences in brain development, and hence in cognitive abilities, is an intriguing one and has become the focus of a great deal of current research (Hussain, Thompson, & Schellenberg, 2002; Schellenberg, 2006b; Schellenberg, Nakata, Hunter, & Tamoto, 2007).

Finally, some research demonstrates that the brain can undergo structural change based on unique experiences even in adulthood. Maguire and colleagues (2000) looked at the structure of the brains of humans with extensive navigational experience—London taxi drivers—and compared these brains with a set of control subjects who did not drive taxis. These researchers found that the posterior hippocampi, which is thought to be associated with spatial representations of the environment, was larger in the taxi drivers than in the control participants. Such findings suggest a remarkable degree of plasticity in the brain structure in response to environmental demands.

Lack of stimulation or exposure to traumatic events, in contrast, can damage the brain and cause it to malfunction. In abused children both the cortex and the *limbic system*—centres in the brain that are involved in emotions and infant–parent attachment—are 20 to 30 percent smaller and have fewer synapses than in non-abused children (Perry, 1997). Techniques, such as *positron-emission tomography*, or PET (see Table 5-1), also show the effects on the developing brain of early deprivation, for example, the unstimulating and unresponsive environment of a Romanian orphanage (Nelson, 2007; see Figure 5-8) These studies show that under such circumstances there is reduced connectivity or communication between regions of the brain (Chugani, Phelps, & Mazziotta, 2002; Eluvathingal et al., 2006) as well as reduced cortical activity involving neurons acting together to solve a cognitive task such as memory or face processing (Parker et al., 2005). These naturalistic experiments illustrate the malleability of the developing brain and its responsiveness to environmental conditions.

For Thought and Discussion

1. What implications does work on brain development and brain plasticity have for the arguments about genetic versus environmental influences on development that we encountered in Chapter 2?

2. One controversial finding that has come out in recent years is that listening to music and receiving music lessons have an influence on children's (and adults') cognitive and spatial abilities, possibly through an impact on brain development. What do you think of this possibility? How would you actually go about testing this idea? How would you control for such aspects as general increased stimulation resulting from being exposed to music or music lessons?

Table 5-1 Techniques for studying human brain function and structure

Technique	What it Shows	Advantages (+) and Disadvantages (−)
EEG (electroencephalograph): Multiple electrodes are pasted to the outside of the head.	Lines that chart the summated electrical fields resulting from the activity of billions of neurons.	+ Detects very rapid changes in electrical activity, allowing analysis of stages of cognitive processing − Provides poor spatial resolution of the source of electrical activity. EEG is sometimes combined with magnetoencephalography (MEG), which localizes electrical activity by measuring magnetic fields associated with it
PET (positron-emission tomography) and SPECT (single-photon emission computed tomography): Positrons and photons are emissions from radioactive substances.	An image of the amount and localization of any molecule that can be injected in radioactive form, such as neurotransmitters, drugs, or tracers for blood flow or glucose use (images indicate specific changes in neuronal activity).	+ Allows functional and biochemical studies + Provides visual image corresponding to anatomy − Requires exposure to low levels of radioactivity − Provides spatial resolution better than that of EEG but poorer than that of MRI − Cannot follow rapid changes (faster than 30 seconds)
MRI (magnetic resonance imaging): Exposes the brain to a magnetic field and measures radiofrequency waves.	Traditional MRI provides high-resolution image of brain anatomy. Functional MRI (fMRI) provides images of changes in blood flow (which indicate specific changes in neural activity). A new variant, diffusion tensor imaging (DTI), shows water flow in neural fibres, thus revealing the "wiring diagram" of neural connections in the brain.	+ Requires no exposure to radioactivity + Provides high spatial resolution of anatomical details (under 1 mm) + Provides high temporal resolution (slower than 1/10 of a second)
TMS (transcranial magnetic stimulation): Temporarily disrupts electrical activity of a small region of brain by exposing it to an intense magnetic field.	Normal function of a particular brain region can be studied by observing changes after TMS is applied to a specific location.	+ Shows which brain regions are necessary for given tasks − Long-term safety not well established

Source: Bernstein et al., 2008.

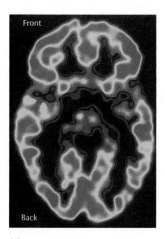
(a)

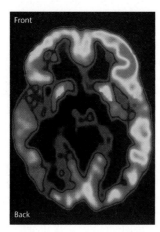
(b)

Figure 5-8

How early deprivation can affect brain activity

In the brain of a normal child (a), positron-emission tomography (PET) reveals many regions of high activity (red), whereas in the brain of an institutionalized Romanian orphan who suffered extreme deprivation from birth (b), there are many fewer such regions and more areas of lesser activity. The degrees of brain activity, from highest to lowest, follow the colour sequence red, yellow, green, blue, and black.

Source: Begley, 1997.

ⓛ3 MOTOR DEVELOPMENT

In this section, we discuss the course of motor development—the development of hand skills, as infants reach and grasp and pick up objects, and locomotion skills, as infants learn to crawl and then to walk.

Hand Skills

Using a finger grasp to pull a puzzle piece out of its place with one hand and with the other to hold a second piece in waiting shows some advanced skill on the part of this 7-month-old baby. On average, infants are 8 months old before they can use this type of grasp.

Reaching out and grasping an object is one of the greatest achievements in the first two years of life (Adolph & Berger, 2006). Even newborns display a grasping reflex and a rudimentary form of reaching—called "prereaching"—that involves uncoordinated "swipes" at objects that babies notice. At about 3 months of age, infants initiate a new and more complex and efficient pattern, namely, *directed reaching* (Thelen et al., 1993; Spencer & Thelen, 2000). By the time they are about 5 months old, they generally succeed in reaching in for an object and successfully grasping it. To achieve this milestone involves muscle growth, postural control, control over the movement of arms and hands, and a variety of perceptual and motor abilities. Only when all parts of the system are ready to work together can infants become competent in reaching and grasping objects (Adolph, 2005, 2008; Thelen & Smith, 2006). This "putting the pieces" together view of how reaching develops is consistent with the dynamic systems view of development that we reviewed in Chapter 1.

One component of the dynamic system is visual perception. If the infant has nothing to look at, there is no incentive to reach out. In experiments with institutionalized infants whose normal environments were severely restricted, researchers showed that enriching infants' visual world by hanging colourful toys over their cribs, providing them with multi-coloured sheets and bumper pads, and ensuring that they were handled more often by caregivers could advance their abilities to attend to objects and to reach for them (White, 1967).

Another component involves the motor ability to grip an object. The frequency and skill with which infants employ various grips improves with age (Adolph & Berger, 2006; Siddiqui, 1995). Grips also depend on the size and shape of the object. Infants vary their grip according to the size and shape of an object and the size of their own hands relative to the object's size (Newell et al., 1989). They use a grip involving the thumb and index finger for small objects, but for large objects they use either all the fingers of one hand or both hands. Four-month-olds rely on touch to determine their grip; 8-month-olds use vision as a guide so they can preshape their hand as they reach for an object.

Over the first year of life, infants' progress in controlling their hands is remarkable. They not only become highly skilled reachers and graspers (Siddiqui, 1995) but they also begin to use objects as tools—for example, a spoon (Barrett, Davis, & Needham, 2007; McCarty, Clifton, & Collard, 2001; Szokolszky & Devánszky, 2008). Moreover, they learn the use of gestures in social communication. For example, at roughly 1 year of age, children are able to follow a parent's pointing finger to the target object rather than focus on the finger alone (Franco & Butterworth, 1996; Goldin-Meadow, 2007). By age 2, they use their hands skilfully in play, for example, building a tower of blocks, and by age 3, they use their hands to scribble with crayons or copy vertical lines on a page.

ⓛ4 Locomotion

The development of locomotion involves three phases or transitions (Thelen & Smith, 1994, 2006). The first of these has long puzzled researchers. When you hold a baby upright and let his feet touch a flat surface, tilting his body slightly from side to side, the baby responds by reflexively moving his legs in a rhythmic stepping motion that resembles walking. But this stepping reflex disappears by the time the infant is about two months old. Not until the second half of the baby's first year does the second transition occur, with the reappearance of stepping movements. In the third, at about 1 year of age, infants begin to walk without support.

Various theories of how walking develops have been offered. Maturational theorists believe it depends on the development of the motor cortex (McGraw, 1940; Zelazo, 1998). Cognitive theorists have suggested that it as a response to cognitive plans or representations that are the consequence of watching other people walk (Zelazo, 1983), as well as of practice in stepping itself (Zelazo, Zelazo, Cohen, & Zelazo, 1993). The most satisfactory explanation, however, is based on Thelen's dynamic systems theory (Thelen, 2000, 2002; Thelen & Bates, 2003; Thelen & Smith, 2006), which suggests that walking skills are determined by the interplay of a variety of emotional, perceptual, attentional, motivational, postural, and anatomical factors. Just as we saw for reaching and grasping, all these components must be "ready," and the developmental context (in this case, the weight of the baby's body in proportion to the strength of the legs) must be right before the infant can walk. According to this theory, the newborn stepping response disappears for a 10-month interval before true walking emerges because of anatomical factors—that is, the baby's size and weight become too much of a load on the emerging motor system, masking the child's stepping capability (Thelen, 1995). If this explanation is right, infants between the ages of two months and 12 months should be able to step as long as they are given the stability and postural support necessary to stretch each leg forwards and back while in an upright position. Thelen (1986; Thelen & Smith, 2006) provided such support by holding infants on a motorized treadmill. Immediately, they performed alternating stepping movements that were remarkably similar to more mature walking.

Upright walking is only the beginning, of course, and by the time children are about 7 years old they have acquired the more complex skills of running, galloping, and hopping (Cratty, 1999; Adolph & Berger, 2006). Running is well established by the time the child is a year and a half (Forrester, Phillips, & Clark, 1993), and galloping emerges at about the same time (Whitall & Clark, 1994). Hopping, which requires balance and strength, emerges between 2 and 3 years (Halverson & Williams, 1985). As with walking, a dynamic systems approach provides the best explanation of this developmental progression. These skills depend on improvements in balance and coordination and on the opportunity for practice (Adolph & Berger, 2006; Bertenthal & Clifton, 1998).

Taking your first steps must be an emotional experience; the joy and excitement mirrored on the faces of both the 11-month-old baby taking those first steps and the child's 7-year-old sister are contagious. Perhaps these positive emotions are also contributing to the baby's slightly advanced ability; on average, children walk alone at about 12 months of age.

How Locomotion May Affect Other Aspects of Development

One important consequence of locomotor development is increased independence. Babies who can crawl or walk can explore their environments more fully and initiate more contact with other people. This new-found independence, in turn, changes the way that others respond to the child. No longer can parents place an infant on a blanket in the middle of the floor, expecting that she will be there when they turn around. Infants can now move at will, leaving behind them a trail of mayhem—torn magazines, overturned coffee cups, broken glass. To prevent this chaos, parents must intervene with distractions or prohibitions. Researchers have observed that early walking is related to increased parent–child interaction and more "testing" of wills between mothers and their children (Biringen, Emde, Campos, & Appelbaum, 1995).

Many researchers have adopted a "perception–action coupling" approach to understanding the growth of such independent mobility (Hofsten, 1989; Pick, 1984; Schmuckler, 1993). According to this view, motor or action systems are functionally interrelated to sensory or perceptual systems such that changes in one aspect influence the development of the other aspect. Researchers have suggested that the onset of locomotion can change the way babies understand their perceptual world (Adolph & Berger, 2006; Campos et al., 2000; Schmuckler & Tsang-Tong, 2000). For example, the onset of crawling brings with it a fear of heights and other spatial abilities (Campos et al., 2000). In one study (Bai & Bertenthal, 1992), researchers found that crawling babies were better than pre-crawling or belly-crawling infants at finding a hidden toy after being moved through the world, suggesting that locomotion helps infants deal better with changes in spatial orientation.

Another illustration of the link between perception and action is provided by experiments on the use of vision in balance control employing a "moving room" (Lee & Aronson, 1974; Lee & Lishman, 1975). The moving room is a room in which the walls and ceiling can be moved back and forth, while the floor itself stays immobile. Many researchers (Delorme, Frigon, & Lagace, 1989; Godoi & Barela, 2008; Lee & Aronson, 1974; Lejeune et al., 2006; Schmuckler, 1997) have demonstrated that infants and young children use the visual input produced by a moving room to control their balance, despite the lack of vestibular information that would typically tell someone about a loss of balance. Schmuckler (1997), for example, found that 3- to 6-year-olds will not only sway back and forth periodically to visual movement but will also do so even when the movement is quite fast, at almost one cycle (a back and forth motion) per second. Bertenthal and Bai (1989) have speculated that self-produced locomotion is critical for infants' use of visual information in such situations, based on their observations that crawling infants, but not similar-age pre-crawling ones, used moving room input to control their balance. Thus, once again we see that perceptual and action systems are inextricably linked in development, with changes in one system related to growth in the corresponding system. Box 5.1 on pages 172 and 173 describes another aspect of perception–action coupling by looking at what happens to children who are at risk due to some developmental disability.

LO5 The Role of Experience and Culture

Although overall limits to motor development may well be set by physical maturation, within those limits, the timing of the onset of various skills may be affected by societal and other factors (Bradley et al., 2001).

Cross-cultural studies have provided us with information about how specific ways of caring for infants can alter their motor development. In general, it seems that when parents or other caretakers give babies special physical attention, including manipulation, massage, exercise, and specific practice of skills, the infants achieve motor milestones somewhat earlier than children not given such care and opportunities. For example, in Zambia, mothers carry their new babies with them everywhere in a sling on their backs; then, when they are able to sit, the mothers leave their infants sitting alone for considerable periods of time, giving them plenty of opportunity to practise motor skills. Zambian babies show early development of motor skills (Hopkins & Westra, 1988). Jamaican mothers regularly massage their infants, stretch their arms and legs, and give them practice in stepping, and their children, too, are motorically advanced (Hopkins & Westra, 1990). In contrast, among the Zinacantecos of Mexico, infants are tightly swaddled for the first three months of life; they have less-advanced motor skills (Greenfield & Childs, 1991). In Chinese families living in small, cramped apartments with uncarpeted floors, parents put their infants on soft featherbeds and pillows to prevent them from hurting themselves and the babies' crawling is restricted by the lack of room to roam (Campos et al., 2000). Some of these infants fail to develop adequate strength in muscle groups critical for crawling and their crawling is delayed.

Among infants in the United States, practice in motor behaviour can hasten walking and other motor skills. Zelazo and colleagues (1972) asked mothers of newborns to give their infants practice in the stepping reflex a few minutes a day. Not only did these babies make more walking responses at 2 to 8 weeks of age, but they walked earlier than a control group of babies who were given no practice (see Figure 5-9). In another study these investigators found that practice in sitting yielded similar results: Babies who were given practice in sitting for three minutes a day were able to sit upright longer than infants in a no-practice control group (Zelazo et al., 1988). Karen Adolph and her colleagues (Adolph, Vereijken, & Shrout, 2003) collected diary records of infants' walking activities. These records showed that walking infants practised keeping balance in an upright stance and locomotion for more than six hours a day, averaging between 500 and 1,500 walking steps per hour, so that by the end of each day, they had taken 9,000 walking steps and travelled the length of 29 football fields. Not surprisingly, infants with more walking experience were the most-skilled walkers. But practice does not make perfect. There are limits to how far infants' motor development can be pushed. No stepping-trained baby has walked at 3 or 4 months of age, for example (Zelazo et al., 1988). Cross-cultural studies have provided us with information about how specific ways of caring for infants can alter their motor development.

These examples of environmental influences on motor development raise another interesting idea—the possibility that aspects of the geographic region in which children are reared may influence motor development. In a direct test of this "seasonality" hypothesis, Benson (1993) looked at over 400 babies born in Denver, Colorado, and observed that babies born between June and November took about three weeks longer to achieve independent mobility than did babies born between December and May. Benson

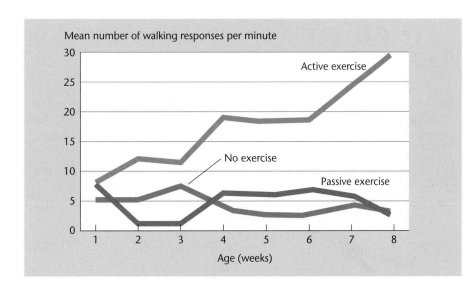

Figure 5-9

Can practice really make perfect?

Newborns given active exercise of the walking reflex showed a clear increase in this response over babies given passive exercise or no exercise at all. The practised babies also walked earlier than the other children in this experiment.

Source: Adapted from Zelazo, Zelazo, & Kolb, 1972.

Box 5.1

Risk and Resilience

BLINDNESS, MOTOR DEVELOPMENT, AND COGNITIVE ABILITIES

Being unable to see puts an infant at risk for many difficulties. As Figure 5-10 shows, blindness retards motor development considerably, especially the baby's first efforts to raise his body with his arms and his attempts to stand up by holding on to furniture, to walk alone, and to reach for objects (Adelson & Fraiberg, 1974). This limited mobility can have some serious consequences: "It lessens [the blind infant's] ability to explore independently, to discover by himself the objective rules that govern things and events in the external world" (Fraiberg, 1977, p. 270).

One subsequent complication of blind infants' delayed motor development, and their decreased independent exploration of the world, can be seen in a variety of cognitive abilities, such as the development of spatial knowledge (Landau, Gleitman, & Spelke, 1981; Landau, Spelke, & Gleitman, 1984; Morrongiello, Timney, Humphrey, Anderson, & Skory, 1995) or what is called "joint attention" (Bigelow, 2003). At St. Francis Xavier University, Ann Bigelow has examined the relation between blindness and such cognitive abilities in a number of contexts, including looking at spatial knowledge in blind and sighted children (Bigelow, 1991a, 1991b, 1991c, 1992a, 1992b, 1996). In one of Bigelow's studies (1991a), blind, visually impaired, and sighted children between about 3 and 7 years of age were asked to hide themselves, a toy, and specific parts of their body from an observer. Bigelow found that the blind children were not as successful at hiding as the other groups, acting as if they did not understand that a covering obstacle had to completely block an observ-

er's view. And in a later study, Bigelow (1996) even found that blind children's understanding of the spatial layout of their own homes was not as good as either sighted or visually impaired children. In this case, blind children's spatial knowledge was based more on how one would move between places, rather than the correct layout. Clearly, the lack of sight has significant consequences for both motor and cognitive abilities and development.

Technology can play a role in building motor capabilities for blind infants. Experimenters in Scotland suggested that an electronic device that produces echoes from nearby objects may help blind babies to "see." The blind infant might learn to use this feedback to judge her distance from an object and even perhaps to assess the object's size and texture. Bower (1979, 1989) had blind infants wear an echo-producing device for several months and found that by using the echo feedback, the babies could judge their distance from objects and even sometimes the objects' size and texture. The infants' reaching ability was improved, and they were able to do things more typical of sighted infants.

Because much research in this area has focused on devices that must be carried and manipulated by the user, the so-called electronic travel aids (ETAs) that have been developed are designed for blind adults. Adults have found ETAs, which use laser or sound-wave technologies, to be useful particularly in enabling them to avoid contact with other pedestrians and to detect the presence of nearby objects (Blasch, Long, & Griffin-Shirley, 1989). Two of the newer sensor devices,

suggested that infants born in the summer or fall months acquired motor skills later than infants born in the winter or spring months because the former group would begin to develop locomotor skills in the winter to early spring (about six to eight months after birth), a time when motor skills might be constrained due to more restrictive clothing, activity-reducing illnesses, and less time for free movement because of shorter days. Seasonality effects have since been observed by other researchers looking at babies born in Osaka, Japan (Hiyashi, 1990, 1992), and in Edmonton, Alberta (Bartlett, 1998). In the latter case, Bartlett found that these seasonality effects failed to occur in a geographic region of more extreme cold, with temperatures ranging from 16°C in July to −14.2°C in January. Bartlett (1998) explains this difference by noting that even though Edmonton is significantly colder than Denver, because the infants examined in this study were from an urban environment, parents may have maintained a more uniform home temperature throughout the year. Thus, this study also highlights the possibility that constraints imposed by the environment can influence motor development.

Figure 5-10

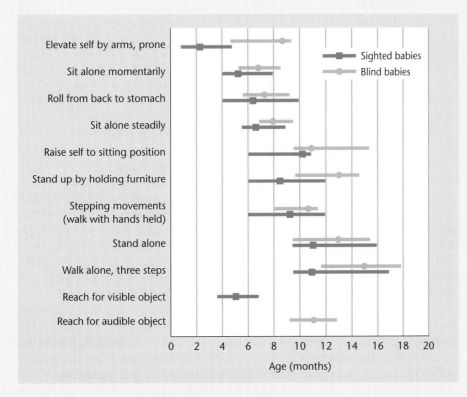

Motor development in blind and sighted babies

Clearly, being sighted helps an infant to develop motor skills, but in some movements, such as rolling over and sitting up, blind babies are not very far behind sighted infants. The squares and circles indicate the average ages at which particular activities emerge in blind and sighted babies; the extent of each line indicates the age range within which babies may begin specific activities.

Sources: Adelson & Fraiberg, 1974; Bower, 1979.

which provide information to the user in synthesized speech, require that places frequented by the public, such as hotels and public buildings, install special transmitters whose signals can be picked up by the device (Bentzen & Mitchell, 1995). Thus, for example, a transmitter in a hotel lobby might, when activated by a scanning sensor, inform the person that "elevators are to your right." For the pre-verbal child, perhaps scaled-down versions of ETAs might be developed, but it is not beyond imagining that for the child who has acquired good language skills, the newer, "talking sign" devices might be adapted to home and school use.

For Thought and Discussion

1. In what way do you think vision is important in reaching? Do you think infants are more likely to reach for an object in the light than in the dark (assuming they can, of course, see the object)?

2. Related to the above question, if you learned that researchers actually did a study looking at how likely infants were to reach in the light versus the dark and found out that infants reached for objects in the light and the dark at the same age, how would you change your view of the role of vision in reaching?

3. How would you apply a systems approach to the development of visually guided reaching? What might be the components? How about for locomotion? What are the components or factors here?

ⓛⓞ6 PHYSICAL GROWTH

cephalocaudal development

The notion that human physical growth occurs from the head downward—that is, from brain and neck to trunk and legs.

proximal-distal pattern

The tendency for human physical development to occur from the centre outward; for example, from internal organs to arms and legs.

The study of physical growth is guided by two classic principles. First, growth is characterized by **cephalocaudal development**—that is, growth occurs from the head downward; the brain and neck develop earlier than do the legs and trunk. Second, growth follows a **proximal-distal pattern**, from the centre outward; the internal organs develop earlier than do the arms and hands. Although most developmentalists simply take these two principles for granted, one recent study identified an intriguing exception to the idea of cephalocaudal development. In a longitudinal study, Galloway and Thelen (2004) found that young infants reached for objects approximately two weeks earlier with their feet than they did with their hands, thus demonstrating more complex motor skills with parts of the body further away from the head (the feet) than body parts closer to the head (the hands).

Height and weight are the two principal measures of overall growth. Babies grow faster in their first half year of life than ever again (National Center for Health Statistics, 2000). They nearly double their weight in the first three months and triple their weight by the end of the first year. As they develop, their shape changes, too, as newborns' top-heavy light-bulb-shaped bodies become increasingly cylindrical, and infants' centre of mass moves from the sternum to below the belly button. The typical fat-bellied toddlers become slender kindergartners (Adolph & Berger, 2006). Although growth appears to follow a smooth and gradual pattern as shown in Figure 5-11, daily observations reveal that growth is episodic rather than continuous (Lampl, Johnson, & Frongillo, 2001). Dramatic growth spurts can occur in a single day followed by days or weeks of no change. Normal healthy babies grow in fits and starts (Adolph & Berger, 2006).

In this section, we discuss the various factors that influence infants' and children's growth in both height and weight, beginning with possible genetic factors and turning next to such environmental factors as nutrition, hygiene and sanitation, and poverty. We also look at evidence that people—at least in more developed countries—are growing taller. Our final discussion in this section focuses on the growing problems of obesity and eating disturbance as well as on methods of preventing and treating these conditions.

Figure 5-11

Male and female growth in height and weight

As they approach puberty, girls tend to gain in height and, to a lesser degree, in weight, faster than boys, but by the age of 14 or 15 years, boys surpass girls on both counts.

Source: National Center for Health Statistics, 1976.

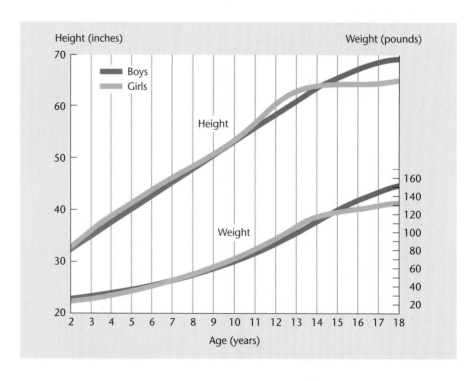

Do Genes Affect Height and Weight?

Although both height and weight can be influenced by environmental factors, research suggests that genetic factors strongly influence these physical characteristics (Rutter, 2006a; Tanner, 1990). Data from the Colorado Adoption Project, a longitudinal study that compares several hundred adoptive and biological parents and their adopted and natural children, indicates that genetic factors may determine as much as two-thirds of the variance in these characteristics (Cardon, 1994). In other research, too, scientists have found a strong relation between the weights of adopted children and their biological parents but no relation between adoptees' and adoptive parents' weights (Stunkard et al., 1986b). Similarly, identical twins are twice as likely to resemble each other in weight as are fraternal twins (Stunkard et al., 1986a). Twins reared apart who did not share a common environment still show marked similarity in weight (Bouchard, 1994).

Being taller than their dance partners is a common experience for girls between the ages of about 11 and 14 years. Boys their age are typically 2 to 3 inches (5–7.5 cm) shorter than they are. These preteens do not seem to mind, though.

Gender has a clear effect on height and weight, as you can see from Figure 5-11. Girls tend to be a bit taller than boys from the age of 2 years until about the age of 9 years, when boys catch up. At about 10½ years of age, girls experience a growth spurt, shooting well up above boys of their own age. At about 14 years, however, girls' height almost plateaus, whereas boys continue to grow taller until they are about 18. The pattern for weight is similar; girls tend to weigh less than boys in the early years and then to exceed them in weight until about age 14, when their weight gain slows down, while boys' gain continues to accelerate (National Center for Health Statistics, 2000; Tanner, 1990).

There are also wide individual differences in maturation rates. Because these differences become particularly obvious at adolescence, it is often assumed that they begin in adolescence. In fact, however, these differences are present at all ages, so early maturers are always ahead of late-maturing peers. Tanner (1978, 1998), an early pioneer in the study of physical growth, coined the term *tempo of growth* to designate this variability in the timing of changes in infants' and children's growth.

The Influence of Environmental Factors

LO 7

Growth is determined not only by genetic factors but also by such environmental influences as nutrition, physical and psychological disorders, and climate (Tanner, 1990). When environmental conditions are favourable, individual growth curves tend to be very similar, but in the presence of one or more unfavourable conditions, such as inadequate nutrition or poor caregiving, growth rates can be seriously depressed (Bradley et al., 1994; Pollitt, 1994). Of interest, too, are the variations in growth rates attributed to differences in nationality, ethnicity, and socio-economic class. There are fairly wide variations across regional areas; for example, peoples in northwestern and western European countries are taller than those in southern Europeans. Within the continent of Africa and among the countries of Central America, there are also substantial variations in height and weight. For example, in one African tribe adults typically grow to seven feet tall, whereas the Pygmies of Zaire, Ruanda, Burundi, and the western coastal areas are on average about four feet tall. Moreover, people vary in growth within the same country; for example, in Brazil and India people in urban areas, where nutrition and standards of living are high, tend to be taller than rural dwellers. In the United States, children in upper-middle-class families are both taller and heavier than children of families living in poverty (Centers for Disease Control, 2007; Martorell, 1984).

NUTRITION   Good nutrition is critical for proper development from infancy to adolescence. In this section, we examine nutrition's part in normal growth and under adverse conditions such as famine. The effects of over- and under-eating are examined as well.

Bottle- versus Breast-feeding   In infancy, one of the first challenges parents face is the choice to feed their new baby breast milk or bottled formula. Although over the last century, ideas about the relative virtues of each have fluctuated—in some decades, experts promoted the bottle, and in other periods, breast-feeding was more popular—we know today that breastfeeding is best for babies' healthy development (Blum, 2000). As Table 5-2 outlines, a host of benefits for both infants and mothers are associated with the choice to breast-feed. These include protection against infectious disease, better development of the brain and nervous system, and a reduction in the likelihood of sudden infant death syndrome (SIDS). Recently, young children in Britain (age 5) and in New Zealand (ages 7 to 13) who were breastfed were found to have higher intelligence than bottle-fed children, but only if the infants had a specific genetic makeup (Caspi et al., 2007). Specifically, children who were genetically predisposed to benefit from fatty acids present in breast milk showed the advantage in IQ; those without this genetic makeup did not benefit from breast-feeding. Although mothers who are better off socio-economically are more likely to breast-feed as well as have smarter children, these findings were evident even after statistically controlling for the contribution of socio-economic factors.

For mothers, breast-feeding is more convenient (no refrigeration or warming is required). It helps women lose the weight gained during pregnancy and delays ovulation. It also promotes closeness between mother and baby. Breast-feeding is particularly important for mothers and children in developing countries. Relative to the incomes of most families in these countries, formula is expensive; because of this, women often dilute the formula, thus endangering the health of their babies. The lack of clean water also often leads to infected formula and increased rates of illness. According to UNICEF (United Nations Children's Fund, 2004), bottle-fed babies in developing countries are 14 times more likely than breast-fed babies to die from diarrhea and four times more likely to succumb to respiratory ailments. If all babies were fed only breast milk for the first six months of life, the lives of an estimated 1.5 million infants would be saved every year, and the health and development of millions of others would be greatly improved.

In the United States, about 60 percent of mothers breast-feed for several months, but after the baby reaches 6 months of age and begins eating some solid foods, this percentage drops sharply. Women who are over 25, of higher socio-economic status, and better educated are more likely to breast-feed than younger, poorer women. But even in this group, returning to employment outside the home reduces the amount of breast-feeding. Some mothers are unable to breast-feed because of medical conditions, such as AIDS or tuberculosis, or because they are being treated for illnesses. Although breast-feeding confers advantages, it is important to note that babies who receive appropriate formula-based bottle nutrition develop normally, especially in Western countries where bottle-feeding is safe.

Nutrition and Physical Growth   Nutrition plays a controlling role in physical growth. Wartime restrictions on food consumption provide clear evidence of this fact. In Europe during the First and Second World Wars, for example, there was a general trend toward less growth. In contrast, in the period between these wars, there was a general increase in growth, especially in weight (Tanner, 1990). Nutritional factors can also affect the age at which children enter puberty; during the Second World War, girls in occupied France on the average did not achieve menarche (the onset of menstruation) until they were 16 years old, approximately three years later than the pre-war norm (Howe & Schiller, 1952). Of course, stress probably contributed to this delay as well.

Studies of people during times of peace have also demonstrated the role of nutrition in growth. In a study in Bogota, Colombia, researchers found that the provision

Table 5-2 Advantages of breast-feeding for infants and mothers

Infants	
Short-Term Benefits of Breast-feeding	**Long-Term Benefits of Breast-Feeding**
Breast milk contains nutritionally balanced ingredients, including proteins, cholesterol, and lactose that, taken together, support development of the brain and nervous system	Breast-fed children have slightly higher IQs than bottle-fed children
Supports appropriate weight gain	Breast-fed children demonstrate better reading comprehension
Strengthens infant's immune system and reduces risk of diarrhea and infectious diseases	Breast-fed children are less likely to have childhood cancer, allergies, or diabetes
Promotes more efficient absorption of iron, lessening likelihood of iron deficiencies	Breast-fed children have denser bones in pre-adolescence
Reduces likelihood of SIDS	
Lessens likelihood of allergies	
Builds denser bones	
Makes shift to solid food easier	
Mothers	
Breast-Feeding	
Builds closeness to her baby	
Promotes faster weight loss after baby's birth	
Delays ovulation (but is not a reliable form of birth control)	
Is convenient	

Sources: Blum, 2000; Caspi et al., 2007; Dewey, 2001; Fredrickson, 1993; Harwood & Fergusson, 1998; Hoppu, Kalliomäki, Laiho, & Isolauri, 2001; Jones, Riley, & Dwyer, 2000; Lifshitz, Finch, & Lifshitz, 1991; Newman, 1995.

of food supplements for entire families from mid-pregnancy until a child was 3 years old effectively prevented severe growth retardation in children at risk for malnutrition (Super et al., 1990). Moreover, the children who received the food supplements remained taller and heavier than control children at 6 years of age, three years after the intervention ended. Equally impressive were the results of a study in rural Bangladesh, in which researchers found that changing traditional unhygienic practices by means of educational and supportive interventions improved children's health, growth, and nutrition (Ahmed et al., 1993). When parents used safer methods of food preparation and waste disposal they lessened food contamination and reduced the incidence of diarrhea, which interferes with the absorption of essential minerals and vitamins.

Finally, research on the effects of poverty in both the United States and other nations highlights the importance of providing nutritional supplements and controlling disease (Pollitt, 1994). **Iron-deficiency anemia**, a condition in which insufficient iron in the diet causes listlessness and may retard children's physical and intellectual development, is common among poor minority children and children in low-income countries, especially countries with little meat in their diets (Conrad, 2006). Interventions in Kenya and Zanzibar involving iron or meat supplements were found to improve these children's rates of growth as well as their motor and mental development (Neumann et al., 2007; Olney et al., 2006)

iron-deficiency anemia

A disorder in which inadequate amounts of iron in the diet cause listlessness and may retard a child's physical and intellectual development.

catch-up growth

The tendency for human beings to regain a normal course of physical growth after injury or deprivation.

CATCH-UP GROWTH   A corrective principle, referred to as **catch-up growth**, operates after children are born. Children who are born small or who experience early environmental injury or deprivation are usually able to catch up with normal physical growth (Emmons et al., 2005). If they are deflected from their genetically governed growth trajectory by acute malnutrition or illness, when the missing food is supplied or the illness terminated, they catch up toward their original curve (Tanner, 1970). However, the degree of catch-up growth the child can achieve will depend on the duration, severity, and timing of the original deprivation and the nature of the subsequent treatment or therapy. In a study of the effects of nutritional supplements following severe malnutrition, researchers found that malnourished infants who had a 5 percent deficit in height were able to catch up, but infants with a 15 percent deficit remained significantly shorter (Graham, 1966). Catch-up growth following severe malnutrition may also be limited to only some aspects of growth. In a 20-year longitudinal study of severely starved children, even a program of nutritional intervention failed to enable full development in head circumference (and presumably brain development) and produced only some catch-up growth in height (Stoch, Smyth, Moodie, & Bradshaw, 1982). This impact of malnutrition on brain development may, in part, account for the intellectual and attentional deficits shown by malnourished children (Neumann et al., 2007; Shonkoff & Phillips, 2000). Timing is also critical in determining the degree of catch-up growth. Pathology and undernourishment early in life can have serious consequences, and children starved in utero usually show only partial catch-up (Pollitt et al., 1992; Tanner, 1990). In general, the earlier and more prolonged the malnutrition, the more difficult it is for interventions to be fully effective in achieving normal growth.

People Are Growing Taller

secular trend

A shift in the normative pattern of a characteristic, such as height or weight, that occurs over a historical time period, such as a decade or century.

According to scientists who have measured bones exhumed from gravesites, between the eleventh and fourteenth centuries, the average Englishman was roughly five feet six inches tall, whereas today the average adult British male is five feet nine inches tall. This is a **secular trend**—a shift that occurs in the normative pattern of a particular characteristic over some historical time period, such as a decade or a century (see Figure 5-12). It is also an average. The same increase in height may not occur at every level of society. For example, if we look at the North American population from the point of view of socio-economic status, we find that most people in the upper 75 percent have probably reached their maximum growth potential (Centers for Disease Control, 2007). People in less-advantaged segments of society will likely continue to make gains. In

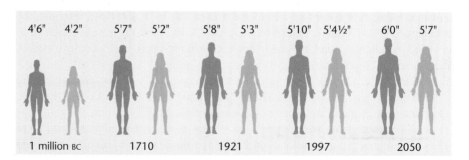

Figure 5-12

Height gains across centuries and millennia

By 1997, the average North American had gained 2½ to 3 inches in height since the early eighteenth century, and expectations are that both men and women will double this gain by 2050. By that time, we'll have become a foot and a half taller than our prehistoric ancestors!

Source: Richard Steckel, Ohio State University, 1997.

Happiness floods the faces of this Saudi Arabian couple as they pose with their son after his graduation ceremonies at a North American college. Towering over his parents, the graduate represents the new generation of young people, who are, indeed, taller than their parents.

other countries, there are different patterns of change. In the Netherlands, for instance, people are continuing to gain in height and weight regardless of socio-economic level; the average Dutch male is now six feet one inch, and Dutch women average five feet eight inches in height (Bilger, 2004). In Japan, England, and Norway, increase in stature has apparently come to a halt (Murata, 2000; Tanner, 1990).

North Americans are not only growing taller but, as a consequence of their added height, their feet are growing longer too, gaining about a third of an inch in each generation. The average university student's grandfather probably wore size seven shoes, whereas today, the average male wears between sizes 9 and 10. And not only are North Americans and their feet increasing in size, but people are achieving these growth increases at earlier ages than in the past. A hundred years ago, people did not attain adult height until their early or mid-20s, but today, many 16- and 17-year-olds are often as tall as, or taller than, their parents.

There are several possible reasons for these historical trends toward greater height. First, health and nutrition have been improved in many countries of the world. Growth-retarding illnesses have come under control, particularly those that strike in the first five years of life, such as *marasmus* (caused by insufficient protein and calories) or *kwashiorkor* (caused by insufficient protein). In many areas, nutritional intake has improved in terms of both quantity of food consumed and balance among essential food groups (Tanner, 1990). Medical care and personal health practices have also improved. Second, socio-economic conditions have generally improved; child labour is less common, and living conditions such as housing and sanitation have improved. Third, the influence of genetic factors has been affected by such things as intermarriage among people of different racial and ethnic backgrounds, which produces increases in height in offspring. In the future, if we experience major changes in the environment brought about by spectacular medical discoveries, natural disasters like famine or global warming, or a substantial increases or decreases in pollution levels, the average height of the population could shift again.

Are We Growing Heavier?
Obesity and Eating Disorders

Children and adults in North America as well as many other places such as England, Western Europe, Japan and Australia are growing heavier (Davies & Fitzgerald, 2008; Fitzgerald, Mousouli, & Davies, 2008). **Obesity**, the condition in which a person's

obesity

A condition in which a person's weight is 30 percent or more in excess of the average weight for his or her height and frame.

weight is 30 percent or more over average weight for his or her height and frame, has been on the rise since the early 1960s (Raynor & Epstein, 2001; see Figure 5-13) when about 5 percent of children were overweight to 2004 when almost 18 percent were obese (National Center for Health Statistics, 2006). This rise has occurred despite the fact that North American children are born into a society that reveres youthful, healthy good looks. Although the preference for tall, slender people over short, overweight people may seem narcissistic, the emphasis on losing weight and keeping fit is based partly on realistic concerns about physical health and the avoidance of illness. Unfortunately, the desire to be attractive and physically fit leads many to a near-obsession with weight-reduction clubs, magazines about weight and diet, and fad diets, and it is young girls who are most likely to suffer from this preoccupation with weight. In a study of 5- to 8-year-old Australian children, nearly 60 percent of the girls wanted a thinner figure, whereas 35 percent of the boys wanted to be thinner. Girls hoped to be thinner as teenagers as well (Lowes & Tiggemann, 2003). Indeed, by mid-adolescence, perhaps 70 to 80 percent of North American girls have been on at least one diet (Attie & Brooks-Gunn, 1989; Barr, 1995; Cowley, 2001). In this section, we look at the continuing North American struggle to be thin and consider the problems of obesity and of eating disorders, such as anorexia and bulimia.

WHY DO CHILDREN GAIN TOO MUCH WEIGHT? In North America, nearly 18 percent of children are obese (National Center for Health Statistics, 2006). Recently in Canada, the prevalence of obesity has increased to about 35 percent in 7- to 13-year-old boys, and 15 percent in 7- to 13-year-old girls (Shields, 2005; Tremblay & Willms, 2000; Katzmarzyk, 2001), and there is evidence for a trend toward obesity in preschool children (Canning, Courage, & Frizzell, 2004). This trend toward obesity varies across different ethnic groups and genders. Over 20 percent of Mexican-American boys and African-American girls are overweight (National Center for Health Statistics, 2006); Asian Americans are the least likely to be overweight.

Why are so many children overweight? One set of factors identified by researchers has to do with the level of caloric intake "enjoyed" by children of this age, combined with a growing trend toward physical inactivity (Auer, Lau, & Reimer, 2001; Katzmarzyk, 2002; Rao, 2006; Tremblay & Willms, 2000). Although the benefits of physical activity have been widely publicized (Health Canada, 1998; Physical Activity and Health, 1996), and a lack of physical activity is associated with childhood obesity (Janssen et al., 2004; Katzmarzyk, Tremblay, Morrison, & Tremblay, 2007), it remains the case that about 62 percent of Canadians are relatively inactive (Katzmarzyk,

Figure 5-13

Overweight (obese) children and adolescents, 1963–2000

Over close to 40 years, obesity (being 30 percent or more over average weight) roughly tripled among both teens and preteens.

Source: National Center for Health Statistics, 2002.

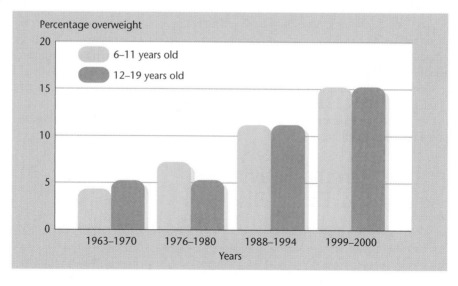

Gledhill, & Shepard, 2000). And, although the reasons why Canadians and Canadian children in particular are inactive remain unclear, researchers have pointed to an obvious influence: "Children are choosing to watch television, surf the Internet and play video games instead of engaging in more active leisure pursuits" (Tremblay & Willms, 2000, p. 1429).

Genetic factors do play a role in obesity. For example, Katzmarzyk, Pérusse, Rao, and Bouchard (1999), using a sample of over 15,000 participants aged 7 to 69 years drawn from the 1981 Canada Fitness Survey, found that the risk for obesity (as measured by the body mass index and a measure of fat distribution) was greater among first-degree relatives than spouses, suggesting a role for genetic factors. Similarly, identical twins are twice as likely to resemble each other in weight as are fraternal twins (Stunkard, Foch, & Hrubeck, 1986a), even when reared apart (Bouchard, 1994; Bouchard, Lykken, Segal, & Wilcox, 1986). Other evidence of the role of inheritance comes from studies of early infant behaviour. Milstein (1980) found that newborn infants with two overweight parents were more responsive to the contrast between a sweet-tasting solution and plain water than were infants of normal-weight parents. Even babies' genetically determined sucking patterns predict later obesity. Moreover, children who are overweight tend to stay that way. Overweight infants tend to become obese children who develop into obese adolescents and continue to be obese into adulthood (Jeffrey, 2001).

Along with these preceding factors, education and income also play a role in obesity. For example, a national health survey found that as income increases, there is a decreasing likelihood that excess weight constitutes a health risk (Health Canada, 1999a)—a finding that has also been observed in the United States (Kumanyika, 1993). Moreover, the chances of being overweight decrease with more education. Canadians with less than a high school education are about one and a half times more likely than university graduates to face a probable health risk due to being overweight.

Finally, there is also evidence that modelling by others strongly affects children's eating behaviours. Parents of obese children encourage them to eat more than their thinner siblings (explaining that they are bigger so they need more food) and offer them eating prompts twice as often as parents of normal-weight children (Klesges, Malott, Boschee, & Weber, 1986; Ray & Klesges, 1993). As Box 5.2 on the following pages shows, teaching children how to recognize when they are hungry and to stop eating when they feel full may help prevent the development of obesity. Rewarding children for eating everything on their plates may teach them to rely on external instead of internal cues in deciding whether to eat and for some children, this leads to eating whenever food is in sight.

Canadian Fitness Resources

Obese children and adolescents often suffer from a variety of physical problems, including asthma, sleep problems, hypertension and diabetes (Beebe et al., 2007; Cruz et al., 2005). They may also run the risk of having high cholesterol levels, especially if they are boys, which can predispose them to high blood pressure and other cardiovascular problems (Labarthe, 1997; Pinhas & Zeitler, 2000). Overweight children suffer psychologically as well, because of body-image disturbances and discrimination by their (thinner) peers (Bierman, 2004; Storch et al., 2007). Peers tease obese kids, exclude them from groups, and choose them last for athletic activities. For their part, because they fear other children will ridicule their bodies, chubby children often seek excuses to avoid gym class and, thus, get less exercise than they should. Overweight adolescents date less and are less likely to be admitted to prestigious colleges than their thinner classmates. Clearly, the costs of being obese can be high.

TREATING OVERWEIGHT CHILDREN   Two ideas seem most promising for controlling children's weight. First, it appears to be important to involve the family—parents and perhaps siblings and peers as well—in any treatment program. Parents often encourage their children's overeating not only by tying eating to external cues but by their own eating habits. Researchers are finding that working with entire families in attempting to reverse these processes are relatively successful (Epstein et al., 1994,

Box 5.2

Child Psychology in Action

LEARNING NOT TO "CLEAN YOUR PLATE"

Parents play a major role in teaching children about eating. They help children learn about what to eat, when to eat it, and how much to eat (Rozin, 1996). Unfortunately, parents may also teach children to rely more on external cues—such as feedback from them or the mere presence of food—than on cues that come from their own bodies that tell them when they are hungry and when they are not. When a child says, "I'm full" and the parent says, "No, finish what's on your plate," the parent is giving a clear message that it is the external cue that is important.

Birch and colleagues (Birch, McPhee, Shoba, Steinberg, & Krehbeil, 1987), at the University of Illinois, showed that children can learn to rely on either internal or external feedback, depending on adult response to their eating behaviour. Twenty-two preschoolers attended a series of special snack sessions over a six-week period. In one group, the adult researchers helped the children focus on their sensations of hunger and fullness and stressed how these internal reminders tell us when to eat and when to stop eating. The children felt their stomachs and discussed how eating changes our feelings of hunger. In a second group, external cues were the focus. A bell rang to signal "snack time," and children were rewarded with such things as stickers for cleaning their plates.

Then, the groups were combined and everyone was given a yogourt snack to eat, after which they were given a chance to eat another snack of cookies and granola bars. Children in the first group, who had been taught to rely on their internal signals, consumed less of the second snack, but children who had learned to depend on external cues, such as rewards and adult urging, ate just as much of the second snack, no matter how full they were. It seems clear that the social context can influence which kinds of cues children learn to rely on in choosing or stopping eating. Other more recent studies with older children show similar counterproductive effects of pressuring children to eat: intake is higher and children's feelings about eating are more negative (Birch, 2006).

This work helps us to understand why children are getting heavier. In recent years, portion sizes have increased, and "supersizing" is common in fast-food establishments. It wouldn't matter if children regulated their food intake so they stopped when they were full, but by the age of 5, children will eat more when portions are larger (Rolls, Engell, & Birch, 2000, and see Figure 5-14). Younger children (3-year-olds) seem to know better; for them, portion size does not affect consumption.

Children can be encouraged to eat more healthily in a number of ways (Birch, 2006; Ray & Klesges, 1993). Allowing children to have more control over their food choices and the amounts they consume may help them learn more about how foods help people

1995; Epstein et al., 1997; Nader, 1993). They have also found that such interventions as reducing the likelihood of stressful interactions with family members at mealtime can help curb overeating (Israel, 1988). In one family-based study, researchers found that by encouraging parents to serve as models of good eating and physical exercise, 34 percent of the children succeeded in losing 20 percent or more of their overweight poundage; at the close of the 10-year study, 30 percent were no longer obese (Epstein et al., 1994). Even school-based peer-tutoring programs show promise as an obesity prevention strategy. Older students (grades 4 to 7) who were taught lessons of healthy living—nutrition, physical activity and healthy body image—were paired with younger students as "Healthy Buddies." Compared to controls, both older and younger children increased their knowledge about healthy living and showed a smaller increase in blood pressure; the older children gained less weight and the younger ones grew taller (Stock et al., 2007).

The second promising idea for controlling children's weight is to increase the physical expenditure of energy in innovative ways (NICHD Child Care Research Network, 2003). We all know that taking it off and keeping it off requires not only watching food intake but also burning off calories as well. A recent study following the "America on

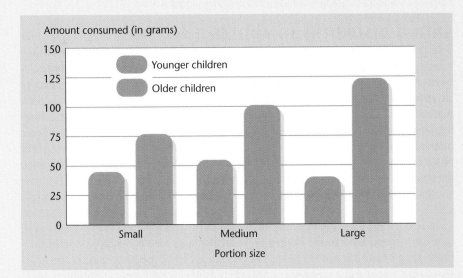

Amount consumed (in grams)

Portion size

Figure 5-14

Do we get smarter with age or not?

Researchers served two groups of children one of three different-size portions of macaroni and cheese at lunch. The 3½-year-old children were not affected by the portion sizes, but among the 5-year-olds, the bigger their portion, the more they ate.

Source: Rolls, Engell, & Birch, 2000.

balance energy. Involving children more in food-related activities such as helping to shop and prepare foods may give them more awareness of the importance of good nutrition. But most important, modelling good eating behaviour for children shows them what and how much to eat. Children are more likely to eat a food when they see an adult eating it. They tend to develop the same food preferences as their parents. If parents eat a balanced and moderate diet, their children are likely to follow suit, but if parents eat large amounts of foods with saturated fatty acid content, children are likely to do the same. Perhaps parents should look at mealtime as an opportunity rather than a challenge. The need to teach their children that healthy eating habits might be just the nudge they need to watch their own diets and keep in shape.

the Move" protocol in which families made two small lifestyle changes—walking an additional 2000 steps per day and reducing calories by replacing sugar with non-caloric sweeteners—found that 7- to 14-year-olds were more likely to maintain or decrease their weight in comparison to children in a control group (Rodearmel et al., 2007).

A study by Leonard Epstein and colleagues at the State University of New York at Buffalo suggests that choice may be important in getting children to increase their level of exercise (Epstein et al., 1995). These researchers gave children two options: They could spend less time in sedentary behaviours, such as watching TV and playing computer games, or they could increase their physical activity by riding an exercise bike or exercising to an aerobics tape. As you can see from Figure 5-15 on the next page, decreasing sedentary activity was more effective in producing weight loss than was increasing specific exercises. Based on significant improvements in fitness among the children who reduced their sedentary activities, the investigators speculate that these children may have substituted other, higher-energy-expenditure activities of their own choice. Parents had been instructed to make easily available such things as skates and bicycles. Not only is increased physical activity helpful for weight loss, it leads to other benefits as well, such as increases in perceived body satisfaction, overall physical self-worth and improved motor skills (Goldfield et al., 2007; Korsten-Reck et al., 2007). In spite of the success of some recent weight-reduction programs for children, maintaining weight loss and preventing weight gains in the first place remain serious challenges. Not only lifestyle issues such as lack of exercise and the widespread availability of high-fat, high-calory fast food make it hard for children to keep their weight in check but also genetic predispositions to become overweight among some children pose a problem, too.

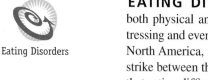

Eating Disorders

EATING DISORDERS IN ADOLESCENCE   Just as obesity can cause both physical and psychological problems, being underweight can also bring on distressing and even life-threatening conditions. The two most common eating disorders in North America, anorexia and bulimia, afflict far more women than men and generally strike between the ages of 10 and the early twenties. Although there is some indication that eating difficulties tend to decline in frequency in the transition to adulthood, a number of women continue to be dissatisfied with their bodies and to indulge in repetitive dieting. Men, on the other hand, who are less affected in adolescence and early adulthood, may begin to gain weight after beginning college/university and for the first time, they may become concerned with dieting and body image.

anorexia nervosa

An eating disorder in which the person, usually a young woman, is preoccupied with avoiding obesity and often diets to the point of starvation.

bulimia nervosa

An eating disorder in which people, usually young women, alternate periods of binge eating with vomiting and other means of compensating for the weight gained.

People with **anorexia nervosa** have an unaccountable dread of being overweight and diet constantly to avoid that state. They see themselves as obese even if they are quite slender and although they may be preoccupied with food and may even hoard it, they eat less and less. Young women, in particular, may lose up to 25 percent of their body weight (some lose even more) and become so weak that they must be hospitalized to correct fluid and electrolyte imbalances. Without continuing intervention, these skeletal creatures, who often have been attractive, bright, and achieving young women, may die from starvation or suicide (Tinsley, 2003).

Bulimia nervosa is an eating disorder in which the person—again, typically a young woman in adolescence or early adulthood—goes through cycles of seemingly uncontrollable binge eating followed by either vomiting or the use of laxatives to compensate for the bingeing and to prevent weight gain. Sometimes, this disorder is seen in young women pursuing activities that stress slimness such as gymnastics, cheerleading, running, figure skating, or ballet (Moreno, 2006; Sherwood et al., 2002). Bulimics like

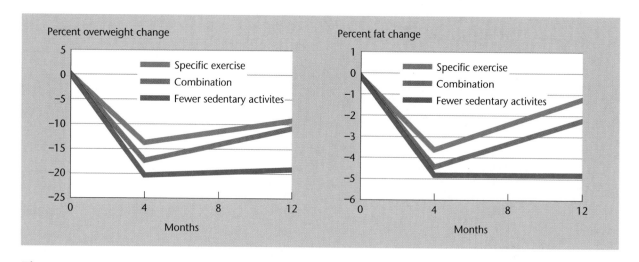

Figure 5-15

Reducing sedentary activities helps reduce weight

Children who spent less time watching TV and playing computer games lost the most weight. Neither a specific exercise regimen nor the combination of exercise and reduction of sedentary activities worked as effectively.

Source: Epstein et al., 1995.

anorexics, risk fluid and electrolyte abnormalities, and the loss of stomach acid through vomiting and the frequent induction of diarrhea can cause other metabolic problems (Mehler, 2003).

Most cases of bulimia emerge during the late teens and early twenties, whereas anorexia may begin at a variety of points throughout adolescence, especially at puberty (Attie & Brooks-Gunn, 1989). Bulimia affects between 1 and 3 percent of adolescent and young women (Moreno, 2006), anorexia probably less than 1 percent (Tamburrino & McGinnis, 2002). Both disorders are more prevalent in industrialized societies, such as Canada, the United States, Australia, Japan, New Zealand, South Africa, and European countries.

Despite some outward similarities, the two disorders are quite different. Unlike anorexics, young women with bulimia rarely diet to the point of starvation and death; anorexics, however, do sometimes engage in bingeing and purging. In contrast to anorexic young women, who tend to be of normal weight before the illness takes hold of them and to be socially withdrawn, bulimics are sometimes obese before the on-set of illness and are typically extroverted and have voracious appetites. Women with both disorders may exhibit symptoms of depression, but whereas bulimics often have poor self-images and low self-esteem, anorexics have a tendency toward *obsessive-compulsiveness* (the tendency to have recurrent obsessions or compulsions to do certain things, both of which take up time and may cause marked psychological distress) perfectionism, and a strong need to control their environment (Fairborn, Cooper, Doll, & Welch, 1999; Haimi et al., 2003). It may be that controlling their food intake is, for some anorexics, the only control they feel able to exert over their lives.

Most anorexics and bulimics are of European descent and relatively high socio-economic status (Benokraitis, 1996). Girls of African descent are less likely to develop eating disorders, in part, because of their lower level of dissatisfaction with their body image relative to white females of the same weight (Moreno, 2006). Girls with eating problems often come from families with histories of eating disorders or of substance abuse (alcohol, marijuana, uppers, downers) (Laporte, Marcoux, & Guttman, 2001). The families of bulimic adolescents are often chaotic, conflict-ridden, and stressed, and family members have difficulty communicating their feelings (Fisher & Brone, 1991; Rodriguez Martin et al., 2005). The families of anorexic girls are often high achieving and protective; mothers are dominating, intrusive, and overbearing and fathers are "emotional absentees" (Carson & Butcher, 1992; Karwautz et al., 2003). The development of eating disorders has also been linked to images prevalent in the media. Vaughan and Fouts (2003), for example, found, in a 6-month-old longitudinal study, that pre-adolescent girls (11 and 12 years of age) who increased their eating disorder symptoms also tended to be those who spent more time looking at fashion magazines. Clearly, the factors underlying the development of eating disorders are both complex and multi-dimensional.

Treating anorexia may require initial hospitalization and physical intervention. Although in-hospital behavioural modification techniques have succeeded in regularizing anorexics' eating behaviour and in achieving weight gain, the effects of this type of therapy seem to be short-lived (Mehler & Crews, 2001). Longer-term psychotherapy that includes the family has had some success (Miller & Pumariega, 2001). However, according to one estimate, fewer than half of adolescents with this disorder make a complete recovery (Zerbe, 1993), and 5 to 10 percent die either from starvation or by overt suicide (American Psychiatric Association, 2000). Treatments for bulimia are generally more successful than treatments for anorexia. A variety of approaches, including individual and family psychotherapy, support groups, nutrition and eating education (recognizing satiety or fullness), and, in cases where depression is evident, anti-depressive medications, have been successful in treating bulimia (Bergh et al., 2002; Mitchell et al., 2001; Tinsley, 2003). Unfortunately, many adolescents never seek treatment for this disorder.

The treatment of anorexia can achieve remarkably successful changes. From this girl's shocking appearance at diagnosis (a), one might not have believed that she could exude the health and happiness her post-treatment image shows (b).

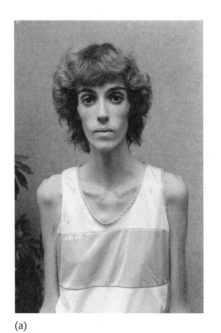

(a)

(b)

For Thought and Discussion

1. What implications does research into environmental influences on physical growth or motor development have for the concept of canalization (discussed in Chapter 2)?

2. In a recent attempt to respond to the rise of childhood obesity, a school in Lethbridge, Alberta, banned the sale of junk food to its students. This school has since received strong resistance to this ban from its school board, who claim that the exclusive arrangement with the retailer of this food (that allowed for the sale of the junk food) provided much-needed revenue to this underfunded school. Do you think that the school had the right to impose such a ban? What do you think about the implications of the school board's response?

LO9 SEXUAL MATURATION

Whereas physical growth, except for one or two growth spurts, is more or less gradual, sexual maturation arrives with rather a flourish. Suddenly, a girl begins to menstruate, a boy has his first ejaculation, and both know or come to know that they are no longer children but young adults, capable both of fully expressing their sexuality and of reproducing their species. **Puberty**, or the onset of sexual maturity, has long been held as a time of stress for the adolescent, when the intensity of new drives and the social pressures for new behaviours and new responsibilities may cause conflict and confusion. In this section, we describe the actual changes that occur with puberty and then explore the question of whether young people are generally experiencing puberty earlier and earlier. We close the section with a discussion of whether maturing earlier or later than one's peers has a significant effect on a young person.

puberty

The onset of sexual maturity.

pituitary gland

A so-called master gland, located at the base of the brain, which triggers the secretion of hormones by all other hormone-secreting, or endocrine, glands.

The Onset of Sexual Maturity

Puberty is marked by a number of growth changes that are triggered when the hypothalamus at the base of the brain stimulates the **pituitary gland** (see Figure 5-16), to

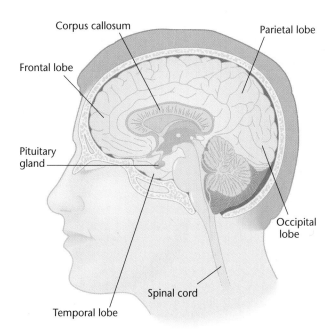

Figure 5-16

The pituitary gland

Cutting through the cerebrum, we can see the location of the pituitary gland, which controls the secretion of important human hormones, including those that stimulate cell growth and replication.

Source: Adapted from Postlethwait & Hopson, 1995.

secrete **hormones**. Hormones are powerful and highly specialized chemical substances produced by the cells of certain body organs and that have a regulatory effect on the activities of certain other organs. In this case, the pituitary gland's hormones cause the *adrenal cortex* (the outer layer of an adrenal gland) and the *gonads* (in males, the testes, and in females, the ovaries) to initiate a growth spurt. As Table 5-3 shows, in girls, this spurt begins with breast development, and in both sexes, the appearance of pubic hair is an early sign of puberty. These characteristics, along with voice change in boys, are considered *secondary sex characteristics*, which are not directly involved in sexual

hormone

A powerful and highly specialized chemical substance that interacts with cells capable of receiving the hormonal message and responding to it.

Table 5-3 Sexual maturation: A timetable

Average Age of Onset	Girls	Boys
10	Breasts (breast buds) begin to develop	
11	Pubic hair appears; it is sparse and slightly pigmented	**Testes and scrotum begin to grow**
12		Pubic hair, lightly pigmented, begins to appear
12 to 13	Underarm hair begins to appear	
13	Breasts continue to enlarge; areola and nipple project above contour of breast	**Spermarche: first ejaculation of semen**
13 to 14	**Menarche: beginning of menstruation**	
14	Pubic hair becomes denser, but area covered is smaller than in adult woman	Underarm and facial hair begin to appear
15	Breasts and pubic hair coverage are fully mature	**Penis, testes are fully developed** Pubic hair coverage is complete; moustache and beard hair begin to grow

Note: Primary sex characteristics are in boldface type.

Sources: Petersen & Taylor, 1980; Tanner, 1978; Turner & Rubinson, 1993.

spermarche

In males, the first ejaculation of semen-containing ejaculate.

menarche

In females, the beginning of the menstrual cycle.

estrogens

Hormones that, in the female, are responsible for sexual maturation.

progesterone

A hormone that, in females, helps regulate the menstrual cycle and prepares the uterus to receive and nurture a fertilized egg.

testosterone

A hormone that, in the male, is responsible for the development of primary and secondary sex characteristics and is essential for the production of sperm.

reproduction. *Primary sex characteristics*, which are involved in the reproductive process and which evolve a few years after the first secondary characteristics appear, include, in males, **spermarche**, or the capability of the testes and associated internal organs to produce sperm-containing ejaculate. In females, primary sex characteristics include the changes in the reproductive organs that culminate with **menarche**, or the beginning of *ovulation*. Each month an egg, released from an ovary, begins its journey through the fallopian tubes to the uterus where, if not fertilized, it is expelled in the menstrual flow.

In female and male adolescents, the rising concentrations of hormones stimulate the development of both primary and secondary sex characteristics. In females, **estrogens** are crucial to the maturation of the reproductive system, including the ovaries, fallopian tubes, and uterus, and to the onset of ovulation and menstruation. **Progesterone** helps regulate the menstrual cycle and readies the uterus for the reception and nurture of a fertilized egg. In males, **testosterone**, the most important of several *androgens*, is essential to the maturation of the penis, testes, and other organs of the reproductive system and to the production of sperm. Male sexual motivation is influenced by testosterone; female sexual motivation is less dependent on hormonal secretions.

As you can see from Table 5-3, even the attainment of secondary sex characteristics is gradual, with menarche and spermarche occurring two to three years after the beginning of the maturation process. Nevertheless, it is because these two later events signal such a marked change in the person, not only physically and physiologically but psychologically, that they are considered a major turning point. For some women, menarche is the "true" or real onset of puberty (Brooks-Gunn & Ruble, 1984).

In industrialized countries, at least, young women have been reaching puberty at earlier ages than before. In the United States, for example, young women in the late 1960s tended to experience menarche a year and a half earlier (at 12.9 years) than their mothers had (at 14.4 years) (Herman-Giddens et al., 1997). As Figure 5-17 shows, in Finland, Norway, and Sweden, the age of menarche dropped roughly three and a half years in a little over a century. This trend to earlier menarche is slowing down in many Western European countries and among middle-class girls in the United States (Helm & Grolund, 1998; Wellens et al., 1990; Wyshak & Frisch, 1982). However, among certain groups (e.g., African-American girls), the onset of menarche is now even earlier: at age 7 or 9 (Freedman et al., 2002; Herman-Giddens et al., 1997; NHLBI, 1992). The reduction in age at menarche has not been uniform around the world. Change has occurred hardly at all among Inuit groups and among only some groups in India (Roche,

Figure 5-17

Decline in the age of menarche

In the Scandinavian countries represented here, the age of onset of menstruation declined considerably over a little more than a century and a half. Although the data for the United Kingdom and the United States do not cover the same time period, their trend suggests that the rate of change in menarche onset in all these countries is fairly similar.

Source: Roche, 1979.

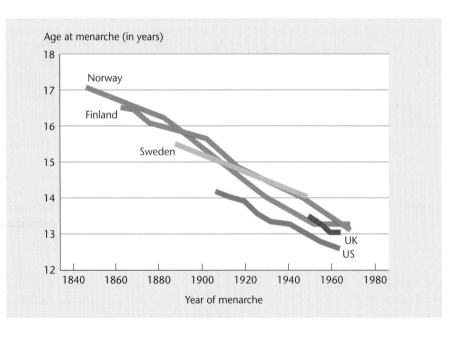

1979), and in Denmark, change has ceased altogether (Helm & Grolund, 1998). In certain underdeveloped countries, such as some parts of New Guinea, the median age is very late: 17.5 to 18.4 years (Malcolm, 1970).

What Determines the Timing of Puberty?

Inheritance plays some role in the timing of menarche; girls whose mothers have matured early tend to mature early themselves. But environmental factors also contribute to this important event. For example, gymnasts, figure skaters, and ballet dancers who practice intensively, perform regularly, and diet to keep fit may delay the onset of menstruation by as much as one year (Brooks-Gunn & Warren, 1985). In one study of French-Canadian gymnasts who were 14 or 15 years old, over half the females had not yet reached menarche (Samela, 1979). After girls reach menarche, their periods may not be regular if they train hard and keep their weight low; for example, runners and gymnasts sometimes stop menstruating, or become *amenorrheic*. Such girls can literally turn their menstrual cycles on and off by stopping and restarting their training regime (Brooks-Gunn & Warren, 1985).

Parent–child relationships can also alter the timing of sexual maturation (Ellis, 2004). In a longitudinal study of family relationships, Steinberg (1987) found that systematic changes in family systems around the time of puberty affected the timing of young people's sexual maturation, and that this maturation also affected family relationships by increasing conflicts between youth and parents. In families where parents and children were emotionally distant, young people tended to reach sexual maturity earlier, whereas the closer parent and child were, the slower the process of maturation seemed to be. Recent research confirms these findings: girls whose mothers and fathers were more supportive toward them in early childhood reached puberty later (Ellis & Essex, 2007); girls who experienced more family conflict and father absence reached menarche earlier (Belsky et al., 2007; Ellis et al., 1999; Moffitt et al., 1992). These findings may be explained by suggesting that stress leads to earlier maturation, or they may also reflect genetic inheritance. For example, statistics show that women who mature early and have children early are likely to become single parents, which exposes their children to more stressful conditions and father absence. Further research is needed to determine the relative contributions of inheritance and the environment to the timing of sexual maturation.

The Effects of Early and Late Maturation   **LO 10**

Does variation in the rate of maturation make a psychological difference for children? To some extent, it depends on gender. For boys, there are some risks and some advantages in maturing early, but for girls the disadvantages clearly outweigh advantages.

Boys who mature early have the advantage of being considered by their peers to be more physically attractive, athletic, masculine and popular; late-maturing boys are viewed as less attractive and masculine, more childish, bossy, talkative, and attention-seeking (Jones & Bayley, 1950). However there is a downside for boys who reach maturity early: Early-maturing boys are more likely to engage in delinquent behaviour; owing to their obvious physical maturity, they are often accepted by, and associate with, older males—leading them to more risk-taking and more externalizing problems (Ge et al., 2001, 2003). Moreover these boys are more likely to experience depressive symptoms during adolescence but these symptoms decrease after several years. Too many temptations before they are ready to evaluate the risks associated with these more mature activities can lead to trouble and elevated sadness for early maturing boys.

For girls the effects of early maturing are more negative, dramatic, and long lasting. Early maturing girls may not be as prepared for the changes in their bodies and body functions as girls reaching puberty on time because their development typically occurs before schools offer health classes and their mothers are less likely to discuss these changes with them (Brooks-Gunn, 1988; Mendle et al., 2007). They tend to have a poorer body image than on-time or late maturers, in part because the weight gains accompanying the onset of maturation violate the cultural ideal of thinness for girls (Graber et al., 1996; Mendle et al., 2007). As you can see from Figure 5-18, the trends for positive body image for girls and boys are almost opposites: Early-maturing boys have a far more positive body image than late-maturing boys; early-maturing girls tend to have negative body images, whereas late-maturing girls have positive self-images. Notice, however, that like boys who mature late, the latest-maturing girls also tend to have problems with body image. Early-maturing girls have been found to have more adjustment or behavioural problems including higher and more sustained levels of depression (Ge et al., 2001; Mendle et al., 2007), higher levels of eating disorders such as bulimia nervosa (Kaltiala-Heino et al., 2001), earlier initiation of substance use such as smoking and drinking (Stice et al., 2001), poorer academic achievement (Stattin & Magnusson, 1990), earlier initiation of sexual activity (Stice et al., 2001; Stattin & Magnusson, 1990), and higher rates of delinquent behaviour (Haynie, 2003). Longitudinal studies in Sweden (Magnusson, 1988, 1996b; Stattin & Magnusson, 1990; Stice et al., 2000) suggest the causes of these patterns. Early-maturing girls had smaller networks of close friends and were more likely to engage in adult behaviours such as smoking, drinking, and sexual intercourse at a younger age than late maturers because they tended to associate with older peers who are closer to them in terms of physical status and appearance.

Of course, although early maturation entails risks, not all early maturers have a poor body image or date, smoke, or drink earlier. Individuals differ in whether they perceive early maturation as "on time" (normal) or "off-time" (deviant), depending on the attitudes, beliefs, and behaviours of their particular reference group. In the final analysis, a girl's adjustment to the changes of puberty probably depend more on the kinds of support, encouragement, and guidance she receives from parents, and the values and expectations of her own particular peer group, than on whether maturation is early, average, or late (Conger & Petersen, 1984).

The impact of the transition to sexual maturity cannot be fully appreciated in isolation from other changes in young people's lives. Some adolescents attend junior high school after grade 6, whereas others stay in elementary school through grade 8 and then go on to high school. Researchers have found that youth moving through the former type of system experience more adjustment difficulties (Wigfield et al., 2006; Rudolph et al., 2001). In addition, some adolescents date early and others delay this step. Simmons and

Figure 5-18

Body image in adolescent girls and boys

For boys, the relation between body image and timing of puberty is a straight line: the sooner the better. Girls tend to have more positive body images the later they mature, but if maturity comes exceedingly late, their body images may suffer.

Source: Tobin-Richards, Boxer, & Petersen, 1984.

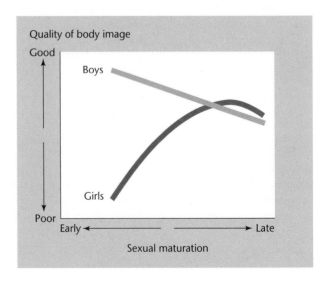

Blyth (1987) found that girls who entered puberty early and at the same time changed schools and started to date had lower self-esteem than other girls. Girls who moved their residences or experienced a major family disruption (divorce, death, remarriage) suffered even more loss in self-esteem and grades, and their participation in extracurricular activities decreased (Simmons et al., 1987). Attending a co-ed school also increases problems for early-maturing girls (Caspi et al., 1993; Ge et al., 1996).

The challenges of coping with multiple and simultaneous life changes are not limited to girls. Boys who experienced sexual maturity accompanied by a variety of other changes, such as change of school, moving to a new neighborhood, or engaging in early dating, had poorer grades and participated less in extracurricular activities than boys who experienced fewer life transitions (Mendle et al., 2007; Simmons et al., 1987). These findings underscore the idea that the impact of the timing of puberty can best be understood in the context of other transitions and illustrate the ability of the environmental context to help or hinder children's abilities to cope with biological change.

Making the Connections 5

There are many links between concepts and ideas in one area of development and concepts and ideas in other areas. Here are some of the connections between ideas in Chapter 5 and discussions in other chapters of this book.

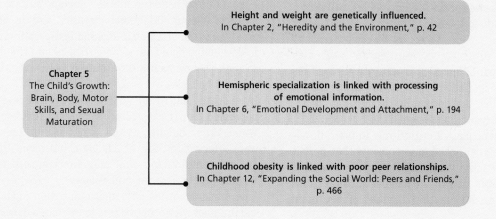

Chapter 5
The Child's Growth: Brain, Body, Motor Skills, and Sexual Maturation

Height and weight are genetically influenced.
In Chapter 2, "Heredity and the Environment," p. 42

Hemispheric specialization is linked with processing of emotional information.
In Chapter 6, "Emotional Development and Attachment," p. 194

Childhood obesity is linked with poor peer relationships.
In Chapter 12, "Expanding the Social World: Peers and Friends," p. 466

SUMMARY

Brain Development in Infancy

- The largest portion of the human brain, the **cerebrum**, is covered by a highly convoluted layer called the **cerebral cortex**. The cortex is divided into a number of regions whose cells control specific functions, such as seeing, hearing, feeling, moving, and thinking.

- In the developing organism, **neuron proliferation** rapidly increases the brain's **neurons**. Although all the brain's neurons are present at birth, many subsequent changes take place in the size of neurons, the numbers of **synapses**, and the production of the surrounding, supportive **glial cells**. These changes, such as **myelination**, increase the speed, efficiency, and complexity of transmissions between neurons.

- **Neural migration** distributes neurons throughout brain regions. The abundance of synapses, formed by **synaptogenesis**, and of neurons is trimmed over time through the processes of **neuronal death** and **synaptic pruning**.

- The human brain is organized in two halves: the two **brain hemispheres** are connected by the **corpus callosum**. The right hemisphere controls the left side of the body and is involved in the processing of visual-spatial information, face recognition, and interpreting emotional expressions. The left hemisphere controls the right side of the body and is important for understanding and using language. Both **hemispheric specialization** and **lateralization** are evident early in infancy and are well developed by age 3 years.

- **Dyslexia**, or difficulty in learning to read, may reflect abnormal lateralization patterns, such as the processing of spatial information on both sides of the brain rather than primarily in the right hemisphere, the normal arrangement.

- The environment plays a critical role in brain development. In rats, enriched environments that permit a great deal of activity and exploration are related to increases in brain size, in the number of connections among neurons, and in the activities of key brain chemicals.

Motor Development

- Research suggests that infants grasp objects in different ways depending on the object's size and shape and the relative size of their own hands. This research indicates that the infant motor system is able to adapt to the demands of a situation.

- The development of walking follows a U-shaped course, beginning with a stepping reflex at birth that disappears in a few months; that is followed by the emergence of independent, voluntary walking a number of months later, usually around the first birthday.

- A dynamic systems approach to explain this pattern suggests that the development of walking depends on the combination of a variety of factors, and when the baby's weight becomes too much of a load on the emerging motor system, stepping ability may be temporarily masked. Cross-cultural studies indicate that environmental influences, such as repeated practice, may either enhance or slow down independent walking.

- The relations among locomotion; other aspects of development, such as perception, social interaction, and problem solving; and environmental forces are complex. In general, the greater a child's motor skills, the more his general development is enhanced.

Physical Growth

- Infants' and children's growth is guided by the two basic principles of cephalocaudal development and proximal-distal pattern. Growth proceeds at different rates during different stages of development.

- Most authorities are agreed today that breast-feeding provides infants with better support for healthy growth than bottle-feeding. Breast-feeding ensures healthy development of the brain and nervous system; it strengthens the infant's immune system and protects against infectious diseases; and it helps build denser bones. Bottle-feeding is especially risky in developing countries, where the cost of formula is so high that women often dilute it with water that may not be clean.

- Inadequate nutrition may result in severely depressed growth rates. During the First and Second World Wars, height, weight, and age of puberty were affected by lack of adequate nutrition. Other environmental factors that may affect growth rates include illness, disease, and climate.

- Environmental influences, such as nutrition and housing, interact with other factors to produce a considerable variation in growth rates. The effects of poverty may be seen in such disorders as **iron-deficiency anemia**, common in minority children and children in less-developed countries.

- Following environmental injury or deprivation, a strong corrective principle appears to operate in the case of physical growth. The degree of **catch-up growth** will depend on such things as the duration, severity, and timing of the deprivation.

- **Secular trends** in many countries show that across evolution, people have become taller. Although in North America people in the most advantaged groups may have reached their maximum potential in height gain, people in other segments of society continue to grow taller.

- Although the problem of **obesity** may begin in infancy and childhood, only about one-quarter of obese infants will remain obese 20 years later. The two critical periods for the development of obesity are during infancy and at about 4 years of age. Recent research indicates that genetic factors may play a role in determining later obesity.

- In addition to physical problems, such as hypertension and diabetes, obese children and adolescents may experience body-image disturbances and may suffer discrimination from peers and adults.

- Eating disorders include **anorexia nervosa**, which may occur early in adolescence and results from reduced intake of calories, and **bulimia nervosa**, which typically occurs in later adolescence and is characterized by food binges and purging through vomiting.

Sexual Maturation

- **Puberty**, the attainment of sexual maturity, is triggered when the **pituitary gland** stimulates other endocrine glands to secrete **hormones**, including **estrogens** and **progesterone** in females and **testosterone** in males, which initiate a growth spurt. This milestone in growth is marked by such changes as the start of breast development and **menarche** in girls, and the enlargement of the testes and **spermarche** in boys. Girls tend to reach menarche earlier in the more advanced countries, but there is still considerable age variation for the onset of menstruation throughout the world.

- The timing of physical maturation can affect the child's social and emotional adjustment. In general, the impact of the timing of puberty is best understood in the context of other transitions, such as school transitions and family disruptions, which may help or hinder the child's ability to cope with biological changes.

- In general, girls mature earlier than boys; on average, major changes occur two years earlier for girls. Although early maturation is usually seen as advantageous for boys, girls sometimes find early maturation stressful, developing poor body images and engaging in so-called adult behaviours.

MCGRAW-HILL CONNECT™—Available 24/7 with instant feedback so you can study when you want, how you want, and where you want. Take advantage of the Study Plan—an innovative tool that helps you customize your learning experience. You can diagnose your knowledge with pre- and post-tests, identify the areas where you need help, search the entire learning package for content specific to the topic you're studying, and add these resources to your personalized study plan. Visit *www.mcgrawhillconnect.ca* to register—take practice quizzes, search the e-book, and much more.

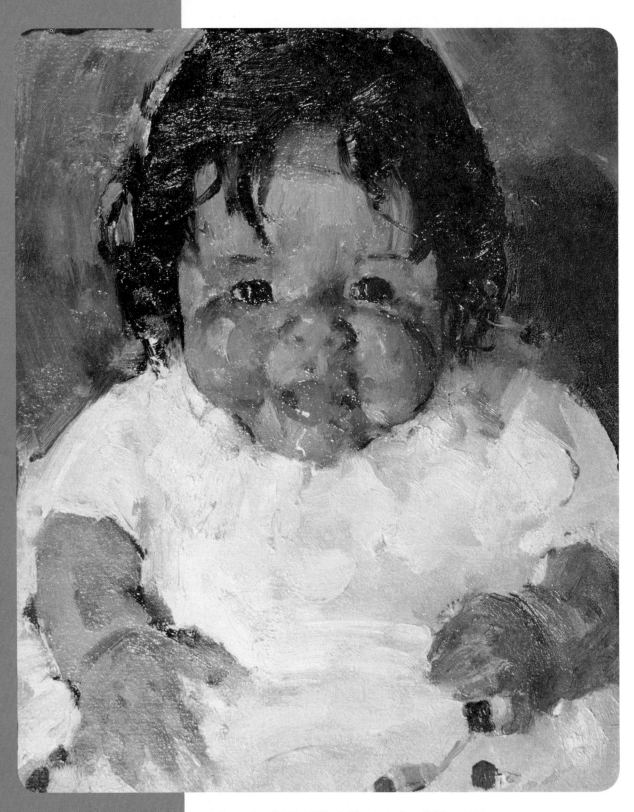

Martha Walter (1875–1976). *California Indian Child*, c. 1920.
David David Gallery, Philadelphia.

Chapter 6

Emotional Development and Attachment

LEARNING OBJECTIVES

After reading this chapter, you should be able to

LO1 Describe the functions of early emotions in children; why are such emotions important?

LO2 Discuss some of the different theoretical perspectives on emotional development.

LO3 Describe positive and negative primary emotions; give examples of each, and discuss the developmental time course for these examples; describe secondary emotions, and discuss the developmental time course for some examples.

LO4 Describe individual differences in emotions.

LO5 Discuss the idea of emotional regulation; what are emotional display rules?

LO6 Discuss how children think about and understand emotions, including the notion of emotional scripts and the recognition of multiple emotions.

LO7 Discuss the major theories of attachment, focusing primarily on ethological theory; identify the main attachment classifications.

LO8 Describe multiple procedures for how attachment can be measured.

LO9 Discuss how attachment is influenced by parental behaviour and infant temperament; state how this course is influenced by parental behaviour and infant temperament; discuss how internal working models influence attachment.

LO10 Discuss the stability of attachment and the consequences of attachment; include the effects of multiple attachments and multiple caregivers on the quality of attachment, including the data on daycare.

Children display a wide range of emotions, even from the time they are infants. Babies communicate their feelings, needs, and desires to others through the expression of emotion. The smiling infant tells others that something is pleasurable to him, and his frown communicates displeasure. Babies also influence the behaviour of other people by their expression of emotions. When a baby smiles, for instance, caregivers are almost sure to approach her, pick her up, talk to her, caress her; when a stranger approaches, on the other hand, her screams are apt to stop the stranger from picking her up. The older child may use smiling as a sign of welcome and express anger as a way of deterring a potential aggressor. In addition to using their own emotions to communicate with and regulate their worlds, children learn to read the emotional signs that other people display. Both processes—the production and the recognition of emotion—are essential to useful interactions with other people, and they enable babies to begin to exert some control over their social world.

We begin this chapter by examining why emotions are important and a variety of theories that help explain emotional development. Next, we explore children's earliest emotional expressions—smiling, laughter, ear, anger, and sadness—in some detail. Then we look at the development of some of the later-developing emotions such as pride, shame, guilt, and jealousy. Next we discuss how children learn to regulate their emotions and how the family contributes to the socialization of different aspects of emotional development. Concluding our discussion of emotion, we explore how the family contributes to the socialization of different aspects of emotional development.

We then turn to the study of attachment, first reviewing several theories of how attachment relationships form and then tracing the evolution of these relationships between infants and parents, siblings, and others.

In the last section of the chapter, we explore the nature and quality of attachment relationships, considering such issues as the role of parenting styles in these relationships and the effects of attachment quality on the child's cognitive and social development as well as on her sense of self. We conclude by examining the important question of the effects of child care and multiple caregivers on the children of working parents. ●

Human Development Laboratories

Canadian Researchers

LO1 EARLY EMOTIONAL DEVELOPMENT

emotions

Subjective reactions to something in the environment that are usually experienced cognitively as either pleasant or unpleasant, that are generally accompanied by physiological changes, and that are often expressed in some form of visible behaviour.

What are **emotions**? Emotions, such as joy, anger, and fear have several important aspects. They are (a) subjective reactions to the environment, (b) usually experienced cognitively as either pleasant or unpleasant, (c) generally accompanied by some form of physiological arousal, and (d) often communicated to others by some behaviour or action. Thus, for example, Becky, her family's newest member, may react to the taste of a different formula with disgust, experiencing it as unpleasant, and if we were to measure her heart rate, we might find that it had accelerated. Moreover, because Becky has not yet learned to hide her emotions, as adults sometimes do, she would undoubtedly let her family know, in no uncertain terms of her displeasure. Watching her wrinkle her face, spit out, and cry, Becky's parents could be pretty certain of the source of her unhappiness.

Why Are Emotions Important?

Emotions have a wide variety of functions in the lives of children. First, as we just noted, emotions are a means of letting others know how we feel. Second, our success in communicating our emotions and in learning to interpret other people's emotions is linked with our social success. Being able to express and interpret emotions is just as important as being able to solve a cognitive problem. Just as we have intellectual or cognitive intelligence, we develop emotional intelligence as well. As Daniel Goleman has documented in his popular book *Emotional Intelligence* (1995), being able to navigate successfully in the world of your own and other people's emotions is a critical ingredient of social and occupational success.

Emotions are linked to children's mental and physical health as well. As we explore in greater detail in the chapter on psychopathology, children who become excessively sad and despondent may develop other problems such as poor concentration and withdrawal from social interaction with others. In extreme cases, such children's self-worth may deteriorate seriously. Physical health suffers, too, when emotional development goes wrong. Children reared in environments in which they are emotionally and socially deprived, such as orphanages, often develop later problems with the management of stress and anxiety. The fact that these children have more difficulty modulating their reactions to stress is revealed by heightened levels of *cortisol* (a biological marker of stress response) that, in turn, may lead to problems of physical health (Gunnar, 2000; Rutter, 2002). Even children reared in ostensibly normal homes may suffer impaired physical health when they are exposed to emotional hostility between their parents (Gottman et al., 1996). Clearly, emotions have a wide range of effects on children's development.

Primary and Secondary Emotions

(LO)2

It is useful to distinguish between primary and secondary emotions. Primary emotions—such as fear, joy, disgust, surprise, sadness, and interest—emerge early in life and do not require introspection or self-reflection. Another set of emotions, the secondary, or self-conscious, emotions—such as pride, shame, guilt, jealousy, and embarrassment—emerge later in development and depend on our sense of self and our awareness of other individuals' reactions to our actions (Lewis, 1998; Saarni et al., 2006). We consider primary emotions first and then we explore secondary emotions.

Perspectives on Emotional Development

A child's emotional development is influenced by many factors: her genetic inheritance, the conditions of the environment into which she is born, her interactions with family members and, later, with peers. These and other factors all play important roles in determining her emotional makeup. In this section, we examine three theoretical perspectives on emotional development: the genetic-maturational, learning, and functionalist perspectives. Each of these three perspectives may be useful in explaining certain aspects of the child's development at certain stages of her life. And as you will see, all views overlap to some degree.

THE GENETIC-MATURATIONAL PERSPECTIVE According to the genetic-maturational view, emotions are best seen as products of biological factors. Individual differences in temperament play a central role in how intensely children react to emotionally arousing situations and in how well they are able to regulate their reactions. And right- and left-brain hemispheres control joy and fear expressions, respectively (see Chapter 2). Twin studies and research with premature infants support the biological underpinnings for the development of emotions. Identical twins show greater similarity than fraternal twins in both the earliest times of their first smiles and the amount of smiling in which each engages (Plomin et al., 1997). Studies of smiling in premature infants support the role of genetic-maturational factors in the onset of smiling. The normal *conceptual age* (age since conception) of a newborn human is 40 weeks, and most full-term babies begin to smile about 6 weeks after they are born, or at a conceptual age of 46 weeks. Premature infants who are born at 34 weeks often do not smile until 12 weeks after birth, which, for them, is also 46 weeks since conception (Dittrichova, 1969). A certain amount of physical maturation and social stimulation must occur before a baby is ready to start smiling. The interplay between genetics and the environment accounts for the timing and form of the behaviour.

A genetic-maturational basis for negative emotions, such as fear, is supported by both twin and cross-cultural studies. Again, identical twins are more similar than fraternal twins in their fear reactions to strangers and in their general degree of inhibitedness (Plomin et al., 1997; Robinson et al., 1992).

THE LEARNING PERSPECTIVE   The learning perspective is particularly useful in explaining individual differences in emotional expression. In general, different emotional expressions have different onsets, frequencies, and intensities in different children. The frequency with which children smile and laugh seems to vary with the nature of the environment in which they are raised (Denham et al., 2007). Parents can help their children learn to manage and understand their emotions by rewarding only certain emotional displays. Or they can interfere by being punitive and by dismissing their children's emotional expressions and experiences (Gottman et al., 1996). Common sense suggests that parents who respond with enthusiasm to their smiling infant will tend to encourage him to smile more. This has in fact been verified in studies showing that when adults, particularly familiar caregivers, respond to a baby's smile with positive stimulation, the child's rate of smiling increases (Denham et al., 2007; Rovee-Collier, 1987).

Learning experiences can also elicit and reinforce fear responses. Recall our example, in Chapter 4, of how a child may become classically conditioned to fear the doctor who gave him a painful shot on his first visit. Children may learn other fears through operant conditioning when one of their own behaviours, such as climbing up on a high ladder, is followed by a punishing consequence, such as a painful fall. And they can learn still other fears simply by observing others. For example, a child may watch her mother react fearfully to a bee or to a large dog and later imitate her mother's reaction (Bandura, 1989). In all these cases, the child's particular set of fears depends on what she has learned.

THE FUNCTIONALIST PERSPECTIVE   The functionalist perspective is a contemporary approach to emotional development (Saarni et al., 2006). According to this theory, emotions serve to help us achieve our goals and adapt to our environment, and it emphasizes the role of emotions in establishing and maintaining social relationships as well as the role that social cues play in regulating our emotional perceptions and expressions. This approach incorporates many features of the learning perspective in a unified view of emotional development.

How does this perspective approach emotional development? It assumes that the purpose of emotion is to help us achieve our goals. We all have goals that we try to reach—for example, to make a new friend, or to stay out of danger. And goals arouse emotions: Joy and hope arise as we anticipate forming a new friendship; fear may engulf us in a scary situation. In both cases, the emotions aroused help us reach our goals. The emotion of fear may lead us to flee the dangerous situation, enabling us to achieve the goal of self-preservation.

The functional approach also recognizes the social nature of emotions. We use information provided by others' emotional signals to guide our own behaviour. For instance, the way someone you view as a potential friend reacts emotionally to your social overture will be a critical determinant of how you feel. If she responds positively and smiles, you'll be happy and carry on, but if she frowns, you'll probably not be pleased and will try to make friends with someone else. So, you evaluate the situation and use the feedback from others as a guide. Finally, memories of the past serve as a guide in shaping how the child will respond emotionally to a situation. Children who have routinely been rebuffed by potential friends will be more wary, whereas children who have been socially successful will be more confident in this situation. In both cases, emotions regulate children's behaviour and enhance their adaptation to their environment.

No single theoretical perspective alone is likely to integrate all aspects of emotional development. Instead, different theories are useful in answering different questions. Emotional responses are shaped by a complex interplay between biological factors and the many forces of the environment that the child experiences. As we look at different aspects of emotional development, we will consider how each of the three perspectives we have examined helps us understand issues of emotional development.

The Development of Emotional Expressions

Most parents pay a great deal of attention to their newborn infants' behaviours and activities, and witnessing displays, such as smiling, frowning, and laughing many times over, they are inclined to agree that infants display a wide range of emotions at a very early age. Ninety-nine percent of mothers said that their 1-month-olds clearly displayed interest; 95 percent of mothers observed joy; 85 percent, anger; 74 percent, surprise; 58 percent, fear; and 34 percent, sadness (Johnson, Emde, Pannabecker, Stenberg, & Davis, 1982). These women based their judgments not only on their babies' behaviours (facial expressions, vocalizations, body movements) but also on the nature of the situations in which those behaviours occurred. For example, a mother who watched her baby staring intently at the mobile above her crib was likely to label the infant's emotion as "interest," whereas she might call the emotion expressed by a gurgling, smiling baby "joy." As you continue through this chapter, you may find it useful to refer to the Turning Points chart on pages 200–201, which offers a brief chronology of the milestones of emotional development in a typical child.

But relying on mothers' judgments may not be the best way to approach the issue. If you are wondering how researchers can distinguish among infants' expressions of all these emotions, the answer is by means of coding systems that pay careful attention to changes in a baby's facial expressions and bodily movements. These systems assign finely differentiated scores to different parts of the face (e.g., lips, eyelids, forehead) and to specific infant movement patterns. Researchers then use these scores to judge whether an infant has displayed a particular emotion (e.g., Izard et al., 1995). Carroll Izard at the University of Delaware and his associates have developed the most elaborate of the coding systems for infant emotional expressions now in use: the Maximally Discriminative Facial Movement, or MAX, coding system.

Infant Facial Coding

DEVELOPMENT OF PRIMARY EMOTIONS

With this general overview of early emotional development as a guide, let's turn to the development of the primary emotions of smiling, laughter, fear, anger, and sadness.

Positive Primary Emotions: Smiling and Laughter

At age 6 months, Liah smiled widely whenever her mother reached down to pick her up; by 12 months, Liah was laughing and giggling every time she and her dad played peeka-boo. What events elicit the smiling and laughter, and what is the developmental course of joy and pleasure? As we have already noted, if you watch closely, you can see smiles

Turning Points

THE EVOLUTION OF EMOTIONAL EXPRESSION AND THE SENSE OF SELF

EARLY WEEKS	• Shows distress by crying
1 MONTH	• Generalized distress; may be irritable by late afternoon
2 MONTHS	• Shows pleasure; mildly aroused by sight of toy; social smile
3 MONTHS	• Excitement and boredom appear; smiles broadly and often; cries when bored; may show wariness and frustration
4 MONTHS	• Laughs, especially at certain sounds; crying lessens; gurgles with pleasure; shows beginnings of anger
5 MONTHS	• Usually gleeful and pleased but sometimes frustrated; shows primitive resistant behaviours; turns head from disliked food; smiles at own image in mirror; some babies may begin to show wariness of strangers
6 MONTHS	• Matches emotions to others—e.g., smiles and laughs when mother does; fear and anger may appear now or later
7 MONTHS	• Fear and anger; defiance; affection; shyness
8 MONTHS	• More individuality in emotional expression; touches and explores body parts
9 MONTHS	• Shows negative emotions when restrained; frowns when annoyed; actively seeks others' comfort when tired; nighttime crying may reappear; recognizes self in mirror; most babies display real fear of strangers
10 MONTHS	• Intense positive and negative emotions; occasionally testy; uses reflection in mirror—e.g., seeing toy in mirror, may move toward toy
11 MONTHS	• Greater variability in emotions; individual temperament is more evident; learning to associate names of body parts; may insist on feeding self
12 MONTHS	• Becomes distressed when others are distressed; cries when something is not to liking; may show signs of jealousy; laughs often at own cleverness; struts/preens when walking; loves to look at self in mirror; wants to show mastery, and plays on own

Note: Developmental events described in this and other Turning Points charts represent overall trends identified in research studies. Individual children vary greatly in the ages at which they achieve these developmental changes.

Sources: Kopp, 1994; Saarni, Campos, & Camras, 2006; Sroufe, 1996.

reflex smile

A newborn infant's smile, which appears to reflect some internal stimulus, such as a change in the infant's level of arousal, rather than an external stimulus, such as another person's behaviour.

even in newborn infants. These **reflex or simple smiles** (Fogel et al., 2006; Wolff, 1987) are usually spontaneous and appear to depend on the infant's internal state, but the exact nature of the internal stimulus is as yet unknown. Whether or not researchers can shed light on the origin of the baby's reflex smiles, these smiles serve a good purpose. Most caregivers interpret these smiles as signs of pleasure, and this gives the caregivers pleasure and encourages them to cuddle and talk to the baby. In this sense, these smiles may

15 MONTHS	• More mood swings; is more caring toward agemates; annoyed by dirty hands; strongly prefers certain clothing; may fret or cry often but usually briefly
18 MONTHS	• Can be restless and stubborn; may sometimes have tantrums; sometimes shy; shows shame; uses adjectives to refer to self; uses objects like a blanket or a favourite stuffed animal to soothe self

21 MONTHS	• Makes some efforts to control negative emotions; can be finicky and exacting; increased efforts to control situations; begins to understand parents' values; refers appropriately to self as good or bad
24 MONTHS	• Can be contrary but also appropriately contrite; responds to others' moods; very intense; may be overwhelmed by changes; can be upset by dreams; refers to self by name; identifies self by gender; talks about self by using I and a verb, such as hurt or need; keen to experience world on own terms; begins to understand emotional display rules
30 MONTHS	• Begins to show shame, embarrassment
36 MONTHS	• Shows guilt, pride

48 TO 60 MONTHS	• Shows increased understanding and use of emotional display rules
72 MONTHS	• Begins to understand how two or more emotions can occur simultaneously

have adaptive value for the baby, ensuring critical caregiver attention and stimulation. Overall, early as well as later smiling helps keep caregivers nearby and, thus, becomes a means of communication and aid to survival (Saarni et al., 2006).

Between 3 and 8 weeks of age, infants begin to smile in response not only to internal events but to a wide range of external elicitors, including social stimuli such as faces, voices, light touches, and gentle bouncing (Sroufe, 1996). Infants are particularly interested in people and faces, and a high-pitched human voice or a combination of voice and face are reliable smile elicitors for babies between 2 and 6 months old. When 3-month-old infants were shown a human face and puppets whose faces varied in their resemblance to a human face, the infants smiled almost exclusively at the human face (Ellsworth et al., 1993), and infants between 2½ and 5 months smile more at their mothers than they do at a toy (Cossett, Pomerleau, Malcuit, & Kaczorowsk, 1996). Babies aren't such gullible little creatures; they know the "real thing" when they see it.

As infants grow older, they tend to smile at different aspects of the human face (Saarni et al., 2006). As we saw in Chapter 4, when 4-week-old babies look at human faces, they tend to focus on the eyes, but by the time they're 8 or 9 weeks old, they examine the mouth as well. Smiling behaviour follows a similar pattern: At first, babies smile at the eyes, then the mouth, and finally the entire face and the facial expression. By the time they are about 3 months old, babies also start to smile more selectively at familiar faces (Camras et al., 1991; Saarni et al., 2006), a fact that lends some support to the notion that smiling has begun to signal pleasure and not just arousal. For example, 3-month-olds show greater increases in smiling when their smiles are reinforced by reciprocal smiles and vocalizations from their mothers than when they are reinforced by equally responsive women who are strangers (Wahler, 1967). These findings are consistent with the learning and functionalist perspectives and suggest that infant smiling becomes more discriminating as babies develop.

A baby's pleasure at watching a familiar face is revealed in other ways as well. For instance, one study found that 10-month-olds generally reserved a special kind of smile for their mothers, rarely offering it to strangers (Fox & Davidson, 1988). These special smiles (called *Duchenne smiles* after Guillaume Duchenne, the French physician who noticed this pattern more than 100 years ago) are likely to involve not just an upturned mouth but wrinkles around the eyes as well, making the whole face seem to light up with pleasure (Ekman, 2003; Ekman et al., 1990). Also, babies display genuine smiles more in interacting with caregivers than when smiling alone (Messinger et al., 2001). And babies show other kinds of smiles during play—the display smile—which is a combination of the Duchenne smile and a jaw drop. This is evident in later phases of tickle games and peekaboo where there has been a buildup of excitement, followed by completion of the play bout (Fogel et al., 2006).

This infant's face clearly has a lot to say! Can you tell which emotion the child is feeling in each picture?

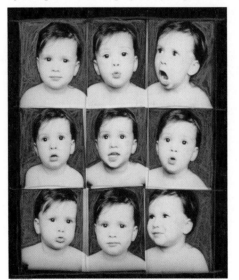

Of course, not all babies smile with equal frequency at their caregivers: There are individual differences in the amount of smiling a baby does. Some of these differences have to do with the social responsiveness of the baby's environment. For example, Israeli infants reared in a family environment smiled more often by the second half-year than infants raised in either a kibbutz (a communal living arrangement—see the "Styles of Caregiving" section) or an institution, where the level of social stimulation is presumably lower (Gewirtz, 1967). Gender is related to babies' smiling: In the newborn period, at least, girls generally show more spontaneous smiles than boys do (Korner, 1974). Nor are gender differences in smiling restricted to infants—teenage girls smile more than teenage boys (LaFrance et al., 2003). This higher rate of smiling has led some observers to suggest that girls may be genetically better prepared for social interaction than boys, because their greater tendency to smile more often draws others to them (Saarni et al., 2006). This view supports the genetic-maturational perspective. On the other hand, parents generally elicit and expect more emotions from girls than boys, which suggests that both genetic and environmental factors need to be considered.

There are national, ethnic, and gender differences in smiling (LaFrance et al., 2003). Compared with their peers in Britain, children and adults in Canada and the United States show larger gender differences in smiling. Perhaps Europeans have less stereotyped views of gender differences and treat boys and girls more similarly than do North Americans. And European-American males and females differ more in their smiling rates than do African Americans, among whom males and females show smaller differences in their smiling behaviour. This ethnicity difference is consistent with the finding that African-American parents treat boys and girls more similarly than European-American parents do (see Chapter 13).

Laughing, at which infants become quite skilled by the time they're 4 months old (Sroufe, 1996), is, if anything, even more useful in maintaining the baby's well-being (Nwokah et al., 1994). If smiling gradually becomes a sign of pleasure, laughter leaves us with little doubt of a baby's positive emotion, and it plays a very important role in caregiver–infant interaction.

What sorts of events elicit laughter across the first year of life? Sroufe and Wunsch (1972), using mothers as their experimental assistants, examined the amount of laughter elicited in babies between 4 and 12 months of age by a wide array of visual, tactile, auditory, and social-behavioural stimuli—for example, a human mask or a disappearing object; bouncing the child on an adult's knee or blowing on the baby's hair; making lip-popping, whispering, or whinnying sounds; and playing peekaboo, covering the baby's face, or sticking out the tongue.

As Figure 6-1 shows, up to about 7 months of age, babies are increasingly likely to laugh at visual, tactile, and social events, but their reactions to auditory stimulation remain stable. Note, however, that the nature of the stimuli that elicit laughter changes as the child develops. From 7 months on, both social and tactile stimuli begin to be less effective, but response to visual stimuli continues to increase. Toward the end of the first year, babies respond more to social games, visual displays, and other activities in which they can participate, such as covering and uncovering the mother's face with a cloth or playing tug-of-war with a blanket. By the end of the first year and throughout the second year, infants increasingly smile and laugh in response to activities that they create themselves (Sroufe, 1996), such as practising their motor accomplishments by pulling themselves to a standing position or laughing after making a jack-in-the-box pop up. As children grow older, laughing increases and becomes more of a social event (La Freniere, 2000; Saarni et al., 2006). In one study of 3- to 5-year-olds, nearly 95 percent of laughter occurred in the presence of other children and adults (Bainum et al., 1984). Acting silly was most often the elicitor of laughter among the nursery school set.

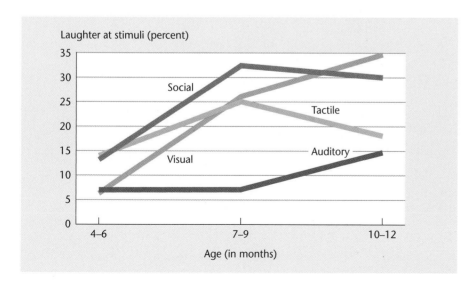

Figure 6-1

What makes children laugh?

Between the ages of 4 months and a year, children are most likely consistently to laugh at visual and social stimuli, such as a disappearing object or playing peekaboo.

Source: From Sroufe & Wunsch, 1972.

Negative Primary Emotions: Fear, Anger, and Sadness

FEAR   Timothy, at the age of 8 months, is exploring some toys in his playpen. He looks up and sees a strange woman standing near, watching him. Timothy turns back to his toys briefly, then again solemnly looks at the stranger, whimpers, turns away, and begins to cry. In the continuing search for regularities in early development, few phenomena have captured as much time, effort, and interest as this type of exchange between an infant and a stranger. Apparently, at the same time that babies are beginning to display signs of positive emotion in smiles and laughter, they are also learning to be fearful of some events and people, especially unfamiliar ones (La Freniere, 2000; Saarni et al., 2006).

The negative emotional response called *fear of strangers* evolves more slowly than the positive emotional expressions we have just discussed. Sroufe (1996) distinguishes two phases in the emergence of fear. At about 3 months of age, Sroufe maintains, infants show *wariness*, in which they respond with distress to an event that includes both familiar and unfamiliar aspects and which they therefore cannot comprehend and assimilate. This argument is consistent with the cognitive perspective on emotional development. By the time they are 7 to 9 months old, babies show true *fear*, which is an immediate negative reaction to an event that has specific meaning for them, such as seeing the face of a total stranger (e.g., "I don't know what this is, and I don't like it").

Even at 4 months of age, babies smile less at unfamiliar adults than they do at their mothers, showing early signs that they recognize familiar people. But they are not yet distressed by the presence of a stranger. In fact, they show great interest in novel people as well as novel objects. Often, they look longer at a stranger than at a familiar person, and if the mother is present, they will frequently look back and forth between her face and the stranger's, as if comparing them. Then, at about 5 months of age, this earlier reaction of gaze and interest starts to be replaced largely by giving a stranger a sober stare. At 6 months, although babies still are most likely to react to strangers with a sober expression, they're also likely to display distress. A distress reaction then gradually increases in frequency over the next half year, and by 7 to 9 months, the earlier wary reactions give way to clear expressions of fear. Figure 6-2 summarizes this progression from interest and exploration to fear over the first year of life (Emde et al., 1976).

Fear of strangers, or **stranger distress**, has become enshrined in the psychological literature as a developmental milestone and at one time was thought to be both

stranger distress

A fear of strangers that typically emerges in infants around the age of 9 months.

Figure 6-2

The onset of stranger distress

At 8 months of age, half the children studied here were showing distress at the appearance of strangers, and within a month or two, this distress reaction was clearly dominant.

Source: Adapted from Emde, Gaensbauer, & Harmon, 1976.

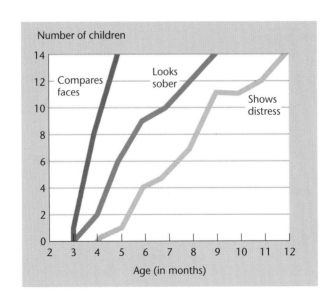

inevitable and universal. Researchers now know that it is neither (La Freniere, 2000; Saarni et al., 2006). Stranger distress emerges at about 7 to 9 months of age in several cultures, including the Hopi Indians (Dennis, 1940) and in Uganda (Ainsworth, 1963). However, in other cultures, such as the Efe (Africa), that emphasize shared caregiving among relatives babies show little stranger fear (Tronick et al., 1992). Moreover, babies are not all alike in their reactions to strangers. For some, greeting and smiling may be a frequent reaction, and fear is not typical while others show fear (Rheingold & Eckerman, 1973).

Whether a baby is fearful of a stranger depends on a host of variables, including who the stranger is, how she behaves, the setting in which the person is encountered, and the child's age (Mangelsdorf et al., 1991), as shown in Table 6-1. Consistent with the functionalist perspective on emotional development, contextual factors help determine the way an infant will react to a stranger. When babies meet strangers in their own homes, they show less stranger fear than when encountering unfamiliar people in an unfamiliar setting such as a researcher's laboratory (Sroufe et al., 1974). Similarly, babies who sit on their mothers' laps while a stranger approaches rarely show any fear, but when they are not in physical contact with their caregiver they may show fear when a stranger approaches (Bohlin & Hagekull, 1993; Morgan & Ricciuti, 1969). And it depends on how the mother reacts to the stranger, too. When a baby sees his mother reacting positively to a stranger, he tends to follow suit and responds much more positively, smiling more, approaching the stranger, and offering his toys (Feinman & Lewis, 1983). Conversely, when the mother adopts a worried look in the presence of a stranger, her baby is apt to cry more and smile less (Boccia & Campos, 1989; Mumme et al., 1996).

These studies illustrate **social referencing** in infants—that is, the process of "reading" emotional cues in other people to help determine how to act in an uncertain situation (Moore & Corkum, 1994; Saarni et al., 2006). Much of this work has been stimulated by the functionalist perspective on emotional development. This social referencing undergoes clear changes over time (Walden, 1991). As infants develop, they are more likely to look at the mother's face than at other parts of her body. Babies between 14 and 22 months old were clearly more aware than 6- to 9-month-old babies that their mother's face was the best source of information (Walden, 1991). Infants grow also in their tendency to check with their mothers before they act. Younger infants often act first and look later, a strategy that could lead to trouble in a dangerous situation. The fact that even infants learn to use others' emotional expressions as a guide to their own actions underscores the importance of emotion for regulating social behaviour (Saarni et al., 2006). Another contextual factor is the degree to which the situation allows the infant some control over the extent and pace of the interaction (Mangelsdorf et al., 1991). When babies could control the noise and movement of a toy monkey or the predictability of the noise (regular vs. erratic) 1-year-olds were less

Somewhere around the age of 7 months, children begin to experience fear, especially in response to unfamiliar people or events. This child clearly does not want the little Dalmatian puppy anywhere near her.

social referencing

The process of "reading" emotional cues in others to help determine how to act in an uncertain situation.

Table 6-1 Factors that alter infant fear of strangers

	More Fear	Less Fear
Context	Unfamiliar setting (e.g., lab)	Familiar setting (home)
	No physical contact with familiar figure; distant from mother or familiar person	Close physical proximity to familiar figure
	Sober or negative emotional reactions to stranger from familiar figure	Positive or encouraging reactions to stranger from familiar figure
Characteristics of stranger	Adult size and features	Child size and features
Behaviour of stranger	Passive and exhibits sober expression	Active, friendly, smiling
Degree of control over strange person or object	Low control and unpredictability	High control and predictability

Perhaps if Mom had not backed away to take a picture, this 1-year old would not have felt so threatened by Santa Claus.

fearful (Gunnar, 1980; Gunnar et al., 1984). The characteristics of the stranger matters, too. Infants are less afraid of children than adults, as Figure 6-3 indicates.

Is it size or facial features of the stranger that matters? When confronted with three strangers, an adult, an adult midget, and a child, the infants were more fearful of the adult midget than the child. Size is less important than faces and babies react more negatively to adult faces than a child's. Unfortunately, a "baby-faced adult" was not available to test this hypothesis. A stranger's behaviour also affects the degree of stranger distress an infant displays (Mumme et al., 1996; Saarni et al., 2006). When confronted by an active, friendly stranger who talks, gestures, smiles, imitates the baby, and offers toys, most 12-month-olds show little fear. In contrast, infants are more apprehensive when confronted by a passive and sober-looking stranger.

separation protest

An infant's distress reaction to being separated from his or her mother, which typically peaks at about 15 months of age.

Some kinds of fear do appear to be universal and are present in all cultures. A common fear in childhood is associated with being separated from one's mother or other familiar caregivers. This fear, called **separation protest**, tends to peak in Western infants at roughly 15 months of age and, as Figure 6-4 shows, displays a remarkably similar timetable in such diverse cultures as those of Guatemala and the Kalahari Desert

Figure 6-3

Proximity and age of a stranger affect babies' reactions

In this study of stranger distress, the gender of a stranger had no effect on infant subjects, but age did. The infants did not perceive the 4-year-old stranger as threatening, but reacted very negatively to both adults. Distance from the infants had relatively little effect on the way they perceived the young stranger, but the closer the adult strangers got, the more intensely the babies showed their distress. In comparison, the infants reacted quite positively both to their own reflections and to their mothers, and this tendency increased with proximity.

Source: Adapted from Lewis & Brooks, 1974.

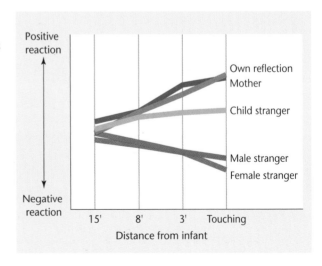

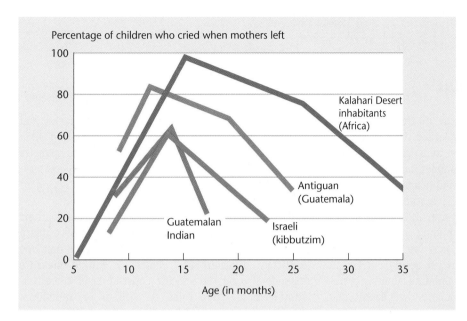

Percentage of children who cried when mothers left

Kalahari Desert inhabitants (Africa)

Antiguan (Guatemala)

Guatemalan Indian

Israeli (kibbutzim)

Age (in months)

Source: From *Infancy: Its Place in Human Development*, by Kagan, J., Kearsley, R. B., and Zelazo, P. R., p. 107, Figure 2.8. Copyright © 1978 by the President and Fellows of Harvard College. Reprinted by permission of the publisher, Harvard University Press, Cambridge, MA.

Figure 6-4

Separation protest

Although children of the four different cultures depicted here varied considerably in the intensity of their protest at their mothers' departure, they all tended to reach a peak of distress at about the same age: between 13 and 15 months.

region in Botswana. As we will see later in the chapter, separation protest also occurs in infants in child care when working parents drop them off at a child-care centre. Although *separation anxiety*, as this fear is also called, generally becomes less and less common in childhood, it sometimes reappears in other forms: Box 6.1 on the following pages describes a study of homesickness among children at camp and suggests some useful ways of coping with this kind of distress.

ANGER AND SADNESS   In early infancy, it is not clear that young infants' emotional expressions are the same as what seem to be analogous adult expressions or even that infants are expressing the same sets of feelings. For example, what looks like anger in a baby may actually represent a generalized state of distress (Camras et al., 1991). Carroll Izard, a pioneer in the study of infant emotion, holds that newborns do express specific emotions (Izard, 1994; Izard et al., 1995). According to Izard, the first negative expressions to appear are *startle*, *disgust* (as in response to bitter tastes), and *distress* (in response to pain) that seems unrelated to external events. However, Izard proposes, not until babies are about 2½ or 3 months old do they begin reliably to display facial expressions of anger, interest, surprise, and sadness (Izard et al., 1995). For example, although few 1-month-olds show anger expressions when their arms are gently restrained, by the time infants are 4 to 7 months old, some 56 percent show clear expressions of anger at this restriction (Stenberg & Campos, 1989). These kinds of early emotions are probably influenced at the outset by genetic-maturational factors. Over time, learning and functional perspectives come into play.

Not unlike adults, infants usually display anger, in response to particular external events (Saarni et al., 2006; Sroufe, 1996). For example, researchers have evoked anger in 7-month-olds by offering them a teething biscuit and then withdrawing it just before it reaches the baby's mouth (Stenberg et al., 1983). Two-month-olds respond with a distress expression to being inoculated by a physician, whereas 6-month-old babies respond to the same stimulus with an expression of anger (Izard, Hembree, & Huebner, 1987). It seems that babies respond to emotional provocations in predictable ways at specific ages (Denham et al., 2007) and anger is elicited by pain and frustration.

Sadness, too, is a reaction to pain, hunger, or lack of control, but occurs less often than anger. Babies become sad when there are breakdowns in parent–infant communication. For example, when a usually responsive caregiver ceases to respond to the babies' social overtures, the infant will exhibit distress and sadness (Tronick et al.,

Box 6.1
Child Psychology in Action

COPING WITH HOMESICKNESS

Homesickness, which is common in the middle and later childhood years, usually arises in settings in which children must stay away from their homes for periods of more than a day. Summer camps, boarding schools, colleges, foster homes, and hospitals are among the sites in which researchers have studied homesickness in children (Thurber & Weisz, 1997). *Homesickness*, which we can define as a longing to be with one's family or regular caregivers, may be expressed in depressive or anxious behaviour; in acting out, as in aggressive behaviour; or in complaints about physiological problems, such as headache, stomachache, and other pains of an ill-defined nature.

How do children cope with homesickness? According to Thurber and Weisz (1997), a child's beliefs about his ability to exert control over a situation strongly determine his choice of coping mechanism. If a child sent to live with relatives in a neighbouring town because of economic distress at home believes he can change his situation, he may exert *primary control* by running away from his aunt's house and returning to his own home. Often, however, a child is unable to change his situation or finds that attempts to do so are unsuccessful and lead only to feelings of helplessness and depression. In this event, a child may instead elect *secondary control*, changing himself or his behaviour in order to adapt to the unwanted situation. Thus, a child placed in a boarding school many kilometres from his home might write letters home every day to feel in touch with his family, or

he might join specific activities in which he had participated at home. A third way of dealing with homesickness is to *relinquish control*, or to give up trying to change things, and seek solace in expressing sadness through some means, such as crying or withdrawing from others.

Because some stressors are controllable and others that are not, coping is sometimes a mix of primary and secondary measures with the child trying first one and then another. The choice of coping measure depends also on the specific constraints of the situation, such as camp rules, as well as on individual characteristics, such as age, perceived ability to control events, and cognitive sophistication.

To study homesickness, Thurber and Weisz (1997) chose two summer camps, one for girls and one for boys, and found that overall, both boys and girls tended to use secondary control methods to cope with homesickness, most often doing something that was fun in order to forget their negative feelings. Among these youngsters, who ranged in age between 8 and 16 years but who were on average 12½, the most homesick were those who were most likely to relinquish control, making little effort to cope with their unhappiness. On the other hand, the least homesick were those who appeared to know how to use different combinations of both primary and secondary methods to cope with whatever unpleasant feelings they had; this group was also the least likely to relinquish control.

2005; Weinberg & Tronick, 1998). In older infants, separation from their mothers or other familiar caregivers can lead to sadness as well. We will explore this issue later in this chapter when we examine how infants develop an attachment bond to adults. Again, just as we saw with positive emotions, anger and sadness are effective emotional signals for eliciting care and comfort from adults and, therefore, serve an important evolutionary function that promotes the survival of the infant.

DEVELOPMENT OF SECONDARY EMOTIONS

In this section, we focus on some of the more complex and nuanced emotions that young children "grow into" over time: pride, shame, guilt, and jealousy.

Girls were more likely to call upon specific coping devices than boys were. However, there was also a significant gender difference in respect to the use of the primary control device of seeking out "someone who could talk with me and help me feel better, like a leader or one of my friends." Although 8- to 10-year-old boys and girls differed little in this regard, from 11 years on, girls were far more likely than boys to use this social-support approach to solving the problem of homesickness (see Figure 6-5). As we suggested earlier in the book and will discuss at greater length in Chapter 13, girls seem to be more socially oriented from early on.

Thurber and Weisz (1997) conclude that useful intervention in homesickness may involve helping children understand that homesickness is not just an unhappy emotion but an emotional reaction to circumstances, some of which are controllable and some of which are not; helping them to distinguish these components of the problem; helping them develop specific coping methods at both primary and secondary levels; showing them how to apply each type of coping method for maximum benefit; and helping them understand why relinquishing control is not effective.

Figure 6-5 Coping with homesickness

When they were homesick, both girls (G) and boys (B) at camp preferred to talk with someone rather than act out in some way in the hope of being sent home. However, this trend was much stronger in girls than in boys.

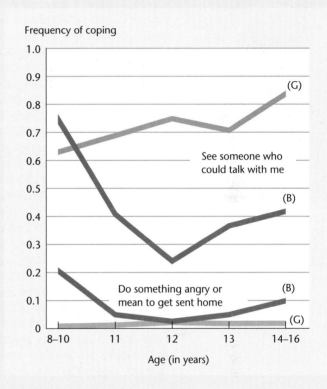

Source: Adapted from Thurber & Weisz, 1997.

More Complex Emotions: Pride, Shame, Guilt, and Jealousy

The appropriate display of more complex emotions, such as pride, shame, guilt, and jealousy, requires the ability to differentiate and integrate the roles of multiple factors in a situation, and often includes the role of personal responsibility. Often called secondary, or "self-conscious" emotions because they rely on the development of self-awareness (Saarni et al., 2006; Tangney, 2003; Tangney & Dearing, 2002), these emotions begin to emerge toward the middle of the second year of life. For example, children may show embarrassment by blushing and turning away and express envy or jealousy by pouting when other children receive more desirable toys (Lewis, 1995; Lewis & Ramsey, 2002). When a child is pleased with her accomplishments, she shows pride, but when

This adolescent is clearly proud and happy at winning a yellow ribbon in the Special Olympics.

she perceives that someone finds her wanting or deficient—perhaps she has failed an easy task—she shows evidence of shame. The feeling of guilt, which requires the development of the sense of personal responsibility and the internalization of some moral standards, emerges a bit later than pride and shame (Tangney, 1998).

PRIDE AND SHAME   Crucial to distinguishing between children's experience of pride or shame is their emerging sense of the differences between "easy" and "difficult" and between "success" and "failure" (Lewis, 2000). Lewis and his colleagues (Lewis, 1992; Lewis, Alessandri, & Sullivan, 1992) found that by the time they were 3 years old, children had learned that they were more likely to feel pride if they succeeded at difficult tasks rather than at easy ones (see also Figure 6-6). They also expressed more shame if they failed an easy task but expressed little shame if they failed a difficult task. Solving a problem that was not particularly difficult elicited joy in these youngsters, but succeeding on a difficult task produced pride. Failing a difficult task caused sadness, but failing an easy task aroused shame (Lewis et al., 1992).

Children's understanding of pride also depends on their ability to entertain multiple emotions—such as pleasure at doing a task well and happiness that others appreciate the accomplishment (Saarni et al., 2006)—and on their sense of personal agency, or effort. To evaluate this understanding, Thompson (1987, 1989) told stories to 7-, 10-, and 18-year-olds involving accomplishments that individuals achieved either by their own efforts or by luck and then asked them questions about the stories. The 7-year-olds used the word "proud" in discussing good outcomes, regardless of whether or not the protagonists in the stories had succeeded through their own efforts. More discriminating, the 10- and 18-year-old subjects realized that "feeling proud" can occur only when good outcomes are the result of a person's own effort, not of luck or chance.

GUILT   It is only gradually that children develop an appreciation of the central role of personal responsibility in their behaviour in relation to other people and, thus, an understanding of guilt. According to Graham, Doubleday, and Guarino (1984), this understanding emerges in middle childhood. Asking 6- and 9-year-old children to describe situations in which they had felt guilty, these researchers found that only the older children had a clear understanding of this emotion and its relation to personal responsibility. For example, even when they had little control over the outcome of a situation, 6-year-olds often described themselves as feeling guilty: "I felt guilty when

Figure 6-6

Pride, shame, and task difficulty

The more difficult the task, the less shame children felt at failing it and the more pride they felt when they succeeded at it.

Source: Lewis, Alessandri, & Sullivan, 1992.

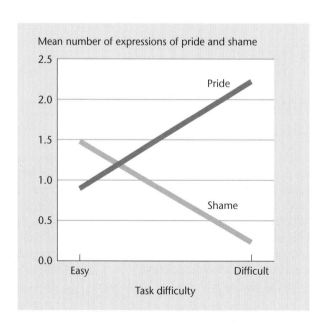

my brother and I had boxing gloves on and I hit him too hard . . . sometimes I don't know my own strength." In contrast, 9-year-olds recognized that to feel guilty, it is critical to be responsible for the outcome of a situation: "I felt guilty when I didn't turn in my homework because I was too lazy to do it." Other studies (Saarni et al., 2006) have reached similar conclusions—namely, that young children focus on simple outcomes, whereas older children, who focus on the role of personal responsibility, understand that unless they themselves caused the outcome they need not feel guilty.

Although we often explore the development of different human capacities, such as emotional expression and cognitive competence, separately, these capacities clearly are mutually interdependent. For example, it is clear that the development of specific emotions is closely entwined with such cognitive advances as the ability to understand causality and, hence, personal responsibility.

JEALOUSY   Jealousy is a common emotion that we all experience. From early childhood, when a sibling gets more parental attention than you do, to adolescence, when you resent your best friend's flirtation with your new romantic partner, you experience jealousy. Indeed, jealousy can occur as early as 1 year of age. In one study, children showed signs of jealousy (e.g., sadness, seeking maternal attention, anger) when mothers directed their attention away from their child toward an infant-sized doll, a newborn infant, or a peer (Case et al., 1988; Hart et al., 1998). Jealousy is a social emotion; it occurs among three people who have established important social relationships. Generally speaking, two people who have been friends for many years don't experience jealousy in interacting with a new acquaintance.

Volling and colleagues (2002) explored jealousy among younger (12 months old) and older (2 to 6 years old) children. When mothers or fathers played with one child and encouraged his sibling to play alone, both younger and older children expressed jealousy of the sibling who received parental attention. Not surprisingly, the way that children express their jealousy changes across development. The researchers found that, in response to a jealousy-provoking scenario, younger children displayed distress, whereas older siblings showed sadness and anger. And jealous reactions are costly: Children who react with jealousy may be less able to focus on their play activities than children who show less jealousy. As in the case of other complex emotions, such as pride and shame, cognitive understanding of emotions helps modify children's jealous reactions. Especially in older siblings, a more sophisticated understanding of emotions may be associated with less jealousy and less disturbed behaviour.

Finally, the experience and expression of jealousy depend on the nature of the relationship in which this unpleasant emotion arises. When children have a secure and trusting relationship with their mothers and fathers, jealousy between siblings is less prevalent. Moreover, when parents are in a positive marriage, children are less likely to show jealous reactions with their siblings. Close relationships between child and parent and between the parents themselves serve as a protective factor in buffering children from jealous reactions.

INDIVIDUAL DIFFERENCES IN EMOTIONS   (LO)4

There are wide individual differences among infants and young children in their readiness to express positive or negative emotions. Babies who are more sociable show less wariness in encounters with strangers than less sociable infants (Bohlin & Hagekull, 1993). Some babies smile more readily and laugh more heartily (La Freniere, 2000). Other babies react more fearfully to new people and events and are more easily angered than other infants. For example, Ricard and Gouin Décarie (1993) had infants confront an unfamiliar object and a stranger with their mother nearby. These researchers found that one group of infants (the "bold" group) approached both the object and the stranger, whereas the second group (the "shy" group) approached the toy only. Similarly, Kagan (1998) identified a subset of children whom he calls "behaviourally inhibited." These children tend to be shy, fearful, and introverted, often avoiding even their peers, and they are more anxious and upset by mildly stressful situations than are other children (Kagan, 1998). Behaviourally inhibited youngsters tend to show atypical physiological reactions—such as rapid heart rates—in stressful situations, and their fearful responses and shyness tend to endure across time, from toddlerhood on into the early school years. However, warm, supportive parents can reduce fearfulness and lessen the likelihood that their children will continue to be abnormally shy and fearful (Gunnar, 1998; Kagan, 1998).

Finally, individual differences in positive and negative emotionality are related to children's adjustment (Lengua, 2002). For example, 10-year-olds who exhibited high levels of negative emotionality (fearfulness and irritability) were more likely to have adjustment difficulties. They tended to be depressed and to have conduct problems. Children who were judged emotionally positive (rated high on smiling and laughing) had high self-esteem and social competence, indicating better adjustment.

For Thought and Discussion

1. In this chapter, we describe two sets of findings on gender differences in emotional development: (i) 6-month-old boys show more emotional expressiveness than girls, yet (ii) girls smile more than boys generally and at their caregivers. How might you reconcile these two sets of findings? What do they tell you about how research might be conducted and how it is compared?

2. Your older brother and his wife have just had a baby, and this newborn seems to smile all the time. Your mother is convinced that her new grandchild of only a few weeks is the happiest baby around. What might you tell your mother about the development of emotional expressiveness in infancy?

3. Researchers used to feel that there were a number of basic emotions but have since backed away from this idea and have begun to propose a much more limited set of infant emotions. What emotions would you say are "fundamental" for an infant? Why these emotions? What purpose might they serve?

RECOGNIZING EMOTIONS IN OTHERS

Another challenge for the developing infant is to learn how to recognize the emotions that other people express. According to Malatesta (1982), between the ages of 3 and 6 months, babies are exposed to others' facial expressions some 32,000 times. Learning to interpret these expressions of emotion presents infants with a formidable task, one that draws on diverse psychological and neural structures (Adolphs, 2002). But during this peak period for face-to-face interaction with parents or other caregivers, facial expressions are an effective way for parents to communicate their feelings and wishes to a child who cannot yet understand speech.

In mother–infant face-to-face interactions, babies may develop the ability to recognize positive emotions such as joy earlier than they can recognize negative emotions such as anger (Izard et al., 1995; Denham et al., 2007). More specifically, babies may develop the ability to recognize joy earlier than they can recognize anger. In one study, infants between 4 and 6 months of age looked longer at a face showing an expression of joy than at one showing anger (La Barbera, Izard, Vietze, & Parisi, 1976). And consistent with the functionalist perspective, recognizing joy before anger has functional value for a baby.

Recognition of joy can provide rewarding and self-enhancing experiences for the infant. Such recognition can also strengthen the mother–infant bond and facilitate mutually rewarding experiences, particularly if the joy recognition leads to joy expression. . . . [In contrast], anger recognition is not adaptive in the first half year of life. It seems reasonable that the threat of an anger expression would call for coping responses that are beyond the capacity of the six month old. (La Barbera et al., 1976, p. 537)

The joy–anger recognition sequence is also consistent with the course of the infant's own emotional displays. As we saw earlier, smiling and laughter emerge before fear (La Freniere, 2000). Review the Turning Points chart on pages 200–201 for an emotional development time frame.

Children, of course, become more discriminating as they develop; 9- to 10-year-olds can discriminate between Duchenne smiles and non–Duchenne smiles more reliably than can 6- to 7-year-olds (Gosselin et al., 2002). Others suggest that adults are even better than children in recognizing Duchenne (or authentic) smiles (Del Giudice & Colle, 2007).

The nature of early experience alters children's ability to recognize emotions, as the learning perspective on emotional development would predict. For example, 3½-month-old infants recognize their mothers' emotional expressions earlier than they recognize such expressions in either fathers or strangers. Moreover, when mothers spent more time interacting directly with their babies, their infants were more successful at recognizing their mothers' emotional expressions (Montague & Walker-Andrews, 2002). However, both the quality and the quantity of interactions between parents and infants make a difference in children's ability to recognize emotions. Abused children who experience high levels of threat and hostility are able to identify anger expressions more easily than non-abused children are, but they are less capable of detecting expressions of sadness (Pollak & Sinha, 2002). The early family environment clearly plays a role in shaping children's abilities to recognize emotions. And culture matters, too. In one study, both Mexican and Chinese children were better than either Euro-American or Australian children in recognizing vocal and/or facial emotional expressions (Cole & Tan, 2007). Both China and Mexico are societies that value group harmony and a focus on others' feelings is one way to achieve this goal.

It is probably harder for babies to learn to recognize expressions of emotions in others than it is for them to learn to express emotions accurately themselves. Citing the fact that around the world, people use similar facial expressions of emotion, some researchers believe that producing these expressions is at least in part genetically determined (Ekman, 1994; Izard, 1994). If this were so, it would help to explain also why both babies and children are more accurate at producing emotional expressions than at interpreting them (Denham, 1998; Field, 1990). Nevertheless, by the time they are 2 or 3, children show production and recognition skills that are positively correlated: Toddlers who send clear emotional signals also tend to be good at identifying emotions (Magai & McFadden, 1995). Both these skills continue to improve with age, probably contributing to the older child's ability to participate more often and more successfully in peer-group activities as well as to more sustained and sophisticated social interactions (Denham, et al., 2007; Saarni et al., 2006).

EMOTIONAL REGULATION AND EMOTIONAL DISPLAY RULES

LO 5

Learning how to regulate the expression of their emotions is a major challenge for infants and children (Cole et al., 2004; Saarni et al., 2006; Thompson, 2006). In this section, we trace the developmental changes in emotional regulation and shifts in children's use of display rules that govern expression of emotions.

Often, humans get their first clue from something they began learning even before they were born: They found that putting their thumbs in their mouths helps to soothe them. From this unintentional act of control, infants move to the more deliberate regulation of their emotions. For example, when they encounter a frightening event they may turn away, place their hands over their faces, or distract themselves by some form of play (Bridges & Grolnick, 1995). Children's methods of emotional control continue to change as they grow older. Mangelsdorf, Shapiro, and Marzolf (1995) found that 6-month-olds who confronted a stranger typically looked away or became fussy, whereas 18-month-olds were more likely to use self-soothing and self-distraction to cope with uncertain or arousing situations.

As infants become toddlers and head toward the preschool years, they learn a variety of strategies for emotional regulation as parents and others start to require them to exert even more control over their emotional expression (Calkins et al., 2002; Diener, Mangelsdorf, McHale, & Frosch, 2002). Under this pressure, gradually, "the intense and unregulated expressions of infancy give way to expressions that are more modulated" (Malatesta, Culver, Tesman, & Shepard, 1989). Several things illustrate this greater self-control over emotions. Emotional expressions become less frequent, less variable and more conventionalized, less distinct, and less intense and exaggerated (La Freniere, 2000; Saarni et al., 2006). For example, a hungry baby may cry in uncontrollable frustration, whereas an older child whose mealtime is delayed will merely pout and complain. And emotional regulation abilities are important predictors of later adjustment (Fox & Calkins, 2003). Children in preschool who were better at regulating their anger showed less externalizing behaviour when they entered school; those who were able to distract themselves by shifting attention away from the frustrating situation were less aggressive and disruptive in kindergarten (Gilliom et al., 2002).

emotional display rules

Rules that dictate which emotions one may appropriately display in particular situations.

At the same time, children begin to learn **emotional display rules** that dictate what emotions to show under what circumstances. This often means learning to separate the visible expression of an emotion from its inner experience. Following various social norms, children 8 to 10 years old learn to smile even when they feel unhappy, to feign distress that is not really felt, or to mask amusement when they know they should not laugh (Garner & Power, 1996; Saarni et al., 2006). Indeed, in a recent study, Ruihe and Guoliang (2006) found that masking and neutralization were the most common strategies employed by students between grade 1 and 5. But children as young as 2 years may show such understanding of display rules for emotions (Lewis & Michaelson, 1985). In their earliest attempts to follow these rules, children typically mirror others' behaviours by simply exaggerating or minimizing their emotional displays. Moreover, children acquire knowledge about display rules before they are proficient regulators of their own emotional displays (Saarni, 1999).

Culture plays an important role in how children appraise situations, communicate emotions, and act on their feelings. Studying three cultural groups—Brahman and Tamang societies in rural Nepal and a rural town in the United States—Cole and colleagues (2002) compared the reactions of children to difficult, emotionally arousing situations. They interviewed grade 2, 4, and 5 students about how they would react to a difficult interpersonal situation, such as someone's spilling a drink on their homework or accusing them falsely of stealing. How would they feel? Would they want others to know their feelings? Why or why not? And what would they do in the situation? As expected, culture clearly influences children's emotional responses. Among the Tamang, a Buddhist group who endorse interpersonal harmony, children were more likely than the other two groups to respond to difficult situations with shame. In contrast, children of the Brahman society, which teaches self-control in social interactions and the careful control of emotions, did not reveal anger or shame in response to their emotionally upsetting problem. Different again were the American children, who were more likely to endorse the display of anger—an emotion consistent with the US value of self-assertion. Children from the States were more problem-focused and action-oriented than the children in the two Nepali groups, who were more accepting of difficult situations and less likely to seek to alter the situation. Clearly, cultural and religious customs and values shape the ways that children react to emotionally upsetting events. Learning to follow cultural display rules seems to be an important developmental accomplishment. It seems that competence in implementing these rules is linked with better social relationships with peers (Parke et al., 2006; Valiente & Eisenberg, 2006).

HOW CHILDREN THINK ABOUT EMOTIONS 🔘6

Not only do children act on their emotions, but they also learn to think about those emotions as well. If we understand how children think about feelings, we are in a better position to understand why they act emotionally.

A child is invited to a birthday party; another child's favourite pet dies; a third child hears a loud, unexpected bang. When do children become able to think and talk about the varying emotional reactions that are likely to accompany these very different kinds of events? When can they understand the coexistence of multiple emotions? When can they empathize with another person, predicting how that person will feel in a given situation? We try to answer these questions in this section.

Matching Emotions to Situations: Emotional Scripts

Over time, children undergo shifts in the ways they express emotions. They develop a more complete understanding of the meanings of emotion terms and of the situations that evoke different kinds of feelings. According to Saarni et al. (2006), this understanding can be seen as a collection of **emotional scripts**, or complex schemes that enable the child to identify the type of emotional reaction that is likely to accompany a particular kind of event.

From a young age, children create a number of such emotional scripts. In a classic study, Borke (1971) told 3- and 4-year-old children simple stories about such things as getting lost in the woods or having a fight or going to a party and asked them to tell her the emotions they thought the characters in the different stories would be likely to feel. The children easily identified situations that would lead to happiness, and they were reasonably good at identifying stories that were linked with sadness or anger. Later research (Cole & Tan, 2007; Levine, 1995) showed that 3- and 4-year-old children could also describe situations that evoked other emotions, such as excitement, surprise, and being scared. Clearly, young children know which emotions go with which situations.

Children's emotional scripts gain in complexity as they mature. For example, 5-year-olds generally understand only those situations that lead to emotions that have a recognizable facial display (e.g., anger, displayed in frowning) or that lead to a particular kind of behaviour (e.g., sadness, displayed in crying or moping about). By the time they are 7, however, children can describe situations that elicit more complicated emotions with no obvious facial or behavioural expressions, such as pride, jealousy, worry, and guilt. And by the time they reach 10 or 14 years of age, children can describe situations that elicit relief and disappointment (Harris, Olthof, Meerum Terwogt, & Hardman, 1987). A similar developmental sequence is found in a variety of cultures, including Britain, the United States, the Netherlands, and Nepal (Harris, 1989). Culture matters: children in the United States react to a request to stop playing and go to bed with anger, but first-graders in Nepal are happy with such a request. In Nepal, children value co-sleeping with adults and so are not upset with the cessation of play (Cole & Tamang, 1998). Finally, as we will see in Chapter 15, autistic children are less proficient in their understanding of emotions compared to normally functioning children (Baron-Cohen, 2001; Balconi & Carrera, 2007; Losh & Capps, 2006).

emotional script

A complex scheme that enables a child to identify the emotional reaction that is likely to accompany a particular sort of event.

Multiple Emotions, Multiple Causes

Another aspect of emotional understanding that develops only gradually is the awareness that one can have more than one feeling at a time and that one can even experience two or more conflicting feelings at the same time. Although toddlers and even young infants show signs of experiencing conflicting feelings, children's ability to understand and express their knowledge of emotions emerges slowly and lags well behind their capacity to experience ambivalent emotions (Arsenio & Kramer, 1992; Pons, Harris, & de Rosnay, 2004; Wintre & Vallance, 1994). According to Harter (Harter, 2006; Harter & Buddin, 1987), children show a clear developmental sequence in their ability to understand multiple and conflicting feelings. From their study of children between the ages of 4 and 12 years, Harter and her colleagues (Harter & Buddin, 1987) derived the five stages of emotional understanding shown in Table 6-2. As you can see, it is not until the fourth stage, at roughly the age of 10, that children begin to be able to conceive of opposite feelings existing simultaneously.

As they develop, children learn to consider more and more aspects of an emotion-related situation, such as the desires, goals, and intentions of the people involved. Children realize that people's emotional expressions are produced by inner states and are not responsive solely to the characteristics of the situation. For example, young children often get angry when someone thwarts, wrongs, or frustrates them, regardless of whether the wrongful act was intentional, but children 7 years and older, like adults, tend to reserve their anger for situations in which they think a person intended to upset them (Levine, 1995). We return to this issue of inferring others' internal mental states in our discussion of theory of mind in Chapter 8.

THE FAMILY'S ROLE IN EMOTIONAL DEVELOPMENT

Families play a major role in children's emotional development. Suzanne Denham (1998), a leading emotions researcher, has outlined three ways in which families influence children's emotions (see Figure 6-7). First, family members' own patterns of emotional expressiveness serve as models for the child's emotional expressiveness.

Table 6-2 Children's understanding of multiple and conflicting emotions

Approximate Ages	Children's Capabilities
4 to 6	Conceive of only one emotion at a time: "You can't have two feelings at the same time."
6 to 8	Begin to conceive of two emotions of the same type occurring simultaneously: "I was happy and proud that I hit a home run." "I was upset and mad when my sister messed up my things."
8 to 9	Describe two distinct emotions in response to different situations at the same time: "I was bored because there was nothing to do and mad because my mom punished me."
10	Describe two opposing feelings where the events are different or different aspects of the same situation: "I was sitting in school worrying about the next soccer game but happy that I got an A in math." "I was mad at my brother for hitting me but glad my dad let me hit him back."
11 on	Understand that the same event can cause opposing feelings: "I was happy that I got a present but disappointed that it wasn't what I wanted."

Source: Based on Harter, 2006; Harter & Buddin, 1987.

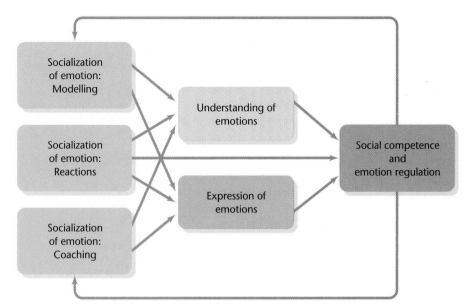

Figure 6-7

A model of emotional socialization

Parental socialization practices lead to changes in understanding and expression of emotions—which, in turn, lead to changes in children's social competence and in their abilities to regulate their emotions.

Source: Denham, 1998.

Second, parents' and siblings' specific reactions to children's emotions encourage or discourage certain patterns of emotional expressiveness. Third, parents often act as emotional coaches by talking about emotions and explaining and exploring children's understanding of their own and other people's emotional responses.

Just as children learn to share toys, to say their ABC's, and sometimes to hit people by watching others, they learn a great deal about how and when to express emotions by watching members of their family:

> *Claire learned about anger and sadness. She witnessed an argument between her mother and father. The mother began to cry out of frustration and sadness over the long-standing, unresolved conflict. Claire watched with eyes wide. Then she got tearful herself.* (Denham, 1998, p. 106)

Families vary in their emotional expressiveness. Some are subdued and restrained in their emotional reactions; others are more demonstrative and engage in more intense and frequent emotional displays. Many studies have shown similarities between parents and their children in both level of emotional expressiveness and types of emotions typically displayed (Eisenberg et al., 2001; Halberstadt et al., 2001). Children who grow up in a positive emotional home with lots of happiness and joy are more likely to exhibit positive emotions (Halberstadt et al., 2001). However, children who are reared in a negative family environment characterized by hostility and conflict are more likely to display negative emotions, such as anger and sadness (Denham et al., 2007; Halberstadt et al., 2001). To take an extreme example, children who have been abused by parents, particularly girls, are more likely to exude shame and less likely to show pride than their non-abused peers; according to Alessandri and Lewis (1996), this reflects the intense and frequent negative feedback these girls receive from their parents. Children can learn both by watching how parents react emotionally to them, as well as by observing how parents and other family members react emotionally to each other. Watching mom and dad argue or siblings squabble or a mother smile at a baby sister are all ways of learning about the world of emotions.

Or, sometimes, parents' reactions contribute to children's emotional repertoire by helping them cope more effectively with their emotions and by improving their understanding of what emotions may appropriately be displayed

> *Stacey's mother bought a new wading pool and had high hope for the fun the family could have. Whether told to wait, get in or get out of the pool, Stacey*

cried and wouldn't be consoled. Nothing could please her. Finally she had a mini-tantrum, lying down on the floor, knocking over a chair, and kicking out at things. Her mother told her she couldn't act like that . . . she let Stacey cry a while and then consoled her, hugging her and discussing what had happened. Then everyone went back to the pool and had a good time! Stacey learned that some intensities and means of expression are not acceptable and that talking about rather than venting feelings can have a positive outcome. (Denham, 1998, p. 107)

And there is evidence that parental reactions are, indeed, important contributions to children's emotional development. Children whose parents help them with their emotions are better able to manage emotional upset on their own and are also more accepted by their peers (Gottman et al., 1996). When parents are punitive or dismissive of their children's emotions, the children are hampered in regulating their own emotions (McDowell & Parke, 2000; Parke et al., 2006; Valiente & Eisenberg, 2006). Dismissive parents may belittle the child's emotion (e.g., "There's no reason for you to be [sad][angry] . . .") or show little interest in how the child is feeling (e.g., "Don't worry about it—go watch TV"). Punitive parents may scold or punish their child for expressing emotions, especially negative ones such as anger or sadness. Dismissive or punitive parents "fail to use emotional moments as a chance to get closer to the child or to help the child learn lessons in emotional competence" (Goleman, 1995, p. 191).

Some parents actively deal with the world of emotions by coaching their children and by discussing emotions with them. Anikka learned about emotions while looking at a picture book with her mother. In the story they read, a new puppy tried to run away into the path of a school bus:

> **Mother:** They were frightened . . . [They] grabbed the dog and brought it to safety. See the worried looks?
> **Anikka:** They look so scared.

Anikka learned some new vocabulary for the emotion of fear, new cues for fear, and a new reason to be fearful—when the safety of a loved one is endangered (Denham, 1998, p. 107).

Parents who are good emotional coaches value emotional expression, are aware of their own emotions, and are willing to help their children with theirs. Help often takes the form of talking about feelings, for children whose parents discuss emotions are better at taking the perspective or viewpoint of others and at understanding their own and others' emotions. For example, in Britain, Dunn and her colleagues at the University of London (Dunn et al., 1995; Dunn & Hughes, 1998) found that 3-year-old children's conversations with their mothers and siblings about feeling states were closely related to the same children's ability, at the age of 6, to understand other people's emotions. Children from families in which there was more discussion of feelings were better able to recognize others' emotions than children raised in families in which feelings were less often discussed (Dunn, 2004). In general, the better a child understands emotions, the more skilled he will be at such social practices as group problem solving and conflict resolution and the more likely he is to be accepted by peers (Denham et al., 2007; Dunn, 2004; Parke & O'Neil, 2000).

It is important to remember that not only parents but also peers and siblings function as socializers of emotion. When children display anger, their peers often respond with anger or rejection (Denham et al., 2007; Fabes et al., 1996). Similarly, siblings often shape children's emotional reactions by their positive or negative responses or by alerting a parent to their siblings' angry emotional outbursts (Denham et al., 2007; Dunn, 1988, 2004). Interactions with siblings also contribute to a child's development of emotional understanding. Pretend play with siblings or friends, often characterized by conflict and other intense emotional experiences, is associated with increased understanding of other people's feelings and beliefs (Dunn & Hughes, 1998; Youngblade & Dunn, 1995).

Finally, as we have often noted, socialization is a two-way process, and parent, peer, and sibling reactions are shaped by the characteristics and behaviour of the children who are the objects of their endeavours. Recall from our discussion in Chapter 2 of temperament how children differ in the intensity of their reactions to events and how easily and quickly they calm themselves. These temperamental differences probably play an important role in the socialization of emotion. Children of difficult temperaments, for example, may require more direct intervention, such as coaching, than children with easy temperaments. Clearly, children play important roles in their own emotional socialization.

Although we often explore the development of different human capacities, such as emotional expression and cognitive competence, separately, these capacities clearly are mutually interdependent. For example, it is clear that the development of specific emotions is closely entwined with such cognitive advances as the ability to understand causality and, hence, personal responsibility. In addition, social influences, such as variations in the style of family interaction, play a role in the way children come to understand emotions both in themselves and in others (Denham, 1998). Children's capacity to experience and show different emotions is closely tied to child-rearing history. As we discussed, children who have been abused, particularly girls, are more likely to display shame and less likely to show pride than their non-abused peers (Alessandri & Lewis, 1998).

THE DEVELOPMENT OF ATTACHMENT

Closely related to emotional development is the development of **attachment**, a strong emotional bond that forms in the second half of the first year between an infant and one or more of the child's regular caregivers. Visible signs of attachment are the warm greetings the child gives her parents when they approach, smiling broadly, stretching out her arms, and her active efforts at contact when picked up, touching her parent's face and snuggling close. Attachment can also be seen in a child's efforts to stay near his parents in an unfamiliar situation, crawling or running to their sides, holding on to a leg. Attachment can also be seen in the distress that older babies show when their parents leave them temporarily; its negative counterpart is expressed in the separation protest (or anxiety) that we discussed earlier.

attachment

A strong emotional bond that forms between infant and caregiver in the second half of the child's first year.

The emergence of attachment is one of the developmental milestones in the first year of life. It is of great interest to researchers not only because it is so intense and dramatic but because it is thought to enhance the parents' effectiveness in the later socialization of their children. Children who have developed an attachment to their parents presumably want to maintain their parents' affection and approval and so are motivated to adopt the standards of behaviour that their parents set for them.

Attachment is such an important and widely studied topic that we devote the rest of this chapter to it. We begin this section with several theories of why attachment develops; we next look at how attachment evolves over the first two years of life and then consider special characteristics of attachment to fathers and to peers. In the last section of the chapter, we discuss variations in the quality of attachment and in the consequences of such variations.

Attachment Theory

Theories of Attachment

 7

A variety of theories have been offered to explain the development of attachment, including psychoanalytic, learning, cognitive developmental, and ethological theory.

Each of these positions makes different assumptions about the variables that are important for the development of attachment and about the processes underlying the development of an attachment relationship.

PSYCHOANALYTIC THEORY   According to Freud's classic **psychoanalytic theory of attachment**, babies become attached to their caregivers because the caregivers are associated with gratification of infants' innate drive to obtain pleasure through sucking and other forms of oral stimulation. On this line of thinking, a woman who breast-feeds her baby is particularly important to her child's oral gratification. The baby becomes attached first to the mother's breast and ultimately to the mother herself. Although this argument from traditional psychoanalytic theory has fallen out of favour today, recent work has attempted to combine psychoanalytic thought with the related disciplines of infancy research, cognitive science, and neuroscience to produce a more workable psychoanalytic theory of attachment (Cristobal, 2003; Diamond, Blatt, & Lichtenburg, 2003). Whether or not this approach truly remains a viable explanation of attachment, the stress placed by psychoanalytic thought on a person's inner needs and feelings and its focus on mother–infant interaction remain important influences in the study of infant attachment.

learning theory of attachment

The theory that infants become attached to the mother because she provides food, or primary reinforcement, and, thus, she acquires secondary-reinforcement properties.

secondary reinforcer

A person or other stimulus that acquires reinforcing properties by virtue of repeated association with a primary reinforcer.

LEARNING THEORY   Like psychoanalytic theory, the **learning theory of attachment** has traditionally associated the formation of mother–infant attachment with the mother's reduction of the baby's primary drive of hunger. Because the mother provides the infant with food, which is a *primary reinforcer*, she herself becomes a **secondary reinforcer**. Presumably, this ability to satisfy the baby's hunger drive forms the basis for infant attachment to the mother or any other caregiver linked to feeding.

Many studies, however, have challenged the view that feeding is critical for the development of attachment. In what is probably the most famous of these, Harry Harlow (Harlow & Zimmerman, 1959) separated infant monkeys from their real mothers and raised them in the company of two surrogate mothers. One "mother" was made of stiff wire and had a feeding bottle attached to it; the other was made of soft terrycloth but lacked a bottle. Especially in moments of stress, the baby monkeys preferred to cling to the cloth "mother," even though she dispensed no food. Attachment to this surrogate mother clearly did not require the reduction of hunger.

Research on human beings tells a similar story. Schaffer and Emerson (1964) found that babies formed attachments to their fathers and other frequently seen adults who played little or no role in the child's feeding. They found that babies whose mothers were relatively unresponsive and distant, except for routine physical care, but whose fathers were attentive and stimulating tended to form paternal attachments, even though they actually spent more time with their mothers (Schaffer & Emerson, 1964).

The central point of the learning theory explanation is that attachment is not automatic; it develops over time as a result of satisfying interactions with responsive adults. As evidence for this view, one study (Sutton, 2001) found that a side effect of a program of behavioural parent training for parents whose children were displaying conduct disorders was that the children became far more attached and loving than they were previously. This serendipitous result suggests that the regularly recurring positive interactions with these adults led to the formation and maintenance of a positive emotional bond. More generally, according to this view, babies are initially attracted to their regular caregivers because they are the most important and reliable sources of these types of stimulation. As interactions with these caregivers continue over weeks and months, infants learn to depend on and to value these special adults in their lives, becoming attached to them.

cognitive developmental view of attachment

The view that to form attachments, infants must differentiate between mother and stranger and must understand that people exist independently of their interaction with them.

COGNITIVE DEVELOPMENTAL THEORY   According to the **cognitive developmental view of attachment**, before specific attachments can occur, the infant not only must be able to differentiate between her mother and a stranger but also must be aware that people still exist even when she cannot see them. That is, she must have developed what Piaget terms *object permanence*, or the knowledge that objects, including people, have a continuous existence apart from her own interaction with them. As we will see in Chapter 8, there is some evidence that children as young as 3.5 months have an awareness of object permanence, although Piaget believed that this awareness did not begin to evolve until about 7 or 8 months of age.

Advances in the infant's cognitive development can also account, in part, for the gradual shift in the ways that attachment is expressed. Physical proximity to attachment figures becomes less important as children grow older. Children are now increasingly able to maintain psychological contact with a parent through words, smiles, and looks. In addition, because they are also able to understand better that separations from a parent are sometimes necessary and are usually temporary, they are less upset by separations. Parents can reduce their children's distress over separations further by explaining the reasons for their departures. In one study, for instance, two 2-year-olds handled separation from their mothers much better when the mothers gave them clear information ("I'm going out now for just a minute, but I'll be right back") than when the mothers left without a word (Weinraub & Lewis, 1977).

ETHOLOGICAL THEORY   Probably the most influential approach to attachment is John Bowlby's **ethological theory of attachment** (1958, 1969, 1973). Both evolutionary theory and observational studies of animals helped shape this theory, and an important early demonstration of the value of the ethological approach was provided by Lorenz's (1952) classic studies of imprinting in ducklings. By the process of **imprinting**, newborn birds and the young of other infrahuman animals can develop an attachment to the first object they see during a brief, critical period after their birth. In Lorenz's case, the young ducklings he studied became attached to Lorenz himself. Bowlby suggested that attachment has its roots in a set of instinctual infant responses that are important for the protection and survival of the species. The infant responses of crying, smiling, sucking, clinging, and following (visually at first and, later, motorically) both elicit the parental care and protection that the baby needs and promote contact between the child and the parents. Just as the infant is biologically prepared to respond to the sights, sounds, and nurturance provided by the parents, so, too, are the parents biologically prepared to respond to these eliciting behaviours on the part of the baby. As a result of these biologically programmed responses, both parent and infant develop a mutual attachment.

The value of Bowlby's position lies in its emphasis on the active role in the formation of attachment played by the infant's early social-signalling systems, such as smiling and crying. Another attractive feature is the theory's stress on the development of mutual attachment, whereby both partners, not just one, become attached (Cassidy, 1999; Thompson, 2006). From this perspective, attachment is a relationship, not simply a behaviour of either the infant or the parent (Sroufe et al., 2005). More controversial is Bowlby's suggestion that these early behaviours are biologically programmed. As we have seen, for example, there is considerable evidence that smiling has social as well as biological origins.

Since Bowlby's original formulation of attachment theory, researchers have broadened the presumed basis for attachment relations to include such aspects as parental sensitivity and responsiveness toward the child. Although offering a richer and more complex perspective on why attachments may form, Goldberg, Grusec, and Jenkins (1999a, 1999b) have proposed a return to a narrower definition of attachment relations, one more in keeping with Bowlby's initial insights. These authors argue that it is important to distinguish the role of the parent as the primary protector from more general aspects of good parenting (a distinction between "security" and "love"; MacDonald, 1999). According to Goldberg, Grusec, and Jenkins, this distinction carries important implications for questions such as how attachment is assessed (which we take up in a moment), as well as for clinical interventions with families, and so on.

ethological theory of attachment

Bowlby's theory that attachment derives from the biological preparation of both infant and parents to respond to each other's behaviours in such a way that parents provide the infant with care and protection.

imprinting

The process by which birds and other infrahuman animals develop a preference for the person or object to which they are first exposed during a brief, critical period after birth.

How Attachment Evolves

Attachment does not develop suddenly and unheralded but rather emerges in a series of steps, moving from a baby's general preference for human beings over inanimate objects to a child's real partnership with his parents. Schaffer (1996) proposes four phases in the development of attachment—these are outlined in Table 6-3. In the first phase, which lasts only a month or two, the baby's social responses are relatively indiscriminate. In the second phase, the baby gradually learns to distinguish familiar from unfamiliar people. However, even though a baby under 6 months of age can make these discriminations between his mother and other caregivers, he does not yet protest when familiar caregivers depart; he is not yet truly attached to these people.

In the third phase, at about 7 months, specific attachments develop. Now the infant actively seeks contact with certain regular caregivers, such as the mother, greeting them happily and often crying when those people temporarily depart. The baby does not show these behaviours to just anyone but only to *specific* attachment figures. When the child passes the 2 years of age and enters toddlerhood (from about 2 to 5 years), the attachment relationship moves into the final phase—the so-called goal-corrected partnership (Bowlby, 1969). At this point, owing to advances in cognitive development, children become aware of others' feelings, goals, and plans and begin to consider these things in formulating their own actions. As Colin (1996) has noted, "the child becomes a partner in planning how the dyad will handle separations" (p. 72).

Attachment to Fathers

Infants develop attachments not only to their mothers but to their fathers and to a variety of other persons with whom they regularly interact, such as siblings or other peers. Moreover, according to several anthropologists (Harkness & Super, 2002; Weisner & Gallimore, 1977), mothers are exclusive caregivers in only about 3 percent of human societies. In as many as 40 percent of societies, mothers are not even the major caregivers. And as we will see later, the quality of attachment relationships can vary greatly (Sroufe et al., 2005).

FATHERS   Today's North American fathers often take a much more active role with their infants than the fathers in past generations did; just like mothers, fathers develop mutual attachments with their babies (Parke, 2002a). Fathers who have the opportunity to interact with their infants in the first few days after infants are born tend to hold, touch, talk to, and kiss them just as much as mothers do (Parke, 1996). And later in their first year of life, the children of these fathers show just as much attachment to their fathers as to their mothers.

Table 6-3

Phases in the development of attachment

Source: Schaffer, 1996.

Name	Age Range (Months)	Principal Features
1. Pre-attachment	0–2	Indiscriminate social responsiveness
2. Attachment-in-the-making	2–7	Recognition of familiar people
3. Clear-cut attachment	7–24	Separation protest; wariness of strangers; intentional communication
4. Goal-corrected partnership	24 on	Relationships more two-sided: children understand parents' needs

But although babies can be strongly attached to their fathers, North American fathers are usually less involved than mothers in an infant's routine care regardless of ethnicity. Fathers of African, Latino, and European descent all show this pattern (Parke et al., 2005). This is true also of grandfathers compared with grandmothers (Smith & Drew, 2002). Significantly, fathers participate more in caregiving when the mother is supportive of the father's involvement and views him as a competent caregiver (Beitel & Parke, 1998). Father involvement in infant care also increases when the mother is less available for such reasons as recovery from a Caesarean section delivery (Pederson, Zaslow, Cain, & Anderson, 1980) or employment outside the home (Coltrane, 1996).

In some cultures, particularly hunter-gatherer societies where the search for food and other necessities requires the efforts of both men and women, fathers may be more likely to share in child care. According to Hewlett (2004), fathers among the Aka, who live in the southern part of the Central African Republic and the northern reaches of the Domestic Republic of Congo, provide more direct care to their babies than do fathers in any other known society. Among the Efe, however, another African forager society (in Congo), child care is considered a woman's responsibility, and although Efe fathers spend a great deal of time with their infants, a relatively small percentage of that time goes into direct child care (Morelli & Tronick, 1992). Among the Agta, in Cagayan, Philippines, a hunter-gatherer society in which women and men share labour and sub-sistence activities almost equally, mothers remain the primary caregivers (Griffin & Griffin, 1992).

In many cultures, fathers have a special role in the infant's development—that of playmate (Lewis & Lamb, 2003). The quality of a father's play with a baby generally differs from a mother's: Fathers engage in more unusual and physically arousing games (especially with their sons), whereas mothers tend to stimulate their babies verbally and to play quieter games, such as peekaboo (Parke, 1996, 2002a). Even when fathers have assumed the role of their babies' primary caregiver, they tend to display this physically arousing style of interaction (Field, 1978; Hwang, 1986). Although North American fathers, as well as fathers in other countries such as Australia, Britain, and Israel (Lamb, 1987; Roopnarine, 2004), spend four to five times more time playing with their infants than caring for them, not all fathers engage in rough-and-tumble play with their children. Fathers in India, Central Africa, and Sweden are apparently less likely to engage in this style of play (Hewlett, 2004; Roopnarine, 2004). Also, fathers who enter parent-hood at a later age (over 35 years) tend to be less physical in their play than younger men are (Neville & Parke, 1997).

Mothers and fathers continue to show these different styles of play as their children grow older, well into the early childhood years (MacDonald & Parke, 1984, 1986). We do not yet know whether these mother–father differences in play mode are the result of biology or experience, but whatever their cause, infants tend to react more positively to a father's style of play than a mother's (Field, 1990; Parke et al., 2005). When given a choice of play partners, 18-month-olds in one study reliably chose their fathers more often than their mothers (Clarke-Stewart, 1978), but perhaps this preference for dads may be less pronounced in contemporary families in which both parents are working and away from their children during day. Probably, children like playing with their fathers because they make more exciting and unpredictable playmates.

Clearly, culture is important in shaping fathering roles but does biology play a role in preparing men for their fatherhood role as well? Mothers, as well as fathers, undergo a variety of hormonal changes during pregnancy and childbirth that makes them sensitive to infant cries and primed for parenthood. Men experienced changes in several hormones, including a drop in testosterone after the birth of the baby when the father has the first opportunity to interact with their new offspring (Storey et al., 2000). Men with lower testosterone were more responsive to infant cues such as crying and held baby dolls longer than men who did not show these hormonal decreases (Fleming et al., 2002). These shifts are especially true for men who were closely involved with

Young North American fathers are particularly likely to engage in rough-and-tumble play with their young sons.

their wives during pregnancy, which suggests that intimate ties between partners during pregnancy may stimulate hormonal changes. This is an important reminder that hormones may alter social behaviour, but social relationships may modify hormonal levels as well. Clearly, fathering is multiply determined with social/cultural, developmental, and even biological factors playing roles in the emergence of fathering and infant–father attachment.

Other Objects of Attachment

Although infants' most significant attachment relationships are usually with fathers and mothers, as Table 6-4 shows, a variety of other individuals are important in the infant's social world, including peers, siblings, and relatives, such as grandparents, aunts, and uncles (Berlin & Cassidy, 1999; Smith & Drew, 2002). Peers can become important attachment figures, even for very young children. For example, one investigator found that in a preschool where some children were transferring to new schools, children who were leaving as well as those left behind experienced a variety of reactions, including increased fussiness, activity level, negative affect, and illness, as well as changes in eating and sleeping patterns (Field, 1986). And as children reach adolescence, they develop attachment relationships with friends and with romantic partners (Collins & Van Dulman, 2006; Furman, 2002). For a discussion of romantic attachments, see Chapter 12.

For Thought and Discussion

1. Is it possible that all the different theoretical approaches to the development of emotion are, in some way or another, correct? How does this possibility change the way you conceive of the role or purpose of developmental theory?

2. Interestingly, attachment is one of the few areas in child development in which a single theory, Bowlby's ethological approach, dominates. In looking at Bowlby's theory, how much does it depend upon, or has it borrowed from, other approaches to attachment? Put differently, what is its relation to psychoanalytic theory? To cognitive developmental theory? And so on.

3. How important do you think specific functions of the caregiver, such as primary protector, caregiver, and feeder, are for the development of attachment? Why? Does an emphasis on these functions eliminate the possibility of attachment to others, such as grandparents, siblings, and the like, who may not play these roles as much in the child's life?

Table 6-4

The breadth of children's attachments

Source: Schaffer, 1996.

Attachment Target	Percentage of Infants Attached	
	Initially	At 18 Months
Mother	95	81
Father	30	75
Grandparent	11	45
Relative other than sibling	8	44
Sibling	2	24
Other child	3	14

THE NATURE AND QUALITY OF ATTACHMENT

Like most aspects of human development, the formation of early attachments is not always uniform from one child to another or from one relationship to the next. Many children form what appear to be highly secure attachments. The important adults in their lives seem to serve as a source of nurturance and affection that gives the youngsters confidence to explore the world and become more independent. For other children, however, attachments seem much less secure and dependable. Researchers describe such variations as differences in the *quality* of attachments.

Before we examine some of the specific factors that may affect the nature and quality of individual child–parent attachments, let us consider a classic body of work that has provided a means of characterizing attachment relationships of different qualities. Mary Ainsworth's studies, based on her concept of the *secure base* and using the so-called Strange Situation, have been replicated many times and in many parts of the world.

Methods of Assessing Attachment Relationships

Attachment Disorders

Proposing that infants organize their attachment behaviour around a particular adult in such a way that they seem to be using the adult as a **secure base** for exploration or a safe haven in the event of distress, Ainsworth made valuable observations of infants' attachment and exploratory behaviour at about 1 year of age (Ainsworth, 1973; Waters, Vaughn, Posada, & Kondo-Ikemura, 1995). The striking differences in the infants' behaviours in what is known as the **Strange Situation**, a carefully worked out scenario in which a mother twice leaves her baby alone or with a stranger and returns twice to be reunited with her child (see Table 6-5 on the next page), enabled Ainsworth to assess the infant–mother relationships and to classify these relationships according to their nature and quality. This procedure is typically used with infants at 8 or 9 months of age. Subsequent research both expanded on Ainsworth's work and added a longitudinal feature, comparing children's behaviour from infancy to young adulthood (Main et al., 2005; Solomon & George, 1999; Sroufe et al., 2005).

As we examine Ainsworth's classification system you may find it useful to look at Table 6-6, which summarizes four categories of attachment relationship: secure, insecure-avoidant, insecure-resistant, and insecure-disorganized attachment. As we note here, the importance of these classifications lies in their value in predicting differences in infants' and children's later emotional, social, and cognitive development. Of the Caucasian, middle-class children studied, Ainsworth classified some 60 to 65 percent as displaying **secure attachment** to their mothers because they readily sought contact with her after the stress of her departure in an unfamiliar setting and were quickly comforted by her, even if initially quite upset. These babies also felt secure enough to explore a novel environment when the mother was present. They did not whine and cling to her but actively investigated their surroundings, as if the mother's presence gave them confidence. In familiar situations, such as the home, these children are minimally disturbed by minor separations from the mother, although they greet her happily when she returns.

Ainsworth classified the remaining children she studied as insecure in one of several ways. Exhibiting **insecure-avoidant attachment** were children who typically showed little distress over the mother's absence in the Strange Situation, at least on her first departure. However, these children actively avoided their mothers on her return: They turned away from her, increased their distance from her, and paid her no attention. After the mother's second departure, during which time many of these babies became visibly upset, they again avoided her on her return. Later researchers have found that this first insecure pattern typically characterizes about 20 percent of North American samples.

secure base

According to Ainsworth, a caregiver to whom an infant has formed an attachment and whom the child uses as a base from which to explore new things and as a safe haven in times of stress.

Strange Situation

A testing scenario in which mother and child are separated and reunited several times and that enables investigators to assess the nature and quality of a mother–infant attachment relationship.

secure attachment

A kind of attachment displayed by babies who are secure enough to explore novel environments, who are minimally disturbed by brief separations from their mothers, and who greet them happily when they return.

insecure-avoidant attachment

A type of attachment shown by babies who seem not to be bothered by their mothers' brief absence but specifically avoid them on their return, sometimes becoming visibly upset.

Table 6-5 The Strange Situation scenario

Episode Number	Persons Present	Duration	Brief Description of Actions
1	Mother, baby, and observer	30 seconds	Observer introduces mother and baby to experimental room, then leaves. (Room contains many appealing toys scattered about.)
2	Mother and baby	3 minutes	Mother is non-participant while baby explores; if necessary, play is stimulated after two minutes.
3	Stranger, mother, and baby	3 minutes	Stranger enters. First minute: stranger silent. Second minute: stranger converses with mother. Third minute: stranger approaches baby. After three minutes: mother leaves unobtrusively.
4	Stranger and baby	3 minutes or less	First separation episode. Stranger's behaviour is geared to that of baby.
5	Mother and baby	3 minutes or more	First reunion episode. Mother greets and/or comforts baby, then tries to settle the baby again in play. Mother then leaves, saying "bye-bye."
6	Baby alone	3 minutes or less	Second separation episode.
7	Stranger and baby	3 minutes or less	Continuation of second separation. Stranger enters and gears behaviour to that of baby.
8	Mother and baby	3 minutes	Second reunion episode. Mother enters, greets baby, then picks baby up. Meanwhile, stranger leaves unobtrusively.

insecure-resistant attachment

A kind of attachment shown by babies who tend to become very upset at the departure of their mothers and who exhibit inconsistent behaviour on their mothers' return, sometimes seeking contact, sometimes pushing their mothers away.

insecure-disorganized attachment

A type of attachment shown by babies who seem disorganized and disoriented when reunited with their mothers after a brief separation.

A second type of insecure relationship is called **insecure-resistant attachment**. Researchers have found that infants who display this type of attachment (and who make up about 10 to 15 percent of North American samples) often become extremely upset when the mother leaves them but are oddly ambivalent toward her when she returns. Intermittently, they seek contact with her and then angrily push her away.

The third type of insecure relationship, identified by later researchers, is called **insecure-disorganized attachment** (Solomon & George, 1999). When babies who display this kind of behaviour are reunited with their mothers in the Strange Situation scenario, they seem disorganized and disoriented. They look dazed, they freeze often in the middle of their movements, or they engage in repetitive behaviours such as rocking. These children also seem apprehensive and fearful of their attachment figures and are unable to cope in a consistent and organized way with distress in the presence of their caregivers. Note that all these attachment classifications reflect the quality of the relationship between the child and the parent, not individual traits of either the child or the parent. Interestingly, as Table 6-6 shows, similar child–parent relationship patterns can be observed in these children and parents when the children are 6 years old (Main & Cassidy, 1988).

Fraley and Spieker (2003) have questioned a fundamental assumption of attachment research—namely, the idea that the different patterns of secure and insecure attachment relations delineated by the Strange Situation truly represent categorically different patterns of behaviour. According to their analyses, Fraley and Spieker (2003) suggest that it might be more appropriate to view individual differences in attachment as being continuous (as opposed to being discontinuous or categorical) in nature, with such differences varying along a single continuum of emotional security. This conception of attachment has met with some skepticism by others (Cassidy, 2003; Sroufe, 2003),

Table 6-6 Children's attachment behaviour in the Strange Situation: A typology

1 Year Old	6 Years Old
Secure Attachment On reunion after brief separation from parents, children seek physical contact, proximity, interaction; often try to maintain physical contact. Readily soothed by parents and return to exploration and play.	On reunion, children initiate conversation and pleasant interaction with parents or are highly responsive to parents' overtures. May subtly move close to or into physical contact with parents, usually with rationale, for example, to seek a toy. Children remain calm throughout.
Insecure-Avoidant Attachment Children actively avoid and ignore parents on reunion, looking away and remaining occupied with toys. May move away from parents and ignore their efforts to communicate.	Children minimize and restrict opportunities for interaction with parents on reunion, looking and speaking only as necessary and remaining occupied with toys or activities. May subtly move away with rationale, for example, to retrieve a toy.
Insecure-Resistant Attachment Although infants seem to want closeness and contact, their parents are not able to alleviate effectively their distress after brief separation. Child may show subtle or overt signs of anger, seeking proximity and then resisting it.	In movements, posture, and tones of voice, children seem to try to exaggerate both intimacy and distress dependency on parents. They may seek closeness but appear uncomfortable, for example, lying in parent's lap but wriggling and squirming. These children sometimes show subtle signs of hostility.
Insecure-Disorganized Attachment Children show signs of disorganization (e.g., crying for parents at door and then running quickly away when door opens; approaching parent with head down) or disorientation (e.g., seeming to "freeze" for a few seconds).	Children almost seem to adopt parental role with parents, trying to control and direct parents' behaviour either by embarrassing or humiliating parents or by showing extreme enthusiasm for reunion or overly solicitous behaviour toward parents.

Sources: Adapted from Ainsworth, Blehar, Waters, & Wall, 1978; Main & Cassidy, 1988; Main & Hesse, 1990; Solomon & George, 1999.

and has opened up the whole question of whether attachment theory actually demands either a continuous or a categorical conception (Waters & Beauchaine, 2003).

Although the Strange Situation is the most widely accepted and most validated means of assessing attachment (Goldberg, 2001), new methods of assessing attachment have been developed in recent years. Relying on the judgments of caregivers who are familiar with the child's behaviour, the **Attachment Q-Sort (AQS)** (Solomon & George, 1999; van IJzendoorn et al., 2004) calls for the mother or other caregiver to sort a set of cards containing phrases that describe the child's behaviour (e.g., "rarely asks for help," "keeps track of mother's location while playing around the house") into sets ranging from those that are most descriptive of the child to those that are least descriptive. The method, which is useful for children between the ages of 1 and 5 years, was designed to facilitate making ratings, in naturalistic settings, of a broad variety of attachment-related behaviours (e.g., secure-base behaviour, attachment-exploration balance, and affective responsiveness). As we will see later, other investigators (Bretherton, 2005; Solomon & George, 1999) have developed later-age assessments of attachment that closely resemble the Strange Situation and permit across-time comparisons between children in infancy and at later ages.

Finally, other innovative procedures for assessing attachment have been developed that do not rely on mother–child separations. The California Attachment Procedure (CAP) focuses on how mothers manage children's fear and upset in response to stressful events such as loud noises or a scary robot instead of maternal separations (Clarke-Stewart et al., 2001). This approach has been used with children at 18 months and more accurately classifies the attachment of children who are accustomed to routine separations from their parents such those involved in child care, a topic we address later in the chapter.

Attachment Q-Sort (AQS)

An assessment method in which a caregiver or observer judges the quality of a child's attachment based on the child's behaviour in natural- istic situations, often includ- ing brief separations from parents.

Box 6.2

Risk and Resilience

ATTACHMENT, INSTITUTIONALIZATION, AND INTERNATIONAL ADOPTION

In many of the affluent, industrialized countries, the number of children available for domestic adoption has been decreasing due to such factors as better and more available birth control, abortion, and the increased acceptance of single parenthood (Goldberg & Marcovitch, 1997; Serbin, 1997). One consequence of this trend has been an increase in international adoption, with families from North America and Western Europe coming forward to adopt infants who have been orphaned or abandoned as a result of conflicts and civil war (Serbin, 1997). Although many point out the advantages, in humanitarian terms, of such adoptions, citing the rather bleak prospects for these children if left in their home countries, international adoption has not received uniform approval around the world. Some of the concerns raised include the ethics of removing a child from his or her home country and culture, the risks related to the child's visible minority status in their new country, and the costs to the original home country of losing their children (Serbin, 1997). Along with these political, social, and economic risks, there are also significant psychological concerns surrounding international adoption. Accordingly, studying the psychological impact of international adoption on the adopted child has become a research topic of growing relevance and importance.

One issue that has been of concern with international adoptions has to do with the formation of attachment relationships in these children. In fact, early research on the attachment of institutionalized children suggested that such children show a variety of behaviours that could be problematic for adoptive parents, such as failure to respond to or initiate social contact (Provence & Lipton, 1962), difficulties forming attachments (Goldfarb, 1945), as well as a variety of cognitive and linguistic deficits (Windsor et al., 2007). Although some of these early conclusions were criticized because they were based on rather descriptive

data derived from fairly small numbers of children (Chisholm, Carter, Ames, & Morison, 1995), recent meta-analyses of the psychological adjustment of adopted children (Wierzbicki, 1993) continue to show that adopted children are at risk for a number of cognitive, social, and emotional problems (Iftene & Nasreen, 2004; MacLean, 2003).

What is known about the possible developmental risks for children adopted internationally? Studies of the impact of international adoption on psychological development have been carried out by researchers around the world (Beckett et al., 2006, 2007; ERA Study Team, 1998). One particularly well-studied case involves work by Elinor Ames and Kim Chisholm and their colleagues at Simon Fraser University, who have been studying the psychological adjustment of Romanian children adopted by Canadian families in British Columbia. Following the overthrow of the Ceausescu totalitarian government in Romania in 1989, large numbers of infants and children were either orphaned or abandoned by their parents, with many of these children ending up in orphanages in which physical care was barely adequate. Because of the media attention devoted to the plight of these children, families from all over the world, including Canada, began to adopt the children, thus providing developmental psychologists with a unique opportunity to study the effects of institutionalization and adoption on a number of aspects of child development.

Given the extreme deprivation suffered by the Romanian adoptees in their homeland, it was not surprising to find that they showed a number of serious medical and psychological problems (Fischer, Ames, Chisholm, & Savoie, 1997; Morison, Ames, & Chisholm, 1995), including eating disorders, sleep problems, stereotypical behaviours (such as rocking back and forth), and sibling and peer relationship problems (Fischer et al., 1997; Marcovitch, Cesaroni, Roberts, & Swanson,

In recent years, researchers have become interested in a number of related questions concerning the formation of attachments. What happens, for example, to attachment when children are orphaned or institutionalized very early in life, and then subsequently adopted. This question is explored in Box 6.2, which focuses on the attachment relations of international adoptees. Another question is whether Ainsworth's model is

1995). Additionally, interviews with the parents of these adoptees revealed that when these children were first adopted (at an average age of about 17 months) they showed a wide array of developmental delays, including deficits in fine-motor, gross-motor, personal-social, and linguistic development. Moreover, cognitive deficits have been found to persist for up to four and a half years years after being adopted (Morison & Ellwood, 2000), and some six and a half years later, the late-adopted Romanian children had higher cortisol levels than the control groups (Gunnar, Morison, Chisholm, & Schuder, 2001). Cortisol levels are important in that cortisol has been associated with stress, and is known to affect, and often suppress, physical growth (Johnson, Kamilaris, Chrousos, & Gold, 1992).

And what about attachment in these children? Chisholm and colleagues (1995) found that relative to the two control groups, these children scored significantly lower in their security of attachment. Moreover, these researchers looked at the presence of what has been called "indiscriminately friendly" (IF) behaviour in these children, which is behaviour that is affectionate and friendly toward all adults, without any caution or fear. In keeping with all the previous results, the Romanian adoptees displayed significantly more IF-type behaviour than either of the control groups. As a striking example of such behaviours, over 60 percent of the parents of the Romanian children judged that these children would typically approach a stranger, and 50 percent said they thought their child would be willing to go home with a stranger. And more recent work suggests that such indiscriminate behaviour is unrelated to whether or not children actually develop a preferred attachment figure (Zeanah, Smyke, & Dumitrescu, 2002).

In a three-year follow-up study (Chisholm, 1998), when these children were about 4½ years old, the adoptees showed somewhat higher percentages of insecure attachments relative to the control groups, although attachment security scores (based on a Strange Situation assessment) no longer differed between the Romanian adoptees and the two control groups. In contrast to this improvement in attachment relations, though, scores of indiscriminate friendliness showed little change in this follow-up.

What are some of the implications of this research on international adoption? One conclusion is that parents who plan to adopt internationally must be aware of, and concerned with, their children's social and emotional development, as well as their medical condition and other developmental delays. Clearly, the experiences these children have faced constitute a risk factor for many aspects of development.

What this work has also demonstrated is a remarkable resiliency among these children, with the environmental change brought about by the international adoption helping these children to overcome much of their early deprivation. Although it is tempting to point out that these children are still somewhat delayed relative to their counterparts in their newly adopted country, it is also true that their level of functioning likely far surpasses same-aged children who remained institutionalized in their host country (Serbin, 1997). Moreover, there have even been reports (Marcovitch et al., 1997; Westhues & Cohen, 1994, 1997) that some subgroups of these Romanian adoptees actually score above the population means in such areas as self-esteem. Generally, this work offers an important and informative window into processes of development that simply could not, due to ethical reasons, be explored in other ways. As such, our knowledge of what contributes to social and emotional risk and resilience in children has been dramatically enhanced.

equally useful in different cultures both within North America and around the world. As Box 6.3 on the next pages discusses, the model does seem to have considerable applicability, although there are wide differences among the ways children of different cultures organize their secure-base behaviour.

Box 6.3

Perspectives on Diversity

ATTACHMENT TYPES IN DIFFERENT CULTURES

Can Ainsworth's Strange Situation be used in cultures other than North America to assess the character of children's relationships with their parents? For example, do *secure, avoidant*, and *resistant* mean the same things in Africa as they do in North America? If mothers and fathers in Norway encourage their young children to develop independence earlier than North American parents, how may this affect the interpretation of "avoidant" behaviour on a child's reunion with parental figures? A number of researchers have addressed these and other questions relating to the universality of Ainsworth's concepts. They have found that, although overall the attachment categories seem to have considerable applicability across cultural groups, important variations do occur in the way infants of different racial-ethnic groups give expression to secure and insecure attachment relationships.

Another important question is the origin of particular attachment behaviours and relationships. According to Thompson (2006), parental solicitude is affected not only by personality factors and personal belief systems but also by such things as the availability of environmental resources and a parent's degree of freedom to care for a child rather than be stressed or exhausted by the effort to obtain the necessities for survival. On this view, all three major types of attachment can be seen as adaptive responses by infants to parental investment patterns. Thus, in assessing attachment behaviours among parents and children in the resource-poor environments found not only in developing countries but also in areas within more developed nations, it is important to consider the many factors that may contribute to attachment behaviour.

Attachment Types within a Culture

Although some researchers have suggested that the patterns of attachment identified by Ainsworth and colleagues (1978) are representative of North America and Europe in both their form and proportions (van IJzendoorn & Kroonenberg, 1988), others have questioned whether these attachment classifications will hold up in cultures having different expectations for infant behaviour (Miyake, Chen, & Campos, 1985; Sagi et al., 1985; Strayer, 1984). As a first pass, one can ask if the various attachment types and measures are even consistent across different subgroups within a particular culture.

In an attempt to explore just this question, Brian Vaughn, Francis Strayer, and some colleagues examined attachment classifications, using the Attachment Q-Sort (AQS) method, in two different sociocultural groups—English-speaking children from Chicago and francophone children from Montreal (Strayer, Verissimo, Vaughn, & Howes, 1995; Vaughn, Strayer, Jacques, Trudel, & Seifer, 1991). These researchers found that despite the differences between these groups with respect to language, ethnic identity, and cultural values, the Q-sorts provided not only valid descriptions of attachment for both groups of children but were also fairly equivalent characterizations of mother–infant attachment in the two groups, although there were some differences in the security of attachment scores between the Chicagoan and Québécois samples. Unfortunately, these researchers could not say whether these differences reflected true variations in attachment security or resulted due to procedural differences in how the studies were run. But what does seem clear from these studies is that at least for different subgroups within a more global North American cultural context, attachment measures and classifications appear fairly robust.

Attachment Types across Cultures

Secure Attachment Relations When babies are accustomed to almost constant contact with their mothers, they may react differently to reunion in the Strange Situation than would be expected on the basis of North American standards. Thus, secure attachments may be present even when infants' behaviour in the Strange Situation at first seems to indicate otherwise.

For example, the Ganda infants Ainsworth herself studied showed more distress in response to brief separations from their mothers than did North American babies, but on investigation it was revealed that brief separations are infrequent in this African society. Ganda mothers leave their babies for hours at a time while they work in their gardens, and other relatives look after the children in their absence (Colin, 1996). Thus, when they left their babies in the experimental situation, the infants expected a long absence and reacted accordingly—a very counterintuitive finding.

In North America, however, most 1-year-olds are encouraged to play with toys, exercise their motor skills, and to nap alone. And whereas few North American parents bring their babies into their own beds, in many parts of the world, it is common for infants to sleep with their parents. For example, babies in Japan usually sleep in the same bed with their mothers, and

parents do not hesitate to take a child into their bed when the youngster cries or asks to be fed (van IJzendoorn & Sagi, 1999). Infants in Japan show much stronger reactions to departure of the mother than North American babies do.

Avoidant-Attachment Relationships In Germany and Sweden, evidence of avoidant relationships is seen more often than in North America, reflecting the fact that parents in these countries tend to stress early independence somewhat more than do North American parents (Colin, 1996; Grossmann et al., 2005). And according to Schaffer (1996), infants in the United Kingdom are also more likely to evidence avoidant relationships than North American babies are, though not as likely as German infants (Grossmann et al., 2005).

In contrast, avoidant reactions are uncommon among Japanese babies, partly because children in Japan are socialized to maintain harmonious personal relationships; ignoring or turning away from someone would be considered rude (Colin, 1996). Moreover, in one Japanese study on reunion, most mothers rushed to pick up their infants before the babies could give any sign that they wanted contact. Presumably, these mothers hurried to alleviate the distress that they assumed their babies were experiencing.

Resistant-Attachment Relationships Japanese and Israeli babies seem more likely than North American infants to show resistant behaviour in both the baby-alone episode of the Strange Situation and in the reunion phase. In the case of the Japanese infants, this may be because they are in close contact with their mothers from the time they are born, including, as we have noted, sharing their parents' beds (Rothbaum et al., 2000). For these infants, the stress of separation seems much greater than it is for North American or European babies.

Babies living on Israeli kibbutzim probably show resistant attachment behaviour in the Strange Situation for different reasons. Although an infant Israeli _kibbutznik_ is usually raised by a hired caregiver (in Hebrew, a _metapelet_), this person is not always highly motivated to engage in infant care—typically having responsibility for three children—and may be unable to respond sensitively to each of them in an optimal fashion (Aviezer et al., 1999; Sagi-Schwartz & Aviezer, 2005). The child customarily spends only a few hours with her parents, at suppertime, and unless she sleeps in her parents' home, she may be watched over at night by a person who must monitor all the babies in the nursery building. As a result, "even secure attachments might be expected often to be tinged with resistance and/or preoccupation with the caregiver, who may often have been unavailable" (Colin, 1996, p. 155).

Can We Rely on the Strange Situation in Cross-Cultural Contexts?

In view of the foregoing findings, we may ask whether the Strange Situation is truly applicable to assessing attachment relationships in babies of other cultures. Given the cultural practices we have described that either neutralize the effects of separation or make it excessively threatening, it can be argued that this measurement device needs revision or replacement.

Does the fact that children from Germany and Sweden who may be well adjusted in terms of their upbringing nevertheless appear to have avoidant—and thus, by definition, insecure—attachment relationships undermine the usefulness of the assessment in those cultures? And perhaps the test situation is just too stressful for Japanese and Israeli babies? Several researchers have argued that as long as the experimenter shortens separation episodes for babies who are highly distressed by the scenario, the procedure probably produces valid classifications across cultures. Or possibly new approaches that we discussed in the text, such as the California Attachment Procedure (CAP), will be useful in cross-cultural studies, since it avoids stressful separation episodes (Clarke-Stewart et al., 2001).

The newer Attachment Q-Sort that we discuss in the text allows for more input by infants' caregivers into the assessment process, but even this device may be culture-bound. Although Posada and colleagues (1995) found considerable overall cross-cultural consistency in their study of mothers' Q-sorts in China, Colombia, Germany, Israel, Japan, Norway, and the United States, they report that sociocultural similarity both within and across cultural groups was modest, and that there is considerable diversity in the ways that children behave in separation situations. The issue of multicultural applicability of attachment-assessment measures may remain unresolved until researchers undertake multiple naturalistic observations of infant–caregiver dyads in many cultures and social contexts (van IJzendoorn & Sagi, 1999).

🔵9 The Parents' Role in the Quality of Attachment

We have said that attachment is a *relationship*, developing out of the interaction between infant and parent. Both parents and infants contribute to the nature of the attachment relationship, and we begin, in this section, by considering the parents' input. We look at babies' contribution to the relationship in the section that follows.

STYLES OF CAREGIVING Ainsworth was the first to describe how parents' styles of interacting with their infants are linked with the kinds of attachment relationships that infants and parents develop. Mothers of securely attached infants, for instance, usually permit their babies to play an active role in determining the onset, pacing, and end of feeding early in life. This behaviour in and of itself does not promote a secure attachment, but it identifies a mother as generally responsive to her baby's needs. The mother of a securely attached infant is also consistently available to her baby; she does not sometimes ignore her baby when he signals a genuine need for her (Belsky, 1999; Braungart-Rieker, Garwood, Powers, & Wang, 2001). This style of parenting, called **sensitive care**, is widely associated with the formation of secure attachments. Moreover, this link between sensitive parenting and attachment security is evident in many cultures such as Australia, Brazil, and South Africa (Harrison & Ungerer, 2002; Posada et al., 2002; Tomlinson et al., 2005).

A number of parenting styles are associated with insecure attachments. Cassidy and Berlin (1994), for example, have found that mothers of babies with an insecure-avoidant type of attachment tend to be *unavailable* and *rejecting*. These mothers are generally unresponsive to their infants' signals, rarely have close bodily contact with them, and often interact with them in an angry, irritable way. And the parents of infants with insecure-resistant attachments exhibit an *inconsistently available* parenting style (Belsky, 1999; Thompson, 2006). Mothers who display this style respond to their babies' needs at times, but at other times they do not, and in general they offer little affection and are awkward in their interactions with their infants.

The most deficient forms of parenting are found among parents whose attachment with their infants is of the insecure-disorganized type; these parents often neglect their babies or abuse them physically. The **approach–avoidance behaviour**—the tendency to show an alternative pattern of approaching a person or object and retreating or escaping from it—that infants with this type of attachment display when reunited with their caregivers in the Strange Situation may actually be an adaptive response, for these babies do not know what to expect (Solomon & George, 1999). Carlson et al. (1989) found that mistreated infants were significantly more likely to develop insecure-disorganized attachments (82 percent) than were children who were not mistreated (19 percent). Another factor often associated with the insecure-disorganized pattern of attachment is maternal depression. Babies of depressed mothers show not only approach–avoidance but also sadness upon reunion. Observations of such mothers with their 6-month-old babies have revealed little mutual eye contact and minimal mutual responsiveness; instead, both mother and baby tended to avert their gaze (Field, 1990; Greenberg, 1999). The presence of a non-depressed caregiver such as a father can, in part, mitigate the negative effects of maternal depression on infant's development (Hossain et al., 1994). Studies of the Dogan, who live in Mali, West Africa, suggest that atypical maternal behaviour, or behaviours that scare or frighten infants, is linked with disorganized attachments—a pattern similar to that found in Europe and North America (Benoit et al., 2001; Goldberg, Benoit, Blokland, & Madigan, 2003; Lyons-Ruth & Jacobvitz, 1999; True, Pisani, & Oumar, 2001). As in the case of abuse, the parent is a source of both comfort and fear, which leads to the infant's disorganized behaviour.

Some of the parent–infant pairs that fail to achieve early **interactive synchrony** also fail to develop a secure attachment in the baby's second half-year of life. Maternal unresponsiveness to infant signals can play an important role in the emergence of an insecure attachment, just as a mother's sensitivity to her baby's needs can help promote secure

sensitive care

Caregiving that is consistent and responsive and that begins by allowing an infant to play a role in determining when feeding will begin and end and at what pace it will proceed.

approach–avoidance behaviour

A pattern of interaction in which the infant or child shows an inconsistent pattern of approaching and retreating from a person or an object.

interactive synchrony

A term that characterizes mother–infant interactions in which the mother constantly adjusts her behaviour to that of her baby, responding to and respecting his signals as to when he is ready for and wants engagement and interaction.

attachment. This has been shown in a series of studies by David Pederson, Greg Moran, and their colleagues at the University of Western Ontario (Madigan et al., 2006, 2007; Moran et al., 2008; Moran & Pederson, 1998; Pederson & Moran, 1995, 1996). For example, Moran and colleagues (2008) recently categorized a large number of mother–infant relationships using the Strange Situation, while simultaneously assessing both maternal sensitivity and atypical maternal behaviour. Moran and his fellow researchers (2008) observed that both maternal sensitivity and atypical maternal behaviour predicted attachment security and the degree of attachment disorganization. These researchers suggested that these two factors—sensitivity and atypical behaviour—more likely reflect a single factor related to the nature of the maternal interaction between mother and child that has a strong impact on the nature of the infants' attachment relationship.

Pederson and Moran

Attachment processes do not cease in infancy, but continue to be important in later phases of development such as adolescence. Just as infants gain comfort from using mother as a secure base, adolescents continue to find value in the quality of the attachment relationship with their mothers. When the mother was supportive and attuned to the adolescent's needs and self-perceptions and when the mother and adolescent were able to maintain their relationship through disagreements, the adolescents' attachment relationship with their mother was more secure (Allen et al., 2003). Just as a secure base allows the infant to begin to explore her physical world, a secure base as expressed by a positive and supportive mother–adolescent relationship allows the adolescent to explore independence in ideas and behaviours. The forms of attachment relationships shift across development, but the fundamental dynamics remain the same.

What can we learn about attachment from infant–parent interactions in other cultures? An interesting comparison can be drawn between North American parenting styles and those of Israeli parents, some of whom live with their families in a *kibbutz*, or communal village, and raise their infant children in group-care arrangements. In all *kibbutzim* (plural of kibbutz), babies stay in the infant-care centre during the day, and in some, they stay in the centre even at night, but in others, they spend the night with their families. Sagi and his colleagues (Sagi, van IJzendoorn, Aviezer, Donnell, & Mayseless, 1994) examined the effects of these contrasting child-rearing arrangements on attachment relationships. Some of their results are summarized in Table 6-7, which shows that infants who slept at home with their families were more likely to develop secure attachments than babies who spent the night in the infant centre. As you can see, among the children who spent the night at home, those in the secure and insecure-resistant attachment groups had proportions similar to those of the North American groups that we have already mentioned. Note that no infants were classified as having insecure-avoidant attachments. Babies reared in kibbutzim rarely exhibit such attachments, for kibbutzim caregivers rarely exhibit rejecting behaviour or pressure children to act independently (Sagi-Schwartz & Aviezer, 2005). Quite recently, the practice of

Attachment Type	Children Who Spent the Night		Total Children
	In the Care Centre	At Home	
Secure	6 (26%)	15 (60%)	21 (44%)
Insecure-avoidant	0	0	0
Insecure-resistant	7 (30%)	2 (8%)	9 (19%)
Insecure-disorganized	10 (44%)	8 (32%)	18 (37%)

Table 6-7

Attachment in children raised in an Israeli kibbutz

Note: Figures in parentheses are percentages.

Source: Adapted from Sagi, van IJzendoorn, Aviezer, Donnell, & Mayseless, 1994.

communal sleeping in kibbutzim has decreased dramatically (Dror, 2001). Virtually all of these collectives now practise home sleeping—an end result that some researchers feel was almost "predestined" from the perspective of attachment theory (Aviezer, Sagi, & van IJzendoorn, 2002).

Of course, relationships between parents and infants do not develop in a vacuum. They are affected by and affect other relationships among family members, as well as relationships outside the home. For example, there is a link between marital adjustment and infant–parent attachment. Secure attachment is more likely when marital adjustment is good (e.g., Doyle, Markiewicz, Brendgen, Lieberman, & Voss, 2000; Goldberg & Easterbrooks, 1984; Thompson, 2006). Although the birth of a child is generally associated with a decline in marital satisfaction (Cowan & Cowan, 2000), mothers whose infants become securely attached usually report less dissatisfaction with their marriages than mothers whose children are insecurely attached. As you will see when we discuss the family in Chapter 11, marital and parent–child relationships are often closely connected.

IS THERE INTERGENERATIONAL CONTINUITY IN ATTACHMENT?
The kind of care that parents received when they were infants is another influence on the quality of attachment that develops between them and their own children (Bretherton & Munholland, 1999; Thompson, 2006). From our mothers and fathers, we all acquire what Bowlby (1973) calls **internal working models** of the self and parents. According to Bowlby, these models are mental representations about oneself, one's own parents, and the styles of interaction that one experienced as a child. Note that it is not the actual experience of the parent when she was an infant that forms this model but rather how she reconstructs or interprets these early experiences. Because of these internal working models, people tend to recreate their own childhood relationships when they themselves become mothers or fathers (Bretherton, 2005).

To investigate this notion of intergenerational continuity, Main and her colleagues (Main et al., 1985, 2005) interviewed 40 middle-class mothers about recollections of their own relationships with their mothers during infancy and childhood. Supporting Bowlby's theory, the mothers' patterns of memories related to the quality of their current attachment relationships with their own infants. As Table 6-8 shows, Main classified the women into three groups: autonomous, dismissing, and preoccupied. The *autonomous* group, who had developed secure attachment relationships with their infants, revealed in their interviews that although they valued close relationships with their parents and others, they were at the same time objective. They tended not to idealize their own parents but had a clear understanding of their relationships with them and were able to describe both their positive and negative aspects even if the relationship was strong enough to overcome any weaknesses. The *dismissing* group, who had avoidant attachment relationships with their babies, had a different set of memories; they dismissed and devalued attachment and frequently claimed that they could not recall incidents from their childhood. On the other hand, the recollections they did report were often of idealized parents: "I had the world's greatest mom!" The third, *preoccupied*, group were the parents of resistant infants. Preoccupied with earlier family attachments, these mothers recalled many conflict-ridden incidents from childhood but could not organize them into coherent patterns.

Intergenerational continuity is not always straightforward, for some children and adults are able to overcome early adversity and insecure attachments and eventually develop satisfying interpersonal relationships with their spouses, partners, and offspring. Several cross-sectional studies have supported the existence of this resilient group of individuals, now called "earned-secure" people (Paley et al., 1999). Roisman and colleagues (2002), who used data from a 23-year longitudinal study, showed that individuals can indeed overcome early problems and develop "secure" attachment relationships. Even though these young adults had negative childhood experiences, those who overcame their past and developed secure internal working models of

internal working model

According to Bowlby, a person's mental representation of herself as a child, of her parents, and of the nature of her interaction with her parents as she reconstructs and interprets that interaction.

Table 6-8 Relationships between mothers' and children's attachment status

| Attachment Category | | Mother–Child Relationship |
Mother	Child	
Autonomous	Secure	Mother's mind not taken up with unresolved concerns about her own experience; mother thus able to be sensitive to child's communications
Dismissing	Insecure-Avoidant	Mother reluctant to acknowledge her own attachment needs and, thus, insensitive and unresponsive to child's needs
Preoccupied	Insecure-Resistant	Mother confused about her attachment history and, thus, inconsistent in her interactions with her child

Sources: Hesse, 1999; Main, Kaplan, & Cassidy, 1985; Schaffer, 1996.

attachment relationships had high-quality romantic relationships in their early twenties. The romantic ties of these earned-secure young adults were comparable to those of individuals who were continuously secure and of higher quality than those of individuals with insecure attachments.

Additional support for intergenerational continuity comes from studies of other racial-ethnic groups and of parents in other countries. When Levine and colleagues (1991) studied a group of largely African-American and Hispanic teen mothers, they found these mothers' attachment interview classifications to be reliable predictors of the attachment classification assigned to their relationships with their infants. And in Germany, Grossmann and colleagues (2005) found strong links between adults' recollections and their attachment relationships with their infants. In Israel, Scharf (2001) found that adolescents who had been reared in a kibbutz communal setting, including overnight sleeping in the kibbutz, differed from family-raised adolescents in their attachment representations or working models of relationships. The kibbutz group had a higher incidence of non-autonomous attachment representations and were less competent at coping with imagined separations than family-reared adolescents. Adolescents in the kibbutz, whose parents had switched to family sleeping arrangements when the children were between ages 3 and 6 did not differ from family-reared adolescents, in terms of attachment representations. This suggests that children's working models can shift in response to changing circumstances (Bretherton, 2005).

Perhaps the most convincing evidence of intergenerational continuity comes from studies of women who have not yet even given birth (Benoit & Parker, 1994; Benoit, Parker, & Zeanah, 1997; Fonagy et al., 1991). Benoit and Parker (1994), for example, interviewed soon-to-be mothers during their pregnancy (and again when their children were 11 months old), as well as the soon-to-be grandmothers, to assess the mothers' and grandmothers' attachment classifications. These attachment classifications were then compared with the infants' attachment (as measured in the Strange Situation) when they reached 12 months. Benoit and Parker found that mothers' attachment during pregnancy predicted both infants' and grandmothers' classifications over 80 percent and 75 percent of the time, respectively. Thus, these authors found strong support for the idea that parental-attachment history influences the attachment relationship between parents and their children. Even more striking: such effects can be transmitted across at least three generations.

The Effect of Infant Temperament

As you learned in earlier chapters, some babies are more difficult to interact with and care for than others. Might this affect the quality of attachments that these infants

Some babies are fussy and difficult, no matter how lovingly parents care for them (a), and others are easygoing right from the start (b).

(a)

(b)

develop? Some investigators have found a link between certain temperamental characteristics in infants and the kinds of relationships they develop with their parents. For instance, Moran and Pederson (1998) found that mothers with insecure-resistant relationships with their infants were more likely to report that their infants were either fussy or difficult (at both 12 and 18 months) than mothers in either secure or insecure-avoidant relationships. Perhaps these early difficulties reflect underlying problems in adaptive mechanisms that continue to influence a child's behaviour and interactions with others as it matures. Similarly, some (Stevenson-Hinde, 2005) suggest that children who are shy and fearful may fail to develop secure attachment due to their inability to openly express their emotions while interacting with their caregivers. We must be cautious in drawing such conclusions, however, because many other researchers have failed to find clear links between early infant temperament and later infant–parent attachment (Thompson, 2006; Vaughn & Bost, 1999).

If infant temperament does have some influence on the development of attachment, that influence is probably mediated by many other factors. A "difficult" infant certainly is not destined to have a poor relationship with her parents. Parents who have a difficult or irritable baby can usually cope successfully if they receive help and support from other family members and friends. When adequate social support is available to the mother, an irritable baby is no more likely to become insecurely attached than a non-irritable one is (Crockenberg, 1981; van den Boom, 1994). If a mother is socially isolated or has poor relationships with other adults, however, she is more likely to have problems fostering secure attachment in a difficult infant (Levitt, Weber, & Clark, 1986). Thus, the effect of temperament on attachment cannot be separated from the influence of the total social context in which the baby is developing (Sroufe, 1996; Thompson, 2006; Vaughn & Bost, 1999).

LO 10 Stability in the Quality of Attachment

There is substantial stability in the quality of attachment from one period of time to another. As you saw earlier in the chapter, among infants tested with their mothers in the Strange Situation, the same attachment patterns were detected both at 12 months and at 6 years of age (Solomon & George, 1999). Recently, Moss and colleagues (Moss et al., 2005) found about 68 percent stability of attachment classifications in a French-Canadian sample from children aged 3½ to 5½ years. The Q-sort method of attachment has been found to be similarly reliable. Symons, Clark, Isaksen, and Marshall (1998), for example, found that Q-sort attachment security scores were stable when measured at 2, 4, and 6 years of age, although, again, the correlation was by no means perfect. Also, Waters and colleagues (2000) found that 72 percent of their sample classified as secure versus insecure in infancy were similarly rated 20 years later in early adulthood—an impressive level of attachment stability across the lifespan. Even in adulthood, attachment representations tend to be relatively stable: 89 percent of couples received similar Adult Attachment Interview classifications before marriage and 18 months later (Crowell et al., 2002).

But general stability in the quality of parent–child relationships does not mean that change is impossible (Waters et al., 2000). In the studies just mentioned, substantial minorities of children with insecure attachments as infants developed better relationships with their parents by school age. This is particularly likely when a child's parents begin to experience less stress in their lives (fewer financial worries, for instance, or less marital tension) and so are able to become more available to their child and to interact in ways that are more responsive to the child's needs (Thompson, Lamb, & Estes, 1982). Alternatively, secure infant–parent attachment relationships can become insecure if the life circumstances of the family deteriorate due to job loss, divorce, illness, or abuse. More infants (44 percent) who later experienced negative life events changed attachment classifications from infancy to adulthood than children (22 percent) in families with no negative events (22 percent) (Waters et al., 2000).

Professional intervention can help improve a troubled parent–child relationship (Bakermans-Kranenburg et al., 2003). In a Dutch study, mothers who were taught to be more sensitive to their infants developed better attachment relationships with them than did the mothers of a control group of infants (van den Boom, 1990). Clearly, attachment relationships continue to develop and are responsive to changes in the behaviour of both parent and child (Thompson, 2006; Waters et al., 2000).

The Consequences of Attachment Quality

Does the quality of early infant–parent attachments have serious implications for the child's development? As you will see, early interactions with attachment figures do indeed seem to shape children's continuing development, particularly their development of cognitive and social skills and a sense of self (Thompson, 2006).

COGNITIVE DEVELOPMENT An early secure attachment appears to be related to more complex exploratory behaviour at 2 years of age (Main, 1973). Moreover, as the child continues to develop, this intellectual curiosity is reflected in an intensified interest in, and enjoyment of, solving problems. This positive approach to problem solving is seldom seen in toddlers who were insecurely attached as infants (Matas, Arend, & Sroufe, 1978; Moss, Gosselin, Parent, Rousseau, & Dumont, 1997).

Moss and her colleagues (Moss et al., 1997), for example, examined securely and insecurely attached 3- and 4-year-olds' collaborative problem-solving interactions during a grocery store planning task. Their results showed that securely attached children were more likely to show task-relevant and metacognitive behaviour and were more goal-directed than were insecurely attached preschoolers. And in later work, Moss and St. Laurent (2001) demonstrated that childhood attachment classifications at 6 years were related to academic performance at 8 years. Secure children achieved higher scores than insecure children on communication, cognitive engagement, and mastery motivation.

Other aspects of cognitive functioning are similarly influenced by mother–infant attachment relations. In a longitudinal study, Symons and Clark (2000) found that attachment security at ages 2 and 5 was related to children's "theory of mind" ability (discussed more in Chapter 8) at 5 years. Cross-culturally, similar findings on the relationship between attachment and theory of mind have been found by researchers in Spain (Arranz, Artamendi, Olabarrieta, & Martín, 2002) and in Reykjavik, Iceland (Jacobsen and Hofmann, 1997). These studies not only underscore the link between the quality of the parent–child relationship and cognitive development but also point out that the success of adult experts in facilitating children's learning, as proposed by Vygotsky, may, at least in part, depend on the quality of the attachment relationship. (We introduced Vygotsky's theory and approach in Chapter 1 and will revisit this theory in more detail in Chapter 8.)

SOCIAL DEVELOPMENT Many studies support the idea that the quality of caregiver–infant relationships for later social development (Sroufe et al., 2005; Thompson, 2006). A recent longitudinal study in which children were traced from infancy to age 19 illustrates the importance of the early attachment for later social behaviour (Carlson et al., 2004; Sroufe et al., 2005). Securely and insecurely attached youngsters developed very different social and emotional patterns. At 4 to 5 years of age, teachers rated securely attached children as showing more positive emotions and as having greater empathy for others and increased ability to initiate, respond to, and sustain interactions with other people. Securely attached children also whined less, were less aggressive, and displayed fewer negative reactions when other children approached them. Not surprisingly, their teachers rated them as more socially competent and socially skilled and as having more friends than other children, and their classmates considered them more popular than others.

At 8 and 12 years of age, the securely attached continued to be rated as more socially competent, more peer-oriented, and less dependent on adults. Moreover, they were more likely to develop close friendships than their less securely attached peers. Attachment history also predicted friendship choices: Children with secure attachment histories were more likely to form friendships with other securely attached peers. At age 19, the socio-emotional functioning of those adolescents with a history of secure attachment was rated higher as well. In comparison with peers who had a history of insecure attachment, these young adults were more likely to have close family relationships, long-term friendships, sustained romantic involvement, higher self-confidence, and greater determination regarding personal goals. Others have found similar links between the quality of early attachment and later school-age peer competence and friendship patterns (Contreras et al., 2000; Schneider et al., 2001). The long-term consequences of attachment security are evident not just in biologically related families but also in families of adopted children. Infants who were adopted before 6 months of age and who developed high-quality infant–mother relationships and secure attachments were better adjusted socially at age 7 (Stams et al., 2002). This work underscores the importance for later adjustment of good early caregiving and suggests that the effect is not simply due to a shared genetic history.

Just as Bowlby argued, the links between attachment and social outcomes are forged by children's internal working models. For instance, Ellen Moss and her colleagues in Montreal (Moss et al., 1997, 1999, 2006) have found that children who have an avoidant–attachment style show *internalizing* behaviour problems such as depression and

Attachment relations have been found to influence any number of aspects of social interaction. In this photo, these children all seem to be interacting positively, a behaviour pattern that has been found to be related to secure parent–child attachment.

self-criticism at ages 5 to 7, and 7 to 9 years. Children with an ambivalent attachment, on the other hand, tended to show more *externalizing*, or aggressive and hostile behaviours. Worst off were those with a disorganized attachment; these children showed both externalizing and internalizing behavioural problems. Other work (Moris, Meesters, & Van Den Berg, 2003) has revealed that even in adolescents, insecure attachments are related to a higher prevalence of internalizing and externalizing symptoms.

Similarly, in their longitudinal study, Sroufe and colleagues (2005) assessed children's cognitive working models of relationships at various times throughout childhood and adolescence. For example, in the preschool years, these researchers evaluated children's relationship expectations, attitudes, and feelings. Securely attached children's relationship models were characterized by expectations of empathy between play partners, a high expectation of sharing during play, and constructive approaches to conflict resolution (e.g., taking turns, seeking adult acceptance, getting another toy). During adolescence (age 12) securely attached children construed their friendships as close, emotionally connected, and skilled in conflict resolution. These investigators showed that cognitive working models and social behaviour mutually influence each other across time. In other words, cognitive representations in the preschool period predict social behaviour in middle childhood; in turn, the representations in middle childhood predict social behaviour at 12 years of age, and these cognitive models predict social outcomes at 19 years of age. Moreover, across time, social behaviour at one point predicts later cognitive representations. For example, social behaviour in middle childhood influences a child's cognitive working models in early adolescence. Figure 6-8 on the next page depicts this pattern of across-time influence between cognitive and behavioural levels. Together, these studies illustrate the interplay among attachment, cognitive understanding, and children's social outcomes.

Emotions play a role in accounting for the links between attachment and social competence, too. For example, attachment to his mother affects the way a child processes emotional information and understands and regulates his emotions. Securely attached children tend to remember positive events more accurately than negative events, whereas insecurely attached children do the opposite (Belsky et al., 1996). And securely attached preschoolers are better at understanding emotions than insecurely attached children (Laible & Thompson, 1998). Finally, Contreras and colleagues (2000) found that securely attached children are better at regulating their emotions, which in turn accounted for their superior social relationships with peers.

In trying to understand children's later social behaviour, it is also important to consider both infant–mother and infant–father attachment relationships (Berlin & Cassidy, 1999; Lamb, 2004). Even very young children often develop distinctly different relationships with each parent. In a study of 1-year-old infants, Main and Weston (1981) classified babies according to whether they were securely attached to both parents, to their mothers but not their fathers, to their fathers but not their mothers, or to neither parent. To determine whether the infants' relationships with their mothers and fathers affected their social responsiveness to other people, Main and Weston observed the infants' reactions to a friendly clown. The infants who were securely attached to both parents were more responsive to the clown than the infants who were securely attached to only one parent and insecurely attached to the other, and the babies who were insecurely attached to both parents were the least sociable of all with the clown. These results suggest that a less-than-optimal relationship with one parent can be compensated for by a better relationship with the other parent, and that it is, therefore, not enough to study just mothers or fathers alone. Viewing the parents as part of a family system is the best way to understand their roles in child development (Parke & Buriel, 2006).

In summary, a healthy attachment to parents facilitates exploration, curiosity, and mastery of the social and physical environments. Early secure attachment also increases the child's trust in other social relationships and permits the later development of mature affectional relationships with peers. Longitudinal studies aimed at specifying the links between early parent–infant interaction and later relationships in adolescence

Figure 6-8

A model of across-time influence of social behaviour and cognitive working models on children's adjustment

This model illustrates the ways that cognitive working models, or representations of relationships, influence each other across development. Together, earlier social behaviours and relationship representations influence social functioning in adolescence. Rectangles contain the specific measures used at each time point.

*PIPS: Preschool Interpersonal Problem Solving Assessment Interview.

Source: Carlson et al., 2004; Sroufe et al., 2005.

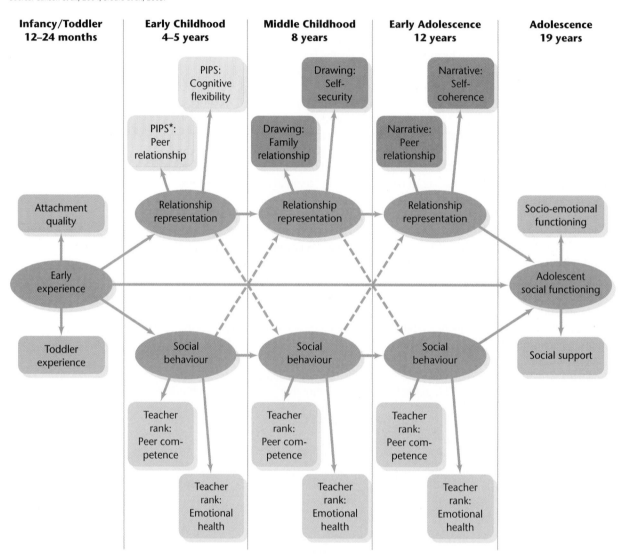

and adulthood will give us more information about the long-term stability of these positive cognitive and social effects of an early secure attachment. Clearly, developmental history leaves its mark (Thompson, 2006).

THE SENSE OF SELF The *sense of self*, or the awareness of the self as differentiated from other people, is crucial to the child's development (Harter, 1998, 2006). As this awareness evolves, it becomes increasingly complicated, incorporating such notions as self-concept, self-esteem, self-confidence, and self-respect, all of which partake of cognitive and social as well as emotional factors.

When do children begin to recognize themselves as being different from other people? Babies as young as 18 weeks of age happily gaze at their reflections in a mirror, but not until they are well past 1 year do they realize that they are looking at a reflection of themselves. A classic method of examining self-identity in the child involves allowing the child to look into a mirror for a bit and then putting a spot of rouge on the child's nose and returning her to the mirror (Brooks-Gunn & Lewis, 1984; Lewis, 1991). We assume that if the child recognizes that the mirror reflection is of herself, she will be likely to touch her nose. Children under 1 year of age seem to believe that the reflection is another child and sometimes touch it or try to look behind the mirror for the other child, but they do not try to touch their noses (Brooks-Gunn & Lewis, 1984). Sometime during the second year of life, children begin to recognize their own images, and by the time they are 2, almost all children give evidence of self-recognition, giggling, showing embarrassment, or acting silly at the sight of their rouged noses (see Figure 6-9). On average, children are 20 months old before they fairly consistently locate or touch the rouge on their noses. Table 6-9 presents the stages in the development of self-awareness in the first two years of life.

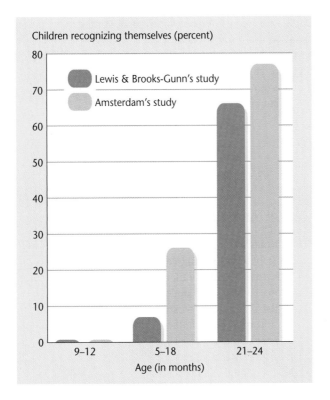

Figure 6-9

What's that on my nose?

When experimenters dabbed rouge on children's noses, in two separate studies the children showed similar behaviour. Those less than a year old did not recognize themselves in the mirror, but by the time they were 2, most children realized that mirror images of children with rouge on their noses were images of themselves.

Source: Lewis & Brooks-Gunn, 1979; Schaffer, 1996.

Age in Months	Behavioural Indications
0–3	Infant shows interest in social objects but does not distinguish between self and other.
3–8	Child's first signs of self-recognition, based on contingency clues (fact that mirror image moves in tandem with child's movements), are tentative and unreliable.
8–12	Notion of self permanence emerges. Child reliably recognizes self based on contingency clues, begins to use feature clues (child's own physical features as seen in video or photograph).
12–24	Basic self categories, such as age and gender, are consolidated. Child reliably recognizes self based on feature clues.

Table 6-9

The early stages of self-awareness

Source: Schaffer, 1996.

Is it possible that the sense of self develops in human children even earlier than 20 months? Some researchers have suggested that infants as young as 3 months may have some sense of self-awareness (e.g., Schaffer, 1996), and others have even suggested that a sense of self develops prenatally, citing the behaviour of some infrahuman creatures that make clear distinctions between themselves and others (Angier, 1997). Still others (e.g., Porges, 1995), however, point out that a considerable difference exists between survival-adapted tendencies to look out for oneself and a real consciousness of that choice or of one's relationship to others.

However these complicated questions may be answered, we do have some evidence that the quality of the child–parent attachment relationship affects the child's developing self-concept. Moreover, the value that one places on the self varies with the quality of attachment (Thompson, 2006). In one study, Cassidy (1988) assessed the attachment relationships of 6-year-olds and the children's self-concepts. Children who were securely attached viewed themselves in a positive way, although they were able to acknowledge their less-than-perfect qualities. In contrast, insecure-avoidant children tended to present themselves as perfect, and insecure-ambivalent children showed no clear pattern of responses. A group of children classified as insecure-controlling (similar to the insecure-disorganized classification discussed earlier) had negative self-concepts. These results strongly suggest that the quality of early attachment is related to the degree to which children view themselves positively and realistically; both of these capacities are important aspects of social adjustment.

MULTIPLE CAREGIVERS AND ATTACHMENT: THE EFFECTS OF CHILD CARE

Currently, in North America, a large number of parents with young children need some form of child care. In 2006, 65 percent of children under the age of 5 had mothers who worked outside the home (Cotter et al., May 10, 2007) and 4 million children *under the age of 5* were being cared for by someone other than the parents (US Bureau of the Census, 2002). Similarly, in Canada, over 67 percent of children (just under 3.5 million) 12 years and under had mothers in the paid workforce, with about 40 percent of these children 5 years or younger (Friendly, Beach, & Turiano, 2002). And based on information from the National Longitudinal Survey of Children and Youth (discussed in Chapter 1), as of 2002/03, about 54 percent of children from 6 months to 5 years of age were cared for by some form of non-parental child care (Bushnik, 2006). And, although many children of working mothers are cared for by their parents, siblings, and other relatives, over 50 percent of children under 5 spend some hours a week in some form of child care—that is, care provided by one or more non-family members in the child's own home, in the caregiver's home, or in an organized child-care facility (see Figure 6-10) (Clarke-Stewart & Allhusen, 2005). It should be stressed that both parents often are forced to work to maintain the economic well-being of the family; thus, placing an infant or child in outside care is often a necessity rather than a choice.

According to John Bowlby, having not only parents but also a number of other caregivers share in caring for an infant may impair the quality of infant attachment. This proposition has been central to the controversy surrounding the advantages and disadvantages of child care for the infant's and young child's social development. There is no evidence that being in child care actually prevents the formation of an attachment between infants and their parents. Children who spend time in child care form close relationships with their mothers and fathers, just as children raised at home do (Clarke-Stewart & Allhusen, 2002, 2005; Lamb & Ahnert, 2006). As we saw earlier, children do show separation protest/anxiety in response to being left by their parents even when they are clearly attached to them.

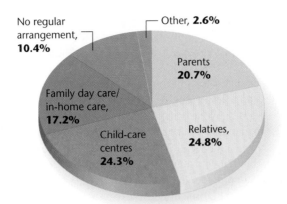

No regular arrangement, **10.4%**

Other, **2.6%**

Parents **20.7%**

Family day care/in-home care, **17.2%**

Child-care centres **24.3%**

Relatives, **24.8%**

Figure 6-10

Who is caring for our preschoolers?

Nearly half of all preschoolers whose mothers worked outside the home were cared for by their parents or other relatives. Fathers account for 17.5 percent and grandparents for 18.6 percent of the relative care.

Source: Clarke-Stewart & Allhusen, 2005; US Bureau of the Census, 2002.

However, some evidence suggests that the *amount of time* children spend in child care does affect the nature of parent–child relationships (NICHD Early Child Care Research Network, 1997, 2005). In an extensive study of 1,300 families in 14 different locations in the United States, researchers found that the more time their children spent in child care, the less sensitive mothers were toward their infants at 6 months of age, at 15 months, and at 3 years of age. The study also found that children in child care were less affectionate toward their mothers at 2 and 3 years of age. These associations, however, were relatively weak. Recent evidence from Israel is consistent with the argument that not only the amount of time in child care but also child-care quality are important to consider in understanding the links between child care and attachment. In a large-scale study of over 750 12-month-old infants, Sagi and his colleagues (2002) found that infants in **centre care**—an arrangement in which children are cared for in a "school-like" environment by professional caregivers—were more likely to be insecurely attached than infants cared for by mothers, other relatives, paid caregivers, or **family child care**—an arrangement in which an individual cares for three or four children in her home. Centre care in Israel is of poor quality and has a high infant–caregiver ratio (i.e., each caregiver must look after a considerable number of infants), characteristics that account for the increased level of attachment insecurity among centre-care infants.

Some earlier studies have suggested that infants who are in child care because their mothers are employed full time—especially babies who begin full-time daycare before they are 1 year old—are more likely to be classified as insecurely attached than infants of unemployed or part-time working mothers (Barglow et al., 1987; Belsky & Cassidy, 1994; Belsky & Rovine, 1988). Again, however, the correlations were not strong. Moreover, in a review of daycare studies, Clarke-Stewart (1989) found that although on average 36 percent of the infants of full-time working mothers became insecurely attached, 29 percent of the infants of non-employed or part-time working mothers also developed insecure attachments.

How might we explain why roughly a third of the babies of working mothers, regardless of whether they are in child care or are cared for at home, develop insecure attachments? It is, of course, possible that child-care babies are somewhat more apt to develop an insecure attachment because their mothers are less available to them or because they interpret her absence as rejection (Barglow et al., 1987; Belsky & Rovine, 1988). However, other explanations are also possible (Clarke-Stewart & Allhusen, 2005; Lamb & Ahnert, 2006). For instance, mothers who dislike caring for a baby (and who, thus, tend to be less sensitive caregivers) may be more inclined than other mothers to take full-time jobs. Or possibly, the stress associated with handling both a baby and work interferes with a working mother's ability to promote secure attachment. These alternative explanations suggest that child care itself may not exert an influence on attachment but rather that something associated with a parent's use of child-care facilities,

centre care

An arrangement in which children are cared for in a "school-like" environment by professional caregivers.

family child care

An arrangement in which an individual cares for three or four children in her home.

such as holding a full-time job, may reduce parental effectiveness at being a consistently sensitive and responsive caregiver. As Clarke-Stewart (1989) has expressed, it may not be that "40 hours of daycare is hard on infants but that 40 hours of work is hard on mothers" (p. 270).

Thus, even with the latest findings on child care, it seems unlikely that child care alone is responsible for a lesser degree of security in these relationships (Clarke-Stewart & Allhusen, 2002). What is more, good child-care providers can sometimes compensate for less than optimal care from parents by giving children an opportunity to form secure attachments outside the home (Howes, 1999; Howes & Ritchie, 2003). Research shows that children with an insecure attachment to their mothers but a secure attachment to a child-care provider tend to be more socially competent than insecurely attached children who have not formed such a strong compensatory relationship outside the family. Interestingly, this positive effect of child care is not restricted to American children; similar findings have been recorded in the Netherlands and in Israel (van IJzendoorn & Sagi, 1999).

Stability of staff may be an important determinant of the quality of the relationship that emerges between care providers and children (De Schipper, Tavecchio, van IJzendoorn, & Linting, 2003). De Schipper and colleagues (2003), for instance, found that children had a greater sense of wellbeing while in child care when the staffing was more stable on a daily basis, and when children had fewer parallel (e.g., multiple) care arrangements. When staff turnover was high, positive caregiving was found to be lower. Clearly, minimizing turnover of staff is important in providing a stable, predictable child-care environment (Lamb & Ahnert, 2006). In addition, a training program aimed at improving the quality of help provided by family child-care can have a real impact on the attachment relationships developed between children and non-parental caregivers.

The higher the level of training of staff members, the more likely children are to develop secure attachment relationships with their caregivers (Clarke-Stewart & Allhusen, 2005). There are other important benefits of training as well. For example, children in high-quality programs are less likely to engage in delinquent and other anti-social behaviour as they grow up, and they are less likely to need special education later on or to be held back in a grade. Kindergarten teachers have estimated that one in three children enters the classroom unprepared to meet its challenges (Lamb & Ahnert, 2006), and inadequate child care for preschoolers may be among the factors responsible for this finding. Another difficulty is that good child care is far more accessible to the affluent than to low-income families (see Figure 6-11). In the United States, this

These infants and toddlers may learn important social and cognitive skills in this multicultural child-care facility. Especially in small centres with favourable staff–child ratios, age-appropriate activities, and responsive caregiving, child care can be a positive and enriching experience for young children.

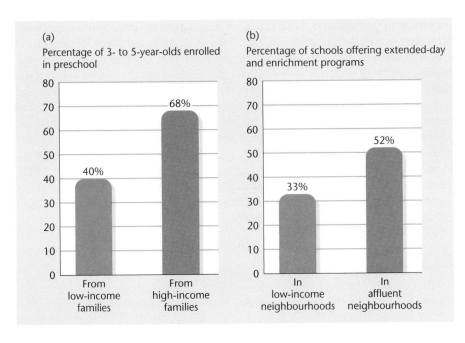

(a)
Percentage of 3- to 5-year-olds enrolled in preschool

(b)
Percentage of schools offering extended-day and enrichment programs

Source: Children's Defense Fund, 1997, 2004.

Child Care in Canada

Figure 6-11

Are child-care and enrichment programs only for the affluent?

Children from high-income families are more likely to be enrolled in preschool (graph a), but they are also more likely to have access to enrichment and before- and after-school programs (graph b).

problem may worsen as a result of the 1996 federal welfare law that brought in a program called Temporary Assistance for Needy Families (TANF), which requires parents of all but the very youngest children to work and, thus, will increase the demand for child-care facilities (Children's Defense Fund, 1997). In Canada, there is no national plan and there are no national guidelines that either regulate or provide funding for child care (Friendly, 2000).

Good quality child care tends to enhance children's language abilities and cognitive skills, and infants with child-care experience adapt more quickly and explore more in an unfamiliar setting (Clarke-Stewart & Allhusen, 2005). These children play more with peers and are more socially competent; they also exhibit more self-confidence and are less fearful of unfamiliar adults (NICHD Network, 2002), especially when they have a secure infant–care provider relationship (Howes & Ritchie, 2003).

At the same time, it's true that child-care children are often reported, at the age of 4½ and in kindergarten, to be more aggressive and less compliant than their home-reared peers. As the amount of time in non-maternal care increased, there was more assertiveness, disobedience, and aggression (NICHD Early Child Care Research Network, 2002, 2003). However, these rates of aggression and non-compliance are within normal ranges and do not indicate that child-care children are, in any sense, socially maladjusted (Lamb & Ahnert, 2006).

One reason for the increased levels of aggression is that extended periods in child care may be stressful for some children. In one study, researchers measured salivary cortisol (levels of cortisol provide an index of stress) in children at child care or at home in the morning and late afternoon (Watamura et al., 2003). At child care, 35 percent of infants and 71 percent of toddlers showed a rise in cortisol across the day; at home, 71 percent of infants and 64 percent of toddlers showed decreases. Children who were better adapted to the child-care context, as evidenced by their greater involvement with peers, exhibited lower cortisol. Similarly, children at child care, who were rated higher in social fearfulness—which may interfere with the ability to play successfully with peers—exhibited higher cortisol levels and larger increases across the day. Clearly, some children fare better and cope more effectively than others with the group life of child care.

Of course, the quality of child care is an important factor as well (Lamb & Ahnert, 2006; Love et al., 2003). Optimal social development, as measured by better relationships with teachers and peers, is more likely to be observed in high-quality child-care centres, where there are smaller groups, lower staff-to-child ratios, more interaction between staff and children, better caregiver training, more space, and better equipment than in poor-quality centres (Clarke-Stewart & Allhusen, 2005). Moreover, the effects of child-care quality seem to continue even after children reach school age. In one study, high-quality preschool child care was related to less child hostility and better orientation to tasks in kindergarten. Poor quality child care, however, coupled with early entry into a facility (before the age of 1 year) was related to a higher level of destructiveness and less consideration for others in kindergarten (Howes, 1999; Howes & Ritchie, 2003). In another study, even four years after being enrolled in high-quality child care, children were rated as friendlier, more inclined toward positive emotions, more competent, and better at resolving conflicts (Vandell, Henderson, & Wilson, 1988). There is no question that child-care quality is associated with children's later social and emotional development, but the long-term effects are greater for disadvantaged children (Clarke-Stewart & Allhusen, 2005).

For Thought and Discussion

1. Given parents' concerns for their children's safety, many parents actively train their children not to approach or talk to strangers under any circumstances. What effect might this have on attachment classifications in the Strange Situation? What are the ethics involved in actually running a Strange Situation procedure, given that you are placing children in a context that many parents want to discourage?

2. Some have suggested that conducting research on international adoption is potentially worrisome, in that knowledge of the possible problems associated with such adoptions might discourage people from actually adopting these children. What do you think of this possibility? How do the advantages of such work (greater knowledge of the plight of these children) relate to the possible disadvantages or problems produced by this work (discouraging potential adoption for these children in need)?

3. Another ethical issue arises in work on the effects of child care on children's attachment. Some have suggested that work attempting to assess the "negative" effects of child care has, in fact, a social and political agenda, in that it might cause women to feel guilty for pursuing careers outside the home instead of staying at home to care for their children. These researchers argue that for any number of reasons, women should and will work outside the home. As such, rather than focusing on whether child care is good or bad for children, more attention needs to be devoted to looking at how to moderate or offset any potential effects of child care. What do you think of this debate? Do you agree that research should take into account these types of ethical considerations? If so, what options are there for addressing such concerns?

Making the Connections 6

There are many links between concepts and ideas in one area of development and concepts and ideas in other areas. Here are some of the connections between ideas in Chapter 6 and discussions in other chapters of this book.

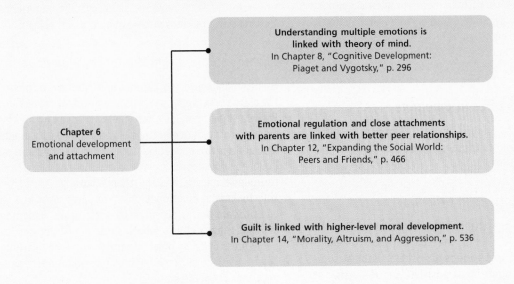

Chapter 6
Emotional development
and attachment

Understanding multiple emotions is linked with theory of mind.
In Chapter 8, "Cognitive Development: Piaget and Vygotsky," p. 296

Emotional regulation and close attachments with parents are linked with better peer relationships.
In Chapter 12, "Expanding the Social World: Peers and Friends," p. 466

Guilt is linked with higher-level moral development.
In Chapter 14, "Morality, Altruism, and Aggression," p. 536

SUMMARY

- Through emotional expression, infants not only communicate their feelings, needs, and wishes to others but even succeed in regulating other people's behaviour.

Early Emotional Development

- Some argue that emotions are learned while others stress the genetic basis of emotions. Some view emotions as cognitively based. According to the functionalist view, emotions serve to help us achieve our goals and adapt to our environment and establish and maintain social relationships as well as regulate our emotional perceptions and expressions. This approach incorporates features of the learning and cognitive perspectives in a unified view of emotional development.

Development of Primary Emotions

- Babies begin expressing both positive and negative primary **emotions** quite early in life. Startle, disgust, and distress are among the first true emotions to appear. Next to emerge is the social smile, in which true pleasure is expressed. Smiling in infants follows a general developmental pattern, beginning with the newborn's **reflex smile**, which depends on the child's internal state. Next, at 4 to 6 weeks of age, come smiles elicited by external events, including social stimuli such as faces and voices. By 12 weeks, infants begin to smile selectively at familiar faces and voices, and their smiles differ depending on the situation. By 4 months of age, infants begin to laugh, and the number and kinds of events that elicit laughter change with their development. Both laughter and smiling may play a critical role in maintaining the proximity of the caregiver to the baby, and this is followed soon thereafter by delight, anger, joy, and surprise. Fear arrives a bit later. Although not all infants develop **stranger distress** in their second half-year, when they do, the fear emerges gradually. Many factors determine how an infant will react to a particular stranger. Babies tend to be less fearful in a familiar setting and when they feel as if they have some control over the situation.

- **Social referencing** helps them interpret emotional cues in other people so as to know how to behave in a new situation. They also are less fearful of unfamiliar children than of unfamiliar adults, and they are less likely to be afraid of friendly, outgoing strangers.

- In general, emotions become more differentiated from one another over time and are more tied to specific situations.

Development of Secondary Emotions

- In the second year of life, more complex secondary emotions such as pride, shame, guilt, and jealousy develop. These emotions rely on the development of self awareness and on the ability to entertain multiple emotions.

Individual Differences in Emotions

- Infants and children differ in their degree of sociability, wariness, and fearfulness as well as their degree of guilt and jealousy.

Recognizing Emotions in Others

- Another challenge that infants confront within the first half year of life is that of learning to recognize emotional expressions in others. Babies' typically easier recognition of positive emotions than of negative ones has functional value, for it strengthens the bond with mothers and other caretakers. In general, children are more proficient at producing than at recognizing emotions, but the two abilities are positively related: Children who are skilled at one are typically skilled at the other.

Emotional Regulation and Emotional Display Rules

- A major challenge for infants is to learn how to regulate their own emotions, to modify or control them when desirable. Gradually emotional expressions become less frequent and less intense. By the preschool years, children begin to follow **emotional display rules**, which dictate what emotions to show under what circumstances.
- Culture affects these rules, and the display of such emotions as anger and shame may be sanctioned in one culture but disapproved of in another.

How Children Think about Emotions

- As children mature they develop an understanding of the meanings of emotion-related terminology and of the situations that trigger particular feelings; each emotional script within this collection helps the child identify the feeling that typically accompanies a given situation. They also learn that they can experience more than one emotion at a time and that two or more such emotions may conflict, and they begin to consider the desires of others in predicting the emotions that others will experience in particular contexts. Learning to differentiate and integrate multiple factors in a situation helps children to understand more complex emotions like pride, guilt, shame, and jealousy, as do both the ability to understand causal sequences and specific experience in discussing feelings with caregivers and others.

The Family's Role in Emotional Development

- Family members, both parents and siblings, influence the child's developing patterns of emotional expression. Parents serve as models for emotional display, and by reacting to a child's emotional expressions both parents and siblings can encourage or discourage such displays. Children whose parents serve as coaches, helping them to understand and manage their emotions, are better able to handle emotional upset on their own and in addition are better accepted by their peers. Belittling or dismissing a child's emotions or punishing her for her expressions may prevent her not only from learning how to manage her own feelings but from understanding other people's emotions

The Development of Attachment

- During the second half of the first year, infants begin to discriminate between familiar and unfamiliar caregivers, and to form **attachments** to the important people in their lives. According to the **psychoanalytic** view, the basis for the mother–infant attachment is oral gratification. The **learning** view stresses the role the mother plays as a **secondary reinforcer**. The **ethological** view stresses the role of instinctual infant responses that elicit the parent's care and protection. Analogous to infant–parent bonding is the process of **imprinting**, which among birds and other infrahuman animals can forge bonds between newborns and anything they see just after their birth. According to the **cognitive developmental view**, the infant must be able to differentiate his mother from a stranger and must be aware that his mother continues to exist even when he cannot see her.
- Attachment emerges over the first 6 to 8 months in a consistent series of steps. The first step, which seems to be innate in newborns, is a preference for other humans over inanimate objects. The second step, which begins soon after birth, is learning to discriminate familiar people from unfamiliar ones. Finally, in the third step, babies develop attachments to specific people. These attachments are revealed in the infants' loud protests when attachment figures depart and their joyous greetings for caregivers when reunited with them.
- Infants develop attachment relationships not only

with their mothers but with their fathers, siblings, peers, and others. In many cultures fathers have the special role of playmate in the development of their babies; fathers' play with infants tends to be physical, whereas mothers' play is quieter and more verbal.

The Nature and Quality of Attachment

- The quality of an infant's attachment can be assessed in a scenario called the **Strange Situation**, in which the child's interactions with the mother are observed under mildly stressful conditions. This scenario evolved out of the notion that infants use the adult to whom they've become attached as a **secure base**. Typically, some 60 to 65 percent of infants are classified by this method as **securely attached** to their mothers, whereas the rest fall into three categories of insecure attachment: **avoidant**, **resistant**, or **disorganized**. Attachment classifications generally remain stable over time unless major changes occur in the lives of family members.
- The **Attachment Q-Sort (AQS)**, a newer method of assessing attachment, makes it possible to rate a broad range of attachment-related behaviours in a naturalistic setting.
- The quality of an infant's attachment to parents is determined by early parent–child interactions. Parents who display **sensitive care**, responding to their infant's needs and giving the baby a sense of control over the environment, seem to have more securely attached infants. **Interactive synchrony** requires that the mother constantly adjust her behaviour to her baby's, engaging him when he is ready and backing off when he is not.
- Parents' **internal working models** of their own experience with their parents are likely to influence their attachment relationships with their babies. Both mothers and fathers who have been classified as autonomous, dismissing, and preoccupied have been shown to be more likely to have secure, avoidant, or resistant infants.
- A baby's temperament may play a role in the quality of the infant–parent attachment, but this occurs probably only in combination with other factors, such as the caregiver's behaviour. Early attachments shape a child's later attitudes and behaviours. Children who were securely attached as infants are more likely than others to see themselves positively, to have high self-esteem, to be intellectually curious and eager to explore, and to have good relationships with peers and others.
- The quality of attachment is relatively stable across time, but changes in the environment may act to improve or lessen that quality, and professional intervention can help improve a troubled attachment relationship. Early secure attachment appears to be related to cognitive advancement and to the development of social skills. In addition, the more secure a child's attachment relationship, the more likely she is to develop a positive self-concept.

Multiple Caregivers and Attachment: The Effects of Child Care

- Although there is no evidence that having multiple caregivers or spending time in a child-care centre prevents the formation of a secure parent–child attachment relationship, some studies have indicated that the amount of time spent in such care is negatively correlated with the sensitivity mothers express toward their children and the affection children show to their mothers. Other studies have indicated that infants of working mothers are slightly more likely to be classified insecurely attached than those of stay-at-home mothers, but the percentage difference is not large. It has been suggested that, rather than the mother's absence, it is the stress of working away from home and also raising a child that interferes with the development of a strong attachment relationship.
- In a **centre care** setting, the quality and stability of child-care centre staff are important ingredients in the security experienced by children in the care of these part-time caregivers. When quality of care is good, children may benefit both cognitively and socially.
- The quality of **family child care** is less certain, depending as it does on the one individual who cares for three or four children in such an arrangement.

Jacob Lawrence (1917–2000). *Library II*, 1960.
Private Collection, New York.

Chapter 7

Language and Communication

LEARNING OBJECTIVES

After reading this chapter, you should be able to

LO1 Describe what language is; define phonology, semantics, grammar, and pragmatics.

LO2 Discuss the nativist, learning, and interactionist approaches to language acquisition, including criticisms of each approach.

LO3 Discuss the critical period hypothesis, as well as evidence both for and against this idea.

LO4 Discuss the implications of the animal language debate, in terms of critical periods and nativist versus empiricist arguments.

LO5 Describe some of the different aspects of the antecedents of language development, including pre-verbal communication, early language comprehension, and babbling.

LO6 Understand the course of semantic development, including how children acquire words, what words they learn first, and errors in early word use.

LO7 Explain how grammar is mastered in language development; include the emergence of modifiers, grammatical categories, questions, and negatives.

LO8 Understand what is meant by the social and creative uses of language; describe pragmatic development, including learning to communicate and learning to listen.

LO9 Define metalinguistic awareness and its development in relation to other language abilities.

LO10 Discuss the nature of bilingual development, as well as the implications for bilingualism on language learning and cognitive development.

Christa and her mother are talking about a recent event, a Halloween party that Christa, who is 19 months old, attended (from Engel, 1995):

Mother: (while looking at a doll clown) You looked like this. Remember the other day we dressed you up like this? Huh? Where'd you go? You went to a party? You went to a Halloween party. Remember? I put pom-poms on your dress?

Christa: Pom-pom.
Mother: Pom-poms. And d'you remember what you got at the party?
Christa: Pom-pom.
Mother: You got pom-poms, yeah. We fixed your pom-poms up when we came home. And what else did you get? A balloon?
Christa: Balloon.
Mother: And the pumpkin.
Christa: Pumpkin, pumpkin, pumpkin.
Mother: (pointing to a pumpkin on the table) There he is.
Christa: Pumpkin. (p. 132)

In this discussion, the mother contributes a large part of the conversation. She introduces the topic, connects it to a shared event, and reminds her child of her experiences. The child participates in several ways. She repeats words the mother uses that are interesting and important to her. She also answers questions, although she is greatly reliant on mother's help in doing so. By participating in this exchange, Christa is learning much about language and how to use it, such as turn taking, the question–answer format, and several new words. She is also learning about the kinds of ideas and events people find interesting to talk about, as well as how to use language to refer to a mental event, in this case a memory of a party.

Early conversations can also involve functional goals. For example, here, 20-month-old Megan and her mother are playing with toys and other objects (from Budwig, 2002):

Megan: I want that one. (lifting the childproof container with the nut inside)
Mother: Oh you want that one, okay.
Megan: (tries to open container, fails) My open that!
Mother: What?
Megan: My open that, mommy. (handing container to mother)
Mother: Wanna open that?
Megan: Yeah.
Mother: (opens container) (p. 77)

Here, the child wants to achieve a goal, but she is unable to do so. She uses language to make her desire known to someone who may be able to help her, her mother, and she and her mother have several exchanges to clarify exactly what it is that Megan wants.

Sometimes, conversations between young children and older children or adults focus on helping children learn language, especially conventional forms of speech in their community. Here is an exchange, observed by Watson-Gegeo and Gegeo (1986), between a 15-year-old Kwara'ae girl in the Solomon Islands and her 27-month-old brother, Fita.

Sister: Then when you're full you just speak like this, "I don't want any more now."
Fita: What?
Sister: "I don't want to eat any more now."
Fita: I don't want?
Sister: Then you just speak as I said, like this, "I don't want any more now."
Fita: I don't want.
Sister: "I'm full now."
Fita: Full now.
Sister: "I'm—I'm full, I don't want to eat any more now."
Fita: Don't want to eat any more now. (pp. 29–30)

Notice how the sister repeats the phrasing and encourages her brother as he repeats after her. Such exchanges help children learn how to communicate information that is important for everyday functioning in socially appropriate ways.

Language Laboratories

Language is one of the most complex systems of rules a person ever learns, yet children in a wide range of different environments and cultures learn to understand and use their native languages in a relatively short period. Their ability to do this strongly suggests that human infants are prepared to respond to the language environment and to acquire language skills. However, biological preparation is insufficient, in that the language abilities the child develops must fit with the community in which she lives. Thus, a crucial part of language learning is the social support provided by others as children learn to speak and use language to accomplish their own goals.

What is **language**? The aspect that most focus on when thinking about language, although admittedly only one small part of language (Turnbull & Carpendale, 1999, 2001), is that it is a system of communication in which words and their written symbols combine in rule-governed ways that enable speakers to produce an infinite number of messages. Learning language serves a wide range of purposes for the developing child. It helps him interact with others, communicate information, and express his feelings, wishes, and views. Children can use language to influence other people's behaviour, to explore and learn about their environment, and to escape from reality by using their imagination (Halliday, 1975). Language also helps children to organize their perceptions, direct their thinking, control their actions, sharpen their memories, and even modify their emotions.

An important part of children's language learning is the development of **communicative competence**, which is the ability to convey thoughts, feelings, and intentions (Haslett, 1997; Hymes, 1972; Schaffer, 1974; Tomasello, 2006). Communication is by definition a two-way process; we send messages to others and receive messages from them. Thus, using **productive language**, we produce communications; using **receptive language**, we receive communications from others.

We start this chapter with an overview of the primary components of language; next, we explore the dominant theories of how language develops in the infant and young child. Then, we discuss the structure of language, including words, sentences, and grammar. After this discussion, we examine how children begin to understand and use language to communicate. Finally, we consider language development for children who are bilingual and learn two languages. ●

language

A communication system in which words and their written symbols combine in various, regulated ways to produce an infinite number of messages.

communicative competence

The ability to convey thoughts, feelings, and intentions in an organized, culturally patterned way that sustains and regulates human interactions.

productive language

The production of speech.

receptive language

Understanding the speech of others.

THE COMPONENTS OF LANGUAGE: PHONOLOGY, SEMANTICS, GRAMMAR, AND PRAGMATICS

Children learn about the sounds, meanings, structures, and uses of language simultaneously. However, for purposes of analysis, scholars divide the study of language into four main areas: phonology, semantics, grammar, and pragmatics.

Phonology, the system of sounds that a particular language uses, includes not only the language's basic units of sound, or **phonemes**, but also rules about how we put phonemes together to form words and rules about the proper intonation patterns for phrases and sentences. Phonemes are considered *basic* units of sound because they are the smallest sound units that affect meaning; changing a phoneme changes the meaning of a word. For example, by changing the initial phoneme in the word *bat*, we can make the very different word *cat*. By changing the middle phoneme, we can

phonology

The system of sounds that a particular language uses.

phoneme

Any of the basic units of a language's phonetic system; phonemes are the smallest sound units that affect meaning.

make yet another word, *bit*. A very important feature of phonologic rules is that they are *generative*, that is, they are applicable beyond the cases on which they are based. A native English speaker, for instance, knows that *kib* is not a word in English, but it is nonetheless a possible sound pattern in the language's system. In contrast, *bnik* is not possible in English.

The study of word meanings and word combinations is called **semantics**. Comprehension of written as well as spoken language requires not only knowledge of specific words and their definitions but also an understanding of how we use words and how we combine them in phrases, clauses, and sentences. Thus, as children mature intellectually, their semantic knowledge continues to grow. Even adults continue to expand their vocabularies to encompass new knowledge. For example, a first-year psychology student must learn a whole new vocabulary of psychological terms.

Grammar describes the structure of a language and consists of two major parts: morphology and syntax. The subfield of grammar studies called **morphology** concentrates on the smallest units of meaning in a language, such as prefixes, suffixes, and root words. These units are called **morphemes**. Rules for altering root words to produce such things as plurals, past tenses, and inflections are part of a language's morphological system. **Syntax** is the aspect of grammar that specifies how words are combined into sentences. For example, each language has syntactic rules for expressing grammatical relations such as negation, interrogation, possession, and the arrangement of subject and order in a statement. The rules of syntax allow us to vary word order so that we are not limited to one way of saying what we mean. For example, we can say, "After class, I went to the library and listened to some music," but the syntactically incorrect sentence, "I listened to some music after class and I went to the library," is ambiguous and unclear.

The fourth component of language, **pragmatics**, consists of rules for the use of appropriate language in particular contexts (Bates, 1999). Thus, pragmatics directly concerns effective and appropriate communication. For example, a child learns that certain forms of language are more appropriate in some situations. A child may have a better chance of getting what she wants if she asks a schoolmate, "May I have one of your crayons?" instead of demanding, "Gimme a crayon!" Researchers in pragmatics study these and other issues, such as how children learn to take turns speaking, to remain silent while others speak, and to speak differently in such different settings as the classroom and the playground.

semantics

The study of word meanings and word combinations, as in phrases, clauses, and sentences.

grammar

The structure of a language; made up of morphology and syntax.

morphology

The study of a language's smallest units of meaning, or morphemes.

morpheme

Any of a language's smallest units of meaning, such as a prefix, a suffix, or a root word.

syntax

The subdivision of grammar that prescribes how words are to be combined into phrases, clauses, and sentences.

pragmatics

A set of rules that specifies appropriate language for particular social contexts.

LO2 THEORIES OF LANGUAGE DEVELOPMENT

As in many other subfields of child psychology, those who study language development debate how much heredity contributes to the development of language and how much children's experiences contribute to the ability to communicate by means of language. Most theorists today hold an interactionist view, recognizing the roles that both biological and environmental factors play in language development. To gain a full understanding of this interactionist approach, which focuses particularly on the role of early caregivers in the child's acquisition of language, we first explore the environmental, or learning, view, and then the biological, or nativist, view.

The Learning View: Claims and Limitations

Traditional learning explanations use the principle of *reinforcement* to explain language development. The learning theorist B. F. Skinner (1957) posited that parents or other caregivers selectively reinforce each of the child's babbling sounds that is most like adult speech. He argued that by giving attention to these particular sounds and showing approval when their baby utters them, parents encourage the child to repeat them.

Language Researchers

Steven Pinker, one of the leading scholars in children's language development, has provided one of the most current, nativist accounts of language development. Building on Noam Chomsky's ground-breaking work, Pinker has written extensively on how children may acquire language, with his work of interest to both laypeople and scholars.

When the child repeats the sounds, the parents or caregivers approve again, and the child, in turn vocalizes these particular sounds more often. Thus, according to Skinner, by giving their greatest approval to the infant's closest approximations to adult speech sounds, parents shape their child's verbal behaviour into what increasingly resembles adult speech. Other learning theorists (Bandura, 1989; Bullock, 1983) propose that the child learns primarily through *imitation* or observational learning. According to this view, the child picks up words, phrases, and sentences directly by imitating what he hears. Then, through reinforcement and *generalization*, or applying what he has learned to new situations, the child learns when it is appropriate or inappropriate to use particular words and phrases.

Learning theory accounts, however, have not fared well as a sole explanation of language acquisition for several reasons. First, the number of stimulus-response connections—that is, specific linkages between a baby's vocalization and a parent's reinforcing response—that would be needed to explain language, even the language of a very young child, is so enormous that a child could not acquire all of them even in a lifetime, not to mention a few short years. Second, naturalistic studies of parent–child interaction fail to support the learning theory account. For example, mothers are just as likely to reward their children for truthful but grammatically incorrect statements as they are to reinforce the children for grammatically correct utterances (Brown & Hanlon, 1970). Parents are concerned to teach their children acceptable behaviour as well as correct language. It is difficult to see, then, how adult reinforcement alone might account for the child's learning of grammar (Brown, 1973; Pinker, 1994).

A third argument against a learning explanation is that we cannot predict the vast majority of language utterances from opportunities to observe specific utterances by others. For example, utterances that are closely tied to environmental cues, such as "Hello," "Watch out!" or "You're welcome" are relatively rare. For most sets of circumstances, language entails more creative responses that can be accounted for by a learning view. Fourth, learning theory accounts have not explained the regular sequence in which language develops. Children in North American culture and other cultures seem to learn the same types of grammatical rules and in the same order. For example, they learn active constructions before passive constructions. They learn to say, "Taisha and Neville prepared the posters for the class presentation" before they learn to say, "The posters for the class presentation were prepared by Taisha and Neville." Finally, the learning explanation basically portrays the child as playing a passive role in language development, although, as evidence we discuss later shows, the child plays an active and creative role in discovering and applying the general rules of language.

For all these reasons, strict learning theory accounts of language acquisition are not considered viable. An alternative explanation—the nativist view—suggest that language acquisition unfolds as a result of the unique biological properties of the human organism.

  ## The Nativist View: Claims and Limitations

Linguist Noam Chomsky (1968), the most influential advocate of the nativist position, proposed that children are born with an innate mental structure that guides their acquisition of language and, in particular, grammar. Chomsky termed this structure a **language-acquisition device (LAD)**.

language-acquisition device (LAD)

Noam Chomsky's proposed mental structure in the human nervous system that incorporates an innate concept of language.

Noam Chomsky, Steven Pinker

Nativists argue that the human child is biologically predisposed to acquire human language. Following this assumption, nativists contend that because language ability is an inherited species-specific characteristic, all languages of the species must display universal features; that is, they must share certain basic characteristics. By examining features such as the sounds used in speaking, the way words are organized in sentences, and how meaning is determined in various languages, investigators have concluded that a set of common principles does underlie all human languages (Slobin, 1985, 1992). For instance, speakers of all languages create a vast number of spoken words by combining a relatively small set of the possible vocal sounds humans can make. Finally, all languages have grammars, and nativists claim that these grammars share certain formal properties as well (e.g., the subject–predicate relationship).

Also, in support of their position, nativists point out that in many different cultures, normal children acquire language relatively quickly and learn it well (Maratsos, 1989; Meisel, 1995; Pinker, 1994). Even in situations in which children receive fragmented and incomplete environmental input, children can learn a language. Thus, nativists argue that the child must be biologically prepared to acquire language. As Box 7.1 on pages 258 and 259 suggests, some of the most striking evidence for the possibility of an innate predisposition for language comes from the study of children who learn language even with restricted input.

Another source of support for the nativist view is evidence that human beings learn language far more easily during a certain critical period of biological development. A **critical period** is a time during which a child is sensitive to a particular environmental stimulus that does not have the same effect when encountered before or after this period. The critical period for language stretches from infancy to puberty. Before puberty, a child may achieve the fluency of a native speaker in any language (or even in two or more languages simultaneously) without special training, but after puberty, it is extremely difficult to learn a first language (see Figure 7-1). Dramatic examples come from several famous case studies. In the winter of 1800, a 12-year-old boy who had lived in the woods near Aveyron, France, was discovered. The boy had no language, and in spite of efforts by Jean Itard at the National Institute for Deaf-Mutes in Paris, the boy was able to learn only a few words. Although no one knows why this boy had difficulty (he may have been impaired at birth), his case raises the question of whether language can be acquired only before puberty (Lane, 1976). In a modern case, 13-year-old "Genie" was discovered to have been kept locked in a room by her mentally ill father from the time she was 18 months of age (Curtiss, 1989; Rymer, 1993). Although Genie was more successful in learning to communicate than the wild boy in France, she never acquired normal language. Further support for the idea of a critical period of language learning is found among young children whose speech is disrupted by brain injury and often recover their language capacity rapidly and completely. If the brain damage occurs after puberty, however, the prognosis for the recovery of language is poorer. Nevertheless, the fact that there is considerable variation, even among adults, suggests that despite the existence of a critical period, other contributions are also important (Goodglass, 1993).

critical period

A specific period in children's development when they are sensitive to a particular environmental stimulus that does not have the same effect on them when encountered before or after this period.

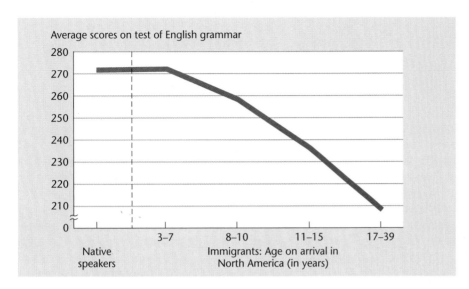

Figure 7-1

It helps to learn a new language early in life

On a test of English grammar, native speakers of Chinese and Korean who had immigrated to North America before they were 7 years old scored as well as native speakers of English. The older the immigrants were when they arrived in North America, the less well they did on the test.

Source: Newport, 1990; redrawn from Johnson & Newport, 1989.

Others, however, have argued against this critical period hypothesis. Ellen Bialystok of Toronto's York University and Kenji Hakuta, at the University of California at Mercedes, have pointed out that according to the critical period hypothesis, there should be a rapid decline in learning at the end of the critical period, which would be consistent with a learning mechanism being "turned off" at a particular age (Birdsong, 1999) and not with a decline after the end of the critical period that would be related to increasing age. According to a re-analysis of data, such as that shown in Figure 7-1, by Bialystok and Hakuta (1994, 1999), English proficiency showed its sharpest decline in language skills with increasing age, a pattern inconsistent with the critical language hypothesis. And more recently, Hakuta, Bialystok, and Wiley (2003; Wiley, Bialystok, & Hakuta, 2005) analyzed data on second-language learning from the 1990 US Census and again failed to find a pattern of learning consistent with the critical period hypothesis. As an alternative to a critical period explanation, these authors propose that the advantage typically shown by children in secondary-language learning could be due to the fact that children have a more nurturing environment, better educational opportunities, receive simplified input, and so on.

Often, people have cited the ability of animals to learn language as evidence against the nativist viewpoint, but the conclusions are mixed (Gomez, 2004). Determining whether animals other than humans learn language depends on the definition of language a scientist uses as well as on the assumptions about what goes on in the human mind when people use language. If one is to define language as a use of symbols as referents, then the average sheepdog is able to learn a language when it learns dozens of whistles for various actions. However, linguists consider many features when defining language, including the understanding of word order ("Bob hit Jim" as opposed to "Jim hit Bob"), and the creation of novel yet understandable speech—for example, by putting together two known words to create a novel meaning. Using these guidelines, there does seem to be some evidence of language in many species, ranging from the African grey parrot (Pepperberg, 2000) to dolphins (Herman & Uyeyama, 1999) and various primate species (Savage-Rumbaugh & Shanker, 1998). Some researchers, such as Kako (1999), argue that their language abilities place these animals at about the level of a 2-year-old human. They are still lacking crucial aspects of language learning such as the use of prepositions and conjunctions. Finally, the assumption that using human language effectively entails understanding the mind and its properties, whether such abilities exist in non-human primates, such as chimpanzees, is difficult to answer (Hermann et al., 2007; Povinelli, Bering, & Giambrone, 2000).

Ellen Bialystok

Box 7.1
Perspectives on Diversity

ARE CREOLE LANGUAGES EVIDENCE OF A UNIVERSAL FIRST GRAMMAR?

The most striking evidence that children may possess an innate program or template for grammar comes from the work of Derek Bickerton (1983, 1990, 2008), who has studied creole languages around the globe. A creole language often arises in a context in which people who speak different languages are thrown together in a single culture. We see this, for instance, in Hawaii, the southeast coast of North America, New Orleans, the Caribbean, the Guyanas, Africa, islands in the Indian Ocean, Indonesia, and the Philippines, where peoples from countries of Asia, Africa, Europe, and the Americas came together to form polyglot societies. Although the adults in these situations craved a common language that could be used to communicate, this language, called *pidgin*, lacked grammatical structure. However, the children in these cultures, regardless of their parents' native languages, used a language derived from pidgin, called *creole*, which had a single structure and linguistic system. Moreover, the creole languages persisted into succeeding generations and in similar form. How could the children of these different racial and ethnic groups have evolved languages that resemble each other if they did not possess some sort of inner template of a universal grammar?

In these multicultural societies, many of which were made up of people who were moved, oftentimes against their will, to perform labour on colonial plantations, communication began with workers' development of a pidgin language, a simplified linguistic system created out of two languages that suddenly come into contact with each other. As Table 7-1 shows, Pidgin lacks grammatical complexity. Its sentences are often no more than strings of nouns, verbs, and adjectives. For this

reason, and because pidgin is highly individualistic, varying from speaker to speaker, its usefulness is limited. Such limitations may be what led children of pidgin speakers to develop the more complex type of communication represented by creole languages.

The language that children in polyglot societies develop is much richer in grammatical structure than pidgin (Bickerton, 1983). And, interestingly, creole languages that develop in different places throughout the world are very similar in their structure, no matter what the contributing languages. Even more remarkably, the speech of first-generation creole-speaking children does not differ from that of later generations of speakers, which suggests that the acquisition of this new language happens very rapidly. Together, the uniformity of language across speakers and geographic locales and the speed of language acquisition argue against any simple explanation, suggesting that children who learn creole are borrowing from the contact language in a haphazard fashion.

What are the implications of these observations for theories of language acquisition? According to Bickerton (1983),

> The evidence from creole languages suggests that first-language acquisition is mediated by an innate device . . . the device provides the child with a single and fairly specific grammatical model. It was only in pidgin-speaking communities, where there was no grammatical model that could compete with the child's innate grammar, that the innate grammatical model was not eventually suppressed. The innate grammar was then clothed in whatever vocabulary was locally available and gave rise to the creole languages heard today. (p. 121)

Like the learning view, the nativist explanation of language development has its limitations. First, few theorists agree about the exact nature of the types of grammatical rules that children learn. In fact, several theorists have offered alternative explanations of the early grammar-acquisition process that differ from Chomsky's original formulation (Maratsos, 1989, 1998; Pinker, 1994; Slobin, 1985). Second, language learning is a gradual process and is not completed as early as nativist accounts would predict. As we will see later in the chapter, specific aspects of grammar continue to develop in the elementary school years and even beyond.

Third, the nativist perspective makes it very difficult to account for the many languages human beings speak throughout the world. Despite the nativist claim that

Table 7-1 Some utterances in Hawaiian pidgin English

Pidgin:	Ifu laik meiki, mo beta make time, mani no kaen hapai.
Direct translation:	If like make, more better die time, money no can carry.
Meaning:	"If you want to build (a temple), you should do it just before you die—you can't take it with you!"
Pidgin:	Aena tu macha churen, samawl churen, haus mani pei.
Direct translation:	And too much children, small children, house money pay.
Meaning:	"And I had many children, small children, and I had to pay the rent."

Source: From Bickerton, 1990.

In 1977, Nicaragua opened its first school for deaf people. In the new school, children and adults were taught to lip read and to speak Spanish. This approach yielded little success, but students were also able to freely engage in gestural communication. Slowly, a rudimentary sign language emerged among the students. As new people of various ages entered the school, they learned this language from their peers. Senghas and Coppola (2001) investigated the complexity of this gestural language in relation to how long individuals were at the school and at what age they entered. If the complex grammar of language was found only among the children, then they could conclude that the knowledge stemmed from innate abilities that are available to the child until she reaches the critical period. If the most complex components of the language were found only in adults learning the new sign language, they could conclude that higher cognitive levels are needed to grasp the hardest parts of language. The investigators found that the most complex patterns of speech originate in children under age 10, and that adults were unable to make use of these structures in comprehension or production. Thus, children were able to create and learn gestures that conveyed complex linguistic structures, whereas adults that were past the critical period were unable to do so. This provides powerful support for the hypothesis that humans are designed to learn language at an early age.

The case is certainly not closed. Some critics like Tomasello (1995) have argued that adult influences may play a role in the emergence of creole English. And others argue that creole languages reveal the common uses of language across cultures rather than simply reflecting properties of the human mind (Jourdan, 1991). Finally, as Hoff (2005) points out, the fact that creole languages developed a long time ago makes it difficult to know exactly what processes underlie them. At this point, it seems that the interactionist position (see page 260), which suggests that both biological factors and environmental influences provide the best account of language acquisition, may offer a viable alternative explanation for the Hawaiian creole findings.

languages possess universal features, how are we to envision features that produce such different grammatical structures and the enormous variety of sound combinations found in the world's languages? Fourth, the nativist view gives the social context of language little recognition. We know from research that takes an interactionist approach to language development that social influences play a much larger role in the process than is proposed in a nativist view (Nelson, 2007). Additionally, the theoretical assertion that language milestones are acquired in a universal stage sequence is not supported by empirical research stemming from an interactionist approach (Nelson, 1988). The communicative context of language development, especially adult–child communication, plays a significant role in the pacing of this developmental process.

It seems likely that human beings are biologically prepared *in some way* for learning language. However, it seems quite unlikely that biological principles can account for all aspects of language development.

The Interactionist View

Most modern theorists of language development take the interactionist view, recognizing that language is learned in the context of spoken language but assuming as well that humans are in some way biologically prepared for learning to speak (Tomasello, 2003). Interactionists are concerned with the interplay between biological and environmental factors in the acquisition of language, and see language learning as the integration of learning in multiple domains (Chapman, 2000). The child's own active role in language development complements the role played by socializing agents like parents (Gallaway & Richards, 1994; Morgan, 1990). "Children are instrumental in the language development process. Not only do they formulate, test, and evaluate hypotheses concerning the rules of their languages, but they also actively compile linguistic information to use in the formulation of hypotheses" (Gallaway & Richards, 1994; Morgan, 1990). In addition, language acquisition is not separate from other aspects of development (Bloom & Tinker, 2001). Rather, language development occurs in a rich behavioural and developmental context in which children try to accomplish meaningful goals and engage in relationships with others. Although biology is considered an important contributor, interactionist theorists today are trying to discover just what this biological contribution is, a pursuit that Bates and Goodman (1999) refer to as determining the "nature of nurture" (p. 33).

In the interactionist view, normal language develops as a result of a delicate balance between parent and child understanding: When parents speak to children in a way that recognizes how much the children already know and understand, they increase enormously their children's chances of comprehending a novel message (Bloom, 1998; Ninio & Snow, 1996; Tomasello, 2006). You will recall from Chapter 1 that Vygotsky proposed this sort of help from older and more experienced people as necessary to children's learning. We will explore Vygotsky's concepts in greater depth in Chapter 8.

FACILITATING CHILDREN'S LANGUAGE DEVELOPMENT

language-acquisition support system (LASS)

According to Jerome Bruner, a collection of strategies and tactics that environmental influences—initially, a child's parents or primary caregivers—provide the language learning child.

An advocate of the social interaction view, Jerome Bruner has proposed that the environment provides the language-learning child with a **language-acquisition support system**, or **LASS** (Bruner, 1983). This view emphasizes the parents' or primary caregivers' role as facilitators of language acquisition (Snow, 1989). When children are very young, parents support their development of language and their comprehension with several strategies. For example, parents often introduce objects to a child to provide a basis for their mutual play and speak about objects and events that are present and easily visible to the child. They also monitor their child's apparent goals or intentions closely, often commenting on them. Although parents do not usually conceive of these tactics as deliberate teaching techniques but as conversations with their children, they are facilitating their children's language learning.

We turn now to a series of techniques that adults use to facilitate language acquisition in young children. These techniques include playing non-verbal games, using simplified speech, and elaborating on and rewording children's own utterances to help them sharpen their communicative skills.

Playing Non-Verbal Games

Parents make some of their first efforts to "converse" with their children in early non-linguistic games, such as peekaboo or pat-a-cake. Children learn some structural features of spoken language, such as turn taking, from these games. At first, young babies are not capable of either initiating or responding in conversations. Parents help them learn this social skill by carrying on more than their share of early dialogues and by waiting for pauses in the infant's vocal or motor behaviour and then inserting an appropriate response. This supportive activity by parents may contribute not only to later give-and-take in conversation but also to social turn taking in play and formal games (Garvey, 1990b).

Using Simplified Speech

Parents' often modify their speech when they talk to infants and children. Typically, they use a simplified style, known as **infant-directed speech**, or **child-directed speech** (also called *motherese*), in which they speak in short, simple sentences that refer to concrete objects and events and that often repeat important words and phrases. In this style of speech, parents also talk more slowly and in higher-pitched voices, enunciate more clearly, exaggerate the pitch contour of their voices, and often end sentences with a rising intonation (Fernald, 1992; Fernald & Morikawa, 1993). The simplified grammar and syntax may help children learn the relations between words and objects and may also give them some understanding of the rules of segmentation—that is, how speech is divided into words, phrases, and sentences. The acoustic variations can help highlight important words. For example, in reading to 14-month-olds, mothers consistently positioned a word that identified a picture ("that's a *shirt*" or "that's a *boy*") at the end of a phrase and spoke in an exaggerated pitch, thus capturing their infants' attention (Fernald & Kuhl, 1987; Fernald & Mazzie, 1991).

Research has shown that newborns and 4-week-olds prefer to listen to infant-directed speech than to adult-directed talk (Cooper & Aslin, 1990) and that babies are equally responsive to this style of communication whether it is used by men or women (Pegg, Werker, & McLeod, 1992). And infants show a preference for infant-directed speech even when it is in a non-native language. For example, when English-learning infants listened to Cantonese, they still appeared to prefer the infant-directed speech in the second language (Werker, Pegg, & McLeod, 1994).

Although exaggerating speech, placing important words at the ends of sentences, and raising pitch and intonation helps adults gain infants' attention, it has other uses as well. According to Janet Werker at the University of British Columbia (McLeod, 1993; Pegg et al., 1992; Werker & McLeod, 1989) and Laurel Trainor at McMaster University (Trainor, Austin, & Desjardins, 2000), such changes in speech also elicit more positive emotions in babies and may actually increase the chances that children will understand the message. But does simplified speech actually facilitate children's language learning? Some research suggests it does help, at least in certain ways. Trainor and Desjardins (2002), for instance, found that the exaggerated pitch contours of motherese increased 6- to 7-month-old infants' abilities to discriminate different vowel sounds. Other work, however, suggests that such simplified speech might not always be beneficial. In one study, children who had progressed beyond the one-word stage were more likely to respond appropriately to an adult form of a command ("Throw me the ball") than to a simplified form ("Throw ball"). As we have seen in other areas of development, a level of complexity that is slightly ahead of children may maximize learning (Hoff-Ginsberg & Shatz, 1982; Sokolov, 1993). When infants or children show signs that they are not comprehending, adults often revert to simpler speech (Bohannon & Warren-Leubecker, 1988). In general, parents adjust their speech to a child's level of linguistic sophistication, using a wider and wider range of words and parts of speech as children mature (Hoff, 2005; Shatz, 1983).

Janet Werker

infant-directed speech or child-directed speech

A simplified style of speech parents use with young children, in which sentences are short, simple, and often repetitive; the speaker enunciates especially clearly, slowly, and in a higher-pitched voice and often ends with a rising intonation. This style of speech is also called *motherese*.

Many games parents play with their young children help toddlers to learn words as well as pragmatic features of conversation, such as turn taking and the meaning of pauses.

Other Influence Techniques

Parents facilitate early communication in several other important ways. Consider the following exchanges between a mother and her child:

Child: Daddy juice.

Mother: Daddy drinks juice.

Child: Give mama.

Mother: Give it to mama.

expansion

A technique adults use in speaking to young children in which they imitate and expand or add to a child's statement.

In the technique of **expansion** illustrated here, the adult imitates and expands or adds to the child's statement. Expanding on children's statements facilitates language development, including vocabulary (Weizman & Snow, 2001). And parents are especially likely to use this expansion strategy after a child has made a grammatical error (Bohannon & Stanowicz, 1988). Moreover, following up on the child's interests and attention is more supportive of learning than switching the child's attention to another topic (Dunham et al., 1993; Tomasello & Farrar, 1986). Brown (1973) has estimated that among middle-class families, about 30 percent of the time, parents' speech to their children is composed of such expansions but that lower-income parents use this technique much less often.

recast

A technique adults use in speaking to young children in which they render a child's incomplete sentence in a more complex grammatical form.

In the technique called **recast**, the adult listener renders the child's incomplete sentence in a more complex grammatical form. For example, when the child says, "Kitty eat," the adult may recast the sentence as a question: "What is the kitty eating?" Through recasting, adults are, in effect, both correcting children's utterances and guiding them toward more appropriate grammatical usage. Some researchers have shown that children whose parents have recast their utterances appear to develop linguistically at a faster rate, using questions and complex verb forms at an earlier age than is common (Nelson, 1989; Nelson, Welsh, Camarata, Butkovsky, & Camarata, 1995). As we do not know how often parents use recasts, we cannot yet say how powerful a role recasting plays in normal language acquisition.

We do know, however, that children often imitate their parents' expansions and recasts, especially when the children's utterances are incorrect. When children's speech is correct, they are unlikely to imitate the adult's speech (Bohannon & Stanowicz, 1988). Perhaps children are more aware of their own mistakes than we recognize.

Is Social Interaction Crucial to Language Development?

Some theorists hold that although social interaction is necessary for language acquisition, the specific devices of expansion, recasting, and imitation may not be necessary. First, no universal pattern characterizes all parents within a cultural group (Hoff, 2005). In fact, there are impressive individual differences among the linguistic environments that parents within a given cultural group provide for their children (Hart & Risley, 1999; Shatz, 1983). In addition, not all cultures use the devices typical of the North American middle class (Minami & McCabe, 1995; Peters, 1983). For example, among the Kaluli of New Guinea and in American Samoa, people speak to the very youngest children as if they were adults (Ochs, 1988; Schieffelin & Ochs, 1987). Evidently, there are forms of interaction that we do not yet entirely understand but that, nevertheless, ensure that children around the world develop language at the same general pace.

The final word on the role of parental influence in language acquisition is not yet in. Those who advocate the interactionist view hold that although the child is biologically prepared for learning language, there is also strong support for the role of environmental input in the child's development of language. For instance, longitudinal research exploring the relation between maternal responsiveness and the achievement by children of language milestones indicates that a mother's responsiveness to her child's activity at 9 and 13 months of age predicts language development (Tamis-LeMonda, Bornstein, & Baumwell, 2001). Maternal responsiveness was defined as any meaningful, positive change in the mother's behaviour within five seconds of a child's action—for example, if the child picked up a cup and the mother said, "That's a cup." Such research suggests that social contributions play an important facilitative role in language acquisition.

For Thought and Discussion

1. How do you think Chomsky's nativist theory of language development would account for learning disabilities related to language development? What does this say about the nature of the language-acquisition device (LAD)?

2. On the basis of our discussion of infants' perceptions of musical properties in Chapter 4, what might be some of the reasons that infants show a preference for infant-directed speech (motherese)?

3. As a parent, do you think you would be more likely to react to the content of your young child's speech or to the grammatical structure?

THE ANTECEDENTS OF LANGUAGE DEVELOPMENT

LO5

Communication skills are not achieved solely by learning words. If we restricted our focus to verbal communication only, we could easily underestimate how early in life communication begins. To fully understand the development of human communication, we must consider the many sounds babies make as well as the many looks, movements, and gestures by which they convey meaning before they can begin to approximate adults' vocalizations. These pre-linguistic achievements are important precursors of actual language use (Adamson, 1995).

Pre-Verbal Communication

Some of infants' earliest communications take place during interactions with their first caregivers (Fogel, 1993; Uzgiris, 1989). Parent and infant often engage in a kind of dialogue of sounds, movements, smiles, and other facial expressions (Hsu & Fogel, 2001, 2003; Lavelli & Fogel, 2002). Smiles, in particular, seem important in helping infants learn how to coordinate vocalizations and to translate expressions into effective communication (Yale et al., 2003). Although these may seem at first glance to be "conversations," a closer look suggests that they be described as "pseudo-conversations" or "pseudo-dialogues" because the adult alone is responsible for maintaining their flow (Schaffer, 1977). Babies have only limited control over the timing of their responses, so adults insert their behaviour into the infants' cycles of responsiveness and unresponsiveness. For instance, a baby gurgles and her mother replies by smiling and speaking to the infant. She first waits for the child's response, but if none is forthcoming, she may prompt the baby by changing her expression, speaking again, or gently touching the child. Such interactions help the infant become a communicative partner by the end of the first year (Golinkoff, 1983; Schaffer, 1977, 1996).

Gestures and expressions play an important role in this process (Goldin-Meadow, 2006). Between 3 and 12 months of age, infants improve greatly in their ability to use gestures to communicate (Fogel, 1993). By at least the time when babies are 3 or 4 months old, adults offer and show things to them, and 6-month-old infants respond with smiles, gestures, movements, and sounds. When babies are about 6 months old, they begin to use a pointing gesture to guide others' attention to things. Surprisingly, it is not until children are a year old that they can follow the point of another person. Through pointing, children receive labels for objects in the distance that interest them and learn a great deal about the world around them (Golinkoff & Hirsch-Pasek, 1999). Some researchers argue that when 12-month-olds point, they are attempting to influence the thinking and action of another person, and thus, reveal an effort to share their intentions with this person (Tomasello et al., 2007).

This type of gesture helps set the stage for learning about language and the communicative process (Goldin-Meadow, 2007). When a pre-verbal infant uses a gesture to call an object to someone's attention, this action has been called a **proto-declarative** (Bates, 1976). When babies can also use gestures to get another person to do something for them it is called a **proto-imperative**; for example, a child may point to a teddy bear on a high shelf to get someone to give it to her (Bates, 1976; Bates, Thal, Whitsell, Fenson, & Oakes, 1989). Other common gestures exhibited by pre-verbal children include reaching, grasping, and staring, and some recent cross-cultural work with Japanese infants suggests that such communicative gestures might be universal (Blake, Osborne, Cabral, & Gluck, 2003).

Recently, some have argued that all of these forms of gestures and pointing are aspects of a more general ability called **joint visual attention**, which is the ability to follow another person's focus or gaze (Butterworth, 1998; Butterworth & Cochran, 1980; Flom, Lee, & Muir, 2007). Although there has been some controversy over whether joint visual attention occurs within the first six months of life (D'Entremont, Hains, & Muir, 1997; Scaife & Bruner, 1975) or not until later in the first year of life (Corkum & Moore, 1995, 1998; Morissette, Ricard, & Gouin-Decarie, 1995), all agree that joint visual attention is a major advance in infants' communicative abilities, important for social interaction and referential communication between infants and their parents (D'Entremont et al., 1997; Moore & D'Entremont, 2001; Tremblay & Rovira, 2007), and possibly necessary for the growth of pointing and other manual abilities (Butterworth, 1998; Butterworth & Grover, 1990) and as a precursor to language acquisition (Blake, 2000; Bruner, 1983).

As children learn language, they often combine words and gestures for more effective communication (Adamson, 1995). A child may point to an object and then comment verbally or gesture to emphasize the meaning of the words. However, children's ability to use and understand gestures may develop independently of verbal language. It is only in the third year of life that children begin to recognize that gestures and language can be part of the same message and that, if they are, they require an integrated response (Bates, 1999; Shatz, 1983). Across time, however, children reduce their use of gestures as they rely increasingly on their verbal skills to communicate their needs and wishes (Adamson, 1995).

Early Language Comprehension

The foundations for receptive language skills begin to emerge early. Well before they are able to speak themselves, babies can attend selectively to certain features of others' speech. In fact, newborns prefer listening to speech or to vocal music than to instrumental music or other rhythmic sounds (Butterfield & Siperstein, 1974). As we saw in Chapter 4, infants quickly become skilled listeners. Even 2-day-old infants can distinguish their mother's voice from the voice of an unfamiliar woman. Moreover, like adults, infants respond with different parts of their brain to speech and non–speech sounds; for example, electrical activity increases in the left half of the brain in response to speech, whereas the right side responds to music (Molfese, 1973; Molfese & Betz, 1988; Neville, 1991).

---

proto-declarative

A gesture that an infant uses to call attention to an object.

proto-imperative

A gesture that either an infant or a young child may use to get someone to do something she or he wants.

joint visual attention

The ability to follow another person's attentional focus or gaze of direction.

CATEGORICAL SPEECH PERCEPTION The finding that infants perceive some consonants categorically is one of the most remarkable discoveries of recent decades (Aslin et al., 1998; Werker & Polka, 1993). Infants hear "one range of acoustic signals all as /p/ and a different range of acoustic signals as /b/ but no acoustic signal is perceived as something in between a /p/ and a /b/" (Hoff, 2005, p. 109). This phenomenon is known as **categorical speech perception**, or the *phoneme boundary effect*. In a classic study of such discriminatory ability, one group of 5-month-old babies listened to 60 repetitions of the sound *bah*, followed by 10 repetitions of *gah*; a second group listened to 60 repetitions of *gah*, followed by 10 *bah* repetitions; and a third group heard only 70 repetitions of *bah* (Moffitt, 1971). The babies in the first two groups showed a marked heart-rate response when the experimenters suddenly presented the new consonant sound, *gah* or *bah*, respectively, which is evidence that the infants perceived the change. This ability to discriminate speech sounds is evident from as early as 1 month of age and holds true for a variety of other consonants, such as *m*, *n*, and *d* (Aslin, 1987; Aslin et al., 1998; Miller & Eimas, 1994). Infants' discrimination abilities rapidly improve, and by the time they are 2 months old, infants can tell the difference between /a/ and /i/. Even more remarkably, 2- to 3-month-old infants can recognize the same vowel even when it is spoken by different people and at different pitches (Marean, Werner, & Kuhl, 1992).

Findings such as these seem to suggest that infants are indeed born with some innate mechanism for perceiving oral language. Others, though, have questioned the universality of infant categorical perception. First, it has been noted that not all infants in such studies show phonetic boundaries. Indeed, in one recent study (Nittrouer, 2001) only about 65 percent of subjects discriminated vowel sounds; this finding, however, has been criticized on both methodological and interpretive grounds (Aslin, Werker, & Morgan, 2002). Moreover, recent research has demonstrated that both adults and infants are, in some cases, sensitive to within category variations in consonant sounds, a result that undermines the notion of categorical perception in the first place (McMurray et al., 2002; McMurray & Aslin, 2005). Finally, although evidence suggests that infants have an innate tendency to look for the boundaries in sound patterns, this tendency is not unique to processing the sounds of speech, nor is it unique to humans. Kuhl and Miller (1975) found that chinchillas categorically perceived the consonants /b/ and /p/. This casts doubt on the idea that humans are uniquely prepared for language acquisition. Instead, categorical speech perception may be simply a property of the mammal's aural system that language simply utilizes (Kuhl et al., 1997; Miller & Eimas, 1994).

BEYOND CATEGORICAL PERCEPTION Categorical speech perception is not the only skill babies exhibit that may help them learn language. In Chapter 4, we discussed a study by DeCasper suggesting that infants may learn some features of language prenatally; recent evidence suggests that infants can identify key properties of their native language's rhythmic organization either prenatally or during the first few days of life (Saffran et al., 2006). For example, 4-day-old French babies increased their sucking rate when listening to French speech as opposed to Russian speech (Mehler et al., 1988), and in another study, infants distinguished the rhythmic properties of their native tongue (Mehler, Dupoux, Nazzi, & Dehaene-Lambertz, 1996).

Whatever innate abilities infants have for perceiving speech sounds, these abilities constantly interact with experience over the language-learning period. Research suggests that as babies develop they lose their ability to distinguish the sounds of languages to which they have not been exposed (Werker, 1989). For example, in an extensive series of studies, Janet Werker and her colleagues have found that English-learning 6- to 8-month-old infants could distinguish between both English and Hindi phonetic contrasts. However, 10- to 12-month-olds (along with older children and adults) failed to distinguish the Hindi contrasts (Werker, Gilbert, Humphrey, & Tees, 1981; Werker & Tees, 1983, 1984). Findings such as these underscore the importance of both innate and experiential factors in the early recognition of speech sounds.

categorical speech perception

The tendency to perceive as the same a range of sounds belonging to the same phonemic group.

In this study, the experimenter is using a head-turn response to test this young infant's ability to discriminate between sounds.

Although babies become highly skilled at discriminating the speech sounds of their native language at an early age, it takes time for them to learn to focus on important sound distinctions in everyday speech. As we have seen, 1-month-old infants can detect the differences between the consonant sounds of *bah* and *gah*, and 2- and 3-month-old infants can recognize the consistency of a speech sound, for example /i/, when pronounced by different speakers (Marean et al., 1992). Learning a language also requires learning which of the many discriminable differences in speech sounds actually signal differences in meanings. Recent evidence suggests that infants can segment fluent speech and recognize words in ongoing speech better and much earlier than we had thought possible—by the end of their first year (Saffran et al., 2006), and perhaps even as early as 6½ to 7 months of age (Thiessen & Saffran, 2003). Research suggests that infants have the capacity to make the kinds of distinctions that indicate word boundaries in the flow of speech (Hohne & Jusczyk, 1994; Morgan, 1994; Morgan & Saffran, 1995; Saffran et al., 1996) and they use a variety of cues, such as strong syllables (e.g., *tar* in *gui•TAR*), pitch, stressed monosyllables (e.g., *cup*, *dog*, or *bike*), a strong syllable followed by a weak one (e.g., *FOWL•er*, *TUR•ban*), and rhythmic properties to help them define the boundaries of words, including pitch and pauses (Jusczyk et al., 1993, 1999; Morgan, 1994; Thiessen & Saffran, 2003).

According to still other work (Aslin, Saffran, & Newport, 1996; Saffran, 2001, 2002, 2003), 8-month-old infants can detect new words in unfamiliar artificial language even when they have no idea what the words mean. Researchers had infants listen to two minutes of nonsense "words" (words such as "tupiro" and "golabu"). Following this exposure, these researchers noted that infants paid more attention to novel nonwords (such as "dapiku" and "tilado"), which contained the same syllables as the familiarization string, but now presented in a different order, than they did to the previously presented words. This finding suggests not only that infants can learn to quickly detect words in an ongoing speech stream, but also that they are able to do so based on the statistical probability of the co-occurrence of various syllables. Subsequent work in this paradigm (Johnson & Jusczyk, 2001; Thiessen & Saffran, 2003) found that infants will use multiple cues to segment such sequences into words, including both statistical probabilities and speech cues such as stress and co-articulation. Generally, it is a good thing that infants have the ability to detect words in sentences because this is how most words are introduced to the young language learner. When researchers Woodward and Aslin (1990) asked mothers to teach new words to their 12-month-olds, the mothers presented their infants with most of the words in sentences. They presented only 20 percent of the words as words alone.

Babbling and Other Early Sounds

It is not just receptive language abilities that develop rapidly in infancy. Babies are actively producing sounds—even though not language—from birth onwards. Anyone who has been awakened in the wee hours of the morning by the sound of a baby happily "talking" to herself knows that infants are neither quiet nor passive. They make a great many sounds, as if "gearing up" for their ultimate production of speech.

The production of sounds in the first year of life follows an orderly four-stage sequence summarized in Table 7-2. Crying, which begins at birth, is an important way of indicating distress and serves as a rudimentary means of communication. **Cooing**, the production of vowel-like sounds, starts at the end of the first month. Cooing, so named because it often consists of *oo* sounds that resemble the sounds pigeons make, often occurs during social exchanges between infant and caregiver. **Babbling**, or producing strings of consonant–vowel combinations, begins in the middle of the first year. Finally, at the close of the first year, **patterned speech** makes its debut. In this pseudo-speech, the child utters strings of "words" that are made up of phonemes in his native language and that sound very much like real speech—including intonation—but are not. These various stages overlap, and even patterned speech and true speech may occur together as the child's first meaningful words begin to appear.

Not only does the early production of sounds follow an orderly sequence, but also the kinds of sounds made at each of the first three stages are quite similar across different language communities. For instance, young Chinese, North American, and Ethiopian babies all babble similar consonant vowel combinations, even though they are exposed to different phonemes in their native languages (Thevenin et al., 1985). Even the early babbling of deaf babies sounds similar to the babbling of babies who can hear (Lenneberg, Rebelsky, & Nichols, 1965), although deaf infants do tend to start babbling later in the first year (Koopmans-van Beinum, Clement, & van den Dikkenberg-Pot, 2001). Deaf infants born to deaf parents who sign (rather than speak) babble with their hands and fingers at the same age as hearing children babble vocally; moreover, their movements show similar structure in terms of syllabic and phonetic patterning (Bloom, 1998; Petitto et al., 2001). These similarities between manual and vocal babbling suggest "a unitary language capacity that underlies human signed and spoken language acquisition" (Petitto & Marenette, 1991, p. 1495). Overall, these findings suggest that the pattern of development of early sounds that infants make is a function of maturational changes in vocal structures and in the parts of the brain that have to do with producing sounds.

In the middle of the second half-year, however, cultural differences in babbling begin to emerge. For instance, babies exposed to one of two different native languages, Arabic or French, which contrast significantly in voice quality and pitch, may begin to show differences in their babbling at around 8 months of age (Ingram, 1989). Even in multilingual homes, such as French–English, infants' babbling begins to sound more like one language than the other (Poulin-Dubois & Goodz, 2001). It seems that babies are now starting to "tune in" to their language environment. Interestingly, the amount

cooing

A very young infant's production of vowel-like sounds.

babbling

An infant's production of strings of consonant–vowel combinations.

patterned speech

A form of pseudo-speech in which the child utters strings of phonemes that sound very much like real speech but are not.

Stage	Begins	Description
Crying	At birth	Signals of distress
Cooing	At about 1 month	*Oo* sounds that occur during social exchanges with caregiver
Babbling	Middle of first year	Strings of consonant–vowel combinations
Patterned speech	Close of first year	Strings of pseudo-words made up of phonemes in native language and that sound like words

Table 7-2

Stages of sound production in the infant's first year

of time exposed to language, not just the baby's physical maturation, appears to be an important factor. Babies who are born prematurely, and who are therefore exposed to language earlier (in terms of their gestational age) than full term babies are, begin complex babbling sooner than the full-term infant (Eilers et al., 1993).

Although, historically, linguists have argued that there is no relation between babies' early vocalizations and subsequent speech (Jakobson, 1968), more recent evidence challenges this view. The babblings of infants over their first year resemble the child's first meaningful words in a variety of ways (Blake & Finke, 1987; Carroll et al., 2003; Oller et al., 1976). Blake and Fink (1987), for example, found that the types of sounds infants make when babbling have some relation to the action in which the infant is engaged, with particular utterances tending to occur in particular contexts. Blake and deBoysson-Bardies (1992) noted similar results in a longitudinal study of both Canadian-English and Parisian-French infants between 9 and 14 months. Thus, a child's early vocalizations are not only orderly in their development but also related to later speech. In terms of the foundations for both receptive and productive language skills, the human infant is very well prepared for learning to talk.

For Thought and Discussion

1. Categorical perception of speech sounds is a fairly robust phenomenon, demonstrable in both infants and adults. What function or purpose do you think it might serve in speech perception?

2. What advantages are there for language learning due to the fact that infants start off perceiving speech contrasts that do not exist in their native language?

3. Researchers have debated for years whether or not infant babbling is actually related to early speech development. What would you take as evidence of this relation? Put differently, if babbling is related to early speech, how might you anticipate seeing this relation?

LO6 SEMANTIC DEVELOPMENT: THE POWER OF WORDS

naming explosion

The rapid increase in vocabulary that the child typically shows at about 1½ years of age.

Despite their early skills in both receptive and productive language, research suggests that children's understanding of language far exceeds their capacity to express themselves clearly (see Figure 7-2). These findings may help to explain the fact that children do not develop their vocabularies in a strictly linear fashion. Like other aspects of development, vocabulary acquisition proceeds in bursts. The **naming explosion** (Bloom et al., 1985) is the rapid increase in vocabulary that most children begin to show at the age of about 1½, when typically they know between 50 and 100 words. Children usually utter their first words between 10 and 15 months (Fenson et al., 1994). In one well-documented case, a 16-month-old learned 44 words in a single week.

By the age of 2, the average child knows approximately 900 root words, and by 6 years, when she is in either kindergarten or grade 1, she knows 8,000. Whether this increase occurs in spurts or more gradually is still under study (Bloom, 2000). Some recent research suggests that, although some children—about 20 percent—display a true spurt or explosion in vocabulary, most children add words gradually (Ganger & Brent, 2004). Whatever the answer here, clearly, the remarkable growth of vocabulary over the first five years of life is a dramatic example of the human capacity for language and communication.

How do children learn words? Imagine that you have taken a job in a foreign country, and your first task is to learn the language. A native of the country points to a dog lying on a rug and says, "Xitf." How do you know whether "Xitf" refers to the dog, the

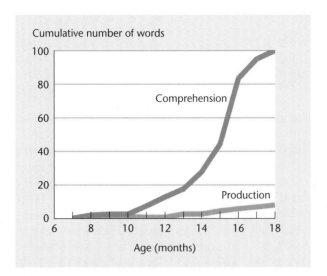

Figure 7-2

**Receptive and productive
language in infants**

Children's comprehension out-
paces their production of words.
On average, children understood
nearly 100 words by the time they
were 18 months old but could
produce only 8 to 10.

Source: Huttenlocher, 1974.

dog's twitching ear, the dog's fur, the fact that the dog is sleeping on the rug, the fact that the dog is the speaker's pet, or indeed, the rug itself? Clearly, the acquisition of object names is no simple matter. Let's look a bit more closely at this issue.

How Children Acquire Words

There are many different views of how children create a linguistic link between the mind and the world (Waxman & Lidz, 2006). Some theorists argue that children simply form an association; others contend that the social aspect of this process is important, and still others take the middle ground. According to Smith (2000), word learning is based on associations combined with attention to perceptual similarity of overall object shape. If a child sees many tables that are often given the label *table*, over time, he will realize that most things with a flat top and four legs get the label *table*.

Another view is that children use mainly social cues from adults to learn what a word labels (Bloom, 2000; Tomasello, 1998). Many findings show that simply hearing a label in the presence of an object is not enough for an infant to learn that the word is a symbol for the object. For example, simply seeing a novel toy on a table and hearing an automated voice saying "glorp" will not cause the child to attach the label "glorp" to the object. Children depend on social cues such as pointing and the speaker's eye gaze.

Still other theorists claim that multiple cues are available to infants for word learning, but how much they depend on each type of cue changes with age (Hollich et al., 2000). In this viewpoint, younger children do rely on perceptual similarity to learn when a word is the correct label for an object, but as they get older they become more dependent on social and linguistic cues. There is evidence that 16-month-olds will not accept a common label for two objects that are extremely different looking, but 20-month-old infants are willing to trust the speaker and give two perceptually distinct objects the same label (Nazzi & Gopnik, 2001).

Although the task of word learning may seem difficult, infants seem to come into the task with some constraints or principles that aid them. (See Box 7.2 on the next pages for a discussion of how even children with mental retardation can learn to use words.) Markman (1989) was the first to introduce the idea of word-learning principles. For example, the *whole object constraint* involves the assumption that a new word refers to the entire object and not to one of its parts or properties. Children as young as 18 months appear to make use of this constraint. For example, when 2-year-old Jamia visits the zoo and hears the word "anteater" for the first time, she assumes that anteater refers to the animal, not its nose, body, or behaviour. Even 12-month-olds associate novel words with whole objects rather than parts of the object (Hollich et al., 2007).

Box 7.2

Risk and Resilience

CHILDREN AT RISK FOR FAILURE TO DEVELOP LANGUAGE

Youth with moderate or severe mental retardation often need extensive and ongoing support in more than one major life activity; one of the most important is communication. Youth with moderate and severe retardation range from those who do learn to speak, although slowly and often with limited success, to those who are unable to develop spoken communicative skills at all, even with considerable speech and language instruction.

Using one of the methods developed by investigators of non-human primate communication, Mary Ann Romski and Rose Sevcik (1996) have shown that youth with moderate and severe retardation who have never developed oral speech can learn to communicate intelligibly with adults and peers. In an approach based on Vygotskian concepts, each of 13 young boys with moderate to severe retardation worked with a partner (a teacher or a parent) who demonstrated to and encouraged the child in using a computerized device that enabled him to select a particular symbol or lexigram, referred to as the *system for augmenting language* (SAL), on a keyboard to produce a single word or phrase (see Figure 7-3). When the child presses a given key, the computer produces a synthesized voicing of the word or phrase and also prints it on a screen. In contrast to some work on facilitated communication, research with children with severe retardation had claimed that such children could learn only with continuous prompting. Romski and Sevcik found, however, that a majority of their participants, 12 years old on average, who used the SAL device learned rapidly to associate symbols with words and phrases. By the end of the two years, most of the participants could both comprehend and produce a majority of the vocabulary words presented to them in instruction sessions. More than half the participants even demonstrated the skill of fast-mapping, a technique by which a child learns to link a new word with a concept they already understand, immediately associating a new name with a new object/symbol.

Romski and Sevcik chose to use arbitrary visual-graphic symbols rather than representational pictures in this work in part because they wanted to study "the process of learning to communicate symbolically" (1996, p. 61). They introduced only a small number of symbols at a time to participants, beginning with a set of 12 symbols relevant to mealtime—symbols for specific foods, drinks, and utensils. The next group of words related to leisure time activities—for example, *ball*, *game*, *magazine*, *television*—and the third group of social-regulative words and phrases included *hello*, *excuse me*, *I want*, and *thank you*. A final group consisted of words tailored to individual participants' needs; for example, they added the word *work* to the lexicon of a participant who had a part-time job.

By the end of the two-year period, all participants had acquired 53 single words or two-word phrases in the first two categories, 16 words or phrases in the third group, and additional words or phrases in the final category. Moreover, many used their lexicons to engage in communication with people in the community without the use of the computer and synthesized speech. Thus, the participants' speech production had to stand on its own. For instance, one youth, classified as severely retarded, went to a music store and requested the assistance of a clerk by asking, "Help tape" and then showed the clerk a photograph of the audiotape he wanted. With tape in hand the youth then said, "Thank you" (Romski & Sevcik, 1996, p. 145).

According to Romski and Sevcik, some parents have been reluctant to offer SAL training to their children because they fear that it will impede the children's efforts to learn to speak. Very few data are available on the outcome of the early use of intervention with speech-output communication devices. Clearly, there is room for a great deal more research in this area. Among other things, we need to know what early predictors, such as specific behaviours, may differentiate children who will not develop speech from those who will. We also need to determine whether early intervention with SAL will not only help children who are at risk of failing to develop language to communicate but perhaps also whether SAL can help provide the cognitive stimulation

After Markman introduced the concept of constraints, researchers began to notice other constraints that children seem to follow in word learning (Merriman & Bowman, 1989; Markman & Hutchinson, 1994). As a result, Hollich and colleagues (2000) have compiled a set of six principles "deemed necessary and sufficient to account for how children get word learning 'off the ground'" within the framework of their emergentist

Figure 7-3

Communicating with a computer and lexigrams

(a) Lexigrams like these, each made up of some combination of the nine elements shown, appear on the upper keypad of the computerized device (b). When a child presses the key for, say, *hot dog*, the words are sounded in synthetic speech and are also printed on the display screen of the computer (lower portion of b).

Source: Adapted from Romski & Sevcik, 1996.

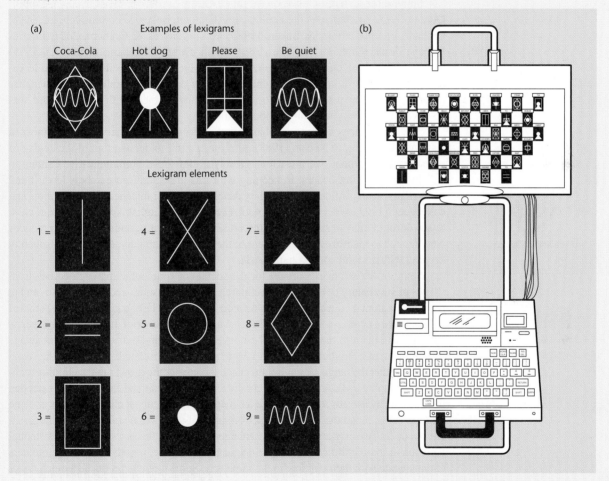

and trigger the motivation that might facilitate their learning of oral speech. Whatever its ultimate usefulness, SAL training has revealed the presence of cognitive capacities in children with mental retardation who, by traditional measures, had been considered only minimally functional. The work suggests that such young people can learn language under the right conditions and can apply it in social interaction and even in useful work.

coalition model (ECM). These principles are less strict than the more nativist view Markman proposed because the principles themselves undergo change with development and because the use of these principles depends on a combination of both inborn biases and word-learning experience.

The six principles begin with the basic necessity to understand language. For example, the first thing a child must understand is the principle of *reference*, or the idea that words stand for objects, actions, and events. Later in development, children come to understand more complex principles such as the *Novel Name-Nameless Category* (abbreviated as *N3C*). Similar to Markman's (1989) *mutual exclusivity bias*, N3C states that upon hearing a novel label, infants assume it labels a novel object over a familiar one. In a representative experiment, the researcher placed four objects in front of a 28-month-old (Golinkoff et al., 1992). Three of the objects were familiar (a ball, a shoe, and keys) and one was unfamiliar (a tea strainer). The experimenter asked for the "glorp." Consistent with N3C, children selected the unnamed object as the referent for "glorp." In a control condition in which no label was used but children were asked to retrieve an object, children selected the unnamed object only at a chance level.

Support for such principles comes from a variety of sources. Work by Diane Poulin-Dubois, Susan Graham, and their colleagues (Graham, Baker, & Poulin-Dubois, 1998a; Graham, Poulin-Dubois, & Baker, 1998b; Poulin-Dubois & Graham, 2007; Poulin-Dubois, Frank, Graham, & Elkin, 1999; Poulin-Dubois, Graham, & Sippola, 1995) has found that these constraints, along with other factors, do play a role in word learning. For example, in keeping with the exclusivity constraint, Graham and colleagues (1998b) found that the tendency to associate a novel object with a novel word was positively related to vocabulary at about two years.

The ECM places a strong emphasis on the necessity for social interaction in word learning. According to Nelson (1988), to acquire a full understanding of the course of semantic development, we must look closely at the social communicative context in which word learning occurs. In keeping with this idea, some researchers have found that parents clearly influence vocabulary development. For instance, Poulin-Dubois and colleagues (1995) videotaped groups of French- and English-speaking parent–child dyads during a play session. These researchers found that parental labelling practices were related to measures of the content of the child's vocabulary, a result very much in keeping with a social context hypothesis.

Diane Poulin-Dubois

Some of the strongest support for the social-environmental approach comes from studies of vocabulary development in children of differing socio-economic classes and in relation to parental education (Huttenlocher et al., 2007). Hart and Risley (1999) studied the language environments of 42 children, ranging in age from 10 months to 3 years, by observing them in their homes. These investigators found that social class, language environment, and children's vocabulary were all highly correlated: The higher the social class, the richer the language environment and the greater the growth in the child's vocabulary (see Figure 7-4). A large study conducted by Weizman and Snow (2001) extended these results by investigating the home language environments of children in low-income families at age 5 and the vocabulary performance of these same children in kindergarten and grade 2. Two important findings emerged. First, the researchers found substantial variation in these children's homes in language experience; not all low-income mothers communicate with their children in the same way. Some mothers produced a much richer language experience for children than others did. Second, children's language experience at home at age 5 was positively related to their later vocabulary performance in school.

Whether language is supported at home or outside the home, social stimulation is important to its development. Three-year-old children who attend daycare centres with stimulating language environments, in which there is much conversation between children and their caregivers, have more words for letters, colours, and shapes—the kinds of words that help prepare them for school—than children who attend programs with fewer conversational opportunities (NICHD Early Child Care Research Network, 2000a).

What Kinds of Words Do Children Learn First?

Analyzing the kinds of words children acquire and the ways in which they use them can give us important information about children's cognitive development and con-

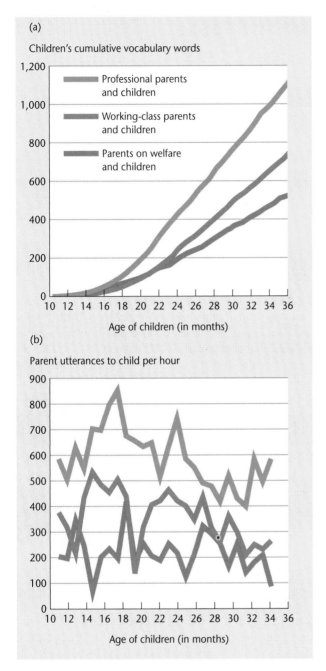

(a)

Children's cumulative vocabulary words

- Professional parents and children
- Working-class parents and children
- Parents on welfare and children

Age of children (in months)

(b)

Parent utterances to child per hour

Age of children (in months)

Figure 7-4

Social class and vocabulary development

Note: The legend in graph (a) also applies to graph (b). (a) Over a period of a little more than two years, children from working-class families (middle to lower socio-economic status) built vocabularies about two-thirds as large as those acquired by children from professional families; children from families who were on welfare acquired vocabularies only half as large as those of the children from more affluent families. (b) The frequencies with which parents in each of the three groups talked to their children correlated quite well with children's vocabulary size. Parents in professional families, whose children had the largest vocabularies, talked to their children the most; parents in working-class families, whose children had the next largest vocabularies, talked a good deal less often; and parents in welfare families, whose children had the smallest vocabularies, talked even less.

Source: Hart & Risley, 1995.

cept formation. Studying the first 50 words learned by a group of 18 young children, Nelson (1973), in a classic study of early word acquisition, classified these words into six categories. Mothers kept diaries of each new word their children produced until the children produced 50 words. On average, children reached the 50-word level by the time they were 1½ years old, but there were a great deal of individual differences. Some infants learned their first 50 words by 15 months, whereas others took 24 months. As Figure 7-5 illustrates on the next page, about 65 percent of the 50 words were naming, or object, words, whereas words denoting action made up only about 14 percent. For Poulin-Dubois and colleagues (1995), comparisons of the word acquisition of French- and English-speaking children generally revealed that both language groups acquired a predominance of names (between 55 and 65 percent) in their first 50 words.

Figure 7-5

Words that children use first

According to the classic work illustrated here, naming, or object, words make up almost two-thirds of the vocabularies of children between 1 and 2 years old.

Source: Based on data from Nelson, 1973.

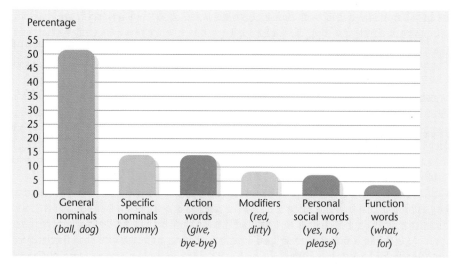

One explanation for why children may learn object words first is that the concepts to which object words refer are simpler than those to which action words refer (Gentner, 1982; Huttenlocher & Smiley, 1987). To learn object words, children must match objects with their appropriate linguistic referents (Gentner, 1982), but to learn action words, or verbs, children must also form an understanding of the connections between objects and actions (Huttenlocher & Lui, 1979). However, some action words are learned more readily than others. Huttenlocher, Smiley, and Charney (1987) found that children are better at learning action words for things they can actually do themselves. For example, a 2-year-old is more likely to learn the word *walk* than *skip* because she is physically able to perform the action of walking.

Some researchers (e.g., Bloom, 1993, 1998) have challenged the assumption that object names predominate in early vocabularies. Studying children who ranged in age from 9 months to 2 years, Bloom found that object words represented only a third of the words the children learned. Similarly, Tardif (1996) found that 21-month-old children learning Mandarin Chinese used equal numbers of verbs and nouns in their speech. In part, this is because in some Asian languages, verbs play a more prominent role in speech and often occur in a prominent place at the end of a sentence (Hoff, 2005). The fact that Japanese mothers spend less time labelling objects than North American mothers may also account for the less pronounced bias toward noun production among Japanese children (Fernald & Morikawa, 1993).

It is important to note that the principles and constraints discussed in object learning must also apply to verb learning. With this in mind, Merriman, Evey-Burkey, Marazita, and Jarvis (1996) investigated children's use of the *mutual exclusivity* bias in verb learning. Two-year-olds watched two people performing actions on a television screen. On one side of the screen an actor performed an action that young children do not have a word for, like rolling his arms in circles. Overall, both actions were equally interesting to the infants, but when the children were asked to "look at the person glorping" they were more likely to look at the novel action. This is similar to Golinkoff and colleagues' (1992) finding that children assumed a novel label applied to a novel object.

Errors in Early Word Use

overextension

The use, by a young child, of a single word to cover many different things.

Errors in children's early word use can help illuminate the learning process. Two such errors are overextension and underextension. In **overextension**, children use a single word to cover many different things. For example, a young child uses the word *doggie* for horses, cows, giraffes, and all sorts of four-legged animals (see Table 7-3 for other examples of children's overextensions).

Word	Referents
Ball	Ball, balloon, marble, apple, egg, wool pom-pom, spherical water tank
Cat	Cat, cat's usual location on top of TV even when absent
Moon	Moon, half-moon-shaped lemon slice, circular chrome dial on dishwasher, ball of spinach, wall hanging with pink and purple circles, half a Cheerio
Snow	Snow, white tail of a spring horse, white flannel bed pad, white puddle of milk on floor
Baby	Own reflection in mirror, framed photograph of self, framed photographs of others
Shoe	Shoe, sock

Table 7-3

Some examples of children's overextensions

Source: From *Language Development*, 3rd Ed., by Hoff (2005).

Rescorla (1980) investigated how and when children between 1 year and 18 months of age overextend words. She found that although about a third of young children's utterances involve overextensions, a relatively small number of different words are included. Rescorla also found that children's overextensions usually show one of three themes or characteristics. First, overextensions can be categorical, meaning children will use one word within a category for another closely related word—for example, they will use the name of one colour for another. Second, the words are used for something perceptually similar, as when a child calls all round objects *balls*. Finally, overextensions can reflect a relationship. For example, a child might use the word *doll* for an empty crib where the doll should be. As children's vocabularies increase, they use fewer overextended words (Bloom, 1993; deVilliers & deVilliers, 1992).

In **underextension**, a less common type of error, children use a single word in a highly restricted and individualistic way. For example, a child may use the word *car* only when she sees her father's yellow Chevy and call all other automobiles, including her mother's green Ford, *trucks* (Bloom, 1993, 1998). The use of underextensions suggests that a child's understanding of a word is too restrictive or limited to a small set of meanings. In speaking with their young children, parents may not initially give every instance of a class of objects its correct name and may thus trigger some word errors. Mervis and Mervis (1982) found that mothers tended to use single nouns to label certain toys and objects; for example, they called both lions and leopards *kitty cats*.

According to some researchers, errors like over- and underextension in early word use are not really errors in the usual sense of the term. As the child's vocabulary is limited, she may try to find the relation between linguistic form and an element of experience—that is, she is not just making an error (Bloom, 1993, 1998). As Bloom notes,

It seems entirely reasonable for the child to use an available word to represent different but related objects—it is almost as if the child were reasoning, "I know about dogs; that thing is not a dog. I don't know what to call it, but it is like a dog." (1976, p. 23)

Gradually, as the child's vocabulary improves and her conceptual categories become stable, her accuracy in the use of words increases.

underextension

The use, by a young child, of a single word in a restricted and individualistic way.

THE ACQUISITION OF GRAMMAR: FROM WORDS TO SENTENCES

 7

In their early years, children acquire an incredible amount of knowledge about language, and the rapidity with which children learn the complexities of language continues

Table 7-4

Speech samples 10 months apart

Source: Adapted from Brown & Bellugi, 1964; McNeill, 1970.

Earlier	Ten Months Later
"What dat?"	"Who put dust on my hair?"
"Where birdie go?"	"You got some beads?"
"Read dat?"	"I broke my racing car."
"Have screw . . . "	"It's got a flat tire . . . when it's got a flat tire it needs to go . . . to the station."
"Get broom . . . "	"The station will fix it."

to fascinate developmentalists. As Table 7-4 shows, in just 10 months, a child may go from barely intelligible speech to clear communication.

In this section, we examine this leap in clarity and sophistication of communication. You may find it helpful to refer to the Turning Points chart on pages 278 and 279 to keep track of the sequence of development encompassed. We begin with the child's use of single-word utterances and then consider the evolution of two-word sentences, the emergence of modifications, such as plurals and possessives, the development of questions and of negating sentences, and the ability to learn how to understand the meaning of others' utterances.

Can One Word Express a Complete Thought?

Are first words simply words? Or are they early attempts to express complete thoughts? When a young child points to a toy airplane on a high shelf and says, "Down," or when he takes a spoon from his mother and says, "Me," is there more to his utterance than meets the ear? In the first case, parents may assume that the child is requesting that the toy be taken down off the shelf; in the second example, they might guess that the child is saying, "I want to do it myself."

Dale (1976) has noted, "First words seem to be more than single words. They appear to be attempts to express complex ideas—ideas that would be expressed in sentences by an adult" (p. 13). The term **holophrase** has been given to such single words that appear to represent a complete thought. Whether or not children are really expressing thoughts in these single-word utterances that could be expressed in sentences—thoughts that include subjects, objects, and actions—remains an unanswered question.

Two-Word Sentences

Somewhere between 1½ and 2 years of age, the child begins to put two words together in what is often called **telegraphic speech**. Like telegrams, these two-word utterances include only the crucial words that are needed to convey the speaker's intent. Although children generally use nouns, verbs, and adjectives, they are likely to omit other parts of speech such as articles and prepositions. Thus, the child's speech is creative and is not merely a copy of adult language. Table 7-5 shows some two-word sentences used by young children speaking either English or one of several other languages (Slobin, 1985). Notice how these two-word phrases resemble one another in terms of the relation between the words, or the basic grammar of language, no matter how different the languages in which they were spoken. This similarity in semantic relations extends to the sign language many deaf people use. As Box 7.3 on pages 282 and 283 shows, in acquiring American Sign Language (ASL), deaf children start out with many of the same word combinations that hearing children produce as they acquire oral language.

holophrase

A single word that appears to represent a complete thought.

telegraphic speech

Two-word utterances that include only the words that are essential to convey the speaker's intent.

Table 7-5 Two-word sentences in several languages

Function of Utterance	Language					
	English	German	Russian	Finnish	Luo	Samoan
Locate, name	*there book*	*buch der* [book there]	*Tosya tam* [Tosya there]	*tuossa Rina* [there Rina]	*en saa* [it clock]	*Keith lea* [Keith there]
Demand, desire	*more milk*	*mehr milch* [more milk]	*yeshchë moloko* [more milk]	*anna Rina* [give Rina]	*miya tamtam* [give me candy]	*mai pepe* [give doll]
Negate	*no wet*	*nicht blasen* [not blow]	*vody net* [water no]	*ei susi* [not wolf]	*beda onge* [my-slasher absent]	*le'ai* [not eat]
Describe event or situation	*Bambi go*	*puppe kommt* [doll comes]	*mam prua* [mama walk]	*Seppo putoo* [Seppo fall]	*odhi skul* [he-went school]	*pá u pepe* [fall doll]
Indicate possession	*my shoe*	*mein ball* [my ball]	*mami cashka* [mama's cup]	*täti auto* [aunt car]	*kom baba* [chair father]	*lole a'u* [candy my]
Modify, qualify (attributive)	*pretty dress*	*milch heiss* [milk hot]	*mama khoroshaya* [mama good]	*rikki auto* [broken car]	*piypiy kech* [pepper hot]	*fa'ali'i pepe* [headstrong baby]
Question	*where ball*	*wo ball* [where ball]	*gde papa* [where papa]	*missä pallo* [where ball]		*fea Punafu* [where Punafu]

Notes: Luo is spoken in Kenya. The order of the two words in each "sentence" is generally fixed in all languages but Finnish, in which children are free to use both orders for some types of utterances.

Source: Adapted from Slobin, 1979.

Why are the early utterances of children similar in terms of the meaning of what they talk about? Language can be viewed as a way of expressing what one knows or understands about the world. As children's capacity for understanding events in the world around them continues to grow, and because children around the world tend to have encounters with similar kinds of basic situations in life, their learning of language is tied to their cognitive development. Such fundamental experiences include the distinction between self and other; the concept of causality; and understanding of objects. Thus, wherever they live, in whatever society, children beginning to speak express similar relationships and events, such as agent–action relations, possessives, and person and object identity. The development of cognitive capacity and the development of language are undoubtedly closely related (Clark, 1983; Carey, 1994).

Learning the Rules

One of the most interesting aspects of early grammar acquisition is the way children learn how to modify the meanings of the words they use, an accomplishment that also

Turning Points

LANGUAGE MILESTONES FROM INFANCY TO MIDDLE CHILDHOOD

BIRTH
- Crying
- Perception of others' speech
- Preference for human voices

1–6 MONTHS
- Decrease in crying
- Makes soft sounds
- Cooing, laughing, gurgling
- Imitates short string of vowel sounds; alternates making sounds with another person
- Making consonant sounds; "says" consonants increasingly often
- Responds to prosodic features of speech (e.g., inflection and pitch)
- Intonations move towards speech patterns heard most often

6–12 MONTHS
- Babbling strings of consonant-vowel combinations
- May babble more in familiar than unfamiliar settings
- Sounds resemble speech
- Increasing preference for own language over unfamiliar language
- Produces sound for familiar toy or object; experiments with sounds
- Babbling has sentence-like quality
- May "say" a word—"bah" for "bottle," "mama" for "mother"
- May say no but doesn't always mean "no"
- May say two or three words; uses same word for category, such as "wah" for both water and milk

Note: Developmental events described in this and other Turning Points charts represent overall trends identified in research studies. Individual children vary greatly in the ages at which they achieve these developmental changes.

Sources: Hoff, 2005; Kopp, 1994; Tomasello, 2006; Waxman & Lidz, 2006.

illustrates the close ties between semantic and grammar development. Roger Brown (1973) of Harvard University, in his classic longitudinal study of Adam, Eve, and Sarah, followed these three children from 2 to 4 years of age and noted, among many other things, that they acquired certain morphemes in a regular order. For example, dur-

12–18 MONTHS	• Sentences usually one word at first
	• Tries hard to make self understood
	• Symbolic gesturing
	• Utterance of first words
	• Imitates words; may repeatedly use a new word
	• May use a few two-word sentences
	• May use adjective to refer to self (good boy)
	• Understanding of naming processes
18–24 MONTHS	• Beginning of naming explosion (average child goes from 50 to 900 words in about six months)
	• Uses two-word sentences
	• Rapid expansion of understanding
24–36 MONTHS	• Decrease in gesturing
	• Disappearance of babbling
	• Increase in use of plurals, past tense, definite and indefinite articles, some prepositions
	• Use of three-word combinations
	• Excellent comprehension
	• Gradually increasing use of sentences to communicate
36–48 MONTHS	• Use of yes/no questions, why questions, negatives, and imperatives
	• Embedding one sentence within another (using clauses)
	• Use of overregularizations
	• Vocabulary increases by about 1,000 words
	• Coordination of simple sentences and use of prepositions
48–60 MONTHS	• Increasingly sophisticated use of pragmatic rules of communication
	• Use of humour and metaphor
5 YEARS AND BEYOND	• Use of more complex syntax
	• Further expansion of vocabulary (to about 14,000 words)
	• Development of metalinguistic awareness
	• Language and Communication

ing this period the children began to use qualifiers that indicate plurality or a possessive relation. Table 7-6 on the next page lists the 14 morphemes that Brown studied in the order in which his young participants acquired them. Although Adam, Eve, and Sarah each acquired these morphemes at different rates of speed, the order in which each child acquired them was the same.

Table 7-6

English-speaking children's first 14 morphemes

Source: Based on Brown, 1973.

	Form	Meaning	Example
1.	Present progressive: -*ing*	Ongoing process	He is sitt*ing* down.
2.	Preposition: *in*	Containment	The mouse is *in* the box.
3.	Preposition: *on*	Support	The book is *on* the table.
4.	Plural: -*s*	Number	The dog*s* ran away.
5.	Past irregular: e.g., went	Earlier in time relative to time of speaking	The boy *went* home.
6.	Possessive: -'*s*	Possession	The girl'*s* dog is big.
7.	Uncontractible copula be: e.g., *are, was*	Number; earlier in time	*Are* they boys or girls? *Was* that a dog?
8.	Articles: *the, a*	Definite/indefinite	He has *a* book.
9.	Past regular: -*ed*	Earlier in time	He jump*ed* the stream.
10.	Third person regular: -*s*	Number; earlier in time	She run*s* fast.
11.	Third person irregular: e.g., *has, does*	Number; earlier in time	*Does* the dog bark?
12.	Uncontractible auxiliary be: e.g., *is, were*	Number; earlier in time; ongoing process	*Were* they at home? *Is* he running?
13.	Contractible copula be: e.g., -'*s*, -'*re*	Number; earlier in time	That'*s* a spaniel.
14.	Contractible auxiliary be: e.g., -'*s*, -'*re*	Number; earlier in time; ongoing process	They'*re* running very slowly.

Notice that the order in which these morphemes are acquired is a sensible one: Simpler morphemes are acquired earlier than more complex ones. For example, plural forms, like -*s*, are learned before the copula (meaning a linking word) *be*. Similarly, Golinkoff, Hirsch-Pasek, and Schweisguth (2001) found that children began to understand morphemes—for example, they learn that -*ing* is a morpheme typically generally used with actions—much earlier than they can produce the same morphemes. In the next two chapters, we will see that this same general principle of progressing from the simple to the more complex characterizes children's cognitive development as well.

Slobin (1985) suggests that children go through four phases in their application of grammatical rules such as the use of plurals. In phase 1, they try but fail. In phase 2, they succeed in memorizing some of the irregular verbs, such as *broke* and *went*, but do not yet acquire a grammatical rule. This kind of learning, of course, is quite inefficient. Imagine how time-consuming it would be if children had to learn separate, specific rules for each new word that they encountered. In Slobin's phase 3, children learn general grammatical rules that can be used with new as well as familiar words. Only in phase 4, however, do children—at 7 or 8 years—finally approach adult usage, recognizing when to apply these rules. A crucial achievement of this last phase is learning when *not* to apply a rule.

Adult language is full of irregularities and other exceptions to the rules. When children are first learning a language, they ignore these irregularities and rigidly apply the rules they learn. In **overregularization** of rules, children apply a rule for forming regularities in cases in which the adult form is irregular and does not follow the rule. For instance, a young child may start out using the words *went* and *came* correctly but, after learning that *-ed* forms the past tense for many verbs, she may begin to use this ending for all verbs, producing *goed* and *comed* (Slobin, 1985). Overregularization is found not only in North America but also in other parts of countries, where children applied the rules they learn broadly to form novel "regularized" words and phrases that do not occur in adult speech (Slobin, 1982).

Despite great interest in overregularization among researchers, questions remain about why and how often children overregularize language in their speech. Additionally, it has been shown that some children are more likely than others to overregularize language (Maratos, 1993), which suggests that children's interest in or skill at the rules of language may vary individually. Finally, some researchers suggest that it is not language development per se that explains overregularization. Rather, memory development may contribute to this behaviour because learning all the complexities and rules of language places great demands on memory. Because young children are developing memory skills at the same time they are developing language, these processes may influence each other, and behaviours such as overregularization may be a result (Marcus, 1995).

overregularization

The mistaken application of a principle of regular change to a word that changes irregularly.

Approaching Formal Grammar

In the third year of life, there is a "grammatical flowering" (deVilliers & deVilliers, 1992, p. 378). Simple sentences start to become subtle and more complex as children show early signs of understanding the rules of adult grammar (Valian, 1986). Among children's many achievements is the beginning use of auxiliary and modal verbs (deVilliers & deVilliers, 1992). *Mode*, or "mood," is the capacity of verbs to convey factual statements, expressions of possibility (e.g., the subjunctive), or imperatives. One of the auxiliary verbs children begin to use at this stage is the verb *to be*, which appears in many English sentence structures and, thus, opens up the possibility of new forms of expression. Children begin to use tenses other than the present: "I kicked it." And they begin to use pronouns and articles and even begin to create complex sentences: "The teddy and doll are gonna play" (deVilliers & deVilliers, 1992, p. 379). Let's take a closer look at two of these grammatical milestones: questions and negatives.

Animated conversations like this one are a sign of the "grammatical flowering" that generally characterizes the third year of life.

Box 7.3

Child Psychology in Action

LANGUAGE LEARNING IN THE DEAF

Deaf children learning American Sign Language (ASL) produce word combinations that are very similar to those that hearing children around the world produce (Goldin-Meadow, 2006; Lederberg, et al., 2000; Meier & Newport, 1990). Compare the examples in Table 7-6 with those in Table 7-5 on pages 280 and 277 respectively. In both the deaf child's phrases and those uttered by hearing children, we see locating and naming, indication of possession, making a demand, and describing modifying. (For the ASL signs representing some of the words in Table 7-7, see Figure 7-6.) Among deaf children, the length of utterances increases steadily, just as it does among hearing children, and like hearing children, those who use sign language tend to overextend (Bellugi, van Hoek, Lillo-Martin, & O'Grady, 1993; Petitto, 1993). Nor are young signing children always accurate, as with the early words of their speaking peers. For example, intending to point to their mouths in signing (which might indicate "speech" or "speaking"), children may miss and point to their chins (which could mean "preference" or "favourite").

Although the steps that children follow in learning language, whether gestural or spoken, are similar, evidence suggests that deaf children may learn sign language faster and earlier than hearing children learn

Table 7-7 Some two-word combinations in a deaf child's signing

Sign	Meaning
Daddy work	"Daddy is at work."
Barry train	"That's Barry's [her brother's] train."
Bed shoes?	(Asking where her slippers are)
Daddy shoe	(Attempting to persuade her father to take off his shoes and play in the sand)

Source: Meier & Newport, 1990.

spoken language. In a longitudinal study of 13 infants raised by deaf parents, Bonvillian and his colleagues (Bonvillian, Orlansky, Novack, & Folven, 1983) found that these children learned their first signs several months earlier than hearing children spoke their first words. And by the age of 17 months, these children began to combine two or more signs, again about two to three months ahead of hearing children.

More recent work, however, argues that the development of timelines for learning spoken and sign lan-

QUESTIONS To express a question, young children may first use an assertion, such as "sit chair" by simply raising their voices at the end to indicate that they are asking a question (deVilliers & deVilliers, 1979). In the latter part of the third year, children begin to ask "wh" questions—those that start with the words what, when, who, why, and which—as well as questions that begin with how.

Between ages 2 and 3 years, children's "wh" constructions may fail to include the auxiliary verb, and they can be heard to say such things as, "Where you going?" A little later, they include the auxiliary without inverting it (Rowland & Pine, 2000, 2003); for example, "Where you are going?" Finally, they incorporate all the rules for producing a "wh" question; for example, "Where are you going?"

An important feature of "wh" questions is that they enable children to learn new things. Callanan and Oakes (1992) asked parents of 3-, 4-, and 5-year-old children to keep diaries over a 2-week period of their children's "why" and "how" questions. They found, as every parent knows, that the frequency of these questions increases over these years. They also found that at all ages, these questions tended to be complex—that is, children rarely asked about the world just by stating "why" or "how." Rather, these questions usually included referents, ideas, and observations—for example, "Why is the sky blue?" or "How does the telephone know which house to call?" Children use their emerging skill at questioning as an important tool for obtaining knowledge. Again,

Figure 7-6

Some signs in American Sign Language

In early two-word communications like those listed in Table 7-7, a deaf child might combine the signs in (a) and (b).

Source: Adapted from Costello, 1983.

(a)

Father, Dad
With the palm of the right hand facing left and fingers up, tap the thumb on the centre of the forehead.

(b)

Work, employment
With both hands in form of fist, tap the heel of the right hand on the back of the left hand, twice.

(c)

Train, railroad
Using the index and middle fingers of both hands, move the right two fingers back and forth several times on top of the left two fingers.

(d)

Shoes
With both hands in the form of fist, hit the thumb sides of both hands together several times.

guages are virtually identical. Pettito (2000), for example, in reviewing her own work, suggests that hearing and deaf children reach the same language milestones at exactly the same pace. Given that spoken and sign languages make use of different modalities, the fact that the developmental trajectories of the two systems are so similar leads Pettito to suggest that infants are sensitive to the patterning and structure of language, regardless of modality. In this case, so long as the environment contains the proper types of patterns, infants will learn and produce these patterns regardless of whether the input is on the hands or in the mouth (Pettito, 2000). Moreover, Pettito and colleagues (2001) found that the bilingual acquisition of either English and French or French and langues des signes Québécoise similarly occurred at the same rates.

we see that language and cognitive development are closely tied, with each serving the other and both together promoting the child's overall progress.

NEGATIVES   Some of the earliest evidence of children's expression of negation comes in non-verbal form, for example, by shaking their heads. The simplest verbal forms involve the word *no* either alone or affixed to the beginning of a phrase—for example, a child may say, "No doggie" to mean "The dog is not here." As children develop, they learn to form different kinds of negatives and three distinct types of negation appear in a particular developmental order (Bloom, 1970; Tager-Flusberg, 1985). First, children are able to express the non-existence of something (e.g., "All gone"), then they become capable of rejecting something (e.g., "No wash hair"), and, lastly, they are able to deny that something is true (e.g., "That not Daddy").

Language researchers have found that these same types of negations appear in the same order in Japanese as in English (Bloom, 1991; Clancy, 1985). As children's language skills develop, more complex forms of negation appear that include auxiliary verbs—for example, "I didn't do it" or "He isn't my friend."

The development of these two types of speech, questions and negatives is only a sample of a wide range of grammatical accomplishments during the preschool years. By 3 years of age, children begin to use complex sentences, and progress is gradual but orderly. At first, children tack on relative clauses; for example, "See the ball that I got." It is only later that they interrupt a main clause with a subordinate clause: they compose utterances like "The owl who eats the candy runs fast" (Slobin, 1985; Maratsos, 1998) and "Where did you say you put my doll?" (deVilliers & deVilliers, 1992, p. 379). Although most fundamental forms of grammar are acquired by 4½ to 5 years of age, the process of grammar acquisition continues to develop through the school years (Maratsos, 1998).

How Children Make Sense of What They Hear

Although we have been discussing language production, it is important to remember that productive and receptive languages are closely linked. Several researchers have shown that at an early age, children are able to understand sentences that are more complex than those they can produce. This understanding is aided by syntax, which provides clues about the meanings of nouns (or object words) and verbs (or action words). For example, some types of verbs appear in some sentences but not others (Hoff, 2005). Verbs such as *hit* and *hug* refer to an action that one person does to another, and therefore, such verbs usually appear in sentences in which the verb is preceded by one noun, the doer of the action, and followed by a different noun, the recipient of the action (e.g., *Joe hugged Molly*). Other verbs, such as those that refer to an action with no recipient (e.g., *laugh* or *slip*) appear in such sentences in which there is just one noun, the doer (e.g., *Paul laughed*). According to Gleitman and her colleagues (Fisher, Hall, Rakowitz, & Gleitman, 1994; Gleitman, 1990), children use a kind of "syntactic bootstrapping" to figure out word meaning. According to this theory, once children learn how to parse utterances into syntactic units, they use this knowledge to distinguish the meaning of verbs they may not yet understand. In other words, they use what they already know about syntax to support, or bootstrap, their learning and comprehension (Naigles, 1990).

According to Goodman (1989), even 1½- to 3½-year-old children use semantic and syntactic cues to identify spoken words. In a sentence completion task, Goodman presented children with spoken sentences and asked them to fill in a final missing noun. For example, to the utterance, "Mommy feeds the _____," children responded "baby." In a word-identification task, children listened to complete sentences and pointed to pictures to identify the final word in each sentence. In one condition of this task, the word called for by the sentence meaning was among those pictured, but the word actually spoken was represented by another picture. For example, children listened to the sentence, "Ann drives the duck" and then looked at pictures of a duck, a truck, a dog, and a book. Although the word spoken was *duck*, the children chose the word *truck*. When the children heard the sentence, "The man sees the duck," however, they chose the duck picture.

Does the ability to use semantic and syntactic information improve with age? Entwisle and Frasure (1974) demonstrated that this is very probably so. Employing a "noisy telephone" technique, in which background noise was used to make auditory material difficult to hear, these researchers asked groups of 6-, 7-, 8-, and 9-year-old children to listen to three sentences. The children were then asked to repeat the sentences as accurately as possible. Because the noise blocked out parts of the sentence, the children had to rely on their knowledge of how sentences are formed generally to fill in the missing words. Here are the sentences:

Bears steal honey from the hive.

Trains steal elephants around the house.

From shoot highways the passengers mothers.

In the *meaningful* first sentence, both semantics and syntax are correct. The *anomalous* second sentence is syntactically correct, although it makes no sense. In the *scrambled* last sentence, both syntax and semantics are jumbled, making this presumably the most

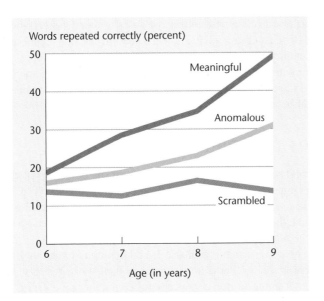

Figure 7-7

Learning to use semantic and syntactic clues

The more syntactic and semantic clues offered by sentences heard against background noise, the more successful children were at repeating the sentences. All children had difficulty with the *scrambled* sentence that lacked any clues, but when clues were present, as in the *meaningful* and *anomalous* sentences, older children made better use of them than did the younger children.

Source: Entwisle & Frasure, 1974.

difficult sentence for children to reproduce. As you can see from Figure 7-7, the older the child, the more she was able to benefit from the available syntactic and semantic clues. At all ages, the more such clues the children had, the better they did; all age groups experienced similar difficulties with the sentence in which these clues were totally absent.

Children's comprehension of many complex constructions remains poorly understood. We still do not know when or how children are able to understand "John was thought by Mary to have been scratched by Sam" (Maratsos, 1983). Children continue to develop in both their production and understanding of complex syntax well beyond the early school years; for example, the differences between a grade 3 English lesson and a university seminar on Shakespeare clearly indicate that both a young person's comprehension and usage continue to develop for many years.

For Thought and Discussion

1. How would the learning theory view explain aspects of word learning, such as the *naming explosion* or *fast-mapping*? What about the nativist approach?

2. At what point in the acquisition of language do you think children begin to understand aspects of humour? What language capabilities are necessary for such understanding?

LEARNING THE SOCIAL AND CREATIVE USES OF LANGUAGE

Language, by its very nature, is a social phenomenon; it enables the child to communicate with other people. What becomes very important as children develop, therefore, is the decision as to what words and phrases to use in differing social situations. The rules for this usage, which we have already identified, are known collectively as *pragmatics*. Speakers have a variety of pragmatic intentions, such as getting people to do things for them and thanking people for their help, and they need to know how to express these intentions appropriately, depending on the situation and the other people involved. When these expressions clearly refer to situations or sequences of events, rather than to just one object or action, we call these expressions **speech acts**.

speech acts

One- or two-word utterances that clearly refer to situations or to sequences of events.

discourse

Socially based conversation.

Communication becomes **discourse**, or socially based conversation, when children are able to listen and respond to another's speech. The latter achievement includes the important ability to recognize one's own lack of understanding and to request additional information. In this section, we begin by looking at some of the rules of pragmatics and then turn to the ways children learn first to communicate and then to be good listeners.

The Rules of Pragmatics

Even when a child has mastered meaning and syntax, she is not yet fully equipped to be an effective communicator. She must learn another set of rules—namely, how to use language appropriate to a given situation. To be an effective speaker requires a complicated set of skills. First, the child must engage the attention of her listeners so that they know that she wants to address them and that they should listen. Second, effective speakers have to be sensitive to listeners' feedback. If children do not know when others fail to understand them or do not know how to change their messages to make themselves clear, they are not going to be very successful communicators. Third, speakers must adjust their speech to the characteristics of their listeners, such as age and cultural and social background. For example, the grade 5 child must learn that in addressing his classmates he can use words and concepts that he cannot use when he makes a presentation to kindergartners. Being a good communicator requires that you adapt your message in consideration of "who the listener is, what the listener already knows, and what the listener needs to know" (Glucksberg, Krauss, & Higgins, 1975, p. 329).

A fourth rule requires that children learn to adjust their speech to suit the situation. Children and adults learn to talk differently on a playground or a street from how they would in a church or a classroom. A fifth guideline points out that communication is a two-way process. To participate in a conversation, one must be not only an effective speaker but also a skilled listener; learning to listen is just as important as learning to speak. A sixth rule underlines the importance of understanding one's own communicative skills, that is, children must learn to evaluate both their own messages and the messages they receive from others for clarity and usefulness. They must also learn to correct their own messages, when necessary, and to let another speaker know when they do not understand the speaker's communication, often specifying the information that they need from the speaker (Glucksberg et al., 1975).

How early do children acquire these various communication skills? How do these skills develop and how do children use them across different situations? We explore these questions next.

Learning to Adjust Speech to Audience

By 2 years of age, children are remarkably adept both at engaging the attention of a listener and at responding to listener feedback. Videotaping ten 2-year-olds in their day-to-day interactions in a nursery school, Wellman and Lempers (1977) recorded 300 referential communicative interactions, in which the communicator's intent was to point out, show, or display a particular object or referent to another child. The results were striking in their demonstration of these children's competence as speakers. The toddlers addressed their listeners when both were either interacting or playing together (82 percent) or when the listeners were at least not involved with someone else (88 percent). The children also directed communications to others when they could see each other (97 percent), when they were physically close to each other (91 percent), and, to a lesser extent, when the listeners were looking directly at them (41 percent). Similarly, the children made sure that when they spoke, they were close to the thing they were talking about (92 percent) and that the listener was also close to the thing referred to (84 percent) to make it more likely that the listener would understand the message.

In light of these precautions, it is not surprising that these young speakers were very effective in engaging their listeners. In fact, 79 percent of messages met with an adequate response from listeners. Moreover, speakers showed an awareness that certain situations were particularly difficult and adjusted their communications accordingly. They communicated more in difficult situations—for example, when there was an obstacle between the listener and the thing referred to. Finally, these children were responsive to feedback from their listeners. For example, more than half the time, when the speakers received no response, they repeated their messages in some form, but they repeated messages only 3 percent of the time when they received an adequate response. In sum, these 2-year-olds were surprisingly sophisticated speakers.

Children as young as 2 years of age learn to adjust their speech when talking with other children of different ages. In several studies (Dunn, 1988; Dunn & Kendrick, 1982b) 2- and 3-year-olds used more repetitions and attention-eliciting words (*hey, hello,* and *look*) when talking to their baby brothers and sisters than they did when addressing their mothers. Researchers (Gelman & Shatz, 1977; Shatz, 1983, 1994) have also found that children make the same kinds of adjustments when they speak to people outside the family. Contrast the following statements directed at an adult and a child (Shatz & Gelman, 1973):

> [*Four-year-old to unfamiliar adult*]: You're supposed to put one of these persons in, see? Then, one goes with the other little girl. And then the little boy. He's the little boy and he drives. And then they back up. And then the little girl has marbles. . . .

> [*Four-year-old to unfamiliar, younger child*]: Watch, Perry. Watch this. He backing in here. Now he drives up. Look, Perry, look here. Those are marbles, Perry. Put the men in here. Now I'll do it. (p.13)

Despite the sophisticated level at which children can often operate, children's communicative competence does face some limitations. Preschoolers, for example, are more effective in a one-to-one conversation; they do less well when they must compete for their turn with adults and other children. Young children are more competent when speaking about single familiar objects that are present in their immediate environment than when speaking about absent objects (absent in time or space) or their own feelings, thoughts, and relationships (Dunn, 1988; Shatz, 1983, 1994).

How do children acquire the ability to converse on an increasingly sophisticated level? Learning the social aspects of language is similar to learning other forms of social behaviour. Children learn by observing people and through direct instruction from parents and teachers (Bandura, 1989; Dunn, 1988). They also learn by listening to people talk about conversations—who said what to whom and how this or that person responded (Miller & Sperry, 1987).

Much of what children learn from parents about the culturally appropriate use of language involves the acquisition of social conventions. For example, one of the child's first lessons in formal communication involves learning how to use polite, socially accepted words and phrases, such as *hello, good-bye, please,* and *thank you* (Grief & Gleason, 1980); these simple social routines are common to all cultures (Schieffelin & Ochs, 1987). Children must also learn when, where, and to whom it is appropriate to express negative feelings and thoughts, such as anger (Miller & Sperry, 1987).

Learning to Listen Critically

To learn from a communication, you must be able to recognize when a message sent to you is not clear. Young children are often unaware that they do not understand a message. In one experiment, Markman (1977) gave children in grades 1 to 3 game instructions that left out critical information that was essential to playing the game. The grade 3 children noticed the inadequacy of the instructions more readily than did the younger

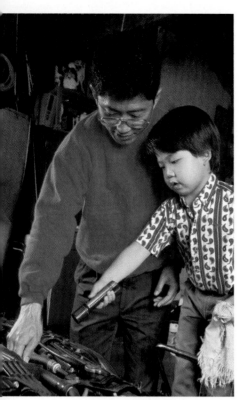

Learning to listen carefully to another's message is an important achievement, and adults can help children learn to attend to objects and events in the environment.

metalinguistic awareness

The understanding that language is a system of communicating with others that is bound by rules.

phonological awareness

The understanding of the sounds of a language and of the properties, such as the number of sounds in a word, related to these sounds.

children; indeed, the latter were generally unaware that information was missing and had to be urged to try to play the game before realizing that they did not know enough to do so.

However, if the task is simple enough, even 3-year-olds can recognize a breakdown in communication. In one study (Ferrier, Dunham, & Dunham, 2000), preschool children at 27 and 33 months talked with a toy robot while playing. During these conversations the robot asked either general (e.g., "what?") or specific (e.g., "Piggy's on the what?") questions in response to what the children said. An analysis of the responses to these queries indicated that in answer to the general question, children at both ages responded by repeating their earlier statement. In response to the more specific question, the older children switched their strategy and responded with a specification, sometimes elaborating on their original statement or providing additional information, or repeating the key constituent component of the statement. The younger children, however, failed to switch the nature of their response, once again simply repeating their original utterance. This type of study suggests that children as young as 3 years old possess the necessary skills for monitoring conversations, such as recognizing when problems occur and knowing how to fix such problems.

Children can be taught to be more effective listeners, but there may be a minimal age at which children can learn to listen critically. Two studies have shown that when 6- to 10-year-old children were encouraged to ask a speaker questions to clarify his communication, they performed more effectively than children who were not given this lesson in listening (Cosgrove & Patterson, 1977; Patterson & Kister, 1981). Because 4-year-olds did not benefit from this instruction suggests this type of listening strategy may be a moderately advanced communication skill.

METALINGUISTIC AWARENESS: KNOWING ABOUT LANGUAGE LO9

An important achievement in language development, and one of the latest to develop, is the understanding of how language works. That is, children become aware that they know language and can think and talk about language itself.

Metalinguistic awareness is the understanding that language is a rule-bound system of communicating. It includes the ability to talk about the various properties and uses of language as well as to monitor language as it is used (Whitehurst & Lonigan, 1998). This understanding and ability emerges well after children are proficient at producing language (Bullinger & Chatillon, 1983).

To test children's understanding of grammar, we can ask children to judge between grammatical and ungrammatical sentences and acceptable and unacceptable syntax. In one investigation, deVilliers and deVilliers (1972), using the clever technique of asking children to teach a puppet to talk correctly, tested children's ability not only to judge but also to correct word order in sentences describing specific actions. Sometimes, the puppet spoke in correct word order: for example, "Eat the cake." At other times, the puppet reversed word order: "Dog the pat." And at still other times, the puppet used correct syntax but described actions that were impossible: "Drink the chair." The children not only told the puppet whether it was right or wrong but also helped the puppet rephrase the "right way." The researchers found a clear relation between the children's level of language development and their metalinguistic awareness; as their ability to produce and comprehend sentences increased, their awareness increased as evidenced by their ability to correct the puppet's "wrong" utterances (deVilliers & deVilliers, 1992).

Phonological awareness is the specific aspect of metalinguistic awareness related to the sounds of language. This understanding includes knowledge of the sounds of language and of properties related to these sounds, such as how many sounds are in a word. Rhyming is a particularly interesting instance of phonological awareness because of the delight children seem to take in discovering that words can rhyme and in learning how to make this happen. Children as young as 2 years of age have been observed making rhymes. Learning and passing on oral rhymes are common in the preschool and early school years. Here is a rhyme that was common among children in England in the early twentieth century (Opie & Opie, 1959):

> *Mrs. White had a fright*
>
> *In the middle of the night*
>
> *She saw a ghost eating toast*
>
> *Half-way up the lamp post*

The fact that a rhyme, like this one, may make little sense does not seem to bother children; it even seems to make it more appealing. Children's interest in and use of rhymes reflects phonological awareness and can help create social connections and enjoyment for children. Phonological awareness also has significance for learning to read. Research has shown that children's phonological awareness before they enter school is positively related to success in reading both in the early grades and later (Goswami & Bryant, 1990).

BILINGUALISM AND LANGUAGE DEVELOPMENT

LO 10

One of the most dramatic changes to occur in North America is the growing presence of significant portions of the population that speak more than one language. Canada became a bilingual nation with the Official Languages Act (law in 1969; enacted in 1988), meaning that all federal government services must be provided in both of the country's official languages, French or English. Such statutes, along with other legislation protecting, for example, Aboriginal languages, laid the groundwork for making Canada not only bilingual, but multilingual as well.

However, **bilingualism**, or the acquisition of learning two languages either simultaneously or sequentially, has also raised a number of important questions for the language-acquisition process. Initially, experts feared that the task of learning two languages might interfere with children's language learning in general. Recent work, though, suggests that this is not the case (Holowka, Brosseau-Lapre, & Pettito, 2002; Pettito & Holowka, 2002; Sundara, Polka, & Molnar, 2008). Children who learn two languages may learn both languages more slowly than some of their peers learning one language; nevertheless, the performance gap disappears as children develop. Moreover, the age at which children begin to learn the two languages is important. Studies of children between 8 months and 2½ years found that bilingual and monolingual children had comprehension vocabularies of about the same size (Pearson, Fernández, & Oller, 1993). In contrast, children who are 5 years or older when they learn to speak two languages have smaller comprehension vocabularies than monolingual children (Bialystok, 1997, 2001; de Houwer, 1995; Hakuta, 1986). Although a bilingual child may have, in each of her languages, a vocabulary that is smaller than a monolingual child's vocabulary, her total production vocabulary—her vocabularies in both languages combined—may be equal in size to the monolingual child's production vocabulary (Pearson et al., 1993).

The way in which two languages are learned differs depending upon whether children learn the languages simultaneously or in sequence. When very young children learn two languages simultaneously, they rely on language sounds, such as consonants, longer than monolingual children do (Fennell et al., 2007). The researchers think that this process may be adaptive in that bilingual children can use the distinct language sounds to help them deal with the cognitive load of learning words in two languages.

bilingualism

The acquisition of two languages.

In addition, research (Hirsch & Kim, 1997) has suggested that when children learn two languages simultaneously, from infancy, the languages share the same brain region (called *Broca's area*) that is responsible for the execution of speech as well as for some grammatical aspects of language. However, when children learn a second language later in childhood or adulthood, this brain region is divided, with a distinct area reserved for the second language. And recently, Kovelman, Baker, and Petitto (2008), using fMRI analyses, found differential brain activation between Spanish-English bilinguals and English monolinguals. Although others have disagreed with the idea that the two languages in bilinguals have separate anatomical representations (Paradis, 1990, 1996) and have differential brain processing, if these findings are valid, we might speculate that they underlie the apparent greater ease of learning a second language early in childhood. Perhaps, future studies will shed more light on this issue.

How do children learn a second language? The most obvious influence on second-language learning is the sociocultural environment (Masgoret & Gardner, 2003), including such factors as the family, the school, and the overall community in which one lives (Caldas & Caron-Caldas, 2000; Gardner & Clément, 1990; Gardner, Masgoret, & Tremblay, 1999). R. C. Gardner of the University of Western Ontario and collaborators (Gardner & Clément, 1990; Gardner, Lalonde, & Pierson, 1983; Gardner et al., 1999), for example, for a number of years have been looking at the types of sociocultural variables that play a role in children's second-language learning. These researchers have identified a number of factors that play a role in such acquisition, including parental encouragement, motivation, and the number of French speakers in the home community. Other researchers (Caldas & Caron-Caldas, 2000) closely examined the impact of home, school, and community on three French–English bilingual children's language preference and found that the greatest impact on choice of language was the community in which the children lived. Interestingly, because these children spent part of their time in English-speaking Louisiana and in French-speaking Quebec, these authors were actually able to track rapid shifts in the children's language choice, often observing changes of between 80 and 90 percent in language preference from one month to the next. Clearly, the cultural influences on language learning and use are quite strong.

In both Canada and the United States, another significant context for language learning involves using the two languages as part of children's academic instruction. In Canada, such French-immersion programs were originally introduced in 1965 in response to the concerns of English-speaking parents in Quebec that their children were not receiving adequate instruction in learning French (Genesee, 1985; Lambert & Tucker, 1972). In French-immersion programs, students receive anywhere from 50 to 100 percent of their school instruction in French. Currently, the most common model nationally is 100 percent immersion from kindergarten through grade 2, and at least 50 percent immersion through the rest of elementary school (Genesee & Gándara, 1999).

Bilingualism

Canada introduced bilingual education programs in 1965, with students receiving up to 50 percent of their daily instruction in French.

What is the impact of immersion programs, or of bilingualism in general, on social, cognitive, and linguistic development? Learning a second language often has specific benefits. Studies have shown that children who learn two languages exhibit any number of cognitive enhancements, such as better concept formation and more flexibility in their thinking (Diaz, 1983, 1985; Goncz & Kodzopeljic, 1991; Rosenbluum & Pinker, 1983). For example, Ellen Bialystok (Bialystok & Majumber, 1998) has found that bilingual children are better than monolingual children at controlling their attention and are less susceptible to distraction while problem solving, although recent work has raised some questions about the strength of this bilingual advantage on metalinguistic development (Bialystok, Majumber, & Martin, 2003). Bilingualism also appears to facilitate the development of metalinguistic awareness (Bialystok, 1991).

Other research, focused more specifically on the impact of immersion programs, also found that such advantages are not limited to just cognitive processing but can also be seen in aspects of social processing and behaviour as well. In a series of studies by Wallace Lambert, Fred Genesee, and others (Genesee & Gándara, 1999; Holobow, Genesee, Lambert, Gastrich, & Met, 1987; Holobow, Genesee, & Lambert, 1991; Lambert, Genesee, Holobow, & Chartrand, 1993), the authors have reported on the effects of French immersion on an array of linguistic, cognitive, and social behaviours. Lambert (1987), for example, reports that in comparison to control children, immersion children have less stereotypical attitudes toward French-Canadians and have more mature and productive social perspectives. Although other work (Holobow et al., 1987, 1991) has tended not to find any differences in academic achievement between immersion and non-immersion students, this research has similarly found that foreign-language immersion tended to diminish the effects of social class background. In a review of the literature relevant to bilingual education programs in Canada and the United States, Genesee and Gándara (1999) found that immersion programs had a positive impact on inter-group attitudes and reduced prejudicial feelings toward members of the other language group. Although Genesee and Gándara admit that these influences were not as substantial, or as long-lasting, as some researchers had hoped, clearly, second-language learning and immersion provides both an advantage and an opportunity for children.

Finally, some recent work has looked at the impact on social factors of education in one's native or heritage language. Wright and Taylor (1995), for instance, looked at self-esteem in groups of Inuit, white, and mixed-heritage kindergartners after receiving education in their native language (English, French, or Inuittut, the heritage language of the Inuit). These researchers found that after one year of instruction in their native language, children showed increases in both personal and collective self-esteem. Thus, an immersion program in one's heritage language clearly seems to promote potentially important social outcomes.

For Thought and Discussion

1. Much of our discussion concerning language development has involved aspects of communication. Yet language has a very important social function as well. How well do current theories of language development (learning theory, nativist theory, interactionist theory) capture the social aspect?

2. What cognitive abilities might underlie the understanding of metalinguistic awareness? More generally, what is the relation between cognition and language?

3. What do you think of the current state of bilingual education in Canada? Given the rise in different language groups over recent years, should bilingual education be expanded to become multilingual education and include more languages?

Making the Connections 7

There are many links between concepts and ideas in one area of development and concepts and ideas in other areas. Here are some of the connections between ideas in Chapter 7 and discussions in other chapters of this book.

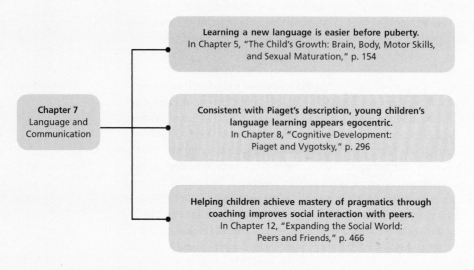

Chapter 7
Language and Communication

Learning a new language is easier before puberty.
In Chapter 5, "The Child's Growth: Brain, Body, Motor Skills, and Sexual Maturation," p. 154

Consistent with Piaget's description, young children's language learning appears egocentric.
In Chapter 8, "Cognitive Development: Piaget and Vygotsky," p. 296

Helping children achieve mastery of pragmatics through coaching improves social interaction with peers.
In Chapter 12, "Expanding the Social World: Peers and Friends," p. 466

SUMMARY

- **Language** serves a variety of purposes for the developing child. It facilitates interpersonal communication, helps organize thinking, and aids in learning. The development of **communicative competence** is an important part of children's language learning.

- Communication requires us to use both **productive language**, transmitting messages to others, and **receptive language**, in which we receive and understand messages others send us.

The Components of Language: Phonology, Semantics, Grammar, and Pragmatics

- The study of language can be divided into four areas: **Phonology** describes a language's systems of sounds, or the way basic sound units, called **phonemes**, are connected to form words. **Semantics** is the study of the meaning of words and sentences. **Grammar**, which describes the structure of a language, includes **syntax** and **morphology; morphemes** are a language's smallest units of meaning. **Pragmatics** consists of rules for the use of appropriate language in particular social settings.

Theories of Language Development

- Learning theory explains language development by the principle of reinforcement or by imitation. Although learning principles seem to be important in modifying language usage, they do not explain how children might acquire the enormous number of reinforcement linkages required to communicate effectively. Neither do they account for the regular sequence of language development, children's creative utterances, or the fact that children learn to speak grammatically even when parents fail to reinforce grammar.

- According to linguist Noam Chomsky's nativist approach to language development, children have an innate **language-acquisition device (LAD)** that enables them to learn language early and quickly. Support for this position comes from the finding of certain universal features in all languages, as well as from evidence that there may be a **critical period** for learning language. Critics point out that there is little agreement about the exact nature of the early grammatical rules that children learn. They also point out that the wealth of variant grammatical and syntactic rules around the world argues against any sort of universality.

- Most modern theorists take an interactionist position, recognizing that children are biologically prepared for language but require extensive experience with expressed language for adequate development. According to this view, children play an active role in acquiring language by formulating, testing, and evaluating hypotheses about their language's rules.

Facilitating Children's Language Development

- In proposing a **language-acquisition support system (LASS)**, Jerome Bruner emphasizes the critical roles of parents and other early caregivers in the child's language development. North American middle-class mothers, in particular, support a child's learning language by playing non-verbal games with them, by using the technique of **expansion** to expand or add to children's statements, and by **recasting** children's incomplete sentences in grammatical form.

The Antecedents of Language Development

- Infants acquire early training in the give and take of conversation through "pseudo-dialogues" with their parents. Using **proto-declaratives** and **proto-imperatives**, young children can call attention to objects and get other people to do things for them.
- Infants' capacity for receptive language begins as early as the first month of life, as demonstrated in their **categorical speech perception**, the ability to discriminate among consonant sounds as well as their ability to recognize some vowel sounds by the age of 2 months.
- Precursors to productive language include **cooing**, **babbling**, and **patterned speech**. Babbling occurs in many cultures, and the babbling of deaf babies is very similar to that of hearing infants.

Semantic Development: The Power of Words

- Children's acquisition of vocabulary proceeds in bursts, the first of these occurring at about a year and a half in the **naming explosion**. To build their vocabularies, children use a number of constraints that make certain narrowing judgments about a new word, such as that it refers only to an object or that it is entirely different from other words they already know.
- Two kinds of errors that children sometimes make in early word use are **overextension**, in which a single word covers many different things. In **underextension**, a child may restrict a word to only one representative of a category.

The Acquisition of Grammar: From Words to Sentences

- The one-word utterances that children begin to produce from about one year on are known as **holophrases** to indicate that these words often appear to represent a complete thought.
- Somewhere between one and two years, children begin to use **telegraphic speech**, which generally includes only nouns, verbs, and adjectives. These two-word communications are semantically similar across cultures and languages, including the sign language used by the deaf.
- At about the age of 3, children begin to form more complex sentences. In the latter part of the third year, the questions they have started to frame begin to include "wh" questions and questions that begin with "how." Negative statements may express recognition that something is absent or has disappeared or rejection or denial of something.
- The process of acquiring grammatic forms and achieving grammatic accuracy continues throughout the elementary school years and to some degree is a lifelong task. Using a kind of "syntactic bootstrapping," children as young as 1 or 2 years old use semantic and syntactic cues to help them understand sentences. This ability improves both as a function of an increasing number of cues and with age.

Learning the Social Uses of Language

- Because language is a social phenomenon, children must learn to raise their level of communication beyond **speech acts** to true **discourse**, which includes a complicated set of skills such as engaging the listener, sensitivity to listeners' feedback, adjusting speech to the characteristics of listeners, how to be good listeners, and how, as listeners, to let others know that their messages are unclear.
- Even preschoolers are remarkably sophisticated speakers, but because they have difficulty tracking multiple speakers and judging when it is their turn to speak, they are more effective on a one-to-one basis than in a group. Children improve their conversational sophistication through direct instruction and by observing/listening to others speak.

Metalinguistic Awareness: Knowing about Language

- When children achieve **metalinguistic awareness**, about the age of 10 years, they can understand that language is a system of rules for communication as well as discuss the properties and uses of language. Although they can use many rules at an early age, they have difficulty separating words from the object or events they represent and grasping the concept that words are elements of language.

- **Phonological awareness** appears earlier. Even preschool children have some understanding of the sounds of language and of how to use these sounds in different ways—for example, in creating rhymes.

Bilingualism and Language Development

- The evidence indicates that **bilingualism**, in which children learn two languages simultaneously, may have specific benefits, such as advanced cognitive skills, more flexibility of thought, and greater acceptance of peers of other cultural backgrounds.

MCGRAW-HILL CONNECT™—Available 24/7 with instant feedback so you can study when you want, how you want, and where you want. Take advantage of the Study Plan—an innovative tool that helps you customize your learning experience. You can diagnose your knowledge with pre- and post-tests, identify the areas where you need help, search the entire learning package for content specific to the topic you're studying, and add these resources to your personalized study plan. Visit *www.mcgrawhillconnect.ca* to register—take practice quizzes, search the e-book, and much more.

Chinese painting, Northern Song dynasty, 1127–1279. *Children playing in an autumn garden*, thirteenth century CE.

National Palace Museum, Taipei.

Chapter 8

Cognitive Development: Piaget and Vygotsky

LEARNING OBJECTIVES

After reading this chapter, you should be able to

LO 1 Define cognition; describe Piaget's model of cognitive development.

LO 2 Describe Piaget's notions of cognitive organization and cognitive adaptation; describe how schemata are modified throughout the lifetime, and the principles used to modify them (assimilation and accommodation).

LO 3 Describe the sensorimotor period and the concept of object permanence; discuss some of the more recent research on infants' abilities in the sensorimotor period, as well as some of the challenges to the idea of a "cognitive" infant.

LO 4 Describe the preoperational period and the capabilities and limitations during the preconceptual and intuitive sub-periods; discuss the general limitations on preoperational thought.

LO 5 Discuss the child's capabilities and limitations during the concrete operational and the formal operational period.

LO 6 Describe how Piaget's ideas have been applied to the development of social cognition.

LO 7 Critically evaluate Piaget's theory, discussing both strengths and limitations of this approach.

LO 8 Discuss Vygotsky's model of cognitive development, including the concepts of elementary and higher mental functions, as well as how the zone of proximal development relates to advances in development.

LO 9 Discuss the roles of culture and language in Vygotsky's theory.

LO 10 Critically evaluate Vygotsky's theory, discussing both strengths and limitations of this approach.

How do we make sense of the world and all the people and objects in it? As adults, we normally take what we know about the world for granted. For example, when was the last time you wondered if an object continues to exist even when you cannot see it? Or when have you stopped to think about at what age and how you came to understand the symbols and gestures that people use to communicate with one another? **Cognition** is the term used to describe the mental activity through which human beings acquire, remember, and learn to use knowledge. Cognition includes many mental processes, such as perception, attention, learning, memory, and reasoning. It is such a broad concept that most of the topics covered in this book have some relation to cognition and its development. After all, human beings are thinking creatures and most of our behaviour reflects this fact. Research on cognitive development focuses specifically on how and when intellectual abilities and knowledge of the world first emerge in childhood and then change as a person grows older.

In this chapter and its companion, Chapter 9, we discuss several different approaches to the study of cognitive development. Here, we describe two of these approaches. First, we explore Jean Piaget's theory of cognitive development, which emphasizes developmental changes in the organization or structure of children's thinking processes. Then we consider Lev Vygotsky's sociocultural theory of cognitive development, which suggests that a child's interactions with the social world produce advances in thinking and understanding. In Chapter 9, we will explore the information-processing approach to cognitive development. This view concentrates on how people use their cognitive abilities to process information and carry out intelligent actions ●

cognition

The mental activity through which human beings acquire and process knowledge.

LO1 PIAGET'S THEORY OF COGNITIVE DEVELOPMENT

Cognitive Development Knowledge

One of the most influential theories of cognitive development is that of the Swiss scientist Jean Piaget (1896–1980). Part of Piaget's influence on the field stems from the fact that his theory raised many interesting questions about intellectual development, which stimulated further research (Piaget, 1926, 1929, 1950, 1985). Piaget's work is not without controversy, and many developmentalists have challenged both his methods and his conclusions. First, we describe Piaget's theory, and then we turn to the main criticisms of this approach.

Piaget began his own scientific research at a considerably younger age than most other people do. His primary interest was biology, and at the age of 10, he published his first scholarly article on the rare albino sparrow. As Piaget continued his studies, his interest in biology continued. However, he also became interested in philosophy, especially the study of knowledge or *epistemology*. As a young man, Piaget pursued these interests by working in Paris in Alfred Binet's laboratory (Piaget, 1952). Binet's team was working on the development of the first intelligence test (discussed in Chapter 10). As he helped Binet to develop standardized IQ tests for children, Piaget made two important observations. First, he noticed that children of the same age tended to get the same answers wrong. Second, he observed that the errors of children of a particular age differed in systematic ways from those of older or younger children. Piaget's theory of cognitive development began to take shape as he thought about these errors; in particular, he thought they revealed distinct age-related ways of thinking and understanding the world. To study children's thinking, Piaget relied on two methods: interviews and observations. In his interviews, he would present the children with a problem to solve or a question to answer and then ask them to explain their thinking. In his observational research, which he used mainly with very young children, including detailed observations of his own children, he would present a problem and then watch how children behaved as they tried to solve it.

Piaget's theory, which became popular in North America in the 1960s, proposed that over development, the child acquires qualitatively new ways of thinking and understanding the world. For developmental psychologists, this theory was an attractive alternative to behaviourism, which was dominant at the time, for it focused on development and was thus based on observations of how children's cognitive abilities change as they grow from infancy to adolescence.

PIAGET'S MAIN TENET: THE CHILD ACTIVELY SEEKS KNOWLEDGE

Piaget argued that children play an active role in acquiring knowledge. Unlike behaviourism, in which children passively wait for information (or stimuli) from their environments, Piaget argued that children actively seek out information. In addition, when children encounter new information, they actively try to fit it in with the knowledge they already possess. In other words, children construct their own understanding. Thus, this theory is referred to as a **constructivist view**.

Children need to develop a lot of knowledge about the world. Piaget was particularly interested in the development of knowledge about logical properties of the world. Piaget set out to discover precisely how children at different points in their development think about how objects work and are related to one another. He felt that children vary in the timing of when they develop this knowledge and, as a result, he provided approximate ages at which these developmental achievements occur. The Turning Points chart on pages 300–301 covers many topics discussed in this chapter and includes a summary of Piaget's descriptions of the milestones of cognitive development.

Cognitive Organization

Piaget believed that, over the course of development, children's knowledge of the world gets organized into increasingly more complex cognitive structures. A *cognitive structure* is not a physical entity in the brain but an organized group of interrelated memories, thoughts, and strategies that the child uses in trying to understand a situation. Piaget built much of his theory around the concept of the **schema** (plural, **schemas**), which is much like a concept. A schema is an organized unit of knowledge, and collectively, schemas form the knowledge base that a person uses to understand and interact with the environment.

As this definition suggests, a key feature of children's developing knowledge is that it is organized. **Organization**, for Piaget, entails the combination of simple mental structures into more complex systems. The organization of the knowledge that children have available at any given point in development enables the child to act on and interpret the world in a particular way. However, over time and with experience, this knowledge changes as the child attempts to understand new information and combine it in some way with their current knowledge. What emerges is a new organization of the child's knowledge, one that builds on the prior organization but extends this knowledge into new and more powerful directions. For instance, newborns possess many basic reflexes, such as sucking, grasping, and looking, all of which help the infant engage with and learn about the world. Initially, these reflexes are used in very specific ways. However, over time and with experience at sucking, for example, this schema changes and the newborn sucks differently on different objects and uses this schema for different purposes, such as exploring objects.

Jean Piaget based much of his theory of children's cognitive development on direct observations and interviews with young children. When he travelled to North America, he often visited with children in nursery schools and the early grades.

 2

constructivist view

The idea that children actively create their understanding of the world as they encounter new information and have new experiences.

schema/schemas

An organized unit of knowledge that the child uses to try to understand a situation; a schema forms the basis for organizing actions to respond to the environment.

organization

Combining simple mental structures into more complex systems.

Turning Points

THE CHILD'S COGNITIVE DEVELOPMENT FROM INFANCY THROUGH LATE CHILDHOOD

1 MONTH
- Becomes more efficient in use of reflexes and can invite stimulation that allows this use; can tell the difference between mother's nipple, the nipple on a bottle, thumb, and a pacifier

2 MONTHS
- Can anticipate: stops crying at sight of mother's breast or the bottle; expects animate behaviour from human beings

3 MONTHS
- Shows recognition memory; reacts to newness with body stiffening; quiets at sight of interesting toy

4 MONTHS
- Repeats actions of own body that are pleasurable and satisfying; can reach out and gently probe objects; will search for partially concealed objects and may grasp notion of object permanence; anticipation becomes immediate—opens mouth at sight of bottle; may be capable of simple categorization

5 MONTHS
- Visually follows an object as it is moved out of direct line of vision; remembers pictures of faces

6 MONTHS
- Learns behaviours of familiar people; may understand physical causality; reacts to changes in familiar events

7 MONTHS
- Explores objects by manipulation; drops objects from heights; may understand the notion of physical support; is more attentive when playing

8 MONTHS
- Likes to make things happen and combines learned behaviours in this effort; searches for completely concealed objects; displays primitive problem-solving abilities; attends to play, shaking, banging, and dangling toys; often mouths toys as a way of exploring

9 MONTHS
- Begins to remember without cues; uses knowledge to solve problems; is aware of cause and effect; recognizes that own actions may affect outcomes; gets other people to make things happen

10 MONTHS
- Explores inside and outside surfaces of toys; repeats play sequences with different toys; investigates textures, designs, or parts of toys; may be able to reason about hidden objects; peers intently at pictures

11 MONTHS
- Uses props as aids (e.g., uses a chair to stand up); is more easily entertained; begins to put knowledge of an "inside" to use (e.g., tries to stack cups)

Sources: Flavell, 1963; Gauvain, 2001b; Kopp, 1994; Siegler & Alibali, 2005.

operations

Schemas based on internal mental activities.

As children grow older and gain experience, they shift gradually from using schemata based on overt physical activities to those based on internal mental activities. Piaget called these mental schemata **operations**. With development, cognitive operations are used to alter and combine schemata to form more complex behaviours. Piaget

1 YEAR	• Searches for objects when they are moved or hidden within sight; actively plans to achieve a goal; comprehensively examines objects; uses imitative learning; deliberately introduces variations into play sequences; recognizes self in mirror
15 MONTHS	• Continues to use systematic trial-and-error learning; is more aware of the functions of objects; may use dolls in play; recognizes and uses more cause-and-effect relationships
18 MONTHS	• Searches for objects even when they have been moved out of own sight; likes to experiment with the properties of objects; thinks in terms of ideas; has better recall memory; has primitive idea of "what should be" (e.g., puts lids on jars); recognizes that others have possessions
21 MONTHS	• To some degree, understands past, present, and future; consistently uses scripts to organize activities into episodes; has some understanding of the idea of categories (e.g., colours)
2 YEARS	• Can think symbolically and use language symbolically; can store mental representations and replay an action long after observing it; can plan problem solving mentally rather than use trial and error; begins to understand conservation; engages in fantasy play; recognizes that family members have specific roles; shows creative problem solving
3 YEARS	• May be able to see the perspectives of others; may grasp conservation of number
4 YEARS	• Begins to realize that others have different perspectives from own; may be able to understand part–whole relations
5 YEARS	• Can respond to scaffolding in the instructional process
7 YEARS	• Can use certain mental operations to solve problems but uses them intuitively, without a clear understanding of how and why they work; has achieved conservation of number, mass, liquid, length; begins to describe self in more abstract terms
8–10 YEARS	• Can anticipate and consider the thoughts of others; achieves conservation of weight
11–12 YEARS	• Achieves conservation of volume; understands reversibility; begins to think deductively; can form concepts of space and time; can sort things in complicated combinations of attributes
12 AND BEYOND	• Thinking becomes logical, more flexible, and capable of abstraction; can apply logic to ideas and problems that violate reality; can entertain many possible solutions for a problem

claimed that when a substantial number of changes in schemata occur, children change from one organized way of understanding to an entirely new way of approaching the world. He described these large-scale organizational changes as stages and suggested that, over the life course, there are four stages of cognitive development. These stages are described in detail in the next major section of the chapter.

Cognitive Adaptation

Piaget proposed that children continually modify their schemas in relation to their own experiences and referred to this process as **adaptation**. Adaptation of a schema is a bit like a two-way street. It always involves determining how new information fits with existing knowledge as well as how existing knowledge may need to change to incorporate new information. To understand a new experience, children at first try **assimilation**; that is, applying their existing schemes to the new experience, they try to apply what they already know, their existing schemas, to the new experience. For example, as babies are confronted with new objects, they try to assimilate those objects to their complex looking-grasping-sucking scheme. In most cases, they are successful, and object after object gets grasped and placed in the mouth.

However, babies will sometimes encounter an object that is hard to assimilate. For example, a large inflated beach ball is very difficult to grasp and suck. Now, the infant must modify her strategy for exploring objects (her looking–grasping–sucking scheme) and adopt a new approach. Using the method of **accommodation**, she may hold the ball in her arms instead of her hands and lick it with her tongue instead of sucking on it. In this way, she has modified an existing scheme to fit the characteristics of the new situation. Assimilation and accommodation work together to organize children's knowledge and behaviour into increasingly complex structures.

THE STAGES OF COGNITIVE DEVELOPMENT

Piaget viewed intellectual growth in terms of progressive changes in children's cognitive structures. Small changes in understanding and interacting with the world eventually result in large-scale changes referred to as **stages of development**. Each stage is qualitatively different from the one that precedes it. Because stages are built through experience, children do not reach these stages at exactly the same age. However, all children pass through the stages in the same order, and no stage can be skipped. This is because the attainments of earlier stages are the building blocks of the later stages. Piaget saw intellectual development as occurring in four main stages: the sensorimotor period, the preoperational period, the period of concrete operations, and the period of formal operations (see Table 8-1). According to Piaget, as children pass through these stages, they change from infants, who are incapable of mental operations and depend on sensory and motor activities to learn about the world, into emerging young adults capable of great flexibility of thought and abstract reasoning.

L03 The Sensorimotor Stage

Dramatic achievements in children's intellectual development occur during the **sensorimotor stage**, which spans approximately the first two years of life. By interacting with their environment in active ways, children build on basic reflexes and, from these origins, form a way of understanding and interacting with the world. By the end of infancy, around 2 years of age, children begin to form mental representations of objects and events and to use this information in developing new behaviours and solving problems.

Because so many cognitive changes occur in the first two years, Piaget divided the sensorimotor period into six substages. One of the major cognitive achievements during the sensorimotor stages is the development of the object concept. We are not born with knowledge of objects. Rather, the child must construct this knowledge over the course of his experience with objects. According to Piaget, over the sensorimotor stage, infants learn about objects, including **object permanence**: the realization that objects continue to exist even when they are out of sight (see Table 8-2). We discuss Piaget's thinking about the development of the object concept in the next several paragraphs, as we describe the six substages of the sensorimotor stage.

Table 8-1 Piaget's stages of cognitive development

Stage	Age Range (in years)	Major Characteristics and Achievements
Sensorimotor period	0–2	Child's thought is confined to action schemes and sensory experiences. Infant differentiates self from other objects; seeks stimulation and prolongs interesting sights and experiences; develops object concept, including object permanence; achieves basic understanding of causality, time, space; grasps means–end relationships; begins to imitate behaviours previously experienced; engages in imaginative play; and late in the stage, shows the beginnings of symbolic thought
Preoperational period	2–7	Child begins to use symbols to represent objects and experiences and to use language symbolically; shows intuitive problem solving. Thinking is semi-logical, characterized by irreversibility, centration, egocentrism, and animism. Child begins to think in terms of classes, sees relations, and grasps concept of conservation of numbers
Period of concrete operations	7–12	Child is capable of logical reasoning, but this ability is limited to physically real and present objects; grasps concepts of the conservation of mass, length, weight, and volume; thinking is now characterized by reversibility, decentration, and the ability to take the role of another; child can organize objects into hierarchical classes (classification) and to place objects into ordered series (seriation)
Period of formal operations	12 and beyond	Child acquires flexibility in thinking as well as the capacities for abstraction and mental hypothesis testing; child can consider possible alternatives in complex reasoning and problem solving

Table 8-2 Acquiring the object concept and an understanding of object permanence

Substage	Age Range (in Months)	Child's Behaviour
1 Basic reflex activity	0–1	Focuses only on objects directly in front of him
2 Primary circular reactions	1–4	Begins to operate on objects with action schemes; initially, this occurs accidentally and then becomes less accidental; looks for a long time at the place where an object disappeared but does not search visually or manually for the object
3 Secondary circular reactions	4–8	Can operate on objects and repeats actions toward objects; can visually anticipate where an object may be; searches for partially concealed objects
4 Coordination of secondary schemata	8–12	Will search for completely hidden objects but has tendency to repeat old actions by searching where objects were previously hidden (A-not-B error)
5 Tertiary circular reactions	12–18	Lots of trial-and-error experimentation with objects and how they move; searches for objects that have been concealed while she was watching but has difficulty if an object is displaced more than once
6 Inventing new means by mental combination	18–24	Object concept is fully developed; child searches and finds objects easily, even if the object has been hidden and displaced many times

SUBSTAGE 1: BASIC REFLEX ACTIVITY (BIRTH TO 1 MONTH)   In

basic reflex activity

An infant's exercise of and growing proficiency in the use of innate reflexes.

the substage of **basic reflex activity**, infants become more proficient in the use of their innate reflexes, such as grasping and sucking. Much of their initial exploration of objects occurs through involuntary reflexive behaviours. However, over the first month of life, many of these involuntary behaviours are replaced by behaviours that are similar in form but are controlled voluntarily. For example, between birth and 1 month of age, the grasping reflex gradually subsides, and in its place, the infant begins to use her hands voluntarily to grab onto objects that come within reach. In terms of the object concept, from birth to 1 month, infants look only at objects that are directly in front of them.

SUBSTAGE 2: PRIMARY CIRCULAR REACTIONS (1 TO 4 MONTHS)

primary circular reactions

Behaviours in which infants repeat and modify actions that focus on their own bodies and that are pleasurable and satisfying.

This substage is called **primary circular reactions** because during this time, infants produce repetitive behaviours that are focused on the infant's own body. Babies begin to repeat and modify actions that they find pleasurable. Often, these actions begin by chance. For example, a baby may accidentally bring a finger close to her mouth and start sucking on it. Finding this behaviour pleasurable, the infant attempts to reproduce the exact behaviour—in this case, by seeking the finger to suck on it again and again. In terms of the object concept, infants display no comprehension that objects have an existence of their own. When a toy vanishes, they do not look for it. In fact, if the toy drops from a child's hand, she will stare at her hand rather than follow the falling object's path to the floor.

SUBSTAGE 3: SECONDARY CIRCULAR REACTIONS (4 TO 8 MONTHS)   Not

secondary circular reactions

Behaviours focused on objects outside the infant's own body that the infant repeatedly engages in because they are pleasurable.

until the infant enters the substage of **secondary circular reactions**, at about 4 months of age, does he become interested in making things happen outside his own body. Secondary circular reactions involve repetitive behaviours focused on external objects, hence the term *secondary*. During this substage, the child's reactions are still circular; that is, he repeatedly engages in behaviours that please him. For example, the infant may shake a rattle, hear an interesting sound, shake the rattle again, and so on. The baby now is capable of combining schemes, such as grasping and shaking, to produce relatively more complex behaviours. In terms of the object concept, the infant begins to show some awareness of the permanence of objects. A child will search visually for an object if its loss interrupts the child's actions, and he will anticipate the path of a moving object by looking at a location where it can be ex-

This 7-month-old child seems quite absorbed in shaking his rattle. With its attachments, the rattle may make more than just one intriguing sound.

pected to appear. The child will search for a partially visible object, but not a covered one, and even if he watches as an object is covered, he will not attempt to retrieve it.

SUBSTAGE 4: COORDINATION OF SECONDARY SCHEMATA (8 TO 12 MONTHS)   In the substage called **coordination of secondary**

coordination of secondary schemata

An infant's combination of different schemes to achieve a specific goal.

schemata, the child develops more sophisticated combinations of behaviours that are directed toward objects and that reflect intentionality. At this point in development, Piaget held, the child is able to plan deliberately to attain a goal. Furthermore, schemas can be combined to reach these goals. For example, the child can now combine a hitting schema with her reaching and grasping schemas to move one toy out of the way so she can reach another. Thus, this substage marks the beginning of problem-solving behaviour.

In terms of the object concept, the child now begins to search for completely concealed objects. However, although the child will search successfully for an object hidden in one location, if the object is moved to another location as the child watches, she will continue to search in the first hiding place. This type of error is referred to as the A-not-B error because the child continues to search in the first hiding place, identified as A, even after, in the child's presence, the object is put in a second spot, identified as B.

SUBSTAGE 5: TERTIARY CIRCULAR REACTIONS (12 TO 18 MONTHS)

In the substage of **tertiary circular reactions**, children begin to experiment with external objects. Children use trial-and-error methods to learn more about the properties of objects and to solve problems. Unlike the earlier substages in which the child repeated *exact* behaviours, infants are now capable of producing *similar* but not exact behaviours. Piaget referred to infants who had acquired this capability, which allows for novel exploration, as "little scientists." For example, children at this age often experiment by deliberately dropping objects from different heights to see what happens to them.

In this substage, the infant finally displays understanding of the permanence of an object hidden from view. But despite this new awareness, these children still have difficulty following more than one displacement of an object. While playing a hiding game with his son, Laurent, Piaget hid his watch repeatedly behind one of two cushions, and Laurent consistently searched for the watch under the correct cushion. However, as Laurent watched, Piaget then placed the watch in a box, put the box behind a cushion, and then secretly removed the watch from the box and put the watch behind the cushion. He then handed the box to Laurent, who opened it and found it empty. Laurent did not search for the watch behind the cushion. Although the type of hiding problem described in the A-not-B error no longer puzzled Laurent, understanding this type of hiding, called *invisible displacement*, was not within his grasp.

SUBSTAGE 6: INVENTING NEW MEANS BY MENTAL COMBINATION (18 TO 24 MONTHS)

It is not until the sixth and last substage of **inventing new means by mental combination**, that the beginnings of **symbolic thought** appear. Children begin to think symbolically and engage in internal, or mental, problem solving. The child can now invent ways to attain a goal by *mentally* combining schemas; he is no longer limited to physically exploring, manipulating, and

tertiary circular reactions

Behaviours in which infants experiment with the properties of external objects and try to learn how objects respond to various actions.

inventing new means by mental combination

In this last stage of the sensorimotor period, children begin to combine schemes mentally, thus relying less on physical trial and error.

symbolic thought

The use of mental images to represent people, objects, and events.

(a)

(b)

At 11 months, this child is already beginning to experiment with dropping things to see what happens to them. From this height, her toy probably did nothing too startling, but it may have moved in interesting ways.

deferred imitation

Mimicry of an action some
time after having observed
it; requires that the child has
stored a mental image of the
action.

acting on objects. Symbolic capabilities are evident in the child's emerging ability to
use language and in **deferred imitation**, in which the child mimics an action some time
after observing it.

Finally, at this last substage, children fully acquire the concept of object permanence. They are able to make inferences about the positions of unseen objects even
when the objects have been hidden or displaced several times.

NEW RESEARCH DIRECTIONS AND EXPLANATIONS OF
KNOWLEDGE IN INFANCY

Piaget's ideas about the development of the
knowledge in infancy, including the object concept, have met with controversy. In all
the tasks he used to study the development of the object concept, Piaget measured only
the child's manual search behaviour. Many investigators have argued that because of
developmental limitations, such as poor hand–eye coordination, some children who have
acquired the object concept may be unable to reveal it in manual search activities.

To study this possibility, Canadian-born researcher Renée Baillargeon (1986, 1993)
designed a task that allowed her to measure the amount of time infants look at a situation involving objects, which she referred to as an event, to try to reveal information
about infants' understanding of objects before they are capable of manually searching
for an object. Baillargeon presented 6- and 8-month-old infants with what seemed to be
an impossible event: One solid object appeared to move through the space occupied by
another solid object. The infant sat in front of a platform on which was an inclined ramp
(see Figure 8-1a). At the bottom of the ramp, directly in front of the infant, was a small
screen that could be raised and lowered. After the screen had been lowered, a small car
rolled down the ramp along a track, disappearing behind the screen and reappearing at
the other side of the screen. This event was repeated until the infant became habituated
to it and stopped looking at the display.

According to the Piagetian
view of object permanence,
this 10-month-old child is
pretty much on track, searching for an object that was
completely concealed. Renée
Baillargeon has demonstrated,
however, that even 3½-month-
old infants may be aware that
objects exist whether or not
they are visible.

Next, the infant saw one of two test events (see Figures 8-1b and 8-1c). Both of
these events were identical to the habituation event except that when the screen was
raised, the infant saw a box placed behind it and then hidden by the lowered screen.
The two test events differed by the placement of the box. In the possible event (Figure
8-1b), the box was placed behind the track, and, therefore, out of the car's path. In the
impossible event (Figure 8-1c), the box was placed on top of the track, directly in the
car's path. This time, when the car disappeared behind the screen and then reappeared,
it looked like it rolled right through the box. (During the impossible event, the box was
actually removed through a door in the back of the stage.)

What did Baillargeon find? Infants looked longer at the impossible event than at
the possible event. And in later studies using the same basic experimental procedure,
Baillargeon and her colleagues (see Baillargeon & Wang, 2002) found that even infants
as young as 3½ months of age could demonstrate an awareness of object permanence
under these conditions. These findings suggest that infants know a great deal more
about objects than Piaget thought they did.

Object permanence may not be the only principle of the physical world that children understand earlier than Piaget thought. There may be some other understandings about the world so fundamental to cognitive development that these, too, appear
very early in life. Developmental psychologists refer to these types of understanding as
core knowledge systems (Spelke, 2000) and examples include some understanding of
physical laws, such as the solidity of objects and what can happen to objects, or *event
knowledge* (Baillargeon & Wang, 2002).

core knowledge systems

Ways of reasoning about
ecologically important objects
and events, such as the solidity and continuity of objects.

Research on early event knowledge has relied primarily on the *violation-of-expectation* method described in Chapter 4. For example, Hespos and Baillargeon (2001)
studied the behaviour of 4½-month-old infants when they were shown two types of
events, one possible and one impossible, regarding the occlusion and the containment
of objects (see Figure 8-2 on page 308). In this experiment, the infants watched as an
object, a tall cylinder, was either lowered behind a screen (the occlusion condition) or

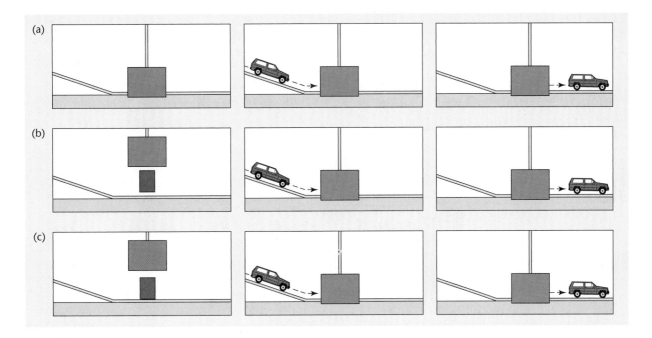

Figure 8-1

Testing infants' grasp of object permanence

(a) As 6- to 8-month-old babies watched, a car rolled down a ramp, disappeared behind a screen and reappeared at the other side. (b) After infants saw the box placed *behind* the ramp, the car again rolled down the ramp, and disappeared and reappeared once again (a possible event). (c) After infants saw the box placed *on* the ramp, where it would obstruct the car's passage, the car once again rolled down the ramp, disappearing and reappearing as before (an impossible event). Babies looked longer at the event in (c) than at the event in (b).

Source: Adapted from Baillargeon, 1986.

lowered inside a container (the containment condition). The investigators studied two types of events, the possible or expected event and the impossible or unexpected event. In the expected events, the objects used to occlude or contain the cylinder were as tall as the cylinder and, therefore, physically able to hide the cylinder from view. In the unexpected events, the objects used to occlude or contain the cylinder were shorter than the cylinder; in fact they were only half as tall as the cylinder. In the unexpected events, the cylinder was, nonetheless, hidden entirely from view in the two hiding conditions (a trap door was used to make this impossible event work). What did the infants do? They looked longer at the unexpected than at the expected events when they were in the occlusion condition but not in the containment condition. In a similar study that included older infants, 7½-month-old infants, but not 5½- or 6½-month-old infants, looked longer at both the unexpected occlusion and containment events (Baillargeon, 2002). These findings suggest that this type of event knowledge develops very early, though it appears gradually over the first year of life.

Studies such as this suggest that infants know more about the world than Piaget proposed. They also indicate that such early achievements develop over time. Infants may learn general principles quite early but be unable for some time to grasp the subtleties of these principles. This argument proposes that infants are biologically prepared to learn certain kinds of information or principles about the world (Gelman & Williams, 1998). This does not necessarily imply that a baby's understanding is innate but rather that the human infant is predisposed to learn some critical features of her environment quite rapidly.

However, it is important to add that other researchers have raised important criticisms of studies that examine early understanding in infancy. Some have argued that

Figure 8-2

Figure 8-2

Exploring infants' knowledge of events

Drawings representing the unexpected test events for the occlusion condition (a) and the containment condition (b). Babies as young as 4½ months looked longer at the unexpected test event in the occlusion condition, but it was not until babies were 7½ months old that they looked longer at the unexpected test event in the containment condition.

Source: Adapted from Baillargeon & Wang, 2002; Hespos & Baillargeon, 2001.

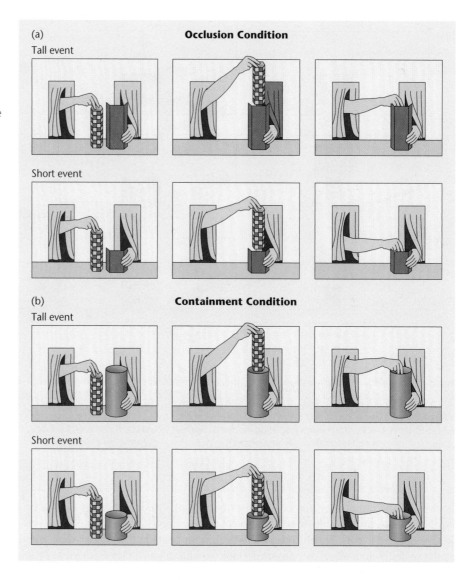

longer looking time indicates that the infant can discriminate between two events but it does not tell us why the infant looks longer at some information than at others (Haith & Benson, 1998). Other psychologists have argued that perceptual processes rather than conceptual processes explain an infant's longer looking at an impossible event (Bogartz et al., 2000; Cashon & Cohen, 2000; Rivera et al., 1999).

Finally, other psychologists have discovered that the knowledge identified in infants on tasks such as those just described is not clearly evident in children between 2 and 3 years of age (Keen, 2003). For instance, in one study toddlers were asked to find a ball after it rolled down a ramp and stopped behind a screen (Berthier et al., 2000), as depicted in Figure 8-3. The ball could be stopped at any one of several locations behind the screen by a movable barrier that protruded above the screen, and, therefore, served as a cue as to where the ball had stopped. To find the ball, the child opened one of the small doors that were in the screen. Children under 3 years of age were unsuccessful at finding the ball. Changes to the display, such as making the small doors transparent, did not help 2-year-olds perform any better on this task (Butler et al., 2002). However, 2½-year-olds performed better with the transparent doors than they had with the opaque doors.

In examining the results from these studies, Keen (2003) points out that in order to solve some of these problems, children need more than object knowledge—they also need to know how to solve problems related to objects, such as searching for objects

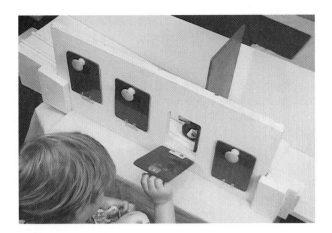

Figure 8-3

Finding objects that have moved into a hidden space

When a ball rolled down a ramp and into one of the spaces behind the screen with the small doors, children had to open the door behind which they thought they would find the ball. The movable barrier that protruded above the screen and that stopped the ball's rolling gave them a clue as to which door led to the ball.

Source: Berthier et al., 2000.

when they are moved. Searching for objects requires that the child be able to create a plan that coordinates her own actions with her predictions about how the object will move. Exactly what young children understand about objects at different ages is a question for future research.

It is clear that the account of infant cognition outlined in Piaget's six sensorimotor substages cannot explain many of the recent findings of early infant capabilities. Although Piaget did not capture the entirety of the young infant's cognitive capacities, he provided the first detailed description of cognitive development in the first two years of life. Moreover, cross-cultural research on the sensorimotor stage supports his general framework. Longitudinal research conducted with Baoulé children between 6 and 30 months of age in Côte d'Ivoire revealed the same six substages Piaget described (Dasen et al., 1978).

Cognition Studies Lab

The Preoperational Stage

The major characteristic of the **preoperational stage** is the child's development of the **symbolic function**, or the ability to use symbols, such as words, images, and gestures, to represent objects and events mentally. This ability to represent experience symbolically continues to evolve throughout the two stages of this period, the preconceptual and the intuitive stages.

THE PRECONCEPTUAL SUBSTAGE (2 TO 4 YEARS) In the **preconceptual substage**, the emergence of symbolic capabilities is evident in children's rapid development of language, their great interest in imaginative play, and their increasing use of deferred imitation. Other important characteristics of children's thinking during this substage are animistic thinking and egocentricity.

The child who demonstrates **animistic thinking** tends to attribute life to inanimate objects. For example, the child may believe that plants feel pain when he picks their flowers or that the wind talks to his friends, the trees. Researchers have questioned Piaget's hypothesis regarding animistic thought, however. For example, Bullock (1985) and others have pointed out that the objects Piaget used to test the limits of children's animistic thought, such as the sun, the moon, and the wind, are often open to magical interpretations. In contrast to Piaget's observations, Massey and Gelman (1988) found that when they used simple and familiar objects, children as young as 4 years old were quite good at deciding whether animate objects, such as mammals, or inanimate objects, such as statues, could move on their own.

Piaget also claimed that children in the preconceptual substage tend to view the world from their own perspective and to have difficulty seeing things from another person's point of view. Piaget called this type of reasoning **egocentrism**. For instance, notice in the previous example that the wind is described as talking to the child's friends.

preoperational stage

In this period, the symbolic function promotes the learning of language; the period is also marked by egocentricity and intuitive behaviour, in which the child can solve problems using mental operations but cannot explain how she did so.

symbolic function

The ability to use symbols, such as images, words, and gestures, to represent objects and events in the world.

preconceptual substage

The first substage of Piaget's preoperational period, during which the child's thought is characterized by animistic thinking and egocentricity.

animistic thinking

The attribution of life to inanimate objects.

egocentrism

The tendency to view the world from one's own perspective and to have difficulty seeing things from another's viewpoint.

To test the child's ability to see things from another person's perspective, Piaget designed what is known as the three-mountain test (see Figure 8-4). Models of three mountains of varying sizes are placed on a square table, and chairs are placed around all four sides of the table. The child is seated in one chair, and the experimenter places a doll in the other three chairs, one at a time, asking the child each time to describe what the doll sees from the three different positions. The child may select one of a set of drawings or use cardboard cutouts of the mountains to construct the doll's views. Piaget found that children could not consistently identify the dolls' view from each of the three locations until they reached the period of concrete operations, when they were 9 or 10 years old.

Piaget's three-mountain task and his interpretations of when children develop perspective-taking skills have been challenged by many researchers on several grounds. First, in his original test, he used simple models of mountains that lacked clear features that could be used to differentiate one view from the next. Second, reconstructing the display or choosing the appropriate drawings, may be beyond the ability of a young child. And third, choosing the correct perspective may simply not be an activity that makes sense to young children. Making two simple changes in Piaget's design, Borke (1975) obtained very different results: (a) The researcher placed familiar things, such as snowcaps, trees, or houses, on the sides of the mountains to make them more distinctive, and (b) he asked children to rotate a small model of the display to present the appropriate view rather than reconstruct the display or choose from drawings. Children as young as 3 were then able to identify the correct perspective from each of the three different positions. Hughes (1975, cited in Donaldson, 1978) tackled another aspect

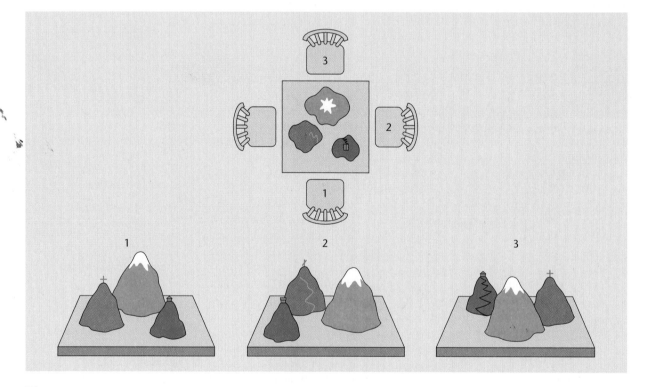

Figure 8-4

Understanding different perspectives: Piaget's three-mountain test

We show Piaget's classic test, which used a tabletop model to represent mountains. As discussed in the text, contemporary researchers have found that young children can better understand the perspectives of dolls or imaginary people sitting in chairs 1 to 3 when the mountains look more realistic, when the children are allowed to rotate small models or the mountains, and when the reason for taking another's perspective is made more meaningful or sensible to children.

of this task, by making the purpose of the task more understandable to the children. Rather than having three mountains, he sat the children at a table on which there were two "walls" that intersected in the middle. Thus, there were four areas or corners of the table; each was set off from the other by these walls (see Figure 8-5). Hughes then introduced two dolls, a child doll and a police doll, and asked each youngster a series of questions about where the child doll could hide so that the police officer could not find her. Most of the children between 3½ and 5 years of age were able to provide correct answers to the questions. These results suggest that when the task is made more comprehensible to children, they are able to perform much better than Piaget claimed.

THE INTUITIVE SUBSTAGE (4 TO 7 YEARS)   Piaget called the second substage of the preoperational stage "intuitive" because, although the child can employ certain mental operations, such as ways of classifying, quantifying, or relating objects, she does not seem to be aware of the principles she has used in performing these operations. In other words, the child in the **intuitive substage** can solve problems with these operations but cannot explain why she solved them in a particular way. In this substage, the child has difficulty understanding part–whole relations, as illustrated in class-inclusion problems, such as the following: A child is given 7 toy dogs and 3 toy cats—a total of 10 animals. If the child is asked whether there are more dogs or more cats, he can answer correctly that there are more dogs. However, if the child is then asked if there are more dogs than there are animals, the child responds that there are more dogs. Piaget proposed that the child is responding incorrectly because he is unable to focus simultaneously on a part of the set of animals (the subset of dogs) and on the whole set of animals.

Developmentalists have criticized Piaget's research on part–whole relations, suggesting that the way he posed his questions confused children. When Smith (1979) used simpler questions that still addressed children's ability to use part–whole relations, such as, "A pug is a kind of dog, but it's not a shepherd. Is a pug an animal?" she found that children as young as 4 displayed knowledge of the part–whole relation between dogs and animals by correctly answering that a pug is an animal. Similar findings have been produced by changing from a verbal to a multiple-choice or forced-choice response format (Boisvert, Standing, & Moller, 1999). Other experimental (Southard & Pasnak, 1997) and computer-simulation work (Mareschal & Shultz, 1999) has even called into question the whole notion of large-scale, readily definable stages for such abilities.

intuitive substage

The second substage of the preoperational period, during which the child begins to solve problems by means of specific mental operations but cannot yet explain how she arrives at the solutions.

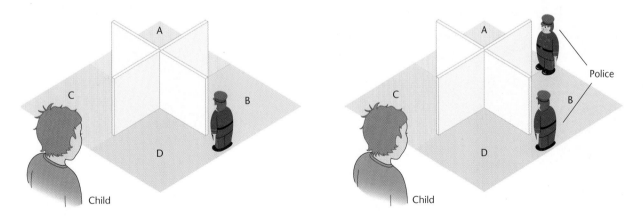

Figure 8-5

Another way to study children's perspective-taking abilities

In this model, Hughes devised four small rooms (A, B, C, and D) from among which a child doll could choose a hiding place where the police doll, from various positions around the model, could not find her. Most children between 3½ and 5 years of age were able to provide correct answers to questions about this scenario.

Source: Donaldson, 1978.

This child's decision as to whether the two glasses hold equal amounts of coloured water will reveal whether he has attained an understanding of the conservation of liquids.

THE MAIN LIMITATIONS OF PREOPERATIONAL THOUGHT

The main limitation in preoperational thinking is that the child is semi-logical. We see one of the most vivid examples of semi-logical thinking when preoperational children perform conservation tasks. To understand **conservation** the child must recognize that even when an object's appearance is altered in some way, the object's basic attributes or properties remain the same. For example, we present the child with two identical glasses, each of which contains the same amount of liquid. The liquid in these glasses is then poured into two other glasses of different sizes, such that one glass is tall and thin and the other glass is short and wide. The result of the pouring is that, although the liquid remains the same in quantity—nothing has spilled or been taken away—the water levels in the tall and short glasses are now different.

Two basic attributes of a physical object, in this case the liquid, are at issue here. One attribute pertains to the identity of the object, which is a qualitative property. To probe a child's understanding of identity in this example, we can ask her, "Is the water in the different-shape glasses the same water that was in the two original glasses of the same shape?" Preoperational children have no difficulty with this question and, therefore, understand *object identity*, a qualitative attribute of objects. The second attribute of a physical object that can be assessed is the quantity of the object—in this case, whether the amount of the liquid before and after the pouring is the same. Preoperational children have great difficulty with object quantity questions and respond that the amounts of liquid in each of the two different-shaped glasses, though previously the same, are now different. Thus, these children can conserve the identity or quality but not the amount or quantity of objects; they are semi-logical.

This semi-logical pattern of reasoning among preoperational children has been demonstrated on a wide range of conservation tasks, such as those involving liquid, mass, volume, and area (see Figure 8-6). What processes may lead the child to make this error in judgment? Piaget proposed that preoperational children's semi-logical reasoning is explained by three characteristics: the inability to understand reversibility, the tendency to focus on the end state of an action and centration, which is closely related to egocentrism.

The child's inability to understand **reversibility** means that the child cannot mentally reverse or undo a given action. For example, preoperational children presented with the liquid-conservation task that we have outlined do not understand that if the water in the tall, thin glass is poured back into the short, wide glass, it will reach the same height it had before. This *inability to reverse a series of mental steps* is evident in many other responses of the child between 2 and 6 years old. For example, an investigator asks a 4-year-old boy,

"Have you a brother?"

The child replies, "Yes."

"What's his name?"

"Jim."

"Does Jim have a brother?"

"No." (Phillips, 1969, p. 61)

The preoperational thinker also tends to have an **ends-over-means focus**; that is, the child focuses on the end states rather than the means by which the end states were obtained. As a result, he tends to overlook the process or transformations by which the change occurs. Again, in the liquid-conservation task, the preoperational child ignores both the experimenter's action of pouring the water from one glass to the other and the rising water level in the glass. Instead, the child focuses on the end state of the process—that is, the high water level in the tall container that now appears different from the water level in the short container.

1. **Number**

Experimenter shows child two rows of plastic chips. Child agrees there are the same number of chips in each row.

Experimenter increases length of one row by adding space between chips (or by squeezing other row) and asks child whether each row still has the same number of chips.

2. **Mass, or substance**

Experimenter presents child with two identical balls of clay or Plasticene. Child agrees that each has the same amount of clay.

Experimenter rolls one ball into breadstick or sausage form and asks child whether the two objects still have the same amount of clay.

3. **Length**

Experimenter places two sticks of equal length before child, who agrees they are of the same length.

Experimenter moves one of the sticks to the right and asks child whether sticks are still of the same length.

4. **Liquids**

Experimenter fills two glasses of the same size and shape to the same level with water. Child agrees each glass has the same amount of water.

Experimenter pours the water in one of the glasses into a taller, thinner glass and asks child if each glass with water in it now contains the same amount of water.

5. **Area**

Experimenter shows child two sheets of cardboard, on each of which square blocks are placed in identical positions. Child agrees that each sheet has the same amount of open (uncovered) area.

Experimenter then scatters the blocks about one of the cardboard sheets and asks child whether the two sheets now have the same amount of open area.

6. **Weight**

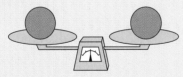   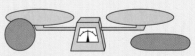

Experimenter places two balls of clay of the same size on a scale and asks the child if they weigh the same.

Experimenter then reshapes one ball and, before replacing it on the scale, asks the child if the two pieces of clay still weigh the same or if one weighs more.

7. **Volume**

Experimenter drops each of two balls of clay of the same size into two glasses of water; the child has already agreed that the glasses have the same amount of water.

Experimenter removes one piece of clay, reshapes it, and, before putting it back into the glass, asks the child if the water level will be higher or lower than or the same as the water level in the other glass.

Figure 8-6

Some Piagetian tests of conservation

These tests are discussed at further length in the text.

Source: Based on Lefrancois, 1973.

centration

Centring one's attention on only one dimension or characteristic of an object or situation.

Finally, **centration** in thinking leads preoperational children to centre their attention on only one dimension of an object or situation. In our test example, children tend to base their reasons for why they think the amount of water in the containers is no longer equal on either the height of the water or the width of the glass. This tendency prevents the child from grasping the notion of conservation, which involves several changes simultaneously.

Cross-cultural studies have found considerable variation in the age at which children acquire the concept of conservation and variation in the ages at which they acquire the concept with respect to various substances (Mishra, 1997; Rogoff, 2003). In Western societies, in general, children achieve conservation of liquids, mass, and length somewhere between the ages of 6 and 7; they can conserve number a little earlier, by about age 6. Understanding conservation of weight, area, and volume takes somewhat longer, emerging, respectively, at about age 9, between 9 and 10, and after age 11. Cultural variation in the onset of these particular conservation abilities has been linked to the experiences children have with these particular abilities in different communities (Dasen, 1975; Gardiner & Kosmitzki, 2008). For example, children who live in communities in Mexico, where adults make clay pots for a living, develop conservation of mass earlier than children who do not live in such communities (Price-Williams et al., 1969). Such patterns raise interesting questions about the connection between cultural practices and the development of cognitive skills (Goodnow et al., 1995).

LO5 The Stage of Concrete Operations

concrete operations stage

Period in which the child acquires such concepts as conservation and classification and can reason logically.

The **concrete operations stage** extends from about the age of 7 to 11 or 12. At this time, children understand reversibility and are able to attend to more than one dimension of a problem at a time. They are able to conserve quantity and to classify or group things in a logical way. However, their thinking at this point is tied to concrete reality; that is, they can solve problems only if the objects necessary for problem solution are physically present. For example, suppose we show a child three kids of varying heights in differently composed pairs. In pair 1, the child sees that Melissa is taller than Zoe, and in pair 2, she sees that Zoe is taller than Fabiana. Without seeing Melissa and Fabiana together, the child can reason that Melissa is taller than both Zoe and Fabiana. If, however, instead of presenting the three girls physically, we present the problem to our participant verbally, as "Melissa is taller than Zoe and Zoe is taller than Fabiana; who is the tallest of the three?" the concrete operational child will have difficulty solving the problem.

Children also make advances in the ability to classify or sort objects according to combinations of several attributes. For example, the child can sort a group of flowers into a major class (types of flowers) and a subclass (flower colours within these types): yellow roses, yellow tulips, yellow daisies, red roses, red tulips, and red daisies (Fischer & Roberts, 1986).

Again, developmentalists have questioned whether the solution to such problems is based on the underlying changes in mental operations that Piaget proposed. Some investigators have suggested that in tests of inference, like judging the relative heights of several sticks based on a verbal statement, what poses difficulty for the concrete operational child is not the lack of physical stimuli but the lack of memory capacity. To test this idea, Bryant and Trabasso (1971) showed that when memory demands of a task are limited, concrete operational children can make logical inferences without having the physical materials present.

Although Piaget thought that the ability to classify develops during the preoperational and concrete operational periods, we now have evidence that even infants can place objects into categories on the basis of perceptual similarities (e.g., Arterberry & Bornstein, 2002; Rakison & Oakes, 2003). Researchers have shown that babies as young as 3 to 4 months old can form categories of animals, such as a category with dogs and cats but not with birds (Cohen & Cashon, 2006; Haith & Benson, 1998; Mareschal, Powell, & Volein, 2003; Mareschal, Quinn, & French, 2002), or categories for even more complex concepts like for spatial relations such as containment and "between" (Casasola, Cohen, & Chiarello, 2003; Quinn et al., 2003). For instance, one study (Behl-Chadra, 1996), using visual preferential looking measures, found that 3- to 4-month-old infants could form a category that included domestic cats, but excluded birds, dogs, and horses. In addition, the babies are able to categorize animals and vehicles based on perceptual similarities and also based on different types of motion—for example, the motion of a dog versus the motion of a car (Arterberry & Bornstein, 2001; Raikson, 2007). Apparently, children can classify objects at a much earlier age and in a more sophisticated fashion than Piaget believed possible.

Researchers who have undertaken cross-cultural studies of Piagetian concepts associated with concrete operations have demonstrated the importance of culture in determining what concepts will be learned and when. This research indicates that cognitive competence is intricately related to the cultural context in which development occurs (Cole, 2006; Rogoff, 2003; Shweder et al., 2006). If we define intelligence as adaptation to the environment, as did Piaget, it is not surprising that cognitive development differs in some ways in cultures with different environments, expectations, and needs. Some cultures emphasize the need to learn certain kinds of concepts while others stress other kinds. Even when cultures emphasize similar concepts, the timing of this emphasis—in terms of when opportunities are provided for children that support the development of these skills—may vary.

Pierre Dasen (1984) has examined these ideas by comparing the performance of children of two very different cultures on tasks of the conservation of liquids and of horizontality (the latter requires the child to understand that when a vessel containing a liquid is tilted at various angles the surface plane of the water will always be horizontal). Dasen found interesting differences on these tasks across these two groups. Whereas 90 percent of Inuit children, of Cape Dorset in Nunavut Territory understood horizontality by the age of 8 (100 percent by age 12), only 60 percent grasped the conservation of liquids even by the age of 15 (see Figure 8-7a on the next page). In contrast, only 50 percent of Baoulé children, of Côte d'Ivoire, understood horizontality by age 15, but 100 percent had an understanding of the conservation of liquids by the age of 10 (see Figure 8-7b). Commenting on these results, Dasen suggests that people develop "those skills and concepts that are useful in the daily activities required" in their eco-cultural settings. The Inuit, who are nomadic hunter-gatherers, value spatial skills and, as a result, acquire ideas like horizontality quite quickly, but they have less experience with quantitative comparisons. The Baoulé, on the other hand, are an agricultural people who, because they produce food, store it, and exchange it in the markets, have considerable experience with quantitative concepts, especially those concepts involved in measurement.

As these results suggest, culture alters the cognitive experiences children have and the *rate* at which children learn certain types of knowledge, including the concepts Piaget described in relation to the stage of concrete operations.

The Stage of Formal Operations

How do thought processes in the **formal operations stage**, which begins at 11 or 12, differ from those typical of the concrete operations stage? Perhaps the most significant changes are in flexibility and complexity of the thought process, the use of mental hypothesis testing, and the ability to entertain many possible alternatives when solving problems (Kuhn & Franklin, 2006).

One particularly interesting change is the ability to think abstractly and understand and even solve problems that have no basis in reality. For example, consider the problem, "If all blue people live in red houses, are all people who live in red houses blue?"

formal operations stage

The period in which the child becomes capable of flexible and abstract thought, complex reasoning, and hypothesis testing.

Figure 8-7

Conservation among Inuit and Baoulé children

Achievement of the concepts of horizontality and the conservation of liquids between the ages of 6 and 15 years among (a) Inuit children of Nunavut Territory and (b) Baoulé children of Côte d'Ivoire.

Source: Adapted from Dasen, 1984.

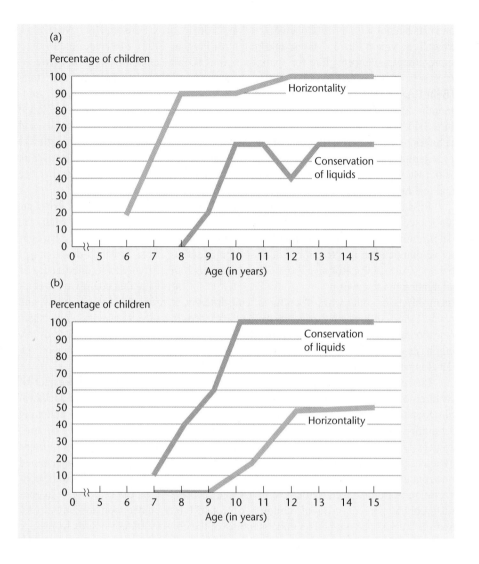

The concrete operational child would have difficulty getting beyond the fact that there is no such thing as blue people. In contrast, the child, or, more accurately, the young adolescent, in the stage of formal operations can move beyond the unrealistic content to focus on applying logical solutions to the question posed. Consequently, in the stage of formal operations, the thinker's understanding and examination of the world is not confined to reality. Rather, young adolescents are able to think of and contrast both real and ideal states of the world. They can consider different ways of arranging the world; for instance, they can think about and discuss philosophical issues such as truth and justice, and they can imagine alternative lifestyles and universes. Not surprisingly, this is the stage when science fiction becomes of interest.

Children in this stage are also able to review several possible alternatives or hypotheses in a problem-solving situation. Inhelder and Piaget (1958) used a task involving a problem in physics to illustrate the differences in problem solving in the stages of concrete and formal operations. In this task, participants are shown an assortment of objects and a container of water and asked to use these materials to find an explanation for why some objects float and others do not. What the children are actually being asked is to derive Archimedes' law of floating bodies, which states that an object will float if its weight per unit (or density) is less than that of water. Thus, if two objects are of equal weight, the larger object is more likely to float than the smaller. Concrete operational children may focus on weight or size as a reason things float or sink; for instance, they may say that the heavier or bigger objects are, the more likely they are to sink. They may even arrive at a double classification that involves the categories large and heavy, large and light, small and heavy, or small and light. However, they are still unable to consider alternatives not directly observable in the physical world. For example, they cannot predict that a large and heavy piece of wood will float even though it is bigger and heavier than a small lead weight.

In contrast, in the formal operations stage, the child can free herself from the obvious cues of weight and size and conceptualize a variety of possible alternatives to arrive at the concept of density. Piaget describes the comments of a child who has just entered the period of formal operations grappling with this kind of problem: "It sinks because it is small, it isn't stretched enough. You would have to have something larger to stay at the surface, something of the same weight and which would have a greater extension" (Inhelder and Piaget, 1958, p. 38).

Developmentalists continue to debate Piaget's notions about cognitive development in this last stage and to search for the best ways to describe the child's thinking at this time (Keating, 1990; Kuhn & Franklin, 2006; Overton & Byrnes, 1991). Actually, not all adolescents or, for that matter, all adults in all societies reach the period of formal operations and achieve the flexibility in problem solving that Piaget associated with this period (Kuhn & Franklin, 2006). Unlike concrete operational thought, which seems to be acquired to some degree in all societies, the attainment of formal operations is strongly influenced by culture (Bond, 1998; Rogoff, 2003). In cultures that do not emphasize symbolic skills or in which educational experiences are limited, the stage of formal operations may occur late in development or may even be absent (Moshman, 1998). Even in Western communities in which symbolic skills and educational attainment are highly valued and available, adolescents and adults are more likely to achieve the capacity for logical abstract reasoning within their particular areas of interest or expertise than in other domains. For instance, abstract thinking has been documented in traditional cultures in tasks of much importance to the group, such as court cases related to land disputes and navigating on the open seas (Gladwin, 1970; Hutchins, 1980). Thomas Gladwin found that seafarers in traditional communities in Micronesia use star charts and other complex techniques to construct elaborate and sophisticated routes that enable them to transverse the ocean and even cross the equator. In addition, scientific training in such subjects as physics, chemistry, and the philosophy of logic has been found to be associated with greater ability to use formal operations (Kuhn & Franklin, 2006). Thus, formal operational thinking is strongly tied to social and cultural experiences.

PIAGETIAN CONCEPTS AND SOCIAL COGNITION

LO6

Although Piaget concentrated on the individual's cognitive development, a number of his ideas have stimulated research on the development of social cognition. His concept of object permanence, for example, has relevance for the development of self-recognition—conceiving of the self as an entity distinct from the environment and other people—and the development of attachment, or a deep emotional connection to another person. Piaget's views on egocentrism and perspective taking also have implications for the development of social cognition. Because understanding of the self and others has tremendous consequences for children's development, we discuss it here.

The Self as Distinct from Others

A central component in the development of social cognition is differentiation of the self from the environment, including other human beings (Harter, 2006). This differentiation process has its roots in early infancy (Rochat, 2001; Rochat & Striano, 2000), when babies "see" people and objects as behaving differently. In fact, young babies seem to expect certain behaviours from people. If you face a 2-month-old child without moving or speaking, the infant will become distressed (Adamsom & Frick, 2003), a finding that has also been replicated cross-culturally (Hsu & Jeng, 2008). Infants even come to expect that other people will behave differently toward people and objects (Legerstee, Barna, & DiAdamo, 2000)—talking is accepted by the infant as a normal mode of interaction with a person and reaching is a typical interaction with an object.

Within the first few months of life, infants also learn to differentiate their own movements from the movements of another person (Rochat & Morgan, 1995; Schmuckler & Fairhall, 2001; Schmuckler & Jewell, 2007). In one study, Schmuckler (1996b) had 5-month-old infants manually explore an unseen object hidden inside a box. While feeling this object, they watched two video monitors, one containing an online picture of their own unseen limb (produced by placing a video camera inside the box), while the other showed a previously recorded videotape of a different infant's hand (see Figure 8-8). In this situation, infants showed that they distinguished between these two displays by looking more at the display of the other child. According to these researchers, the fact that infants can discriminate between the two displays indicates a form of self-recognition early in life, which could act as the beginning of the child's developing self-concept.

With development, the child's view of herself becomes more differentiated. As we saw in Chapter 6, very young infants will gaze at their reflections in a mirror, but it is not until the second year of life that children recognize their own images in a mirror. Recall that Piaget said children achieve a full understanding of object permanence some time between the ages of 1½ and 2 years, about the same time that they first see

Figure 8-8

Experiment showing that infants distinguish their own movements from others

A schematic drawing of the experimental set-up used by Schmuckler and colleagues (Schmuckler, 1996; Schmuckler & Fairhall, 2001). Infants place a limb (e.g., their hand) inside a box containing a video camera. This camera then provides an online image of the child's limb to one of the two video monitors, while the other monitor shows the limb of a different child. Using the set-up, these researchers were able to demonstrate that even 5-month-old infants appeared to distinguish their own movements from those of another child.

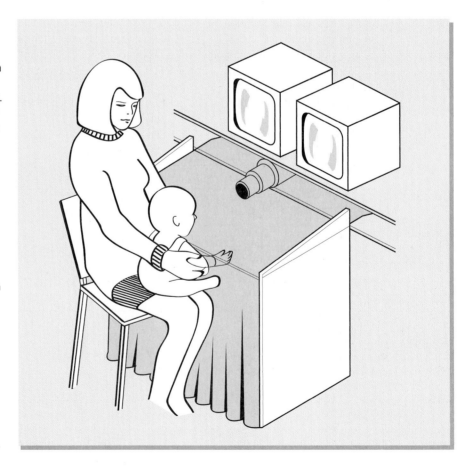

their mirror images as themselves. An understanding of object permanence may be a prerequisite for self-recognition.

Also, with development, the child's view of herself includes more information about the self, such as values, motives, intentions, and other psychological experiences. Whereas preschool children (age 5 or younger) tend to define themselves mainly by physical attributes or favourite activities (e.g., *I'm 4 years old; I like to swim*) at around 7 or 8 (Piaget's stage of concrete operations), children begin to describe themselves in more complex terms that focus on abilities and interpersonal characteristics, such as *smart* and *nice* (Harter, 2006). The growing ability to think in the abstract allows the adolescent (from 11 or 12 onwards) to create a more integrated and complex view of the self and his role in society (Harter, 2006).

Role Taking: Understanding Others' Perspectives

With development, children become less egocentric and more able to understand the thoughts and perspectives of others (Yuill & Pearson, 1998). Some developmentalists argue that the shift away from an egocentric orientation underlies improved communication skill as well as the development of moral standards and prosocial behaviours (Eisenberg et al., 2006; Harter, 2006). The development of these skills is basic to the child's socialization, and we will return to this topic in greater detail in Chapter 14.

Selman and his colleagues have linked cognitive development and social perspective taking over a series of five distinct stages (see Table 8-3) (Selman, 1980; Selman & Byrne, 1974; Selman & Jacquette, 1978). These stages begin with the child's egocentric behaviour and then proceed into more complex social understanding and reasoning. As children move through these stages, they learn not only to differentiate between their own perspectives and those of others but to understand others' views and the relations

Table 8-3

Role taking: Developing the ability to take different perspectives

Stage 0 Egocentric Perspective
The child does not distinguish his own perspective from that of others nor recognize that another person may interpret experiences differently.

Stage 1 Differentiated Perspective
The child realizes that she and others may have either the same or a different perspective. Although she is concerned with the uniqueness of each person's cognitions, she cannot judge accurately what the other person's perspective may be.

Stage 2 Reciprocal Perspective
Because the child can see himself from another's perspective and knows the other person can do the same thing, he can anticipate and consider another's thoughts and feelings.

Stage 3 Mutual Perspectives
Now the child can view her own perspective; a peer's perspective; and their shared, or mutual perspective, from the viewpoint of a third person. For example, she can think of how a parent, teacher, or other peer might view both her and her friend's perspectives as well as their mutual perspective.

Stage 4 Societal or In-Depth Perspectives
Children (and adults) can see networks of perspectives, such as the societal, Conservative Party, or African-Canadian point of view. People understand that these varying perspectives not only exist in awareness but involve deeper, perhaps unconscious, representations, such as feelings and values.

Source: Adapted from Selman & Jacquette, 1978.

between those views and their own. Although there are normative patterns in the development of perspective taking, some children develop these abilities earlier than others (see Figure 8-9). What kinds of factors are related to these individual differences? As we discuss in Chapter 14, some studies have found positive relations between prosocial behaviour, such as helping and sharing, and role-taking skills (Eisenberg, 1992; Eisenberg et al., 2006).

Theory of Mind

theory of mind

Understanding of the mind and how it works.

The area of study known as **theory of mind** focuses on when and how children come to understand the mind. This research covers topics ranging from the development of the ability to distinguish appearance from reality to children's understanding of dreams, beliefs, intentions, desires, and deception (Baird & Astington, 2005; Harris, 2006). Researchers are also interested in when and how children come to think of the self and other people as psychological beings.

A number of studies have explored when it is that children begin to understand the thinking of other people. A task that has been used often to study this question is the *false-belief task* (Wimmer & Perner, 1983), which involves telling a child a story and then asking him what a character in the story thinks. For example, the child will be told a story about a young boy named Maxi who puts his candy in a cupboard in the kitchen and then goes into another room to play. When Maxi is off playing, his mother moves his candy from the cupboard to a drawer. After a while, Maxi returns and wants his candy. At this point, the researcher would ask the child where Maxi will look for his candy. Older preschoolers, 4- to 5-year-old children, typically say that Maxi will search in the cupboard, indicating that they assume Maxi will look where he believes the candy is, not where they themselves know the candy to be. In other words, they attribute a belief, or mental state, to Maxi and use this belief as a basis for their response. To answer in this way, the child needs to hold two understandings or representations of

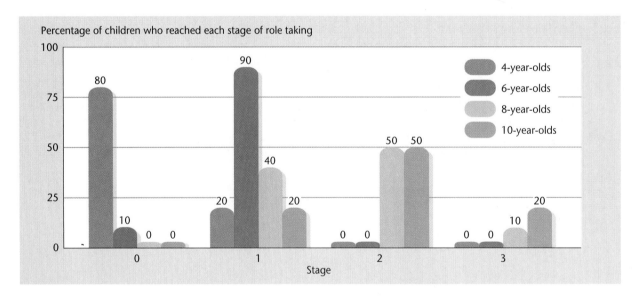

Figure 8-9

Role taking at different ages

Between the ages of 4 and 6 years, children take the enormous step of moving from egocentricity to a differentiated perspective. From here on, progress in appreciating others' views is less dramatic but steady.

Source: Based on Selman & Byrne, 1974.

the situation in his mind simultaneously: what the child himself knows to be true and what Maxi believes to be true. Three-year-old children respond quite differently; they say that Maxi will look for the candy in the drawer where his mother put it. In other words, the child has his own belief about where the candy is based on his knowledge and he is unable to separate his understanding from the mental state of the child in the story. Thus, the child's answer represents his own belief about where the candy is.

These results suggest that our understanding of mental states, and the role these states play in guiding behaviour, develops over the years of early childhood. Although this basic pattern of results has been replicated in a wide range of studies (Wellman et al., 2001), the findings have been contested on a number of grounds (Mitchell, 1997). Some investigators have also pointed out that there may be a difference between the development of a theory of mind in relation to fictional information, as in pretend play, and the development of an understanding of states of knowledge, such as false beliefs (Lillard, 1993). At present, it appears that this complex ability originates early in life, and it exists in almost all people—the main exception being children with autism (Baron-Cohen, 2000; Lillard, 2006). It seems that human beings have a special ability to identify with other human beings as mental agents with needs, desires, and intentions that guide their behaviour. The potential for interacting with, and learning from, others that this capability makes possible is profound (Carpendale & Lewis, 2006; Tomasello et al., 2005).

More recently, researchers have been finding that young children's inability to deal with false belief situations is not as straightforward as the early research suggested. Michael Chandler and Suzanne Hala (Chandler & Hala, 1995; Hala & Chandler, 1996), for example, propose that if children are given a personal interest in understanding the mental states of others, even 3-year-olds are able to demonstrate a grasp of the possibility of false beliefs.

According to these researchers, the problem with the more typical false-belief situation as outlined above is that children simply hear about (or watch) a previously unknown story character who has a false belief. In contrast, Chandler and Hala believe that a critical factor for children's understanding of false belief is whether the goal in creating a false belief is in keeping with their own personal interests, as opposed to simply being a bystander who happens to see a false-belief situation created.

To test this idea, Chandler and Hala (1994; Hala & Chandler, 1996) ran a series of experiments in which the children were involved themselves in moving the hidden object by playing a hiding game with two experimenters. When one of the experimenters left the room, the child was encouraged by the remaining experimenter to move the object from its current location to a new one, thus becoming an active participant in producing a false belief. Under these conditions, Chandler and Hala report that even 3-year-olds correctly predict that the second experimenter will mistakenly think the object still resides in its original location.

Leaving aside the issue of whether children's knowledge of other people's mental states undergoes its most dramatic change at 3 versus 4 to 5 years, what does seem clear is that between the ages of 3 and 5 years, children begin to understand that people have mental representational states. Children of this age think of the mind as a recorder that simply copies information from the world, with beliefs created by what we see, hear, and touch (Lalonde & Chandler, 2002). It is not until children are 6 to 7 years old, though, that they begin to appreciate beliefs as interpretations of the world and that people can interpret the same thing differently (Carpendale & Chandler, 1988), although there has been some recent evidence that even adults, if tested with sensitive enough measures, can show problems with false-belief reasoning (Birch & Bloom, 2007). Although there is still some debate as to the exact interpretative nature of the understanding of representations at young ages (Carpendale & Chandler, 1996), it seems clear that children do understand the notion of representational states.

Do Sociocultural Experiences Influence the Development of Social Cognition?

Although Piaget's theory has implications for research on the development of social cognition, Piaget's own theoretical development along these lines was limited. In addition, research indicating that the development of social cognition may be modified by social and cultural factors also challenges the links between Piaget's theory and the development of social cognition (Cole, 2006; Dasen, 1984). For instance, from early to middle childhood, children's self-constructs become increasingly aligned with the values of their cultural community, such as in terms of the roles and preferences they have. Along these lines, North American children of European descent tend to describe their memories in relation to their own feelings and experiences and Chinese-Canadian children tend to emphasize social roles and responsibilities (Wang, 2004).

Although most research on children's theory of mind has been conducted with children in Western, middle-class communities in which discussions about the mind and what people think are common, research has examined both social and cultural contributions to the development of a theory of mind. Children in Western middle-class communities are often encouraged by their parents to talk about the mind (e.g., when parents ask children what they or others are thinking about). However, some styles of parenting, a topic covered in Chapter 11, may affect this development. Vinden (2001) found lower rates of social understanding among North American children of European descent who had authoritarian parents. Siblings may also play an important role in this developmental process.

Perner and colleagues (1994) showed that young children who have more siblings with whom they interact perform better on false-belief tasks. However, the ages of the siblings matter. Children with siblings (who are not their twin) performed better on theory of mind tasks than children who were twins and had no other siblings (Cassidy et al., 2005). The extent to which children in immigrant Latino families who informally translate for their parents in their negotiations with doctors, employers, or government officials is related to theory of mind as well. This cultural brokering experience may increase children's awareness of the mental states of others and the links between mental states and social behaviour—central aspects of theory of mind (Harris, 2006).

Are changes in children's understanding of mind universal? That is, do these changes appear in all cultures? Avis and Harris (1991) conducted a study of children's reasoning about people's beliefs and desires in the Baka community, hunter-gatherers who live in central Africa. The researchers found that by 5 years of age, most of the children they studied were able to predict correctly what an adult would find in a container that they had left for a moment and that, while they were gone, had been emptied. These results are consistent with other findings that show successful performance by preschool-age children in non-Western communities on theory of mind tasks (Harris, 2006). Although variation both within and across cultures in the development of theory of mind have been shown (Lillard, 1998), the research indicates that during childhood an important set of capabilities known as theory of mind develops and that cultural experiences around the world support this process.

For Thought and Discussion

1. What do you think of Baillargeon's evidence of object permanence in young infants? Are the abilities that she describes for young infants the same in crucial respects to the types of capabilities in which Piaget was interested? In what way are they the same or different? And even if one accepts the possibility that object permanence is achieved earlier than Piaget suggested, does this necessarily mean that this ability is innate, as Baillargeon and others would have one believe?

2. As suggested in the text, a number of researchers have challenged the idea that infants have sophisticated cognitive abilities. This raises the general question of what one should take as evidence for cognitive competency. Is it critical that infants show such abilities in the same way as adults? Do they need to verbalize such knowledge? Do they need to act on such knowledge in some way?

3. Do you think that recognizing one's own movement on a television screen actually demonstrates knowledge of the self? How is such preferential looking related to self-concept?

AN EVALUATION OF PIAGET'S THEORY

Piaget's theory has a valuable place in the study of cognitive development. However, like every theory, it has strengths and limitations, which we review as a prelude to our overall assessment of the theory.

Strengths of the Theory

In Chapter 1, we pointed out that theories are useful for two reasons: They integrate a wide array of information and they lead to new research by stimulating hypotheses and defining new areas of study. Piaget's theory achieved both these goals. With his stage model and his underlying concepts, such as schemas, cognitive organization, and adaptation, Piaget integrated a broad spectrum of concepts of the physical world—such as conservation, classification, and number—into a single theory. In addition, Piaget's theory has stimulated an enormous amount of research. According to Miller (2002), the most important ideas that Piaget introduced to the field are that the child actively seeks and constructs knowledge, that cognitive development unfolds over a series of qualitatively different stages, and that in the first two years of life, cognition is based on the child's perceptual-motor system.

Piaget was an extraordinary observer of human behaviour. His observations described behaviours that continue to intrigue developmental psychologists. Why do infants behave as if objects disappear when they go out of sight? Why do preschoolers not conserve the quantities of substances when their shapes or appearances are altered? Why is it that school-age children can think logically about problems, even difficult problems, but when these problems are abstract (concrete materials are not available), they cannot use their skills at logical thought?

Limitations of the Theory

DID PIAGET JUDGE THE CHILD'S ABILITIES ACCURATELY?

As we discussed, a great deal of research has suggested that infants and children may know a lot more than Piaget thought. In other words, Piaget may have underestimated the timing or onset of children's cognitive abilities. For instance, infants seen to understand some aspects of object permanence quite early (Cohen & Cashon, 2006) and many children in the preoperational and concrete operational periods seem to be more cognitively advanced than Piaget's theory would suggest (Halford & Andrews, 2006). However, it remains an open question whether showing cognitive abilities at an earlier age than Piaget proposed represents a major challenge to his theory. After all, Piaget was less concerned with the age of onset of the abilities he studied than with their order of appearance.

Before leaving this issue, it should be noted that others have risen to the defence of Piaget's theory. According to these researchers, it is important to realize that although some researchers have had great success in demonstrating that children younger than those predicted by Piaget will actually solve many of these puzzles when the task is changed and "simplified," one concern with such changes is that making the task easier sometimes actually transforms the task into one that is quite different and that can be solved with a different form of reasoning.

As an example, think back to Borke's (1975) study on egocentrism that we discussed earlier. According to Michael Chapman, a well-known Piagetian scholar from the University of British Columbia, Borke's simplification of Piaget's task allows children to solve this problem by observing which object is closest to the observer and then turning the array until that object is close to themselves (Chapman, 1988). According to Chapman, this reasoning is simply different from that investigated by Piaget, who wished to explore children's abilities to produce different perspectives by transformations of left, right, back, and front. Similar objections regarding how changing the nature of the task actually changes the type of reasoning required to solve the task can be offered for Gelman's work on conservation of number that we discussed earlier or for Bryant and Trabasso's (1971) exemplary work on classification (Chapman, 1988).

DOES COGNITIVE DEVELOPMENT PROCEED IN STAGES?

According to Piaget, children's cognitive development undergoes qualitative shifts from one stage to another, and these stages are presumed to follow each other in an invariant order. Moreover, the child cannot proceed to the next stage until she has mastered the ways of thinking characteristic of the current stage she is in.

Recent evidence (Siegler & Alibali, 2005) suggests that cognitive development may not occur in the stage-like steps that Piaget proposed. How we describe changes in children's thinking, and whether or not they are called stages, depends in large measure on the way in which change is studied. The focus of a study and especially the length of time between two or more measurement points are important. For example, if we evaluate a child's abilities at six-month intervals or even years apart, changes in these abilities may seem discontinuous, as Piaget found. However, if we look closely at the changes that occur within a shorter period of time, an hour or a day or even across several weeks—let's say as a child tries to solve a particular problem—we find that the child's progress appears more gradual and continuous.

One difficulty in knowing for sure whether cognitive development is best described as a series of stages is due to the fact that children in the concrete operational stage do not acquire the ability to conserve all types of substances at the same age. This unevenness in development, which Piaget called **horizontal décalage** (the French word *décalage* can be translated as "time lag"), is problematic for his stage theory. The idea of a stage implies that the child in a particular stage should be consistent in her thinking across similar types of problems. Piaget proposed that horizontal décalage reflects the differing degrees of abstraction required to understand the conservation of particular objects or substances. For example, he suggested that conserving mass requires the fewest abstract operations, whereas conserving volume requires the most; as a result, conservation of mass is acquired earlier.

Interestingly, findings from studies in which conservation tasks have been changed to be more accessible to children show that if we present children with simpler ver-

horizontal décalage

The term Piaget used to describe unevenness in children's thinking within a particular stage; for example, in developing an understanding of conservation, children conserve different objects or substances at different ages.

sions of these tasks or teach them to attend to all the relevant aspects of the task, they can often demonstrate their understanding of conservation. For instance, in the study in Mexico of the children of potters, mentioned previously, those children who initially performed poorly on conservation tasks that were conducted with materials unfamiliar to them went on to perform quite well on a test of conservation of mass when they were dealing with familiar materials, such as the clay and other substances used in making pottery (Price-Williams et al., 1969). To test the notion that failure to conserve may occur because the child attends to some irrelevant aspect of the stimulus, such as shape, length, or height, Jerome Bruner (1966) presented preoperational children with a modification of Piaget's liquid-conservation task. As the experimenters poured the water from the short glass to the tall glass, they placed a screen in front of the tall glass. When the distracting changes in the height and width of the water column were not visible to the children, most were able to conserve. In sum, if a task is simplified or made more comprehensible, children can conserve at earlier ages than Piaget suspected. This type of research suggests that Piaget's notion of stages requires further study and explanation.

HOW DOES THE SOCIO-EMOTIONAL AND CULTURAL CONTEXT OF COGNITIVE DEVELOPMENT FIT WITH PIAGET'S THEORY?

Although Piaget's theory did not include social, emotional, and cultural contributions to cognitive development in any central way, research indicates that cognitive development, including Piagetian-based concepts, may be modified by cultural, social, and other experiential factors (Cole, 2006; Dasen, 1984). We discussed contributions of the social and cultural context to many aspects of Piaget's theory. Except in his theory of children's moral development (see Chapter 14), Piaget also did not consider children's emotional states and emotional development in relation to cognitive development. Additionally, in spite of Piaget's pessimism about the child's ability to proceed more quickly through the stages as a result of instruction, the evidence is now clear that active intervention, such as training in problem-solving strategies—a specialized form of social experience, can accelerate cognitive development (Gelman & Baillargeon, 1983; Siegler & Alibali, 2005).

Despite these theoretical limitations, Piaget's ideas have relevance to both education and counselling, which may, in turn, affect children's social and emotional functioning. There is a long history of connections between Piaget's theory and educational practice. Piaget admired the ideas of Maria Montessori, especially her views on the close relation between thought and action (Lillard, 2005). He drew on these ideas in his theory and even conducted many of his observations of young children's thinking at a modified Montessori school in Switzerland. In addition, approaches to child counselling may be informed by Piaget's ideas. Consider how Piaget's theory could be helpful in counselling a young child who is struggling with his parents' divorce or a parent's death. Would a preoperational child be likely to interpret such situations egocentrically and perhaps blame himself for his parents' divorce? Or would a preoperational child, because of limited understanding of the distinction between what is real and what is not, be prone to wishful thinking, perhaps believing that if he just wished hard enough, his deceased parent would come back to life? Although Piaget did not deal directly with such issues, clearly, an understanding of the capabilities and limitations associated with the different stages of thinking that he described could help guide an educator or therapist as she works with children in need.

Overall Assessment

Despite these new findings and their resulting criticisms, Piaget's theory has had an enormous impact on the study of the child's development of cognitive skills. In fact, his theory was a major force in introducing cognition into developmental research in the latter half of the twentieth century (Beilin, 1992). Although his theorizing and methodology were sometimes flawed, Piaget asked, and answered, important questions in innovative ways, and his ideas have stimulated a vast amount of research and theorizing by other behavioural scientists. If one test of the worth of a theory is its ability to generate interesting ideas for further study, Piaget's theory, without question, passes this test with flying colours.

For Thought and Discussion

1. Even if Piaget got all the ages wrong in his theory, does this necessarily mean that his theory is flawed? What, in fact, is the critical aspect of Piagetian theory—the ages or the sequential process?

2. How critical is it that Piaget did not specifically address such subjects as shame and guilt? Is Piaget obligated to apply this theory to as many areas as possible? More generally, is it important that a theory apply widely, across many different areas?

3. Given all that you know about Piaget, does cognitive development proceed in stages, or is it continuous? What evidence can you provide for each answer?

Lev Vygotsky, shown here, is another developmental theorist who was interested in children's thinking. Although Vygotsky's work has been relatively unknown in the West until recent times, his ideas represent an important challenge to Piagetian thought and have proven influential, particularly in educational contexts.

Lev Vygotsky

VYGOTSKY'S SOCIOCULTURAL THEORY OF COGNITIVE DEVELOPMENT LO8

The developmental theory put forth by Russian psychologist Lev S. Vygotsky (1896–1934) focuses on the influence of the social and cultural world on cognitive development (Vygotsky, 1978). Vygotsky's interest in the sociocultural context of cognitive development was undoubtedly informed by his own experience growing up in the early twentieth century, which was a time of tumultuous social change in Russia (Kozulin, 1990). When Vygotsky was young, Czar Nichoas ruled Russia and the social divisions within the society were clearly marked. These divisions had enormous effects on the lives of the Russian people, and Jews, like Vygotsky, were treated particularly badly. In 1917, the year Vygotsky graduated from Moscow University, the Russian Revolution began and the entire society was in upheaval. After the revolution, as Vygotsky launched his career as a psychologist and developed his theory, civil war and famine ravaged the country, and the entire social structure of the nation changed dramatically. Although some aspects of Vygotsky's life improved, others did not. At the time of his death at age 37 from tuberculosis, he had fallen into political disfavour in Stalinist Russia and his work was banned. As a result, it was not until the late 1970s that psychologists in North America and other parts of the world began to explore Vygotsky's ideas (Wertsch & Tulviste, 1992).

Vygotsky's view of cognitive development is called a sociocultural approach because it proposes that cognitive development is largely the result of children's interaction with more experienced members of their culture, such as parents, teachers, and older children. As the child and her partners solve problems together, the child has opportunities to participate in actions that extend beyond her current individual capabilities. Through these experiences, the child learns to function on her own in a more advanced intellectual way. Although Vygotsky held that each child is born with a set of innate capabilities, such as attention, perception, and memory, he believed that input from the child's social and cultural worlds, in the form of interactions with more experienced adults and peers, directs these basic capabilities toward more complex, higher-order cognitive functions. Because this theory puts great emphasis on the role of social interaction in cognitive development, Vygotsky held that language has a particularly important effect on the child's intellectual development.

Vygotsky was especially interested in the social and cultural processes that support cognitive development. He described changes in the ways that children interact with other people as well as with the psychological tools and symbol systems of a culture that can be used to support and extend cognition, which he called **mediators**. Across development, children begin to learn to use different types of mediators—such as language, counting, mnemonic devices, algebraic symbols, art, and writing. Mediators permit the child to become more effective in solving problems and understanding the world. For Vygotsky, what was particularly important about mediators is that they come from, and thereby represent, the social and cultural context of development. As the child develops competence with these mediators and comes to use them in her thinking process, her thinking is increasingly aligned with the social and cultural context in which growth occurs. This enables the child to act effectively in her environment and interact in understandable and meaningful ways with other people in her culture.

We begin by discussing Vygotsky's notion of mental functions. Here, we will see how mediators enable the child to move to new levels of psychological processing. We then examine Vygotsky's concept of the *zone of proximal development*, a concept that expands on his idea that children learn through social interaction and has given rise to concepts such as scaffolding and guided participation. Lastly, we explore the influence of culture on children's cognitive development, learning, and use of language.

mediators

According to Vygotsky, psychological tools and signs, such as language, counting, mnemonic devices, algebraic symbols, art, and writing.

Elementary and Higher Mental Functions

In Vygotsky's theory, an important change in children's cognitive development occurs between elementary and higher mental functions. **Elementary mental functions**, such as basic attention, perception, and involuntary memory, are biological and emerge spontaneously. With development, elementary mental functions are transformed into **higher mental functions**, such as voluntary attention and intentional remembering. These functions involve the coordination of several cognitive processes. They also invite the use of mediators, such as language and other cognitive tools and symbol systems that children learn to use as they interact with other people in their culture.

Vygotsky's discussion of memory illustrates the difference between these two types of mental function. The elementary form of memory is constructed of images and impressions of events. It is similar to perception; it is also unintentional and the environment directly influences its content. The higher form of memory involves the use of signs to mediate memory functions; for instance, the child may write something down to help him remember it. Thus, he uses literacy as a tool to extend basic memory processes. Mediational systems, like language and other tools that aid intelligent action, such as literacy, are products of culture (Cole, 2006). Children learn to use these tools through the assistance of people in their culture who are more experienced than the child in their use. For Vygotsky, culture provides children with mediators that enable them to transform elementary mental functions into higher-level cognitive skills.

elementary mental functions

Functions which the child is endowed with by nature, including attention, perception, and memory.

higher mental functions

Functions that rely on mediators that have become increasingly sophisticated through the child's interaction with his environment.

The Zone of Proximal Development

Vygotsky's interest in the social origins of cognitive development led him to be less concerned with children's individual intellectual capabilities at a particular point in time than he was with the child's potential for intellectual growth through social experience (Daniels et al., 2007). To assess and describe this potential, Vygotsky proposed the notion of the **zone of proximal development (ZPD)**. The ZPD is defined as the difference between a child's "actual developmental level as determined by independent problem solving" and his "potential development as determined through problem solving under adult guidance or in collaboration with more capable peers" (Vygotsky, 1978, p. 86). The child's zone is, essentially, his region of sensitivity to learning in a particular area of cognitive development. When support for learning is targeted at the child's zone

zone of proximal development (ZPD)

According to Vygotsky, the difference between the developmental level a child has reached and the level she is potentially capable of reaching with the guidance or collaboration of a more skilled adult or peer.

of proximal development, the child's level of competence in this area changes through this social experience. The concept of the zone of proximal development is twofold: First, it describes how cognitive development may arise from social interaction with more skilled partners. Second, it provides a method of assessing children's intellectual potential under optimal conditions—that is, conditions tailored to the child's specific learning needs and built on the child's present capabilities.

Developmental researchers have demonstrated the value of this approach to cognitive development in studies of children's learning in many areas, including attention, memory, problem-solving skills, and planning. This research shows that children's understanding and cognitive skills can indeed be improved when adults or more skilled peers provide children with appropriate support for learning (Brown & Campione, 1998; Gauvain, 2001b; Rogoff, 1998). This is because when a child and a more skilled partner work together within a child's zone of proximal development, the child has the opportunity to engage in more advanced cognitive activities than she could undertake on her own. More experienced partners are able to describe or break down a cognitive activity, such as planning a series of errands, in ways that make it more understandable and accessible to the learner. More experienced partners also may model new strategies for solving the problem and encourage and support the child's involvement in the more difficult parts of the problem. Finally, the more experienced partner may take on or assume some of the more difficult parts of the problem so that the learner can concentrate on other aspects. For example, when an adult and child work together on a task that involves planning and carrying out errands in a model grocery store, the adult may keep track of how many errands have been planned, thereby allowing the child to concentrate on the best way to organize the remaining errands (Gauvain, 1992). In the study described in Box 8.1 on pages 330 and 331, children planned a series of errands with the help of an adult or a peer. Children learn different things when they collaborate with an adult versus a peer partner. Whereas adults provide children with more opportunities to learn about a task, peers can help children learn how to negotiate and share activities. The skills that can be obtained from both adult–child and peer interactions are important to social and cognitive development.

Vygotsky's theory has had considerable impact in the fields of psychology and education (Scrimsher & Tudge, 2003; Tudge & Scrimsher, 2003). **Scaffolding**, a form of instruction inspired by Vygotskian thinking, is a process by which the teacher adjusts the amount and type of support he offers to fit with the child's learning needs over the course of an interaction. In a classic demonstration, Wood, Bruner, and Ross (1976) taught 3- and 5-year-olds to build a pyramid out of interlocking wooden blocks through both verbal and physical scaffolding. This scaffolding involved modelling the steps, encouraging the child to put the blocks in the right places, and segmenting the task into more easily understood steps. By careful monitoring of each child's progress, the teacher was able to constantly adjust the task to make it manageable for the child and provide assistance when needed. In scaffolding, which has been demonstrated in a variety of tasks by later researchers (Kermani & Brenner, 2001; Pratt, Kerig, Cowan, & Cowan, 1988; Rogoff, 1990, 1998), as the child becomes more skilled, the teacher gradually reduces the amount of support he provides as the child becomes more skilled, so that the child can eventually do the task competently on her own.

One example of the application of these ideas to the classroom comes from the research or Annemarie Palincsar and Ann Brown (1984), who introduced an instructional technique called **reciprocal instruction** that is based on the zone of proximal development. This tutoring approach helps children in reading comprehension by having the learner collaborate with tutors who help children develop skills critical to comprehension, such as explication and elaboration. Brown and colleagues (Brown, 1994; Brown & Campione, 1998) have also developed a related classroom application called the **community of learners**. In this approach, children work together on sustained or long-range class projects, and the teacher serves as an expert guide who facilitates the process. The

scaffolding

Based on Vygotsky's thought, an instructional process in which the teacher continually adjusts the amount and type of support he offers as the child continues to develop more sophisticated skills.

reciprocal instruction

A tutoring approach based on the ideas of the *zone of proximal development* and *scaffolding*.

community of learners

An approach to classroom learning in which adults and children work together in shared activities, peers learn from each other, and the teacher serves as a guide.

teacher in the community of learners has two roles: one as a scaffolding agent for the students and the other as a participant in the learning process. The students, who vary in knowledge and ability, actively help each other and learn through their interchanges. A similar model has been applied in science education in Japan. Kobayashi (1994) describes a system that involves discussion among students in a classroom. Finally, arrangements for learning through social processes can occur outside school. Cole and his colleagues (1996) developed one of the most impressive and extensive programs for this sort, called the Fifth Dimension. This after-school, computer-based program was designed so that children could learn during collaborative activities that incorporate engaging and important cultural tools into a challenging but fun setting.

The zone of proximal development and related ideas describe children's learning in instructional situations. However, much of children's learning occurs as they participate in cultural activities. To describe this type of learning, Rogoff (1990) introduced the concept of **guided participation**. This approach highlights the fact that adults regularly support learning in the context of everyday activities by directing children's attention to, and involvement in, these activities. Sometimes, these activities are child-focused, such as in play or an organized game, but oftentimes they are adult activities in which the primary purpose is not to instruct children but to carry out the activity itself. In one form of guided participation, learning through **intent community participation**, Rogoff and her colleagues (2003) describe how children seek out ways to participate in authentic activities of their community alongside more experienced cultural members. For example, as a mother tries to bake a cake, her child may ask if he can help. The mother may agree and then structure the task in a way that gives the child some real responsibility in the activity, such as stirring the ingredients that the mother has assembled. She then carefully supervises the child and provides assistance when needed. In this example, the child initiates participation and engages in the activity as a meaningful participant—that is, his actions, though guided by the adult, contribute in meaningful ways to the activity. Over time, if the child remains interested in, and continues to be involved in, baking cakes with his mother, the nature of the child's involvement and the mother's actions will both change as the child's competence increases. Thus, over the course of participation, as a child's roles and responsibilities change, her understanding of the activity also changes. For Rogoff (2003), intent community participation is one of the most prevalent forms of children's learning.

The Role of Culture

An important feature of Vygotsky's approach is his emphasis on the role of culture in cognitive development (Cole, 2006). Culture provides the institutions and social settings that support and direct cognitive development. In these settings, particular ways of identifying and solving problems are emphasized along with the tools that aid problems solving. In every culture, both symbolic tools, such as language and mathematics, and material tools, such as pencil, paper, and computers, are used to support intelligent action. Once certain cultural tools become incorporated into intelligent action, it is difficult to imagine how the activity would occur without such tools. Think for a moment about how you would remember your class material without the cultural tool of literacy, which mediates your learning and remembering in the classroom. There is cultural variation in the tools that support cognitive development. For example, in cultures in which verbal explanation is highly valued, activities such as oral narratives and storytelling assume a great deal of importance and are part of children's cognitive development in that community (Heath, 1998).

Vygotsky stressed that any attempt to assess children's cognitive development must consider the cultural context. He claimed that if we ignore the culturally specific nature of children's learning, we run the risk of seriously underestimating children's

guided participation

Learning that occurs as children participate in activities of their community and are guided in their participation by the actions of more experienced partners in the setting.

intent community participation

Children's participation in the authentic activities of their community with the purpose of learning about the activity.

Culture plays an important role in the types of information that are taught to children and how they learn to use such information. So, for these children, what they are learning and how they are learning it will vary depending on where in the world they live.

Box 8.1

Child Psychology in Action

ADULT PARTNERING GUIDES CHILDREN IN EFFICIENT PLANNING

Do children solve a planning problem more efficiently when given guidance by a more skilled partner? According to Vygotsky, children should do better under these conditions. To find out, Radziszewska and Rogoff (1988) asked 9-year-olds to plan an errand in collaboration with either another 9-year-old or a parent as a partner.

Partners were given a map of an imaginary town (see Figure 8-10) and two lists of errands and were asked to plan a trip to obtain materials for a school play (e.g., to buy uniforms from the theatrical supplies store, paint brushes from the paint shop or the shopping centre, and so on). Partners were asked to plan an efficient route to save gas; this undertaking required that the participants decide from which stores to purchase the needed supplies and then develop a plan that incorporated all of these stores in sequence, without backtracking or other unnecessary travel.

Adult–child dyads were better planners than peer–child dyads. The adult–child couples planned longer sequences of moves (average of 4.9 stores per move) than the peer–child couples (average of 1.3 stores per move). Nearly half the adult–child dyads planned the whole route at the onset, whereas none of the peer–child dyads showed this kind of careful planning. Children learned other helpful strategies when they worked with an adult, such as exploring the map of the town before making any moves and marking stores that they wished or did not wish to shop at with different colours. Of great importance was the children's active involvement in the planning decisions, which the adults often verbalized to help the children's understanding. In contrast, peer partners often dominated the decision-making process, ignored their co-workers, and communicated very little.

Not only did children plan better with an adult, but they were able to transfer what they had learned to later planning tasks that they did by themselves. In a later independent planning task, children who had worked with adults planned more efficient routes (20 percent shorter) than children who had previously planned with a peer.

As Vygotsky predicted, "children appear to benefit from participation in problem-solving with the guidance of partners who are skilled in accomplishing the task at hand" (Rogoff, 1990, p. 169).

intellectual capabilities. Indeed, many cross-cultural studies have documented that children learn highly sophisticated and complex cognitive skills important in their culture (Cole, 2006; Rogoff, 2003). These skills are conveyed to children largely through social experiences. Social interactions with more experienced cultural members are especially important because these people are the most immediate representatives in children's lives of culturally organized ways of thinking and acting (Gauvain & Perez, 2006). Researchers have studied several social processes that promote children's learning of culturally valued skills, such as observational learning (Morelli et al., 2003), the social regulation of attention in infancy (Bornstein et al., 1991; Martini & Kirkpatrick, 1981), deliberate efforts to transfer knowledge from more to less experienced partners (Serpell & Hatano, 1997), social coordination during joint cognitive activity (Rogoff, 1998), and cognitive socialization through conversation and joint narratives (Mullen & Yi, 1995). Taken together, this research suggests that social opportunities for children's learning appear in many forms and that culture determines the frequency and manner with which these processes occur.

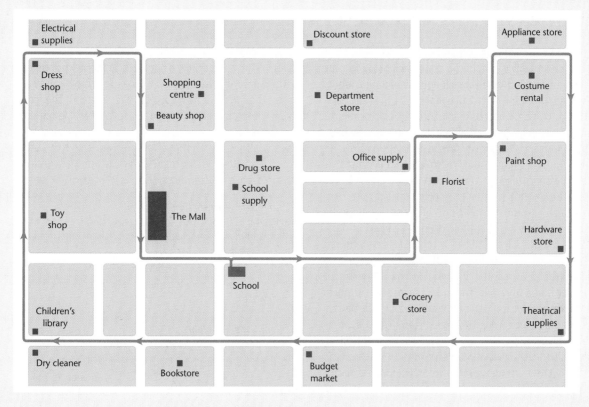

Figure 8-10   How adult guidance can help children plan efficiently

This map of an imaginary town shows the efficient route an adult–child pair planned for acquiring all the materials they would need to prepare for and stage a school play.
Source: Radziszewska & Rogoff, 1988.

Vygotsky's theory not only leads us to an appreciation of different cultures and their values but it also connects cultural values and practices directly to cognitive development. Mathematics provides an interesting example of this kind of link. Findings from research of the mathematics skills of children in Brazil who work as street vendors are discussed in Box 8.2 on the next page. As this box shows, the children's daily interaction with addition and subtraction, as well as their lack of formal schooling, has led them to develop ways of performing mathematical functions that work for them in their daily activities but that affect their ability to deal with mathematical concepts in an academic setting. If, as Vygotsky insisted, we take culture into account in evaluating such children's cognitive skills, we must recognize the sophistication of their competence, which certainly exceeds what we might have expected. Studies such as these underscore the importance of considering the cultural context in our examination and evaluation of children's cognitive development.

Box 8.2

Risk and Resilience

STREET MATH AND SCHOOL MATH IN BRAZIL

Most of us use mathematics and numerical reasoning every day of our lives. People calculate the costs of items in the supermarket, divide a snack equally among friends, and estimate how far it is to school and other destinations. In most cases, people learn the necessary skills in elementary school, but not all children or adults have the opportunity to acquire a formal education. How do those without that opportunity perform such daily tasks? As the study we discuss here illustrates, even without formal training and in the face of hardship and risk, children demonstrate an amazing ability to develop the cognitive skills needed for their everyday functioning.

Carraher, Schliemann, and Carraher (1988) studied young vendors on the streets of Brazilian cities. These children, who are usually between 9 and 15 years of age, sell all kinds of goods, including coconuts, oranges, and other fruits, as well as candy and sweets, to pedestrians and riders of public transportation. The researchers were interested in the ability of these children to solve mathematical problems. After all, they reasoned, success at their trade relied on mathematical skill. Oftentimes, the children sold items in bulk, such as three oranges for 10 cruzados (the monetary unit in Brazil), but if a customer wanted only two oranges, the seller would need to figure out a fair price or risk losing the sale (Saxe, 1991). Also, because inflation is rampant in Brazil, the prices on a given day may be different from the prices the previous day. As a result, there is no fixed pricing scheme for the children to memorize. To study these children's skills at mathematical calculations, the experimenters presented five young vendors, ranged in age from 8 to 15 years, with either a familiar commercial transaction between a vendor and a customer or a similar mathematics problem presented as it would be in school.

The young vendors revealed striking differences in their abilities to perform the two different types of tasks. On the familiar commercial transaction, the children were correct 98 percent of the time, but when the same problems were presented in the form of a school exercise, the percentage of correct answers dropped to 37. One notable difference in the children's solutions was in the method they used: They solved the commercial problem mentally but resorted to pencil and paper to solve the school-like problem. They also used different problem-solving strategies in the two situations. The following protocol from one of the children illustrates these differences (Nunes & Bryant, 1996):

Commercial Transaction Problem
Customer: I'll take two coconuts. (Each coconut costs 40 cruzados, and the customer pays with a 500-cruzado bill.) What do I get back?

Child Vendor (before reaching for the customer's change): Eighty, ninety, one hundred, four hundred and twenty.

School-Type Problem
Test Question: What is 420 plus 80?

Child's Response: The child writes 42 plus 8 underneath and obtains 130 as a result. She apparently proceeds as follows: She adds the 8 and the 2, carries the 1, and then adds 1 1 4 1 8, obtaining 13. With the 0 already in the sum, she gets 130. (Note that the child is confusing multiplication and addition rules).

The child has approached the same problem (420 + 80) in two distinctly different ways. On the street, she uses an "add-on" strategy efficiently to arrive at the correct answer, whereas in the academic setting she applies strategies learned in school incorrectly. As Vygotsky would have predicted, this study shows the importance of context for understanding cognitive development. It also illustrates how cognitive tools or mediators—in this case, mathematical symbols or strategies—are integrated with thinking. Finally, it demonstrates the resilience of children at risk and their ability to survive and learn even complex cognitive skills despite the lack of opportunity for formal schooling.

The Role of Language

Language plays a central role in Vygotsky's approach to cognitive development. It provides children with access to the ideas and understandings of other people, and also enables them to convey their own ideas and thoughts to others. Moreover, language, which is a cultural product, is the primary cultural tool that mediates individual mental functioning. Once children learn to use language, it gradually becomes incorporated into their thought processes.

EGOCENTRIC SPEECH AS A COGNITIVE AID For Vygotsky, thought and speech are independent in early development. However, around the second year of life, they begin to join together when children start to use words to label objects. Within a year, speech assumes two forms: social, or communicative, speech and egocentric speech (also called "private speech"). For Vygotsky, **egocentric speech** is a form of self-directed monologue by which the child instructs herself in solving problems. Egocentric speech is a cornerstone for the subsequent development of higher psychological processes (Feigenbaum, 2002), and becomes a tool for intellectual growth that allows the child to become a more effective and skilled learner. For example, in his efforts to solve a dinosaur puzzle, a child might say, "First, I'll put the tail piece here, then the claw goes over here and the head right there." By age 7 or 8, this form of speech becomes internalized in the thought processes and becomes **inner speech**, a form of internal monologue that guides intelligent functioning. This view is quite different from Piaget's ideas about egocentrism and egocentric speech.

For Piaget, egocentric speech is a mental limitation of the preoperational stage in which the child's self-focused way of thinking leads children to explain natural phenomena in reference to the self—for example, by claiming that the moon follows the child home at night. The egocentric child, in Piaget's view, makes no effort to adapt his point of view in a way that makes it understandable to others. Moreover, unlike Vygotsky, who considered egocentric speech as one step in the path of the development of internalized knowledge, Piaget thought that egocentric speech served no useful cognitive function. Finally, Piaget suggested that egocentric speech diminishes at the end of the preoperational period, as the child's perspective-taking abilities improve, whereas Vygotsky thought that this kind of speech becomes internalized as thought.

Who is right? Most of the evidence favours Vygotsky's version. For example, children use more private or self-speech when they work on a difficult cognitive task (e.g., Patrick & Abravanel, 2000); as a result, their performance improves, suggesting that children use this form of speech as a cognitive aid (Berk, 1992; Berk et al., 2006). In addition, in a longitudinal study of the developmental sequence of this kind of speech, Bivens and Berk (1990) found that egocentric speech does shift from external (audible, self-directed speech) to internal (silent, self-directed speech) between 7 and 10 years of age, thus supporting Vygotsky's view. As Vygotsky stated, language seems to serve as a tool for regulating cognition as well as for communicating.

USING THE ZONE OF PROXIMAL DEVELOPMENT IN TEACHING LANGUAGE Vygotsky's notion of the zone of proximal development (ZPD) is the basis for the theory of instruction adopted by the Kamehameha Early Education Program, or KEEP, that is in operation in Hawaii, Arizona, and Los Angeles. In this program, minority public-school children receive language instruction as well as instruction in other subjects, all based on the ZPD concept (Au, 1997; Gallimore & Tharp, 1999). This program is learner-centred (Bransford et al., 1999) in that it was designed to incorporate the knowledge, skills, values, and beliefs that learners bring to the classroom and their lessons. The KEEP program was particularly concerned with how the cultural practices that Hawaiian children experience at home could be incorporated into the classroom. For example, the Native Hawaiian tradition of storytelling was used to develop the classroom practice of "talk-story," an approach to literacy instruction in which the teacher and the children jointly produce narratives about the focus of the day's lessons (Au & Jordan, 1981). This approach emphasizes social participation, along with story creation and comprehension, and its use has been related to improvements in the standardized reading scores of Native Hawaiian children.

---

egocentric speech

According to Vygotsky, a form of self-directed dialogue by which the child instructs herself in solving problems and formulating plans; as the child matures, this becomes internalized as *inner speech*.

inner speech

Internalized egocentric speech that continues to direct and regulate intellectual functioning.

The KEEP teacher uses modelling, questioning, and feedback, all of which are part of the methods of scaffolding and reciprocal instruction (Palincsar & Brown, 1984). For example, in the following exchange, a teacher uses repetition, rewording, and expansion as she questions the child and seeks to clarify his statement (Tharp & Gallimore, 1988, p. 143):

Child: Probably, probably have snow on the . . . stuff and . . . thing, thing was heavy and thing fall.

Teacher: Oh, you mean there might be so much snow and ice on the plane that it couldn't fly?

Through these instructional techniques, children in the KEEP program are aided as they learn to use language as tool in the school setting. This program builds on the cultural experiences children have when they enter school, rather than ignoring this rich foundation of learning. Based on their research at KEEP, Tharp and Gallimore (1988) argue that minority or other "non-standard dialect speakers" can benefit greatly from opportunities to converse throughout goal-oriented activities with a responsive yet uncritical teacher who speaks standard English. As Tharp and Gallimore point out, however, this kind of teaching is not common in North American schools.

LO10 AN EVALUATION OF VYGOTSKY'S THEORY

Vygotsky's approach offers a perspective of cognitive development that emphasizes the culturally organized and socially mediated nature of this development. As such, it overcomes some of the limitations of Piaget's focus on cognitive development as an individual or solitary endeavour.

Strengths of the Theory

Vygotsky's theory has helped to make developmental psychologists more aware of the importance of the immediate social contexts of learning and cognition. In particular, through the notion of the zone of proximal development and the related concepts of scaffolding and guided participation, this approach has pointed to new ways of assessing children's cognitive potential and of teaching reading, mathematics, and writing. Reciprocal instruction, the community of learners model, the Fifth Dimension, and the KEEP program are excellent examples of the application of these principles to educational settings. In addition, Vygotsky's approach has increased our appreciation of the profound importance of culture in cognitive development. This approach is particularly useful in multi-ethnic societies, like Canada and the United States, in that it provides a theoretical base for examining the ways that children of different cultural and ethnic traditions approach cognitive tasks and schooling. Vygotsky's theory also provides a way of conceptualizing the role played by tools of thinking in cognitive development. This theory addresses how tools such as literacy and numerical systems, which are products of culture, get passed on across generations and become incorporated into the ways children learn to think and solve problems as they grow.

Does Vygotsky's Theory Describe Developmental Change?

microgenetic change

Changes associated with learning that occur over the time of a specific learning experience or episode.

Although Vygotsky's work has recently inspired a great deal of research activity, his theory has several limitations, largely pertaining to its explanation of development. Although the approach emphasizes change over time in a specific learning experience, or **microgenetic change**, and the role of long-term historical influences on intellectual development as embodied in cultural practices and tools, this approach is not very specific in relation to age-related, or *ontogenetic*, change. Vygotsky did not provide a detailed description of how children's thinking changes with age (Miller, 2002). This approach also does not describe how changes in physical, social, and emotional capabilities contribute to changes in children's cognitive abilities.

Overall Assessment

In a sense, Vygotsky left developmental psychology a unique framework for thinking about cognitive development rather than a fully specified theory. Filling in the details of this theoretical position remains a challenge for the future. However, for now, most developmentalists agree that this approach offers a unique understanding of human cognition and that it holds great promise as a way of thinking about cognitive development in social and cultural contexts.

For Thought and Discussion

1. What is the relation between Vygotsky's notion of the zone of proximal development and the more typical ideas related to learning theory?

2. Given the central role that culture plays in so many cognitive abilities, what implications do such findings have for the generality of theories of cognitive development? Put differently, is Piaget's or Vygotsky's theory truly applicable across different cultures?

3. Vygotsky believed that language acquisition plays a critical role in cognitive development. Given that language acquisition occurs at the same time as other developmental acquisitions, how might you actually demonstrate an influence of language on cognition?

Making the Connections 8

There are many links between concepts and ideas in one area of development and concepts and ideas in other areas. Here are some of the connections between ideas in Chapter 8 and discussions in other chapters of this book.

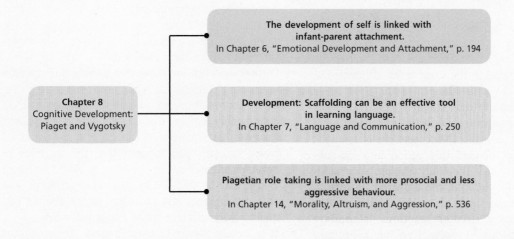

Chapter 8
Cognitive Development:
Piaget and Vygotsky

The development of self is linked with infant-parent attachment.
In Chapter 6, "Emotional Development and Attachment," p. 194

Development: Scaffolding can be an effective tool in learning language.
In Chapter 7, "Language and Communication," p. 250

Piagetian role taking is linked with more prosocial and less aggressive behaviour.
In Chapter 14, "Morality, Altruism, and Aggression," p. 536

SUMMARY

- **Cognition** is the mental activity and behaviour that allows us to understand the world. A variety of theories have been proposed to explain the pattern of cognitive development seen in children.

Piaget's Theory of Cognitive Development

- Piaget's theory concentrates on the cognitive capabilities of children of different ages. Piaget based his theory of observations on his own and other children as they answered questions during structured and unstructured interviews.

Piaget's Main Tenet: The Child Actively Seeks Knowledge

- According to Piaget, children actively seek out information and adapt it to the knowledge and conceptions of the world that they already have. Children organize their knowledge into increasingly complex cognitive structures called **schemas.**
- Children possess many different schemes, and these change as children develop. In the newborn, the schemes take the form of innate reflexes and reaction patterns, such as sucking. As the child grows and gains experience, the schemes shift from motor activities to mental activities called **operations.**
- Piaget suggested that schemes are modified according to the principles of **organization** and **adaptation.** Organization is the predisposition to combine simple physical or psychological structures into more complex systems. Adaptation involves the processes of **assimilation**, or fitting new experiences into current cognitive schemes, and **accommodation**, or adjusting current schemes to fit the new experiences.

The Stages of Cognitive Development

- Piaget divided intellectual development into four unique periods that are indicative of the changes in children's cognitive structures. All children go through the stages in the same order, although not necessarily at the same ages.
- During the **sensorimotor stage**, a child makes the transition from relying on reflexes to using internal representation, which is the cornerstone of symbolic thought. Piaget divided this period into six substages, during which the child develops such abilities as **symbolic thought** and **deferred imitation.** Throughout these substages, which include **reflex activity**, **primary circular reactions**, **secondary circular reactions**, **coordination of secondary**

schemata, **tertiary circular reactions**, and **inventing new means by mental combination**, children gradually come to understand object permanence.
- The major developmental milestone during the **preoperational stage** is the development of the **symbolic function**, or the ability to use symbols, such as words, images, and gestures, to represent objects and events. Piaget divided this stage into the **preconceptual substage** and the **intuitive substage.**
- The most important acquisition of the preoperational period is an elementary understanding of the notion of **conservation.** Typically, the child learns to conserve number at the end of this period but cannot yet conserve other characteristics, such as mass and volume. The concept of **horizontal décalage** explains this unevenness of children's cognitive achievements.
- Piaget believed that three characteristics of preoperational thought limit children's thinking. The first is the child's inability to understand **reversibility**, or the notion that all logical operations are reversible. The second is the tendency to focus on the end states of a change rather than on the process of transformation. The third characteristic is **centration**, or focusing on only one dimension of a problem.
- During the **concrete operational stage** children acquire the ability to perform tasks such as conservation of various substances and characteristics, classification, and seriation.
- Children in the **formal operations stage** can use flexible and abstract reasoning, test mental hypotheses, and consider multiple possibilities for the solution to a problem.

An Evaluation of Piaget's Theory

- Piaget's theory integrates and illuminates a broad spectrum of diverse issues revolving around children's understanding and use of knowledge, and it has stimulated an enormous amount of research. Among the most significant of Piaget's ideas are that children actively construct their knowledge of the world and that the errors they make provide important clues about their thinking.
- Current evidence indicates that infants and children grasp many concepts, such as object permanence, causality, conservation, and the perspectives of another, considerably earlier than Piaget thought. Others, however, have questioned the use of more simplified tasks. Research also suggests that the sequence of development may not be invariant as Piaget believed, that it may be modified by cultural experiences, and that development may not occur in the distinct and qualitatively different stages Piaget proposed.
- It is largely thanks to Piaget's work, however, that

the field of cognitive development owes its ascendancy. Despite flaws in his theorizing and methods, Piaget asked and proposed answers to important questions in an innovative way, stimulating the work of other investigators.

Vygotsky's Sociocultural Theory of Cognitive Development

- Vygotsky's theory emphasizes the critical role played by the social world in facilitating the child's development. According to his theory, children internalize thought processes that first occur through interaction with others in the social environment. Qualitative transitions between **elementary mental functions** and **higher mental functions** occur because of shifts in the use of **mediators**, such as language and other symbols. The acquisition and use of language play a primary role in children's developing intellectual abilities.
- Vygotsky's interest in the child's potential for intellectual growth led him to develop the concept of the **zone of proximal development**. This concept has led to the use of **scaffolding**, an instructional process in which the teacher adjusts the amount and type of support offered to the child to suit the child's abilities.

- Language plays an important role in Vygotskian theory. As children begin to use social speech, **egocentric speech**, and **inner speech**, they learn to communicate and to form thoughts and regulate intellectual functions.

An Evaluation of Vygotsky's Theory

- Vygotsky drew attention to the importance of the social context in which learning and the evolution of cognitive skills take place and to the influence of peers and adults on the child's development. He pointed out that the particularities of a given culture determine the nature and manner of functioning of the societal institutions that influence how children think and learn.
- Vygotsky's theory does not provide the richness of detail that Piaget's approach offers, and he did not provide the kinds of specific tools for research that Piaget's many tests and experiments have given us. Vygotsky's approach offers only a general outline of cognitive development; in its emphasis on the social and cultural aspects of learning and cognition, however, it challenges future researchers to explore the role of context in greater depth.

Christian Pierre (b. 1962). *Modern Madonna, 1996.*
Private Collection.

Chapter 9

Cognitive Development: The Information-Processing Approach

LEARNING OBJECTIVES

After reading this chapter, you should be able to

LO 1 Characterize the information-processing approach to cognitive development.

LO 2 Discuss the main assumptions of the information-processing approach.

LO 3 Describe different information-processing models.

LO 4 Describe the developmental changes in the processes of encoding, representation, strategy construction, automatization, and generalization. Include the influence of changes in executive control strategies and world knowledge on children's cognition.

LO 5 Discuss developmental changes in attention and memory.

LO 6 Discuss developmental changes in problem solving, deductive and transitive reasoning, hierarchical categorization, and numerical reasoning.

LO 7 Define metacognition and discuss the various components of metacognitive knowledge. Evaluate the information-processing approach to cognitive development.

Every day of their lives, children engage in activities that require thinking: deciding what to wear, remembering to take their homework to school, solving problems on a math assignment, or trying to understand why their best friend is angry with them. In this chapter, we focus on the cognitive skills that children use during these activities as well as the way these skills change over the course of childhood. We examine approaches to cognitive development that are based on an information-processing view of cognition (Munakata, 2006), which views human beings as possessing an array of cognitive processes that help them to understand and make use of the information they get from their experiences in the world.

The information-processing approach originated in the study of adult cognition, and several approaches to cognitive development are based on this perspective. One approach, the *multi-store model*, focuses on the steps that the mind goes through as information is processed. Another approach, called a *connectionist view*, examines cognitive processing as a system of connections of the neural network that makes up the human brain. Another approach involves combining many of Piaget's ideas with focusing on cognitive processing rather than on stages of development. As we will see, this view, referred to as a *neo-Piagetian approach*, proposes that the stage-related changes that Piaget described are brought about by changes in the ways children process information.

After describing the multi-store, connectionist, and neo-Piagetian approaches, we explore several basic cognitive abilities and discuss how these abilities changes with development. We begin by describing changes in attention, and then we consider memory and the child's developing competence in storing and retrieving information. Following this, we discuss children's increasing ability to solve various kinds of problems, including children's developing skill at using strategies to help them solve problems. Finally, we look at children's knowledge of their own mental capabilities, referred to as *metacognition*.

As you study this chapter, keep in mind that the many different theories and approaches to cognitive development discussed in this chapter and Chapter 8 are not necessarily competing with one another. In many cases, the theories address different aspects of cognitive development. To date, no single theory of cognitive development explains all of mental functioning and its development. Although such a theory is a goal of the field at large, researchers realize that the human cognitive system is extremely complex and that no single theory may be able to explain this entire process. ●

ⓛ1 INFORMATION-PROCESSING THEORY

information-processing approach

A perspective on cognition and cognitive development in which the human mind is likened to a computer, processing information from the environment through perception and attention (input), encoding it in memory (storage and retrieval), and applying information to the solution of problems (software).

Information-processing approaches to the study of cognition often use the computer as an analogue for describing how the human mind works. Like the computer, the human mind is seen as an organized system that processes information through a series of logical rules or steps. Information from the environment, or input, initially enters the cognitive system through the processes of perception, which we discussed in Chapter 4, and attention. This information is encoded into some symbolic form so that it can be examined mentally. Then it is either expelled because it is no longer needed or saved so that at some later point it can be retrieved and used for thinking or solving problems. Like the computer, the mind is limited in both the amount and type of information it can process. Finally, just as the computer can be made into a better information processor by making changes in its hardware (e.g., microchips) and its software (programming), so are human thinkers able to become more cognitively skilled through changes in their brains and sensory systems (hardware) and in the rules and strategies of thinking (software) that they learn over the course of development.

A primary quality of the human cognition system is its flexibility. Human thinking can be adapted to many different situations. However, the human cognitive system has two main limitations: the amount of information that it can process at one time and the speed with which it can process information. In fact, computers can process information much faster than the human mind. Does this mean that the human mind is less effective at processing information than a computer? No, the rapid-fire speed of the computer reflects its singular design: to solve specific types of problems in the way it is programmed to solve them. In contrast, when the human mind solves problems, it has the flexibility to consider a broad range of factors and as a result it takes longer to do the job. In essence, the human mind is a truly unique kind of information-processing system with vast problem solving potential.

There are four basic assumptions that are shared by all psychologists who study cognitive development using the information-processing perspective. After discussing these assumptions, we will describe some of the most well-known approaches

Basic Assumptions of the Information-Processing Approach

LO2 LO3

According to Siegler and Alibali (2005), the information-processing approach is characterized by several main assumptions. First, *thinking is information processing*. In other words, mental activity involves taking information into the mind and operating on it in ways that make it usable. In terms of cognitive development, this assumption directs attention to questions about how thinking processes, such as attending to and remembering information, change as children get older.

A second assumption is that there are *mechanisms or processes of change that underlie the processing of information*. For instance, with development, children become better able to represent or encode information in their minds, and this mechanism helps them solve problems more effectively. The four key mechanisms of information processing—encoding, strategy construction, automatization, and generalization—are discussed in more detail later in the chapter. Together, these mechanisms help bring about change in children's cognitive skills.

Information-processing theory also assumes that cognitive development is a *self-modifying process*. In other words, the child uses the strategies she has acquired from earlier problem solutions to modify her responses to a new problem. In this way, children play an active role in their own cognitive development.

Another assumption of an information-processing approach is that *careful task analysis* is crucial. According to this view, in addition to the child's own level of development, the task or problem situation itself influences the child's cognitive performance. Careful task analysis, coupled with accurate observation of a child's performance on the task, can reveal much about how children of different ages understand and solve problems. Careful task analysis often involves *error analysis*, or attending to the errors children make. These errors can be especially enlightening about development when they are similar across the same age group of children. Such analysis often relies on a method called **microgenetic analysis**, which involves very detailed examination of how a child solves a problem over a single learning episode or over several episodes that occur close in time (Siegler, 2006). This method is rather like a film in slow motion as the investigator observes in detail the way a child arrives at a problem solution.

microgenetic analysis

A very detailed examination of how a child solves a problem.

Taken together, these four assumptions form the basis of an information-processing perspective. In the next section, we discuss some of the approaches or models that are derived from an information-processing perspective and that guide research on cognitive development.

Information-Processing Models

Several types of approaches or models are used to describe cognition from an information-processing perspective. Here, we discuss three models that have been influential to the study of cognitive development. These are the multi-store model, connectionist models, and the neo-Piagetian model.

THE MULTI-STORE MODEL This model describes how information enters and flows through the mind as it is processed (Atkinson and Shiffrin, 1968). It describes this process in terms of the various types of storage units that are involved and, hence, the name **multi-store model** (see Figure 9-1 on the next page). As an initial step, we

multi-store model

A model of information processing in which information is depicted as moving through a series of processing units—sensory register, short-term memory, and long-term memory—in each of which it may be stored, either fleetingly or permanently.

Figure 9-1

A multi-store model of information processing

A model of information processing that describes the flow of information through various stores of the cognitive system.

Source: Based on Atkinson & Shiffrin, 1968.

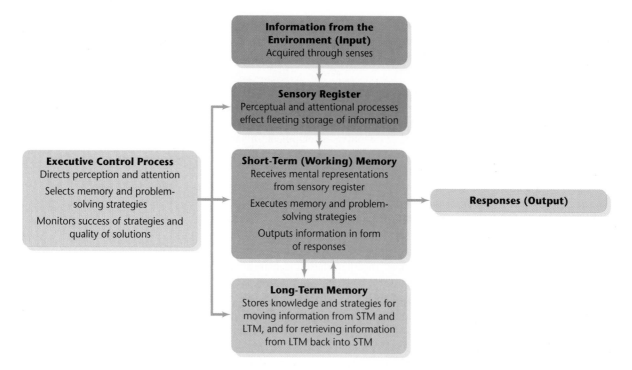

sensory register

The mental processing unit that receives information from the environment and stores it fleetingly.

short-term memory/ working memory

The mental processing unit in which information may be stored temporarily; the "workspace" of the mind, where a decision must be made to discard information or to transfer it to permanent storage in *long-term memory*.

long-term memory

The mental processing unit in which information may be stored permanently and from which it may later be retrieved.

acquire information from the environment through the **sensory register**. Although the information in the sensory register is stored in its original form—that is, images are stored visually, sounds aurally, and so forth—this storage is very brief. Sperling (1960) showed that the sensory register can store visual sensory information for only one second! In addition, this sensory capacity changes little over development: Research has shown, for example, that 5-year-olds and adults have the same time limitations on their ability to store sensory information (Morrison, Holmes, & Haith, 1974; Siegler, 1998), although there is some evidence that auditory sensory storage does change across infancy and childhood (Cheoud et al., 2002; Cowan, Nugent, Elliot, & Saults, 2000).

In the next step of processing, information in the sensory register is transformed, or encoded, into a mental representations and then placed in the storage area referred to as **short-term memory** or **working memory**. Short-term memory can best be thought of as the conscious "workspace" of the mind (Bjorklund, 2005); it is limited in the number of meaningful units or chunks of information it can hold at any one time, as well as how long it can hold this information without any active effort to retain the data. Without a specific effort, such as rehearsal, we generally lose information from short-term memory within 15 to 30 seconds. Although we might often try to get around this limitation, it has functional value, in that it allows us to respond to a rather continuous flow of incoming information. This ability to use active strategies like rehearsal to keep information in short-term memory improves with age. For example, the faster a child can rehearse a piece of information—let's say, a new word—the more information can be retained (Hitch & Towse, 1995). Figure 9-2 shows how older children's more rapid response enables them to remember more words.

Long-term memory is the term used to describe knowledge that is retained over a long period of time. It contains information about objects, events, rules, types of problems and ways to solve them, and general knowledge about the world, such

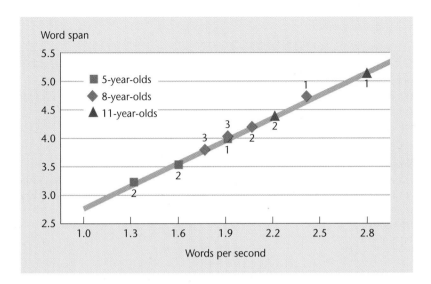

Figure 9-2

Memory skills improve with age

Experimenters asked children in three age groups to memorize a list of words. The older the child, the faster she could pronounce the words in rehearsing them and the more words she could retain in working memory. For example, 11-year-olds could pronounce 2.8 words per second and could remember about five words, whereas 5-year-olds at best could pronounce 1.9 words per second and could remember about four words.

Source: Siegler & Alibali, 2005.

a vocabulary and what flowers smell like. In addition, long-term memory stores the strategies for building new knowledge, such as ways of encoding, representing, and retaining information. Information transferred from short- to long-term memory can be retained for an indefinite period of time.

The multi-store model has directed research in cognitive development in a number of ways. In particular, this research has examined changes in short-term memory and the way these changes influence the development of long-term memory or the knowledge base.

CONNECTIONIST MODELS   An alternative approach to how information is processed is described in **connectionist models**. These models emphasize the biological components of information processing, referred to as neural networks. In this approach, information is described as an elaborate set of neural connections and thinking involves processing of information as it spreads throughout the network, or what is referred to as *parallel distributed processing* (McClelland, Rumelhart, & Hinton, 2003; Rumelhart & McClelland, 1987; Thomas & McClelland, 2008).

In terms of cognitive development, psychologists who adopt this approach are interested in how these neural connections are organized, how they change over the course of development, and how different connections are activated as a child thinks and solves problems (Elman et al., 1998). Researchers have attempted to simulate various aspects of cognitive development using connectionist ideas, including language learning, object knowledge, and conceptual development (MacWhinney, 1996; Munakata et al., 1997; Plunkett et al., 1997). The contributions that developmental psychologists can make to this approach are important in that a full understanding of neural networks will require a description of how these networks change with development.

NEO-PIAGETIAN INFORMATION-PROCESSING MODELS   There are also **neo-Piagetian theories** of information processing. These theories attempt to integrate Piaget's ideas with that of an information-processing perspective. According to Robbie Case (1992, 1998; Case & Mueller, 2001) of the University of Toronto, the proponent of one of these theories, the stage-like development of cognition described by Piaget is based on improvements in memory capacity and executive control, two features of an information-processing system. Like Piaget, Case divides development into four stages (see Table 9-1 on the next page). Each of these stages entails an increasingly sophisticated **executive control structure**, which is a "mental blueprint or plan for solving a class of problems." An executive control structure has three components (Case, 1984): a representation of the problem, a representation of the goal of the problem, and a representation of a strategy for attaining the goal. Table 9-1 provides examples

connectionist models

Information-processing approaches that describe mental processes in terms of the interconnections of the neural network.

neo-Piagetian theories

Theories of cognitive development that reinterpret Piaget's concepts from an information-processing perspective.

executive control structure

According to Case, a mental blueprint or plan for solving a class of problems.

Table 9-1 Case's stages of cognitive development

	Examples of Mental Representations and Operations
Sensorimotor Control Structures (Birth to 1½ Years) Infants' mental representations are linked to their physical movement. Their executive control structures are combinations of physical objects and motor actions.	A child sees a frightening face (sensory) and runs out of the room (motor).
Relational Control Structures (1½ to 5 Years) Children's representations include knowledge of relationships among objects, people, and events. They also include durable, concrete internal images on which they can act. Children's executive control structures now include cause-and-effect statements and explicit goal structures.	The child produces a mental image of the frightening face (representation) he saw the day before and draws a picture of it (acting on representation).
Dimensional Control Structures (5 to 11 Years) Children begin to extract significant dimensions from the physical world. They become able to use logical processes in comparing two dimensions, such as distance, number, and weight. They can represent stimuli abstractly and can act on these representations with simple transformations.	A child may realize that two friends don't like each other (abstract representation) and may tell them that they could all have more fun if they were all friends (simple transformation).
Abstract Control Structures (11 to 18½ Years) Building on the dimensional control structures of the preceding stage, children begin to use abstract systems of thought that allow them to perform higher-order reasoning tasks and more complex transformations of information.	The child may realize that such direct attempts to create friendships rarely succeed (abstract representation) and, so, may not tell her friends what she proposed but instead plan activities in which they will all engage with the hope that greater familiarity and contact will produce the desired relationships (complex transformation).

Sources: Case, 1985, Siegler, 1998.

of how developmental changes in the executive control system lead to different ways of processing information about the world. Case's synthesis of Piagetian and information processing theories can be used to account for many different aspects of development that neither theory can adequately explain alone. In fact, Case and his colleagues (Case & Griffin, 1990; Case, Okamoto, Henderson, & McKeough, 1993; Okamoto & Case, 1996) have applied this theory to a variety of different tasks and domains, including scientific reasoning (Marini, 1992), music sight reading (Capodilupo, 1992), solving math problems (Kalchman, Moss, & Case, 2001), telling time, and handling money.

LO 4 Cognitive Processes: What Are They? How Do They Contribute to Development?

cognitive processes

Ways that the human mental system operates on information.

As children grow and develop, they become more skilled and efficient in using **cognitive processes**, which are the mechanisms or ways that the human mental system operations on information. Thus, the information-processing perspective is focused on gradual and quantitative changes in mental functioning. Our discussion focuses on the four cognitive processes that change with development: encoding and representation, the construction of strategies, automatization, and generalization. These four processes are critical to the development of the information-processing system.

ENCODING AND REPRESENTATION   A massive amount of information enters the human information-processing system every day. Rather than try to retain and store every bit of information in the form in which we experience it, we encode, or change into mental representations, only the information we consider relevant. If this **encoding** process is efficient, crucial information is obtained, but if it is inefficient, critical information may be lost. As we will see later, the ability to attend to relevant information often determines what information is retained and what information is lost.

Mental representation is the term used to describe information that is stored mentally in some form (e.g., verbal, pictorial, procedural). A mental representation depends on the child's understanding that one thing (e.g., a word such as *chair*) can stand for or "represent" something else (e.g., an actual chair). Some developmentalists have proposed that changes in the type and complexity of mental representations underlie much of cognitive development (Bjorklund, 2005). Of particular interest to psychologists is the representation called a *script*, which reflects a particular event or series of events that are based on common experiences of daily life. Scripts are used to understand new events and to generate predictions about how those events will unfold.

STRATEGIES   The development and use of strategies are some of the most important changes that occur in children's thinking over childhood (Pressley & Hilden, 2006). **Strategies** are conscious cognitive or behavioural activities that are used to enhance mental performance. An example of strategy use appears in children's counting. When we present younger children with an addition problem like 3 + 14, they will attempt to solve it by using the *count-all* strategy, counting from 1 up to the first term of the problem (i.e., 3) and then continuing to count the number of the second term (i.e., 14 more) until they arrive at the answer of 17. Older children, in contrast, will use a more efficient strategy known as the *min rule*. Using this strategy to solve the problem, a child will begin counting from the larger of the two addends (14) and continue upward, adding the amount of the smaller number, thus counting "14, 15, 16, 17" to arrive at the answer (Siegler, 1987).

The main purpose of a strategy is to decrease the load on the child's information-processing system by increasing the efficiency of each process and, thus, freeing up space for the various tasks necessary for solving the problem. Another way to increase the efficiency of the information-processing system is to automatize certain aspects of the solution process.

AUTOMATIZATION   **Automatization** involves making behaviours that once were conscious and controlled into unconscious and automatic ones. A good example of automatization is an adult learning to drive a car with a stick shift. At first, every shifting of the gears is slow and strained, with the driver concentrating on each aspect of shifting to do it right. With practice, however, the driver can shift gears quickly and efficiently, unaware of the individual steps involved and often unaware of shifting altogether. In the same way, the child who has developed a memorization strategy for calculating multiplication problems is able, in time, to use this strategy without thinking about it (Siegler & Alibali, 2005). For example, a child who has memorized the mathematic formula that 2 + 2 = 4 can use this stored knowledge to answer the question, "What is 2 + 2?" In contrast, a child who has not memorized the formula may have to stop, think, and perhaps count on his fingers ([1 + 1] + [1 + 1]) to figure out the answer.

GENERALIZATION   Initially, the strategies that children develop to solve a given problem tend to be quite specific to the task at hand. Through the process of **generalization**, children apply a strategy learned while solving a problem in one situation to a similar problem in a new situation. Generalization does not happen overnight, though, and children may need to gain familiarity with the use of a rule, using it many times over, before they can successfully generalize it to new situations. Suppose, for example, that the child who used the min rule in the earlier addition problem had arrived at this solution in school. Coming home after school she finds that her mother

encoding

The transformation of information from the environment into a lasting mental representation.

mental representation

Information stored in some form (e.g., verbal, pictorial) in the cognitive system after the person has encountered it in the environment.

strategies

Conscious cognitive or behavioural activities that are used to enhance mental performance.

automatization

The process of transforming conscious, controlled behaviours into unconscious and automatic ones.

Using objects of different shapes, colours, and sizes (sometimes called manipulatives) can help children in the early grades to learn to count, do simple arithmetic problems, and sort objects into categories.

generalization

The application of a strategy learned while solving a problem in one situation to a similar problem in a new situation.

has bought some jelly beans, and she decides to count the jelly beans so that she and her brother will have the same number of candies. Even though she applied the min rule successfully at school, now that she is presented with a set of concrete objects—a different situation—she may revert to the less-sophisticated and more time-consuming strategy of counting all the items. However, with time and experience, the more general use of a strategy across problem situations occurs.

The Roles of the Executive Control Process and the Knowledge Base in Information Processing

executive control process

A cognitive process that serves to control, guide, and monitor the success of a problem-solving approach a child uses.

All the processes we have discussed help children increase their efficiency in absorbing information. It is also important to know when to use them and to monitor their use to make sure they are effective. The **executive control process** guides the child in the selection and use of such strategies. Between the ages of 3 and 12, brain systems that develop—in particular, changes in the prefrontal cortex—are central to the development of the executive control process. Over the years, the child's executive process shows dramatic development. Whereas the preschooler may apply a single ineffective strategy to a variety of tasks and not change course, the 12-year-old is able to master a wide range of intellectual tasks and use strategies that are suited to the problem at hand. Toward the end of this chapter, we take up this topic again when we discuss metacognition, which relies on the executive control process.

One critical feature of information processing that we have yet to discuss is the role of knowledge itself (Keil, 2006). A child's knowledge base, in particular his familiarity with the domain or type of problem he is trying to solve, plays a major role in his abilities to process information and solve problems (Pressley & Hilden, 2006). Research has shown that when children are given problems in an area in which they know a great deal, they will equal, and even surpass, the performance of less-knowledgeable adults (Bédard & Chi, 1992; Chi, 1978).

To study this topic, Michelene Chi (1978) tested both children and adults on their ability to recall either a set of numbers or specific chess-piece positions. The children were experienced chess players, but the adults had only a basic understanding of the game. Chi found that although the grade 3 and grade 8 children could not remember as many numbers as the adults on an immediate recall test, and needed more viewings to reach perfect recall, they far surpassed the adults in remembering chess-piece positions (see Figure 9-3). Chi concluded that the children's knowledge of chess played an

Figure 9-3

Knowledge and children's memory

In this test of the hypothesis that amount of knowledge plays a greater role in memory than simple memory capacity, young chess players recalled more chess-piece positions than non-chess-playing adults could (a), and they needed many fewer trials than the adults to reach perfect recall (b).

Source: Chi, 1978.

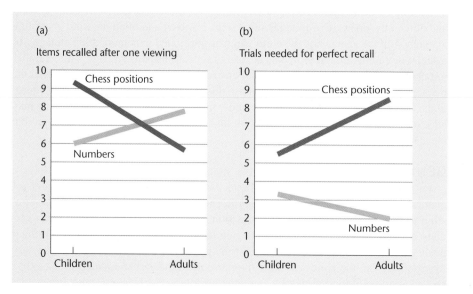

important role in their memory performance and that the adult's superiority in recalling numbers may have reflected their generally greater familiarity with number systems. These results suggest that expertise can enhance cognitive processing in children in a familiar domain but that this expertise does not influence performance in other domains. These results challenge stage-like views of cognitive development. It appears that when children have expertise in a domain, they function at a more advanced level (or stage) in this domain than they do when they are thinking about problems outside that domain.

DEVELOPMENTAL CHANGES IN SOME SIGNIFICANT COGNITIVE ABILITIES

 LO 5

In this section, we consider what has been learned about the development of some important cognitive abilities when they have been studied using an information-processing approach. These abilities include attention, planning, memory, problem solving, and reasoning. From an information-processing perspective, each of these abilities plays an important role in how information is organized and operated on.

Attention

A group of children in the same situation do not necessarily take in the same information. Each child's **attention** may be focused on different aspects of the environment. Attention involves the identification and selection of particular sensory input for more detailed processing. For example, one child in a classroom who is focusing on the teacher will hear and understand the lesson, but another child, more interested in a whispered message from a classmate may focus on that sound and regard the teacher's voice as background noise. How children's experiences affect them depends on what aspects of a situation children attend to and what meaning this information has for them. Attention is a complex process that changes substantially with development. Children have difficulty controlling their attention when they are young. As they develop, the control they have over their attention increases.

attention

The identification and selection of particular sensory input for more detailed processing.

CONTROL OF ATTENTION   Very young children can sustain their attention for only short periods, but this ability increases steadily over time (Johnson, 2002; Ruff

Attention is important in learning to read. Children respond best to material that is appropriate to their age level, and at about 3 years of age, they begin making marked gains in their ability to focus their attention.

Figure 9-4

Attention in the face of distracters

In the third year of life, children are already showing some skill at being able to focus their attention when distracting information is present.

Source: From Ruff & Rothbart, 1996.

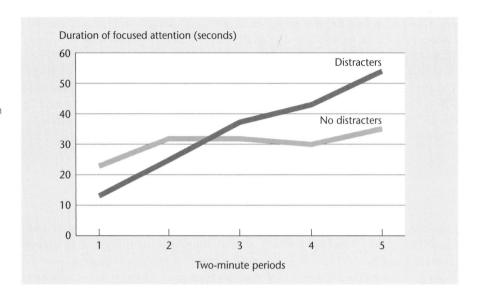

& Capozzoli, 2003; Ruff & Lawson, 1990). Even over the first year of life, there are a number of changes in the focus and duration of attention. Between 2 and 3 months of age, the focus of the infant's attention shifts from the external contours of objects toward the internal features. From 3 to 9 months of age, infants show increasing control over their attention, and by 9 months of age, infants can use attention to solve simple problems such as getting toys from behind barriers (Willatts, 1990). Over the first few years of life, the duration of attention increases and distractibility decreases. Ruff and Capozzoli (2003) found that 10-month-olds were far more distractible than 26- and 42-month-olds when playing with toys. The youngest group responded more frequently and looked longer at distracters, which in this case were images and sounds from a video player, than the older children. Interestingly, some of the 42-month-old children increased their attentional focus in the presence of the distracters. This pattern suggests that children as young as 42 months of age may be less distractible when an activity fully engages their attention. Although this may sound surprising, research with preschool- and school-age children shows that distraction can sometimes facilitate children's performance. For example, Turnure (1970) found that preschoolers did better on a learning task when they listened to sounds that had nothing to do with the task, such as a recording of a children's song (see Figure 9-4). Other research (Higgins & Turnure, 1984; Humphrey, 1982) suggests that older, school-age children perform better on learning tasks when there are visual or auditory distracters present than when they are not present. These results suggest that even preschoolers are learning to hone their attention to relevant information when distracting information is present. The accompanying Turning Points chart describes these and other advances in children's cognitive skills.

LEARNING TO ATTEND TO WHAT IS RELEVANT To learn, a child must acquire the attentional strategy known as **selective attention**, in which the child focuses on the relevant aspects of the environment and ignores the irrelevant features. Shifts in selective attention are evident as early as 2 to 3 months of age. Whereas neonates may look longer at an object just because it is larger or brighter than another object, by 2 to 3 months of age, infants begin to select what to look at based more on the form or pattern of the information (Ruff & Rothbart, 1996). As children get older, the ability to attend selectively increases and enhances children's ability to learn (Richards & Anderson, 2004).

Research has shown that in the school years, children improve markedly in their ability to focus their attention on relevant information. In one study, investigators

selective attention

A strategy in which a person focuses on some features of the environment and ignores others.

Turning Points

SOME COGNITIVE ACHIEVEMENTS AS SEEN FROM THE INFORMATION-PROCESSING VIEW

AT BIRTH
- Infant's brain weighs one-quarter of adult brain weight; it has 100 to 200 billion neurons and 2,500 synapses for every neuron
- Baby generally assumes fetal position

1 YEAR
- Has limited attentional capacity; can attend to a toy for only a few seconds
- May have a rudimentary understanding of categories

2 YEARS
- Has increased attentional capacity; will spend more than eight seconds with a single toy
- Can use external supports, such as landmarks to find hidden toys
- May be able to use basic category labels to help remember things
- May be able to draw very simple analogies
- Relies on scripts of familiar events

3 YEARS
- Can use two rules in combination
- Often distracted by other things while watching TV but, when attention is fully engaged, may be quite attentive to a program
- May be able to use fairly sophisticated analogies in solving a problem
- Understands relationship between scale models and real objects

4 YEARS
- With a meaningful context and guidance in using simple strategies, can focus attention on relevant aspects of the environment and apply the information gained to a task
- Can combine two or more rules into a higher-order rule
- Knows that long lists are harder to remember than short lists
- Understands that if you try harder on a more difficult task, you may succeed

5 YEARS
- Can memorize four units in a digit-span test
- Understands that thinking has content, that it is different from both perception and knowing, and that only people (and perhaps some other animate organisms) can think; can sometimes infer thinking in others if the evidence is strong

6 YEARS
- Begins to find audio content of TV programs as interesting as visual content
- With enough cues, may be able to plan a very effective strategy of attention

7 YEARS
- With training, may score as well on a test of recall as 12-year-olds

10 YEARS
- Becomes more selective in searching for information needed to make decisions

11 YEARS
- Begins to spend less time processing irrelevant information

12 YEARS
- Can memorize six or seven units in a digit-span test

Note: Developmental events described in this and other Turning Points charts represent overall trends identified in research studies. Individual children vary greatly in the ages at which they achieve these developmental changes.

Sources: Flavell, Miller, & Miller, 1993; Siegler, 1998.

(Miller & Seier, 1994) gave children a study period in which they could open up any of the boxes in which objects had been placed to help them remember the location of the target objects (animals). There were pictures of cages on the doors of the boxes containing animals and pictures of houses on the doors of the boxes holding household objects (see Figure 9-5). Older children (8-year-olds) focused on the first set of boxes and ignored the second set. However, the youngest children (3-year-olds) looked equally at both kinds of boxes during the study period. Modifying their attentional strategies paid off. The older children remembered more than the younger and less-selective children did. In short, older children used more selective search strategies, whereas younger children used more exhaustive methods. Subsequent work (Woody-Dorning & Miller, 2001) examined individual differences in the use of such memory strategies, and found that the strategy effectiveness (how well it worked) was well predicted by other measures of memory capacity.

As Figure 9.6 shows, the processing of relevant information increases steadily throughout the elementary and high school years. However, even preschoolers will use the relevance of items as a guide when they encode and process information (Blumberg et al., 2005). The processing of irrelevant information, however, increases slightly until the age of 11 or 12 and then decreases rapidly. Overall, children show increasing efficiency in how they use attention in processing information.

ATTENTION AND PLANNING One of the reasons that older children are better at using their attentional skills is that they develop a plan of action to guide their attention as they solve problems. With development, the ability to attend selectively combines with **planning**, which is the deliberate organization of a sequence of actions oriented toward achieving a goal, and enables the child to solve increasingly more complex problems.

A classic study by Elaine Vurpillot (1968) illustrated the coordination of attention and planning using the drawings of houses shown in Figure 9-7. Suppose you were asked to determine whether each pair of houses was identical. How might you

planning

The deliberate organization of a sequence of actions oriented toward achieving a goal.

Figure 9-5

Paying attention to what is important

All the children in this study initially looked inside every box, finding animals in those with cages on their doors and household items in the boxes that displayed houses. When researchers asked 3-year-olds to recall where animals were, they opened "house" doors as well as "cage" ones, but 8-year-olds ignored the irrelevant house boxes and checked only the cage ones.

Source: Miller & Seier, 1994.

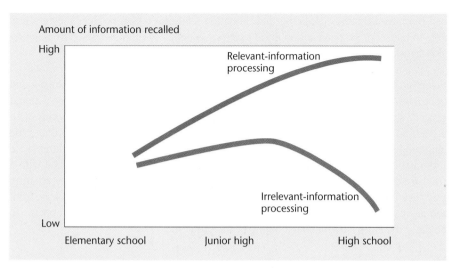

Figure 9-6

Children's changing attention to relevant and irrelevant information

Children steadily increase their attention to relevant information, but their concern with irrelevant information weakens and drops off quickly after junior high school.

approach this problem? Probably, you would compare the six pairs of corresponding windows in each pair of houses until you found a pair in which the objects displayed did not match. If all the pairs matched, you would conclude that the houses were identical. When Vurpillot (1968) administered this task to children, she found that younger children were far less likely than older children were to apply a systematic plan to get the necessary information. Filming the children's eye movements as they made their comparisons, she found that younger children tended to look at the windows randomly and even made judgments without ever looking at the windows that were different.

Should we conclude from this research that the young child is unable to plan an efficient strategy of attention? Not necessarily. In a study with preschool-age children, Miller and Aloise-Young (1995) gave the children (ages 3 to 4) a task that required them to open doors to reveal two arrays of pictures and then to determine if the arrays were the same or different. When the task was embedded in an engaging story context, the children were able to attend to the appropriate contextual information and plan their solution more effectively. However, even in meaningful contexts, preschoolers

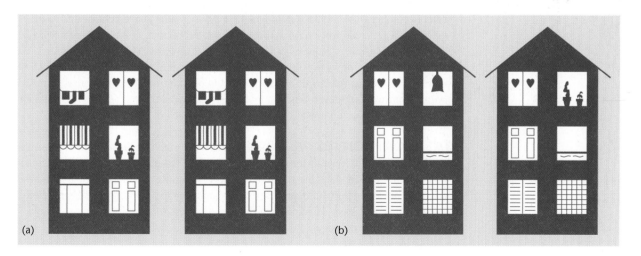

Figure 9-7

A test of children's ability to gather and filter information

How quickly can you perform a task given to young children—to determine which pair of houses, either pair (a) or pair (b), is identical?

Source: Vurpillot, 1968.

can run into difficulty regulating their attention while they plan because they are less able to inhibit or suspend action during activity, a behaviour that is critical to planning (Kochanska et al., 2000).

Planning is often done in social situations and, as we saw in Chapter 8, Vygotsky's theory considers social and cognitive development as closely linked. To explore social contributions to the development of planning, Gauvain and Rogoff (1989) used a model grocery store to compare the planning behaviour of 5- and 9-year-olds working with a peer, an adult, or alone. The older children were better at planning ahead, and the children who planned in advance of action devised more efficient routes. Children were more likely to use attentional strategies and plan efficiently when they worked with a peer or adult partner, especially when the partners shared task responsibility. Sharing responsibility for carrying out a task helps children understand the problem from the perspective of another person. Learning about the thinking of another appears to enhance the child's own understanding of the problem.

Memory

Memory of one of the most extensively studied topics in cognitive development. An interest in human memory is not surprising if one considers what memory is. Everything you know, you remember in some way. Thus, the terms *memory* and *knowledge* are interchangeable. Acts of memory range from rapid-fire, basic processes, such as face recognition, to the recall of complex knowledge systems and events, such as the rules of chess and how a family coped with a tragic event.

There are several different types of memory (Schneider & Bjorkland, 1998). As we have discussed, short-term (or working) memory is the conscious area of memory. Long-term memory is where we store knowledge that we retain for long periods of time. Long-term memory encompasses a vast array of information. It includes all the world knowledge and facts a person possesses, which is called **semantic memory**. It also includes knowledge of specific events or **episodic memory** (Bauer, 2006). Much of the latter is autobiographical in nature, for it includes memories of important events or experiences that have happened to an individual. Later, we discuss the development of autobiographical memory, which has been the topic of a great deal of research.

The act of remembering can be either intentional or unintentional. Much of everyday experience involves unintentional forms of remembering. It is rarely necessary to exert effort to recall such things as language (e.g., vocabulary) and behavioural routines (e.g., how to get ready for school in the morning). In contrast, intentional memory, also called *explicit memory*, requires effort to store and retrieve. Much of the research on memory development focuses on the strategies children use to remember information intentionally such as rehearsal, organization, and elaboration. The three areas of memory that improve with development are (1) basic capacities; (2) strategies that enhance memory; and (3) world knowledge. We will discuss each of these aspects in turn.

BASIC CAPACITIES   Basic memory capacities include the amount of information that can be held in short-term memory, referred to as memory span; the efficiency of memory processing; and the speed of this processing. Research has shown that these basic capacities—in particular, processing efficiency and processing speed—are related to each other and have an impact on the effectiveness of working memory (Bayliss et al., 2005; Demetriou et al., 2002).

Memory Span   Suppose you are asked to repeat a sequence of numbers beginning with three digits and then progressively more numbers are added. Eventually, you will be unable to repeat all the numbers correctly, for the sequence will have exceeded your **memory span** for this kind of information. The amount of information that a person can keep in short-term memory at any one time is limited, but the limit changes with

semantic memory

All the world knowledge and facts a person possesses.

episodic memory

Memory for specific events, often autobiographical in nature.

memory span

The amount of information one can hold in short-term memory.

development. For example, memory for a series of numbers (digit span) is about eight units for college/university students, six or seven units for 12-year-olds, and four units for 5-year-olds (Brener, 1940; Starr, 1923). Several explanations have been proposed regarding this age-related change. Juan Pascual-Leone (1980, 1989) of York University in Toronto argues that this growth in children and adolescents demonstrates that the capacity of working memory increases over time (i.e., that actual changes in the brain improve basic memory capability so that the child has more "room" to remember things). Others argue that there is no solid evidence for a capacity change as children develop (e.g., Dempster, 1985) and that young children can remember more items from lists of things that interest them (e.g., toys). Such findings demonstrate that interest or motivation plays a role in memory span, and capacity changes may not be necessary to explain changes associated with age (Lindberg, 1980).

Another explanation for older children's and adults' greater memory span is that they use one or more strategies that help them organize such information in a way that facilitates remembering it (Chi, 1976). In particular, the older person may "chunk" the information into smaller, more easily remembered groups of numbers (Miller, 1956), although it is worth noting that the number of such chunks that one can hold has come under debate (Cowan, 2001). Thus, whereas the young child may not be able to remember the sequence 1 8 6 7 1 9 9 9 2 0 0 2 because it is too long, the adult can recall the sequence because she chunks the numbers into meaningful groups: 1867 (the date of Confederation), 1999, and 2002 (the date that the Canadian men's hockey team won Olympic gold over the United States). Notice that world knowledge, which increases with age, enables this ability to chunk.

If this child is dialling a telephone number from memory, she is probably demonstrating a greater memory span than is common among children her age.

Processing Efficiency   The first time a child uses a memory strategy, such as chunking, it takes up a fair amount of space in working memory. However, with practice, some memory processing becomes automatic, and as a result, space in working memory becomes available to work on other problems or strategies. Robbie Case (1996) proposes that one of the important development changes in basic memory is that the memory system, or what he calls *executive processing space*, becomes more efficient (Demetrious, Christou, Spanoudis, & Platsidou, 2002); recently, a similar argument has been proposed by Pascual-Leone and his colleagues to explain changes in working memory (Roncadin, Pascual-Leone, Rich, & Dennis, 2007).

Case (1985) attributes the child's increasing efficiency to two factors: streamlining of executive control structures (e.g., as the result of strategies such as chunking and automatization) and biological maturation, such as changes in the myelination of the axons of neurons in such a way as to increase the efficiency of neural firing and, presumably, the efficiency of brain function. Although Case's position on the role of biological maturation in cognitive development has yet to be fully tested (Siegler & Alibabli, 2005), his emphasis on the role of increasing efficiency in the use of memory is consistent with research findings on memory development.

Processing Speed   Processing speed, which is often assessed by reaction time, is the time it takes an individual to carry out a given mental act, such as recognizing a stimulus or reading a word. Processing speed is connected with processing efficiency; the more efficient a process, the quicker it is. Kail (1995, 2000, 2003) has demonstrated that speed of processing increases linearly with age from childhood to early adulthood.

Developmental changes in processing speed are similar for tasks that are very different from one another, such as reading comprehension, mental addition, retrieving names from memory, and visual search (Kail, 1995). According to Kail, the fact that we see developmental changes in processing speeds in many different tasks with widely varying task components and requirements suggests that change in processing speed is a fundamental aspect of cognitive development. We also know that processing speed is not simply due to practice. With development, children increase the speed with which they accomplish tasks that they encounter regularly and those that they rarely encounter (and, therefore, have little opportunity to practise) (Kail, 1995; Miller & Vernon, 1996, 1997). Finally, Kail and Park (1994) found the same relation between processing speed and age in Korean children and North American children, which suggests that this may be a universal developmental process, although, clearly, more research needs to be conducted to confirm this possibility.

MEMORY STRATEGIES   Memory strategies are deliberate procedures that help people carry out memory-related tasks. Because what can be held in short-term memory is limited, if we want to remember something that exceeds these limitations, it is critical to use some technique or strategy. The ability to store and retrieve information efficiently from long-term memory also relies on strategies. People use a wide range of strategies to remember. Some of these strategies involve external supports such as taking notes in lectures or writing appointments on calendars. Other memory supports are purely mental (e.g., repeating that attractive person's name to yourself several times). Adults commonly use three memory strategies: rehearsal, organization, and elaboration. Developmentalists have studied these three strategies to determine when and how they emerge in childhood and what role they may play in enhancing children's memory.

Although researchers tend to study these strategies separately, children often use more than one strategy at a time (Schneider & Bjorkland, 1998; Siegler, 1996). Children's use of multiple strategies was demonstrated in a study by Coyle and Bjorkland (1997). They presented grade 2, 3, and 4 children with sets of words (e.g., *house, pencil, carrot, bean, dog, book, cat, potato*) that could be organized into categories such as vegetables, animals, or school-related items. Although the number of strategies children used to organize the words increased with age (see Figure 9-8), even grade 2 children used a variety of strategies.

Rehearsal   One of the simplest strategies is to repeat the information to be remembered, either mentally or out loud. This is called **rehearsal**. Research has shown that the spontaneous use of rehearsal to aid memory increases with age (Bebko, 1979; Flavell, Beach, & Chinsky, 1966; Lehmann & Hasselhorn, 2007). For example, younger children will repeat the items to be remembered only once or twice when more repetitions are needed, and they are less likely to repeat earlier items (Naus, 1982). However, even young children can employ and benefit from rehearsal strategies if instructed to use them (Gill, Kiecan-Aker, Roberts, & Fredenburg, 2003; Keeney, Cannizzo, & Flavell, 1967).

rehearsal

A memory strategy in which one repeats a number of times, either mentally or orally, the information one wants to remember.

Figure 9-8

More strategies, more memory

In a memory task, the oldest children used more strategies and recalled more words. Quite a few of the youngest children used multiple strategies, but their recall was less accurate.

Source: Coyle & Bjorklund, 1997.

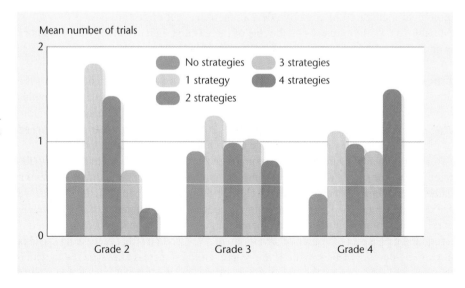

In a classic study, John Flavell and his colleagues (Flavell et al., 1966) showed a series of pictures to a group of children ranging from kindergarten to grade 5 and asked them to recall the sequence in which an experimenter pointed to a subset of the pictures. Watching the children's lip movements for a sign that they were rehearsing by naming the pictures to themselves, the researchers found that the children who used spontaneous rehearsal had better memory for the pictures. They also found that the use of such rehearsal increased dramatically with age. Whereas only about 10 percent of kindergarten children rehearsed the names of the objects in the pictures, more than 60 percent of grade 2 children and over 85 percent of grade 5 children did so. Later research by Ornstein, Naus, and Liberty (1975) modified this finding by showing that it was not the frequency of rehearsal that predicted performance differences in younger and older children. Rather, the style of rehearsal, which differs in younger and older children, explains the age differences in performance. Younger children are more likely to rehearse each item one at a time as it is presented to them. Older children are more likely to rehearse each item in a group with previously rehearsed items. It seems that the use of a more cumulative rehearsal strategy is more effective in aiding memory of items in a list. Although younger children can be trained to use a cumulative rehearsal strategy (Cox, Ornstein, Naus, Maxfield, & Zimler, 1989), older children are more likely to use this strategy spontaneously (Lehmann & Hasselhorn, 2007).

To perform well in a spelling bee, a person needs to know a lot of words. What memory strategies may be most effective for learning such information? Obviously, rehearsal can be a powerful tool in this context, providing the child with lots of practice in how to spell specific words.

Organization When we store information, we reorganize and reconstruct it to make it more meaningful and, thus, easier to remember. How does the process of actively altering and rebuilding information change as children get older? An answer to this question is found in research on **organization**, or the process of imposing an order on the information to be remembered using categories and hierarchical relations.

organization

Ordering information to be remembered by means of categorization and hierarchical relationships.

Over time, children make increasing use of organization to help them remember. The spontaneous use of organization to facilitate memory appears late in elementary school (Hasselhorn, 1992). By grade 4, most children use organizational strategies, such as categorizing and sorting (Bjorklund, 2005; Rakison & Oakes, 2003). Suppose that we present a series of cards containing pictures of a *sweater, hat, apple, orange, jeans, sandwich, gloves, coat, milk,* and *dress* to children of different ages. Older children would be more likely than younger ones to form the cards into two groups of similar objects: *apple, orange, sandwich,* and *milk* as food items and *sweater, hat, jeans, gloves, coat,* and *dress* as items of clothing (Schneider & Bjorklund, 1998). Children who use this strategy would be better able to recall the items in a subsequent test (Best, 1993; Best & Ornstein, 1986).

Are we to assume that young children are incapable of learning to use categorization? No, indeed. Children as young as 2 or 3 years old have been found to use basic category labels that help them remember (Waxman, Shipley, & Shepperson, 1991). Also, recall from Chapter 8 that assistance from more skilled people, such as parents or teachers, may enhance a child's cognitive performance. Researchers have been able to teach children as young as 7 to use organizational strategies like categorization. For example, Ackerman (1996) prompted 7- and 12-year-olds to categorize a set of words (e.g., *horse, pig,* and *cow*) by asking them, "Are all of these animals?" Older children generally recalled more than younger ones did, but with training, 7-year-olds did as well as their older peers.

Finally, children's engagement in a task can also influence the use of this strategy. Guttentag (1995) presented grade 3 children with pictures of common objects to be recalled (25 pictures in 5 categories) and used these measures to explore how active participation (being allowed to place the pictures themselves) related to children's use of an organizational strategy. Active participation led children to use the organizational strategy and thereby facilitated their recall.

Elaboration   The strategy of **elaboration** involves adding to the information we want to remember to make it more meaningful and, thus, easier to remember. This is a useful strategy because, although it might seem to add to the information burden, we are much more likely to remember something that is meaningful to us (Kee, 1994; Schneider & Bjorklund, 1998). The Peanuts cartoon in Figure 9-9 shows how Charlie Brown elaborates the numbers of his locker combination with famous major league baseball players' numbers to provide a meaningful context for three seemingly random numbers. As with other strategies, children are more likely to use elaboration when they get older.

Even preschoolers and young children can be trained to use elaborative techniques, however (e.g., Brown & Pipe, 2003; O'Sullivan & Pressley, 1984; Pressley & Hilden 2006), and others have found that simply inducing children to form elaborations can influence their memory. Eileen Wood, from Wilfrid Laurier University, and Teena Willoughby, from the University of Waterloo, and their colleagues (Willoughby, Wood, & Kraftcheck, 2003; Wood, Willoughby, Bolger, Younger, & Kaspar, 1993; Wood, Willoughby, McDermott, Motz, Kaspar, & Ducharme, 1999), for example, have investigated the use of "elaborative interrogation" in which children (or adults for that matter; Willoughby et al., 2003) are asked questions about information they have learned that forces them to elaborate on this information. In one study (Wood et al., 1993), researchers found that grade 5 children remembered more facts about animals when they were asked to explain "why" these facts might be true of a particular animal, relative to groups in which the students either simply rehearsed the facts or were given elaborative information provided by the experimenter. Thus, actively generating elaborations also has a positive influence on memory.

elaboration

A memory strategy in which one adds to information to make it more meaningful and, thus, easier to place in long-term memory.

Figure 9-9

Charlie Brown's elaboration strategy

Source: PEANUTS reprinted by permission of United Feature Syndicate, Inc.

Why Do Young Children Not Use Strategies? Why do young children fail to use strategies to help them remember? There are three explanations as to why young children fail to use strategies that older children and adults find so useful. First, children may possess a **mediation deficiency**. This suggests that they simply cannot make use of strategies for incorporating information into long-term storage. The fact that children can be taught to use such strategies, however, makes this proposal seem unlikely.

A second explanation proposes that young children have a **production deficiency**. The suggestion here is that, although they may know certain strategies for remembering, they are unable to generate and use these strategies spontaneously. This raises the question of what young children do while they are trying to remember something. Although the strategies that young children use may not be the same strategies that older children and adults use, and although they are not always effective, they are nonetheless strategic acts by the child to remember. For example, DeLoache and Brown (1983) observed children as young as 18 months of age as they tried to remember the hiding place of a toy in their own home after a brief waiting period. Although some of the strategies children used aided memory, such as staring or pointing at the hiding location during the entire waiting period, others were less effective, such as repeating the name of the toy over and over with little or no attention to the hiding place. Thus, even young children can produce memory strategies spontaneously, but the complexity and effectiveness of their strategies are limited in comparison to the strategies of older children.

Finally, some researchers have suggested a third explanation—namely that the children have a **utilization deficiency** (Bjorklund, Miller, Coyle, & Slawinski, 1997; Miller, 1990, 2000; Miller & Seier, 1994; Salatas Waters, 2000). When they are in the early phases of strategy acquisition—for example, when learning how to rehearse—children may produce an appropriate strategy spontaneously but be unable to profit from using it. To illustrate, in one study, 9- and 10-year-old children were trained in the use of organizational memory strategies for remembering items in a list, such as sorting items into categories (Bjorklund, Schneider, Cassel, & Ashley, 1994). Later, when the children were tested on their memory for the items, the children showed that they had retained the strategies they had been taught in the training session. However, despite the use of these strategies, their memory for the items decreased. In other words, they used the strategies but the strategies did not facilitate their memory of the items.

Children's ability to benefit from memory strategies may reflect a trade-off between the costs and benefits of using the strategy (Miller, Seier, Probert, & Aloise, 1991). When a strategy is newer and a less practised skill—as is often the case for younger children—using the strategy may consume much mental effort. Therefore, children may opt sometimes not to use it or to use it only haphazardly. As children become more adept at strategizing, the costs decrease while the benefits increase. With practice, then, children learn to use a new strategy to aid memory (Coyle & Bjorklund, 1997). In addition, children's ability to use different memory strategies is based on any number of factors. Box 9.1 on the next page, for instance, describes an example of how strategy use can vary with the language ability of the child.

KNOWLEDGE OF THE WORLD What children know about the world in general influences what they understand about a present event and what they will remember about it later. We saw an example of the effects of **world knowledge** on children's memory in our discussion of Michelene Chi's work with child chess experts and adult novices. Chi and others have further documented the differing cognitive performances of novices and experts (Bedard & Chi, 1992; Chase & Simon, 1973; Chi, 1978; Chi & Koeske, 1983; Chi & Slotta, 1993).

Children obtain knowledge of the world in many ways: from their own experiences, through formal and informal instruction, and via information they obtain from their society and family. This knowledge also influences their memory abilities. Research based on Vygotsky's sociocultural view of development has focused on society's role in

mediation deficiency

Inability to use strategies to store information in long-term memory.

production deficiency

Inability to generate and spontaneously use memory strategies that one knows.

utilization deficiency

Inability to use a memory strategy that one knows.

world knowledge

What a child has learned from experience and knows about the world in general.

Box 9.1

Risk and Resilience

MEMORY SKILLS AND STRATEGIES IN CHILDREN WHO ARE DEAF

The abilities to remember information and to retrieve this information in appropriate situations are so important in our daily lives that it is really no surprise that these abilities and their development have been the subject of extensive investigation over the years. Of course, this interest in memory and cognitive processing has typically focused on children and adults who have all their perceptual and cognitive faculties "intact" or functioning within a normal range. This raises the obvious question of the nature of memory skills and cognitive abilities in populations that, for one reason or another, are at risk in some way. One area that has been examined is deaf children's memory and their use of various memory strategies.

In fact, research on the memory skills of children who are deaf reveals an interesting dichotomy. On the one hand, a number of researchers have seen that deaf children show significantly more problems than hearing children with tests of short-term memory that involve verbal material or sequential processing (Bebko, 1984; Bebko & McKinnon, 1990; Chen, 1974; Wallace & Corballis, 1973). On the other hand, some studies suggest that deaf children do as well, or possibly even better, than hearing children when the short-term memory task involves visual or spatial processing (Blair, 1957; O'Conner & Hermelin, 1976). Although the reason for this difference is ultimately unclear, one suggestion is that it is tasks that can be most easily accomplished by spontaneous verbal rehearsal that produce the greatest differences between hearing and deaf children.

The fact that it is verbal tasks that appear to produce this difference between hearing and deaf children provides a nice example of a production deficiency. In this case, deaf children may be simply unable to produce the appropriate memory strategy in the verbal and sequential contexts. In an exploration of the use of rehearsal strategies in young children, James Bebko (1984) of York University showed a sequence of easily recognized matched cards (e.g., red, green, blue) to groups of deaf children and then looked at the amount of spontaneous rehearsal of these sequences engaged in by the children during a delay period. Bebko saw that the deaf children's spontaneous use of rehearsal did not

appear until relatively late, about 10 to 13 years of age, whereas rehearsal typically appears much earlier, at about 7 to 8 years, in hearing children (Flavell et al., 1966). Interestingly, though, when the deaf children were induced to rehearse the sequences, their memory was as good, if not better, than the hearing subjects.

Given that deaf children benefit just as much as hearing children from rehearsal, why don't they spontaneously use this strategy? One possibility, and an idea proposed by Bebko (1984), is the difference in linguistic environments of hearing and deaf children. Hearing children are immersed in their native language from birth; in contrast, because diagnosis of deafness (and subsequent language intervention) often does not occur until much later (by, say, 3 years of age), deaf children experience a significant delay in their language experience and training, which could be related to spontaneous rehearsal. Bebko and McKinnon (1990) tested this hypothesis directly by deriving language experience scores for deaf children based on the number of years they had received language training and found that language experience was a virtually perfect mediator of the relation between age and rehearsal. And in a further test of this idea, Bebko, Bell, Metcalfe-Haggert, and McKinnon (1998) found that not only was language proficiency an important predictor of rehearsal use, but measures of the degree to which deaf children use language automatically was also an important contributing factor to the use of rehearsal.

Such findings have a number of educational implications. For example, given that deaf children can remember information as well as hearing children once this information has been encoded well, efforts to aid memory in deaf children will likely be more effective if they focus on how one should try to remember (i.e., the processes of memory) rather than emphasizing what is to be remembered (i.e., its content). Another implication is if it is true that linguistic experience plays a critical role here, then interventions will be particularly effective if they focus on the language environment of the child. In this case, the timing may be critical, with early language intervention playing a central role in memory processing.

children's use of memory strategies and their memory performance (Gauvain, 2001b). Unfortunately, a great deal of cross-cultural research investigating children's memory processes has applied experimental techniques commonly used in Western society to non-Western populations. As a result, children in non-Western communities, who are less familiar with these techniques, often perform poorly on them (Cole, 1996; Rogoff, 2003). However, when memory tasks draw on children's knowledge base, for example, when they are presented in culturally familiar contexts, children in non-Western cultures perform as well as, or better than, children tested in the North America.

Meaningfulness and Goals   Rogoff and Waddell (1982) presented 9-year-old Mayan children in Guatemala and 9-year-old North American children with a memory task. The children watched as 20 familiar objects were placed into a model of a town that contained familiar landmarks (each model was appropriate to the culture of the group being tested). These objects were placed in their culturally appropriate locations—for example, boats on lakes and furniture in houses. The objects were then removed from the display, and after a short delay, the children were asked to recreate the display they had seen prepared. Rogoff and Waddell found that the Mayan children performed slightly better than the North American children did.

What led to the Mayan children's advantage? Rogoff (2003) speculates that the performance of the North American children was hampered by the fact that about a third of them tried to use the strategy of rehearsal. However, this strategy, which is often taught in North American schools, is best suited to memorizing unrelated lists of objects; it may have been only minimally effective in this spatial-reconstruction task. In contrast to the North American children, the Mayan children appeared to rely on the look of the display; they used the spatial relations of the objects to organize their memory, which seems to have enhanced their performance.

In another study designed to explore how the goal of the activity affects children's memory, researchers (Mistry et al., 2001; Rogoff & Mistry, 1990) enlisted the help of the parents of a group of 4-year-olds. In the "lab" condition, parents presented their children with 10 pictures of lunch-related items such as cheese, bread, juice and a napkin. After repeating the names of all 10 items, they asked the children to go to the experimenter at the other side of the room and tell her all the items they remembered. In the "lunch" condition, parents told the children that they were making a bag lunch and needed all the ingredients from the "grocer" (played by the experimenter). The parent showed the child the pictures of the 10 items, and the child then went to the "grocer" and asked for the items. On average, children in the lab condition remembered only 2.7 items, whereas children in the lunch condition remembered 5.3 items. It seems that a clear and meaningful goal for the activity is important to children's remembering.

These findings echo Vygotsky's (1978) view that memory in everyday life occurs in the course of meaningful, goal-directed activities. In other words, to remember something in and of itself is rarely our goal. Instead, we usually remember something so that we can do something else. For example, we remember the items on a list so that we can assemble them for an event, like a meal. Frequently, when memory is tested in laboratory situations, remembering in and of itself is the goal of the activity. Therefore, children who have more experience with activities in which memory functions as a goal in and of itself, which is frequent in school settings, do better on such tasks than children who have less experience with school. But when a laboratory task is designed to resemble a more everyday type of memory activity—one in which remembering is used to carry out a meaningful, goal-directed activity—the difference in memory performance between children who have much versus little experience with school is reduced or eliminated.

Meaningfulness may not always elicit optimal remembering in children, however. Consider the question of children's reliability as witnesses in the courtroom. Often, the cases in which children serve as witnesses involve domestic conflict or, worse, domestic

Box 9.2
Child Psychology in Action

SHOULD YOUNG CHILDREN TESTIFY IN COURT?

How accurate can children be when asked to give testimony in a court of law? Research has indicated that suggestion by others, especially adults, as well as the distinctiveness of their memories, and so on, strongly influence a young child's reporting of past events (Bruck et al., 2006). Several investigators have explored this issue by having children listen to brief stories and then following the presentation with the introduction of inaccurate information (e.g., Ceci et al., 1987; Doris, 1991; Marche & Howe, 1995; Ornstein, Larus, & Clubb, 1992). In general, these researchers have concluded that young children are more often affected by inaccurate information than are older children and that interviewing children expertly is a crucial factor in such investigations (Bigelow, 2000).

Steve Ceci from Cornell University, Maggie Bruck from McGill University, and their colleagues (Bruck et al., 2002; Ceci & Bruck, 1998; Ceci et al., 1998) undertook an extensive series of studies to explore these effects of suggestion on children's memory. In one study, the experimenters engaged preschool children in a game similar to "Simon Says." A month later, an interviewer talked with each child about the activity. In one condition of the experiment, the interviewer was accurately informed about what happened during the activity, and in the other, the interviewer was given false information. When the interviewer was accurately informed, the children's recall was 93 percent accurate. However, when she was misinformed, 34 percent of children 3 to 4 years old and 18 percent of children 5 to 6 years old corroborated false statements about what had happened during the experiment itself. The experimenters concluded that the younger the child, the more likely he or she was to be influenced by false information.

One important limitation to the type of study just described is that the kind of material that children are asked to remember is not especially emotionally charged. Unfortunately, however, the most common situations under which children are actually asked to testify tend to be traumatic situations, such as may occur in cases of physical or sexual abuse. And it is the traumatic nature of the situation that most of us intuitively think would have an important influence, either for good or ill, on children's memories. Accordingly, a number of researchers have attempted to investigate children's memory for traumatic events as well.

Carole Peterson from Memorial University and her colleagues (Howe et al., 1994, 1995; Peterson, 1999, 2002; Peterson & Bell, 1996; Peterson & Parsons, 2005; Peterson et al., 2004, 2007; Peterson & Whalen, 2001) have conducted a series of studies looking at 1- to 13-year-old children's memories for traumatic events, comparing memory immediately after the event to up to five years later. In one study (Howe et al., 1995), these investigators examined 30-, 36-, and 48-month-old infants' memories for injuries requiring emergency-room treatment. To explore this question, an experimenter interviewed children, and their parents, a few days after these children were seen in the emergency room for treatment of such injuries as broken limbs, cuts requiring stitches, dog bites, and so on. At this first interview, children were simply asked to tell the experimenter what happened when they got hurt and were also provided with some open-ended questions such as, "Who was with you when you got hurt?" and "Who took you to the hospital?"

Six months later, these children were interviewed again using the same procedure (parents were asked to not rehearse the incident with their children over this six-month period). These researchers then analyzed the children's responses, assessing their accuracy and looking for intrusions in their reports.

The percentage of children who added some piece of information that did not actually occur, at both the initial and six-month interview, is shown in Figure 9-10, and reveals that at all ages, a significant number of children made intrusion errors. Interestingly, however, those children who made such intrusions recalled the same amount of correct information as the children

and/or child abuse that is sometimes of a sexual nature. Although these situations are highly meaningful to children, as Box 9.2 suggests, other factors, such as the influence of inaccurate suggestions by others and repeated questions may undermine memory performance (Eisen, Goodman, & Quas, 2002).

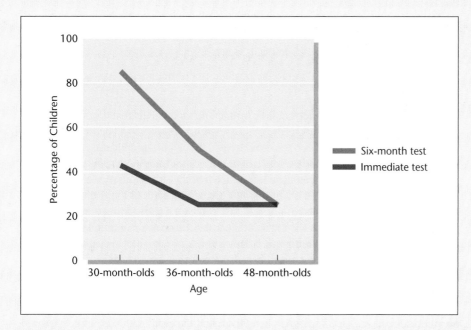

Figure 9-10

Children's memory for traumatic events

Percentage of preschoolers who exhibited at least one intrusion error in their recall of a traumatic event at their immediate interview (3–5 days later; blue line) and their interview 6 months later (red line).

who did not make any intrusions. Thus, the good news is that although other events can intrude between a traumatic event and its recall, these intrusions do not seem to interfere with children's abilities to correctly recall details of the event. The bad news, though, is that these intrusions often involve similar events and, thus, may lead to the confusion or blending of the intrusions and the actual events themselves.

Why do such errors occur? In an attempt to examine this question, Peterson and her colleagues have found that the format of the questions has an impact on recall—children show much poorer recall when ask questions in a yes/no format, as opposed to using *wh-* questions (who, where, or what) (Fivush et al., 2002; Peterson & Grant, 2001; Peterson & Biggs, 1997; Peterson et al., 1999). Peterson et al. (2007) also found that parents who were more elaborative in discussing these incidents with their children had children who

remembered more of the event during an initial interview and up to two years later.

Research in the 1990s has moved beyond description to focus on the mechanisms that may account for children's ability to recall events accurately. Some cognitive mechanisms include strength of memory, semantic knowledge, knowledge of scripts, and linguistic comprehension. Socio-emotional factors also play a role, such as avoiding punishment or embarrassment, keeping promises made to others, eschewing personal gain if it involves being deceitful, and social pressure. As we have repeatedly noted, cognitive and social factors operate together in accounting for the kinds of effects we have discussed here. Finally, this work reminds us that the lines between basic and applied research are often blurred. Although the research reviewed tells us about children's testimony, it also informs us about children's cognitive and social development.

Knowledge of the Self: Autobiographical Memory Here is how 5-year-old Ben explained to his teacher how his 2½-year-old brother Graeme sustained a bloody but minor cut to the head.

Teacher: What did you do over the holidays?

Ben: There was an accident.

Teacher: Oh, what happened?

Ben: My brother jumped on the bed and cut his head on the table. And then, after he cut his head, then the paramedics came and two fire trucks and an ambulance.

Teacher: Oh, how awful! Then what happened?

Ben: Mommy went with him to the hospital in the ambulance. I stayed home with Nana.

In this example, an adult, the child's teacher, elicited details that brought out more information about the event from the child's memory. She also defined an emotional context and steered the child along as he recounted the story. The child used the occasion to describe the aspects of the event that were important and understandable to him. He used the **narrative form**, an account of an event that is temporally sequenced and conveys meaning (Bruner, 1990). In his narrative, he described the event, as well as information about himself, his family, and his own experience during the event. Even though what Ben said is brief, he makes it clear that this was an emotionally arousing experience for him. Even a short narrative may have deep meaning or value for a child (Engel, 1995). This value is enhanced because memories such as this one are personal in an interesting way: They define an individual's own history. Because there are often social contributions to these memories as children discuss them with others, this history is shaped by other people who inform the child about what aspects of his memory are interesting or important to remember. Given that the event in this example garnered interest and attention from an adult, it may increase the likelihood of Ben's retelling the story and therefore rehearsing it, which will help him remember the event. Even the interpretations of others regarding an event may become part of the memory if the retelling triggers a certain response. For instance, if a child describes an experience that adults find amusing, the event may then be remembered not only in terms of the actions and the sequences of these actions, but also in terms of its effect on others.

A person's memories about things that happened to her at a specific time or place are part of the person's **autobiographical memory** (Bauer, 2006). Autobiographical memory emerges in the early years of life, when a child is about 2½-years old, and it develops substantially over the preschool years (Nelson & Fivush, 2004). Autobiographical memories are linked in both process and content to children's social experiences (Fivush et al., 2006). Researchers estimate that during family interaction, discussion of past events occurs as often as five to seven times an hour (Fivush et al., 1996). Parents talk directly to children about the past. Parents also talk to each other about the past in the presence of their children. Early in the child's life, shared memories are mostly one-sided, with the parent taking on much of the responsibility for reminiscing. But by the age of 3, children's contributions increase and their memories begin to endure rather well. In fact, children as young as 3 years of age can remember specific event information over a fairly long time period (Fivush & Hamond, 1989).

Shared conversations about the past also help children have better memory for the event (Haden et al., 2001). The fact that these conversations typically tie these memories to something of personal significance helps children acquire knowledge about themselves, other people, and the world in which they live (Engel & Li, 2004). This type of personal storytelling or shared reminiscence is not unique to particular families or cultures. This practice is culturally widespread and helps to communicate cultural values to children. Psychologists have observed interesting cultural variations in these conversations. Wang (2004) asked preschool and early-school-age Chinese and North American children to recount four autobiographical events. She found that the memo-

narrative form

A temporally sequenced account that conveys meaning about an event.

autobiographical memory

A collection of memories of things that have happened to a person at a specific time or place.

ries of the North American children included lots of personal details that emphasized the child's own experiences and feelings. In contrast, the Chinese children recalled memories that concentrated on social aspects of their lives, such as interactions with people and daily routines. These patterns are consistent with different emphases on autonomy and social connections and with the parenting styles in these two cultural communities, which have been studied by Ruth Chao. We take a close look at the difference between groups of children from more similar milieus—Canada and Italy—in Box 12.3, "Perspectives on Diversity: Cross-Cultural Variations in Children's Peer Relationships," on page 498.

During social interaction, children learn much about what to remember, how to formulate their memories, and how to retain them in a retrievable form (Bauer, 2006). These conversations also help children learn how to cope with difficult or emotional experiences such as an asthma attack or a hurricane or other environmental disaster (Fivush & Sales, 2004).

Such shared memory experiences carry much import in young children's lives (Nelson, 2007). They contribute to the development of the self, and thereby help create what Nelson (1996) calls the historical self. They also contribute to the cultural self in that shared memories reflect the values and practices of the culture in which development occurs. Finally, they give children the opportunity to rehearse these memories and, in so doing, to learn some very important things about the process of remembering.

Problem Solving and Reasoning

Every day, people try to achieve many and varied goals. Some of these are modest, such as having a good breakfast. Some are grand, such as completing a long project at school or work. To reach these goals, people organize their actions in ways that are directed toward meeting their goals. **Problem solving** is the processing of identifying an action goal and delineating steps or means to reach this goal. Problem solving is a central feature of human intelligence. In fact, some psychologists equate problem solving with thinking. An important feature of problem solving is overcoming obstacles that interfere with reaching the goal. Thus, problem solving usually involves a goal and one or more obstacles that need to be overcome to reach this goal.

problem solving

The identification of a goal and of steps to reach that goal.

During children's development, their problem-solving abilities become more sophisticated; the strategies they possess become better developed and they acquire new strategies (Garton, 2004; Klahr, 2000). To illustrate the impact these changes have on children's problem-solving abilities, we examine development in four areas of problem solving: solving problems by using rules that guide thinking; solving problems by analogy, or using information from one problem to solve another; using cognitive tools, such as the structure of routine behaviours or forms of representations, to solve problems, and solving problems by deductive reasoning. We also discuss another type of reasoning that plays an important role in cognitive development and problem solving: numerical reasoning.

RULE-BASED PROBLEM SOLVING Some types of problems are solved by applying rules that describe the properties or elements of the problem. An interesting aspect of the development of problem-solving skills is that children learn the various rules to solve problems at different points in childhood. This is because the rules often vary in complexity, so younger children understand and apply the simpler rules of the problem whereas older children understand and apply the more complex rules. This developmental change lends itself well to observational analysis of the development of skills in rule-based problem solving and Robert Siegler (1983, 1991) has conducted research examining this development. This research uses the balance scale task developed by Inhelder and Piaget (1958), in which there is a balance beam with weights on either side of the fulcrum. Children are asked to predict which way a balance with

Piaget believed that children had to reach the stage of formal operations before they could solve complex problems, such as measuring and calculating relative weights. Later researchers, such as Robert Siegler, have found that younger children may be able to solve such problems if they have enough information.

different weights placed at different distances from the fulcrum will tilt when supports holding up the arms of the beam are released. As you can see from Figure 9-11, what makes this a difficult problem is the need to consider two dimensions at the same time: both the number of weights on each side of the balance's fulcrum and the distance from the fulcrum at which each set of weights lies. Based on their observations of children of different ages, researchers (Klahr & Siegler, 1978; van Rijn et al., 2003) have described four rules that children apply at various points in development as they go about solving the problem:

Rule I: The side with more weights is heavier.

Rule II: If weights on both sides are equal, the side whose weights are farther from the fulcrum is heavier.

Rule III: If one side has more weights but the other's weights are farther from the fulcrum, you have to guess at the answer.

Rule IV: Weights × distance from fulcrum equals *torque*; the side with greater torque is heavier.

Siegler (1976, 1981) found that 3-year-olds do not to use rules at all; about half of 4-year-olds used rule I, and all 5-year-olds used rule I. Among 9-year-olds, roughly half used rule II and half used rule III, and 13- and 17-year-olds almost always used rule III. Interestingly, although rule IV embodies the reasoning Piaget attributed to the child in the period of formal operations, only a minority of university students even used it! When Siegler analyzed the task carefully to try to discover why young children couldn't solve many of the balance-scale problems, he hypothesized that perhaps limited memory and/or lack of knowledge were at fault. When he allowed children to continue viewing the original balance arrangement (low memory demand) and gave them direct, detailed, and repeated instructions (knowledge), those as young as 5 were often able to solve the problems. In this case, social support or scaffolding, as research based on Vygotsky's ideas would predict, led to better task performance (Gauvain 2001a).

SOLVING PROBLEMS BY ANALOGY Suppose that you are trying to learn how to use a personal computer and are having difficulty understanding how all the directories and files are organized. In this situation, drawing an analogy between the workings of the computer and that of an office filing system may be helpful. The computer can be thought of as a filing cabinet, and files are the documents inserted in the drawers of the cabinet.

Figure 9-11

Balance-scale problems and strategies for solving them

Using Robert Siegler's rule IV will get you the correct answers on all of these problems. Interestingly, your next best chance to get as many correct answers as possible is to use rule II. Why? Answers to problems are upside down below.

Problems 1 and 6: balance; problems 2–5: left down

Source: From Siegler, Robert S., Alibali, Marth W., *Children's Thinking*, 4th edition, 2005. Adapted and reprinted by permission of Pearson Education, Inc., Upper Saddle River, NJ.

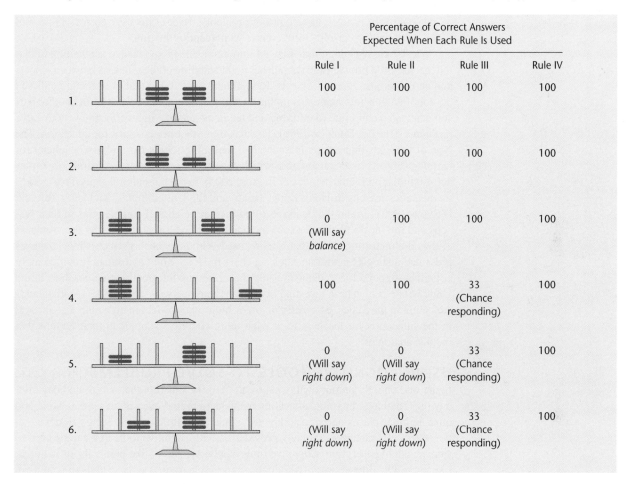

	Percentage of Correct Answers Expected When Each Rule Is Used			
	Rule I	Rule II	Rule III	Rule IV
1.	100	100	100	100
2.	100	100	100	100
3.	0 (Will say *balance*)	100	100	100
4.	100	100	33 (Chance responding)	100
5.	0 (Will say *right down*)	0 (Will say *right down*)	33 (Chance responding)	100
6.	0 (Will say *right down*)	0 (Will say *right down*)	33 (Chance responding)	100

The use of *analogy*—or the inference that if two or more objects or situations resemble each other in some respects, they are likely to resemble each other in yet other respects—is a powerful problem-solving strategy (Holyoak, 2005). In an analogy, there is one situation that is more familiar and one that is less familiar. When individuals use an analogy to help them solve a problem, they draw an inference between the *source analogue*, or the familiar situation, and the *target analogue*, or the unfamiliar situation (Gentner & Holyoak, 1997). Sometimes, children and adults find it difficult to either think or to make use of analogies (Gick & Holyoak, 1980, 1983; Kim & Choi, 2003). One reason may be that when analogies are presented in the classic form of A:B as C:? (e.g., "foot is to leg as arm is to what?"), the important relations that need to be evaluated in the analogy may be unclear.

However, when simpler relations are used, even infants are able to use them to solve a problem (Goswami, 2001). For instance, Chen, Sanchez, and Campbell (1997) showed that 13-month-olds can use the perceptual similarity of different tools, such as boxes, cloths, and strings, to pull toys closer to play with them. Using perceptual similarity is a very simple type of analogical reasoning, however—recognizing deeper relations across two pairs of objects is more difficult. Research has shown that young children can demonstrate reasoning involving deeper relations provided the relational information is clear and little distracting information is present (Richland et al., 2006). For instance, in a study with preschoolers, pictures represented the A, B, and C terms of the analogy—for example, chocolate (A):melted chocolate (B) as snowman (C):? (Goswami & Brown, 1990). The investigator would then show children five picture choices, one of which was of a melted snowman, and children would be asked to choose the picture that best represented the answer (D). Three-year-olds were correct 52 percent of the time on these types of problems, 4-year-olds were correct 89 percent of the time, and 5-year-olds were correct 99 percent of the time.

Analogical reasoning may play an important role in knowledge acquisition in that it helps the child broaden and deepen her understanding of the relations between objects and across similar types of objects. Researchers have found that even though children do not often generate analogies on their own, that cognitive support from another person can lead a child into identifying and using an analogy in an effective way to solve problems (Chen & Daehler, 1989). This has important implications for education. The type of relations that occurs in analogical reasoning seems particularly beneficial for learning subjects like mathematics, which require the application of abstract principles across similar problems (Novick & Bassok, 2005). In a cross-cultural analysis of grade 8 mathematics lessons in Hong Kong, Japan, and the United States, Richland, Zur, and Holyoak (2007) found that teachers often include relational comparisons in their lessons and the most effective lessons included cognitive supports such as the vividness of the relational comparison that is being used. Although teachers in the three countries presented analogies at similar rates, teachers in Hong Kong and Japan provided more cognitive supports for students in using this relational information than teachers in the United States did. These investigators suggest that one way to strengthen mathematics education in the States, especially in junior high school when many youth lose interest in the subject, is for teachers to provide more cognitive support in their lessons that include analogies.

USING COGNITIVE TOOLS TO SOLVE PROBLEMS

If we had to figure out, entirely on our own, what to do in every situation that is repeated day after day (e.g., bathing, dressing, and eating meals) and to find our way to school, work, and other familiar places anew each day, we would have little time or energy to devote to new events and activities. Society provides us with cognitive tools that can be used to support intelligent action. Cognitive tools can be symbolic, like numerals, or material, like maps. Over the course of childhood, children learn to use these tools to help them solve problems. Psychologists refer to these types of external aids as cognitive tools because they function in the same way that a tool like a hammer does when you try to build something. A tool is an extension of your action (Lockman, 2000). It enables you to carry out an activity that you could not carry out in the same way or at all without the use of the tool. Sociocultural psychologists are particularly interested in the understanding and use of cognitive tools because such tools are products of a culture, they mediate cognitive activity, and they are passed on to children socially through the efforts of more experienced members of the culture (Olson & Cole, 2006; Sternberg & Preiss, 2005).

To illustrate the important role that cognitive tools play in intellectual development, we concentrate on three particular tools: scripts, cognitive maps, and symbolic representations. We use these three types of cognitive tools to show how important such tools are to cognitive functioning and its development

Scripts   One way that people deal with everyday situations is by forming scripts for many routine activities. **Scripts** provide basic outlines of what one can expect in a particular situation and what one should do in that situation, allowing people to carry out many routine behaviours efficiently and almost automatically (Fivush, 2002; Nelson, 1993; Schank & Ableson, 1977).

script

A mental representation of an event or situation of daily life, including the expected order in which things happen and how one should behave in that event or situation.

Even infants and toddlers learn to organize their representations of routine events such as bathing and feeding along script-like lines (Bauer & Wewerka, 1997). Bauer and her colleagues (Bauer & Dow, 1994; Bauer & Mandler, 1992) have shown that by the end of the first year, infants use temporal order information in recalling events. For example, these researchers presented infants with a familiar sequence, such as giving a teddy bear a bath (*put teddy in the tub, "wash" teddy with a sponge, "dry" teddy with the towel*). Not only were infants able to reproduce the familiar sequence with a high degree of accuracy, but they were also able to do this with novel events as well (*make a rocking horse move with a magnet*). This research suggests that the central aspect of the script—that is, the ability to represent events in temporal order—is learned very early in life (Bauer et al., 2000).

One of the ways researchers have demonstrated early understanding of scripts is to observe what a child does when a routine event is changed and thereby violates the expectations of a script. Even very young children find such changes confusing and disconcerting (Bauer & Wewerka, 1997). In fact, young children are more rigid in their applications of scripts than older children and adults (Wimmer, 1980). For example, when asked to recall stories, young children will eliminate inconsistent elements of a story to preserve the expected sequence of events or to add events that they were expecting to happen but that did not (Fivush et al., 1996; Myles-Worsley et al., 1986). Moreover, if you present 20-month-olds with an incorrect sequence (e.g., *dry, wash, put teddy bear in tub*), they sometimes correct the order to the real-life script (*wash* before *dry*). When the order of a well-understood script is violated, toddlers often say, "That's so silly."

In addition to organizing behaviour, what other roles might scripts play in cognitive development? Scripts help children remember over a long period. In one instance, kindergarten children visited a museum, a special event for youngsters. Not only did the children develop and remember a general museum script when questioned six weeks and one year later, but they were able to remember details of their personal museum visit at these times as well (Fivush et al., 1984). The children could distinguish the general from the personal script, and the general script appeared to helps them remember personal experiences better by providing a way to organize specific memories. By 8 years of age children even know which social scripts are appropriate for dealing with parents, friends, siblings, and teachers (Bigelow et al., 1996).

Scripts also function as a cognitive tool by freeing up space in the information-processing system so that an individual can pay attention to new or unexpected information that might come up within the course of a routine activity. As such, scripts function as a tool that helps to organize children's memory and expectations of events and, over the course of development, they are increasingly part of the information that guides children's behaviour.

Cognitive Maps   Just as children need to be able to negotiate their way through routine events, so too they must find their way through the spatial environment. Even very young children manage to manoeuvre their way through familiar places, avoiding obstacles and barriers in their paths (Heth & Cornell, 1980; Kingsnorth & Schmuckler, 2000; Schmuckler, 1996a). Spatial cognition—that is, the processing of visual information and spatial relations—is critical to human functioning (Newcombe & Huttenlocher, 2003). Many cognitive tools have been devised to support spatial thinking, including maps, directions, and, most recently, global positioning systems (GPS) in automobiles. Children learn to use tools to aid their understanding and use of spatial information, and this capacity changes throughout childhood. For example, young children often interpret symbolic representations, such as the symbols used on maps, quite literally: They may assume that the outline of an airplane on a map means that there's a real airplane, rather than an airport, at that location (Downs & Liben, 1986). As children grow, they become better able to use this kind of information

This child's script for her visit to the Calgary Zoo will help her remember the animals she saw and the things she learned about them for a long time after.

accurately to negotiate new surroundings (Liben, 1999; Uttal, 2000). Parents and other more experienced cultural members play important roles in helping children learn to use maps and other tools (Gauvain, 1993).

As children mature, they also become more skilful at constructing mental and physical maps of places they know (home, school, and neighbourhood) and routes they have travelled. They do this with the aid of **cognitive maps** (Tolman, 1948), which are mental representations of the spatial relations within a physical or geographical place—for example, a playground or a town. According to Siegel and his colleagues (Anooshian & Siegel, 1985; Siegel & White, 1975), children develop the ability to form cognitive maps in three steps (see Table 9-2). First, they learn to recognize specific landmarks, acquiring *landmark knowledge*. Next, they put several landmarks together to form *route knowledge* (Cornell, Heth, & Skoczylas, 1999; Heth, Cornell, & Flood, 2002). Finally, children acquire the ability to combine routes into an understanding of the spatial relations, referred to as a cognitive or *mental map*.

Landmark learning emerges early in life, and changes with development. On simple tasks, 3-year-old children can use landmarks to search for an object (Newcombe et al., 1998). Over the course of childhood, children get better at identifying and using landmarks (Cornell, Heth, & Broda, 1989; Cornell, Heth, & Rowat, 1992; Heth, Cornell, & Alberts, 1997). For example, Edward Cornell and Donald Heth and their colleagues at the University of Alberta (Cornell et al., 1989, 1992; Heth et al., 1997) have looked at the impact of explicit instructions to pay attention to landmarks on children's route finding. In one study, Cornell and colleagues (Cornell et al., 2001), observed children between 6 and 12 years of age as they travelled through the neighbourhoods around their homes, where they were allowed to roam on their own (referred to as their *home range*; see Figure 9-12). The experimenters observed the visual scanning that children used during their travel in the home range along with the distance and the duration of these walks. The researchers undertook this study because of a request from the police in Edmonton, who wanted information about how children move about in their home range. They thought this knowledge would help them in searching for a lost or missing child. As you'll see in Figure 9-12, they especially wanted to know how children of different ages travel around their neighbourhoods when they are on their own. When children get lost, their ability to find their way home may depend on the visual scanning they do while they walk, how far they travel, and how long they are willing to walk (Cornell & Hill, 2006; Heth & Cornell, 2007).

Cornell and his colleagues (2001) found that the distance and length of time a child would travel on his own increased significantly from 6 to 12 years of age. As children get older, they are more likely to try new routes and to travel beyond the limits of where their parents expect them to travel. Older children scan the environment more than younger children as they travel and they pay more attention to landmarks. In fact,

cognitive map

A cognitive representation of the spatial layout of a physical or geographical place.

Cornell and Heth

Table 9-2

Developing understanding of space and cognitive maps

Source: Siegel & White, 1975.

Step 1	Using Landmark Knowledge	Children use landmarks, such as the yellow house or the red fire hydrant, to help orient themselves in space.
Step 2	Using Route Knowledge	Children can integrate several landmarks (e.g., yellow house, red hydrant, and blue mailbox) into a sequence that forms a route through space that leads unfailingly to the baseball diamond or the nearby store.
Step 3	Developing Mental Maps	Children can create an overall mental or cognitive map of a familiar area that incorporates landmarks and routes learned earlier.

Figure 9-12

The home range

This overview map shows the child's home (H) and his or her intended destination (ID). The "crow's flight" is the distance identified by the solid line to the ID, and the actual path the child took to the ID is identified by the dashed line. Notice that because the child cannot walk through barriers in the environment, the child's path of travel is longer than the crow's flight distance. If a boy or girl was reported as lost or missing, this information would be used by police to create a search plan for the child.

Source: Cornell, Hadley, Sterling, Chan, & Boechler, 2001.

8-year-olds are quite knowledgeable about the landmarks in their home range, but this information is not as well integrated with way-finding information as it is for 12-year-olds. For example, 12-year-olds, but not 8-year-olds, will attend to the location of landmarks in relation to intersections and other choice points on their routes.

For children throughout the world, from early to middle childhood, the home range expands considerably, and children often travel outside the areas their parents expect them to visit (Munroe, Munroe, & Brasher, 1985). Thus, the development of spatial skills that may facilitate children's way-finding is critical to children's ability to explore their environments safely and to adults' capacity to help their children when needed.

Symbolic Tools or Representation   As Judy DeLoache (1995, 2000, 2002a, 2002b) has argued, becoming a proficient symbol user is a universal developmental task, and being able to use symbols is a great aid in solving real-world problems (DeLoache, 2004). One of the most basic forms of symbolic representation involves understanding notational systems.

Probably the most obvious notational system that children learn involves the use of print (Bialystok, 2000; Bialystok & Luk, 2007; Bialystok & Martin, 2003). Bialystok (2000), for example, examined 3- to 5-year-old children's use of notations by showing children a card containing a notation and explaining what the notation said. This notation was a word, a picture that indicated what the object was, or a number that indicated an amount. When they had the notation to use to solve problems, all the children found problem solving easy when the notation was either a picture or a number, but not when it was a word. According to Bialystok, these results suggest that children's problems in using symbolic representations stem from how these representations refer to meanings. More recent work has found a common neuropsychological mechanism for understanding the symbolic function of print. Although previous work has typically observed unique patterns of brain activation for individuals reading alphabetic and Asian languages (Tatsuno & Sakai, 2004; Xue et al., 2004), Bialystok and Luk (2007) found comparable patterns of brain activation in 4-year-old children learning to read Cantonese in Hong Kong and English in Canada. According to these authors, these findings point to an important cognitive universal in the development of literacy in children—namely, the understanding of the symbolic function of print.

Symbolic representation has also been studied by looking at children's use of symbolic tools, such as scale models and pictures (DeLoache, Pierroutsakos, & Uttal, 2003; Pierroutsakos & DeLoache, 2003). In a classic study, DeLoache (1987) showed children who were 31 and 39 months old a furnished, normal-sized living room and a miniature model of the same room, complete with furniture. She also showed them a normal-sized doll and a miniature version of the doll. She hid the tiny doll in the model room while the children watched and then asked the children to find the larger version of the doll in the life-sized living room, explaining that it was hidden in the same place in that room as the miniature doll was in the model room. Figure 9-13 shows these steps in another similar study in which DeLoache used toy dogs instead of toy dolls.

The older children had no problem finding the doll, but the younger children could not do so. DeLoache proposed that the problem for the younger children was their inability to form a *dual representation*. That is, they could not conceive of the model room both as an object in its own right and as a representation of the larger, real room. To test this hypothesis, DeLoache and her colleagues (DeLoache et al., 1997) presented two groups of children with different accounts of the hidden doll problem. Both groups saw the full-size room and the doll hidden in this room. The researchers then presented the model room to the first group and hid the miniature doll. To the second group, however, they explained that "a shrinking machine" had shrunk the full-size room and then the researchers revealed the small, model room. The 2½-year-old children in this study had no difficulty finding the miniature doll in the "shrunken" room. DeLoache and her colleagues suggest that the shrunken room version of the task was easier for the children because it did not require them to understand that the small room stood for or represented the large room symbolically. Thus, the children in the second group did not need to understand the *relation* between two objects—the large and small rooms, as

(a) Hiding toy in model

(b) Finding toy dog in room

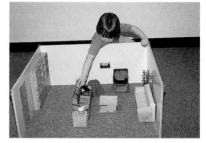
(c) Finding toy in model

Figure 9-13

A room is a room, but is it the same room?

In a series of classic experiments, Judy DeLoache has tested the ability of young children to conceive of a model room not only as a representation of a full-sized room but as an object in itself. (a) DeLoache hides a small toy dog in a scale-model room while a 3-year-old child watches. (b) The child retrieves a normal-sized toy dog from the analogous place in the full-sized room. (c) The child retrieves the small toy dog from its hiding place in the scale-model room.

Source: Courtesy of Judy S. DeLoache, University of Illinois at Urbana–Champaign.

children in the first group did. Instead, children in the second group had only to recognize the room in its new, "shrunken" form.

For DeLoache and colleagues (DeLoache et al., 1997; DeLoache & Smith, 1999), the notion that very young children may not be capable of dual representation has several practical implications. It may be that teaching basic mathematic concepts by using blocks of different sizes to represent different numerical quantities may present difficulty for very young children. Similarly, using anatomically correct dolls when interviewing young children about possible sexual abuse may not be as effective as psychologists have thought. Finally, there is substantial development in the preschool years in children's understanding and use of information represented in one symbolic form which is then presented or tested in another form—for example, viewing a video or a picture and then finding an object in a real space based on this information (Troseth et al., 2004). Experience with media, especially experiences that emphasize the connection between what is represented in the media and reality, helps even very young children use media as sources of information about the real world (DeLoache et al., 2004).

DEDUCTIVE REASONING   Piaget placed great emphasis on children's ability to perform tasks based on logical reasoning, such as conservation and class inclusion. These tasks rely on children's ability to use a form of logic called **deductive reasoning**, although others have pointed to alternatives that could explain performance on such tasks (e.g., Chapman & Carpendale, 1999; Rabinowitz, Howe, & Saunders, 2002). When individuals use deductive reasoning, they come to a conclusion based on a set of premises or statements that have already been laid out. A syllogism is a type of deductive reasoning problem that includes a major premise, a minor premise, and a conclusion. For example: All virtues are good. Kindness is a virtue. Therefore, kindness is good. Researchers have studied several types of deductive reasoning problems with children. We concentrate on three of these: propositional logic, transitive reasoning, and hierarchical categorization. Each of these types of reasoning makes important contributions to mature thinking. However, as we shall see, they take a while to develop and children often find problems based on deductive reasoning difficult.

deductive reasoning

Logical thinking that involves reaching a necessary and valid conclusion based on a set of premises.

Propositional Logic   In **propositional reasoning**, the logic of a statement is evaluated based on the information in the statement alone, as in a syllogism. For example, the Russian psychologist Alexander Luria (1976) tested the propositional reasoning of adults who had varying experiences with schooling and literacy by using the following syllogism:

propositional reasoning

Logical thinking that involves evaluating a statement or set of statements based on the information in the statement alone.

> In the Far North, where there is snow, all bears are white.
>
> Novaya Zemlya is in the Far North and there is always snow there.
>
> What colours are the bears there? (p. 108)

Piaget considered logical syllogisms such as this quite difficult and claimed that solving them required formal operational thinking. However, simpler versions of logical syllogisms were presented to 4- and 5-year-old children by Hawkins and her colleagues (1984). Here's an example of these syllogisms.

> Pogs wear blue boots.
>
> Tom is a pog.
>
> Does Tom wear blue boots? (p. 587)

The children in this study performed very well on these types of syllogisms—for example, by stating that Tom wears blue boots because he is a pog, which suggests that some of the basic skills needed for deductive reasoning of the type that is tapped in logical syllogisms may start to appear in the late preschool years.

TRANSITIVE REASONING   One of Piaget's classic reasoning tasks involves **transitive inference**, or the mental arrangement of things along a quantitative dimension. Recall from Chapter 8 that children younger than 6 or 7 could not deduce that Melissa was taller than Fabiana when given the information "Melissa is taller than Zoe, and Zoe is taller than Fabiana." Piaget attributed this failure to an inability to use the logic of transitive inference. An alternative hypothesis, proposed by Halford (2006), is that children do understand transitive inference but either use an incorrect strategy to solve this kind of problem or the memory load is too great, and, therefore, it interferes with their performance. One strategy young children use is to assume that the most recently mentioned object is also the largest; in this case, the strategy leads them to an incorrect inference. Another strategy is to assume automatically that one of the given objects is longer than the others, regardless of what the experimenter actually said (Brainerd & Reyna, 1990). Both these strategies reduce the child's memory load but often lead to erroneous conclusions. Children often fail to remember and use information correctly and effectively in transitive inference tasks (Rabinowitz et al., 1994). However, when a transitive inference task is presented in a simple or familiar form—for example, when children are asked to arrange the mama, papa, and baby bears in the Goldilocks story in order of their size—even 4-year-old children do well (Goswami, 1995).

HIERARCHICAL CATEGORIZATION   The organization of concepts into levels of abstraction that range from the specific (e.g., *dog*) to the general (e.g., *animal*) is called **hierarchical categorization**, or class inclusion. It is one thing to know that there are dogs and there are collies; a much more sophisticated appreciation of categorization is required to understand that a collie is a kind of dog, such that all collies are dogs but not all dogs are collies. Some evidence suggests that even very young children are capable of forming categories based on hierarchical relations (Haith & Benson, 1998; Klahr & Wallace, 1976; Mandler, 1998; Trabasso et al., 1978).

   Rakison and his colleagues (Rakison & Butterworth, 1998a, 1998b; Rakison & Cohen, 1999) examined 1- to 2-year-old's knowledge of hierarchical relations using a method called *sequential touching*, or *inductive categorization* (Rakison, 2005, 2007), which takes advantage of young children's tendency to touch and manipulate objects within their grasp. Looking at 14-, 18-, and 22-month-old infants, these authors investigated infants' abilities to distinguish between basic-level (e.g., cows and cars) and superordinate (e.g., animals and vehicles) categories. For example, Rakison and Butterworth (1998b) found that all infants readily distinguished between classes of objects that had different parts (e.g., legs versus wheels), whereas only the oldest infants distinguished between objects that may have contained similar parts (e.g., both animals and furniture

have legs). Thus, it appears that even infants have some knowledge of class-inclusion relations and can use this information to form categories for familiar objects (Mandler, 1998).

   What could infants as young as 1 year use as a basis to form categories? Two factors have been hypothesized to affect children's ability to form hierarchical categories. First, objects that form a category have perceptual similarities (Rakison & Butterworth,

Researchers have found intriguing ways of demonstrating categorization abilities in young children. One method, shown in this picture, involves looking at how children actually touch and manipulate a series of objects. Using this procedure, researchers have found that even 1- to 2-year-old children can distinguish different hierarchically organized categories.

1998a, 1998b; Rakison & Cohen, 1999; Rakison & Oakes, 2003), and young children may take advantage of this in forming categories (Rosch & Mervis, 1975; Rosch, Mervis, Gray, Johnson, & Boyes-Braem, 1976). For example, most dogs have four legs and a furry coat and they bark.

Second, people use labels to denote category membership, which helps children associate words with different objects (Gelman & Markman, 1987; Yoshida & Smith, 2003; Waxman & Gelman, 1986). Language development, especially names or labels for objects, is a second factor that contributes to the ability of children to categorize objects hierarchically. Markman and Hutchinson (1984) gave 2- to 3-year-old children a set of three objects and asked the children to sort the objects "where they belong," sometimes labelling objects and sometimes giving them no labels. When the experimenters did not label an object—for example, a police car—the children put it with either a same-physical-category object (another car) or a same-thematic-category object (a police officer), apparently at random. When the experimenters did apply labels to objects, they used nonsense words rather than an object's real name. For example, they referred to the police car as a *daz*. Given this label, most of the children placed the police car with another car, apparently seeing both as having the same category membership. Other researchers have replicated this effect (e.g., Mandler, 1998), and some have reported similar findings using Japanese words instead of nonsense syllables (Waxman & Gelman, 1986).

In summary, children's ability to form hierarchical categories is evident from a very young age. This ability, together with other deductive reasoning skills, contributes in significant ways to how children think and solve problems.

NUMERICAL REASONING   The ability to think about and use numbers to reason and solve problems is an important developmental achievement that has significant implications for children's success at school (Geary, 2006). Children begin to master some critical principles of counting at an astonishingly early age. Rochel Gelman and Charles Gallistel (1978) have studied what preschool children do and do not understand about number systems. Based on their findings, they proposed five basic principles of counting that lead to children's competence with numbers (Gelman & Gallistel, 1978):

1. The one-one principle: each object should be counted once and only once.
2. The stable-order principle: always assign the numbers in the same order.
3. The cardinal principle: a single number can be used to describe the total of a set.
4. The abstraction principle: the other principles apply to any set of objects.
5. The order-irrelevance principle: the order in which objects are counted is irrelevant.

A simple example will show these principles in action. Suppose we show a child 10 pennies, placed in a row, and ask her to count them. Pointing to each one, she proceeds to count them aloud, "1, 2, 3, 5, a, b, c, 10, 15, 12." When she finishes, we ask her to count them again, starting from the other end. Again she counts all 10 of the pennies, counting each one once and only once. "How many pennies are there?" we ask. "Twelve" is her confident reply. We then ask her to count 10 marbles. She repeats, "1, 2, 3, 5, a, b, c, 10, 15, 12." Again, we ask, "How many?" "Twelve."

Can we say that this child understands numbering and counting? On the basis of the principles outlined above, the answer is yes. Despite her use of an unconventional number sequence, she does seem to understand the critical principles of counting. She assigned only one number to each of the objects and always assigned the numbers in the same order, showing that she understood the one-one and stable-order principles. She had no problem switching the order in which she counted the objects, and she didn't mind counting both pennies and marbles, demonstrating her command of the

Perspectives on Diversity

IT'S EASIER TO COUNT IN CHINESE THAN IN ENGLISH!

Chinese-speaking children may have an advantage over English-speaking children when it comes to counting. According to Miller and colleagues (Miller, Smith, Zhu, & Zhang, 1995), the Chinese language offers a more consistent "base-10" naming system than the system used in English does; this may make it easier for young children to learn to count.

As Miller and associates point out, the base-10 Arabic system of numbering (1, 2, 3 . . . 10, 11, 12 . . . , etc.) is now used throughout the world, but names for numbers in different languages reflect older and sometimes more complex number systems. These researchers divided the number naming systems of both (Mandarin) Chinese and English into four segments of interest: 1 to 10; 11–19, 20–99, and 100 and above. In the first segment, Chinese and English do not differ in difficulty of learning, the authors propose, for both languages require children to master an unordered sequence of names. There is no way to predict, for example, that *jiu* follows *ba* or that *nine* follows *eight*. In the second segment, however, Chinese follows a consistent base-10 rule (e.g., in Mandarin Chinese, the number 11 is called, literally, "ten-one"), whereas the English system is inconsistent and mixed: the names *eleven* and *twelve* seem to bear no relation to *one* and *two*, and the names for 13 through 19 both place unit values before the tens values and modify the names of both (*thirteen*, *fif-teen*).

Between 20 and 99, both languages follow a base-10 approach in naming, except that Chinese uses unmodified unit and tens names (e.g., "two-ten-four," for 24), whereas English modifies the first unit name—but not the second—and the tens names (e.g., *twen-ty-four*). Finally, above 100, the naming systems in both languages are fairly consistent in using the base-10 format, with only a few exceptions.

Based on an early study in which they found some differences in mathematical skills favouring Chinese over North American children entering school for the first time, Miller and colleagues formulated several hypotheses. If these differences, in fact, reflected a more easily comprehended number naming system, then (1) Chinese children should show substantial skills advantages after all children begin to learn to count above 10, (2) North American children should have more trouble with counting in the teens than Chinese children, and (3) differences should generally be related to the system of number names and should not involve other aspects of counting. Engaging 99 Chinese children and 98 North American children—all between 3 and 6 years old—in a series of tasks that involved abstract counting, these investigators confirmed their predictions. As you can see from Figure 9-14, there were no substantial differences between the two groups in counting up to 10, but as children began to count in the teens, a significant difference between Chinese and North American children emerged. This differential ability was evident until both groups began to count in the 100s, where they again performed similarly. Chinese children were somewhat more successful in counting actual displays of between 14 and 17 objects, but they did not differ from North American children in their ability to solve simple mathematical problems or to count arrays of 10 or fewer objects. Although this finding might seem to violate the researchers' third prediction, it is consistent with

order-irrelevance and abstraction principles. When asked how many objects there were, she replied, "Twelve," showing that she understood the cardinal principle. Children may be competent in some or all of these principles at different points in their development. For example, a 3-year-old may grasp the one-one principle and the cardinal principle. However, he may be able to apply the stable-order principle only to sets with five or fewer members. Finally, other research has suggested that infants and children use numbers before they understand counting principles (Lipton & Spelke, 2003; Siegler, 1998; Wynn, 1992).

Recently, researchers have suggested that children and adults may use different cognitive processes when counting small groups, as opposed to large groups (Gelman & Corres, 2001; Revkin et al., 2008; Sophian & Crosby, 2008; Trick, 2008; Trick & Pylyshyn, 1994). According to Lana Trick, when counting sets of four items or fewer, one

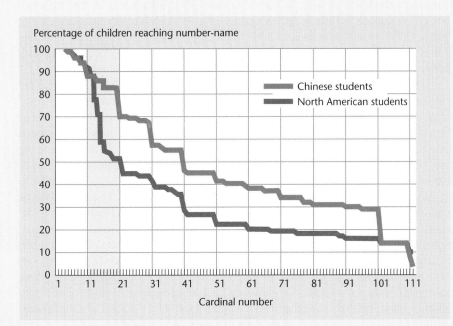

Percentage of children reaching number-name

— Chinese students
— North American students

Cardinal number

Figure 9-14

Abstract counting in Chinese and English

The coloured band at the left of the graph highlights the teens (11–19) when Chinese and North American children begin to diverge in counting skills, possibly owing to the non-base-10 structure of English names for these numbers.

Source: Miller, Smith, Zhu, & Zhang, 1995.

the notion that North American children will have the greatest difficulty with number naming in the teens.

Given that neither the Chinese nor the English language is likely to change its number-naming system, how can we help North American children acquire counting skills more efficiently and effectively? According to Miller and colleagues, obstacles that the English system presents can interfere with such math operations as arithmetic carrying and borrowing. Other studies have suggested not only that Chinese children display more sophisticated addition strategies when they first enter school but also that counting strategies for certain kinds of problems predict adult performance on those problems. Although these researchers suggest that it may be important both to familiarize North American children with Arabic numerals at an earlier age and to emphasize use of the digits over the use of number words, they also point out that this approach might interfere with other methods used to teach Western children the tens-structured addition method. Perhaps the answer lies in both parents and teachers—in the Vygotskian style—offering more encouragement to children to learn math skills.

makes use of a preattentive process called **subitizing**, in which the quantities involved in these sets are simply grasped effortlessly, accurately, and quite rapidly. For sets of five items or larger, however, one must count the items, with counting being an effortful, error-prone, and relatively slow process. Interestingly, these researchers (e.g., Trick et al., 1996) have found that there are different developmental processes involved in subitizing versus counting on the basis of the fact that subitizing makes only small demands on spatial attention, whereas counting requires fairly sophisticated spatial attention.

Researchers have studied when children develop skills in other areas of numerical and mathematical reasoning, including enumeration, number facts, arithmetic, word problems, and number relations (De Corte & Verschaffel, 2006). Evidence has also accumulated showing that Asian children display better mathematical skills than North American children (Lytton, 2000). Box 9.3 suggests that, as seen in Chinese and North

subitizing

A preattentive process in which sets of four items or fewer are counted or understood effortlessly, accurately, and quite rapidly.

American children, this difference may begin to emerge very early in life and may reflect verbal as well as quantitative abilities.

EXECUTIVE FUNCTION Some researchers have tried to explain children's performance on a variety of cognitive tasks and reasoning problems in terms of increasing executive functions that have to do with developments in the prefrontal cortex (Frye, Zelazo, & Burack, 1998; Zelazo & Frye, 1998; Zelazo, Frye, & Rapus, 1996; Zelazo, Müller, Frye, & Marcovitch, 2003). These researchers suggest that at about the age of four years, children begin to apply rule-based reasoning to a variety of problems, with the rule to be applied dependent on the particular conditions of the problem.

A typical example of children's rule-based approach is seen in a task called the dimensional change card sort (see Figure 9-15). In this task, children are shown two target cards and are asked to sort a series of test cards, each of which matches one of the target cards on one dimension (e.g., colour) and the other target card on a second dimension (e.g., shape), into two groups according to one dimension (e.g., match the cards according to colour). After performing this task for a while, children are told to stop matching according to colour and to start matching according to shape. Similar to Piaget's classic demonstrations of perseveration in the A-not-B task, 3-year-old children continue to sort by the first dimension (colour) even when asked to switch to using the second dimension (shape), and even though they are told the new rule on every trial. Moreover, if asked about the rules regarding how the cards should be sorted, children even answer correctly, although when told to go ahead and sort the cards they perseverate in their response (Zelazo et al., 1998, 2003). According to these researchers, these children know the various rules they are to use in sorting these cards but have difficulty reflecting on the rule pairs and their relations (Zelazo, 1997, 1998) and have difficulties actually formulating what should be done (Jacques, Zelazo, Kirkham, & Semcesen, 1999).

Figure 9-15

The dimensional card sort

Sample stimuli used in the dimensional card-sort task. In this procedure, children are first instructed to match cards according to one dimension, such as shape, and are then told to match cards according to a second dimension, such as colour.

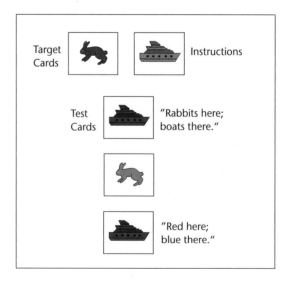

<hr>

For Thought and Discussion

1. Because of the issues and potential problems associated with the information processing approach, many psychologists resist abandoning other approaches (Piaget, Vygotsky) totally. How might you coherently combine these theoretical perspectives? Can you simply borrow from one versus the other approach when necessary and appropriate?

2. What do you think of the reliability of children as eyewitnesses? How about the ethics involved in having children testify? Does this work have any relevance to the recent debate over repressed memories in childhood?

METACOGNITION

LO 7

As cognitive beings, we do not just remember things, solve problems, and form concepts—we have an awareness of the strengths and limitations of our cognitive processing and of the way we control or regulate it to achieve such mental feats. In other words, we know about knowing (Flavell et al., 1995b). These two components of **metacognition**—knowledge about knowing and control of cognitive functioning—are interrelated and act on each other (Brown, 1975). The child's understanding of her cognitive abilities and processes and of the task situation will influence the strategies she uses in her learning. In turn, her abilities and her experience in learning will contribute to her knowledge about cognition and to her success or failure on cognitive tasks. Consequently, metacognitive skills have significant implications for children's success in the classroom (Bransford et al., 1999).

There are a number of developmental changes in metacognition. The child's own awareness of how much he knows and is able to remember changes with age. Older children have a more realistic and accurate picture of their own and others' memory abilities than do younger children (Flavell, 1985; Flavell et al., 1970; Yussen & Berman, 1981). An older child recognizes, for example, that he doesn't learn well when tired or anxious.

In this section, we examine two important areas of research on metacognition: children's knowledge of tasks, and their knowledge of specific strategies for learning and remembering. The development of a theory of mind, which we discussed in Chapter 8, is also directly related to metacognition. The limitations in young children's understanding of the mind that are related to the types of metacognitive abilities discussed here are listed in Table 9.3

metacognition

The individual's knowledge about knowing and her control of cognitive activities.

Knowledge about the Task

The ability to monitor one's comprehension is critical for a wide range of problem-solving and communication tasks. Do I understand the directions to get to the party tomorrow? Do I understand the instructions for this week's science project? To process information effectively, the child has to be sensitive to her present state of knowledge so that she can seek out the information she needs to further her understanding.

Young Children . . .
• Underestimate the amount of thinking they and others do.
• Do not understand the concept of a "stream of consciousness."
• Fail to appreciate that someone sitting quietly and not obviously "doing" something might be engaging in mental activity.
• Do not understand that such activities as looking, listening, or reading involve thinking. When someone is engaged in such an activity, preschoolers do not automatically understand that the person's mind is active. Similarly, they do not recognize that they have been thinking when engaging in these kinds of activities.
• Cannot infer what another person might be thinking about, even when they realize the person is thinking.
• Fail to understand that when you focus attention on one thing, you are often not able to think about other things.
• Have difficulty saying, when asked, whether they were thinking or what they were thinking about, even when their responses are prompted and facilitated.
• Tend to understand thinking in terms of its products rather than in terms of the process of thinking itself.

Table 9-3

Limitations on young children's metacognition

Source: Flavell, Green, & Flavell, 1995b.

One way that children get information about their present state of understanding is by monitoring their task performance. To study this type of knowledge, Markman (1977, 1979) assessed children's ability to monitor their comprehension of task instructions. In one study, Markman (1977) gave children in grades 1, 2, and 3 inadequate instructions for playing a card game. The experimenter dealt each child four cards, which had letters on them, and explained the game:

We each put our cards in a pile. We both turn over the top card in our pile. We look at the cards to see who has the special card. Then, we turn over the next card in our pile to see who has the special card this time. In the end, the person with the most cards wins the game. How would you like to try to play this game with these instructions?

The experimenter made no mention either of what the "special card" might be or of how one acquired more cards. The grade 1 children were far less likely to realize the inadequacy of the instructions than were the grade 2 and 3 children, who asked for more instructions before attempting to play the game. One-quarter of the grade 1 children never asked a question, and most recognized that a problem existed only when they were asked to repeat the instructions or when they began to flounder in playing the game.

Another aspect of knowledge of a task is an understanding of task demands. Do children realize that some things are harder to learn than others? Apparently, yes. Even 4-year-olds know that a long list of objects is harder to remember than a very short list and that success on the harder task is more likely if one makes a greater effort (Wellman, 1978; Wellman et al., 1981). Many kindergartners and grade 1 children know that it would be easier to relearn information (e.g., a list of birds) that one had forgotten than to learn it for the first time. Of course, younger children are not aware of some aspects of memory; for example, only older children appreciate that it is easier to retell a story in their own words than to repeat it verbatim, a realization that is relevant to children's courtroom testimony (Bruck et al., 2006; Kurtz & Borkowski, 1987).

Knowledge about Strategies

Children know a great deal more about using strategies in memorizing than we might think. They seem particularly sensitive to the value of external aids to memory: for example, leaving your books where you will see them in the morning and writing notes to yourself. According to Lovett and Pillow (1995), even children who were not yet literate suggested the latter ploy. Children are also aware of the value of associations in memory (e.g., remembering your mother's age by adding 30 to your own) (Wellman, 1977). As children grow older, their understanding of what strategy is appropriate increases (O'Sullivan, 1996), and sometimes, they reveal a rather sophisticated understanding of memory strategies.

How can we define the relation between metacognition and performance on cognitive tasks? Unfortunately, this relation is not straightforward (Miller & Weiss, 1981). Some situations, for example, are more likely to engage the child's metacognitive activity than are others. Carr and Jessup (1995) found that children from grades 1 to 3 who understood which strategy they were using employed some strategies more correctly when solving math problems. But it is important to remember that even adults do not always apply strategies they know to be effective in situations where they would be useful. It is unrealistic to expect the child to always act at an optimal level of cognitive functioning.

AN EVALUATION OF THE INFORMATION-PROCESSING APPROACH

Like all theories, the information-processing approach to cognitive development has strengths and weaknesses. On the plus side, one of its major strengths is its precision in breaking down cognitive processing into component operations. Accordingly, information processing has provided detailed and accurate descriptions of how children of many ages perceive and attend to the world around them, learn and memorize information in the world, solve problems, and so on.

The information-processing view also, however, has its limitations. Ironically, one of its problems stems from its central strength. Unfortunately, breaking down cognitive processing into its constituent components produces difficulties when attempting to integrate these separate pockets of knowledge into any kind of broad, comprehensive theory. Put another way, this view leads to many small theories about particular abilities that are difficult to combine, rather than to a general theory of cognition or cognitive development.

There are also problems with the computer metaphor that is central to information processing. One problem is that just because a person can write a computer program that is meant to model children's thinking in some domain, it does not mean that children actually think in this fashion, even if the computer and the children produce similar responses. And related to this problem, it is easily possible to write different computer programs that produce the same result—how, then, does one decide between these programs? And finally, although the computer analogy is powerful, it must be remembered that because computers only manipulate symbols, the symbols in and of themselves are actually meaningless. Instead, it is the human observer who is using the program that attaches meanings to these symbols. This problem, called the *symbol grounding problem*, suggests that computers simply do not process information in the same way as people do; thus, as a model of human cognition, information processing has some real limitations.

Regardless of these issues, this approach has contributed significantly to our knowledge and understanding of a wide array of cognitive changes, and researchers working within this tradition continue to generate a wealth of important and insightful experimental results.

For Thought and Discussion

1. What do you think Piaget would say about research on children's theory of mind? How different is this work from Piaget's own interests in egocentrism and animism?

2. What would Piaget think of the information-processing approach to the study of cognition?

3. One way of summarizing the research on development of cognitive abilities from an information-processing perspective is that children simply get better (e.g., have more focused attention, longer memory spans, more knowledge about thinking, and so on) with age. If this is true, what does this say about information processing as a developmental theory?

Making the Connections 9

There are many links between concepts and ideas in one area of development and concepts and ideas in other areas. Here are some of the connections between ideas in Chapter 9 and discussions in other chapters of this book.

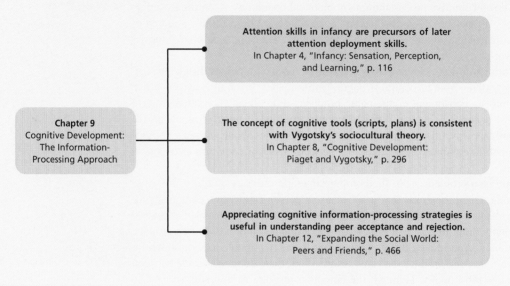

Attention skills in infancy are precursors of later attention deployment skills.
In Chapter 4, "Infancy: Sensation, Perception, and Learning," p. 116

Chapter 9
Cognitive Development: The Information-Processing Approach

The concept of cognitive tools (scripts, plans) is consistent with Vygotsky's sociocultural theory.
In Chapter 8, "Cognitive Development: Piaget and Vygotsky," p. 296

Appreciating cognitive information-processing strategies is useful in understanding peer acceptance and rejection.
In Chapter 12, "Expanding the Social World: Peers and Friends," p. 466

SUMMARY

Information-Processing Theory

- The **information-processing approach** to cognitive development views the human mind as a system that processes information according to a set of logical rules and limitations similar to those with which a computer is programmed. Researchers using this perspective try to describe and explain changes in the processes and strategies that lead to greater cognitive competence as children develop.

- Several basic assumptions of information-processing approaches are present to some degree in all views on cognitive development. These assumptions are that thinking is information processing, mechanisms of change are important to describe, the cognitive system is self-modifying, and careful task analysis will aid researchers in examining the information-processing system. One type of task analysis used in this perspective is microgenetic analysis, which examines how children solve problems in close detail.

- The **multi-store model** of information processing proposes that information enters the system through the **sensory register** and is encoded and stored in either **short-term memory** or **long-term memory**. **Connectionist models** propose that memory is based on the interconnections of information in neural net-

works in the brain. **Neo-Piagetian theories** attempt to apply information-processing ideas to explain Piaget's stage-related changes.

- The basic structures of the information-processing system do not change with development; instead, development occurs through changes in the speed and efficiency of the processes one applies to the information. Four cognitive processes considered to be important in development are **encoding** and **mental representation**, **strategies**, **automatization**, and **generalization**. Some theorists also posit an **executive control process** that monitors, selects, and organizes the various **cognitive processes** applied to information. In addition, knowledge plays a critical role in children's abilities to encode and represent information.

Developmental Changes in Some Significant Cognitive Abilities

- As children mature, they can control and focus their **attention** for longer periods. In addition, older children are better than younger children at **selective attention**, whereby they modify their attention to fit task requirements. Older children also implement more systematic plans to focus their attention when gathering needed information, especially when **planning** a course of action, although younger children can make use of attention-focusing strategies when these are provided to them.

- Memory development is studied extensively, both in terms of **semantic memory**, which includes all the knowledge and facts about the world a child has, and **episodic memory**, which includes memory for specific events. Our **memory span**, or the amount of information we can hold in short-term memory, improves between infancy and adulthood. Some researchers suggest that this is due to the development of increased capacity based on changes in the brain. Others suggest that the difference is due to greater efficiency in the cognitive system.

- The spontaneous use of verbal **rehearsal** as a memory strategy increases with age. Although even young children can use rehearsal as a strategy, if instructed to do so, they fail typically to generalize the strategy to new tasks. Another strategy that improves with age is **organization**, in which children use categorization and hierarchical relations to process and store information. As with rehearsal, young children can successfully learn to use this strategy, if instructed to do so.

- **Elaboration**—a strategy that involves adding to information to make it more meaningful and, thus, easier to remember—appears to aid children's retention. The fact that elaboration improves recall, despite the increase in informational load that it involves, underlines the importance of meaning in memory.

- **World knowledge**, or what the person has learned about the world from past experiences, influences what the person will understand and remember about a present event. Evidence for the role of world knowledge comes from studies indicating that experts remember more than novices do.

- **Problem solving** involves a high level of information processing because it mobilizes perception, attention, and memory to reach a solution. Over the course of cognitive development in young people, rule-based problem solving changes as children use different and more complex rules to guide their problems solving on logical tasks. Although **analogy** is a powerful tool in problem solving, young children and even adults often have difficult recognizing and using analogies. **Cognitive tools**, such as scripts, cognitive maps, and symbolic representations, aid thinking—with development, children increasingly use these tools to solve problems.

- **Scripts** of routine activities provide children with basic outlines of how events occur in many familiar situations. Children also use **cognitive maps** to negotiate their way through their surroundings. Very young children also develop the ability to understand and use **symbolic representations**, such as maps, models, and pictures, which represent objects or places in the real world.

- **Deductive reasoning** develops later in childhood. Though simple versions of such tasks have shown some early evidence of **propositional reasoning**, **transitive inference**, and **hierarchical categorization**.

- Children's numerical reasoning reflects their developing competence with numbers, which includes five basic principles of counting that develop during the preschool years. Counting skills may to some degree reflect the number-naming system of a child's native language.

Metacognition

- **Metacognition** refers to the individual's knowledge and control of cognitive activities. Metacognitive knowledge, which develops over childhood, includes the child's knowledge about the self, her theory of mind, and her knowledge about the task and about specific strategies.

- Although young children understand how some features of a task may influence memory, even grade 1 children are not good at monitoring their comprehension of information about a task. Young children are aware of the importance of memory strategies, and they are particularly sensitive to the use of external memory cues. However, older children have a more accurate and realistic view of their own memory abilities, and they are able to separate their own beliefs and desires from reality.

An Evaluation of the Information-Processing Approach

- On the plus side, information processing is precise about the cognitive processes involved in component operations. On the minus side, this approach is problematic in terms of integrating the different component processes into a coherent theory, and it poses questions about the validity of the computer metaphor.

Anonymous. *Wolfgang Amadeus Mozart as a child at the pianoforte,* eighteenth century.

Mozart House, Salzburg, Austria.

Chapter 10

Intelligence and Achievement

LEARNING OBJECTIVES

After reading this chapter, you should be able to

LO 1 Discuss different theories of intelligence, including the factor analytic approach, information-processing models such as Sternberg's theory of successful intelligence, and Gardner's theory of multiple intelligences.

LO 2 Describe various means for testing intelligence, including intelligence tests used in infancy and throughout development.

LO 3 Discuss how one goes about constructing measures of intelligence; understand aspects of intelligence test construction including norm-referenced assessments, standardization, test validity and reliability, and the stability of intelligence.

LO 4 Discuss why people might differ in intelligence, including factors such as the heritability of intelligence and the importance of environmental factors.

LO 5 Discuss the impact of ethnicity and social class on intelligence.

LO 6 Describe the effects of emotion, motivation, and academic context on achievement.

LO 7 Present evidence concerning the effectiveness of cognitive intervention strategies designed to aid cognitive development.

LO 8 Discuss intellectual giftedness and mental retardation.

What do you think intelligence is? People generally agree that three behaviours are central to intelligence: problem-solving ability, verbal ability, and social competence. How do these three behaviours fit in with the scientific definition of intelligence? In this chapter, we will answer this question by describing how scientists define and measure intelligence. We will also identify the biological and experiential factors that affect intelligence and its development, and discuss how these factors may be modified to improve intelligent behaviour.

In this third chapter on cognitive functioning, we take a slightly different perspective. In Chapters 8 and 9, we were concerned with cognition in general, and we were more interested in similarities among people than in their differences. In this chapter, however, we want to examine how individuals use their cognitive skills. To do this, we look at individual intelligence and why people appear to differ in intelligence and cognitive achievements. We discuss such questions as, "Are differences in intelligence caused by genetic factors, by environmental influences, or both?" "Are these differences permanent, or can they be changed?" We then consider the matter of achievement, examining various factors that affect children's performance on intelligence tests and in the schoolroom. Then, after considering the results of some interventions to improve cognitive functioning, we look at intellectual giftedness and mental retardation and conclude with some ideas about creativity in young children. ●

LO1   THEORIES OF INTELLIGENCE

In attempting to formulate useful theories of intelligence, scientists have focused on three primary issues: whether intelligence is unitary or multi-faceted; whether it is determined by genetic or environmental factors; and whether it predicts academic success and success outside school. The first of these questions, which was hotly debated in the early years of the twentieth century, asked whether intelligence has many components and a person can be intelligent in some but not all of these components. Today, it is generally accepted that intelligence is multi-faceted and that both genetic and environmental influences contribute to a person's intelligence. The argument is far from over, however, for now investigators concentrate on such issues a whether heredity is more influential than environment or the other way around and the degree to which inherited factors that contribute to intelligence may be altered by environmental conditions.

The third question asks how important intelligence, as measured by IQ tests, is in predicting children's and adults' success in school and in real-life situations. Is it useful in predicting academic success, job stability, and general good health and adjustment? Throughout the chapter, we find answers to these and other questions, but we also raise more questions. Let's look now at several ways scientists have devised to understand what intelligence is.

Intelligence Theory

The Factor Analytic Approach

To many people, it may seem obvious that intelligence has many components. We all know we are better—or smarter—at some things than at others. Early investigators believed that intelligence is a unitary or single ability that affects everything a person does. To test this idea, researchers have performed **factor analysis** on intelligence test performances of large samples of people. This approach is a statistical procedure that can determine which of several factors, or scores, are closely related to one another without overlapping each other's contribution. An early researcher who used factor analysis, Charles Spearman (1927), proposed that intelligence is composed of a **general factor (g)** and a number of **specific factors (s)**. Spearman regarded g as general mental energy, or ability that was involved in all cognitive tasks, and he saw s factors as factors unique to particular tasks. A person with a high g would be expected to do generally well on all tasks. Variations in her performance on different tasks could be attributed to the possession of varying amounts of s factors.

This unitary concept of intelligence was challenged by Lewis Thurstone (1938) who proposed that seven primary skills comprise intelligence: *verbal meaning*, *perceptual speed*, *reasoning*, *number*, *rote memory*, *word fluency*, and *spatial visualization*. More recently, Carroll (1993, 1997) and other researchers (Johnson et al., 2004) have confirmed the existence of a general factor of cognitive ability. It seems that people who

factor analysis

A statistical procedure used to determine which of a number of factors or scores are both closely related to each other and relatively independent of other groups of factors or scores.

general factor (g)

General mental energy or ability that is involved in all cognitive tasks.

specific factors (s)

Factors that are unique to particular cognitive tasks.

do well on one kind of cognitive test (e.g., reading comprehension) are likely to do well on other such tests (e.g., listening comprehension or folding paper into specific shapes, as in Japanese origami). However, individuals still vary in their competence across different domains, such as vocabulary knowledge, basic mathematic skills, or the ability to discriminate musical pitch. In other words, children vary both in overall level of intellectual ability and in how skilled they are in specific aspects of cognitive functioning.

The Information-Processing Approach: Sternberg's Triarchic Theory

Information-processing researchers focus on the processes involved in intellectual activity. They argue that to understand intelligence, we must assess how individuals use information-processing capabilities, such as memory and problem-solving skills, to carry out intelligent tasks (Das, 2004).

Sternberg's (1985, 2001, 2005) **triarchic theory of intelligence** is an important example of this approach. As the name implies, it proposes three major components of intelligent behaviour: information-processing skills, experience with a given task or situation, and the ability to tailor one's behaviour to the demands of a context. These three components work together in organizing and guiding intelligent behaviour. *Information-processing skills*, which we discussed in Chapter 9, are required to encode, store, and retrieve varying kinds of information. *Experience*, the second component of Sternberg's model, considers how much exposure and practice an individual has had with a particular intellectual task. For example, if two children perform similarly on a mathematics test of long division but one child has never studied this topic and the other child has studied it for several years, we would make different judgments about these children's relative intelligence based on their performance on this test (Sternberg et al., 1993).

Context, Sternberg's third component, recognizes that intelligence cannot be separated from the situation in which it is used. Because people must function effectively in many different environments, they must be able both to adapt to the requirements of a situation and to select and arrange situations to meet their own abilities and needs (Sternberg, 1985). Thus, one dimension on which the intelligence of a particular behaviour can be measured is its suitability and effectiveness in a particular setting (Ceci, 1996; Sternberg & Wagner, 1994). For example, consider how the young Brazilian street vendors we discussed in Chapter 8 were able to adapt their understanding of mathematics to the contexts in which they used these skills.

More recently, Sternberg expanded his triarchic theory into a theory of **successful intelligence**, which considers intelligence in relation to the ability of an individual to meet his own goals and those of his society (Sternberg, 2001). Successful intelligence requires three abilities: analytical, creative, and practical. *Analytical abilities* include those taught and tested in most schools and universities, such as reasoning about the best answer to a test question. *Creative abilities* are involved in devising new ways of addressing issues and concerns. *Practical abilities* are used in everyday activities, such as work, family life, and social and professional interactions. Much of the practical knowledge we use is tacit. It is not explicitly formulated and it is rarely taught directly to children; instead, it is learned by observing others (Sternberg & Wagner, 1993). Nonetheless, this kind of practical, **tacit knowledge**, which is often referred to as common sense, is shared by many people and guides intelligent behaviour (Cianciolo et al., 2006). Table 10-1 on the next page displays an example of a test item that Sternberg and his colleagues use to measure tacit knowledge in university study behaviour. Sternberg (2001) found that tacit knowledge of this sort, though not associated with IQ score, predicted the salaries and job performance of adult workers.

Applications of Sternberg's triarchic theory to school curricula have shown success in helping children learn academic material (Grigorenko et al., 2006) and in helping

triarchic theory of intelligence

A theory that proposes three major components of intelligent behaviour: information-processing skills, experience with a particular situation, and the ability to adapt to the demands of a context.

successful intelligence

The ability to fit into, mould, and choose environments that best fulfill the demands of one's society and culture and one's own needs and desires (includes analytical, creative, and practical abilities).

tacit knowledge

Implicit knowledge that is shared by many people and that guides behaviour.

Table 10-1

Tacit knowledge: A sample test question

Source: Adapted from Sternberg & Wagner, 1993.

University Life
You are enrolled in a large introductory lecture course. Requirements consist of three exams and a final. Please indicate how characteristic (on a scale of 1 to 5, from least to most characteristic) it would be of your behaviour to spend time doing each of the following if your goal were to receive an A in the course:
_____ attend class regularly
_____ attend optional weekly review sessions with the tutorial assistant
_____ read assigned text chapters thoroughly
_____ take comprehensive class notes
_____ speak with the professor after class and during office hours

adolescents improve their scores on university entrance examinations (Stemler et al., 2006). Moreover, children who were instructed with curricula based on the triarchic theory reported enjoying the material more than children taught the same information in a traditional fashion. The work of these researchers suggests that this approach to intelligence, when applied in the class setting, may benefit children's learning and also enhance their motivation to learn.

Gardner's Theory of Multiple Intelligences

theory of multiple intelligences

Gardner's multi-factorial theory that proposes eight distinct types of intelligence.

Howard Gardner (2004) has proposed a **theory of multiple intelligences**. He suggests that human beings possess eight kinds of intelligence: *linguistic*, *logical-mathematical*, *spatial*, *musical*, *bodily kinesthetic*, *intrapersonal*, *interpersonal*, and *naturalist* (see Table 10-2). He has also suggested a possible ninth form, which he called *spirituality* or *existential intelligence* (Gardner, 1999). Three of the types of intelligence—linguistic, logical-mathematical, and spatial—are similar to the kinds of abilities that are assessed in traditional intelligence tests. The remaining types have been much less widely studied, yet, according to Gardner, they are equally important to human functioning. For example, interpersonal intelligence may be particularly important to a parent, a nurse, or a teacher; bodily kinesthetic intelligence may greatly facilitate the performance of a dancer or tennis player.

According to Gardner, each type of intelligence has its own developmental course in terms of perception, learning, and memory (Connell et al., 2003). For example, linguistic intelligence emphasizes verbal and memory abilities and generally develops over years of educational experience, whereas bodily kinesthetic intelligence, which emphasizes understanding of body mechanisms and its coordination with perceptual abilities, may appear quite early in life and be less dependent on experience. In addition, Gardner suggests, a single individual can display different combinations of these intelligences, and different cultures or periods of history may emphasize or value some of these forms of intelligence more than others. In this way, Gardner's view of intelligence corresponds with the ideas presented in the domain-specific views of intelligence discussed by evolutionary psychologists (recall our discussion of evolutionary psychology in Chapter 1).

Gardner's theory has its critics, however. Some have pointed out that Gardner's intelligences may not all be separate entities; that is, some may be closely tied to others, whereas others may be distinct (Carroll, 1993; Weinberg, 1989). Others, such as Klein (1997, 1998), point out that Gardner's theory is somewhat circular. For instance, if one poses the question, "Why is Michael a good dancer?" Gardner's answer is that Michael is a good dancer because of his high bodily kinesthetic intelligence. But, then, if one looks at the definition of bodily kinesthetic intelligence, it is virtually a definition of dance. In other words, Michael is a good dancer because he is a good dancer (Klein, 1997). Also, few efforts have been made to evaluate Gardner's theory rigorously using standard assessment techniques or to develop tests based directly on the theory (Benbow & Lubinski, 1996; Sternberg & Wagner, 1994).

Table 10-2 Gardner's theory of multiple intelligences

Type of Intelligence/Description	Examples
Linguistic: Sensitivity to word meanings; mastery of syntax; appreciation of the ways language can be used	Poet, teacher
Logical-mathematical: Understanding of objects, symbols, the actions that can be performed on them, and the interrelations among these actions; ability to operate in the abstract and to identify problems and seek explanations	Mathematician, scientist
Spatial: Accurate perception of visual world; ability to transform perceptions and mentally recreate visual experience; sensitivity to tension, balance, and composition; ability to detect similar patterns	Artist, engineer, chess player
Musical: Sensitivity to musical tones and phrases; ability to combine tones and phrases into larger rhythms and structures; awareness of music's emotional aspects	Musician, composer
Bodily kinesthetic: Skilled and graceful use of one's body for expressive or goal-directed purposes; ability to handle objects skilfully	Dancer, tennis player, actor
Intrapersonal: Access to one's own feeling life; ability to draw on one's emotions to guide and understand behaviour	Novelist, psychotherapist, actor
Interpersonal: Ability to notice and distinguish among others' moods, temperaments, motives, and intentions; ability to act on this knowledge	Political or religious leader, parent, teacher, psychotherapist
Naturalist: Ability to understand living things and to use this knowledge productively	Biologist, naturalist

Sources: Gardner, 1983, 1999; Torff & Gardner, 1999

These caveats aside, Gardner's theory has been used to improve public education (Kornhaber & Gardner, 2006). Most notably, Gardner's work with Harvard University's Project Zero has resulted in more individualized and varied instruction through the use of different curricula aligned with his multiple intelligences. Also, Gardner, Sternberg, and their colleagues collaborated on the Practical Intelligence for Schools (PIFS) program, designed to teach the tacit knowledge needed to succeed in school. These programs appear to be successful (Williams et al., 2002), and have been shown to bring about positive effects on student motivation, achievement, and behaviour (Gardner, 1999; Sternberg, 2001).

Building a model out of Tinkertoys, as this North American child is doing (a), illustrates Howard Gardner's spatial intelligence. Playing an indigenous flute, like this Quechan child from Peru is doing (b), illustrates Gardner's musical intelligence.

(a)   (b)

For Thought and Discussion

1. What do you think is a reasonable definition of intelligence? How much of your own, personal assessment of someone's intelligence is driven by "academic" factors, such as reasoning, memory ability, or vocabulary, and how much is driven by such factors as common sense, interpersonal skills, creativity, musical ability, and so on?

2. One problem in designing tests to measure something such as intelligence is that they often literally create the construct, which does not exist under other circumstances, in the process of attempting to measure it. Do you actually think there is such a thing as intelligence? If you believe it exists, do you think it is measurable?

(LO2) TESTING INTELLIGENCE

intelligence quotient (IQ)

An index of the way a person performs on a standardized intelligence test relative to the way others her age perform.

Although psychologists have become increasingly interested in the *processes* that contribute to intellectual functioning, the study and testing of intelligence have traditionally focused on its *products*—that is, on the specific knowledge and skills displayed on intelligence tests. On the basis of such tests, researchers have developed the **intelligence quotient (IQ)**, an index of the way a person performs on a standardized intelligence test relative to the way others her age perform. Although the term IQ is widely used, it is often misunderstood: Many people think IQ is innate and does not change. But research has shown that IQ *can* change over the lifespan, for it can be modified by experience.

In discussing intelligence and intelligence testing, it is important to remember that we can only *infer* intellectual capacity from the results of an IQ test. Although we assume that capacity and performance are related, we can measure only performance. Moreover, there is always some discrepancy or gap between capacity and performance owing to the particular circumstances of a performance, such as the precise construction of a test or the test taker's emotional state during the test. How we interpret or explain the gap ends up being crucial to our evaluations of our own and other people's intelligence, a topic we discuss later in the chapter when we consider achievement motivation (Dweck, 2000; 2006).

Why do we need to measure intelligence? There are three primary purposes in intelligence testing: predicting academic performance, predicting performance on the job, and assessing general adjustment and health (Flanagan & Harrison, 2005). The earliest intelligence tests were designed to meet the first of these goals, and most existing intelligence tests, such as the Binet and Wechsler scales, predict academic achievement quite well. Predicting how well a person will succeed at a job is the second goal of intelligence testing, and according to Gottfredson (1997), such measures are the most powerful predictors of overall work performance. A third use of intelligence testing is in assessing people's general adjustment and health. The Bayley, Stanford-Binet, and Wechsler tests that we discuss in this section can detect signs of neurological problems, mental retardation, and emotional distress in infants and children as well as in adults.

culture-fair test

A test that attempts to minimize cultural biases in content that might influence the test taker's responses.

Unfortunately, traditional tests do not make predictions as accurately for some groups in our society as for others (Neisser et al., 1996). Many critics, for example, have pointed out that these tests often require knowledge that children with fewer advantages than others may not have. As a result, intelligence tests may unfairly classify some people or groups of people as less intelligent than they actually are. For some years, researchers have been attempting to develop what are known as **culture-fair tests**, which attempt to exclude or minimize the kind of experientially or culturally biased content in IQ tests that could prejudice test takers' responses. The Raven Progressive Matrices test, which requires people to identify, distinguish, and match patterns of varying complexity, and the Kaufman test, which we discuss shortly, are culture-fair tests.

We begin this section with a brief discussion of infant intelligence and then examine the two tests that are most widely used for testing IQ beyond the years of infancy—the Stanford-Binet tests and the Wechsler scales. Next, we examine the relatively new Kaufman test—it attempts to measure the processes by which people acquire information and solve problems. We then turn to how intelligence tests are constructed, including the ways psychologists develop norms for test scoring and the kinds of procedures they adopt to ensure the validity and reliability of their tests. We conclude the section by considering the relative stability of intelligence as well as what factors may effect changes in intelligence over time.

Measuring Infant Intelligence

The **Bayley Scales of Infant Development (BSID)**, are probably the best known and most widely used of all infant development tests (Bayley, 1969, 1993). Because these tests were designed to be used with the very young, they include non-verbal test items chosen for their ability to measure specific developmental milestones. The Bayley scales are used with infants and children between 1 month and 3½ years of age, and they are generally used to assess children suspected to be at risk for abnormal development. For example, the Bayley *mental* scale includes such things as looking for a hidden object and naming pictures, whereas the *motor* scale includes such items as grasping ability and jumping skills. Although these scales are useful in identifying infants at risk for unhealthy development, the Bayley scales and other older tests of infant intelligence are poor predictors of later cognitive levels. This may be because they rely primarily on sensorimotor measures. The Bayley scales are somewhat more reliable with older children.

Newer tests, such as the Fagan test, measure information-processing skills. The **Fagan Test of Infant Intelligence** assesses processes such as encoding the attributes of objects, seeing similarities and differences between objects, and forming and using mental representations (Fagan, 1992). You will recall that in Chapter 4, we discussed habituation and the infant's tendency to pay attention to what is novel in his environment. Based on this notion, the Fagan test examines an infant's intelligence by measuring the amount of time the infant spends looking at a new object compared with the time he spends looking at a familiar object (Fagan et al., 1991). Using a set of 20 photographs of human faces, arranged in pairs, the examiner begins by showing a baby one photograph of the first pair for 20 seconds. Then, the examiner pairs that photograph with its mate, showing the baby the two photos together for 5 seconds, and then again for another 5 seconds, this time reversing the two photos left to right (to avoid any tendency for the infant to "choose" one side). The score the infant receives is made up of the total time he spends looking at the novel photograph throughout a presentation of all 10 pairs. In research on whether infants from different cultures would be equally adept at this task, Fagan and his colleagues found that there were practically no differences between the average scores obtained by nearly 200 infants representing European Americans, African Americans, Bahrainians, and Ugandans, suggesting that the test is culture-fair. Although the Fagan test predicts later cognitive development better than older tests, the correlations with later development remain weak to moderate (Sternberg et al., 2001; Tasbihsazan et al., 2003). However, infant tests are primarily used for diagnostic screening to determine a child's need for early-intervention services.

The Stanford-Binet Test

The **Stanford-Binet test** is the modern version of the test devised in the early twentieth century by Binet and Simon to identify children who were unable to learn in traditional classroom settings and who would benefit from special education.

Bayley Scales of Infant Development (BSID)

Non-verbal tests that measure specific developmental milestones and that are generally used with children who are thought to be at risk for abnormal development.

Fagan Test of Infant Intelligence

A test of how infants process information, including encoding attributes of objects and seeing similarities and differences across objects.

Stanford-Binet test

The modern version of the first major intelligence test; emphasizes verbal and performance skills.

Binet and Simon believed that intelligence was malleable and that children's academic performance could be improved with special programs (Binet, 1909/1973; Jarvin & Sternberg, 2003; Siegler, 1992; Sternberg & Jarvin, 2003). Critics of earlier psychologists who had tried to assess intelligence by measuring simple sensory or motor responses, Binet and Simon tested higher mental functions, such as comprehension, reasoning, and judgment, as well as skills taught in school, such as recalling details of a story. In addition, because they recognized that as children grow they become able to solve increasingly complex problems, Binet and Simon built into their test age-related changes in children's learning with the aim of tapping children's competence at different age levels.

mental age

An index of a child's actual performance on an intelligence test as compared with her true age.

Binet originated the concept of **mental age**, which is an index of a child's actual performance level as contrasted with her true age. Thus, if a 6-year-old child gets as many items correct as the average 7-year-old, the 6-year-old's mental age is 7 years; that is, she performs as well as a 7-year-old child. The mental age concept was later captured in the intelligence quotient, for which the German psychologist William Stern devised the following formula:

$$IQ = MA/CA \times 100$$

where IQ equals mental age (MA) divided by chronological age (CA), multiplied by 100. Thus, if a child's mental age equalled her chronological age, she would be performing like an average child of her true age and her IQ would be 100. If her performance were superior to other children her age, her IQ would be above 100. If it were inferior, her IQ would be less than 100.

Today's Stanford-Binet test is an updated version of the Binet-Simon test. It includes language and mathematics skills as well as other indexes of intelligent performance. The extent to which experience in school influences performance on this test is not completely clear.

The Wechsler Scales

Wechsler Intelligence Scales

Three intelligence tests for infants, children, and adults that yield separate scores for verbal and performance IQ as well as a combined IQ score.

The **Wechsler Intelligence Scales**, developed by David Wechsler (1952, 1958), include the Wechsler Preschool and Primary Scale of Intelligence (WPPSI), the Wechsler Intelligence Scale for Children (WISC), and the Wechsler Adult Intelligence Scale (WAIS). These tests yield separate verbal and performance IQ scores as well as a combined, full-scale IQ score. The most recent update of the WISC, which is the fourth version (Wechsler, 2003), includes items related to how children process information, focusing on memory, strategy use, and processing speed. Such items were added because they may be less influenced by experience with school or certain cultural or economic factors. The descriptions of the WISC subtests from this recent version are shown in Table 10-3.

deviation IQ

An IQ score that indicates the extent to which a person's performance on a test deviates from agemates' average performance.

Rather than use mental age as a basis for estimating intelligence, Wechsler created the **deviation IQ**, which, like the Binet IQ, takes 100 as an average score. The deviation IQ is based on extensive testing of people of different ages and on the statistical computation of mean scores for each age group. In computing these average scores, psychologists use a statistic called the *standard deviation* to identify the extent to which non-average scores deviate from the norm. As a result, an individual's score may be at the mean, or it may be one or more standard deviations above or below the mean. This test has been standardized around the world, and has been normalized with a Canadian sample (Saklofske, Hildebrand, Reynolds, & Willson, 1998; Saklofske, Hildebrand, & Gorsuch, 2000; Saklofske, Caravan, & Schwartz, 2000; Saklofske, Tulsky, Wilkins, & Weiss, 2003; Weiss, Saklofske, Prifitera, Chen, & Hildebrand, 1999).

Table 10-3 The Wechsler Intelligence Scale for Children, Fourth Edition (WISC-IV)

Subtests	Descriptions and Some Examples	Skills Thought to Tap
Similarities	The child is asked to tell how paired words are alike (e.g., *How are a cup and a glass alike?*).	Concept formation; categorization
Vocabulary	The child is asked to define each word in a list of words of increasing difficulty.	Concept formation; long-term memory; vocabulary
Comprehension	A series of questions ask the child to explain why certain actions or practices are desirable (e.g., *What should you do if you lose a friend's toy?*).	Factual knowledge; long-term memory; intellectual interest
Information	For each item, the child answers questions that address a broad range of general knowledge topics (e.g., *How many days are there in a week?*).	Factual knowledge; long-term memory; intellectual interest
Word reasoning*	The child is given successive clues and asked to identify the common concept being described in a series of clues (e.g., *"This is squishy and full of holes"* or *"You use it to wash things with"*).	Verbal abstraction and comprehension; analogic and general reasoning ability; integration and synthesis of different types of information; domain knowledge; generation of alternative concepts
Block design	The child is shown a model of a red-and-white design or a picture of it and is asked to recreate the design, using blocks whose sides are red, white, or half red and half white.	Visual-motor coordination; concept formation; pattern recognition; spatial ability
Picture concepts*	The child is presented with two or three rows of pictures of familiar objects and must choose one from each row to form a group with a common characteristic (e.g., *things to eat or things to play with*).	Fluid reasoning; abstract categorical ability
Matrix reasoning*	The child looks at an incomplete matrix, a grid of four equal-size squares in which all but three of the squares are filled with designs. The child must look then at a separate display of five possible designs and choose the one that will complete the matrix.	Visual information processing; abstract reasoning skills
Picture completion	The child is asked to look at a series of pictures and, for each one, to point out what is missing from the picture (e.g., *a car with a missing wheel; a rabbit with a missing ear*).	Visual organization; perceptual reasoning; concentration
Digit span	The examiner says several sequences of digits, each longer than the preceding one, and the child is asked to repeat them either in the order in which the examiner said them or in reverse order (e.g., *2-7-4; 3-1-9-6; 8-4-2-7-5*).	Mental alertness and attention; cognitive flexibility; short-term memory
Letter–number sequencing*	The examiner reads to the child a sequence of letters and numbers and asks the child to recall the numbers (in ascending order) and the letters (in alphabetical order).	Working memory—sequencing, mental manipulation, attention, short-term auditory memory, visual-spatial imaging, processing speed
Arithmetic	The child is asked to solve, without physical aids such as pencil and paper, arithmetic problems that the examiner presents orally. The test is timed.	Working memory; mathematical skills
Cancellation*	The child is shown an array of pictures of objects and asked to find and mark every picture of a certain class of objects as fast as possible (the test is timed) (e.g., *in any array of pictures of miscellaneous things, such as flowers, furniture items, animals, cleaning implements, the child might be asked to find and mark all pictures of animals*).	Visual selective attention; processing speed

* Subtests marked with an asterisk are new to the WISC in its fourth edition.

Source: Items similar to those in *The Wechsler Intelligence Scale for Children*, Fourth Edition (WISC-IV).

The Kaufman Assessment Battery for Children

Kaufman Assessment Battery for Children (K-ABC)

An intelligence test designed to measure several types of information-processing skills as well as achievement in some academic subjects.

The **Kaufman Assessment Battery for Children (K-ABC)** measures several types of information-processing skills grouped into two categories (Kaufman & Kaufman, 1983, 2006): *sequential processing* (solving problems in a step-by-step fashion) and *simultaneous processing* (examining and integrating a wide variety of materials in the solution of a problem). The test also assesses achievement in academic subjects, such as vocabulary and arithmetic, and efforts have been made to design the test items (many non-verbal) to be culture-fair. In addition, the test designers used a wide and representative sample of many North American cultural and socio-economic groups in establishing norms for the test. An interesting innovation is that if a child fails early items on a subscale, the examiner teaches the child how to complete these items before the child does the rest of the subtest. According to the designers of the test, this ensures that no child who is capable of learning an unfamiliar task receives a failing score on it.

LO3 Constructing Measures of Intelligence

psychometrician

A psychologist who specializes in the construction and use of tests designed to measure various psychological constructs, such as intelligence, motivation, achievement orientation, and personality characteristics.

When a **psychometrician**, or test constructor, designs an intelligence test, she is guided by a particular theory of intelligence. For example, if the theory emphasizes information processing, the items will be designed to tap processing functions, speed, and the strategies a person uses to solve a problem. Certain goals and principles, however, are shared by all constructors of intelligence tests. These goals and principles include how the norms for a test are established, how the test is standardized, and the importance of determining a test's validity and reliability.

DEVELOPMENT OF NORMS AND STANDARDS

test norms

Values or sets of values that describe the typical performance of a specific group of people.

A person's performance on an intelligence test is always described in relation to the performance on the same test of others in a particular group; the person, then, is described as either average, above average, or below average in relation to other group members. **Test norms** are the values that describe the typical test performance of a specific group of people.

Age is a particularly critical factor when setting norms for children's test performance. Although children generally improve their test performance as they grow older, their score relative to the scores of other children of their age continues to be the significant factor in evaluating their intellectual development.

Psychometricians do not agree on whether comparison groups in intelligence testing should be equated based on such factors as level of education, socio-economic class, or gender. Nevertheless, in evaluating test performance, we should always consider how closely the attributes and experiences of the person being tested approximate those of the group that was used to establish the test norms. For example, it would be inappropriate to use the same set of norms in evaluating the performance of children raised in an isolated New Guinea tribal community without access to formal schooling that we use to evaluate the performance of white, middle-class North American children. And as we will discuss later, norms for the latter group may not be appropriate even for the children of minority groups in Canada or the United States.

standardization

The process by which test constructors ensure that testing procedures, instructions, and scoring are identical on every testing occasion.

Because the conditions under which a test is administered may influence performance, it is extremely important that we subject a test to **standardization**, which means that on every testing occasion, the procedures that examiners follow, the instructions they give to examinees, and test scoring are identical, or as nearly so as possible.

TEST VALIDITY AND RELIABILITY

For any test to provide useful information about an individual, it must be valid; that is, it must measure what it claims to measure. It also must be reliable; that is, an individual's scores must be consistent over different times of measurement.

In establishing the **validity** of an intelligence test, psychometricians must often link performance on the test with some other measure, called a criterion. Criterion validity is the extent to which a test is associated with a specific criterion that is believed to be associated with the skills being tested. The most frequently used criteria are achievement test scores, grades in school, teachers' ratings of cognitive ability, and performance on other intelligence tests. Intelligence tests are much more successful in predicting school performance than in predicting things like creativity or social skills. Additionally, intelligence test scores are more closely related to mathematical problem solving and reading comprehension than to ability in drama, art, or music.

Reliability—the extent to which a test yields consistent results over time or successive administrations—is also critical for evaluating the utility of an intelligence test. To be useful, a test's scores must not fluctuate unpredictably from one administration to another. This is because a chief goal of these tests is to *predict* the individual's performance *beyond a single administration of the test*. Although reliability captures how much a test is useful across administrations, a related but broader issue is that of the stability of intelligence, to which we turn next.

Stability of Measured Intelligence

Is intelligence an absolute quality that remains stable over time, or can it change as a function of experience? To answer this question, we need to understand many things about intelligence, intelligence testing, and the limitations of intelligence measures. Tests like the Binet and Wechsler scales, which focus on the products of intelligence and measure current performance, have generally demonstrated that IQ scores are not stable over time but fluctuate. As investigators have begun to use newer tests that focus on the processes of intelligent functioning, however, the evidence for stability has been mounting.

In this section, we review longitudinal studies in which children have been tested repeatedly over long periods to examine the stability of intellectual functioning over time. We also address a second, related question: Are the average intelligence levels within a population stable across time?

As we will see, the evidence to date suggests that there is both stability and change in intellectual functioning over time. This finding highlights a third question: Can intelligence be changed by purposeful effort? Throughout the rest of the chapter, we explore the many ramifications of this important issue.

PREDICTIVE VALUE OF INFANT TESTING   Most of our information on the consistency of performance on intelligence tests derives from longitudinal studies in which children—in some cases as young as 1 month old—have been repeatedly tested over time. Some of these studies include the Berkeley Guidance Study, the Berkeley Growth Study, and the Fels Longitudinal Study, in which individuals were followed for periods of time ranging from 20 to 50 years. These and other early research studies found no significant relation between intelligence test scores recorded in infancy and those attained later in childhood or even adulthood (see Figure 10-1 on the next page; see also Honzik, 1983; Lewis, 1983; McCall et al., 1972).

More recent research using infant tests that largely focus on information-processing abilities, especially attentional processes, has found higher correlations with later cognitive measures (e.g., Fagan, 1992; Rose & Feldman, 1995). Within attentional processes (which we described in Chapter 4), these studies have followed habituation and recovery in particular. Recall that habituation is the infant's ability to discontinue attending to a stimulus after several presentations, and **recovery** is the infant's ability to recognize a totally new stimulus.

What kinds of correlations are found between measures of infant attentional processes and later IQ scores? Fagan and his colleagues found significant but moderate

validity

The extent to which a test actually measures what it claims to measure.

reliability

The degree to which a test yields consistent results over successive administrations.

recovery

The ability to recognize a new stimulus as novel and to direct attention to it instead of a familiar stimulus.

Figure 10-1

Predicting IQ scores

The height of each curve represents the degree to which children's early intelligence test scores were correlated with their Stanford-Binet IQ scores when they were 8 years old. The longer the time lapse between earlier and later testing, the less predictive value the earlier score had. Notice that in the Berkeley Growth and Stockholm studies, the earliest scores were actually negatively correlated with later ones.

Source: Honzik, 1976, 1983.

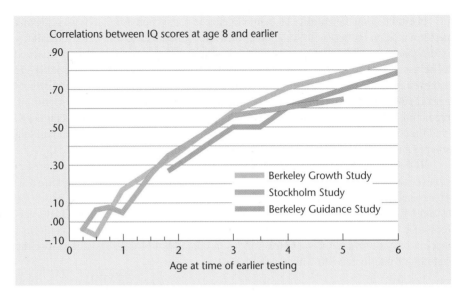

Correlations between IQ scores at age 8 and earlier

— Berkeley Growth Study
— Stockholm Study
— Berkeley Guidance Study

Age at time of earlier testing

correlations between infants' attention at 7 months of age and their intellectual functioning at 3 and 5 years (Fagan et al., 1991). Bornstein and Sigman (1986) also found moderately strong relations between such attentional measures in infants and the scores children achieved on intelligence tests at ages 3 to 6. Other researchers have found similar relations (Smith et al., 2002), sometimes extending even into adulthood (DiLalla et al., 1990; Rose et al., 1989). However, not all studies show such positive relations (Tasbihsazan et al., 2003).

Although we may be tempted to conclude that early individual differences in attention reflect genetic predispositions, the child's environment and other personal characteristics may be influential. In fact, one study found that attentional processing in 5-month-olds was related to the responsivity of the infants' mothers (Bornstein & Tamis, 1986). Differences in attentional processing in infants may also reflect variation stemming from other factors, such as child temperament (Karass & Braungart-Rieker, 2004). Thus, parental behaviours and the child's own emotionally related characteristics may well have a significant impact on infant intelligence.

CHANGES IN CHILDREN'S IQ OVER TIME   Most research indicates that from the middle years of childhood onwards, intelligence tests are fairly reliable predictors of later performance on such tests. For example, Honzik, MacFarlane, and Allen (1948) found a correlation of 0.70 between children's IQs at ages 8 and 18. Nonetheless, there is also evidence of variability in children's IQs. Many of the children tested in the Fels study, mentioned earlier, shifted considerably upward in IQ scores between the ages of 2½ and 17 (McCall et al., 1973). One of every three children scored higher by some 30 points, and one in seven shifted upward more than 40 points. On rare occasions, individuals have improved their IQ performance as much as 74 points. Investigators have also observed that high-IQ children are likely to show greater amounts of change than low-IQ children.

Some of the variability in IQ scores reflects the fact that different children develop cognitively at different rates of speed, just as they experience physical growth in spurts and at different ages (Garlick, 2003; Kanaya, Ceci, & Scullin, 2005). These variations in cognitive development affect the reliability of IQ scores. Experiential factors may also contribute to changes in IQ. Stressful life events, such as parental divorce or death or a change in schools, can cause at least temporary disruptions in cognitive performance. Indeed, children who show the most dramatic changes in IQ over time have often experienced major changes in their life circumstances, such as foster-home placement or a serious illness (Honzik, 1983).

In addition to examining the stability of individual IQ scores over time, some researchers have studied the stability of the average IQ for a group over time. Examining studies of different populations throughout the developed world between 1932 and 2002, J. R. Flynn (1987, 2007) found that the average IQ score in these nations increased by about 15 points during this time; this trend is known as the **Flynn Effect**. Gains were observed in measures tapping problem-solving ability but not in measures involving learned material. For example, using data from the Scottish Mental Surveys of 1932 and 1947, researchers at the universities of Edinburgh and Aberdeen (Deary et al., 2000; Deary et al., 2004; Starr et al., 2000; Whalley & Starr, 2001) compared performance on IQ-type measures at age 11 with performance on these same tests at age 80 (Deary et al., 2004). These researchers observed a general increase in test performance across this time, and also found that scores on these tests strongly correlated across time. The explanations for such gains in the group average are still being debated; they range from improved nutrition, changes in testing formats and procedures, exposure to technology and media, and possibly enriched home and school environments (Neisser, 1998).

Some of the variability demonstrated in IQ scores reflects the fact that, just as with physical growth, children develop cognitively at different rates. Interestingly, studies suggest that most changes in IQ are likely to occur at the ages of 6 and 10 years. Some researchers have proposed that a change at the age of 6 years may be associated with the shift at about that age to higher levels of abstract reasoning and conceptual ability as described by Piaget and his followers, and possibly a shift from a preschool to a school environment for children. Reasons for the shift at the age of 10 are less clear.

Flynn Effect

The general trend toward an increase in average IQ test scores across subsequent generations of the twentieth century.

For Thought and Discussion

1. If you had to design an intelligence test, what would your test contain? How would you go about measuring those aspects you think are most important? Is your test culture-fair?

2. Recently, the Canadian Psychological Association published norms for the WAIS-III (the Wechsler Adult Intelligence Scale). Interestingly, Canadian raw scores are significantly higher than US scores; so, ironically, in the course of standardizing these scores, Canadian IQs will actually appear to drop (to bring them in line with the US scores). Put differently, Canadians will suddenly seem to have lower IQs because they are smarter. What does this say about the process of testing intelligence and/or interpreting intelligence scores?

3. Much of the research on measuring intelligence finds that processing speed seems to correlate with other IQ measures. What are the implications and underlying assumptions of such a relation? What does this say about the importance of environmental versus genetic factors on intelligence?

WHY DO PEOPLE DIFFER IN MEASURED INTELLIGENCE?

LO 4

Closely related to the question of the stability of intelligence is one of the most controversial issues in the study of human intellectual functioning: how individual differences in intelligence develop. The modern controversy on this issue was touched off over 40 years ago when psychologist Arthur Jensen (1969) claimed that as much as 80 percent of differences in IQ among people was attributable to genetic, or inherited factors, and only a small proportion of differences to social-environmental factors.

In this section, we review some of the research on the side of heredity and then we examine the evidence for the role of social and environmental factors in intelligence.

Because the issue of the effects of ethnic and social-class differences on intelligence is so important, we have reserved much of our discussion of this topic for a major section, starting on page 400, entitled "Ethnicity, Social Class, and Intellectual Performance."

How Much of Intelligence Is Inherited?

As we saw in our Chapter 2 discussions of the relative roles of heredity and environment in the development of many human characteristics, there is considerable support for the importance of heredity in intelligence. Most estimates of the heritability of intelligence—that is, the proportion of the variability in intelligence attributable to genetic factors—have supported a figure of about 40 to 50 percent for middle-class North Americans of European ancestry (McGue & Bouchard, 1987; Plomin, 1990a; Plomin & Petrill, 1997). This suggests that the remaining 50 to 60 percent of the variability is a function of environmental factors, both social (family, peers, school) and non-social (dietary and disease factors, toxins, pollutants). Many psychologists disagree with this more or less 50–50 proposition, however. Some, such as Douglas Wahlsten (1990, 1994a, 1994b, 1999, 2000, 2002; Wahlsten & Gottlieb, 1997), criticize this approach on both biological and statistical grounds, pointing out there is no evidence that heredity and environment are truly separate. Because this assumption is a prerequisite to parcelling out the effects of genes from the environment, it is simply not possible to assign percentages to the roles of genetic and environmental factors (Wahlsten, 2000, 2002). Others, like Stephen Ceci (1996), hold that the estimates of the heritability of intelligence are too high, whereas others, such as Jensen, insist that they are too low. Still others argue that these estimates depend on the match and the interaction between genetic potential and environmental opportunities (Dickens & Flynn, 2001).

The 1994 publication of Richard Herrnstein and Charles Murray's *The Bell Curve*, which argued that intelligence is, in part, genetically based, rekindled this argument among students of intelligence. (The book's title refers to the bell-shaped curve that, for psychometricians, represents the tendency of scores or measures of a given characteristic to cluster in the middle of a range, with extreme highs and lows at either end.) The book also aroused the concern of many laypeople who, to at least some degree led by the media, understood the book not only to attribute most of the variability in IQ to inheritance but to suggest that IQ is relatively unchangeable.

In an effort to correct these and other misunderstandings of theory and research on intelligence, a number of investigators, in both books (e.g., Fish, 2002) and in the pages of academic journals like *Intelligence* and *The Alberta Journal of Educational Research*, have attempted to respond to many of the issues raised by Herrnstein and Murray (1994). One recurrent concern expressed in many of these commentaries involves the often-noted problem that many of the notions of intelligence employed in this work, as well as the actual measures of IQ themselves, have serious cultural biases that render such results potentially problematic. In addition, some authors (e.g., Barrow, 1995; Devlin, Fienberg, Resnick, & Roeder, 2002; Fancher, 1995; Horn, 2002; Hout, 2002) point out that many of Herrnstein and Murray's assumptions are simply unproven (e.g., the assumption that a normal distribution curve must underlie intelligence), and that much of the evidence provided by these authors as supporting heritability is either inaccurate or interpreted incorrectly.

VIEWS THAT EMPHASIZE THE HERITABILITY OF IQ   The measures of intelligence used in studies to support arguments for high levels of heritability in IQ are often based on traditional views of intellectual functioning. For instance, Arthur Jensen (1969, 1993), the most outspoken proponent of the heritability position, proposes two types of learning, both inherited but each clearly distinct from the other. **Associative learning** (*level I learning*) is lower-level learning involving such skills as short-term memory, rote

Douglas Wahlsten

associative learning

According to Jensen, lower-level learning tapped in tests of such things as short-term memorization and recall, attention, rote learning, and simple associative skills. Also called *level I learning*.

learning, attention, and simple associative skills. For example, we might ask a child to look at a group of familiar objects and then later to recall these objects. **Cognitive learning** (*level II learning*) is higher-level learning involving abstract thinking, symbolic processes, conceptual learning, and the use of language in problem solving. An example of cognitive learning is the ability to answer such questions as the following:

What should be the next number in the following series? 2, 3, 5, 8, 12, 17, . . .

How are an apple and a banana alike?

Most intelligence tests measure predominantly cognitive abilities. Some, however, include items that tap associative learning ability. Jensen suggests that associative learning is equally distributed across all people but that level II learning is more concentrated in middle-class groups and North American groups of European lineage than in working-class or North American groups of African lineage. And some scholars claim, because people tend to marry within their own groups, the differences between cognitive learning across populations, as measured in IQ tests, will tend to increase over time (Herrnstein, 1971; Herrnstein & Murray, 1994).

These conclusions have been called into question by studies comparing the IQs of people with differing numbers of genetic markers for African ancestry. Such studies have found no association between the number of markers of African ancestry and IQ (Nisbett, 1998). In addition, Williams and Ceci (1997) have shown that the IQ gap between racial groups has been decreasing, rather than increasing. Further complicating this issue is the fact that in highly multicultural countries such as Canada, many people have mixed ancestries and, thus, who is included in each group can vary depending on how one is classified.

CULTURE AND INHERITANCE Comparing intelligence scores across groups is a complex process. It is inappropriate to use estimates of the heritability of intelligence obtained from one group in interpreting findings based on the study of another group unless it can be demonstrated that the critical contributions from the environment to support the development of IQ are present across these groups. This is because environmental conditions will influence the extent to which an inherited ability can be expressed. Let's take as an example a person's height, a physical characteristic of human beings that, when children have good nutrition and are immunized against serious diseases, is essentially the result of inheritance (Kagan, 1969). Because the majority of North Americans are well nourished, the genes associated with height express themselves fairly directly in the actual height of a child. However, all inherited characteristics interact with environmental forces to some degree, and so does height. In cultures with extremely adverse health and/or nutritional factors, the genetic contributions to physical stature are lessened relative to more advantageous situations. This is why most starving children, if they live to adulthood, remain small of stature regardless of the typical height of the ethnic groups to which they belong.

In the same fashion, heritability measures for middle-class North American families with reasonably similar backgrounds and life circumstances may be quite different from such measures for minority or working-class groups whose circumstances may differ dramatically from those of the former group. In short, genes depend on the environment for their expression (Moore, 2001). Poor nutrition, disease, and stress due to a variety of factors—for example, economic deprivation, overcrowded living quarters, homelessness, abuse, civil unrest, war—may overwhelm and, thus, minimize the genetic contribution to intelligence and intellectual performance (Garcia Coll, 1990; Huston et al., 1994; Neisser, 1998).

THE MALLEABILITY OF INHERITED CHARACTERISTICS
Finding evidence for genetic influences on intelligence in a population does not suggest that differences among individuals are unchangeable (Plomin & Petrill, 1997). Consider

cognitive learning

According to Jensen, higher-level learning tapped in tests of such things as abstract thinking, the use of symbolic processes, conceptual learning, and the use of language in problem solving. Also called *level II learning*.

some other kinds of developmental differences, such as blindness and deafness, which we know in some cases are influenced by genetic factors. The fact that these conditions may be genetically induced has not interfered with the ability of special-education programs to help affected children. And as we noted earlier, the gap between the scores of African North American and European North American students on IQ tests and tests of achievement in mathematics and reading have narrowed substantially over the last few decade (Hauser, 1998). Moreover, some recent research has shown that when characteristics of the home environment are taken into account, the gap narrows still further (Brooks-Gunn et al., 2003).

Environmental Factors

Even strong advocates for the genetic basis of human intelligence understand that children are brought up in circumstances that range from the most favourable to the most destructive (Sternberg & Grigorenko, 2001). Furthermore, most scholars recognize that the quality and amount of stimulation offered to children in these varying conditions affect their intellectual development. In this section, we consider some of the factors that can affect the child's intellectual abilities before or during birth; in addition, we explore the important influences of the family, the school and peer culture, and the community.

PREGNANCY AND BIRTH   As we pointed out in Chapter 3, such factors as poor maternal nutrition can have highly influential and lasting effects on a child. Moreover, an extensive body of research details the negative effects on intellectual development of such things as maternal disease (e.g., AIDS) or a mother's alcoholism or addiction to other drugs. In addition, events attending the process of birth, like oxygen deprivation, can have destructive effects on a child's mental functioning. Deficits or defects traced to such factors are considered **congenital**, meaning that they occur during gestation or at birth. Rather than genetic in origin, they are either transmitted directly from the mother to the fetus or result from events during the birth process.

congenital

Describing deficits or defects that the child incurs in the womb or during the birth process.

THE FAMILY   The child's first social environment, which is usually the family, has important influences on her intellectual functioning (Grigorenko & Sternberg, 2001; Rodgers, 2001). A supportive, warm home environment that encourages a child to become self-reliant, to express her curiosity, and to explore has been linked to higher intellectual functioning (Petrill & Deater-Deckard, 2004). Parents who are emotionally and verbally responsive to their children, who provide a variety of learning experiences, and who encourage their children's interest in and efforts at learning tend to have children with higher IQ scores (Bradley et al., 2001; Wachs, 2000). It is important to note, however, that such family environments do not uniformly produce high-achieving children. Recall from Chapter 2 that even though children in the same family have many shared environmental influences, they are also subject to non-shared environmental stimuli that may counteract other influences and affect their intellectual development (Reiss et al., 2000; Rutter, 2006b). Moreover, because the home environment tends to be influenced by inherited intelligence factors, the ways in which the family environment is related to children's intellectual functioning are complex.

SCHOOLS AND PEER GROUPS   Although more years of school and higher-quality education are related to increases in intelligence scores, the flip side is also true: deficits in education may cause IQ scores to decline (Ceci, 1996; Ceci & Williams, 1997). Declines in intellectual skills have been associated with lack of formal education, dropping out, and too much time off from school. Numerous studies have also shown that children who have attended a high-quality preschool have higher skill levels than children who have not, even when the two groups are similar in socio-economic status, family environment, and prior skill levels (Wachs, 2000).

Poor and minority students in inner city and rural neighbourhoods often face a substantial disadvantage in school quality compared to those in wealthier areas. In addition, these students, due to a variety of environmental factors, are likely to enter school with no preschool experience and with lower levels of skills as compared to their middle-class peers. Furthermore, disadvantaged students tend to fall further behind as they progress into middle and high school (Molfese & Martin, 2001; Turkheimer et al., 2003). Cultural differences and negative teacher attitudes may also hinder adjustment and learning (Comer, 1996, 2004; Eccles, 2007).

Peers also influence children's attitudes toward, and success in, school. For example, one study found that peer groups of Asian-American students supported each others' academic pursuits and participated in education-related activities such as studying together (Steinberg et al., 1992). In contrast, some researchers have reported anti-academic attitudes among African-American students (Ogbu, 1988). Because of the strong adolescent need to belong in a peer culture, the effect of negative feedback from their peers may often outweigh parental encouragement of academic achievement (Steinberg et al., 1992). Sometimes, African-American children who succeed in school choose strategies to hide or camouflage their true attitudes toward schoolwork and their actual efforts to achieve academic success (Fordham & Ogbu, 1986). For example, a student may excel in athletics or take on a role, such as class comedian, to disguise his intellectual pursuits.

This mother is using marbles and printed numbers to encourage her son in learning to match number symbols and names with quantities of actual objects.

THE COMMUNITY The community as a cultural unit may have significant effects on a child's cognitive and intellectual development. For example, studies have shown that children living in isolated circumstances, such as rural areas, score lower on IQ tests than do children in nearby villages or in metropolitan areas (Ceci, 1991; Flynn, 1987). Similarly, economically disadvantaged areas of modern cities are often associated with slowed intellectual development. The poor diets, unsafe housing, and high levels of community violence and unemployment that characterize impoverished areas may all contribute to less adequate cognitive functioning (Bronfenbrenner et al., 1996; Garbarino, 1995; Evans, 2003; Pollitt, 1994).

It is important to stress, however, that in some cases, environments stimulate and help children to develop abilities that are sophisticated, highly adaptive, and meaningful in their specific circumstances (Sternberg et al., 2007). Intelligence tests devised to reveal intellectual capabilities in varying cultural contexts, such as regions in Africa (Serpell & Haynes, 2004) and the Eastern Mediterranean-Middle East (Gulgoz & Kagitcibasi, 2004), have been helpful in identifying how the construct of intelligence can be construed and measured in different cultural settings. This research indicates that concepts of intelligence can differ widely across cultures and that social factors, such as responsibility and sensitivity toward the family or community, are an important component of many of these conceptions. In recent years, the idea of social intelligence has even risen in prominence in discussions of intelligence in North America (Goleman, 2006). Finally, other research has revealed intelligent actions that people carry out in their cultures and that are rarely tapped in typical tests of intelligence. Children living in remote communities in Newfoundland and Labrador, for example, were found to have highly developed perceptual and motor abilities that were useful in their setting, although their verbal and reasoning skills—less important in that setting—were below average (Burnett, Beach, & Sullivan, 1963). Similarly, the Pulawat islanders of Micronesia, who have little formal education or technology, have developed a navigational system that reveals a complex understanding of the relations among direction, winds, tides, and currents and that enables them to sail long distances out of the sight of land. Nevertheless, these skilled navigators would not perform well either on a standard test of intelligence despite the fact that their navigational skills evidence high levels of intelligence. Observations like these show us how important it is to analyze intellectual performance within the individual's cultural context (Ceci, 1996; Hutchins, 1996).

For Thought and Discussion

1. Given what you have read about attempts to separate genetic from environmental factors, what do you think about the idea of a "heritability estimate"? Is it possible to truly think about the independent influences of these factors, or are they too closely linked to one another to ever really be separated?

2. On the basis of how you answered the question above, are there ethical considerations that might arise from your position on this issue? What are the ethical implications of books, such as *The Bell Curve*, that seem to take a definite stance on issues like this?

3. Finally, what are some of the developmental implications of these ideas on the separability of genetic and environmental factors? What type of developmental change might you expect if abilities are driven by environmental versus genetic influences?

LO5 ETHNICITY, SOCIAL CLASS, AND INTELLECTUAL PERFORMANCE

Research has found relations between ethnicity and social class and intellectual performance. *Social class* is a broad term that includes such variables as education, occupation, and income. The term *socio-economic status* (SES) is often used to refer to a combined assessment of these three variables (Benokraitis, 1998). Because these factors are frequently associated with each other, researchers tend to study them together. However, because they are closely associated, researchers often find it very difficult to disentangle one factor from another—for example, the effects of having a particular occupation from being poor.

Ethnicity presents particular problems of measurement and analysis because researchers tend to lump subcultures together. Thus, a study of "Asians" or "Asian Canadians" may include Chinese, Filipinos, Indians, Japanese, Koreans, and Vietnamese as one group, and, as a result, the study will mask important differences among these groups. Another problem related to both ethnicity and social class is that researchers' assumptions may influence the kinds of questions they ask and the way they ask them. For example, many studies of Asian North Americans ask why children of this group are successful in school, whereas many studies of African North Americans may ask why children of this group perform poorly. Scholars working in this area recommend research that focuses on each group's strengths as well as on the areas in which each could improve (Spencer, 2006).

With these constraints on existing research in mind, let's look at three main sets of explanations for the differences in IQ and intellectual performance observed among various ethnic and socio-economic groups. The first set proposes that existing standardized tests are inappropriate for lower-class and minority children. The second set focuses specifically on the role that socio-economic factors play in intellectual performance. The third set explores how parent–child interactions may differ among social classes and racial and ethnic groups.

Are Intelligence Tests Biased against Minority Groups?

Those who argue that existing tests of intelligence are biased against a sizable group of the North American population point out that the most widely used tests were standardized on European North American middle-class people (Valencia & Suzuki, 2001). They maintain that for this reason, test items do not accurately measure the problem-solving abilities appropriate to the circumstances in which some members of ethnic groups live. These tests, their detractors insist, draw on the language, experience, and values of middle-class European North Americans. For example, the vocabulary used on traditional IQ tests often differs from the dialect or even language some children use every day. On this view, some researchers have argued that minority children's lower verbal scores may reflect cultural bias, not lack of intelligence. In support of this position, tests such as the Kaufman battery, aimed at minimizing cultural bias, show less difference between the scores of African North American and European North American children than do standard IQ tests.

     In his concept of **stereotype threat**, Claude Steele (1997) has offered yet another explanation for poor performance on IQ tests among ethnic minority youth. According to Steele, people are aware of the stereotypes that society holds about their particular groups—for example, the stereotype that certain ethnic groups are intellectually inferior to other ethnic groups. In situations in which this stereotype can be tested, Steele believes that individuals from the group for which there is a negative stereotype have self-doubt and worry about confirming the stereotype in their test performance. This self-doubt has the effect of hurting the individual's performance, which, in turn, confirms the stereotype. Stereotype threat has been found in children as young as 6 years of age and by age 10 most children are aware of broadly held social stereotypes regarding certain stigmatized minority groups such as African Americans and Latinos (McKown & Weinstein, 2003). Moreover, children in these minority groups are more aware of the stereotypes than children who are not in these groups. And, as Steele (1997) predicted, children in these minority groups who are aware of the stereotypes performed less well on cognitive tasks when they were told the purpose was to test their ability.

ETHNIC GROUPS MAY EXCEL IN DIFFERENT AREAS   One criticism of IQ tests is that they fail to measure the ability to cope with the everyday activities and problems of life with which people must contend. Following up on this criticism, Mercer (1971) studied a large group of children and young adults whose IQ scores classified them as mentally retarded. Mercer tested these individuals in their adaptive abilities—that is, their abilities to perform skills required for such things as self-care (e.g., dressing), household tasks (e.g., shopping, cooking), holding a job, and travelling alone to and from their jobs. The results were amazing: 90 percent of the African-American children and 60 percent of the Latino children who had IQs below 70 (i.e., these children scored in the lowest range of measured intelligence, the bottom 3 percent, traditionally labelled "mentally defective") *passed* Mercer's test, but every European American child with an IQ below 70 *failed* it! The disturbing implications of these findings were that minority children are far more likely than European North American children to be inappropriately classified as mentally retarded—a label that will have a pervasive effect on their life experiences and on others' expectations of them.

     On the theory that members of various groups may show different patterns of abilities on tests, one classic studied compared the verbal skills, reasoning, and numerical abilities of middle- and lower-class African-American, Chinese-American, Jewish, and Puerto Rican children between about 6 and 7 years of age (Lesser et al., 1965). G. S. Lesser and his colleagues found that these four groups did indeed have different

stereotype threat

Being at risk of confirming a negative stereotype about the group to which one belongs.

profiles of ability scores. In general, Jewish and Chinese-American children scored higher on these tests than did African-American and Puerto Rican children; African-American children showed greater verbal abilities than Chinese-American children and scored better on reasoning than Puerto Rican children; and Puerto Rican children scored slightly above African Americans on numerical and spatial abilities. Social class influenced score levels for all groups; however, differences in score level due to socio-economic factors were greatest for African Americans, suggesting that social class disadvantages had a relatively greater impact on these children. These and other findings (e.g., Neisser, 1996; Williams, 1998) have led some investigators to reason that under-standing the relation between ethnicity and performance on intelligence tests requires examining achievement levels on different kinds of cognitive skills and not just at overall IQ levels.

The Effect of Context and Cultural Background on Intellectual Performance

Not only may traditional intelligence tests be biased in their content and approach, but the conditions under which they are administered to minority children of lower socio-economic status may also have interfered with these children's ability to perform (Spencer, 2006). Recall that the newer information-processing approaches to intelligence testing have pointed to the importance of context in children's intellectual performance (Das, 2004). Researchers influenced by these ideas have tried to familiarize children with the test environment and test materials, to encourage them on various tasks, and to use material rewards, such as candy, to motivate performance. These efforts have been successful with some low-income and minority group children; in fact, they have been significantly more successful with economically deprived children than with middle-class children (Zigler et al., 1982). These findings support the view that intelligence tests do not measure the competencies of low-income and ethnic minority children as well as they measure the abilities of middle-class European North American children.

Understanding the relations of ethnicity and intellectual performance has also been informed by studies that look at how cultural background and experiences contribute to performance on achievement tests. In recent years, both scholarly and lay publications have documented a trend in North American students' academic performance that is disturbing to many. These reports have warned that in mathematics and science, and

This 6-year-old child is studying the WISC Picture Arrangement task, which requires her to put an array of picture cards in order so that "they tell a story."

even in the language arts, North American students are falling behind students in other countries, particularly in Asia (Martin et al., 2004). Research, such as that conducted by Harold Stevenson and his colleagues (described in Box 10.1 on the next pages) that followed groups of North American, Chinese, and Japanese students from grades 1 through 11, raises many provocative questions about the influence of cultural values and practices on intellectual performance and academic achievement (Chen et al., 1995; Stevenson & Stigler, 1992). One question is whether patterns of interaction in Asian North American families can explain the high levels of performance frequently shown by Asian North American children (Lytton, 2000). Whereas African North American, European North American, and Latino North American parents also value education highly, their children typically do not experience the same level of academic success seen in Asian North American families. Asian North American parents strongly support their children's academic achievement (Chao, 2001). They hold high expectations for their children's education and also tend to convey the idea that academic achievement is part of children's duty to parents. Asian North American families often strictly monitor the time their children spend on homework and in free play. In addition, they frequently profess the belief that effort will be rewarded (Slaughter-Defoe et al., 1990). This research suggests that the critical family factors determining the different patterns of achievement across diverse ethnic groups merit further study.

Social-Class Influences on Intellectual Performance

Separating social class from intelligence and achievement is enormously challenging. If non-genetic factors contribute roughly 50 percent of the variation in IQ scores and intellectual performance, it is important to do this to gain a better understanding of intellectual development. In this section, we look at some research efforts to isolate social-class factors in intellectual performance.

SOCIAL-CLASS FACTORS AND CUMULATIVE RISK   Investigators throughout the world have described differences in performance on standardized tests among children from various social-class groups (Huang & Hauser, 1998; Neisser et al., 1996). In the United States, children in the lower socio-economic classes score 10 to 15 IQ points below middle-class children (Brody, 1992). These differences are generally observed by grade 1 and remain consistent throughout the school years (Kennedy, 1969; Moffitt et al., 1993). However, when factors such as family conditions and home environment are taken into account, the differences in scores are reduced somewhat (Brooks-Gunn et al., 2003). Longitudinal research in Scotland has revealed similar patterns, in that children in families from the lowest social class group in the study had IQ scores in the years of middle childhood that were significantly lower than children in families from higher SES groups (Lawlor et al., 2005).

The concept of **cumulative risk** may help us understand the significance of the effects of socio-economic factors on intelligence and intellectual performance. If in the life circumstances of a given child only one of the many risk factors that may compromise healthy development, such as poverty, is present, many other factors in that child's environment may outweigh the risk that one factor poses for her. However, as more and more negative factors are added to the child's life experience, her risk of poor outcomes will increase (Carmody et al., 2006; Sameroff & Fiese, 2000). To test this notion, Sameroff and colleagues (Sameroff et al., 1987, 1993) identified specific environmental factors that are likely to present risks to children's cognitive development (see Table 10-4 on page 407) and then, among 215 4-year-old African-American, European-American, and Puerto Rican children, examined the links between these risks and IQ scores. As you can see in Figure 10-5 on page 407, the findings were striking. Children

cumulative risk

The notion that risk factors in children's life circumstances have cumulative negative effects on their intellectual performance.

Box 10.1

Perspectives on Diversity

MAKING THE GRADE IN JAPAN, TAIWAN, AND THE UNITED STATES

The declining academic achievement of North American children has received substantial attention from the media. What can psychology tell us about children's academic achievement? Longitudinal studies by Harold Stevenson and his associates (Chen et al., 1995; Stevenson et al., 1993; Stevenson et al., 1990) have now provided evidence that in the earliest months of grade 1, children in the United States already lag behind other children in academic achievement. Thus, although differences in academic performance may well reflect varying educational systems, the fact that these differences appear when children have had little exposure to formal education suggests that more is involved than inadequate educational practices.

Over a 10-year period, Stevenson and colleagues administered tests of reading and mathematic ability to groups of grade 1, 5, and 11 children in classrooms in two US metropolitan areas (Minneapolis, Minnesota, and Fairfax County, Virginia), in two East Asian cities (Beijing, China, and Taipei, Taiwan), and in Japan (Sendai). The US students included four cultural groups—European, Chinese, African, and Latino Americans—although not all these groups were represented in every study. In each study, the researchers interviewed teachers, students, and students' mothers on a variety of topics, such as the value of education, beliefs about learning, attitudes toward school, and family involvement in children's schoolwork.

In one study, there were noticeable differences in reading-test scores among seven groups of students even in grade 1 (see Figure 10-2). In grade 1, Japanese students scored highest, followed fairly closely by Asian-American, Taiwanese, and European-American students; African-American and Latino-American students scored the lowest. By grade 5, Taiwanese and European-American students had jumped ahead of Japanese and Asian

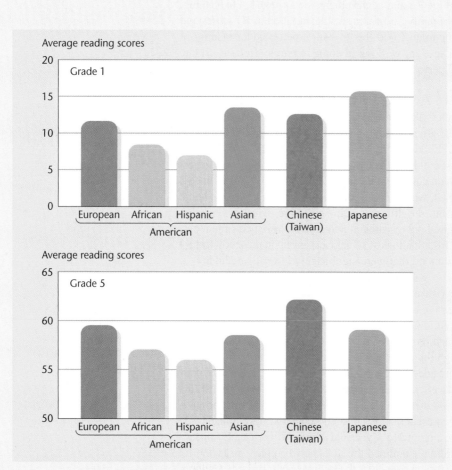

Average reading scores

Figure 10-2

Reading scores in China, Japan, and the United States

Across both grade 1 and 5, Chinese and Japanese students tended to do better in reading than any of the US cultural groups. In grade 1, Asian-American students ran second to Japanese students but, for some reason, dropped down by grade 5. In grade 5, Chinese students took top honours, but European Americans, Japanese, and Asian Americans, ranking in that order, all had very close scores. The relations among European-, African-, and Hispanic-American students remained fairly stable from grades 1 to 5; these groups scored from higher to lower, respectively.

Source: Adapted from Chen, Stevenson, Hayward, & Burgess, 1995.

Americans. Once again, US students scored considerably below others on a mathematics test, and between grades 1 and 5, these differences became more pronounced (see Figure 10-3). At both times, Chinese (Beijing, Taiwan) and Japanese students had the highest scores, Asian Americans following close behind.

What could be contributing to these results? Stevenson and his colleagues found no evidence that the US children had lower intellectual levels, and parental education levels argued, if anything, in favour of European American students. However, there were marked differences in parents' beliefs, their reported activities with their children, and the evaluations they made of their children and their educational systems. Chinese and Japanese mothers generally viewed academic achievement as the child's most important pursuit. Once children entered school, Chinese and Japanese families mobilized to help their children and to provide an environment conducive to achievement. Japanese mothers, in particular, were likely to see themselves as kyoiku mamas, that is, "education moms" responsible for assisting, directing, and supervising their children's learning.

American mothers were less likely to be involved in helping their children with homework than mothers in other groups. They tended to put more emphasis on the role of innate ability in school performance and less on the role of effort. Mothers in all three countries viewed their children's academic performance as above average but, as Figure 10-4 shows, mothers in the United States voiced the most positive views about their children's scholastic achievement and experience, even though they were aware of the country's low rank in comparative studies of children's performance.

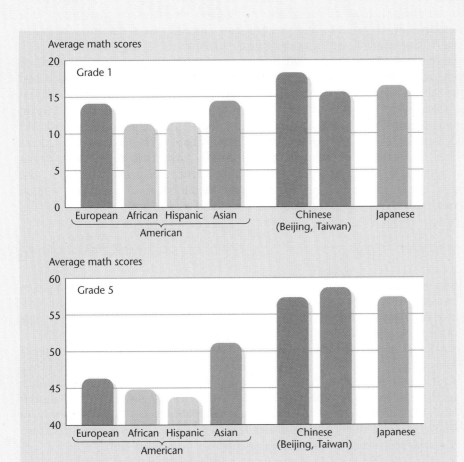

Figure 10-3

Mathematics skills in China, Japan, and the United States

As in reading, Chinese and Japanese students outscored US students in math. Although the differences were small in grade 1, they were large in grade 5, and Asian-American students clearly led their US peers.

Source: Adapted from Chen, Stevenson, Hayward, & Burgess, 1995.

(continued)

Box 10.1   (continued)

Perspectives on Diversity

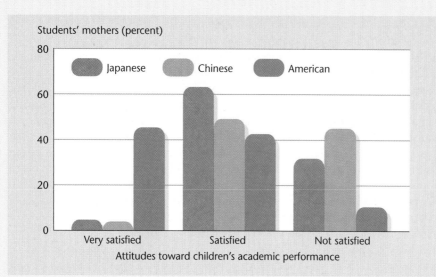

Students' mothers (percent)

Japanese   Chinese   American

Attitudes toward children's academic performance

Figure 10-4

Mothers' attitudes toward their children's academic performance

In 1990, more Japanese and Chinese mothers than US mothers were "satisfied" with their children's academic performance. However, more than 40 percent of US mothers but fewer than 5 percent of Chinese and Japanese mothers were "very satisfied."

Source: Stevenson, Chen, & Lee, 1993.

Children in the United States spend significantly less time on homework and reading for pleasure and more time playing and doing chores than Japanese or Taiwanese children do. In one study, only 17 percent of grade 1 and 28 percent of grade 5 Taiwanese children did chores, in contrast to 90 percent and 95 percent of US grades 1 and 5 children, respectively. When researchers asked one Taiwanese mother why she did not assign her children chores, she replied, "It would break my heart. Doing chores would consume time that the child should devote to studying."

Mothers in the States appeared to be more interested in their children's general cognitive development than in their academic achievement per se, attempting to provide the children with experiences that fostered cognitive growth (Stevenson et al., 1990). These mothers reported reading more frequently to their young children, taking them on excursions, and accompanying them to more cultural events than did Chinese or Japanese parents (Stevenson et al., 1993).

What might be done to help improve US students' competitive status? Some school districts have moved toward lengthening the academic year, which has traditionally been much shorter than the school year in Asian countries. The shorter schoolday in the United States may also contribute to the fact that US students spend more time than Asian students in extracurricular pursuits, including sports, socializing, and dating. But if Stevenson and his colleagues are right, intervention needs to begin earlier and at home.

with only one risk factor had verbal IQ scores well above average; an IQ of 115 is considered "bright normal." As the number of environmental risk factors increased, however, IQ scores dropped, and children whose life circumstances included seven or eight of the risk factors had IQs 30 points lower, putting them in the "dull normal" range.

Social class did not appreciably affect these findings. The presence of several risk factors was associated with low IQs in families of both low and high socio-economic status. However, any one of these factors was more likely to be present in low-income families than in families with more financial advantages. A follow-up study (Sameroff et al., 1993) of 152 of the same families when the children were 13 years old revealed a similar pattern: a 30- to 35-point IQ difference between the children whose risks were few (high end) and those who confronted many risk factors (low end).

These findings argue for the notion that children who confront multiple risk factors face potential declines in their performance on intelligence tests (Grissmer et al.,

Table 10-4

Major risk factors that endanger children's cognitive development

Source: Sameroff, Seifer, Baldwin, & Baldwin, 1993.

Poor maternal mental health
High maternal anxiety
Low maternal education
Head of household either unemployed or in unskilled occupation
Father absent from family
Minority-group membership
Family in which there are more than four children
High incidence of stressful events, such as illness, job loss, or death in the family

1998). The findings also allow us to hypothesize that in the absence of such risk factors, children should achieve higher test scores. Psychologists have tested this hypothesis by studying African-American children who were adopted by economically well-off European-American parents (Scarr & Weinberg, 1976). As you can see from Figure 10-6 on the next page, adopted African-American children achieved scores some 20 points above the national average for African-American children, and the younger they were at adoption, the higher their scores were. Follow-up studies (Scarr, 1997, 1998; Weinberg et al., 1992) found that the adoptees experienced a gain in IQ similar to the gains of the biological offspring of the adoptive parents. Although the adoptees' IQ scores more closely resembled their biological parents than their adoptive parents, their higher scores and continued gains reveal the strong influence that environment has on IQ and on the long-term maintenance of gains in IQ.

SOCIAL CLASS AND PARENT–CHILD INTERACTIONS Several investigators have suggested that maternal behaviour differs across social classes and may differentially affect children's intellectual performance in the school setting. For instance, middle-class mothers were more likely than lower-income mothers to speak in response to their babies' vocalizations (Hart & Risley, 1995; Lewis & Wilson, 1972), and their infants tended to stop vocalizing and listen when their mothers spoke. In contrast, lower-income children were more likely to continue vocalizing when their mothers were speaking (Lewis & Freedle, 1973). Some scholars have suggested that

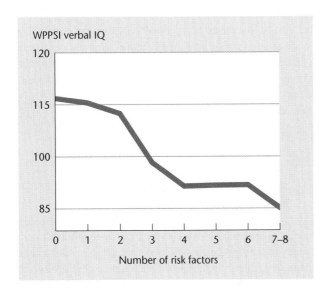

Figure 10-5

Risk and intellectual performance

This graph dramatically illustrates the relationship between risk factors associated with poverty and intellectual performance. The more risk factors such as hunger, poor clothing, and family stress in the lives of these 4-year-olds, the lower were their scores on the Wechsler Preschool and Primary Scale of Intelligence (WPPSI).

Source: Sameroff, Seifer, Baldwin, & Baldwin, 1993.

Figure 10-6

How do children adopted into middle-class European-American homes fare?

Both African-American and European-American children adopted into middle-class European-American homes obtained IQ scores that were substantially above the national averages for their respective groups. We do not know why the European Americans fared somewhat better than the African Americans.

Source: Adapted from Scarr & Weinberg, 1976.

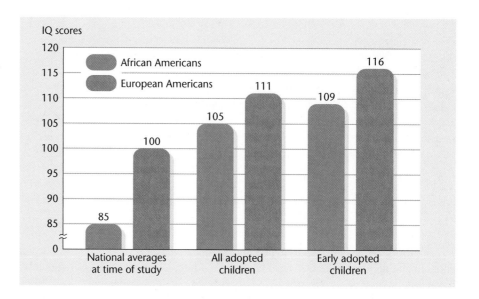

these early differences in the way infants attend to their mothers' speech may be related to later differences in the ease with which children learn from verbal information (Hoff, 2005).

Barnard, Bee, and Hammond (1984) found that mothers who had gone beyond a high-school education were more highly involved with their infants than mothers who had not finished high school; these differences, measured at several intervals before the children reached age 2, were significantly related to the children's IQ scores at age 4. Specific behaviours that are important include reading to young children before they enter school. On average, 73 percent of young children whose mothers graduated from university were read to every day by a family member, compared with 60 percent of children whose mothers had some years of university, 49 percent of children whose mothers finished high school without any further education, and 42 percent of children whose mothers had not finished high school (Federal Interagency Forum on Child and Family Statistics, 2007). These different rates are significant, in that reading with an adult in the preschool years is associated with better reading achievement in elementary school (Bus et al., 1995).

In China, where there are relatively small differences in income across groups of people who vary in education, Tardif (1993) found that less-educated parents used more imperatives with their toddlers than did better-educated mothers. This style of interaction is likely to be associated with poorer cognitive development. Finally, many researchers have argued that stress, presumably more commonly experienced by lower-income parents than by their middle-class counterparts, may directly influence parental styles of interaction—for example, lower-income parents may be more concerned with discipline at the expense of positive emotional communication (Goldstein, 1990; Hess & Shipman, 1967; McLoyd et al., 2005).

LO 6 ACHIEVEMENT, MOTIVATION, AND INTELLECTUAL PERFORMANCE

achievement motivation

A person's tendency to strive for successful performance, to evaluate her performance against standards of excellence, and to feel pleasure at having performed successfully.

Children's academic performance is affected not only by their experiences in the family, school, peer group, and community, but also by their own **achievement motivation**— that is, their tendency to strive for successful performance, to evaluate their performance against specific standards of excellence, and to experience pleasure as a result of having performed successfully (Wigfield et al., 2006). Variations in achievement motivation and intellectual performance are often related to a child's emotions and opinions of himself as a person and a learner—in short, to the sense of self (Dweck, 2000; 2006). Some children have negative feelings about specific learning tasks and may be convinced of their inability to learn in certain areas. Sometimes, a child's feelings and beliefs about his ability to succeed are sufficiently negative that they distract the learner from the task itself and may prevent him from learning (Bransford et al., 1999).

Researchers have identified two different response patterns among children working on a challenging task at which they could fail (Heckhausen & Dweck, 1998). In an early study, children from grades 5 and 6 attempted to solve a series of difficult problems that resembled a game of Twenty Questions (Diener & Dweck, 1978). At first, the children were able to solve the problems, but then the experimenter presented several very hard problems that they failed. Some children maintained or even improved their level of performance despite failure on some of the hard problems; the researchers labelled these children mastery-oriented because they were focused on gaining skill or mastery at the problems. In contrast, other children tended to give up easily or to show marked performance deterioration when working on challenging problems; the researchers labelled these children as helpless.

When mastery-oriented children performed poorly, they expressed neutral or even positive emotions, attributed their failure to insufficient effort rather than to lack of ability, and maintained high expectations for future success. Helpless children, on the other hand, expressed negative emotions such as frustration, blamed their own lack of ability for their performance, and expressed low expectations for future performance.

What might cause different children to react so differently to the same task? Helpless and mastery-oriented children do not differ in their actual ability levels; rather, they *think* differently about ability and achievement (Dweck, 2006; Heckhausen & Dweck, 1998; Kamins & Dweck, 1999). Mastery-oriented children tend to have *learning goals*. In other words, they are more concerned with improving their skills and learning new things than they are with specific judgments of their ability. Children who show the helpless pattern, on the other hand, tend to have *performance goals*; that is, they are concerned with "looking smart," obtaining positive judgments, and avoiding negative judgments of their ability. Dweck and her colleagues have proposed that these different goals are associated with different beliefs about intelligence itself. That is, mastery-oriented children tend to hold an *incremental* view of intelligence, viewing intelligence as a body of skills and knowledge that can be increased with effort. In contrast, helpless children tend to hold an *entity* view of intelligence, believing, if implicitly, that intelligence is a fixed and unchangeable entity that people possess in varying degrees.

Dweck suggests that the two views of intelligence and the two goals orient children to react very differently to achievement tasks. As Table 10-5 on the next page illustrates, when children are successful at tasks, they do not appear to differ in their behaviour; even children with an entity view and performance goals are likely to show the mastery-oriented pattern. However, when children fail at a task, their different views of intelligence lead to different behaviours. Under these circumstances, mastery-oriented children may interpret their failure as an indication that they must work harder to learn more, whereas helpless children may see failure as evidence of their lack of ability and may give up. Of course, different situations can elicit different responses, and mastery-oriented children may occasionally show helpless responses when examiners or others put a lot of stress on performance goals (Dweck, 2001; 2006; Heckhausen & Dweck, 1998).

Experience in the family in the preschool years may affect the development of these views of performance (Eccles, 2007). Children whose parents encouraged more mastery-oriented behaviour from them as toddlers, for example by promoting independence and persistence in solving problems, show more mastery-oriented behaviours later on when they enter school (Pomerantz et al., 2005). In contrast, some environmental conditions may even promote helplessness in children. In research on rural children

Table 10-5 Views of intelligence, goal orientations, and behaviour patterns for high and low performance levels

View of Intelligence	Goal Orientation	Present Performance Level	Behaviour Pattern
Entity (intelligence is fixed)	**Performance** (to gain positive, avoid negative judgments of competence)	High	**Mastery oriented** (seeking challenge, persistence)
		Low	**Helpless** (avoiding challenge, low persistence)
Incremental (intelligence is malleable)	**Learning** (to increase competence)	High	**Mastery oriented** (seeking challenge that fosters learning, persistence
		Low	**Master oriented** (seeking challenge that fosters persistence)

Source: Dweck, 2001; Dweck & Leggett, 1988.

in upstate New York, Gary Evans (2003) found that children living in poverty who experienced a number of physical stresses, such as crowding and poor-quality housing, and psychosocial stresses, such as family turmoil or violence, were more likely to behave in a helpless manner when presented with a challenging puzzle task than were poor children who had fewer stresses in their lives.

Culture may also play a role. Chen and Stevenson (1995) found that European-American students tended to endorse "having a good teacher" as the most important factor in their performance in mathematics, whereas Asian students reported that "studying hard" was the most important factor (see Figure 10-7). Chen and Stevenson and their colleagues (Chen & Stevenson, 1995; Stevenson, 2001; Stevenson, Lee, & Mu, 2000) found that, compared with Asian students and their parents, European-American students had lower standards for their academic work, and their parents more often attributed their children's performance to innate ability.

Finally, the timing of certain school-related experiences may affect children's achievement or their motivation to achieve. Traditionally, the first eight years of

Figure 10-7

To study hard, or to be taught well—is there a question?

When researchers asked Chinese and Japanese high school students in their own countries, and Asian- and European-American students in the United States, to choose among several factors that may affect students' academic performance, the majority chose either "studying hard" or "having a good teacher." Within these choices, the Japanese and Chinese students were far more likely to choose the first of these factors, whereas the US high-school students were much more likely to choose the second.

Source: Chen & Stevenson, 1995.

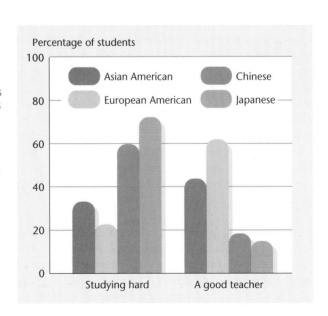

elementary school (or nine, including kindergarten) and the four years of high school were arranged in two separate segments. However, in recent years, the first six years of elementary school are grouped together, followed by two years of junior high or middle school (grades 7–8), followed by four years of high school (grades 9–12). Research suggests that such organizational variations make a difference in children's academic experience. Simmons, Blyth, and McKinney (1984) compared students moving from grade 6 to 7 in an eight-year elementary school and in a junior high school where this transition involved moving to a new school. In comparison to the grade 7 children who stayed in elementary school, the junior high-schoolers had lower self-concepts, were less involved in activities and clubs, and perceived themselves as less integrated into their school and peer groups (Roeser et al., 2000). For preadolescents and adolescents, the onset of puberty, the start of dating, or some disruption in family life may make the burden of shifting to a new school especially heavy. Consistent with the concept of cumulative risk, Simmons and her colleagues (1987) found that children, especially girls, who were undergoing three or more transitions had lower self-esteem, participated less in extracurricular activities, and had lower grade-point averages.

One important new Canadian program is the Ontario Early Years Centres. The centres are places where parents and other caregivers can talk with early-years professionals, along with other parents and caregivers, about any questions or concerns they might have. These centres also provide information about programs and services that are available to young children in their communities.

COGNITIVE INTERVENTION STUDIES

As we have seen, a sizable number of factors contribute to a child's intellectual functioning. When some of these factors are negative and impede children's intellectual development, as well as their ability and motivation to use their intellectual powers to grow and prosper, can we alter them and improve a child's intellectual functioning? Cognitive intervention studies are designed to address this question.

Head Start and Similar Programs

Beginning in the 1960s, researchers and policymakers have implemented a great many programs aimed at modifying the development of learning-disabled or economically deprived children. Some *preventive* programs were designed to prevent the decline in cognitive skills that was theorized to occur in preschool children who were relatively disadvantaged in society; other *interventionist*, or remedial, programs focused on school-aged children who already had demonstrated learning difficulties. One of the most well-known cognitive intervention programs is **Head Start**—begun in 1965, it is for severely economically deprived preschoolers. This program is intended to provide 3- and 4-year-old children with daily preschool, and it originally included social services, medical care, and health education for parents. However, funding cuts starting in the 1970s eliminated a number of the parent services, and many eligible children cannot be accommodated in the preschool component in some areas. Box 10.2 on pages 412 and 413 describes a recent Canadian initiative in Head Start. One especially ambitious Canadian intervention program is the Better Beginnings, Better Futures project, a 25-year primary prevention program (Nelson et al., 2005; Peters, 1994, 2005). In a recent evaluation of this program by Ray Peters of Queen's University and his colleagues (Peters, Petrunka, & Arnold, 2003), these researchers noted significant gains in both children's and parents' social-emotional functioning and physical health over the first five years of the project. Other notable Canadian intervention efforts include the Ontario Early Years program; the Staying on Track project, which assesses the impact of regular visits by public health nurses to families with infants and young children in Brockville, Ontario (Landy, Peters, Arnold, Allen, Brookes, & Jewell, 1998); and, most recently, the Human Early Learning Partnership of British Columbia (Hertzman & Williams, 2009; Kershaw, Irwin, Trafford, & Hertzman, 2005). This last program has been particularly effective in assessing the school readiness and performance of children; it uses the Early Development Instrument (EDI; Janus &

Head Start

A federally funded program, started in the United States, that provides disadvantaged young children with preschool experience, social services, and medical and nutritional assistance.

Canadian Head Start Programs
Ontario Early Years Centres Program
Better Beginnings, Better Futures Project
Human Early Learning Partnership of British Columbia

Box 10.2

Risk and Resilience

ABORIGINAL HEAD START

Since its beginnings in the 1960s, Head Start programs have been focused primarily in the United States. In more recent years, however, this program has extended into Canada, with the inception of the Aboriginal Head Start (AHS) program, which began in May 1995 and receives $22.5 million of funding each year. As with the parent program, the goal of this initiative is to offer early-childhood development intervention, and maintain a program that provides First Nations, Inuit, and Métis children with the opportunity to develop capabilities, attitudes, and the confidence to achieve in school.

Currently, there are about 140 AHS sites across Canada in nine provinces and the three territories. Approximately 4,500 children are enrolled in the AHS, with a primary emphasis on 3- to 5-year-old Aboriginal children and their families. Thirty percent of these projects are located in urban centres, 21 percent in remote locations, and 49 percent in non-remote locations where less than 50,000 people live. Of the children participating in this program, 44 percent are First Nations, 22 percent are Métis, and 34 percent are Inuit (Health Canada, 2000a).

Aboriginal Head Start programming in these communities is organized around six components, shown in Table 10-6. Although all the AHS sites offer programming in each of these areas, the different sites do vary in deciding how to make an impact in each. Nevertheless, the vision is the same for all such programs: to provide high-quality intervention to Aboriginal children and their families.

How do these programs hope to make a positive impact in each of the different component areas? In general, the approach is to provide Aboriginal children with a positive sense of themselves, a desire for learning, and, hopefully, the opportunities to develop successfully. Programming in culture and languages, for example, attempts to provide children with a positive sense of themselves as Aboriginal children, and to enhance cultural and language revival, with the goal that children will learn their respective languages and participate in their communities' culture. Many of the sites do this by providing instruction in English and at least one Aboriginal language. In their attempts to encourage school readiness, children are encouraged to ask questions, are praised for their accomplishments, and receive instruction in alphabet and number recognition, and so on. And in such areas as health promotion and nutrition, parents and caregivers receive information that enables them to take control of and improve their health and the health of their children, as well as to provide snacks and meals to children, and to teach them to distinguish between healthy food and junk food.

Of course, one of the key issues with any early-intervention program is its success in improving the chances for normal, healthy development in its target population. How has the AHS program fared in this "bottom line" evaluation? According to some (Health Canada, 2000a), AHS has had an impressive beginning, in that a number of communities have developed facilities and begun operational programs. As for program evaluation, there are two main components to this project, the first involving a *process evaluation* and the second an *impact evaluation*. The goal of the former is to collect demo-

Offord, 2007), which asks teachers to report on their students across five different domains (physical, social, emotional, communication, and language and cognitive skills).

Studies have shown that children have higher scores on IQ and other ability measures immediately after these programs end, whether the programs are preventive or interventionist (McLoyd et al., 2005). In the early grades, Head Start children show higher cognitive and social skills than similar children not involved in the program (Brooks-Gunn, 1995; Lee et al., 1990).

Long-term studies have shown other effects that last well into adulthood. Compared to similar children who did not participate in the program, Head Start children scored higher on achievement tests and were less likely to have been held back in a grade, placed into special education, or to have engaged in criminal behaviour. They were more likely to have graduated from high school and attended university, and they had higher earnings as adult workers (Barnett et al., 1992; Lazar & Darlington, 1982).

Table 10-6 The six programming components of Aboriginal Head Start

1. Culture and language	Provide children with a positive sense of themselves as Aboriginal children.
2. Education and school readiness	Encourage children to take initiative in learning, and provide them with enjoyable opportunities to learn.
3. Health promotion	Empower parents, guardians, and caregivers to increase control over their health, and to encourage practices for self-care.
4. Nutrition	Ensure that children receive food that will help them meet their nutritional needs, and educate parents about the relationships between nutrition and the ability to learn, and physical and mental development.
5. Social support	Make families aware of, and aid them in, accessing available resources and community services that will make an impact on their quality of life.
6. Parental involvement	Support the parents' and family's role as children's teachers, help parents gain a deeper understanding of their children, and promote the development of parents as role models for children in their community.

Source: Based on Health Canada (2000a).

graphic and descriptive data from each AHS site about its participants, activities, needs, and finances. Data such as these are useful in explaining and promoting the program within and outside government.

The goal of the impact evaluation is to describe the changes in children, parents, and communities that have occurred as a result of taking part in this program, and to look at all six program components described earlier. The impact evaluation for this program began in 2002, but has, unfortunately, not yet made its findings publicly available.

One concern is that the evaluation procedures used must be culturally sensitive, and employ methods and measures relevant for the testing of Aboriginal children. As we have seen throughout this chapter, many of the available testing procedures have been developed with urban, middle-class children in mind and do not take into account the experiences or values of Aboriginal families and children. In sum, there is a lot of work yet to do to even evaluate the effectiveness of this intervention effort.

Characteristics of Successful Intervention Programs

The earlier intervention programs start and the longer they continue, the more successful they are likely to be (Ramey & Ramey, 1992, 2006). Table 10-7 on page 414 lists seven principles on which the most effective intervention programs have been based. Children from impoverished settings who do not benefit from early-intervention efforts suffer a significant loss in both cognitive and social-emotional development during the second and third years of life (Blair et al., 1995). Moreover, it is not very likely that children can ever achieve a complete catch-up in these areas of development, although later-intervention programs can effect some gains.

Intervention endeavours that focus on improving both the parent–child relationship and the family's natural support systems, and that place the child in an

Table 10-7 Seven principles of successful early-intervention programs

Principle	Description
1. Timing	Interventions should begin during the first two years of life and continue at least until children enter kindergarten, and they should engage families earlier rather than later.
2. Intensity	The more intensive the intervention—that is, the greater the number of hours per day, days per week, and weeks per year during which intervention activities take place—the more positive the program's effects, particularly in families in which parents have the lowest education levels and during the first five years of the child's life.
3. Direct provision of learning experiences	Intervention programs that offer services directly to the child rather than through an intermediary, such as a parent or a home visitor, are more successful than others.
4. Breadth	The broader the spectrum of services provided and the more routes used to enhance children's development, the more successful the program.
5. Recognition of individual differences	Programs must recognize the varying needs of individuals. In the lives of poor families, numerous reasons may account for one individual's failure to do well; thus, individualization of treatment interventions is very important.
6. Environmental maintenance of development	Unless poor or at-risk children are supported in multiple domains of development beyond the preschool years, they will not develop the skills, motivation, health, and resources needed to succeed in school settings. Two-generation programs may, by helping parents, create the support system children need to make academic progress.
7. Cultural appropriateness and relevance of intervention strategies	To be valued, used, and incorporated into participants' everyday lives, interventions must be culturally relevant and welcome to family and child. Because individuals within cultures vary greatly, stereotyping cultures will lead to failure.

Source: Based on Ramey, Ramey, Gaines, & Blair, 1995; Ramey & Ramey, 1998, 2006.

two-generation program

A program of early cognitive intervention that extends help to parents as well as to their children.

educationally stimulating program, are among the most successful (Hyson et al., 2006; Slaughter, 1988; Smith, 1995). Almost as successful are programs that actively involve low-income parents in their children's education (Powell, 2006). In some cases, mothers are employed as teaching aides in preschool centres; in others, program staffers visit mothers in their homes and instruct and support them in their educational activities with their children. Some successful programs offer support that stretches beyond the home and preschool environments. The goal of these **two-generation programs** is to support both parents and children as they try to improve their futures (Stipek & McCroskey, 1989). They enable parents to take advantage of community resources in furthering their own education, getting job training, and finding work, or strengthening family relationships and family functioning through supportive social relationships (Ramey & Ramey, 2006; Smith, 1995).

For Thought and Discussion

1. Given the evidence that many intelligence tests are biased against minorities, what do you think of the practice of adjusting test scores in an attempt to account for such bias? Does this introduce another bias of its own?

2. Although there is evidence that intelligence tests vary with the social class of the child, it is a category that can encompass many possible differences (e.g., economic, educational). Which of the possible factors that go into social class do you think are the critical ones?

BEYOND THE NORMS: GIFTEDNESS AND MENTAL RETARDATION

Children vary greatly in the rate and manner in which they learn. Some children are exceptionally talented, learning much faster than their classmates, whereas others function at significantly lower intellectual levels than their peers. Traditionally, specialists in intelligence testing have held that an IQ score above 130 signals **intellectual giftedness**; a score below 70, coupled with a person's difficulty in coping with age-appropriate activities in everyday life, indicates **mental retardation**. Finally, some children, many of whom have normal or even high intelligence levels, have specific difficulties that interfere with learning, such as speech or language impairments or reading disabilities like dyslexia. These children are identified as having **learning disabilities**. We look first at the evidence on giftedness and then at the contemporary view of retardation and the prospects of leading fulfilling lives for those who fall into this category. Then, we examine children with learning disabilities.

The Intellectually Gifted

Do children who are intellectually gifted burst upon society, speaking when they are only a year old, solving problems in calculus at the age of 2 years? Not usually. Often, however, gifted children show special interests and talents quite early, and they apply themselves to these interests with enthusiasm and perseverance (Winner, 2006). But are the cognitive processes these children use unique or different from what older children use? Veronica Dark and Camilla Benbow (1993) suggest the processes that underlie the cognitive feats of gifted children are not unique; it is simply that such children use their cognitive skills more efficiently than the rest of us. For example, gifted children seem to be able to process information more rapidly than others.

The question of how to educate and encourage exceptionally bright and talented children is controversial (Sternberg, 2006; Winner, 2006). Should these children be permitted to begin school early? Should they skip grades? Some argue that these sorts of steps are necessary to maintain an exceedingly bright child's interest and motivation. However, critics worry that these efforts may meet the child's intellectual needs at the expense of her social and emotional development, especially in terms of experiences and relationships with peers. Education alternatives for gifted children include enrichment programs, which attempt to provide these children with extra stimulation without advancing them to higher grades. In another type of program, the school sets up a special subject or activity meant to enrich the educational lives of a group of intellectually talented students—for example, a special class in science or social studies. A third type of enrichment program offers gifted students instruction in creative writing or foreign languages or opportunities for study in the arts, such as painting and dance. Although some argue that the "enrichment" offered by these types of programs may be mostly busywork unrelated to the child's talent, enrichment programs influenced by Howard Gardner's notion of multiple intelligences are proliferating. These programs are designed to nurture the specific talents of gifted children (Moran & Gardner, 2006).

Children with Intellectual Deficits

We first encountered mental retardation in Chapter 2, when we discussed three specific disorders that are accompanied by serious intellectual deficits: Down syndrome, phenylketonuria (PKU), and fragile X syndrome. Down and fragile X syndromes, you will recall, are chromosomal disorders, whereas the cause of PKU is the lack of a specific enzyme for processing phenylalanine. Mental retardation resulting from genetic or other factors that are clearly biological is referred to as *organic* retardation (Hodapp &

intellectual giftedness

A characteristic defined by an IQ score of 130 or over; gifted children learn faster than others and may show early exceptional talents in certain areas.

mental retardation

A characteristic defined by an IQ score below 70 and the inability to cope adequately with age-appropriate activities in everyday life.

learning disabilities

Deficits in one or more cognitive processes important for learning.

Dykens, 2006). Intellectual deficits that derive from factors surrounding the birth process (such as lack of sufficient oxygen) and those resulting from conditions of infancy or childhood (such as infections, traumas, or lack of nurturance) are considered *familial* retardation. In general, organic retardation is more severe than familial retardation.

Mental retardation is diagnosed by two basic measures: assessments of the child's mental functioning and of the child's adaptive behaviour (American Association of Mental Retardation, 2002). Traditionally, an IQ score below 70, together with adaptive behaviour deficits, has indicated mental retardation. Each of four IQ score ranges reflects an increasingly serious degree of retardation: mild mental retardation, IQ 55 to 70; moderate retardation, IQ 40 to 54; severe retardation, IQ 25 to 39; and profound retardation, IQ below 20 or 25. In addition, according to the guidelines of the American Association on Mental Retardation (2002), to be classified as mentally retarded, children must show deficits in their abilities to function in the real world. Young children who can dress themselves, find their way around the neighbourhood, and use the telephone, for example, are less likely to be identified as mentally retarded than are children with the same IQs who do not exhibit these practical competencies.

By far, the majority of mentally retarded people—some 95 percent—can learn and hold jobs of more or less complexity and can live in the community. Children with mild retardation (about 85 percent of all retarded children) usually acquire social and communicative skills during the preschool years and may be indistinguishable from other children until they reach their teens, at which time they may begin to have difficulty with more advanced academic work. Children who are moderately retarded (about 10 percent) generally acquire communication skills in early childhood, and although they can benefit from vocational training, they are limited in their grasp of academic subjects. Young people in both these groups may join the workforce and live in supervised settings or, in some cases, independently. Children with severe retardation (3 to 4 percent of all retarded children) may learn to speak and communicate but rarely progress beyond reading a few words. Finally, children with profound retardation (1 to 2 percent) may learn communicative skills and some self-care. Both of the latter groups can learn to do some simple tasks with close supervision; at present, young people in both these groups must live in supervised settings.

Whether the competencies of any or all of these groups of mentally retarded children can be improved has yet to be determined. Researchers at the Language Research Center in Georgia have succeeded for the first time in enabling non-speaking severely and moderately retarded youngsters to communicate intelligibly with adults and peers using a computerized keyboard device, and have begun to explore the use of this device with 1½- to 3½-year-old children at risk of failing to develop language. And as we mentioned in Chapter 2, with caring parenting that includes extra stimulation and training, many children with Down syndrome can lead very productive lives (Hodapp, 2002).

Children with Learning Disabilities

Not all children learn at the same pace or in the same way. Some learn faster than their classmates, but others with various learning disabilities may learn more slowly. Of the more than 5 million US children classified as disabled, a little more than 50 percent are considered learning disabled, about 20 percent have speech or language difficulties, about 9 percent are emotionally disturbed, about 12 percent are mentally retarded, and about 8 percent have various other kinds of handicaps (US Department of Education, 1997). Children identified as learning disabled are a very heterogeneous group in terms of the types of cognitive and social abilities they possess (National Joint Committee on Learning Disabilities, 1994). The diversity among learning-disabled children makes it particularly difficult to know exactly what types of interventions are most useful for this group.

A major question in recent years has been whether these "special-needs" children should be placed in separate classes or integrated into regular classrooms. Many schools have adopted the approach of **inclusion** (also called *integration* or *mainstreaming*), in which children of all ability levels are included in the same classroom. Other schools have placed children with learning disabilities and other special needs in separate, special-education classes. The success of these different approaches is still being debated (Berninger, 2006). Some argue that inclusion programs enhance the academic achievement of learning-disabled children (Buysse & Bailey, 1993), whereas others argue that such programs put children at risk for peer rejection or inappropriate labelling (Weissberg & Greenberg, 1998).

inclusion

A policy by which children of all abilities levels, whether learning disabled, physically handicapped, or mentally retarded, are included in the same classroom.

CREATIVITY

The nature of creativity and its relation to intelligence have long been of interest to psychologists. Some investigators, like Robert Sternberg, see intelligence and creativity as intertwined, but others, such as Howard Gardner, see clear distinctions between the two. In this section, we first look at some efforts aimed at definitions and theories of creativity and then at some evidence on the distinctions between creativity and intelligence. We then consider children's creative behaviours and conclude with some thoughts on how to encourage creativity in children.

Definitions and Theories

Defining creativity is about as hard as defining intelligence; both are multi-faceted qualities that vary as a function of personal characteristics (which are both inherited and learned), the context in which they are exercised, the risk factors that may inhibit them, and the environmental supports that may encourage and sustain them. The key to creativity is the notion of *uniqueness*. Most people—including most psychologists—would agree that the creative product is novel. In some way, it is unlike anything else in its class. But most authorities, such as Gardner (2006), also agree that a truly creative idea or product must be characterized by *usefulness*. It must be of benefit in some area of life, whether that be astrophysics, the visual arts (e.g., painting, sculpture), household products, literature, microbiology, music, or another field of human endeavour. And still others argue that knowledge is crucial. For instance, Keegan (1996) discusses how Charles Darwin amassed an enormous body of knowledge of natural history before he offered his ideas about evolution to the world.

The Relationship between Creativity and Intelligence

Are IQ and creativity related? **Creativity** is defined as the ability to solve problems, create products, or pose questions in a way that is different (novel) from the approaches that most other people use (Gardner, 2006). To explore the relation of creativity to IQ, Wallach and Kogan (1965) administered WISC subtests and other intelligence tests, as well as a set of tasks designed to tap creative modes of thinking, to a group of grade 5 children, both genders in equal numbers. The researchers found only minimal correlations between "correct" answers on the intelligence tests and answers judged creative on the more open-ended tasks. These results suggested that the intelligent person excels at *convergent thinking*, or thinking with the goal of recognizing or remembering specific information or solving traditional problems for the correct answers, and the creative person excels at *divergent thinking*, or thinking that is imaginative and seeks

creativity

The ability to solve problems, create products, or pose questions in a way that is novel or unique; also, the ability to envision new problems not yet recognized by others and to come up with solutions to them.

variety, novelty, and uniqueness. Thus, although highly creative people tend to be above average in intelligence, a higher IQ does not predict creativity (Gardner, 2006). Clearly, the true relation between creativity and intelligence has yet to be determined. One thing people do agree on, however, is that both are desirable characteristics.

Are Children Creative?

According to some psychologists, very young children are not capable of true creativity. Although we know that children are capable of gathering significant bodies of knowledge, psychologists who specialize in creativity, such as Mark Runco (1996), hold that because young children often cannot distinguish reality and fantasy, children cannot be truly creative until they reach preadolescence and can make this distinction. However, others point out that even though young children are not creative in the full sense of the term, their play—especially fantasy or pretend play—gives children a chance to practise the kind of divergent thinking that can lead them someday to invent new things or ideas (Moore & Russ, 2006; Russ, 2003). Lev Vygotsky also thought that play facilitated creativity: "The child's play activity is not simply a recollection of past experience but a creative reworking that combines impressions and construct-forming new realities addressing the needs of the child" (1930/1967, p. 7).

If children may eventually be capable of creativity, are there ways that this creativity can be fostered or encouraged? Formal school instruction tends to be focused on learning specific content, passing tests, and advancing in grade. According to Robert Albert (1996), a number of researchers have identified a period from middle childhood through preadolescence when early signs of creativity seem to disappear as children concentrate on well-organized (and thus well-controlled) learning skills. Divergent thinking simply does not have much opportunity to flourish in the classroom. However, outside of school, parents can contribute by encouraging their children's creative impulses (Russ, 2003).

For Thought and Discussion

1. How well do current theories of intelligence, or intelligence tests, assess and explain creativity? In your own personal theory of intelligence, how much importance do you place on creativity?

2. What do you think the function of creativity is in intellectual development? What cognitive abilities are necessary for creativity? Is language a prerequisite? How about reasoning?

3. In a classic study by Lewis Terman (1954), he found that a large group of intellectually gifted children were advanced in any number of ways, including having precocious motor development in infancy, having fewer than the average cases of psychological disturbances as children and adults, and reporting higher occupational and marital satisfaction than the average number of adults. Do such results actually demonstrate that intellectual giftedness leads to a better life? What other factors might account for these differences?

Making the Connections 10

There are many links between concepts and ideas in one area of development and concepts and ideas in other areas. Here are some of the connections between ideas in Chapter 10 and discussions in other chapters of this book.

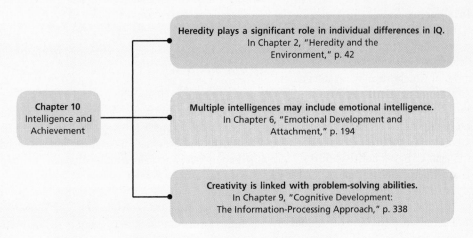

Chapter 10
Intelligence and Achievement

Heredity plays a significant role in individual differences in IQ.
In Chapter 2, "Heredity and the Environment," p. 42

Multiple intelligences may include emotional intelligence.
In Chapter 6, "Emotional Development and Attachment," p. 194

Creativity is linked with problem-solving abilities.
In Chapter 9, "Cognitive Development: The Information-Processing Approach," p. 338

SUMMARY

Theories of Intelligence

- It is generally agreed that intelligence is composed of multiple abilities and is not a single, general construct. Contemporary intelligence specialists have confirmed the existence of a general factor of cognitive ability derived from Spearman's original **general factor (g)**. This modern middle-ground position, which also recognizes Spearman's concept of **specific factors (s)**, holds that children may vary both in overall intellectual power and in their proficiency in specific aspects of cognitive functioning.

- An information-processing approach to intelligence, Sternberg's **triarchic theory of intelligence** holds that intelligent behaviour is built on information-processing skills, experience with particular kinds of tasks and problems, and the abilities to adapt to a particular context, or environment, and to shape others to one's needs.

- Gardner's **theory of multiple intelligences** suggests that each of eight kinds of intelligence has its own developmental path and is guided by different forms of perception, learning, and memory. Each type of intelligence is likely to characterize individuals and cultures with particular interests and endeavours, and a single individual may possess one or more types.

Testing Intelligence

- Specialists in intelligence testing have generally described intelligence by means of an **intelligence quotient (IQ)**. However, it is important to remember that what is measured on an IQ test is performance; capacity cannot be directly measured.

- Intelligence tests have three primary purposes: predicting academic performance, predicting performance on the job, and assessing general adjustment and health. Although traditional tests predict school performance better than anything else, they have been criticized as unfair to minority groups, and efforts have been made to develop **culture-fair tests**.

- The widely used **Bayley Scales of Infant Development (BSID)**, designed for infants and very young children, measure certain developmental milestones and are generally used with children who are thought to be at risk of suffering abnormal development.
- The early intelligence test developed by Binet and Simon focused on verbal and problem-solving abilities. The **Stanford-Binet test** is a US adaptation of Binet's test.
- The **Wechsler Intelligence Scales** are probably the most commonly used intelligence tests today. Their scoring is based on a **deviation IQ**, or the relation between an individual's score and the distribution of scores for the group of which he or she is a member.
- The **Kaufman Assessment Battery for Children** also attempts to be culture-fair. Examiners teach a child who fails an item how to solve it before moving on to the next item.
- Intelligence tests must have both **validity** and **reliability**. Test constructors may examine for these characteristics by splitting a test's items and comparing each half with the other or by comparing the results of one administration with those of another on another date. IQ scores can and do fluctuate. Early studies indicated that scores on intelligence tests during infancy did not predict later childhood or adulthood intelligence, but recent research suggests that measures of infant attention may be related to IQ scores during early childhood. After about age 8, prediction of intelligence becomes more accurate. The rate of mental growth varies among children, however, so that IQ scores are more stable for some than others.

Why Do People Differ in Measured Intelligence?

- Most estimates of the heritability of intelligence have indicated that 40 to 50 percent of the variability in intelligence among middle-class European North Americans is due to genetic factors.
- Many psychologists continue to debate the heritability of intelligence, some holding that it is less than 50 percent, others that it is more. Arthur Jensen proposes two types of learning, both inherited—**associative learning** and **cognitive learning**. According to Jensen, all people share the first type of learning, but the second type is more prevalent among certain racial-ethnic groups.

- When we estimate heritability among people within a specific cultural or ethnic group, our estimates of heritability will be higher because such people, by definition, share some characteristics that are both inherited and environmental. Conversely, it is inappropriate to apply heritability indexes based on one group to members of another.
- Significant environmental factors that affect the child's intellectual functioning include events during pregnancy and the child's birth that can result in **congenital** defects; also, the interpersonal relationships that the child develops with family members, teachers, peers, and members of the community at large can have an impact.

Ethnicity, Social Class, and Intellectual Performance

- According to those who hold that intelligence tests are biased against members of minority groups, the content of standard IQ tests is drawn from European North American middle-class language, vocabulary, experience, and values and, thus, may be inappropriate for other groups.
- Context is an important factor in children's intellectual performance. Testing conditions, such as unfamiliar surroundings and European North American examiners, may be deleterious to the performance of lower-income and minority children.
- The concept of **cumulative risk** suggests that the more negative aspects of poverty and deprivation a child experiences, such as poor nutrition and homelessness, the more likely he or she is to score poorly on a test of intellectual skills.
- Varying styles of parent–child interactions in different social classes may influence a child's development of verbal and cognitive skills. Studies indicate that early differences in mothers' use of language and infants' attention to their mothers' speech may account for later differences in the use of verbal information.
- Research indicates that multicultural and cross-cultural differences in parents' attitudes and enthusiasm for education may affect children's performance on academic tasks. Chinese and Japanese students have been found to perform at a higher intellectual level, particularly in mathematics, than Asian-American students who, in turn, score higher than European-American, African-American, and Latin-American students.

Achievement Motivation and Intellectual Performance

- Children's intellectual performance is influenced by their own **achievement motivation**, the emotions they associate with learning tasks, the ways they view themselves and their abilities and their responses to success and failure.

- In one approach to understanding achievement motivation, children who see themselves as helpless tend to give up easily or show deterioration when working hard on problems. In contrast, mastery-oriented children use failure feedback to maintain or improve their performance. Helpless children may hold an *entity* view of intelligence, whereas mastery-oriented children may hold an *incremental view*.

Cognitive Intervention Studies

- Many programs have been launched aimed at modifying the development of learning-disabled or economically deprived children. One of the most well known and successful is **Head Start**. The findings with respect to maintenance of gains achieved in initial years in this and other programs are mixed. Almost all programs, whether preventive or interventionist, have reported short-term gains in academic performance, but some others have reported a loss over time of the initial advances.

- Keys to long-term success may be in involving children within the first two years of their lives, continuing intervention efforts at least until children enter kindergarten, and offering **two-generation programs**, in which educational, occupational, health, and counselling services are provided to the children's parents as well.

Beyond the Norms: Giftedness and Mental Retardation

- Whether or not to advance children who display intellectual giftedness to higher grades in school remains a controversial topic, although some such programs have shown considerable success. While some voice concerns that advancement will socially isolate gifted young children, others hold that such children are advanced socially as well as intellectually.

- Only 4 to 6 percent of children afflicted with **mental retardation** must live under close supervision throughout their lives. We do not yet know to what degree the intellectual competencies of these children can be improved, although some studies have shown that mentally retarded children who do not speak can learn to communicate through the computerized use of visual symbols.

- More than half the children with special-education needs are identified as having specific learning disabilities that interfere with cognitive processing in some way. Schools differ in terms of how these children are integrated in the classroom; some schools place children with learning disabilities in classes with normally functioning children and other schools separate these children into special-education classes.

Creativity

- The defining features of creativity are uniqueness and usefulness. The relationship between creativity and intelligence continues to be debated, but a current theory suggests that the sources of creativity lie in intelligence and motivation as well as in a willingness to meet challenges, overcome obstacles, and take risks.

- Because children lack the knowledge base required to evince true creative efforts, some psychologists believe that creativity begins only in preadolescence. Others, however, hold that young children have novel ideas, engage in creative acts, and use play to practice divergent thinking.

Faith Ringgold (b. 1930). *Tar Beach*, 1988.

Solomon R. Guggenheim Museum, New York.

Chapter 11

The Family

LEARNING OBJECTIVES

After reading this chapter, you should be able to

LO1 Describe the family systems perspective and the basic principles of the ecological systems perspective as applied to families.

LO2 Discuss the relationships between the marital system and the parent–child system.

LO3 Identify how parents socialize their children during early childhood.

LO4 Discuss the dimensions of emotionality and control as they relate to parents' relationships with their children; identify Baumrind's typology of parenting behaviours and the likely outcomes for children with parents of each type.

LO5 Describe how family functioning is related to the number, sex, and spacing of the children; discuss the research relating birth order to parent–child interactions, sibling interactions, and personality characteristics.

LO6 Explain how social class and ethnicity are related to socialization; discuss research findings on the relationships between child-rearing differences and social class and ethnicity.

LO7 Discuss changes in the North American family in recent years and the impact of these changes on children.

LO8 Cite characteristics often associated with abusive families and their members; discuss the consequences of child abuse.

The family is both the earliest and the most sustained source of social contact for the child. What is a family? It is a social unit in which the adult partners or spouses and the children share economic, social, and emotional rights and responsibilities as well as a sense of commitment or identification with each other. Even though many contemporary families have new and different structures, family relationships remain the most intense and enduring of all interpersonal and social bonds. Family members share not only their memories of the past but also their expectations of future shared events and experiences. It is largely this continuity over time that makes the family relationship qualitatively different from the shorter-lived relationships children have with playmates and friends, teachers, neighbours, and, later in life, co-workers. Children carry their memories of past family interactions in their perceptions and feelings about family members and in the standards they hold, not only for family behaviour but for the behaviour of people in general.

In the child's earliest years, her sole interpersonal relationships may be with her parents, and parents generally present cultural beliefs, values, and attitudes to their children in a highly personalized and selective fashion. Clearly, parents' own personalities, family backgrounds, attitudes, values, education, religious beliefs, socio-economic status, and gender influence the way they socialize their children. However, parents play a crucial role in this **socialization** process, ensuring that their child's standards of behaviour, attitudes, skills, and motives conform as closely as possible to those regarded as desirable and appropriate to her role in society. We will see in the next few chapters that peers, schools, churches, the media, and other forces also contribute importantly to a child's socialization. From the moment of birth, however, "whether the child is wrapped in a pink or blue blanket, swaddled and placed on a cradleboard . . . nestled in a mobile-festooned bassinet, indulged by a tender mother, or left to cry it out by a mother who fears spoiling the child, socialization has begun" (Hetherington & Morris, 1978, p. 3).

We begin this chapter by examining the family system from the ecological theory perspective described in Chapter 1. We explore several subsystems of the family—including the relationships between and among marital partners, parents, children, and siblings—and examine how the family as a whole contributes to the child's socialization. We then look at the effects of social class, socio-economic status, and ethnicity on the family and its role as socializing agent. In addition, we explore some of the major changes in the structure and functioning of the North American family that have occurred in recent decades. In a majority of families today, both parents work outside the home, a change that can have important effects on the child's development. In addition, there is enormous diversity in the way modern families are structured; some are headed by a single and/or divorced parent, some families are blended by divorce and remarriage, and still other families are headed by gay or lesbian parents. In some families, partners are becoming parents at later ages; in other families, parents cherish adopted children. We also consider the development of children born to teenaged parents who are often unwed mothers. We end the chapter with an examination of the causes and consequences of the tragedy of child abuse. ●

socialization

The process by which parents and others ensure that a child's standards of behaviour, attitudes, skills, and motives conform closely to those deemed appropriate to her role in society.

Canadian Researchers

ⓛ1 THE FAMILY SYSTEM

It is not uncommon for people to view socialization as a process by which parents modify children's behaviour, but it would be more accurate to think of this phenomenon as a process of mutual shaping. That is, parents do indeed influence and direct their children, but their children also influence them and, in fact, play an active role in their own socialization (Bronfenbrenner & Morris, 2006; Kuczynski & Parkin, 2007). In a complex system in which members are interdependent, changes in structure or the altered behaviour of a single family member can affect the functioning of the entire system. Moreover, families do not function in isolation; they are influenced by the larger physical, cultural, social, and historical settings and events around them. And families are not static; they change over time. Every family member, from the youngest infant to the oldest adult, is changing all the time, and these changes are reflected in family relationships.

The Family

The Ecological Systems Perspective

The view of the family as an interdependent system that functions as a whole has two principal origins: the realization by psychotherapists that to change the behaviour of a troubled child, one usually must change the family system as well (Minuchin, 2001); and Bronfenbrenner's ecological theory. This position is concerned both with the relations between the child and the many nested systems within which he develops, as well as with the relations among these systems themselves, from the familiar microsystem to the larger social and cultural setting of the macrosystem (Bronfenbrenner & Morris, 2006). The key here is that the contexts in which children are embedded are not only backdrops to development, but they actually play important roles in developmental trajectories.

To refresh your memory, look back at Table 1-2 (see Chapter 1), which used the family system to illustrate several important principles of dynamic systems theory. We learned there that a system is *complex* and *organized*; that it has an ongoing *identity* of its own; and that, although it maintains a certain *stability* over time, it must also be capable of *morphogenesis*, adapting to changes both within the system and outside of it. In addition, a system demonstrates *equifinality* as time goes by, developing many similarities with other systems like it, even though such systems (e.g., families in different cultures) may express these similarities in different ways.

In addition, we need to consider one or two other principles that govern system functioning. *Interdependency* explains why the functioning of the family system is not always smooth. Because each family member and family subsystem influences and is influenced by each other member and subsystem, both co-operative behaviour and hostile or anti-social behaviour may have widespread effects on the system as a whole. Parents who have a good relationship with each other are more likely than not to be caring and supportive with their children, and, in turn, the latter are likely to be co-operative and responsible. On the other hand, parents whose marriages are unhappy may become irritable with their children, and the children may exhibit anti-social behaviour that may, in turn, intensify problems in the parents' relationship.

Families tend to attain equilibrium, or *homeostasis*, in their functioning and to become resistant to forces that might alter this balance. This can be useful, when routines and rituals help establish a sense of family history, identity, and tradition, making interactions easier and more comfortable. On the other hand, adaptability is the central criterion of a well-functioning family; when family members are unbending in the face of parental dissension or family distress over an aggressive child, routines can solidify and intensify negative patterns of interaction (Dishion & Bullock, 2002; Katz & Gottman, 1997). In these circumstances, members may make no effort to communicate rationally, defuse anger, protect others, or solve problems and may become locked into a pattern of interaction that promotes or sustains maladaptive behaviour in one or more family members. Resistance to change can prevent parents or other family members from recognizing problems and can cause members to blame all family difficulties on one child, who becomes the scapegoat for everyone else.

Finally, families have *boundaries* that vary in how permeable or vulnerable they are to outside influences. A well-functioning family tends to have permeable boundaries that allow members to maintain satisfying relationships both within and outside the family itself (Kerig, 2008). If families are too rigidly bounded, members may have difficulty disengaging appropriately from the family—for example, in adolescence, when

This family is clearly pleased with their snow sculpture. Such shared activities can reinforce family members' interdependency and increase positive and supportive feelings among them.

starting university, when marrying, or in time of need, making use of resources outside the family. Such families may have few positive community contacts and social supports, and may be more likely than others to perceive their children in a negative light and to be punitive and inconsistent with them (Wahler & Dumas, 1987). On the other hand, families whose boundaries are too permeable can be vulnerable to disruptions by external forces, such as intrusive in-laws or peer groups whose behaviour is at odds with the family's own standards.

LO2 The Marital System

Both partners in a marriage, or other form of committed relationship, make up the marital system, the first and founding subsystem within the family system. Although the marital system still predominates in contemporary society, there are now other forms of committed arrangements between adult partners, such as civil unions and cohabitation by domestic partners. Many of the principles that we will describe probably apply equally to marital and other forms of stable couple arrangements. However, at this time, we know considerably less about these newer relationships than about the more traditional marriage. The nature of the partners' relationship with one another unquestionably has a clear impact on their children (Bouchard & Lee, 2000). Indeed, a relationship that is satisfactory to both adult partners is often regarded as the cornerstone of good family functioning. Directly or indirectly, it facilitates effective parenting, good sibling relationships, and the healthy development of all the family's children.

HOW DOES THE MARITAL RELATIONSHIP AFFECT CHILDREN?

As we have suggested, when partners offer each other emotional and physical support and comfort, the likelihood that they will provide the same kind of support and caring to their children, is greatly increased. Research has shown that when partners are mutually supportive, they are more involved with their children, and their relationships with their children demonstrate affection, sensitivity, and competent child-rearing practices (Cowan & Cowan, 2002, 2008; Katz & Gottman, 1997).

One study (Ehrenberg, Gearing-Smil, Hunter, & Small, 2001), for example, found that the amount of shared parenting engaged in by couples predicted their marital satisfaction, parental competence, and closeness to their children, although the actual division of child-care tasks was unrelated to these dimensions. Moreover, couples who share child care and household chores have more time for playful and pleasurable interactions with their children and increase their chances of witnessing developmental milestones, such as a child's first words or steps. Couples who co-operate in caring for their children also help each other shoulder some of the special burdens that new parents experience, such as 2:00 a.m. feedings, changing dirty diapers, and soothing a crying or sick child.

Conflict between partners, however, can have seriously negative effects on both parents and children (Cummings & Merrilees, 2008; Grych & Fincham, 2001). Even when a family's children are infants or preschool age, conflict between parents has been found to reflect insecure attachments of the children to both parents (Frosch et al., 2000; see also Chapter 6). Studying school-age children, Katz and Gottman (1993, 1996) found that not only the level of conflict but also the way adult partners manage their conflict can have deleterious effects on a couple's children. Within families whose marital partners typically confronted conflicts with hostility, belligerence, and contempt, children tended to display more aggressive and acting-out behaviour than other children. In addition, fathers who had an angry and withdrawn style of dealing with marital disputes had children who were more likely to be depressed than other children.

The effect of marital conflict on children can take one of two pathways: direct and indirect (Cummings & Merrilees, 2008; Grych & Fincham, 2001). Children may be affected by such conflict *indirectly* when marital difficulties cause parents to change their child-rearing practices or interact differentially with their children (Jenkins, Rasbach,

& O'Conner, 2003). In Katz and Gottman's study (1997), parents in conflicted marriages had a poor parenting style that was characterized as cold, unresponsive, angry, and deficient in providing structure and setting limits; the children of these couples tended to display a lot of anger and non-compliance in interacting with their parents. Children may also be affected *directly* by marital conflict when they are actual witnesses to arguments and fights. In a series of studies by Mark Cummings and his colleagues (see Figure 11-1), children witnessed interactions between adult actors behaving like two parents in a home setting. For example, the actors might disagree about which movie to watch or who will wash the dishes. The more frequent and violent the conflict and the more often the arguments were about something a child had done or said, the more likely the children were to show distress, shame, and self-blame (Cummings et al.,

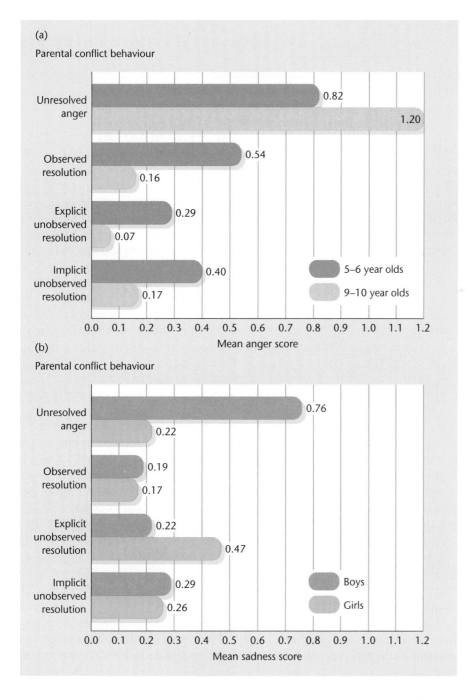

Figure 11-1

How children respond to parental conflict

(a) Parents' failure to resolve an angry conflict was the most likely behaviour to arouse children's anger and caused the most displays of anger in older children. (b) Such a failure was also more likely to trigger sadness in boys, but girls were more likely to be sad when parents resolved a conflict out of their presence and made only a brief reference to it later (explicit, unobserved resolution).

Source: Adapted from Cummings, Simpson, & Wilson, 1993.

2002; Frosch & Mangelsdorf, 2001). Moreover, when the actors failed to settle their dispute, the children expressed more anger and distress than when the actors resolved a conflict. Fighting in front of the kids has never been a good idea, but if partners handle their discussions constructively, showing respect for one another's opinions and expressing mutual warmth and support, they can reduce the harmful effects that their argument may have on their children. Moreover, they can model healthy conflict negotiation for their children. Finally, Papp, Cummings, and Goeke-Morey (2002) observed that, contrary to what one expects, although more marital conflicts occur when children are absent, the couples themselves tend to be more negative and destructive when children are actually present.

Boys are much more susceptible to the negative effects of family disharmony than are girls. Why should this be so? It seems that boys are more likely to be directly exposed to parental bickering and physical abuse than girls are (Hetherington & Stanley-Hagan, 2002). Parents quarrel more often and their quarrels are longer in the presence of their sons. If parents begin to disagree when daughters are present, they are more likely to raise their eyebrows, nod in the direction of the child, and mutter, "We'll talk about this later." Parents are simply more protective of daughters than of sons. Moreover, in response to parents' marital difficulties, boys tend to display more *externalizing*, or aggressive and anti-social, behaviour and girls tend to show more *internalizing*, or shy and withdrawn, behaviour.

IMPACT OF A NEW BABY ON THE MARITAL/PARTNER SYSTEM   Just as the relationship between marital partners affects their responses to their children, the presence and behaviour of a child influences the marital relationship. The most immediate effect—especially after the birth of a couple's first child—is a shift toward a more traditional division of labour between husband and wife, even when the initial role arrangement was egalitarian (Cowan & Cowan, 2000). Despite the changes that have occurred in gender roles in recent decades, an implicit assumption seems to be that the role of the mother with young children is in child care and homemaking, the role of the father is in providing for the family (Parke, 2002a). Sometimes, a father will take time from his job to be with his wife and newborn, but that time hardly ever exceeds two weeks. In families where both partners have worked outside the home, the wife is most likely to give up her job. Thus, not surprisingly, marital satisfaction declines more markedly in women than in men after the birth of a couple's first child (Cowan & Cowan, 2000). Fathers' marital satisfaction also takes a dive but more slowly; it may be only gradually that men become aware of the restrictions a baby imposes on their lives and realize that they are no longer the central focus of their wives' attention. In general, mothers get more of the responsibilities of raising a child, but they also often experience more of the pleasures (Coltrane, 1996).

Children can influence the relationship between their parents in other ways. For example, kids who are temperamentally difficult or handicapped in some way may often contribute to heightened family stress that may translate into marital conflict. Couples who were satisfied with their relationship before the child's birth weather such pressures reasonably well, and their relationships show fewer disruptions than those of couples who were experiencing dissension before a child's arrival. Thus, although the presence of a difficult child may be enough to fragment a fragile marriage (Hogan & Msall, 2002), the birth of a child rarely destroys a good marriage. However, because becoming parents does pose risks to a young family, intervention programs have been designed to strengthen couple relationships and reduce the adverse consequences of the transition to parenthood.

LO3 LO4 The Parent–Child System

Most parents have some beliefs about the qualities they would like to see their children develop and the child-rearing methods that ought to encourage them. There are many paths to the development of positive as well as negative social behaviours, however, and there is no magic child-rearing formula. Parents have to try to adapt their methods to each child's temperament and needs and to the demands of the culture, but it is important to keep in mind that individual children may develop very differently within the same family situation (Grusec & Davidov, 2007). It is also important to remember that, as we saw in Chapter 3 (Box 3-3), even in adverse environments some children seem to be relatively resilient (Cicchetti & Toth, 2006; Luthar et al., 2000).

HOW PARENTS SOCIALIZE CHILDREN Attachment between parent and infant, as we discussed in Chapter 6, forms the foundation for later family relationships. Although socialization begins at birth, it seems to become more conscious and systematic as the child achieves greater mobility and begins to use formal language. Parents cuddle and pet the child and praise her for all sorts of achievements that parents and society regard as desirable, such as learning to use a spoon, naming objects, and repeating new words. On the other hand, whereas up to now parents have accepted and even indulged a number of "cute" behaviours, all of a sudden, the air rings with "No!" "Don't!" and "Stop!" as children climb out of their cribs, totter to the head of the stairs, and discover the grand fun that can be had with the pots and pans so conveniently stored in cabinets at their own level. Practising their new-found motor skills and exploring the world around them become real trials when playpen bars restrain exploration and parents make serious attempts at toilet training.

In teaching their children social rules and roles, parents rely on several of the learning principles we discussed earlier. For example, they use *reinforcement* when they explain acceptable standards of behaviour and then praise or discipline their children according to whether they conform to or violate these rules. Parents also teach their children by *modelling* behaviours they want the children to adopt. An important difference between these two approaches is that whereas parents knowingly use reinforcement techniques, observational learning may occur by chance. As a result, the modelled behaviour may not always be what they want to produce. Suppose a child sees a churchgoing, platitude-spouting, moralizing parent lie about his golf score, cheat on his income tax, bully his children, and pay substandard wages to a household helper from the neighbourhood. Do you think the child will emulate his parent's hypocritical words or his actual behaviour? The "do as I say, not as I do" approach to socialization does not work.

Parents also manage aspects of their children's environment that will influence their social development. They choose the neighbourhoods and home in which the child lives, decorate the child's room in a masculine or feminine style, provide the child with toys and books, and manage the child's television viewing. They also promote the child's social life and activities by arranging social events and enrolling the child in such activities as sports, art, music, and other social- and skill-enhancement programs (Ladd & Pettit, 2002; Parke & Buriel, 2006).

DIMENSIONS OF PARENTAL BEHAVIOUR Parenting patterns and styles tend to reflect two primary dimensions of behaviour. The first revolves around emotionality. Parents may be warm, responsive, and child-centred in their approach to their offspring, or they may be rejecting, unresponsive, and essentially uninvolved with their children and more focused on their own needs and wishes. The second dimension concerns the issue of control. Parents may be very demanding of their children, restricting their behaviour, or they may be permissive and undemanding, pretty much allowing the child to do as she wishes. We discuss some aspects of these two dimensions and then consider four parental patterns of behaviour to which they contribute.

Emotionality Parental *emotionality is* crucial in the socialization process. When a parent is warm and loving, the child is likely to want to maintain the parent's approval and to be distressed at any prospect of losing the parent's love (Baumrind, 1991a; Grusec

Warm and loving parents tend to have children who are secure, feel good about themselves, and return their parents' affection.

& Davidov, 2007). If a parent is cold and rejecting, however, the threat of withdrawal of love is unlikely to be an effective mechanism of socialization. From such a parent, what has the child to lose? Physical punishment, too, is more effective in the hands of warm parents, again probably because the child wants to conform to his parents' standards. But also, the child knows from experience that his parents are involved and concerned with his well-being and that they will give him information about socially acceptable alternative behaviours. The child with rejecting parents has no such expectation. It is easier to learn the rules of the game if someone not only tells you what they are but also explains why you should play that way (Holden, 1997; Holden & Hawk, 2003).

Warmth and nurturance are likely to be associated with parental responsiveness to the child's needs. Loving parents make children feel good about themselves, dispelling anxiety and building their sense of security and their self-esteem. Children with such parents are more likely to learn and to accept and internalize parental standards than are children of rejecting parents (Kochanska & Murray, 2000). The high levels of tension and anxiety that are likely to be associated with hostile parents and frequent physical punishment may make it very difficult for the child to learn the social rules that the parent is attempting to teach.

Control   The goal of socialization is to enable the child to regulate her own behaviour and to choose socially responsible alternatives. Although the process of socialization does involve mutual influence between parents and children, the parent usually has more control than the child in their interactions. Two types of control have been identified: behavioural and psychological control (Barber, 2002). Behavioural control involves setting reasonable rules and parental use of suggestions, reasoning, and possible alternative courses of action as well as monitoring of children's activities. When moderate levels of behavioural control are used (consistency of discipline, use of the minimum amount of pressure necessary to change the child's behaviour, and encouragement for the child to view her compliance as self-initiated), children are more likely to co-operate and to adopt or internalize their parents' standards (Barber & Harmon, 2002; Holden & Hawk, 2003) than when parents are either overly controlling or lax and permissive. Psychological control involves the use of emotion-directed tactics such as guilt or shame induction, withdrawal of love or affection, or ignoring or discounting a child's feelings. This type of control often leads to lower self-esteem, higher anxiety, and possibly, depression (Barber & Harmon, 2002). And, in the long run, the child might actually adopt these types of power-assertive techniques when she becomes a parent. Covell, Grusec, and King (1995), for example, found that mothers who were categorized as power assertive in disciplining their 3- to 5-year-old children had mothers who also used power assertion when their children were 3 to 5 years old. Box 11.1 on pages 432 and 433 describes, in more detail, some ideas related to parental discipline of children, including one of the ultimate power-assertion techniques: corporal punishment.

Age plays an important role in children's responses to discipline. As children grow older, they resist being controlled and manipulated by others, and self-reinforcement for appropriate social behaviour becomes increasingly important. Even older preschool children try to negotiate with their parents:

Child: "I'll do it after I finish my painting. All right?"

Parent: "How about if you and I do it together?"

As the child gains in social and cognitive competence and becomes more autonomous, parents rely increasingly on reasoning, and the child engages more and more in active bargaining (Kuczynski & Parkin, 2007). This gradual shift from control by parents and others to self-control becomes critical for the child as he moves out of the home. Parents' opportunities to monitor and control the child's activities directly decline markedly in the elementary school years and even more in adolescence (Mounts, 2000).

In a somewhat different perspective on disciplining children, Grusec and Goodnow (1994a, 1994b; Grusec, Goodnow, & Kuczynski, 2000) suggest that rather than view the effects of discipline in terms of the particular method employed, parents' effective socialization of the child is due to the child's interpretation of the methods of the parent, the parent–child relationship, and the goals of the parent. In this case, the child's socialization is based on his accurate perception of the parent's message (which is influenced by such factors as consistent signals from the parent and the message being clear and understandable) and his acceptance of this message (which is influenced by such factors as whether the parent's behaviour is seen by the child as appropriate given his misdeed and how much the child feels that value is self-generated). Moreover, these authors note that parents often employ techniques other than power assertion and reasoning to discipline children (e.g., humour, irony, and drama) and that an adequate theory of controlling children must address the function served by these behaviours as well.

PARENTING STYLE   Family systems theorists would argue that what is important in a child's socialization is not any particular parental dimension of behaviour but the overall combination of these behaviours. The four parenting styles shown in Figure 11-3 on page 434—authoritative, authoritarian, permissive, and uninvolved—are composed of different combinations of the warm-responsive/rejecting-unresponsive and the restrictive-demanding/permissive-undemanding dimensions that we have discussed. They also reflect research that has explored the relations between each parenting style and children's emotional, social, and cognitive development. In a now-classic study, Baumrind (1967) linked the first three of these styles with specific and quite distinctive patterns of children's interactions with their parents. Maccoby and Martin (1983) extended the Baumrind typology, adding the fourth, "uninvolved" parenting style.

Baumrind (1967, 1991a) identified three parenting styles based on parental interviews and observations of parents interacting with their children both at home and in the laboratory. They are shown in Figure 11-4 at the bottom of page 434; in turn, she observed the children in preschool and again in adolescence to discover the links between parental styles and child behavioural patterns. **Authoritative parenting** was correlated with the behaviour of the energetic-friendly children who exhibited positive emotional, social, and cognitive development. Authoritative parents were not intrusive and permitted their children to have considerable freedom. At the same time, they imposed restrictions in areas in which they had greater knowledge or insight, and they were firm in resisting children's efforts to get them to acquiesce to their demands. In general, warmth and moderate restrictiveness, with the parents expecting appropriately mature behaviour from their children and setting reasonable limits, but also being responsive and attentive to their needs, were associated with the children's development of self-esteem, adaptability, competence, internalized control, popularity with peers, and low levels of anti-social behaviour. Authoritative parenting continued to be associated with positive outcomes for adolescents, as it was with younger children; responsiveness and firm parent–child relationships were especially important in the development of competence in sons.

In contrast, **authoritarian parenting** was linked with the behaviour of conflicted-irritable children, who tended to be fearful, moody, and vulnerable to stressors. These parents were rigid, power assertive, harsh, and unresponsive to their children's needs. In these families, children had little control over their environment and received little gratification. Baumrind proposed that these children often felt trapped and angry but also fearful of asserting themselves in a hostile environment. Authoritarian child-rearing had more negative long-term outcomes for boys than for girls. Sons of authoritarian parents were low in cognitive and social competence. Their academic and intellectual performance was poor. They were unfriendly and lacked self-confidence, initiative, and leadership in their relations with peers.

Finally, **permissive parenting**, although it appeared to have produced reasonably affectionate relationships between parents and children, was correlated with children's impulsive-aggressive behaviour. Excessively lax and inconsistent discipline and encouragement of children's free expression of their impulses were associated with the development of uncontrolled, non-compliant, and aggressive behaviour in children.

authoritative parenting

Parenting that is warm, responsive, and involved yet unintrusive, and in which parents set reasonable limits and expect appropriately mature behaviour from their children.

authoritarian parenting

Parenting that is harsh, unresponsive, and rigid, and in which parents tend to use power-assertive methods of control.

permissive parenting

Parenting that is lax and in which parents exercise inconsistent discipline and encourage children to express their impulses freely.

Box 11.1
Child Psychology in Action

PHYSICAL DISCIPLINE VERSUS CHILD ABUSE

What is the best way to discipline your child? Ask any parent and she will give you any number of possible strategies, ranging from reasoning and talking with the child to withholding or taking away privileges to the use of actual physical punishment. Although the majority of such parental disciplinary techniques are not especially controversial, this last one—the use of physical punishment—has become a hot topic of debate in recent years (Benjet & Kazdin, 2003; Donnelly & Straus, 2005; Gershoff, 2002; Holden, 2002; Kazdin & Benjet, 2003). Although most would agree that parents have a right, and indeed a responsibility, to properly discipline their children, whether or not it is appropriate for parents to use physical means to accomplish this goal is a much more problematic question. One of the main considerations in the use of physical punishment is that it is often difficult to know where to draw the line between appropriate punishment and what might be considered by some to be child abuse. Drawing this distinction, though, is important not only in terms of how parents are to control their children but also in its implications for the health and welfare of children in the short term and possibly the long term.

Probably the most common forms of physical discipline for children involve slapping or spanking (what is called "corporal punishment"). Because some researchers have demonstrated that physical discipline produces compliance (e.g., Roberts, 1988; Roberts & Powers, 1990), some have suggested that it might actually be beneficial for children (Larzelere, 1996, 2000), at least in the short term. In the long term, however, corporal punishment seems to have some negative effects. Some studies, for example, have found that it is related to higher levels of aggression and lower levels of mental health (Gershoff, 2002), as well as depression and suicide (DuRant, Cadenhead, Pendergrast, Slavens, & Linder, 1994; Turner & Finkelhor, 1996). Others (Baumrind, Larzelere, & Cowan, 2002), however, argue that these undesirable outcomes are more a result of inept parenting than of corporal punishment

itself, and hence, a blanket injunction against spanking is simply not warranted.

Given that corporal punishment has the potential to do serious harm to children, one factor that has arisen in the debate over its use and appropriateness involves the legal issue of parents' rights to discipline their children in a manner in which they see fit versus children's rights not to be harmed (Durrant, 2000). What is the legal status of physical discipline? According to the Criminal Code of Canada, parents can use physical force to discipline their children, provided that this force is reasonable in the particular circumstances (Durrant, 2000); a principle upheld in the Supreme Court of Canada decision rendered on January 30, 2004. Interestingly, the Supreme Court set some guidelines for spanking, including a prohibition on spanking teenagers and children under 2 years old, a banning of instruments to spank with, and so on.

Worldwide, however, there is a strong movement to end corporal punishment (Straus, 2008). UNICEF has declared it a violation of its charter of children's rights, and the European Union has called on its member nations to prohibit corporal punishment (Straus, 2008). In one of the strongest stances, Sweden, in 1979, became the first country to legally prohibit all forms of corporal punishment by parents and other caregivers. This move toward abolishing corporal punishment grew out of a concern for children's welfare and culminated in the addition to the parents' code (of Sweden) of a paragraph that explicitly bans the use of "physical punishment or other injurious or humiliating treatment of children" (Durrant, 2000).

What has the impact of this legal prohibition of corporal punishment been on societal attitudes and child development? Work by Joan Durrant of the University of Manitoba and her colleagues (Durrant, 1999, 2000; Durrant & Olsen, 1997) has observed that according to Swedish national opinion polls, support for corporal punishment has dropped markedly since the 1960s (see Figure 11-2), starting at over 50 percent support in 1965

---

uninvolved parenting

Parenting that is indifferent and neglectful and in which parents focus on their own needs rather than on their children's needs.

Figure 11-4 summarizes Baumrind's findings on some major dimensions of parents' behaviours; parents of the energetic-friendly children scored highest on all these dimensions during both home and laboratory observations.

The fourth type, **uninvolved parenting**, identified by Maccoby and Martin (1983), characterized parents who were indifferent to or actively neglected their children and were "motivated to do whatever is necessary to minimize the costs in time and effort

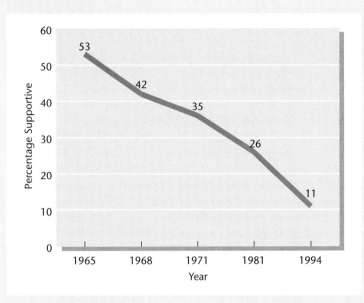

Figure 11-2 Support for corporal punishment

The percentage of Swedish citizenry who voiced support for corporal punishment from 1965 to 1994. Spanking was legally abolished in Sweden in 1979.
Source: Durrant, J. E. (1999). Evaluating the success of Sweden's corporal punishment ban. *Child Abuse and Neglect*, 23, 443–448.

and declining to 11 percent in 1994. More importantly, the rate of criminally caused child deaths, an unequivocal indicator of violence against children, has not increased since the mid-1970s; since 1975, one in four children die as a result of abuse. Ultimately, violence against children has decreased dramatically in Sweden, with corporal punishment infrequent and child abuse fatalities extremely rare (Durrant & Janson, 2005). As for the effect on child development, Durrant (2000) also found that the rate of adolescent involvement in criminal activities, such as theft, selling drugs, and using drugs or alcohol, as well as in violent crimes, such as assault or rape, has generally decreased (the only exception being the rate of assault, which actually increased between these two cohorts). According to Durrant, Swedish youth are functioning better today than they were before the ban was passed, suggesting that the prohibition on corporal punishment has not lead to Swedish youth becoming undersocialized due to a lack of discipline.

What is the current status of corporal punishment? In some ways, it appears as though the public's attitude is turning against such disciplinary measures, as evidenced by the Swedish ban and recent attempts in Canada to prohibit physical punishment. Yet, the prevalence of corporal punishment is clearly not on the decline. In the United States, between 70 and 90 percent of parents have administered physical punishment at some time (Durrant, 2000; Saadeh, Rizzo, & Roberts, 2002); in Canada, estimates of corporal punishment are about 75 percent (Ateah & Parkin, 2002). In some areas, such as the Caribbean (and specifically Jamaica), harsh disciplinary practices are widespread (Smith & Mosby, 2003). One possibility for the continuing prevalence of corporal punishment is that there may, in fact, be a growing dissociation between attitudes and the social acceptability of punishment and actual parenting practices. Unfortunately, the implications and effects of such a possible dissociation are simply not known.

of interaction with the child" (p. 48). Uninvolved parents are parent-centred, rather than child-centred; they focus on their own needs. Particularly when a child is older, these parents fail to monitor her activity or to know where she is, what she is doing, or who her companions are. This parenting pattern is sometimes found in mothers who are depressed (Goodman & Gotlib, 2002) and in people under the stress of such things as marital discord or divorce (Hetherington & Kelly, 2002). Their own anxiety and

Figure 11-3

Parenting styles

Although recent multicultural and cross-cultural studies suggest that these four parenting styles are not universally applicable, the essential characteristics and qualities on which they were based remain valid measures of behaviour in many settings. New research may further refine these categories and add qualifying information based on cultural variations.

Source: From *Handbook of child psychology*, 4th ed. (E. M. Hetherington, Ed.) by Maccoby, E. E. and Martin, J. A., Socialization in the context of the family: Parent-child interaction. Copyright © 1983 John Wiley & Sons Limited. Reprinted with permission.

	Emotionality	
	Warm, responsive	Rejecting, unresponsive
Control — Restrictive, demanding	Authoritative	Authoritarian
Control — Permissive, undemanding	Permissive	Uninvolved

emotional neediness may drive some parents to pursue self-gratification at the expense and neglect of their children's welfare (Patterson & Capaldi, 1991). Table 11-1 summarizes the characteristics of parents who display the four parenting styles as well as the kinds of behaviours that the children of each group of parents manifest.

Parental involvement plays a crucial role in the development of both social and cognitive competence in children. In infants, lack of parental involvement is associated with disruptions in attachment (Thompson, 2006), and among preschool children, poor monitoring combined with coercive discipline predicted conduct problems in African-American boys and girls at age 6 (Kilgore et al., 2000). In older children, it is associated with impulsivity, aggression, non-compliance, moodiness, and low self-esteem (Baumrind, 1991a). In a kind of "double whammy," children of uninvolved parents tend not only to be socially incompetent, irresponsible, immature, and alienated from their families but also to show disruptions in cognitive development, achievement,

Figure 11-4

Dimensions of parental behaviour and children's characteristics

Parents of energetic-friendly children get higher scores on all four dimensions measured—control, demands for mature behaviour, communication, and nurturance—based on observations of children and parents at home.

Source: Adapted from Baumrind, 1967.

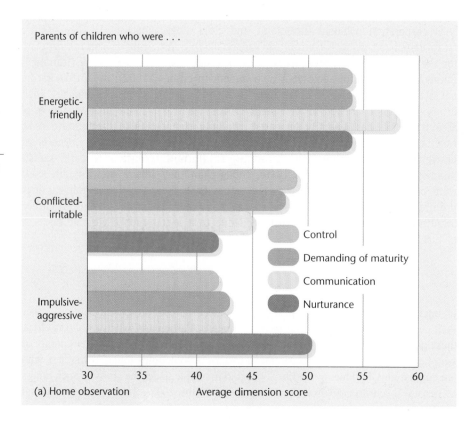

(a) Home observation

Table 11-1 Relation between parenting styles and children's characteristics

Parenting Style	Children's Characteristics
Authoritative Parent Warm, involved, responsive; shows pleasure in and support of child's constructive behaviour; considers child's wishes and solicits her opinions; offers alternatives Sets standards, communicates them clearly, and enforces them firmly; does not yield to child's coercion; shows displeasure at bad behaviour; confronts disobedient child Expects mature, independent, age-appropriate behaviour Plans cultural events and joint activities	**Energetic-Friendly Child** Cheerful Self-controlled and self-reliant Purposive, achievement oriented Shows interest and curiosity in novel situations Has high energy level Maintains friendly relations with peers Co-operates with adults; is tractable Copes well with stress
Authoritarian Parent Shows little warmth or positive involvement Does not solicit or consider child's desires or opinions Enforces rules rigidly but does not explain them clearly Shows anger and displeasure; confronts child regarding bad behaviour and uses harsh, punitive discipline Views child as dominated by anti-social impulses	**Conflicted-Irritable Child** Moody, unhappy, aimless Fearful, apprehensive; easily annoyed Passively hostile and deceitful Alternates between aggressive behaviour and sulky withdrawal Vulnerable to stress
Permissive Parent Moderately warm Glorifies free expression of impulses and desires Does not communicate rules clearly or enforce them; ignores or accepts bad behaviour; disciplines inconsistently; yields to coercion and whining; hides impatience, anger Makes few demands for mature, independent behaviour	**Impulsive-Aggressive Child** Aggressive, domineering, resistant, non-compliant Quick to anger but fast to recover cheerful mood Lacks self-control and displays little self-reliance Impulsive Shows little achievement orientation Aimless; has few goal-directed activities
Uninvolved Parent Self-centred, generally unresponsive, neglectful Pursues self-gratification at expense of child's welfare Tries to minimize costs (time, effort) of interaction with child Fails to monitor child's activity, whereabouts, companions May be depressive, anxious, emotionally needy Vulnerable to marital discord, divorce	**Neglected Child** Moody, insecurely attached, impulsive, aggressive, non-compliant, irresponsible Low self-esteem, immature, alienated from family Lacks skills for social and academic pursuits Truancy, association with troubled peers, delinquency and arrests, precocious sexuality

Sources: Baumrind, 1967, 1991a; Hetherington & Clingempeel, 1992; Karavasilis, Doyle, & Markiewicz, 1998; Maccoby & Martin, 1983.

and school performance (Baumrind, 1991a; Hetherington & Stanley-Hagan, 2002). Adolescents and young adults whose parents are uninvolved are likely to be truant, to spend time on the streets with troublesome peers, to be precociously sexually active, to have drinking problems, and to be delinquent (Dishion & Bullock, 2002).

CHALLENGES TO THE PARENTING STYLES APPROACH Other investigators have challenged the parenting style approach, asserting that more research is needed on several fronts. First, some have suggested that we need to identify more clearly the components of each style that contribute to its relative effectiveness or ineffectiveness in respect to the child's development. Second, some authorities propose giving greater attention to how much the child's temperament and behaviour influence the parent's style (Bates & Pettit, 2007; Kochanska, 1997). Finally, recent work has raised serious questions about the generalizability of these styles across

Box 11.2

Perspectives on Diversity

PARENTAL CHILD-REARING STYLES CARRY DIFFERENT MEANINGS IN DIFFERENT CULTURES

In North America, there may be more than one explanation for why children of Asian descent outstrip children of European backgrounds and other cultural groups in academic performance. As we discuss elsewhere, Steinberg and his colleagues (1991, 1992) have proposed that the character of the peer groups with whom Asian and other students identify and socialize makes the difference, with Asian students, on average, being more supportive of academic achievement. According to Ruth Chao (1994, 2001), however, other, much earlier factors in children's lives may also be at work. It seems likely that the supportive Asian peer group is reflecting a kind of child-rearing that has no real North American equivalent.

In response to the finding that Chinese parents score high on North American psychologists' "authoritarian" scales, Chao points out that *authoritarian* does not mean in Chinese what it means in English. Thus, when Chinese parents get such high scores, they may be expressing behavioural patterns that are quite different from the North American patterns that illustrate the authoritarian concept. Moreover, this culturally based difference may hold also for parents from other Asian cultures who espouse such Confucian principles as family unity and respect for elders and may help explain why Asian North American stu-

dents typically do better in school that other North American students.

Whereas the North American concept of authoritarianism is associated with many negative beliefs, attitudes, and behaviours (see Table 11-1 on page 435), the Chinese style of parenting characterized by the concepts of *chiao shun* ("training") and *guan* ("to govern") requires a high degree of involvement with the child, physical closeness to the child, and devotion—mainly by the mother—of a great amount of time and effort. These concepts subsume teaching or educating children, focusing particularly on children's performance in school (for it is the Chinese belief that education is the key to success), and also connote "loving" and "caring for" the children. In this sense, *chiao shun* and *guan* are antithetical to the concept of authoritarianism as it is defined in Western society. As Ruth Chao (1994) suggests, the seemingly restrictive behaviours that cause Asian parents to get high scores on Western scales may be equated with parental concern, caring, and involvement, and Asian parental control may reflect a more organizational effort designed to keep the family running smoothly and to foster family harmony.

If, in fact, the concepts of authoritarian and authoritative parenting actually differ between cultures, then

socio-economic or ethnic/cultural groups (Chao, 1994, 2001; Rudy & Grusec, 2001). There are two primary issues: Do all groups use the parenting styles we have identified to the same degree, and are the advantages and disadvantages of each style for the child's development similar across groups? The answer to both these questions seems to be no.

For one thing, neighbourhoods make a difference in children's development, not only by confronting them with physical and social challenges that may or may not be beneficial but by determining the kinds of socialization strategies parents adopt (Ceballo & McLoyd, 2002; Leventhal & Brooks-Gunn, 2000). For example, although an authoritative child-rearing style may promote social and academic competence in children living in low-risk environments, it may not work in other situations. Several studies have found that poor minority parents who used more authoritarian child-rearing practices, especially those who lived in dangerous neighbourhoods, had better-adjusted children than those who relied on authoritative strategies (Furstenberg et al., 1999; Parke et al., 2008b). Parental social integration into the neighbourhood may also be an important predictor of more adequate parenting practices (Furstenberg et al., 1999; Steinberg et al., 1995). The more socially integrated the parents, the more vigilant they may be about their children's behaviour, although this probably holds true only when families reside in neighbourhoods where "good parenting" is the norm.

There are also reports of differences cross-culturally (Chao, 1994, 2001; Chao & Kim, 2000; Chao & Tseng, 2002; Rudy & Grusec, 2001, 2006). Rudy and Grusec

it is an open question as to the relation between parenting style and child adjustment in Chinese society. According to Xinyin Chen of the University of Western Ontario, in Chinese culture, just as in North American society, what is really important are the meanings of these different approaches, with authoritative parenting also leading to well-adjusted children and authoritarian parenting related to more significant problems in children's socialization (Chen, Dong, & Zhou, 1997). Moreover, according to Chen, the focus on broad categories of parenting style ignores both the specific dimensional components of a particular style that are important for parent–child relations and the cultural context of such behaviours. For instance, is there a logical connection between a collectivist orientation, such as found in Chinese culture, and authoritarian parenting (Liu et al., 2005).

Chen and his colleagues have examined these ideas in a number of ways (Chen et al., 1997, 2000). In one study, Chen's group (1997) looked at a set of 8-year-old grade 2 children and their parents living in Beijing, China. These researchers assessed both the social adjustment and academic achievement of these children as a function of parental child-rearing style. They observed that authoritarian parenting for both mothers and fathers was correlated positively to children's

aggression and was negatively related to such social measures as peer preferences and sociability, and such academic-performance measures as distinguished studentship and school achievement. In contrast, an authoritative parenting style showed virtually the reverse pattern—it was negatively correlated with aggression, and positively correlated with both social adjustment and academic achievement. And in a subsequent study (Chen et al., 2000), the researchers found that authoritative attitudes by Chinese mothers were associated positively with such child-management strategies as *reasoning* and negatively with such techniques as *reprimands*. In contrast, the reverse pattern was observed for maternal authoritarian parenting.

What is striking about these studies, of course, is that these patterns of results are exactly what one might predict based on Baumrind's (1967, 1971) original analyses of the impact of different parenting styles on child development and socialization. Accordingly, even though the cultural emphasis on parental authority and obedience in Chinese society makes Chinese parents look more authoritarian and less authoritative than North American parents, there is nevertheless individual variation in parenting practices among Chinese parents. And it is this variability that is significant for child development.

(2006), for instance, found no links between authoritarian parenting and negative feeling about the child or lack or warmth in Middle Eastern families in Canada, whereas the ties between this style and negativity and low warmth were evident for Anglo-Canadian parents. Moreover, authoritarian parenting was associated with higher child self-esteem for Middle Eastern but not Anglo children. Similarly, in Chinese families, child-rearing appears to be more authoritarian, but some have argued that there are major differences between the North American and Chinese conceptions of *authoritarian* and that the application of such a style to Chinese parents may be ethnocentric and misleading (see the accompanying Box 11.2). According to Ruth Chao (1994, 2001), the child-rearing styles described here reflect a North American perspective that emphasizes an individualistic view of childhood socialization and development; we revisit Chao's views in the section on cultural patterns in child-rearing. In summary, it is important to consider contextual and cultural issues in developing new concepts of parenting styles.

The Co-Parenting System 5

Although parents often act separately in dealing with a child, mothers and fathers sometimes *co-parent* as a team. **Co-parenting**, in which spouses coordinate their child-rearing practices with one another, ideally working as a team, can take many forms. In a family where the mother and father's co-parenting patterns reflect warmth,

co-parenting

Parenting in which spouses work together as a team, coordinating their child-rearing practices with each other; co-parenting can be co-operative, hostile, or characterized by different levels of investment in the parenting task.

437

co-operation, cohesion, and child-centeredness, there may be a high degree of family harmony (McHale, 2008; McHale et al., 2002). On the other hand, parents who are hostile may actively compete against one another, and, in some cases, spouses may invest different amounts of time and energy in the parenting task, leading to an imbalance between the amounts of involvement each parent has with the child. These different co-parenting patterns have been observed across a range of studies with infants, preschoolers, and school-age children and in both European North American and African North American families (Brody, Flor, & Neubaum, 1998; Fivaz-Depeursinge & Corboz-Warnery, 1999).

Gatekeeping is one form of co-parenting in which one parent limits or controls the other parent's level of participation. For example, if a mother assumes that women are biologically a better fit for parenting than men, she may set up subtle barriers that limit the father's involvement in the care of an infant (Beitel & Parke, 1998). And, in fact, maternal encouragement has been found to influence fathers' involvement with their infant children (Schoppe-Sullivan et al., 2008). Moreover, there are clear links between early co-parenting dynamics and later indices of a child's social adaptation. McHale and Rasmussen (1998) found that hostile-competitive co-parenting during infancy was related to aggression in children. When there were large discrepancies between the input of each parent, parents rated children as displaying anxiety. Other researchers have found links between problematic family alliances in the first year and insecure mother–child attachments and, in the preschool years, behaviour problems such as acting out or withdrawal (McHale, 2008). As Figure 11-5 illustrates, the impact of the co-parenting subsystem on children is independent of the effects of either the parent–child relationship or the marital relationship. This suggests that co-parenting makes a unique contribution to children's development.

The Sibling System

In Canada, the majority of families with children have more than one of them (Statistics Canada, 2007b). The number of children, their gender, the space of years between childbirths, and the relations among a family's children greatly affect the functioning of the entire family unit. These factors affect not only parent–child interactions but also the relations among *siblings*, or sisters and brothers. In fact, most children probably spend more time in direct interaction with their siblings than with their parents or other significant

Figure 11-5

Family systems and children's socialization

This model proposes that the family unit itself is a subsystem of the overall family system with as important an influence on children's socialization as the influence wielded by parent–child, marital, co-parenting, and sibling subsystems.

Source: From *Handbook of personal relationships*, 2nd ed. (S. Duck, Ed.) by Parke, R. D., and O'Neil, R., p. 56. Copyright © 1997 John Wiley & Sons Limited.

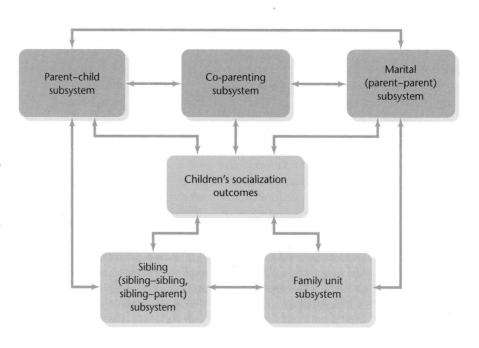

people in their lives (Dunn, 2007; Larson & Verma, 1999). Interactions between siblings provide plenty of opportunities for learning about positive and negative behaviours, and the emotional intensity of these exchanges may be greater than that of exchanges with other family members and friends (Bigelow et al., 1996; Katz et al., 1992).

HOW ARE SIBLINGS AFFECTED BY BIRTH ORDER?   A child's position in the family—that is, whether she is the first-born or a later-born child—affects her, her siblings, her parents, and the interactions among all family members. Each child's experience is different, but the experience of the first-born child is unique. She is the only child who reigns supreme in the love and attention of her parents until she is displaced by the birth of a new baby with whom she now must share her parents' affection. The only child, of course, enjoys his parents' exclusive attention all his life. First-born children are generally more adult-oriented, helpful, and self-controlled than their siblings, and also tend to be more studious, conscientious, and serious, to excel in academic and professional endeavours (Herrera et al., 2003; Zajonc, 2001; Zajonc & Mullally, 1997), and to hold more positions of political leadership (Andeweg & Van Den Berry, 2003) (see Figure 11-6). Indeed, first-borns are overrepresented in Who's Who and among Rhodes scholars and eminent North Americans in the fields of letters and science.

Interestingly, however, research has found that it is second-born sons who support innovative theories in major scientific controversies related to such issues as evolution, whereas first-born sons support the status quo (Sulloway, 1995). In one study, Salmon and Daly (1998) found that middle-born university students were significantly different from both first- and last-borns in a number of ways. For example, first- and last-borns were much more likely than middle-borns to use kinship to describe themselves, to turn to their parents in times of need, and to nominate their mother as the person to whom they felt closest. In keeping with this result, Marleau and colleagues (2006) recently observed that second-born children had more positive interactions with their mothers than first-born children, and showed fewer internalized behaviour problems. In fact, others have noted a downside to being born first, with such children tending to be more fearful and anxious than their siblings, to experience more guilt, and to have more

Figure 11-6

Birth order and academic and occupational achievement

This research showed a clear positive relation between a person's rank in the family and her degree of achievement in academic endeavours and in working or professional life.

Source: Adapted from Herrera et al., 2003.

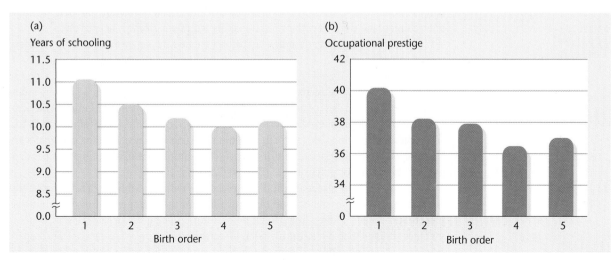

difficulty coping with stressful situations. It may be that the greater expectations and demands parents typically place on their first-borns are responsible for some of these less-desirable characteristics.

Although the only child has sometimes been called a "spoiled brat," research findings suggest that in many ways, the only child has advantages over other children—especially children in families with three or more siblings—in becoming a well-adjusted adult. An only child is exposed to the same high level of parental demands as other first-borns, but does not have to adapt to displacement and competition with siblings. Like first-borns, the only child tends to be a high achiever, sustained by her close relationship with her parents, but she tends to be less anxious and to show more personal control, maturity, and leadership (Falbo & Polit, 1986). In social relations both outside and inside the home, solo children seem to make more positive adjustments than children who are involved in sibling rivalry.

BIRTH ORDER, PARENT–CHILD, AND SIB–SIB INTERACTIONS

As one might expect, based on family systems theory, introducing a new sibling into the family changes the dynamics of relationships among family members. The parents, to a great extent, determine whether the first-born child will find seriously distressing the changes wrought by the arrival of a sibling (Dunn, 2007; Teti, 2002). If a mother continues to be responsive to the needs of the older child and helps him to understand the feelings of the younger child, intense sibling rivalry is unlikely to occur (Howe & Ross, 1990). And if a father becomes increasingly involved with his first-born child, this can also counter the child's feelings of displacement and jealousy. In fact, one positive effect of the birth of a second child may be that a father participates more in child care (Kramer & Ramsburg, 2002; Parke, 2002a). Friends, too, can serve as buffers in this potentially stressful transition. Kramer and Gottman (1992) found that preschoolers who had good friendships showed less upset than children who did not get along well with friends. Moreover, these preschoolers were more accepting and behaved more positively toward their new sibling.

Do siblings themselves notice that parents treat them differently? Yes, they do. In addition, as we saw in Chapter 2, differential reactions by siblings to parental treatment form the non-shared environmental experiences that help us understand how siblings grow up to be quite different from each other. And such differential parental treatment can, for a disfavoured sibling, have adverse effects such as heightened sibling rivalry and increased stress (Dunn, 2007). At the same time, children's own interpretation of differential treatment by parents may defuse such effects. As Kowal and Kramer (1997) found in their study of 11- to 13-year-old siblings, only 25 percent of adolescents viewed parental treatment as unfair or capricious. The majority accepted it and understood that age, needs, and personal attributes of their siblings accounted for their parents' behaviour. Only when siblings did not understand or tolerate parental differential treatment did they view their relationships with their siblings negatively.

Older siblings in large families are often assigned the supervisory and disciplinary roles that parents play in smaller families. According to Edwards and Whiting (1993), girls are more likely than boys to fulfill such roles; a first-born 12-year-old girl in a large family may warm bottles, burp babies, change diapers, and soothe a squalling infant with the alacrity and skill of a young mother. In African-American and Latino-American families, older siblings, especially females, often serve as caregivers (Harwood et al., 2002; Zukow-Goldring, 2002). In other cultures, such as Polynesia, sibling caregivers are common (Wiesner, 1993), and in still others—for example, Mexico—siblings rather than parents, are the major play partners (Zukow-Goldring, 2002).

Birth order also affects a child's interactions with his siblings. The eldest child is often expected to assume some responsibility for the younger sibling who has displaced him. Older siblings may function as tutors, managers, or supervisors of their younger siblings' behaviour during social interactions and may also act as gatekeepers who extend or limit siblings' opportunities to interact with other children outside the family (Edwards & Whiting, 1993; Parke & Buriel, 2006). Parents are likely to restrain or punish the eldest child for showing signs of jealousy or hostility toward a younger sibling and to protect and defend the younger child. On the other hand, the eldest child is dominant and more competent and can either bully or help and teach younger offspring. So it is not surprising that older children tend to show both more antagonistic behaviour, such as hitting, kicking, and biting, and more nurturant, prosocial behaviour toward their younger siblings (Dunn, 2007; Teti, 2002).

Eldest children focus on parents as their main sources of social learning, whereas younger children use both parents and older siblings as models and teachers (Dunn, 2007). Younger siblings, even infants as young as a year old, tend to watch, follow, and imitate their older siblings (Pepler et al., 1982). Nor does their influence stop when children enter school, as 70 percent of children report getting help with homework from siblings, especially from older sisters (Zukow-Goldring, 2002). Older siblings can sometimes serve as deviant or negative influences, encouraging early sexual activity, drug use, or delinquency in their brothers or sisters (East, 1996; Garcia et al., 2000) (see also Chapter 14, page 536). Sibling relationships change with age. In adolescence, early overt sibling rivalry and ambivalence may diminish and intimacy may arise in which a sibling serves as the most trusted confidant and source of emotional support. In concerns about appearance, peer relations, social problems, and sexuality, siblings can often communicate more openly with each other than with peers or parents (Dunn, 2007). Female siblings often become closer over the lifespan.

When older children are secure in their parents' affection, they often make good teachers and guides for their younger siblings.

The Family Unit as an Agent of Children's Socialization: Family Stories and Rituals

Although we need to focus on marital, parent–child, and sibling influences on children's socialization, we must not fail to recognize the important role the family unit itself plays as an agent of socialization (Parke, 1988). As systems theory emphasizes, the properties, functions, and effects of the family unit cannot necessarily be inferred by analyzing only family subsystems (Minuchin, 2001). Families as units change across development and develop distinct *styles* of responding to events, and *boundaries*, all of which provide differing socialization contexts for the developing child (Kerig, 2008; McHale, 2008). Families also develop stories and rituals—activities in which all family members share—and these help transmit family values and roles, reinforcing the uniqueness of the family as a unit.

Through *family stories*, family members may transmit family-of-origin experiences across generations by telling stories and sharing memories, in this way shaping contemporary interaction between family members. Parents can teach their children about the importance of their grandparents and other members of the extended family through stories. Take the story this mother told to her 4-year-old child:

> *When I was a little girl I lived with my grandfather and grandmother. Grandpa had a big, comfy chair, and I would crawl up on his lap, and he would tell me stories. And one of my favorite things was to comb Grandpa's hair. One day I decided to comb his hair, but he didn't know that I had some little ponytail holders and some pins, and I put little curls all on the top of his head, and he fell asleep. And when he woke up he had the prettiest curls you ever saw all over his head, and he didn't even mind. Wasn't that nice?* (Fiese & Bickham, 2004, p. 268)

The child learns through this story about the acceptance and playfulness of grandparents.

Fiese (1990) found that mothers who told stories of their own childhood that emphasized affiliative, nurturant, and playful themes engaged in more turn-taking and reciprocal interactions with their children. On the other hand, mothers who told stories of either achievement or rejection were less engaged and, when they interacted with their children, more intrusive and directive.

This photograph illustrates an important weekly ritual in Jewish families, which involves the Sabbath lighting of the Friday night candles. Virtually all families have such traditions and rituals.

People have known for decades of the importance of *family rituals* in family life, but it is only recently that researchers have recognized the socialization function of these rituals (Fiese, 2006). Family rituals range from formal and intricate religious observances such as a first communion or a bat or bar mitzvah, to less articulated daily-interaction patterns, such as the kind of greeting family members give to someone returning home. Researchers have found, for example, that children who came from families who were able to preserve family rituals such as dinner and holiday routines were less likely to become alcoholics as adults and that adolescents from families who attach more meaning to their rituals tend to have higher self-esteem than other children (Fiese, 2006; Pratt & Fiese, 2004). Rituals offer a powerful clue to the nature and quality of family functioning and have clear protective advantages for the child.

In sum, stories and rituals show us that families function not just as collections of individuals but also as true systems. Moreover, families differ from one another in special ways, much the way individuals differ from each other. In a sense, just as each individual develops a unique personality, so do families develop ways of interacting that give them a unique signature or identity.

For Thought and Discussion

1. The issues of physical discipline and child abuse have received a great deal of public attention because of some recent legal actions, such as in the case of some tourists in Alberta who had a child's parents apprehended because the parents spanked him in the parking lot of a mall, or in the case of the children who were removed from their parents' care because their religion encourages corporal punishment. What do you think the role of government is in such cases? Is government interfering with appropriate and reasonable parental disciplinary techniques, or is it truly protecting the rights of the child? More generally, what do you think of the issue of corporal punishment? Is it child abuse? Would you spank your child?

2. What do you think of the evidence suggesting that the dimensions of parenting, and the impact of these dimensions, may vary as a function of culture? In your own experience, have you noticed any cross-cultural differences?

3. Do you believe the findings on birth order and aspects of personality and development? If so, what factors may underlie such influences?

SOCIAL CLASS, ETHNICITY, AND SOCIALIZATION

No culture is entirely homogeneous. Subgroups within a culture may have their own particular values, attitudes, and beliefs as well as different problems to cope with. Any or all of these differences may be reflected in the unique goals of socialization and methods for achieving it.

Poverty and Powerlessness

Both scholarly and lay writers have focused much attention, in recent years, on the differences between the life situations of families of the lower and middle social classes in North American culture. Of particular importance is the prevalence of children living in poverty and under extremely unfavourable circumstances. In both Canada and the United States, the number of children living in poverty or in low-income families rose from the 1970s to the 1990s to roughly 20 percent, or about 1.5 million children in Canada and over 13 million in the United States (Brooks-Gunn, Britto, & Brady, 1999; Duncan & Brooks-Gunn, 2000; Health Canada, 1999a). The good news is that in the last few years, Canadian child poverty rates have dropped to just over 1 million, or 15.6 percent; the bad news is that this decline has essentially stabilized, and, more strikingly, that this is the same level of poverty as in 1989, despite the unprecedented economic growth of the 1990s (Campaign, 2000, 2008). Although the most obvious differences between the lower and middle classes are seen in the indicators of socio-economic status—income, education, and occupation—other related and pervasive features of the lives of the lower and middle classes may be more directly relevant to the socialization process (e.g., dangerous neighbourhoods, chronic stress).

Child Poverty

ECONOMIC HARDSHIP   Powerlessness is a basic problem of the poor. The poor have less influence over the society in which they live and are less likely than members of the middle class to be treated adequately and with appropriate concern by social organizations. The poor receive fewer public services, and their lack of power, information, and educational and economic resources restricts the options available to them. The poor have little choice when it comes to occupations and housing and little contact with other social groups; they are vulnerable to job loss, financial stress, and illness and subject to impersonal, bureaucratic decisions in the legal system and in social institutions, such as welfare agencies. Agents of law, social workers, educators, and others are more likely to violate the individual rights of lower-income citizens than those of middle-class people.

According to McLoyd and her colleagues (McLoyd et al., 2001; McLoyd et al., 2006), in view of the multiple stresses, few resources, and little social power possessed by poor parents, it is not surprising that many experience considerable psychological distress, feel helpless, insecure, and controlled by external forces, and are unable to support and nurture their children adequately (see Figure 11-7 on the next page). Nor is it only poor families who suffer in this way. As Conger and Elder (1994) have shown, families at a variety of income levels who suffer economic stress of any kind are more likely than non-stressed families to experience depression and marital conflict and to be harsh with their children. Moreover, the effects of economic stress on family functions have been documented in families of many ethnic derivations, such as European North American, African North American, and Mexican-American families. White families in the Midwest of the United States who lost their family farms in the recession of the late 1980s, poor African-American families in rural Georgia, and economically stressed Latino families in California in the mid-1990s all showed similar responses to economic hardship (Brody et al., 2002; Conger & Dogan, 2007; Parke et al., 2004). Similar effects

Figure 11-7

How economic stress can lead to children's adjustment problems

Adverse economic conditions may combine with personal financial stressors to create worry and insecurity in parents, which can lead to family conflict that may interfere with children's and adolescents' healthy adjustment.

Source: Adapted from Conger, Conger, Elder, Lorenz, Simons, & Whitbeck, 1992.

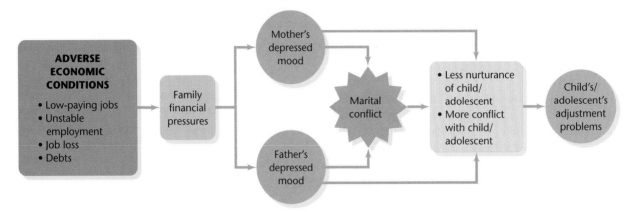

of economic hardship have been observed worldwide in countries such as Romania, Australia, Britain, and Brazil as well (Robila & Krishnakumar, 2005). Clearly, economic hardship affects families regardless of race, ethnicity, or nationality.

The mutual assistance and support among the poor themselves often relieves this dismal picture. Perhaps the very stresses that highlight their powerlessness lead working-class families to form extensive support networks of kin, friends, and neighbours; such networks are particularly common among economically deprived African-American families (Brody et al., 1996; Gadsden, 1999) and Latino families (Coltrane et al., 2007). These systems provide families not only with emotional support but also with unpaid services that could not be purchased. Families and friends render each other mutual assistance in fulfilling emergency needs in times of unemployment, childbirth, illness, and death, as well as in the day-to-day needs of family life (Coltrane et al., 2007).

THE IMPACT OF POVERTY ON CHILDREN   How does poverty affect children's development? First, poor children face more risks to physical health than do children of affluent families: Poor children are 1.9 times more likely to have low birthweight, 2.8 times more likely to have inadequate prenatal care, 3.5 times more likely to suffer lead poisoning, 1.7 times more likely to die during childhood, 2.0 times more likely to endure a short-term hospital stay, and 8 times as likely to have had too little food some time in the last four months. In short, being poor is bad for a child's health (Children's Defense Fund, 2007; Duncan & Brooks-Gunn, 2000). Nor is poverty helpful for children's achievement, as those in poverty are twice as likely to be held back in a grade and 3.5 times as likely to drop out of high school (Children's Defense Fund, 2007). Poor children are 1.3 times more likely to suffer emotional or behavioural problems, 6.8 times more likely to suffer child abuse or neglect, and over 2.2 times more likely to encounter violent crime.

The timing of poverty matters. Being poor in early childhood is much more detrimental than being poor in middle childhood or adolescence (McLoyd et al., 2006). A $10,000 increment to income over the first five years of life for children in low-income families is associated with nearly a threefold increase in the chances of finishing high school. Increasing income later in childhood was less effective in producing a change (Duncan et al., 1998). Poverty affects children through several pathways: First, the quality of the home environment differs in poor and non-poor families (Bradley et al., 2001). Children in poor homes have fewer physical resources (books, toys, educational games, and computers); they also receive fewer learning opportunities and less cognitive stimulation (parents less often read to children or engage in other developmentally appropriate activities) than children in non-poor homes. Second, the quality of care young children receive outside the home also matters, and poor children are often placed in poorer-quality child-care settings. Third, poverty and economic stress are linked with parent–child conflict; this leads to lower grades and impairs emotional and social development. Fourth, poor families often live in high-risk neighbourhoods characterized by social disorganization (crime, unemployment, low parental supervision) and limited resources (fewer playgrounds, after-school programs, child-care and health-care facilities); such poor neighbourhoods can adversely affect children's development (Leventhal & Brooks-Gunn, 2000). Finally, poor parents often suffer more physical and emotional problems that impair their parenting abilities. Children suffer as a result of this reduced parental competence.

We have painted a bleak picture of the impact of poverty on children, but there is some good news: The effects of poverty are sometimes reversible. Recent evidence based on experimental studies in which families received supplemental income suggests that an increase in family income is linked with improvement in poor children's school engagement and social behaviour (Morris & Gennetian, 2003). How do recent changes in welfare policies affect children's development? As a result of legislation in the 1990s, welfare-reform efforts have been directed at reducing family dependence on welfare and at increasing families' participation in the workforce. Researchers have found that when reforms increased work opportunities and provided the kinds of financial support that led to a net gain in income for working families, children achieved higher levels of school performance and showed more positive social behaviour. In contrast, welfare reforms that mandated work but did not result in an overall financial gain had few effects on children (Morris et al., 2001). However, when decreased dependence on welfare is linked with increased income, children were found to exhibit fewer problem behaviours and to perform better in school, and mothers were less depressed and reported less domestic violence (Gennetian & Miller, 2002).

Cultural Patterns in Child-Rearing

In general, social-class differences in family relations are more marked than variations based on race or ethnicity (Parke & Buriel, 2006). However, because race and social class do tend to be related, separating these factors has often been difficult; minorities are overrepresented in poorer and less-educated families. Unfortunately, investigators have often treated ethnic groups that vary greatly in terms of socio-economic, cultural, and linguistic characteristics as if they were homogeneous, and not recognized the great variability within such groups. Moreover, each group contains subgroups, within which there is great individual variation (Parke & Buriel, 2006).

Parents' and children's behaviours must always be understood in the context of the meanings and values of the individual's particular socioculture (McLoyd et al., 2006; Parke & Buriel, 2006). For example, in socializing their children, many ethnic minorities place greater emphasis than the European North American population does on the continuity of their ethnic values and worldviews and on social interdependence. In many groups, we see reflections of such interdependence in the role played by the **extended family**—the family inclusive of grandparents, aunts, uncles, nieces, and nephews—in many groups (McLoyd et al., 2005). This emphasis on interdependence is also reflected in concerns with co-operation, obligation, sharing, and reciprocity, which contrasts with North American ideals of self-reliance and competition. On the other hand, North American parents from Chinese and other Asian-American subcultures, who also emphasize family co-operation and obligation, encourage self-sufficiency and achievement even more than do European North American parents (Chao & Tseng, 2002). Once again, we must always know what group we are talking about when we make general statements.

extended family

Typically, a family that includes many relatives, such as grandparents, aunts, uncles, nieces, and nephews, within the basic family unit of parents and children.

Both the nuclear and the extended family are important in Asian cultures, which emphasize sharing and co-operation in both good times and bad.

Different parenting styles are found among many subcultural groups, but the effects of these styles seem to vary among some groups. Studying more than 20,000 high school students who were from varying ethnic and class backgrounds, Steinberg and colleagues (1992) found that in the United States, in families of European, African, and Asian descent, authoritative parenting had similar benefits in promoting better psychosocial adjustment and minimizing depression and delinquency in adolescents. However, these researchers found that the relationship specifically between authoritative parenting and school performance was less consistent for African and Asian North American adolescents than for European and Hispanic adolescents (Steinberg et al., 1995). European and Latino North American adolescents were more likely to benefit academically from authoritative parenting than were African or Asian North American adolescents. In North America, within the African and Asian subcultures, adolescents with authoritative parents did not show greater academic achievement than those with non-authoritative parents. How can these findings be explained?

(LO7) THE CHANGING FAMILY STRUCTURE

The North American family has been changing for some years now, and although some have predicted the demise of the family, it seems more accurate to say that family forms and family members' roles are becoming more varied. Most children still live in families with two parents who have been married only to each other. However, the proportion of **traditional nuclear families**—composed of two parents and children, with the father as the sole breadwinner—has declined drastically. What are some of the main changes in family structure and functioning that are occurring?

According to the 2006 Canadian Census, the average household size in Canada is at about 3.0 people. The average number of children in all families (including those families without children) is about 1.1, and for just those families with children it is about 1.8. There are a greater number of single-adult households. This is attributable, in part, to late marriages, declining birth rates (see Figure 11-8) and remarriage rates, and an increase in the number of elderly people living alone.

There are more single-parent households today than in earlier times, primarily because of the rising divorce rate and secondarily because more unmarried women are having children. The divorce rate doubled between 1960 and 1985; it is estimated that 40 to 50 percent of marriages today will end in divorce and that 60 percent of these divorces will involve children. In 2006, nearly 28 percent of children under 18 years of age lived with a single parent, but this figure was much higher for some ethnic groups (see Figure 11-9). One-third of children will experience the remarriage of one or both of their parents,

traditional nuclear family

The traditional family form, composed of two parents and one or more children, in which the father is the bread-winner and the mother the homemaker.

Figure 11-8

The changing birth rate in Canada, from the 1920s through the 1990s

Source: Anne Milan, "One Hundred Years of Families," *Canadian Social Trends*, Spring, 2000: 4.

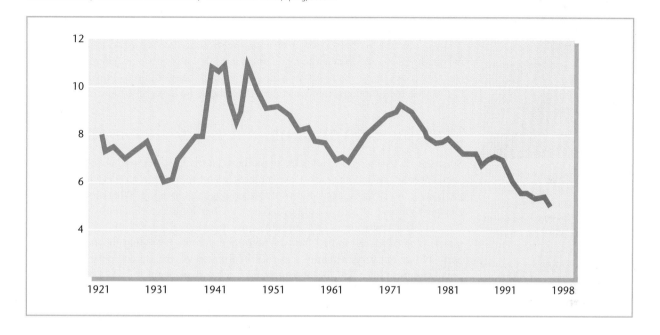

and 62 percent of remarriages end in divorce. Thus, more parents and children are undergoing multiple marital transitions and rearrangements in family relationships.

The proportion of out-of-wedlock births is currently at about 26 percent in Canada (Statistics Canada, 2006a), with this rate varying by ethnic group. In the United States (the relevant data for Canada is not tabulated), 70 percent of African Americans had babies out of wedlock; among Native Americans, the percentage was 57; in the Latino community, 43; for European Americans, 25; and among Asians and Pacific Islanders, 16 (Children's Defense Fund, 2007). Contrary to popular wisdom, more than twice as many unmarried mothers are over 20 years old, not under 20. We examine teenage parenthood later in this chapter.

The number of working mothers has increased also. In Canada, by 2005, 65 percent of married women with children under the age of 3 years were employed, and 70

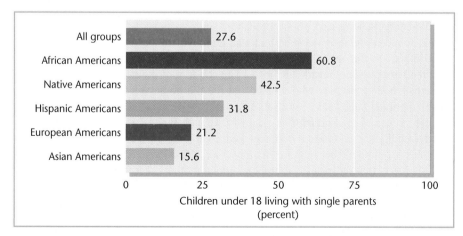

Figure 11-9

Children living with single parents, 1996

As with children living in poverty (see Figure 11-7 on page 444), children living with a single parent are much more likely to vary as a function of ethnic group. Although information for Canada is not available, in the United States, African-, Native-, or Hispanic-American children are more likely to be living with a single parent than are European- or Asian-American children.

Source: Based on Children's Defense Fund, 1997.

Although mothers still shoulder most of the responsibility for homemaking, there has been a shift in Western societies to men taking on more household chores. Interestingly, the change is associated with any number of positive effects on children's attitudes.

percent of women with children between 3 and 5 years were also working (Statistics Canada, 2006a). The employment of single mothers is very much influenced by the age of the child; 46 percent of single-parent women with children younger than 3 are employed outside of the home, compared with 63 percent of women with children between 3 and 5 years and 75 percent of women with children between 6 and 15 years (Statistics Canada, 2006a).

We look first, in this section, at changes in the family that are associated with maternal employment, and then at the kinds of changes that unwed single parenting, divorce, and remarriage bring about. As we will see, although many children of divorce continue to live with their mothers, joint custody arrangements have become more common.

Parental Employment and Child Development

Since the 1970s, increasing numbers of mothers, particularly of preschool children, have been entering the labour market. As mothers spend more time on the job and less in the home, family roles and patterns of functioning are changing. What are some of the changes that have already occurred, and how do they influence children's behaviour?

One shift may be a growing similarity between the roles of the mother and father. When children more often see both their parents providing for the family and participating actively in family and child-rearing tasks, the stereotypical roles of the breadwinning father and the homemaking mother may begin to fade away (Pleck & Masciadrelli, 2004). Note, however, that although paternal participation increases in dual-career families, currently, mothers are still doing most of the child care and housework (Coltrane, 2000).

Working mothers report that time is their scarcest and most valued resource. Both working mothers and their school-aged children complain that the mothers have too little time to spend with their children (Booth et al., 2002; Perry-Jenkins et al., 2000). However, greater father involvement may compensate for some of these problems. In both dual-earner and single-earner families, high father involvement is associated with higher IQ and achievement test scores, as well as with greater social maturity (Gottfried et al., 2002).

Children of working mothers have more egalitarian views of gender roles (Hoffman, 2000; Hoffman & Youngblade, 1999), and children in middle-class families whose mothers are employed have higher educational and occupational goals. Daughters are less likely to display traditional feminine interests and characteristics and more often perceive the woman's role as involving freedom of choice, satisfaction, and competence; daughters themselves are career and achievement oriented, independent, and assertive and have high self-esteem (Hoffman, 2000). The sons of working mothers, in contrast to sons of unemployed mothers, not only perceive women as more competent but view men as warmer and more expressive.

What are the long-term effects of maternal employment? Gottfried and colleagues (2002) found no relation between maternal employment and children's development from infancy to the age of 12 and concluded that no sleeper effects were associated with mothers working outside the home. The children of mothers who were full-time homemakers and mothers who worked outside the home were similar in cognitive, socio-emotional, academic, motivational, and behavioural domains from infancy through adolescence. Research has shown that such factors as parental involvement and the quality of the home environment were clearly linked to children's development, regardless of mothers' occupation (Bradley et al., 2001; Parke & Buriel, 2006).

It appears that individual differences among mothers seem likely to be more significant for children's development than whether the mothers worked outside the home or were full-time homemakers. Mothers who derive a sense of satisfaction and self-efficacy from their homemaking role, and working mothers who enjoy their employment, both show more positive relations with their husbands and with their children than unhappy homemakers who would like to be employed (Hoffman, 2000). However, mothers and fathers both display more negative feelings and behaviour toward their children when their attitudes toward maternal employment and the wife's work status are not congruent (Hoffman, 2000).

Despite many predictions to the contrary, studies have indicated that with adequate alternative child care, maternal employment does not usually have detrimental effects on children. It is important, however, that in evaluating the effects of maternal employment we consider all relevant factors, such as the mother's reasons for working, her level of job satisfaction, the demands her employment may place on other family members, the attitudes of these family members toward her employment, and the quality of the substitute care and supervision provided for the children.

WORK STRESS AND CHILDREN'S ADJUSTMENT What determines how parental employment affects a child's development? It is not just whether one parent or the other works; the nature of the work situation determines the effects of parental employment on a child's development. As we have seen, maternal employment per se does not put children at risk. However, parents' experience of stress on the job may take its toll on children, spouses, and marriages (Crouter & Bumpus, 2001). Fathers who worked in a high-stress occupation, air traffic control, withdrew from their wives and were more irritable with their children after a stressful day (Repetti, 1989, 1996). Similarly, mothers were more likely to withdraw from their children after particularly stressful work days (Repetti & Wood, 1997). Finally, children of mothers who work non-standard schedules (evening, night, or rotating shifts) have poor early cognitive and language development (Han, 2005). In sum, it is not merely working or not working that matters, but the conditions under which adults work that make a difference in their children's lives.

SELF-CARE: THE CASE OF LATCHKEY CHILDREN The need for child care, which we discussed earlier (see Chapter 6), does not stop when children enter school, and it is a cause of concern for working parents. In the United States, over 2 million children care for themselves without the benefit of parental supervision. Approximately 20 percent of 6- to 12-year-olds are **latchkey children**, who must let themselves into their homes because one or both parents are at work elsewhere (Urban Institute, 2000). Not surprisingly, self-care increases with age, and by adolescence, many children are in self-care at least some of the time. What are the effects of unsupervised care? On the positive side, self-care places greater demands on children for responsibility and maturity (Belle, 1999). And some children appreciate the positive aspects of being left on their own.

As one child noted, the best things about her unsupervised arrangement are "being able to come home. Being able to have unstructured time. Being able to relax after school. Having flexibility. Being able to decide last minute to play with another friend . . ." (Belle, 1999, p. 87). But, for children, there is a downside to being left on their own. Children who are left unsupervised are at higher risk for a variety of problems, such as increased delinquency and anti-social behaviour, poorer grades, heightened stress, and greater substance abuse (Belle, 1999). And the risks of leaving children unsupervised are not lost on parents. As one mother fretted, "It puts more pressure on me worrying about what she's doing in the afternoon. From 3 p.m. on I can't be totally relaxed. I'm thinking about whether she's home doing homework" (Belle, 1999, p. 87).

What helps reduce the risks associated with self-care? *Distal monitoring*, in which parents check in by phone, can be useful, as can devising clear rules and expectations about permitted activities, friends, and places (Belle, 1999). Perhaps the most helpful alternative is after-school care programs. Children who are enrolled in high-quality after-school programs during the elementary school years benefit in many ways. They have better grades, avoid drugs and delinquency, and have better relationships with their peers (NICHD Early Child Care Research Network, 2004a; Vandell, Pierce, & Dadisman, 2005). And parents feel better, too: "Justin's after-school program relieves

One reason some latchkey schoolchildren come home to empty houses is a lack of sufficient child-care and after-school programs.

latchkey children

Children who must let themselves into their homes after school because a parent or both parents are working outside their home.

me of the fear of him being caught on the streets unattended. He's playing with a selected group of kids. He's not . . . [strapped] to the TV. I feel so comfortable with the program and teachers" (Belle, 1999, p. 88).

Just as we saw in the case of child care for younger children, quality is the key. Poorly supervised and disorganized after-school programs can be detrimental to children's development (Vandell et al., 2005). In short, parents need to be careful to choose quality after-school care.

Marital Transitions

We need to view divorce and remarriage not as discrete events but as steps in a transition that will modify the lives and development of parents and children. Children's experiences in earlier family situations will moderate their response to this transition. The response of family members to divorce and to life in a single-parent family is generally a function of the quality of family life that preceded the separation and divorce. In like fashion, the response to remarriage will be shaped by experiences in the earlier marriage and the subsequent, single-parent household. Both divorce and remarriage force a restructuring of the household and changes in family roles and relationships (Clarke-Stewart & Brentano, 2006; Hetherington & Kelly, 2002).

Although divorce is sometimes a positive solution to destructive family functioning, for many family members, the transition period following separation and divorce is highly stressful. During the first year after a divorce, parents' feelings of distress and unhappiness, troubled parent–child relationships, and children's social and emotional adjustment tends to get worse (Hetherington, 2006). In the second year, however, when families are adapting to their new single-head-of-household status, many parents experience a dramatic improvement in their sense of personal well-being, interpersonal functioning, and family relations. In the long run, children in stable, well-functioning single-parent households are better adjusted than children in conflict-ridden nuclear families.

Some researchers have suggested that when parents delay divorcing—sometimes in the hope of protecting their children—those children show behavioural problems long before the divorce finally takes place. Moreover, these problems may be greater than those of children whose parents have some difficulties but remain in their marriage (Clarke-Stewart et al., 2000). It is possible that children respond adversely to the acrimony and conflict in a stressed marriage, particularly when it is suppressed, or behavioural problems in children may exacerbate difficulties in a troubled marriage and help to precipitate a divorce.

DIVORCE AND THE SINGLE-PARENT HOUSEHOLD What are the most important effects of divorce on children? When divorce leads, as it usually does, to children living in single-parent households, how does the family's lifestyle and functioning differ? What kinds of stresses are single-parent households more likely to encounter than nuclear families? Can a single parent cope with all that two parents have handled up to now? Does the single parent have time to be a parent?

When divorced parents and their children do not experience additional stresses following divorce, more are coping reasonably well by the second or third year after a divorce. However, one-parent, mother-headed households are at increased risk of encountering multiple stresses that make it difficult to raise children successfully, and, in fact, a period of diminished parenting often follows a divorce (Hetherington & Stanley-Hagan, 2002). Custodial mothers may become self-involved, erratic, uncommunicative, non-supportive, and inconsistently punitive in dealing with their children. They may also fail to control and monitor their children's behaviour adequately. Not uncommonly, children reciprocate in the immediate aftermath of divorce by being demanding, non-compliant, and aggressive or by whining and being overly dependent.

Divorced mothers and sons are particularly likely to engage in escalating, mutually coercive exchanges. Some desperate divorced mothers have described their relationships with their children right after a divorce as "declared war," "a struggle for survival," or "like getting bitten to death by ducks." Although inept parenting is most marked in the first year following divorce—parenting improves markedly in the second year—problematic parenting is more likely to be sustained with sons, especially temperamentally difficult sons, than with daughters. Divorced mothers and their daughters are likely to form very close relationships eventually, although mothers may have to weather their daughters' acting-out behaviour during adolescence (Hetherington & Kelly, 2002). Despite this information, Wolchik and colleagues (2000) have found that when divorced mothers are high in warmth and consistent in their discipline, 8- to 15-year-olds had fewer adjustment problems than their peers in less warm and consistent families.

Non-custodial as well as custodian parents can continue to play a significant role in their children's development. When divorced parents agree on child-rearing methods and maintain a reasonably friendly attitude toward each other, frequent visits between the children and the non-custodial parent may be associated with positive adjustment and self-control in the children. When the mother has custody, such visits are particularly helpful for sons. When there is continued conflict between parents, however, especially conflict in which the child feels caught in the middle or when the parent is a non-authoritative parent or is poorly adjusted, frequent contact between the non-custodial parent and the child may be associated with disruptions in the child's behaviour (Buchanan & Heiges, 2001; Buchanan et al., 1991). Clearly, what counts is the quality of the contact with a non-custodial parent and the exposure of the child to conflict and stress.

FAMILY INTERACTION IN REMARRIED FAMILIES Family members' experiences in their original family setting greatly affects their response to remarriage. For divorced women, remarriage is the most common route out of poverty, and a new partner may give a custodial mother not only economic but also emotional support as well as help in child-rearing.

Children sometimes resist the arrival of a step-parent, creating stress in the new marital relationship. Sons, who have often been involved in coercive relationships with their custodial mothers, may have little to lose and much to gain from a relationship with a caring stepfather. Daughters, on the other hand, may feel the intrusion of stepfathers into their close relationships with their mothers as more threatening and disruptive. Among preadolescent children, divorce seems to have more adverse consequences for boys and remarriage seems to be more difficult for girls. Adolescents, regardless of gender, have a particularly difficult time accepting a parent's remarriage (Hetherington & Stanley-Hagan, 2002).

In general, neither stepmothers nor stepfathers take as active a role in parenting as biological parents (Clarke-Stewart & Brentano, 2006). Indeed, many stepfathers are rather like polite strangers with their stepchildren, hesitating to become involved in controlling or disciplining them. Stepmothers, who walk into the maternal role, are forced to take a more active role in disciplining children than stepfathers are (Cherlin & Furstenberg, 1994). This may in part explain the finding that children are more resistant and have poorer adjustment in stepmother families (Cherlin & Furstenberg, 1994; Hetherington et al., 1998). In addition, a child's age at the time of a parent's remarriage will affect both the child's attitude toward the new marriage and the likelihood that he will develop any kind of problem behaviour. Although we have been focusing on the effects of divorce and remarriage on parent–child relations, sibling relations also are often disrupted. More antagonistic, non-supportive relations are found among siblings in divorced and remarried families than among those in non-divorced families (Conger & Conger, 1996; Dunn & Davies, 2000; Hetherington et al., 1998). These adverse effects are most marked for male siblings, whereas some pairs of female siblings serve as mutual supports in coping with their parents' marital transitions.

CHILDREN IN DIVORCED AND REMARRIED FAMILIES   Over time, most boys and girls adjust reasonably well to their parents' marital transitions. Exhibiting remarkable resilience, some children actually become stronger through coping with divorce and remarriage. In fact, only about 25 percent have long-term problems (Hetherington & Kelly, 2002). Authoritative parenting is associated with more positive adjustment in children in divorced and remarried families, just as it is in non-divorced families. If divorce reduces stress and conflict and leads to better functioning on the part of the custodial parent, or if the child's loss of an uninvolved or incompetent father eventually results in the acquisition of a more accessible, responsive father figure, the child often benefits in the long run from divorce and remarriage. Preadolescent boys, in particular, may benefit from a close, caring relationship with a stepfather.

The most common reported problem behaviours found in children of divorced and remarried families are aggressive, non-compliant, anti-social behaviour; a decline in prosocial behaviours; and disruptions in peer relations (Clarke-Stewart & Brentano, 2006; Hetherington et al., 1998). And the age of the child when the parent divorces also plays a role in the child's subsequent adjustment. Pagini, Boulerice, Tremblay, and Vitaro (1997), for example, found that children whose parents divorced before they were 6 years old showed more behaviour problems, including anxiety, hyperactivity, and oppositional behaviour, than children who were older than 6 years when their parents divorced. Adolescence seems to trigger adjustment problems (depression, substance abuse, precocious sexuality) in both boys and girls in divorced and remarried families (Hetherington & Kelly, 2002). Problems in academic achievement, school adjustment, and school dropout are greater for boys than for girls in divorced families.

What are the long-term effects of divorce and remarriage on a family's children? Over the long haul, boys continue to experience major problems. One long-term longitudinal project, the Montreal Longitudinal study, conducted by Pagini, Tremblay, Vitaro, Kerr, and McDuff (1998) looked at delinquency in over 400 French-Canadian boys. This study found that boys between 12 and 15 years of age who experienced the remarriage of a parent showed more delinquency, especially through activities involving physical violence (fighting, coercion) and theft. And more recently, Pagini, Larocque, Vitaro, and Tremblay (2003) found that children of divorced mothers who remained divorced were even more likely to be aggressive toward their mothers. Other national survey studies suggest that divorce is related to several negative outcomes (Amato, 2000, 2001; McLanahan & Sandefur, 1994). The risk of dropping out of high school was twice as high for children of divorced families as it was for children in intact families (see Figure 11-10), and failing to finish school will likely reduce future employment and educational opportunities. Perhaps the most dramatic evidence of the long-term effects of divorce comes from a study of the predictors of longevity (Freidman et al., 1995). In a follow-up investigation of a group of gifted children originally studied by Lewis Terman in the 1920s, individuals who experienced parental divorce during childhood were likely to die sooner than those whose parents stayed married. Although these individuals were more likely themselves to divorce as adults, even after taking this into account, parental divorce was still a predictor of premature death. Achieving a sense of personal satisfaction in life and avoiding the smoking habit helped to lessen the link between parental divorce and mortality (Martin et al., 2005). Clearly, divorce has long-term consequences, although the mechanisms by which divorce alters longevity are still not clearly understood.

CHILD CUSTODY   Although mothers more commonly gain custody after a divorce, the traditional doctrine of sole custody has been re-examined. Perhaps children and ex-spouses would all benefit if joint custody was always an option in divorce cases involving children: "At its best, joint custody presents the possibility that each family member can 'win' in post-divorce life" (Thompson, 1994, p. 17). Neither mother

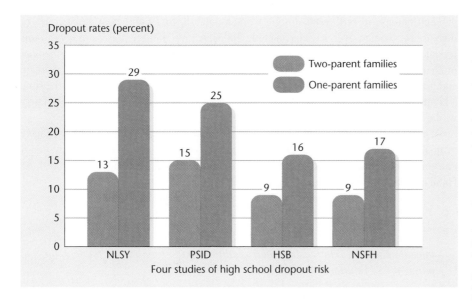

Dropout rates (percent)

Four studies of high school dropout risk

■ Two-parent families
■ One-parent families

NLSY: 13, 29
PSID: 15, 25
HSB: 9, 16
NSFH: 9, 17

Figure 11-10

Education and one-parent families

As measured in four separate studies, the risk of dropping out of high school was twice as high for children living in one-parent families (including stepfamilies) as for those living with two parents (NLSY = National Longitudinal Survey of Youth; PSID = Panel Study of Income Dynamics; HSB = High School and Beyond Study; NSFH = National Survey of Families and Households).

Source: From *Growing up with a single parent*, by McLanahan, S. and Sandefur, G., "The Risk of Dropping Out of High School," p. 41. Copyright © 1994 by the President and Fellows of Harvard College. Adapted by permission of the publisher, Harvard University Press, Cambridge, MA.

nor father is identified as a better or worse parent, and mothers and fathers each win a significant future role in the lives of their children. Perhaps even more important, the children win.

Joint custody takes two main forms. In **joint legal custody**, both mother and father retain and share responsibility for decisions concerning their children's lives, but the children usually reside with one parent. Under a **joint physical custody** arrangement, the children live with each parent for certain periods throughout the year. Although the length and timing of these periods vary, it is expected that children will have physical access to both parents on a regular basis.

Joint custody works best when conflict between parents decreases and when children do not "feel caught" in the middle (e.g., as a messenger) between warring parents (Buchanan et al., 1996). Older adolescents and girls were more likely to feel caught in the between-parents squeeze. Adolescents with stronger feelings against being caught between the estranged parents were more likely to experience depression and anxiety and to engage in more deviant behaviour (e.g., smoking, drug use, fighting, cheating, stealing) than were adolescents who experienced more interparental co-operation (Buchanan & Heiges, 2001).

The degree of parental conflict, rather than custody arrangement itself, seems to be the best predictor of children's adjustment (Buchanan & Heiges, 2001; Goodman et al., 1998). Joint custody is clearly not a panacea for divorced families or divorced fathers in particular. Fathers' influence and contact with their children seems less governed by custody arrangements than by other factors, such as geographic distance and relationship with the ex-spouse. In the long run, the advantage of joint custody may be its "symbolic value to parents and children" (Emery, 1988). It may offer a sign to fathers that they retain some rights and obligations as a parent and a message to their children that their fathers are still part of their larger family and a significant figure in their lives. At the same time, it is evident that joint custody is not a problem-free solution, especially if interparental conflict continues after divorce (Buchanan & Heiges, 2001). Evaluations are needed of the long-term impact of differing types of custody arrangements on children as well as on their parents.

LATE-TIMED PARENTHOOD People are not only marrying later today than in earlier times (three or four years later than they did in the 1950s) but they are also becoming first-time parents at later ages. Between 1991 and 2003, there was a 12

joint legal custody

A form of child custody in which both parents retain and share responsibility for decisions regarding the child's life but which generally provides for the child to reside with one parent.

joint physical custody

As in joint legal custody, parents make decisions together regarding their child's life, but they also share physical custody, the child living with each parent for a portion of the year.

percent increase in birth rates among women aged 30 to 39 and even higher rates of increase for women over 40 (Martin et al., 2005). Although there may be many reasons for later parenthood, important factors are doubtless the widespread employment of mothers outside the home, more flexibility in gender roles for both men and women, and greater availability of support services such as child care. In addition, by the time a couple is in their thirties, they have usually completed their education and are fairly well established in their careers.

Delaying the decision to become parents sometimes means that a couple will have difficulty in conceiving (Henig, 2004), and, in fact, older prospective parents are major consumers of the new reproductive technologies (see Box 2.2 on pages 59 and 60). As Hahn and DiPietro (2001) note,

> *Research on the effects of reproductive technologies has been fueled by the speculation that the emotional distress associated with previous infertility and the unusual form of transition to parenthood may influence a [formerly] infertile couple's relationship, their quality of parenting and, ultimately, the parent–child relationship.* (p. 37)

Research to date suggests that children born via the technique of donor insemination, for example, function as well as conventionally born children (Golombok, 2006; Patterson & Hastings, 2007). And recent study of the technique of surrogacy suggests not only that the offspring of surrogate mothers develop well but also that these children may benefit from parent–child relationships that are even more positive than many that occur in naturally conceived families. In part, this may be due to the eagerness of couples who must make extraordinary efforts to become parents (Golombok et al., 2004).

For both mothers and fathers, the age of onset of parenting is linked with both parenting practices and knowledge. Between the teen years and 30, increasing the age of first-time motherhood is related to greater satisfaction and higher parenting knowledge as well as higher sensitivity and language stimulation in regard to their 20-month-olds. However, after the age of 30, few links with age were found, and some aspects of parenting are immune from age, such as parental investment and social play (Bornstein & Putnick, 2007). By age 30, mothers may be sufficiently settled in terms of their cognitive and emotional development that further shifts in their parenting are unlikely.

The older father, with more flexibility and freedom in balancing the demands of work and family, is three times more likely than a younger father to have regular responsibility for some part of a preschool child's daily care (Daniels & Weingarten, 1988). Moreover, the older father may be generally more involved in the parental role and may experience more positive affect associated with child-rearing (NICHD Early Child Care Research Network, 2000b). The fact that younger fathers tend to engage in more strenuous physical play with their children and that older fathers tend to use more cognitive mechanisms in their play may reflect less stereotypical views of men's and women's roles in parenting as much as a lessening of physical energy (Neville & Parke, 1997).

As family systems theory would predict, greater participation by fathers in caring for and playing with their children may help facilitate the more enjoyable and productive relations that older mothers enjoy with their children. Clearly, the timing of first parenthood is a powerful organizer of both maternal and paternal roles. Future investigations of marital and parenting interaction patterns need to consider this timing as well as other factors.

Adoption: Another Route to Parenthood

Couples choose adoption for many reasons: Some are unable to conceive a child; some are older and, thus, at risk of suffering some of the problems we discussed in Chapter

2; others may wish to avoid a family-related genetic disorder. In the United States, 2 to 4 percent of children are adopted (Stolley, 1993). Twenty or thirty years ago, people commonly adopted infants born in North America. Today, however, because contraceptive methods are more effective, abortion is more available, and young unwed mothers often keep their babies, couples are more likely to find their little adoptees in other countries and/or among the numbers of developmentally at-risk infants and children. In 2006, approximately 1,500 children were adopted in Canada from abroad (Adoption Council of Canada, 2007), and in the United States, nearly 22,000 foreign-born children were adopted. Currently, babies are most often adopted from China, Haiti, South Korea, Russia, and Ethiopia (Adoption Council of Canada, 2007).

How do adopted children fare in terms of their development? There are two perspectives on this issue. According to one view, adoption is a protective measure if it removes an infant or child from adverse social conditions such as long-term foster care or institutional environments such as orphanages. Children who are able to escape these poor rearing environments through adoption have better developmental outcomes than children who remain in deprived and non-stimulating environments (Kreppner et al., 2007; Rutter, 2002). The success of adoption as an intervention, however, depends on a variety of factors, perhaps most importantly, on the age of the adopted child. Children who are adopted at any early age out of adverse circumstances fare better than those who remain for longer periods in such circumstances. Early adolescents who were adopted from the infamous Romanian orphanages before they were 6 months old were similar to British adoptees who had not suffered early deprivation (Kreppner et al., 2007). This suggests that a normal family environment can help adopted children catch up and develop normally. On the other hand, many adopted children have not necessarily suffered the extreme adversity that characterized institutionalized Romanian infants. In spite of this difference, adopted children are at greater risk of having psychological problems, including hyperactivity, externalizing behaviour, academic troubles, and learning disabilities (Brodzinsky & Pinderhughes, 2002).

Several factors affect an adopted child's relative risk for developmental problems: being a boy; being older at the time of placement; and having had more adverse prior experiences, such as multiple placements in foster care or being abused or neglected, are all linked with poorer adjustment. At the same time, the vast majority of adoptees fall within the range of normal development, and the differences between the progress of adopted and biological children are often small (van London, Juffer, & van IJzendoorn, 2007). For most adopted children, and for most couples who adopt, the benefits clearly outweigh the risks.

Gay and Lesbian Parents

Another recent change in the North American family is the greater numbers of lesbian and gay parents. Although we have only estimates at the moment, most authorities believe that there are somewhere between 1 and 5 million lesbian mothers and between 1 and 3 million gay fathers in the United States, and that gay or lesbian parents are rearing between 6 and 14 million children (Patterson & Hastings, 2007).

Families with gay or lesbian parents are diverse. The largest group of children with gay or lesbian parents are those who were born to one of the parents before they established their same-gender relationship—that is, in the context of a previous heterosexual relationship or marriage. Within this group, there are two primary variations: When one of the child's biological parents declares a same-gender sexual preference and the couple divorce, the gay or lesbian parent may then form a new, same-sex relationship in which the partners together care for the child. In another arrangement, a gay or a lesbian couple who do not have children may choose to become parents. One partner in a lesbian relationship may choose to bear a child through donor insemination. Or the couples may adopt a child.

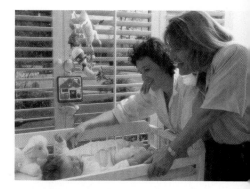

Lesbian partners who choose to become parents tend to share child-rearing and home-making tasks more equally than heterosexual couples.

Figure 11-11

Lesbian parents and paid employment

Among lesbian parents, (a) biological mothers spent less time in paid employment (only 40 percent worked a full week) and more time in child care, whereas (b) nearly three-quarters of non-biological mothers were engaged in full-time employment.

Source: Adapted from Patterson, 1995.

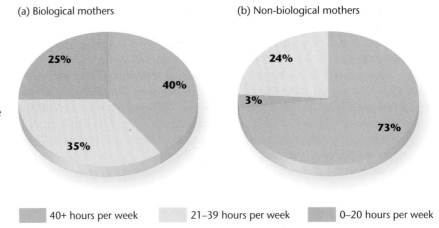

(a) Biological mothers   (b) Non-biological mothers

■ 40+ hours per week   ■ 21–39 hours per week   ■ 0–20 hours per week

Research suggests that heterosexual mothers and lesbian mothers who have divorced their heterosexual partners differ little in terms of self-concept, general happiness, and overall adjustment (Patterson & Hastings, 2007). We know less about divorced gay fathers because only a small minority of these men are granted custody of their children or live with them (Patterson, 2004). Most of our knowledge of gay and lesbian parenting comes from studies of couples who, after establishing their relationship, chose to become parents. Research that compared these couples' households with heterosexual households found that both gay and lesbian couples tended to share household duties more equally (Solomon et al., 2004). Among lesbian partners, biological mothers appeared to be more involved in child care and non-biological mothers to spend longer hours in paid employment (see Figure 11-11). At the same time, children in lesbian families, as with those in heterosexual families, were likely to be better adjusted when both partners shared child care more or less equally, and lesbian parents were also likely to be more satisfied (Patterson & Hastings, 2007).

What about the children? Children of lesbian mothers develop in a normal fashion and do not have any greater emotional or social problems—including peer relationships and relationships with adults—than other children, nor is there any appreciable evidence of altered gender roles among lesbian parents' children (Wainright & Patterson, 2008) (see also Chapter 13). In similar fashion, the great majority of gay fathers' children grow up to be heterosexual adults. Nor are children of gay fathers victims of sexual abuse or at any significant disadvantage in comparison with children of heterosexual fathers. Although gay fathers undoubtedly face prejudice and discrimination, children have described their relationships with gay fathers as warm and supportive (Patterson, 2004).

Teenage Pregnancy: Children Having Children

Why do teenagers have babies out of wedlock? Teenagers are initiating sexual behaviour earlier and people generally are marrying later (Maticka-Tyndale, 2001; Milan, 2000). For adolescent parents, poverty, being socially and economically disadvantaged, having models (parents and other adults) who also have children out of wedlock, and growing up too soon all play particularly important roles in early teen pregnancy (Moore & Brooks-Gunn, 2002). Early sexual activity leads not just to unplanned pregnancies but to declining school achievement and to sexually transmitted diseases (STDs). Teenagers have the highest STD rates of any age group, and one-fifth of all AIDS cases start in adolescence (Tinsley et al., 2004).

How many teen pregnancies are there in a year? As Figure 11-12 shows, the rate of teenage pregnancy in Canada has been decreasing since the 1990s, a current rate (as of

2005) of 25.6 for every 1,000 females under 20 years of age (McKay, 2006; Statistics Canada, 2007a). This was substantially less than in the United States, which (as of 2002) had a teenage pregnancy rate of 75.4 for every 1,000 women (Guttmacher Institute, 2006). Cultural and geographic factors contribute to differences in teen pregnancy rates In Canada, the rates tend to be higher in the North and in the Prairie provinces (*The Daily*, 2000, October). Moreover, many of these teenage pregnancies end in births (Maticka-Tyndale et al., 2000; Wadhera & Millar, 1997), with minority teens one and a half to two times as likely as European-Canadian teens to bear children. Altogether, in Canada, the birth rate for teenagers under 20 years of age was about 20 per 1,000 women, compared with 18 in Australia, 28 in the United Kingdom, and 30 in New Zealand. The United States tops this group, with about 46 births per 1,000 women to teenage mothers (Foundation for Child Development, 2007). Although almost a quarter of teenage mothers are married and another third have fairly stable relationships with the fathers of their babies, more than half face personal, economic, and social problems that make it very difficult for them to support and care for their children (Wakschlag et al., 2001). As a result, these babies have poor prospects, largely because of the economic constraints most teen mothers confront, and the younger the mother, the greater the risk:

> *During the preschool years, signs of delays in cognitive development begin to emerge and tend to grow more evident as the children age. Preschool children of teen mothers also tend to display higher levels of aggression and less ability to control impulsive behaviour. By adolescence, children of teen mothers have, on the whole, higher rates of grade failure and more delinquency. . . . They also become sexually active earlier [and have] a greater likelihood of pregnancy before age 20.* (Children's Defense Fund, 1998, p. 98)

According to one estimate, the sons of teen mothers are 13 percent more likely than others to be incarcerated, and daughters are 22 percent more likely to become teen mothers themselves (Children's Defense Fund, 2004). The negative effects on children are to some degree due to the less effective caregiving provided by teen mothers: they are less warm and provide less verbal and cognitive stimulation than more mature mothers. Although fathers sometimes either marry or give support, many are unable to provide economic help or sometimes fail to get involved (Moore & Brooks-Gunn, 2002). Even the younger sisters of teenage mothers can be affected by the early arrival of a nephew or niece. Often, they must take time away from schoolwork to help care for the child, and they are at increased risk for drug and alcohol use and for becoming pregnant themselves (East & Jacobson, 2001). Teen parents and their children pay huge

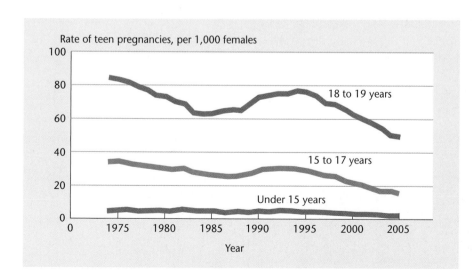

Figure 11-12

Canadian teen pregnancy rates as a function of age

This graph shows the rate of teenage pregnancies, per 1,000 females, for young adults under 15 years of age, between 15 and 17 years, and between 18 and 19 years.

Source: Statistics Canada (2007a). *Table 106-9002—Pregnancy outcomes by age group, Canada, provinces and territories, annual.* CANSIM (database).

prices, and society pays in lost productivity and in the need to provide public care and services for disadvantaged children.

PREVENTION AND INTERVENTION   Teenagers whose parents are educated and financially secure as well as warm and responsive to their children have a better chance at avoiding teen pregnancy (Moore & Brooks-Gunn, 2002). A family's active involvement with religious beliefs and practices also is a protective factor that can help avoid early sexual activity and child-bearing among the children. The use of contraceptives by teenagers who have initiated sexual activity can, of course, prevent pregnancy as well as serious and life-threatening sexual diseases. Fortunately, the rate at which teenagers use contraceptives has been increasing, but so has the number of young people who are sexually active.

Once an unwed teen has become a parent, what are her options for avoiding some of the negative effects we have discussed? Marriage is one of the most important routes out of poverty, largely because of the husband's income, but the divorce rate for this group is high. The failure of such marriages may be due to the immaturity of the young people and their inability to judge what makes for a good life partner.

Other factors help improve the outcomes for teen mothers, such as getting a good education and limiting future births. In addition, when the children of unwed mothers have good-quality relationships with their fathers, they tend to achieve higher educational levels and to be less subject to depression and less likely to be imprisoned for misbehaviours or crimes (Moore & Brooks-Gunn, 2002). Particularly for African North American children, having a stepfather join the family seems to have positive effects, increasing the likelihood that the children will be successful in life. In any event, if the mother's situation changes for the better, particularly if she moves off welfare, becomes economically independent, acquires more education, or enters a stable marriage before her child becomes an adolescent, the child's adjustment and academic performance may be enhanced (Moore & Brooks-Gunn, 2002).

For Thought and Discussion

1. In many ways, the influence of social class on child socialization tends to centre on economic differences. Are there aspects of social class that can be separated from economic effects? Given that ethnicity is also related to economic level, are there influences of ethnicity that can be seen as separate from economic effects?

2. One current trend in the outcome of divorce negotiation is joint custody arrangements. What do you think are the pluses and minuses of such arrangements? Are they confusing, or do children manage to get the best (and maybe the worst) of both worlds?

3. Another recent trend in society has been an increase in the number of parents who have children later in life (in their late thirties to forties), and research suggests that these parents may interact differently with their children. What reasons can you think of for such a trend? What role might economic factors play here?

LO8 CHILD ABUSE WITHIN THE FAMILY

Family Violence

Although it is difficult to obtain precise figures on how many children in Canada and the United States suffer from maltreatment, it is estimated that every year, between 1 and 3 million children are physically or psychologically abused and that the majority of these children are abused by family members (Child Trends, 2007). In the United States, in 2005, Child Protective Services dealt with approximately 3 million cases of child abuse, about 900,000 of which were substantiated (Child Trends, 2007). In Canada, in 2003, there were an estimated 235,315 child-maltreatment investigations, or 38.33 investigations per 1,000 children, with 49 percent of these investigations, or 114,607 child investigations, substantiating the maltreatment (Trocmé et al., 2005). Of the remaining cases, about 12 percent of them were suspected but not confirmed, and 38 percent were unsubstantiated. In the United States, 16.5 percent of these children were infants or toddlers and another 13.5 percent were 4 to 7 years old (US Department of Health and Human Services, 2007). Of the different types of abuse, the most common was neglect, comprising 30 percent of the substantiated cases in Canada and 63 percent of the cases in the States, followed by physical abuse, 24 percent in Canada and 17 percent in the States; sexual abuse accounted for 3 percent in Canada and 9 percent in the States (Child Trends, 2007; Trocmé et al., 2005). Because many instances of child abuse are not even reported or are discovered only after abuse has continued for a long time or the child is dead, these figures are conservative. In 2005, more than 1,300 children died in the United States as a result of child abuse—almost four children every day (Centers for Disease Control and Prevention, 2005).

What can possibly lead to this inhuman treatment of children? Some of the contributing risk factors lie in the characteristics of parents and their abused children, some are attributable to ecological factors, such as the quality of the neighbourhood and available support systems, and still others are related to the life experiences and stresses that family members encounter. Abuse is unlikely to occur when only one risk factor is at play. It is the presence of multiple risk factors and of interaction among them that often leads to abuse, especially when the family and the children have few protective advantages such as a warm and caring marital relationship, a supportive social network, accessible community resources, high intelligence, education, good health, and adaptability (Azar, 2002; Cicchetti & Toth, 2006). Many African North Americans, Indian/Alaskan and Pacific Islanders still live under such stressful conditions—poverty, substandard housing, lack of educational opportunities, and poor health—and it is in these groups that we find the most cases of child maltreatment (see Figure 11-13). Asian and European North Americans—who tend not to live in circumstances of this sort—have many fewer cases of child abuse. Interestingly, Hispanic families have relatively low rates of child abuse, in part due to a higher number of two-parent families and a strong sense of familism or commitment to family well-being. As we will see in looking at

Figure 11-13

Child maltreatment rates (per 1,000) by race and Hispanic origin

Child abuse is more common in some ethnic groups than others. At present, in the United States, the families in which children are most commonly mistreated tend to be African American, Native American, and non-Hispanic Pacific Islanders; people in these groups often find it difficult to obtain good jobs, typically receive low wages, and often live in areas where delinquency and crime are more common.

Source: Adapted from US Department of Health and Human Services, 2007.

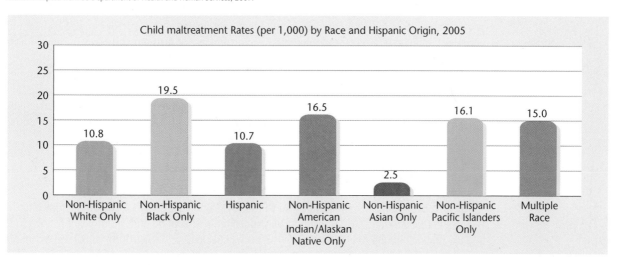

child abuse, ethnic differences of these kinds and other stress-related factors, such as single parenthood, probably account for some of these variations among subcultures.

Abused Children and Their Parents

Most students reading this book probably think that no one they know would ever abuse a child or that only someone who is really mentally ill would inflict grievous physical harm on defenceless children. However, although chronic maltreatment is most likely to occur in economically deprived, poorly educated families, child abusers are found in all social classes and in all religious, racial, and ethnic groups. In addition, there is little evidence that severe mental illness or specific personality traits consistently distinguish abusive parents from non-abusive parents. Shocking as it may seem, mothers are frequently the persons who abuse children. Why might this happen? For one thing, some mothers feel locked into a stressful family situation, and mothers generally spend a good deal more time with a child than do other family members (Azar, 2002; Cicchetti & Toth, 2006).

Certain characteristics of the child and family are also associated with maltreatment of children. Child physical abuse is more likely to occur in large families and to children under the age of 3. A higher-than-normal incidence of birth anomalies, physical and intellectual deviations, irritability, negativism, and other behaviours that parents often find exasperating are seen in many of these children. **Sexual abuse** occurs from infancy through adolescence; for females, the peak onset occurs between 7 and 8 years of age, and for boys, the peak onset is in the years just before puberty. Female children are four times more likely to be victims of sexual abuse than male children (Azar, 2002; Feerick et al., 2006).

Two factors most commonly associated with abusive behaviour are a distressed, often sexually unsatisfying marriage and the abuse of one or both marital partners by his or her own parents. Although incompetent, abusive parenting may to some extent be transmitted across generations (Azar, 2002; Grusec et al., 1991), young parents are not locked into their own parents' style of parenting. Only about a third of parents who were abused when they were young will abuse their own children (Cicchetti & Toth, 2006). Mothers who break this intergenerational cycle are more likely to have had a warm, caring adult in their background, to have established a close marital relationship, and at some time to have received therapy (Egeland et al., 1988).

Abusive parents are likely to have unrealistic beliefs about parent–child relationships and to respond less appropriately to their children's behaviour than do non-abusive parents. They often expect their children to perform in a manner far beyond what is normal for their stage of development or to exhibit levels of independence and self-control that are unlikely in children of their ages (Azar, 2002; Feerick et al., 2006). Compared with non-abusive mothers, abusive mothers show fewer positive behaviours toward the children and more severe negative behaviours, such as threatening commands, strong criticism, and physical punishment (Cicchetti & Toth, 2006). And the behaviour of abusive parents is unpredictable and less contingent on the type of behaviour the child exhibits (Azar, 2002). A mother's response may not distinguish between a tantrum or a task well done or between a smiling or a crying baby (Frodi & Lamb, 1980). They seem to be experiencing both the crying baby and the pleasant, happy baby as emotionally aversive. We have spoken earlier of the importance of parents accurately reading and responding to children's cues. This distorted perception of the child's behaviour must greatly increase the stress and confusion in already disturbed parent–child relationships.

The Ecology of Child Abuse

Recognizing that individuals and families do not operate in a social vacuum but are embedded in a variety of important social contexts outside the family can improve our understanding of child abuse (Azar, 2002; Cicchetti & Toth, 2006). This level of analy-

sexual abuse

Inappropriate sexual activity between an adult and a child for the perpetrator's pleasure or benefit; the abuse may be direct (sexual contact of any type) or indirect (exposing a child to pornography or to the live exhibition of body parts or sexual acts).

sis—Bronfenbrenner's exosystem—includes neighbourhoods and communities as well as schools, workplaces, peer groups, and religious institutions. The social support and guidance that these contexts provide can alter parental attitudes, knowledge, and their child-rearing practices, which, in turn, may modify the likelihood of abuse.

First, poverty makes a difference. Although violence against children occurs in all social classes, it is greater in poor families (Duncan & Brooks-Gunn, 2000). Several reasons have been suggested: Among them are the stressors associated with being poor, the greater number of single-parent families who live in poverty, the violence that often pervades poor neighbourhoods, and limited access to social services. Although physical abuse and neglect both have been linked with poverty, sexual abuse has not and appears to be more common in middle-class families.

Closely linked with poverty as a factor in abuse is unemployment. Several studies have clearly shown that unemployment is related to rates of child abuse (e.g., Krishnan & Morrison, 1995). Krishnan and Morrison (1995), for example, used an ecological perspective to predict the rates of child maltreatment in Alberta. Although a number of variables, including population change, location in the northwest region, and the percentage of the population that was Native, were correlates of the rate of child abuse, the unemployment rate was the single most important factor in predicting maltreatment. Of course, the processes underlying this link are still not clear, with such factors as stress, frustration, and increased contact between parents and children all potentially contributing to the possible connection between job loss and child abuse.

Neighbourhoods matter, too. Some neighbourhoods serve a protective or buffering function against abuse, whereas others seem to exacerbate the family's risk for abuse. Protective or low-risk neighbourhoods have more social resources, and the families tend to use these resources—friends, neighbours, and relatives, as well as community centres—for advice, guidance, and physical and financial assistance in a balanced and reciprocal fashion. High-risk neighbourhoods are less friendly places; people rely on each other for guidance and support less often and tend to exploit each other more when they do exchange goods and services. Such neighbourhoods are physically run down, dangerous, and experience highly volatile levels of residency (Leventhal & Brooks-Gunn, 2000; Parke et al., 2008b). And child abuse rates—even after controlling for race and poverty levels—are higher in the high-risk neighbourhoods (Garbarino & Sherman, 1980).

Broad cultural changes in North American society may play a role in the emergence of abusive patterns. For example, increased divorce rates, increased mobility, limited availability of daycare, lack of medical coverage, and lack of paid family leave at the birth of a child may increase stress that may, in turn, contribute to abuse. A widespread indifference to violence or even acceptance of violence as a solution to social problems, including our culture's general acceptance of the physical punishment of children (as discussed in Box 11.1 on pages 432 and 433), may contribute to the rise in child abuse in North American society. Child abuse is relatively uncommon in cultures like that of the Chinese, who rarely punish children physically. Thus, the cultural approval of violence, such as spanking in child-rearing, may sometimes combine with caregivers' lack of social, economic, and emotional resources to produce child abuse.

In summary, no single factor leads to child abuse. It involves complex interactions among dysfunctional family relationships, multiple stressful experiences, a disorganized or non-supportive environment, and cultural values that tolerate or justify aggression and physical punishment.

Children's Rights

Consequences of Abuse

The consequences of abuse are, in a word, devastating. More than 1,300 children die each year; 65 percent of these children die as a direct result of physical abuse, and another 36 percent die from the consequences of neglect. And it is the youngest children who are most likely to die from abusive treatment: 77 percent of all the children who died from abuse or neglect in 2001 were younger than 4 years of age (Coser & Cohen, 2003). If abused or neglected children do not die, they may suffer brain dysfunction, neuromotor handicaps, physical defects, stunted growth, and mental retardation. Abuse can slow intellectual development and cause psychosocial problems as well (Guterman, 2001).

Even as infants, abused children show less secure attachment and more noncompliant, resistant, and avoidant behaviour toward their mothers (Cicchetti & Toth, 2006; Lyons-Ruth & Jacobvitz, 1999). Moreover, abused children are more likely to have problems in regulating their emotions, tend to show less prosocial behaviour and empathy, and are more aggressive with their peers and more likely than non-abused children to be rejected by their classmates (Bolger & Patterson, 2001; Howe & Parke, 2001; Shields et al., 2001). In infancy and early childhood, sexually abused children, particularly girls, often display bedwetting problems (called *enuresis*). Abused boys are more likely to have somatic complaints, such as stomachache. Both boys and girls display inappropriate sexual behaviour and have higher anxiety and social withdrawal. Among sexually abused children, delays in cognitive and academic development are common as well (Trickett & Putnam, 1998).

As abused children advance through the school year, they tend not only to show problems in relations with peers, teachers, and caregivers but they also tend to have academic problems and low self-esteem, to exhibit behaviour problems, and, not surprisingly, to be depressed and withdrawn (Cicchetti & Toth, 2006). Problems are greater if abuse begins early (prior to age 5) rather than later (Keiley et al., 2001). Most abused children do not become delinquents or violent offenders. Long-term effects of abuse are most likely to be found if children remain in low-income socio-economic environments with multiple stresses and few supports available (Cicchetti & Toth, 2006). In sexually abused children, it is common to find inappropriate sexual behaviour directed toward themselves or other children and adults, play and fantasy with sexual content, earlier menarche and onset of sexual activity, as well as sexual and obesity problems in adulthood (Centers for Disease Control and Prevention, 2005; Noll et al., 2009; Vigil et al., 2005). Higher rates of fears, nightmares, aggressive behaviour, behaviour problems, and self-injurious behaviour have also been found (Cicchetti & Toth, 2006; Noll et al., 2006). Finally, more learning problems and poorer academic performance, as well as a greater number of attention-deficit hyperactivity disorder (ADHD) problems, have been found in sexually abused children (Feerick et al., 2006).

Prevention of Child Abuse

A variety of strategies help reduce rates of abuse (Golden, 2000; Thompson, 1995). First, increasing parents' understanding of children's developmental timetables reduces unrealistic expectations about children's progress. Second, teaching parents nonpunitive disciplinary tactics, such as timeout and reasoning, can help decrease abuse rates. Third, providing support networks, both formal and informal, to reduce the isolation of abusing families is helpful. And fourth, as some argue, another way to lessen the incidence of child abuse in our society may be to change our tendency to tolerate and even justify the use of violence in dealing with interpersonal and social problems (Donnelly & Straus, 2005; Thompson, 1995).

For Thought and Discussion

1. Given the various levels of factors that all contribute to child abuse, is it actually possible to determine the individual influences of each of these different levels? What impact might this have on interventions and/or treatment?

2. Clearly, one of the primary underlying factors related to child abuse is poverty. Given the importance of poverty, what possible steps might be taken to break the cycle of abuse?

Making the Connections 11

There are many links between concepts and ideas in one area of development and concepts and ideas in other areas. Here are some of the connections between ideas in Chapter 11 and discussions in other chapters of this book.

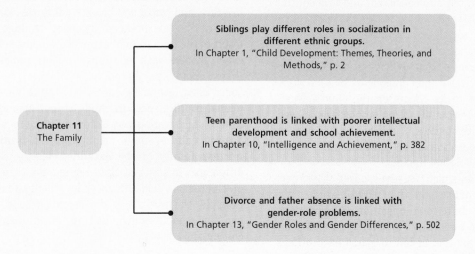

Chapter 11
The Family

Siblings play different roles in socialization in different ethnic groups.
In Chapter 1, "Child Development: Themes, Theories, and Methods," p. 2

Teen parenthood is linked with poorer intellectual development and school achievement.
In Chapter 10, "Intelligence and Achievement," p. 382

Divorce and father absence is linked with gender-role problems.
In Chapter 13, "Gender Roles and Gender Differences," p. 502

SUMMARY

- The family is both the earliest and the most sustained source of social contact for the child. The beliefs and values of the culture are filtered through the parents, and their interpretation is influenced by the parents' personalities, religion, social class, education, and gender.
- Parents, siblings, peers, and teachers are major agents of **socialization**. They may influence the child by directly teaching standards, rules, and values; by providing role models; by making attributions about the child; and by creating the environment in which the child lives.

The Family System

- The family is a complex system involving interdependent members whose functioning may be altered by changes in the behaviour of one member, by relationships among family members, and by changes over time. In addition, family functioning is influenced by the larger physical, cultural, and social setting in which the family lives.
- The functioning of the marital system, parent–child system, and sibling system are interrelated and influ-

ence children's adjustment. A satisfying marital relationship is often regarded as the basis of good family functioning, which directly or indirectly affects interactions with the children.

- Marital conflict is associated with negative feelings and behaviours directed toward the children and with disruptions in children's social and cognitive competence.
- Children have an impact on the marital relationship. Both mothers and fathers report declines in marital satisfaction following the birth of their first child, but fathers are slower to express such declines than are mothers.
- Parents begin to consciously and systematically socialize their child during the second year by saying "no" to some behaviours and by praising other behaviours. They also teach social rules directly, serve as models with whom the child may identify or imitate, and choose the environment and social life that their child will experience.
- Parental warmth and responsiveness are regarded as important to socialization, and some degree of parental control is necessary for positive social development. The goal should be the child's learning of self-regulation rather than continuing external control by the parents.

- The interaction of the dimensions of warmth and responsiveness with those of permissiveness and control creates a four-way typology: **authoritative**, **authoritarian**, **permissive**, and **uninvolved parenting**. Baumrind found that authoritative parenting involving high-warmth responsiveness and communication, but also consistent and firm control and high-maturity demands, led to the most positive emotional, social, and cognitive development in children and adolescents.
- Critics of Baumrind's typology have cited the need to identify more clearly the components of each style that contribute to its effects on the child's development, to pay more attention to the role played by the child's temperament and behaviour, and to scrutinize the question of the generalizability across cultures of the original findings.
- **Co-parenting**, in which, ideally, spouses or partners take a team approach in their child-rearing practices, can contribute to co-operation, cohesiveness, and harmony in the family. However, if parents compete with one another or fail to match each other's investment of time and energy in the work of parenting, the children may react with aggression, anxiety, or other kinds of problem behaviour.
- The functioning of the family is affected by the number of children, their gender, and the space of years between childbirths. As family size increases, parents and children have less opportunity for extensive contact, but siblings experience more contact.
- Variations in interactions with parents and siblings have been associated with birth order. First-born children often show emotional and behavioural problems after the birth of a sibling, but the outcome is mediated by the mother's reaction and efforts to include the first-born and by the father's involvement.
- First-borns are more adult oriented, helpful, self-controlled, conforming, and anxious than their siblings, and they tend to excel in academic and professional achievement. Although solo children experience many of the same parental demands of first-borns, they do not have to compete with siblings. Thus, they tend to be higher in achievement, but lower in anxiety, and make more positive adjustments in social relations both within and outside of the home.
- Eldest children are typically expected to assume some responsibility for the younger children. This leads both to antagonistic behaviour and to more nurturant behaviour toward younger siblings.
- The family unit is a distinct family subsystem and is responsible for the development and perpetuation of family stories and rituals, which transmit values, teach family roles, and reinforce the family's uniqueness.

Social Class, Ethnicity, and Socialization

- In addition to obvious differences in income, education, and occupation, lower-income and middle-class families may differ in other ways. Poor families generally experience little power within all the systems that they encounter, leading them to feel helpless, insecure, and controlled by external forces. However, the stresses experienced by poor families often result in the formation of extensive support networks which involve both emotional support and services that cannot be purchased.
- Social class, ethnicity, race, and culture have been related to differences in child-rearing. Among other things, child-rearing may differ according to whether a given cultural group emphasizes the **traditional nuclear family** or the **extended family**. Specific differences in styles of child-rearing and their effect on children are also influenced by other systems—for example, the workplace, the neighbourhood, peers, and the school—which, in turn, are influenced by culture and society.

The Changing Family Structure

- In recent years, family roles and forms have become more varied. As the number of working mothers has increased, the average size of households has decreased. Single-parent households have increased, due largely to rising divorce rates and increases in out-of-wedlock births.
- The overall effects of rising maternal employment have been related to the mother's reason for working, the mother's satisfaction with her role, the demands placed on other family members, the attitudes of the other family members, and the quality of substitute care provided for the children. If each of these is positive, maternal employment not only has no detrimental effects on children but instead may have specific positive effects, especially for girls.
- Divorce, life in a one-parent family, and remarriage should be viewed as part of a series of transitions that modify family roles and relationships. In the first year following divorce, the children in single-parent households tend to be more disturbed, but in the long run, most are able to adapt to their parents' divorce.
- Family interactions immediately following divorce are characterized by inept parenting on the part of custodial parents—usually mothers—and distressed, demanding, non-compliant behaviour on the part of children. These effects seem to last longer and to be more negative for preadolescent sons than for daughters.

- Children's responses to remarriage vary depending on the previous family experience, but the age at which the remarriage occurs is associated with the child's acceptance of the new parent. For adolescents, anti-social behaviour, depression and anxiety, school problems, and disruptions in peer relations have been associated with divorce and remarriage. In pre-adolescence, boys show the most negative responses to divorce and girls the most lasting resistance to remarriage.

- Although in nearly 75 percent of divorce and custody cases the children reside with the mother, a divorced couple may select either **joint legal custody** or **joint physical custody** arrangements.

- People are marrying and becoming parents later today than in earlier years, and there are some positive aspects to later parenthood, such as being better established in careers, feeling more responsible, and being more flexible about family roles.

- Gay and lesbian families are becoming increasingly common. The children of gay and lesbian couples develop as children of heterosexual marriages do, in that they generally adopt heterosexual lifestyles and their concepts of gender roles do not differ from those of children of heterosexual parents.

- Although on the decline, births to unwed adolescent mothers more than tripled between the 1960s and the 1990s. The younger the mother, the more likely the child is to experience cognitive and eventual academic deficits. Children of teen mothers are more likely to have behavioural problems, to have less self-control, and to show more anti-social behaviour, such as drug abuse and delinquency.

Child Abuse within the Family

- In 2005 in the United States, nearly 1 million cases of child abuse or neglect were substantiated, another two million cases were reported, and the number of unreported incidents was unknown. In Canada in 2003, there were 114,607 substantiated cases of child maltreatment. The severe abuse of children is most likely to occur in the presence of multiple risk factors and in the absence of such protective advantages as community resources, good health, high intelligence, education, and a supportive social network.

- Child abuse is more likely to occur in large families, to children under age 3, and to children with physical and intellectual deficits or who exhibit excessive fussiness and crying. Parents in abusive families often are socially isolated and have unrealistic beliefs about young children's abilities and about the parent–child relationship.

- Parents who abuse their children are frequently involved in a distressed marriage; have been abused by their own parents; and are unemployed, poorly educated, and economically deprived. No single factor leads to abuse. It is a product of the interactions among family characteristics, non-supportive environments, and cultural values that tolerate aggression and physical punishment as well as poverty, unemployment, and high-risk, dangerous neighbourhoods.

- The devastating consequences of child abuse include less secure attachment in infants; problems with emotional regulation and aggressive behaviour in toddlers; poor relations with peers and adults; academic problems, and low self-esteem as children get older; brain dysfunction; mental retardation; neuromotor deficits; physical handicaps—and death.

MCGRAW-HILL CONNECT™—Available 24/7 with instant feedback so you can study when you want, how you want, and where you want. Take advantage of the Study Plan—an innovative tool that helps you customize your learning experience. You can diagnose your knowledge with pre- and post-tests, identify the areas where you need help, search the entire learning package for content specific to the topic you're studying, and add these resources to your personalized study plan. Visit *www.mcgrawhillconnect.ca* to register—take practice quizzes, search the e-book, and much more.

www.mcgrawhillconnect.ca

Pavel Kuznetsov (1878–1968). *Pushball*.

Chapter 12

Expanding the Social World: Peers and Friends

LEARNING OBJECTIVES

After reading this chapter, you should be able to

LO 1 Identify and describe developmental trends in peer interactions; describe the roles of peers in socialization.

LO 2 Discuss the typical assessment of peer status; identify the major factors that determine acceptance by peers.

LO 3 Identify the consequences of rejection by peers and ways in which parents and teachers facilitate social skills to promote peer acceptance.

LO 4 Describe trends in the development of friendship.

LO 5 Discuss differences in the amount and kind of influence exerted by parents and peers on children.

LO 6 Discuss the process of peer-group formation, organization, and functioning.

LO 7 Cite different functions of the peer group in a variety of cultures.

We have become increasingly aware, in recent years, of how important people outside the family are in socializing children. The roles that peers, friends, and teachers play in this process have gained significance as more and more mothers work outside the home and as preschool care and education have become more prevalent. In this chapter, we focus on how children's friends and peers contribute to their socialization.

Children's relationships with their peers differ from relations with their parents in several ways. In general, relations with peers are less enduring than those with family, especially parents. Interactions among agemates are freer and more egalitarian. This greater fluidity offers children the opportunity for a new kind of interpersonal exploration. In particular, it facilitates the growth of social competence, encourages a sense of social justice, and opens the way for children to form relationships with people outside the family (Dunn, 2004).

We start out by looking at the child's first encounters with peers in early infancy. We then examine the special roles peers play in children's socialization, such as modelling behaviours for each other. Next, we consider the many factors that affect children's acceptance by peers, such as the ability to interact with others smoothly. We explore the kinds of problems that children can face in peer relationships and consider some ways of resolving them. We then explore the roles of parents, teachers, and others in promoting children's acceptance by peers and look at the ways children make friends. Then, we turn to children's behaviours in groups, examining the way children form "pecking orders" and cliques, or groups of friends that are often exclusive. Finally, we look at some cultural differences in peer relationships. Throughout these discussions, we will see changes over time in children's relations with their peers—changes that are reflected in our Turning Points chart on page 470. ●

Canadian Researchers

LO 1 HOW PEER INTERACTIONS BEGIN: DEVELOPMENTAL PATTERNS

Interactions with peers begin to shape children's behaviour at an early age. Even in their earliest months, babies begin to react to each other, and when children begin to utter their first words and phrases, social interaction really gets under way. Gradually, children spend increasing amounts of time with peers, and by the time they are 3 years old, toddlers generally prefer interaction with peers to that with adults (Dunn, 2004).

Infancy: First Social Encounters

Babies are very curious about each other. In their first six months of life, they touch and look at each other and are surprisingly responsive to each other's behaviour. If one child cries, another may cry too. But these early responses cannot be considered truly social in the sense of the infant's seeking and expecting a response from another child. It is not until the second half of the first year that infants begin to recognize a peer as a social partner (Brownell, 1990; Dunn, 2004). Between 6 and 12 months of age, an infant will start trying to influence another child by vocalizing, by looking at or waving at the child, or by touching him. At this age infants even show the ability to interact in groups, and to be involved with more than one person at the same time (Selby & Bradley, 2003). Although babies do hit and push sometimes, a considerable amount of social behaviour among the baby crowd is friendly (Eckerman & Didow, 1988; Rubin et al., 2006). Here is a classic example:

> Larry sits on the floor, and Bernie turns and looks toward him. Bernie waves his hand and says "da," still looking at Larry. He repeats the vocalization three more times before Larry laughs. Bernie vocalizes again, and Larry laughs again. Then, the same sequence of one child saying "da" and the other laughing is repeated 12 more times before Bernie turns away from Larry and walks off. Bernie and Larry become distracted at times during the interchange. Yet, when this happens, the partner reattracts attention either by repeating his socially directed action or by modifying it, as when Bernie both waves and says "da," re-engaging Larry. (Mueller & Lucas, 1975, p. 241)

As children develop competence in interacting with peers, they shift toward increased social play and exhibit a clear preference for playing with peers rather than adults. In a classic study of social play in children between 10 months and 2 years of age, Eckerman, Whatley, and Kutz (1975) found that older children engaged in significantly more social play than younger ones, but were less interested than the younger children in playing with their mothers and more interested in playing with peers.

Social exchanges with mothers differ from those with peers (Dunn, 2004; Rubin et al., 2006; Vandell & Wilson, 1987). Babies find mothers more reliable and more responsive than infants. Exchanges with mothers are longer and more sustained, but the interchanges may be a bit one-sided. Mothers tend to bear the larger responsibility for maintaining the interaction, whereas in exchanges between infant peers, the two partners contribute more equally. Mothers make it easy; peers make you work for your social life!

Social Exchange among Toddlers

Between the ages of 1 and 2, children make gains in locomotion and language that increase the complexity of their social exchange (Dunn, 2004; Rubin et al., 2006). During this period, they develop the capacity to engage in complementary social interaction (Howes, 1987). That is, partners take turns and exchange roles in their play so that, for example, Jason may play "hider" and Samantha "seeker," and then Samantha may hide while Jason seeks. Peers begin to imitate one another's activity, and to show awareness that they are being imitated (Eckerman, 1993). Now, too, when children engage in positive social interactions, they are more likely to smile or laugh or display other kinds of appropriate positive affect (Mueller & Brenner, 1977), and their interactions last longer (Ross & Conant, 1992).

In the late toddler period (25 to 36 months), the child's main social achievement is the ability to share meaning with a social partner (Dunn, 2004):

> *When children communicate meanings, they know how to play a particular game, for example, being pulled in or pulling a wagon, the signal or invitation to begin the game (eye gaze, plus run to wagon), the signal to switch roles ("my turn" plus a tug) and how to communicate that they share this knowledge. . . . Children's communication of meaning makes possible a wider range of games and variations on the themes of games, as well as early forms of pretend play.* (Howes, 1987, p. 260)

Table 12-1 summarizes Parten's (1932) classic description of the types of play that characterize the social exchanges of 2½ to 4 year olds. The complexity of toddlers' play increases over age: solitary play and parallel play diminish as the child grows older, and associative and co-operative play both increase in frequency. There is, of course, overlap: some 4-year-olds are still engaging in solitary play, while some precocious 2½-year-olds are busily engaged in co-operative play bouts.

Table 12-1

Types of play in preschool-age children

Solitary play
Children play by themselves and generally ignore other children who are near. About half of 2-year-olds engage in this type of play.

Parallel play
Two children play in similar activities, often side by side, but do not engage one another. This type of play is common in 2-year-olds but diminishes by the time a child is 3 or 4 years old.

Associative play
Children play with other children but do not necessarily share the same goals or agendas. They share toys and materials, and they may even react to or comment on another child's ongoing activities (e.g., sharing paints or remarking on another child's art work). However, they are still not fully engaged with each other in a joint project. This type of play is commonly seen in 3- and 4-year-olds, less often in 2-year-olds.

Co-operative play
At age 3–4, children begin to engage in this sophisticated type of play in which they co-operate, reciprocate, and share common goals. Some examples of co-operative play are building a sand castle, drawing a picture together, and playing a fantasy game in which characters interact with each other.

Turning Points

PEER RELATIONSHIPS AND THE DEVELOPMENT OF FRIENDSHIPS

0–6 MONTHS	• Touches and looks at another infant and cries in response to the other's crying
6–12 MONTHS	• Tries to influence another baby by looking, touching, vocalizing, laughing, or waving • Interactions with other infants are generally friendly, but may sometimes hit or push another
13–24 MONTHS	• Begins to adopt complementary behaviour (e.g., taking turns, exchanging roles) • Social play increases throughout this period • Begins to engage in imaginative play
25–36 MONTHS	• In play and other social interaction, begins to communicate meaning, such as inviting another to play or signalling that it's time to switch roles • Begins to prefer peer over adult companions
3 YEARS	• Begins to engage in complex co-operative and dramatic play • Starts to prefer same-sex playmates
4 YEARS	• Shares more with peers than 3-year-olds do • May engage in fantasy play that's designed to master specific fears
4½ YEARS	• Begins to have longer play sequences and is more willing to accept roles other than the protagonist
6 YEARS	• Reaches a peak in imaginative play
3–7 YEARS	• Main friendship goal is coordinated and successful play
7 YEARS	• Shows stable preference for same-sex playmates
7–9 YEARS	• Expects friends to share activities, offer help, be physically nearby
8–12 YEARS	• Main goal of friendship is to be accepted by one's same-sex peers
9–11 YEARS	• Expects friends to accept and admire her and to be loyal and committed to the relationship • Is likely to build friendships on the basis of earlier interactions
11–13 YEARS	• Expects genuineness, intimacy, self-disclosure, common interests, and similar attitudes and values in friends • Emergence of cliques
13–16 YEARS	• Important friendship goal: understanding of the self; beginnings of cross-gender relationships, often in group contexts • Development of crowds in the high-school years
16–18 YEARS	• Expects friends to provide emotional support; increase in dyadic romantic ties and development of exclusive romantic alliances

Note: Developmental events described in this and other Turning Points charts represent overall trends identified in research studies. Individual children vary greatly in the ages at which they achieve these developmental changes.

Sources: Collins & Van Dulmen, 2006; Dunn, 2004; Ladd, 2005; Rubin, Bukowski, & Parker, 2006.

As children develop, negative exchanges and conflict increase as well (Dunn, 2004; Hay & Ross, 1982; Rubin et al., 2006). In fact, socializing and getting into conflicts seem to go together. As Brown and Brownell (1990) found, toddlers who frequently initiated conflicts with peers were also the most sociable and the most likely to initiate interactions. It takes a little time to learn to manage your social interchanges effectively.

As children become familiar with each other, their early peer interactions tend to develop into relationships. In a **relationship**, two acquaintances share an ongoing succession of interactions that continues over time and that affects each other (Dunn, 2004; Rubin et al., 2006). That is, in every encounter between the partners, both their history of past interactions and their expectations of future interactions influence the nature and course of events. Hildy Ross from the University of Waterloo and her colleagues (Ross et al., 1992) have found that toddlers develop relationships that are based on both positive and negative exchanges. In their simple give-and-take exchanges, these young peers display an elementary form of friendship. Interestingly, children between the ages of 1 and 2 develop preferences for particular playmates: it is a clear sign of early friendship formation that not just any other child will do. And these early social choices of special friends are not temporary: 50 to 70 percent of early friendships last over a year, and in some cases, over several years (Dunn, 2004; Howes, 1996). Nor are early relationships limited to just dyads: even 2-year-olds can interact in a three-toddler group and exhibit not just dyadic but triadic, or three-way, interchanges as well (Ishikawa & Hay, 2006). Clearly, toddlers are capable of more complex social exchanges than we previously thought. We explore the topic of friendship in some detail later in the chapter.

relationship

A succession of interactions between two people who know each other that is altered by their shared, past interactions and that also affects their future interactions.

Preschool and Elementary School Society

As children move into preschool and elementary school, they continue to seek out and engage in more and more peer interactions. With whom do children of various ages spend time? In their study of social interaction, Ellis and colleagues (1981) found that the 400 children they observed were alone 26 percent of the time, with other children 46 percent, and with adults and peers 15 percent of the time. As Figure 12-1 shows, over time, children spend more hours with child companions and fewer with adults. These trends continue into adolescence, when children grow into spending less time with family and more time either alone or with friends (Larson, 1997).

Larson (1997) found that among both European-American and African-American preadolescents and adolescents, talking with peers increased dramatically between the ages of 10 and 15. Interestingly, when Larson (Larson & Verma, 1999) compared US, Korean, and Japanese twelfth graders, they found that the US teens spent more than

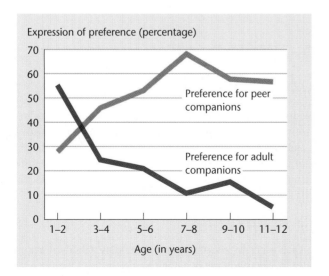

Figure 12-1

Peers preferred

At about the age of 2½ years, children begin to prefer other children as companions over adults, and their choice of adults for companionship dwindles rapidly over time.

Source: Ellis, Rogoff, & Cromer, 1981.

Figure 12-2

Girls/boys aren't so bad after all

This study showed that (a) both girls and boys in elementary and middle school generally chose same-sex others for companions; (b) beginning in grade 9, the amount of time children spent with opposite-sex friends increased significantly, especially for girls, who mature earlier than boys.

Source: Richards, Crowe, Larson, & Swarr, 1998.

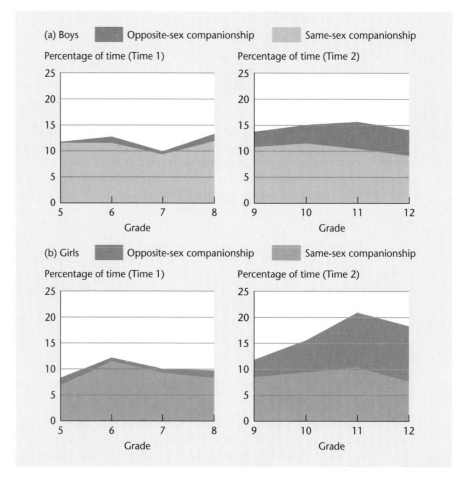

twice as much time each day talking with each other (2.5 hours per day) than did the Korean and Japanese teens (1.0 hours per day).

The kinds of peers children choose to spend time with change also. Age becomes a more important factor; for example, companionship with peers of the same age grows over time. Gender, too, begins to matter. Up to age 3 or 4, children choose same- and opposite-sex companions, but after this, both boys and girls prefer same- to opposite-gender play partners. Adolescence, of course, heralds a reversal, as cross-gender friendships begin to blossom once again (Richards et al., 1998; Rubin et al., 2006) (see Figure 12-2).

HOW DO PEERS HELP TO SOCIALIZE CHILDREN?

Peers play a role in socializing children, just as families do. Peers offer a perspective quite different from that of the family—the perspective of equals who share common abilities, goals, and problems. How does the peer group influence the child's development? In many of the same ways parents do—through modelling, reinforcement, and social comparison and by providing opportunities for learning and socializing.

Modelling Behaviours

Peers influence each other by serving as social models. Children acquire knowledge behaviours simply by observing the behaviour and actions of their peers. For example,

Colin is spending his first day at a new school. Through observing the other students, he rapidly learns that children are expected to stand when the teacher enters the room, that it is risky to shoot spitballs, and that he should avoid contact with the big, grumpy kid because he is the class bully. Colin may also learn new social skills by modelling, or imitating, Melissa and Tom, who appear to be the class leaders and more socially skilled than some other members of the group (Grusec & Abramovitch, 1982).

Children also imitate older, more powerful, and more prestigious peer models (Bandura, 1989; Rubin et al., 2006). But imitation serves other purposes besides rule learning. It can often be an important way of maintaining social interaction. As Eckerman (1993; Eckerman & Peterman, 2001) suggests, even in 2-year-olds, imitation sustains joint play between partners and leads to more sophisticated forms of play in social games, and, ultimately, to the generation of verbal communication (Didow & Eckerman, 2001).

As we will see, in many cultures, siblings are primary caregivers for infants and toddlers. This allows the young child to learn from peers of different age groups. Some observers have suggested that the rigid age grading common to many Western institutions such as schools and sports organizations may alter or at least limit children's opportunities to learn. What do you think?

Teaching and Reinforcing

As children develop, they begin to reinforce their peers' behaviours. To *reinforce* is to pay attention to another's behaviour, to praise or criticize it, or to share in it. No one knows this better than parents—especially parents of adolescents—who often bemoan the fact that their children ignore wise parental advice and instead listen to, and emulate, their peers. As the concept of "peer pressure" implies, childhood and adolescent peers can convince their compatriots to take risks and engage in deviant behaviour. Clearly, peers' influence can be harmful as well as beneficial. Throughout the preschool years, peers are increasingly likely to reinforce each other: One study found that 4-year-olds praised, attended to, or shared with their peers more than 3 year olds did (Charlesworth & Hartup, 1967). And reciprocity begins to grow, as nursery schoolers reinforce the same peers who reinforce them (Hartup, 1983). The notion that peer reinforcement in the form of attention and approval affects a child's behavioural patterns has considerable research support. Peers' differential reinforcement can produce significant changes in the target child's behaviour (Furman & Gavin, 1989; Rubin et al., 2006).

Children respond to negative reinforcement, too. Just think of the looks and comments an adolescent who wears the wrong clothes is likely to elicit or of the reactions preschoolers are likely to get if they play with toys generally regarded as meant for the opposite sex. Peers can quickly whip an errant child into shape by giving looks, offering biting comments, or ostracizing the child from the group (Lamb & Roopnarine, 1979).

Interaction with peers also provides an opportunity for specific instruction and learning (Ladd, 2005; Zarbatany et al., 1990). In Western cultures, one can see this in school games and sports and in tutorial arrangements, in which children teach each other and acquire new skills together. In some other cultures, such as those of India, Kenya, and Mexico, both older peers and siblings teach and are caregivers for younger children (Maynard, 2002; Rogoff, 2002; Whiting & Edwards, 1988).

Social Comparison and the Developing Self

Peers may help a child develop her self-image and self-esteem by providing standards against which to measure herself. There are few objective ways to rate one's own characteristics, abilities, and values, and children turn to other people, particularly to peers, for help. Through **social comparison**, children watch and talk with their peers and then use what they have learned to evaluate themselves.

social comparison

The process of evaluating one's characteristics, abilities, values, and other qualities by comparing oneself with others, usually one's peers.

Children build self-esteem, in part, by comparing their own characteristics, abilities, and skills with those of their peers.

Research has shown that in the early elementary school years, children display a marked increase in their use of social comparison, with the peer group as a means of self-evaluation (Harter, 2006; Ruble, 1987; Zarbatany et al., 1990). And the child's self-image and self-acceptance are closely associated with how she is received by her peers. This social-comparison process helps the child define her own self-image and self-esteem (Harter, 2006). How well children think they "stack up" against their peers plays a major role in the development of their self-esteem. If you think you are as good as your peers, your self-esteem is high, but if you see yourself as falling short, your self-esteem suffers.

How do we choose the particular person with whom we want to compare ourselves? It is likely that if a child wants to know how good a fighter he is, he thinks about how he has done in neighbourhood scuffles and how tough his peers seem to think he is; he does not compare himself with Georges Laraque or Tie Domi. If a child wants to evaluate her reading ability, she most probably compares herself with other children in her class; she is pretty unlikely to judge herself by how many words her mother can read or by how rapidly her teacher reads. As a basis for self-definition, the peer group is unequalled.

For Thought and Discussion

1. In what context do you think children learn many of the social skills needed to conduct successful peer interactions? Who do you think is the principal figure that children use to practise such skills? What does this say about the interconnectedness of development (e.g., the relation between, say, family and peers or peers and the neighbourhood)?

2. Although researchers talk about, and have obtained evidence of, peer interaction in infancy, these interactions are limited in many (obvious) ways. This raises the issue of how best to define peer interaction. Put differently, what behaviours qualify as true exchanges between peers?

LO2 PEER ACCEPTANCE

Children place enormous significance on being accepted by peers, and peer acceptance is of great importance to children's social development. Interacting with peers is the child's first experience of social behaviour beyond the family, and when this experience is positive, it can lay the foundation for healthy adult social behaviour. In this section, we look first at the way psychologists study children's status among their peers and at their discoveries about the factors that affect children's judgments of others. Then, we examine the way children are affected by their peers' view of them and interactions with them. Based on our findings here, we go on to consider how we can promote healthy social interactions in children.

How Do We Study Peer Acceptance?

sociometric technique

A procedure for determining children's status within their peer group in which peers nominate others whom they like best or least or rate each child in the group for her likeability or desirability as a companion.

A common way of studying peer acceptance is to assess the status of children in a specific peer group. To do this, developmental psychologists generally use **sociometric techniques** in which they ask children to rate peers on scales of aggressiveness or helpfulness or to compare peers as to likeability or to identify those whom they like best (Ladd, 2005; Poulin & Dishion, 2008).

Why do psychologists ask children, rather than teachers or other adults, to provide them with data on children's peer status? First, as insiders in the group, peers see a wider range of relevant behaviours than do adults. Second, peers have extended and varied experience with each other. And third, by gathering data from many individuals who have interacted with the child who is the subject of study, we prevent any single individual's view from dominating our results.

Let's look at a method of study called the *nominations technique*, in which an investigator begins by asking each child in a group to name a specific number (usually three) of peers whom he likes "especially" and the same number of peers whom he does not like "very much." Next, the investigator sums the scores of all the "like most" and "like least" choices and assigns children to one of several groups. **Popular children** are those who have received the greatest number of positive nominations and the fewest negative ones. Children whom their peers judge as popular are friendly and assertive but not disruptive or aggressive. When they join a play group, they do it so smoothly that the ongoing action can continue without interruption (Black & Hazen, 1990; Newcomb et al., 1993). Children like this are good at communication; they help set the rules and norms for their groups, and they engage in more prosocial behaviour than less popular children.

Not all popular children fit this profile. Some children who are perceived as popular are also characterized as athletic, cool, dominant, arrogant, and both physically and relationally aggressive. These children and adolescents may wield high levels of social influence even though their actions are often manipulative in nature (Cillessen & Mayeux, 2004; Cillessen & Rose, 2005; Rodkin et al., 2000). In short, there is more than one pathway to popularity.

Average children receive some of both types of nominations, but are neither as well liked as popular peers nor as disliked as peers in other categories. **Neglected children** are isolated, often friendless children but are not necessarily disliked by their classmates; they receive few like or dislike votes. And children termed neglected are less aggressive, less talkative, and more withdrawn. **Controversial children** receive many positive nominations but also a lot of negative ones. **Rejected children** receive many negative nominations. **Aggressive rejected children** are characterized by aggressiveness, poor self-control, and behavioural problems, although their self-perceptions are not poor (Hymel et al., 1993). **Non-aggressive rejected children** tend to be anxious, withdrawn, and socially unskilled (Bierman et al., 1993; French, 1990; Ladd, 2005; Parkhurst & Asher, 1992), and have been found to perceive themselves as less competent (Verschueren & Marcoen, 2002). Children can be rejected for different reasons; they, in turn, are capable of responding to rejection in different ways (Schneider, 2000).

However, as we saw in our discussion of popular children, aggressive children who are competent and develop social networks are unlikely to be rejected and may even be popular (Cairns & Cairns, 1994; Rubin et al., 2006).

Factors That Affect Peer Status

What factors influence children's appraisals of one another? Research suggests that probably the single most significant factor is a child's cognitive and social skills—his ability to initiate interactions with others, to communicate effectively and interact comfortably with them, to be responsive to others' interests and behaviours, and to cooperate with others in play and school activities (Coie, Dodge, & Kupersmidt, 1990; Rubin et al., 2006; Schneider, 2000). In this section, we focus first on exploring these kinds of skills and the ways in which children develop them.

We will also have to look, however, at some less crucial factors in peer acceptance that are as influential with children as they are with adults. When people meet others, especially for the first time, they are likely to base their initial appraisals of the person on such superficial characteristics as name or physical appearance, or even enduring characteristics such as race, gender, or age. Unfortunately, children often do this, too.

popular children
Children who are liked by many peers and disliked by very few.

average children
Children who have some friends but are not as well liked as popular children.

neglected children
Children who tend to be socially isolated and, though they have few friends, are not necessarily disliked by others.

controversial children
Children who are liked by many peers but also disliked by many.

rejected children
Children who are disliked by many peers and liked by very few.

aggressive rejected children
Rejected children who are characterized by high levels of aggressive behaviour, low self-control, and behavioural problems.

non-aggressive rejected children
Rejected children who tend to be withdrawn, anxious, and socially unskilled.

ACQUIRING SOCIAL-COGNITIVE SKILLS

Think about how you react when new people join a group of which you are a member. What do you think of a person who smiles in a friendly way and asks you about yourself and the group? What do you think of someone who stands on the edge of the group and makes no effort to approach anyone? Which person would you be most likely to chat with or invite to join you in a particular activity? Probably, the first, although, of course, there are always extenuating circumstances.

In the same way, the child who asks new acquaintances for information (e.g., "Where do you live?"), offers information (e.g., "My favourite sport is soccer"), or invites another child to join in an activity (e.g., "Wanna help me build this fort?") is well on the way to being accepted by the group (Rubin et al., 2006). On the other hand, the child who tries to initiate social interaction by hovering about a group silently or by making inappropriate or aggressive remarks is likely losing friends before she even gets started. To feel comfortable approaching a new social situation, a child needs to want to interact with others, to feel confident that she has something useful to contribute to the group, and to be interested in learning what others in the group are like—what their interests are and what they think about many things.

PROCESSING AND ACTING ON SOCIAL INFORMATION

Approaching a new social situation is similar to solving a cognitive problem or puzzle. A child approaching the new group of peers needs to understand others' communications clearly, to interpret their behaviour accurately, to formulate his own goals and strategies based on these interpretations, to make useful decisions, to communicate clearly to others, and to try out and then evaluate his strategies. This is quite a large order, especially for a young child, and some are better at it than others. To examine the interplay of these complicated functions in a social situation, Crick and Dodge (1994) devised the model of social information processing illustrated in Figure 12-3. Although the model stresses the cognitive steps in evaluating problems that a child confronts when interacting with others, it is important to remember that individual biological predispositions, such as a tendency to be impulsive, also play a role in accounting for variations in the decision-making process (Dodge & Pettit, 2003). As we study a child's progress through this scheme of processing, we will see that at every one of the six steps outlined, the child must make a decision or take an action that may be accurate or inaccurate, helpful or unhelpful.

Vimala, 7 years old and quite socially competent, approaches two children playing a board game. She notices that one of the girls smiles at her in a friendly way (step 1, encodes cues). She concludes that the girl would like her to play too (step 2, interprets cues), and decides that she wants to make friends (step 3, clarifies goals). Next, she reviews possible actions to further her goal—smile back, ask to join in—and consider how the girls might react to each possible choice (step 4, reviews actions/responses). Vimala decides to make a friendly comment about the girl's game (step 5, decides). Just then, the smiling girl looks up again, and Vimala smiles back and says, "Looks like fun" (step 6, acts). The girls invite her to play the next game.

Now replace Vimala with Christopher, 6 years old and less competent socially. Christopher sees two boys playing, but because he is looking at their sneakers, he misses the friendly look one boy gives him (step 1, encodes the wrong cues). Christopher decides that the boys are unfriendly (step 2, incorrectly interprets cues) and wonders what he might do. He thinks of some hostile things—ask the boys why they do not invite him to play, call them mean—fails to consider how they might react (steps 3 and 4, fails to clarify goal and review possible acts and responses). Christopher decides on the latter approach (step 5, decides) and blurts out, "You two are really selfish not to let me play!" (step 6, acts). It is no great surprise that the boys ignore him and move off.

Using these models, Dodge (1986) and co-workers compared 5- to 7-year-old children who were rated either socially competent or socially incompetent by their teachers and peers. They presented children with a video of situations similar to the ones just

Joining a group of peers who are already friends with one another is often difficult. Self-confidence, persistence, and the ability to adopt a new strategy when another has not worked are all helpful in this regard.

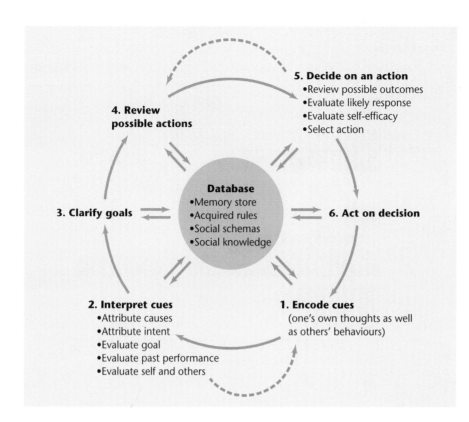

Figure 12-3

An information-processing model of children's social behaviour

This model outlines the way children perceive and interpret a social situation, decide what they want to achieve in that situation, choose a behaviour they think likely to accomplish their goal, and act on their decisions (steps 1–6). Note that the child's "database" consists of memories of other situations and acts, learned rules of social behaviour, and his general social knowledge. As the double arrows indicate, the child's thinking and action both draw on the database and contribute to it. The dashed-line arrows point out that the child may refer back to the preceding step and perhaps change his plan for the one he's about to take.

Source: Adapted from Crick & Dodge, 1994.

described in which a child is trying to join the play of two other children, and asked their participants about what they would do in each of five stages (the researchers omitted step 3 in this study). Predicting that children of various levels of competence would respond differently, the researchers found just that. The incompetent children were less likely to notice and interpret the cues correctly, generated fewer competent responses, chose less appropriate responses, and, in the next phase of the experiment, were less skilled at actually enacting or carrying out the behaviour. The researchers then asked the children to participate in an actual peer-group entry task with two peers from their classroom. Measures at each of the five stages in the model predicted children's competence and success at this task; children who understood what to do were better at the real task of gaining entry into the peer group (see Figure 12-4 on the next page). These studies provide strong support for the role of cognitive factors in understanding children's social relationships with peers. Deficits in social understanding can lead to poor social relationships. In this case, thought and action are clearly linked.

Let's look at some of these steps in more detail, since other experts have found support for many of the components of the Crick and Dodge model. First, rejected children, especially aggressive ones, tend to view others in hostile terms and to make hostile attributions about other peers' intentions (Burks et al., 1999). Second, not all children have the same goals and strategies in social situations. Chung and Asher (1996) suggest that one needs to be aware of one's goals in a social situation and to have the ability to devise a few strategies to achieve those goals. Not surprisingly, certain kinds of social goals tend to be accompanied by certain kinds of strategies. For example, children who want to have relationships with others are more likely to use prosocial strategies in interacting with their peers. On the other hand, children who want to control others may choose hostile and coercive strategies.

Why do some children develop positive goals and strategies and others negative goals and behaviours? One important explanation is that children differ in the way they perceive themselves and in the way they explain why they are sometimes successful at a task and sometimes unsuccessful.

Figure 12-4

Social competence and social-processing skills

Children who were more socially competent and better adjusted displayed fewer deficits in their ability to process cues and other information in social situations than children who were socially incompetent.

Source: Adapted from Dodge et al., 1987.

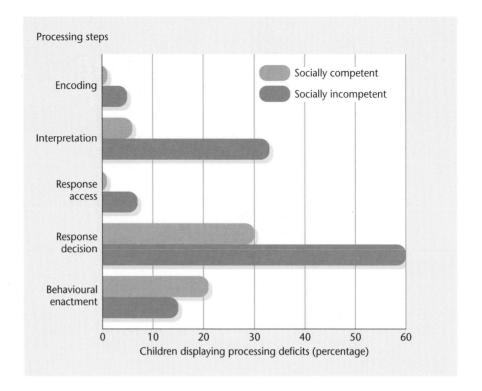

Clearly, a child who thinks that she did not succeed at something because she just did not try hard enough may well try again, but the child who believes that there is something lacking within herself may give up. Dweck, who has conducted extensive research on children's implicit theories of personality, suggests that one way to circumvent the latter kind of thinking is to prevent the child from seeing a task or problem as a measure of her ability and instead to focus the child's attention on just trying out something new and possibly useful (Dweck, 2006).

In a study testing this notion, Erdley and colleagues (1997) told children that they were trying out for membership in a pen-pal club, and they divided the children into a learning-goal group and a performance-goal group. The researchers told the children in the first group that the important thing was that the task would help them "practise and improve" their ways of making friends. "So think of it as a chance to work on your skills," they continued, "and maybe learn some new ones." They told the children in the second group that what they were interested in was "how good" they were at striking up new friendships: "Think of it as a chance for you to see how good you are at making friends."

The children given the learning goal were more persistent and, ultimately, more successful than the children given the performance goal. The latter were much more likely to give up (Dweck, 2006; Ladd, 2005). This work is consistent with Bandura's social self-efficacy theory that we outlined in Chapter 1.

It is important to recognize that the relations between the information-processing steps in the model and actual behaviour with peers are reciprocal. Although we assume that biased processing of social information leads to maladaptive social behaviour and poor peer acceptance, the model recognizes that maladaptive behaviour over time can lead to the development of social-information-processing deficits as well (Gifford-Smith & Rabiner, 2004). For example, Dodge and his colleagues (2003) found that children who were rejected by peers in kindergarten became, as the researchers predicted, less competent social processors in grades 2 and 3. The experience of early peer rejection, either by confirming biased processing patterns or by limiting a child's ability to acquire necessary social experience, leads to greater cognitive deficits which, in turn, contribute to maladaptive behaviour and less acceptance by peers.

BEAUTY MAY BE ONLY SKIN DEEP, BUT IT'S WAY COOL When they encounter someone new, children are just as likely as adults to base their impressions on the person's physical appearance. As you will recall from Chapter 4, when newborns view pictures of unfamiliar faces that have been judged "attractive" and "unattractive," they look more at the attractive ones (Langlois et al., 2000; Slater et al., 2000). And 3-year-olds show the same preference, choosing attractive over unattractive faces (Langlois, 1985).

People in general tend to attribute positive qualities to those who are physically attractive, and children and adolescents go right along with this tendency (Hawley et al., 2007; Langlois et al., 2000). Children expect to find characteristics such as friendliness, willingness to share, fearlessness, and self-sufficiency in good-looking peers and often think unattractive children are likely to be aggressive, anti-social, and mean. Teenagers, almost uniformly prefer good-looking partners, viewing unattractive ones as unacceptable.

Have our expectations that attractive people will demonstrate positive characteristics and behaviour any basis in reality? Langlois and her colleagues (2000) confirmed many of these expectations and underscored that beauty and attractiveness may be more important than we thought. Attractive children are judged more positively (higher on social appeal, adjustment, and interpersonal competence) than unattractive children—even by those who know them. You get treated better if you are attractive, too. The more attractive children were treated more positively and less negatively by others, even by people who were familiar with these children. Finally, attractive children were more popular, better adjusted, and even displayed greater intelligence. Perhaps it is time to re-evaluate our cultural myths: Beauty is more that just skin deep after all (Langlois et al., 2000).

Timing of puberty matters as well. Recall from Chapter 6 that boys who are early maturers tend to be more readily accepted by older peers. On the down side, this leads to more risk taking and problem behaviours as well (Ge et al., 2002). Early-maturing girls, on the other hand, have a smaller network of close friends and more adjustment problems that on-time or late maturing females (Stice et al., 2001).

"WE LIKE TO HAVE (BOYS) (GIRLS)" Preschoolers Jake and Danny are playing on the big swing, and Laura runs up, calling excitedly, "Can I get on?" "No!" says Jake, emphatically, "We don't want you on here. We only want boys on here." When researcher Zick Rubin asks why boys will not play with Laura, Jake replies simply, "Because we like boys—we like to have boys" (Leaper, 1994). Up to the age of 7, children are usually willing to play with peers of either gender, but as you see, even in the preschool years, gender discrimination can occur.

The tendency to gender-exclusivity increases throughout elementary school (Maccoby, 1998), and it's not until early adolescence that children once again choose opposite-gender companions—this time, as dates. There are exceptions, but they often operate underground. For example, a boy and girl may spend time together in church work or in neighbourhood activities but they keep their friendship a secret from their classmates (Gottman, 1986; Thorne, 1986). Too bad, say some researchers, for cross-gender play can introduce boys and girls to a broader range of behavioural styles and activities (Rubin, 1980). It can expand their pool of potential friends and "promote a better understanding of the qualities that are shared by both sexes" (Rubin, 1980, p. 104).

Grade 3 and 4 children who had cross-gender friendships as well as same-gender friendships were among the most well accepted, socially skilled children in the group (Kovacs et al., 1996). In contrast, children whose primary friendships, or only friendships, were with opposite-sex peers were less well accepted, judged less skilled academically and socially, and tended to report lower self-esteem. Similarly, others have found that boys who had girls in their friendship networks reported greater intimacy with their same-gender best friends (Zarbatany et al., 2000).

One reason elementary-school children tend to choose same-gender playmates is the traditional difference in preferred activities. Boys spend a lot of time playing team sports, whereas girls may prefer less organized activities, such as walking and talking. As girls' participation in team sports continues to grow, however, perhaps playmate choices will change, too.

Recently, McDougall & Hymel (2007) examined children's own beliefs about same- and cross-gender friendships by interviewing grades 3, 6, 9, and 12 children about their conceptions regarding such relationships. The researchers found that children do view these relationships differently, with students more commonly expecting mutual liking, similarity, loyalty, and intimacy from their same-sex friendships, and emphasizing issues of having a good character, being nice, and not harming a friend's ego in cross-gender friendships. Interestingly, these conceptions were largely found to hold across the different ages in this study. Overall, and as these authors suggest, the topic of cross-gender friendships requires a great deal more research and thought to fully appreciate the significance of these relationships for children's development.

Finally, it is important not to exaggerate the differences in peer relationship styles of boys and girls (Underwood, 2004). Boys and girls participate in both co-operative and competitive activities. Team sports, for example, foster both types of goals. And as we will see in Chapter 14, girls can be as aggressive as boys but generally express aggression differently. In addition, recent work has questioned the claim that boys' and girls' social networks are different in size or structure; for example, girls and boys are equally likely to be central members of their respective cliques (Bagwell et al., 2000; Cairns & Cairns, 1994). There are many similarities in the behaviours of boys and girls in their respective peer relationships.

WHAT'S IN A NAME? OR AN AGE?   Children learn very quickly what given names are popular among their peers and thus "acceptable," and often they may think another child's name "funny" or worry that their own name is odd. As a result, they are more likely to be friendly to a peer with a name that is familiar to them, such as Michelle or Jason, than to a child with a name that is currently out of favour, such as Horace or Myrtle (Rubin et al., 2006). Few children realize that name trends change constantly.

In Western societies, play groups, especially those of young children, tend to be age graded. North American children spend most of their time with same-age peers, playing less than a third of the time with children who are more than two years older or younger than themselves (Ellis et al., 1981). In contrast, in many other cultures, older children often play with younger ones as well as care for and teach them (Edwards, 1992; Whiting & Edwards, 1988; Zukow-Goldring, 2002).

Across the continents of Africa, Asia, and North America, even young children seem to understand that older and younger peers serve different functions. Typically, children expect to play with agemates and younger peers and to get help from older peers (Edwards & Lewis, 1979; Rubin et al., 2006).

The bottom line, however, is that children's typical preference for play with same-age peers does serve a special role in social development. After all, children share interests most closely with those who are at similar points in their cognitive, emotional, social, and physical development (Maccoby, 1998), and it is largely their peers with whom they are interacting on a continuing basis in their schooling, their work, and their communities.

ⓛⓞ3 Consequences of Being Unpopular

To understand the consequences of being rejected by peers, we need to take a closer look at how children actually express their rejection of others. Then, we consider the short- and long-term consequences of being rejected, including the stability of peer status over time.

Children are creative and cruel in the ways they reject the children whom they dislike. Sometimes, children exclude others from their group or activities; sometimes, children bully or dominate others in the classroom. Or children can be sneaky, telling another child that they dislike a third child. In more direct action, children can deny others access to other people or objects; for example, children may not let a preschooler play on a swing or slide. Also, children can directly attack a disliked peer, either verbally or physically.

Many rejected children, especially those who are not aggressive, tend to be victimized by their classmates. In Box 12.1 on the next pages, we discuss this problem, looking at the issue of bullying.

SHORT- AND LONG-TERM CONSEQUENCES OF REJECTION
Being unpopular among peers can lead to both short-term and long-term problems (Hymel et al., 2002; McDougall et al., 2001). Loneliness among children is one of the primary results of being rejected or ignored, and it has many faces (see Table 12-2). Unpopular children report feeling lonely and socially dissatisfied (Asher & Paquette, 2003; Bukowski et al., 2007; Cassidy & Asher, 1992). Research suggests that although neglected children may be no lonelier than average children, rejected children are much more likely than average or neglected children to feel lonely (see Figure 12-6 on page 484). Being actively disliked by many of one's peers can lead to strong feelings of social isolation and alienation, although non-aggressive rejected children are likely to feel lonelier than aggressive rejected children (Parkhurst & Asher, 1992). Often, rejected or disliked children are seen as "easy marks" by others and, thus, become victims of other children (Boivin et al., 2001), and being verbally and physically victimized by peers rather that merely rejected is associated with even greater degrees of loneliness (Klesner, 2002; Kochenderfer & Ladd, 1996; Ladd, 2005).

As social relationships change, feelings of loneliness can change, too. Renshaw and Brown (1993) tracked a group of Australian children in grades 3 through 6 for a year and found that those who showed considerable increases in loneliness over time were those who lost friends, became less accepted by peers, and made more remarks about how hard it was for them to make friends. However, even after victimization ceases, children often continue to feel lonely even when they are no longer being harassed by their peers (Kochenderfer-Ladd & Wardrop, 2001). It helps, though, to have at least one friend. Rejected children who have a stable friendship with just one other child may feel less lonely than rejected and totally friendless children (Parker & Asher, 1993; Sanderson & Siegal, 1991).

What are the long-term consequences for a child who is accepted by only a few of his peers? According to Asher and his co-workers (Asher & Paquette, 2003; Parker & Asher, 1987), these consequences are poor achievement, school avoidance, and loneliness. These researchers found that children who were poorly accepted by their peers were less co-operative in the classroom than well-accepted children and were also more likely to drop out of school entirely and to develop patterns of criminal activity. Moreover,

Girl, Grade 6	**Why did that make you feel lonely?**
"Today, everybody's going to Mary Ann's party in the group. I'm sort of the one that gets left behind. I'm not invited to the party, so I won't do anything on the weekend. Anywhere the whole group goes, I don't."	"I'm just the person that gets left back. Maybe they don't realize that I get left, that I'm there, but it happens all the time."
Boy, Grade 5	**Why did that make you feel lonely?**
"I was living in Greenvalley. It was a Sunday. All the stores were closed, I had no money. Jason, a friend, had to go to his aunt's. I decided to call on Jamie, but no one was home. I went to turn on the TV and only church stuff was on. I went upstairs to play with my toys, but it was so boring. The dog was behind the couch, so I didn't want to bother him. Mom was sleeping. My sister was babysitting. It wasn't my day."	"There was no one to talk to or play with, nothing to listen to."

Table 12-2

Loneliness is not having anyone around

Source: Hayden, Turulli, & Hymel, 1988.

Box 12.1

Risk and Resilience

BULLIES AND VICTIMS: LIFE ON THE PLAYGROUND

Some children are not only the regular targets of other children's wrath, but they also, unfortunately, often remain victims over the course of the school years (Khatri, Kupersmidt, & Patterson, 1994). Who are these children that peers target to victimize, tease, or attack? Some children may, unwittingly, send implicit signals that they are unlikely to defend themselves. These children may cry easily, may exhibit anxiety, or they may appear weak (Hodges & Perry, 1999). They tend to lack self-esteem and self-confidence, and they are often without a sense of humour. And again, without realizing it, they may encourage their attackers by being submissive, by not being very good at persuading others, or by giving in to a bully's demands and surrendering possessions (Crick et al., 1999; Juvonen et al., 2003).

Who are bullies, and how does bullying change developmentally? In a recent study, Debra Pepler from York University and Wendy Craig from Queen's University and their colleagues (Pepler et al., 2006) examined bullying in a large cross-sectional sample of almost 1,900 children from grade 6 through grade 12. Based on self-reports of bullying and sexual harassment of peers, these researchers found that bullying peaked around the school transition (moving from junior to senior high), and decreased by the end of high school. Boys reported more bullying than did girls, as well as more incidents of sexual harassment. In addition, adolescents who bullied were more likely to show other forms of relationship aggression.

Bullying

What can we do to help prevent bullying? Pepler and Craig (2000) advocate a systemic approach to dealing with bullying, in which action is taken at many different levels. Figure 12-5 outlines this systemic perspective, in which interventions occur not only at the level of the bully and the victim, but also within the school system and within the peer group itself, and include parental involvement. This approach emphasizes that changes must occur with the help of all individuals involved (the bully, victim, peers, parents, school staff, and community), recognizing the roles and responsibilities of each and the fact that attitudes must change within the school system toward bullying (Pepler and Craig, 2000). As such, an overall school policy is essential for addressing, and thereby preventing, bullying. Moreover, based on the work of Pepler and colleagues (2006), bullying seems to be at least partly a relationship problem, and, as such, prevention programs might focus on curtailing the use of power and aggression in adolescent relationships.

Bullying has, unfortunately, become quite common today, and some kids are continually picked on by others. Here is a typical bullying situation, as it not only involves a bully and a victim, but also a number of children who participate as onlookers to the aggressive acts.

chronically victimized children in late elementary school were more depressed at the age of 23 and more susceptible to being harassed by peers at work or school (Olweus, 2003). Even children who are shy and withdrawn follow a different life-course pattern than do less shy children (Caspi et al., 1988). Shy children tend to be slower than non-shy children in establishing careers, marrying, or becoming parents (Caspi et al., 1988).

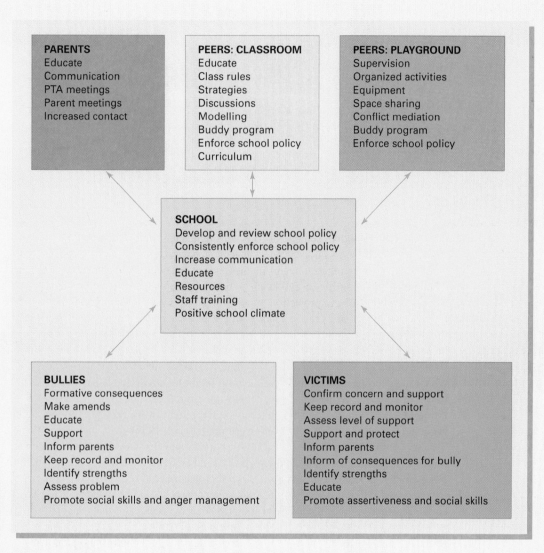

Figure 12-5

A systemic approach to bullying: Overview of strategies

Source: Pepler & Craig (2000). *Making a Difference in Bullying (Report #60)*. Lamarsh Centre for Research on Violence & Conflict Resolution.

CAN PEER STATUS CHANGE? Unfortunately, social standing tends to remain stable across time and in different situations. One short-term longitudinal study (Hardy et al., 2002) found that the social status of Canadian children moving from elementary to middle school (grades 6 to 7) remained stable, particularly for rejected children. Looking more long-term, in a study by Coie and Dodge (1983), both popular and neglected children were fairly stable in their social standing over a five-year span. Interestingly,

Figure 12-6

Loneliness and peer status

In this study, being rejected triggered considerably more loneliness than being either popular or average—or even than being neglected.

Source: Asher et al., 1984.

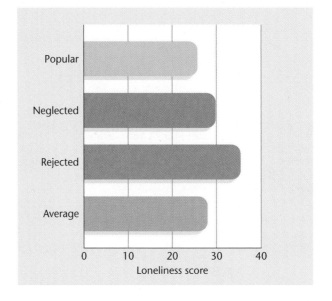

reputational bias

Children's tendency to interpret peers' behaviour on the basis of past encounters with and feeling about them.

though, popular children sometimes lost their high status, and neglected children occasionally gained some social acceptance. In general, however, once a child was rejected, she was more likely than others to maintain this status over a considerable time span. It seems that poor peer relationships in childhood do have implications for later adjustment.

The stability of peer rejection appears to be even greater among kindergartners than the stability of any other category of peer acceptance (Parke et al., 1997). In part, this is the result of **reputational bias**, or the tendency of children to interpret peers' behaviour on the basis of their past encounters with and feelings about these children (Hymel et al., 1990). When we ask children to judge negative behaviour of a peer whom they earlier liked or disliked, they are likely to excuse the behaviour of a peer they earlier liked, giving her the benefit of the doubt, but not to excuse a peer they did not like. Reputation colours children's interpretations of peers' actions and helps account for the stability of behaviour over time (Hymel, 1986).

Reputation, however, is not the only component in peer-status stability. The behaviour and characteristics of the children who have experienced rejection are important, too. For example, Coie and colleagues (1990) found that when boys were brought together into new and different social groups (whose members had no knowledge of the boys' earlier reputations), they tended to be assigned the same peer status they had had before. This was as true of boys who had been considered popular as of those who had been rejected (Coie & Kupersmidt, 1983). As we said earlier, although peers' judgments of other children are often bound by relatively superficial and unimportant factors, like physical appearance, it is largely children's social skills that determine their social status. Clearly, we need to find ways to help children with lower status improve these skills and gain greater acceptance among their peers.

PROMOTERS OF PEER ACCEPTANCE: PARENTS AND TEACHERS

The task of increasing peer acceptance among children is huge. We need to help socially isolated or rejected children to gain peer acceptance. We need to lessen the loneliness that results from being less popular than others. We need to encourage children who are "popular" or "average" in social status to be more generous toward their less socially adept peers—to make a greater effort to understand these peers and to find ways of including them in social groups.

Some believe that early training in social skills may eventually help developing children to find ways to celebrate strengths in one another and offer support for each others' weaknesses. Who is to provide this training? It must rest with parents and teachers, the prime members of Hilary Clinton's (1996) "village," one that ultimately must encompass all of society.

Parents can draw on a variety of resources in helping their children develop healthy peer relationships (Parke et al., 2002). As Figure 12-7 shows, they start as trusted partners with whom their children can begin to acquire skills of social interaction. Recall from Chapter 6 that secure attachments to parental figures can form the basis for later social competence (Schneider et al., 2001; Sroufe et al., 2005). In addition, researchers have found clear relations between parents' specific ways of interacting with their children and the children's social behaviour with their peers. Parents of well-accepted children interacted in a positive and agreeable manner with their children and were concerned with the child's feelings as well as their own. In contrast, parents of rejected children exhibited more negative and controlling behaviours with their children (Clark & Ladd, 2000; Parke et al., 2004).

In extreme cases, parents who abuse a child often prevent the child from developing healthy peer relationships. For example, Bolger and Patterson (2001) found that preadolescents who were chronically abused were more likely to be rejected by their peers. As Figure 12-8 on the next page shows, the more extensive the abuse, the more likely a child was to be rejected by her peers. Moreover, maltreated children, especially if the abuse occurred in the preschool years, had difficulty forming and maintaining friendships. Neglected children were more likely to be social isolates who had infrequent contact with peers (Bolger et al., 1998; Garbarino & Kostelny, 2002). As we saw in Chapter 11, being abused can cause a child to exhibit aggressive behaviour with others, and it was the elevated levels of aggression that accounted for the links between chronic maltreatment and peer rejection. Other work (Shields et al., 2001) suggests that the inability of many maltreated children to regulate their emotions often leads peers to

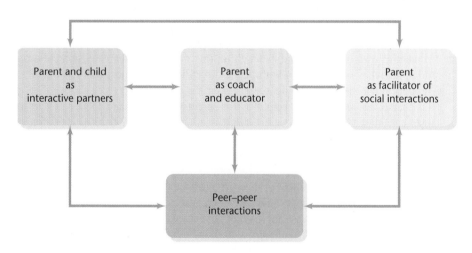

Figure 12-7

How parents help their children develop peer relationships

Children learn social behaviours by interacting with their parents, through their parent's coaching and other educational methods, and through their parents' facilitation of opportunities for interaction with peers. The upper, two-way arrows symbolize the reciprocal relationship of the parent–child interactive experience (parent as coach) and parents' decisions about opportunities for social interaction; those experiences about ways to further improve their children's peer interaction, and those decisions, affect each other. The lower two-way arrows signal that children's experience in peer interaction provides feedback to parents and children on useful adjustments in social-interaction patterns.

Source: Parke & Buriel, 2006.

Figure 12-8

Abused children are often rejected

In this study, not only were children who had been abused found to be often rejected by their peers, but the longer the abuse continued, the more likely these children were to be rejected by others.

Source: Bolger & Patterson, 2001.

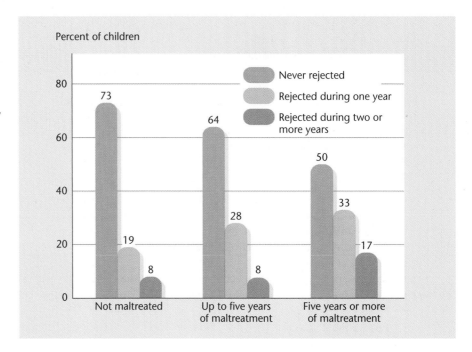

reject them. Finally, prior abuse in the family also makes it more likely that children, especially boys, will be victimized by their peers (Schwartz et al., 1997).

Parents Are Coaches

Parents can also prepare their children for successful and satisfying social relationships through specific coaching, or teaching (Ladd & Pettit, 2002; Parke et al., 2002). In coaching, parents teach a child a general concept or strategy and give examples of successful behaviours and then guide the child through multiple rehearsals of a particular action. Following that, they review both concept and rehearsal to show the child how to evaluate his own behaviour and its result. In this way, parents can advise a child on helpful approaches in interaction with peers, direct him to the most useful strategies, and support him as he tries new ideas.

Of course, coaching is most helpful when parents themselves are socially adept. In an Australian study (Finnie & Russell, 1988; Russell & Finnie, 1990), researchers found clear differences between the coaching methods mothers of children of high social status and those of children of lower status used when their children were confronted with a peer problem. The former generally used positive approaches (e.g., suggesting that a child propose a third, positive alternative action when she and another child cannot agree) and more rule-oriented strategies (e.g., suggesting that a child propose turn taking instead of fighting over a particular toy). In contrast, the mothers of low-status children tended to suggest avoidance strategies (e.g., that a child ignore unfriendly behaviour) or non-specific tactics (e.g., "just get to know the children"). When they actually joined in the children's activities, the two groups of mothers showed different degrees of skilfulness. For example, the first group encouraged communication among the children generally and actively helped their own children to join in conversation. The second group, however, often took control of a game, disrupted the children's play patterns, or simply avoided supervising the group.

Parents Are Social Arrangers

Another way parents can influence their child's relations with peers is by providing opportunities for peer interaction (Ladd, 2005; Ladd & Pettit, 2002). The first step in this effort is often finding housing in a neighbourhood where children are likely to find suitable playmates and where there are good facilities for children's play. Like many other things that help children grow and develop, a good neighbourhood is generally more accessible to families at the higher socio-economic levels. But even affluent neighbourhoods differ. One parent told researchers,

> *Just look at this street—kids, swing sets, swimming pools everywhere. It's a kid's paradise. That's one of the main reasons we moved. Before, we were in another section of town. We had a beautiful house, but there weren't many kids to play with.* (Rubin & Sloman, 1984, p. 231)

Socio-economic factors can affect friendship patterns in surprising ways. In one study, Medrich (1981) discovered that friendships were more abundant and easy in a low-income neighbourhood than in a more affluent one. In the well-to-do community, friends often lived so far apart that, typically, parents chauffeured their children to pre-planned social events. In contrast, in the low-income inner-city neighbourhood, friends were abundant and nearby, and children's play tended to be more spontaneous and frequent. In the first neighbourhood, children were selective in their friendships; many had only one or two friends whom they chose because they had "something in common." In the second neighbourhood, children typically had four or five close friends and spent considerable time in large groups.

Thus, the physical environment can sometimes counteract other factors in the endeavour to help kids get to know one another. And even in dangerous and unsafe neighbourhoods, parents can protect their children by monitoring their activities and choices of peers (Brody et al., 2001; O'Neil et al., 2001; Parke et al., 2008b).

Because 2-year-olds are unequipped to find playmates without their parents' help, being good social arrangers is particularly important for parents of these very young children. Parents can schedule visits between young friends and enroll their children in organized activities, and then, of course, transport their children to and from such visits and gatherings (Ladd & Pettit, 2002). And this effort pays off. Comparing the social activities of children whose parents were good arrangers with those of children whose parents did not facilitate peer contacts, Gary Ladd and colleagues (Ladd, 2005; Ladd & Golter, 1988) found that boys in the first group had a clear advantage. They had a larger range of playmates and more frequent play companions outside school than boys in the second group. Girls in both groups were equally well accepted by their peers, but peer acceptance for boys was greater for those whose parents initiated peer contacts.

Teachers Can Facilitate Healthy Social Interaction

Teachers can help lonely or socially awkward children improve their people skills and increase their acceptance among their peers. We should note, though, that not every child who appears to be unpopular needs intervention. According to Coie and Dodge (1983), many neglected children become socially competent and accepted over time. And there is nothing intrinsically wrong about solitary play, a common form of play among 2-year-olds, as we saw earlier in this chapter. Often, a child who plays alone simply has a passion for certain types of experiences and activities. The time a child spends with Lego sets or paints or the computer may or may not produce the next Frank Lloyd Wright or Picasso or Bill Gates, but in any case, the child may become socially competent.

Studying a group of preschoolers, however, Rubin (1982; Rubin & LeMare, 1990) found that the children who often engaged in simple repetitive activities like banging on the table, whether alone or close to other children, tended to be less socially competent. Similarly, children who engaged in solitary dramatic play (e.g., pretending to be Spider-Man all by oneself) were not very socially skilled either. And at greatest risk for later social adjustment problems were rejected children.

Teachers and parents often act as coaches, encouraging children to include others in their play and helping them to settle disputes.

Using coaching techniques, Murphy and Schneider (1994b) coached unpopular grade 5 children on the importance of showing behaviours that are liked by peers. After this training, the children were encouraged to display these behaviours to specific children in their class with whom they wished to be friends. In a subsequent assessment, these target children reported liking the children who had been coached and also said that they felt that these children liked them more. As such, the training program was effective in enabling the unpopular children to make friends. Similar work has been conducted by Ladd and colleagues (Ladd, 1981, 2005; Mize & Ladd, 1990), who have explored ways to improve the social relationships of unpopular grade 3 children.

In addition to improving the lonely child's skills and behaviours, Asher and Hopmeyer (2001) suggest changing elements in the child's environment so as to reduce or eliminate conditions that may be hindering her development of good social skills. For example, in a Norwegian study (Olweus, 1993, 2000), researchers persuaded a school to lower its tolerance for bullying and succeeded in altering classroom inter-actions, such as encouraging teachers to offer public praise to lonely children. These investigators also propose altering class organization patterns: one possibility is to use the homeroom pattern of elementary grades in secondary schools in order to avoid the constant changing from room to room. Another is "looping," in which one teacher stays with a given class for several years as the classmates move up in grade level.

Interventions of the sort we have described are not undertaken only with young children. Programs have targeted preadolescents who were not well accepted by peers and who were either aggressive or isolated (Bienert & Schneider, 1995). When interventions were tailored to children's specific deficits (i.e., training was designed to reduce either isolation or aggression), both groups of children gained in peer group acceptance. More recently, prevention programs aimed at both parents and peers have been found to be helpful as well (Conduct Problems Prevention Research Group, 2004). We review these programs in Chapter 14.

For Thought and Discussion

1. Say you are a researcher doing work on peer acceptance, and you adopt a sociometric technique by having children rate their classmates as to likeability. When presenting this research at a conference, another researcher questions the validity of your measures. How might you go about confirming, or supporting, your ratings? What does this say about the use of sociometric techniques more generally?

2. Given all the different, and sometimes extraneous, factors that appear to influence peer acceptance, how important is interpersonal behaviour? Put differently, and as an example, what happens when you have an attractive child who behaves aggressively toward his peers?

3. On the basis of what you have read about interpersonal acceptance, what might be important in trying to help children who have problems with their peers? What would you focus on if you were to design an intervention program?

LO4 WHEN PEERS BECOME FRIENDS

friendship

A reciprocal commitment between two people who see themselves as relative equals.

In our discussions so far, we have focused on how well children are accepted by their classmates or peer group. Although this group perspective is an important one, children also develop close, dyadic relationships with a few peers that we call friendships. The essentials of a **friendship**, according to Hartup (1989), are reciprocity and commitment between people who see themselves more or less as equals. As the following exchange indicates, young children do not always find it easy to define a friend. Here is one child's attempt:

Interviewer: Why is Caleb your friend?

Tony: Because I like him.

Interviewer: And why do you like him?

Tony: Because he's my friend.

Interviewer: And why is he your friend?

Tony (with mild disgust): Because—I—choosed—him—for—my—friend. (Rubin, 1980, p. 11)

Expectations and Obligations of Friendship

Children do have certain expectations about relationships with friends (Dunn, 2004; Schneider, 2000). And these expectations about friends seem to progress over time in three stages. Note, in the following list, that the expectations that emerge at each stage do not disappear with the next; in fact, those shown in italics tend to increase with age (Bigelow, 1977; Bigelow & LaGaipa, 1975):

1. **Reward–cost stage (grades 2–3):** Children expect friends to *offer help*, *share common activities*, provide stimulating ideas, be able to join in organized play, *offer judgments*, *be physically nearby*, and be demographically similar to them.

2. **Normative stage (grades 4–5):** Children now expect friends to *accept* and *admire* them, to bring *loyalty and commitment* to a friendship, and to express similar values and attitudes toward rules and sanctions.

3. **Empathic stage (grades 6–7):** Children begin to expect *genuineness* and the *potential for intimacy* in their friends; they expect friends to understand them and to be willing to engage in **self-disclosure** or **restrictive disclosure**; they want friends to accept their help, to share *common interests*, and to hold similar attitudes and values.

self-disclosure or restrictive disclosure

The honest sharing of information of a very personal nature, often with a focus on problem solving; a central means by which adolescents develop friendships.

One important aspect of friendship that changes with age is children's restrictive disclosures about themselves. According to research done at Lakehead University by Ken Rotenberg and his colleagues (Rotenberg, 1995a, 1995b; Rotenberg & Morgan, 1995; Rotenberg & Sliz, 1988), as children become older, they become more willing to tell their friends (relative to non-friends) more highly personal information about themselves. But it is not just that they say more to their friends, however. The amount of low personal information that is relayed to friends versus non-friends does not vary. And, of course, one critical aspect of sharing information is that children must trust that their friends will keep their secrets. This issue of *trustworthiness* (Betts & Rotenberg, 2007, 2008; Rotenberg et al., 2005, 2008) has been found to be related to peer acceptance and to children's school-related adjustment.

The obligations of friendship change as well (Bigelow et al., 1996, 1999). Studying 10- to 17-year-olds, Youniss and his colleagues (Smollar & Youniss, 1982; Youniss, 1980) found that friendship obligations undergo marked shifts over adolescence. Although 80 percent of the 10- to 11-year-olds thought friends should "be nice to one another and help each other," only 11 percent of the 16- to 17-year-olds indicated that this was a central obligation. In contrast, 62 percent of the 16- to 17-year-olds thought that providing emotional support was important, but only 5 percent of the 10- to 11-year-olds agreed. Reasons change, too. Young children view obligations as important "so he'll be nice to you, too" or "to keep the relation going good." Obligations are important to older children because they will benefit the other person ("because she'll be happier if you do") or because they define the relationship ("That's what friends are supposed to do"). Gender is also a factor: females at all ages are more likely than males to be concerned with emotional assistance and to stress reasons based on benefiting the other person (Ladd, 2005; Schneider, 2000).

Unfortunately, there is no clear evidence that these expectations always translate into action. What children—and many adults—say they expect and what they do are not highly related. Nor are friendships always smooth and everlasting. Fights often occur, friends can and do hurt each other, and friendships do end. In Box 12.2 on page 492, we discuss a particularly unhappy kind of relationship in which two people develop mutual antipathy rather than friendship. In the next section, we explore how children make friends and how they behave with their friends.

Making Friends

Although psychologists and others have studied children's peer relations for many decades, we still find it difficult to answer a simple question: How do children become friends? Gottman and his colleagues (Gottman, 1983; Gottman & Parker, 1986; Parker & Gottman, 1989) tried to provide an answer in a series of studies of children ranging in age from 3 to 7 years. These researchers set tape recorders in children's homes and listened while some children played with their best friends and other children played with strangers. The study found that friends communicated more clearly, disclosed information about themselves more, had more positive exchanges, established common ground more easily, and were able to resolve conflict more effectively than strangers. Interestingly, unacquainted children who got along well and were rated as more likely to become friends scored higher on these dimensions than others in the stranger group.

Studies with other samples of children at varying ages confirm many of these findings. Not surprisingly, children spend more time with friends and express more positive affect with them than with non-friends (Dunn, 2004; Ladd, 2005; Schneider, 2000). They share more with their friends (Jones, 1985), although, when friends are tough competitors, sharing with each other may decrease somewhat (Berndt, 1986). Being friends does not mean never disagreeing (Hartup, 1996; Laursen et al., 1996). In fact, friends disagree more than non-friends, but their conflicts are less heated and they are more likely to stay in contact after an argument than non-friends (Hartup et al., 1988). Friends are more likely to resolve conflicts in an equitable way and to ensure that the resolution preserves the friendship (Bowker et al., 2006; Hartup, 1996; Laursen et al., 1996), and are more likely to change their own opinions after disagreeing with a friend than with a non-friend (Aboud, 1989). And friends, of course, are more intimate and self-disclosing with each other than with acquaintances (Simpkins & Parke, 2001). Friends are more knowledgeable about each other than about non-friends; they know each other's strengths and secrets as well as their wishes and weaknesses (Dunn, 2004; Ladd, 2005; Schneider, 2000). As someone once said, "A friend is someone who knows our faults but doesn't give a damn!"

Friendships Change over Time

How do friendship patterns change across development? Parker and Gottman (1989) suggest that the goals and central processes involved in successful friendship formation shift across ages. For young children (ages 3 to 7 years), the goal of peer interaction is coordinated play with all the social processes organized to promote successful play. In the second developmental phase—the 8- to 12-year period—the goal changes from playful interaction to a concern with being accepted by one's same-gender peers. Children are concerned with the norms of the group, figuring out which actions will lead to acceptance and inclusion and which to exclusion and rejection. The most salient social process in middle childhood is **negative gossip**, which involves sharing some negative information about another child. When it works well, the partner responds with interest, more negative gossip, and even feelings of solidarity.

One study found, for example, that in some schools, girls kept "slam books" in which nasty things were written by each girl about other girls (Giese-Davis, cited by Gottman, 1986). Here is an example of two girls, Erica and Mikaila, gossiping about another girl, Katie:

> **Erica:** Katie does lots of weird things. Like, every time she makes a mistake, she says, "Well, sorry." (Sarcastic tone)
>
> **Mikaila:** I know.
>
> **Erica:** And stuff like that.
>
> **Mikaila:** She's mean. She beat me up once. (Laughs) I could hardly breathe, she hit me in the stomach so hard.
>
> **Erica:** She acts like . . .
>
> **Mikaila:** She's the boss. (Gottman, 1986)

As we will see in Chapter 14, gossip sometimes expresses hostility. Girls tend to use this kind of relational aggression rather than the forms of physical aggression that boys more commonly use. In the third developmental period (13 to 17 years of age), the focus shifts to the understanding of self. Self-exploration and self-disclosure are the principal social processes this time, and they are accompanied by intense honesty and a lot of problem solving. Table 12-3 summarizes these developmental periods.

Losing Friends

Friendships, like most everything else in life, change over time. Children form new friendships and lose, renew, and replace friendships—sometimes as quickly as within days or weeks, and sometimes over a span of years (Dunn, 2004). To study changes in friendship patterns, Parker and Seal (1996) studied 216 children, ages 8 to 15, at a summer camp. Within this larger group, these researchers identified different subgroups based on common patterns in friendships. Some children readily formed new

Table 12-3 How friendship patterns develop

	Early Childhood (3 to 7 years old)	Middle Childhood (8 to 12 years old)	Adolescence (13 to 17 years old)
Primary concerns	To maximize excitement, entertainment, and affect through play	To be included by peers; to present oneself to others in a positive way	To explore oneself—to come to know oneself, define oneself
Main processes and purposes of communication	To coordinate play; to escalate and de-escalate play activity; to talk about activities; to resolve conflict	To share negative gossip with others	To disclose oneself to another or others; to solve problems
Emotional development	Learning to manage arousal during interaction	Acquiring rules for showing feelings; rejecting sentiment	Getting logic and emotion together; understanding the implications of emotions for relationships

Source: Adapted from Gottman & Mettetal, 1986.

Box 12.2

Child Psychology in Action

WHEN "LOVE THY NEIGHBOUR" FAILS: PEERS AS MUTUAL ENEMIES

Peer interaction can have a dark side, as studies of peer rejection and bullying reveal. A relationship that clearly partakes of this dark aspect of social behaviour is that of **mutual antipathy**—a situation in which two or more children dislike or even hate each other (Parker & Gamm, 2003). Some mutual antipathies involve children of the same sex; others occur between opposite-gender children. What effect do such relationships have on children's social adjustment?

In one study of North American third-grade children, 65 percent of the students reported at least one same-sex mutual antipathy, and some children had as many as three (Hembree & Vandell, 2000). Such relationships of mutual dislike are found in older children as well. In a study of Dutch children, Abecassis and colleagues (2002) found that grade 5 and grade 8 children reported mutual antipathies. In this case, boys were more likely to have these kinds of relationships than girls. And, not surprisingly, among children at many ages, rejected and controversial children were more likely to be involved in these kinds of relationships than were popular and average children. Sadly, mutual antipathies can have very negative effects on both children's and adolescents' developmental outcomes: The more numerous the same-sex antipathies a child is involved in, the poorer her socio-emotional adjustment and academic performance (Hembree & Vandell, 2000).

During preadolescence, all children with same-sex antipathies are more likely than those without such relationships to be anti-social and to fight and bully or be victimized. In contrast, the effects of mixed-sex antipathies (boy/girl dislikes and is disliked by girl/boy) differ between boys and girls. Boys with these problems tend to be anti-social, but in girls, anti-social behaviour does not seem to be linked with mixed-sex antipathies. Instead, girls in mixed-sex antipathies were less socially skilled and less prosocial; they had fewer friends, they were more likely to be victimized, and they reported more somatic and depressive symptoms.

Moreover, having enemies in preadolescence foreshadows later problems in adolescence. Boys who had same-sex mutual antipathies at age 10 were more likely, three years later in adolescence, to exhibit addiction and delinquency and to have more somatic complaints and less support from friends (Abecassis et al., 2002). For girls, same-sex antipathies in preadolescence predicted lower achievement scores in adolescence. Cross-gender antipathies in preadolescence were not related to adolescent outcomes for either boys or girls.

Moreover, children hold distorted views of their enemies more that their views of other peers. Ten-year-olds in Estonia attributed more hostility and expected hostile responses when the partner was an enemy than a neutral peer. In other words, the context of a mutual antipathy even modifies our perception of another's intent and behavioural strategies (Peet et al., 2007).

Having friends is clearly a protective factor in children's development. Having enemies, on the other hand, puts children at risk for later problems. Just as it isn't good for countries to have enemies, it's not good for children, either. "Love thy neighbour" is clearly a better policy for countries and children alike.

mutual antipathy

A relationship of mutual dislike between two people.

relationships but whose social ties showed little stability. These children were considered playful teasers and were always up on the latest interesting gossip, but they were also aggressive, bossy, and untrustworthy. Other children added new relationships and kept existing ones. These children were neither bossy nor easily pushed around.

Another group of children often broke up friendships but failed to replace these relationships. These children were caring, shared with others, and, engaged in playful teasing, yet they were often judged to be "show-offs." Others maintained a stable pool of friendships but added no new ones. The girls in this group were known for honesty, and the group members in general were less apt to tease others; at the same time, they were less caring than others. Finally, some children made no friends at all throughout the summer. These children were perceived by others as timid, shy, and as preferring to play alone. And as we might expect, these children were lonelier than others.

Gender is a factor in the stability of children's peer relationships. Benenson and

Christakos (2003) found that girls' closest same-sex friendships appeared more fragile and less lasting than those of boys. Based on their study of 10- to 15-year-olds, these researchers suggest that the tendency of girls to form close relationships with each other in isolation from a larger group may jeopardize these relationships in a way not seen in boys' friendships. Boys' same-sex friendships are more often embedded in a larger group of relationships, which provides a kind of safety net. The easy recourse to third-party mediators, allies, and alternative partners helps keep boys' friendship ties intact.

Although the greater intimacy expressed in girls' friendships may be rewarding, it may also place the friendships at greater risk. Girls may be more likely to worry that a relationship might end or to feel that they have done something to damage a friendship. In girls' friendships, there is more "co-rumination" or excessively discussing personal problems than in boys' friendships (Rose, 2002). Moreover, higher co-rumination is linked with more depression and anxiety in girls while not in boys (Rose et al., 2007). When things go wrong, girls may intensify the problem by divulging intimate secrets about their partners to others, and this betrayal may hasten the demise of a friendship. Boys, on the other hand, seem to be less intimate with one another, less likely to divulge personal information about their partners, and, when problems arise, more likely to confront their partners directly (Rose & Rudolph, 2006).

The Pros and Cons of Friendship

For most children, having friends is a positive accomplishment. As we saw earlier in the chapter, peers and friends provide support, intimacy, and guidance. Children with friends are less lonely and depressed (Asher & Paquette, 2003; Dunn, 2004), and even their long-term outcomes are better. Bagwell and colleagues (1998) found that grade 5 children who had a reciprocated best friendship were better adjusted at the age of 23. Compared with friendless children, these individuals experienced less depression, were less likely to exhibit delinquent behaviour, did better in university, and had more fruitful relationships with family and peers. Having a childhood friendship forecasts more successful adult development.

Not all friendships are beneficial—they may pose risks as well as offer protective factors (Bagwell, 2004). Even rejected children form friendships, but they often choose as friends other rejected (and often aggressive) classmates. Moreover, compared with the friendships of non-rejected/non-aggressive children, the friendships of rejected children are often of poorer quality—that is, they tend to be less satisfying, less intimate, and more likely to be conflict-ridden (Poulin et al., 1999). Rejected children who are friends often encourage each other's deviant behaviour, such as cheating on tests, acting aggressively with others, and using/abusing substances (Bagwell, 2004). Thus, it is important to consider the common activities that form the basis of a friendship in addition to the quality of the relationship. We return to this issue in Chapter 15 when we explore the role of peers and friends in the development of psychological difficulties.

The Romantic Relationship: A Developmental Milestone

Andrew Collins, a student of adolescence, has observed that "popular culture is suffused with images of the dreaminess, preoccupation, shyness, self-consciousness and sexual awakening of adolescents in love" (Collins, 2003). Many dismiss romantic relationships as no more than flings or even a fiction of popular culture. If they've no developmental significance, why, then, should we discuss adolescent romantic relationships? Let's examine some of the myths that surround these kinds of relationships and try to separate fact from fancy.

Romantic ties form earlier than some people believe, as these preteens illustrate.

peer-group network

The cluster of peer acquaintances who are familiar with and interact with one another at different times for common play or task-oriented purposes.

TEENAGE LOVE AFFAIRS REALLY DO MATTER   Here are four commonly held mistaken ideas about adolescent romantic relationships.

Myth 1: Adolescent romantic relationships are transitory. According to this belief, these relations are superficial.

Reality: Adolescent romantic relationships are neither uncommon nor transitory. In one study, 25 percent of 12-year olds, nearly 50 percent of 15-year olds, and 70 percent of 18-year olds reported having a romantic relationship within the preceding 18 months (Carver et al., 2003). And a surprising percentage of adolescents in dating relationships reported that their relationships had lasted 11 months or more. Among adolescents 14 and under, 20 percent reported a similar length of relationship history, and 60 percent of 17- and 18-year olds indicated that their romantic ties lasted nearly a year or longer (Carver et al., 2003).

Myth 2: Adolescent romantic relationships are trivial. Even if romantic ties last a fair amount of time, they are of little significance to adolescent development.

Reality: Adolescent romantic alliances are quite significant in adolescent functioning and possibly in longer-term outcomes. As we all know, romance has its costs as well as its rewards. Adolescents in romantic relationships report more conflict, have more mood swings, and experience more symptoms of depression (Laursen, 1995; Joyner & Udry, 2000), especially around a breakup. But there are positive outcomes associated with romantic relationships, too. Being in such a relationship is linked with a feeling of self-worth, a sense of competence, and a feeling that one is part of a **peer-group network** (Connolly et al., 2004; Kirtler et al., 1999).

On the other hand, early dating with a large number of different partners may forecast relationships of poorer quality in young adulthood (Collins, 2003; Collins & Van Dulmen, 2006). Although these studies suggest that quality, timing, and duration of relationships are all possible determinants of the long-term consequences of adolescent romantic ties, one recent report found no link between adolescent romantic involvement and adult adjustment (Roisman et al., 2004). Although the short-term significance of adolescent romance is clear, the verdict on its long-term significance for adult functioning is not yet in.

Myth 3: Romantic relationships do not differ from other relationships. According to this myth, these relationships simply mirror relationships with family members, friends, and other peers.

Reality: It is true that the quality of family relationships and same-sex friendships are often predictive of the quality of romantic ties. Conger and colleagues (2000) found that nurturant parenting during adolescence predicted the quality of romantic relationships five years later; a close parent–adolescent relationship was linked with a better-quality romantic relationship. Neither sibling nor marital relationship quality predicted romantic ties. On the other hand, inadequate parenting (insufficient monitoring of child behaviour, inconsistent discipline) is related to increased risk of that child showing aggressive and violent behaviour toward a future romantic partner (Capaldi & Clark, 1998; Simons et al., 1998). Clearly, quality of the parent–child relationship is an important predictor of the quality of children's later romantic alliances.

Myth 4: Romantic relationships are important mainly as harbingers of problem behaviour. According to this myth, early dating and especially early sexual activity are linked with a variety of behavioural problems, such as drug use and classroom difficulties.

Reality: This is partly true, but mainly teens who date at an early age are likely to develop behaviour problems (Davies & Windle, 2000). Delaying dating until it is more normative and until the adolescent is more mature—at 15 or 16—is associated with reduced risk for later problems. Dating many different partners can also increase risk for behavioural problems, such as acting out and aggression. Male and female adolescents who dated many partners between the ages of 12 and 16 showed an increase in behavioural problems compared to those who dated fewer people (Zimmer-Gembeck et al., 2001).

CHANGES IN ROMANTIC ALLIANCES OVER TIME   Adolescents at all ages develop romantic ties but the romantic experience changes between early and late adolescence (Collins, 2003). Just as the frequency of romantic involvement increases across development, the length of time in a specific relationship also increases. Among 14- to 15-year olds, 35 percent were in relationships that lasted 11 months or more, whereas 55 percent of those 16 or older were in long-term relationships (Carver et al., 2003).

The peer group plays a major role in partner choice among young adolescents. You date partners that your peer network approves of or views as "cool." Appearance, clothes, status, and other superficial features guide young adolescents' choices, but older adolescents focus more on characteristics that underlie intimacy and compatibility, such as personality, values, and particular interests (Zani, 1993). Among older adolescents, there is more interdependence between partners in romantic relationships (Laursen & Jensen-Campbell, 1999). Older adolescents are more likely than younger ones to compromise with their partners as a way of solving problems.

PARENTS OR PEERS? WHO ARE MOST INFLUENTIAL?

LO5

Many writers have seen preadolescence and adolescence as highly stressful periods during which children are buffeted by the often conflicting behavioural standards of parents and friends. Others have argued that these standards conflict far less frequently than is suggested and that, in fact, there is often remarkable agreement between parental and peer values (Brown & Huang, 1995; Collins et al., 2000; Vandell, 2000). A better question than whether peers or adults are more influential is, "Under what conditions and with what behaviours are peers or adults influential?"

Peers and parents each have their own areas of expertise. Although peers are not generally the best advisors on occupational choices, parents are not the best source for the latest and best music recordings and videos. Peers exert more influence on teens' styles of interpersonal behaviour, their selection of friends, and their choices of fashion and entertainment. Parents have more impact on their teenager's academic choices, their job preferences, and their future aspirations (Hartup, 1996). For example, Brian Bigelow and Run Min Zhou, from Laurentian University (Bigelow & Zhou, 2001), found that parents and children across a range of ages, from elementary school to high school, tend to place similar emphases on school performance. According to these authors, students' school goals are embedded within the parent–child relationship and are scaffolded by it.

Much of a child's behaviour reflects a mix of peer and parental influences (Elder & Conger, 2000; Ladd, 2005). Studying the use of marijuana, Kandel (1973) found that among teenagers whose best friends were non-users but whose parents were users, only 17 percent smoked marijuana. If friends used drugs, however, and parents did not, 56 percent of adolescents reported using marijuana. When both parents and peers were users, 67 percent of the adolescents used marijuana. Similar findings have been reported for alcohol, tobacco, and other forms of illegal drugs and for early and risky sexual behaviour (Dishion et al., 2000; Mounts & Steinberg, 1995). Thus, drug use by parents and peers had a combined impact on adolescents' use of marijuana.

Authoritative parents who maintain close relationships with their children help them to resist peer pressure more effectively.

In sum, the beliefs that parental influence is soon replaced by peer influence and that parenting really does not matter are very simply wrong. Although parental influence wanes as peer influence increases, both parents and peers play a significant role in determining the child's and adolescents' social development.

LO6 BEYOND DYADIC FRIENDSHIPS: THE FORMATION OF GROUPS

As popular TV reality shows such as *Big Brother* or *Survivor* illustrate, people form alliances and pacts and make other kinds of social connections to overcome obstacles and to reach common goals. In similar fashion, children form alliances and develop group structures with common goals and rules of behaviour. Group structures are quite different from dyadic friendships but are another way that children can achieve their social goals.

Groups usually develop a hierarchical structure that identifies and characterizes the relationship of each member of the group to each other member and facilities member interaction (Hawley, 2007). Inevitably, some group members are identified as dominant, and their leadership roles clearly differ from the roles of the other children in the group.

Dominance Hierarchies

dominance hierarchy

An ordering of individuals in a group from most to least dominant; a "pecking order."

Children in a group will a **dominance hierarchy**, or "pecking order," even in preschool. In fact, Hawley and Little (1999) found clear evidence of a social dominance hierarchy in children aged 1.4 to 3.2 years. Although preschool children tend to perceive their own positions as a bit higher in the pecking order than they really are, they become increasingly accurate at judging their own status in the early school years (Hawley, 1999, 2007; Strayer, 1984). Moreover, although preschool children's dominance hierarchies are simpler and more loosely differentiated than those of older children, as these children age, they tend to agree in identifying group status structures (Hawley, 1999). Other evidence suggests that dominance hierarchies emerge very quickly. In a study by Pettit and colleagues (1990), within the first 45 minutes of contact, unacquainted boys from grades 1 and 3 began to develop a coherently organized social structure.

What functions do hierarchies serve? First, they reduce aggression among the group members who establish non-aggressive means of resolving conflict. For example, a high-ranking member may use a threatening gesture to keep a lower-ranking group member in line. In fact, aggression is rarely seen in a group with a well-established hierarchy (Hawley & Little, 1999). A second purpose is to help divide the tasks and labour of the group, with worker roles being assumed by the lower-status members and leadership roles going to the more dominant members. Third, dominance hierarchies determine the allocation of resources—especially limited resources (Charlesworth, 1988; Hawley, 2007). Rank has its privileges in the nursery school set as among adolescents (Charlesworth & Dzur, 1987; Savin-Williams, 1987). In a study of adolescent summer campers, Savin-Williams (1987) found that the dominant teens "frequently ate the bigger piece of cake at mealtimes, sat where they wanted to during discussions and slept in the preferred sleeping sites during camp-outs (near the fire)—all scarce resources at summer camp" (p. 934). Clearly, dominance hierarchies play important roles in regulating interaction, but as is often the case, the ones at the top of the hierarchy seem to benefit the most.

Cliques and Crowds

clique

A voluntary group formed on the basis of friendship.

In middle childhood, kids begin to form **cliques**, voluntary groups based on friendship (Schneider, 2000). A clique may range in size from three to nine children, and members usually are of the same gender and same race (Kindermann et al., 1995). By the time children are 11 years old, most of their interaction with peers is in the context of the clique. Membership in cliques enhances children's psychological well-being and ability to cope with stress (Rubin et al., 2006), just as social acceptance and friendship are buffers against loneliness. Cliques are evident in adolescence as well but decline across the high-school years (Shrum & Cheek, 1987), when they are superseded by *crowds*.

A **crowd** is a collection of people who share attitudes or activities that define a particular stereotype—for example, *jocks*, *brains*, *eggheads*, *loners*, *burnouts*, *druggies*, *populars*, and *nerds*—and who may or may not spend much time together (Brown & Klute, 2003). Crowd affiliation is assigned by consensus of the peer group; adolescents do not select it themselves (Rubin et al., 2006). The salience of crowds probably peaks in grade 9 or 10 and decreases through the end of high school (Brown, 1990; Brown & Huang, 1995). Those who are in the populars or jocks crowds experience a drop in internalizing problems between childhood and adolescence while the brains, a less popular group, experience an increase in internalizing problems (Prinstein & LaGreca, 2002). Like friendships, peer groups are not always beneficial to participants; for example, as we will see in Chapter 14, gang membership is often linked with delinquency and other negative outcomes. In late adolescence, crowds tend to disband and are replaced by mixed-sex cliques or romantically oriented couples, as we saw in our exploration of romantic ties.

crowd

A collection of people whose shared attitudes or activities have been designated by a stereotypical term, such as *populars* or *nerds*.

PEER GROUPS IN DIFFERENT CULTURES

Are peers equally important in all cultures or in all parts of one culture? Is North America a uniquely peer-oriented culture? Even within cultures, patterns of peer interaction may differ; for example, comparison of urban and rural peers indicates that Israeli children reared in rural kibbutzim are more co-operative and supportive than city-reared children (Schneider, 2000). For another view of cultural variations among peer relations, see Box 12.3 on the next page.

In some countries, peers play a more influential role, but in others, the family and adult agents are more important. Compared with North American youth, adolescents in Japan spend less time with peers and more time at home (Rothbaum et al., 2000). In Japan, parental values play a more prominent role than peer values in the formation and structure of adolescent peer groups than in the United States (Rothbaum et al., 2000). Similarly, in Latino cultures, children are more family oriented and less influenced by peers (DeRosier & Kupersmidt, 1991). In Mexico and Central America, parents often maintain this family orientation by directly discouraging peer interaction (Ladd, 2005; Schneider, 2000).

There are even cultural differences in the factors that contribute to the formation of cliques. For example, an adolescent's academic achievement or standing is a stronger determinant of clique membership in China than it is in the Western World (Chen et al., 2003). In North America, as we saw earlier, a wider range of factors, from academic achievement to athletic prowess to deviant orientation influence clique membership.

For Thought and Discussion

1. How universal is the concept of dominance hierarchy? Does this reflect North American society, or would you expect to see this in cultures around the world?

2. Researchers have shown that overcontrolling parents tend to have adolescents who have both internalizing and externalizing problems. Why do you think this might be the case? What are the mechanisms that may underlie this relation?

Box 12.3

Perspectives on Diversity

CROSS-CULTURAL VARIATIONS IN CHILDREN'S PEER RELATIONSHIPS

Many of our discussions of cross-cultural diversity have compared societies varying greatly in terms of ideology (collectivist versus individualist), such as are found in Asian countries relative to North American and Western European countries. Is it necessary to have such widely varying societies in order to uncover cultural influences? How about differences between societies within the same general cultural milieu?

Over the years, Barry Schneider at the University of Ottawa and his colleagues have been interested in how parental attitudes and peer interactions may vary across cultural groups (Chen et al., 2007). They have examined variations in numerous Muslim communities in France (Alles-Jardel et al., 2002), as well as differences between Canadian and Italian children (Schneider et al., 1997, 2000) and between Canadian and Taiwanese children (Benjamin et al., 2001). Work with Canadian and Italian children (Schneider et al., 1997, 2000), for instance, has focused on friendship quality and stability, the influence of conflict, and conflict resolution among third and fourth graders. Looking at the stability of Italian and Canadian children's friendships, Schneider and colleagues (1997a) found that, relative to Canadian children, after one year, fewer of the friendships among Italian children had ended, and that these friendships were marked by less conflict. In keeping with this result, Schneider's group (2000) found that Canadian and Italian children differed in their reactions to a conflict situation (e.g., how to share a chocolate egg with a toy inside). Although the Canadian children made more proposals as to how to resolve this conflict, they were actually less efficient in arriving at a potential solution than were the Italian children.

According to these researchers, both sets of findings could have been due to a cultural difference between Italian and Canadian children, in that in Italian society, children (and adults) are much more involved with extended families than are English Canadians, with these strong kinship bonds possibly facilitating children's knowledge of the importance of high-quality relationships with other people. Also, in Italy, parents and other adults explicitly incorporate reasoning about interpersonal relationships into children's socialization and engage in what is called *discussions*, or *living debate* (Corsaro & Maynard, 1996), which might also teach children how to resolve conflict with their friends.

In other ways, of course, Canadians and Italians are quite similar both in the manner of childhood peer interactions and in parental beliefs about children's behav-

iour. For example, Attili and colleagues (1997) have found that the proportions of Italian children who are judged as popular and rejected by their peers are roughly comparable to those found in North America, and the consequences of social rejection, in terms of increased aggression and less prosocial behaviour, were also similar. Moreover, Italian and Canadian children show comparable gender differences in expressions of physical aggression, with boys displaying more physical aggression than girls (Tomada & Schneider, 1997). Canadian and Italian parents' reactions to aggression also appear to be similar. Schneider and colleagues (1997a) asked Italian and Canadian mothers of 7-year-olds about how they would react to instances of aggression and social withdrawal in children, and in many ways, the reactions of both sets of mothers were quite similar. Both Italian and Canadian mothers indicated that they would use moderate to high levels of power assertion in response to aggression, and low to moderate power assertion in response to social withdrawal, although even in this context, there were some subtler differences in the strength of mothers' emotional reactions to aggression and social withdrawal.

Clearly, then, there are some striking cross-cultural similarities between Canada and Italy, as well as some fascinating, and often subtle, differences between the two cultures. Such results suggest that in our efforts to understand peer relationships, we obviously need to recognize the broader cultural contexts in which these relationships are embedded. Even more than a cautionary tale, though, cross-cultural comparisons provide a final test of the generality of our conceptions, and our theories, of child development (Schneider, 1998), giving us insight into exactly how our notions of development are inextricably bound to cultural values within our society.

Children in all cultures spend time with peers, but the nature of their interactions may differ. Chinese children, for example, are less aggressive and more co-operative than are North American children.

Making the Connections 12

There are many links between concepts and ideas in one area of development and concepts and ideas in other areas. Here are some of the connections between ideas in Chapter 12 and discussions in other chapters of this book.

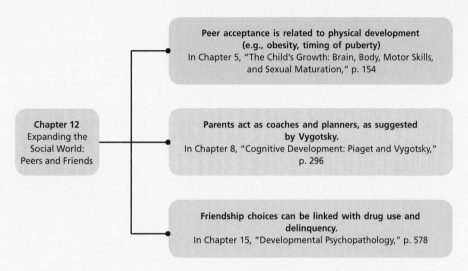

Chapter 12
Expanding the
Social World:
Peers and Friends

Peer acceptance is related to physical development (e.g., obesity, timing of puberty)
In Chapter 5, "The Child's Growth: Brain, Body, Motor Skills, and Sexual Maturation," p. 154

Parents act as coaches and planners, as suggested by Vygotsky.
In Chapter 8, "Cognitive Development: Piaget and Vygotsky," p. 296

Friendship choices can be linked with drug use and delinquency.
In Chapter 15, "Developmental Psychopathology," p. 578

SUMMARY

- Children's interactions with peers are freer and more egalitarian than their interactions with their parents. They allow for more interpersonal experimentation, and children take on a new kind of interpersonal sensitivity to the feelings of others.

How Peer Interactions Begin: Developmental Patterns

- During the second half of the first year, infants begin to recognize peers as social partners and attempt to influence one another by such means as vocalizing and touching.
- In the early toddler period, peers begin to exchange both turns and roles during social interactions; in the late toddler period, a major achievement is the ability to share meaning with a social partner. As children's competence with peers develops, they begin to form true **relationships**.
- After about age 7, children are more likely to choose same-sex rather than opposite-sex play partners; this remains the case until adolescence, when interest in the opposite sex begins.

How Do Peers Help to Socialize Children?

- The peer group influences the development of the child using many of the same techniques that parents do, such as modelling and reinforcement. Children acquire a wide range of knowledge and a variety of responses by observing and imitating the behaviours of their peers. Imitation may serve as a way to both learn social rules and maintain social interaction.
- Peers reinforce one another with increasing frequency throughout the preschool years, and reinforcement commonly is reciprocated.
- Peers also serve as standards against which children evaluate themselves. Research indicates that the use of **social comparison** with the peer group as a means of self-evaluation increases dramatically in the early elementary school years. Comparing oneself with others forms one building block for one's self-image and self-esteem.

Peer Acceptance

- Researchers assess peer status with **sociometric techniques**, in which children identify peers they like and those they do not like. On the basis of these nominations, children have been classified as **popular** (those who receive many positive but few negative nominations), **rejected** (those who receive many negative but few positive nominations), **neglected** (those who receive few nominations in either direction), and **average** (those who have some friends but not as many as the popular group).

- **Controversial** children are liked by many peers but also disliked by many. Rejection occurs for a variety of reasons: **non-aggressive rejected** children tend to be withdrawn and to lack social skills; **aggressive rejected children** have low self-control and exhibit aggressive and other problem behaviours.

- Popular children engage in more prosocial behaviour and help set the norms for a group, whereas rejected children are often aggressive, aversive, and socially unskilled. Neglected children are less talkative and more withdrawn.

- For a child to interact effectively with others, she needs self-confidence, persistence, and the ability to try a new approach when another has been unsuccessful. A model of the cognitive decision-making process describes six steps that children must negotiate in social interaction: Children must evaluate a social situation, assess other children's behaviour, decide what their own goals in a situation are and how they may best achieve them, decide on certain actions, and act on their decisions. Children who show social competence and are not overly aggressive use this process most successfully.

- Achieving such competence may be difficult for children who approach social interactions with a focus on their inadequacies and the belief that they cannot change their own abilities and behaviours. In addition, when children attribute the causation of events to factors outside themselves, they may believe they can have no effect on a situation and not try their best.

- In general, children prefer spending time with peers of the same age and same gender. Although age preferences may be due to the age grading of many institutions in our society, some research suggests that children would choose same-age playmates on their own. Segregation by gender is clearly self-imposed, and it seems to be related to differences in the interests and play patterns of girls and boys. Until the onset of adolescence, opposite-sex friendships are somewhat rare.

- Children often form first impressions of others on the basis of appearance. By age 3, children distinguish attractive from unattractive children in the same way that adults do, and they attribute more negative characteristics to children judged to be unattractive.

- Being unpopular among peers can lead to both short- and long-term problems. Unpopular children (especially rejected ones) feel lonely and socially dissatisfied, and they are more likely to drop out of school and develop criminal behaviour patterns. Peer victimization can take a heavy toll on children; having at least one friend can reduce the loneliness this may cause.

- Social standing tends to remain stable across time and situations, showing the most stability for rejected children. Some programs designed to help these children by shaping socially desirable behaviour through reinforcement and coaching in social skills have proved beneficial. Although not all unpopular children need help in peer interactions, rejected children clearly can benefit from intervention. Loneliness, a common result of being rejected or ignored, can be lessened if a rejected child has at least one stable friendship.

Promoters of Peer Acceptance: Parents and Teachers

- Parents play an important role in promoting a child's peer relations. They serve as partners with whom the child acquires social skills that help him interact with other children by giving advice and support, reinforcing useful behaviours, modelling strategies for conduct with peers. They provide opportunities for peer interaction through their choice of neighbourhood and their willingness to schedule visits with friends (especially for preschoolers). But a child who is abused by parents may develop aggressive behaviours with peers and, thus, incur their rejection.

- Teachers can play an important role in helping children improve their social skills. Good results have been gained through coaching children in more effective ways of communicating and in change conditions of children's environment, such as penalizing bullies and using the home-room pattern at the secondary level.

When Peers Become Friends

- Children develop **friendships** with only a few peers. Expectations of a friend change during the elementary school years from simply someone who shares activities to someone who can also be told secrets and will be understanding.

- Studies indicate that the goals of friendship appear to change with development. For young children (ages 3 to 7 years), the goal is coordinated play, while for older children (ages 8 to 12), the goal is establishing group norms and being accepted by peers. By adolescence (ages 13 to 17), the focus shifts to understanding the self, making **self-disclosure** a critical component of friendship.

- Although children who are friends often disagree and fight, they tend to communicate more clearly, disclose themselves more, exchange more information, establish more common ground, and become able to resolve conflicts more effectively than strangers.
- Over time, children form new friendships and lose or replace old friendships. A child's personal characteristics may influence her ability to form and keep friendships.
- Romantic involvements are different from family and other relationships and can have positive effects of the adolescents' development. Although the teenager may experience more conflict and more mood swings, she may also gain a sense of competence, heightened self-worth, and a feeling of belonging to the peer group.

Parents or Peers? Who Are Most Influential?

- Parents and peers each have their own areas of expertise and influence in children's lives. Peers have more influence in the preadolescent and adolescent years, when they have a lot of impact on such things as selection of friends, styles of dress, and choices of entertainment. Parents have greater impact on academic choices and work, on job preferences, and on a child's aspirations for the future.
- Activities such as using drugs and engaging in other risky behaviours are less attractive to teenagers with authoritative parents who are warm and supportive, who encourage their kids in education and grant them psychological autonomy, but who also demand that they conform to rules of behaviour. And teens whose parents do not possess these qualities may be particularly susceptible to negative peer influence.

Beyond Dyadic Friendships: The Formation of Groups

- In addition to friendships, children form groups whose members share common goals and rules of conduct. Such groups are usually hierarchically organized to identify members' relationships with one another and to facilitate interaction. **Dominance hierarchies** within groups are apparent even among preschoolers, and a "pecking order" appears to develop within a short time of first contact.
- Within groups of children, hierarchies serve the purposes of resolving conflict, dividing up tasks, and allocating resources.
- In middle childhood, kids may form **cliques**, which enhance their well-being and ability to cope with stress. Later, children may be assigned by their peers to **crowds**, whose salience decreases by the end of high school.

Peer Groups in Different Cultures

- Within and between cultures, patterns of peer interaction differ. Varying socialization concepts and practices give peers more or less influence on children. In Mexico and Central America, for example, family influences remain strong throughout adolescence.

Berthe Morisot (1841–1895). *The Children of M. Gabriel Thomas*, 1894.
Musée d'Orsay, Paris.

Chapter 13

Gender Roles and Gender Differences

LEARNING OBJECTIVES

After reading this chapter, you should be able to

LO 1 Describe the process of gender typing, including learning gender roles and gender stereotypes; describe current gender-role standards and stereotypes, and discuss how these vary over time and across cultures.

LO 2 Identify gender differences in development, including the real, equivocal, and mythical differences discussed in the text.

LO 3 Detail the role of biological factors in the development of gender roles; discuss the results of John Money's research, as well as its problems; describe the relation between biology and cognitive abilities, gender differences, and cultural expectations.

LO 4 Discuss the role of cognitive factors in the development of gender roles, including cognitive developmental and gender-schema theories.

LO 5 Discuss various social and situational factors that contribute to gender-role typing, including the family, parental characteristics, media, peers, and teachers and the schools; discuss the impact of gender stereotyping on career aspirations.

LO 6 Explain the concept of androgyny and how it has been studied.

In most societies, males and females behave differently, are viewed and treated differently, and play distinctive roles. At the same time, there are many situations in which males and females behave alike, receive equal treatment from others, and play similar roles. The challenge for psychologists is to determine how these similarities and differences originate in the developing child and to articulate the processes that contribute to gender-specific patterns of behaviour.

Five primary theories, most of them discussed in Chapter 1, have been used to explain these patterns. First, in his psychoanalytic theory, Sigmund Freud proposed that the child, through a process of **identification**, acquired either feminine or masculine traits and behaviours by identifying with the same-sex parent. Freud noted that children's developing curiosity about their own bodies, around the ages of 5 or 6, alerts

identification

The Freudian notion that children acquire gender identity by identifying with and imitating their same-sex parents.

Canadian Researchers

them to differences in the sexual anatomy of males and females. This observation formed the basis for his proposal that this period was critical to the formation of gender identity. Second, cognitive social learning theory suggested that children acquire gender identification both through parents' direct guidance and encouragement and by imitating parents and other people. According to this view, children understand gender quite early, and the fact that parents behave differently toward their male and female babies from the moment of birth may be influential in this understanding. Third, gender-schema theory, an information-processing approach, proposes that children as young as 2½ begin to develop their own naive theories about gender differences and gender-appropriate behaviours. Fourth, in his, cognitive developmental theory, Lawrence Kohlberg asserted that children categorize themselves as male or female on the basis of physical and behavioural clues and then proceed to behave in gender-appropriate ways. According to Kohlberg, it is not until children are about 6 or 7 years old that they make stable gender-typed choices. Finally, evolutionary approaches to psychology have stressed the principles of natural selection and adaptation.

These concepts were applied to gender-related behaviours, especially behaviours that increase the likelihood that a person's genes will be passed across generations (Buss, 2003, 2007; Geary, 2006). To be able to pass genes from one generation to the next, individuals need to have mating strategies that enhance their reproductive success. According to Buss (2000), males and females use different strategies to achieve reproductive success. Males have developed aggressive and competitive skills in order to compete successfully with other males in attracting mates. Females have developed strategies for attracting and keeping males who are able to provide resources, including protection, for their offspring. These two sets of strategies complement each other and have led to the evolution of gender differences in both humans and other animals. Other biological factors also contribute to differences in female and male attitudes and behaviours, such as specific hormones and levels of those hormones, as well as male–female differences in brain lateralization. As we have stressed throughout this book, most human characteristics are products of the interplay between genetic and environmental forces, and gender behaviour is no exception.

We begin this chapter by examining some standards of female and male behaviour common to the North American culture and take a brief look at some quite different cross-cultural behaviours. We then consider some actual patterns of gender differences and ask how stable these patterns are over the life course. We then turn to the issue of biological influences in gender behaviour. Next, we explore cognitive factors, And we then consider the influences on gender behaviour of parental teaching, reinforcement, and modelling and of the social forces represented by peer groups, schools, and the media. Next, we examine children's development of sexual orientation and preference for same- or opposite-sex individuals. We conclude with a brief look at androgyny, the quality of possessing within oneself both masculine and feminine psychological characteristics. ●

LO 1   DEFINING SEX AND GENDER

Traditionally, the word *gender* has been used to refer to cognitive and social differences, and *sex* refers to biological and physiological differences, but it is often difficult to separate these issues. For this reason, we use the terms interchangeably, except when we are discussing primary or secondary sex characteristics or sexual behaviour.

The process by which children acquire the values, motives, and behaviours viewed as appropriate to their gender in a specific culture, referred to as **gender typing**, is a multi-dimensional concept (Ruble et al., 2006). Children begin by developing **gender-based beliefs** about what behaviours are appropriate. These beliefs are derived largely from **gender stereotypes**, which are the beliefs that members of an entire culture hold about the attitudes and behaviours that are acceptable and appropriate for each sex. These stereotypes prescribe the ways males and females should be and should act. **Gender roles** are composites of the distinctive behaviours that males and females in a culture actually exhibit and, thus, are essentially the reflections of a culture's gender stereotypes. Early in life, children develop a **gender identity**, or a perception of themselves as either masculine or feminine and as having characteristics and interests that are appropriate to their sex. And children develop **gender-role preferences**, or desires to possess certain gender-typed characteristics. Children's choices of toys and of play partners reflect these preferences. Finally, in late childhood or adolescence, children develop **sexual preferences** and are attracted to same- or opposite-sex individuals.

GENDER-ROLE STANDARDS AND STEREOTYPES

When children are still young infants, parents and other agents of socialization attempt systematically to teach them standards for behaviour that are gender based and to shape different behaviours in boys and girls (Maccoby, 2000). In fact, this process starts immediately after a baby's birth when parents give the baby a name and bring her or him home to a nursery often decorated in gender-typed ways—flowered bumper pads and pale, beribboned lampshades or bright-coloured curtains with sports or outer-space themes. Parents dress male and female children in distinctive clothes, style their hair in different ways, select toys and activities for them that they deem appropriate, promote children's association with same-gender playmates, and often react negatively when children behave in ways they consider gender inappropriate.

Cultures are internally quite consistent with regard to their standards of "appropriate" gender-role behaviour. We do not use the term *appropriate* to mean "desirable"; we mean what people in general think is appropriate—what is typical and generally accepted. In North American society, the male role is seen, stereotypically, as charged with controlling and manipulating the environment. Men are expected to be independent, assertive, dominant, and competitive in social and sexual relations. The female role is seen as emotionally supporting the family. Women are expected to be relatively passive, loving, sensitive, and supportive in family and social relationships. In general, people regard the expression of warmth in personal relationships, the display of anxiety under pressure, and the suppression of overt aggression and sexuality as more appropriate for women than for men (Ruble et al., 2006). Despite the concerns with gender equality initiated by the women's movement, major change in societal stereotyping has been slow. Males have become less likely to endorse personality traits such as toughness and aggression (Spence & Buckner, 2000). However, the world of work remains stereotypically gendered (Liben & Bigler, 2002). Both children and adults still tend to think of mechanics and doctors as male and librarians and nurses as female. These stereotypical roles are widespread not only in North American culture but also in a wide range of societies from Middle and South America, Europe, Africa, Asia, and Oceania (Wade & Tavris, 1999; Williams & Best, 1990). However, there are variations among countries, with more tradition-bound cultures such as Middle Eastern nations (Saudi Arabia, Iraq) and some Asian societies (Taiwan) adhering to more rigid stereotypes for the two sexes. In one study, for example, 8- to 10-year-old Taiwanese children were more committed to maintaining gender-role stereotypes than were more westernized Israeli children (Lobel et al., 2001).

gender typing

The process by which children acquire the values, motives, and behaviours considered appropriate for their gender in their particular culture.

gender-based beliefs

Ideas and expectations about what is appropriate behaviour for males and females.

gender stereotypes

Beliefs that members of a culture hold about how females and males ought to behave, that is, what behaviours are acceptable and appropriate for each.

gender roles

Composites of the behaviours actually exhibited by a typical male or female in a given culture; the reflection of a gender stereotype in everyday life.

gender identity

The perception of oneself as either masculine or feminine.

gender-role preferences

Desires to possess certain gender-typical characteristics.

sexual preferences

The preference for same- or opposite-sex romantic partners.

Gender Identity

Despite the changes that have occurred in recent years in men's and women's roles in society, gender-stereotypical roles are still widespread. In Japan, some women continue to teach their daughters to perform the formal and highly ritualized tea ceremony, and in the Philippines, some men train their sons in traditional male skills. Here, a young boy learns the blacksmith trade.

Within North America, the strength of these standards also varies with ethnicity. Some evidence suggests that African-American families are more likely to socialize children without strict boy–girl gender-role distinctions, and the children are less likely to hold stereotypic views about women (Leaper et al., 1998). These families value early independence for both boys and girls, and they make fewer gender distinctions in deciding who is to carry out which family roles and tasks (Gibbs, 1989). They encourage girls to be aggressive and assertive and boys to express emotion and nurturance (Allen & Majidi-Abi, 1989; Basow, 1992). Among Mexican Americans, gender-role socialization standards for boys and girls are much more clearly differentiated (Coltrane & Adams, 2008).

Age affects gender-role expectations as well. Young children between 3 and 6 years old are especially rigid in their gender stereotyping (Ruble et al., 2006). As they develop, they become more flexible in their attitudes about a variety of concepts, including gender issues (Blakemore, 2003).

Education also affects gender-role standards and stereotypes (Ruble et al., 2006). University-educated women are more likely than less educated females to perceive the feminine role as involving independence and desire for achievement. This difference trickles down to their children. Boys and girls with mothers who are employed in skilled occupations and professions are more likely than children whose mothers are full-time homemakers to think that acquiring an education and having a profession are appropriate for women and that it is also all right for men to assume housekeeping and child-care tasks. At the same time, researchers have found that even educated men maintain more stereotyped gender-role standards than do women.

Adult men and women also differ in their views of gender typing in children. It is common to find that fathers are more concerned than mothers with their children maintaining behaviours appropriate to their sex (Ruble et al., 2006), although some researchers have suggested that mothers and fathers may play more similar roles in gender typing than previously thought (Lytton & Romney, 1991). Still, almost all North Americans, regardless of gender, age, and education, continue to view aggression as more characteristic of men and interpersonal sensitivity as more common in women (Dodge et al., 2006).

ⓛⓞ2 GENDER DIFFERENCES IN DEVELOPMENT

How accurately do gender stereotypes reflect differences in the actual gender role behaviours of males and females? As Table 13-1 shows, although clear gender differences have been found in some characteristics, others have been found only occasionally, and still others have never been observed. As you examine the table in detail, keep in mind that even for the differences that have been observed consistently, the characteristics of males and females overlap. Some males are more compliant, verbal, and interested in the arts than some females. Some women are stronger than the average male.

Table 13-1 Gender differences: Real or myth?

Some gender differences are real . . .

Physical, Motor, and Sensory Development

At birth, girls are physically and neurologically more advanced. They walk earlier, and they attain puberty earlier. Boys have more mature muscular development and larger lungs and heart, and at birth they are less sensitive to pain. With increasing age, boys become superior at activities involving strength and gross motor skills. On the other hand, male fetuses are more likely to be miscarried, and boys have a higher rate of infant mortality and are more vulnerable to many hereditary anomalies, malnutrition, and disease. In terms of physical and physiological vulnerability, females are clearly not the weaker sex.

Cognitive Development

From infancy through the early school years, girls display superior verbal abilities, including vocabulary, reading comprehension, and verbal creativity. During middle childhood and adolescence, gender differences are either non-existent or very small. From about the age of 10 years, boys display greater visual-spatial ability, which is involved in such tasks as manipulating objects in two- or three-dimensional space, reading maps, or aiming at a target. Beginning at about age 12, boys tend to excel in mathematics, especially mathematical reasoning.

Social and Emotional Development

Even in early social play, boys are more often the aggressors and the victims of aggression, particularly physical aggression. Girls tend to use more indirect forms of aggression, such as excluding another child from social interaction. As early as age 2, girls are more likely to comply with the demands of parents and other adults. Boys are more variable in their responses to adult direction. We do not find gender differences in compliance consistently in peer relations, although preschool boys are less likely to comply with girls' demands than with boys' demands, and are less likely to comply than girls are with partners of either gender. Girls are more nurturant toward younger children.

Atypical Development

Boys are more likely to have genetic defects, physical disabilities, mental retardation, reading disabilities, speech defects, and school and emotional problems.

Some are found only sometimes . . .

Activity Level

Many studies find no gender differences in activity level. When they do find differences, it is usually boys who are more active than girls.

Dependence

Younger children do not display gender differences in dependency. Older girls and women tend to rate themselves as more dependent, but this is probably changing.

Fear, Timidity, and Anxiety

Again, young children do not exhibit consistent gender differences in timidity. Older girls and women report themselves as being more fearful, and males are more likely to involve themselves in physically risky recreations and occupations. On the other hand, many women today are in dangerous occupations (e.g., firefighting, high-steel construction) and enjoy risky sports (e.g., mountain climbing, hang gliding, triathlon).

Exploratory Activity

Studies do not find consistent gender differences in exploratory activity. A number of studies of early exploratory activity have found boys to be more venturesome and curious and likelier to attack barriers that intervene between themselves and a desirable object.

Vulnerability to Stress

Findings over the last decade suggest that males may be more vulnerable to family disharmony and interpersonal stress, as evidenced by a higher rate of boys in child guidance clinics. However, we need further research to draw firm conclusions.

Orientation to Social Stimuli

Some evidence indicates that infant girls may orient to faces more than boys and may recognize their mother's face at an earlier age.

(continued)

Table 13-1 continued   Gender differences: Real or myth?

Others are myths . . .
Sociability Boys and girls are equally social; they spend as much time with others and are equally responsive to others. There is no gender difference in the need for love and attachment. Males and females are equally capable of nurturance, although girls and women do more of the actual care of children, relatives, and friends.
Suggestibility and Conformity Girls and boys do not differ in suggestibility or in the tendency to conform to standards of a peer group or to imitate the responses of others.
Learning Style Boys and girls are equally good at rote learning and simple repetitive tasks. They also display similar skills in tasks involving the inhibition of previously learned responses and in complex cognitive tasks. Girls and boys are equally responsive to visual and auditory stimuli.
Achievement Girls and boys generally display equal levels of achievement motivation. Under neutral conditions, girls are often more achievement oriented than boys are, but in a competitive situation, boys are likelier to exhibit enhanced achievement motivation than are girls.
Self-Esteem Boys and girls do not differ in self-esteem. However, girls rate themselves as more competent in social skills, and boys view themselves as stronger and more powerful.
Verbal Aggressiveness and Hostility Girls and boys engage equally in verbal aggression but use different approaches: girls tend to gossip and exclude others; boys are more directly verbally assaultive.

Sources: Dodge et al., 2006; Halpern, 2004; Halpern et al., 2007; Hyde, 2005; Hyde & Linn, 1998; Hyde & Plant, 1995; Leaper & Friedman, 2007; Maccoby, 1998; Maccoby & Jacklin, 1974; Ruble et al., 2006; Underwood, 2003, 2004; Wigfield et al., 2006

Developmental Patterns of Gender Typing

Children develop gender-typical behaviour patterns at an early age (Ruble et al., 2006). Even before they can tell us about their gender-based preferences, infants and toddlers clearly express their choices through their looking behaviour. Using techniques that we described in Chapter 4, Lisa Serbin and her colleagues (Serbin et al., 2001) found that from a very young age, boys and girls differ in their preferences for dolls and cars, and can recognize gender-inconsistent events, such as a man putting on lipstick (Serbin et al., 2002). As Figure 13-1 shows, by the time they were a year old, girls had begun to show a greater preference for dolls than boys did, and this gender difference was even stronger by the time the children were 1½ to 2 years old. In contrast, boys showed much stronger preferences for vehicles such as cars and trucks than girls did by the ages of 1½ and 2. In a study of 1- to 3-year-olds in a daycare centre, boys and girls expressed their preferences for gender-appropriate toys (O'Brien et al., 1983). However, girls more often than boys also played with gender-inappropriate toys. Why do you suppose girls are more likely to play with a truck than boys are to cuddle a doll? Let's look at some of the reasons.

Western culture is basically male oriented, and the masculine role is associated with greater esteem, more privileges, and higher status. The male role is more clearly defined, and there is greater pressure for boys than for girls to conform to narrow gender-appropriate standards. Boys are also more likely to be "systematizers," who focus on trying to understand and organize a specific domain (e.g., cars), than girls, who are less focused on a particular set of interests (Baron-Cohen, 2003). In addition, boys are more likely to develop "extremely intense interests" in some objects and activities than are girls, and these passionate interests of boys are often gender stereotyped (e.g., vehicles, machines, trains) (DeLoache et al., 2007). Moreover, boys' preference for gender-stereotyped toys

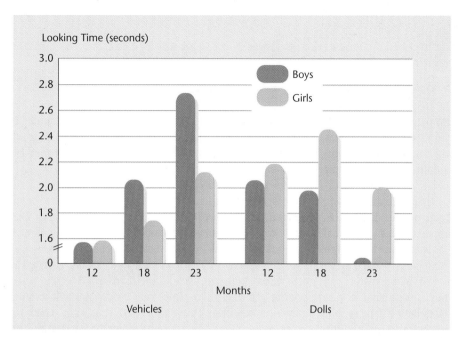

Figure 13-1

Toddlers prefer to look at gender-reflective toys

By 18 months, boys and girls prefer to look at gender-reflective toys. Boys prefer looking at vehicles and girls prefer to look at dolls.

Source: Serbin et al., 2001.

remained consistent across a wide age range (5 to 13), whereas girls' interest in play with gender-stereotyped toys decreased as they grew older (Cherney & London, 2006).

Although the situation is changing, boys shy away from things that are "for girls," fearing derision from other boys, whereas girls may want to do things that are regarded as higher status. Parents and peers condemn boys for acting like sissies—crying, retreating in the face of aggression, wearing feminine apparel, or playing with dolls. In contrast, we tend to accept a girl's occasional temper tantrum and rough-and-tumble play, and her wearing jeans or playing with trucks. In fact, one survey found that more that 50 percent of women and girls described themselves as being or having been tomboys, participating in sports, and playing with "boys'" toys at some point during childhood (Morgan, 1998).

Even though many girls engage in masculine activities, boys and girls do develop distinctive patterns of interest that are consistent with gender stereotypes. In a national survey of more than 2,000 children between the ages of 7 and 11, Zill (1986) found that boys liked guns, boxing, wrestling and karate, team sports, and fixing and making things more than girls did. In contrast, girls enjoyed playing with dolls, sewing, cooking, dancing, and looking after younger children more than boys did. More recent studies of girls in middle childhood and adolescence have found that girls spend more time in feminine leisure activities (dance, handicrafts, art, writing stories and letters) than in masculine activities (competitive sports, hunting, fishing, building) (McHale et al., 2004). Parents and others encourage these patterns of interest in a variety of ways, including in the assignment of household tasks. Even in the twenty-first century, girls are more likely to make beds, clean, prepare meals, wash dishes, and do laundry. Boys are more likely to fix things, take out the garbage, and mow lawns (Coltrane & Adams, 2008). As we will see, a variety of theoretical perspectives can account for these findings. Unfortunately, as Box 13.1 suggests on the next pages, parents and others in society also differentially encourage and discourage certain academic interests in boys and girls, which may be detrimental to children in the long run.

Stability of Gender Typing

Although children develop masculine and feminine interests and behaviours early, as we have noted, many girls participate in both female and male pursuits during childhood.

Box 13.1

Child Psychology in Action

WILL WE LET COMPUTERS WIDEN THE GENDER GAP?

Computers are becoming commonplace in classrooms, but are boys and girls benefiting equally from this technological revolution? Studying many types of computer activities available to children, including home use of a computer and in courses at school, after-school clubs, and summer camps, Mark Lepper (1985; Lepper & Gurtner, 1989) found large gender differences in girls' and boys' use of these opportunities. In formal computer programs, there were as many as five to ten boys for every girl, and this difference in participation rates increased as activities became more costly and effortful. In California schools, boys outnumbered girls in introductory programming classes by a 2:1 ratio, but in advanced programming classes, the ratio was as high as 10 to 15 boys for each girl.

What may be the reasons for this gender gap? The computer field—like the fields of math and science—has long been dominated by males, in large part because of the myth that males are more capable than females in technical subjects. Thus, the computer science field has few female role models. Computer labs in schools are often competitive, noisy, and high-activity environments in which boys may feel more comfortable than girls. Many girls view computing as a socially isolated activity and find the negative stereotypes of computer users as unflattering and unfeminine

(Schott & Selwyn, 2000). In fact, grade 6 and grade 8 children depicted computer users as male and wearing glasses, consistent with the prominent stereotypes of the male computer nerd (Mercier et al., 2006).

The kinds of software that are often used to introduce students to computers also seem to have been written for boys (Subrahmanyam et al., 2001). The most common themes of games are war and violence and male-centred sports such as football. Even the titles of specifically educational games may turn girls off: *Alien Addition, Demolition Division*. It is not surprising, therefore, to find that boys play electronic games more often than girls, and that they tend to make more gender distinctions about the acceptability of these games for either boys or girls (Cherney & London, 2006). According to Funk and Buchman (1996), although most grade 4 and 5 students thought boys and girls could play video games, boys were considerably more likely than girls to say that playing video games was not an acceptable activity for girls. Boys clearly spent more time than girls at such games, and they were a good deal more likely than girls to describe video-game playing as their favourite activity. A number of boys also said that girls who spent a lot of time playing video games were not popular and that, if girls wanted to be popular, they ought not to play such

With the onset of puberty, however, there is a movement back toward strict gender typing (Larson & Richards, 1994; McHale et al., 2004). In one study, girls who claimed to be tomboys indicated that at about age 12, they began to adopt more traditionally feminine interests and behaviours owing to pressures from both parents and peers and to their own increasing interest in romantic relationships (Burn et al., 1996; see also Chapter 12).

In spite of these developmental fluctuations in gender typing, individual children who are strongly masculine or feminine during childhood tend to be more masculine or feminine during adulthood (Kagan & Moss, 1962). Boys who were interested in competitive games, activities that required gross motor skills, and such things as mechanics, and girls who were interested in cooking, sewing, reading, and non-competitive games were involved in similar gender-typical activities in adulthood. The stability of gender-typed characteristics was related to cultural acceptance, however. When a characteristic was congruent with such gender-role standards, it led in adulthood to similar behaviour; for example, a girl who was very dependent on others in childhood might become a secretary. But when a characteristic was incongruent with cultural standards, it tended not to remain stable from childhood to maturity; a boy who was dependent on others in childhood might become an entrepreneur.

games—especially "the fighting games." Few girls agreed with these statements by boys; as many as a third held that fighting games were okay for girls. This result is consistent with research that suggests females are more flexible than males in their attitudes toward gender roles.

Can we change gender differences in attitudes toward computers? In one study, Judith Bernhard (1992) assessed an intervention program designed to modify gender-related attitudes toward computer programming and use in which preschool boys and girls received training in a computer-programming language (LOGO) for six weeks. Relative to a control group, the girls did not show any more positive attitudes toward computer use after this training program—both training and control groups saw computers as being more appropriate for girls than they did before the training program. However, Bernhard also found that despite the fact that the boys and girls received equivalent instruction during the training period, the boys actually completed more computer-related tasks than did the girls in a post-training assessment. One possible explanation is that the boys might have gone into the training with better initial skills than the girls did (although both groups were equivalent regarding the presence of computers in the home). Clearly, then, intervention programs aimed at narrowing the gender gap in computer use must address both gender-related attitudes as well as differences in initial experiences and skill.

One problem in this regard is that although computers have many varied uses, schools often present computers as mathematical tools. Computer labs are often found in the math department, and math teachers supervise their use. Inasmuch as girls have long been socialized into believing that they cannot do math as well as boys, this arrangement both keeps girls away from computers and reinforces the myth. The ultimate result is to turn girls ever further away from careers in math and science (Shea et al., 2001). However, according to recent trends, the gender gap in computer use may be closing, partly because of the expanding range of applications that are available, including email, chat rooms, and educational pursuits.

Recent data suggests that girls' and boys' attitudes toward computers are equalizing (North & Noyes, 2002), and that they show equivalent levels of computer usage and are equally confident in their computer skills. But they still differ in the type of usage they favour; for example, girls often use computers for social contact, whereas boys play games (Subrahmanyam et al., 2001).

During adulthood, most people's masculine or feminine behaviour remains stable. In one longitudinal study, researchers found that 54 percent of adults continued to be rated similarly by observers over a 10-year period in terms of masculinity or femininity (Hyde et al., 1991). However, gender roles may shift as adults meet the demands of new situations and circumstances. One of the most important transitions is parenthood. Even among egalitarian couples committed to the equal sharing of household tasks, the onset of parenthood generally heralds a return to traditional gender roles (Cowan & Cowan, 2000; Parke, 2002a). In these roles, women exhibit more **expressive characteristics**—they are more nurturant, concerned with feelings, and child oriented. Men exhibit more **instrumental characteristics**—they are more task and occupation oriented. Women tend to become more autonomous as they get older but return to a more feminine gender-role orientation in old age, perhaps because they become less self-sufficient and have a greater need for help (Hyde et al., 1991; Maccoby, 1998).

expressive characteristics

Presumably typical of females, these characteristics include nurturance and concern with feelings.

instrumental characteristics

Presumably typical of males, these characteristics include task and occupation orientation.

Gender Differences in Abilities

There are modest gender differences in abilities but also many similarities (Hyde, 2005). Boys tend to be more skilled than girls at manipulating objects, constructing

Figure 13-2

Boys' and girls' understanding of horizontal and vertical relations

Between the ages of about 8 or 9 years to roughly 16 or 17 years, boys tend to make correct predictions of changes in horizontals and verticals following tilt, whereas girls are more likely to predict the results incorrectly. In general, boys seem to be more skilled at visual-spatial tasks.

Source: Liben & Golbeck, 1980.

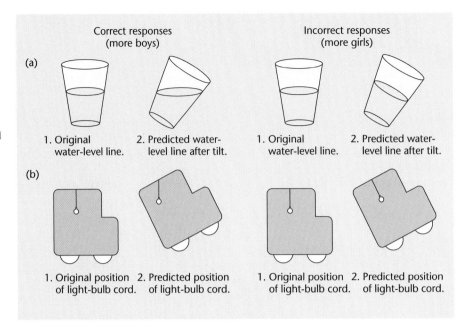

three-dimensional forms, and mentally manipulating complex figures and pictures (Choi & Silverman, 2003). In grades 3 to 11, boys are more likely than girls to make correct judgments of visual-spatial relations, as Figure 13-2 illustrates (Liben, 1991). However, this is not always the case: few gender differences in spatial abilities are found among children in poor families, which suggests that these differences are at least to some extent determined by environmental opportunities (Bower, 2005). Male superiority in math is generally restricted to performance in geometry, a form of mathematics that requires spatial visualization skills (Hyde, 2005). In fact, girls do better in computational skills than boys, and there are no gender differences in girls' and boys' performance on tests of basic math knowledge or algebra, which are less reliant on spatial ability than geometry (Halpern, 2004; Hyde et al., 1990). Moreover, boys' math superiority only surfaces in the high-school years, probably because of the lower expectations of teachers and parents for girls' math skills (Hyde, 2005). Girls tend to speak and write earlier and to be better at grammar and spelling than boys (Halpern, 2000). Boys are more likely to suffer from social and communicative difficulties; autism is four times more common in boys than in girls (Baron-Cohen, 2003).

For Thought and Discussion

1. Given the prevalence of gender-role stereotypes in North American society, how possible is it to conduct research on this issue without the sex of the experimenter influencing the research in some way? How might you get around this problem?

2. Differences between the sexes are often treated as "facts" arising from any number of potential sources. In recent years, however, a number of writers have questioned this idea and have instead suggested that the concept of gender is actually a social construction arising out of assumptions and social influences. How important is the socio-cultural context in our basic concepts of gender?

3. Where do you think many of the cultural myths in gender differences come from? If there is no actual evidence for them, why do people believe they exist?

BIOLOGICAL FACTORS IN GENDER DIFFERENCES

The differences between males and females are to some extent rooted in biology. Research on the influence of biological factors on gender differences has focused on hormonal function and brain lateralization. Refer back to Chapter 5 if you need to refresh your understanding of these concepts.

Hormones and Social Behaviour

Hormones are powerful and highly specialized chemical substances produced by cells of certain body organs and have a regulatory effect on the activities of certain other organs. Those hormones associated with sexual characteristics and with reproductive functions are found in differing concentrations in males and females from infancy through adulthood. Among male hormones, called androgens, testosterone is the principal and most potent one. Women's principal hormones are various forms of estrogen and progesterone. The differences in the concentrations of these hormones are not great in boys and girls of preschool and elementary school age, but they become quite pronounced after puberty.

Both the prenatal and pubertal periods are critical in terms of the effect of hormonal action on the development of human beings (Hines, 2004). In the prenatal period, fetal testosterone is the major determinant of the anatomic sex of the fetus, and hormones organize the fetus's biological and psychological predispositions to be masculine or feminine. The surge in hormones during puberty activates these early predispositions.

The effects of hormones have been demonstrated in animal studies. When pregnant monkeys were injected with testosterone, their offspring were females that exhibited masculine behaviours such as threatening gestures and rough-and-tumble play (Young et al., 1967). When male hormones were injected into female monkeys after birth, they also become more assertive, sometimes even attaining prime dominance status in their monkey troop (Wallen, 1996). In human case studies, girls who were exposed to high levels of androgens prenatally exhibited masculine behaviours and interests—even if they were raised as girls (Hines, 2004). They sought out boys as playmates and chose toys usually preferred by boys. The greater the girl's exposure to androgen when a fetus, the stronger were her preferences for masculine play and activities. In other human case studies, genetic males born without a penis or with a very small one who underwent sex reassignment surgery and were raised as girls exhibited typical male behaviour such as rough-and-tumble play and had many male friends (Reiner & Gerhart, 2004). Although there is still no clear answer concerning the relative influences of biology and environmental factors, it is evident that biology plays an important role in gender-role development (Berenbaum, 2006).

Probably the most dramatic example of the relative roles of social experience and hormonal factors is demonstrated in the classic studies of John Money and his colleagues from Johns Hopkins University (Money, 1987; Money & Annecillo, 1987; Money & Ehrhardt, 1972). These investigators studied prenatal hormonal anomalies, such as high levels of androgen in a female fetus, which results in masculinizing the female child, and causing mistaken sexual identity. Money and his colleagues found that if such a child were reassigned to her correct feminine role early in development, these girls experienced normal psychosexual development. According to Money, findings such as these suggest that gender roles are highly dependent on social factors, and that there is a critical period for the establishment of gender-role identity.

Money's theories about sexual reassignment have been challenged, however. Probably the most well-known, and most dramatic, challenge has arisen out of the

John/Joan case (Colapinto, 2000). In 1967, 8-month-old Canadian David Reimer accidentally had his penis amputated during a circumcision, and his parents decided, after consulting with Money, that David should undergo sex-change surgery and be raised as a girl (named Brenda). Although this case was, for many years, hailed as evidence of the importance of social context and experience in gender identity, there was one fundamental problem. Despite being raised as a girl, as well as eventually receiving female hormone treatments, Brenda never felt comfortable as a girl and insisted she was a boy. By her teenage years, and after learning what had happened, Brenda refused to continue living as a girl. She stopped taking her hormonal treatments, and eventually underwent extensive surgeries (including the construction of an artificial penis) to switch her gender back to that of a male. David eventually married, although his marriage was, over the years, a difficult one. And in a truly sad ending to this story, David Reimer, in May 2004, took his own life. Case studies, such as this one, which virtually everyone would agree represents a serious failure of Money's theories, raise anew the importance of both genetic and environmental factors in gender identity.

Hormones and Cognitive Skills

Researchers have suggested that at a critical period in prenatal development, sex hormones may determine a fetus's brain organization, and this, in turn, may lead to gender differences in males' and females' verbal and spatial skills. Support for this suggestion comes from studies showing that when prenatal androgen levels in female fetuses are exceptionally high, girls have better visual-spatial skills than other girls (Hines, 2004; Hines et al., 2003). Other methods of assessing prenatal hormone concentrations, including analysis of umbilical cord blood, amniotic fluid, maternal serum during pregnancy, and finger-length ratios also show masculinizing effects of prenatal androgens on spatial abilities, especially at high doses of androgens (Cohen-Bendahan et al., 2005). Other evidence for sex differences on spatial abilities has been provided by Irwin Silverman of York University and Jean Choi at the University of Lethbridge, who have demonstrated that children as young as 9 years of age exhibit sex differences in route-learning and other navigational strategies (Choi & Silverman, 2003; Silverman & Choi, 2005, 2006). According to these authors, males employ a more Euclidean, or orientation strategy that features distances, vectors, and cardinal directions such as north, northeast, or 90°, whereas females are more likely to employ topographical or landmark strategies, including using relative directions such as right, in front of, or behind. However, even if researchers have established a biological basis for such gender differences in spatial abilities, this does not mean that these abilities were unaffected by culture or unmodifiable by the environments (Berenbaum, 2006; Ruble et al., 2006). Hormonal differences between males and females may contribute to their spatial abilities, but environmental factors modify these biologically influenced patterns of differences between males and females.

Brain Lateralization and Gender Differences

Another biological difference between males and females that may contribute to differences in cognitive abilities is the extent to which brain functioning is organized across the two cerebral hemispheres. As we discussed in Chapter 5, in most people, the right hemisphere is more involved in processing spatial information and the left hemisphere in processing verbal information. However, there is some evidence that men's brains are more lateralized than women's (Halpern, 2000); that is, their hemispheres are more specialized than women's. Men whose left hemispheres are damaged are more likely than women with left-hemisphere damage to experience verbal deficits, and men whose right hemispheres are damaged show more spatial deficits than women with right-hemisphere damage (Halpern, 2000). Studies using brain-imaging techniques that detect blood flow in the brain as people perform different cognitive tasks confirm the greater lateralism among men. In a task in which men and women were asked to decide if nonsense words rhymed, both left and right sides of women's brains were activated; in men, however, only the left hemisphere was activated (Shaywitz et al., 1995). Even infants show this gender difference in patterns of brain activation in a word-comprehension task (Hines, 2004).

Biological Programming and Cultural Expectations

Researchers have asked what role biological "programming" plays in shaping both gender-role standards and gender typing. For example, are women's abilities to have and to breast-feed a baby related to some kind of biological programming that causes girls to be more responsive than boys to the sights and signals of infants and children? Investigators have found that by the age of 4 or 5, girls interact more with babies and, when asked to care for a baby, are more likely to engage actively, whereas boys are inclined to watch the baby passively (Berman, 1987; Blakemore, 1990). These observations are consistent with the evolutionary theoretical perspective; it argues that females are more committed to parental activities than males. Similarly, evolutionary theory suggests that males' greater visual-spatial ability is rooted in the distant past, when males' major activity was hunting (Choi & Silverman, 2003; Geary, 2006; Silverman et al., 2007; Silverman & Choi, 2006).

These behavioural tendencies, however, could as easily be due to cultural expectations. In adolescents and adults, they are more apparent when people know that someone is observing them (Berman, 1987). When experimenters have used subtle measures of responsiveness to an infant's crying, such as changes in blood pressure, electrical skin conductance, or other responses of the autonomic nervous system, they have not detected any differences in mothers' and fathers' responses to an infant's crying (Lamb, 2004). Biological programming notwithstanding, culture has a considerable impact on males' and females' behaviour toward infants and children. Similarly, males' superior visual-spatial ability is fostered by culture, as boys are encouraged more often than girls to play with toys that involve spatial abilities, such as building sets, and to undertake mathematical and scientific endeavours (Beal, 1994). Experience with blocks, models, and video games, moreover, enhances spatial skills (Subrahmanyam et al., 2001).

COGNITIVE FACTORS IN GENDER TYPING   **LO**4

Biology and culture are not the only determinants of gender typing. Children's own understanding of gender roles and rules contributes to the process of gender-role acquisition (see the Turning Points chart on the next pages for a general outline of the development of gender roles and gender typing). In this section, we explore two cognitive approaches to gender typing: Kohlberg's cognitive developmental theory and an information-processing approach called gender-schema theory.

Kohlberg's Cognitive Developmental Theory

In his **cognitive developmental theory of gender typing**, Lawrence Kohlberg (1966) proposed that children's differentiation of gender roles and their perception of themselves as more like same-sex rather than opposite-gender models begins very early. Children, using physical and behavioural clues such as hairstyle or playing with trucks, categorize people, including themselves, as male or female; they then find it rewarding to behave in a gender-appropriate manner and to imitate same-gender models. For example, the girl's

cognitive developmental theory of gender typing

Kohlberg's theory that children use physical and behavioural clues to differentiate gender roles and to gender-type themselves very early in life.

Turning Points

DEVELOPMENT OF GENDER ROLES AND GENDER TYPING

FROM BIRTH	• Father typically greets male infant with something like "Hey, Tiger" and female infant with "Hello, little darlin'" or some such expression • Parents typically set the stage for gender typing by dressing baby and decorating nursery in pink or blue • Parents select gender-appropriate toys, promote contact with same-sex playmates, react disapprovingly when child displays behaviour that's "inappropriate" for gender • Other adults describe boys as "strong," "active" and girls as "sweet," "cuddly"
1 YEAR	• Child may recognize male and female faces as belonging to two distinct categories
18 MONTHS OR YOUNGER	• Fathers are more likely to gender-type children than mothers
2 YEARS	• Child can correctly label own gender but has limited understanding of gender identity and its wider implications • As they approach 3 years of age, children begin to grasp concept of gender identity
3 YEARS	• Children understand that they themselves, along with other children, belong to a gender class • They have developed clear preferences for gender-appropriate toys by this time
3–6 YEARS	• Children of this age range are more gender-stereotypical than adults
4 YEARS	• Children who grasped gender identity early (before 27 months) have greater knowledge of gender-role stereotypes

Note: Developmental events described in this and other Turning Points charts represent overall trends identified in research studies. Individual children vary greatly in the ages at which they achieve these developmental changes.

Sources: Beal, 1994; Golombok & Fivush, 1994; Leaper & Friedman, 2007; Maccoby, 1998; Ruble et al., 2006.

thinking goes something like this: "I am a girl because I am more like my mother and other girls than like boys; therefore, I want to dress like a girl, play girl games, and feel and think like a girl." Consistency between children's actual gender, the way they see themselves, and their behaviours and values is critical in sustaining self-esteem.

Kohlberg believed that children go through three phases in gaining an understanding of gender. First, between the ages of 2 and 3, they acquire basic gender identity, recognizing that they are either male or female. Second, by the age of 4 or 5, they acquire the concept of **gender stability**, accepting that males remain male and females remain female. The little boy no longer thinks he might grow up to be a mommy, and the little girl gives up her heady hopes of becoming Spider-Man. Third, by about the age of 6 or 7, children acquire the notion of **gender constancy**, recognizing that superficial changes in appearance or activities do not alter gender. Even when a girl wears jeans or plays football, or when a boy wears long hair or has a burning interest in needlework, she or he recognizes—and peers recognize, too—that gender remains the same.

Researchers who have tested Kohlberg's theory around the world have confirmed that both boys and girls acquire gender identity first, an understanding of stability next, and, finally, an appreciation of constancy (Martin & Little, 1990; Slaby & Frey, 1975).

gender stability

The notion that gender does not change; males remain male and females remain female.

gender constancy

The awareness that superficial alterations in appearance or activity do not alter gender.

516

4–5 YEARS	• Children begin to understand the concept of gender stability but do not grasp it fully until about the age of 7 years
	• Children 4 years and younger tend to rely more on gender schemas than do children 5 years and older
	• By 4½ years of age, children spend three times as much time with same-sex play-mates as with other-gender peers
	• Girls interact more with babies and in a more active way than boys do
5 YEARS	• Few children this age show knowledge of traits
4–6 YEARS	• Boys are more likely than girls to congregate in same-sex groups
6½ YEARS	• Children spend 11 times as much time with same-sex playmates as with other-gender children
6–7 YEARS	• Children now understand gender stability and also grasp gender constancy
7–11 YEARS	• Children develop distinct patterns of interest in activities that are consistent with cultural gender stereotypes
8 YEARS	• Most children display knowledge of gender-typed traits
8–13 YEARS	• Studies of children in this age range suggest that female brains may be more bilaterally organized than male brains

Working-class children and kids in non-industrialized cultures generally reach these milestones about a year later than middle-class North American children do (Frey & Ruble, 1992).

Some researchers have suggested that the process by which children come to recognize males and females as distinct categories probably has its origins in early infancy—well before babies can understand labels and language. Some studies (Poulin-Dubois et al., 1994) have found that 9- and 12-month-old infants show intermodal knowledge of gender by correctly matching female voices to female faces (although male voices and faces were not matched), and that by 1½ to 2 years, infants understand gender stereotypes for both conventional (e.g., a tiara versus a fire hat) and metaphorical (e.g., a cat versus a bear) objects (Eichstedt et al., 2002). Such findings suggest that the process of understanding gender begins earlier than Kohlberg originally thought.

With increasing age, understanding of gender improves. By 18 months, children can match both male and female faces and voices (Poulin-Dubois, Serbin, & Derbyshire, 1998), and their ability to actually label genders, such as "boy" and "girl," appears by about 2 years, although they still have a very limited understanding of gender identity (Fagot & Leinbach, 1992). Young children have some understanding of gender words. Poulin-Dubois and colleagues (1998), for example, found that 18-month-old girls (but not boys) matched male and female voices with the labels *man* and *lady*. Children also recognize that some activities and objects are associated with each sex (e.g., wearing neckties versus wearing skirts). It is not until they are about 3 years of age, however, when kids grasp the concept that they themselves, along with other children, belong to a gender class or group. Considerably later (around age 7), children have a complete understanding of gender constancy. Consider the following exchange between two preschool boys. Jeremy, who wore a barrette to nursery school, was accused by Leo of being a girl because "only girls wear barrettes." Jeremy pulled down his pants to show that he really was a boy. His young classmate replied, "Everyone has a penis; only girls wear barrettes" (Bem, 1983, p. 607). Clearly, he did not yet understand gender constancy.

Genital knowledge is an important determinant of gender constancy (Ruble et al., 2006). Bem (1989, 1993) showed preschool children anatomically correct photos of a nude boy and a nude girl and then showed the youngsters pictures of the same children dressed in either clothing appropriate to their own gender or clothing appropriate to the opposite gender. Even when boys wore dresses or girls wore pants, nearly 40 percent of the children correctly identified the gender of the child. When Bem then tested the preschoolers' understanding of genital differences between the sexes, she found that nearly 60 percent of the children who possessed genital knowledge, but only 10 percent of children who lacked it, had gender constancy.

Kohlberg's theory was not entirely accurate in predicting that children would behave in more gender-typed ways after they fully understood gender constancy. However, research has shown that children who had developed gender identity engaged in more gender-typed play at age 2 than children who gained gender identity later; the boys were more likely to play with trucks and trains, and the girls more likely to be in the doll corner (Fagot & Leinbach, 1989). Girls who had acquired gender stability chose to play with other girls more than did girls who acquired gender stability later (Smetana & Letourneau, 1984). Five-year-old children who understood gender constancy were more attentive to same-sex characters on television than were children with less understanding of gender constancy, as shown in Figure 13-3 (Luecke-Aleksa et al., 1995).

Gender-Schema Theory: An Information-Processing Approach

gender-schema theory

The notion that children develop schemas, or naive theories, that help them to organize and structure their experience related to gender differences and gender roles.

According to **gender-schema theory**, children develop *schemas*, or naive theories, about gender that help them to organize and structure experience related to gender differences and gender roles (Bem, 1998; Martin & Ruble, 2004). These schemas tell the child what kinds of information to look for in the environment and how to interpret such information. Martin and Halverson (1983) demonstrated the importance of gender-role schemas by showing 5- and 6-year-olds pictures of males and females involved in activities that were either gender consistent (e.g., a boy playing with a train) or gender inconsistent (e.g., a girl sawing wood). A week later, the researchers asked the children to recall the pictures. When they were asked to recall gender-inconsistent pictures, children tended to distort information by changing the gender of the actor—presumably because they had

These children do not seem worried that either rock climbing, stereotypically a male activity, or baking, more traditionally a female task, will alter their gender identities; they have grasped the notion of gender constancy.

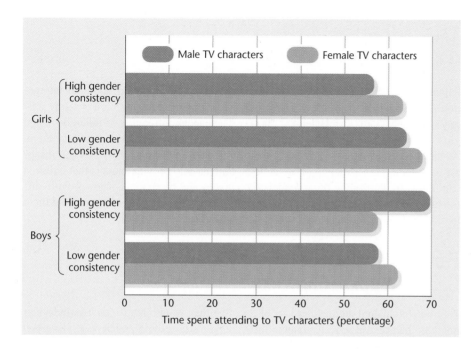

Figure 13-3

Gender constancy and attention to television characters

Grasping the concept of gender constancy led both boys and girls to pay more attention to same-sex characters on television. Because both girls and boys who have not yet grasped this concept tend to pay more attention to female characters, constancy did not alter girls' viewing patterns very much, although it reversed the boys' patterns.

Source: Based on Luecke-Aleska, Anderson, Collins, and Schmitt, 1995.

schemas for what was gender appropriate. Some children are particularly "gender schematic" and are more attentive to gender cues (Signorella et al., 1993). They are the ones who display better memories for gender-consistent information and are more likely to distort gender-inconsistent information (Levy, 1994; Lobel et al., 2000). The degree to which children rely on gender schemas in interpreting their social world changes with age (Ruble et al., 2006). Preschool children rely more on gender schemas than elementary school children because older children have more complete and elaborate knowledge of gender roles, attach less importance to these roles, and are less rigid in applying their knowledge.

Children develop schemas through their own perceptions (boys wearing camouflage) and based on information provided by parents, peers, and cultural stereotypes ("boys don't wear pink"). They use these gender schemas to evaluate and explain behaviour. For instance, when they were told about a child who spilled some milk, children evaluated the behaviour more negatively if the child was a boy—because of the stereotype that boys are bad (Giles & Heyman, 2004; Heyman & Giles, 2006). They appraised the risk of injury as higher for girls than for boys because of the stereotype that girls are fragile—even though boys actually incur more injuries than girls do (Morrongioello et al., 2000). The links between gender schemas and the child's own behaviour are presumed to occur through selective attention to, and memory for, own-sex relevant information and through motivation to be like same-sex others.

For Thought and Discussion

1. Given that all biological effects on human behaviour must occur within a social context, what do you think is the influence of this context on our interpretations of biologically based gender differences? Are such differences "real," or are they still observed (and judged) within an implicit social framework?

2. Popular culture, in recent years, has seen a number of backlashes at research on gender, claiming that men are often forgotten in such work or are simply treated as unimportant. Is research on gender necessarily about women, or is the idea of gender research broader than this? What would be some examples of a broader conception of gender research?

3. Why would brain differences as a function of sex be important in understanding human behaviour? What assumptions does such research make?

(LO)5 THE INFLUENCE OF FAMILY ON GENDER TYPING

Parents have a significant impact on children's gender development, acting as interaction partners, direct instructors, and providers of opportunities to learn sex-role attitudes and behaviours (McHale et al., 2003). They speak differently to infant boys and girls, hold and move them differently, and choose different clothes and toys for them. As children grow, parents encourage them in gender-appropriate activities and disapprove of their gender-inappropriate actions. Parents also provide models that children can follow in developing their gender-role choices and behaviours. They provide different opportunities for boys and girls to learn sex-typed behaviours by enrolling them in different activities, clubs, and sports (Leaper & Friedman, 2007).

Parents' Influence on Children's Gender-Typed Choices

Well before children are making lists of toys that they would like for their birthdays or holidays, parents are actively shaping their children's tastes and preferences. Have you ever compared the bedrooms of girls and boys? Researchers have recorded the kinds of toys, decorations, furniture, and even the curtains and bedspreads that adorn the bedrooms of boys and girls between 1 month and 6 years of age (Pomerleau et al., 1990; Rheingold & Cook, 1975). Boys' rooms contained more vehicles, machines, army equipment, soldiers, and sports equipment. In contrast, girls' rooms were more likely to house dolls and floral-patterned and ruffled furnishings. Boys' toys were more action oriented; girls' toys were less action oriented and more family focused. There was little difference between children's rooms in the 1970s and 1990s. Parents also subtly shape their children toward "appropriate" gender roles by the way they dress them. When a group of researchers watched 1- to 13-month-olds in a shopping centre, they found baby girls in pink, puffed sleeves, ruffles, and lace. Boys wore blue or red but few bows, barrettes, or ribbons (Shakin et al., 1985). Gender-typed clothing serves not only to announce a child's gender but to ensure that even strangers will respond to the child in gender- appropriate ways.

Parents' Behaviour toward Girls and Boys

Both mothers and fathers tend to behave differently with their sons and daughters, but fathers are especially likely to treat them differently (Leaper & Friedman, 2007).

INFANTS AND TODDLERS   From earliest infancy, parents are likely to view their sons and daughters as different. They describe their newborn daughters as smaller, softer, cuter, more delicate, and more finely featured than their sons. Fathers, even if they have only seen and not yet handled their infants, are more extreme than mothers in emphasizing the size, strength, coordination, and alertness of sons versus the fragility and beauty of daughters (Rubin et al., 1974; Stern & Karraker, 1989). These predictions are consistent with predictions from an evolutionary theoretical approach to gender differences, which emphasizes strength and competitiveness in boys and nurturance in girls (Geary, 1998). Researchers have found that adult strangers will play in more masculine ways with a baby that they have been led to believe is a boy and in a gentler fashion with an infant they think is a girl, regardless of the infant's actual gender.

Fathers are more likely to play and talk with infant sons than with daughters, especially when the new babies are first-borns (Parke, 2002a; Schoppe-Sullivan et al., 2006). As children grow older, fathers spend more time in play with male toddlers, and they watch and touch them more. They indulge in rough-and-tumble antics with male infants and may talk with them in a kind of macho way, saying things like "Hey, tiger!" or "What's up, bud?" (Parke, 2002a). Fathers are more likely to cuddle their infant daughters gently than to engage in active play with them. Mothers tend to treat female and male babies pretty much the same way (Leaper, 2002; Lytton & Romney, 1991; Siegel, 1987). Both parents, however, are more verbally responsive to girls; they talk to them more, and they use more supportive and directive speech with daughters than they do with sons (Leaper & Friedman, 2007; Leaper et al., 1998).

This pattern of differences in mothers' and fathers' interactions with sons and daughters suggests that the social forces involved in gender-role typing begin at birth and that fathers, through their markedly different treatment of boys and girls, may play a more important role in the gender-typing process than mothers do.

OLDER CHILDREN   As children grow older, parents more actively encourage and reinforce them for behaving in a gender-stereotypical manner. Langlois and Downs (1980) observed how mothers and fathers reacted to their 3- and 5-year-old girls' and boys' play, purposely manipulating the children's choices of toys. Both "masculine" toys, such as soldiers and a gas station, and "feminine" toys, such as a dollhouse and kitchen utensils, were available to the children, but the researchers specifically told them to play with toys that were either gender-appropriate or not. They then recorded parents' reactions to their children's choices of toys, mothers in one session, and fathers in another. Fathers consistently exerted pressure on their children—both boys and girls—to play with gender-typical toys. They were also quite consistent in rewarding both sons and daughters for play with gender-appropriate toys and in punishing them for play with opposite-gender toys. With daughters, mothers took the same approach, but their responses to their sons were inconsistent. They sometimes punished and other times rewarded them for playing with opposite-gender toys.

These findings are consistent with other evidence that reveals men are more likely than women to gender-type toys and to purchase them, especially for boys (Fisher-Thompson, 1990). They are also consistent with the view that the father is the principal agent of gender-role socialization and that the mother is less influential in this process (Parke, 2002a).

When we meet an infant for the first time, we often use clothing to judge the child's gender. If the beruffled infant in pink and the baby in the blue sailor outfit changed clothes, would you be just as likely to judge the first a girl and the second a boy?

Another difference in the way parents treat girls and boys is that they are more protective of girls' than of boys' physical well-being. Parents tend to encourage dependence and close family ties in girls and to put more emphasis on independence, early exploration, achievement, and competition in boys (Rubin et al., 2006). They have similar expectations for boys' and girls' independence and maturity in relation to such safe activities as tidying up rooms, putting away toys or clothes, or getting dressed, but they treat boys and girls differently in areas where there are greater risks. Parents generally think that boys should be able to play away from home without telling parents where they are, run errands in the neighbourhood, cross the street alone, use sharp scissors, and indulge in other venturesome activities at an earlier age than girls. Parents are also less likely to pick up or supervise boys after school. Moreover, parents often communicate these messages directly. Pomerantz and Ruble (1998) found that parents were more likely to tell sons specifically that they were free to do certain activities than they were to grant such freedoms to daughters. In Box 13.2 on the next page, we take a closer look at gender differences in children's risk-taking behaviour and how parents may or may not tacitly encourage such activities.

Not all cultural groups make these gender-based distinctions. Many psychologists are concerned, however, that among those groups that do tend to gender-type their children along traditional lines, girls may suffer. Restricting girls' freedom more than boys' may lead girls to lack feelings of self-efficacy and to discourage them from exploring their worlds and taking intellectual and creative risks. Under these conditions, girls may continue to be more likely than boys to conform to cultural norms and values; clearly, this may sometimes be useful, but it may also be detrimental (Ruble et al., 2006).

Parents' gender-differentiated behaviours often seem to be associated with an interest in their children's achievement. Fathers, who are particularly prone to differentiate

Box 13.2

Risk and Resilience

GENDER DIFFERENCES IN INJURIES: CHILDREN'S RISK TAKING AND PARENTAL PERCEPTIONS

In most industrialized countries, including Canada and the United States, the leading cause of childhood death and of visits to hospital emergency rooms is accidental injury (Canadian Institute of Child Health, 1994; Morrongiello et al., 2008). The frequency of injury, however, is not the same among all children; instead, boys are much more likely to sustain a serious injury than are girls (Canadian Institute of Child Health, 1994; Morrongiello, 1996; Morrongiello & Dawber, 1999). Although it is not clear exactly why boys have more injuries than girls do (Morrongiello, 1996), contributing factors to this difference could be that boys are more active than girls (Eaton, 1989), that boys engage in more risk-taking behaviour than girls do (Rivara et al., 1982), and, most interestingly, that boys are more likely to believe that they will not get hurt when engaging in risky behaviour (Morrongiello, 1997; Morrongiello & Rennie, 1998). And what is even more striking, parental judgments of risk-taking situations involving their young children also vary according to the sex of the child, as do the ways in which parents communicate potentially dangerous situations to their children (Mondschein et al., 2000; Morrongiello & Dawber, 1999, 2000).

Barbara Morrongiello, of the University of Guelph, and her colleagues have examined gender differences in children's risk-taking behaviour, as well as parental reactions to such behaviour. In one series of studies (Morrongiello, 1997; Morrongiello et al., 2000; Morrongiello & Rennie, 1998; Hillier & Morrongiello, 1998), these researchers looked at whether children's perceptions of the riskiness of certain behaviours truly varied with gender, as well as the children's own recognition of such risky situations. Hillier and Morrongiello (1998), for example, found that although 6- to 10-year-old children were all able to discriminate between varying degrees of risk across different situations, boys deemed activities lower risk than did girls, and that boys based their judgments on the perceived severity of an injury ("how might I get hurt") whereas girls based their judgments on perceived vulnerability ("will I get hurt"). Subsequently, Morrongiello and colleagues (2000) found that both boys and girls rated boys as being less likely to sustain injury than girls, even though the boys and girls were engaged in exactly the same activity. So,

children truly do have gender biases in the assessment of risk.

Not only do children exhibit these gender biases, but parents both expect them (Morrongiello & Dawber, 1999, 2000; Morrongiello & Hogg, 2004) and respond differentially to injuries to their sons and daughters (Morrongiello & Hogg, 2004; Morrongiello et al., 2004). Morrongiello and Hogg (2001, 2004), for instance, asked parents to imagine their reactions to an injury to their school-aged children caused by children's misbehaviour. Prior to the injury, parental reactions to their children varied with the gender of the child, with mothers expressing concerns over safety to their daughters and concerns over discipline to their sons. After the injury, parents expressed a greater degree of concern for injuries to their daughters than their sons, and felt that the sons' risky behaviour resulted from unchangeable characteristics, whereas the daughters' misbehaviour was due to factors that the parents could have influenced. Thus, not only do parents expect riskier behaviour from sons versus daughters, but they also believe that they have greater influence on risk taking involving their daughters than involving their sons.

And there is even evidence that parents show gender differences in their expectations for basic aspects of their child's motor ability, with such differences evident at least as early as when the child can first move himself or herself around. Karen Adolph at New York University and her colleagues (Mondschein et al., 2000) observed mothers of 11-month-old infants as they estimated their infants' abilities to crawl up and down steep and shallow slopes and found that mothers of girls consistently underestimated their child's performance, whereas mothers of boys consistently overestimated their child's abilities. When actually tested on the slopes, however, girls and boys showed no difference in their ability to traverse them.

Clearly, parents are sending different messages to their sons and daughters about what they expect them to be able to do, and children are picking up on these messages. As a consequence, ensuring that children remain safe and free of injury may be more difficult for our sons than for our daughters; boys truly do seem to be more at risk for injury, serious or otherwise, than girls.

between boys and girls in this regard, are more likely to stress the importance of a career or occupational success for sons than for daughters (Block, 1983; Hoffman, 1977). Differential treatment of boys and girls is particularly marked in the area of mathematical and scientific achievement (DeLisi & McGillicuddy-DeLisi, 2002). For example, parents are likely to encourage boys more often than girls to work on math or science-related activities at home (Eccles et al., 2000). In one study, even when families visited a science museum, parents were more likely to explain interactive exhibits to their sons than to their daughters (Crowley et al., 2001). In another study, fathers of sons used more explanations and scientific vocabulary than fathers of daughters when instructing their child on a physical science task (Tenenbaum & Leaper, 2003).

Fathers of girls seem to be less concerned with performance and more concerned with interpersonal interactions with their daughters (Block, 1983). Even mothers, when reading bedtime stories, teach their boys more than their girls. They supply unfamiliar names for sons ("Look, here's a giraffe. Can you say giraffe?"), whereas with daughters, they emphasize enjoying the time spent with them (Weitzman et al., 1985). These parental behaviours are not lost on children. Eccles and colleagues (Eccles et al., 1998; Wigfield et al., 2006) found that when they controlled for children's actual skills in English, math, and sports, the children's performance and perception of their own competence matched their parents' stereotyped expectations. The good news is that girls do better when their parents endorse more gender-egalitarian attitudes and are more balanced in their treatment of boys and girls (Leaper & Friedman, 2007; Updegraff et al., 1996).

When One Parent Is Absent

Particularly because the father plays such an important role in gender typing, we might expect that children from families in which the father is absent would show disruptions in gender typing. When fathers are permanently gone because of divorce or death, when they are temporarily absent or unavailable because of occupational demands or wartime service, and when they simply show little interest in their children, young boys especially may have problems with gender identity and gender role (Ruble et al., 2006). Disruptions in gender roles are most likely if the separation has occurred when the child was very young (Hetherington, 1966). As children get older and have wider social contacts, other models such as peers, siblings, surrogate fathers, teachers, and people in the mass media, can mitigate the effects of father absence on gender-role adoption (Ruble et al., 2006).

The effect of parental absence on gender typing in girls is minimal. However, parental absence may have a delayed effect on girls' gender typing in adolescence. Father absence may cause adolescent daughters to have difficulties relating to other males; these difficulties may take different forms for daughters of widows and of divorcees. Adolescent girls from divorced homes have been observed to be more sexually precocious and assertive with males, whereas girls whose mothers were widowed were characterized as excessively anxious about sexuality and as shy and uncomfortable around males (Hetherington, 1972, 1991a; Newcomer & Udry, 1987).

Following girls in the United States and New Zealand from age 5 to 18, Ellis and colleagues (2003) found that father absence (due to divorce or unmarried motherhood) was associated with elevated risk of early sexual activity and adolescent pregnancy. Moreover, girls who suffered father absence early in life had the highest rates of sexual activity and pregnancy (see Figure 13-4 on the next page). These links between father absence and sexual behaviour were still evident even after the researchers controlled for adverse family and economic conditions, such as poverty, exposure to violence, inadequate parental guidance, and lack of supervision.

What explains these relations between father absence and female sexual risk taking? According to social learning, daughters learn to feel competent and to value and acquire the social skills necessary for effective heterosexual relationships by interacting with warm, responsive, masculine fathers who reward and enjoy their daughters' femininity. The father-absent girls not only lacked positive male models, but may have been exposed to irresponsible dating and repartnering on the part of their mothers, which may have encouraged earlier sexual behaviour.

According to the evolutionary perspective, girls in homes without a father tend to view male parental investment in families as unreliable and unimportant (Ellis & Bjorklund, 2005; Ellis & Essex, 2007; Geary, 1998, 2006). As a result, these girls are more likely to be casual in their sexual encounters and, thus, risk pregnancy. Mothers can moderate the effects of father absence on their daughters, however. Women who cast their former husbands and their relationships with them in a positive light, and who themselves demonstrate emotional stability, can lessen the deleterious effects of father absence.

Gender Roles in Children of Gay and Lesbian Parents

Studies of children growing up in a gay or lesbian household have challenged the importance of the father's contribution to gender typing (Golombok et al., 2003). Children reared in lesbian families do not differ in gender-role behaviour from children reared in heterosexual households (Golombok et al., 2003). Boys and girls in lesbian homes choose traditionally gender-oriented toys, activities, and friends. Nor is there any evidence that children reared in lesbian households are likely to develop a gay or a lesbian sexual orientation (Patterson & Hastings, 2007).

Similarly, recent evidence suggests that boys raised by gay fathers are largely heterosexual in their sexual orientations and that this is so regardless of how long the sons lived with their gay fathers (Bailey et al., 1995; Patterson, 2004). As we discussed in Chapter 11, the socio-emotional adjustment of children in lesbian households seems

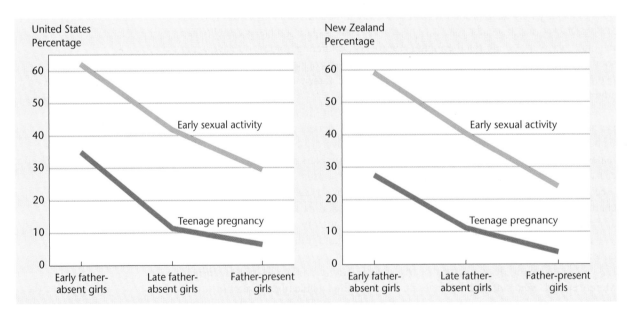

Figure 13-4

The effects of father absence or presence on girls' early sexual activity and teen pregnancy

Teenage girls in both the United States and New Zealand were far more likely to engage in early sexual activity when, at an early age, they were bereft of their fathers, and even girls who lost their fathers later in their development were more likely to engage in such activity than girls whose fathers were consistently present. A similar pattern was found for rates of teenage pregnancy.

Source: Ellis et al., 2003.

very similar to that of children reared in traditional families. Research in this area has raised important questions about the role of environmental and biological influences on the development of gender-related orientations and behaviours. Although fathers do appear to have the greater role in gender-role typing, these studies suggest that children can learn gender roles in a variety of family arrangements.

Siblings as Gender Socialization Agents

Siblings as well as parents can influence children's gender choices, attitudes, and behaviours. In a longitudinal study, researchers assessed whether the gender-role attitudes, leisure activities, and personality qualities of first-born children predicted these same outcomes in their second-born siblings, two years later (McHale et al., 2001). They found that older siblings did indeed influence younger siblings' gender typing. Moreover, the links between siblings' attributes were stronger than the links between a child's attributes and those of the mother or father. Also, second-born children were more likely to model their older, first-born siblings than the other way around.

The sex of the older sibling matters, too. Children with sisters tend to develop more feminine qualities, whereas those with brothers generally develop more masculine qualities (Rust et al., 2000). In one study, brother–brother pairs engaged in more stereotypically masculine play (e.g., play with balls, vehicles, or toy weapons); sister–sister or older sister–younger brother pairs engaged in more feminine play (e.g., art activities, doll play, playing house) (Stoneman et al., 1986). Children who had an older sibling of the other sex also had less stereotypical gender-role concepts.

EXTRAFAMILIAL INFLUENCES ON GENDER ROLES

Families are the first among the many social forces to play a role in shaping our gender-linked behaviours. As children get older, influences outside the family become increasingly important. Among the earliest of these forces are books and television. Peers and teachers also have considerable impact on a child's gender roles. In this section, we explore some of the forces that may contribute to children's amazingly clear distinctions about what is gender appropriate and inappropriate, "boyish" or "girlish."

Books and Television

Although there has been pressure within educational circles for more egalitarian treatment of boys and girls, children's literature, schoolbooks, and television programs still contain many gender stereotypes. There has been a shift toward more equal representation of boys and girls in children's books over the past few decades, but boys still appear more often in titles and in pictures than girls do (Gooden & Gooden, 2001; Purcell & Stewart, 1990). And a recent analysis of children's books (Hamilton et al., 2006) has confirmed that these findings have not varied much over the years—there are still twice as many male titles and main characters as there are female, and male characters appear 53 percent more often in pictures in these books. Moreover, books still often show females as more passive, dependent, and engaged in a narrower range of occupations than men, and they tend to show males as more assertive and action oriented (Hamilton et al., 2006; Turner-Bowker, 1996). This gender stereotyping is evident even in books labelled as "non-sexist" (Diekman & Murnen, 2004). Males are not immune from stereotyping, however. According to Anderson and Hamilton (2005), an analysis of fathers in children's books reveals that they are under-represented in such books, and when they do appear, they are withdrawn and ineffectual parents.

Males on television are more likely than females to be depicted as aggressive, decisive, professionally competent, rational, stable, powerful, and tolerant. Females tend to be portrayed as warmer, more sociable, more emotional, and happier. When women on television are aggressive, they are also often seen as inept or unsuccessful, and they are more likely to be shown as victims than as initiators of violence. This is true for prime time as well as children's television programming. Even in prime time shows, females are less likely to be leading characters and more likely to be in comedy roles, to be married or about to be married, and to be younger than males (Huston & Wright, 1998; Comstock & Scharrer, 2006)—although there is a trend, as in books, toward depicting women in a wider range of occupational roles (Coltrane, 1998; Douglas, 2003; Coltrane & Adams, 2008). In fact, according to one survey, only 4 percent of female TV characters were portrayed as homemakers (Heintz-Knowles, 2001).

Even in television commercials, males more often portray authorities and make more voice-over comments about a product's merit. Women are likelier to play the role of the consumer, displaying interest in product demonstrations (Coltrane, 1998). When women are shown as experts, they are likely to be discussing food products, laundry, soap, or beauty aids. These trends have been identified in the United States and Canada, as well as in other countries around the world (Best & Williams, 1993; Singer & Singer, 2001).

The likelihood that these stereotypical presentations of male and female roles have a real impact on children is underscored by findings revealing that children who are heavy television viewers are more likely to have stereotypical notions of gender and race and to show conformity to culturally accepted gender-role typing (Berry, 2000; Ward & Friedman, 2006). When television was first introduced in a small town in British Columbia (see the discussion of natural experiments on page 30 in Chapter 1), analysts recorded marked increases in traditional gender attitudes (Kimball, 1986; MacBeth, 1996). Moreover, experimental studies of TV advertisements that were targeted either to boys (action toys) or to girls (dolls, fashion, beauty) showed that the ads shaped children's toy requests (Robinson et al., 2001). The specific programs children watch may be guided by their gender schemas, and what they watch may shape their gender beliefs (Leaper & Friedman, 2007).

Television can also be used to change children's gender-role stereotypes. In one study, 5- and 6-year-olds who were shown a cartoon in which the characters played non-traditional roles (girls helped boys build a clubhouse) subsequently expressed less conventional gender-role attitudes (Davidson et al., 1979). Similarly, *Freestyle*, a television series that tried to counteract children's gender and ethnic stereotypes, was moderately successful in increasing children's acceptance of non-traditional gender-typed behaviours. For example, 9- to 12-year-old viewers were more accepting of girls who participated in athletics and mechanical activities and of boys who engaged in nurturant activities (Johnston & Ettema, 1982). However, the effects of most TV-based interventions have been relatively modest and short-lived and are more effective with younger than with older children (Bigler & Liben, 1992; Comstock & Scharrer, 2006). It will probably take a lot more change in books and television, and the larger popular culture, to alter gender-role stereotypes and attitudes.

Peers, Gender Roles, and Gender Segregation

Peers often serve as enforcers of society's gender-role standards, and they may also help to define them. In these roles, peers may also help the individual children define themselves and their gender identities (Leaper & Friedman, 2007; Rose & Rudolph, 2006). Observing 200 preschoolers at play over several months' time, Fagot (1985a) found that peers displayed marked reactions when children violated appropriate gender-role behaviour patterns. Boys who played with dolls rather than trucks had a tough time; their classmates criticized them five to six times more often than they heckled children who conformed. Peers were not as harsh in their treatment of girls who would rather play firefighter than nurse, though; they tended to ignore rather than criticize these girls. When same-sex peers rewarded children for appropriate gender-role behaviour, the children tended to persist longer in the rewarded type of activity. Boys respond to feedback from boys, whereas girls are more receptive to feedback from other girls. This pattern of responsiveness can lead to gender segregation which, in turn, may provide additional opportunities to learn accepted gender roles (Fagot, 1985a; Maccoby, 1998).

On any school playground, you can see that children have a very strong tendency to associate and play with other children of their same sex. When children are 4½ years old, they spend nearly three times as much time with same-sex play partners as with children of the other sex. By age 6½, children spend 11 times as much time with same-gender as with opposite-gender partners (Maccoby, 1998). Gender segregation is particularly marked for boys (Benenson et al., 1997). Children also like same-gender peers better than opposite-gender peers and are less likely to behave negatively toward them (Underwood et al., 2001).

Martin and Fabes (2001) followed preschoolers throughout the school year. They found not only an increase in gender segregation but also increasing gender differences in activities when children were in same-gender groups. The more time boys spent with other boys, the more active they became. They engaged in more and more rough-and-tumble play and overt aggression, spent less time with or near adults, and seemed to have more fun. In contrast, girls in groups with other girls showed a drop in activity level, their aggressive behaviour lessened, and they spent more time in proximity to adults. Consistent with these findings is the fact that preschool boys choose high activity level friends while girls choose low activity friends; in short, children choose friends who suit the level of activity that is within their comfort zone (Gleason et al., 2005). Similarly, girls are less competitive with their friends than are boys (Schneider et al., 2005).

These differences in boys' and girls' groups led Maccoby (1998) to suggest a couple of reasons for gender segregation. First, girls view boys' rough-and-tumble play style and their competition-dominance orientation as aversive; as a result, girls avoid interactions with boys. Second, girls find it difficult to influence boys. They influence one another successfully using their preferred method of making polite suggestions, but these tactics are not very effective with boys, who prefer more direct demands. Girls find it aversive to try to interact with children who are unresponsive, and they avoid such partners.

Gender segregation in childhood is evident across many cultures, ranging from Canada and the United States to India and Africa. It occurs without specific adult encouragement, guidance, or pressure. Although earlier parental influence may play a role in setting the process in motion, children spontaneously choose same-gender play partners. Individual children may differ in terms of their masculinity or femininity, or in their grasp of gender stability and gender constancy, but most show the same preference for same-gender playmates (Powlishta, 1989). Thus, from preschool onwards, children live in segregated play worlds that, in turn, nurture and encourage separate styles of interaction that are distinctly male and female. This **self-socialization** as children spontaneously hang out with same-sex playmates and adopt conventionally gender-appropriate behaviour is another way that boys and girls learn gender roles. Of course, gender segregation is not permanent; by adolescence, interest in opposite-sex partners is in full swing (Larson et al., 2002).

self-socialization

The child's spontaneous adoption of conventionally gender-appropriate behaviour.

Schools and Teachers

Teachers and the schools deliver a number of gender-related messages to children (Leaper & Friedman, 2007; Ruble et al., 2006). For one thing, the structure of the school system is predominantly male; men hold many more positions of power, such as principal and superintendent, whereas the teaching staff is predominantly female. In addition, teachers sometimes structure classroom activities by gender and provide differential reinforcements and punishments to boys and girls. In this section, we consider the differential impact of the school culture and environment on girls and boys, and we explore some specific effects of teachers' attitudes and practices.

THE SCHOOL CULTURE   Although teachers often seem to pay more attention to boys than to girls, the general culture of the classroom and the school in some ways favours girls. The school system tends to frown upon the independent, assertive, competitive, and boisterous qualities that parents and the culture have encouraged in boys from infancy. Girls, who are more verbally oriented, are generally better behaved and more adept at following rules, and typically experience greater acceptance from teachers who—at least in the early grades—are likely to be females. Is it surprising, then, that from the start, girls tend to like school more than boys and perform better in their academic work? For many boys, school may not be a happy place. They feel that their teachers like them less than girls, and they have more difficulty adjusting to school routines. They create more problems for teachers and elicit more criticism from them, and, most importantly, they often perform at a level that is not only lower than their female classmates' but well below their own abilities (McCall et al., 2000; Ruble et al., 2006).

If boys perceive school to be a gender-inappropriate institution, they may be less motivated and interested in school-related activities than girls, who are likely to view school as consistent with their own gender-role identity. Girls outperform their male peers in the early grades, especially in reading; some surveys have found that boys are between three and six times as likely as girls to experience problems in learning to read (Halpern, 2000; Lummis & Stevenson, 1990).

However, although girls have an advantage in the early grades, this has a short-lived effect. Girls' achievement levels actually decline as they grow older, and by university, girls are more likely to be underachievers than are boys (Eccles et al., 1993; Wigfield et al., 2006). The kinds of conforming and dependent behaviours that schools encourage in girls may, in the long run, be detrimental. Dependency is negatively related to intellectual achievement. Independence, assertiveness, and non-conformity are much more likely to lead to creative thinking and problem solving and to high levels of achievement in both girls and boys (Dweck, 2001, 2006). The many conflicting messages that girls receive in the school years can put them at risk, if not for failure, then for less than satisfying lives.

Over the years, psychologists have found that public achievement, particularly in competitive activities, is often threatening to girls and women. Some girls cope with their conflict about achievement by concealing their abilities, particularly from boys (Ruble et al., 2006). For example, a girl may tell a male peer that she received lower grades than she actually did in a course they both attend. Or she may lower her effort, intentionally performing below her capabilities. And even women who are highly successful professionals sometimes seek to disguise their achievements by appearing *superfeminine*; they may try not only to be super-career-women but also super wives, super mothers, and super volunteers. What boy or man would try to hide his ambition and his accomplishments from others? However, if girls can find support from their peer group for their interest in science, their expectations for science achievement will increase (Stake & Nickens, 2005).

Finally, gender stereotyping can influence students' career aspirations (Wigfield et al., 2002). Given the general shift in North American society toward increasing acceptance of non-traditional occupations, one might expect that high-school students' occupational goals would show similar changes. Interestingly, however, studies done in both Canada and the United States suggest otherwise (Lupaschuk & Yewchuk, 1996, 1998; Papageorgiou, 1982). Lupaschuk and Yewchuk (1998), for example, interviewed students in grades 4 through 12 in rural Alberta and asked them how their life would

Teachers often resort to segregating a child from the rest of the class for a period of time as a way of controlling unruly behaviour. Many more boys than girls get the "time-out" treatment.

change if they suddenly woke up tomorrow and discovered they had changed gender. Of the varying responses given to this fantastical question, 50 to 80 percent felt that a change in gender would precipitate a change in career aspirations, with many of the males suggesting that their career options would be more limited, less prestigious, and less rewarding. Clearly, gender-role stereotyping continues to be a major factor in one's attitudes toward occupational aspirations, even in subtle form, for a number of school children.

IMPACT OF TEACHERS' ATTITUDES AND BEHAVIOURS

Even in the preschool years, teachers respond differently to boys and girls, often reacting to boys and girls in gender-stereotypical ways (Duffy et al., 2001; Einarsson & Granstroek, 2002; Fagot, 1985a). Researchers have found that teachers interrupt girls more frequently than boys during conversations and pay more attention to boys' assertive behaviour than to girls' pushing and shoving (Hendrick & Stange, 1991). They respond to girls' social initiatives, such as talking and gesturing, more than to these same behaviours in boys. Also, although teachers may encourage boys to engage in quiet activities rather than aggressive and rough-and-tumble play, they criticize them for cross-gender behaviours (e.g., dressing up or playing with dolls) more than they criticize girls for cross-gender play (Fagot, 1985a).

Not surprisingly, differential teacher attention has an impact. Fagot (1985a) found that nine months after she first observed a group of preschoolers, clear gender differences had emerged. Girls talked to the teacher more and boys exhibited a higher level of assertiveness. Although educators once believed that increasing the number of male teachers would counteract female teachers' apparently differential treatment of boys and girls, Fagot (1985b) discovered that both male and female teachers reacted more positively to children involved in stereotypical female gender-role behaviours, such as art activities and helping others, regardless of the child's gender.

Teachers also influence how well children do in different school subjects. They encourage boys more than girls in mathematical pursuits and stress literature more for girls (Shepardson & Pizzini, 1992; Wigfield et al., 2006). Children pick up on teachers' belief that math is a field for males. Even before high school, boys have greater interest in, and higher expectations for, success in math and science than girls, whereas girls have more interest and self-perceived competence in reading and writing than boys (Evans et al., 2002). Eccles (2007) found that 668 children in grades 5 through 12 thought boys were better at math and could make more use of it than girls, despite the fact that these children displayed no gender differences in their actual mathematics performance. Nor is this only a North American issue; recently, European researchers (Muzzatti & Agnoli, 2007) found that grade 4 and 5 Italian boys are more confident than girls in their math abilities in spite of the girls having similar abilities. As they get older, girls express a decreased liking for mathematics and, lacking any positive reinforcement for studying math, are more likely than boys to drop math during their high-school years (Shea et al., 2001). In contrast, boys' course-enrolment decisions reflect their past performance; if they have done well in math, they continue to take math courses. It seems that educators may need further education about children's educational skills and potential capabilities.

SEXUAL ORIENTATION AND IDENTITY

Most adolescents develop a heterosexual orientation, but a small percentage of children and adolescents realize that they prefer members of their own sex as romantic partners. According to recent estimates (Rotherman-Borus & Langabeer, 2001), between 3 and 6 percent of adolescents identify themselves as gay, lesbian, or bisexual. These are only estimates, for awareness of one's sexual orientation and of one's attraction to same-sex partners comes at different times to different individuals. For some, this occurs in early or middle childhood, but others reach adulthood before recognizing their same-sex preferences. The recognition that one prefers a member of the same sex as a romantic partner is often a gradual process that is marked by a series of milestones. Many gay or lesbian adults report recalling that as children, they had feelings that differed from those of their peers (Bailey & Zucker, 1995). Some children as early as grade 4 express doubts about their heterosexuality (Egan & Perry, 2001; Carver et al., 2004). These children responded more negatively to such questions as, "Some girls (boys) definitely think they'll get married one day" or "Some girls (boys) definitely think that they will be a mother (father) one day." Compared with children more confident in their heterosexuality, young people who questioned their sexual identify reported more impaired self-concepts. They expressed less interest in activities stereotypically linked to their own gender, such as babysitting for girls and building model planes and cars for boys. In addition, they were more likely to feel different from others of their sex and to express dissatisfaction with their own gender assignment. Interestingly, the patterns were similar for both boys and girls.

Across-time analyses suggested the sexual questioning leads to impaired self-concepts rather than the other way around. There is great variability in when sexual questioning begins: studies (e.g., Savin-Williams & Diamond, 2000) suggest that it can start in early and middle childhood, but, for some, it may not begin until considerably later. This is especially true for women; a significant minority shift toward a lesbian orientation after being heterosexual or even after motherhood (D'Augelli & Patterson, 2001; Rotherman-Borus & Langabeer, 2001). Although studies of sexual questioning by children suggest that the process of achieving a sexual identity and orientation starts early, this does not mean that all children who have questions about their sexual orientation will necessarily grow up to be gay or lesbian. At the same time, gay and lesbian adults often report that such questioning is part of their childhood history (Bailey & Zucker, 1995). In addition, cross-typed behaviour (e.g., boys playing with dolls) is often found in the childhood of gay men.

According to Savin-Williams (1998; Savin-Williams & Cohen, 2004), the next step in the journey toward full acceptance of minority sexual identity is "test and exploration." During this phase, the youth becomes ambivalent about same-sex preferences and begins tentatively to explore these feelings. Next, during the identity-acceptance phase, young people begin to accept their orientation and preferences for individuals of the same sex. They may share their sexual preferences with family and friends and may act on those preferences. Adolescent boys begin to label themselves as gay by age 13 and to engage in sex with other boys by age 15. Boys and girls, however, follow slightly different developmental pathways. Boys act first and label later, whereas girls do the opposite. Boys have sexual encounters with other males and only later label themselves as gay, whereas girls identify themselves as lesbians and later engage in sexual encounters with other females (Savin-Williams & Diamond, 2000).

Identity integration is the final milestone in this identity process. At this juncture, gay, lesbian, and bisexual individuals accept their orientation and acknowledge their identity to others in their family, school, and community. About 55 percent of university students of either sex disclosed their sexual identity to their parents; a decade ago, only 45 percent disclosed such information (Savin-Williams & Ream, 2003). And young people are disclosing themselves earlier than in the past—at age 17 instead of in the mid-twenties, as they did a decade ago (D'Augelli, 2006). Mothers are more accepting of their son's or daughter's gay/lesbian orientation than are fathers (D'Augelli, 2006). Moreover, ethnicity and religion are important predictors of acceptance. Some ethnic minorities—especially Asian and Latino minorities—are less tolerant than European North Americans of non-heterosexual orientations (Dube et al., 2001). Similarly, some members of conservative religious groups are less likely to be accepting of sexual-minority youth (D'Augelli, 2006). There is considerable prejudice in many parts of society toward non-heterosexuals, and many (20 to 40 percent) experience discrimination, rejection, and outright verbal and even physical hostility (D'Augelli, 2006). On occasion, gay teenagers have actually been killed by others owing simply to their sexual preferences. The widely publicized October 1998 murder of Matthew Shepard in Laramie, Wyoming, led to protests by those who sought to raise awareness of the potential consequences of anti–gay and lesbian beliefs and behaviour.

What are the origins of same-sex preferences? Both biological and environmental causes have been proposed. Some genetic evidence supports the notion that identical twins are more likely to show similar sexual orientations than are fraternal twins (Bailey et al., 1993). Other studies (Hamer et al., 1993) suggest that variations in DNA may make it more likely that some boys will develop same-sex preferences.

Family experiences doubtless play a role in this process as well. Distant or hostile relationships with parents of the same gender may lead children to reject behaviour typically associated with their same-gender parents (McConaghy & Silove, 1992; Bailey et al., 1995). Indeed, gay men have recalled distant relationships with their fathers, whereas lesbian women have reported poorer ties with their mothers. The gender of one's siblings may contribute to gay or lesbian identity. Boys who are born later in the family and who have a larger-than-usual number of older brothers are more likely to develop same-sex attraction (Blanchard et al., 1995). However, as we saw earlier in this chapter, there is little support for the view that gay and lesbian parents will produce gay and lesbian children (Patterson & Hastings, 2007). In short, none of these theories has received extensive support, and viewpoints that emphasize multiple pathways to gay/lesbian identity and that involve both environmental and biological factors are likely to be the most fruitful in helping us understand this topic.

ANDROGYNY

LO6

Many psychologists believe that traditional ideas of masculinity and femininity have been socially and psychologically destructive. To speak and act as if each individual person is either "masculine" or "feminine" in interests, attitudes, and behaviours makes little sense when we know that in reality, most people possess a combination of characteristics that we have traditionally viewed as either masculine or feminine. Any person, male or female, can be tender and nurturant with children, professionally successful, fiercely competitive on the tennis court, and an excellent cook. Many people are **androgynous**; that is, they possess a notable number of both masculine and feminine psychological characteristics (Bem, 1981, 1993, 1998; Spence & Buckner, 2000). Children, as well as adults, can be androgynous, and these children are less likely to make stereotypical choices of play, activities, and occupations (Harter et al., 1998; Hebert, 2000); they are better adjusted and more creative, too (Norlander et al., 2000). Children who are either masculine or androgynous in their gender identity tend to have higher self-esteem than those with a feminine gender identity (Boldizar, 1991; Ruble et al., 2006). Children who are both accepting of themselves as typical of their own sex and feel that it is okay to cross gender boundaries are better adjusted than those who are not secure in their gender role (Carver et al., 2004; Egan & Perry, 2001).

Can children be taught to be more androgynous? Can children learn that fashion models and firefighters can be either males or females? As the following exchange illustrates, the task may not be easy. A psychologist overheard her 4-year-old son trying to explain her occupation to a young friend:

Son: My mother helps people. She's a doctor.

Friend: You mean a nurse.

Son: No. She's not that kind of doctor. She's a psychologist. She's a doctor of psychology.

Friend: I see. She's a nurse of psychology.

androgyny

A normal state of being for many people who possess a notable number of both masculine and feminine psychological characteristics. Children who are more androgynous make less stereotypical play and activity choices.

Work by Bigler and Liben (1990, 1992) does suggest that children can learn to use fewer stereotypes. Using 10 occupations that children view as typically masculine (e.g., dentist, farmer, construction worker) or feminine (e.g., beautician, flight attendant, librarian), the researchers tried to lessen children's stereotyping of these work roles. First, they taught the children that gender is irrelevant. Then they focused the children's attention on two other ways of looking at job appropriateness: liking a job and having the skills needed for the job. For example, construction workers must like to build things, and they must acquire the skills to drive big machines. The investigators gave the children practice problems for which they had to specify why the job (e.g., construction worker) was a good match for the person. If the children based their answers on gender rather than on interest or skills they received corrective feedback. In a control group, children participated in a discussion about the roles of specific occupations within the community, with no emphasis on gender stereotyping. Children in the experimental group later gave more non-stereotypical answers not only for the occupations involved in the lessons but also for a range of other occupations. For instance, when they were asked who could do various specific activities, such as police work and nursing, they gave more "both men and women" responses. Children in the control group still argued that "girls can't be firefighters!"

Consistent with gender-schema theory, Bigler and Liben found that children in the experimental intervention exhibited better recall of counter-stereotypical information in a later memory test. Although children in both the experimental and control groups remembered stories about Frank the firefighter and Betty the beautician, children who were in the experimental group remembered stories about Larry the librarian and Ann the astronaut far better than did children in the control group. These findings suggest that even children's ways of thinking about gender roles can be modified.

multi-schematic children

Children who hold more than one gender schema for responding to the world.

Some parents and schools are working toward the goal of reducing gender typing (Bigler, 1995). In open preschools, where the staff consciously attempt to minimize gender stereotyping, children spend more time in mixed-gender groups and less time engaged in conventional gender-typical activities than do children in traditional schools. In non-traditional preschools, children of both sexes are likely to be playing house and refuelling their toy trucks (Bianchi & Bakeman, 1983). Clearly, gender roles and attitudes are modifiable. Such children are **multi-schematic**, holding more than one gender schema for responding to the world. Some cultures, such as in Sweden, have made a commitment to gender equality, and the opportunities to observe males and females engaging in non-gender-stereotyped behaviours have resulted in some increases in androgynous attitudes among children (Coltrane & Adams, 2008; Tennebaum & Leaper, 2002). Attitudes toward gender roles are changing slowly and they will likely continue to change as more and more individuals cross gender lines.

For Thought and Discussion

1. As an experiment, go to a park one day and watch parents playing with their children. Do parents truly treat their sons and daughters differently in play? How about in risk-taking behaviours? If so, where do you think such differences come from?

2. For another experiment, think about the characters in different movies (or television shows) you have seen. How different are the roles of the male and female characters in these media presentations? What types of occupations do men and women typically have? Are there differences in these occupations as a function of gender? How about in how men and women are generally portrayed? Are they seen as strong, aggressive, humble, self-effacing, and so on? What might such differences say about the images of men and women our culture portrays?

3. How likely is it that our society will truly embrace the idea of androgyny? Do you think it is easier for one or the other sex to be androgynous in our society? What does this say about the concept of androgyny more generally?

Making the Connections 13

There are many links between concepts and ideas in one area of development and concepts and ideas in other areas. Here are some of the connections between ideas in Chapter 13 and discussions in other chapters of this book.

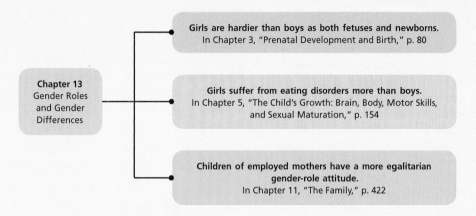

Chapter 13
Gender Roles and Gender Differences

Girls are hardier than boys as both fetuses and newborns.
In Chapter 3, "Prenatal Development and Birth," p. 80

Girls suffer from eating disorders more than boys.
In Chapter 5, "The Child's Growth: Brain, Body, Motor Skills, and Sexual Maturation," p. 154

Children of employed mothers have a more egalitarian gender-role attitude.
In Chapter 11, "The Family," p. 422

SUMMARY

Defining Sex and Gender

- Both biological and psychological factors influence gender-based behaviours. There are five principal psychological explanations of gender-linked behavioural patterns: Freudian theory's process of **identification**, **cognitive social learning theory**, Kohlberg's **cognitive developmental theory**, **gender-schema theory**, and **evolutionary theory**.
- The process by which children acquire the values, motives, and behaviours viewed as appropriate for males and females within a culture is called **gender typing**. Children develop **gender-based beliefs**, largely on the basis of **gender stereotypes**; the latter are reflected in **gender roles**. Children adopt a **gender identity** early in life.

Gender-Role Standards and Stereotypes

- Both within and across different cultures, we find great consistency in standards of desirable gender-role behaviour. Males are expected to be independent, assertive, and competitive; females are expected to be more passive, sensitive, and supportive.
- There is some variation in cultural gender-role standards, with standards varying depending on ethnic-

ity, age, education, and occupation. For example, black families are less likely to adhere to strict gender-role distinctions when socializing their children, whereas Hispanic families are more likely to highlight gender differences.
- Divergence between cultures is also clearly seen. However, even within groups, individual differences in the strength of stereotypes often outweigh group characteristics.

Gender Differences in Development

- Of the many traditionally held differences between the behaviours of males and females, some are real, some are found only inconsistently, and some are downright mythical.
- Girls are more physically and neurologically advanced at birth. Boys have more mature muscular development but are more vulnerable to disease and hereditary anomalies. Girls excel early in verbal skills, but boys excel in visual-spatial and math skills. Boys' superior mathematic abilities reflect only a better grasp of geometry, however, which depends on visual-spatial abilities. Boys are more aggressive, and girls more nurturant. Boys have more reading, speech, and emotional problems than girls.

- More equivocal are gender differences in activity level, dependency, timidity, exploratory activity, and vulnerability to stress. There are no gender differences in sociability, conformity, achievement, self-esteem, or verbal hostility.
- Although differences exist, the overlap between the distributions is always greater than the differences between them. In addition, noting the existence of the differences does not tell us why they exist. Clearly, girls and boys have many different experiences and opportunities as they develop, and these may lead to divergent outcomes or highlight existing differences.
- Children develop gender-typical patterns of behaviour and preferences before they are 2 years old. Girls tend to conform less strictly to gender-role stereotypes than do boys, possibly because parents and teachers exert greater pressure on boys to adhere to the masculine role. Although some boys and girls receive support for cross-gender behaviour, most are encouraged to behave according to traditional stereotypes.
- Gender-typed interests tend to remain stable from childhood to maturity. However, gender roles fluctuate across the life course as adults change to meet the demands of new situations and circumstances, such as child-rearing. When they become parents, women tend to show more **expressive characteristics** in parenthood and men more **instrumental characteristics**.

Biological Factors in Gender Differences

- Biological factors that are thought to shape gender differences include hormones and lateralization of brain function. Hormones may organize a biological predisposition to be masculine or feminine during the prenatal period, and the increase in hormones during puberty may activate that predisposition. In addition, social experience may alter the levels of such hormones as testosterone.
- Gender differences in the brain's organization may be reflected in the greater lateralization of brain functioning in males, which may help explain male success at spatial tasks. It may also explain female tendencies to be more flexible than males and to better withstand injury to the brain.
- Exceptionally high prenatal androgen levels in females may be correlated with greater visual-spatial skills later on. Environmental factors also influence both sexes' development of traditional and non-traditional gender-based abilities and interests.

Cognitive Factors in Gender Typing

- Cognitive factors in children's understanding of gender and gender stereotypes may contribute to their acquisition of gender roles. Kohlberg's three-stage cognitive developmental theory of gender typing suggests that children begin by categorizing themselves as male or female, then feel rewarded by behaving in gender-consistent ways. To do this, they must develop gender identity, gender stability, and gender constancy.
- Gender-schema theory suggests that children need only basic information about gender to develop mental schemas that help them organize their experiences and form rules concerning gender. Some children are more "gender schematic" than others.

The Influence of Family on Gender Typing

- Families play an active role in gender-role socialization in the way they organize their children's environment. They dress boys and girls differently, give them different toys to play with, and furnish their bedrooms differently. In addition, parents—especially fathers—treat girls and boys differently. Parents tend to see boys as stronger, even at birth, and to treat them more roughly and play with them more actively than with girls. As children grow older, parents protect girls more and allow them less autonomy than boys. Parents also expect boys to achieve more than girls in the areas of mathematics and careers.
- Because the father plays such a critical role in the development of children's gender roles, his absence may be related to disruptions in gender typing. Father's absence has been associated with teenage daughters' early sexual activity and pregnancy. The earlier in her life that a girl's father becomes absent, the higher her risks are for both of these conditions. There is no evidence of differences in the gender roles of boys and girls raised in gay or lesbian families. Most children in these families grow up to have heterosexual orientations.
- Siblings can have an important impact on each other's gender socialization. Younger siblings tend to model their older siblings' behaviours; in addition, the sex of the older sibling may determine the character of his or her play with a younger sibling. This situation can result in the younger sibling's development of more or less stereotypical gender-role concepts.

Extrafamilial Influences on Gender Roles

- Male and female roles are portrayed in gender-stereotypical ways in many children's books and on television. Males are more likely than females to be portrayed as aggressive, competent, rational, and powerful in the workforce. Females are more often portrayed as involved primarily in housework or caring for children.

- Females are less likely to portray leading characters on TV, and male characters are overrepresented in children's books—although some change toward greater equality has occurred in recent years. Children who are heavy TV viewers hold more gender-stereotypical views. A few attempts to use television to change gender stereotypes have been successful, but the effects typically have been modest and short-lived.

- Children are likely to react when other children violate gender-typical behaviours, and boys' cross-gender behaviours are especially likely to meet with negative reactions from peers. Reactions from peers typically result in changes in behaviour, particularly if the feedback is from a child of the same sex. This pattern of responsiveness may lead to gender segregation, which, in turn, provides opportunities to learn gender-typical roles. In doing **self-socialization**, children spontaneously adopt gender-appropriate behaviour.

- Teachers also treat girls and boys differently. Because schools emphasize quiet and conformity to rules, girls tend to enjoy school more and perform better than boys in the early grades. Even in preschool, teachers, who often react to children in gender-stereotypical ways, tend to criticize boys more than girls. If young boys perceive school as gender inappropriate, they may be less motivated to participate in school activities. This may, in part, explain the higher rate of learning problems found in boys in the early grades. The kinds of conforming and dependent behaviours encouraged in girls may be detrimental to their later academic success.

Sexual Orientation and Identity

- Most adolescents develop a heterosexual orientation, but a small minority identify themselves as gay, lesbian, or bisexual. Awareness of gender preferences may begin in early childhood or be delayed until adolescence. The identity process involves several steps, from an initial questioning of one's sexual identity to a final phase of identity integration.

- Disclosure is often accompanied by initial negative reactions from family and friends, but varies by ethnicity and religious beliefs.

- Genetic and hormonal factors, as well as family influences, may contribute to the development of same-sex preferences.

Androgyny

- Most people are not strictly feminine or masculine but possess both masculine and feminine characteristics. Children who are more **androgynous** make less stereotypical play and activity choices. Children who have masculine or androgynous characteristics are likely to have higher self-esteem than those who have traditionally feminine characteristics.

- Children of non-conventional parents who place a high value on gender egalitarianism are less gender-typical in their beliefs about possible occupations for males and females, although they are no different from other children on play preferences and knowledge of cultural gender typing. Such children are **multi-schematic**, holding more than one gender schema for responding to the world. Research interventions and the experience of non-traditional preschools clearly indicate that children's gender stereotypes can be modified or eliminated.

MCGRAW-HILL CONNECT™—Available 24/7 with instant feedback so you can study when you want, how you want, and where you want. Take advantage of the Study Plan—an innovative tool that helps you customize your learning experience. You can diagnose your knowledge with pre- and post-tests, identify the areas where you need help, search the entire learning package for content specific to the topic you're studying, and add these resources to your personalized study plan. Visit *www.mcgrawhillconnect.ca* to register—take practice quizzes, search the e-book, and much more.

Illustration in the border of a page of Latin text from the Luttrell Psalter:
A boy stealing cherries from a tree. c. 1300–c. 1340.
British Library, London.

Chapter 14

Morality, Altruism, and Aggression

LEARNING OBJECTIVES

After reading this chapter, you should be able to

LO 1 Explain and evaluate Piaget's and Kohlberg's theories of moral development, and be able to compare and contrast the two theories.

LO 2 Discuss the relation between moral judgments and social rules, and moral judgments and moral behaviour.

LO 3 Describe the behavioural side and the affective sides of morality.

LO 4 Describe the development of altruism and prosocial behaviour, including changes in eliciting cues and expressions; discuss the various biological and environmental determinants of prosocial development.

LO 5 Discuss prosocial reasoning.

LO 6 Trace developmental changes in aggression, including gender differences and the stability of aggression.

LO 7 Discuss the role of biology in aggression; identify influences on aggression, including parental practices and control techniques used by others.

Anyone who spends time observing children in the classroom or on the playground must be impressed by the great diversity of children's behaviour. Some children play together co-operatively, help or share with others, and try to soothe classmates who have broken toys or scraped knees. Other children are involved in one altercation after another—successive bouts of name calling, quarrelling, shoving, and pushing, with occasional bursts of more violent physical fighting. You can also watch children during an exam; some are whispering or peeking surreptitiously at a neighbour's exam paper or stealthily slipping out crib notes concealed in their desks. Others sit with their brows furrowed in focused attention, trying to solve the problems on the exam.

What contributes to such marked variations in children's behaviour toward one another and in their apparent attitudes toward ethical issues? How do moral values and behaviours develop in the young child? How does the child become capable of self-control, resistance to temptation, and personal sacrifices for the welfare of others? In this chapter, we trace the course of moral development, the evolution of altruistic behaviours, and the development and control of aggression. We begin by discussing two of the most important theories of moral development: those of Jean Piaget (1896–1980) and Lawrence Kohlberg (1927–1987). We examine the relation between moral judgment and moral actions and the consistency of these behaviours across situations and over time. We then explore the development of prosocial and altruistic behaviours, asking how early these behaviours begin, how they change, and how parents influence them. Finally, we consider the topic of aggression, raising a number of issues: How does aggression develop? How does it change in form and frequency? How do biological and environmental factors, such as the family, influence the development of aggressive behaviours? And how can we control aggression most effectively? ●

LO1 AN OVERVIEW OF MORAL DEVELOPMENT

Canadian Researchers

In every culture, one of the most basic tasks of socialization is communicating ethical standards to the developing child and shaping and enforcing the practice of "good" behaviours. Although the specific values and behaviours regarded as desirable vary among cultures, every society has a system of rules about the rightness and wrongness of certain behaviours. Adults expect children to learn these rules, and to experience satisfaction when conforming to them and emotional discomfort or guilt when violating them.

Initially, parents control the young child's behaviour largely through immediate external factors, such as displeasure or punishment. As children mature, however, they begin to regulate their own behaviour by means of internalized standards of conduct. They become able, in the absence of external restraints, to exert self-control. Through *internalization*, children incorporate others' ideas and beliefs into their own concepts of themselves, thus developing personal standards of conduct. Many psychologists believe that internalization is the fundamental and essential process in the development of morality.

Psychological research has focused on the development of three basic components of morality: cognitive, behavioural, and emotional. The cognitive component involves knowledge of ethical rules and judgments of the "goodness" or "badness" of various acts. The behavioural component refers to people's actual behaviour in situations that invoke ethical considerations. The emotional component focuses on people's feelings about situations and behaviours that involve moral and ethical decisions. As we will see, these same three components can help us understand the development of altruism and of aggression.

In general, studies of moral behaviour in children have investigated activities that most adults consider wrong, such as cheating, lying, failing to delay gratification, resisting temptation, or controlling aggressive behaviour. More recently, researchers have studied positive behaviours, such as sharing, helping, co-operating, and performing prosocial or altruistic acts. Studies of the emotional dimension of morality have also traditionally focused on negative aspects, such as feelings of guilt after a transgression, but more recent work has focused on positive emotions such as **empathy** for other people's misfortunes or distress (Eisenberg et al., 2006). The particular theory a researcher embraces generally determines the specific aspect of moral development she explores. Cognitive theories drive investigations of moral judgments, learning theories provide the underpinning for studies of ethical behaviours, and psychoanalytic theories underlie examinations of the affective components of morality.

empathy

The capacity to experience the same emotion that someone else is experiencing.

COGNITIVE THEORIES OF MORAL DEVELOPMENT

Jean Piaget and Lawrence Kohlberg have offered alternative explanations for the acceptance and development of moral standards. Piaget's explanations involved many of his principles and processes of cognitive growth we discussed in Chapter 8. Indeed, both Piaget and Kohlberg consider moral development to be essentially an aspect of cognitive development.

Piaget's Cognitive Theory of Moral Development

Piaget proposed a cognitive-developmental theory of moral development in which the child's moral concepts evolve in an unvarying sequence through three stages. The first *premoral stage* lasts until about the age of 5; the *stage of moral realism* lasts from roughly 6 to 10 years of age; and the third stage, *morality of reciprocity* or *autonomous morality*, lasts from about age 11 onwards. According to Piaget, mature morality includes both an understanding and acceptance of social rules and a concern for equality and reciprocity in human relationships; these qualities form the basis of justice. Piaget investigated children's developing moral judgment in two main ways: by studying how children change their attitudes toward rules in common games and by examining the way they change their judgments of the seriousness of transgressions over time.

LEARNING THE RULES OF MORAL BEHAVIOUR   Preschool children are in the **premoral stage**; they show little concern for, or awareness of, rules. In games like marbles, they do not try to play systematically with the intention of winning but seem rather to gain satisfaction from manipulating the marbles and finding out how they can be used in different ways. By the time they are 5 years old, however, children move into the stage of **moral realism**, in which they develop great concern and respect for rules that come from authority, usually their parents, and see rules as immutable—unchanging and not to be questioned. In this stage, what Piaget calls *moral absolutism* prevails. If we ask children of this age if children in other countries could play marbles with different rules, they will assure us that they could not. We see a similar rigidity in the way that children approach social interactions, frequently falling back on a "my mommy says" ploy to solve disputes.

In addition, young children subscribe to the notion of **immanent justice**. They see any deviation from the rules as inevitably resulting in punishment. Someone or something is going to get you, one way or another! Such retribution might take the form of accidents or mishaps controlled by inanimate objects or by a higher power. A child who has lied to her mother may later fall off her bike, skin her knees, and think, "That's what I get for lying to Mom." In this stage, children also evaluate the seriousness of an act solely in terms of its consequences; they do not take the perpetrator's intentions into account. The two factors that contribute to young children's moral realism are their *egocentrism*—their inability to subordinate their own experiences and to perceive situations as others may—and their *immature way of thinking*, which leads them to confuse external reality with their own thought processes and subjective experiences.

Piaget believed that a **morality of reciprocity** begins to emerge in children at about the age of 11. Children's moral judgments are now characterized by the recognition that social rules are arbitrary agreements that can be questioned and changed. They realize that obedience to authority is neither necessary nor always desirable and that violations of rules are not always wrong or inevitably punished. In judging another's behaviour, children consider the other's feelings and viewpoint. In this stage, children believe that if behaviour is to be punished, the punishment should be related to both the wrongdoer's intentions and the nature of the transgression. The punishment, the child

premoral stage

Piaget's first stage of moral development, in which the child shows little concern for rules.

moral realism

Piaget's second stage of moral development, in which the child shows great respect for rules but applies them quite inflexibly.

immanent justice

The notion that any deviation from rules will inevitably result in punishment or retribution.

morality of reciprocity

Piaget's third stage of moral development, in which the child recognizes that rules may be questioned and altered, considers the feelings and views of others, and believes in equal justice for all.

Starting to play formal games is one of the ways in which children, like these Moroccan boys, learn the meaning of rules. However, rules may vary across different cultures.

thinks, should also be of such a nature that it somehow makes up for the harm done or helps teach the wrongdoer to behave better in the future. Children in this stage also believe in "equalitarianism"—that is, they believe there should be equal justice for all.

Some of the shifts in attitude from moral realism to moral reciprocity are vividly illustrated in Piaget's account of his investigations, *The Moral Judgment of the Child* (1932). Piaget would read paired stories to a child and then ask the child if the children in each story were equally guilty, which child was the naughtier, and why.

Story I.

A little boy who is called John is in his room. He is called to dinner. He goes into the dining room. But behind the door there [is] a chair, and on the chair there [is] a tray with 15 cups on it. John couldn't have known that there was all this behind the door. He goes in, the door knocks against the tray, "bang" to the 15 cups, and they all get broken!

Story II.

Once there was a little boy whose name was Henry. One day, when his mother was out, he tried to get some jam out of the cupboard. He climbed up on a chair and stretched out his arm. But the jam was too high up and he couldn't reach it and have any. But while he was trying to get it, he knocked over a cup. The cup fell down and broke. (Piaget, 1932, p. 122)

Clearly, Henry tried to deceive his mother. But the child in the stage of moral realism regards John as less ethical because he broke more cups, even though John's act was an accident and unintentional. In contrast, René, who is 10 years old, shows signs that he has reached the stage of moral reciprocity by responding that the child who wanted to take the jam was naughtier. When asked if it makes any difference that the other child broke more cups, René replies, "No, because the one who broke 15 cups didn't do it on purpose" (Piaget, 1932, p. 130).

EVALUATION OF PIAGET'S THEORY   How well has Piaget's theory fared since 1932? In industrialized Western countries, such as Canada, the United States, the United Kingdom, France, Greece, Switzerland, across a wide range of populations and social classes and among both genders, investigators find regular age trends in the development of moral judgment from moral realism to moral reciprocity. However, the findings in other cultures are less consistent. For example, Havinghurst and Neugarten (1955) found that among the people of ten Native North American tribes, the belief in immanent justice increased rather than decreased over time. Also, only two of the ten groups showed the predicted shift toward greater flexibility with age in the conception of rules.

Although research on moral development lends support to the general developmental sequence, it also suggests that Piaget underestimated the cognitive capacities of young children. In judging the behaviour of others, even 6-year-old children are able to consider an actor's intentions when the situation is described in a way that they can comprehend. For example, when Chandler and colleagues (1973) presented stories to 6-year-olds by video rather than orally, the younger children responded to the intentions of the actors as well as older children did. Viewing the scenarios probably helps younger children by providing them with more information, such as facial expressions that signal emotional states; these additional clues can help younger ones better infer the actor's intentions.

Another methodological shortcoming in Piaget's early studies may help account for his underestimation of young children's ability to make moral judgments. Piaget always mixed action outcome with actor intention. Thus, he invariably required children to judge whether a child who causes a small amount of damage in the service of bad intentions is "worse" than a child who causes a large amount of damage but has good intentions. When researchers present stories in which good and bad intentions can be evaluated separately from good and bad outcomes, even elementary-school children can use intentions as a basis for judgment (Bussey, 1992; Helwig et al., 2001; Zelazo et al., 1996). For example, if the case of the broken cups is presented with a focus on intention (the child breaks cups *trying to help his mother* or *trying to sneak a cookie*) but the outcome is the same for all stories (the child breaks six cups), children have no trouble understanding the role of intention. By cleverly creating variations on these basic stories, researchers have been able to isolate factors that affect moral judgment. Just as in real life, many issues influence children's judgments about rightness and wrongness, about whether or not the consequences of actions are positive or negative and whether the consequences are intended or accidental (Helwig, 2008).

The "simple" tasks that Piaget devised more than half a century ago have become much more complicated today. Clearly, there are many more factors to consider in understanding moral reasoning than simply intentions and consequences. In the next section, we will see that Kohlberg has offered a more complex approach to the study of moral judgment.

Kohlberg's Cognitive Theory of Moral Development

Lawrence Kohlberg (1969, 1985) based his theory of moral development on Piaget's theory, but he refined and expanded the stages and extended the age periods covered. Like Piaget, Kohlberg believed that the child's cognitive capabilities determine the evolution of her moral reasoning and that moral development builds on concepts grasped in preceding stages.

To test his theory, Kohlberg began by interviewing boys between the ages of 10 and 16 years, presenting them with a series of moral dilemmas in which they had to choose either to obey rules and authority or to ignore such regulatory forces and respond to the needs and welfare of other people instead. Here is a representative story presented to Kohlberg's young participants:

> *Heinz needs a particular expensive drug to help his dying wife. The pharmacist who discovered and controls the supply of the drug has refused Heinz's offer to give him all the money he now has, which would be about half the necessary sum, and to pay the rest later. Heinz must now decide whether or not to steal the drug to save his wife, that is, whether to obey the rules and laws of society or to violate them to respond to the needs of his wife. What should Heinz do, and why?*

On the basis of his findings, Kohlberg formulated a series of three broad levels of moral development and subdivided these into six stages. Each stage was based not only on participants' choices of either an obedient or a need-serving act but on the reasons participants gave and on the ways they justified their choices. Table 14-1 on the next page presents these levels and stages of moral development. Kohlberg argued that although the sequence of all six stages is fixed—that is, all people pass through the stages in the same order—they may occur in different people at different ages. Moreover, many people may never attain the highest level of moral judgment, and even some adults continue to think in immature terms.

Kohlberg saw behaviour at the **pre-conventional level** as based on the desire to avoid punishment and gain rewards (see Table 14-1, Level I , on the next page). At level II, the **conventional level**, although children identify with their parents and conform to what they regard as right and wrong, what they have internalized is the motive to conform, not the notion of ethical standards. It is only at level III, the **post-conventional level**, that moral judgment is rational and internalized and that conduct is controlled by an internalized ethical code that is relatively independent of others' approval or castigation. At this level, moral conflict is resolved in terms of broad ethical principles, and violating these principles results in guilt and self-condemnation.

pre-conventional level

Kohlberg's first level of moral development, in which he views the child's behaviour as based on the desire to avoid punishment and gain rewards.

conventional level

Kohlberg's second level of moral development, in which the child's behaviour is designed to solicit others' approval and maintain good relations with them. The child accepts societal regulations unquestioningly and judges behaviour as good if it conforms to these rules.

post-conventional level

Kohlberg's third level of moral development, in which the child's judgments are rational and his conduct is controlled by an internalized ethical code that is relatively independent of the approval or disapproval of others.

Table 14-1 Kohlberg's theory of moral development

Level I Pre-conventional Morality	
Stage 1 Obedience and punishment orientation	To avoid punishment, the child defers to prestigious or powerful people, usually the parents. The morality of an act is defined by its physical consequences.
Stage 2 Naive hedonistic and instrumental orientation	The child conforms to gain rewards. The child understands reciprocity and sharing, but this reciprocity is manipulative and self-serving rather than based on a true sense of justice, generosity, sympathy, or compassion. It is a kind of bartering: "I'll lend you my bike if I can play with your wagon." "I'll do my homework now if I can watch the late-night movie."
Level II Conventional Morality: Conventional Rules and Conformity	
Stage 3 Good-boy morality	The child's good behaviour is designed to maintain approval and good relations with others. Although the child is still basing judgments of right and wrong on others' responses, he is concerned with their approval and disapproval rather than with their physical power. To maintain goodwill, he conforms to families' and friends' standards. However, the child is starting to accept others' social regulations and to judge the goodness or badness of behaviour in terms of a person's intent to violate these rules.
Stage 4 Authority and morality that maintain the social order	The person blindly accepts social conventions and rules and believes that if society accepts these rules, they should be maintained to avoid censure. He now conforms not just to other individuals' standards but to the social order. This is the epitome of "law and order" morality, involving unquestioning acceptance of social regulations. The person judges behaviour as good according to whether it conforms to a rigid set of rules. According to Kohlberg, many people never go beyond this conventional level of morality.
Level III Post-conventional Morality: Self-Accepted Moral Principles	
Stage 5 Morality of contract, individual rights, and democratically accepted law	People now have a flexibility of moral beliefs that they lacked in earlier stages. Morality is based on an agreement among individuals to conform to norms that appear necessary to maintain the social order and the rights of others. However, because this is a social contract, it can be modified when people within a society rationally discuss alternatives that might be more advantageous to more members of the society.
Stage 6 Morality of individual principles and conscience	People conform both to social standards and to internalized ideals. Their intent is to avoid self-condemnation rather than criticism by others. People base their decisions on abstract principles involving justice, compassion, and equality. This is a morality based on respect for others. People who have attained this level of development will have highly individualistic moral beliefs that may, at times, conflict with rules accepted by the majority of a society. According to Kohlberg, among the non-violent activist students who demonstrated in the mid- to late 1960s against the Vietnam War, more had attained the post-conventional level of morality than had non-activist students.

Source: Kohlberg, 1969.

In Kohlberg's studies (Colby & Kohlberg, 1987; Kohlberg, 1985), young children gave more pre-conventional (Level I) responses and older children gave more post-conventional responses (see Figure 14-1). Although, as we have said, Kohlberg predicted no specific level of response at any specific age, the general sequence of stages is followed in these participants' responding. The sequence should be invariant across cultures, Kohlberg asserted, although the ultimate level attained may vary among cultures and for individuals within the same society. Once a person has attained a high level of moral cognition, especially stage 6, he will typically not regress and go back to earlier stages.

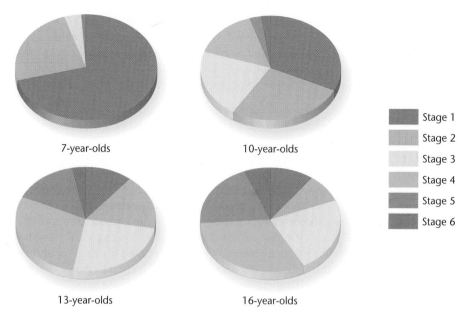

Figure 14-1

Use of Kohlberg's six stages of moral reasoning and judgment

Most 7-year-olds responded at Level I (Stages 1 and 2), although a very few offered some Level III (Stage 5) responses. The 10-year-olds showed the most regular pattern. In descending order of frequency, they gave Stages 1, 2, 3, 4, 5, and 6 responses. Among 16-year-olds, the most common responses were at Level II (Stages 3 and 4). Quite a few participants responded at Level III (Stages 5 and 6), but there were also some Level I responses.

Source: Adapted from Kohlberg, 1969.

7-year-olds

10-year-olds

13-year-olds

16-year-olds

Stage 1

Stage 2

Stage 3

Stage 4

Stage 5

Stage 6

MORAL DEVELOPMENT IN GIRLS AND WOMEN Have you noticed that the participants in Kohlberg's initial work (although not, admittedly, in his subsequent research) were boys, not girls? A lot of women did! Feminists contend that Kohlberg's theory was biased against females. Carol Gilligan, the foremost spokesperson for this view, argued eloquently in her book *In a Different Voice* (1982) that Kohlberg failed to take account of possible differences in the moral orientations of females and males. Citing the fact that women usually score lower than men on Kohlberg's tests, Gilligan (1982) pointed out that "the very traits that traditionally have defined the 'goodness' of women are those that mark them as deficient in moral development" (p. 18). Researchers have rated most women's moral judgments on these tests at Stage 3, the stage in which morality is conceived in terms of goodness and badness. In this stage, the person is motivated primarily to maintain the goodwill and approval of others, although she is beginning to accept the notion of social regulations and to judge behaviours in terms of whether people conform to or violate these rules.

According to Gilligan, Kohlberg's theory, based as it was on the study of boys and men, fails to account for gender-based differences. For example, women tend to take a more caring and interpersonal approach to moral dilemmas, whereas men tend to emphasize less clearly personal values as individual rights and principles of justice. Consider how two children—a boy and a girl—responded to the question, "Should Heinz steal the drug to save his wife's life?"

Jake, age 11:

> *For one thing, a human life is worth more than money, and if the druggist only makes $1,000, he is still going to live, but if Heinz doesn't steal the drug, his wife is going to die. [Why is life worth more than money?] Because the druggist can get a thousand dollars from rich people with cancer, but Heinz can't get his wife again. [Why not?] Because people are all different and so you couldn't get Heinz's wife again.* (Gilligan, 1982, p. 26)

Jake's response emphasizes logic and the balance between life and property rights, according to Gilligan, a masculine orientation.

Amy, age 11:

> *Well, I don't think so. I think there might be other ways besides stealing it, like if he could borrow the money or make a loan or something, but he really*

shouldn't steal the drug—but his wife shouldn't die, either. If he stole the drug, he might save his wife then, but if he did, he might have to go to jail, and then his wife might get sicker again, and he couldn't get more of the drug, and it might not be good. So, they should really just talk it out and find some other way to make the money. (Gilligan, 1982, p. 28)

Instead of focusing on the issues of property or law, Amy focuses on the impact the theft might have on Heinz, his wife, his wife's condition, and their relationship—an interpersonal orientation to morality.

Others have found support for Gilligan's claim of separate moral orientations for males and females. Lollis and colleagues (1996) looked at moral orientation in parent–child interactions in the context of settling fights between siblings over property. These researchers found that regardless of the gender of the child, mothers used more care than justice orientations, whereas fathers displayed slightly more justice than care orientations (although Walker, 1996, has criticized these findings on empirical grounds). And when asked to recall real-life dilemmas, women were more likely to recall ones that concerned personal relationships, whereas men recalled more impersonal kinds of dilemmas. Interestingly, when men and women were asked to respond to the same real-life dilemmas, both sexes focused more on caring than justice (Walker et al., 1995). Other studies using both hypothetical and real-life situations have yielded no clear pattern of gender differences (Jaffe & Hyde, 2000; Knox et al., 2004; Turiel, 2006).

Although there is some basis for Gilligan's contention that there may be different orientations to morality, we have little evidence of a gender bias in moral reasoning (Turiel, 2006). Reviewing data from more than 10,000 research participants, Lawrence Walker from the University of British Columbia (1988, 2006) found little support for the notion that females and males differ in the levels of their moral judgments, although Walker would agree that Kohlberg's emphasis on a justice orientation is a somewhat restricted view of morality (Walker et al., 1999). At the same time, Gilligan (1993) argues that the caring and interpersonal perspective should be added to the understanding of moral reasoning in all people. Moreover, evidence from neural-imaging studies suggests that different parts of the brain may be involved in decision making about issues of justice and care regardless of gender (Robertson et al., 2007). Interestingly, this view has received some support from cross-cultural studies. Consider, for example, the research described in Box 14.1 on pages 546 and 547.

EFFECTS OF SOCIAL INTERACTIONS ON MORAL DEVELOP-
MENT   Kohlberg emphasized the importance for the child's moral development of social interactions that involve role-taking opportunities, and following his lead, researchers devised educational programs to foster the development of moral judgment. Designed for classroom use, these programs focus on peer discussion of controversial moral issues and practise exploring solutions to moral dilemmas and negotiating with others. These educational interventions did foster moral judgment and promote closer links between judgments and behaviour (Youniss & Yates, 1997).

Children's moral judgments are also advanced when their parents use consistent disciplinary techniques that involve reasoning and explanation, when they initiate discussion of the feelings of others, and when they promote a democratic family-discussion style (Hoffman, 1984; Parke, 1977; Walker et al., 2000).

Children's understanding of moral rules begins at a very early age. Observing family interactions, Judy Dunn (1987, 1989) and her colleagues found that children showed the beginnings of moral understanding and rapid increases in understanding between the ages of 2 and 3. As early as 16 months, mothers and children engaged in "moral dialogues" about rules, with children often nodding, shaking their heads, or providing verbal answers to their mothers' inquiries about rules.

Ella (21 months): [At table, throws toy to floor, a previously forbidden act. Looks at mother.]

Mother: No! What's Ella?

Child: Bad bad baba.

Mother: A bad bad baba.

By 36 months, in nearly a third of their disputes, children produced justifications for their actions. These justifications might invoke the child's own wants, needs, or feelings ("But, I need that"), a social rule ("That doesn't belong to you"), the feelings of others ("Rachel will be cross if you do that"), or consequences of actions ("You'll break it if you do that").

EVALUATION OF KOHLBERG'S THEORY Kohlberg's theory of moral judgment received more support than Piaget's. The notion that children proceed through the stages of moral judgment in an invariant fashion received general support (Rest et al., 2000; Turiel, 2006; Walker et al., 2000). In one study, participants were asked to make judgments about moral dilemmas over a 20-year period (Colby et al., 1983). All but two participants moved from lower to higher stages, and no one skipped stages. Although the vast majority stopped at Stage 4, a few (10 percent) continued to develop their moral reasoning in their twenties, reaching Stage 5 in young adulthood (see Figure 14-3 on page 548). None, however, reached Stage 6. The dominant pattern of responding of moral reasoning in most adults appears to be conventional (Level II, Stage 3 or 4). In other work, participants who were exposed to a model's reasoning about a moral dilemma at a stage above or a stage below their own stage of moral development preferred the more advanced reasoning (Rest et al., 2000; Turiel, 2002, 2006).

Research has generally supported the sequencing of stages. However, a related criticism of Kohlberg's theory is that people often show a remarkable inconsistency in their moral judgments (Carpendale, 2000; Carpendale & Krebs, 1992, 1995; Denton & Krebs, 1990). For example, when judging moral dilemmas involving a business situation (Carpendale & Krebs, 1992, 1995) or drinking and driving (Denton & Krebs, 1990), participants use reasoning at a lower stage than normal, usually at about Stage 2 (Carpendale, 2000), an inconsistency in moral reasoning generally thought to be incompatible with Kohlberg's theory. Carpendale (2000) has argued for a modification of Kohlberg's theory emphasizing the idea that moral reasoning is a process of coordinating different perspectives of a moral dilemma, as opposed to simply focusing on the application of rules. This idea, which, according to Carpendale, was actually drawn from Piaget's theory of moral development, allows for inconsistency in moral reasoning because individuals may be constrained or restricted in their ability to consider the different perspectives. According to Krebs and Denton (2005), who attempted to revise Kohlberg's theory to accommodate a host of discrepant findings, this theory is simply poorly equipped to account for the ways in which people make moral decisions in their everyday lives.

How does the theory fare in cross-cultural studies? In Turkey (Nisan & Kohlberg, 1982), Taiwan (Lei & Cheng, 1989), and Israel (Snarey et al., 1985), studies showed that individuals, regardless of their cultural background, developed through the stage sequence in the same manner. On the other hand, some research evidence suggests the possibility of cultural bias. For example, Lee, Cameron, Xu, Fu, and Board (1997) found differences in Chinese and Canadian children's judgments of lying and truth telling reflective of an emphasis on self-effacement and modesty in Chinese culture. Similarly, Baek (2002) observed differences in moral reasoning between Korean and British children, with Korean children employing traditional Korean concepts that

Box 14.1

Perspectives on Diversity

JUSTICE VERSUS INTERPERSONAL OBLIGATIONS: INDIA AND THE UNITED STATES

The debate about the significance of a caring and interpersonal perspective for a model of moral reasoning may have broader implications than Gilligan foresaw when she first challenged Kohlberg's model of moral development. Cross-cultural research that has pitted interpersonal obligations against justice obligations has revealed significant differences between the choices American and Hindu Indian children and adults make in the face of moral dilemmas (Baron & Miller, 2000; Miller & Bersoff, 1992, 1999). Whereas more than four-fifths of Indian children and adults endorsed interpersonal considerations in judging moral dilemmas, little more than a third of US schoolchildren and adults did.

Kohlberg's model is based on a philosophical tradition that sees obligations to care for others as subordinate to obligations based on justice, fairness, the Golden Rule. Concerns for the welfare of others are matters of interpersonal responsibility and personal choice. In Miller's research, American children indicated they believe that only justice obligations, and not helping behaviour, should be rule governed. Hindu Indian children and adults saw helping others as fully moral—that is, as involving a sense of objective obligation and as being within the scope of legitimate regulation.

Comparing groups of grade 3 and grade 7 children and university-aged adults in New Haven, Connecticut, and in Mysore, a city in southern India, Miller and her colleagues asked participants to rate the undesirability of single incidents in which people were described as breaching either justice or interpersonal obligations. In this phase of the study, the researchers endeavoured to adjust their examples so as to ensure that participants considered all incidents to be of the same or nearly the same degree of importance. In the second phase of the study, the researchers presented participants with fully described conflict situations in which the respondents could fulfill one kind of behavioural

obligation (justice or interpersonal) only by violating the other. Here is one of the conflict situations presented to US participants:

Ben was in Los Angeles on business. When his meetings were over . . . Ben planned to travel to San Francisco . . . to attend [his best friend's wedding]. He needed to catch the very next train if he was to be on time for the ceremony, as he had to deliver the wedding rings. However, Ben's wallet was stolen in the train station. He lost all his money as well as his ticket to San Francisco. . . . He approached several officials as well as passengers . . . and asked them to loan him money to buy a new ticket. But . . . no one was willing to lend him the money he needed. While Ben was sitting on a bench trying to decide what to do next, a well-dressed man sitting next to him walked away for a minute . . . Ben noticed that the man had left his coat unattended. Sticking out of the man's coat pocket was a train ticket to San Francisco. Ben knew that he could take the ticket and use it to travel to San Francisco on the next train. He also saw that the man had more than enough money in his coat pocket to buy another train ticket.

In this example, participants were asked to decide which of the following two alternative actions Ben should choose:

1. *Ben should not take the ticket from the man's coat pocket*—even though it means not getting to San Francisco in time to deliver the wedding rings to his best friend.

2. *Ben should go to San Francisco to deliver the wedding rings to his best friend*—even though it means taking the train ticket from the other man's coat pocket.

As Figure 14-2 shows, Indian participants at all age levels were more than twice as likely to decide in favour of the interpersonal alternatives than were the American participants. The more serious the breach of an

simply could not be mapped into Kohlberg's system of morality. Finally, Kohlberg's focus on individual rights and obligations may lead to underestimates of moral development in other cultures or may exclude some culturally unique domains of morality (Shweder, 1999; Shweder et al., 1998; Snarey & Hooker, 2006; Wainryb, 2006).

People's moral judgments also differ depending on the way questions are presented. When an issue is couched in abstract form, rather than embedded in a realistic description of a particular situation of conflict, respondents are more likely to support the default position (Helwig, 2003, 2006). For example, when children were asked whether

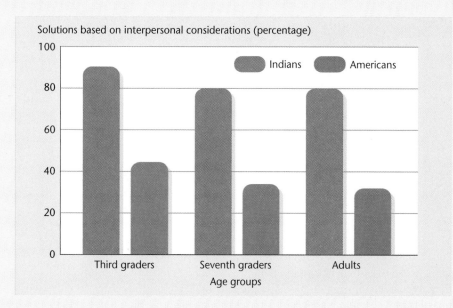

Solutions based on interpersonal considerations (percentage)

Indians   Americans

Third graders   Seventh graders   Adults

Age groups

Figure 14-2

Moral dilemmas and interpersonal-versus-justice considerations

In every age group, Hindu Indians were far more likely than Americans to cite interpersonal considerations in deciding on solutions to moral dilemmas.

Source: Based on Miller & Bersoff, 1992.

obligation, the more likely the Hindu Indians were to switch to a justice choice, but even in these circumstances, the Indians clearly preferred the interpersonal alternatives. Indians also tended to categorize their recommendations as moral imperatives whether they opted for justice or interpersonal alternatives. Americans, however, tended to describe an interpersonal alternative as a personal-moral or personal-choice decision. When Americans and Indians considered life-threatening situations, they both viewed helping others as moral issues; they disagreed, however, when the dilemmas were less extreme. It seems that Indians tend to view helping others in fully moral terms no matter how minor the issue, which is more compatible with the view of morality Gilligan originally proposed as more "feminine."

Kohlberg's model specifies that at Stage 6, "individuals conform both to social standards and to internalized ideals [and] . . . make decisions that are based on abstract principles that include compassion . . . [evidencing] a morality that is based upon a respect for others" (see Table 14-1 on page 542). This formulation certainly does not seem to rule out the so-called interpersonal concerns. Moreover, as we have noted in the text, many researchers who have used Kohlberg's model have failed to find the gender differences that early research detected. The Hindu religion holds that all life is sacred, and the Hindu Indian culture emphasizes "social duties as the starting point of society" (Miller & Bersoff, 1992, p. 552). These views are not greatly different from those that many in Western society have attributed to a "feminine" perspective. It seems likely that caring and interpersonal moral reasoning is not feminine but, rather, a view of morality that differs from a moral perspective based on the concept of justice and individual rights.

they endorsed freedom of speech and religion, nearly all said they did. However, when they were asked the same question in a context in which these freedoms conflicted with other liberties, such as freedom from physical and psychological harm, results were quite different. Fewer children endorsed freedom of speech. Moral judgments involve the need to balance competing moral issues and Kohlberg's original stories oversimplified the nature of the dilemmas people face in everyday moral decision making. History also shapes people's views of morality. Events—whether they are protracted ones such as the civil rights movement or sudden and horrific ones like the 9/11 attacks on New

Figure 14-3

How does moral reasoning evolve into adulthood?

Although Level I reasoning was significant in preadolescence, Stage 1 disappeared in the teens and Stage 2 had virtually disappeared by age 30. At age 36, Level II, Stage 4 reasoning was the most common, and Level III was barely represented, with a small percentage of Stage 5 responses.

Source: Adapted from Colby, Kohlberg, Gibbs, and Lieberman, 1983.

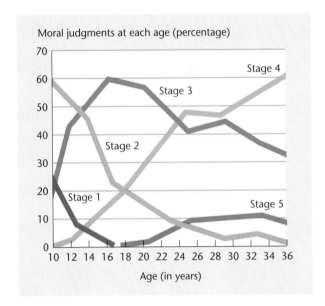

York City and the Pentagon—sensitize people to issues of fairness and justice (Turiel, 2002, 2006; Wainryb & Pasupathi, 2008).

In spite of criticisms and limitations, Kohlberg's pioneering work revolutionized the way that we think about moral development. Due to his influence, cognitive judgment and understanding are central concerns of a contemporary approach to the issue of morality.

LO 2 Distinguishing Moral Judgments from Other Social Rules

social-convention rules

Socially based rules about everyday conduct.

Children must learn many rules for behaviour. At the same time that they learn moral rules against cheating, lying, and stealing, they learn many other **social-convention rules**: table manners, kinds of dress, modes of greeting, forms of address, and other rules of social etiquette. According to Elliot Turiel (1983, 1998, 2006; Helwig & Turiel, 2002), children make clear distinctions between these two kinds of rules. In one study of preschool-aged children, researchers asked children how wrong it would be to hit someone, to lie, or to steal (moral rules), and how wrong it would be to address teachers by their first names, for a boy to enter a girl's bathroom, or to eat lunch with one's fingers (social-convention rules) (Nucci & Turiel, 1978). Children and adolescents from grade 2 to university consistently viewed the moral violations as more wrong than the violations of social convention. Even children as young as 3 can distinguish moral issues from social-convention issues (Smetana & Braeges, 1990; Yau & Smetana, 2003). Children view moral violations as more wrong because they result in harm to another and violate norms of justice and others' rights, whereas they see deviations from social conventions as impolite or disruptive (Turiel, 2006).

Children agree that moral issues are fixed, absolute, and invariant across cultures and that social conventions are arbitrary and relative and vary across communities and cultures (Helwig, 2006; Turiel, 2002, 2006; Wainryb, 2006). When asked if it would be acceptable to steal in a country that had no laws against stealing, children as young as 6 thought it was wrong to steal. However, they thought that people in different countries could play games by different rules (Turiel et al., 1988). In many countries, including Brazil, India, Indonesia, Korea, Nigeria, and Zambia, children and adolescents judge moral issues differently from social-convention issues (Turiel, 2002, 2006; Wainryb, 2006).

Children's differential between moral and conventional rules has implications for another aspect of moral development—the development of tolerance. Children are intolerant of moral violations, but they often tolerate not only divergent social conventions but also different psychological and religious beliefs (e.g., "that the way to be really good friends with people is never to tell them how you feel about anything"; "that there are 38 gods"; or "that only people who die on Tuesday become angels") (Wainryb et al., 2001).

How do children learn to distinguish between moral and other transgressions? Children learn from their parents at a very early age that the consequences of eating your spaghetti with your hands or spilling your milk or wearing your sweater inside out are different from taking your brother's toy or pulling your kid sister's hair. Mothers of 2-year-olds responded to social-convention violations with rules about social order and social regulation that focused on the disorder that the act created ("Look at the mess that you made!"). They responded to moral transgressions by focusing on the consequences of the acts for other's rights and welfare or by making perspective-taking requests ("Think about how you would feel if you were hit!") (Smetana, 1995, 2006).

Parents influence adolescents as well as young children. Teenagers understand and accept that parents may legitimately regulate their moral behaviour (Smetana, 1995, 2006). They even accept some parental regulation of social-convention matters (Smetana, 2005), although they view parental regulation of moral issues as more legitimate (Smetana & Asquith, 1994; Smetana & Daddis, 2002; Smetana & Gaines, 1999). However, adolescents do not agree that parents have a right to regulate personal matters such as appearance, friendship choices, and spending decisions. Conflicts most often arise in this area, and they arise increasingly as the adolescent grows older (Smetana, 2000). Conflicts that mix social-convention issues and personal issues—for example, cleaning one's own room affects the entire home—are more intense (Smetana et al., 2003).

Other socializing agents, including teachers and peers, play a part, too. Smetana (1997) found that 2- and 3-year-olds in a child-care centre reacted more emotionally and retaliated more often in the face of moral transgressions than when confronting social-convention transgressions. The 3-year-olds were likely to make statements about rights ("That's not fair," or "The rules say you can't do that"), a major accomplishment. In sum, children can distinguish among different kinds of violations and can do so at a surprisingly early age.

This child is demonstrating a serious violation of moral rules—he is shoplifting candy from this store. According to Kohlberg's theory, such a violation of moral rules should be evident to children at virtually all ages, although possibly for different reasons.

Do Moral Judgments Always Lead to Moral Behaviour?

The maturity of a child's moral judgments does not necessarily predict how the child will actually behave; moral judgments and moral behaviour are often unrelated, especially in young children (Blasi, 1983; Straughtan, 1986). Often, children's behaviour is impulsive and not guided by rational and deliberate thought (Burton, 1984; Walker, 2004). A child may have reached Kohlberg's Stage 3, the level of "good-girl morality," and be concerned with maintaining parental approval. She may even be able to tell a researcher that it is wrong to hit young children because they do not really know what they are doing (Batson & Thompson, 2001; Batson et al., 2002). However, when her younger brother breaks her favourite toy, she may kick him. Thought does not always guide action.

In older children and adults, moral judgments and moral behaviour may be linked (Kochanska et al., 2002). People who have reached Kohlberg's Level III (Stages 5 and 6) are less likely to cheat than those at lower levels, less likely to inflict pain on others, and more likely to endorse free speech and due process and to oppose capital punishment (Gibbs et al., 1995; Judy & Nelson, 2000; Kohlberg & Candee, 1984). Nevertheless, as we noted earlier, relatively few people may reach Stage 6 in Kohlberg's moral hierarchy.

There are relatively few towering moral figures such as Martin Luther King, Jr., or Mother Teresa among us.

Rest and colleagues (2000) proposed a four-step process involved in executing a moral action (this process is reminiscent of Dodge's information-processing approach to social interaction discussed in Chapter 12). In Step 1, the child interprets the situation in terms of how other people's welfare could be affected by his possible actions. In Step 2, the child figures out what the ideally moral course of action would be, given the possibilities in Step 1. In Step 3, the child decides what to do, and finally, in Step 4, the child actually performs the action chosen. So far, we have considered Steps 1 and 2; in the next section, we explore Steps 3 and 4.

LO3 THE BEHAVIOURAL SIDE OF MORAL DEVELOPMENT

In this section, we focus on the action, or behavioural, component of moral judgment—deciding what to do and doing it.

Self-Regulation and the Delay of Gratification

self-regulation

Children's ability to control behaviour on their own without reminders from others.

One goal in socializing children is to help them achieve **self-regulation**, or the ability to control behaviour on their own, without reminders from others. For moral development, children must also learn to inhibit or direct their actions to conform to moral rules. Life is full of temptations, traps, and tugs that try to pull young children away from moral courses of action. Children's ability to resist these forces is a consequence of both their own emerging cognitive and representational capacities and the guidance that parents, siblings, and other socializing agents provide.

control phase

According to Kopp, the first phase in learning self-regulation, when children are highly dependent on caregivers to remind them about acceptable behaviours.

How does this capacity to monitor and regulate one's own behaviour develop? According to Kopp (1982, 2002), it begins with a **control phase**, when 12- to 18-month-old children first initiate, maintain, modulate or cease acts when an adult makes a demand. In this phase, children are highly dependent on the caregiver for reminder signals about acceptable behaviours. In the **self-control phase**, children gain the ability to comply with caregiver expectations in the absence of external monitors. Presumably, this is because the development of representational thinking and recall memory permits these children to remember the family rules and routines. In the **self-regulation phase**, children become able to use strategies and plans to direct their behaviour and to aid them in resisting temptation and to **delay gratification**. Kopp demonstrated these developmental changes by showing children attractive objects such as a toy telephone and telling them not to touch the objects right away. Children who were 18 months old were able to wait only 20 seconds, the 24-month-olds waited 70 seconds, and the 30-month-olds waited nearly 100 seconds before touching the attractive but forbidden objects (Vaughn et al., 1984). Kopp and other researchers extended the study of self-regulation through the preschool period and confirmed the progression in self-control (Kochanska et al., 2001; Kopp, 2002).

self-control phase

Kopp's second phase in learning self-regulation, when the child becomes able to comply with caregiver expectations in the absence of the caregiver.

self-regulation phase

The third phase in Kopp's model of learning self-regulation, when children become able to use strategies and plans in directing their own behaviour and capable of delaying gratification.

delay gratification

Putting off until another time possessing or doing something that gives one pleasure.

Although all children progress from control by others through self-control to self-regulation, some progress more rapidly and achieve higher levels of control than others. Some children reach the self-regulation phase by 4 or 5 years, whereas others continue to rely on adult control to comply with rules. Children who are self-regulators have a stronger sense of "moral self"; they endorse and internalize parental values and rules, and they make conscious efforts to control their behaviour, even when it requires giving up or postponing pleasurable outcomes (Kochanska, 2002a; Kochanska et al., 2001). When they were infants, self-regulators were better at inhibiting their actions. Moreover, there is a relation between verbal abilities and self-control. Cournoyer and colleagues

(1998) tested 18- and 22-month-old francophone infants and found that children's language development was significantly related to their self-control at 24 months.

The development of self-control is also promoted by the actions of parents and other caregivers. Consistent and carefully timed punishment, as well as the provision of a rationale for compliance, help increase resistance to temptation (Kuczynski, 1983; Kuczynski, Marshall, & Shell, 1997; Parke, 1977). It also helps when mothers shift their control strategies from physical techniques such as distraction to verbal modalities such as explanations, bargaining, and reprimands as the child grows older and distraction techniques decrease (Kochanska, 2002b; Kuczynski et al., 1987; Murray & Kochanska, 2002). This adjusted parental input heightens the child's own abilities to use verbally based control strategies (Kopp, 2002). In addition, models who follow the rules, such as siblings and peers, are often effective in reducing cheating in young children (Bandura, 1989; Grusec et al., 1979), particularly if they display alternative acceptable behaviour while they resist breaking the rules (Bussey & Perry, 1977). Moreover, a mutually responsive orientation involving co-operation and shared positive affect between mother and child aids in conscience development. Children who, as toddlers, enjoyed this kind of mother–child or father–child relationships developed a higher level of **conscience**—internalized values and standards of behaviour—at 3 and 5 years of age than children in less mutually responsive parent–child relationships (Kochanska et al., 2008; Kochanska & Murray, 2000).

Because children differ in temperament, it is not surprising that although, overall, a positive mother–child relationship is linked with strong conscience development in young children, different parental disciplinary strategies are effective with different children. Kochanska (1995, 1997) found that for children who were relatively fearful as 2-year-olds, mothers' gentle discipline that de-emphasized power was correlated with evidence of conscience in the preschool period, whereas, for relatively fearless children, parental strategies that focused on positive motivation promoted higher levels of self-control.

This boy may be trying to guess what is in the packages or just itching to start tearing off the paper—or both! Learning to delay gratification is a significant part of self-regulation.

conscience

The child's internalized values and standards of behaviour.

The Affective Side of Morality

The development of moral behaviour also involves emotions. We have all experienced "feeling bad" when we break a rule. We may feel remorse, or shame, or guilt. Do children have these same emotional reactions? Kochanska and her colleagues (2002) tested young children at 22, 33, and 45 months. They presented each child with an object that belonged to the experimenter (e.g., a favourite stuffed animal the experimenter had kept from her childhood or a toy she had assembled herself) and asked the child to be very careful with it. However, the objects had been "rigged" and fell apart as soon as a child began to handle them. Even at 22 months, children "looked" guilty when the mishap occurred—they frowned, froze, or fretted. At older ages, children were better at masking their guilty reactions—they expressed fewer overt negative emotions. Instead, guilt leaked out in the form of subtle signs such as changes in posture, squirming, hanging the head, and other indications of arousal and upset. When they were later tested at 56 months, the children who had displayed more guilty reactions were less likely to play with forbidden toys than children who had not shown any guilty feelings.

Girls in Kochanska's study displayed more guilt than boys. Other researchers have reported similar gender differences in middle childhood (Zahn-Waxler, 2000). Perhaps this reflects the fact that girls are expected to adhere more closely to rules than are boys and, thus, may experience more upset when they violate them.

Children who displayed more guilt in the Kochanska study were also more fearful in scary situations, such as climbing a ladder, falling backward on a trampoline, or interacting with a clown. In other research, as well, 6- and 7-year-old children who were fearful as infants were rated by their parents as more prone to guilt and shame (Rothbart et al., 1994). Analyses of Kochanska's data suggested that fearful temperament contributes to guilt proneness, which in turn serves to inhibit children's tendency to violate rules. In contrast, fearless children do not experience remorse, guilt, or shame if they violate rules, and because they feel no guilt, the lack of guilt does not deter them from future rule violations.

Consistency across Situations and Time

Are children consistent in their moral behaviour across situations? In an extensive investigation of moral behaviour in children, Hartshorne and May (1928) gave 11,000 school-aged children the opportunity to cheat, steal, and lie in a wide variety of situations: athletics, social events, the school, the home, alone, or with peers. There was a high degree of consistency in individual children's behaviour (Burton, 1963, 1984). Each child had a general predisposition to behave either morally or immorally in a variety of situations. The more similar the situations, the more consistent was the child's behaviour. In markedly different situations, other variables such as fear of detection, peer support for deviant behaviour, and the importance of the outcome for the child affected the likelihood that the child would cheat.

For Thought and Discussion

1. Some have argued that Piaget did actually believe that children understand intentions. As evidence, look closely at what young René says following the stories about John and Henry. René clearly does make a response indicating an understanding of intention: "He didn't do it on purpose." Accordingly, this is why Piaget chose to combine intentions and outcomes. If true, what does this say about the criticisms often directed toward Piaget? Are they still as valid if this was a conscious decision as opposed to a methodological mistake?

2. Many researchers have argued that the fact few, if any, adults ever reach Kohlberg's Stage 6 can actually be seen as a flaw in his theory. Exactly why might this be considered a flaw? Is this a reasonable criticism?

3. Even if there is little support for the claims of gender differences in moral reasoning, what do you think of Gilligan's arguments for an alternative "interpersonal orientation of caring" approach to morality? Do you think such an orientation characterizes men's and women's moral reasoning? Does it do so equally? If not, what might be the differences?

LO4 THE EVOLUTION OF PROSOCIAL AND ALTRUISTIC BEHAVIOURS

prosocial behaviour

Behaviour that is designed to help or benefit other people.

altruistic behaviour

Intrinsically motivated behaviour that is intended to help others without expectation of acknowledgment or concrete reward.

altruism

An unselfish concern for the welfare of others.

Prosocial behaviour is voluntary behaviour that is intended to benefit another. It may be motivated by egoistic, other-oriented, and practical concerns (Eisenberg, 2003; Grusec et al., 2002). **Altruistic behaviour** is also voluntary behaviour that is designed to help someone else. However, what distinguishes **altruism** is an unselfish concern for the welfare of other people. Altruistic behaviour is the willingness to help another without any thought of compensation. Altruistic acts are motivated by internalized values, goals, and self-rewards rather than by the expectation of concrete or social rewards (Eisenberg et al., 2006). Prosocial behaviour includes sharing and co-operating with others, helping or caring for them, sympathizing and comforting them in times of distress and need, and performing acts of kindness. Prosocial behaviour can also encompass actions designed to help groups of people, societies, nations, and even the world. When people act altruistically, however, they do so without thought for their own immediate welfare, without expectation of reciprocity or acknowledgment (often acting anonymously), and sometimes even at the sacrifice of their own longer-term needs and wishes. According to Eisenberg and colleagues (2006), we see the beginnings of prosocial behaviour in very young children, whereas truly altruistic behaviour occurs only later on.

How Prosocial Behaviour Evolves

As the Turning Points chart shows on page 554, the roots of prosocial behaviour appear in infancy, when children show things to others or share toys. Rheingold and her colleagues found that among 12- to 18-month-old children, showing and giving toys to a variety of adults (mothers, fathers, and strangers) is very common (Hay, 1979, 1994; Rheingold et al., 1976). Children engage in these early sharing activities without prompting or direction and without being reinforced by praise.

CHANGES IN PROSOCIAL BEHAVIOURS Sharing and showing are not the only ways in which young children reveal their capacity for prosocial action. From an early age, children engage in a variety of other behaviours, such as caring for siblings, helping adults with housework, or comforting another in distress (Hastings et al., 2007). Children between 10 and 12 months old typically become agitated or cry in response to another child's distress, but they make little effort to help the other child. By the time they are 13 or 14 months old, however, they often approach and comfort another child in distress. This comforting, though, may not be specific to the source of distress. By 18 months of age, children not only approach a distressed person but also offer specific kinds of help. For example, they may offer a toy to a child with a broken toy or a Band-Aid to a mother with a cut finger. By age 2, children engage in a wide range of prosocial actions, including verbal advice ("Be careful"), indirect helping (getting their mother to retrieve the baby's rattle), sharing (giving food to a sister), distraction (closing a picture book that has made their mother sad), and protection or defence (trying to prevent another from being injured, distressed, or attacked) (Garner et al., 1994; Lamb & Zakhireh, 1997; van der Mark et al., 2002).

Children do not always show prosocial reactions to others' distress, and indeed, they sometimes laugh or behave aggressively or even become distressed themselves (Lamb & Zakhireh, 1997; Radke-Yarrow & Zahn-Waxler, 1983; Zahn-Waxler et al., 1992b). However, based on a meta-analysis of many relevant studies, Eisenberg and colleagues (2006) found clear evidence that as children grow older, they are generally more likely to engage in prosocial behaviours. Specifically, prosocial behaviour increases from infancy and the preschool years through middle childhood to adolescence. Prosocial behaviour not only increases with age, it also increases with cognitive maturation, and has been found to be related to language abilities for boys (Bouchard et al., 2008). Toddlers who display self-recognition are more empathic and prosocial (Zahn-Waxler et al., 2001); preschool children who are able to take another person's perspective are more prosocial (Zahn-Waxler et al., 1995). Prosocial behaviour also increases as children learn to detect other people's emotional cues and realize that they need help (Eisenberg et al., 2006).

STABILITY AND STYLES OF PROSOCIAL BEHAVIOUR
Baumrind (1971) measured preschool children's nurturant and sympathetic behaviours toward peers and then assessed these behaviours in the same children five or six years later. These behaviours were moderately stable between the two ages; children who behaved more prosocially at age 4 were likelier to behave prosocially at age 9. Other longitudinal studies have told a similar story (e.g., Eisenberg et al., 2002). Children's tendencies to donate to needy children, to assist an adult (e.g., by helping pick up paper clips), and to offer others help are consistent across all of elementary school (Eisenberg et al., 2006). During adolescence, prosocial behaviour toward peers is relatively stable

Volunteering their time, for example, by working in a food drive to help people who are less fortunate than themselves, is an excellent way for young people to learn about pro-social behaviour.

Turning Points

PROSOCIAL AND ALTRUISTIC BEHAVIOUR

BIRTH–6 MONTHS
- Responds positively to others (smiles, laughs with others)
- Participates in social games (e.g., peekaboo)
- Reacts emotionally to others' distress (crying or general upset)

6–12 MONTHS
- Takes an active role in social games
- Exhibits sharing behaviours
- Displays affection to familiar persons

12–24 MONTHS
- Refines ability to point with index finger
- Complies with simple requests
- Indicates knowledge of rules of co-operative games
- Shows knowledge of caregiving skills
- Comforts people in distress
- Participates in adults' work, household tasks
- Shows and gives toys to adults

24–36 MONTHS
- Draws person's attention to objects with words as well as gestures
- Exhibits increasingly well-planned caregiving and helping behaviours
- Verbally expresses own intentions to help and knowledge of tasks
- Gives helpful verbal advice
- Tries to protect others

3–ABOUT 7 YEARS
- Is hedonistically motivated to perform prosocial acts

3–11 YEARS
- Recognizes others' needs even when they conflict with own needs

6–17 YEARS
- Justifies prosocial or non-prosocial behaviour by reference to stereotypical notions of good and bad and considerations of approval and acceptance from others

10–17 YEARS
- Empathizes with others and feels pride or guilt about consequences of own actions

14–17 YEARS
- May justify helping or not helping by internalized values and by concern with the rights and dignity of others
- May believe in individual and social obligations, the equality of all individuals, and may base self-respect on living up to own values and accepted norms

Note: Developmental events described in this and other Turning Points charts represent overall trends identified in research studies. Individual children vary greatly in the ages at which they achieve these developmental changes.

Sources: Based on Eisenberg, Fabes, & Spinrad, 2006; Hay & Rheingold, 1983.

(Wentzel et al., 2004), as is young adults' valuing of concern for others (Pratt et al., 2003). Similar longitudinal findings have been observed cross-culturally in a sample of Chinese children/young adults (Chen et al., 2002).

Children have different styles of expressing their prosocial intentions, however. Researchers studying 2-year-olds' reactions when their mothers cried after reading a sad story in the newspaper observed a number of different reactions (Radke-Yarrow & Zahn-Waxler, 1983). One child tensed up and fought back her tears. Another asked, "What's wrong, Mommy?" A third tore up the newspaper that made her mother cry. As these very different reactions illustrate, infants and children develop their own styles of dealing with others' distress. Some children are very emotional and get upset. Others are cool and reflective and appear to approach the situation more cognitively, inspecting, exploring, and asking questions. Still others are aggressive or defensive—for example, hitting the person who made the baby cry. Children's prosocial styles also tend to be stable across time. These researchers observed stability in style from age 2 to age 7 in about two-thirds of the children they studied.

Are Girls More Prosocial than Boys?

Gender differences vary depending on the type of prosocial behaviour (Eisenberg et al., 2006; Fabes & Eisenberg, 1996). Although girls tend to be generally more oriented toward helping others than boys are, the reality is more complex (Grusec et al., 2002). Differences are greatest for kindness and consideration; girls consistently express more of these kinds of prosocial behaviours than boys do. Girls are also more **empathic** than boys (Zahn-Waxler et al., 2001), especially as they get older (Eisenberg et al., 2006). That is, girls have a greater capacity to experience the emotions that others feel. Girls are also slightly higher than boys in instrumental helping, comforting, sharing, and donating, but gender differences in these behaviours are less dramatic.

empathic

Able to experience the same emotion that someone else is experiencing.

Of note, gender differences are more pronounced in data derived from self-reports and the reports by family members and peers than in data gathered by observational techniques (Grusec et al., 2002; Hastings et al., 2005). This suggests that some gender differences reflect people's conceptions of what boys and girls are *supposed* to be like rather than how they actually behave (Eisenberg et al., 2006; Hastings et al., 2007). Parents do stress the importance of politeness and prosocial behaviour more for daughters than for sons (Maccoby, 1998). Moreover, when girls behave prosocially, parents attribute such behaviours to inborn tendencies, whereas they attribute boys' prosocial behaviours to the influences of the environment and socialization. These findings do not mean that gender differences are *only* in the eye of the self or the beholder; rather, the cultural stereotypes and beliefs that girls are made of "everything nice" contribute to gender differences that researchers have found (Hastings et al., 2007).

Determinants of Prosocial Development

Like most behaviours, prosocial behaviour has both biological and environmental determinants.

BIOLOGICAL INFLUENCES   Some evolutionists argue that human beings have a biological predisposition to respond with empathy and are biologically prepared to engage in prosocial behaviour (Sober & Wilson, 1998). As evidence of this, helping and sharing are seen among many infrahuman animals; for example, Preston and de Waal (2002) report both empathy and consoling behaviour in chimpanzees. A similar argument has been made by Dennis Krebs of Simon Fraser University (Krebs, 2000, 2005, 2008; Krebs & Janicki, 2004). According to Krebs, moral development and prosocial behaviour are best seen from the perspective of evolutionary biology, in which it is adaptive for children and adults to co-operate with one another (Krebs & Janicki, 2004).

There is also evidence that individual differences in prosocial behaviour may have a genetic basis. Identical or monozygotic twins are more alike in prosocial behaviour

(Davis et al., 1994) than are fraternal or dizygotic twins. Other studies of identical twins underscore the combined role of genetic and environmental factors in the development of children's prosocial behaviour (Hastings et al., 2005). For example, in a study of identical preschool-age twins, Deater-Deckard and colleagues (2001) found that both genetic and environmental factors (e.g., maternal supportive or punitive behaviours) contributed to children's prosocial behaviour. Further support for the genetic basis of prosocial behaviour comes from the study of children with genetic abnormalities. Children who have Williams syndrome (marked by loss of the long arm of chromosome 7) are more sociable, empathic, sympathetic, and prosocial than children who do not have Williams (Mervis & Klein-Tasman, 2000; Semal & Rosner, 2003).

Researchers are beginning to isolate the neurological roots of prosocial behaviour. For example, studies using the neuroimaging PET scan reveal that neural structures associated with emotions (in particular, the *amygdala*) were more activated in response to sad than to neutral stories (Decety & Chaminade, 2003).

Temperament may play a role in the likelihood of children's sympathetic behaviour, just as it appears to influence children's undesirable responses. For example, highly inhibited 2-year-olds became more upset by another's distress than their less inhibited peers (Young et al., 1999). Similarly, children who can regulate their emotions better, as indexed by measures of heart rate, are more likely to exhibit comforting behaviour (Eisenberg et al., 1996b).

In sum, a variety of biological factors—evolutionary, genetic, neurological, and temperamental—predispose children to behave prosocially. These biological influences interact with the environment in determining how prosocial a child will be.

ENVIRONMENTAL INFLUENCES Environmental factors affecting children's willingness to behave prosocially include the family, peers, and mass media. Laboratory studies in which children see people donate to or share with others, as well as real-life situations in which parents, peers, and others model prosocial behaviours, demonstrate that children acquire prosocial behaviours through social learning (Eisenberg et al., 2006; Hart & Fegley, 1995). Daughters whose mothers are sensitive to their emotions, who try to find out why they feel bad and listen to them when they are anxious and upset, display more prosocial behaviour; for example, they will comfort an infant in distress (Eisenberg et al., 1993). The way that mothers talk about emotions matters, too. Preschoolers whose mothers explain their own feelings when they are sad display more prosocial behaviour (Denham, 1998; Denham et al., 2007). In addition, children who have opportunities to engage in prosocial actions, by volunteering at homeless shelters, for example, develop more prosocial attitudes and behaviour (Johnson et al., 1998; Metz et al., 2003; Pratt et al., 2003).

As we discuss in Box 14.2, parents' child-rearing practices also contribute to children's prosocial behaviours by acting as models or directly encouraging and shaping prosocial behaviours (Grusec & Dix, 1986; Hastings et al., 2007). Parents who use power-assertive techniques (e.g., physical punishment) and little reasoning and who show less warmth are unlikely to have altruistic children. In a study in the Netherlands, Dekovic and Janssens (1992) found that democratic parenting (parenting that is warm, supportive, and demanding and that provides guidance and positive feedback) was linked to more prosocial behaviour in children as rated by both teachers and peers. And in a meta-analysis of five studies that looked at families in Ontario and British Columbia, Roberts (1999) found that children's prosocial behaviours were related to parents' tolerant, non-punitive reactions to emotional distress. When parents were negative and controlling and intolerant of children's distress, children were less empathic and prosocial (Asbury et al., 2003; Strayer & Roberts, 2004). And recently, Paul Hastings from Concordia University and his colleagues (2007) found that mothers' authoritative parenting style predicted both boys' and girls' prosocial actions toward peers; fathers' parenting, although similarly styled, was more weakly related to prosocial behaviour.

Box 14.2

Child Psychology in Action

HOW PARENTS CAN TEACH CHILDREN PROSOCIAL BEHAVIOUR

To find out how children learn to react in helpful ways when they have caused distress in another person or when they see another person suffering, Carolyn Zahn-Waxler and her colleagues (1979, 1992) devised a clever scheme. They trained mothers of 18-month-olds to tape-record their children's reactions to others' distress that the children themselves either caused or witnessed. The mothers recorded both the children's and their own behaviour over a 9-month period during which observers occasionally visited the home to check on the accuracy of the mothers' records. The researchers also asked the mothers to simulate distress from time to time. For example, mothers might pretend to be sad (sobbing for 5 to 10 seconds), to be in pain (bumping their feet or heads, saying, "Ouch!" and rubbing the injured parts), or to suffer respiratory distress (coughing/choking).

How did the children respond to others' distress? Overall, whether they had hurt someone else or merely witnessed another person's distress, they reacted in a helpful fashion about a third of the time. However, some children responded in most distress situations (between 60 and 70 percent), whereas some failed to respond at all.

Mothers' reactions to their own children's harmful behaviour toward others, as well as to the sight of another person's distress, were related to their children's helpful behaviour in distress situations. Some mothers linked a child's behaviour with its consequences for the child's victim; the children of these mothers were more likely to respond in a helpful way when they caused harm to someone. These mothers

might say, for example, in a clear but objective manner, "Tom's crying because you pushed him." Other mothers' discussions of distress situations had strong emotional overtones, and these explanations appeared to be even more effective. The children of these mothers were more likely to intervene in bystander situations when they did not cause any harm but saw that someone else was upset. These mothers might say something like, "You must never poke anyone's eyes" or "When you hurt me, I don't want to be near you. I am going away from you."

Other studies have confirmed these findings. For example, children of mothers who pointed out a peer's personal distress in an affectively charged manner reacted in a sad fashion (Denham et al., 1994). However, some maternal tactics were ineffective in encouraging prosocial behaviour. For example, physical restraint (simply moving away from the child or moving her away from a victim), physical punishment (a mother might have reported, "I swatted him a good one"), or unexplained prohibitions ("Stop that!") may even interfere with the development of prosocial behaviour. These researchers also found that when mothers showed anger as they delivered their disciplinary reasoning and tried to induce guilt in children, preschoolers were unlikely to engage in parent-directed prosocial actions.

Prosocial and altruistic behaviour can begin early, and parents play an important role. They can facilitate and encourage the child's emerging altruistic behaviours by helping children to make connections between their own actions and other people's emotional states. Altruism truly does begin at home.

Parents who explicitly model prosocial behaviour and provide opportunities for children to perform these actions may be particularly successful in promoting altruism (Eisenberg et al., 2006). A common way parents provide opportunities for learning prosocial behaviour is by assigning children responsibility for household tasks. Even 2-years-old will help adults in a variety of tasks such as sweeping, cleaning, and setting tables (Rheingold, 1982). Allowing children to help in these ways may be important for their prosocial development. Nor are the effects limited to young children. McLellan and Youniss (2003) found that adolescent volunteering was more common when the parents engaged in volunteer activities. Adolescents even modelled the types of voluntary services in which their parents engaged, such as working in a homeless shelter or working for an environmental cause.

Peers also act as models and shapers of children's prosocial behaviour. In one study, preschoolers who were exposed to prosocial peers at the beginning of the school year engaged in more prosocial peer interactions later in the year (Fabes et al., 2002). However, in general, children who were less prosocial spent their time with other less prosocial children, whereas highly prosocial children played together. As a result of this "prosocial segregation," children who are low in prosocial behaviours have few chances to learn more prosocial practices from their prosocial peers. Moreover, pre-schoolers who initiated more altruism received more altruism from their peers a year later, although the converse was not true. Only the state of being the recipient was not related to increases in receiving altruistic behaviour from peers. Acting as a participant in being helpful and kind likely leads to reciprocity of prosocial acts from peers (Persson, 2005).

Television and Prosocial Behaviour   Television may also teach prosocial behaviours (Comstock & Scharrer, 2006; Mares & Woodard, 2007). Researchers have assessed the impact of *Mister Rogers' Neighborhood*, *Barney & Friends*, *Sesame Street*, and other programs focused on understanding the feelings of others, expressing sympathy, and helping. Children who watched these programs not only learned the specific prosocial content of the programs but were also able to apply that learning to other situations involving peers. In comparison with children who watched shows with neutral content, they learned general rules about prosocial behaviour (Friedrich & Stein, 1973; Huston & Wright, 1998; Singer & Singer, 2001). This was especially true for young children from middle- to upper-class families whose parents watched the programs with them and encouraged their altruistic behaviour (Mares & Woodward, 2001).

CROSS-CULTURAL PERSPECTIVES   In some cultures, children are given more responsibility for taking care of siblings and performing household tasks (Eisenberg et al., 2006). What effect does this have? Cross-cultural studies of children from a wide range of societies—in Mexico, Japan, India, and Kenya—suggest that children who perform more domestic chores and spend more time caring for their infant brothers, sisters, and cousins are more altruistic (Whiting & Edwards, 1988; Whiting & Whiting, 1975). Similar results have been found in cultures that stress communal values, such as the Aitutaki of Polynesia, the Papago Indian tribe in Arizona, and many Asian cultures (Chen, 2000; Eisenberg et al., 2006; Zaff et al., 2003). Further evidence of the role of culture comes from studies of children raised in Israeli kibbutzim, which stress prosocial and co-operative values. Children reared in these communal settings are more prosocial than city-reared peers (Aviezer et al., 1994). Mexican-American children are more prosocial than European-American children (Knight et al., 1982). However, as they become teenagers and more acculturated to North American norms, they report less prosocial behaviour (de Guzman & Carlo, 2004).

LO5 Prosocial Reasoning

prosocial reasoning

Thinking and making judgments about prosocial issues.

Prosocial behaviour shifts in form and expression across development. These changes reflect changes in **prosocial reasoning**, which in turn reflect changes in children's cognitive development. Nancy Eisenberg and her colleagues at Arizona State University (Eisenberg et al., 1999, 2001b, 2006) proposed a model of the development of prosocial reasoning that is similar to the Kohlberg model of the development of moral reasoning. To test the model, they devised a number of hypothetical dilemmas. Here is a sample:

> *One day a girl named Mary was going to a friend's birthday party. On her way she saw a girl who had fallen down and hurt her leg. The girl asked Mary to go to her house and tell her parents so the parents could come and take her to the doctor. But if Mary did run and get the child's parents, she would be late to the birthday party and miss the ice cream, cake, and all the games. What should Mary do? Why?*

Eisenberg and her colleagues tested groups of children when they were 4½ and 11½ years old and again in early adulthood. As the children matured, they became less egocentric and more other-oriented, and they became more capable of abstract reasoning about prosocial dilemmas. The first type of reasoning, shown in Table 14-2, was **hedonistic reasoning**, in which children based their decision to perform a prosocial act on the promise of material reward. This type of reasoning decreased with age. The second type of reasoning was **needs-oriented reasoning**. This was still a relatively simple type of reasoning in which children expressed concern for the needs of others, even though these needs conflicted with their own. It peaked in middle childhood and then levelled off. The higher types of reasoning listed in the table were empathic and prosocial—they all increased with age. Hedonistic reasoning was related to less sharing and empathy; needs-oriented reasoning was related to more prosocial behaviour; prosocial reasoning was related to more prosocial behaviour that required some cognitive reflection (Carlo et al., 2003).

Some researchers have suggested that delay of gratification and prosocial behaviour might be related to children's theory of mind and executive function abilities, along with a concern for the future self. According to Chris Moore, John Barresi, and their colleagues (Lemmon & Moore, 2007; Moore & Lemmon, 2001; Moore et al., 1998;

hedonistic reasoning

Making a decision to perform a prosocial act on the basis of expected material reward.

needs-oriented reasoning

Reasoning in which children express concern for others' needs even though their own needs may conflict with the needs of others.

Table 14-2 Evolution of prosocial reasoning

Level	Age Group	Orientation	Mode of Prosocial Reasoning
1	Preschoolers and younger elementary schoolchildren	Hedonistic, self-focused	Child is concerned with self-oriented consequences rather than moral considerations. Decision to help or not help another is based on consideration of direct gain to self, future reciprocity, and concern for people to whom the child is bound by affectional ties.
2	Preschoolers and elementary schoolchildren	Recognition of needs of others	Child expresses concern for the physical, material, and psychological needs of others even if these needs conflict with her own. Concern is expressed in the simplest terms, without verbal expressions of sympathy, evidence of self-reflective role taking, or reference to internalized affect, such as guilt.
3	Elementary and high-school students	Seeking others' approval and acceptance	Child uses stereotypical images of good and bad persons and behaviours and considerations of others' approval and acceptance in justifying prosocial or non-helping behaviours.
4	Older elementary and high-school students	(a) Empathic	Child's judgments include evidence of sympathetic responding, self-reflective role taking, concern with the other's humanness, and guilt or positive affect related to the consequences of his actions.
	Minority of high-school-age children	(b) Transitional (empathic and internalized)	Child's justifications for helping or not helping involve internalized values, norms, duties, or responsibilities, and may refer to the necessity of protecting the rights and dignity of other persons. These ideas, however, are not clearly stated.
5	Only a small minority of high-school students and virtually no elementary schoolchildren	Strongly internalized	Child's justifications for helping or not helping are based on internalized values, norms, or responsibilities, the desire to maintain individual and societal contractual obligations, and the belief in the dignity, rights, and equality of all individuals. Child also construes her self-respect as based on living up to her own values and accepted norms.

Source: Adapted from Eisenberg, Lennon, & Roth, 1983.

Thompson et al., 1997), changes in prosocial behaviour during preschool occur because children become capable of future-oriented reasoning, which itself relies on children's abilities to represent a future mental state (an aspect of theory of mind) and to inhibit responses to the immediate situation (an aspect of executive function) in favour of what will happen in the future. In a test of this relation, Lemmon and Moore (2007) gave 3- and 4-year-olds a choice between a smaller immediate reward of one sticker and a delayed larger reward of between two and five stickers. These authors found that although 3-year-olds showed no tendency to delay gratification to receive a larger reward, 4-year-olds' choices reflected the value of the delayed reward, a result demonstrating that future-oriented responding reflects a growth in concern with the future self.

Beliefs about appropriate behaviour toward others are grounded in bodies of religious and philosophical thought that have deep roots in the history of the culture. Not surprisingly, therefore, researchers have found that there are cultural differences in prosocial reasoning, and there are differences in prosocial behaviour. For example, in Asian countries, people take a more collective approach to social and interpersonal behaviour than do people in Western nations, placing the emphasis on the welfare of the group or nation rather than the individual. In these cultures, ties of responsibility and reciprocity may be more binding than they are in the West. In Germany and Israel, children are more likely than North American children to emphasize direct reciprocity, whereby children expect to receive similar payback for their prosocial actions (Eisenberg et al., 1985); in Brazil, urban adolescents are less likely to use high-level prosocial reasoning than North American teens (Eisenberg et al., 2001). Clearly, cultural values not only shape prosocial behaviours but organize the ways people think about their prosocial obligations to others.

For Thought and Discussion

1. Just as with morality, one can question whether prosocial and altruistic behaviour is a personality trait (and, hence, consistent) or situation dependent (and, hence, inconsistent). How would you design an experiment to look at this question? Would you focus on reasoning, behaviour, or both?

2. How important are models for prosocial behaviour? Do you think children can learn to act prosocially simply by watching others act that way? Can you think of an example from your own life in which you have seen such an influence? What theory of development would support this effect?

LO6 THE DEVELOPMENT OF AGGRESSION

aggression

Behaviour that intentionally harms other people by inflicting pain or injury on them.

Aggression is the opposite of prosocial behaviour; traditionally, it refers to behaviour that is intended to and does harm to other people by inflicting pain or injury on them. Recently, however, this definition has been expanded by some researchers to include behaviour toward animals and inanimate objects (Halperin et al., 2002, 2003). The notion of intention is crucial, for we need to separate acts of aggression from the actions taken by parents in disciplining their children and from the action of doctors and dentists who must at times cause pain to preserve physical health. What distinguishes painful actions of these kinds from acts of aggression is that their intention is not to cause pain or harm but to better the condition of others. For decades, psychologists have puzzled over the knotty problem of aggression. Why do some children attack others? Why do some adults cheat, rob, and attack, and murder others? Do patterns of aggression change over time, and if so, how? What roles do families, peers, and the mass media play in the development of aggression? Most important, how can we control aggression in our children?

How Aggressive Behaviour Develops in Children

A visit to a preschool and a stopover at an elementary school playground reveal some striking age differences in the form and frequency of aggressive behaviour. (The Turning Points chart on page 563 offers a brief outline of how aggression changes over time.) Preschool children are more likely to quarrel and fight over toys and possessions; this is **instrumental aggression**, and some have recently argued (Tremblay, 2000; Tremblay et al., 1999) that such physical aggression is related to later aggressive behaviour, an argument that has found empirical support (Zhang et al., 2003). Older children are more likely to exhibit **hostile aggression**—personally oriented aggressive acts in which a child criticizes, ridicules, tattles on, or calls the person names (Dodge et al., 2006). This shift may occur as older children acquire a greater ability to infer the intentions and motives of others (Ferguson & Rule, 1980). When an older child recognizes that a peer wants to hurt him, he is more likely to retaliate by a direct assault on the tormentor than by an indirect attack on the aggressor's possessions.

Despite children's gradually improved ability to infer intent, individual children differ in how accurately they can "read" another person's intentions. Some children, especially those who are highly aggressive, have more difficulty judging other people's intentions. We can apply the information-processing model of social behaviour (discussed in Chapter 12) to aggressive behaviour (Crick & Dodge, 1994). This is especially helpful in ambiguous situations, when children's intentions are not clearly either aggressive or prosocial. In such situations, boys who are rated by their classmates as more aggressive are likely to react in a hostile way—as if the other person intended to be aggressive. Aggressive boys see the world as a threatening and hostile place. The reason for their negative views may be based on their experience: they not only commit more unprovoked aggressive acts, but they are also the targets of more aggressive attacks (Dodge & Frame, 1982). Researchers have found that aggressive children make more hostile attributions about other people's behaviour in studies of children of European, African, and Latino backgrounds (Graham & Hudley, 1994; Guerra & Huesmann, 2003). And they have found that the bias continues on into adolescence (Van Oostrum & Howard, 1997).

The kinds of aggression children display can be characterized in other ways. Some children act aggressively only in response to being attacked, threatened, or frustrated, displaying **reactive aggression**. These children are particularly likely to misinterpret others' intentions (Poulin & Boivin, 2000). Other children—playground bullies—show **proactive aggression**, using force to dominate another person or to threaten another in order to gain a prized object or possession. They may be accurate in reading others' intentions, but the focus, nonetheless, is dominating them. Like instrumental aggression, proactive aggression generally decreases across development. For example, in one study, "hits others" occurred in 70 percent of the children observed when they were 2 or 3 years old, but it declined to 20 percent by ages 4 and 5 and to 12 percent by grade 3 (NICHD Early Child Care Research Network, 2004b).

The ways children express their aggression also change over development. Toddlers rely more on physical attacks; older children, with their improved communication skills, are likely to be aggressive verbally rather than physically (Dodge et al., 2006). This developmental shift is due not only to increased verbal skills but also to changes in adult expectations and rules. Most adults become less tolerant of physical aggression as children mature but are more likely to ignore a "battle of words"—even among older children. A few older children continue to express aggression physically, however; they fist-fight at age 8, vandalize at age 12, and commit homicide at age 18 (Dodge et al., 2006).

Although, in general, the level of aggression declines as children grow older and learn to solve problems and conflicts through more socially acceptable means, individual differences in aggressiveness are quite stable over time (Ledingham & Schwartzman,

instrumental aggression

Quarrelling and fighting over toys and possessions.

hostile aggression

Aggressive behaviour directed at another person, including criticizing, ridiculing, and name calling.

reactive aggression

Aggression in response to attack, threat, or frustration.

proactive aggression

The use of force to dominate another person or to bully or threaten others.

1984; Moskowitz et al., 1985), and those who are particularly aggressive in childhood are likely to remain so into adulthood (Dodge et al., 2006). In one study of more than 600 individuals originally seen at 8 years of age, researchers found that the more aggressive 8-year-olds were, at age 30, still more aggressive than their peers (Bushman & Huesmann, 2001; Huesmann et al., 1984). The boys who were rated in childhood as aggressive were more likely as adults to have moving traffic violations, to have been arrested for drunk driving, and to have abused their wives; both boys and girls who were rated as aggressive as children were more likely to have criminal convictions by the age of 30 years (see Figure 14-4). In other longitudinal studies as well, young children who were ill-tempered at age 3 had more problems with aggression six years later (S. B. Campbell, 2000); ill-tempered girls also experienced more marital instability later in life and were less adequate and more ill-tempered mothers (Caspi et al., 1987; Kokko & Pulkkinen, 2000). Clearly, an early pattern of aggressive behaviour leaves its mark.

Gender Differences in Aggression

Although there are few gender differences in aggression in infancy, by the time they are toddlers, boys are more likely than girls to instigate and be involved in aggressive incidents (Loeber & Hay, 1993; Maccoby & Jacklin, 1980). This gender difference is evident not only across North American socio-economic groups but also across cultures such as the United Kingdom, Switzerland, Ethiopia, Kenya, India, the Philippines, Mexico, New Zealand, and Japan (Broidy et al., 2003; Dodge et al., 2006; Whiting & Whiting, 1975). Boys' and girls' aggressive patterns differ in important ways. Boys are more likely than girls to retaliate after being attacked (Darvill & Cheyne, 1981),

Figure 14-4

The correlation between childhood aggression and adult criminal behaviour

Among males, the correlation between highly aggressive behaviour in childhood and number of criminal convictions in later life was 0.75, which is extremely high. The same correlations for boys who showed little or only moderate aggressiveness in childhood were much lower, as were all the correlations for females between aggressiveness in childhood and criminal convictions in adulthood. Note, however, that among females, we see the same tendency of rising correlations as the degree of early aggression escalates.

Source: Adapted from Huesmann, Eron, Lefkowitz, & Walder, 1984.

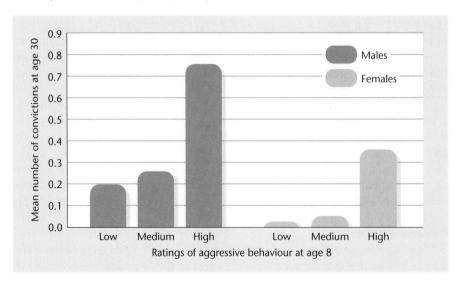

Turning Points

THE DEVELOPMENT OF AGGRESSIVE BEHAVIOUR

INFANCY: 0–2 YEARS
- Infants express anger and frustration
- They show some early signs of aggression (pushing, shoving)
- Temperamental differences in irritability predict later aggression

PRESCHOOL YEARS: 2–5 OR 6 YEARS
- Children encouraged by family members in anti-social behaviour may later begin to display seriously aggressive behaviour
- Children in this age group tend to display instrumental aggression, to fight over toys and possessions, and to rely on the physical expression of aggression
- Even in the preschool period, girls exhibit more verbal and relational aggression, excluding and gossiping about others, whereas boys are more physical

6–7 YEARS
- Children display hostile aggression, using criticism, ridicule, name calling, and tattling, as they begin to infer and to judge the intentions of others
- Instrumental aggression decreases

7–10 YEARS
- The difference between boys' reliance on physical aggression and girls' reliance on relational aggression becomes more marked
- However, in both boys and girls, physical aggression gradually declines and verbal aggression becomes more common
- Aggressive children may begin to do poorly in school and to be rejected by peers
- In the fourth or fifth grade, parental monitoring becomes particularly important to deter delinquency and vandalism

ADOLESCENCE
- Aggressive children select aggressive and deviant peer groups
- Among some youths, vandalism, use of guns, and delinquency increase
- Gender differences are marked: rates of delinquency and violent behaviour are much higher among boys than girls
- Hormonal changes, such as rising levels of testosterone, are associated with increases in reactive aggression in boys; individual differences in hormonal levels are important determinants of the levels of aggression

Note: Developmental events described in this and other Turning Points charts represent overall trends identified in research studies. Patterns of aggressive behaviour vary greatly among individual children (see especially "The Family as a Training Centre for Aggression" on page 567).

Sources: Coie & Dodge, 1998; Crick et al., 1998; Dodge, Coie, & Lynam, 2006; Ostrov and Crick, 2006; Underwood, 2004.

and they are more likely to attack a male than a female (Barrett, 1979). Boys are more physically confrontational, and their expressions of physical aggression are more frequent than those of girls (Broidy et al., 2003; Ostrov & Crick, 2006). Boys are less likely than girls to engage in negative self-evaluation, they are less likely to anticipate parental disapproval for acting aggressively, and they are also more likely to approve of aggression (Huesmann & Guerra, 1997; Perry et al., 1989).

In attempting to resolve conflicts, girls tend to use such strategies as verbal objection and negotiation, methods that may make the escalation of a quarrel into overt aggression less likely (Eisenberg et al., 1994). This doesn't mean that girls are not aggressive but rather that they use different tactics in achieving their goals. Especially in the elementary school years, girls often use what is called **relational aggression**, or the damaging or destruction of interpersonal relationships (Ostrov & Crick, 2006; Underwood, 2003). In this mode, girls attempt to exclude peers from group participation, besmirch other girls' reputations, and gossip about each other's negative attributes. Researchers have found that girls may choose social ostracism rather than direct confrontation (Goodwin, 2002). As girls enter adolescence, they tend to make increasing use of the aggressive strategy of excluding others from social cliques (Crick et al., 1999, 2004; Underwood, 2003; Xie et al., 2005). Although relational aggression becomes more common as girls get older, even preschool girls show significantly more relational aggression and are less overtly aggressive than boys (Crick et al., 1997).

Relational aggression is significantly related to social and psychological maladjustment; boys and girls who engage in this type of aggression are more likely to be rejected by their peers, both in North America and in Italy (Crick et al., 2004; Ostrov & Crick, 2006; Tomada & Schneider, 1997). Although this kind of aggression may be less overt, other children notice it, and they ostracize those who engage in it—thus creating a "mean girls" vicious cycle. More girls than boys view this type of aggression as hurtful and, indeed, view it as being equally hurtful as physical aggression (Galen & Underwood, 1997; Underwood, 2003). Boys tend to view physical aggression as more hurtful than relational aggression. Table 14-3 and Figure 14-5 illustrate some of the differences between these two types of aggression and between girls' and boys' use of these behaviours.

Gender differences in aggression become more salient as children develop. Marked male–female differences in aggressive behaviour are evident in adolescence and adulthood (Moffitt et al., 2001). As Figure 14-6 shows, approximately five times as many adolescent boys as girls are arrested for violent crimes (e.g., robbery, aggravated assault, criminal homicide), although in recent years, the number of females found guilty of such crimes has increased (Cairns & Cairns, 1994; Moffitt et al., 2001). However, although males are still more likely than females to be the victim of a violent crime, the gender gap has closed over the past three decades from 45 percent to less than 10 percent, as Figure 14-7 on page 566 illustrates (Bureau of Justice, 2006).

LO7 Origins of Aggressive Behaviour

The theme of the interplay between biological and environmental influences reappears once again as we explore the causes of aggressive behaviour.

relational aggression

Damaging or destroying interpersonal relationships by such means as excluding another or gossiping about or spoiling another's reputation.

Table 14-3

Some characteristics of overt and relational aggression in schoolchildren

Source: Based on Crick, 1997; Ostrov & Crick, 2006.

Overt Aggressors	Relational Aggressors
Hit, kick, punch other children	Try to make other children dislike a certain child by spreading rumours about her
Say mean things to insult others or put them down	When angry, get over it by excluding another person from group of friends
Tell other children that they will beat them up unless the children do what they say	Tell friends that they will stop liking them unless the friends do what they say
Push and shove others	When angry at a person, ignore him or stop talking to him
Call other children mean names directly	Try to keep certain people out of their own group during activity or play time

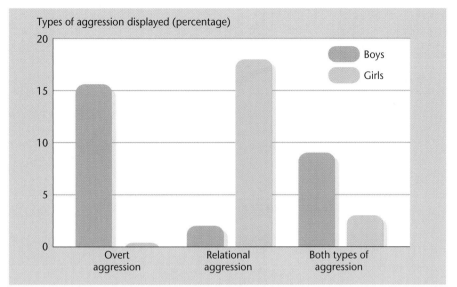

Figure 14-5

Aggression in boys and girls
Boys and girls do not differ greatly in the amount of aggression they express, but they express it in quite different ways.

Source: Based on Crick & Grotpeter, 1995.

THE ROLE OF BIOLOGY Aggression has a biological basis. Studies of twins give some support to a role for genetic factors in aggression (Dionne et al., 2003; Rhee & Waldman, 2002). Dionne and her colleagues found that, according to parents' ratings of aggressive behaviour, 18-month-old Canadian identical twins were more similar than non-identical twins. Studies of adolescents have similar findings. Responding to a questionnaire about aggression that contained such items as "Some people think that I have a violent temper," identical twins rated themselves as more similar than did

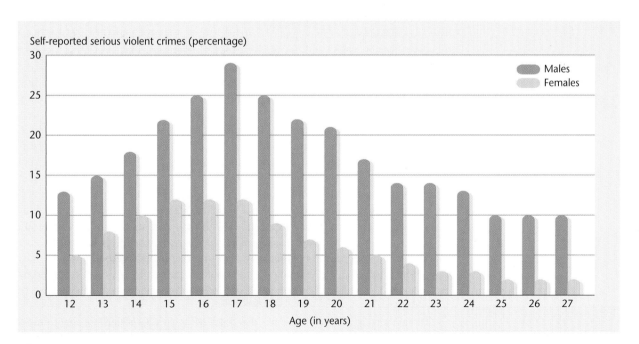

Figure 14-6

Serious violent crime among adolescents and young adults: Self-reports

Serious violent offences (SVOs), which include aggravated assault (assault with intent to commit a crime), robbery, and rape, rise sharply between the ages of 12 and 17. Although more males than females commit violent offences, girls are likely to get involved in criminal behaviour when they are about two years younger than boys (age 14 versus 16).

Source: Coie & Dodge, 1998.

Figure 14-7

Violent crime rates by gender of victim

Violent crime rates have declined for both male and females victims, and the gender gap has decreased as well.

Source: Bureau of Justice Statistics, 2006.

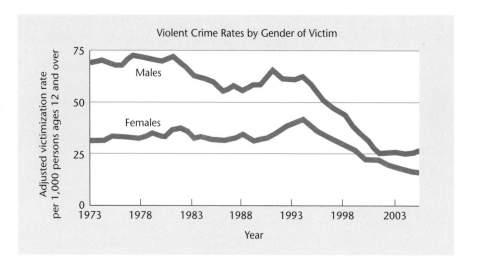

non-identical twins (Gottesman & Goldsmith, 1994). Researchers in the Netherlands, Sweden, and Britain have obtained similar results (Eley et al., 1999; Van Den Oord et al., 1994).

There are links between hormones and aggression, too. Looking at preschool children, Sanchez-Martin and colleagues (2000) found that testosterone levels were positively correlated with the amount of aggression shown in children's social interactions for young boys. And the evidence is even clearer in adolescence, when hormone levels rise (Moeller, 2001; Ramirez, 2003). A study of 15- to 17-year-old boys in Sweden (Olweus et al., 1988) found a link between testosterone and aggression. Boys whose blood showed higher levels of testosterone rated themselves as more likely to respond aggressively to provocations and threats from others. In these cases, the hormone seems to have a direct effect on the aggressive behaviour. Boys with high blood levels of testosterone were also more impatient or irritable, which, in turn, increased their readiness to engage in unprovoked and destructive kinds of aggressive behaviour (e.g., to start fights or say rude or hostile things without being provoked).

Research by Tremblay and his Canadian colleagues (1998) found another link between testosterone and aggression. In this study, testosterone was related to body mass, which in turn was linked to increased physical aggression. Even when researchers controlled for child-rearing practices, these hormonal effects held. Boys rated as tough and social leaders had the highest testosterone levels, although they were not necessarily higher in everyday aggression. Tough, dominant boys, however, may be more likely to respond aggressively to provocation by lower-status peers. Hormones may affect aggression in girls as well (Brook et al., 2003). Levels of hormones, especially estradiol, that increase during puberty were positively linked with adolescent girls' expressions of anger and aggression during interactions with their parents (Inoff-Germain et al., 1988). Interestingly, other work has suggested that there may be reciprocal effects; that is, dominance or success in conflict may lead to a rise in testosterone levels (Schaal et al., 1996). For example, winning a judo contest leads to increases in testosterone levels, but losing results in a drop in levels of this hormone (Dodge et al., 2006; McCaul et al., 1992).

Researchers have also examined the links between aggression and neurotransmitters, chemical compounds that can facilitate or inhibit the transmission of neural impulses within the central nervous system (Moeller, 2001). *Serotonin*, a neurotransmitter that is involved in emotional states and the regulation of emotion, has been linked with aggression in both humans and animals (Herbert & Martinez, 2001). In a two-year-study, Kruesi and colleagues (1992) found a negative relation between the severity of children's physically aggressive behaviour and levels of the neurotransmitter serotonin; the lower the level of serotonin, the higher the level of aggression. However, a combination of low levels of serotonin and a history of family conflict was evident in the most violent offenders, a reminder that the environment and biological factors operate together (Moffitt & Caspi, 2006). Similarly, Marks and colleagues (2007) found that individuals who were at biological risk for aggression, based on their degree of serotonin responsiveness, were particularly vulnerable to the impact of social adversity and risk, displaying more aggression and delinquency.

Temperament also may be linked with aggressive behaviour. Infants with difficult temperaments—those who are irritable, whiny, unpredictable, hard to soothe, and prone to negative affect—are more likely to develop aggressive behaviour patterns at later ages (Rothbart & Bates, 2006).

Biological factors do not act independently of the social environment, of course; their influence on aggressive behaviour is exacerbated under certain conditions, such as a provoking and threatening situation or a high-risk and conflict-ridden environment (Dodge et al., 2006; Raine, 2002). A Swedish study of adopted children illustrates the joint contributions of biology and environment (Cloninger et al., 1978, 1982). When both the child's biological and adoptive parents were criminals, 40 percent of the adopted boys were likely to engage in criminal acts. If just the biological parent was a criminal, the percentage declined to 12; if just the adoptive parent was a criminal, it declined to 7 percent. If neither parent was a criminal, the proportion of adopted males who engaged in criminal acts dropped to 3 percent. A similar gene–environment interaction was found for girls.

A study of more than 4,000 males in Denmark also illustrates the combined effects of biology and environment on aggression. In this study, a combination of birth complications and early rejection by the mother predicted that adolescents would be involved in violent crime by the time they were 19 years old. Among the young offenders who had experienced both risk factors, 40 percent became violent, whereas only 20 percent of those who experienced only one risk factor committed violent crimes (Raine & Liu, 1998). Finally, a study of Australian 15-year-olds tells a similar story: The most aggressive adolescents were those who were exposed to both biological risks (e.g., maternal smoking during pregnancy, low birthweight, and difficult temperament) and environmental risks (e.g., poverty, harsh discipline, family instability) (Brennan et al., 2003). This cross-national evidence clearly argues for the view that biology and social environments operate together to produce aggressive children. Next, we take a closer look at the environmental side of this issue.

THE FAMILY AS A TRAINING CENTRE FOR AGGRESSION

Parents clearly play a role in children's aggressive tendencies. Although most parents do not view themselves as giving aggression tutorials, some parents deliberately teach their children, especially boys, to "defend" themselves or to "be a man" (Anderson, 1998). African-American families are also likely to encourage daughters to be assertive and defend themselves. But this is not the only way children learn aggression from their parents. When parents argue or fight with one another and, especially, fail to resolve their conflicts in positive ways, they may well be giving implicit instruction to their children. In addition, parents' typical control tactics may contribute to their children's aggression. Parents who use physical punishment, especially inconsistently, are likely to have aggressive, hostile children (Cohen & Brook, 1995; Gershoff, 2002; Patterson, 2002). Physical punishment is especially likely to lead to aggressive behaviour when the parent–child relationship lacks warmth (Caspi & Moffitt, 2006; Deater-Deckard & Dodge, 1997) or when parents are abusive (Landsford et al., 2002). The link between physical punishment and aggression is clearer in European-American families than in African-American families (Deater-Deckard et al., 1996; Landsford et al., 2002).

Since the 1970s, Gerald Patterson's Social Learning Center in Eugene, Oregon, has been one of the world's leading research institutions devoted to understanding the origins of aggressive behaviour and devising ways of treating children with aggression problems. Researchers there have found that the family environments of aggressive and

Whether her parents have spanked her or spanked a sibling in her presence, this little girl has clearly got the message that misbehaviour is to be punished severely.

non-aggressive children are strikingly different (Patterson, 1982, 2002). Aggressive children's parents tend to be erratic and inconsistent in their use of punishment for deviant behaviours and ineffective in rewarding their children for prosocial behaviours. They punish their sons more often, even when the children are behaving appropriately. Such inept parenting practices often lead to cycles of mutually coercive behaviour. Children are not passive victims in this sort of process; they often develop behaviour patterns in which they quite purposely use aversive behaviours—such as whining and being difficult or committing directly aggressive acts—to coerce parents into giving them what they want. Children learn that such coercive behaviours can help them control the behaviour of other family members, including that of siblings. When sibling pairs engage in coercive exchanges, especially if the older sibling is already delinquent, the younger sibling is more likely to become delinquent, too (Slomkowski et al., 2001). A combination of rejecting parenting and sibling conflict is an especially potent recipe for later conduct disorders (Garcia et al., 2000). The most appropriate model of discipline recognizes that parents, siblings, and children all influence one another and all contribute to the development of aggression.

Parents not only influence their own children; their influence often continues across generations. To evaluate whether hostile parenting increases the risk of aggressive behaviour in the next generation was the goal of a study by Scaramella and Conger (2003). These researchers examined patterns of parent–adolescent interaction and then re-examined these same adolescents when they became parents themselves. The investigators found that adolescents who received hostile parenting were more likely to repeat this style of angry and coercive parenting with their 2-year-olds. In turn, their toddlers exhibited more problem behaviours, including aggressive acts. Cross-generational continuity was not inevitable, however. One factor that affected cross-generation consistency was the 2-year-old's emotional reactivity (i.e., how much the child reacted to parental control with an angry emotional reaction). In families in which the young child was high in negative emotional reactivity, there was continuity in hostile parenting from one generation to the next, but when the child was less emotionally reactive, there was no link across generations. This illustrates again the interplay between biology (temperament) and parenting in determining an aggressive outcome.

Families not only contribute directly to their children's aggressive tendencies through the control tactics they use but also shape the development of aggression indirectly. When parents fail to monitor their children's whereabouts, activities, and social contacts, this can be an important determinant of whether children will develop aggressive behaviour. Some parents are fully aware of their children's activities, problems, and successes and can report accurately what their children are doing, whom they are with, and where they are. Other parents are largely oblivious to their children's lives. They do not know if their children are hanging around on street corners, whether they are habitual truants or involved students, or whether their child is the friendly neighbourhood drug dealer. Lack of parental monitoring is associated with high rates of delinquency (Patterson, 2002; Pettit et al., 2001). Children's development of aggressive behaviours may depend as much on parents' awareness of activities in the surrounding community and their efforts to control negative aspects of these activities as on direct parental child-rearing practices. Training parents to use more effective disciplinary techniques and to increase their monitoring of their children's activities may help reduce aggressive behaviour (Reid et al., 2002).

Monitoring children's friends and activities is not just the parents' job, though; it is a shared responsibility between parents and children (Kerr & Stattin, 2000). The ability to monitor relies on the extent to which children share information about their activities and choices of companions with their parents. As Laird and colleagues (2003) found, monitoring is higher and anti-social behaviour is less likely when parents and adolescents spend more time together and have a more enjoyable relationship, and when adolescents view monitoring as an appropriate parenting activity.

Patterson and colleagues showed that children progress from aggression problems in early childhood to full-fledged delinquency in adolescence (see Figure 14-8). A negative trajectory starts as a consequence of the early experience of poor parental disciplinary practice and lack of monitoring (Patterson et al., 1989). When these children enter school, two things typically happen: their peer group rejects them and they experience academic failure (Buhs & Ladd, 2001; Ladd, 2005; Ladd et al., 1999). In late childhood and early adolescence, these now anti-social children may seek out deviant peers who, in turn, provide further training in anti-social behaviour and opportunities for delinquent activities (Coie, 2004; Dishion et al., 2001). Among adolescents, aggression is, in some cases, not only tolerated but admired and viewed as "cool" (Cillessen & Mayeux, 2004). In spite of their status among peers, anti-social youth are more likely to be school dropouts, to experience marital problems, and to end up in jail (Patterson & Bank, 1989).

If the family environment is already encouraging anti-social behaviour before children are 5 or 6 years old, they are more likely to develop serious and persistent delinquent behaviour than if they start on the deviancy road at a later age—in middle to late adolescence (Dishion et al., 2001; Moffitt, 2003). These late starters may have avoided the social rejection and school failure common among early starters, as well as early family encouragement of anti-social behaviour. Early starters also may be at greater risk owing to biological factors. Children who experience perinatal or birth complications, maternal illness during pregnancy, poor infant temperament, limited language understanding, and deficits in executive functioning—combined with social risks such as poverty—are the most likely to be aggressive adolescents at age 15 (Brennan et al., 2003). Early starters are also ten times more often boys than girls (Moffitt, 2003; Moffitt et al., 2001).

TELEVISION VIEWING, VIDEO GAMES, AND AGGRESSION

Exposure to aggressive role models on television can increase children's aggressive behaviour (Bushman & Huesmann, 2001; Comstock & Scharrer, 2006). Heavy doses of TV violence can also affect children's attitudes, leading them to view violence as an acceptable and effective way to solve interpersonal conflict (Bushman & Huesmann, 2001). Children learn that violence works, for both the good guys and the bad guys—it gets things done (Dominick & Greenberg, 1972). Similar findings have also been found in Australia, Finland, Britain, Israel, the Netherlands, and Poland (Bushman & Huesmann, 2001; Huesmann & Miller, 1994).

Frequent viewers of TV violence may also become immune to onscreen mayhem (i.e., they show less emotional reaction when viewing televised aggression; Cantor,

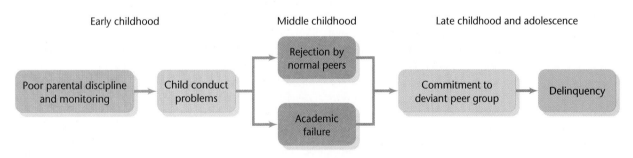

Figure 14-8

Evolution and progression of anti-social behaviour

Note that parents, peers, and school all play a role in the evolution of anti-social behaviour, but at different stages in the child's development.

Source: Adapted from Patterson, DeBarshyshe, & Ramsey, 1989.

2000) and indifferent to real-life violence (Drabman & Thomas, 1976). Exposure to TV violence affects children differently depending on their cognitive abilities. Children who were told that a violent film clip was real (a newsreel of an actual riot) later reacted more aggressively than children who believed that the film was a Hollywood production (Atkin, 1983). As children develop and are able to make the fiction–reality distinction, many TV programs may have less impact (Bushman & Huesmann, 2001).

Nor is television the only culprit. Video and computer games may influence aggressive behaviour as well (Comstock & Scharrer, 2006; Sherry, 2007). The most notorious case of this was the 1999 Columbine High School incident in Colorado, in which two students shot numerous schoolmates. The shooters were described as being "obsessed with the violent video game *Doom*—in which the players try to rack up the most kills— and played it every afternoon" (Glick et al., 1999). This incident does not prove the case, but empirical evidence clearly suggests that violent video games can increase aggression (Anderson et al., 2007; Krahe & Moller, 2004) as well as produce desensitization to actual violence (Carnagey et al., 2007b), just as TV violence has been shown to do.

Lastly, we are beginning to understand the neurological underpinnings of exposure to media violence (Carnagey et al., 2007a). Recent neuroimaging studies using MRI techniques (see Chapter 5) found that some regions of the brain (such as the prefrontal cortex) are less activated when children are exposed to violent rather than non-violent scenes from movies (Murray et al., 2006) or violent video games (Weber et al., 2006). This brain region is related to reduced activation of neural mechanisms associated with self-control which may, in part, aid in explaining why exposure to violence increases aggression.

PEERS, GANGS, AND NEIGHBOURHOODS Peers, especially deviant peers, can encourage other children's aggressive tendencies. Researchers have found that if a child's friends engage in disruptive behaviour (e.g., disobedience or truancy), the child was more likely to engage in either overt delinquent behaviour (e.g., fighting) or covert delinquent behaviour (e.g., stealing) both concurrently and a year later (Keenan et al., 1995; Thornberry et al., 2003). In Box 14.3 on pages 572 and 573, we describe in detail the path to juvenile delinquency and the role peers may play in such a course. Similarly, association with gangs is likely to increase violent activity (Thornberry et al., 2003). Individuals in a gang are three times more likely to engage in violent offences than are those not in a gang (Craig et al., 2002; Spergel et al., 1989). Joining a gang increases a child's illegal and violent activities, and leaving one decreases these activities (Craig et al., 2002; Thornberry et al., 2003; Zimring, 2000).

Other environmental conditions such as living in a poor, high-crime neighbourhood will increase aggression, but these effects are generally due to changes in family functioning that are associated with poverty or unemployment. Several researchers have found that poor African-American mothers who experienced stress and lack of social support were more likely to display ineffective and coercive parenting; this, in turn, led to aggressive behaviour in their children and greater gang involvement (Farver et al., 2005; Guerra et al., 1995; Tolan et al., 2003).

Control of Aggression

How can we control aggression in our children? One of the most commonly offered solutions, and yet one whose beneficial effects have been seriously questioned, is the notion of *catharsis*, popularly known as letting off steam.

THE CATHARSIS MYTH One of the most persistent beliefs about aggression is that if people have ample opportunity to engage in aggressive acts, whether in actuality or symbolically, a process known as **catharsis**, they will be less likely to act on hostile aggressive urges. Presumably, aggressive urges build up in an individual, and unless this accumulating reservoir of aggressive energies is drained, a violent outburst will occur.

catharsis

Presumably, discharging aggressive impulses by engaging in actual or symbolic aggressive acts that do not impinge on another person.

The implications are clear: Provide people with a safe opportunity to behave aggressively and the likelihood of anti-social aggression will be lessened. In clinical circles, there is widespread belief in catharsis. People are often encouraged to express aggression in group-therapy sessions. There are punching bags in many wards in mental hospitals and Bobo dolls, pounding boards, and toy guns and knives in many play-therapy rooms.

Advice columnists in the media have sometimes propagated a similar view. For example, Ann Landers once advised a reader that "hostile feelings must be released" and went on to recommend that children be taught to vent their anger against furniture rather than against other people. Another reader replied,

> *I was shocked at your advice to the mother whose three-year-old had temper tantrums. . . . My younger brother used to kick the furniture when he got mad. . . . He is 32 years old now and still kicking the furniture. . . . He is also kicking his wife, the cat, the kids, and anything else that gets in his way. . . . Why don't you tell mothers that children must be taught to control their anger? This is what separates civilized human beings from savages.*

In many juvenile gangs, violence is common, both within gangs as a way of controlling their members and between gangs to protect their "turf."

The research evidence on the value of catharsis tends to support the advice column's reader. Most studies suggest that aggressive experiences may promote rather than "drain off" aggressive urges. In a classic test of the issue, Mallick and McCandless (1966) allowed grade 3 children to shoot a toy gun after being frustrated by a peer who interfered with a task they were working on. Another group of children were allowed to work on arithmetic problems after the peer upset them. Then, all the children were given a chance to express their aggression toward the peer who had upset them. Whether the children shot the toy gun or worked on math problems, after being frustrated by the peer, made little difference in their aggression. Thus, catharsis appeared to be insufficient to reduce aggression. Similar findings have been found for adults by Bushman and his colleagues who used a variety of direct measures of aggression (Bushman, 2002; Bushman et al., 2001a; Bushman et al., 2001b).

COGNITIVE MODIFICATION STRATEGIES   According to the social information-processing approach to aggression, aggressive children may behave in a hostile and inappropriate fashion because they are **socially unskilled**: that is, they are not very skilled at solving interpersonal problems (Dodge et al., 2006). In several studies, researchers who asked children and adolescents to come up with solutions to conflict problems in social situations found that aggressive participants in the studies offered fewer solutions than their non-aggressive peers (Crick & Dodge, 1994; Gifford-Smith & Rabiner, 2004). Moreover, the proposals aggressive children and adolescents made for resolving social disputes were generally less effective than the solutions less aggressive individuals offered.

socially unskilled
Being unskilled at solving interpersonal problems.

Making aggressive children and adolescents aware of the negative consequences of aggression for themselves and others through modelling and explanations can reduce aggression, and teaching and encouraging children to use alternative problem-solving behaviours, such as co-operation or turn taking, have also been found to reduce aggression (Chittenden, 1942; Guerra et al., 1997). One study found that teaching children how to read another person's behaviour more accurately—specifically, helping them to reduce, if not wholly give up, their biases toward making hostile attributions about other people and their behaviour—led to a decrease in aggression among African-American boys (Hudley & Graham, 1993). This approach is especially effective with reactively aggressive children, who are poor at reading other people's intentions. Empathy and sympathy also play important roles in the control of aggression. There is a clear link among sympathy, empathy, and lower levels of aggression in children as well as less delinquency in adolescents (Laible et al., 2000; Strayer & Roberts, 2004). Training children and adolescents to be more empathic and sensitive to the views and feelings of other individuals can be an effective way of controlling aggression (Chandler, 1973; Guerra et al., 1997).

Box 14.3

Risk and Resilience

THE ROAD TO DELINQUENCY

One of the most common fears of parents of aggressive children is that their child will gradually grow from being physically aggressive into juvenile delinquency as they hit their teenage years. Although such fears are often portrayed as somewhat old-fashioned and stereotyped, the research on the stability of aggression across the lifespan does nothing to dispel such concerns. And, in fact, this issue is so pervasive that investigating the relation between aggression in childhood and subsequent delinquency later in life, as well as looking at the factors that put a child at risk for subsequent delinquency, have occupied a great deal of researchers' time and energy.

Richard Tremblay, Frank Vitaro, Linda Pagini, Mara Brendgen and a host of other researchers at the University of Montreal have, for a number of years, been exploring the factors related to the development of delinquency in young boys. These researchers have been making use of long-term longitudinal data of French-speaking children from Montreal and throughout other areas in Quebec. This project, which began in the 1980s, has been following a sample of low socioeconomic children, from kindergarten onwards, assumed to be at high risk, assessing the relation between behaviours in young childhood and later conduct disorders, and attempting to identify factors that might be predictive of behaviour problems later in life.

In one project, for example, Nagin and Tremblay (1999) looked at a sample of over 1,000 boys who were assessed repeatedly from 6 to 15 years of age and found four distinct developmental trajectories of physical aggression, shown in Table 14-4. The researchers found a systematic increase in incidents of self-reported violence, theft, and serious delinquency at 17 years of age as children increased from low to high levels of aggression, with these results suggesting that aggressive kindergarten children were most prone to chronic violence later in life.

Subsequent work by Côté and colleagues (Côté et al., 2002a, 2002b, 2006) has examined the link between childhood behavioural dimensions and adolescent conduct disorders using a longitudinal sample of over 1,000 children. Côté and colleagues (2002a), for instance, had teachers rate the behaviours of these children between kindergarten and grade 6, and then used these ratings to categorize children into groups based on three behavioural dimensions: hyperactivity, fearfulness, and helpfulness. In this work, the researchers found that when boys were hyperactive, either on their own or in combination with unhelpfulness and/or fearfulness, they were more likely to display conduct disorders. In contrast, girls had a risk for conduct disorders only when they were both hyperactive and unhelpful.

Côté and colleagues, and many others, have also observed that deviant friends can play a role in the adoption of delinquent behaviours (Agnew, 1991; Elliot, 1994; Elliot, Huizinga, & Ageton, 1985), although any number of factors can moderate this influence. In one study, for example, Vitaro, Brendgen, and Tremblay (2000) assessed three potential mediators of the link between a child's delinquency and the delinquency of friend-personal factors, such as the child's attitude toward delinquency, familial factors, such as parental attachment, and social factors, such as the characteristics of their friends. These researchers observed that

Some psychologists are putting these findings into practical use. Curricula have been developed to improve the social problem-solving skills of aggressive children, and some success has been reported in studies in both the United States and Sweden (Stevahn et al., 2000; Weissberg & Greenberg, 1998). Researchers found that when teachers taught lessons in conflict resolution to the grade 1 and 6 students, these children were less aggressive over time (Aber et al., 2003). The children made fewer hostile attributions, showed fewer conduct problems, and exhibited less aggressive behaviour and more prosocial behaviour.

AGGRESSION PREVENTION: A MULTI-PRONGED APPROACH As we have stressed, many factors influence aggression and as a result, we need to consider many variables to change levels of aggression. We conclude the chapter with a brief description of one national experiment in controlling aggression, known as Fast

although delinquency of children was related to the deviancy of their friends, such delinquency was moderated by parental attachment and by children's own attitudes toward delinquency, with such attitudes distinguishing between adolescents who could be swayed by their friends into committing deviant acts and adolescents who resisted delinquent temptations. Thus, simply making the "wrong kind" of friends, as many parents fear, in preadolescence and adolescence does not necessarily spell disaster for a child.

Of course, one of the hopes in knowing about the various factors that place a child at risk for delinquency is that it will be possible to actually devise some form of intervention to help such children. And, in fact, the Montreal group has turned their attention also to just such a program (Gatti, Tremblay, & Larocque, 2003; Lacourse et al., 2002; Tremblay et al., 1995; Vitaro et al., 1999). In one such program (Tremblay et al., 1995), disruptive kindergarten boys received a two-year prevention program consisting of home-based parent training and school-based social-skills training, and boys were then assessed in mid-adolescence. The results of this study revealed that children participating in the various training regimens showed significantly less delinquency, relative to a control group of boys. And in a subsequent analysis of the intervention program, Vitaro and colleagues (1999) found that the positive influences of associating with less deviant friends varied depending on whether the child's delinquency had been reduced by the intervention program.

What becomes clear from these findings is that any number of factors can play a role in the link between children's aggressiveness early in life and their subsequent delinquency later in adolescence. The ability to follow such a large group of children, as is made possible by this long-term longitudinal study, provides invaluable insight into these complex relations and allows for the assessment of not only what is important in the development of delinquency but also what can prevent it.

Table 14-4 Developmental trajectories of physical aggression

Chronic Physical Aggression Trajectory	4%	Boys who continually displayed physical aggression throughout childhood and adolescence
High-Level Declining Trajectory	28%	Boys who showed high levels of aggression in kindergarten, but declined afterwards
Moderate-Level Declining Trajectory	52%	Boys who showed moderate aggression in kindergarten and then declined afterwards
Low Trajectory	17%	Boys with generally low levels of aggression

Source: Nagin & Tremblay, 1999.

Track (Foster, Jones, & Conduct Problem Prevention Research Group, 2006). In four US cities, over 200 grade 1 children from poor, and mostly minority, families, were exposed to a variety of interventions to help prevent aggressive and anti-social behaviour. Another 200 children served as the control group. Children in the intervention group participated in a program to help them with social problem solving, emotional understanding, and communication and to teach them how to regulate their actions in the face of frustrating events. For the children with the most serious problems (10 percent of the group) there was a more intensive program involving academic tutoring, extra social-skills training, and a parental intervention designed to improve parenting skills. It worked. Children in the intervention group were less aggressive, improved academically, and developed better social-emotional skills. Moreover, peer relationships improved; children got along better and were better liked by their peers. Parents benefited, too: Their parenting skills improved and they were more involved in school-related activities. By the end of grade 3, 37 percent of the children in the program had no aggression problems—and 27 percent of the control group also had no such problems. The positive effects persisted through grade 5 according to a recent report (Foster, Jones, & Conduct Problem Prevention Research Group, 2006). Clearly, by mounting a broad-based assault on aggression, children's anti-social behaviour can be reduced.

For Thought and Discussion

1. Although girls are often thought of as less physically aggressive than boys, recent events such as the beating of one girl by a gang of girls in British Columbia suggest that such gender differences may not be as true as one would initially believe. Do you think that girls are actually becoming more physically aggressive? If they are, what factors might be leading to this increase?

2. Research on the supermale, or men with an XYY chromosome pattern, has produced mixed data as to whether such biological differences truly lead to increased aggression. What would you take as evidence for such an effect? What do such results say about biological influences on aggression?

3. Given what you have read about the impact of peers on social development (Chapter 12), how important is the peer group in leading to violence and delinquency? What role(s) do peers actually play in this process?

Making the Connections 14

There are many links between concepts and ideas in one area of development and concepts and ideas in other areas. Here are some of the connections between ideas in Chapter 14 and discussions in other chapters of this book.

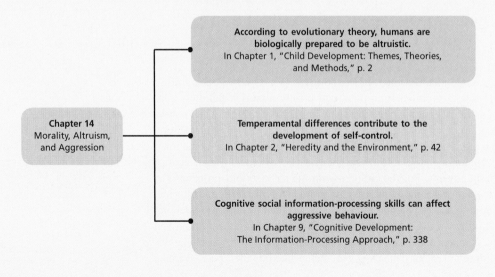

Chapter 14
Morality, Altruism, and Aggression

According to evolutionary theory, humans are biologically prepared to be altruistic.
In Chapter 1, "Child Development: Themes, Theories, and Methods," p. 2

Temperamental differences contribute to the development of self-control.
In Chapter 2, "Heredity and the Environment," p. 42

Cognitive social information-processing skills can affect aggressive behaviour.
In Chapter 9, "Cognitive Development: The Information-Processing Approach," p. 338

SUMMARY

An Overview of Moral Development

- The socialization of moral beliefs and behaviour is one of the main tasks in all cultures. Psychological research has focused on the three basic components of morality: cognitive, behavioural, and emotional.

Cognitive Theories of Moral Development

- Jean Piaget proposed a three-stage approach; the **premoral stage**, the stage of **moral realism**, and the stage ruled by a **morality of reciprocity**, also called *autonomous morality*. Moral absolutism and a belief in **immanent justice** characterize moral realism. In contrast, children in the stage of reciprocity recognize the arbitrariness of social rules and intentionality in their moral judgments.

- Lawrence Kohlberg proposed a theory of the development of moral judgment in which each of three levels contains two stages. The order of development is fixed and invariant and movement is generally from lower levels—the **preconventional** and **conventional levels**—toward higher ones. Moral judgments continue to develop into adulthood, but few individuals reach the most advanced, **post-conventional level**.

- Gilligan proposed that Kohlberg's model emphasizes a more masculine orientation, focusing on rights and logic, whereas an interpersonal and caring orientation may more accurately describe women's moral reasoning and judgments.

- Piaget emphasized the role of peers, and Kohlberg emphasized the importance of varied opportunities for role taking in the development of moral judgments. Data suggest that a combination of consistent discipline, involving reasoning and explanation, and concern with the feelings of others tends to produce more mature moral judgments in children. There is also evidence that maturity of moral reasoning is related to cognitive maturity.

- Kohlberg's theory may be flawed in some ways. The theory's third level is controversial; relatively few people reach this level and, in particular, the sixth stage of moral reasoning. In addition, cross-cultural research suggests that Kohlberg's theory is culture-bound.

- **Social conventional rules**, such as table manners and forms of address, are distinct from moral rules and follow a different developmental course; in fact, children learn quite early to distinguish these kinds of rules from each other. Moral judgments do not always lead to moral behaviour, particularly among very young children.

The Behavioural Side of Moral Development

- **Self-regulation**, the ability to inhibit one's impulses and to behave in accordance with social or moral rules, proceeds through three stages—the **control phase**, the **self-control phase**, and the **self-regulation phase**. In the latter phase, children become capable of **delaying gratification**.

- Self-control or moral behaviour is strongly influenced by situational factors. As the elements of situations and types of behaviour assessed become more similar, moral conduct becomes more consistent. The development of **conscience** is linked with children's achievement of self-regulatory capacities. Both self-regulation and the development of conscience are linked with mother–child relationships that are positive, responsive, and co-operative.

- Some evidence indicates that children's early ability to regulate their behaviour is related to later social and cognitive competence.

The Evolution of Prosocial and Altruistic Behaviours

- Prosocial behaviour begins very early; helping, sharing, and exhibiting emotional reactions to the distress of others occur in the first and second years of life. **Altruism** may also appear quite early.

- Parents influence the emergence of **altruism** or **altruistic behaviour** by their direct teaching in "distress" situations, by providing models, and by arranging for opportunities to behave in prosocial ways. Role playing and **empathy** both contribute to the development of altruism and helping behaviour.

- Girls tend to be more prosocial than boys, but gender differences depend on the type of prosocial behaviour being expressed. Such differences are largest for expressions of kindness and consideration.

- Evidence of helping and sharing behaviour in infrahuman animals leads some scientists to believe that evolution has prepared both humans and animals for prosocial behaviour.

- Environmental factors, including the family, the mass media, and general cultural influences affect prosocial and altruistic behaviours, but children probably learn such behaviours most often from modelling parental behaviours.

- Children's prosocial reasoning evolves over time through a number of stages including **hedonistic reasoning** and **needs-oriented reasoning**, as values and norms become increasingly internalized.

The Development of Aggression

- **Aggression** undergoes important developmental shifts. Younger children show more **instrumental aggression**, whereas older children display more person-oriented or **hostile aggression**. Children's ability to correctly infer intent in others may account, in part, for these shifts. **Proactive aggression**, which is used to dominate another person, decreases across development more than **reactive aggression**, which occurs in response to being attacked.

- The expression of aggression changes over time, becoming more verbal as children mature. Clear gender differences in aggression are evident, with boys instigating and retaliating more than girls. Girls are more likely to use **relational aggression** than boys are, who are more likely to use physical aggression. Aggression is moderately stable over age for both sexes.

- Certain parental disciplinary practices, especially ineffectual and erratic physical punishment, contribute to high levels of aggression in children. Lack of parental monitoring of children is another contributor to later aggressive behaviour or even serious delinquency.

- Biological influences on aggression include genetic, temperamental, and hormonal factors. All of these factors find expression in interaction with the environment.

- Association with deviant peers can increase the possibility that a child will engage in aggressive or delinquent activities. Poverty and high-crime neighbourhoods can also promote aggressive behaviour.

- **Catharsis** theory, the belief that behaving aggressively against a safe target can reduce aggression in other parts of life, has been seriously challenged by research evidence. Strategies that involve cognitive modification may be more successful. Some aggressive children who are **socially unskilled** may be helped to learn more prosocial behaviours through teaching them how to read others' behaviour more accurately and encouraging them to be more sensitive to the views and feelings of others.

- Increasing children's awareness of the harmful effects of aggression is an effective control technique. Altering the environment by reducing crowding and providing adequate numbers of toys and playthings, including toys that are non-aggressive in nature, may also reduce aggression.

Donald Martin (20th Century). *Stripes.*

Chapter 15

Developmental Psychopathology

LEARNING OBJECTIVES

After reading this chapter, you should be able to

LO1 Discuss the concept of abnormality; describe a medical approach to abnormality, along with different notions of abnormality as deviation from an expected value; and discuss the idea of the social judgment of the child.

LO2 Describe factors involved in classifying child psychopathology; distinguish between the diagnostic and empirical approach to such classifications.

LO3 Identify the differences between undercontrolled and overcontrolled disorders.

LO4 Describe some different forms of conduct disorders in development; outline approaches to treating conduct disorders.

LO5 Describe attention deficit/hyperactivity disorder (ADHD); discuss the different potential factors underlying this disorder; outline different forms of treatment for ADHD.

LO6 Discuss depression in childhood; describe some of the different categories of causes of childhood depression; describe different treatments for childhood depression.

LO7 Describe the characteristics of autistic spectrum disorder; discuss the causes of autism, and the possible treatments of autistic disorder.

Throughout the first 14 chapters of this book, we have focused on the development of the normal child. In this chapter, we turn to an intriguing but often painful and poorly understood area of development: psychological disorders of childhood. Shifting our focus from the normal to what is considered abnormal, we pursue an understanding of why some children develop problems that require special treatment and intervention. We address such questions as, "What is 'abnormal'?" "How have psychologists defined abnormality?" "What is unique about a developmental approach to psychopathology?"

"How do risk factors, vulnerabilities, and protective processes interact to promote or protect against the development of abnormal behaviour?" "How should we classify the psychological disorders of childhood?"

Some of the psychological disorders we discuss are not uncommon; others are relatively rare. Problems such as attention deficit/hyperactivity disorder, in which children appear unable to control their own behaviour and are excitable, in constant motion, and generally disruptive, is one of the most common childhood disorders. Problems such as autistic disorder, in which children evidence extreme disturbances that invade many spheres of functioning, are, fortunately, much less common.

In discussing these and other disorders, we ask what causes these problems and how we can treat them effectively. We also consider efforts to prevent children from developing serious psychological disturbances. To introduce you to the topics of this discussion and to illustrate the range of problems that children can exhibit, we offer the following brief case studies:

Victor: Victor had always been a handful. As an infant, he cried frequently, woke up at all hours, and soon gave up his afternoon nap in favour of exploring tabletops and other forbidden territories. As a toddler, he raced around from dawn until dark, always seeming to run when others walked. When he was 4, one of his favourite games was scrambling onto the roof of the family car and fearlessly diving off into his father's tired arms. During times like these, Victor's parents would try to discipline him by reasoning with him, but that tactic rarely worked. Instead, they would tolerate—and often secretly enjoy—his antics until they reached their limit, at which point they found it necessary to simply force Victor to comply. Although Victor exhausted them, his parents never considered him to have a real problem—until he started school. At the end of first grade, Victor's principal called his parents in for a conference. The principal told them that Victor wasn't paying attention in class, was consequently falling behind in his work, and required more supervision than his teacher said she could give. In addition, his antics in the classroom were distracting other children and disrupting the entire class. The principal suggested that Victor's parents talk to their pediatrician about how to do something to change his behaviour before he started the second grade. If not, the school was going to consider placing Victor in their "resource room" next year—a special class for "emotionally disturbed" children.

Emily: Emily was beginning to worry her mother. She was a very well-behaved and helpful 12-year-old, but to her mother, Emily seemed unhappy. She really didn't have any close friends, and her mother wondered why the phone wasn't constantly ringing for Emily as it had for her when she was Emily's age. To her mother, Emily seemed to be spending too much of her time alone in her room and not enough time socializing. More than that, her mother was concerned about Emily's schoolwork. Her straight A's in sixth grade had slipped down to mostly B's and even one C for the first term in her new junior high school, and Emily had dropped out of the one activity that her mother thought she really seemed to enjoy: orchestra. Her mother tried to talk with Emily about how she was feeling, but when she tried to approach her, Emily got angry at her mother for "bugging her" and ran to her room in tears. Emily's mother blamed the child's unhappiness on Emily's father and their divorce six years earlier. But what could she do about that now?

Pauli: *Pauli was becoming a source of grave concern to his parents. At age 3, he had not yet spoken his first word, and they could not ignore his unusual behaviour. He spent hours every day sitting and spinning a top that he had played with since he was 2, and he became violently upset if the toy was taken away from him. Pauli showed no interest in other children and would jerk away from his mother or father if they tried to give him a hug. Even as an infant Pauli had resisted being held and stiffened at physical contact, and his mother could not remember a time when they had really cuddled. She commented that holding Pauli was more like holding a log than a baby since he did not mould or cling to her shoulder the way most babies do. His rejection of his parents didn't seem to be one of anger; instead, it almost seemed as if it were physically painful for Pauli to be touched by someone. Although Pauli had been an exceptionally good baby, his failure to speak and his endless repetitive play gradually became more and more distressing to his parents. The pediatrician's calm reassurances when Pauli was younger had now ceased, and he suggested that Pauli be taken for an evaluation at a special hospital for exceptional children in a city over 300 kilometres away. Pauli's parents were frightened by this possibility. Would they be asked to leave him at the hospital, and, if so, for how long?*

All three of these children are exhibiting behaviour that concerns their parents. Victor's loving parents could tolerate and even appreciate his boundless energy, but his uncontrolled activity is causing trouble for him, his teacher, and his classmates in school. Does Victor have a special problem that differentiates him from his peers and may require special attention? Should he be placed in a special classroom? His teacher seems to think so. As for Emily, her apparent unhappiness may be a problem, but we do not really know how she feels about herself and her life. Is she feeling depressed, helpless, and angry at her mother and father for getting divorced? Or is she going through a "stage," feeling confused and lonely as she enters puberty? Perhaps Emily is simply experiencing the normal feelings of a quiet girl who is going through a transition to a new school. Of the three children, Pauli is especially disturbing. But why is he behaving in this unusual manner? Is Pauli suffering from some sort of an emotional problem, or is he perhaps mentally retarded? We will meet Victor, Emily, and Pauli again as we explore the complexities of developmental psychopathology. ●

THE DEVELOPMENTAL APPROACH TO PSYCHOPATHOLOGY

When a child appears to be experiencing unusual psychological distress, to understand and help this young person, we need to invoke principles of what is called developmental psychopathology. *Psychopathology* is the study of disorders of the *psyche*—that is, of the mind. **Developmental psychopathology**, which combines the study of psychopathology with the study of development, involves the investigation of the origins, course, changes, and continuities in disordered or maladaptive behaviour over the individual's lifespan. The principles of developmental psychopathology are applicable to people of all ages as people change throughout the lifespan. Life transitions—such as graduation, a new job, marriage, childbirth, divorce, and retirement—all have their effects on people's functioning and have the potential to create shifts in developmental trajectories. Here, of course, we are concerned with the usefulness of these principles for understanding the special influences that biological, emotional, social, and environmental factors have on the young developing person.

developmental psychopathology

The investigation of the origins, course, changes, and continuities in disordered or maladaptive behaviour over a person's lifespan.

Depressive episodes are not uncommon in teenage girls and may well be linked to the changes of puberty and the stresses and challenges of adolescence. When depression lingers and is associated with expressions of guilt, low self-worth, or suicidal ideation, however, knowledgeable adults need to intervene to prevent the adolescent from sinking into self-destructive behaviours such as the abuse of drugs and alcohol.

The unique approach of *developmental* psychopathology is embodied in four basic principles (Cicchetti & Toth, 2006; Cummings et al., 2000). First, because child disorders occur in a developing organism, *we must take into account the role of development in interpreting the symptoms, searching for the origins, and understanding the course of any given disorder.* The frequency and patterns of symptoms in behaviour disorders vary across the course of development. For example, children may suffer depression as they move from preadolescence to adolescence. Although there are no gender differences in the incidence of depression among preadolescents, depression increases notably in adolescent girls. Depression in young children is typically characterized by social withdrawal and a *dysphoric* (unhappy, dejected, anxious, and/or self-doubting) mood. However, childhood depression is often masked by other, more strictly behavioural symptoms such as hyperactivity, bedwetting, learning problems, and anti-social behaviour. Children—especially those between the ages of about 8 and 11—do not manifest the general slowing of mental and physical activity or the motivational deficits that depressed adults typically do (Gelfand & Drew, 2003). In depressed adolescents, suicidal thoughts, which are quite uncharacteristic of younger children, begin to appear, and the depressed adult's symptoms of low self-worth, guilt, depressed mood, negative self-attributions, and inactivity also emerge (Goodman & Gotlib, 2002; Klein & Wender, 2005). The increase in depression and suicidal behaviour at adolescence is probably associated with the onset of pubertal changes, advances in cognitive development, and the many stresses and adaptive challenges young people encounter in this developmental period (Hammen, 1997, 2002).

Second, *psychopathology in a child must be viewed in relation both to children's normal development and to the major developmental tasks and changes that occur as children mature.* By definition, psychopathology involves deviations from normal behaviour, and developmental psychopathology involves deviations from normal attainments of people of the same age as the person under consideration. A critical issue is how to distinguish between developmental disruptions within the normal range and those reflecting more serious disordered behaviour (Rutter, 1996, 2003). As we will see, all children have some problems at some times in their lives, and at some points in development, certain problems occur with such frequency as to be regarded as normal. For example, although temper tantrums would be viewed as somewhat deviant in adolescents, they are common in 2-year-olds.

Third, *developmental psychopathology includes the earliest precursors of disordered behaviour.* Although psychopathology is less clearly defined and less stable in younger children than in adults, early behaviours are often associated with later disturbances. Two such warning signs are non-compliant behaviours and rejection by peers. These two precursors of later anti-social behaviour may also be related. Young children who are resistant, coercive, non-conforming, and confrontational with parents are also likely to be insensitive, unskilled, aggressive, and, hence, unaccepted in peer relations. Peer rejection is often associated with extreme shyness and social anxiety, which often leads to depression by itself, anti-social behaviour by itself, or both depression and anti-social behaviour. Thus, although early non-compliance and rejection by peers are not necessarily pathological, they can be associated with more serious later conduct disorders such as stealing, setting fires, drug abuse, and physical violence (Dishion et al., 2000; Gelfand & Drew, 2003).

The fourth principle is that *there are multiple pathways to both normal and abnormal behaviour over the course of development* (Cicchetti & Toth, 2006). Many factors—genetic, environmental, and experiential—interact to deflect a child either into a deviant trajectory or back into a normal developmental pathway. To the degree that we can identify risk factors of all sorts in the young child, we may be able to prevent children from following an abnormal path.

What Is Abnormal?

Defining abnormal psychological behaviour is no easy task. Many cultural, societal, ethnic, and personal values affect what we consider normal and abnormal, and all of these values vary across regions, nations, and subcultures within nations. However, because some behaviour is so unusual that it causes great distress either to the child or to those with whom she interacts, or places one or more people in danger, we need at least a working definition. We begin with the medical approach to defining and classifying psychological disorders. Then we look at two common views: abnormality as different from most common behaviours and abnormality as different from what we hold as ideal behaviour. We then consider the fact that disorders in children are often judged by the adults who are closest to them. And, finally, we consider how likely it is that childhood disorder will continue into adulthood.

The Medical Model

We can borrow from medical science—more specifically, the field of psychiatry—ideas about the causes and treatments of emotional problems. Unfortunately, however, this leads many people to believe that such behaviours reflect some form of *disease* of the mind analogous to a physical illness. Indeed, the medical model generally assumes that the psychological disorder—like a physical disease—resides within the individual and results from abnormal physiological or *intrapsychic* (mental) processes. Most child psychologists believe that the medical model is insufficient for explaining abnormal child behaviour. They argue that what we call developmental psychopathology is better thought of as a collection of problems in living that are caused by environmental circumstances. At the same time, however, it is important to recognize that problems such as *autism* and *attention deficit/hyperactivity disorder* have genetic roots, even though the expression of these and other disorders may be influenced by environmental conditions (Pennington, 2005).

Abnormality as Deviation from the Average

The term *abnormal* literally means "away from normal"; therefore, one way of defining abnormality is to view as abnormal any behaviours or feelings that differ in some degree from the average. This method of defining abnormality is referred to as the *statistical model.* Although there are problems with this definition of abnormality, it is often used as a guide to what constitutes deviance. For example, part of the definition of mental retardation offered by the American Association of Mental Retardation (AAMR) is that children are retarded if their IQ test scores are two standard deviations below average. On the Wechsler Intelligence Scale for Children–Revised, a score of 100 is average, and one standard deviation is equal to 15 points; by this rule, an IQ score of less than 70 indicates mental retardation.

The statistical model may seem appealing because it is so clear-cut, but things are not so simple. Although it may work for intelligence, which is measured on a numerical scale and can be either lower than normal or higher, it does not work for a concept like normality–abnormality. There is no statistically measurable average. Moreover, deviation from a mean can go in either direction. By this rule, if we were to consider an IQ of 100 "normal," we would have to consider scores of both 69 and 131 "abnormal." Most people would be reluctant to call superior cognitive functioning a sign of abnormality. Another problem with the statistical model is that it gives us no guidance as to how much of a difference is abnormal and under what circumstances differences matter. Why choose two standard deviations below the mean to determine mental retardation—why not one? Or three?

Abnormality as Deviation from the Ideal

An alternative to the statistical model is to define abnormality as a deviation from the ideal. This model identifies an ideal healthy personality and claims that deviations from this ideal are abnormal. The main problem with this approach is the question of how to define the ideal healthy personality. Personality theorists such as Freud have suggested guidelines for the ideal personality, but who is to say they are right? What do you consider to be ideal? Are you willing to say that anyone who falls short of this ideal is abnormal? Are you prepared to accept someone else's judgment of what ideal functioning is? Your parents' definition perhaps? The answers to these questions are clearly in doubt. To define such an ideal seems too big a task for anyone, no matter how brilliant or how highly regarded.

Elements of this concept of abnormality, however, are seen in our definitions of psychopathology. In Western cultures, people are expected to work hard, to love forever, and to be happy in achieving these two goals. When someone falls short of these cultural criteria, we become concerned. However, in Eastern cultures, other ideals may prevail. Box 15.1 discusses some differences in how adults in the United States and Thailand perceive the significance of childhood behaviour problems. This cross-cultural study demonstrates clearly that implicit ideals affect cultural definitions of abnormality.

The Social Judgment of Child Psychopathology

Consider the following brief case history:

> Tom lives with his aunt and cousin and is enrolled in elementary school. He often skips school, however, because he hates it, and he frequently sneaks out of the house at night to meet friends. Just before he ran away from home, Tom was gloomy and felt desperate. He was a forsaken, friendless boy, he said; nobody loved him. When they found out what they had driven him to do, perhaps they would be sorry. He had tried to do right and get along, but they would not let him. They had forced him to it at last; he would lead a life of crime.

What can you conclude from this very brief account about the normality or abnormality of Tom's behaviour? Does Tom differ enough from the average to be considered abnormal according to the statistical model? Certainly, he deviates from many people's ideals, including, we might presume, the ideals of some of the people with whom Tom interacts. Put yourself in the position of a psychologist who has been asked to evaluate Tom's general adjustment. Are you suspicious that he is exhibiting some form of developmental psychopathology, or are you more inclined to dismiss his behaviour as nothing to worry about?

In weighing your decision, you should know that Tom is actually Mark Twain's Tom Sawyer. At the time Twain created this character in 1876, Tom was certainly not meant to be psychopathological or even abnormal. Just the opposite: Tom represented the ideal all-American boy. He was hardly a candidate for psychotherapy. But taken out of context and viewed by today's standards, Tom seems quite deeply troubled as he proposes to leave his home, quit school, and take up a clearly deviant lifestyle. Had someone with a degree of authority heard his thoughts, he might well have been judged abnormal and remanded for treatment or rehabilitation. Clearly, something other than a child's behaviour in any given situation affects people's social judgments as to what constitutes abnormal behaviour.

In general, people's view of abnormality depends on their individual and cultural values. What is abnormal are those behaviours, thoughts, and feelings that a group of individuals agree are deviant. Although this view may be preferable to others, you can easily see that it, too, has problems. For example, different groups of people use different criteria to define abnormality, and these criteria may conflict.

Because children rarely refer themselves for formal help but rather are identified by an adult as disturbed and in need of the attention of mental health professionals, psychologists must constantly be alert to factors other than the child's behaviour itself. Thus, therapists must always ask themselves, "Has this child really a problem or has the

Box 15.1

Perspectives on Diversity

THAI AND NORTH AMERICAN VIEWS ON CHILD BEHAVIOUR PROBLEMS

Cultural values may determine whether adults consider a child's psychological problems to be serious enough to require professional help. John Weisz and his colleagues (Lambert et al., 1989; Weisz et al., 1988, 1995) investigated adults' concern about overcontrolled and undercontrolled child behaviour problems in Thailand and North America. The teachings of Thai Buddhism propose that some unhappiness in life is inevitable, that all things change for the better, and that an individual's behaviour on any given occasion is not reflective of an unchanging personality.

North Americans view children's problems as more serious. In schools, colleges, and universities, and every day in the media, North Americans are exposed to theories and ideas about child psychology, child-rearing, and deviant behaviour. In Weisz's research parents, teachers, and psychologists in the United States and Thailand read vignettes describing two children, one with symptoms of overcontrolled behaviour (e.g., shyness, fearfulness, depression, worrying, and dependency) and the other with problems of undercontrol (e.g., aggression, cruelty, disobedience, and lying). The adults were asked to rate each child on the seriousness of the problems, their level of concern about the problems, whether the children's behaviour would improve over time, and which child had a greater need for professional help.

As Figure 15-1 shows, consistent with their beliefs, Thai people rated both children's behaviours as less serious and worrisome and more likely to improve than the US adults judged them. Cross-national differences were less extreme in psychologists' responses than in the responses of parents and teachers, perhaps because their professional training exposed them to these childhood problems more often. Childhood psychopathology is to some extent in the eye of the beholder, and the beholder's perspective is modified by cultural context.

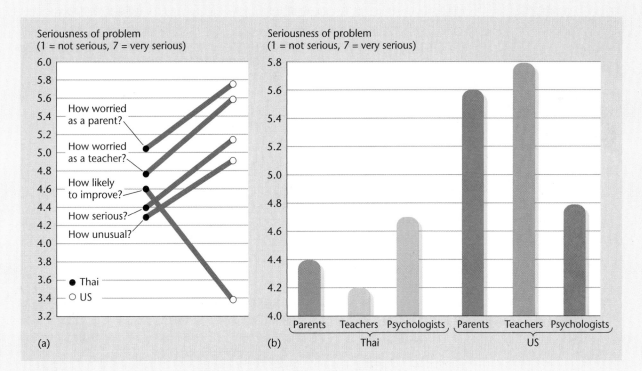

Figure 15-1

Are Thai children's problem behaviours less of a problem?

Rating the seriousness of children's problems (several behaviours combined) on a scale of 1 to 7 (from "not serious" to "very serious"), in general, Thai adults thought such behaviours less problematic than did North American adults (a). Asked, "How serious is this child's problem?" Thai parents and teachers differed from Western ones, but in both parts of the world, psychologists' ratings were similar (b).

Source: Weisz et al., 1988.

adult who has referred him to me a distorted view of the child for some reason?" Three sets of factors that may subtly influence a referring adult's perception are the characteristics of the child, the characteristics of the adult, and contextual influences.

CHARACTERISTICS OF THE CHILD   Parents and other adults are more likely to perceive behaviour as deviant if it occurs in boys, in children who have been temperamentally difficult infants, in unattractive children, and in children with a history of other forms of deviance (Cummings et al., 2000; Rothbart & Bates, 2006). In addition, people are less likely to judge a behaviour displayed by a socially skilled child as abnormal than they are if the child is socially unskilled (Gelfand & Drew, 2003). One reason that Tom Sawyer would not likely be judged as having a psychological problem is that he has other, positive qualities. He's smart and attractive, and although his Aunt Polly often tweaks him by the ear, not even she can get really angry at him.

CHARACTERISTICS OF THE REFERRING ADULT   Characteristics of the adult who identifies a child as disturbed also determine whether the opinion should be trusted. Anyone, including teachers and health professionals, can express a view about a child that, although it may reveal something real about the child's behaviour, also says something about the adult. Although it might seem that parents would know their children better than anyone, not uncommonly, parents have a distorted view of their children's behaviour and of their progeny's need for psychological help (Bradley & Peters, 1991). Parents who are depressed or abusive are likely to report their children's behaviour as more negative than observations of the child's actual behaviour suggest (Cicchetti & Toth, 2006; Hammen, 2005). In one study, researchers examined abusive parents' attributions about the causes of their children's positive and negative behaviours (Bauer & Twentyman, 1985). They showed mothers a series of photographs of either their own child or an unfamiliar child acting in a variety of social situations in which children were either (a) transgressing against each other, (b) engaged in a play situation that had a destructive outcome, or (c) involved in a competitive situation that had an ambiguous outcome. They then asked the mothers questions that required them to evaluate the children's behaviour and also asked them to explain why they thought the children acted as they did.

Consistent with other research (Azar, 2002), abusive mothers expressed negative expectations of their own children. They attributed their children's transgressions or failures to internal, stable causes—that is, they saw them as reflecting continuing traits and, thus, as likely to be repeated. On the other hand, when their own children were successful and when other children were the transgressors or failed at a task, these mothers attributed the other children's behaviours to external, unstable causal factors. They implied that these behaviours were specific to the particular situation and, therefore, unlikely to be repeated. Non-abusive mothers offered almost the exact opposite pattern of causal explanations: They emphasized their children's positive attributes as leading to success, and they suggested that either special circumstances or unusual behaviours were the causes of their children's transgressions. Similarly, other work (Bradley & Peters, 1991) found that abusive parents showed a greater tendency to identify behaviour as problematic, and minimized their own contributions to negative parent–child interactions.

These findings indicate that adults' judgments of children's behaviour involve complex processes. It is not enough for a therapist to help a parent see a child as behaving in a more positive way; the parent also must attribute the child's behaviour to internal, stable causes. For example, if a parent who has referred a child to a psychologist concludes that the child is doing better "only because he is in therapy," the parent is unlikely to maintain a positive view of the child. Ultimately, the goal must be for the parent to see the child as doing better as a result of internal, stable factors: It's "because he's basically a good kid."

THE CHILD'S ENVIRONMENT The context in which adults observe a child's behaviour also influences their judgments of psychopathology. They may judge the same behaviour differently according to the demands of different situations. Victor's parents judged his inattentive and overactive behaviour tiresome, but they accepted it in their home. When Victor began school, however, the demands and stricter standards of the classroom context led teachers to judge his behaviour as being abnormal. Victor's behaviour did not change, but the setting in which it occurred did.

Contextual influences on the evaluation of children's psychological adjustment include still other factors. For example, a child's social background, race, and prior behaviour can create contexts that influence the way adults judge a behaviour. Such factors often lead people to tag children with value-laden labels: "retarded," "a child from a broken home," "delinquent," "high risk." Unfortunately, such labels can create a context in which others perceive and respond to the child's behaviour in a way that has adverse consequences. When arrested for similar offences as youths, for example, lower-class minorities are more likely than middle-class whites to be sent to court or juvenile hall (Dodge et al., 2006; Moeller, 2001).

Continuity over Time

Whether or not a particular behaviour problem is viewed as abnormal also depends on the child's age and the probability that the behaviour will continue over time and be manifested in some form of adult disorder (Rutter, 1996). Some problems, such as bedwetting, thumb-sucking, temper tantrums, and tics, decline with age; others, such as nail-biting, increase from early childhood to adolescence; still others, such as disturbing dreams and nightmares, peak in preadolescence at about age 10 and then decline (Gelfand & Drew, 2003). Table 15-1 on the next page displays some problem behaviours that, when they occur at the ages indicated, are fairly common among normal children and, thus, not necessarily indicative of serious trouble. However, some problem behaviours are cause for concern. As we will see, childhood disorders such as hyperactivity, autism, and overly aggressive and anti-social behaviours are more likely to be associated with later adult dysfunction (Dodge et al., 2006; Gelfand & Drew, 2003).

Caspi and colleagues (1987) studied the stability of behaviour in children who at age 8 had been identified as having an irritable social interactional style, manifested in temper tantrums, explosiveness, and verbal abuse. Boys who were irritable school-age children were, 30 years later, undercontrolled, moody, and unsociable. As adults they were also less dependable, less ambitious, and less productive, as reflected in erratic work patterns and downward occupational mobility. For both males and females, early explosive, ill-tempered behaviour was associated with marital problems and divorce, and for women, with marriage to a man of low socio-economic status and with an irritable, inept parenting style.

For Thought and Discussion

1. Which of the different definitions of abnormality is most convincing to you? What makes this more convincing than the other definitions?

2. In this chapter, we describe a number of different criteria or dimensions for determining when behaviour is abnormal. Given all of these different dimensions, how might one combine them to make a determination of abnormality? Are there any specific dimensions that you believe are more compelling or diagnostic? Why or why not?

Table 15-1 Common problem behaviours of children and adoloescents

Problem Behaviour	1½–2 years	3–5 years	6–10 years	11–14 years	15–18 years
Inattentiveness	x				
Demanding attention constantly	x	x			
Refusal to do things when asked	x	x			
Overactivity	x	x	x		
Specific fears	x	x	x		
Temper tantrums	x	x	x	x	
Negativism		x			
Oversensitivity		x	x		
Lying		x	x		
Jealousy			x	x	
Excessive reserve			x	x	
Moodiness				x	
School achievement problems			x	x	x
Skipping school					x
Cheating on exams					x
Depression					x
Drinking					x
Smoking					x
Drug misuse					x
Early sexual activity					x
Trespassing					x
Shoplifting					x
Other minor law violations					x

Source: Adapted from Gelfand, Jensen, & Drew, 1997.

LO2 CLASSIFYING CHILD PSYCHOPATHOLOGY

Given our many problems in defining abnormal child behaviour, it is not surprising that psychiatrists (physicians who specialize in psychological disorders), psychologists, and others disagree over how to classify the different forms of developmental psychopathology. Until fairly recently, childhood psychological problems were viewed as variations of recognized adult disorders, and the diagnostic categories developed for adults were applied to children as well (Achenbach, 1995). The irony of viewing disturbed children as "munchkins with adult problems" is striking, for most theories of mental and emotional disturbance view psychological functioning during adult life as *a product of child development*.

Although many authorities argue that the seeds of abnormal development are sown in childhood, researchers and others have spent far less time studying abnormal behaviour in children than adult psychological disorders. In recent years, we have seen an increasing interest in the psychological problems unique to childhood. We look next at two important means of assessing and classifying childhood psychopathology: the *diagnostic approach* and the *empirical method*.

The Diagnostic Approach

The diagnostic approach to assessing and classifying psychopathology is rooted in the medical tradition. In medicine, a **diagnosis** is useful or valid if it conveys information about the **etiology**, or cause, of a disorder, about its likely course, or about the kind of treatment likely to be effective in curing or alleviating it. Because the classification of childhood psychopathology is still in its infancy, many diagnostic categories devised to characterize specific disorders are based largely on description—including such things as patterns of behaviour and specific kinds of thoughts and feelings—and few can make firm statements about either etiology or treatment.

The diagnostic classification system most widely used in the field of psychiatry has been compiled by the American Psychiatric Association (APA). The current *Diagnostic and Statistical Manual* (American Psychiatric Association, 2000) is the fourth classification scheme that APA has developed (it is commonly referred to as *DSM-IV*). Table 15-2 on the next page displays some examples of *DSM* categories that relate specifically to childhood disorders. This section has grown considerably over nearly 60 years since *DSM-I* was published in 1952—a sign of the increased interest in psychological disorders of childhood. Today, *DSM-IV* contains 43 diagnostic categories applicable to children, 41 more than were included in *DSM-I*. Inasmuch as this change reflects a trend away from viewing children as little adults, it is to be applauded.

DSM-IV is not without its critics, however (Campbell, 1998, 2002). Perhaps its biggest problem is that many of its diagnostic categories are neither valid nor reliable (Beutler & Malik, 2002). **Diagnostic reliability** is a measure of how often two or more clinicians arrive independently at the same diagnosis of a particular disorder. Without reliability, no system of classification can be valid. If two psychologists cannot agree, for example, on whether a child is clinically depressed, we cannot learn much about depression in childhood. If psychologist Smith decides that Emily, one of the children we discussed at the beginning of the chapter, suffers from depression, but psychologist Jones determines that Emily is merely experiencing the normal ups and downs of pre-adolescence, we learn nothing.

In one study, researchers found that diagnosticians within a large hospital and medical centre agreed easily on a diagnosis of depression, but when diagnostic results in sites across North America were compared, agreement was poor (Keller et al., 1995). Even when a physician or other professional diagnoses the same person on two occasions, six months apart, the two diagnoses may differ (Carson, 1991). One study found that clinicians diagnosing depression in a child agreed only about 40 percent of the time, far below an acceptable level of diagnostic reliability (Cantwell et al., 1979). On the other hand, the diagnostic reliability of some of *DSM-IV*'s categories—such as the diagnosis of attention deficit/hyperactivity disorder, is acceptably high. The psychiatric profession is endeavouring to improve the reliability of the *DSM*'s diagnostic categories and has developed training guides for diagnosticians (Ottosson et al., 2002).

The Empirical Method

An alternative to the diagnostic approach is the empirical or rating-scale method (Achenbach, 1997; Achenbach & Rescorla, 2007). Using this method, an adult who is familiar with a child who displays signs of emotional disturbance—usually a parent or a teacher—rates a large number of problem behaviours according to whether and to what degree the child displays the behaviours. Investigators then use statistical techniques

diagnosis

The identification of a physical or mental disorder on the basis of symptoms and of knowledge of the cause or causes of the disorder and its common course. A diagnosis may also include information about effective forms of treatment.

etiology

In medicine and psychiatry, the cause or causes of a specific disorder.

diagnostic reliability

A measure of how often two or more clinicians arrive independently at the same diagnosis of a particular disorder.

Table 15-2   Some examples of *DSM-IV*'s "Disorders Usually First Diagnosed in Infancy, Childhood, or Adolescence"

Mental Retardation	**Attention-Deficit and Disruptive Behaviour Disorders**
Mild mental retardation	Attention deficit/hyperactivity disorder
Moderate mental retardation	Conduct disorder
Severe mental retardation	Oppositional defiant disorder
Profound mental retardation	**Feeding and Eating Disorders of Infancy or Early Childhood**
Learning Disorders	Rumination disorder (regurgitation and rechewing of food)
Reading disorder	**Tic Disorders (stereotyped motor movements or vocalizations)**
Mathematics disorder	
Disorder of written expression	Tourette's disorder (multiple tics)
	Chronic motor or vocal tic disorder
Motor Skills Disorder	
Developmental coordination disorder	**Elimination Disorders**
	Encopresis (incontinence of feces)
Communication Disorders	Enuresis (bed-wetting)
Expressive language disorder	
Phonological disorder (difficulties in articulating speech)	**Other Disorders of Infancy, Childhood, or Adolescence**
	Separation anxiety disorder
Stuttering	Selective mutism
Pervasive Developmental Disorders	Reactive attachment disorder of infancy or early childhood
Autistic disorder	Stereotypic movement disorder
Rett's disorder (usually associated with severe or profound mental retardation)	
Childhood disintegrative disorder (usually associated with severe mental retardation)	

Source: Based on American Psychiatric Association, 2000.

to determine which problem behaviours are associated with one another. There is considerable overlap among the classifications arrived at by the diagnostic and the empirical methods, but there are also many disparities (Achenbach, 1995). Researchers may also have peers rate the likelihood that other children will engage in risky behaviours (Tinsley et al., 1997). Because peers influence children's risky behaviour, this approach is a particularly useful way of identifying children and adolescents at risk for harmful behaviours such as smoking and using alcohol and other drugs. Moreover, the empirical approach has been useful in describing child problems in other ethnic groups in a variety of cultures (Rescorla et al., 2007a, 2007b).

Both classification methods generally agree on the broader, major categories, such as "mental retardation," but often disagree—both with each other and within their own systems—on narrower subcategories, such as "mild mental retardation" and "moderate mental retardation" (see Table 15-2). The finer the distinction one tries to draw between collections of symptoms and behaviours, the more difficult the task. If symptoms and behaviours were always exactly the same, with enough study, it should be possible to draw these distinctions once and for all. But human beings are infinitely variable—so the work goes on.

LO3 SOME PSYCHOLOGICAL DISORDERS THAT AFFECT CHILDREN

It is useful to discuss some representative child disorders in terms of the degree to which they reflect the nature of the control children exert over their behaviour. In

undercontrolled disorders, the child fails to control behaviour in such a way as to suit the demands of a given environment. Examples of undercontrolled behaviours include non-compliance, disobedience, rule violation, and aggression. Although these behaviours hurt the child, they are initially most disturbing to other people around the child. Because undercontrolled behaviours are defined largely by this negative impact on others, and because most childhood psychological disorders are defined by adults' social judgments, it is not surprising that undercontrolled behavioural disorders are the most frequently reported of all the psychological problems of childhood. In this section, we discuss two of these types of disorders: conduct disorders and attention deficit/hyperactivity disorder.

In contrast to undercontrolled disorders, **overcontrolled disorders** involve withdrawal from others, anxiety, depression, and a lack of spontaneity. Overcontrolled children seem restrained in the way they relate to others. *Phobias* (excessive fears) may cause considerable discomfort for some children and their families; fortunately, research indicates that 80 percent of children's phobias disappear within two years, even without treatment (Gelfand & Drew, 2003). (Table 15-3 lists some fears that are common at different stages of normal development.) However, some fears and phobias are longer lasting, persisting across the lifespan. These include *acrophobia* (fear of heights) and fear of physical illness. Anxiety disorders characterized by a general apprehensiveness and low self-confidence also can last into the adult years (Ollendick & King, 1998).

As an example of overcontrol, we will discuss childhood depression. This disorder is not listed in Table 15-2 because the *DSM-IV* covers depression in childhood in its discussion of *mood disorders* in adults. It also covers the expression in children of anxiety and phobias under the adult category of *anxiety disorders*. For several reasons, it is often difficult to identify overcontrolled problems in children. Because the definition of childhood psychopathology depends on an adult's social judgment, and because it is much more difficult for adults to evaluate children's inner feelings (e.g., sadness) than it is to judge their overt behaviour (e.g., aggression), the diagnostic labels for overcontrolled disorders are often vague and controversial. It is also the case that undercontrolling and overcontrolling behaviours often occur together. For example, the child who acts out and displays aggression may also experience depression and use drugs. So, even though we discuss them separately, keep in mind that "bad things" often go together (Kim et al., 2003). **Comorbidity** is the term used to describe this co-occurrence of two or more problem behaviours (Pennington, 2005).

Although the problems of delinquency, hyperactivity, and depression are serious, some children exhibit even more marked forms of psychological distress that do not

undercontrolled disorders

A group of psychological disturbances in which a child appears to lack self-control and to act out in a variety of ways, through such behaviours as non-compliance, disobedience, and aggression.

overcontrolled disorders

A group of psychological disturbances in which a child withdraws from others, lacks spontaneity, and generally appears to be an unhappy child.

comorbidity

The co-occurrence of two or more problem behaviours.

Ages	Fears
0–12 months	Loss of support; loud noises; unexpected, looming objects; strangers
12–24 months	Separation from parent; injury; strangers
24–36 months	Separation from parent; animals, especially large dogs; darkness
36 months–6 years	Separation from parent; animals; darkness; strangers; bodily harm
6–10 years	Imaginary beings; snakes; injury; darkness; being alone
10–12 years	Social evaluations; school failure; thunderstorms; ridicule; injury; death
Adolescence	Peer rejection; school failure; war and other disasters; family issues; future plans (especially in boys)

Table 15-3

How children's fears wax and wane

Source: From Gelfand & Drew, *Understanding Child Behavior Disorders*, 4th ed. Copyright © 2003, Wadsworth, a part of Cengage Learning, Inc. Reproduced by permission (www.cengage.com/permissions).

pervasive developmental disorders

Childhood disorders characterized by gross deficits in many areas of cognitive, emotional, and social development that are linked with severe and pervasive impairment of social interaction and communication skills.

really fit under either the overcontrolled or undercontrolled designations. The term **pervasive developmental disorders** describes a collection of disorders characterized by gross deficits in many areas of cognitive, emotional, and social development that are linked with severe and pervasive impairment of social interaction and communication skills (American Psychiatric Association, 2000). Children with these kinds of disorders are extremely disturbed. Although these disorders have sometimes been referred to as *psychoses* (broadly, disturbances in which the person's functioning is so maladaptive that she is said to be out of touch with reality), the unusual behaviours seen in these children are even more general and incapacitating than those in most psychoses.

Pervasive developmental disorders have often been confused with schizophrenia, a common and seriously incapacitating disorder that, like some of these disorders, is characterized by loss of contact with reality. However, schizophrenia is also characterized by hallucinations, delusions, and other kinds of thought disorders not found in the pervasive developmental disorders. In addition, these two kinds of disorder have very different ages of onset: The pervasive developmental disorders are evident in the first few years of life, whereas schizophrenia most commonly emerges in late adolescence or early adulthood. Schizophrenia is not found with any great frequency in children.

A bit later in this chapter, we discuss one of the most widely known pervasive developmental disorders: autism (also known as *early infantile autism* and *childhood autism*). Autism has been one of the most baffling of childhood disturbances, but, as we will see, some progress has been made in treating the children who suffer from it.

LO4 Conduct Disorders

conduct disorder

A disorder characterized by a repetitive and persistent pattern of behaviour in which a young person violates the basic rights of others or major age-appropriate societal norms or rules.

delinquency

Juvenile behaviour in violation of the law.

A **conduct disorder** is characterized by a repetitive and persistent pattern of behaviour in which a child or adolescent violates the basic rights of others or major age-appropriate societal norms or rules (American Psychiatric Association, 2000). (See Table 15-4 for the *DSM-IV* description of conduct disorders.) Thus, it is a disorder of *undercontrol*. More than three times as many boys as girls are reported to exhibit conduct disorders (American Psychiatric Association, 2000; Moffit et al., 2001; Reid et al., 2002).

When rule breaking involves a violation not just of norms or others' rights but of the law, the youth is said to be *delinquent*. **Delinquency** is not a psychological term but is the legal designation for juvenile behaviour that violates the law. Juveniles can

Table 15-4

DSM-IV-TR diagnostic criteria for conduct disorder

Source: Reprinted with permission from the *Diagnostic and Statistical Manual of Mental Disorders*, copyright © 2000, American Psychiatric Association.

Repetitive and persistent pattern of behaviour in which the basic rights of others or major age-appropriate societal norms or rules are violated, as manifested by the presence of three (or more) of the following criteria in the past 12 months, with at least one criterion present in the past 6 months:

Aggression to People and Animals
1. Often bullies, threatens, or intimidates others
2. Often initiates physical fights
3. Has used a weapon that can cause serious physical harm to others (e.g., a bat, brick, broken bottle, knife, gun)
4. Has been physically cruel to people
5. Has been physically cruel to animals
6. Has stolen while confronting a victim (e.g., mugging, purse snatching, extortion, armed robbery)
7. Has forced someone into sexual activity

Destruction of Property
8. Has deliberately engaged in fire setting with the intention of causing serious damage
9. Has deliberately destroyed others' property (other than by fire setting)

be judged delinquent for two types of offences. A youth may be charged with a **status offence**, such as possession of alcohol, if she is under the age at which drinking is legal. **Criminal offences** are illegal acts, regardless of the age of the individual; those committed by juveniles accounted for 17 percent of all criminal arrests and 16 percent of arrests for serious violent crime in 1999 (Children's Defense Fund, 2001). The good news, however, is that the arrest rate for juveniles has dropped since 1995 (see Figure 15-2). The juvenile murder arrest rate has declined even more rapidly, dropping over 55 percent since the late 1980s (Children's Defense Fund, 2001).

DSM-IV considers *substance-related disorders* a category separate from the disorders diagnosed in childhood—largely because drug abuse is a serious and pervasive problem among adults. However, we discuss substance abuse here because, among children and adolescents, this problem—again, one of undercontrol—has been and continues to be the cause of much concern.

Substance abuse is the excessive use of legal or illegal drugs in such a way as to interfere with one or more important areas of functioning in life. Table 15-5 on the next page lists the *DSM-IV* criteria for a diagnosis of substance abuse. Nearly half of the students in the United States have tried an illegal drug before they graduate from high school (Johnston et al., 2007). However, trends in adolescents' use of both legal and illegal drugs are declining, primarily in the use of alcohol and illicit drugs such as marijuana, cocaine, heroin, and hallucinogens. Between 2002 and 2004, drug use among 12- to 17-year-olds declined 9 percent overall, but a category that showed an increase was non-medical use of prescription drugs. Young adults aged 18 to 25 had the highest rates of substance abuse (National Institute on Drug Abuse, 2006). Greater awareness of the harmful effects of drugs and better and more widely available treatment programs have both probably contributed to the decline in drug use. A troubling trend in North America is that those who use drugs may be starting at younger ages (Hotton & Haans, 2004; Johnston et al., 1997). Using data from Canada's National Longitudinal Survey of Children and Youth (NLSCY), and as shown in Figure 15-3 on the next page, Hotton and Haans (2004) found that even 12-year-olds had used drugs, and that by the age of 13 and 14 years, children were using marijuana and hallucinogens, and sniffing glue. In addition, the average age of first use of marijuana, hallucinogens, glue, and other drugs varied between 12 and 14 years. Alcohol use began even earlier, with 17 percent of 12-year-olds reporting that they had taken at least one drink, with an average age of first use at 12.4 years. Similar trends have been found in the United States (Leshner, 2001). In both countries, boys were considerably more likely to drink regularly and to use illicit drugs than girls, but girls were just as likely as boys to smoke cigarettes.

status offence

Illegal behaviour committed by an underage offender.

criminal offence

An illegal act.

substance abuse

The excessive use of legal or illegal drugs in such a way as to interfere seriously with one or more important areas of functioning in life: work, intimacy with another, or general interpersonal and social relations.

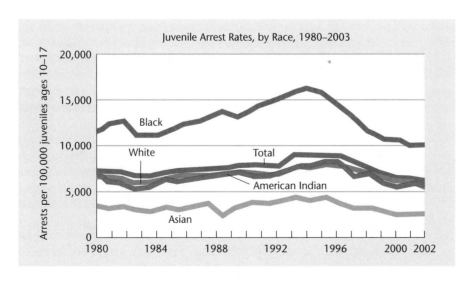

Figure 15-2

Young people and arrest rates for violent crimes by race

Beginning in the 1980s, arrests of youth aged 10 to 17 for violent crimes (robbery, aggravated assault, rape, or murder) peaked in the mid-1990s, and the rate of these arrests began to drop to a lower level than two decades ago for all racial groups.

Source: Juvenile Offenders and Victims: 2006 National Report (2006). U.S. Department of Justice, Office of Justice Programs, Washington, DC.

Table 15-5

DSM-IV-TR criteria for substance abuse

A. A maladaptive pattern of substance use leading to clinically significant impairment or distress, as manifested by one (or more) of the following, occurring within a 12-month period:

(1) Recurrent substance use resulting in a failure to fulfill major role obligations at work, school, or home (e.g., repeated absences or poor work performance related to substance use; substance-related absences, suspensions, or expulsions from school; neglect of children or household)

(2) Recurrent substance use in situations in which it is physically hazardous (e.g., driving an automobile or operating a machine when impaired by substance use)

(3) Recurrent substance-related legal problems (e.g., arrests for substance-related disorderly conduct)

(4) Continued substance use despite having persistent or recurrent social or interpersonal problems caused or exacerbated by the effects of the substance (e.g., arguments with spouse about consequences of intoxication, physical fights)

B. The symptoms have never met the criteria for Substance Dependence for this class of substance.

Table 15-6 lists some factors that, in general, influence children's use of drugs. One of the best predictors of smoking is whether the child's best friend smokes (Gritz, 2004). In addition, children who are undercontrolled, impulsive, risk taking, moody, and who overreact to minor frustrations are more likely to become frequent drug users (Epstein et al., 2001). Heavy drug use by parents and peers is related to children's use of alcohol and marijuana (Claes et al., 2005; Hotton & Haan, 2004; Smith, 2001; Willis & Yeager, 2003). Also related to marijuana use are poor academic records, truancy, minor delinquency, and the desire to experiment. Finally, the more peers in the school who use tobacco and alcohol, the more opportunities there are for other children to begin to use these substances and the more they do so (Cleveland & Wiebe, 2003). If a youth uses marijuana to resolve psychological problems rather than as a response to social situations, he is likely to go on to use hard drugs (Gelfand & Drew, 2003). Those who start their drug careers early (before age 15) are at the highest risk for developing a serious drug problem and for continuing to use drugs into adulthood (Hawkins et al., 1997). A close relationship with a responsible, stable family that strongly disapproves of their use of drugs helps to buffer adolescents against drug abuse (National Institute on Drug Abuse, 2006).

Figure 15-3

The prevalence of substance use in Canada as a function of age, 1998–99

Demonstrating a disturbing trend, children in Canada are starting to use drugs and alcohol at earlier ages. As seen here, even 12-year-olds have tried alcohol and marijuana, and by 15 years of age, children have used a wide assortment of substances.

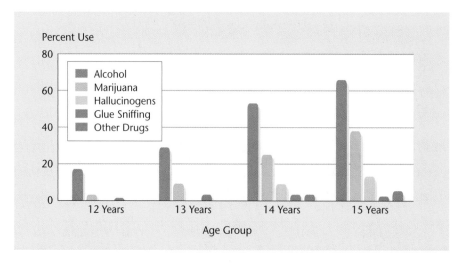

Table 15-6 Some characteristics of young users and non-users of drugs

	Users	Non-users
Cultural Influences		
Attitudes toward drug use	Acceptance	Low acceptance
Drug use in society	High exposure	Low exposure
Contextual and Neighbourhood Influences		
Crime	High crime	Low crime
Employment	Unemployment	Low unemployment
Schools	Inadequate schools	Adequate schools
Availability of drugs	Readily available drugs	Drugs are not readily available
Educational and career opportunities	Lack of legitimate opportunities	Legitimate opportunities available
Family Influences		
Drug use	Parents are users (especially mothers)	Parents do not use drugs
Religion	Not religious	Religious faith
Values	Non-traditional values	Traditional values
Family conflict	More family conflict	Less family conflict
Siblings	Siblings are users	Siblings do not use drugs
Peer Influences		
Drug use	Best friend is user	Best friend does not use drugs
Peer power	Peers are more influential	Peers are less influential
Individual Factors		
Opportunity	Opportunity to take drugs	No opportunity to take drugs
History	Good experiences with drugs	Unpleasant drug experiences
Adjustment	Possible adjustment problems	Possible superior adjustment
Attitude toward authority	More rebellious and questioning	More conforming
Attitude toward deviance	More tolerant of deviance	Less tolerant of deviance
Deviance	More deviant behaviour	More conforming behaviour
Attitude toward school achievement	Less concerned about school achievement	More concerned about school achievement
Self-esteem	Low self-esteem and low self-efficacy	High self-esteem and self-efficacy
Mood	Depressed mood	Not depressed
Coping skills	Poor coping skills	Adequate coping skills
Biological susceptibility to drug addiction	Higher biological susceptibility to drug addiction	Low biological susceptibility to drug addiction

Sources: Based on Gelfand & Drew, 2003; Gelfand et al., 1997; Petraitis, Flay, & Miller, 1995.

TREATING CONDUCT DISORDERS The most successful approaches to treatment for conduct disorders have employed social learning and behavioural techniques (Reid et al., 2002). Parents can be trained to teach and reinforce appropriate behaviour and to use non-reinforcement and **time out**—removing children from a situation or context in which they are acting inappropriately until they are able and ready to act in an appropriate manner—to suppress undesirable behaviours. These approaches have been found to reduce rates of conduct disorders among aggressive, delinquent boys (Cavell et al., 2007; Patterson, 2002) as well as to reduce disruptive behaviour in classrooms (Walker, 1995). A variety of prevention programs involving parent training, home visits, social-skills training, academic tutoring, and classroom intervention have produced promising results (Foster, Jones, & Conduct Problems Prevention Research Group, 2006; Patrikakou et al., 2005; Kress & Elias, 2006; Weissberg & Greenberg, 1998; see also "Aggression Prevention: A Multi-pronged Approach," in Chapter 14 of this book). Ducharme, Atkinson, and Poulton (2000), for instance, describe a compliance

time out

Removing children from a situation or context in which they are acting inappropriately until they are able and ready to act appropriately.

training program in which parents make increasingly demanding requests of children at a graduated pace. This program produced improvements in children's compliance that were maintained up to six months after the treatment. And others have suggested that an ecological, multi-system intervention method can be effective in treating serious juvenile offenders (Henggeler et al., 1992, 2007).

Despite the great concern over youth substance abuse, our social policies and intervention programs have not dealt effectively with this problem. Even the best-run programs—which typically involve detoxification, total abstinence from a drug, and intensive educational and counselling efforts over a period of weeks or months—have recidivism rates that can range as high as 70 percent (Newcomb & Bentler, 1989). In the case of tobacco use, for example, Shiffman (1993) estimated that one treatment program produced abstinence from smoking for one year in about 38 percent of the young people in the program; thus, 60 to 70 percent of those in treatment had relapsed by the end of that year. However, more recent intervention programs are beginning to report better and longer-lasting results in reducing drug abuse among adolescents (Liddle & Rowe, 2006). As Table 15-7 shows, drug-abuse treatment involving either in-patient residential or out-patient programs can be effective for reducing drug use and criminal activity and improving school performance for adolescents (Hser et al., 2001; Grella, 2006). Moreover, prevention efforts to reduce substance use in preadolescence can be successful in stemming the onset and level of substance use (Spoth et al., 2003). Evaluation of a family-based prevention program aimed at reducing the use of alcohol and tobacco among grade 6 to 10 children suggests that the incidence of this sort of problem can be reduced (Guyll et al., 2004; Spoth et al., 2001). The investigators taught families in the program a variety of skills including the following:

1. Increased prosocial involvement in the family.
2. Improved parenting and child-management practices.
3. Increased ability of children to resist peer pressure.
4. Reduced family conflict.
5. More frequent expression of positive emotion among family members.

Compared with children of families in the control group, which was not offered treatment, children in the treatment group were slower to begin using alcohol and tobacco and, at the end of a four-year period, exhibited less overall substance use.

attention deficit/hyperactivity disorder (ADHD)

A childhood disorder characterized by a persistent pattern of inattention and hyperactivity or impulsivity that far exceeds such behaviours observed in children at comparable levels of development.

ⓛ5 Attention Deficit/Hyperactivity Disorder

Some authorities question whether conduct disorders differ from the disorder called attention deficit/hyperactivity disorder. The essential feature of **attention deficit/hyperactivity disorder (ADHD)** is a persistent pattern of inattention and hyperactivity

Table 15-7

Behaviour of adolescents before and one year after treatment

Sources: Grella, 2006; Hser, Grella, Hubbard et al., 2001.

	Before	After
Drug Use		
Weekly marijuana use	80.4%	43.8%
Heavy drinking	33.8%	20.3%
Hallucinogen use	31.0%	26.8%
Stimulant use	19.1%	15.3%
School Performance		
Regular attendance	62.6%	74.0%
Grades (average or better)	53.4%	79.6%
Criminal activities		
Any illegal act	75.6%	52.8%
Any arrest	50.3%	33.9%

or impulsivity that is far in excess of such behaviours observed in children at comparable levels of development (American Psychiatric Association, 2000; see also Table 15-8 for the *DSM* criteria for the diagnosis of ADHD). Another problem of under-control, ADHD leads to difficulties in the home, the classroom, and the peer group (American Psychiatric Association, 2000; Barkley, 2000). A variety of studies have demonstrated that hyperactive children not only run into conflict with adults in their environment but perform more poorly than other children in school, present serious classroom-management problems to the teacher, have difficult peer relations, and often think of themselves as being "no good" (S. B. Campbell, 2000). Perhaps even more important, in at least 60 percent of these children, some ADHD-related problems persist into adolescence and early adulthood (Weiss et al., 1999). Attention deficit disorders occur more frequently and are more sustained in boys than in girls (American Psychiatric Association, 2000).

CHARACTERISTICS OF THE DISORDER Victor exemplifies children with this disorder, who display overactivity, poorly sustained attention, impulsivity, deficits in verbal and visuospatial memory, and problems with adherence to instructions and rules (Barkley, 2000; Brocki et al., 2008; Reiff & Tippins, 2004). Probably the most marked symptom that parents and teachers notice about hyperactive children is their inappropriately high activity level. In free-play situations, hyperactive children are no more active than other children. But in structured situations like the classroom, which demand controlled, task-oriented behaviour, their activity is conspicuous (Barkley, 1998). They fidget, tap their feet, poke their neighbours, and talk out of turn. A child who is engaged in the same amount of motor activity but who is diligently working is judged by the teacher to be normally active (Gelfand & Drew, 2003). The hyperactive child's behaviour disturbs peers and disrupts the class, which may help account for the fact that 50 to 60 percent of ADHD children are rejected by their peers (Henker & Whalen, 1999). Interestingly, when teachers have good knowledge about ADHD, they show more helpful behaviours and perceptions toward the students with this disorder; unfortunately, they also expect these children to be more disruptive in the classroom, and report less confidence in their abilities to manage ADHD students (Ohan et al., 2008).

Criterion	Description
Criterion A	The essential feature of attention-deficit/hyperactivity disorder is a persistent pattern of inattention and/or hyperactivity-impulsivity that is more frequent and severe than is typically observed in individuals at a comparable level of development.
Criterion B	Some hyperactive-impulsive or inattentive symptoms that cause impairment must have been present before age 7 years, although many individuals are diagnosed after the symptoms have been present for a number of years.
Criterion C	Some impairment from the symptoms must be present in at least two settings (e.g., at home and at school or work).
Criterion D	There must be clear evidence of interference with developmentally appropriate social, academic, or occupational functioning.
Criterion E	The disturbance does not occur exclusively during the course of a pervasive developmental disorder, schizophrenia, or other psychotic disorder and is not better accounted for by another mental disorder (e.g., mood disorder, anxiety disorder, dissociative disorder, or personality disorder).

Table 15-8

DSM-IV-TR definition of ADHD

Source: Reprinted with permission from the *Diagnostic and Statistical Manual of Mental Disorders*, copyright © 2000, American Psychiatric Association.

A prime characteristic of hyperactive children is their inability to attend for long or to stay with a specific activity or task, particularly one that requires them to sit quietly and concentrate.

psychostimulant medications

Drugs, such as amphetamines and caffeine, that increase alertness and attention as well as psychomotor activity.

The inappropriate activities often associated with ADHD tend to diminish during adolescence. However, there is some evidence that increased neuroticism and decreased agreeableness continue to characterize many adolescents with ADHD (Miller et al., 2008). Even when the inappropriate activity decreases, however, other problems still persist (Weiss et al., 1999). One of the most persistent problems is *inattention*, which becomes especially problematic in school, where teachers may have to expend considerable effort to keep these children focused on a task (S. B. Campbell, 2000). Another persistent problem experienced by some hyperactive children is *impulsivity* (Waschbusch et al., 2006). Hyperactive children often seem to act before they think. Impulsivity can be seen in the frequent accidents of the preschooler and the poorly thought out test answers of the school-age child. It may continue into adult life, where more frequent changes in residence and a higher incidence of automobile accidents are found among formerly hyperactive children (American Psychiatric Association, 2000; S. B. Campbell, 2000).

Children with attention deficit/hyperactivity disorder also find it difficult to follow rules such as, "When your little brother takes one of your toys, don't hit him, or you will be sent to your room," because they have problems *tracking* contingencies (Barkley, 1998). As a result of all these problems, it is not surprising that hyperactive children tend to do poorly in school. They typically function one to two years below grade level despite normal IQs (Barkley, 1998; Pisecco et al., 2001). Box 15.2 describes a number of potential deficits in cognitive functioning that have been found to be associated with ADHD.

CAUSAL FACTORS IN ADHD   What is the cause of this frustrating collection of problems and how can we help hyperactive children? Research on this topic has been complicated because so many explanations for the etiology and treatment of attention deficit/hyperactivity have been offered. Of the more credible explanations of ADHD, one suggests that the problem has a biological origin and another implicates the environment.

Biological Factors   For years, the leading biological explanation of attention deficit/hyperactivity suggested that this particular cluster of problems was caused by some form of *minimal brain dysfunction*. Supporting this explanation, computer-imaging techniques such as computed tomography (CT) and magnetic resonance imaging (MRI) scans have revealed brain abnormalities in several areas (Casey, 2001; Schmajuk et al., 2006). Another biological aspect is evident in the effect of **psychostimulant medications**—drugs such as caffeine, amphetamines, or methylphenidate (one brand name is Ritalin) (Whalen, 2001). These medications increase attention and, as a result, reduce extraneous activity, enabling the child to focus on a task and complete it. Today, psychostimulants are a common treatment for ADHD children, some of whom refer to these medications as their "arithmetic pills" (Gelfand & Drew, 2003). At present, the most popular biological hypothesis is that ADHD is a genetic disorder. Evidence suggests that activity level is more similar between normal monozygotic twins than between dizygotic twins (Luca et al., 2007; Plomin, 1990).

Psychological Factors   As an alternative to biological explanations of ADHD, some researchers have suggested that attention deficit/hyperactivity is environmentally caused. Diverse social and familial stressors such as poverty, low levels of education, marital discord and disruption, household disorganization, and inept parenting have all been associated with ADHD (S. B. Campbell, 2000). Research focused on parent–child relations has found that the mothers of hyperactive children generally are more controlling and intrusive and less affectionate and reinforcing than the mothers of normal children. However, most investigators think that excessive parental control and lessened affectional response are likely reactions to attention deficit/hyperactivity, rather than its cause (Barkley, 2000). Although a mother's intrusive, non-reinforcing behaviour

Box 15.2

Child Psychology in Action

COGNITIVE IMPLICATIONS OF ATTENTION DEFICIT/HYPERACTIVITY DISORDER

Attention deficit/hyperactivity disorder (ADHD) has been estimated to affect between 5 and 10 percent of the school-age population (Nolan et al., 2001; Scahill & Schwab-Stone, 2000). Given this percentage, approximately 2 to 3 children in every class of 30 will have ADHD, meaning that it is one of the most common mental health disorders present in an educational context. Over the past few decades, there has been an increasing recognition that children with ADHD can be characterized as having deficits in various aspects of cognitive processing, as opposed to, for example, motor restlessness (Corkum et al., 1996; Corkum & Siegel, 1993).

In an attempt to better understand the implications of this disorder, researchers have thus focused on exploring the impact of ADHD on different cognitive abilities. Penny Corkum from Dalhousie University and her collaborators (Corkum et al., 1996, 2008; Corkum & Siegel, 1993; Mullane & Corkum, 2007; Penny et al., 2009) have, over the years, been exploring the relation between ADHD and cognitive processing. For instance, one cognitive function that has been the focus of investigation involves the problems ADHD children have in sustaining attention (Atkins et al., 1985; Schachar et al., 1986). One means of examining sustained attention makes use of the *continuous performance task* (CPT; Connors, 2000), and involves a vigilance task in which a series of stimuli, typically letters or numbers, are presented to an observer, who is asked to respond to a specific target stimulus (e.g., a single letter, Y or a sequence of letters, BY; Corkum & Siegel, 1993). Using the CPT, Corkum and colleagues (1996) were able to demonstrate that children with ADHD showed a deficit in sustained attention over time, although this deficit could not be accounted for based on motivational factors.

More recently, researchers have explored the possibility of impairments in executive functions (EF) as a core

deficit in children with ADHD (Barkley, 1997; Biederman et al., 2004). According to a theory proposed by Barkley (1997), the EFs of working memory, reconstitution (the ability to synthesize information in problem solving), self-regulation of internal states, and internal speech are all mental abilities that enable self-control in the child and, thus, underlie the lack of sustained attention and hyperactive and impulsive nature of children with ADHD. In support of this hypothesis, Mullane and Corkum (2007) examined the performance of children with ADHD on the Wisconsin Card Sorting Test, which assesses working memory. Two working-memory tests were employed—a counting procedure in which children counted yellow dots from a field of blue and yellow dots arranged randomly on a card, and a backwards digit-span test in which children had to repeat backwards an increasing number of digits presented by an experimenter. In keeping with previous findings (Martinussen et al., 2005), these researchers observed that children with ADHD did perform more poorly on tests of working memory, with this deficit arising from a problem with children's ability to maintain the use of a particular rule or procedure.

In follow-up work, Corkum and colleagues (2008) compared whether the Vygotskyian concept of private speech displayed during problem-solving tasks differed between children with ADHD and control subjects. In support of the previous findings emphasizing differences in EFs, these researchers found that children with ADHD did produce more external private speech than control children, although, surprisingly, there was no difference in internal private speech. Overall, however, these findings lend support to Barkley's (1997) theory, with ADHD children demonstrating deficits across a range of executive functions. And more generally, of course, findings such as these have important clinical implications for both educators and parents concerning the nature of the disorder in ADHD.

may initially be a reaction to a hyperactive child, in time her reaction may exacerbate the child's problems. Attention deficit/hyperactivity appears to be a disorder with multiple causes (Kieling et al., 2008; Mash & Johnston, 2005; Waschbusch et al., 2006). Brain damage may cause ADHD in some instances, and inheritance, environmental lead poisoning, or dietary agents may explain other cases. It also seems likely that some children's attention deficit/hyperactivity is exacerbated by the specific environments in which they are reared.

TREATING ATTENTION DEFICIT/HYPERACTIVITY DISORDER

At this time, there is little doubt that psychostimulant medication (e.g., Ritalin) improves the behaviour of about 80 percent of all ADHD children, at least in the short term (Cunningham, 1999; Mehta et al., 2001). Improvement is quite rapid and noticeable to parents and teachers, who quickly become advocates of the medication approach. The impact of psychostimulants is so dramatic that it is estimated that between 2 and 9 percent of North American schoolchildren receive such medication (Corkum et al., 2008; Habel et al., 2005). However, many observers object to the use of these medications, citing concerns that range from the philosophical stance that altering children's behaviour with drugs is inappropriate to questions about the side effects of psychostimulants, which include suppression in the rate of physical growth, irritability, insomnia, weight loss, and abdominal pain (Barkley, 2000; Gelfand & Drew, 2003).

The major alternative treatment available for ADHD is **behaviour therapy**, a psychological intervention based on social learning principles, primarily reinforcement. In traditional behaviour therapy programs, parents and teachers are taught to identify and monitor various specific, troublesome aspects of the hyperactive child's behaviour (e.g., not completing class assignments on time) and to systematically reward the child for making improvements in the targeted problem area (Hardman et al., 2002). In related behaviour therapy programs, teachers and parents also work directly with the child in an attempt to teach cognitive self-control strategies.

To address the ongoing controversy of whether drugs, psychosocial intervention, or both are the best way to treat children with ADHD, the National Institute of Mental Health launched the Multimodal Treatment Study of Children with ADHD (MTA). This study was a large clinical trial (Jensen et al., 2001; Wells, 2001) involving nearly 600 children aged 7 to 9 with a primary diagnosis of ADHD, who were randomly assigned to one of four treatment conditions. One group received only medication; a second group received only psychosocial treatment consisting of parent training, teacher consultation, and cognitive-behavioural and behavioural treatments aimed at fostering academic, social, and sports skills. Children in the third group received a combination of both medication and psychosocial treatment, whereas those in the fourth group received only routine treatment from their community pediatrician or the school. Results indicated that children in all four groups improved after the 14 months of treatment and 10 months of follow-up. Not only did ADHD symptoms decrease, but symptoms of oppositional defiant disorder and internalizing symptoms decreased as well. Moreover, social skills, academic achievement, and parent–child relationships improved. But not all treatments were equally effective. Children receiving medication or the combined treatment (medication and psychosocial intervention) showed greater improvement than those receiving psychosocial treatment alone or community treatment, especially in ADHD symptoms. Additionally, children in the combined group showed the most impressive improvement on other measures, such as oppositional symptoms, internalizing symptoms, social skills, and reading achievement. Recent analyses of the MTA (Jensen et al., 2007; Swanson et al., 2008a, 2008b) have qualified these results somewhat. A three-year follow-up (Jensen et al., 2007) of the children (at this point between 10 and 13 years of age) in this study found that, in contrast to the earlier findings, there were no observable differences among the various groups on any of the outcome measures assessed. According to these researchers, the fact that none of the groups differed may have arisen due to age-related declines in ADHD, changes in the intensity of the medication taken, starting or stopping medication altogether, or possibly other factors not even considered.

behaviour therapy

A psychological form of treatment, often used in treating conduct disorders, that is based on such learning principles as reinforcement and social learning.

depression in childhood

Like adult depression, a mood disorder often manifested in a downbeat mood and loss of interest in familiar activities but also likely to be expressed as irritability and crankiness. Difficulty concentrating or focusing on tasks and concomitant drops in school grades are not uncommon, and children with depression often complain of physical problems such as headaches or stomachaches.

LO6 Depression in Childhood

Depression in childhood—an overcontrolled disorder—is diagnosed when a child has seemed downbeat or has lost interest or pleasure in nearly all activities for at least two weeks. The dominant mood may be one of irritability and crankiness rather than sadness and dejection. Family members often notice social withdrawal or neglect of activities the child formerly enjoyed—for example, a child who used to enjoy playing soccer may begin to make excuses not to practise. Emily was suffering from many of these symptoms. Depression often interferes with appetite and eating, and parents may note a failure of the child to make normal or expected weight gains. Another common effect of depression is an impaired ability to think, to concentrate, or to focus on a task; a precipitous drop in grades may signal depressive problems in a child or adolescent. Somatic complaints (e.g., headache, stomachache) are not uncommon in depressed children. Table 15-9 lists some behaviours that are common in depressed children and adolescents.

To be judged clinically depressed, a child must display changes in cognitive functioning and behaviour. Possible changes in cognitive functioning include guilt and feelings of worthlessness, complaints about inability to concentrate, slowed thinking, and recurrent thoughts of death and suicide. Depression in childhood is low in frequency (1.7 percent), in part because of the difficulty of reliably diagnosing it (Gelfand & Drew, 2003). The fact that professionals diagnose depression in children more frequently as children grow older probably reflects both that difficulty and the fact that depressive disorder is experienced at its fullest only when the child's cognitive capacities reach the stage of formal operations. As Figure 15-4 on the next page shows, depression is rarely diagnosed among children under the age of 10, but the diagnosis rises in frequency quite dramatically among adolescent females from the age of 15 and continues to rise into adulthood. The diagnosis rises for males as well at about 15 but levels off at about 18. Nearly twice as many girls as boys experience depression (Goodman & Gotlib, 2002; Hammen, 2005).

A very serious consequence of the increased rate of depression during adolescence is a concomitant increase in the rate of suicide. Although suicide is rare among children younger than 12, it is estimated to be the third leading killer of adolescents, following car accidents and homicide (Berman et al., 2005; Centers for Disease Control and Prevention, 2007). Among university students, it is the second leading cause of death;

Behaviours	
Infants	Sadness, crying, apathy, motor retardation, failure to thrive, vomiting, irritability, developmental delays, feeding or sleeping difficulties
Toddlers and preschoolers	Irritability, social withdrawal, negative self-image, peer problems, anxiety, phobias, weeping, loss of interest or pleasure in usual activities, loss of appetite, sleep disturbances, changed activity rates, failure to thrive, aggression, self-endangering behaviours, somatic disorders including urinary and fecal incontinence, asthma, eczema, desire to die
Schoolchildren	Irritability, loss of interest or pleasure in usual activities, fatigue, somatic complaints, sleeping and eating disturbances, changed activity rates, guilt, low self-esteem, sudden schoolwork problems, aggression, decreased ability to concentrate, phobias, anxiety, separation anxiety problems, depressed facial expression, suicidal thoughts
Adolescents	Disturbed sleep, appetite or weight changes, changed activity rates, fatigue, loss of interest or pleasure in usual activities, self-devaluation, difficulty in concentrating, indecisiveness, anxiety, phobias, somatic disorders, excessive emotional dependency, withdrawal, reckless behaviour, suicidal thoughts or attempts

Table 15-9

Depressive behaviours in children and adolescents

Figure 15-4

Clinical depression among children and adolescents

Clinical, or serious, depression is not seen often among children, but beginning at about the age of 15, it is diagnosed in a considerable number of young people. About twice as many females as males are found to be seriously depressed, and depression continues to rise slowly as young women enter adulthood.

Source: Hankin et al., 1998.

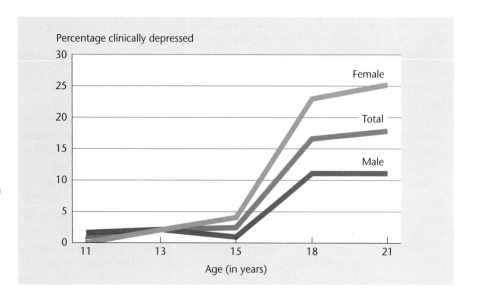

about 10,000 individuals attempt suicide and of those, 1,000 succeed each year. Roughly 3 percent of older adolescent girls and 1 percent of boys make at least one serious suicide attempt. About 17 percent of high-school students seriously considered suicide; 13 percent made specific suicide plans (Centers for Disease Control and Prevention, 2007). Females are much more likely to attempt, but also fail, at suicide than are males. One reason is that females more often use such methods as overdosing with drugs or poisons or suffocation, whereas males tend to use methods that have faster and surer results, such as shooting, or explosives.

Culture plays a role in suicide as well as age and gender. Suicide rates are high in countries such as Japan, where there is a long history of viewing suicide as an honourable option. In Muslim and Catholic countries, where suicide is viewed as a violation of religious teachings, rates are low. In North America, Native youth have high rates of suicide; one study found the rate to be five times higher than the rate for youth in the general population (Chandler et al., 2003). Many factors, including poverty, loss of their traditional culture, limited educational and job opportunities, and alcohol and drug use, contribute to these elevated rates. Among inner-city African North American and Latino North American gangs, suicide rates are rising as well (Rotherman-Borus et al., 2000). Although depression and suicide are often linked, they do not always go together (Jellinek & Snyder, 1998). In one large study of adolescents, 42 percent of those who attempted suicide did *not* have a history of depression (Andrews & Lewinsohn, 1992). Suicide is related to a general sense of overwhelming hopelessness, although it also may result from the accumulation of adverse life events such as family conflicts; loss of a family member due to illness, death, or divorce; breakups or problems in romantic relationships or friendships; school failure; being apprehended in a delinquent, forbidden, or embarrassing act or situation; or real or imagined mental or physical illness (Jellinek & Snyder, 1998). Similarly, Peter and colleagues (2008) found that suicidal ideation among Canadian youth was related to factors such as the ability to communicate feelings, negative attachment to parents, bullying or abuse, and the presence of deviant peers. Adolescents who attempt suicide often feel they have no source of emotional support. They frequently are alienated from their families and may have had disruptions or losses in close relations with girlfriends, boyfriends, or other peers that give them an increasing sense of isolation and helplessness.

CAUSES OF CHILDHOOD DEPRESSION   Theories of the etiology of depression are abundant. Like many human disorders, depression is very likely caused by multiple factors. Thus, in discussing biological, social and psychological, and cognitive theories, we look not for one answer but for many, and we seek to learn how such contributing factors interact.

Biological Theories   Biological theories of the cause of depression have focused more on adults than on children (Taube-Schiff & Lau, 2008). Although a causal role has not been demonstrated, evidence has linked depression among adults with low levels of chemicals that facilitate the transmission of neural impulses (Jacobs, 2004). Similar biochemical evidence has not been consistently obtained in depressed children (Wicks-Nelson & Israel, 2000). However, by the age of 3, children of chronically depressed parents showed lower activation in a variety of brain regions than children of non-depressed mothers (Embry & Dawson, 2002). Infants of mothers who were depressed, but whose depression improved, showed normal brain activity at 3 years of age. This suggests that environmental factors play a role in early depression and in early brain development as well. It seems likely that environmental factors play a considerable role in childhood depression (Cummings et al., 2000). The relative contributions of family interaction and genetic influences remain an open question (Gotlib et al, 2006; Hops, 2001; Silberg et al., 2001).

Social and Psychological Theories   One of the earliest theories of the causes of childhood depression linked it to the loss of maternal affection or failure to form a secure attachment (Bowlby, 1960). Although some research has supported this position, other factors, such as parental conflict, maternal depression, negative life events, lack of effective social supports, and, especially for girls, problems with peers and unpopularity, have been linked with depression in children (Cummings et al., 2000; Hammen, 2005).

The link between depression in parents and children has received considerable attention in the research literature. Depression is more likely to occur in children of clinically depressed parents (Cicchetti & Toth, 2006; Goodman & Gotlib, 2002). Indeed, children of depressed parents are at risk for higher rates not only of depression but of a wide range of other disorders such as anxiety, academic failure, ADHD, and conduct disorders, especially if the parent's depression is chronic or sustained (Elgar et al., 2007; Embry & Dawson, 2002; Hammen, 2005; Weissman et al., 1997). Although twin and adoption studies indicate that this association between depression in children and parents may be in part genetic, other studies show that the experiences of children with a depressed mother may differ from those with a non-depressed mother. Depressed mothers are more tense, disorganized, resentful, and ambivalent, and less sensitive, communicative, and affectionate with their children (Cummings et al., 2000; NICHD Early Child Care Research Network, 1999). Furthermore, they are likelier to perceive their children's behaviour negatively (Hammen, 2005). It is not surprising, then, that children of depressed mothers are likelier to be insecurely attached, fearful, and lower in self-esteem and to have problems in subsequent social relations (Cicchetti & Toth, 2006; Lyons-Ruth et al., 2002).

It is not just mothers who contribute to children's depression. Jacob and Johnson (1997) found that both paternal and maternal depression were associated with child depression. As family systems theory would predict, when one parent is depressed, the marital relationship suffers, and this, in turn, leads to inadequate parenting. Peers can play a role in children's mental health, too. Elementary schoolchildren who were socially anxious (shy, inhibited) and who were excluded by their peers were at higher risk for depression than non-anxious and better-accepted classmates (Gazelle and Ladd, 2003). Life stressors also contribute to depression (Hammen, 2005). Finally, cultural expectations emphasizing achievement, success, and wealth may contribute to the emergence of depression if children fail to meet these expectations. Box 15.3 on the next pages discusses this and other problems facing even affluent youth in North American society.

A mother's depression and listlessness may lead the child to become depressed later on. Disruption in early attachment, as well as modelling, may contribute to the link between parent and child depression.

Box 15.3

Risk and Resilience

DOES A CULTURE OF AFFLUENCE PROTECT CHILDREN AND YOUTH FROM THE RISK OF PSYCHOPATHOLOGY?

In many Western cultures, such as those of Canada and the United States, affluence and the acquisition of material goods are revered. But does wealth buy happiness and protect children from developing psychological problems?

> According to surveys, in spite of historical trends that show that Americans have far more luxuries than they had in the 1950s, with twice as many cars per person and microwave ovens, VCRs, air conditioners, and color TVs, they are no more satisfied with their lives. (Diener, 2000; cited by Luthar, 2003)

The divorce rate has doubled. Teen suicide has tripled. Depression rates have soared. This conjunction of material prosperity and social recession has been called *the American Paradox* (Myers, 2000). From a Canadian perspective, we could just as easily call this *the North American Paradox*.

But what about children? Are they not better off growing up in the relative affluence of suburban life, as compared with children and adolescents who grow up in poverty in the inner cities? Are suburban youth not happier and less likely to suffer from psychological problems such as depression, delinquency, and substance abuse? A study of nearly 1,000 US teenagers revealed a negative relation between parents' socio-economic status and ado-

lescents' happiness (Csikszentmihalyi & Schneider, 2000). Rich youth are not only less happy, but they may be at risk for a variety of mental health problems. It is not just the poor, the disadvantaged, and members of minority cultures who are at risk for psychopathology. Also, privileged children from wealthy homes tend to be at risk for alcohol and illegal drug abuse.

Suniya Luthar (Luthar, 2003, 2006a; Luthar & Latendresse, 2005) has directed her attention to the high cost of affluence for North American youth. In a sample of grade 10 students in an affluent suburban community, she found that suburban youth reported significantly higher levels of anxiety symptoms, and of cigarette, alcohol, marijuana, and hard-drug use than did their economically disadvantaged, inner-city peers. Compared with national samples, more than one in five suburban girls (22 percent) reported clinically significant depressive symptoms—rates three times as high as those in normative samples (7 percent). Rates of clinically significant anxiety among boys (22 percent) and girls (26 percent) were higher than national average rates for boys (17 percent) and girls (21 percent). Similarly, when compared with national samples, affluent young people displayed a higher frequency of substance abuse, particularly of alcohol and among girls (72 percent during

---

learned helplessness

A kind of behaviour that results from the belief that one is helpless to control the events in one's world.

Cognitive Theories   An alternative theoretical explanation of depression invokes the concept of **learned helplessness**, a kind of behaviour that results from the belief that one is helpless to control the events in one's world (Seligman, 1974). The learned helplessness theory of depression proposes that depressed people not only experience feelings of helplessness but also attribute their failures in controlling the world to enduring personal shortcomings. Essentially, this cognitive theory asserts that people become depressed when they perceive themselves as having failed to achieve desired outcomes in their lives (Garber & Martin, 2002).

TREATING CHILDHOOD DEPRESSION   Children and adolescents with depressive disorders benefit from a wide range of interventions (Abela & Hankin, 2008). Antidepressant drugs such as fluoxetine (Prozac) and sertraline (Zoloft) are widely prescribed and somewhat effective. In one study, 56 percent of children with major depression improved with Prozac compared with only 33 percent of a placebo control group (Emslie et al., 1997). Unfortunately, antidepressant drugs are dangerous, and an overdose can be lethal (Gelfand & Drew, 2003). In 2004, the US government began to require that warning labels accompany these antidepressant drugs in light of the increased risk of suicide associated with their use in a small percentage of adolescents. However, the rates of suicide showed a sharp increase at the same time that the

the past year versus 61 percent in normative samples) and of illicit drug use among affluent boys (rates of 59 versus 38 percent).

Moreover, the reasons for substance use differed for rich and poor adolescents. For affluent teens, substance use and maladjustment (anxiety, depression) were related, whereas there were no links between adjustment and drug use among poor adolescents. Affluent adolescents appear to use drugs as a way of "self-medicating" in order to relieve their anxiety and depression. This is particularly troubling because adolescents who use drugs as mood regulators are more likely to continue to be regular users in later adolescence and adulthood (Zucker et al., 1995). Moreover, peer groups in affluent, suburban settings were more likely than inner-city peer groups to endorse substance use among boys. Peer popularity was linked with high substance use among boys of higher socio-economic status, but among inner-city boys, it was not linked.

There are several reasons for these patterns. First, affluent youth are under high pressure to achieve, and that pressure takes its toll on their adjustment. Adolescents who were rated high in perfectionistic strivings had elevated distress and delinquency scores that, in turn, were linked with substance use. Second, ado-

lescents' lack of closeness to their mothers was linked to distress, delinquency, and substance abuse for both boys and girls. Third, minimal after-school supervision was related to girls' distress, delinquency, and substance abuse. In sum, the combination of excessively high expectations and isolation from adults in wealthy families puts affluent youth at risk of having drug and alcohol problems. Clearly, being rich is not a protective factor, and it may be a risk factor for these forms of developmental ills.

Are there factors that protect children from the parental and peer pressures that affluent children may encounter? There are three types of factors that can do this: positive abilities in the child (high intelligence, high self-esteem), a supportive family environment (even one warm and supportive parent), and helpful individuals outside the family (in schools, peer groups, or places of worship) (Luthar, 2006b, Werner, 1995). The effect of these protective factors is not automatic, however. Protection does not lie in the availability of supportive resources but in the child's use of them. Thus, children's own strengths make an extremely important contribution to the resilience they show in the face of risk and to whether they develop as healthy children or become plagued by psychological problems.

use of antidepressants among adolescents declined, which suggests that parents need to be aware of warning signs of suicide whether their teens are on antidepressant drugs or not (Center for Disease Control and Prevention, 2007).

Cognitive behaviour therapy is one of the most effective approaches for treating depression in adolescents (Hammen, 2005). This type of therapy is typically conducted in small groups of three to eight adolescents twice a week over a number of weeks. The goals are to reduce the teenagers' self-consciousness and feelings of being different and to provide them with strategies such as relaxation techniques and self-control tactics to help them control their dark moods. The therapy also emphasizes positive strategies such as improving peer relations, setting realistic goals, and learning how to get more fun out of activities. Results have been impressive. In one series of studies, between 54 and 67 percent of treated adolescents no longer met the *DSM* criteria for depression (Clarke et al., 1992; Lewinsohn & Rohde, 1993). Among teenagers with similar depressive problems who were on a waiting list for therapy and served as controls, only 5 to 48 percent no longer met the criteria. Unfortunately, nearly one-third of adolescents treated with cognitive behaviour therapy experienced recurrence within two years (Birmaher et al., 2000).

Prevention programs have been effective in reducing depression, too. In one study, children at risk for depression were given training in cognitive and problem-solving skills (Gillham et al., 1995). Two years later, when researchers evaluated these children, they found fewer depressive symptoms than in a control group.

cognitive behaviour therapy

A group therapy technique particularly useful in treating depression in adolescents. Therapeutic goals include reducing self-consciousness and feelings of being different and teaching strategies for dealing with depressive moods and for acquiring a more positive outlook and improving social interactions.

🔵7 Autism Spectrum Disorders

autistic disorder

A disorder in which children's ability to communicate and interact socially is seriously impaired; children with autism have specific language deficiencies, demonstrate a need for sameness in their environment, and often engage in repetitive and stereotyped kinds of behaviours.

Autism has the following puzzling and disturbing characteristics:

- *Extreme autistic aloneness*, expressed as a lack of interest in other people that sometimes appears to be an actual aversion to contact with other human beings.

- *Language abnormalities*, ranging from non-speech to repeating others' exact words rather than replying or engaging in conversation.

- *Attempts to preserve sameness* in the environment that may lead to repetitive behaviours or total and extended concentration on something like a spinning top.

Pauli displayed many of these behaviours.

Asperger's disorder shares some of the social and affective deficits associated with autism. However, children with Asperger's do not show significant language delays and are often able to progress in school at a satisfactory rate (Bennett et al., 2008; Pennington, 2005; Volkmar et al., 2004). Currently, autism and Asperger's syndrome are viewed as part of a broader diagnostic category of autism spectrum disorders (ASD).

How prevalent are these disorders? Although a decade ago, estimates ranged from 4 to 5 per 10,000 individuals (American Psychiatric Association, 2000; Patterson & Rafferty, 2001), rates of ASD have increased, owing not only to better detection but also to the use of broader diagnostic criteria that increase the number of children being labelled as part of the autistic spectrum (Baron-Cohen, 2007). Current estimated rates of ASD range between 3 and 7 for every 1,000 children between ages 3 to 10, which suggests that this is a more common disorder than was previously thought (Centers for Disease Control, 2007). These disorders are more common in boys than in girls; the ratio is 3 to 5 boys to 1 girl (American Psychiatric Association, 2000).

It is difficult to imagine just how disturbed an autistic child is, but once you have observed one of these less fortunate children, the memory will last forever. If two children with autism are placed side by side in a room full of toys, chances are that they will ignore each other. They seem to prefer inanimate objects to human interaction. Autistic children often avoid eye contact with others and fail to modulate social interaction in any way. Often, they appear to be unaware of other people and even of themselves. Some autistic children seem not to recognize themselves as independent social beings (Dawson et al., 1998). Children normally develop the ability to recognize their mirror images as themselves around the age of 2. Children with autism show deficits in self-recognition. When researchers in one study showed autistic children a mirror, 31 percent failed to demonstrate recognition of their mirror images (Spiker & Ricks, 1984). These children also were likely to lack speech. However, even the children who showed self-recognition demonstrated little emotional response—unlike normal children.

Children with autism often fail to develop a useful means of communication with others, whether verbal or nonverbal. Such children may be highly resistant to change and to new patterns of behaviour. At the same time, because these children often seem to prefer inanimate objects to human interaction, psychologists are exploring the approach of teaching children with autism to communicate by means of a computer.

Researchers using subtle measures of attention, such as heart rate, have shown that autistic children are aware of the presence of other people, (Baron-Cohen, 1995). However, they may not reflect this knowledge in their overt behaviour. Many autistic children manifest a lack of attachment and empathy in social relations. They also seem unable to understand that mental states such as knowledge, beliefs, and expectations exist and are connected to people's behaviour (Baron-Cohen, 1995, 2003; Konstantareas, 2006; Siegler & Alibali, 2005). This lack of a theory of mind makes it difficult for autistic children to anticipate and predict others' responses and, thus, makes it hard for them to engage in effective social interactions. Most autistic children fail to develop normal friendships and become social isolates (American Psychiatric Association, 2000; Baron-Cohen, 2003).

Children with autism display deficits in both non-verbal and verbal communication. They have difficulty understanding facial expressions of emotion and integrating or using gestures such as those meaning "be quiet" or "come here" or "look" (Baron-Cohen, 2003, 2007). They are less likely than non-autistic children to respond when called by name or to respond to an adult's point and gaze (Dawson et al., 2004). They display less attention to the distress of another person. In addition, some 50 percent of

autistic children never develop meaningful, useful speech, and most others have limited and sometimes bizarre means of verbal expression.

Many children with autism master only a few of the tasks necessary to function in the world and need constant help with feeding, dressing, toileting, and cleaning. Although their senses function adequately when tested, children with autism behave as if they have sensory deficits. For example, they spend their time engaging in **obsessive self-stimulatory behaviour** such as repetitively spinning objects, switching lights on and off, or flapping their hands in front of their eyes (Pennington, 2005). It is thought that the primary purpose of this bizarre-appearing behaviour may be to provide sensory stimulation.

Some children with autism show a type of intelligence traditionally associated with the *savant*. This is a person who has some unusual talent—particularly in the area of mathematical and computer abilities—such as being able to quickly and accurately predict the day of the week on which some date far in the future will fall. Some children with autism perform feats showing remarkable memory, such as being able to repeat television commercials verbatim. However, about 70 percent of children with autism score in the retarded range on commonly used measures of intelligence, and this below-average performance is quite stable over time (Kauffman, 2001).

CAUSES OF AUTISM
At present, the cause of autism is unknown. Some investigators once suggested that the cause might be of psychological origin and attributed the disorder to parents who were cold and aloof. Scientists who held this view described parents of children with autism as "refrigerator parents" who thawed out just long enough to conceive a child. Such assertions were unfounded and have created unnecessary guilt and anxiety among the parents of children with autism. If these parents seem somewhat distant from their children, it is most likely to be a reaction to their child's social aversion. Furthermore, the onset of the disorder comes so early in life that it hardly seems likely a disorder as severe as autism could be caused by parents' "unconscious rejection" of their child.

Currently, it is almost universally accepted that autism has a biological cause yet to be specified. Twin studies have implicated genetics, finding a higher incidence of the disorder in monozygotic than in dizygotic twins (Nigg & Goldsmith, 1994; Rutter, 2007). In one study, the concordance rate for autism in monozygotic twins was 60 percent, whereas for dizyotic twins, it was only 5 percent (Bailey et al., 1995), indicating that autism is one of the most heritable of psychiatric disorders. In addition, a larger percentage of families than would be expected by chance (2 percent) have two or more children with autism. Chromosomal abnormalities have also been found in some children with autism (Drew et al., 1996) as well as alterations in brain chemistry (Dawson & Sterling, 2007).

Although biology is clearly a factor in the development of autism, environmental factors play a role as well. There are wide differences in autistic symptoms within monozygotic twin pairs, which suggests that environmental influences play a role in shaping the form that autism will assume (Pennington, 2005; Rutter, 2007). It has also been suggested that exposure to toxic metals such as mercury may contribute to or trigger autism. Research on this important topic is continuing.

TREATING AUTISTIC DISORDER
Autism is a difficult disorder to treat. Professionals treating children with autism have increasingly used medications—especially those designed to reduce serotonin levels—but although such medications have shown moderate success in reducing some problem behaviours, such as hyperactivity, they have not succeeded in dealing with the core symptoms, primarily self-injurious behaviour (Myers, 2007). Moreover, these medications are often accompanied by adverse side effects (Drew & Hardman, 2000). Of the host of treatments tried, **operant behaviour therapy** appears to be most effective (Clarke, 2001; McEachin et al., 1993). By carefully monitoring the autistic child's behaviour, and by systematically rewarding appropriate behaviour with such things as food, operant-behaviour-therapy programs have been quite successful in teaching children with autism basic self-care

obsessive self-stimulatory behaviour

Behaviour common in children with autism in which they engage in repetitive actions that seemingly have no purpose.

operant behaviour therapy

A form of behaviour therapy in which behaviour is carefully monitored and consistently rewarded with such things as food.

skills. Unfortunately, though, these time-consuming treatments usually leave children with autism still performing well below the normal range (Clarke, 2001). Such techniques have not been successful in teaching generalizable language skills (Cantwell et al., 1978; Lovaas & Smith, 1988). Teaching sign language rather than oral speech, intervening at earlier ages, involving parents in training programs, and working with children in their natural environment are more effective (Clarke, 2001).

For Thought and Discussion

1. What are the implications of the fact that the different methods of classifying child psychopathology, the diagnostic and empirical approaches, sometimes disagree in terms of their classifications? To your mind, does this undermine the reliability of these classifications?

2. One of the interesting aspects of the *DSM-IV* classification system is that it is organic. That is, the system is continually being updated and changed, with some disorders added, others deleted, and still others modified in certain ways. What are the implications of such a changing system for our understanding of psychopathology? Does the fact that the system can change like this have any significance for how we understand abnormality more generally?

3. All of the various disorders discussed (conduct disorders, attention deficit/hyperactivity disorders, depression, autism spectrum disorders) have multiple proposed causes. Do you believe that these are all-or-none, or can more than one potential cause be responsible for the disorder? If multiple causes are possible, why might some causes be operating in some cases, but other causes in other situations?

Making the Connections 15

There are many links between concepts and ideas in one area of development and concepts and ideas in other areas. Here are some of the connections between ideas in Chapter 15 and discussions in other chapters of this book.

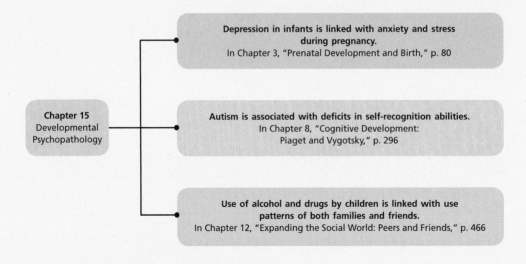

Chapter 15
Developmental
Psychopathology

Depression in infants is linked with anxiety and stress during pregnancy.
In Chapter 3, "Prenatal Development and Birth," p. 80

Autism is associated with deficits in self-recognition abilities.
In Chapter 8, "Cognitive Development:
Piaget and Vygotsky," p. 296

Use of alcohol and drugs by children is linked with use patterns of both families and friends.
In Chapter 12, "Expanding the Social World: Peers and Friends," p. 466

SUMMARY

- Children exhibit a wide array of problem behaviours, some of which are relatively common and others quite rare. Many of these behaviours are marked by either a lack of control or excessive internalizing of troublesome issues.

The Developmental Approach to Psychopathology

- **Developmental psychopathology** involves the study of the origins, changes, and continuities in maladaptive behaviour over the lifespan. The four basic principles of developmental psychopathology are (1) the role of development must be considered in interpreting the symptoms of a disorder and in seeking to understand its origins and course; (2) psychopathology must be viewed in relation both to the child's normal development and to the developmental tasks of children of her age; (3) the earliest precursors of disordered behaviour must be studied; and (4) there are multiple pathways to both normal and abnormal behaviour.

What is Abnormal?

- Most researchers and clinicians think that developmental psychopathology is best thought of as problems in living. The medical model's view of problems as pathological may obscure the role of social judgments that depend on cultural and individual values. The statistical model views as abnormal any behaviours or feelings that differ from the average. Abnormality may also be defined as "deviation from the ideal."
- Children are usually referred to mental health professionals by their parents or other adults, and factors other than the child's behaviour may influence the referring adult's judgment about the child. Three kinds of factors that may influence the adult's perceptions are the child's characteristics, characteristics of the referring adult, and characteristics of the child's environment.
- Whether or not a particular behaviour is viewed as normal depends on the child's age and the likelihood that it will continue over time. Some problems, such as bedwetting, decline with age; others, such as nightmares, increase until adolescence and then decline. However, some childhood disorders are associated with later adult dysfunction.

Classifying Child Psychopathology

- Two major ways of assessing and classifying developmental psychopathology are the *diagnostic approach* and the *empirical method*. Diagnoses are based on descriptions of clusters of behaviours and disturbing thoughts or feelings classified into various diagnostic categories. A **diagnosis** must convey information about the **etiology** and course of a disorder to be useful. The most widely used diagnostic classification system is the American Psychiatric Association's *DSM-IV*. Although this system has been revised several times, it still presents problems of reliability and validity.
- **Diagnostic reliability** is crucial in a classification system. The empirical approach involves having adults familiar with the child rate a large number of problem behaviours and then use statistical techniques to determine which disorders are related.
- **Undercontrolled disorders**, such as conduct and attention deficit/hyperactivity disorders, are the most frequently reported of all psychological problems of childhood and have considerable impact on the child's social environment. **Overcontrolled disorders**, such as childhood depression, have a greater effect on children themselves, who bottle up their feelings and concerns. Children with **pervasive developmental disorders** such as autism are characterized by gross deficits and extreme disturbances.

Some Psychological Disorders that Affect Children

- Children with either socialized or unsocialized **conduct disorders** repeatedly violate the rights of others or age-appropriate societal norms. Children who violate the law are termed **delinquent** and run the risk of being charged with either **status** or **criminal offences**. Young offenders commit a sizable percentage of major offences, and they are also often the victims of violent crime. **Substance abuse**, one kind of conduct disorder, began an upswing in the 1990s. European North American youths are more likely than Latino or African North American adolescents to use legal and illegal drugs, although the data may not include youths who are dropouts or absent from school. Personal factors, such as anxiety and depression, are significant causes of drug abuse, and the common pathway to abuse starts with legal drugs such as alcohol and tobacco.
- Behavioural techniques, including reinforcement of appropriate behaviour and the **time-out** method, are among the most successful treatments for conduct disorders. Prevention programs that involve both family and school show promise.

- **Attention deficit/hyperactivity disorder (ADHD)**, often not diagnosed until children enter the structured environment of school, is characterized by overactivity, impulsivity, poor attention, and difficulties with rule-governed behaviour. Although the inappropriate activity of hyperactive children tends to diminish with age, some problems may persist, resulting in poor academic performance.
- Biological influences on aggression include genetic, temperamental, and hormonal factors. All of these factors find expression in interaction with the environment.
- Biological explanations for this disorder include minimal brain damage and a genetic component. Environmental explanations, such as dysfunctional parent–child interaction patterns, have received some research support. At present, it appears that hyperactivity may have multiple causes. It is often treated by **psychostimulant medications**, **behaviour therapy**, or a combination of the two.
- **Depression in childhood** may be characterized by downcast mood, changes in cognitive functioning such as inability to concentrate, behavioural signs such as irritability and crankiness, and such physical problems as loss of appetite and weight loss. Depression in children is hard to diagnose because children may not be able or willing to talk about feelings of overwhelming sadness until they have reached a certain level of cognitive maturity.
- Diagnoses of depression increase dramatically in adolescence, as does the rate of suicidal thinking and actual suicide attempts. A number of causes of depression have been hypothesized. Biological theories emphasize genetic and biochemical causes. Social and psychological theories suggest such causes as maternal depression and parental conflict. Cognitive theories suggest that feelings of personal inadequacy, or **learned helplessness**, may lead to depression. Antidepressant drugs and **cognitive behaviour therapy** are effective treatments for childhood depression.

- The most widely recognized pervasive developmental disorder is **autistic disorder**, which is characterized by a lack of interest in other people, various language abnormalities, and an intense desire to preserve sameness in the environment. **Obsessive self-stimulation** may be seen as an effort to control sensory stimulation.
- Children with autism sometimes exhibit specific talents in mathematics or the ability to repeat television commercials verbatim, but they score in the retarded range on IQ tests.
- The cause of autism is thought to be biological. Treatment, which has included medication and **operant behaviour therapy**, has met with limited success. Although treatment allows the children to develop many skills they would not otherwise acquire, their range of abilities remains quite limited.

www.mcgrawhillconnect.ca

Epilogue

Throughout this book, we have reviewed the results of many studies of children's development. Beginning in our first chapter, we have described and critiqued theories that attempt to explain and interpret the detailed and highly complex information amassed by theorists and researchers in their effort to understand child development. We have also identified and discussed the themes of development that we introduced in Chapter 1. Although psychology's understanding of children's development is vast, much remains that we do not yet understand. As society and culture change, the process of development also changes. As is true in any field of science, our information is constantly expanding and changing. Child development is a vibrant and exciting area of study, and we are sure you will agree that advancing our knowledge and understanding of the field can contribute substantially to the betterment of society and to the healthy development of children everywhere.

We realize that much of the information discussed in this book will be re-examined and modified in the near future. With this in mind, we have identified some broad principles that characterize, first, our views on the current state of psychology's knowledge about child development and, second, our ideas about knowledge that is on the horizon. In this connection, we make some suggestions about what the field needs to do with respect to both building theory and selecting the kinds of research methods that will make it possible to secure this developing knowledge.

Michael Escoffery (contemporary). *Circle of Love* (1996). Private collection.

OUR KNOWLEDGE OF CHILD DEVELOPMENT AT PRESENT

1. **The child is competent.** Recent years have seen a dramatic change in our view of the capacities of children. Scientists once viewed infants and young children to be helpless, passive creatures who, with limited sensory, perceptual, and social capacities, were simply awaiting the imprint of the adult world. In contrast, today's child psychologists view children as competent and active beings who, from an early age, possess a wide range of perceptual, motoric, cognitive, and social capacities. For example, recent research on early concept development suggests that infants have a greater understanding of the world than was previously realized.

2. **The child's behaviour is organized.** From the very beginning of children's lives, organization is evident in their behaviour. Actions such as sucking and looking are not disorganized reflexes or reactions but highly structured response patterns that enable even newborns to interact with, and to learn from, the social and physical world. Behavioural organization is evident throughout life; for example,

recent research indicates that, with development, children process information in more organized and strategic ways.

3. **The different aspects of psychological development are interdependent.** Although developmentalists often focus on distinct areas of growth such as social, emotional, physical, linguistic, and cognitive development, all of these areas overlap and exert mutual influence on each other. Recent research that integrates social, emotional, and cognitive development has revealed ways in which these aspects of development contribute to and shape each other over time.

4. **The child's behaviour has multiple causes.** Current understanding of development stresses that most behaviours have multiple causes and that causation often involves interaction among biological, environmental, and experiential factors. For example, how and when genetic predispositions are expressed depend on the environmental conditions in a child's life.

5. **There is no single pathway to normal or abnormal development.** Children may take alternative routes to normal development; no single pathway is necessarily the "best" one to follow. It is a well-established observation that individual adults who are intellectually and socially competent often have reached their goals by very different routes. Children's development is profoundly influenced both by varying kinds of experiences and by the timing of these experiences. At one time or another, a child may confront a risk with greater or lesser resilience. Moreover, these same principles hold true with respect to development that is less than ideal: Children whose lives become dysfunctional to one degree or another may reach this state by a variety of pathways.

6. **The child's development is generally continuous but is marked by periods of more rapid and dramatic changes.** These periods of change are often marked by the onset of biological and social changes, such as puberty and school transitions, or by unexpected or non-normative events, such as the loss of a friendship, a parent, or parental employment—or even the occurrence of a natural disaster. In addition, the characterization of development as continuous or discontinuous depends, in part, on how closely we look. A detailed examination reveals that even though developmental progress is, in the main, quite gradual, periods of rapid developmental advance sometimes occur. For example, children have rapid periods of growth and weight followed by periods of little or no change.

7. **Development is a lifelong process.** Although we focus in this book on the development of the child, it is important to recognize that the adults who are influential in a child's development continue to learn and grow throughout their own lives—physically, socially, emotionally, and cognitively. As human beings in every stage of the life cycle, we respond to, learn from, and change through experiences of many kinds. So, to understand children, we need to recognize that their development occurs in the context of the continuing development experienced by their parents, teachers, and by other socializing agents.

8. **The child influences other people.** As children grow, they influence the behaviour of the adults and children with whom they interact. Even infants play an active role in modifying the behaviours of their parents and others by smiling and crying. As children get older and they interact with parents and other adults in problem-solving activities, the behaviours children display inform more experienced partners as to how to help children participate in ways that support their learning needs. Now widely accepted, this *bidirectional* view of development underscores the fact that children play an influential part in their own development.

9. **The child's behaviour varies across situations and settings.** One important feature of human behaviour is the ability to adapt to the demands of different

situations. The same child may behave in numerous ways with different people or in different situations—in the home, the laboratory, the school, or the peer play group. We need, then, to study children in multiple settings and to exercise caution in generalizing our interpretations of children's behaviours from one situation to another.

10. **The child's behaviour is influenced by social systems.** The child is embedded in a variety of systems, and the members of these systems influence one another's behaviour. Social systems range from the smaller and more immediate, such as the family or the peer group, to the larger and more remote, such as the school, the community, the media, or the greater society. The child may have considerable influence in smaller systems but often has less control in larger ones.

11. **Child development occurs in a cultural context.** Cultural contributions to development are important and complex. In multicultural societies like Canada, because cultural systems range from the ethnic neighbourhood to the broader culture of the society at large, children experience a number of cultural influences. In other societies, in which most members share a similar cultural background, this cultural context greatly influences the developing child. In all types of cultural settings, tensions among the generations may evolve as elders expect younger people to carry on valued cultural traditions and the young may resist these expectations. To achieve a full understanding of child development, we need to pay attention to both *intercultural* and *intracultural* variations in children's experience.

12. **Children develop in a historical context.** As social conditions shift, children and families undergo changes that alter their behaviour. The experiences of children who grew up in the Great Depression of the 1930s differed dramatically from those of children growing up in the twenty-first century. The changes in gender roles that occurred in the mid- and late-twentieth century have greatly affected family lifestyles. When both parents work outside the home and household labour is divided differently, children's lives are altered, too. As contact with cultures around the world continues to increase through media, travel, immigration, trade, and other forms of globalization, these experiences will undoubtedly have a huge influence on child development in the Western World. One of the aims of child psychology is to examine these and other changes so as to determine how they affect children's behaviour.

KNOWLEDGE ON THE HORIZON

1. **Child psychologists need to employ multiple research methods.** In examining the complex and multi-faceted aspects of children's development, we cannot rely on any single research method. A wide variety of methods, including naturalistic observations, laboratory and field experiments, self-reports, clinical studies, genetic and neurological measures, and standardized tests, can provide us with different types of information about children. In addition, we need to gather information from the many different people who interact with children, including parents, peers, and teachers. With the information that each of these people can provide and the unique perspectives that each offers, we will gain a broader and deeper understanding of the developing child.

2. **Child psychologists need multiple samples.** To fully understand how children grow and develop, we need to select multiple samples in our research. Doing so will enable us to capture the cultural and ethnic richness—the diversity—of children's development, both within Canada and throughout the world.

3. **Child psychologists need multiple theories of development.** Theories like those of Piaget, Freud, and Vygotsky—theories that attempt to provide a full and comprehensive account of development—have inspired a great deal of useful research. Contemporary psychologists believe, however, that the complex and multi-determined nature of development requires us to explain smaller pieces of the developmental puzzle before we attempt to assemble an all-encompassing theory. Thus, today's developmental psychologists are likelier to advance theories of more specific phenomena—such as gender typing, memory function, aggression, or language development—than to formulate the kinds of grand theories that were put forward during much of the twentieth century.

4. **A full understanding of child development will require a multi-disciplinary effort.** Many scientific disciplines besides child psychology contribute in important ways to our understanding of children. For example, anthropology provides a cross-cultural perspective on child socialization, and sociology offers a societal viewpoint on the systems and institutions that children experience. Pediatrics illuminates the role of physical health in the child's development, while clinical psychology and psychiatry offer an understanding of deviant and abnormal development. Also, history views children's development through the lens of time. Multi-disciplinary approaches are increasingly common in studies of children's development, as they are in other areas of scientific study.

5. **Child development research influences, and is influenced by, social policy.** As we have stressed throughout this book, research in child development and the application of its findings are closely linked. For example, basic research on the importance of development of children's early environment stimulated government efforts (e.g., Aboriginal Head Start and the Human Early Learning Partnership of British Columbia, among others) and the growth of child-care programs. Child psychologists are actively involved in issues of concern to society, such as poverty, problems of family breakdown, schooling that accommodates different cultural styles of learning, and the influence of violent and sexual content on television and in other media, including the Internet, on the growing child. It is both an opportunity and a responsibility for experts in the child development field to contribute to the formation and evaluation of social policy that improves the lives of children.

Glossary

accommodation Modifying an existing way of responding to the environment to fit the characteristics of a new experience. Page 302

achievement motivation A person's tendency to strive for successful performance, to evaluate her performance against standards of excellence, and to feel pleasure at having performed successfully. Page 408

acquired immune deficiency syndrome (AIDS) A viral disease that attacks the body's immune systems; transmitted to a fetus or newborn by the *human immunodeficiency virus (HIV)*, this disorder weakens the child's immune system and may ultimately cause death. Page 102

active genetic–environmental interaction A kind of interaction in which people's genes encourage them to seek out experience compatible with their inherited tendencies. Page 67

adaptation The individual's tendency to adjust to environmental demands. Page 302

age cohort People born within the same generation. Page 17

age of viability The age of 22–26 weeks from conception, by which point the fetus's physical systems are well enough advanced that it has a chance at survival if born prematurely. Page 86

aggression Behaviour that intentionally harms other people by inflicting pain or injury on them. Page 560

aggressive rejected children *Rejected* children who are characterized by high levels of aggressive behaviour, low self-control, and behavioural problems. Page 475

allele An alternative form of a gene; typically, a gene has two alleles, one inherited from the individual's mother and one from the father. Page 48

alphafetoprotein assay (AFP) A blood test performed prenatally to detect such problems as Down syndrome,

the presence of multiple embryos, and defects of the central nervous system. Page 61

altruism An unselfish concern for the welfare of others. Page 552

altruistic behaviour Intrinsically motivated behaviour that is intended to help others without expectation of acknowledgement or concrete reward. Page 552

amniocentesis A technique for sampling and assessing fetal cells for indications of abnormalities in the developing fetus; performed by inserting a needle through the abdominal wall and into the amniotic sac and withdrawing a small amount of the amniotic fluid. Page 60

amniotic sac A membrane containing a watery fluid that encloses the developing organism, protecting it from physical shocks and temperature changes. Page 85

androgyny A normal state of being for many people who possess a notable number of both masculine and feminine psychological characteristics. Children who are more androgynous make less stereotypical play and activity choices. Page 531

animistic thinking The attribution of life to inanimate objects. Page 309

anorexia nervosa An eating disorder in which the person, usually a young woman, is preoccupied with avoiding obesity and often diets to the point of starvation. Page 184

approach-avoidance behaviour A pattern of interaction in which the infant or child shows an inconsistent pattern of approaching and retreating from a person or an object. Page 232

assimilation Moulding a new experience to fit an existing way of responding to the environment. Page 302

associative learning According to Arthur Jensen, lower-level learning tapped in tests of such things as short-term memorization and recall, attention, rote learning, and simple

associative skills. Also called *level I learning*. Page 396

attachment A strong emotional bond that forms between infant and caregiver in the second half of the child's first year. Page 219

Attachment Q-Sort (AQS) An assessment method in which a caregiver or observer judges the quality of a child's attachment on the basis of the child's behaviour in naturalistic situations, often including brief separations from parents. Page 227

attention The identification and selection of particular sensory input for more detailed processing. Page 347

attention deficit/hyperactivity disorder (ADHD) A childhood disorder characterized by a persistent pattern of inattention and hyperactivity or impulsivity that far exceeds such behaviours observed in children at comparable levels of development. Page 596

auditory localization The ability to determine from where in space a sound is originating. Page 134

authoritarian parenting Parenting that is harsh, unresponsive, and rigid, and in which parents tend to use power-assertive methods of control. Page 431

authoritative parenting Parenting that is warm, responsive, and involved yet unintrusive, and in which parents set reasonable limits and expect appropriately mature behaviour from their children. Page 431

autistic disorder A disorder in which children's ability to communicate and interact socially is seriously impaired; children with autism have specific language deficiencies, demonstrate a need for sameness in their environment, and often engage in repetitive and stereotyped kinds of behaviours. Page 606

autobiographical memory A collection of memories of things that have happened to a person at a specific time or place. Page 362

automatization The process of transforming conscious, controlled behaviours into unconscious and automatic ones. Page 345

autosomes The 22 paired non-sex chromosomes in males and females that determine the development of most body structures and attributes. Page 46

autostimulation theory The theory that during REM sleep the infant's brain stimulates itself and that this, in turn, stimulates early development of the central nervous system. Page 122

average children Children who have some friends but are not as well liked as popular children. Page 475

babbling An infant's production of strings of consonant–vowel combinations. Page 267

basic reflex activity An infant's exercise of and growing proficiency in the use of innate reflexes. Page 304

Bayley Scales of Infant Development (BSID) Non-verbal tests that measure specific developmental milestones and that are generally used with children who are thought to be at risk for abnormal development. Page 389

behaviourism A school of psychology that holds that theories of behaviour must be based on direct observations of actual behaviour and not on speculations about such unobservable things as human motives. Page 12

behaviour therapy A psychological form of treatment, often used in treating conduct disorders, that is based on such learning principles as reinforcement and social learning. Page 600

bilingualism The acquisition of two languages. Page 289

Brazelton Neonatal Assessment Scale A scale used to measure an infant's sensory and perceptual capabilities, motor development, range of states, and ability to regulate these states. The scale also indicates whether the brain and the central nervous system are properly regulating autonomic responsivity. Page 125

bulimia nervosa An eating disorder in which people, usually young women, alternate periods of binge eating with vomiting and other means of compensating for the weight gained. Page 184

caesarean delivery The surgical delivery of a baby, whereby the baby is removed from the mother's uterus through an incision made in her abdomen and uterus; also known as Caesarean section. Page 105

canalization The genetic restriction of a phenotype to a small number of developmental outcomes, permitting environmental influences to play only a small role in these outcomes. Page 64

case study method A form of research in which investigators study individual persons. Page 30

catch-up growth The tendency for human beings to regain a normal course of physical growth after injury or deprivation. Page 178

categorical speech perception The tendency to perceive as the same a range of sounds belonging to the same phonemic group. Page 265

catharsis Presumably, discharging aggressive impulses by engaging in actual or symbolic aggressive acts that do not impinge on another person. Page 570

centration Centring one's attention on only one dimension or characteristic of an object or situation. Page 314

centre care An arrangement in which children are cared for in a "school-like" environment by professional caregivers. Page 243

cephalocaudal The pattern of human physical growth in which development begins in the area of the brain and proceeds downward, to the trunk and legs. Page 85

cephalocaudal development The notion that human physical growth occurs from the head downwards— that is, from brain and neck to trunk and legs. Page 174

cerebral cortex The covering layer of the cerebrum that contains the cells that control specific functions, such as seeing, hearing, moving, and thinking. Page 156

cerebrum The two connected hemispheres of the brain. Page 156

child development A field of study that seeks to account for the gradual evolution of the child's cognitive, social, and other capacities first by describing changes in the child's observed behaviours and then by uncovering the processes and strategies that underlie these changes. Page 4

chlamydia Probably the most widespread bacterial sexually transmitted disease; can cause pneumonia or a form of conjunctivitis in a pregnant woman's baby. Page 102

chorionic villi sampling A technique for sampling and assessing cells withdrawn from the chorionic villi, which are projections from the chorion that surrounds the amniotic sac; cells are withdrawn either through a tube inserted into the uterus through the vagina or through a needle inserted through the abdominal wall. Page 60

chromosomes Thread-like structures, located in the central portion, or nucleus, of a cell, that carry genetic information to help direct development. Page 44

chronosystem In Bronfenbrenner's ecological theory, the time-based dimension that can alter the operation of all other levels, from microsystem through macrosystem. Page 17

classical conditioning A type of learning in which individuals learn to respond to unfamiliar stimuli in the same way they are accustomed to respond to familiar stimuli if the two stimuli are repeatedly presented together. Page 12

clique A voluntary group formed on the basis of friendship. Page 496

co-dominance A genetic pattern in which heterozygous alleles express the variants of the trait for which they code simultaneously and with equal force. Page 48

cognition The mental activity through which human beings acquire and process knowledge. Page 298

cognitive behaviour therapy A group therapy technique particularly useful in treating depression in adolescents. Therapeutic goals include reducing self-consciousness and feelings of being different and teaching strategies for dealing with depressive moods and for acquiring a more positive outlook and improving social interactions. Page 605

cognitive developmental theory of gender typing Lawrence Kohlberg's theory that children use physical and behavioural clues to differentiate gender roles and to gender-type themselves very early in life. Page 515

cognitive developmental view of attachment The view that to form attachments, infants must differentiate between mother and stranger and must understand that people exist independently of their interaction with them. Page 220

cognitive learning According to Arthur Jensen, higher-level learning tapped in tests of such things as abstract thinking, the use of symbolic processes, conceptual learning, and the use of language in problem solving. Also called *level II learning*. Page 397

cognitive map A cognitive representation of the spatial layout of a physical or geographical place. Page 368

cognitive processes Ways that the human mental system operates on information. Page 344

cognitive social learning theory A learning theory that stresses learning by observation and imitation mediated by cognitive processes and skills. Page 13

colic A prolonged period of unexplained crying in an infant. Page 124

communicative competence The ability to convey thoughts, feelings, and intentions in an organized, culturally patterned way that sustains and regulates human interactions. Page 253

community of learners An approach to classroom learning in which adults and children work together in shared activities, peers learn from each other, and the teacher serves as a guide. Page 328

comorbidity The co-occurrence of two or more problem behaviours. Page 591

concrete operations stage Period in which the child acquires such concepts as conservation and classification and can reason logically. Page 314

conduct disorder A disorder characterized by a repetitive and persistent pattern of behaviour in which a young person violates the basic rights of others or major age-appropriate societal norms or rules. Page 592

congenital Describing deficits or defects that the child incurs in the womb or during the birth process. Page 398

connectionist models Information-processing approaches that describe mental processes in terms of the interconnections of the neural network. Page 343

conscience The child's internalized values and standards of behaviour. Page 551

conservation The understanding that altering an object's or a substance's appearance does not change its basic attributes or properties. Page 312

constructivist view The idea that children actively create their understanding of the world as they encounter new information and have new experiences. Page 299

control group In a formal experiment, the group that is not exposed to the treatment, that is, the independent variable. Page 28

control phase According to Kopp, the first phase in learning self-regulation, when children are highly dependent on caregivers to remind them about acceptable behaviours. Page 550

controversial children Children who are liked by many peers but also disliked by many. Page 475

conventional level Kohlberg's second level of moral development, in which the child's behaviour is designed to solicit others' approval and maintain good relations with them. The child accepts societal regulations unquestioningly and judges behaviour as good if it conforms to these rules. Page 541

converging operations A research strategy, in which a variety of research techniques are used to investigate or converge upon a particular experimental or research result. Page 26

cooing A very young infant's production of vowel-like sounds. Page 267

coordination of secondary schemata An infant's combination of different schemes to achieve a specific goal. Page 304

co-parenting Parenting in which spouses work together as a team, coordinating their child-rearing practices with each other; co-parenting can be co-operative, hostile, or characterized by different levels of investment in the parenting task. Page 437

core knowledge systems Ways of reasoning about ecologically important objects and events, such as the solidity and continuity of objects. Page 306

corpus callosum The band of nerve fibres that connects the two hemispheres of the brain. Page 162

correlational method A research design that permits investigators to establish relations among variables as well as the strength of those relations. Page 27

creativity The ability to solve problems, create products, or pose questions in a way that is novel or unique; also, the ability to envision new problems not yet recognized by others and to come up with solutions to them. Page 417

criminal offence An illegal act. Page 593

critical period A specific period in children's development when they are sensitive to a particular environmental stimulus that does not have the same effect on them when encountered before or after this period. Page 256

crossing over The process by which equivalent sections of homologous chromosomes switch places randomly, shuffling the genetic information each carries. Page 46

cross-sectional method A method of research in which researchers compare groups of individuals of different age levels at approximately the same point in time. Page 32

crowd A collection of people whose shared attitudes or activities have been designated by a stereotypical term, such as *populars* or *nerds*. Page 497

culture-fair test A test that attempts to minimize cultural biases in content that might influence the test taker's responses. Page 388

cumulative risk The notion that risk factors in children's life circumstances have cumulative negative effects on their intellectual performance. Page 403

deductive reasoning Logical thinking that involves reaching a necessary and valid conclusion based on a set of premises. Page 371

deferred imitation Mimicry of an action some time after having observed it; requires that the child has stored a mental image of the action. Page 306

delay gratification Putting off until another time possessing or doing something that gives one pleasure. Page 550

delinquency Juvenile behaviour in violation of the law. Page 592

deoxyribonucleic acid (DNA) A ladder-like molecule that stores genetic information in cells and transmits it during reproduction. Page 46

dependent variable The variable, or factor, that researchers expect to change as a function of change in the independent variable. Page 29

depression in childhood Like adult depression, a mood disorder often manifested in a downbeat mood and loss of interest in familiar activities but also likely to be expressed as irritability and crankiness. Difficulty concentrating or focusing on tasks and concomitant drops in school grades are not uncommon, and children with depression often complain of physical problems such as headaches or stomachaches. Page 600

deviation IQ An IQ score that indicates the extent to which a person's performance on a test deviates from age-mates' average performance. Page 390

developmental psychopathology The investigation of the origins, course, changes, and continuities in disordered or maladaptive behaviour over a person's lifespan. Page 581

diagnosis The identification of a physical or mental disorder on the basis of symptoms and of knowledge of the cause or causes of the disorder and its common course. A diagnosis may also include information about effective forms of treatment. Page 589

diagnostic reliability A measure of how often two or more clinicians arrive independently at the same diagnosis of a particular disorder. Page 589

diethylstilbestrol (DES) A synthetic hormone once prescribed to pregnant women to prevent miscarriages but discontinued when cancer and pre-cancerous conditions were detected in the children of such women. Page 94

direct observation A method of observation in which researchers go into settings in the natural world or bring participants into the laboratory to observe behaviours of interest. Page 24

discourse Socially based conversation. Page 286

dizygotic Characterizing fraternal twins, who have developed from two separate fertilized eggs. Page 70

dominance hierarchy An ordering of individuals in a group from most to least dominant; a "pecking order." Page 496

dominant Describing the more powerful of two alleles in a heterozygous combination. Page 48

Down syndrome A form of chromosome abnormality, in which the person suffers disabling physical and mental development and is highly susceptible to such illnesses as leukemia, heart disorders, and respiratory infections. Page 54

dynamic systems theory A theory that proposes that individuals develop and function within systems and that studies the relationships among individuals and systems and the processes by which these relationships operate. Page 14

dyslexia A term for the difficulties experienced by some people in reading or learning to read. Page 164

ecological theory A theory of development that stresses the importance of understanding not only the relationships between the organism and various environmental systems but the relations between such systems themselves. Page 16

ecological validity The degree to which a research study accurately represents events and processes that occur in the natural world. Page 29

ego In Freudian theory, the rational, controlling component of the personality, which tries to satisfy needs through appropriate, socially acceptable behaviours. Page 10

egocentric speech According to Vygotsky, a form of self-directed dialogue by which the child instructs herself in solving problems and formulating plans; as the child matures, this becomes internalized as *inner speech*. Page 333

egocentrism The tendency to view the world from one's own perspective and to have difficulty seeing things from another's viewpoint. Page 309

elaboration A memory strategy in which one adds to information to make it more meaningful and, thus, easier to place in long-term memory. Page 356

elementary mental functions Functions which the child is endowed with by nature, including attention, perception, and memory. Page 327

embryo The developing organism between the second and eighth weeks of gestation; the period of the embryo comprises the differentiation of the major physiological structures and systems. Page 85

emotional display rules Rules that dictate which emotions one may appropriately display in particular situations. Page 214

emotional script A complex scheme that enables a child to identify the emotional reaction that is likely to accompany a particular sort of event. Page 215

emotions Subjective reactions to something in the environment that are usually experienced cognitively as either pleasant or unpleasant, that are generally accompanied by physiological changes, and that are often expressed in some form of visible behaviour. Page 196

empathy/empathic The capacity to experience the same emotion that someone else is experiencing. Pages 538 and 555

encoding The transformation of information from the environment into a lasting mental representation. Page 345

ends-over-means focus Consideration of only the end state of a problem in evaluating an event; failure to consider the means by which that end state was obtained. Page 312

episodic memory Memory for specific events, often autobiographical in nature. Page 352

estrogens Hormones that, in the female, are responsible for sexual maturation. Page 188

ethological theory A theory that holds that behaviour must be viewed and understood as occurring in a particular context and as having adaptive or survival value. Page 18

ethological theory of attachment Bowlby's theory that attachment derives from the biological preparation of both infant and parents to respond to each other's behaviours in such a way that parents provide the infant with care and protection. Page 221

etiology In medicine and psychiatry, the cause or causes of a specific disorder. Page 589

evocative genetic–environmental interaction The expression of the gene's influence on the environment through an individual's inherited tendencies to evoke certain environmental responses. Page 67

evocative influences When inherited tendencies evoke certain responses from others, thus shaping their social environment. Page 75

evolutionary psychology An approach which holds that critical components of psychological functioning reflect evolutionary changes and are critical to the survival of the species. Page 18

executive control process A cognitive process that serves to control, guide, and monitor the success of a problem-solving approach a child uses. Page 346

executive control structure According to Robbie Case, a mental blueprint or plan for solving a class of problems. Page 343

exosystem In Bronfenbrenner's ecological theory, the collection of settings that impinge on a child's development but in which the child does not play a direct role. Page 17

expansion A technique adults use in speaking to young children in which they imitate and expand or add to a child's statement. Page 262

experimental group In a formal experiment, the group that is exposed to the treatment, that is, the independent variable. Page 28

expressive characteristics Presumably typical of females, these characteristics include nurturance and concern with feelings. Page 511

extended family Typically, a family that includes many relatives, such as grandparents, aunts, uncles, nieces, and nephews, within the basic family unit of parents and children. Page 445

external validity The degree to which the results of an experiment can be easily generalized outside the immediate context of the study. Page 25

factor analysis A statistical procedure used to determine which of a number of factors or scores are both closely related to each other and relatively independent of other groups of factors or scores. Page 384

fagan test of infant intelligence A test of how infants process information, including encoding attributes of objects and seeing similarities and differences across objects. Page 389

family child care An arrangement in which an individual cares for three or four children in her home. Page 243

fetal alcohol spectrum disorder (FAsd) An umbrella term used to describe the range of effects associated with prenatal exposure to alcohol. Page 91

fetal alcohol syndrome (FAS) A disorder exhibited by infants of alcoholic mothers and characterized by stunted growth, a number of physical and physiological abnormalities and, often, mental retardation. Page 91

fetus The developing organism from the third month of gestation through delivery; during the fetal period, development of bodily structures and systems becomes complete. Page 86

field experiment An experiment in which researchers deliberately create a change in a real-world setting and then measure the outcome of their manipulation. Page 29

Flynn Effect The general trend toward an increase in average IQ test scores across subsequent generations of the twentieth century. Page 395

formal operations stage The period in which the child becomes capable of flexible and abstract thought, complex reasoning, and hypothesis testing. Page 315

fragile X syndrome A form of chromosome abnormality, more common in males than in females, in which an X chromosome is narrowed in some areas, causing it to be fragile and leading to a variety of physical, psychological, and social problems. Page 57

friendship A reciprocal commitment between two people who see themselves as relative equals. Page 488

gender-based beliefs Ideas and expectations about what is appropriate behaviour for males and females. Page 505

gender constancy The awareness that superficial alterations in appearance or activity do not alter gender. Page 516

gender identity The perception of oneself as either masculine or feminine. Page 505

gender-role preferences Desires to possess certain gender-typical characteristics. Page 505

gender roles Composites of the behaviours actually exhibited by a typical male or female in a given culture; the reflection of a gender stereotype in everyday life. Page 505

gender-schema theory The notion that children develop schemas, or naive theories, that help them to organize and structure their experience related to gender differences and gender roles. Page 518

gender stability The notion that gender does not change; males remain male and females remain female. Page 516

gender stereotypes Beliefs that members of a culture hold about how females and males ought to behave, that is, what behaviours are acceptable and appropriate for each. Page 505

gender typing The process by which children acquire the values, motives, and behaviours considered appropriate for their gender in their particular culture. Page 505

gene A portion of DNA that is located at a particular site on a chromosome and that codes for the production of certain kinds of proteins. Page 47

general factor (g) General mental energy or ability that is involved in all cognitive tasks. Page 384

generalization The application of a strategy learned while solving a problem in one situation to a similar problem in a new situation. Page 345

genital herpes A common viral infection spread through sexual contact; if contracted by an infant during birth, it can cause blindness, motor abnormalities, mental retardation, and a wide range of neurological disorders. Page 102

genotype The particular set of genes that a person inherits from her parents. Page 44

gestation The carrying of an embryo or fetus during pregnancy, usually for nine months in humans. Page 85

glial cell A nerve cell that supports and protects neurons and serves to encase them in sheaths of *myelin*. Page 158

gonorrhea A sexually transmitted bacterial infection, which in a pregnant woman, can cause blindness in her infant; normally treatable with antibiotics. Page 101

goodness of fit A measure of the degree to which a child's temperament is matched by her environment. The more effectively parents and other agents of socialization accept and adapt to the child's unique temperament, the better this "fit." Page 75

grammar The structure of a language; made up of morphology and syntax. Page 254

guided participation Learning that occurs as children participate in activities of their community and are guided in their participation by the actions of more experienced partners in the setting. Page 329

habituation The process by which an individual reacts with less and less intensity to a repeatedly presented stimulus, eventually responding only faintly or not at all. Page 132

Head Start A federally funded program, started in the United States, that pro-vides disadvantaged young children with preschool experience, social services, and medical and nutritional assistance. Page 411

hedonistic reasoning Making a decision to perform a prosocial act on the basis of expected material reward. Page 559

hemispheres The two, left and right, halves of the brain's cerebrum. Page 162

hemispheric specialization Differential functioning of the two cerebral hemispheres; for example, the control of speech and language by the left hemisphere and of visual-spatial processing by the right. Page 162

hemophilia A disorder caused by an X-linked recessive gene, in which the blood fails to clot; found more often in males than in females. Page 49

heritability factor A statistical estimate of the contribution made by heredity to a particular trait or ability. Page 68

heterozygous Describing the state of an individual whose alleles for a particular trait from each parent are different. Page 48

hierarchical categorization The organization of concepts into levels of abstraction that range from the specific to the general. Page 372

higher mental functions Functions that rely on mediators that have become increasingly sophisticated through the child's interaction with his environment. Page 327

holophrase A single word that appears to represent a complete thought. Page 276

homozygous Describing the state of an individual whose alleles for a particular trait from each parent are the same. Page 48

horizontal décalage The term Piaget used to describe unevenness in children's thinking within a particular stage; for example, in developing an understanding of conservation, children conserve different objects or substances at different ages. Page 324

hormone A powerful and highly specialized chemical substance that interacts with cells capable of receiving the hormonal message and responding to it. Page 187

hostile aggression Aggressive behaviour directed at another person, including criticizing, ridiculing, and name calling. Page 561

human behaviour genetics The study of the relative influences of heredity and environmental forces on the evolution of individual differences in traits and abilities. Page 68

Huntington disease A genetically caused, fatal disorder of the nervous system that begins in mid-adulthood and is manifested chiefly in uncontrollable, spasmodic movements of the body and limbs and eventual mental deterioration. Page 61

id In Freudian theory, the person's instinctual drives; the first component of the personality to evolve, the id operates on the basis of the pleasure principle. Page 10

identification The Freudian notion that children acquire gender identity by identifying with and imitating their same-sex parents. Page 504

immanent justice The notion that any deviation from rules will inevitably result in punishment or retribution. Page 539

imprinting The process by which birds and other infrahuman animals develop a preference for the person or object to which they are first exposed during a brief, critical period after birth. Page 221

inclusion A policy by which children of all ability levels, whether learning disabled, physically handicapped, or mentally retarded, are included in the same classroom. Page 417

independent variable The variable, or factor, that researchers deliberately manipulate in a formal experiment. Page 29

infant-directed speech/child-directed speech A simplified style of speech parents use with young children, in which sentences are short, simple, and often repetitive; the speaker enunciates especially clearly, slowly, and in a higher-pitched voice and often ends with a rising intonation. Also called *motherese*. Page 261

infant state A recurring pattern of arousal in the newborn, ranging from alert, vigorous, wakeful activity to quiet, regular sleep. Page 120

information-processing approach A perspective on cognition and cognitive development in which the human mind is likened to a computer, processing information from the environment through perception and attention (input), encoding it in memory (storage and retrieval), and applying information to the solution of problems (software). Page 340

information-processing approaches Theories of development that focus on the flow of information through the child's cognitive system and particularly on the specific operations the child performs between input and stimulus phases. Page 13

informed consent Agreement to participate in a research study that is based on a clear and full understanding of the purposes and procedures of that study. Page 37

inner speech Internalized egocentric speech that continues to direct and regulate intellectual functioning. Page 333

insecure-avoidant attachment A type of attachment shown by babies who seem not to be bothered by their mothers' brief absence but specifically avoid them on their return, sometimes becoming visibly upset. Page 225

insecure-disorganized attachment A type of attachment shown by babies who seem disorganized and disoriented when reunited with their mothers after a brief separation. Page 226

insecure-resistant attachment A kind of attachment shown by babies who tend to become very upset at the departure of their mothers and who exhibit inconsistent behaviour on their mothers' return, sometimes seeking contact, sometimes pushing their mothers away. Page 226

instrumental aggression Quarrelling and fighting over toys and possessions. Page 561

instrumental characteristics Presumably typical of males, these characteristics include task and occupation orientation. Page 511

intellectual giftedness A characteristic defined by an IQ score of 130 or over; gifted children learn faster than others and may show early exceptional talents in certain areas. Page 415

intelligence quotient (IQ) An index of the way a person performs on a standardized intelligence test relative to the way others her age perform. Page 388

intent community participation Children's participation in the authentic activities of their community with the purpose of learning about the activity. Page 329

interactive synchrony A term that characterizes mother–infant interactions in which the mother constantly adjusts her behaviour to that of her baby, responding to and respecting his signals as to when he is ready for and wants engagement and interaction. Page 232

intermodal perception The use of sensory information from more than one modality to identify a stimulus; also, the apprehension of a stimulus already identified by one modality by means of another. Page 145

internal working model According to Bowlby, a person's mental representation of herself as a child, of her parents, and of the nature of her interaction with her parents, as she reconstructs and interprets that interaction. Page 234

intuitive substage The second substage of the preoperational period, during which the child begins to solve problems by means of specific mental operations but cannot yet explain how she arrives at the solutions. Page 311

inventing new means by mental combination In this last stage of the sensorimotor period, children begin to combine schemes mentally, thus relying less on physical trial and error. Page 305

iron-deficiency anemia A disorder in which inadequate amounts of iron in the diet cause listlessness and may retard a child's physical and intellectual development. Page 177

joint legal custody A form of child custody in which both parents retain and share responsibility for decisions regarding the child's life but which generally provides for the child to reside with one parent. Page 453

joint physical custody As in joint legal custody, parents make decisions

together regarding their child's life, but they also share physical custody, the child living with each parent for a portion of the year. Page 453

joint visual attention The ability to follow another person's attentional focus or gaze of direction. Page 264

Kaufman Assessment Battery for Children (K-ABC) An intelligence test designed to measure several types of information-processing skills as well as achievement in some academic subjects. Page 392

Klinefelter's syndrome A form of chromosome abnormality, in which a male inherits an extra X sex chromosome, resulting in the XXY pattern, and has many feminine physical characteristics as well as language deficits and, sometimes, mental retardation. Page 57

laboratory experiment A research design that allows investigators, through controlling variables and treatments and assigning participants randomly to treatments, to determine cause and effect. Page 28

language A communication system in which words and their written symbols combine in various, regulated ways to produce an infinite number of messages. Page 253

language-acquisition device (LAD) Chomsky's proposed mental structure in the human nervous system that incorporates an innate concept of language. Page 256

language-acquisition support system (LASS) According to Jerome Bruner, a collection of strategies and tactics that environmental influences—initially, a child's parents or primary caregivers—provide the language-learning child. Page 260

lanugo A fine, soft hair that covers the fetus's body from about the fifth month of gestation on; may be shed before birth or after. Page 86

latchkey children Children who must let themselves into their homes after school because a parent or both parents are working outside their home. Page 449

lateralization The process by which each half of the brain becomes specialized for the performance of certain functions. Page 162

learned helplessness A kind of behaviour that results from the belief that one is helpless to control the events in one's world. Page 604

learning disabilities Deficits in one or more cognitive processes important for learning. Page 415

learning theory of attachment The theory that infants become attached to the mother because she provides food, or primary reinforcement, and, thus, she acquires secondary-reinforcement properties. Page 220

lifespan perspective A theory that sees development as a process that continues throughout the life cycle, from infancy through adulthood and old age. Page 17

longitudinal method A method of research in which investigators study the same people repeatedly at various times in the participants' lives. Page 33

long-term memory The mental processing unit in which information may be stored permanently and from which it may later be retrieved. Page 342

macrosystem The system that surrounds the microsystem, mesosystem, and exosystem, and that represents the values, ideologies, and laws of the society or culture. Page 17

maturation A genetically determined process of growth that unfolds naturally over a period of time. Page 6

mediation deficiency Inability to use strategies to store information in long-term memory. Page 357

mediators According to Vygotsky, psychological tools and signs, such as language, counting, mnemonic devices, algebraic symbols, art, and writing. Page 327

meiosis The process by which a germ cell divides to produce new germ cells with only half the normal complement of chromosomes; thus, male and female germ cells (sperm and ovum) each contain only 23 chromosomes so that when they unite, the new organism they form will have 46 chromosomes, half from each parent. Page 45

memory span The amount of information one can hold in short-term memory. Page 352

menarche In females, the beginning of the menstrual cycle. Page 188

mental age An index of a child's actual performance on an intelligence test as compared with her true age. Page 390

mental representation Information stored in some form (e.g., verbal, pictorial) in the cognitive system after the person has encountered it in the environment. Page 345

mental retardation A characteristic defined by an IQ score below 70 and the inability to cope adequately with age-appropriate activities in everyday life. Page 415

mesosystem The interrelations that occur among the components of the microsystem with which the child interacts. Page 17

metacognition The individual's knowledge about knowing and her control of cognitive activities. Page 377

metalinguistic awareness The understanding that language is a system of communicating with others that is bound by rules. Page 288

microgenetic analysis A very detailed examination of how a child solves a problem. Page 341

microgenetic change Changes associated with learning that occur over the time of a specific learning experience or episode. Page 334

microsystem In Bronfenbrenner's ecological theory, the context in which children live and interact with the people and institutions closest to them, such as parents, peers, and school. Page 17

miscarriage The natural or spontaneous end of a pregnancy before the infant is capable of survival outside the womb and generally defined in humans as prior to 20 weeks gestation. Page 85

mitosis The process in which a body cell divides in two, first duplicating its chromosomes so that the new, daughter cells contain the usual 46 chromosomes. Page 46

modifier genes Genes that exert their influence indirectly, by affecting the expression of still other genes. Page 50

monozygotic Characterizing identical twins, who have developed from a single fertilized egg. Page 70

moral realism Piaget's second stage of moral development, in which the child shows great respect for rules but applies them quite inflexibly. Page 539

morality of reciprocity Piaget's third stage of moral development, in which the child recognizes that rules may be questioned and altered, considers the feelings and views of others, and believes in equal justice for all. Page 539

morpheme Any of a language's smallest units of meaning, such as a prefix, a suffix, or a root word. Page 254

morphology The study of a language's smallest units of meaning, or morphemes. Page 254

multi-schematic children Children who hold more than one gender schema for responding to the world. Page 532

multi-store model A model of information processing in which information is depicted as moving through a series of processing units—sensory register, short-term memory, and long-term memory—in each of which it may be stored, either fleetingly or permanently. Page 341

mutual antipathy A relationship of mutual dislike between two people. Page 492

myelination The process by which glial cells encase neurons in sheaths of the fatty substance *myelin*. Page 159

naming explosion The rapid increase in vocabulary that the child typically shows at about 1½ years of age. Page 268

narrative form A temporally sequenced account that conveys meaning about an event. Page 362

national survey A method of sampling in which a very large, nationally representative group of people are selected for a particular study. Page 22

natural experiment An experiment in which researchers measure the results of events that occur naturally in the real world. Page 30

needs-oriented reasoning Reasoning in which children express concern for others' needs even though their own needs may conflict with the needs of others. Page 559

negative gossip Sharing with a peer some negative information about another child. Page 491

neglected children Children who tend to be socially isolated and, though they have few friends, are not necessarily disliked by others. Page 475

neonate A newborn baby. Page 118

neo-Piagetian theories Theories of cognitive development that reinterpret Piaget's concepts from an information processing context. Page 343

neural migration The movement of neurons within the brain that ensures that all brain areas have a sufficient number of neural connections. Page 159

neuron A cell in the body's nervous system, consisting of a cell body, a long projection called an axon, and several shorter projections called dendrites; neurons send and receive neural impulses, or messages, throughout the brain and nervous system. Page 158

neuron proliferation The rapid proliferation of neurons in the developing organism's brain. Page 158

neuronal death The death of some neurons that surround newly formed synaptic connections among other neurons. Page 159

niche picking Seeking out or creating environments that are compatible with one's own (genetically based) predispositions. Page 67

non-aggressive rejected children Rejected children who tend to be withdrawn, anxious, and socially unskilled. Page 475

non-shared environment A set of conditions or activities that is experienced by one child in a family and not shared with another child in the same family. Page 70

nucleotide A compound containing a nitrogen base, a simple sugar, and a phosphate group. Page 47

obesity A condition in which a person's weight is 30 percent or more in excess of the average weight for his or her height and frame. Page 179

object permanence The notion that entities external to the child, such as objects and people, continue to exist independently of the child's seeing or interacting with them. Page 302

observer bias The tendency of researchers/observers to be influenced in their judgments by their knowledge of the hypotheses guiding the research. Page 30

obsessive self-stimulatory behaviour Behaviour common in children with autism in which they engage in repetitive actions that seemingly have no purpose. Page 607

operant behaviour therapy A form of behaviour therapy in which behaviour is carefully monitored and consistently rewarded with such things as food. Page 607

operant conditioning A type of learning in which learning depends on the consequences of behaviour; rewards increase the likelihood that a behaviour will recur, whereas punishment decreases that likelihood. Page 12

operations Schemes based on internal mental activities. Page 300

organization (a) Combining simple mental structures into more complex systems. (b) Ordering information to be remembered by means of categorization and hierarchical relationships Pages 299 (a) and 355 (b)

overcontrolled disorders A group of psychological disturbances in which a child withdraws from others, lacks spontaneity, and generally appears to be an unhappy child. Page 591

overextension The use, by a young child, of a single word to cover many different things. Page 274

overregularization The mistaken application of a principle of regular change to a word that changes irregularly. Page 281

ovum The female germ cell, or egg. Page 44

passive genetic–environmental interaction The interactive environment created by parents with particular genetic predispositions who encourage the expression of these tendencies in their children. Page 67

patterned speech A form of pseudo-speech in which the child utters strings of phonemes that sound very much like real speech but are not. Page 267

peer-group network The cluster of peer acquaintances who are familiar with and interact with one another at different times for common play or task-oriented purposes. Page 494

perception The interpretation of sensations in order to make them meaningful. Page 129

permissive parenting Parenting that is lax and in which parents exercise inconsistent discipline and encourage children to express their impulses freely. Page 431

pervasive developmental disorders Childhood disorders characterized by gross deficits in many areas of cognitive, emotional, and social development that are linked with severe and pervasive impairment of social interaction and communication skills. Page 592

phenotype Created by the interaction of a person's genotype, or genetic makeup, with the environment; the visible expression of the person's particular physical and behavioural characteristics. Page 44

phenylketonuria (PKU) A disease caused by a recessive allele that fails to produce an enzyme necessary to metabolize the protein phenylalanine; if untreated immediately at birth, it damages the nervous system and causes mental retardation. Page 53

phoneme Any of the basic units of a language's phonetic system; phonemes are the smallest sound units that affect meaning. Page 253

phonological awareness The understanding of the sounds of a language and of the properties, such as the number of sounds in a word, related to these sounds. Page 288

phonology The system of sounds that a particular language uses. Page 253

Piagetian theory A theory of cognitive development that sees the child as actively seeking new information and incorporating it into his knowledge base through the processes of assimilation and accommodation. Page 11

pituitary gland A so-called master gland, located at the base of the brain, which triggers the secretion of hormones by all other hormone-secreting, or endocrine, glands. Page 186

placenta A fleshy, disc-like structure formed by cells from the lining of the uterus and from the zygote, and that, together with the *umbilical cord*, serves to protect and sustain the life of the growing organism. Page 85

planning The deliberate organization of a sequence of actions oriented toward achieving a goal. Page 350

plasticity The capacity of the brain, particularly in its developmental stages, to respond and adapt to input from the external environment. Page 165

popular children Children who are liked by many peers and disliked by very few. Page 475

post-conventional level Kohlberg's third level of moral development, in which the child's judgments are rational and his conduct is controlled by an internalized ethical code that is relatively independent of the approval or disapproval of others. Page 541

pragmatics A set of rules that specifies appropriate language for particular social contexts. Page 254

preconceptual substage The first substage of Piaget's preoperational period, during which the child's thought is characterized by animistic thinking and egocentricity. Page 309

pre-conventional level Kohlberg's first level of moral development, in which he views the child's behaviour as based on the desire to avoid punishment and gain rewards. Page 541

premoral stage Piaget's first stage of moral development, in which the child shows little concern for rules. Page 539

preoperational period In this period, the symbolic function promotes the learning of language; the period is also marked by egocentricity and intuitive behaviour, in which the child can solve problems using mental operations but cannot explain how she did so. Page 309

preterm A term describing a premature baby born before its due date and whose weight, although less than that of a full-term infant, may be appropriate to its gestational age. Page 108

primary circular reactions Behaviours in which infants repeat and modify actions that focus on their own bod-

ies and that are pleasurable and satisfying. Page 304

proactive aggression The use of force to dominate another person or to bully or threaten others. Page 561

problem solving The identification of a goal and of steps to reach that goal. Page 363

production deficiency Inability to generate and spontaneously use memory strategies that one knows. Page 357

productive language The production of speech. Page 253

progesterone A hormone that, in females, helps regulate the menstrual cycle and prepares the uterus to receive and nurture a fertilized egg. Page 188

propositional reasoning Logical thinking that involves evaluating a statement or set of statements based on the information in the statement alone. Page 371

prosocial behaviour Behaviour that is designed to help or benefit other people. Page 552

prosocial reasoning Thinking and making judgments about prosocial issues. Page 558

proteins Proteins are fundamental components of all living cells, and are any of a group of complex organic molecules containing carbon, hydrogen, oxygen, nitrogen, and usually sulphur, and that are composed of one or more chains of amino acids. Page 47

proto-declarative A gesture that an infant uses to call attention to an object. Page 264

proto-imperative A gesture that an infant or a young child may use to get someone to do something she or he wants. Page 264

proximal-distal The pattern of human physical growth wherein development starts in central areas, such as the internal organs, and proceeds to more distant areas, such as arms and legs. Page 85

proximal-distal pattern The tendency for human physical development to occur from the centre outwards; for example, from internal organs to arms and legs. Page 174

psychoanalytic theory of attachment The Freudian theory that babies

become attached first to the mother's breast and then to the mother herself as a source of oral gratification. Page 220

psychodynamic theory Freud's theory that development, which proceeds in discrete stages, is determined largely by biologically based drives shaped by encounters with the environment and through the interaction of three components of personality—the id, ego, and superego. Page 10

psychometrician A psychologist who specializes in the construction and use of tests designed to measure various psychological constructs, such as intelligence, motivation, achievement orientation, and personality characteristics. Page 392

psychosocial theory Erikson's theory of development that sees children developing through a series of stages largely through accomplishing tasks that involve them in interaction with their social environment. Page 11

psychostimulant medications Drugs, such as amphetamines and caffeine, that increase alertness and attention as well as psychomotor activity. Page 598

puberty The onset of sexual maturity. Page 186

random assignment The technique by which researchers assign individuals randomly to either an experimental or a control group. Page 28

range of reaction The notion that the human being's genetic makeup establishes a range of possible developmental outcomes, within which environmental forces largely determine how the person actually develops. Page 63

reactive aggression Aggression in response to attack, threat, or frustration. Page 561

recast A technique adults use in speaking to young children in which they render a child's incomplete sentence in a more complex grammatical form. Page 262

receptive language Understanding the speech of others. Page 253

recessive Describing the weaker of two alleles in a heterozygous combination. Page 48

reciprocal instruction A tutoring approach based on the ideas of the *zone of proximal development* and *scaffolding*. Page 328

recovery The ability to recognize a new stimulus as novel and to direct attention to it in preference to a familiar stimulus. Page 393

reflex A human being's involuntary response to external stimulation. Page 118

reflex smile A newborn infant's smile, which appears to reflect some internal stimulus, such as a change in the infant's level of arousal, rather than an external stimulus, such as another person's behaviour. Page 200

rehearsal A memory strategy in which one repeats a number of times, either mentally or orally, the information one wants to remember. Page 354

rejected children Children who are disliked by many peers and liked by very few. Page 475

relational aggression Damaging or destroying interpersonal relationships by such means as excluding another or gossiping about or spoiling another's reputation. Page 564

relationship A succession of interactions between two people who know each other that is altered by their shared, past interactions and that also affects their future interactions. Page 471

reliability The degree to which a test yields consistent results over successive administrations. Page 393

REM and non-REM sleep REM, or rapid-eye-movement, sleep is characterized by rapid, jerky movements of the eyes and, in adults, is often associated with dreaming; infants spend 50 percent of their sleep in REM activity, whereas adults spend only about 20 percent. This activity is absent in the remaining, non-REM sleep. Page 122

representativeness The degree to which a sample actually possesses the characteristics of the larger population it represents. Page 22

reputational bias Children's tendency to interpret peers' behaviour on the basis of past encounters with and feeling about them. Page 484

respiratory distress syndrome A condition of the newborn marked by laboured breathing and a bluish discolouration of the skin or mucous membranes, and which often leads to death. Page 86

reversibility The notion that one can reverse or undo a given operation, either physically or mentally. Page 312

Rh factor incompatibility A condition in which an infant's Rh negative blood opposes his mother's Rh positive blood, and threatens fetuses in second and third trimesters and later births when the mother's body has had time to produce antibodies that will attack fetal blood cells. Page 101

sample A group of individuals who are representative of a larger population. Page 22

scaffolding Based on Vygotsky's thought, an instructional process in which the teacher continually adjusts the amount and type of support he offers as the child continues to develop more sophisticated skills. Page 328

schema/schemas An organized unit of knowledge that the child uses to try to understand a situation; a schema forms the basis for organizing actions to respond to the environment. Page 299

scientific method The use of measurable and replicable techniques in framing hypotheses and collecting and analyzing data to test a theory's usefulness. Page 21

script A mental representation of an event or situation of daily life, including the expected order in which things happen and how one should behave in that event or situation. Page 366

secondary circular reactions Behaviours focused on objects outside the infant's own body that the infant repeatedly engages in because they are pleasurable. Page 304

secondary reinforcer A person or other stimulus that acquires reinforcing properties by virtue of repeated association with a primary reinforcer. Page 220

secular trend A shift in the normative pattern of a characteristic, such as height or weight, that occurs over a historical time period, such as a decade or century. Page 178

secure attachment A kind of attachment displayed by babies who are secure enough to explore novel environments, who are minimally disturbed by brief separations from their mothers, and who greet them happily when they return. Page 225

secure base According to Ainsworth, a caregiver to whom an infant has formed an attachment and whom the child uses as a base from which to explore new things and as a safe haven in times of stress. Page 225

selective attention A strategy in which a person focuses on some features of the environment and ignores others. Page 348

self-control phase According to Kopp, the second phase in learning self-regulation, when the child becomes able to comply with caregiver expectations in the absence of the caregiver. Page 550

self-disclosure/restrictive disclosure The honest sharing of information of a very personal nature, often with a focus on problem solving; a central means by which adolescents develop friendships. Page 489

self-regulation Children's ability to control behaviour on their own without reminders from others. Page 550

self-regulation phase The third phase in Kopp's model of learning self-regulation, when children become able to use strategies and plans in directing their own behaviour and capable of delaying gratification. Page 550

self-report Information that people provide about themselves, either in a direct interview or in some written form, such as a questionnaire. Page 23

self-socialization The child's spontaneous adoption of conventionally gender-appropriate behaviour. Page 527

semantic memory All the world knowledge and facts a person possesses. Page 352

semantics The study of word meanings and word combinations, as in phrases, clauses, and sentences. Page 254

sensation The detection of stimuli by the sensory receptors. Page 129

sensitive care Caregiving that is consistent and responsive and that begins by allowing an infant to play a role in determining when feeding will begin and end and at what pace it will proceed. Page 232

sensorimotor stage Piaget's first stage of cognitive development, during which children move from purely reflexive behaviour to the beginnings of symbolic thought and goal-directed behaviours. Page 302

sensory register The mental processing unit that receives information from the environment and stores it fleetingly. Page 342

separation protest An infant's distress reaction to being separated from his or her mother, which typically peaks at about 15 months of age. Page 206

sequential method A research method that combines features of both the cross-sectional and the longitudinal methods. Page 35

sex chromosomes In both males and females, the 23rd pair of chromosomes, which determine the individual's gender and are responsible for sex-related characteristics; in females, this pair normally comprises two X chromosomes; in males, an X and a Y chromosome. Page 48

sexual abuse Inappropriate sexual activity between an adult and a child for the perpetrator's pleasure or benefit; the abuse may be direct (sexual contact of any type) or indirect (exposing a child to pornography or to the live exhibition of body parts or sexual acts). Page 460

sexual preferences The preference for same- or opposite-sex romantic partners. Page 505

shape constancy The ability to perceive an object's shape as remaining constant despite changes in its orientation and the angle from which one views it. Page 143

shared environment A set of conditions or experiences that is shared by children raised in the same family with each other; a parameter commonly examined in studies of individual differences. Page 70

short-term memory/working memory The mental processing unit in which information may be stored temporar-

ily; the "workspace" of the mind, where a decision must be made to discard information or to transfer it to permanent storage, in *long-term memory*. Page 342

sickle cell anemia A disorder, caused by a recessive gene, in which the red blood cells become distorted when low in oxygen, causing fatigue, shortness of breath, and severe pain, and posing a threat to life from blockage of crucial blood vessels. Page 54

size constancy The tendency to perceive an object as constant in size regardless of changes in its distance from the viewer and in the image it casts on the retinas of the eyes. Page 142

small for date A term describing a premature baby that may be born close to its due date but who weighs significantly less than would be appropriate to its gestational age. Page 108

social comparison The process of evaluating one's characteristics, abilities, values, and other qualities by comparing oneself with others, usually one's peers. Page 473

social referencing The process of "reading" emotional cues in others to help determine how to act in an uncertain situation. Page 205

social-convention rules Socially based rules about everyday conduct. Page 548

socialization The process by which parents and others ensure that a child's standards of behaviour, attitudes, skills, and motives conform closely to those deemed appropriate to his or her role in society. Page 424

socially unskilled Being unskilled at solving interpersonal problems. Page 571

sociocultural theory A theory of development, proposed by Lev Vygotsky, that sees development as evolving out of children's interactions with more skilled others in their social environment. Page 15

sociometric technique A procedure for determining children's status within their peer group in which children nominate others whom they like best or least or rate each child in the group for her likeability or desirability as a companion. Page 474

specific factors (s) Factors that are unique to particular cognitive tasks. Page 384

speech acts One- or two-word utterances that clearly refer to situations or to sequences of events. Page 285

spermarche In males, the first ejaculation of semen-containing ejaculate. Page 188

stages of development Comprehensive, qualitative changes over time in the way a child thinks. Page 302

standardization The process by which test constructors ensure that testing procedures, instructions, and scoring are identical on every testing occasion. Page 392

Stanford-Binet Test The modern version of the first major intelligence test; emphasizes verbal and performance skills. Page 389

status offence Illegal behaviour committed by an underage offender. Page 593

stereoscopic vision The sense of a third spatial dimension produced by the brain's fusion of the separate images contributed by both eyes, each of which reflects the stimulus from a slightly different angle. Page 141

stereotype threat Being at risk of confirming a negative stereotype about the group to which one belongs. Page 401

Strange Situation A testing scenario in which mother and child are separated and reunited several times and that enables investigators to assess the nature and quality of a mother–infant attachment relationship. Page 225

stranger distress A fear of strangers that typically emerges in infants around the age of 9 months. Page 204

strategies Conscious cognitive or behavioural activities that are used to enhance mental performance. Page 345

structural-organismic perspective Theoretical approaches that describe psychological structures and processes that undergo qualitative or stage-like changes over the course of development. Page 10

structured observation A form of observation, in which researchers structure a situation so that behaviours they wish to study are more likely to occur. Page 25

subitizing A preattentive process in which sets of four items or fewer are counted or understood effortlessly, accurately, and quite rapidly. Page 375

substance abuse The excessive use of legal or illegal drugs in such a way as to interfere seriously with one or more important areas of functioning in life: work, intimacy with another, or general interpersonal and social relations. Page 593

Successful intelligence Ability to fit into, mould, and choose environments that best fulfill the demands of one's society and culture and one's own needs and desires (includes analytical, creative, and practical abilities). Page 385

sudden infant death syndrome (SIDS) SIDS refers to the sudden and unexpected death of an otherwise apparently healthy infant under 1 year of age. The death usually remains unexplained after all known and possible causes of death have been ruled out. Page 122

superego The personality component that is the repository of the child's internalization of parental or societal values, morals, and roles. Page 10

symbolic function The ability to use symbols, such as images, words, and gestures, to represent objects and events in the world. Page 309

symbolic thought The use of mental images to represent people, objects, and events. Page 305

synapse A specialized site of intercellular communication where information is exchanged between nerve cells, usually by means of a chemical *neurotransmitter*. Page 159

synaptic pruning The brain's disposal of the axon and dendrites of a neuron that is not often stimulated. Page 159

synaptogenesis The forming of synapses. Page 159

syntax The subdivision of grammar that prescribes how words are to be combined into phrases, clauses, and sentences. Page 254

syphilis A sexually transmitted bacterial disease that today can usually be treated with antibiotics but, when untreated in the pregnant woman, can lead to miscarriage or blindness, mental retardation, or other physical abnormalities in her baby. Page 102

tacit knowledge Implicit knowledge that is shared by many people and that guides behaviour. Page 385

telegraphic speech Two-word utterances that include only the words that are essential to convey the speaker's intent. Page 276

temperament The individual's typical mode of response to the environment, including such things as activity level, emotional intensity, and attention span; used particularly to describe infants' and children's behaviours. Page 73

teratogen An environmental agent, such as a drug, medication, dietary imbalance, or polluting substance, that may cause developmental deviations in a growing human organism; most threatening in the embryonic stage but capable of causing abnormalities in the fetal stage as well. Page 86

tertiary circular reactions Behaviours in which infants experiment with the properties of external objects and try to learn how objects respond to various actions. Page 305

test norms Values or sets of values that describe the typical performance of a specific group of people. Page 392

testosterone A hormone that, in the male, is responsible for the development of primary and secondary sex characteristics and is essential for the production of sperm. Page 188

thalidomide A drug once prescribed to relieve morning sickness in pregnant women but discontinued when found to cause serious malformations of the fetus. Current controversy surrounds possible use in treating symptoms of such diseases as AIDS, cancer, and leprosy. Page 94

theory of mind Understanding of the mind and how it works. Page 320

theory of multiple intelligences Gardner's multi-factorial theory that proposes eight distinct types of intelligence. Page 386

time out Removing children from a situation or context in which they are acting inappropriately until they are able and ready to act appropriately. Page 595

toxoplasmosis A parasitic disease acquired by eating undercooked meat or by making contact with feces in handling cat litter. Page 101

traditional nuclear family The traditional family form, composed of two parents and one or more children, in which the father is the breadwinner and the mother the homemaker. Page 446

transitive inference The mental arrangement of things along a quantitative dimension. Page 372

triarchic theory of intelligence A theory that proposes three major components of intelligent behaviour: information-processing skills, experience with a particular situation, and ability to adapt to the demands of a context. Page 385

Turner syndrome A form of abnormality of the sex chromosomes found in females, in which secondary sex characteristics develop only if female hormones are administered and in which abnormal formation of internal reproductive organs leads to permanent sterility. Page 57

two-generation program A program of early cognitive intervention that extends help to parents as well as to their children. Page 414

ultrasound A technique that uses sound waves to visualize deep body structures; commonly used to reveal the size and structure of a developing fetus. Popularly called ultrasound. Page 61

umbilical cord A tube that contains blood vessels that carry blood back and forth between the growing organism and its mother by way of the placenta; it carries oxygen and nutrients to the growing infant and removes carbon dioxide and waste products. Page 85

undercontrolled disorders A group of psychological disturbances in which a child appears to lack self-control and to act out in a variety of ways, through such behaviours as non-compliance, disobedience, and aggression. Page 591

underextension The use, by a young child, of a single word in a restricted and individualistic way. Page 275

uninvolved parenting Parenting that is indifferent and neglectful and in which parents focus on their own needs rather than on their children's needs. Page 432

utilization deficiency Inability to use a memory strategy that one knows. Page 357

validity The extent to which a test actually measures what it claims to measure. Page 393

visual acuity Sharpness of vision; the clarity with which fine details can be discerned. Page 135

visual cliff An apparatus that tests an infant's depth perception by using patterned materials and an elevated, clear glass platform to make it appear that one side of the platform is several feet lower than the other. Page 141

visual preference method A method of studying infants' abilities to distinguish one stimulus from another by measuring the length of time they spend attending to different stimuli. Page 132

Wechsler Intelligence Scales Three intelligence tests for infants, children, and adults that yield separate scores for verbal and performance IQ as well as a combined IQ score. Page 390

world knowledge What a child has learned from experience and knows about the world in general. Page 357

X-linked genes Genes that are carried on the X chromosome and that may have no analogous genes on the Y chromosome in males. Page 49

zone of proximal development (ZPD) According to Vygotsky, the difference between the developmental level a child has reached and the level she is potentially capable of reaching with the guidance or collaboration of a more skilled adult or peer. Page 327

zygote The developing organism from the time of the union of the sperm and the egg to about the second week of gestation; the period of the zygote is comprised of the implantation of the fertilized egg in the wall of the uterus. Page 82

References

Abbeduto, L., Warren, S. F., & Connors, F. A. (2007). Language development in Down syndrome: From the prelinguistic period to the acquisition of literacy. *Mental Retardation and Developmental Disabilities Research Reviews, 13,* 247–261.

Abecassis, M., Hartup, W. W., Haselager, G., Scholte, R., & van Lieshout, C. F. M. (2002). Mutual antipathies in middle childhood and adolescence. *Child Development, 73,* 1543–1556.

Abel, E. L. (1998). *Fetal alcohol abuse syndrome.* New York: Plenum.

Abela, J. R. Z., & Hankin, B. L. (2008). Cognitive vulnerability to depression in childhood and adolescents: A developmental psychopathology perspective. In J. R. Z. Abela & B. L. Hankin (Eds.), *Handbook of depression in children and adolescents* (pp. 35–78). New York: Guilford.*

Abela, J. R. Z., & McGirr, A. (2007). Operationalizing cognitive vulnerability and stress from the perspective of the hopelessness theory: A multi-wave longitudinal study of children of affectively ill parents. *British Journal of Clinical Psychology, 46,* 377–395.*

Aber, J. L., Brown, J. L., & Jones, S. M. (2003). Developmental trajectories toward violence in middle childhood: Course, demographic differences and response to school-based interventions. *Developmental Psychology, 39,* 324–348.

Abitz, M., Damgaard-Nielsen, R., Jones, E. G., Laursen, H., Graem, N., & Pakkenberg, B. (2007). Excess of neurons in the human newborn mediodorsal thalamus compared with that of the adult. *Cerebral Cortex, 17,* 2573–3578.

Aboud, F. E. (1989). Disagreement between friends. *International Journal of Behavioral Development, 12,* 495–508.*

Abramovitch, R., Freedman, J. L., Henry, K., & Van Brunschot, M. (1995). Children's capacity to agree to psychological research: Knowledge of risks and benefits and voluntariness. *Ethics and Behavior, 5,* 25–48.*

Achenbach, T. M. (1995). Developmental issues in assessment, taxonomy and diagnosis of child and adolescent psychopathology. In D. Cicchetti & D. J. Cohen (Eds.), *Developmental psychopathology, Vol. 1: Theory and methods* (pp. 57–82). New York: Wiley.

Achenbach, T. M. (1997). What is normal? What is abnormal? Developmental perspectives on behavioral and emotional problems. In S. S. Luthar, J. A. Burack, D. Cicchetti & J. R. Weisz (Eds.), *Developmental psychopathology perspectives on adjustment, risk and disorder* (pp. 93–114). New York: Cambridge University Press.

Achenbach, T. M. & Rescorla, L. A. (2007). *Multicultural Understanding of Child and Adolescent Psychopathology: Implications for Mental Health Assessment.* New York: Guilford.

Ackerman, B. P. (1996). Induction of a memory retrieval strategy by young children. *Journal of Experimental Child Psychology, 62,* 243–271.

Adair, J. G. (2001). Ethics of psychological research: New policies: continuing issues; new concerns. *Canadian Psychology, 42,* 25–37.*

Adams, J. A. (1989). Newborns' discrimination among mid- and long-wavelength stimuli. *Journal of Experimental Child Psychology, 47,* 130–141.*

Adams, J. A. (1996). Further explorations of human neonatal chromatic-achromatic discrimination. *Journal of Experimental Child Psychology, 60,* 344–360.*

Adams, J. A., & Courage, M. L. (1998). Human newborn colour vision: Measurement with chromatic stimuli varying in excitation purity. *Journal of Experimental Child Psychology, 68,* 22–34.*

Adams, J. A., Courage, M. L., & Mercer, M. E. (1994). Systematic measurement of human neonatal colour vision. *Vision Research, 34,* 1691–1701.*

Adams, R. J., & Courage, M. L. (2002). A psychophysical test of the early maturation of infants' mid- and long-wavelength retinal cones. *Infant Behavior and Development, 25,* 247–254.*

Adamson, L. B. (1995). *Communication development during infancy.* Madison, WI: Brown & Benchmark.

Adamson, L. B., & Frick, J. E., (2003). The still face: A history of a shared experimental paradigm. *Infancy, 4,* 451–473.

Adelson, E., & Fraiberg, S. (1974). Gross motor development in infants blind from birth. *Child Development, 45,* 114–126.

Adler, S. A., & Haith, M. M. (2003). The nature of infants' visual expectations for event context. *Infancy, 4,* 389–421.*

Adler, S. A., Haith, M. M., Arehart, D. M., & Lanthier, E. C. (2008). Infants' visual expectations and the processing of time. *Journal of Cognition and Development, 9,* 1–25.

Adolph, K. E. (2005). Learning to learn in the development of actions. In J. Lockman, J. Rieser & C. A. Nelson (Eds.), *Minnesota symposium on child psychology* (Vol. 33, pp. 91–133). Mahwah, NJ: Erlbaum.

Adolph, K. E. (2008). Learning to move. *Current Directions in Psychological Science, 17,* 213–218.

Adolph, K. E., & Berger, S. A. (2006). Motor development. In W. Damon & R. L. Lerner (Gen. Ed.), & D. Kuhn & R. Siegler (Eds.), *Handbook of child psychology: Vol. 2: Cognition, perception, and language* (pp. 161–213). New York: Wiley.

Adolph, K. E., Vereijken, B., & Shrout, P. E. (2003). What changes in infant walking and why. *Child Development, 74,* 475–497.

Adolphs, R. (2002). Recognizing emotion from facial expressions: Psychological and neurological mechanisms. *Behavioral and Cognitive Neuroscience Reviews, 1,* 21–62.

Adoption Council of Canada. (2007, January 10, 2009). Statistics. Retrieved January 10, 2009, from http://www.adoption.ca/statistics.htm

Affleck, G., Tennen, H., & Rowe, J. (1990). Mothers, fathers and the crisis of newborn intensive care. *Infant Medical Health Journal, 11,* 12–25.

Agnew, R. (1991). The interactive effects of peer variables on delinquency. *Criminology, 29,* 47–72.

Ahmed, N. U., Zeitlin, M. F., Beiser, A. S., Super, C. M., & Gershoff, S. N. (1993). A longitudinal study of the impact of behavioural change intervention on cleanliness, diarrhoeal morbidity and growth of children in rural Bangladesh. *Social Science and Medicine, 37,* 159–171.

Ainsworth, M. D. (1963). The development of infant-mother interaction among the Ganda. In D. M. Foss (Ed.), *Determinants of infant behavior* (Vol. 2, pp. 67–104). New York: Wiley.

Ainsworth, M. D. (1973). The development of infant-mother attachment. In B. Caldwell & H. Ricciuti (Eds.), *Review of child development research* (Vol. 3). Chicago: University of Chicago Press.

Ainsworth, M. D., Blehar, M., Waters, E., & Wall, S. (1978). *Patterns of attachment.* Hillsdale, NJ: Erlbaum.

Albert, R. S. (1996, Summer). Some reasons why childhood creativity often fails to make it past puberty into the real world. In M. A. Runco (Ed.), *Creativity from childhood through adulthood: The developmental issues* [Special issue]. *New Directions for Child Development,* No. 72, 43–56.

Aldwin, C. M., & Werner, E. E. (2007). *Stress, coping, and development: An integrative perspective* (2nd ed.). New York: Guilford Press.

Allen, J. P., McElhaney, K. B., Land, D. J., Kuperminic, G. P., Moore, C. W., O'Beirne-Kelly, H., et al. (2003). A secure base in adolescence: Markers of attachment security in the mother-adolescent relationship. *Child Development, 74,* 292–307.

Alles-Jardel, M., Schneider, B. H., & Boutry, V. (2002). Friendship and attitudes toward school among children of two Muslim communities in Marseille. *Early Education and Development, 13,* 221–35.*

Als, J., Gilkerson, L., Duffy, F. H. McAnulty, G. B., Buehler, D. M., Vandenber, K., et al. (2003). A three-center, randomized, controlled trial of individualized developmental care for very low-birthweight preterm infants: Medical, neurodevelopmental, parenting, and caregiving effects. *Journal of Developmental & Behavioral Pediatrics, 24,* 399–408.

Amato, P. (2000). The consequences of divorce for adults and children. *Journal of Marriage and the Family, 62,* 1269–1287.

Amato, P. R. (2001). Children of divorce in the 1990's: An update of Amato & Keith (1991) meta-analysis. *Journal of Family Psychology, 13,* 355–370.

American Academy of Pediatrics Report. (2000). Task for on infant sleep position and Sudden Infant Death: Report at year 2000. *Pediatrics: American Academy of Pediatrics, 105,* 650–656.

American Association of Mental Retardation. (2002). *Mental retardation: Definition, classification, and systems of supports* (10th ed.). Annapolis, MD: Author.

American Medical Association. (1992, December). *Report to the Consumer Product Safety Commission on infant walkers.* Nashville, TN: American Medical Association.

American Psychiatric Association. (2000). *Diagnostic and statistical manual of mental disorders* (*4th ed., Text Revision).* Washington, DC: American Psychiatric Association.

American Psychological Association. (1992). Ethical principles of psychologists: Code of conduct. *American Psychologist, 44,* 1597–1611.

Anderson, C. A., Gentile, D. A., & Buckley, K. E. (2007). *Violent video game effects on children and adolescents: Theory Research, and Public Policy.* New York: Oxford University Press.

Anderson, D. A., & Hamilton, M. C. (2005). Gender role stereotyping of parents in children's picture books: The invisible father. *Sex Roles, 52,* 145–151.

Anderson, G. C. (1995). Touch and the kangaroo care method. In T. M. Field (Ed.), *Touch in early development* (pp. 35–51). Mahwah, NJ: Erlbaum.

Anderson, P., Doyle, L. W., Callahan, C., Carse, E., Casalaz, D., Charlton, M. P., et al. (2003). Neurobehavioral outcomes of school-age children born extremely low birth weight or very preterm in the 1990s. *Journal of American Medical Association, 289,* 3264–3272.

Anderson, P. et al. (1993). Moderate drinking and health: A joint policy statement based on the International Symposium on Moderate Drinking and Health, Toronto, ON, April 30–May 1. Ottawa, ON: Canadian Centre on Substance Abuse.*

Andeweg, R. B., & Van Den Berg, S. (2003). Linking birth order to political leadership: The impact of parents of sibling interaction? *Political Psychology, 24,* 605–624.

Ando, J., Suzuki, A., Yamagata, S., Kijima, N., Makeawa, H., Ono, Y., et al. (2004). Genetic and environmental structure of Cloninger's temperament and character dimensions. *Journal of Personality Disorders, 18,* 379–393.*

Andrews, J. A., & Lewinsohn, P. M. (1992). Suicidal attempts among older adolescents: Prevalence and co-occurrence with psychiatric disorders. *Journal of American Academy of Child and Adolescent Psychiatry, 31,* 655–662.

Angier, N. (1997). Evolutionary necessity or glorious accident? Biologists ponder the self. *The New York Times,* April 22, p. C21.

Anisfeld, M. (1991). Neonatal imitation. *Developmental Review, 11,* 60–97.

Anneken, K., Konrad, C., Dräger, B., Beritenstein, C., Kennerknecht, I., Ringelstein, E. B., et al. (2004). Familial aggregation of strong hmeispheric language lateralization. *Neurology, 63,* 2433–2435.

Anooshian, L. J., & Siegel, A. W. (1985). From cognitive to procedural mapping. In C. J. Brainard & M. Pressley (Eds.), *Basic process in memory development: Progress in cognitive development research* (pp. 47–101). New York: Springer-Verlag.

Antonarakis, S. E., & Down Syndrome Collaborative Group. (1991). Parental origin of the extra chromosome in trisomy 21 as indicated by analysis of DNA polymorphisms. *New England Journal of Medicine, 324,* 872–876.

Arranz, E., Artamendi, J., Olabarrieta, F., & Martin, J. (2002). Family context and theory of mind development. *Early Child Development and Care, 172,* 9–22.

Arsenio, W. F., & Kramer, R. (1992). Victimizers and their victims: Children's conceptions of mixed emotional consequences of moral transgressions. *Child Development, 63,* 915–927.

Arterberry, M. E., & Bornstein, M. H. (2001). Three-month-old infants' categorization of animals and vehicles based on static and dynamic features. *Journal of Experimental Child Psychology, 80,* 333–346.

Arterberry, M. E., & Bornstein, M. H. (2002). Infant perceptual and conceptual categorization: The roles of static and dynamic stimulus attributes. *Cognition, 86,* 1–24.

Asbury, K., Dunn, J. F., Pike, A., & Plomin, R. (2003). Nonshared environmental influences on individual differences in early behavioral development: A monozygotic twin differences study. *Child Development, 74,* 933–943.

Asher, S. R., & Hopmeyer, A. (2001). Loneliness in childhood. In G. G. Baer, K. M. Minke & A. Thomas (Eds.), *Children's needs: Development, problems and alternatives* (pp. 279–292). Silver Spring, MD: National Association of School Psychologists.

Asher, S. R., Hymel, S., & Renshaw, P. D. (1984). Loneliness in children. *Child Development, 55,* 1456–1464.

Asher, S. J., & Paquette, J. A. (2003). Loneliness and peer relations in childhood. *Current Directions in Psychological Science, 12,* 75–78.

Aslin, R. N. (1987). Visual and auditory development in infancy. In J. Osofsky (Ed.), *Handbook of infant development* (2nd ed.). New York: Wiley.

Aslin, R. N., Jurczyk, P. W., & Pisoni, D. B. (1998). Speech and auditory processing during infancy: Constraints on and precursors to language. In W. Damon (Gen. Ed.), D. Kuhn, & R. Siegler (Vol. Eds.), *Handbook of child psychology: Vol. 2. Cognition, perception and language.* New York: Wiley.

Aslin, R. N., Werker, J. F., & Morgan, J. L. (2002). Innate phonetic boundaries revisited. *Journal of the Acoustical Society of America, 112,* 1257–1260.*

Ateah, C. A., & Parkin, C. M. (2002). Childhood experiences with, and current attitudes toward, corporal punishment. *Canadian Journal of Community Mental Health, 21,* 35–46.*

Atkin, C. (1983). Effects of realistic TV violence vs. fictional violence on aggression. *Journalism Quarterly, 60,* 615–621.

Atkins, M. S., Pelham, W. E., & Licht, M. H. (1985). A comparison of objective classroom measures and teacher ratings of attention deficit disorder. *Journal of Abnormal Child Psychology, 13,* 155–167.

Atkinson, D., Gourdeau, M., & Sauvageau, F. (1991). *Summary and analysis of various studies on violence and television.* Ottawa: Canadian Radio, Television and Telecommunications Commission.*

Atkinson, R. C., & Shiffrin, R. M. (1968). Human memory: A proposed system and its control processes. In K. W. Spence & J. Spence (Eds.), *Advances in the psychology of learning and motivation: research and theory* (Vol. 2). New York: Academic.

Attie, I., & Brooks-Gunn, J. (1989). Development of eating problems in adolescent girls: A longitudinal study. *Developmental Psychology, 25,* 70–79.

Attili, G., Vermigli, P., & Schneider, B. H. (1997). Peer acceptance and friendship patterns among Italian school children within a cross-cultural perspective. *International Journal of Behavioral Development, 21,* 277–288.*

Atweh, G. F. e. a. (1999). Sustained induction of fetal hemoglobin by pulse butyrate therapy in sickle cell disease. *Blood, 6,* 1790–1797.

Au, K. H. (1997). A sociocultural model of reading instruction: The Kamehameha Elementary Education Program. In S. A. Stahl & R. A. Hayes (Eds.), *Instructional models in reading* (pp. 181–202). Hillsdale, NJ: Erlbaum.

Au, K., & Jordan, C. (1981). Teaching reading to Hawaiian children: Finding a culturally appropriate solution. In H. Tureba, G. Guthrie, & K. Au (Eds.), *Culture and the bilingual classroom: Studies in classroom*

Auer, R., Lau, D., & Reimer, R. (2001). Obesity in Canadian children. *CMAJ, 164,* 1563.*

Auerbach, R. P., Abela, J. R. Z., & Ho, M.-H. R. (2007). Responding to symptoms of depression and anxiety: Emotion regulation, neurtocism, and engagement in risky behaviors. *Behaviour Research and Therapy, 45,* 2182–2191.*

Aviezer, O., Sagi, A., Joels, T., & Ziv, Y. (1999). Emotional availability and attachment -representations in kibbutz infants and their mothers. *Developmental Psychology, 35,* 811–821.

Aviezer, O., Sagi, A., & van IJzendoorn, M. H. (2002). Balancing the family and the collective in raising children: Why communal sleeping in Kibbutzim was predestined to end. *Family Process, 41,* 435–454.

Aviezer, O., van IJzendoorn, M. H., Sagi, A., & Schuengel, C. (1994). "Children of the dream" revisited: 70 years of collective early child care in Israeli Kibbutzim. *Psychological Bulletin, 116,* 99–116.

Avis, J., & Harris, P. L. (1991). Belief-desire reasoning among Baka children: Evidence for a universal conception of mind. *Child Development, 62,* 460–467.

Axia, G., Bonichini, S., & Benini, F. (1999). Attention and reaction to distress in infancy, a longitudinal study. *Developmental Psychology, 35,* 500–504.

Azar, S. T. (2002). Parenting and child maltreatment. In M. Bornstein (Ed.), *Handbook of parenting* (Vol. 4, pp. 361–388). Mahwah, NJ: Erlbam.

Baek, H. J. (2002). A comparative study of moral development of Korean and British children. *Journal of Moral Education, 31,* 373–391.

Baer, J. S., Sampson, J. D., Barr, H. M., O'Connor, P. D., & Streissguth, A. P. (2003). A 21-year longitudinal analysis of the effects of prenatal alcohol exposure on young adult drinking. *Archives of*

General Psychiatry, 60, 377–385.

Bagwell, C. L. (2004). Friendships, peer networks and antisocial behavior. In J. B. Kupersmidt & K. A. Dodge (Eds.), *Children's peer relations* (pp. 37–57). Washington, DC: American Psychological Association.

Bagwell, C. L., Coie, J. D., Terry, R. A., & Lochman, J. E. (2000). Peer clique participation and social status in preadolescence. *Merrill-Palmer Quarterly, 46,* 280–305.

Bagwell, C. L., Newcomb, A., & Bukowski, W. M. (1998). Preadolescent friendships and peer rejection as predictors of adult adjustment. *Child Development, 69,* 140–153.

Bai, D. L., & Bertenthal, B. I. (1989). *The role of self-produced locomotion in the development of object localization skills.* Unpublished manuscript, University of Virginia.

Bailey, A., LeCouteur, A., Gottesman, I., Bolton, P., Simonoff, E., Yuzda, F. Y., et al. (1995). Autism as a strongly genetic disorder: Evidence from a British twin study. *Psychological Medicine, 25,* 63–77.

Bailey, J., Bobrow, D., Wolfe, M., & Mikach, S. (1995). Sexual orientation of adult sons of gay fathers. Special Issue: Sexual orientation and human development. *Developmental Psychology, 31,* 124–129.

Bailey, J. M., Pillard, R. C., Neale, M. C., & Agyei, Y. (1993). Heritable factors influence sexual orientation in women. *Archives of General Psychiatry, 50,* 217–223.

Bailey, J. M., & Zucker, K. J. (1995). Childhood sex-typed behavior and sexual orientation: A conceptual analysis. *Developmental Psychology, 31,* 43–55.

Baillargeon, R. (1986). Representing the existence and the location of hidden objects: Object permanence in 6- and 8-month-old infants. *Cognition, 23,* 21–41.

Baillargeon, R. (1993). The object concept revisited: New directions in the investigation of infants' physical models of. In C. E. Granrud (Ed.), *Visual perception and cognition in infancy.* Hillsdale, NJ: Erlbaum.

Baillargeon, R. (1994). How do infants learn about the physical world? *Current Directions in Psychological Science, 3,* 133–140.

Baillargeon, R. (2002). The acquisition of physical knowledge in infancy: A summary in eight lessons. In V. Goswami (Ed.), *Blackwell handbook of childhood cognitive development* (pp. 47–83). Malden, MA: Blackwell Publishers.

Baillargeon, R., & Wang, S. (2002). Event categorization in infancy. *Trends in Cognitive Sciences, 6,* 85–93.

Bainum, C. K., Lounsbury, K. R., & Pollio, H. R. (1984). The development of laughing and smiling in nursery school children. *Child Development, 55,* 1946–1957.

Baird, J. A., & Astington, J. W. (2005). The development of the intention concept: From the observable world to the unobservable mind. In R. R. Hassin, J. S. Uleman & J. A. Bargh (Eds.), *The new unconscious. Oxford series in social cognition and social neuroscience* (pp. 256–276). New York, NY: Oxford University Press.*

Bakeman, R., & Gottman, J. (1997). *Observing Behavior* (2nd ed.). New York: Cambridge University Press.

Bakermans-Kranenburg, M. J., van IJzendoorn, M. H., & Juffer, F. (2003). Less is more: Meta-analyses of sensitivity and attachment interventions in early childhood. *Psychological Bulletin, 129,* 195–215.

Baldwin, J. M. (1890). Origin of right or left handedness. *Science, 16,* 247–248.*

Baldwin, J. M. (1891). Suggestion in infancy. *Science, 17,* 113–117.*

Baldwin, J. M. (1892). Origin of volition in childhood. *Science, 20,* 286–287.

Baldwin, J. M. (1894). Imitation: A chapter in the natural history of consciousness. *Mind, 3,* 25–55.

Baldwin, J. M. (1930). James Mark Baldwin. In C. Murchison (Ed.), *A history of psychology in autobiography* (Vol. 1, 1–30). New York: Rinehart & Winston.

Ball, W. A., & Tronick, E. (1971). Infant responses to impending collision: Optical and real. *Science, 171,* 818–820.

Baltes, P. B., Linderberger, U., & Staudinger, U. M. (2006). Life span theory in developmental psychology. In W. Damon & R. M. Lerner (Gen. Ed.), & R. M. Lerner (Ed.), *Handbook of child psychology: Vol. 1. Theoretical models of human development* (6th ed., pp. 569–664). New York: Wiley.

Bandstra, E. S., Morrow, C. E., Anthony, J. C., Accornero, V. H., & Fried, P. A. (2001). Longitudinal investigation of task persistence and sustained attention in children with prenatal cocaine exposure. *Neurotoxicology and Teratology, 23,* 545–559.*

Bandura, A. (1989). Social cognitive theory. In R. Vasta (Ed.), *Annals of child development: Six theories of child development* (Vol. 6). Greenwich, CT: JAI Press.

Bandura, A. (1997). *Self-efficacy.* New York: W. H. Freeman.

Bandura, A. (2001). Social cognitive theory: An agentic perspective. *Annual Review of Psychology, 57,* 1–26.

Banish, J. T. (1998). Integration of information between the cerebral hemispheres. *Current Directions in Psychological Science, 7,* 32–37.

Banks, M. S., & Salapatek, P. (1983). Infant visual perception. In M. H. & J. Campos (Eds.), *Handbook of child psychology; biology and infancy.* New York: Wiley.

Banks, M. S., & Shannon, E. (1993). Spatial and chromatic visual efficiency in human neonates. In C. Granrud (Ed.), *Visual perception and cognition in infancy* (pp. 1–46). Hillsdale, NJ: Erlbaum.

Banks, M. S., Aslin, R. N., & Letson, R. D. (1975). Sensitive period for the development of human binocular vision. *Science, 190,* 675–677.

Barber, B. K. (Ed.). (2002). *Intrusive parenting: How psychological control affects children and adolescents.* Washington, DC: American Psychological Association.* Washington, DC: American Psychological Association.

Barber, B. K., & Harmon, E. (2002). Parental psychological control of children and adolescents. In B. K. E. Barber (Ed.), *Intrusive parenting: How psychological control affects children and adolescents* (pp. 15–52). Washington, DC: American Psychological Association.

Barglow, P., Vaughn, B. E., & Molitor, N. (1987). Effects of maternal absence due to employment on the quality of infant-mother attachment in a low-risk sample. *Child Development, 58,* 945–954.

Baringa, M. (1996). Learning defect identified in the brain. *Science, 273,* 867–868.

Barker, R. G., & Gump, P. V. (1964). *Big school, small school.* Stanford, CA: Stanford University Press.

Barkley, R. A. (1997). Behavioral inhibition, sustained attention, and executive functions: Constructing a unifying theory of ADHD. *Psychological Bulletin, 121,* 65–94.

Barkley, R. A. (1998). *Attention deficit/hyperactivity disorder: A handbook for diagnosis and treatment* (2nd ed.). New York: Guilford Press.

Barkley, R. A. (2000). *Taking charge of ADHD.* New York: Guilford.

Barnard, K. E., & Bee, H. L. (1983). The impact of temporally patterned stimulation on the development of preterm infants. *Child Development, 54,* 1156–1167.

Barnard, K. E., Bee, H. L., & Hammond, M. A. (1984). Home environment and cognitive development in a healthy, low-risk sample: The Seattle study. In A. W. Gottfried (Ed.), *Home environment and early cognitive development* (pp. 117–149). Orlando, FL: Academic.

Baron, J., & Miller, J. G. (2000). Limiting the scope of moral obligations to help: A cross-cultural investigation. *Journal of Cross-Cultural Psychology, 31,* 703–725.

Baron-Cohen, S. (1995). *Mindblindness: An essay on autism and theory of mind.* Cambridge, MA: MIT Press.

Baron-Cohen, S. (2000). Theory of mind and autism: A fifteen year review. In S. Baron-Cohen, H. Tager-Flusberg & D. J. Cohen (Eds.), *Understanding other minds* (pp. 3–20). Oxford: Oxford University Press.

Baron-Cohen, S. (2001). Theory of mind and autism: A review. *International Review of Research in Mental Retardation, 23,* 169–184.

Baron-Cohen, S. (2003). *The essential difference: The truth about the male and female brain.* New York: Basic Books.

Baron-Cohen, S. (2007). The rise of autism and the digital age. *The World Question Center 2007,* New York: Edge Foundation.

Barr, H. M., Streissguth, A. P., Darby, B. L., & Sampson, P. D. (1990). Prenatal exposure to alcohol, caffeine, tobacco and aspirin: Effects on fine and gross motor performance in 4-year-old children. *Developmental Psychology, 26,* 339–348.

Barr, R. G. (1990). The normal crying curve: What do we really know? *Developmental Medicine and Child Neurology, 32,* 356–362.*

Barr, R. G., Hopkins, B., & Green, J. A. (Eds.). (2000). *Crying as a sign, a symptom, and a signal: Clinical, emotional and developmental aspects of infant and toddler crying.* New York: Cambridge University Press.*

Barr, R. G., Konner, M., Bakeman, R., & Adamson, L. (1991). Crying !Kung San infants: A test of the cultural specificity hypothesis. *Developmental Medicine and Child Neurology, 33,* 601–610.*

Barr, R. G., Pantel, M. S., Young, S. N., Wright, J. H., Hendricks, L. A., & Gravel, R. (1999). The response of crying newborns to sucrose: Is it a "sweetness" effect? *Physiology and Behavior, 66,* 409–417.*

Barr, R. G., & Young, S. N. (1999). A two-phase model of the soothing taste response: Implications for a taste probe of temperament and emotional regulation. In M. Lewis & D. Ramsey (Eds.), *Soothing and stress* (pp. 109–137). Mahwah, NJ: Erlbaum.*

Barr, S. I. (1995). Dietary attitudes and behavior in urban high school students: Implications for calcium intake. *Journal of Adolescent Behavior, 16,* 458–464.*

Barrett, D. E. (1979). A naturalistic study of sex differences in children's aggression. *Merrill-Palmer Quarterly, 25,* 193–203.

Barrett, T. M., Davis, E. F., & Needham, A. (2007). Learning about tools in infancy. *Developmental Psychology, 43,* 352–368.

Barrow, R. (1995). Keep them bells a-tolling. *Alberta Journal of Educational Research. Special Issue: Canadian Perspectives on the Bell Curve, 41,* 289–296.*

Bartlett, D. J. (1998). The influence of geographic region on the seasonality of early motor development. *Infant Behavior and Development, 21,* 591–601.*

Bates, D., Thal, D., Whitsell, K., Fenson, L., & Oakes, L. (1989). Integrating language and gesture in infancy. *Developmental Psychology, 25,* 1004–1019.

Bates, E. (1976). *Language and context: The acquisition of pragmatics.* New York: Academic Press.

Bates, E. (1999). On the nature of language. In R. Levi-Montalcini, D. Baltimore, R. Dulbecco, & F. Jacob (Series Eds.), and O. E. Bizzi, P. Calissano, & V. Vorterra (Vol. Eds.), *The brain of Homo sapiens.* Rome: Giovanni Trecami.

Bates, E., & Goodman, J. (1999). On the emergence of grammar from the lexicon. In B. MacWhinney (Ed.), *The emergence of language* (pp. 29–80). Mahwah, NJ: Erlbaum.

Bates, J., & Pettit, G. (2007). Temperament, parenting, and socialization. In J. Grusec & P. Hastings (Eds.), *Handbook of socialization* (pp. 153–177). New York: Guilford Press.

Bates, J. E. (2001). Adjustment style in childhood as a product of parenting and temperament. In T. D. Wachs & G. A. Kohnstamm (Eds.), *Temperament in context* (pp. 173–200). Mahwah, NJ: Erlbaum.

Batson, C. D., & Thompson, E. R. (2001). Why don't moral people act morally? Motivational considerations. *Current Directions in Psychological Science, 10,* 54–57.

Batson, C. D., Thompson, E. R., & Chen, H. (2002). Moral hypocrisy: Addressing some alternatives. *Journal of Personality and Social Psychology, 83,* 330–339.

Bauer, P. J. (1996). What do infants recall of their lives? *American Psychologist, 51,* 29–41.

Bauer, P. J. (2002). Long-term recall memory: Behavioral and neurodevelopmental changes in the first 2 years of life. *Current Directions in Psychological Science, 11,* 137–141.

Bauer, P. J. (2006). Event memory. In W. Damon & R. M. Lerner (Gen. Ed.), & D. Kuhn & R. Siegler (Eds.), *Handbook of child psychology: Vol. 2. Cognition, perception, and language* (6th ed., pp. 373–425). New York: Wiley.

Bauer, P. J. (2007). Recal in infancy: A neurodevelopmental account. *Current Directions in Psychological Science, 16,* 142–146.

Bauer, P. J., & Dow, G. A. (1994). Episodic memory in 16- and 20-month-old children: Specifics are generalized but not forgotten. *Developmental Psychology, 30,* 403–417.

Bauer, P. J., & Mandler, J. M. (1992). Putting the horse before the cart: The use of temporal order in recall of events by one-year-old children. *Developmental Psychology, 28,* 441–452.

Bauer, P. J., & Wewerka, S. S. (1997). Saying is revealing: Verbal expression of event memory in the transition from infancy to early childhood. In P. W. van den Broek, P. J. Bauer & T. Bourg (Eds.), *Developmental spans in event comprehension and representation: Bridging fictional and actual events* (pp. 139–168). Hillsdale: Erlbaum.

Bauer, P. J., Wenner, J. A., Propnik, P. L., & Wewerka, S. S. (2000). Parameters of remembering and forgetting in the transition from infancy to childhood. *Monographs of the Society for Research in Child Development, 65,* v–204.

Bauer, W. D., & Twentyman, C. T. (1985). Abusing, neglecting, and comparison mothers' responses to child-related and non-child-related stressors. *Journal of Consulting and Clinical Psychology, 53,* 335–343.

Baum, S. R., Pell, M. D., Marc, C. L., & Gordon, J. K. (2001). Using prosody to resolve temporary syntactic ambiguities in speech production: Acoustic data on brain-damaged speakers. *Clinical Linguistics and Phonetics, 15,* 441–456.*

Baumeister, A. A. (1967). The effects of dietary control on intelligence in phenylketonuria. *American Journal of Mental Deficiency, 71,* 840–847.

Baumrind, D. (1967). Child care practices anteceding three patterns of preschool behavior. *Genetic*

Psychology Monographs, 75, 43–88.

Baumrind, D. (1971). Current patterns of parental authority. *Developmental Psychology Monographs, 1,* 1–103.

Baumrind, D. (1991a). Effective parenting during the early adolescent transition. In P. A. Cowan & E. M. Hetherington (Eds.), *Family transitions* (pp. 111–164). Hillsdale, NJ: Erlbaum.

Baumrind, D., Larzelere, R. E., & Cowan, P. A. (2002). Ordinary physical punishment: Is it harmful? Comment on Gershoff (2002). *Psychological Bulletin, 128,* 539–579.

Bayley, N. (1969). *Bayley scales of infant development.* New York: Psychological Corporation.

Bayley, N. (1993). *Bayley scales of infant development* (revised ed.). New York: Psychological Corporation.

Bayliss, D. M., Christopher, J., Baddeley, A. D., Gunn, D. M., & Leigh, E. (2005). Mapping the developmental constraints on working memory span performance. *Developmental Psychology, 41,* 579–597.

Beal, C. R. (1994). *Boys and girls: The development of gender roles.* New York: McGraw-Hill.

Bebko, J. M. (1979). Can recall differences among children be attributed to rehearsal effects? *Canadian Journal of Experimental Psychology, 33,* 96–105.*

Bebko, J. M. (1984). Memory and rehearsal characteristics of profoundly deaf children. *Journal of Experimental Child Psychology, 38,* 415–428.*

Bebko, J. M., & McKinnon, E. E. (1990). The language experience of deaf children: Its relation to spontaneous rehearsal in a memory task. *Child Development, 61,* 1744-1752.*

Bebko, J. M., Bell, M. A., Metcalfe-Haggert, A., & McKinnon, E. E. (1998). Language proficiency and the prediction of spontaneous rehearsal in children who are deaf. *Journal of Experimental Child Psychology, 68,* 51–69.*

Bédard, J., & Chi, M. T. H. (1992). Expertise. *Current Directions in Psychological Science, 1,* 135–139.

Beebe, D. W., D., L., Zeller, M., McCabe, M., MacLeod, K., Daniels, S. R., et al. (2007). Sleep in overweight adolescents: Shorter sleep, poorer sleep quality, sleepiness, and sleep-disordered breathing. *Journal of Pediatric Psychology, 32,* 69–79.

Begley, S. (1997). How to build a baby's brain. *Newsweek Special Issue.* Spring/Summer, 28–32.

Behl-Chadha, G. (1996). Basic-level and superordinate-level categorical representation in early infancy. *Cognition, 60,* 105–141.

Beilin, H. (1992). Piaget's enduring contribution to developmental psychology. *Developmental Psychology, 28,* 191–204.

Beitel, A. H., & Parke, R. D. (1998). Parental involvement in infancy: The role of maternal and paternal attitudes. *Journal of Family Psychology, 12,* 268–288.

Bell, S., & Ainsworth, M. D. (1972). Infant crying and maternal responsiveness. *Child Development, 43,* 1171–1190.

Belle, D. (1999). *The after-school lives of children.* Mahwah, NJ: Erlbaum.

Bellugi, U., Van Hoek, K., Lillo-Martin, D., & O'Grady, L. (1993). The acquisition of syntax and space in young deaf signers. In D. Bishop & K. Mogford (Eds.), *Language development in exceptional children* (pp. 132–149). Hove, England: Erlbaum.

Belsky, J. (1999). Interactional and contextual determinates of attachment security. In J. Cassidy & P. R. Shaver (Eds.), *Handbook of attachment* (pp. 249–264). New York: Guilford.

Belsky, J., & Cassidy, J. (1994). Attachment: Theory and evidence. In M. Rutter, D. Hay, & S. Baron-Cohen (Eds.), *Developmental principles and clinical issues in psychology and psychiatry.* Oxford: Blackwell.

Belsky, J., & Rovine, M. (1988). Nonmaternal care in the first year of life and infant-parent attachment security. *Child Development, 57,* 1224–1231.

Belsky, J., Steinberg, L. D., Houts, R. M., Friedman, S. L., DeHart, G., Cauffman, E., et al. (2007). Family rearing antecedents of pubertal timing. *Child Development, 78,* 1302–1321.

Bem, S. L. (1981). Gender schema theory: A cognitive account of sex typing. *Psychological Review, 88,* 354–364.

Bem, S. L. (1983). Gender schema theory and its implications for child development: Raising gender-aschematic children in a gender-schematic society. *Signs: Journal of Women in Culture and Society, 8,* 598–616.

Bem, S. L. (1989). Genital knowledge and gender constancy in preschool children. *Child Development, 60,* 649–662.

Bem, S. L. (1993). *The lenses of gender: Transforming the debate on sexual inequality.* New Haven, CT: Yale University Press.

Bem, S. L. (1998). *An unconventional family.* New Haven, CT: Yale University Press.

Benbow, C. P., & Lubinski, D. J. (Eds.) (1996). Intellectual talent: Psychometric and social issues. Baltimore: Johns Hopkins University Press.

Benenson, J. F., & Christakos, A. (2003). The greater fragility of females' versus males' closest same-sex friendships. *Child Development, 74,* 1123–1129.

Benenson, J. F., Apostoleris, N. H., & Parnass, J. (1997). Age and sex differences in dyadic and group interaction. *Developmental Psychology, 33,* 538–543.

Benjamin, W. J., Schneider, B. H., Greenman, P. S., & Hum, M. (2001). Conflict and childhood friendship in Taiwan and Canada. *Canadian Journal of Behavioural Science, 33,* 203–211.*

Benjet, C., & Kazdin, A. E. (2003). Spanking children: The controversies, findings, and new directions. *Clinical Psychology Review, 23,* 197–224.

Benloucif, S., Bennett, E. L., & Rosenzweig, M. R. (1995). Norepinephrine and neural plasticity: The effects of Xylamine on experience-induced changes in brain weight, memory and behavior. *Neurobiology of Learning and Memory, 63,* 33–42.

Bennett, T., Szatmari, P., Bryson, S., Volden, J., Zwaigenbaum, L., Vaccarella, L., et al. (2008). Differentiating autism and Asperger syndrom on the basis of language delay or impairment. *Journal of Autism and Developmental Disorders, 38,* 616–625.*

Benoit, D., Madigan, S., Lecce, S., Shea, B., & Goldberg, S. (2001). Atypical maternal behavior toward feeding-disordered infants before and after intervention. *Infant Mental Health Journal, 27,* 611–626.*

Benoit, D., & Parker, K. C. H. (1994). Stability and transmission of attachment across three generations. *Child Development, 65,* 1444–1456.*

Benoit, D., Parker, K. C. H., & Zeanah, C. H. (1997). Mothers' representations of their infants assessed prenatally: Stability and association with infants' attachment classifications. *Journal of Child Psychology & Psychiatry & Allied Disciplines, 38,* 307–313.*

Benokraitis, N. V. (1996). *Marriages and families: Changes, choices, and constraints* (2nd ed.). Upper Saddle River, NJ: Prentice Hall.

Benokraitis, N. V. (1998). Personal communication.

Benson, E. S. (2004). Behavior genetics: Meet molecular biology. *Monitor on Psychology, 35,* 42–45.

Benson, J. B. (1993). Season of birth and onset of locomotion: Theoretical and methodological implications. *Infant Behavior and Development, 16,* 69–81.

Bentley, D. B. (1996). Genomic sequence information should be released immediately and freely in the public domain. *Science, 274,* 533–534.

Bentur, Y., & Koren, G. (1991). The three most common occupational exposures reported by pregnant women: An update. *American Journal of Obstetrics and Gynecology, 165,* 429–437.*

Bentzen, B. L., & Mitchell, P. A. (1995). Audible signage as a wayfinding aid: Verbal landmark versus talking signs. *Journal of Visual Impairment & Blindness, 88,* 494–505.

Berenbaum, S. A. (2006). Psychological outcome in children with disorders of sex development: Implications for treatment and understanding typical development. *Annual Review of Sex Research, 17,* 1–38.

Berg, S. J., & Wynne-Edwards, K. E. (2002). Salivary hormone concentration in mothers and fathers becoming parents are not correlated. *Hormones and Behavior, 42,* 424–436.*

Bergh, C., Brodin, J., Lindberg, G., & Södersten, P. (2002). Randomized controlled trial of a treatment for anorexia and bulimia nervosa. *Proceedings of the National Academy of Sciences, 99,* 9486–9491.

Berk, L. E. (1992). Children's private speech: An overview of theory and the status of research. In R. M. Diaz & L. E. Berk (Eds.), *Private speech: From social interaction to self-regulation* (pp. 17–53). Hillsdale, NJ: Erlbaum.

Berk, L. E., Mann, T. D., & Ogan, A. T. (2006). Make-believe play: Wellspring for development of self-regulation. In D. G. Singer, R. M. Gollnkoff & K. Hirsh-Pasek (Eds.), *Play=learning: How play motivates and enhances children's cognitive and social-emotional growth.* New York: Oxford University Press.

Berlin, L. J., & Cassidy, J. (1999). Relations among relationships: Contributions from attachment theory and research. In J. Cassidy & P. R. Shaver (Eds.), *Handbook of attachment* (pp. 688–712). New York: Guildford.

Berman, A. L., Jobes, D. A., & Silverman, M. M. (2005). *Adolescent Suicide: Assessment and intervention* (2nd ed.). Washington, DC: American Psychological Association.

Berman, P. W. (1987). Children caring for babies: Age and sex differ-

ences in response to infant signals and to the social context. In N. Eisenberg (Ed.), *Contemporary topics in developmental psychology.* New York: Wiley.

Bernhard, J. K. (1992). Gender-related attitudes and the development of computer skills: A preschool intervention. *Alberta Journal of Educational Research, 38,* 177–188.*

Berninger, V. W. (2006). A developmental approach to learning disabilities. In W. Damon & R. M. Lerner (Gen. Ed.), & K. A. Renninger & I. E. Siegel (Eds.), *Handbook of child psychology: Vol. 4. Child psychology in practice* (6th ed., pp. 420–452). New York: Wiley.

Berndt, T. J. (1986). Sharing between friends: Contexts and consequences. In E. C. Mueller & C. R. Cooper (Eds.), *Process and outcome in peer relationships.* New York: Academic.

Berry, G. (2000). Multicultural media portrayals and the changing demographic landscape: The psychosocial impact of television representations on the adolescent of color. *Journal of Adolescent Health, 275,* 57–60.

Bertenthal, B., & Bai, D. L. (1989). Infants' sensitivity to optical flow for controlling posture. *Developmental Psychology, 25,* 936–945

Bertenthal, B. I., Campos, J. J., & Kermoian, R. (1994). An -epigenetic perspective on the development of self-produced locomotion and its consequences. *Current Directions in Psychological Science, 3,* 140–145.

Bertenthal, B. I., & Clifton, R. K. (1998). Perception and action. In W. Damon (Gen. Ed.) & D. Kuhn & R. Siegler (Vol. Eds.), *Handbook of child psychology: Vol. 2, Cognition, perception, and language* (pp. 51–102). New York: Wiley.

Bertenthal, B. I., Proffitt, D. R., & Cutting, J. E. (1984). Infant sensitivity to figural coherence in biomechanical motions. *Journal of Experimental Child Psychology, 37,* 213–230.

Bertenthal, B. I., Proffitt, D. R., & Kramer, S. J. (1987). The perception of biomechanical motions. Implementation of various processing constraints. *Journal of Experimental Psychology. Human Perception and Performance, 13,* 577–585.

Berthier, N. E., DeBlois, S., Poirier, C. R., Novak, J. A., & Clifton, R. K. (2000). Where's the ball? Two- and three-year-olds reason about unseen events *Developmental Psychology, 36,* 394–401.

Best, D. L. (1993). Inducing children to generate mnemonic organizational strategies: An examination of long-term retention and materials. *Developmental Psychology, 29,* 324–336.

Best, D. L., & Ornstein, P. A. (1986). Children's generation and communication of mnemonic organizational strategies. *Developmental Psychology, 22,* 845–853.

Best, D. L., & Williams, J. E. (1993). A cross-cultural viewpoint. In A. E. Beall & R. J. Sternberg (Eds.), *The psychology of gender.* (pp. 215–248). New York: Guilford Press.

Betts, L. R., & Rotenberg, K. J. (2007). Trustworthiness, friendships and self-control: Factors that contribute to young children's school adjustment. *Infant and Child Development, 16,* 491–508.

Betts, L. R., & Rotenberg, K. J. (2008). A social relations analysis of children's trust in their peers across the early years of school. *Social Development, 17,* 1039–1055.

Beutler, L. E., & Malik, M. L. (2002). *Rethinking the DSM: A psychological perspective.* Washington, DC: American Psychological Association.

Bialystok, E. (1997). Effects of bilingualism and biliteracy on children's emerging concepts of print. *Developmental Psychology, 33,* 429–440.

Bialystok, E. (2000). Symbolic representation across domains in preschool children *Journal of Experimental Child Psychology, 76,* 173–189.*

Bialystok, E. (2001). *Bilingualism in development: Language, literacy, and cognition.* New York: Cambridge University Press.*

Bialystok, E., & Hakuta, K. (1994). *In other words: The science and psychology of second-language acquisition.* New York, NY: Basic Books.*

Bialystok, E., & Hakuta, K. (1999). Confounded age: Linguistic and cognitive factors in age differences for second language learning. In D. Birdsong (Ed.), *Second language acquisition and the critical period hypothesis* (pp. 161–181). Mahwah, NJ: Erlbaum.*

Bialystok, E., & Luk, G. (2007). The universality of symbolic representation for reading in Asian and alphabetic languages. *Bilingualism: Language and Cognition, 10,* 121–129.*

Bialystok, E., & Majumder, S. (1998). The relationship between bilingualism and the development of cognitive processes in problem solving. *Applied Psycholinguistics, 19,* 69–85.*

Bialystok, E., Majumder, S., & Martin, M. M. (2003). Developing phonological awareness: Is there a bilingual advantage? *Applied Psycholinguistics, 24,* 27–44.*

Bialystok, E., & Martin, M. M. (2003). Notation to symbol: Development in children's understanding of print. *Journal of Experimental Child Psychology, 86,* 223–243.*

Bianchi, B. D., & Bakeman, R. (1983). Patterns of sex typing in an open school. In M. B. Liss (Ed.), *Social and cognitive skills: Sex roles and children's play.* New York: Academic.

Bickerton, D. (1983). Creole languages. *Scientific American, 249,* 116–122.

Bickerton, D. (1990). *Language and species.* Chicago, IL: University of Chicago Press.

Biederman, J., Monuteaux, M. C., Doyle, A. E., Weidman, L. J., Wilens, T. E., Ferrero, F., et al. (2004). Impact of executive function deficits and attention deficit/hyperactivity disorder (ADHD) on academic outcomes in children. *Journal of Consulting and Clinical Psychology, 72,* 757–766.

Bienert, H., & Schneider, B. H. (1995). Deficit-specific social skills training with peer-nominated aggressive--disruptive and sensitive-isolated preadolescents. *Journal of Clinical Child Psychology, 24,* 287–299.

Bierman, K. (2004). *Peer rejection: Causes and consequences.* New York: Guildford.

Bierman, K. L., Smoot, D. L., & Aumiller, K. (1993). Characteristics of aggressive-rejected, aggressive (nonrejected), and rejected (nonaggressive) boys. *Child Development, 64,* 139–151.

Bigelow, A. E. (1991a). Hiding in blind and sighted children. *Development and Psychopathology, 3,* 301–310.*

Bigelow, A. E. (1991b). Spatial mapping of familiar locations in blind children. *Journal of Visual Impairment and Blindness, 3,* 301–310.*

Bigelow, A. E. (1991c). The effects of distance and intervening obstacles on visual inference in blind and sighted children. *International Journal of Behavioral Development, 14,* 273–283.*

Bigelow, A. E. (1992a). Blind children's ability to predict what another sees. *Journal of Visual Impairment and Blindness, 86,* 181–185.*

Bigelow, A. E. (1992b). Locomotion and search behavior in blind infants. *Infant Behavior and Development, 15,* 179–189.*

Bigelow, A. E. (1996). Blind and sighted children's spatial knowledge of their home environments. *International Journal of Behavioral Development, 19,* 797–816.*

Bigelow, B. J. (1977). Children's friendship expectations: A cognitive-developmental study. *Child Development, 48,* 246–253.*

Bigelow, B. J. (2000). On the assessment of children in suspected child sexual abuse in light of Daubert and Frye: Limitations of profiles and interviews as scientifically grounded evidence. *Journal of Forensic Sciences, 45,* 573–581.*

Bigelow, B. J., & LaGaipa, J. J. (1975). Children's written descriptions of friendship: A multidimensional analysis. *Developmental Psychology, 11,* 857–858.*

Bigelow, B. J., Tesson, G., Lewko, J. H. (1996). *Learning the rules: The anatomy of children's relationships.* New York, NY: The Guilford Press.*

Bigelow, B. J., Tesson, G., Lewko, J. H. (1999). The contextual influences of sibling and dating relations on adolescents' personal relations and their close friends, dating partners, and parents: The Sullivan-Piaget-Hartup hypothesis considered. In J.A. McLellan & M. J. V. Pugh (Eds.), *The role of peer groups in adolescent social identity: Exploring the importance of stability and change. New directions for child and adolescent development, No. 84* (pp. 71–86). San Francisco, CA: Jossey-Bass.*

Bigelow, B. J., & Zhou, R. M. (2001). Relational scaffolding of school motivation: Developmental continuities in students' and parents' ratings of the importance of school goals. *The Journal of Genetic Psychology, 162,* 75–92.*

Bigler, R. S. (1995). The role of classification skill in mode-rating environmental influences on children's gender stereotyping: A study of the functional use of gender in the classroom. *Child Development, 68,* 530–548.

Bigler, R. S., & Liben, L. S. (1990). The role of attitudes and interventions in gender-schematic processing. *Child Development, 61,* 1440–1452.

Bigler, R. S., & Liben, L. S. (1992). Cognitive mechanisms in children's gender stereotyping: Theoretical and educational implications of a cognitive-based intervention. *Child Development, 63,* 1351–1363.

Bilger, B. (2004, April 5). The height gap. *New Yorker,* 38–45.

Binet, A. (1909/1973). *Les idées modernes sur les enfants.* Paris: Flammarion.

Birch, E. E. (1993). Stereopsis in infants and its developmental relation to visual acuity. In K. Simons (Ed.), *Early visual development: Normal and abnormal* (pp. 224–236). New York: Oxford University Press.

Birch, L. L. (2006). Child feeding practices and the etiology of obesity. *Obesity Research, 14,* 343–344.

Birch, L. L., McPhee, L., Shoba, B. C., Steinberg, L., & Krehbeil, R. (1987). "Clean up your plate." Effects of child feeding practices on the conditioning of meal size. *Learning & Motivation, 18,* 301–317.

Birch, S. A. J., & Bloom, P. (2007). The curse of knowledge in reasoning about false beliefs. *Psychological Science, 18,* 382–386.*

Birdsong, D. (1999). Introduction: Why and why nots of the critical period hypothesis for second language learning. In D. Birdsong (Ed.), *Second language acquisition and the critical period hypothesis.* Mahwah, NJ: Erlbaum.

Biringen, Z., Emde, R. N., Campos, J. J., & Appelbaum, M. I. (1995). Affective reorganization in the infant, the mother, and the dad: The role of upright locomotion and its timing. *Child Development, 66,* 499–514.

Birmaher, B., Brent, B. A., Kolko, D., Baugher, M., Bridge, J., Holder, D., et al. (2000). Clinical outcome after short-term psychotherapy for adolescents with major depressive disorder. *Archives of General Psychiatry, 57,* 29–36.

Bjorklund, D. F. (2005). *Children's thinking: Developmental function and individual differences* (4th ed.). Belmont, CA: Wadsworth.

Bjorklund, D. F., Miller, P. H., Coyle, T. R., & Slawinski, J. L. (1997). Instructing children to use memory strategies: Evidence of utilization deficiencies in memory training studies. In D. F. Bjorklund & P. H. Miller (Eds.), *New themes in strategy development.*

Bjorklund, D. F., & Pelligrini, A. D. (2002). *The origins of human nature: Evolutionary developmental psychology.* Washington, DC: American Psychological Association.

Bjorklund, D. F., Schneider, W., Cassel, W. S., & Ashley, E. (1994). Training and extension of a memory strategy: Evidence for utilization deficiencies in the acquisition of an organizational strategy in high- and low-IQ children. *Child Development, 65,* 951–965.

Black, B., & Hazen, N. (1990). Social status and patterns of communication in acquainted and unacquainted preschool children. *Developmental Psychology, 26,* 379–387.

Black, J. E., & Greenough, W. T. (1998). Developmental approaches to the memory process. In J. Martinez & R. Kesner (Eds.), *Neurobiology of learning and memory.* New York: Academic Press.

Black, J. E., Jones, T. A., Nelson, C. A., & Greenough, W. T. (1998). Neuronal plasticity and the developing brain. In N. E. Acessi & J. T. Clyde & S. I. Harrison & E. Eth (Eds.), *Handbook of child and adolescent psychiatry* (Vol. 6, pp. 31–53). New York: Wiley.

Black, M., Schuler, M., & Nair, P. (1993). Prenatal drug exposure: Neurodevelopmental outcome and parenting environment. *Journal of Pediatric Psychology, 18,* 605–620.

Blair, C., Ramey, C. T., & Hardin, M. (1995). Early intervention for low birthweight premature infants: Participation and intellectual development. *American Journal of Mental Retardation, 99,* 542–554.

Blair, F. (1957). A study of the visual memory of deaf and hearing children. *American Annals of the Deaf, 102,* 254–263.

Blake, J. (2000). Routes to child language: Evolutionary and developmental precursors. New York: Cambridge University Press.*

Blake, J., & de Boysson-Bardies, B. (1992). Patterns in babbling: A cross-linguistic study. *Journal of Child Language, 19,* 51–74.*

Blake, J., & Dolgoy, S. J. (1993). Gestural development and its relation to cognition during the transition to language. *Journal of Nonverbal Behavior, 17,* 87–102.*

Blake, J., & Fink, R. (1987). Sound-meaning correspondences in babbling. *Journal of Child Language, 14,* 229–253.*

Blake, J., Osborne, P., Cabral, M., & Gluck, P. (2003). The development of communicative gestures in Japanese infants. *First Language, 23,* 1–20.*

Blakemore, J. (1990). Children's nurturant interactions with their infant siblings: An exploration of gender differences and maternal socialization. Sex Roles, 22, 43–57

Blakemore, J. E. O. (2003). Children's beliefs about violating gender norms: Boys shouldn't look like girls, and girls shouldn't act like boys. *Sex Roles, 48,* 411–418.

Blanchard, R., Zucker, K. J., Bradley, S. J., & Hume, C. S. (1995). Birth order and sibling sex ration in homosexual male adolescents and probably pre-homosexual feminine boys. *Developmental Psychology, 31,* 22–30.*

Blasch, B. B., Long, R. G. & Griffin-Shirley, N. (1989). Results of a national survey of electronic travel aid use. *Journal of Visual Impairment & Blindness, 82,* 449–453.

Blasi, A. (1983). Moral cognition and moral action: A theoretical perspective. *Developmental Review, 3,* 178–210.

Blass, E., Ganchrow, J. R., & Steiner, J. E. (1984). Classical conditioning in newborn humans 2–48 hours of age. *Infant Behavior and Development, 7,* 223–234.

Blatz, W. E. (1938). *The five sisters: A study of child psychology.* Toronto: McClelland & Stewart.*

Blatz, W. E., Chant, N., Charles, M. W., Fletcher, M. I., Ford, N. H., Harris, A. L., MacArthur, J. W., Mason, M., & Millichamp, D. A.(1937). *Collected studies on the Dionne quintuplets.* Toronto: University of Toronto Press.*

Bloom, L. (1970). *Language development: Form and function in emerging grammars.* Cambridge, MA: MIT Press.

Bloom, L. (1991). *Language development from two to three.* New York: Cambridge University Press.

Bloom, L. (1993). *The transition from infancy to language.* New York: Cambridge University Press.

Bloom, L. (1998). Language acquisition in its developmental context. In W. Damon (Gen. Ed.), R. Siegler, & D. Kuhn (Vol. Eds.), *Handbook of child psychology: Vol. 2. Cognition, perception, and language* (5th ed., pp. 309–370). New York: Wiley.

Bloom, L., & Tinker, E. (2001). The intentionality model and language acquisition. *Monographs of the Society for Research in Child Development, 66*(4), Serial No. 267.

Bloom, L., Lifter, K., & Broughton, J. (1985). The convergence of early cognition and language in the second year of life: Problems in conceptualization and measurement. In M. Barrett (Ed.), *Single word speech.* London: Wiley.

Bloom, P. (2000). *How children learn the meaning of words.* Cambridge, MA: The MIT Press.

Blum, L. M. (2000). *At the breast: Ideologies of breastfeeding and motherhood in the contemporary United States.* Boston: Beacon Press.

Blumberg, F. C., Torenberg, M., & Randall, J. D. (2005). The relationship between preschoolers' selective attention and memory for location strategies. *Cognitive Development, 20,* 242–255.

Boccia, M., & Campos, J. (1989). Maternal emotional signals, social referencing, and infants' reactions to strangers. In N. Eisenberg (Ed.), *Empathy and related emotional responses: New directions for child development* (pp. 25–49). San Francisco: Jossey-Bass.

Bogartz, R. S., Shinsky, J. L., & Shilling, T. H. (2000). Object permanence in five-and-a-half-month-old infants? *Infancy, 1,* 403–428.

Bohannon, J. N., III, & Stanowicz, L. (1988). The issue of negative evidence: Adult responses to children's language errors. *Developmental Psychology, 24,* 684–689.

Bohannon, J. N., III, & Warren-Leubecker, A. (1988). Recent developments in child-directed speech: We've come a long way, baby talk. *Language Sciences, 10,* 89–110.

Bohlin, G., & Hagekull, B. (1993). Stranger wariness and sociability in the early years. *Infant Behavior and Development, 16,* 53–67.

Boismier, J. D. (1977). Visual stimulation and wake-sleep behavior in human neonates. *Developmental Psychobiology, 10,* 219–227.

Boisvert, M., Standing, L., & Moller, L. (1999). Successful part-whole perception in young children using multiple-choice tests. *The Journal of General Psychology, 160,* 167–180.*

Boivin, M., Hymel, S., & Hodges, E. V. E. (2001). Towards a process view of peer rejection and harassment. In J. Juvonen & S. Graham (Eds.), *Peer harassment in school: The plight of the vulnerable and victimized* (pp. 265–289). New York, NY: Guildford Press.*

Boldizar, J. P. (1991). Assessing sex typing and androgyny in children: The children's sex role inventory. *Developmental Psychology, 27,* 505–515.

Bolger, K. E., & Patterson, C. J. (2001). Developmental pathways from child maltreatment to peer rejection. *Child Development, 72,* 549–568.

Bolger, K. E., Patterson, C., & Kupersmidt, J. B. (1998). Peer relationships and self-esteem among children who have been maltreated. *Child Development, 69,* 1171–1197.

Bond, T. G. (1998). Fifty years of formal operation research: The empirical evidence. *Archives de Psychologie, 66,* 221–238.

Bonvillian, J. D., Orlansky, M. D., Novack, L. I., & Folven, R. J. (1983). Early sign language acquisition and cognitive development. In D. R. Rogers & J. A. Sloboda (Eds.), *The acquisition of symbolic skills.* New York: Plenum.

Booth, C. L., Clarke-Stewart, K. A., Vandell, D. L., McCartney, K., & Owen, M. T. (2002). Childcare usage and mother–infant "quality time." *Journal of Marriage and Family, 64,* 16–26.

Borke, H. (1971). Interpersonal perception of young children: Egocentrism or empathy. *Developmental Psychology, 5,* 263–269.

Borke, H. (1975). Piaget's mountains revisited: Changes in the egocentric landscape. *Developmental Psychology, 11,* 240–243.

Bornstein, M. H., & Putnick, D. L. (2007). Chronological age, cognitions, and practices in European American mothers: A multivariate study of parenting. *Development Psychology, 43,* 850–864.

Bornstein, M. H., & Sigman, M. D. (1986). Continuity in mental development from infancy. *Child Development, 57,* 251–274.

Bornstein, M. H., & Tamis, C. (1986). *Origins of cognitive skills in infants.* Paper presented at the International Conference on Infant Studies, Los Angeles.

Bornstein, M. H., Tal, J., & Tamis-LeMonda, C. S. (1991). Parenting in cross-cultural perspective: The United States, France, and Japan. In M. H. Bornstein (Ed.), *Cultural approaches to parenting* (pp. 69–90). Hillsdale, NJ: Erlbaum.

Bouchard, C. (1994). *The genetics of obesity.* Boca Raton, FL: CRC Press.

Bouchard, C., Cloutier, R., Gravel, F., & Sutton, A. (2008). The role of language skills in perceived prosociality in kindergarten boys and girls. *European Journal of Developmental Psychology, 5,* 338–357.*

Bouchard, G., & Lee, C. M. (2000). The marital context for father involvement with their preschool children: The role of partner support. *Journal of Prevention and Intervention in the Community, 20,* 37–53.*

Bouchard, T. J., & McGue, M. (1981). Familial studies of intelligence: A review. *Science, 212,* 1055–1059.

Bouchard, T. T., Lykken, D. T., Segal, N. L., & Wilcox, K. J. (1986). Development in twins reared apart: A test of the chrono-genetic hypothesis. In A. Demirijian (Ed.), *Human growth: A multidisciplinary review* (pp. 299–310). London: Taylor & Francis.

Bower, B. (2005). Mental meeting of the sexes: Boys' spatial advantage fades in poor families. *Science News, 168,* 323–324.

Bower, T. G. R. (1979). Visual development in the blind child. In V. Smith & J. Keen (Eds.), *Visual handicap in children.* Clinics in Development Medicine, No. 73. London: Lippincott.

Bower, T. G. R. (1989). *The rational infant: Learning in infancy.* San Francisco: Freedman.

Bowker, J. C. W., Rubin, K. H., Burgess, K. H., Booth-LaForce, C., & Rose-Krasnor, L. (2006). Behavioral characteristics associated with stable and fluid best friendship patterns in childhood. *Merrill-Palmer Quarterly, 52,* 671–693.

Bowlby, J. (1958). The nature of the child's tie to his mother. *International Journal of Psychoanalysis, 39,* 350–373.

Bowlby, J. (1960). Grief and mourning in infancy and early childhood. *The Psychoanalytic Study of the Child, 15,* 9–52.

Bowlby, J. (1969). *Attachment and loss: Vol. 1. Attachment.* New York: Basic Books.

Bowlby, J. (1973). *Separation and loss.* New York: Basic Books.

Boyum, L., & Parke, R. D. (1995). Family emotional expressiveness and children's social competence. *Journal of Marriage and the Family, 57,* 593–608.

Brackbill, Y., McManus, K., & Woodward, L. (1985). *Medication in maternity: Infant exposure and maternal information.* Ann Arbor, MI: University of Michigan Press.

Bradley, E. J., & Peters, R. D. (1991). Physically abusive and nonabusive mothers' perceptiosn of parenting and child behavior. *American Journal of Orthopsychiatry, 61,* 455–460.*

Bradley, R. H., Corwyn, R. F., Burchinal, M., McAdoo, H. P., & Garcia-Coll, C. T. (2001). The home environments of children in the United States, Part II: Relations with behavioral development through age thirteen. *Child Development, 72,* 1868–1886.

Bradley, R. H., Whiteside, L., Mundfrom, D. J., Casey, P. H., Kelleher, K. J., & Pope, S. K. (1994). Early indications of resilience and their relation to experiences in the home environments of low birthweight, premature infants living in poverty. *Child Development, 65,* 346–360.

Brainerd, C. J., & Reyna, V. F. (1990). Inclusion illusions: Fuzzy trace theory and perceptual salience effects in cognitive development. *Developmental Review, 10,* 365–403.

Bransford, J. D., Brown, A. L., & Cocking, R. R. (1999). *How people learn: Brain, mind, experience, and school.* Washington, DC: National Academy Press.

Braungart-Rieker, J. M., Garwood, M. M., Powers, B. P., & Wang, X. (2001). Parental sensitivity, infant affect and affect regulation: Predictors of later attachment. *Child Development, 72,* 252–270.

Brazelton, T. B., Nugent, J. K., & Lester, B. M. (1987). Neonatal behavioral assessment scale. In J. Osofsky (Ed.), *Handbook of infancy* (2nd ed., pp. 780–817). New York: Wiley.

Brener, R. (1940). An experimental investigation of memory span. *Journal of Experimental Psychology, 33,* 1–19.

Brennan, P. A., Hall, J., Bor, W., Najman, J. M., & Williams, G. (2003). Integrating biological and social processes in relationship to earl-onset persistent aggression in boys and girls. *Developmental Psychology, 39,* 309–323.

Bretherton, I. (2005). In pursuit of the working model construct and its relevance ot attachment relationships. In K. E. Grossmann, K. Grossmann & E. Waters (Eds.), *Attachment from infancy to adulthood* (pp. 13–47). New York: Guilford.

Bretherton, I., & Munholland, K. A. (1999). Internal working models in attachment relationships: A construct revisited. In J. Cassidy & P. R. Shaver (Eds.), *Handbook of attachment* (pp. 89–114). New York: Guilford.

Bridges, L. J., & Grolnick, W. S. (1995). The development of emotional self-regulation in infancy and early childhood. In N. Eisenberg (Ed.), *Social development. Review of personality and social psychology* (pp. 185–211). Thousand Oaks, CA: Sage.

Briones, T. J., Klintsova, A. Y., & Greenough, W. T. (2004). Stability of synaptic plasticity in adult rat visual cortex induced by complex environment exposure. *Brain Research, 1018,* 130–135.

Brocki, K. C., Randell, D. K., Bohlin, G., & Kerns, K. A. (2008). Working memory in school-aged children with attention-deficit/hyperactivity disorder combined type: Are deficits modality specific and are they independent of impaired inhibitory control? *Journal of Clinical and Experimental Neuropsychology, 30,* 749–759.*

Brockington, I. (1996). *Motherhood and mental health.* Oxford, England: Oxford University Press.

Brody, G., Flor, D., & Neubaum, E. (1998). Coparenting process and child competence among rural African-American families. In M. Lewis & C. Feiring (Eds.), *Families, risk, and competence* (pp. 227–343). Mahwah, NJ: Erlbaum.

Brody, G. H., Dorsey, S., Forehand, R., & Armistead, L. (2002). Unique and protective contributions of parenting and classroom processes to the adjustment of African-American children living in single-parent families. *Child Development, 73,* 274–286.

Brody, G. H., Ge, X., Conger, R., Gibbons, F. X., Murry, V. M., Gerrard, M., et al. (2001). The influence of neighborhood disadvantage, collective socialization and parenting on African American children's affiliation with deviant peers. *Child Development, 72,* 1231–1246.

Brody, G. H., Stoneman, Z., & Flor, D. (1996). Parental religiosity, family processes, and youth competence in rural, two-parent African American families. *Developmental Psychology, 32,* 696–706.

Brody, N. (1992). *Intelligence* (2nd ed.). San Diego, CA: Academic Press.

Brodzinsky, D. M., & Pinderhughes, E. (2002). Parenting and child development in adoptive families. In M. Bornstein (Ed.), *Handbook of parenting* (Rev. ed., Vol. 1, pp. 279–311). Mahwah, NJ: Erlbaum.

Broidy, L. M., Nagin, D. S., Tremblay, R. E., Bates, J. E., Brame, B., Dodge, K. A., et al. (2003). Developmental trajectories of childhood discipline behaviors and adolescent delinquency: A six-site, cross-national study. *Developmental Psychology, 39,* 222–245.*

Bronfenbrenner, U. (1979). *The ecology of human development.* Cambridge, MA: Harvard University Press.

Bronfenbrenner, U., & Morris, P. (2006). The ecology of developmental processes. In R. M. Lerner (Gen. Ed.), & W. Damon & R. M. Lerner (Eds.), *Handbook of child psychology: Vol. 1: Theoretical models of human development* (6th ed., pp. 89–165). New York: Wiley.

Bronfenbrenner, U., McClelland, P., Wethington, E., Moen, P., & Ceci, S. J. (1996). *The state of Americans: This generation and the next.* New York: Free Press.

Brookes, H., Slater, A., Quinn, P., Lewkowicz, D. J., Hayes, R. A., & Brown, E. (2001). Three-month-old infants learn arbitrary auditory-visual pairings between voices and faces. *Infant and Child Development, 10,* 75–82.

Brooks-Gunn, J. (1988). Antecedents and consequences of variations in girls' maturational timing. *Journal of Adolescent Health Care, 9,* 1–9.

Brooks-Gunn, J. (1995). Children in families in communities: Risk and intervention in the Bronfenbrenner tradition. In P. Moen, G. H. Elder, & K. Lüscher (Eds.), *Examining lives in context* (pp. 467–519). Washington, D.C.: American Psychological Association.

Brooks-Gunn, J., Berlin, L. J., Leventhal, T., & Fuligni, A. S. (2000). Depending on the kindness of strangers: Current national data initiatives and developmental research. *Child Development, 71,* 257–268.

Brooks-Gunn, J., Britto, P. J. R., & Brady, C. (1999). Struggling to make ends meet: Poverty and child development. In M. E. Lamb (Ed.), *Parenting and child development in "nontraditional" families* (pp. 279–304). Mahwah, NJ: Erlbaum.

Brooks-Gunn, J., Klebanov, P. K., Smith, J., Duncan, G. J., & Lee, K. (2003). The black-white test score gap in young children: Contributions of test and family characteristics. *Applied Developmental Science, 7,* 239–252.

Brooks-Gunn, J., & Lewis, M. (1984). The development of early visual self-recognition. *Developmental Review, 4,* 215–239.

Brooks-Gunn, J., & Ruble, D. N. (1984). The experience of menarche from a developmental perspective. In J. Brooks-Gunn & A. C. Petersen (Eds.), *Girls at puberty: Biological, psychological and social perspectives.* New York: Plenum.

Brooks-Gunn, J., Smith, J., Berlin, L. J., & Lee, K. (2001). Family-work: Welfare changes, parenting, and young children. In G. K. Brookins (Ed.), *Exits from poverty.* New York: Cambridge University Press.

Brooks-Gunn, J., & Warren, W. P. (1985). The effects of delayed menarche in different contexts: Dance and nondance students. *Journal of Youth and Adolescence, 14,* 285–300.

Bronfenbrenner, U., & Morris, P. (2006). The ecology of developmental processes. In R. M. Lerner (Gen. Ed.), & W. Damon & R. M. Lerner (Eds.), *Handbook of child psychology: Vol. 1: Theoretical models of human development* (6th ed., pp. 89–165). New York: Wiley.

Brown, A. L. (1975). The development of memory: Knowing, knowing about knowing, and knowing how to know. In H. W. Reese (Ed.), *Advances in child development and behavior* (Vol. 10, pp. 103–152). New York: Academic Press.

Brown, A. L. (1994). The advancement of learning. *Educational Researcher, 23,* 4–12.

Brown, A. L., & Campione, J. (1990). Communities of learning and thinking, or a context by any other name. In D. Kuhn (Ed.), *Developmental perspectives on teaching and learning thinking skills: Contributions in human development* (Vol. 21, pp. 108–126). Basel: Karger.

Brown, A. L., & Campione, J. C. (1997). Designing a community of young learners: Theoretical and practical lessons. In N. M. Lambert & B. L. McCombs (Eds.), *How students learn: Reforming schools through learner-centered education* (pp. 153–186). Washington, DC: American Psychological Association.

Brown, A. L., & Campione, J. C. (1998). Designing a community of young learners: Theoretical and practical lessons. In N. M. Lambert & B. L. McCoombs (Eds.), *How students learn: Reforming schools through learner-centered education* (pp. 153–186). Washington, DC: APA.

Brown, B. B. (1990). Peer groups and peer cultures. In S. S. Feldman & G. R. Elliott (Eds.), *At the threshold* (pp. 171–196). Cambridge, MA: Harvard University Press.

Brown, B. B., & Huang, B. (1995). Examining parenting practices in different peer contexts: Implications for adolescent trajectories. In L. J. Crockett & A. C. Crouter (Eds.), *Pathways through adolescence: Individual development in relation to social contexts.* Mahwah, NJ: Erlbaum.

Brown, B. B., & Klute, C. (2003). Friends, cliques, and crowds. In G. R. Adams & M. D. Berzonski (Eds.), *Blackwell handbook of adolescence* (pp. 330–348). Malden, MA: Blackwell.

Brown, D., & Pipe, M. E. (2003). Individual differences in children's event memory reports and the narrative elaboration technique. *Journal of Applied Psychology, 88,* 195–206.

Brown, E., & Brownell, C. (1990). *Individual differences in toddlers' interaction styles.* Paper presented at International Conference on Infant Studies, Montreal.

Brown, R. (1973). *A first language: The early stages.* Cambridge, MA: Harvard University Press.

Brown, R., & Bellugi, U. (1964). Three processes in the child's acquisition of syntax. In E. G. Lenneberg (Ed.), *New directions in the study of language.* Cambridge, MA: MIT Press.

Brown, R., & Hanlon, C. (1970). Derivational complexity and order of acquisition in child speech. In J. Hayes (Ed.), *Cognition and the development of language* (pp. 11–54). New York: Wiley.

Brown, R. E., Murdoch, T., Murphy, P. R., & Moger, W. H. (1995). Hormonal responses of male gerbils to stimuli from their mate and pups. *Hormones and Behavior, 28,* 474–491.

Brownell, C. A. (1990). Peer social skills in toddlers: Competencies and constraints illustrated by same age and mixed-age interaction. *Child Development, 61,* 838–848.

Bruck, M., Ceci, S. J., & Hembrooke, H. (2002). The nature of children's true and false narratives. *Developmental Review, 22,* 520–534.*

Bruner, J. S. (1966). On cognitive growth. In J. S. Bruner, R. R. Olver, & P. M. Greenfield (Eds.), *Studies in cognitive growth.* New York: Wiley.

Bruner, J. S. (1983). *Child's talk; Learning to use language.* New York, NY: Norton.

Bruner, J. (1990). *Acts of meaning.* Cambridge, MA: Harvard University Press.

Bryant, P. E., & Trabasso, J. (1971). Transitive inferences and memory in young children. *Nature, 232,* 456–458.

Bryden, M. P. (1982). *Laterality.* New York: Academic.*

Bryden, M. P. (1988). Does laterality make any difference? Thoughts on the relation between asymmetry and reading. In D. L. Molfese & S. J. Segalowitz (Eds.), *Brain lateralization in children* (pp. 509–525). New York: Guilford Press.*

Bryden, M. P., & MacRae, L. (1989). Dichotic laterality effects obtained with emotional words. *Neuropsychiatry, Neuropsychology & Behavioral Neurology, 1,* 171–176.*

Buchanan, C. M., & Heiges, K. L. (2001). When the conflict continues after the marriage ends: Effects of postdivorce conflict on children. In J. Grych & F. D. Fincham (Eds.), *Interpersonal conflict and child development* (pp. 337–362). New York: Cambridge University Press.

Buchanan, C. M., Maccoby, E. E., & Dornbusch, S. M. (1991). Caught between parents: Adolescents' experience in divorced families. *Child Development, 62,* 1008–1029.

Buchanan, C. M., Maccoby, E. E., & Dornbusch, S. M. (1996). *Adolescents after divorce.* Cambridge, MA: Harvard University Press.

Bukowski, W. M., Brendgen, M., & Vitaro, F. (2007). Peers and socialization: Effects on externalizing and internalizing problems. In J. E. Grusec & P. D. Hastings (Eds.), *Handbook of socialization: Theory and research* (pp. 355–381). New York: Guilford.*

Bruck, M., Ceci, S. J., & Principe, G. F. (2006). The child and the law. In W. Damon & R. M. Lerner (Gen. Ed.), & K. A. Renninger & I. E. Siegel (Eds.), *Handbook of child psychology: Vol. 4. Child*

psychology in practice (6th ed., pp. 776–816). New York: Wiley.*

Budwig, N. (2002). A developmental-functionalist approach to mental state talk. In E. Amsel & J. P. Byrnes (Eds.), *Language, literacy, and cognitive development* (pp. 59–86). Mahwah, NJ: Erlbaum.

Bugental, D., & Grusec, J. E. (2006). Socialization processes. In W. Damon & R. M. Lerner (Gen. Ed.), & N. Eisenberg (Ed.), *Handbook of child psychology: Vol. 3. Social, emotional, and personality development* (6th ed., pp. 89–165). New York: Wiley.*

Bugental, D. B., & Happaney, K. (2004). Predicting infant maltreatment in low-income families: The interactive effects of maternal attributions and child status at birth. *Developmental Psychology, 40,* 234–243.

Buhs, E. S., & Ladd, G. W. (2001). Peer rejection as an antecedent of young children's school adjustment: An examination of mediating processes. *Developmental Psychology, 37,* 550–560.

Bukowski, W. M., Brendgen, M., & Vitaro, F. (2007). Peers and socialization: Effects on externalizing and internalizing problems. In J. E. Grusec & P. D. Hastings (Eds.), *Handbook of socialization: Theory and research* (pp. 355–381). New York: Guilford.*

Bullinger, A., & Chatillon, J. (1983). Recent theory and research of the Genevan school. In P. H. Mussen (Ed.), *Handbook of child psychology* (Vol. 3). New York: Wiley.

Bullock, D. (1983). Seeking relations between cognitive and social-interactive transitions. In K. W. Fischer (Ed.), *Levels and transitions in children's development: New directions in child development.* San Francisco: Jossey-Bass.

Bullock, D., & Merrill, L. (1980). The impact of personal preference on consistency through time: The case of childhood aggression. *Child Development, 51,* 808–814.

Bullock, M. (1985). Animism in childhood thinking: A new look at an old question. *Developmental Psychology, 21,* 217–225.

Burack, J. A. & Enns, J. T. (1997). *Attention, development and psychopathology* (pp. 123–146). New York, NY: Guildford Press.*

Burden, M. J., Jacobson, S. W., & Jacobson, J. L. (2005). Relation of prenatal alcohol exposure to cognitive processing speed and efficiency in childhood. *Alcoholism: Clinical and Experimental Research, 29,* 1473–1483.

Bureau of Justice Statistics. (2006). Violent crime rates declined for both males and females since 1994

from http://www.ojp.usdoj.gov/bjs/.

Burks, V., Laird, R., Dodge, K., Pettit, G., & Bates, J. (1999). Knowledge structures, social information processing, and children's aggressive behavior. *Social Development, 8,* 220–236.

Burnett, A., Beach, H. D., & Sullivan, A. M. (1963). Intelligence in a restricted environment. *Canadian Psychologist, 4,* 126–136.

Burns, G. W., & Bottino, P. J. (1989). *The science of genetics* (6th ed.). New York: Macmillan.

Burns, K. A., Deddish, R. B., Burns, K., & Hatcher, R. P. (1983). Use of oscillating waterbeds and rhythmic sounds for premature infant stimulation. *Developmental Psychology, 19,* 746–751.

Burton, R. V. (1963). The generality of honesty reconsidered. *Psychological Review, 70,* 481–499.

Burton, R. V. (1984). A paradox in theories and research in moral development. In W. M. Kurtines & J. L. Gewirtz (Eds.), *Morality, moral behavior, and moral development.* New York: Wiley.

Bus, A. G., van IJzendoorn, M. H., & Pellegrini, A. D. (1995). Joint book reading makes for success in learning to read: A meta-analysis on intergenerational transmission of literacy. *Review of Educational Research, 65,* 1–21.

Bushman, B. J. (2002). Does venting anger feed or extinguish the flame? Catharsis, rumination, distraction, anger and aggressive responding. *Personality and Social Psychology Bulletin, 28,* 724–731.

Bushman, B. J., Baumeister, R. F., & Phillips, C. M. (2001). Do people aggress to improve their mood? Catharsis beliefs, affect regulation opportunity, and aggressive responding. *Journal of Personality and Social Psychology, 81,* 17–32.

Bushman, B. J., Baumeister, R. F., & Stack, A. D. (2001). Catharsis, aggression, and persuasive influence: Self-fulfilling or self-defeating prophecies. *Journal of Personality and Social Psychology, 76,* 367–376.

Bushman, D., & Huesmann, L. R. (2001). Effects of televised violence on aggression. In D. Singer & J. Singer (Eds.), *Handbook of children and the media* (pp. 223–254). Thousand Oaks, CA: Sage.

Bushnik, T. (2006). *Child Care in Canada* (Catalogue no. 89-599-MIE—No. 003). Ottawa: Statistics Canada.*

Busjahn, A., & Hur, Y.-M. (2006). Twin registries: An ongoing success story. *Twin Research and Human Genetics, 9,* 705–706.

Buss, D. (2000). Evolutionary psychology. In A. Kazdin (Ed.), *Encyclopedia of psychology.* Washington, DC: American Psychological Association and Oxford University Press.

Buss, D. (2003). *The evolution of desire: Strategies of human mating.* New York: Basic Books.

Buss, D. (2007). *Evolutionary psychology: The new science of the mind* (2nd ed.). New York: Basic Books.

Bussey, K. (1992). Lying and truthfulness: Children's definitions, standards and evaluative reactions. *Child Development, 63,* 129–137.

Bussey, K., & Perry, D. G. (1977). The imitation of resistance to deviation: Conclusive evidence for an elusive effect. *Developmental Psychology, 13,* 438–443.

Butler, S. C., Berthier, N. E., & Clifton, R. K. (2002). Two-year-olds' search strategies and visual tracking in a hidden displacement task. *Developmental Psychology, 38,* 581–590.

Butterfield, E. C., & Siperstein, G. N. (1974). Influence of contingent auditory stimulation upon non-nutritional suckle. In *Proceedings of the Third Symposium on Oral Sensation and Perception: The Mouth of the Infant.* Springfield, IL: Charles C. Thomas.

Butterworth, G. (1998). What's special about pointing in babies. In F. Simion & G. Butterworth (Eds.), *The development of sensory, motor and cognitive capacities in early infancy: From perception to cognition* (pp. 171-190). East Sussex, England: Psychology Press Ltd.

Butterworth, G., & Cochran, E. (1980). Towards a mechanism of joint visual attention in human infancy. *International Journal of Behavioral Development, 3,* 253–272.

Butterworth, G., Franco, F., McKenzie, B., Graupner, L., & Todd, B. (2002). Dynamic aspects of visual event perception and the production of pointing by human infants. *British Journal of Developmental Psychology, 20,* 1–24.

Butterworth, G., & Grover, L. (1990). Joint visual attention, manual pointing and preverbal communication in human infancy. In M. Jeannerod (Ed.), *Attention and performance XIII.* Hillsdale, NJ: Erlbaum.

Buysse, V., & Bailey, D. B. (1993). Behavioral and developmental outcomes in young children with disabilities in integrated and segregated settings: A review of comparative studies. *Journal of Special Education, 26,* 434–461.

Cairns, R. B., & Cairns, B. D. (1994). *Lifelines and risks: Path-*

ways of youth in our time. Cambridge, England: Cambridge University Press.

Cairns, R. B., & Cairns, D. B. (2006). The making of developmental psychology. In W. Damon & R. M. Lerner (Gen. Ed.), & R. M. Lerner (Ed.), *Handbook of child psychology: Vol. 1: Theoretical models of human development* (6th ed., pp. 89–165). Hoboken, NJ: John Wiley.

Caldas, S. J., & Caron-Caldas, S. (2000). The influence of family, school, and community on bilingual preferences: Results from a Louisiana/Québec case study. *Applied Psycholinguistics, 21,* 365–381.*

Calkins, S. D., Dedmon, S. E., Gill, K. L., Lomax, L. E., & Johnson, L. M. (2002). Frustration in infancy: Implications for emotion regulation, physiological processes, and temperament. *Infancy, 3,* 175–194.

Callanan, M. A., & Oakes, L. M. (1992). Preschoolers' questions and parents' explanations: Causal thinking in everyday activity. *Cognitive Development, 7,* 213–233.

Campaign 2000. (2008). *Campaign 2000 report card on child and family poverty in Canada 2008.* Toronto: Campaign 2000.*

Campbell, F. P., Pungello, E. P., Miller-Johnson, S., Burchinal, M., & Ramey, C. T. (2001). The development of cognitive and academic abilities: Growth curves from an early childhood educational experiment. *Developmental Psychology, 37,* 231–242.

Campbell, S. B. (1998). Developmental considerations in child psychopathology. In T. Ollendick & M. Hersen (Eds.), *Handbook of child psychopathology* (3rd ed., pp. 1–35). New York: Plenum.

Campbell, S. B. (2000). Developmental perspectives on attention deficit disorder. In A. Sameroff & M. Lewis & S. Miller (Eds.), *Handbook of child psychopathology* (2nd ed., pp. 383–401). New York: Plenum.

Campbell, S. B. (2002). *Behavior problems in preschool children: Clinical and developmental issues* (2nd ed.). New York: Guilford.

Campos, J. J., Anderson, D. I., Barbu-Roth, M. A., Hubbard, E. M., Hertenstein, M. J., & Witherington, D. (2000). Travel broadens the mind. *Infancy, 2,* 149–219.

Campos, J. J., Bertenthal, B., & Kermonian, R. (1992). Early experience and emotional development: The emergence of wariness of heights. *Psychological Science, 3,* 61–64.

Campos, J. J., Hiatt, S., Ramsey, D., Henderson, C., & Svejda, M. (1978). The emergence of fear on the visual cliff. In M. Lewis & L. Rosenblum (Eds.), *The origins of affect.* New York: Plenum.

Campos, J. J., Langer, A., & Krowitz, A. (1970). Cardiac responses on the visual cliff in prelocomotor human infants. *Science, 170,* 196–197.

Campos, R. P. (1989). Soothing-pain elicited distress in infants with swaddling and pacifiers. *Child Development, 60,* 781–792.

Camras, L. A., Malatesta, C., & Izard, C. (1991). The development of facial expressions in infancy. In R. Feldman & B. Rime (Eds.), *Fundamentals of nonverbal behavior.* New York: Cambridge University Press.

Canada Council (1977). *20th Annual report: The Canadian Council.* Ottawa, ON: Author.*

Canadian Institute of Child Health (1994). *The health of Canada's children: A CICH profile, 2nd Edition.* Ottawa, CA: Canadian Institute of Child Health.*

Canfield, R. L., & Haith, M. M. (1991). Young infants' visual expectations for symmetrical and asymmetrical sequences. *Developmental Psychology, 27,* 198–208.

Canning, P. M., Courage, M. L., & Frizzell, L. M. (2004). Prevalence of overweight and obesity in a provincial population of Canadian preschool children. *Canadian Medical Association Journal, 171,* 240–242.*

Cantor, N. (2000). Life task -problem solving: Situational affordances and personal needs. In E. T. Higgins, A. W. Kruglanski, & W. Arie (Eds.), *Motivational science: Social and personality perspectives. Key reading in social psychology* (pp. 100–110). New York: Psychology Press.

Cantwell, D. P., Baker, L., & Rutter, M. (1978). Family factors. In M. Rutter & E. Schopier (Eds.), *Autism: A reappraisal of concepts and treatment* (pp. 269–296). New York: Plenum Press.

Cantwell, D. P., Russell, A. T., Mattison, R., & Will, L. A. (1979). A comparison of *DSM-II* and *DSM-III* in the diagnosis of childhood psychiatric disorders. *Archives of General Psychiatry, 36,* 1208–1228.

Capaldi, D., & Clark, S. (1998). Prospective family predictors of aggression toward female partners for at-risk young men. *Developmental Psychology, 34,* 1175–1188.

Capodilupo, A. M. (1992). A neo-structural analysis of children's response to instruction in the sight-reading of musical notation. In R. Case (Ed.), *The mind's staircase: Exploring the conceptual underpinnings of children's thought and knowledge* (pp. 99–115). Hillsdale, NJ: Erlbaum.*

Capron, C., & Duyme, M. (1989). Assessment of effects of socioeconomic status on IQ in a cross-fostering study. *Nature, 340,* 552–554.

Cardon, L. R. (1994). Height, weight, and obesity. In J. C. DeFries, R. Plomin, & D. W. Fulker (Eds.), *Nature and nurture during middle childhood* (pp. 46–65). Oxford: Blackwell.

Carey, G. (1994). Genetics and violence. In A. J. Reis, K. A. Miczek, & J. A. Roth (Eds.), *Understanding and preventing violence* (pp. 21–58). Washington, DC: National Academy Press.

Carlson, V., Cicchetti, D., Barnett, D., & Braunwald, K. (1989). Disorganized/ disoriented attachment relationships in maltreated infants. *Developmental Psychology, 25,* 525–531.

Carmichael, M. (2004). Have it your way: Redesigning birth. *Newsweek,* May 10, 70–71.

Carmody, D. P., Bendersky, M., Dunn, S. M., DeMarco, J. K., Hegyi, T., Hiatt, M., et al. (2006). Early risk, attention, and brain activation in adolescents born preterm. *Child Development, 77,* 384–394.*

Carnagey, N. L., Anderson, C. A., & Bartholow, B. D. (2007a). Media violence and social neuroscience: New questions and new opportunities. *Current Directions in Psychological Science, 16,* 178–182.

Carnagey, N. L., Anderson, C. A., & Bushman, B. J. (2007b). The effect of videogame violence on physiological desensitization to real-life violence. *Journal of Experimental Social Psychology, 43,* 489–496.

Carpendale, J., & Lewis, C. (2006). *How children develop social understanding.* Malden, MA: Blackwell.

Carpendale, J. I., & Chandler, M. (1996). On the distinction between false belief understanding and subscribing to an interpretive theory of mind. *Child Development, 67,* 1686–1706.*

Carpendale, J. I. M. (2000). Kohlberg and Piaget on stages and moral reasoning. *Developmental Review, 20,* 181–205.*

Carpendale, J. I. M., & Krebs, D. L. (1992). Situational variation in moral judgment: An a stage or on a stage? *Journal of Youth and Adolescence, 21,* 203–224.*

Carpendale, J. I. M., & Krebs, D. L. (1995). Variations in level of moral judgment as a function of type of dilemma and moral choice. *Journal of Personality, 63,* 289–313.*

Carr, M., & Jessup, D. L. (1995). Cognitive and metacognitive predictors of mathematics strategy use. *Learning and Individual Differences, 7,* 235–247.

Carraher, T. N., Schliemann, A. D., & Carraher, D. W. (1988). Mathematical concepts in everyday life. *New Directions for Child Development, 41,* 71–87.

Carroll, J. B. (1993). *Human cognitive abilities: A survey of factor analytic studies.* New York: Cambridge University Press.

Carroll, J. M., Snowling, M. J., Hulme, C., & Stevenson, J. (2003). The development of phonological awareness in preschool children. *Developmental Psychology, 39,* 913–923.

Carson, R. C. (1991). Dilemmas in the pathway of the *DSM-IV. Journal of Abnormal Psychology, 100,* 302–307.

Carson, R. C., & Butcher, J. N. (1992). *Abnormal psychology and modern life* (9th ed.). New York: HarperCollins.

Carter, C. S., Freeman, J. H., & Stanton, M. E. (1995). Neonatal medial prefrontal lesions and recovery of spatial delayed alternation in the rat: Effects of delay interval. *Developmental Psychobiology, 28,* 269–279.

Carver, K., Joyner, K., & Udry, J. R. (2003). National estimates of adolescent romantic relationships. In P. Florsheim (Ed.), *Adolescent romantic relations and sexual behaviors* (pp. 23–56). Mahwah, NJ: Erlbaum.

Casasola, M., Cohen, L. B., & Chiarello, E. (2003). Six-month-old infants' categorization of spatial relations. *Child Development, 74,* 679–693.

Case, R. (1984). The process of stage transition: A neo-Piagetian view. In R. Sternberg (Ed.), *Mechanisms of cognitive development.* New York: Freeman.*

Case, R. (1985). *Intellectual development: Birth to adulthood.* New York: Academic.*

Case, R. (1992). Neo-Piagetian theories of child development. In R. J. Sternberg & C. A. Berg (Eds.), *Intellectual development,* (pp. 161–196). New York: Cambridge University Press.*

Case, R. (1996). Modeling the dynamic interplay between general and specific change in children's conceptual understanding. In R. Case & Y. Okamoto (Eds.), The role of central conceptual structures in the development of children's thought. *Monographs of the Society for Research in Child Development, 61,* Serial No. 246 Nos. 1 & 2, 156–188.*

Case, R. (1998). The development of conceptual structures. In W. Damon (Series Ed.), & D. Kuhn & R. S. Siegler (Vol. Eds.), *Handbook of child psychology: Vol. 2, Cognition, perception, and language* (5th ed., pp. 745–800). New York: Wiley.

Case, R., & Griffin, (1990). Child cognitive development. The role of central conceptual structures in the development of scientific and social thought. In C. A. Hauert (Ed.), *Developmental psychology: Cognitive, perceptuo-motor and neuropsychological perspectives.* Amsterdam: North Holland.*

Case, R., Hayward, S., Lewis, M., & Hurst, P. (1988). Toward a neo-Piagetian theory of cognitive and emotional development. *Developmental Review, 8,* 1–51.

Case, R., & Mueller, M. P. (2001). Differentiation, integration, and covariance mapping as fundamental processes in cognitive and neurological growth. In J. L. McClelland & R. S. Siegler (Eds.), *Mechanisms of cognitive development: Behavioral and neural perspectives. Carnegie Mellon symposia on cognition* (pp. 185–219). Mahwah, NJ: Erlbaum.*

Case, R., Okamoto, Y., Henderson, B., & McKeough, A. (1993). Individual variability and consistency in cognitive development: New evidence for the existence of central conceptual structures. In R. Case & W. Edelstein (Eds.), *The new structuralism in cognitive development: Theory and research on individual pathways.* Basel: Karger.*

Casey, B. J. (2001). Disruption of inhibitory control in developmental disorders: A mechanistic model of implicated frontostriatal circuitry. In J. McClelland & R. Siegler (Eds.), *Mechanisms of cognitive development* (pp. 327–349). Mahwah, NJ: Erlbaum.

Cashon, C. H., & Cohen, L. B. (2000). Eight-month-old infants' perception of possible and impossible events. *Infancy, 1,* 429–446.

Casiro O. G., et al. (1994). Public awareness of the risks of drinking alcohol during pregnancy: The effects of a television campaign. *Canadian Journal of Public Health, 85,* 23–27.*

Caspi, A., Elder, G. H., & Bem, D. J. (1987). Moving against the world: Life course patterns of explosive children. *Developmental Psychology, 23,* 308–313.

Caspi, A., Elder, G. H., & Bem, D. J. (1988). Moving away from the world: Life-course patterns of shy children. *Developmental Psychology, 24,* 824–831.

Caspi, A., Lyman, D., Moffitt, T. E., & Silva, P. A. (1993). Unraveling girls' delinquency: Biological, dispositional and contextual contributions to adolescent misbehavior. *Developmental Psychology, 29,* 19–30.

Caspi, A., Sugden, K., Moffitt, T. E., Taylor, A., Craig, I. W., Harrington, H., et al. (2003). Influence of life stress on depression: Moderation by a polymorphism in the 4-HTT gene. *Science, 301,* 386–389.

Caspi, A., Williams, B., Kim-Cohen, J., Craig, I. W., Milne, B. J., Poulton, R., et al. (2007). Moderation of breastfeeding effects on the IQ by genetic variation in fatty acid metabolism. *Proceedings of the National Academy of Sciences, 104,* 18860–18865.

Cassidy, J. (1988). Child-mother attachment and the self in six-year-olds. *Child Development, 59,* 121–135.

Cassidy, J. (1999). The nature of the child's ties. In J. Cassidy & P. R. Shaver (Eds.), *Handbook of attachment: Theory, research, and clinical applications.* New York: Guildford.

Cassidy, J. (2003). Continuity and change in the measurement of attachment: Comment on Fraley and Spieker (2003). *Developmental Psychology, 39,* 409–412.

Cassidy, J., & Asher, S. R. (1992). Loneliness and sociometric status among young children. *Child Development, 63,* 350–365.

Cassidy, J., & Berlin, L. J. (1994). The insecure/ambivalent pattern of attachment: Theory and research. *Child Development, 65,* 971–991.

Cassidy, K. W., Fineberg, D. S., Brown, K., & Perkins, A. (2005). Theory of mind may be contagious, but you don't catch it from your twin. *Child Development, 76,* 97–106.

Castral, T. C., Warnock, F., Leite, A. M., Haas, V. J., & Scochi, C. G. S. (2008). The effects of skin-to-skin contact during acute pain in preterm newborns. *European Journal of Pain, 12,* 464–471.

Cathey, L. T. (2006). Stress reactivity and regulation in infancy: Indicators, correlates, and methods of soothing. *Stress, Trauma and Crisis: An International Journal, 9,* 161–173.

Cavallini, A., Fazzi, E., Viviani, V., Astori, M. G., Zaviero, S., Bianchi, P. E., & Lanzi, G. (2002). Visual acuity in the first two years of life in healthy term newborns: An experience with the Teller Acuity Cards. *Functional Neurology: New Trends in Adaptive and Behavioral Disorders, 17,* 87–92.

Ceballo, R., & McLoyd, V. (2002). Social support and parenting in poor, dangerous neighborhoods. *Child Development, 73,* 1310–1321.

Ceci, S. J. (1991). How much does schooling influence general intelligence and its cognitive components? A reassessment of the evidence. *Developmental Psychology, 27,* 703–720.

Ceci, S. J. (1996). *On intelligence: A bioecological treatise on intellectual development (expanded edition).* Cambridge, MA: Harvard University Press.

Ceci, S. J., & Bruck, M. (1998). Children's testimony: Applied and basic issues. In W. Damon (Gen. Ed.), I. Sigel & K. A. Renninger (Vol. Eds.), *Handbook of child psychology: Vol. 4* (pp. 713–774). New York: Wiley.

Ceci, S. J., Leichtman, M. D., & White, T. (1998). Interviewing preschoolers' remembrance of things planted. In D. P. Peters (Ed.), *The child witness in context cognitive, social and legal perspectives.* Holland: Kluwer.

Ceci, S. J., Ross, D. F., & Toglia, M. P. (1987). Suggestibility of children's memory: Psycholegal implications. *Journal of Experimental Psychology: General, 116,* 38–49.

Ceci, S. J., & Williams, W. M. (1997). Schooling, intelligence, and income. *American Psychologist, 52,* 1051–1058.

Centers for Disease Control and Prevention. (2005). Child maltreatment: Fact sheet. Retrieved April 11, 2005, from http://www.cdc.gov/ncpic/factsheets/cmfacts.htm.

Centers for Disease Control and Prevention. (2007). *Morbidity and Morality.* Weekly Report (Sept. 8, 2007). Teen CDC: Atlanta GA. .

Chabris, C. F. (1999). Prelude or requiem for the "Mozart Effect"? *Nature, 400,* 826–827.

Chandler, M., & Hala, S. (1994). The role of personal involvement in the assessment of early false-belief skills. In C. Lewis and D. Mitchell (Eds.), *Origins of an understanding of mind* (pp. 403–426). Mahwah, NH: Erlbaum.*

Chandler, M. J. (1973). Egocentrism and antisocial behavior: The assessment and training of social perspective taking skills. *Developmental Psychology, 9,* 326–332.

Chandler, M. J., Greenspan, S., & Barenboim, C. (1973). Judgments of intentionality in response to videotaped and verbally presented moral dilemmas: The medium is the message. *Child Development, 44,* 315–320.

Chandler, M. J., Lalonde, C. E., Sokol, B. W., & Hallett, D. (2003). Personal persistence, identity development, and suicide. *Monographs of the Society for Research on Child Development, 68,* (1, Serial No. 273).

Chang, H. W., & Trehub, S. E. (1977). Infants' perception of grouping in auditory patterns. *Child Development, 48,* 1666–1670.*

Chao, R. (2001). Extending research on the consequences of parenting style for Chinese Americans and European Americans. *Child Development, 72,* 1832–1843.

Chao, R., & Tseng, V. (2002). Parenting of Asians. In M. H. Bornstein (Ed.), *Handbook of parenting: Vol. 4: Social conditions and applied parenting* (2nd ed., pp. 59–93). Mahwah, NJ: Erlbaum.

Chao, R. K. (1994). Beyond parental control and authoritarian parenting style: Understanding Chinese parenting through the cultural notion of training. *Child Development, 65,* 1111–1119.

Chao, R. K., & Kim, K. (2000). Parenting differences among immigrant Chinese fathers and mothers in the United States. *Journal of Chinese Societies, 1,* 71–91.

Chapman, M. (1988). *Constructive evolution: Origins and development of Piaget's thought.* New York: Cambridge University Press.*

Chapman, M., & Carpendale, J. M. (1999). Constructivism and the problem of reality. *Journal of Applied Developmental Psychology, 20,* 31–43.*

Charlesworth, R., & Hartup, W. W. (1967). Positive social reinforcement in the nursery school peer group. *Child Development, 38,* 993–1002.

Charlesworth, W. (1988). Resources and resource acquisition during ontogeny. In K. MacDonald (Ed.), *Sociobiological perspectives on human development.* New York: Springer-Verlag.

Charlesworth, W., & Dzur, C. (1987). Gender comparison of preschoolers' behavior and resource utilization. *Child Development, 58,* 191–200.

Charlton, A. (1994). Children and passive smoking: A review. *Journal of Family Practice, 38,* 267–277.

Chase, W. G., & Simon, H. A. (1973). The mind's eye in chess. In W. G. Chase (Ed.), *Visual information processing.* New York: Academic.

Chen, C., & Stevenson, H. W. (1995). Motivation and mathematics achievement: A comparative study of Asian-American, Caucasian-American and East Asian high school students. *Child Development, 66,* 1215–1234.

Chen, C., Stevenson, H. W., Hayward, C., & Burgess, S. (1995). Culture and academic achievement: Ethnic and cross-national differences. In P. Pintrich & M. Maehr (Eds.), *Advances in motivation and achievement: Vol. 9. Culture, race, ethnicity, and motivation.* New York: Plenum.

Chen, K. (1974). Free recall learning of deaf and hearing subjects. *Journal of General Psychology, 91,* 155–156.

Chen, X. (2000). Growing up in a collectivist culture: Socialization and socioemotional development in Chinese children. In A. L. Comunian & U. P. Gielen (Eds.), *Human development in cross-culture perspective* (pp. 331–353). Padua, Italy: Cedam.

Chen, X., Chang, L., & He, Y. (2003). The peer group as context: Mediating and moderating effects on relations between academic achievement and social functioning in Chinese children. *Child Development, 74,* 710–727.*

Chen, X., Dong, Q., & Zhou, H. (1997). Authoritative and authoritarian parenting practices and social and school performance in Chinese children. *International Journal of Behavioral Development, 21,* 855–873.*

Chen, X., French, D., & Schneider, B. H. (Eds.). (2007). *Peer relationships in cultural context.* New York: Cambridge University Press.*

Chen, X., Liu, M., Li, B., Cen, G., Chen, H., &Wang, L. (2000). Maternal authoritative and authoritarian attitudes and mother-child interactions and relationships in urban China. *International Journal of Behavioral Development, 24,* 119–126.*

Chen, X., Liu, M., Rubin, K. H., Cen, G., Gao, X., & Li, D. (2002). Sociability and prosocial orientation as predictors of youth adjustment: A seven-year longitudinal study in a Chinese sample. *International Journal of Behavioral Development, 26,* 128–136.*

Chen, Z., & Daehler, M. W. (1989). Positive and negative transfer in analogical problem solving by 6-year-old children. *Cognitive Development, 4,* 327–344.

Chen, Z., Sanchez, R. P., & Campbell, T. (1997). From beyond to within their grasp: The rudiments of analogical problem solving in 10- and 13-month-olds. *Developmental Psychology, 33,* 790–801.

Cheoud, M., Ceponiené, R., Leppänen, P., Alho, K., Kujala, T., Renlund, M., Fellman, V., & Näätänen, R. (2002). The auditory sensory memory trace decays rapidly in newborns. *Scandanavian Journal of Psychology, 43,* 33–39.

Cherlin, A. J., & Furstenberg, F. F. (1994). Stepfamilies in the United States: A reconsideration. *Annual Review of Sociology, 20,* 359–381.

Cherney, I. D., & London, K. (2006). Gender-linked differences in toys, television shows, computer games, and outdoor activities of 5- to 13-year-old children. *Sex Roles, 54,* 717–726.

Chi, M. T. H. (1976). Short term memory limitations in children: Capacity or processing deficits? *Memory and Cognition, 4,* 559–572.

Chi, M. T. H. (1978). Knowledge structures and memory development. In R. S. Siegler (Ed.), *Children's thinking: What develops?* Hillsdale, NJ: Erlbaum.

Chi, M. T. H., & Koeske, R. D. (1983). Network representation of a child's dinosaur knowledge. *Developmental Psychology, 19,* 29–39.

Chi, M. T. H., & Slotta, J. D. (1993). The ontological coherence of intuitive physics. *Cognition & Instruction, 10,* 249–260.

Child Trends. (2007). *Facts at a glance.* Publication 2007–12. Washington, DC: Author.

Children's Defense Fund. (1997). *The state of America's children: Yearbook 1997.* Washington, DC: Children's Defense Fund.

Children's Defense Fund. (1998). *The state of American's children: Yearbook 1998.* Washington, D. C., author.

Children's Defense Fund. (2001). *The state of America's children: 2001.* Washington, DC: Author.

Children's Defense Fund. (2004). *The state of America's children.* Washington, DC: Children's Defense Fund Press.

Children's Defense Fund. (2007). *The state of America's children.* Washington, DC: Children's Defense Fund Press.

Chilsholm, K. (1998). A three year follow-up of attachment and indiscriminate friendliness in children adopted from Romanian orphanages. *Child Development, 69,* 1092–1106.*

Chisholm, K., Carter, M. C., Ames, E. W., & Morison, S. J. (1995). Attachment security and indiscriminately friendly behavior in children adopted from Romanian orphanages. *Development and Psychopathology, 7,* 283–294.*

Chisholm, J. S. (1963). *Navajo infancy: An ethological study of child development.* New York: Aldine.

Chittenden, G. E. (1942). An experimental study in measuring and modifying assertive behavior in young children. *Monographs of the Society for Research in Child Development, 7* (Serial No. 31).

Choi, J., & Silverman, I. (2003). Processes underlying sex differences in route-learning strategies in children and adolescents. *Personality and Individual Differences, 34,* 34.*

Chomsky, N. (1968). *Language and mind.* New York: Harcourt, Brace & World.

Chugani, H. T., Phelps, M. E., & Mazziotta, J. C. (2002). Positron emission tomography study of human brain functional development. In M. H. Johnson, Y. Munakata & R. Gilmore (Eds.), *Brain development and cognition: A reader* (2nd ed., pp. 101–116). Malden, MA: Blackwell Publishing.

Chung, T., & Asher, J. R. (1996). Children's goals and strategies in peer conflict situations. *Merrill Palmer Quarterly, 42,* 125–147.

Cianciolo, A. T., Matthew, C., Sternberg, R. J., & Wagner, R. K. (2006). Tacit knowledge, practical intelligence, and expertise. In K. A. Ericsson, N. Charness, P. J. Feltovich & R. R. Hoffman (Eds.), *The Cambridge handbook of expertise and expert performance* (pp. 613–632). New York: Cambridge University.

Cicchetti, D., & Toth, S. L. (2006). Developmental psychopathology and preventive intervention. In W. Damon & R. M. Lerner (Gen. Ed.), & K. A. Renninger & I. E. Siegel (Eds.), *Handbook of child psychology: Vol. 4. Child psychology and practice* (6th ed., pp. 497–547). New York: Wiley.

Cicero, T. J. (1994). Effects of paternal exposure to alcohol on offspring development. *Alcohol Health and Research World, 18,* 37–41.

Cillessen, A. H. N., & Mayeux, L. (2004). From censure to reinforcement: Developmental changes in the association between aggression and social status. *Child Development, 75,* 147–163.

Cillessen, A. H. N., & Rose, A. J. (2005). Understanding popularity in the peer system. *Current Directions in Psychological Science, 14,* 102–105.

Claes, M., Lacourse, E., Ercolani, A.-P., Pierro, A., Leone, L., & Presaghi, F. (2005). Parenting, peer orientation, drug use, and antiscoial behavior in late adolescence: A cross-national study. *Journal of Youth and Adolescence, 34,* 401–411.*

Clancy, P. (1985). Acquisition of Japanese. In D. I. Slobin (Ed.), *The cross-linguistic study of language acquisition: Vol. 1. The data* (pp. 323–524). Hillsdale, NJ: Erlbaum.

Clark, E. V. (1983). Meanings and concepts. In P. H. Mussen (Eds.), *Handbook of child psychology* (Vol. 3). New York: Wiley.

Clark, K. E., & Ladd, G. W. (2000). Connectedness and autonomy support in parent-child relationships: Links to children's socioemotional orientation and peer relationships. *Developmental Psychology, 36,* 485–498.

Clarke, D. J. (2001). Treatment of schizophrenia. In A. Dosen & K. Day (Eds.), *Treating mental illness and behavior disorders in children and adults with mental retardation* (pp. 183–200). Washington, DC: American Psychiatric Press.

Clarke, D. J. (2001). Treatment of schizophrenia. In A. Dosen & K. Day (Eds.), *Treating mental illness and behavior disorders in children and adults with mental retardation* (pp. 183–200). Washington, DC: American Psychiatric Press.

Clarke, G., Hops, H., Lewinsohn, P. M., & Andrews, J. (1992). Cognitive-behavioral group treatment of adolescent depression: Prediction of outcome. *Behavior Therapy, 23,* 341–354.

Clarke-Stewart, K. A. (1978). And daddy makes three: The father's impact on mother and young child. *Child Development, 49,* 466–478.

Clarke-Stewart, K. A. (1989). Infant day care: Maligned or malignant? *American Psychologist, 44,* 266–273.

Clarke-Stewart, K. A., & Allhusen, V. D. (2002). Nonparental caregiving. In M. Bornstein (Ed.), *Handbook of parenting* (2nd ed., pp. 215–252). Mahwah, NJ: Erlbaum.

Clarke-Stewart, K. A., & Allhusen, V. D. (2005). *What we know about childcare.* Cambridge, MA: Harvard University Press.

Clarke-Stewart, K. A., & Brentano, C. (2006). *Divorce: Causes and consequences.* New Haven, CT: Yale University Press.

Clarke-Stewart, K. A., Goodens, F. A., & Allhusen, V. D. (2001). Measuring infant-mother attachment: Is the Strange Situation enough? *Social Development, 10,* 143–169.

Clarke-Stewart, K. A., Vandell, D. L., McCartney, K., Owen, M. T., & Booth, C. (2000). Effects of parental separation and divorce on very young children. *Journal of Family Psychology, 14,* 304–326.

Cleveland, H. H., & Wiebe, R. P. (2003). The moderation of adolescent to peer similarity in tobacco and alcohol use by school levels of substance abuse. *Child Development, 74,* 279–291.

Clifton, R. K. (1992). The development of spatial hearing in human infants. In L. A. Werner & E. W. Rubel (Eds.), *Developmental psychoacoustics,* APA science volumes (pp. 135–157). Washington, DC: American Psychological Association.

Clinton, H. R. (1996). *It takes a village.* New York: Simon & Schuster.

Cloninger, C. R., Christiansen, K. O., Reich, T., & Gottesman, I. I. (1978). Implications of sex differences in the prevalences of antisocial personality, alcoholism, and criminality for familial transmission. *Archives of General Psychiatry, 35,* 941–951.

Cloninger, C. R., Sigvardsson, S., Bohman, M., & van Knoring, A. L. (1982). Predisposition to petty criminality in Swedish adoptees: II. Cross-fostering analyses of gene-environmental interactions. *Archives of General Psychiatry, 39,* 1242–1247.

Cochi, S. L., Edmonds, L. E., Dyer, K., Grooves, W. L., Marks, J. S., Rovira, E. Z., Preblud, S. R., & Orenstein, W. A. (1989). Congenital rubella syndrome in the United States, 1970–1985: On the verge of elimination. *American Journal of Epidemiology, 129,* 349–361.

Cohen, L. B., & Cashon, C. H. (2006). Infant cognition. In W. Damon & R. M. Lerner (Gen. Ed.), & D. Kuhn & R. S. Siegler (Eds.), *Handbook of child psychology: Vol. 2. Cognition, perception, and language* (6th ed., pp. 214–251). New York: Wiley.

Cohen, P., & Brook, J. S. (1995). The reciprocal influence of punishment and child behavior disorder. In J. McCord (Ed.), *Coercion and punishment in long-term perspectives* (pp. 154–164). New York: Cambridge University Press.

Cohen-Bendahan, C. C. C., van de Beek, C., & Berenbaum, S. A. (2005). Prenatal sex hormone effects on child and adult sex-typed behavior: Methods and findings. *Neuroscience & Biobehavioral Reviews. Special Issue: Prenatal Programming Of Behavior, Physiology And Cognition, 29,* 353–384.

Coie, J. D., & Dodge, K. A. (1983). Continuities and changes in children's social status: A five-year longitudinal study. *Merrill-Palmer Quarterly, 29,* 261–282.

Coie, J. D., & Dodge, K. A. (1998). Aggression and antisocial behavior. In W. Damon (Gen. Ed.), & N. Eisenberg (Vol. Ed.), *Handbook of child psychology: Social, emotional, and personal development* (Vol. 3, pp. 779–862). Wiley: New York.

Coie, J. D., Dodge, K. A., & Kupersmidt, J. (1990). Peer group behavior and social status. In S. R. Asher & J. D. Coie (Eds.), *Peer rejection in childhood.* New York: Cambridge University Press.

Coie, J. D., & Kupersmidt, J. B. (1983). A behavioral analysis of emerging social status in boys' groups. *Child Development, 54,* 1400–1416.

Colapinto, J. (2000). *As nature made him: The boy who was raised as a girl.* Harper Collins.

Colby, A., & Kohlberg, L. (1987). *The measurement of moral judgment* (Vols. 1–2). New York: Cambridge University Press.

Colby, A., Kohlberg, L., Gibbs, J., & Lieberman, M. (1983). A longitudinal study of moral judgment. *Monographs of the Society for Research in Child Development, 48* (Serial No. 200).

Cole, M. (1996). *Cultural psychology: A once and future discipline.* Cambridge, MA: Harvard University Press.

Cole, M. (2006). Culture and cognitive development in phylogenetic, historical and ontogenetic perspective. In W. Damon & R. L. Lerner (Gen. Ed.), & D. Kuhn & R. Siegler (Eds.), *Handbook of child psychology: Vol. 2. Cognition, perception, and language* (6th ed., pp. 636–683). New York: Wiley.

Cole, P. M., Bruschi, C. J., & Tamang, B. L. (2002). Cultural differences in children's emotional reactions to difficult situations. *Child Development, 73,* 983–996.

Cole, P. M., Martin, S. E., & Dennis, T. A. (2004). Emotion regulation as a scientific construct: Methodological challenges and directions for child development research. *Child Development, 75,* 317–333.

Cole, P. M., & Tamang, B. L. (1998). Nepali children's ideas about emotional displays in hypothetical situations. *Developmental Psychology, 34,* 640–646.

Cole, P. M., & Tan, P. Z. (2007). Emotion socialization from a cultural perspective. In J. E. Grusec & P. Hastings (Eds.), *Handbook of socialization* (pp. 516–542). New York: Guildford.

Colin, V. L. (1996). *Human attachment.* New York: McGraw-Hill.

Collins, W. A. (2003). More than myth: The developmental significance of romantic relationships during adolescence. *Journal of Research on Adolescence, 13,* 1–24.

Collins, W. A., Maccoby, E. E., Steinberg, L., Hetherington, E. M., & Bornstein, M. H. (2000). Contemporary research on parenting: The case for nature and nurture. *American Psychologist, 55,* 218–232.

Collins, W. A., & Repinski, D. J. (2001). Parents and adolescents as transformers of relationships: Dyadic adaptation to developmental changes. In J. R. M. Gerris (Ed.), *Dynamics of parenting* (pp. 428–444). Leuven, Belgium: Garant.

Collins, W. A., & Van Dulman, M. (2006). The course of true love(s): Origins and pathways in the development of romantic relationships. In A. C. Crouter & A. Booth (Eds.), *Romance and sex in adolescence and emerging adulthood: Risks and opportunities* (pp. 63–86). Mahwah, NJ: Lawrence Erlbaum.

Coltrane, S. (1996). *Family man: Fatherhood, housework, and gender equity.* New York: Oxford University Press.

Coltrane, S. (1998). *Gender and families.* Thousand Oaks, CA: Pine Forge Press.

Coltrane, S. (2000). Research on household labor: Modeling and measuring the social embeddedness of routine family work. *Journal of Marriage and the Family, 62,* 1208–1233.

Coltrane, S., & Adams, M. (2008). *Gender and families* (2nd ed.). Lanham, MD: Rowan & Littlefield.

Coltrane, S., Parke, R. D., Schofield, T. J., Tusha, S., Chavez, M., & Shoon, L. (2007). Mexican American families and poverty. In D. R. Crane & T. B. Heaton (Eds.), *Handbook of families and poverty* (pp. 161–180). Thousand Oaks, CA: Sage.

Comer, J. (1996). Improving psycho-educational outcomes for African American children. In M. Lewis (Ed.), *Child and adolescent psychiatry: A comprehensive textbook* (pp. 176–201). Baltimore: Williams & Wilkins.

Comer, J. (2004). *Leave no child behind: Preparing today's youth for tomorrow's world.* New Haven, CT: Yale University Press.

Comstock, G., & Scharrer, E. (2006). Media and pop culture. In W. Damon & R. M. Lerner (Gen. Ed.), & K. A. Renninger & I. E. Sigel (Eds.), *Handbook of child psychology: Vol. 4. Child psychology in practice* (6th ed.). New York: Wiley.

Conduct Problems Prevention Research Group. (2004). The Fast Track experiment: Translating the developmental model into a prevention design. In J. B. Kupersmidt & K. A. Dodge (Eds.), *Children's peer relations: From development to intervention* (pp. 181–208). Washington, DC: American Psychological Association.

Conel, J. L. (1967). *The postnatal development of the human cerebral cortex* (Vols. 1 & 8). Cambridge, MA: Harvard University Press. (Original work published 1939.)

Conger, J. J., & Petersen, A. C. (1984). *Adolescence & youth* (3rd ed.). New York: Harper & Row.

Conger, R. D., & Conger, K. J. (1996). Sibling relationships. In R. L. Simons et al., (Ed.), *Understanding differences between divorced and intact families* (pp. 104–124). Thousand Oaks, CA: Sage.

Conger, R. D., Conger, K. J., Elder, G. J., Jr., Lorenz, F. O., Simons, R. L., & Whitbeck, L. B. (1992). A family process model of economic hardship and adjustment of early adolescent boys. *Child Development, 63,* 526–541.

Conger, R. D., Cui, M., Bryant, C. M., & Elder, G. H. (2000). Competence in early adult romantic relationships: A developmental perspective on family influences. *Journal of Personality and Social Psychology, 79,* 224–237.

Conger, R. D., & Dogan, S. J. (2007). Social class & socialization in families. In J. E. Grusec & P. Hastings (Eds.), *Handbook of socialization* (pp. 433–460). New York: Guilford.

Conger, R. D., & Elder, G. H. (Eds.). (1994). *Families in troubled times: Adapting to change in rural America.* New York: Aldine.

Connell, M. W., Sheridan, K., & Gardner, H. (2003). On abilities and domains. In R. J. Sternberg & E. L. Grigorenko (Eds.), *Perspectives in the psychology of abilities, competencies and expertise* (pp. 126–155). New York: Cambridge University Press.

Connolly, J. A., Craig, W., Goldberg, A., & Pepler, D. (2004). Mixed-gender groups, dating, and romantic relationships in early adolescence. *Journal of Research on Adolescence, 14,* 185–207.*

Connor, P. D., Sampson, P. D., Bookstein, F. L., Barr, H. M., & Streissguth, A. P. (2001). Direct and indirect effects of prenatal alcohol damage on executive function. *Developmental Neuropsychology, 18,* 331–354.

Connors, C. K. (2000). *The Connors' continuous performance test II.* Toronto, Canada: Multi-Health Systems Inc.

Conrad, M. E. (2006). Iron Deficiency Anemia. Retrieved 28 November, 2007, from http://www.emedicine.com

Contreras, J. M., Kerns, K., Weimer, B. L., Genzler, A. L., & Tomich, P. C. (2000). Emotional regulation as a moderater of association between mother-child attachment and peer relationships in middle childhood. *Journal of Family Psychology, 14,* 111–124.

Cooper, R. P., & Aslin, R. N. (1990). Preference for infant-directed speech in the first month after birth. *Child Development, 61,* 1584–1595.

Coovadia, H. (2004). Anitretroviral agents – how best to protect infants from HIV and save their mothers from AIDS. *New England Journal of Medicine, 351,* 289–292.

Coren, S. (1992). *The left-hander syndrome: The causes and consequences of left-handedness.* New York: Free Press.*

Corkum, V., & Moore, C. (1995). Development of joint visual attention in infants. In C. Moore & P.J. Dunham (Eds.), *Joint attention: Its origins and role in development* (pp. 61–83). Hillsdale, NJ: Erlbaum.*

Corkum, P. V., Humphries, K., Mullane, J. C., & Theriault, F. (2008). Private speech in children with ADHD and their typically developing peers during problem-solving and inhibition tasks. *Contemporary Educational Psychology, 33,* 97–114.*

Corkum, P. V., Schachar, R. J., & Siegel, L. S. (1996). Performance on the continuous performance task and the impact of reward. *Journal of Attention Disorders, 1,* 114–121.*

Corkum, P. V., & Siegel, L. S. (1993). Is the continuous performance task a valuable research tool for use with children with Attention-Deficit-Hyperactivity disorder? *Journal of Child Psychology and Psychiatry, 34,* 1217–1239.*

Cornell, E. H., Hadley, D. C., Sterling, T. M., Chan, M. A., & Boechler, P. (2001). Adventure as a stimulus for cognitive development. *Journal of Environmental Psychology, 21,* 219–231.

Cornell, E. H., Heth, C. D., & Broda, L. S. (1989). Children's wayfinding: Response to instructions to use environmental landmarks. *Developmental Psychology, 25,* 755–764.*

Cornell, E. H., Heth, C. D., & Rowat, W. L. (1992). Wayfinding by children and adults: Response to instructions to use look-back and retrace strategies. *Developmental Psychology, 28,* 328–336.*

Cornell, E. H., & Hill, K. A. (2006). The problem of lost children. In C. Spencer & M. Blades (Eds.), *Children and their environments: Learning, using and designing spaces* (pp. 26–41). New York: Cambridge University Press.*

Corsaro, W. W., & Maynard, D. W. (1996). Format trying in discussion and argumentation among Italian and American children. In D.I. Slobin, J. Gerhardt, A. Kryatzis, & J. Guo (Eds.), *Social interaction, social context, and language* (pp. 157–174). Mahwah, NJ: Lawrence Erlbaum.

Corter, C., & Fleming, A.S. (1995). Psychobiology of maternal behavior in human beings. In M. Bornstein (Ed.), *Handbook of parenting, Vol. 2, Biology and Ecology of Parenting* (87–116). Hillsdale, NY: Erlbaum.*

Coser, C., & Cohen, J. (2003). *America's babies.* Washington, DC: Zero to Three Press.

Cosgrove, J. M., & Patterson, C. J. (1977). Plans and the development of listener skills. *Developmental Psychology, 13,* 557–564.

Cosmides, L., & Tooby, J. (1987). From evolution to behavior: Evolutionary psychology as the missing link. In J. Dupre (Ed.), *The latest and best essays on evolution and optimality* (pp. 277–306). Cambridge, MA: MIT Press.

Cossette, L., Pomerleau, A., Malcuit, G., & Kaczorowski, J. (1996). Emotional expressions of female and male infants in a social and non-social context. *Sex Roles, 35,* 693–709.*

Costello, E. (1983). *Signing: How to speak with your hands.* New York: Bantam.

Côté, S., Tremblay, R. E., Nagin, D. S., Zoccolillo, M., & Vitaro, R. (2002a). Childhood behavior profiles leading to adolescent conduct disorder: Risk trajectories for boys and girls. *Journal of the American Academy of Child and Adolescent Psychiatry, 41,* 1083–1094.*

Côté, S., Tremblay, R. E., Nagin, D. S., Zoccolillo, M., & Vitaro, R. (2002b). The development of impulsivity, fearfulness, and helpfulness during childhood: Patterns of consistency and change in the trajectories of boys and girls. *Journal of Child Psychology and Psychiatry and Allied Disciplines, 43,* 609–618.*

Côté, S. M., Vaillancourt, T., LeBlanc, J. C., Nagin, D. S., & Tremblay, R. E. (2006). The development of physical aggression from toddlerhood to pre-adolescence: A nation wide longitudinal study of Canadian children. *Journal of Abnormal Child Psychology, 34,* 71–85.*

Courage, M. L., & Adams, J. A. (1990). Visual acuity assessment from birth to three years using the acuity card procedures: Cross-longitudinal samples. *Optometry and vision science, 67,* 713–718.*

Courage, M. L., & Howe, M. L. (1998). The ebb and flow of infant attentional preference: Evidence for long-term recognition memory in 3-month-olds. *Journal of Experimental Child Psychology, 70,* 26–53.*

Cournoyer, M., Solomon, C. R., & Trudel, M. (1998). I speak then I expect: Language and self-control in the young child at home. *Canadian Journal of Behavioral Science, 30,* 69–81.*

Covell, K., Grusec, J. E., & King, G. (1995). The intergenerational transmission of maternal discipline and standards for behavior. *Social Development, 4,* 32–43.*

Cowan, C. P., & Cowan, A. (2001). *When partners become parents: The big life change for couples.* Mahwah: Erlbaum.

Cowan, C. P., & Cowan, P. A. (2000). *When partners become parents: The big life change for couples.* Mahwah, NJ: Erlbaum.

Cowan, N., Nugent, L. D., Elliot, E. M., & Saults, J. S. (2000). Persistence of memory for ignored lists of digits: Areas of developmental constancy and change. *Journal of Experimental Child Psychology, 76,* 151–172.

Cowan, P. A., & Cowan, C. P. (2002). What an intervention design reveals about how parents affect their children's academic achievement and behavior problems. In J. G. Borkowski & S. L. Ramey & M. Bristol-Power (Eds.), *Parenting and the child's world* (pp. 75–98). Mahwah, NJ: Erlbaum.

Cowan, P. A., & Cowan, C. P. (2008). From prevention science to public policy: How working with couples fosters children's development. In M. Schultz, M. K. Pruett, P. K. Kerig & R. D. Parke (Eds.), *Feathering the nest: Couples relationships, couples interventions, and children's development.* Washington, DC: American Psychological Association.

Cowley, G. (2001). General XXL. In K. L. Freiberg (Ed.), *Human Development 01/02* (29th ed., pp. 120–121). Guilford, CT: Duskin/McGraw-Hill.

Cox, B. C., Ornstein, P. A., Naus, M. J., Maxfield, D., & Zimler, J. (1989). Children's concurrent use of rehearsal and organizational strategies. *Developmental Psychology, 25,* 619–627.

Coyle, T. R., & Bjorklund, D. F. (1997). Age differences in, and consequences of, multiple and variable-strategy use on a multi-trial sort-recall task. *Developmental Psychology, 33,* 372–380.

Craig, W. M., Pepler, D. J., & Atlas, R. (2000). Observations of bullying in the playground and in the classroom. *School Psychology International, 21,* 22–36.*

Craik, F. I. M., & Salthouse, T. A. (Eds.) (2000). *The handbook of aging and cognition* (2nd ed.). Mahwah, NJ: Lawrence Erlbaum Associates.*

Cratty, B. J. (1999). *Movement behavior and motor learning.* Ann Arbor, MI: Books on Demand.

Crick, N. R. (1997). Engagement in gender normative versus nonnormative forms of aggression: Links to social-psychological adjustment. *Developmental Psychology, 33,* 610–617.

Crick, N. R., Casas, J. F., & Mosher, M. (1997). Relational and overt aggression in preschool. *Developmental Psychology, 33,* 579–588.

Crick, N. R., & Dodge, K. A. (1994). A review and reformulation of social information-processing mechanisms in children's social adjustment. *Psychological Bulletin, 115,* 74–101.

Crick, N. R., & Grotpeter, J. K. (1995). Relational aggression, gender, and social-psychological adjustment. *Child Development, 66,* 710–722.

Crick, N. R., Ostrov, J. M., Appleyard, K., Jansen, E. A., & Casas, J. F. (2004). Relational aggression in early childhood: "You can't come to my birthday party unless." In M. Puttalaz & K. L. Bierman (Eds.), *Aggression, antisocial behavior, and violence among girls* (pp. 71–89). New York: Guilford.

Crick, N. R., Wellman, N. E., Casas, J. F., O'Brien, K. M., Nelson, D. A., Grotpeter, J. K., & Markon, K. (1998). Childhood aggression and gender: A new look at an old problem. In D. Bernstein (Ed.), *Nebraska symposium on motivation* (Vol. 44). Lincoln: University of Nebraska Press.

Crick, N. R., Werner, N. E., Casas, J. F., O'Brien, K. M., Nelson, D. A., Grotpeter, J. K., & Markon, K. (1999). Childhood aggression and gender: A new look at an old problem. *Nebraska symposium on motivation, 44,* 75–141.

Cristobal, E. (2003). The psychoanalytic process in the light of attachment theory. In M. Cortina & M. Marrone (Eds.), *Attachment theory and the psychoanalytic process* (pp. 335–355). London: Whurr Publishers.

Crockenberg, S. B. (1981). Infant irritability, mother responsiveness and social support influences on the security of infant-mother attachment. *Child Development, 52*, 857–865.

Črnčec, R., Wilson, S. J., & Prior, M. (2006). The cognitive and academic benefits of music to music: Facts and fictions. *Educational Psychology, 26*, 579–594.

Crouter, A. C., & Bumpus, M. F. (2001). Linking parents' work stress to children's and adolescents' psychological development. *Current Directions in Psychological Science, 10*, 156–159.

Crowell, J. A., Treboux, D., Gao, Y., Fyffe, C., Pan, H., & Waters, E. (2002). Assessing secure base behavior in adulthood: Development of a measure, links to adult attachment representations and relations to couples' communication and reports of relationships. *Developmental Psychology, 38*, 679–693.

Crowley, K., Callahan, M. A., Tennenbaum, H. R., & Allen, E. (2001). Parents explain more often to boys than to girls during shared scientific thinking. *Psychological Science, 12*, 258–261.

CRTC (1996). Public Notice CRTC 1996–36, Policy on violence in television programming. Ottawa: Canadian Radio, Television and Telecommunications Commission.*

Cruz, M., Shaibi, G., Weigensberg, M., Spruijt-Metz, D., & et al. (2005). Pediatric obesity and insulin resistance: Chronic diseases risk and implications for treatment and prevention beyond body weight modification. *Annual Review of Nutrition, 25*, 435–468.

Csikszentmihalyi, M., & Schneider, B. (2000). *Becoming adult: How teenagers prepare for the world of work.* New York: Basic Books.

Cummings, E. M., Davies, P., & Campbell, S. (2000). *Developmental psychopathology and family process.* New York: Guilford.

Cummings, E. M., Goeke-Morey, M. C., & Graham, M. A. (2002). Interparental relations as a dimension of parenting. In S. L. Ramey & M. Bristol-Power (Eds.), *Parenting and the child's world* (pp. 251–264). Mahwah, NJ: Erlbaum.

Cummings, E. M., & Merrilees, C. E. (2008). Identifying the dynamic processes underlying links between marital conflict and child adjustment. In M. Schultz, M. K. Pruett, P. Kerig & R. D. Parke (Eds.), *Feathering the nest: Couples relationships, couples interventions, and children's development.* Washington, DC: American Psychological Association.

Cummings, E. M., Simpson, K. S., & Wilson, A. (1993). Children's responses to interadult anger as a function of information about resolution. *Developmental Psychology, 29*, 978–985.

Cunningham, C. E. (1999). In the wake of the MTA: Charting a new course for the study and treatment of children with attention-deficit hyperactivity disorder. *Canadian Journal of Psychiatry, 44*, 999–1006.

Cunningham, F. G., MacDonald, P. C., & Grant, N. F. (1993). *Williams obstetrics.* Norwalk, CT: Appleton & Lange.

Curtiss, S. (1989). The independence and task-specificity of language. In M. H. Bornstein & J. S. Bruner (Eds.), *Interaction in human development* (pp. 105–138). Hillsdale, NJ: Erlbaum.

D'Augelli, A. R. (2006). Developmental and contextual factors and mental health among lesbians, gay, and bisexual youths. In A. Omoto & H. Kurtzman (Eds.), *Sexual orientation and mental health: Examining identity and development in lesbian, gay, and bisexual people* (pp. 37–53). Washington, DC: American Psychological Association.

D'Augelli, A. R., & Patterson, C. (Eds.). (2001). Lesbian, gay and bisexual identities among youth: Psychological perspectives. New York: Oxford University Press.

D'Entremont, B., Hains., S.M.J., & Muir, D.W. (1997). A demonstration of gaze following in 3- to 6-month-old infants. *Infant Behavior and Development, 20*, 569–572.*

Dale, P. S. (1976). *Language development: Structure and function* (2nd ed.). New York: Holt.

Daniels, H., Cole, M., & Wertsch, J. V. (2007). *The Cambridge companion to Vygotsky.* Cambridge, UK: Cambridge University Press.

Daniels, P., & Weingarten, K. (1988). The fatherhood click: The timing of parenthood in men's lives. In P. Bronstein & C. P. Cowan (Eds.), *Fatherhood today: Men's changing role in the family* (pp. 36–52). New York: Wiley.

Dannemiller, J. L., & Stephens, B. R. (1988). A critical test of infant pattern perception models. *Child Development, 59*, 210–216.

Dark, V. J., & Benbow, S. P. (1993). Cognitive differences among the gifted: A review and new data. In D. K. Detterman (Ed.). *Current topics in human intelligence,* Vol. 3. Norwood, NJ: Ablex.

Darvill, D., & Cheyne, J. A. (1981). *Sequential analysis of response to aggression: Age and sex effects.* Paper presented at the biennial meeting of the Society for Research in Child Development, Boston.

Darwin, C. (1872). *The expression of emotions in man and animals.* London: John Murray

Das, J. P. (2004). Theories of Intelligence: Issues and Applications. In G. Goldstein, S. R. Beers & M. Hersen (Eds.), *Comprehensive handbook of psychological assessment, Vol. 1: Intellectual and neuropsychological assessment* (pp. 5–23). New York: Wiley.

Dasen, P. R. (1975). Concrete operational development in three cultures. *Journal of Cross--Cultural Psychology, 6*, 156–172.

Dasen, P. R. (1984). The cross-cultural study of intelligence: Piaget and the Baoulé. *International Journal of Psychology, 19*, 407–434.

Dasen, P. R., Inhelder, B., Lavallée, M., & Retschitzki, J. (1978). *Naissance de l'intelligence chez l'enfant Baoulé de Côte d'Ivoire.* Berne, Switzerland: Hans Huber.

Davey, M., Eaker, D. G., & Walters, L. H. (2003). Resilience processes in adolescents: Personality profiles, self-worth and coping. *Journal of Adolescent Research, 18*, 347–362.

Davidson, E. S., Yasuna, A., & Tower, A. (1979). The effects of television cartoons on sex role stereotyping in young girls. *Child Development, 50*, 597–600.

Davidson, R. J. (1994). Temperament, affective style, and frontal lobe asymmetry. In G. Dawson & K. W. Fischer (Eds.), *Human behavior and the developing brain.* New York: Guilford Press.

Davies, H. D., & Fitzgerald, H. E. (Eds.). (2008). *Obesity in childhood and adolescence, Vol. 1: Medical, biological, and social issues.* Westport, CT: Praeger Publishers.

Davies, P. T., & Cummings, E. M. (2006). Interparental discord, family process, and developmental psychopatholoy. In D. Chicchetti & D. J. Cohen (Eds.), *Developmental psychopathology, Vol. 3: Risk, disorder, and adaptation* (2nd ed., pp. 86–128). Hoboken, NJ: Wiley.

Davies, P. T., & Windle, M. (2000). Middle adolescents' dating pathways and psychosocial adjustment. *Merrill-Palmer Quarterly, 46*, 90–118.

Davis, M. H., Luce, C., & Kraus, S. J. (1994). The heritability of characteristics associated with dispositional empathy. *Journal of Personality, 62*, 369–391.

Dawson, G. (1994). Development of emotional expression and regulation in infancy. In G. Dawson & K. W. Fischer (Eds.), *Human behav-ior and the developing brain.* New York: Guilford Press.

Dawson, G., Meltzoff, A. N., Osterling, J., & Rinaldi, J. (1998). Neuropsychological correlates of early symptoms of autism. *Child Development, 19*, 1276–1285.

Dawson, G., & Sterling, L. (2007). Autism Spectrum Disorders. In M. Haith & J. Benson (Eds.), *Encyclopedia of Infant and Early Childhood Development.* Oxford, UK: Elsevier.

Dawson, G., Toth, K., Abbott, R., Osterling, J., Munson, J., Estes, A., et al. (2004). Early social attention impairments in autism: Social orienting, joint attention, and attention to distress. *Developmental Psychology, 40*, 271–283.

Day, N. L., Cornelius, M., Goldschmidt, L., Richardson, G., Robles, N., & Taylor, P. (1992). The effects of prenatal tobacco and marijuana use on offspring growth from birth through 3 years of age. *Neurotoxicology and Teratology, 14*, 402–414.

Day, N. L., & Richardson, G. A. (1994). Comparative teratogenicity of alcohol and other drugs. *Alcohol Health and Research World, 18*, 42–48.

de Boo, G. M., & Kolk, A. M. (2007). Ethnic and gender differences in temperament, and the relationship between temperament and Depressive and Aggressive mood. *Personality and Individual Differences, 43*, 1756–1766.

de Guzman, M. R. T., & Carlo, G. (2004). Family, peer, and acculturative correlates of prosocial development among Latino youth in Nebraska. *Great Plains Research, 14*, 185–202.

de Heering, A., Turati, C., Rossion, B., Bulf, H., Goffaux, V., & Simion, F. (2008). Newborns face recognition is based on spatial frequencies below 0.5 cycles per degree. *Cognition, 106*, 444–454.

de Houwer, A. (1995). Bilingual language acquisition. In P. Fletcher & B. MacWhinney (Eds.), *The handbook of child language* (pp. 219–250). Oxford: Basil Blackwell.

Dean, R. S., & Anderson, J. L. (1997). Lateralization of cerebral function. In A. M. Horton & D. Wedding & J. Webster (Eds.), *The neuropsychology handbook* (Vol. 1, pp. 138–139). New York: Springer-Verlag.

Deary, I. J., Whalley, L. J., Lemmon, H., Crawford, J. R., & Starr, J. M. (2000). The stability of individual differences in mental ability from childhood to old age: Follow-up of the 1932 Scottish mental survey. *Intelligence, 28*, 49–55.

Deary, I. J., Whiteman, M. C., Starr, J. M., Whalley, L. J., & Fox, H. C. (2004). The impact of childhood intelligence on later life: Following up the Scottish mental surveys of 1932 and 1947. *Journal of Personality and Social Psychology, 86,* 130–147.

Deater-Deckard, K., & Dodge, K. A. (1997). Externalizing behavior problems and discipline revisited: Nonlinear effects and variation by culture, context, and gender. *Psychological Inquiry, 8,* 161–175.

Deater-Deckard, K., Dodge, K. A., Bates, J. E., & Pettit, G. S. (1996). Physical discipline among African American and European American mothers: Links to children's externalizing behaviors. *Developmental Psychology, 32,* 1065–1072.

Deater-Deckard, K., Pike, A., Petrill, S. A., Cutting, A. L., Hughes, C., & O'Connor, T. G. (2001). Nonshared environmental processes in social-emotional development: An observational study of identical twin differences in the preschool period. *Developmental Science, 4,* F1–F6.

DeCasper, A., & Fifer, W. (1980). Of human bonding: Newborns prefer their mothers' voices. *Science, 12,* 305–317.

DeCasper, A. J., & Spence, M. (1986). Newborns prefer a familiar story over an unfamiliar one. *Infant Behavior and Development, 9,* 133–150.

DeCasper, A. J., & Spence, M. (1991). Auditory mediated behavior during the perinatal period. A cognitive view. In M. Weiss & P. Zelazo (Eds.), *Newborn attention.* Norwood, NJ: Ablex.

Decety, J., & Chaminade, T. (2003). Neural correlates of feeling sympathy. *Neuropscyhologia, 41,* 127–138.

DeCorte, E., & Verschaffel, L. (2006). Mathematical thinking and learning. In W. Damon & R. M. Lerner (Gen. Ed.), & K. A. Renninger & I. E. Siegel (Eds.), *Handbook of child psychology: Vol. 4. Child psychology in practice* (6th ed., pp. 103–152). New York: Wiley.

Dekovic, M., & Janssens, J. M. (1992). Parents' child-rearing style and child's sociometric status. *Developmental Psychology, 28,* 925–932.

Delahunty, K. M., McKay, D. W., Noseworthy, D. E., & Storey, A. E. (2007). Prolactin responses to infant cues in men and women: Effects of parental experience and recent infant contact. *Hormones and Behavior, 51,* 213–220.

DeLisi, R., & McGillicuddy--DeLisi, A. V. (2002). Sex differences in mathematical abilities and achievement. In A. V. McGillicuddy & R. DeLisi (Eds.), *Biology, society and behavior: The development of sex differences in cognition* (pp. 155–182). Westport, CT: Ablex.

DeLoache, J. S. (1987). Rapid change in symbolic functioning of very young children. *Science, 238,* 1556–1557.

DeLoache, J. S. (1995). Early understanding and use of symbols: The model model. *Current Directions in Psychological Science, 4,* 109–113.

DeLoache, J. S. (2000). Dual representation and young children's use of scale models. *Child Development, 71,* 329–339.

DeLoache, J. S. (2002a). Early development of the understanding and use of symbolic artifacts. In U. Goswami (Ed.), *Blackwell handbook of child cognitive development* (pp. 206–226). Malden, MA: Blackwell Publishers.

DeLoache, J. S. (2002b). The symbol-mindedness of young children. In W. Hartup & R. A. Weinberg (Eds.), *Child psychology in retrospect and prospect: In celebration of the 75th anniversary of the Institute of Child Development. The Minnesota symposia on child psychology* (Vol. 32, pp. 73–101). Mahwah, NJ: Erlbaum.

DeLoache, J. S., & Brown, A. L. (1983). Very young children's memory for the location of objects in a large-scale environment. *Child Development, 54,* 888–897.

DeLoache, J. S., Miller, K., & Rosengren, K. (1997). The credible shrinking room: Very young children's performance in symbolic and non-symbolic tasks. *Psychological Science, 8,* 308–314.

DeLoache, J. S., Pierroutsakos, S. L., & Uttal, D. H. (2003). The origins of pictorial competence. *Current Directions in Psychological Science, 12,* 114–118.

DeLoache, J. S., Simcock, G., & Macari, S. (2007). Planes, trains, automobiles—and tea sets: Extremely intense interests in very young children. *Developmental Psychology, 43,* 1579–1586.

DeLoache, J. S., & Smith, C. M. (1999). Early symbolic representation. In I. E. Siegel (Ed.), *Development of mental representation: Theories and applications* (pp. 61–86). Mahwah, NJ: Erlbaum.

Delorme, A., Frigon, J., & Lagace, C. (1989). Infants' reactions to visual movement of the environment. *Perception, 17,* 667–673.*

Demetriou, A., Christou, C., Spanoudis, G., & Platsidou, M. (2002). The development of mental processing: Efficiency, working memory, and thinking. *Monographs of the Society for Research in Child Development, 67,* vii–154.

Demo, D. H., Allen, K. R., & Fine, M. A. (Eds.). (2000). *Handbook of family diversity.* New York: Oxford University Press.

Dempster, F. N. (1985). Proactive interference in sentence recall: Topic similarity effects and individual differences. *Memory and Cognition, 13,* 81–89.

Denham, S. (1998). *Emotional development in young children.* New York: Guilford.

Denham, S. A., Bassett, H. H., & Wyatt, T. (2007). The socialization of emotional competence. In J. E. Grusec & P. Hastings (Eds.), *Handbook of socialization* (pp. 516–542). New York: Guilford Press.

Denham, S. A., Renwick-DeBardi, S., & Hewes, S. (1994). Emotional communication between mothers and preschoolers: Relations with emotional competence. *Merrill-Palmer Quarterly, 40,* 488–508.

Dennis, W. (1940). Does culture appreciably affect patterns of infant behavior? *Journal of Social Psychology, 12,* 305–317.

Denton, K., & Krebs, D. L. (1990). From the scene to the crime: The effect of alcohol and social context on moral judgment. *Journal of Personality and Social Psychology, 59,* 242–248.*

DeRosier, M., & Kupersmidt, J. B. (1991). Costa Rican children's perceptions of their social networks. *Developmental Psychology, 27,* 656–662.

deVilliers, P. A., & deVilliers, J. G. (1972). Early judgments of semantic and syntactic acceptability by children. *Journal of Psycholinguistic Research, 1,* 299–310.

deVilliers, P. A., & deVilliers, J. G. (1979). *Early language.* Cambridge, MA: Harvard University Press.

deVilliers, P. A., & deVilliers, J. G. (1992). Language Development. In M. E. Lamb & M. H. Bornstein (Eds.), *Developmental psychology: An advanced textbook* (3rd ed.). Hillsdale, NJ: Erlbaum.

Devlin, B., Fienberg, S. E., Resnick, D. P., & Roeper, K. (2002). Intelligence and success: Is it all in the genes? In J. M. Fish (Ed.), *Race and intelligence: Separating science from myth* (pp. 355–368). Mahwah, NJ: Erlbaum.

DeVries, M., & Sameroff, A. J. (1984). Culture and temperament: Influences on temperament in three East African Societies. *American Journal of Orthopsychiatry, 54,* 83–96.

Diamond, D., Blatt, J. J., & Lichtenberg, J. (2003). Prologue. *Psychoanalytic Inquiry. Special Issue: Attachment Research and Psychoanalysis III: Further Reflections on Theory and Clinical Experience, 23,* 1–11.

Diaz, R. M. (1983). Thought and two languages: The impact of bilingualism on cognitive development. *Review of Research in Education, 10,* 23–54.

Diaz, R. M. (1985). Bilingual cognitive development: Addressing three gaps in current research. *Child Development, 56,* 1376–1388.

Dickens, W. T., & Flynn, J. R. (2001). Heritability estimates versus large environmental effects: The IQ paradox resolved. *Psychological Review, 108,* 346–369.

Didow, S. M., & Eckerman, C. O. (2001). Toddler peers: From nonverbal coordinated action to verbal discourse. *Social Development, 10,* 170–188.

Diego, M., Field, T., & Hernandez-Reif, M. (2008). Temperature increases in perterm infants during massage therapy. *Infant Behavior and Development, 31,* 149–152.

Diekman, A. B., & Murner, S. K. (2004). Learning to be little women and little men: The inequitable gender equality of nonsexist children's literature. *Sex Roles, 50,* 373–385.

Diener, C. I., & Dweck, C. S. (1978). An analysis of learned helplessness: Continuous changes in performance, strategy and achievement cognitions following failure. *Journal of Personality and Social Psychology, 36,* 451–462.

Diener, E. (2000). Subjective well-being: The science of happiness and a proposal for a national index. *American Psychologist, 55,* 34–43.

Diener, M. L., Mangesdorf, S. C., McHale, J. L., & Frosch, C. A. (2002). Infants' behavioral strategies for emotion regulation with fathers and mothers: Associations with emotional expressions and attachment quality. *Infancy, 3,* 153–174.

Dietrich, K. N., Berger, O. G., Succop, P. A., Hammond, P. B., & Bornschein, R. L. (1993). The developmental consequences of low to moderate prenatal and postnatal lead exposure: Intellectual attainment in the Cincinnati Lead Study cohort following school entry. *Neurotoxicology and Teratology, 13,* 37–44.

DiLalla, L. F., Thompson, L. A., Plomin, R., Phillips, K., Faga, J. F., Haith, M. M., et al. (1990). Infant predictors of preschool and adult IQ: A study of infant twins and their parents. *Developmental Psychology, 26,* 759–769.

DiMatteo, R., & Kahn, K. L. (1997). Psychosocial aspects of childbirth. In S. J. Gallant & G. P. Keita & Royak-Shaier (Eds.), *Health care for women: Psychological, social, and behavioral influences* (pp. 175–186). Washington, DC: American Psychological Association.

Dionne, G., Tremblay, R. E., Boivin, M., Laplante, D., & Perusse, D. (2003). Physical aggression and expressive vocabulary in 19-month-old twins. *Developmental Psychology, 39,* 261–273.*

DiPietro, J. A. (2004). The role of prenatal maternal stress in child development. *Current Directions in Psychological Science, 13,* 71–74.

DiPietro, J. A., Novak, M. F., Costigan, K. A., Atella, L. D., & Reusing, S. P. (2006). Maternal psychological distress during pregnancy in relation to child development at age 2. *Child Development, 77* (573–587).

Dishion, T., & Bullock, B. M. (2002). Parenting and adolescent behavior: An ecological analysis of the nurturance hypothesis. In J. G. Borkowski & S. L. Ramey & M. Bristol-Power (Eds.), *Parenting and the child's world* (pp. 231–249). Mahwah, NJ: Erlbaum.

Dishion, T. J., Poulin, F., & Burraston, B. (2001). Peer group dynamics associated with matrogenic effects in group interventions with high-risk adolescents. In D. W. Naigle & C. A. Erdley (Eds.), *The role of friendship in psychological adjustment* (pp. 79–92). San Francisco: Jossey-Bass.

Dishion, T. J., Poulin, F., & Medici Skaggs, N. (2000). The ecology of premature autonomy in adolescence: Biological and social influences. In K. A. Kerns & A. M. Neal-Barnett (Eds.), *Family and peers: Linking two social worlds* (pp. 27–45). Westport, CT: Praeger.

Dittrichova, J. (1969). The development of premature infants. In R. J. Robinson (Ed.), *Brain and early development.* London: Academic.

Dodge, K. A. (1986). A social information processing model of social competence in children. In M. Perlmutter (Ed.), *The Minnesota Symposium on Child Psychology: Vol. 18* (pp. 77–125). Hillsdale, NJ: Erlbaum.

Dodge, K. A., Coie, J. D., & Tremblay, R. E. (2006). Aggression. In W. Damon & R. M. Lerner (Gen. Ed.), & N. Eisenberg (Ed.), *Handbook of child psychology: Vol. 3: Social, emotional, and personality development* (6th ed., pp. 719–788). New York: Wiley.*

Dodge, K. A., & Frame, C. L. (1982). Social cognitive biases and deficits in aggressive boys. *Child Development, 53,* 620–635.

Dodge, K. A., Landsford, J., Burks, V., Bates, J., Pettit, G. S., Fontaine, R., et al. (2003). Peer rejection and social information processing factors in the development of aggressive behavior problems in children. *Child Development, 74,* 374–393.

Dodge, K. A., & Pettit, G. S. (2003). A biopsychological model of the development of chronic conduct problems in adolescence. *Developmental Psychology, 39,* 189–190.

Dodge, K. A., Pettit, G. S., McClaskey, C. L., & Brown, M. M. (1987). Social competence in children. *Monographs of the Society for Research in Child Development, 51* (2, Serial No. 213).

Dombrowski, M. A. S., Anderson, G. C., Santori, C., Roller, C. G., Dagliotti, F., & Dowling, D. A. (2000). Kangaroo skin-to-skin care for premature twins and their adolescent parents. *American Journal of Maternal/Child Nursing, 25,* 92–94.

Dominick, J. R., & Greenberg, B. S. (1972). Attitudes toward violence: The interaction of television exposure, family attitudes, and social class. In G. A. Comstock & E. A. Rubenstein (Eds.), *Television and social behavior: Television and adolescent aggressiveness* (Vol. 3, pp. 314–335). Washington, DC: Government Printing Office.

Donaldson, M. (1978). *Children's minds.* New York: Norton.

Dodge, K. A., Landsford, J., Burks, V., Bates, J., Pettit, G. S., Fontaine, R., et al. (2003). Peer rejection and social information processing factors in the development of aggressive behavior problems in children. *Child Development, 74,* 374–393.

Dodge, K. A., & Pettit, G. S. (2003). A biopsychological model of the development of chronic conduct problems in adolescence. *Developmental Psychology, 39,* 189–190.

Dodge, K. A., Pettit, G. S., McClaskey, C. L., & Brown, M. M. (1987). Social competence in children. *Monographs of the Society for Research in Child Development, 51*(2, Serial No. 213).

Donnelly, M., & Straus, M. (Eds.). (2005). *Corporal punishment of children in theoretical perspective.* New Haven, CT: Yale University Press.

Doris, J. (Ed.). (1991). *The suggestibility of children's recollections.* Washington, DC: American Psychological Association.

Douglas, W. (2003). *Television families.* Mahwah, NJ: Erlbaum.

Downs, R. M., & Liben, L. S. (1986). Children's understanding of maps. In P. Ellen & C. Thinus-Blanc (Eds.), *Cognitive processes and spatial orientation in animal and man: Vol. 1. Neurophysiology of spatial knowledge and developmental aspects.* Dordrecht, The Netherlands: Martinius Nijhoff.

Doyle, A. B., Markiewicz, D., Brendgen, M., Lieberman, M., & Voss, K. (2000). Child attachment security and self-concept: Associations with mother and father attachment style and marital quality. *Merrill-Palmer Quarterly, 46,* 514–536.*

Drabman, R. S., & Thomas, M. H. (1976). Does watching violence on television cause apathy? *Pediatrics, 52,* 329–331.

Drew, C. J., & Hardman, M. L. (2000). *Mental retardation: A life cycle approach* (7th ed.). Columbus, OH: Merrill.

Drew, C. J., Hardman, M. L., & Logan, D. R. (1996). *Mental retardation: A life cycle approach* (6th ed.). New York: Macmillan.

Driscoll, M. C. (2007). Sickle cell disease. *Pediatric Review, 28,* 259–268.

Dror, Y. (2001). *History of Kibbutz education: Practice into theory.* Frankfurt: Peter Lang.

Dube, E. M., Savin-Williams, R., & Diamond, L. M. (2001). Intimacy development, gender, and ethnicity among sexual minority youth. In A. R. D'Augelli & C. J. Patterson (Eds.), *Lesbian, gay, and bsexual identities among youth: Psychological perspectives* (pp. 128-182). New York: Oxford University Press.

Dubowitz, L., & Dubowitz, V. (1981). *The neurological assessment of the preterm and full-term newborn infant.* Philadelphia: Lippincott.

Ducharme, J. M., Aktkinson, L., & Poulton, L. (2000). Success-based, noncoercieve treatment of oppositional behavior in children from violent homes. *Journal of the American Academy of Child and Adolescent Psychiatry, 39,* 995–1004.*

Duffy, J., Kelly, W., & Walsh, M. (2001). Classroom interactions: Gender of teacher, gender of student, and classroom subject. *Sex Roles, 49,* 579–593.*

Duncan, G., & Brooks-Gunn, J. (2000). Family parenting, welfare reform and child development. *Child Development, 71,* 188–195.

Duncan, G., Young, W., Brooks-Gunn, J., & Smith, J. R. (1998). How much does childhood poverty affect life choices of children? *American Sociological Review, 63,* 406–423.

Dunham, P. J., Dunham, R., & Curwin, A. (1993). Joint-attentional states and lexical acquisition at 18 months. *Developmental Psychology, 29,* 827–831.

Dunn, J. (1987). The beginning of moral understanding. In J. Kagan and S. Lamb (Eds.), *The emergence of morality in young children.* Chicago: University of Chicago Press.

Dunn, J. (1988). *The beginnings of social understanding.* Cambridge, MA: Harvard University Press.

Dunn, J. (1989). *The beginnings of social understanding.* Cambridge, MA: Harvard University Press.

Dunn, J. (2004). *Children's friendships.* Oxford, UK: Blackwell.

Dunn, J. (2007). Siblings and socialization. In J. E. Grusec & P. Hastings (Eds.), *Handbook of socialization* (pp. 309–327). New York: Guilford.

Dunn, J., & Davies, L. (2000). Sibling relationships and interpersonal conflict. In J. Grych & F. F. Fincham (Eds.), *Interparental conflict and child development* (pp. 273–290). New York: Cambridge University Press.

Dunn, J., & Hughes, C. (1998). Young children's understanding of emotions within close relationships. *Cognition and Emotion, 12,* 171–190.

Dunn, J., & Hughes, C. (2001a). "I got some swords and you're dead!" Violent fantasy, antisocial behavior, and moral sensibility in young children. *Child Development, 72,* 491–505.

Dunn, J., & Hughes, C. (2001b). Young children's understanding of emotions within close relationships. *Cognitive and Emotion, 12,* 171–190.

Dunn, J., & Kendrick, C. (1982b). The speech of two- and three-year-olds to infant siblings: "Baby talk" and the context of communication. *Journal of Child Language, 9,* 579–595.

Dunn, J., Brown, J. R., & Maguire, M. (1995). The development of children's moral sensibility: Individual differences and emotional understanding. *Developmental Psychology, 31,* 649–659.

Dunn, J., & Plomin, R. (1991). Why are siblings so different? The significance of differences in sibling experiences within the family. *Family Process, 30,* 271–283.

DuRant, R. H., Cadenhead, C., Pendergrast, R. A., Slavens, G., & Linder, C. W. (1994). Factors associated with the use of violence among urban Black adolescents. *American Journal of Public Health, 84,* 612–617.*

Durrant, J. E. (1999). Evaluating the success of Sweden's corporal punishment ban. *Child Abuse & Neglect, 23,* 443–448.*

Durrant, J. E. (2000). Trends in young crime and well-being since the abolition of corporal punishment in Sweden. *Youth & Society, 31,* 437–455.

Durrant, J. E., & Janson, S. (2005). Legal reform, corporal punishment and child abuse: The case of Sweden. *International Review of Victimology, 12,* 139–158.*

Durrant, J. E., & Olsen, G. M. (1997). Parenting and publish policy: Contextualizing the Swedish corporal punishment ban. *Journal of Social Welfare and Family Law, 19,* 443–461.*

Duyme, M. (1988). School success and social class: An adoption study. *Developmental psychology, 24,* 203–209.

Dweck, C. S. (2000). *Self-theories.* Philadelphia: Taylor & Francis.

Dweck, C. S. (2001). Caution - Praise can be dangerous. In K. L. Frieberg (Ed.), *Human development 01/02* (29 ed., pp. 105–109). Guilford, CT: Duskin/McGraw-Hill.

Dweck, C. S. (2006). *Mindset: The new psychology of success.* New York: Random House.

Dweck, C. S., & Leggett, E. L. (1988). A social-cognitive approach to motivation and personality. *Psychological Review, 95,* 256–273.

Dzakpasu, S., Mery, L. S., & Trouton, K. (1998). Alcohol and pregnancy. *Canadian Perinatal Surveillance System Fact Sheet.* Health Canada, Laboratory Centre for Disease Control.*

Dzinas, K. (2000). Founding the Canadian Psychological Association: The perils of historiography. *Canadian Psychology, 41,* 205–212.*

East, P. L. (1996). The younger sisters of childrearing adolescents: Their attitudes, expectations, and behaviors. *Child Development, 67,* 953–963.

East, P. L., & Jacobson, J. L. (2001). The younger siblings of teenage mothers: A follow-up of their pregnancy risk. *Developmental Psychology, 37,* 254–264.

Eaton, W. (1989). Are sex differences in child motor activity level a function of sex differences in maturational status? *Child Development, 60,* 1005–1011.

Eccles, J. (2007). Families, schools and developing achievement-related motivation and engagement. In J. Grusec & P. Hastings (Eds.), *Handbook of socialization* (pp. 665–691). New York: Guilford.

Eccles, J. S., Freedman-Doan, C., Frome, P., Jacobs, J., & Yoon, K.

S. (2000). Gender socialization in the family: A longitudinal approach. In T. Ecker & H. Trautner (Eds.), *The developmental social psychology of gender* (pp. 333–365). Mahwah, NJ: Erlbaum.

Eccles, J. S., Jacobs, J., Harold, R., Yoon, K. S., Abreton, A., & Freedman-Doan, C. (1993). Parents' and gender-role socialization during the middle childhood and adolescent years. In S. Oskamp & M. Costanzo (Eds.), *Gender issues in contemporary society* (pp. 59–83). Newbury Park, CA: Sage.

Eccles, J. S., Wigfield, A., & Schiefele, U. (1998). Motivation to succeed. In W. Damon (Gen. Ed.) & N. Eisenberg (Vol. Ed.), *Handbook of child psychology: Vol. 3 Social, emotional, and personality development* (5th ed.). New York: Wiley.

Eckerman, C. O. (1993). Imitation and toddlers' achievement of co-ordinated action with others. In J. Nadel & L. Camaioni (Eds.), *New perspectives in early communicative development* (pp. 116–156). New York: Routledge.

Eckerman, C. O., & Didow, S. M. (1988). Lessons drawn from observing young peers together. *Acta Paeditrica Scandinavica, 77* (Suppl. 344), 55–70.

Eckerman, C. O., & Peterman, K. (2001). Peers and infant social/communicative development. In J. G. Bremner & A. Fogel (Eds.), *Blackwell handbook of infant development* (pp. 326–350). Malden, MA: Blackwell Publishers.

Eckerman, C. O., Whatley, J. L., & Kutz, S. L. (1975). Growth of social play with peers during the second year of life. *Developmental Psychology, 11,* 42–49.

Edwards, C. P. (1992). Cross-cultural perspectives on family-peer relations. In R. D. Parke & G. W. Ladd (Eds.), *Family-peer relationships: Modes of linkage* (pp. 285–316). Hillsdale, NJ: Erlbaum.

Edwards, C. P., & Lewis, M. (1979). Young children's concepts of social relations: Social functions and social objects. In M. Lewis & L. A. Rosenblum (Eds.), *The child and its family: Genesis of behavior* (Vol. 1). New York: Plenum.

Edwards, C. P., & Whiting, B. B. (1993). "Mother, older sibling, and me": The overlapping roles of caregivers and companions in the social world of two- and three-year-olds in Ngeca, Kenya. In K. MacDonald (Ed.), *Parent-child play: Descriptions and implications* (pp. 305–329). Albany, NY: State University of New York Press.

Egan, S. K., & Perry, D. G. (2001). Gender identity: A multidimen-

sional analysis with implications for psychosocial adjustment. *Developmental Psychology, 37,* 451–463.

Egeland, B., Jacobvitz, D., & Sroufe, L. A. (1988). Breaking the cycle of abuse. *Child Development, 59,* 1080–1088.

Ehrenberg, M. F., Gearing-Smil, M., Hunter, M. A., & Small, B. J. (2001). Childcare task division and shared parenting attitudes in dual-earner families with your children. *Family relations: Interdisciplinary journal of applied family studies. Special Issue, 50,* 143–153.*

Eichstedt, J. A., Serbin, L. A., Poulin-Dubois, D., & Sen, M. G. (2002). Of bears and men: Infants' knowledge of conventional and metaphorical gender stereotypes. *Infant Behavior and Development, 25,* 296–310.*

Eilers, R. E., Oller, D. K., Levine, S., Basinger, D., Lynch, M. P., & Urbano, C. (1993). The role of prematurity and socioeconomic status in the onset of canonical babbling in infants. *Infant Behavior & Development, 16,* 297–315.

Einarsson, C., & Granstroek, K. (2002). Gender-biased interaction in the classroom: The influence of gender and age in the relationship between teacher and pupil. *Scandanavian Journal of Psychology, 46,* 117–127.

Eisen, M., Goodman, G., & Quas, J. (2002). *Memory and suggestibility in the forensic interview.* Hillsdale, NJ: Erlbaum.

Eisenberg, N. (1992). *The caring child.* Cambridge, MA: Harvard University Press.

Eisenberg, N. (2003). Prosocial behavior, empathy, and sympathy. In M. H. Bornstein & L. Davidson (Eds.), *Well-being: Positive development across the life-span* (pp. 253–265). Mahwah, NJ: Erlbaum.

Eisenberg, N., & Fabes, R. A. (1998). Prosocial development. In W. Damon (Gen. Ed.) & N. Eisenberg (Vol. Ed.), *Handbook of child psychology: Vol. 3. Social, emotional, and personality development.* 9th ed. (pp. 701–778). New York: Wiley.

Eisenberg, N., Fabes, R. A., Carlo, G., Speer, A. L., Switzer, G., Karbon, M., & Troyer, D. (1993). The relations of empathy-related emotions and maternal practices to children's comforting behavior. *Journal of Experimental Child Psychology, 55,* 131–150.

Eisenberg, N., Fabes, R. A., Guthrie, I. K., & Murphy, B. C. (1996b). The relations of regulation and emotionality to problem behavior in elementary school children. Development & Psychopathology, 8, 141–162.

Eisenberg, N., Fabes, R. A., & Murphy, B. C. (1996a). Parents' reactions to children's negative emotions: Relations to children's social competence and comforting behavior. *Child Development, 67,* 2227–2247.

Eisenberg, N., Fabes, R. A., Nyman, M., Bernzweig, J., & Pinuelas, A. (1994). The relations of emotionality and regulation to children's anger-related reactions. *Child Development, 65,* 109–128.

Eisenberg, N., Fabes, R. A., & Spinrad, T. (2006). Prosocial development. In W. Damon (Gen. Ed.), & N. Eisenberg (Ed.), *Handbook of child psychology: Vol. 3. Social, emotional and personality development* (6th ed., pp. 646–718). New York: Wiley.

Eisenberg, N., Boehnke, K., Schuhler, P., & Silbereisen, R. K. (1985). The development of prosocial behavior and cognitions in German children. *Journal of Cross-Cultural Psychology, 16,* 69–82.

Eisenberg, N., Guthrie, I. K., Murphy, B. C., Cumberland, A., & Carlo, G. (1999). Consistency and development of prosocial dispositions. *Child Development, 70,* 1370–1372.

Eisenberg, N., Guthrie, I. V., Cumberland, A., Murphy, B. C., Shepard, J. A., Zhou, Q., & Carlo, G. (2002). Prosocial development in early adulthood: A longitudinal study. *Journal of Personality and Social Psychology, 82,* 993–1006.

Eisenberg, N., Lennon, R., & Roth, K. (1983). Prosocial development: A longitudinal study. *Developmental Psychology, 19,* 846–855.

Eisenberg, N., Zhou, Q., & Koller, S. (2001). Brazilian adolescents' prosocial moral judgments and behavior: Relations to sympathy, perspective taking, gender-role orientation, and demographic characteristics. *Child Development, 72,* 518–534.

Ekman, P. (1994). Antecedent events and emotion metaphors. In P. Ekman & R. J. Davidson (Eds.), *The nature of emotion* (pp. 146–149). New York: Oxford University Press.

Ekman, P. (2003). *Emotions revealed.* New York: Times Books.

Ekman, P., Davidson, R., & Friesen, W. V. (1990). The Duchenne smile: Emotional expression and brain physiology. *Journal of Personality and Social Behavior, 58,* 342–353.

Ekman, P., Friesen, W. V., O'Sullivan, M., Chan, A., Diacoyanni-Tarlatzis, I., Heider, K., Krauss, R., LeCompte, W. A., Pitcairn, T., Ricci Bilti, P. E.,

Scherer, K., Tomita, M., & Tzavaras, A. (1987). Universals and cultural differences in the judgements of facial expressions of emotion. *Journal of Personality and Social Psychology, 52,* 712–717.

Elder, G. H., & Conger, R. D. (2000). *Children of the land.* Chicago, IL: University of Chicago Press.

Elder, G. H., & Shanahan, J. J. (2006). The life course and human development. In W. Damon & R. M. Lerner (Gen. Ed.), & R. M. Lerner (Ed.), *Handbook of child psychology: Vol. 1. Theoretical models of human development.* New York: Wiley.

Eldredge, L., & Salamy, A. (1988). Neurobehavioral and neurophysiological assessment of healthy and "at risk" full-term infants. *Child Development, 59,* 186–192.

Eley, T. C., Lichtenstein, P., & Stevenson, J. (1999). Sex differences in the etiology of aggressive and nonaggressive antisocial behavior: Results from two twin studies. *Child Development, 70,* 155–168.

Elgar, F. J., Mills, R. S. L., McGrath, P. J., Waschbusch, D. A., & Brownbridge, D. A. (2007). Maternal and paternal depressive symptoms and child maladjustment: The mediating role of parental behavior. *Journal of Abnormal Child Psychology, 35,* 943–955.*

Elliot, D. S. (1994). Longitudinal research in criminology: Promise and practice. In E.G.M. Weitekamp & H.-J Kerner (Eds.), *Cross-national longitudinal research on human development and criminal behavior* (pp. 189–201). Dordrecht, The Netherlands: Kluwer Academic.

Elliot, D. S., Huizinga, D., & Ageton, S. S. (1985). *Explaining delinquency and drug use,* Beverly Hills, CA: Sage.

Elliot, M. R., Reilly, S. M., Drummond, J., & Letourneau, N. (2002). The effect of different soothing interventions on infant crying and on parent-infant interaction. *Infant Mental Health Journal, 23,* 310–328.*

Ellis, B. J. (2004). Timing of pubertal maturation in girls: An integrated life history approach. *Psychological Bulletin, 130,* 920–958.

Ellis, B. J., Bates, J. E., Dodge, K. A., Fergusson, D. M., Horwood, L. J., Pettit, G. S., et al. (2003). Does father absence place daughters at special risk for early sexual activity and teenage pregnancy? *Child Development, 74,* 801–821.

Ellis, B. J., & Bjorklund, D. F. (Eds.). (2005). *Origins of the social mind: Evolutionary psychology and child development.* New York: Guilford Press.

Ellis, B. J., & Essex, M. J. (2007). Family environments, adrenarche, and sexual maturation: A longitudinal test of a life history model. *Child Development, 78,* 1799–1817.

Ellis, B. J., McFadyen-Ketchum, S., Dodge, K. A. Pettit, G. S., & Bates, J. E. (1999). Quality of early family relationships and individual differences in the timing of pubertal maturation in girls: A longitudinal test of an evolutionary model. *Journal of Personality and Social Psychology, 77,* 387–401.

Ellis, S., Rogoff, B., & Cromer, C. (1981). Age segregation in children's social interactions. *Developmental Psychology, 17,* 399–407.

Ellsworth, C. P., Muir, D. W., & Hains, S. M. J. (1993). Social competence and person-object differentiation. An analysis of the still face effect. *Developmental Psychology, 29,* 63–73.

Elman, J. L., Bates, E. A., Johnson, M. H., Karmiloff-Smith, A., Parisi, D., & Plunkett, K. (1998). *Rethinking innateness: A connectionist perspective on development.* Cambridge, MA: MIT Press.

Embry, L., & Dawson, G. (2002). Disruptions in parenting related to maternal depression: Influences on children's behavioral and psychobiological development. In J. G. Borkowski, S. Ramey, & M. Bristol-Power (Eds.), *Parenting and the child's world* (pp. 203–213). Mahwah, NJ: Erlbaum.

Emde, R. N., Gaensbauer, T. J., & Harmon, R. J. (1976). Emotional expression in infancy: A biobehavioral study. *Psychological Issues* (Vol. 10, No. 37). New York: International Universities Press.

Emery, R. E. (Ed.). (1988). *Marriage, divorce and children's adjustment.* Newbury Park, CA: Sage.

Emmons, J. A. M., Boerama, B., Baron, J., & Wit, J. M. (2005). Catch-up growth: Testing the hypothesis of delayed growth plate senesnecne in humans. *Journal of Pediatrics, 14,* 843–846.

Emory, E. K., Schlackman, L. J., & Fiano, K. (1996). Drug-hormone interactions on neurobehavioral responses in human neonates. *Infant Behavior and Development, 19,* 213–220.

Emslie, G. J., Rush, A. J., Weinberg, W. A., Kowatch, R. A., Hughes, C. W., Carmody, T., et al. (1997). A double-blind, randomized, placebo-controlled trial of fluoxitine in children and adolescents with depression. *Archives of General Psychiatry, 54,* 1031–1037.

Engel, S. (1995). *The stories children tell: Making sense of the narratives of childhood.* New York: Freeman.

Engel, S., & Li, A. (2004). Narratives, gossip, and shared experience: How and what young children know about the lives of others. In J. M. Lucariello, J. A. Hudson, R. Fivush & P. J. Bauer (Eds.), *The development of the mediated mind: Sociocultural context and cognitive development* (pp. 151–174). Mahwah, NJ: Erlbaum.

Entwisle, D. R., & Alexander, K. L. (1987). Long-term effects of cesarean delivery on parents' beliefs and children's schooling. *Developmental Psychology, 23,* 676–682.

Entwisle, D. R., & Frasure, N. E. (1974). A contradiction resolved: Children's processing of syntactic cues. *Developmental Psychology, 10,* 852–857.

Environics Research Group. (2006). *Alcohol use during pregnancy and awareness of Fetal Alcohol Syndrome and Fetal Alcholo Spectrum Disorder* (Report no. POR-05-57). Toronto.*

Epstein, J. A., Griffin, K. W., & Botvin, G. J. (2001). Risk taking and refusal assertiveness in a longitudinal model of alcohol use among inner-city adolescents. *Prevention Science, 2,* 193–200.

Epstein, L. H., Saelens, B. E., Myers, M. D., & Vito, D. (1997). Effects of decreasing sedentary behaviors on activity choice in obese children. *Health Psychology, 16,* 107–113.

Epstein, L. H., Valoski, A. M., Vara, S., McCurley, J., Wisniewski, L., Kalarchian, M. A., Klein, K. R., & Shrager, L. R. (1995). Effects of decreasing sedentary behavior and increasing activity on weight change in obese children. *Health Psychology, 14,* 109–115.

Epstein, L. R., Valoski, A., Wing, R. R., & McCurley, J. (1994). Ten-year outcomes of behavioral family-based treatment for childhood obesity. *Health Psychology, 13,* 373–383.

Erdley, C. A., Cain, K. M., Loomis, C. C., Dumas-Hines, F., & Dweck, C. S. (1997). Relations among children's social goals, implicit personality theories, and responses to social failure. *Developmental Psychology, 33,* 263–272.

Evanoo, G. (2007). Infant crying: A clinical conundrum. *Journal of Pediatric Health Care, 21,* 333–338.

Evans, D. W., & Gray, F. L. (2000). Compulsive behavior in individuals with Down syndrome: Its relation to mental age level, adaptive and maladaptive behavior. *Child Development, 71,* 288–300.

Evans, E. M., Schweingruber, H., & Stevenson, H. W. (2002). Gender differences in interest and knowledge acquisition: The United States, Taiwan and Japan. *Sex Roles, 47,* 153–167.

Evans, G. (2004). The environment of childhood poverty. *American Psychologist, 59,* 77–92.

Evans, G. W. (2003). A multi-methodological analysis of cumulative risk and allostatic load among rural children. *Developmental Psychology, 39,* 924–933.

Fabes, R. A., Martin, C. L., & Hanish, L. D. (2002). *The role of sex segregation in young children's prosocial behavior and disposition.* Paper presented at the Groningen Conference on Prosocial Dispositions and Solidarity, Groningen, Netherlands.

Fagan, J. F., III. (1992). Intelligence: A theoretical viewpoint. *Current Directions in Psychological Science, 1,* 82–86.

Fagan, J. F., III, Drotar, D., Berkoff, K., Peterson, N., Kiziri-Mayengo, R., Guay, L., Ndugwa, C., & Zaidan, S. (1991). The Fagan Test of Infant Intelligence: Cross-cultural and racial comparisons. *Journal of Developmental and Behavioral Pediatrics, 12,* 168.

Fagot, B. I. (1985a). Beyond the reinforcement principle: Another step toward understanding sex role development. *Developmental Psychology, 21,* 1097–1104.

Fagot, B. I. (1985b). Changes in thinking about early sex role development. *Developmental Review, 5,* 83–98.

Fagot, B. I., & Leinbach, M. D. (1989). The young child's gender schema: Environmental input, internal organization. *Child Development, 60,* 663–672.

Fagot, B. I., & Leinbach, M. D. (1992). Gender-role development in young children: From discrimination to labeling. *Developmental Review, 13,* 205–224.

Fairborn, C. G., Cooper, A., Doll, H. A., & Welch, S. L. (1999). Risk factors for anorexia nervosa: Three integrated case-control comparison. *Archives of General Psychiatry, 56,* 468–476.

Falbo, T., & Polit, D. F. (1986). Quantitative review of the only child literature: Research evidence and theory development, *Psychological Bulletin, 100,* 176–189.

Fales, C. L., Knowlton, B. I., Holyoak, K. J., Geshwind, D. H.,

Swerdloff, R. S., & Gonzalo, I. G. (2003). Working memory and relational reasoning in Klinefelter syndrome. *Journal of the International Neuropsychological Society, 9*, 839–846.

Fancher, R. E. (1995). The Bell Curve on separated twins. *Alberta Journal of Educational Research. Special Issue: Canadian Perspectives on the Bell Curve, 41*, 265–270.*

Fantz, R. (1963). Pattern vision in newborn infants. *Science, 140*, 296–297.

Farver, J. A., Xu, Y., Eppe, S., Fernandez, A., & Schwartz, D. (2005). Community violence, family conflict, and preschoolers' socioemotional functioning. *Developmental Psychology, 41*, 160–170.

Federal Interagency Forum on Child and Family Statistics. (1997). Washington, DC: U.S. Government Printing Office.

Federal Interagency Forum on Child and Family Statistics. (2007). America's Children: Key National Indicators of Well-Being 2007. Retrieved December, 2008, from http://www.childstats.gov/pdf/ac2007/ac_07.pdf.

Feerick, M. M., Knutson, J. F., Trickett, P. K., & Flanzer, S. (2006). *Child abuse and neglect: Definitions, classifications, and a framework for research.* Maryland: Brookes Publishing.

Feigenbaum, P. (2002). Private speech: Cornerstone of Vygotsky's theory of the development of higher psychological processes. In D. Robbins & A. Stetsenko (Eds.), *Voices within Vygotsky's non-classical psychology: Past, present, future* (pp. 161–174). Hauppauge, NY: Nova Science Publishers.

Feinman, S., & Lewis, M. (1983). Social referencing at ten months: A second-order effect on infants' responses to strangers. *Child Development, 54*, 878–887.

Feiring, C., & Lewis, M. (1987). The ecology of some middle class families at dinner. *International Journal of Behavioral Development, 10*, 377–390.

Feldman, R. (2007). Maternal-infant contact and child development: Insights from the kangaroo intervention. In L. L'Abate (Ed.), *Low-cost approaches to promote physical and mental health: Theory, research, and practice* (pp. 323-351). New York: Springer Science + Business Media.

Feldman, R., & Eidelman, A. I. (2003). Skin-to-skin contact (kangaroo care) accelerates autonomic and neurobehavioral maturation in preterm infants. *Developmental Medicine and Child Neurology, 45*, 274–281.

Feldman, R., Weller, A., Sirota, L., & Eidelman, A. I. (2002). Skin-to-skin contact (kangaroo care) promotes self-regulation in premature infants: Sleep-wake cyclicity, arousal modulation, and sustained exploration. *Developmental Psychology, 38*, 194–207.

Fenaughty, A. M., & MacKinnon, D. P. (1993). Immediate effects of the Arizona alcohol warning poster. *Journal of Public Policy and Marketing, 12*, 69–77.

Fennell, C. T., Byers-Heinlein, K., & Werker, J. F. (2007). Using speech sounds to guide word learning: The case of bilingual infants. *Child Development, 78*, 1510–1525.*

Fenson, L., Dale, P. S., Reznick, J. S., Bates, E., Thal, D. J., & Pethick, S. J. (1994). Variability in early communicative development. *Monographs of the Society for Research in Child Development, 59*, (Serial No. 242).

Ferguson, T. J., & Rule, B. G. (1980). Effects of inferential sex, outcome severity and basis of responsibility on children's evaluations of aggressive acts. *Developmental Psychology, 16*, 141–146.

Fernald, A. (1992). Meaningful melodies in mothers' speech to infants. In H. Papousek, U. Jurgens, & M. Papousek (Eds.), *Nonverbal communication: Comparative and developmental approaches.* Cambridge, England: Cambridge University Press.

Fernald, A., & Kuhl, P. K. (1987). Acoustical determinants of infant preference for motherese speech. *Infant Behavior and Development, 10*, 279–293.

Fernald, A., & Mazzie, C. (1991). Prosody and focus in speech to infants and adults. *Developmental Psychology, 27*, 209–221.

Fernald, A., & Morikawa, H. (1993). Common themes and cultural variations in Japanese and American mothers' speech to infants. *Child Development, 64*, 636–637.

Ferrier, S., Dunham, P., & Dunham, F. (2000). The confused robot: Two-year-olds' responses to breakdowns in communication. *Social Development, 9*, 337–347.*

Fidler, D. J., & Nadel, L. (2007). Education and children with Down syndrome: Neuroscience, development, and intervention. *Mental Retardation and Developmental Disabilities Research Reviews, 13*, 262–271.

Field, T. M. (1978). Interaction behaviors of primary versus secondary caretaker fathers. *Developmental Psychology, 14*, 183–184.

Field, T. M. (1986). Affective responses to separation. In T. B. Brazelton & M. W. Yogman (Eds.),

Affective development in infancy. Norwood, NJ: Ablex.

Field, T. M. (1990). *Infancy.* Cambridge, MA: Harvard University Press.

Field, T. M. (Ed.). (1995). *Touch in early development.* Mahwah, NJ: Erlbaum.

Field, T. M. (2001). Massage therapy facilitates weight gain in preterm infants. *Current Directions in Psychological Science, 10*, 51–54.

Field, T., Diego, M., & Hernandez-Reif, M. (2007). Massage therapy research. *Developmental Review, 27*, 75–89.

Fiese, B. H. (1990). Playful relationships: A contextual analysis of mother-toddler interaction and symbolic play. *Child Development, 61*, 1648–1656.

Fiese, B. H. (2006). *Family routines and rituals.* New Haven, CT: Yale University Press.

Fiese, B. H., & Bickham, N. L. (2004). Pin-curling grandpa's hair in the comfy chair: Parents' stories of growing up and potential links to socialization in the preschool years. In M. W. Pratt & B. H. Fiese (Eds.), *Families, stories, and the life course* (pp. 259–278). Mahwah, NJ: Erlbaum.

Fifer, W. P., & Moon, C. (1989). Auditory experience in the fetus. In W. P. Smotherman & S. R. Robinson (Eds.), *Behavior of the fetus* (pp. 175–187). Caldwell, NJ: Telford Press.

Finnie, V., & Russell, A. (1988). Preschool children's social status and their mothers' behavior and knowledge in the supervisory role. *Developmental Psychology, 24*, 789–801.

Fischer, K. W., & Lazerson, A. (1984). A summary of parental development. In K. W. Fischer & A. Lazerson, *Human development* (p. 117). New York: Freeman.

Fischer, K. W., & Roberts, R. J. (1986). A developmental sequence of classification skills and errors in preschool children. Unpublished manuscript, Harvard University.

Fischer, L., Ames, E.W., Chisholm, K., & Savoie, L. (1997). Problems reported by parents of Romanian orphans adopted to British Columbia. *International Journal of Behavioral Development, 20*, 67–82.*

Fisher, C., Hall, D. G., Rakowitz, S., & Gleitman, L. (1994). When it is better to receive than to give: Syntactic and conceptual constraints on vocabulary growth. In L. Gleitman & B. Landau (Eds.), *The acquisition of lexicon* (pp. 333–376). Cambridge, MA: MIT Press/Elsevier.

Fisher, C. B., & Brone, R. J. (1991). Eating disorders in adolescence. In R. M. Lerner, A. C. Petersen, & J.

Brooks-Gunn (Eds.), *Encyclopedia of Adolescence* (Vol. 1). New York: Garland.

Fisher, C. B., Jackson, J. F., & Villaruel, F. A. (1998). The study of African American and Latin American children and youth. In W. Damon (Series Ed.), & R. M. Lerner (Vol. Ed.), *Handbook of child psychology: Vol. 1. Theoretical models of human development* (5th ed., pp. 1145–1207). New York: Wiley.

Fisher-Thompson, D. (1990). Adult gender typing of children's toys. *Sex Roles, 23*, 291–303.

Fitzgerald, H. E., Mousouli, V., & Davies, H. D. (Eds.). (2008). *Obesity in childhood and adolescence, Vol. 2: Understanding development and prevention.* Westport, CT: Praeger Publishers.

Fivaz-Depeursinge, E., & Corboz-Warnery, A. (1999). *The primary triangle: A developmental systems view of fathers, mothers, and infants.* New York: Basic Books.

Fivush, R. (2002). Scripts, schemas, and memory of trauma. In N. L. Stein & P. J. Bauer (Eds.), *Representation, memory, and development: Essays in honor of Jean Mandler* (pp. 53–74). Mahwah, NJ: Erlbaum.

Fivush, R., Haden, C., & Reese, E. (1996). Remembering, recounting, and reminiscing: The development of autobiographical memory of social context. In D. C. Rubin (Ed.), *Remembering our past: Studies in autobiographical memory* (pp. 341–359). Cambridge, England: Cambridge University Press.

Fivush, R., Haden, C. A., & Reese, E. (2006). Elaborating on elaborations: Role of maternal reminiscing style in cognitive and socioemotional development *Child Development, 77*, 1568–1588.

Fivush, R., & Hamond, N. R. (1989). Time and again: Effects of repetition and retention interval on two year olds' event recall. *Journal of Experimental Child Psychology, 47*, 259–273.

Fivush, R., Hudson, J., & Nelson, K. (1984). Children's long-term memory for a novel event: An exploratory study. *Merrill-Palmer Quarterly, 30*, 303–316.

Fivush, R., Peterson, C., & Schwartzmueller, A. (2002). Questions and answers: The credibility of child witnesses in the context of specific questioning techniques. In M. Leisen (Ed.), *Memory and suggestibility in forensic interview. Personality and clinical psychology series* (pp. 331–354). Mahwah, NJ: Erlbaum.*

Fivush, R., & Sales, J. M. (2004). Children's memories of emotional events. In D. Reisberg & P. Hertel (Eds.), *Memory and emotion* (pp. 242–271). New York: Oxford University Press.

Flanagan, D. P., & Harrison, P. L. (Eds.). (2005). *Contemporary intellectual assessment: Theories, tests, and issues.* New York: Guildford Press.

Flavell, J. H. (1963). *The developmental psychology of Jean Piaget.* Princeton, NJ: Van Nostrand.

Flavell, J. H. (1985). *Cognitive development.* Englewood Cliffs, NJ: Prentice-Hall.

Flavell, J. H., Beach, D. R., & Chinsky, J. M. (1966). Spontaneous verbal rehearsal in a memory task as a function of age. *Child Development, 37,* 283–299.

Flavell, J. H., Friedricks, A. G., & Hoyt, J. D. (1970). Developmental changes in memorization processes. *Cognitive Psychology, 1,* 324–340.

Flavell, J. H., Green, F. L., & Flavell, E. R. (1995b). Young children's knowledge about thinking. *Monographs of the Society for Research in Child Development, 60,* 243–256.

Flavell, J. H., Miller, P. H., & Miller, S. A. (1993). *Cognitive development* (3rd ed.). Englewood Cliffs, NJ: Prentice-Hall.

Fleming, A. S., & Corter, C. (1988). Factors influencing maternal responsiveness in humans: Usefulness of an animal model. *Psychoneuroendocrinology, 13,* 189–212.*

Fleming, A. S., Corter, C., Stallings, J., & Steiner, M. (2002). Testosterone and prolactin are associated with emotional responses to infant cries in new fathers. *Hormones and Behavior, 42,* 399–413.*

Fleming, A. S., Ruble, D., Krieger, H., & Wong, P. Y. (1997). Hormonal and experiential correlates of maternal responsiveness during pregnancy and the puerperium in human mothers. *Hormones and Behavior, 31,* 145–158.*

Fleming, A. S., Steiner, M., & Anderson, V. (1987). Hormonal and attitudinal correlates of maternal behavior during the early postpartum period. *Journal of Reproductive and Infant Psychology, 5,* 193–205.*

Flynn, J. R. (1987). Massive IQ gains: What IQ tests really measure. *Psychological Bulletin, 101,* 171–191.

Flynn, J. R. (2007). *What is intelligence? Beyond the Flynn effect.* Cambridge, UK: Cambridge University Press.

Fogel, A. (1993). *Developing through relationships: Origins of communication, self, and culture.* Chicago: University of Chicago Press.

Fogel, A., Hsu, H., Shapiro, A. F., Nelson-Goens, G. C., & Secrist, C. (2006). Effects of normal and perturbed play on the duration and amplitude of different types of infant smiles. *Developmental Psychology, 42,* 459–473.

Fordham, S., & Ogbu, J. V. (1986). Black students' school success: Coping with the burden of acting white. *Urban Review, 18,* 176–206.

Forrester, L. W., Phillips, S. J., & Clark, J. E. (1993). Locomotor co-ordination in infancy: The transition from walking to running. In G. J. P. Savelsbergh (Ed.), *The development of coordination in infancy* (pp. 359–393). Amsterdam: Elsevier.

Foundation for Child Development. (2007). *2007 Child well-being index (CWI) special focus report on international comparisons.* New York: Foundation for Child Development.

Fox, N. A. (1991). If it's not left, it's right: Electroencephalograph asymmetry and the development of emotion. *American Psychologist, 46,* 863–872.

Fox, N. A., & Calkins, S. (2003). The development of self-control of emotions: Intrinsic and external influences. *Motivation and Emotion, 27,* 7–26.

Fox, N. A., Calkins, S. D., & Bell, M. A. (1994). Neural plasticity and development in the first two years of life: Evidence from cognitive and socioemotional domains. *Development and Psychopathology, 6,* 677–696

Fox, N. A., & Davidson, R. J. (1988). Patterns of brain electrical activity during facial signs of emotion in 10-month-old infants. *Developmental Psychology, 24,* 230–236..

Fraiberg, S. (1977). *Insights from the blind.* New York: Basic Books.

Fraley, R. C., & Spieker, S. J. (2003). Are attachment patterns continuously or categorically distributed? A taxometric analysis of strange situation behavior. *Developmental Psychology, 39,* 387–404.

Francis, P. L., Self, P. A., & Horowitz, F. D. (1987). The behavioral assessment of the neonate: An overview. In J. Osofsky (Ed.), *Handbook of infancy* (2nd ed.). New York: Wiley.

Francks, C., Maegawa, S., Lauren, J., Abrahams, B., & et al. (2007). LRRTMI on chromosome 2p12 is a maternally suppressed gene that is associated with handedness and schizophrenia. *Molecular Psychiatry, 12,* 1120–1139.

Franco, F., & Butterworth, G. (1996). Pointing and social awareness: Declaring and requesting in the second year. *Journal of Child Language, 23,* 307–336.

Frank, D. A., Augustyn, M., Knight, W. G., Pell, T., & Zuckerman, B. (2001). Growth, development, and behavior in early childhood following prenatal cocaine exposure: A systematic review. *Journal of the American Medical Association, 285,* 1613–1625.

Freedman, D. G. (1974). *Human infancy: An evolutionary perspective.* Hillsdale, NJ: Erlbaum.

Freedman, D. S., K., K. L., Serdula, M. K., Dietz, W. H., Srinivasan, S. S., & Berenson, G. S. (2002). Relations of age at menarche to race, time period, and anthropometric dimension: The Bogalusa heart study. *Pediatrics, 110,* e43.

Freiberg, K. L., Tualy, K., & Crassini, B. (2001). Use of an auditory looming task to test infants' sensitivity to sound pressure level as an auditory distance cue. *British Journal of Developmental Psychology, 19 (pt. 1),* 1–10.

Freidman, H. S., Tucker, J. S., Schwartz, J. E., Tomlinson-Keasey, C., Martin, L. R., Wingard, D. L., & Criqui, M. H. (1995). Psychosocial and behavioral predictors of longevity. *American Psychologist, 50,* 69–78.

Freidman, J. M., & Polifka, J. E. (1996). *The effects of drugs on the fetus and the nursing infant.* Baltimore, MD: Johns Hopkins University.

French, D. C. (1990). Heterogeneity of peer rejected girls. *Child Development, 61,* 2028–2031.

Frey, K. S., & Ruble, D. N. (1992). Gender constancy and the "cost" of sex-typed behavior: A test of the conflict hypothesis. *Developmental Psychology, 28,* 714–721.

Frick, W. B. (1999). Flight into health: A new interpretation. *Journal of Humanistic Psychology, 3,* 58–81.

Fried, P. A. (2002). Conceptual issues in behavioral teratology and their application in determining long-term sequelae of prenatal marijuana exposure. *Journal of Child Psychology, Psychiatry and Allied Disciplines, 43,* 81–102.*

Fried, P. A., James, D. J., & Watkinson, B. (2001). Growth and pubertal milestones during adolescence in offspring prenatally exposed to cigarettes and marijuana. *Neurotoxicology and Teratology, 23,* 431–436.*

Fried, P. A., & Smith, A. M. (2001). A literature review of the consequences of prenatal marijuana exposure: An emerging theme of deficiency in executive functioning. *Neurotoxicology and Teratology, 23,* 1–11.*

Fried, P. A., & Watkinson, B. (1990). 36- and 48-month neurobehavioral follow-up of children prenatally exposed to marijuana, cigarettes, and alcohol. *Journal of Developmental and Behavioral Pediatrics, 11,* 49–58.*

Fried, P. A., & Watkinson, B. (2000). Visuoperceptual functioning differs in 9- to 12-year-olds prenatally exposed to cigarettes and marijuana. *Neurotoxicology and Teratology, 22,* 11–20.*

Fried, P. A., & Watkinson, B. (2001). Differential effects on facets of attention in adolescents prenatally exposed to cigarettes and marijuana. *Neurotoxicology and Teratology, 23,* 421–430.*

Fried, P. A., Watkinson, B., & Gray, P. (1999). Growth from birth to early adolescence in offspring prenatally exposed to cigarettes and marijuana. *Neurotoxicology and Teratology, 21,* 513–525.*

Fried, P. A., Watkinson, B., & Gray, R. (1998). Differentiating effects on cognitive functioning in 9- to 12-year-olds prenatally exposed to cigarettes and marijuana. *Neurotoxicology and Teratology, 20,* 293–306.*

Fried, P. A., Watkinson, B., & Gray, R. (2003). Differential effects on cognitive functioning in 13- to 16-year-olds prenatally exposed to cigarettes and marijuana. *Neurotoxicology and Teratology, 25,* 427–436.*

Fried, P. A., Watkinson, B., & Gray, R. (2006). Neurocognitive consequences of cigarette smoking in young adults - a comparison with pre-drug performance. *Neurotoxicology and Teratology, 28,* 517–525.

Friedman, J. M., & Polifka, J. E. (1996). *The effects of drugs on the fetus and the nursing infant.* Baltimore: Johns Hopkins University Press.

Friedrich, L. K., & Stein, A. H. (1973). Aggressive and prosocial television programs and the natural behavior of preschool children. *Monographs of the Society for Research in Child Development, 38* (Serial No. 151).

Friendly, M. (2000). Childcare and Canadian federalism in the 1990s: Canary in a coal mine. Childcare Resource and Research Unit, Occasional Paper 11, Toronto.*

Friendly, M., Beach, J., & Turiano, M. (2002). *Early childhood education and care in Canada, 2001, 5th Edition.* Toronto: Childcare Resource and Research Unit.*

Frodi, A. M., & Lamb, M. E. (1980). Child abusers' responses to infant smiles and cries. *Child Development, 51,* 238–241.

Frosch, C. A., & Mangelsdorf, S. C. (2001). Marital behavior, parenting behavior and multiple reports of preschoolers' behavior problems: Mediation or moderation. *Developmental Psychology, 37,* 502–519.

Frosch, C. A., Mangelsdorf, S., & McHale, J. L. (2000). Marital behavior and the security of preschool-parent attachment relationships. *Journal of Family Psychology, 14,* 1438–1449.

Frye, D., Zelazo, P. D., & Burack, J. A. (1998). Cognitive complexity and control: I. Theory of mind in typical and atypical development. *Current Directions in Psychological Science, 7,* 116–121.*

Fuligni, A. J. (1997). The academic achievement of adolescents from immigrant families: The roles of family background, attitudes, and behavior. *Child Development, 68,* 351–363.

Fuller, B. F. (2001). Infant gender differences regarding acute established pain. *Clinical Nursing Research, 11,* 190–203.

Funk, J. B., and Buchman, D. D. (1996). Children's perceptions of gender differences in social approval for playing electronic games. *Self Roles, 35,* 219–232.

Furman, W. (2002). The emerging field of adolescent romantic relationships. *Current Directions in Psychological Science, 11,* 177–180.

Furman, W., & Gavin, L. A. (1989). Peers influence on adjustment and development. In T. J. Berndt & G. W. Ladd (Eds.), *Peer relationships in child development.* New York: Wiley.

Furstenberg, F. F., Cook, T., Eccles, J. S., Elder, G. H., & Sameroff, A. (1999). *Managing to make it.* Chicago: University of Chicago Press.

Furstenberg, F. F., Jr., Levin, J. A., & Brooks-Gunn, J. (1990). The children of teenage mothers: Patterns of early childbearing in two generations. *Family Planning Perspectives, 22,* 54-60.

Gadsden, V. L. (1999). Black families in international and cultural perspective. In M. E. Lamb (Ed.), *Parenting and child development in "nontraditional" families* (pp. 221-246). Mahwah, NJ: Erlbaum.

Galen, B. R., & Underwood, M. K. (1997). A developmental investigation of social aggression among children. *Developmental Psychology, 33,* 589–600.

Gallaway, C., & Richards, B. J. (1994). *Input and interaction in language acquisition.* Cambridge: Cambridge University Press.

Gallimore, R., & Tharp, R. (1999). Teaching mind in society: Teaching, schooling, and literate discourses. In P. Lloyd & C. Fernyhough (Eds.), *Lev Vygotsky: Critical assessments: The zone of proximal development* (Vol. III, pp. 296–330). Florence, KY: Taylor and Francis.

Galloway, J. C., & Thelen, E. (2004). Feet first: Object exploration in young infants. *Infant Behavior and Development, 27,* 107–112.

Ganger, J., & Brent, M. R. (2004). Reexamining the vocabulary spurt. *Developmental Psychology, 40,* 621–632.

Garbarino, J. (1982). Sociocultural risk: Dangers to competence. In C. Kopp & J. Krakow (Eds.), *Child development in a social context* (pp. 630–685). Reading, MA: Addison-Wesley.

Garbarino, J. (1995). *Raising children in a socially toxic environment.* San Francisco: Jossey-Bass.

Garbarino, J., & Kostelny, K. (2002). Parenting and public policy. In M. Bornstein (Ed.), *Handbook of parenting: Vol 3.* (rev. ed., pp. 419–436). Mahwah, NJ: Erlbaum.

Garbarino, J., & Sherman, D. (1980). High-risk neighborhoods and high-risk families: The human ecology of child maltreatment. *Child Development, 51,* 188–198.

Garber, J., & Mardin, N. C. (2002). Negative cognitions in offspring of depressed parents: Mechanisms of risk. In S. H. Goodman & I. N. Gotlib (Eds.), *Children of depressed parents* (pp. 121–154). Washington, DC: American Psychological Association.

Garcia, M. M., Shaw, D. S., Winslow, E. B., & Yaggi, K. E. (2000). Destructive sibling conflict and the development of conduct problems in young boys. *Developmental Psychology, 36,* 44–53.

Garcia-Coll, C. T. (1990). Developmental outcome of minority infants: A process-oriented look into our beginnings. *Child Development, 61,* 270–289.

Gardiner, H. W., & Kosmitzki, C. (2008). *Lives across cultures.* Boston: Pearson.

Gardner, H. (1983). *Frames of mind: The theory of multiple intelligences.* New York: Basic Books.

Gardner, H. (1999). *Intelligence reframed: Multiple intelligences for the 21st century.* New York: Basic Books.

Gardner, H. (2004). *Frames of mind: The theory of multiple intelligences.* New York: Basic Books.

Gardner, H. (2006). *Multiple intelligences: New horizons.* New York: Basic Books.

Gardner, R. C., & Clément, R. (1990). Social psychological perspectives on second language acquisition. In H. Giles & W.P. Robinson (Eds.), *Handbook of language and social psychology* (pp. 495–517). West Sussex, UK: Wiley.*

Gardner, R. C., Lalonde, R. N., & Pierson, R. (1983). The socio-educational model of second-language learning: An investigation using LISREL causal modeling. *Journal of Language and Social Psychology, 2,* 51–65.*

Gardner, R. C., Masgoret, A. M., & Tremblay, P. F. (1999). Home background characteristics and second language learning. *Journal of Language and Social Psychology, 18,* 419–437.*

Gardner, R. J. M., & Sutherland, G. R. (1996). *Chromosome abnormalities and genetic counseling* (2nd ed.). Oxford: Oxford University Press.

Garlick, D. (2003). Integrating brain science research with intelligence research. *Current Directions in Psychological Science, 12,* 185–189.

Garner, P. W., Jones, D. C., & Palmer, D. (1994). Social cognitive correlates of preschool children's sibling caregiving behavior. *Developmental Psychology, 30,* 905–911.

Garner, P. W., & Power, T. G. (1996). Preschoolers emotional control in the disappointment paradigm and its relation to temperament, emotional knowledge and family expressiveness. *Child Development, 67,* 1406–1429.

Garrett, A. S., Menon, V., Mackenzie, K., & Reiss, A. (2004). Here's looking at you kid: Neural systems underlying face and gaze processing in fragile X syndrome. *Archives of General Psychiatry, 61,* 281–288.

Garton, A. F. (2004). *Exploring cognitive development: The child as problem solver.* Malden, MA: Blackwell.

Garvey, C. (1990a). *Children's talk.* Cambridge, MA: Harvard University Press.

Gatti, V., Tremblay, R. E., & Larocque, D. (2002). Civic community and juvenile delinquency: A study of the regions of Italy. *British Journal of Criminology, 43,* 22–40.*

Gauvain, M. (1992). Social influences on the development of planning in advance and during action. *International Journal of Behavioral Development, 15,* 377–398.

Gauvain, M. (1993). The development of spatial thinking in everyday activity. *Developmental Review, 13,* 92–121.

Gauvain, M. (2001a). Cultural tools, social interaction, and the development of thinking. *Human Development, 44,* 126–143.

Gauvain, M. (2001b). *The sociocultural context of cognitive development.* New York: Guilford Press.

Gauvain, M., & Perez, S. M. (2006). The socialization of cognition. In J. E. Grusec & P. D. Hastings (Eds.), *Handbook of socialization: Theory and research* (pp. 588–613). New York: Guildford.

Gauvain, M., & Rogoff, B. (1989). Collaborative problem solving and children's planning skills. *Developmental Psychology, 25,* 139–151.

Gazelle, H., & Ladd, G. W. (2003). Anxious solitude and peer exclusion: A diathesis-stress model of internalizing trajectories in childhood. *Child Development, 74,* 257–278.

Ge, X., Brody, G., Conger, R., Simons, R., & Murry, V. M. (2002). Contextual amplification of pubertal transition effects on deviant peer affiliation and externalizing behavior among African-American children. *Developmental Psychology, 38,* 42–54.

Ge, X., Conger, R., & Elder, G. H. (1996). Coming of age too early: Pubertal influences on girls' vulnerability to psychological distress. *Child Development, 62,* 3386–3400.

Ge, X., Conger, R., & Elder, G. H. (2001). The relation between puberty and psychological distress in adolescent boys. *Journal of Research on Adolescence, 11,* 49–70.

Ge, X., Conger, R. D., & Elder, G. H. (2001). Pubertal transition, stressful life events, and the emergence of gender differences in adolescent depressive symptoms. *Developmental Psychology, 37,* 404–417.

Ge, X., Kim, I. J., Brody, G. H., Conger, R. D., Simons, R. L., Gibbons, F. X., & Cutrova, C. E. (2003). It's about timing and change: Pubertal transition effects on symptoms of major depression among African American youths. *Developmental Psychology, 39,* 430–439.

Geary, D. C. (1998). *Male, female: The evolution of human sex differences.* Washington, DC: American Psychological Association.

Geary, D. C. (2006a). Development of mathematical understanding. In W. Damon & R. M. Lerner (Gen. Ed.), & D. Kuhn & R. S. Siegler (Eds.), *Handbook of child psychology: Vol. 2. Cognition, perception, and language* (6th ed., pp. 777–810). New York: Wiley.

Geary, D. C. (2006b). Evolutionary developmental psychology: Current status and future directions. *Developmental Review, 26,* 113–119.

Gelfand, D. M., & Drew, C. J. (2003). *Understanding child behavior disorders* (4th ed.). Belmont, CA: Wadsworth

Gelman, R., & Baillargeon, R. (1983). A review of some Piagetian concepts. In J. H. Falvell & E. M. Markman (Eds.), *Handbook of child psychology: Cognitive development* (Vol. 3). New York: Wiley.

Gelman, R., & Corres, S. (2001). Counting in animals and humans. In E. Dupoux (Ed.), *Language, brain, and cognitive development: Essays in honor of Jacques Mehler* (pp. 279–301). Cambidge, MA: The MIT Press.

Gelman, R., & Gallistel, C. R. (1978). *The child's understanding of number.* Cambridge, MA: Harvard University Press.

Gelman, R., & Shatz, M. (1977). Appropriate speech adjustments: The operation of conversational restraints on talk to two year olds. In M. Lewis & L. Rosenblum (Eds.), *Interaction, conversation and the development of language.* New York: Wiley.

Gelman, R., & Williams, E. (1998). Enabling constraints for cognitive development and learning: Domain specificity and epigenesis. In W. Damon (Series Ed.), & D. Kuhn & R. Siegler (Vol. Eds.), *Handbook of child psychology: Vol. 2. Cognition, perception and language* (5th ed., pp. 575–630). New York: Wiley.

Gelman, S. A., & Markman, E. M. (1987). Young children's inductions from natural kinds: The role of categories and appearances. *Child Development, 58,* 1532–1541.

Genesee, F. (1985). Second language learning through immersion: A review of U.S. programs. *Review of Educational Research, 55,* 541–561.*

Genesee, F., & Gándara, P. (1999). Bilingual education programs: A cross-national perspective. *Journal of Social Issues, 55,* 665–685.*

Gennetian, L. A., & Miller, C. (2002). Children and welfare reform: A view from an experimental welfare program in Minnesota. *Child Development, 73,* 601–620.

Gentner, D. (1982). Why nouns are learned before verbs: Linguistic relativity versus natural partitioning. In S. A. Kuczaj II (Ed.), *Language development: Vol. 2. Language, thought, and culture* (pp. 301–332). Hillsdale, NJ: Erlbaum.

Gentner, D., & Holyoak, K. J. (1997). Reasoning and learning by analogy: Introduction. *American Psychologist, 52,* 32–34.

Gershoff, E. T. (2002). Corporal punishment by parents and associated child behaviors and experiences: A meta-analytic and theoretical review. *Psychological Bulletin, 128,* 538–579.

Gesell, A. L. (1928). *Infancy and human growth.* New York: Macmillan.

Gesundheit, B., Grisaru-Soen, G., Greenberg, D., Levtzion-Korach, O., Malkin, D., Petric, M., et al. (2004). Neonatal genital herpes simplex virus type 1 infection after Jewish ritual circumcision: Modern medicine and religious tradition. *Pediatrics, 114,* e259–e263.*

Gewirtz, J. L. (1967). The course of infant smiling in four child-rearing environments in Israel. In B. M. Foss (Ed.), *Determinants of infant behavior* (Vol. 3, pp. 105–248). London: Methuen.

Gewirtz, J. L., & Peláez-Nogueras, B. F. (1992). Skinner's legacy to human infant behavior and development. *American Psychologist, 47,* 1411–1422.

Gibbs, J. C., Potter, G. B., & Goldstein, A. P. (1995). *The EQUIP program: Teaching youth to think and act responsibly through a peer helping approach.* Champaign, IL: Research Press.

Gibbs, J. T. (1989). Black American adolescents. In J. T. Gibbs & L. N. Huang (Eds.), *Children of color.* San Francisco: Jossey-Bass.

Gibson, E. J., & Walk, R. D. (1960). The "visual cliff." *Scientific American, 202,* 64.

Gick, M. L., & Holyoak, K. J. (1980). Analogical problem solving. *Cognitive Psychology, 12,* 306–355.

Gick, M. L., & Holyoak, K. J. (1983). Schema induction and analogical transfer. *Cognitive Psychology, 15,* 1–38.

Gifford-Smith, M. E., & Rabiner, D. L. (2004). Social information processing and children's social adjustment. In J. Kupersmidt & K. A. Dodge (Eds.), *Children's peer relations: From development to intervention to policy: A festschrift to honor John D. Coie.* Washington, DC: American Psychological Association.

Giles, J. W., & Heyman, G. D. (2004). When to cry over spilled milk: Young children's use of category information to guide inferences about ambiguous behavior. *Journal of Cognition and Development, 5,* 359–382.

Gill, C., Kiecan-Aker, J., Roberts, T., & Fredenburg, K. A. (2003). Following directions: Rehearsal and visualization strategies for children with specific language impairment. *Child Language Teaching and Therapy, 19,* 85–101.

Gillham, J. E., Reivich, K. J., Jaycox, L. H., & Seligman, M. E. (1995). Prevention of depressive symptoms in schoolchildren: Two-year follow-up. *Psychological Science, 6,* 343–351.

Gilligan, C. (1982). *In a different voice.* Cambridge, MA: Harvard University Press.

Gilligan, C. (1993). Woman's place in man's life cycle. In A. Dobrin (Ed.), *Being good and doing right: Readings in moral development* (pp. 37–54). Lanham, MD: University Press of America.

Gilliland, F. D., Li, Y.-F., & Peters, J. M. (2001). Effects of maternal smoking during pregnancy and environmental tobacco smoke in asthma and wheezing in children. *American Journal of Respiratory and Critical Care Medicine, 163,* 429–436.

Gilliom, M., Shaw, D., Beck, J. E., Shonberg, M., & Lukon, J. L. (2002). Anger regulation in disadvantaged preschool boys: Strategies, antecedents, and the development of self-control. *Developmental Psychology, 38,* 222–235.

Giusti, R. M., Iwamoto, K., & Hatch, E. E. (1995). Diethylstilbestrol revisited: A review of the long-term health effects. *Annals of Internal Medicine, 122,* 778–788.

Gladwin, T. (1970). *East is a big bird.* Cambridge, MA: Harvard University Press.

Gleason, T. R., Gower, A. L., Hohmann, L. M., & Gleason, T. C. (2005). Temperament and friendship in preschool-aged children. *International Journal of Behavioral Development, 29,* 336–344.

Gleitman, L. (1990). The structural sources of verb meanings. *Language acquisition, 1,* 3–55.

Glick, D., Keene-Osborn, S., Gegax, T. T., & et al. (1999). Anatomy of a massacre. *Newsweek,* May 3, p. 24.

Glucksberg, S., Krauss, R., & Higgins, E. T. (1975). The development of referential communication skills. In F. D. Horowitz (Eds.), *Review of child development research* (Vol. 4). Chicago: University of Chicago Press.

Godoi, D., & Barela, J. A. (2008). Body sway and sensory motor coupling adaptation in children: Effects of distance manipulation. *Developmental Psychobiology, 50,* 77–87.

Goldberg, S. (2001). Attachment assessment in the strange situation. In L. T. Singer & P. J. Zeskind (Eds.), *Biobehavioral assessment of the infant* (pp. 209–229). New York: Guildford.*

Goldberg, S., Benoit, D., Blokland, K., & Madigan, S. (2003). Atypical behavior, maternal representations, and infant disorganized attachment. *Development and Psychopathology, 15,* 239–257.*

Goldberg, S., & DiVitto, B. (2002). Parenting children born prematurely. In M. H. Bornstein (Ed.), *Handbook of parenting* (2nd ed., Vol. 1, pp. 329–354). Mahwah, NH: Erlbaum.*

Goldberg, S., Grusec, J. E., & Jenkins, J. M. (1999a). Confidence in protection: Arguments for a narrow definition of attachment. *Journal of Family Psychology, 13,* 475–483.*

Goldberg, S., Grusec, J. E., & Jenkins, J. M. (1999b). Narrow view of attachment or broad view of protection? Rejoinder to the commentaries. *Journal of Family Psychology, 13,* 504–507.*

Goldberg, S., & Marcovich, S. (1997). International adoption: Risk, resilience, and adjustment (Introduction to the special section). *International Journal of Behavioral Development, 20,* 1–2.*

Golden, O. (2000). The federal response to child abuse and neglect. *American Psychologist, 55,* 1050-1053.

Goldfarb, W. (1945). Effects of psychological deprivation in infancy and subsequent stimulation. *American Journal of Psychiatry, 102,* 18–33.

Goldfield, G. S., Mallory, R., Parker, T., Cunningham, T., Legg, C., Lumb, A., et al. (2007). Effects of modifying physical activity and sedentary behavior on psychosocial adjustment in overweight/obese children. *Journal of Pediatric Psychology, 32,* 783–793.

Goldin-Meadow, S. (2006). Nonverbal communcation: The hand's role in talking and thinking. In W. Damon & R. M. Lerner (Gen. Ed.), & D. Kuhn & R. Siegler (Eds.), *Handbook of child psychology: Vol. 2: Cognition, perception, and language* (pp. 336–371). New York: Wiley.

Goldin-Meadow, S. (2007). Pointing sets the stage for language learning and creating language. *Child Development, 78,* 741–758.

Goldsmith, H. H., Aksan, N., Essex, M., Smider, N. A., & Vandell, D. L. (2001). Temperament and socioemotional adjustment to kindergarten: A multi-informant perspective. In T. D. Wachs & G. A. Kohnstamm (Eds.), *Temperament in context* (pp. 103-138). Mahwah, NJ: Erlbaum.

Goldstein, N. (1990, January). *Explaining socioeconomic differences in children's cognitive test scores.* Unpublished manuscript, Malcolm Weiner Center for Social Policy, J. F. Kennedy School of Government, Harvard University.

Goleman, D. (1995). *Emotional intelligence.* New York: Bantam Books.

Goleman, D. (2006). *Social intelligence: Beyond IQ, beyond emotional intelligence.* New York, NY: Bantam.

Golinkoff, R. M. (1983). The preverbal negotiation of failed messages: Insights into the transition period. In R. M. Golinkoff (Ed.), *The transition from prelinguistic to linguistic communication* (pp. 57–78). Hillsdale, NJ: Erlbaum.

Golinkoff, R. M., & Hirsh-Pasek, K. (1999). *How babies talk.* New York: The Penguin Group.

Golinkoff, R. M., Hirsh-Pasek, K., Bailey, L. M., & Wenger, N. R. (1992). Young children and adults use lexical principles to learn new words. *Developmental Psychology, 28,* 99–108.

Golinkoff, R. M., Hirsh-Pasek, K., & Schweisguth, M. A. (2001). A reappraisal of young children's knowledge of grammatical morphemes. In J. Weissenborn & B. Hoehle (Eds.), *Approaches to bootstrapping: Phonological, syntactic, and neurophysical aspects of early language acquisition.* Amsterdam: John Benjamins Publishing Co.

Golombok, S. (2006). New family forms. In A. Clarke-Stewart & J. Dunn (Eds.), *Families count: Effects of child and adolescent development* (pp. 273–298). New York: Cambridge University Press.

Golombok, S., & Fivush, R. (1994). *Gender development.* New York: Cambridge University Press.

Golombok, S., Murray, C., Jadva, V., MacCallum, F., & Lycett, E. (2004). Families created through surrogacy arrangements: Parent-child relationships in the first year of life. *Developmental Psychology, 40,* 400–411.

Golombok, S., Peppy, B., Burston, A., Murray, C., Mooney-Somers, J., Stevens, M., & Golding, J. (2003). Children with lesbian parents: A community study. *Developmental Psychology, 39,* 20–33.

Gomez, J. C. (2004). *Apes, monkeys, children, and the growth of mind.* Cambridge, MA: Harvard University Press.

Goncz, L., & Kodzopeljic, J. (1991). Exposure to two languages in the preschool period: Metalinguistic development and the acquisition of reading. *Journal of Multilingual and Multicultural Development, 12,* 137–142.

Gooden, A. M., & Gooden, M. A. (2001). Gender representation in notable children's picture books: 1995-1999. *Sex Roles, 45,* 89–101.

Goodglass, H. (1993). *Understanding aphasia.* New York: Academic Press.

Goodman, G. S., Emery, R. E., & Haugaard, J. J. (1998). Developmental psychology and law: Divorce, child maltreatment, foster care, and adoption. In W. Damon (Gen. Ed.), I. E. Sigel, & K. A. Renninger (Vol. Eds.), *Handbook of child psychology: Vol. 4. Child psychology in practice* (pp. 775–874). New York: Wiley.

Goodman, J. C. (1989). *The development of context effects of spoken word recognition.* Doctoral dissertation. The University of Chicago.

Goodman, S. H., & Gotlib, I. N. (Eds.). (2002). *Children of depressed parents.* Washington, DC: American Psychological Association.

Goodnow, J. J., Miller, P. J., & Kessel, F. (1995). *Cultural practices as contexts for development.* San Francisco: Jossey-Bass.

Goodwin, M. H. (2002). Exclusion in girls' peer groups: Ethnographic analysis of language practices on the playground. *Human Development, 45,* 392–415.

Gormally, S., Barr, R. G., Wertheim, L., Alkawaf, R., Calinoiu, N., & Young, S. N. (2001). Contact and nutrient effects on newborn infant pain responses. *Developmental Medicine and Child Neurology, 43,* 23–38.*

Gosselin, P., Perron, M., Legault, M., & Campanella, P. (2002). Children's and adults' knowledge of the distinction between enjoyment and non-enjoyment smiles. *Journal of Nonverbal Behavior, 26,* 83–108.

Goswami, U. (1995). Transitive relational mappings in 3- and 4-year-olds: The analogy of Goldilocks and the Three Bears. *Child Development, 66,* 877–892.

Goswami, U. (2001). Cognitive development: No stages please - we're British. *British Journal of Psychology, 92,* 257–277.

Goswami, U., & Brown, A. L. (1990). Higher-order structure and relational reasoning: Contrasting analogical and thematic relations. *Cognition, 36,* 207–226.

Goswami, U., & Bryant, P. (1990). *Phonological skills and learning to read.* Hillsdale, NJ: Erlbaum.

Gotlib, I. N., Joorman, J., Minor, K. L., & Cooney, R. E. (2006). Cognitive and biological functioning in children at risk for depression. In C. Turhan (Ed.), *Biology of personality and individual differences* (pp. 353–382). New York: Guilford.

Gottesman, I. I. (1963). Genetic aspects of intelligent behavior. In N. Ellis (Ed.), *Handbook of mental deficiency: Psychological theory and research.* New York: McGraw-Hill.

Gottesman, I. I., & Goldsmith, H. H. (1994). Developmental psychopathology of antisocial behavior: Inserting genes into its ontogenesis and epigenesis. In C. A. Nelson (Ed.), *Threats to optimal development: Integrating biological, psychological, and social risk factors* (pp. 69–104). Hillsdale, NJ: Erlbaum.

Gottfredson, L. S. (Ed.). (1997). Intelligence and social policy [Special issue]. *Intelligence, 24,* 1–320.

Gottfried, A. E., Gottfried, A. W., & Bathurst, K. (2002). Maternal and dual-earner employment status and parenting. In M. Bornstein (Ed.), *Handbook of parenting* (Rev. ed., pp. 207–230). Mahwah, NJ: Erlbaum.

Gottlieb, G. (1991). Experiential canalization of behavioral development theory. *Developmental Psychology, 27,* 4–13.

Gottlieb, G. (1992). *Individual development and evolution: The genesis of novel behavior.* New York: Oxford University Press.

Gottlieb, G., & Lickliter, R. (2004). The various roles of animal models in understanding human development. *Social Development, 13,* 311–325.

Gottman, J., Katz, L., & Hooven, C. (1996). *Meta-emotion.* Mahwah, NJ: Erlbaum.

Gottman, J. M. (1983). How children become friends. *Monographs of the Society for Research in Child Development, 48* (Serial No. 201).

Gottman, J. M. (1986). The world of coordinated play: Same and cross-sex friendship in young children. In J. M. Gottman & J. G. Parker (Eds.), *The conversations of friends.* New York: Cambridge University Press.

Gottman, J. M., & Mettetal, G. (1986). Speculations on social and affective development: Friendship and acquaintanceship through adolescence. In J. M. Gottman & J. G. Parker (Eds.), *The conversations of friends.* New York: Cambridge University Press.

Gottman, J. M., & Parker, J. G. (Eds.). (1986). *The conversations of friends.* New York: Cambridge University Press.

Gould, E., Reeves, A. J., Graziano, M. S., & Gross, C. G. (1999). Neurogenesis in the neocortex of adult primates. *Science, 286,* 548–555.

Graber, J. A., Petersen, A. C., & Brooks-Gunn, J. (1996). Pubertal processes: Methods, measures and models. In J. A. Graber, J. Brooks-Gunn, & A. C. Petersen (Eds.), *Transitions through adolescence.* Mahwah, NJ: Erlbaum.

Graham, G. G. (1966). Growth during recovery from infantile malnutrition. *Journal of the American Medical Women's Association, 21,* 737–742.

Graham, S., Doubleday, C., & Guarino, P. A. (1984). The development of relations between perceived controllability and the emotions of pity, anger and guilt. *Child Development, 55,* 561–565.

Graham, S., & Hudley, C. (1994). Attributions of aggressive and non-aggressive African--American male early adolescents: A study of construct accessibility. *Developmental Psychology, 30,* 365–373.

Graham, S. A., Baker, R. K., & Poulin-Dubois, D. (1999a). Infants' expectations about object label references. *Canadian Journal of Experimental Psychology, 52,* 103–113.*

Graham, S. A., Poulin-Dubois, D., & Baker, R. K. (1999b). Infants' disambiguation of novel object words. *First Language, 18,* 149–164.*

Granger, D. A., Serbin, L. A., Schwartzman, A. E., Lehoux, P., Cooperman, J., & Ikera, S. (1998). Children's salivary control, internalising behavior problems, and family environment: Results from the Concordia Longitudinal Risk Project. *International Journal of Behavioral Development, 22,* 707–728.*

Granrud, C. E. (2006). Size constancy in infants: 4-month-olds' responses to physical versus retinal image size. *Journal of Experimental Psychology: Human Perception and Performance, 32,* 1398–1404.

Grantham-McGregor, S. M., Powell, C. A., Walker, S. P., & Hines, J. H. (1991). Nutritional supplementation, psychological stimulation and mental development of stunted children: The Jamaican study. *Lancet, 338,* 1–5.

Graves, S. B. (1993). Television, the portrayal of African-Americans, and the development of children's attitudes. In G. L. Berry & J. K. Asamen (Eds.), *Children and television: Images in a changing socio-cultural world* (pp. 179–190). Newbury Park, CA: Sage.

Green, C. D. (2002). Toronto's "other" original APA member: James Gibson Hume. *Canadian Psychology, 43,* 35–43.*

Green, C. D. (2004). The hiring of James Mark Baldwin and James Gibson Hume at the University of Toronto in 1889. *History of Psychology, 7,* 130–153.*

Greenberg, M. (1999). Attachment and psychopathology. In J. Cassidy & P. R. Shaver (Eds.), *Handbook of attachment* (pp. 419–456). New York: Guilford.

Greenfield, P. M., & Childs, C. P. (1991). Developmental continuity in biocultural context. In R. Cohen & A. W. Siegel (Eds.), *Context and development* (pp. 135–160) Hillsdale, NJ: Erlbaum.

Greenough, W., & Black, J. E. (1999). Experience, neural plasticity, and psychological development. In N. A. Fox, L. A. Leavitt, & J. G. Warhol (Eds.), *The role of early experience in infant development* (pp. 29–40). Newark, NJ: Johnson & Johnson Pediatric Institute.

Grella, C. E. (2006). The Drug Abuse Treatment Outcome Studies: Outcomes with adolescent substance abusers. In H. A. Liddle & R. C. L. (Eds.), *Adolescent substance abuse: Research and clinical issues* (pp. 148–173). New York: Cambridge.

Grief, E. B., & Gleason, J. B. (1980). Hi, thanks, and goodbye: More routine information. *Language in Society, 9,* 159–166.

Griffin, P. B., & Griffin, M. B. (1992). Fathers and childcare among the Cagayan Agta. In B. Hewlett (Ed.), *Father-child relations: Cultural and biosocial contexts* (pp. 297–320). New York: Aldine de Gruyther.

Grigorenko, E. L., & Sternberg, R. J. (Eds.). (2001). *Family-environment and intellectual functioning: A life-span perspective.* Mahwah, NJ: Erlbaum.

Grigorenko, E. L., Sternberg, R. J., & Strauss, S. (2006). Practical intelligence and elementary-school teacher effectiveness in the United States and Israel: Measuring the predictive power of tacit knowledge. *Thinking Skills and Creativity, 1,* 14–33.

Gritz, E. R. (2004). Smoking and friendship influence in three ethnic groups. *Nicotine and Tobacco Research, 11,* 109–115.

Gross, R. T., Spiker, D., & Haynes, C. W. (Eds.). (1997). *Helping low birthweight and premature infants. The Infant Health and Development Program.* Stanford, CA: Stanford University Press.

Grossmann, K. E., Grossmann, K., & Kindler, H. (2005). Early care and the roots of attachment and partnership representations: The Bielefeld and Regensburg Longitudinal studies. In K. E. Grossmann, K. Grossmann & E. Waters (Eds.), *Attachment from infancy to adulthood* (pp. 98–136). New York: Guilford.

Grusec, J. E., & Abramovitch, R. (1982). Imitation of peers and adults in a natural setting: A functional analysis. *Child Development, 53,* 636–642.*

Grusec, J. E., Covell, K., & Paucha, P. (1991). *Intergenerational transmission of discipline styles and associated belief systems.* Paper presented at the meetings of the Society for Research in Child Development. Seattle, WA.*

Grusec, J. E., & Davidov, M. (2007). Socialization in the family: The role of parents. In J. E. Grusec & P. Hastings (Eds.), *Handbook of socialization* (pp. 284–308). New York: Guilford.*

Grusec, J. E., Davidov, M., & Lundek, L. (2002). Prosocial and helping behavior. In P. K. Smith & C. H. Hart (Eds.), *Blackwell handbook of childhood social development* (pp. 457–474). Malden, MA: Blackwell Publishers.*

Grusec, J. E., & Dix, T. (1986). The socialization of prosocial behavior: Theory and reality. In C. Zahn-Waxler, E. M. Cummings, & R. Ioannotti (Eds.), *Altruism and aggression.* New York: Cambridge University Press.*

Grusec, J. E., & Goodnow, J. J. (1994a). Impact of parental discipline methods on the child's internalization of values: A reconceptualization of current points of view. *Developmental Psychology, 30,* 4–19.*

Grusec, J. E., & Goodnow, J. J. (1994b). Summing up and looking to the future. *Developmental Psychology, 30,* 29–31.*

Grusec, J. E., Goodnow, J. J., & Kuczynski, L. (2000). New directions in analyses of parenting contributions to children's acquisition of values. *Child Development, 71,* 205–211.*

Grusec, J. E., Kuczynski, L., Rushton, P., & Simutis, Z. M. (1979). Learning resistance to temptation through observation. *Developmental Psychology, 15,* 233–240.*

Grych, J., & Fincham, F. F. (Eds.). (2001). *Interparental conflict and child development: Theory, research, and application.* New York: Cambridge University Press.

Gubernick, D. J., & Nelson, R. J. (1989). Prolactin and paternal behavior in the biparental California mouse, *Peromyscus californicus. Hormones and Behavior, 23,* 203–210.

Gubernick, D. J., Wright, S. L., & Brown, R. E. (1993). The significance of father's presence for offspring survival in the monogamous California mouse, *Peromyscus californicus. Animal Behavior, 46,* 539–546.

Guerra, N. G., Eron, L. D., Huesmann, L. R., Tolan, P. H., & Van Acker, R. (1997). A cognitive-ecological approach to the prevention and mitigation of violence and aggression in inner-city youth. In D. P. Fry & K. Bjorkqvist (Eds.), *Cultural variation in conflict resolution: Alternatives to violence* (pp. 199–213). Mahwah, NJ: Erlbaum.

Guerra, N. G., & Huesmann, R. (2003). A cognitive–ecological model of aggression. *Revue Internationale de Psychologie Sociale, 17,* 177–203.

Guerra, N. G., Huesmann, L. R., Tolan, P. H., Van Acker, R., & Eron, L. D. (1995). *Correlates of environmental risk for aggression among inner-city children: Implications for preventive interventions.* Unpublished manuscript. University of Illinois at Chicago.

Gulgoz, S., & Kagitcibasi, C. (2004). Intelligence and intelligence testing in Turkey. In R. J. Sternberg (Ed.), *International handbook of intelligence* (pp. 248–269). New York: Cambridge University Press.

Gunnar, M. (1998). Quality of early care and buffering of neuroendocrine stress reactions: Potential effects on the developing human brain. *Preventive Medicine, 27,* 208–211.

Gunnar, M. (1980). Control, warning signals and distress in infancy. *Developmental Psychology, 16,* 281–289.

Gunnar, M., Leighton, K., & Peleaux, R. (1984). *The effects of temporal predictability on year-old infants' reactions to potentially frightening toys.* Unpublished manuscript, University of Minnesota, Minneapolis.

Gunnar, M. R. (2000). Early adversity and the development of stress reactivity and regulation. In C. A. Nelso (Ed.), *The Minnesota symposia on child psychology: Vol. 31. The effects of early adversity on neurobehavioral development* (pp. 163–200). Mahwah, NJ: Lawrence Erlbaum.

Gunnar, M. R., Malone, S. M., Vance, G., & Fisch, R. O. (1985). Coping with aversive stimulation in the neonatal period: Quiet sleep and plasma cortisol levels during recovery from circumcision. *Child Development, 56,* 824–834.

Gunnar, M. R., Morison, S. J., Chisholm, K., & Schuder, M. (2001). Salivary cortisol levels in children adopted from Romanian orphanages. *Development and Psychopathology, 13,* 611–628.*

Gusella, J. F., Wexler, N. S., Conneally, P. M., Naylor, S. L., Anderson, M. A., & Tanzi, R. E. (1983). A polymorphic DNA marker genetically linked to Huntington's disease. *Nature, 306,* 234–238.

Gusella, J. L., & Fried, P. A. (1984). Effects of maternal social drinking and smoking on offspring at 13 months. *Neurobehavioral Toxicology and Teratology, 6,* 13–17.*

Guterman, N. B. (2001). *Stopping child maltreatment before it starts: Emerging horizons in early home visitation services.* Thousand Oaks, CA: Sage Publications.

Guttag, R. E. (1995). Mental effort and motivation: Influences on children's memory strategy use. In F. E. Weinert & W. Schneider (Eds.), *Memory performance and competencies: Issues in growth and development* (pp. 207–224). Mahwah, NJ: Erlbaum.

Guttmacher Institute. (2006). *U. S. teenage pregnancy statistics: National and state trends and trends by race and ethnicity.* New York: Guttmacher Institute.

Guyll, M., Spoth, R. L., Chao, W., Wickrama, K. A. S., & Russell, D. (2004). Family-focused risk moderations of substance use trajectories. *Journal of Family Psychology, 18,* 293–201.

Habel, L. A., Schaefer, C. A., & Levine, P. (2005). Treatment with stimulants among youths in a large California health plan. *Journal of Child Psychology and Adolescent Psychopharmacology, 15,* 62–67.

Haden, C. A., Ornstein, P. A., Eckerman, C. O., & Didow, S. M. (2001). Mother-child conversational interactions as events unfold: Linkages to subsequent remembering. *Child Development, 72,* 1016–1031.

Hahn, C., & DiPietro, J. A. (2001). In vitro fertilization and the family: Quality of parenting, family functioning, and child psychosocial adjustment. *Developmental Psychology, 37,* 37–48

Haimi, K. A., et al. (2003). Obsessions and compulsions in anorexia nervosa subtypes. *International Journal of Eating Disorders, 33,* 308–319.

Haith, M. M., & Benson, J. (1998). Infant cognition. In W. Damon (Gen. Ed.), D. Kuhn, & R. Siegler (Vol. Eds.), *Handbook of child psychology: Vol. 2. Cognition, perception and language.* New York: Wiley.

Haith, M. M., Bergman, T., & Moore, M. J. (1977). *Eye contact* *and face scanning in early infancy.* Unpublished manuscript. University of Denver: Denver, Colorado.

Haith, M. M., Hazen, C., & Goodman, G. S. (1988). Expectation and anticipation of dynamic visual events by 3.5-month-old-babies. *Child Development, 59,* 467–479.

Hakuta, K. (1986). *Mirror of language: The debate on bilingualism.* New York: Basic Books.

Hakuta, K., Bialystok, E., & Wiley, E. (2003). Critical evidence: A test of the critical-period hypothesis for second-language learning. *Psychological Science, 14,* 31–38.*

Hala, S., & Chandler, M. (1996). The role of strategic planning in accessing false-belief understanding. *Child Development, 67,* 2948–2966.*

Halberstadt, A. G., Denham, S. A., & Dunsmore, J. C. (2001). Affective social competence. *Social Development, 10,* 79–119.

Halford, G. S., & Andrews, G. (2006). Reasoning and problem solving. In W. Damon & R. L. Lerner (Gen. Ed.), & D. Kuhn & R. S. Siegler (Eds.), *Handbook of child psychology: Vol. 2. Cognition, perception, and language* (6th ed., pp. 557–608). New York: Wiley.

Halliday, M. A. K. (1975). *Learning how to mean: Exploration in the development of language.* London: Arnold.

Halperin, J. M., McKay, K. E., Grayson, R. H., & Newcorn, J. H. (2003). Reliability, validity, and preliminary normative data for the children's aggression scale-teacher version. *Journal of the American Academy of Child and Adolescent Psychiatry, 42,* 965–971.

Halperin, J. M., McKay, K. E., & Newcorn, J. H. (2002). Development, reliability, and validity of the children's aggression scale-parent version. *Journal of the American Academy of Child and Adolescent Psychiatry, 41,* 245–252.

Halpern, D. F. (2000). *Sex differences in cognitive abilities* (3rd ed.). Mahwah, NJ: Erlbaum.

Halpern, D. F. (2004). A cognitive-process taxonomy for sex differences in cognitive abilities. *Current Directions in Psychological Science, 13,* 135–139.

Halpern, D. F., Benbow, C. P., Geary, D. C., Gur, R. C., Hyde, J. S., & Gernsbacher, M. A. (2007). The science of sex differences in science and mathematics. *Psychological Science in the Public Interest, 8,* 1–51.

Halverson, C. F., & Deal, J. E. (2001). Temperamental changes, parenting and the family context. In T. D. Wachs & G. A. Kohnstamm (Eds.), *Temperament in context* (pp. 61-80). Mahwah, NH: Erlbaum.

Halverson, L. E., & Williams, K. (1985). Developmental sequences for hopping over distance: A prelongitudinal screening. *Research Quarterly for Exercise and Sport, 56,* 37–44.

Hamer, B. H., Hu, S., Magnuson, V. L. Hu, N., & Pattatucci, A. M. L. (1993). A linkage between DNA markers on the X chromosome and male sexual orientation. *Science, 261,* 311–327.

Hamilton, M. C., Anderson, D., Broaddus, M., & Young, K. (2006). Gender stereotyping and under-representation of femal characters in 200 popular children's picture books: A twenty-first century update. *Sex Roles, 55,* 757–765.

Hammen, C. (1997). *Depression.* Washington, DC: Brunner/Mazel.

Hammen, C. (2002). Context of stress in families with depressed parents. In S. H. Goodman & I. Gotlib (Eds.), *Children of depressed parents* (pp. 175–202). Washington, DC.: American Psychological Association.

Hammen, C. (2005). Stress and depression. *Annual Review of Clinical Psychology, 1,* 293–319.

Han, W. (2005). Maternal nonstandard work schedules and child cognitive outcomes. *Child Development, 76,* 137–154.

Hankin, B. L., Abramson, L. Y., Moffit, T. E., Silva, P. A., McGee, R., & Angell, K. E. (1998). Development of depression from preadolescence to adulthood: Emerging gender differences in a 10 year longitudinal study. *Journal of Abnormal Psychology, 107,* 128–140.

Hanna, E., & Meltzoff, A. N. (1993). Peer imitation by toddlers in laboratory, home, and day-care contexts: Implications for social learning and memory. *Developmental Psychology, 29,* 701–710.

Hannon, E. E., & Johnson, S. P. (2005). Infants use meter to categorie rhythms and melodies: Implications for musical structure learning. *Cognitive Psychology, 50,* 354–377.

Hannon, E. E., & Trehub, S. E. (2005). Metrical categories in infancy and adulthood. *Psychological Science, 16,* 48–55.*

Hardman, M. L., Drew, C. J., & Egan, M. W. (2002). *Human exceptionality: Society, school and family* (7th ed.). Newton, MA: Allyn & Bacon.

Hardy, C. L., Bukowski, W. M., & Sippola, L. K. (2002). Stability and change in peer relationships during the transition to middle-level school. *The Journal of Early Adolescence, 22,* 117– 142.

Harkness, S., & Super, C. (1995). Culture and parenting. In M. Bornstein (Ed.), *Handbook of parenting* (2nd ed., pp. 253–280). Hillsdale, NJ: Erlbaum.

Harkness, S., & Super, C. M. (2002). *Culture and parenting.* Mahwah, NJ: Lawrence Erlbaum.

Harlow, H. F., & Zimmerman, R. R. (1959). Affectional responses in the infant monkey. *Science, 130,* 421–432.

Harris, P. L. (1989). *Children and emotion.* New York: Basil Blackwell.

Harris, P. L. (2006). Social cognition. In W. Damon & R. L. Lerner (Gen. Ed.), & D. Kuhn & R. Siegler (Eds.), *Handbook of child psychology: Vol. 2: Cognition, perception, and language* (6th ed., pp. 811–858). New York: Wiley.

Harris, P. L., Olthof, T., Terwogt, M., & Hardman, C. E. (1987). Children's knowledge of the situations that provide emotions. *International Journal of Behavioral Development, 10,* 319–343.

Harrison, L. J., & Ungerer, J. A. (2002). Maternal employment and infant-mother attachment security at 12 months postpartum. *Developmental Psychology, 38,* 758–773.

Hart, B., & Risley, T. R. (1995). *Meaningful differences in the everyday experience of young American children.* Baltimore, MD: Brookes.

Hart, B., & Risley, T. R. (1999). *The social world of children learning to talk.* Baltimore: Paul Brooks.

Hart, D., & Fegley, S. (1995). Prosocial behavior and caring in adolescence: Relations to self-understanding and social judgment. *Child Development, 66,* 1346–1359.

Hart, S., Field, T., DelValle, C., & Letourneau, M. (1998). Infants protest their mothers attending to an infant-size doll. *Social Development, 7,* 54–61.

Harter, S. (1998). The development of self-representations. In W. Damon (Gen. Ed.) & N. Eisenberg (Vol. Ed.), *Handbook of child psychology: Vol. 3. Social, emotional & personality development* (pp. 553–618). New York: Wiley.

Harter, S. (2006). The self. In W. Damon & R. L. Lerner (Gen. Ed.), & N. Eisenberg (Ed.), *Handbook of child psychology: Vol. 3. Social, emotional, and personality development* (pp. 505-570). New York: Wiley.

Harter, S., & Buddin, B. J. (1987). Children's understanding of the simultaneity of two emotions: A five-stage developmental acquisition sequence. *Developmental Psychology, 23,* 388–399.

Harter, S., Waters, P., & Whitesell, N. R. (1998). Relational self-worth: Differences in perceived worth as a person across interpersonal contexts among adolescents. *Child Development, 69,* 756–766.

Hartshorn, K. (2003). Reinstatement maintains a memory in human infants for 1 1/2 years. *Developmental Psychobiology, 42,* 269–282.

Hartshorne, H., & May, M. S. (1928). *Moral studies in the nature of character: Vol. 1. Studies in deceit; Vol. 2. Studies in self-control; Vol. 3. Studies in the organization of character.* New York: Macmillan.

Hartup, W. W. (1983). Peer relations. In P. H. Mussen (Ed.), *Handbook of child psychology* (Vol. 4). New York: Wiley.

Hartup, W. W. (1989). Social relationships and their developmental significance. *American Psychologist, 44,* 120–126.

Hartup, W. W. (1996). The company they keep: Friendships and their developmental significance. *Child Development, 67,* 1–13.

Hartup, W. W., Laursen, B., Stewart, M. I., & Eastenson, A. (1988). Conflict and the friendship relations of young children. *Child Development, 59,* 1590–1600.

Harwood, R., Leyendecker, B., Carlson, V., Asencio, M., & Miller, A. (2002). Parenting among Latino families in the United States. In M. Bornstein (Ed.), *Handbook of parenting* (Rev. ed., Vol. 4, pp. 21–46). Mahwah, NJ: Erlbaum.

Haslett, B. B. (1997). Basic concepts: Communication, cognition, and language. In B. B. Haslett & W. Samter (Eds.), *Children communicating: The first five years.* Mahwah, NJ: Erlbaum.

Hasselhorn, M. (1992). Task dependency and the role of category typicality and metamemory in the development of an organizational strategy. *Child Development, 63,* 202–214.

Hastings, P., Rubin, K., & DeRose, L. (2005). Links among gender, inhibition, and parental socialization in the development of prosocial behavior. *Merrill Palmer Quarterly, 51,* 501–527.*

Hastings, P. D., Utendale, W. T., & Sullivan, C. (2007). The socialization of prosocial behavior. In J. Grusec & P. Hastings (Eds.), *The handbook of socialization* (pp. 638–664). New York: Guilford.*

Havinghurst, R. F., & Neugarten, B. L. (1955). *American Indian and white children.* Chicago: University of Chicago Press.

Hawkins, D. L., Pepler, D. J., & Craig, W. M. (2001). Naturalistic observations of peer interventions in bullying. *Social Development, 10,* 517–527.*

Hawkins, J., Graham, J. W., Maguin, E., Abbott, R., Hill, K. G., & Catalane, R. F. (1997). Exploring the effects of age of alcohol use initiation and psychosocial risk factors on subsequent alcohol misuse. *Journal of Studies on Alcohol, 58,* 280–290.

Hawkins, J., Pea, R. D., Glick, J., & Scribner, S. (1984). "Merds that laugh don't like mushrooms": Evidence for deductive reasoning by preschoolers. *Developmental Psychology, 20,* 584–594.

Hawley, P. H. (1999). The ontogenesis of social dominance: A strategy-based evolutionary perspective. *Developmental Review, 19,* 97–132.

Hawley, P. H. (2007). Social dominance in childhood and adolescence. In P. H. Hawley, T. D. Little & P. Rodkin (Eds.), *Aggression and adaptation: The bright side to bad behavior.* Mahwah, NJ: Erlbaum.

Hawley, P. H., Johnson, S. E., Mize, J. A., & McNamara, K. A. (2007). Physical attractiveness in preschoolers: Relationships with power, status, aggression and social skills. *Journal of School Psychology, 45,* 499–521.

Hawley, P. H., & Little, T. D. (1999). On winning some and losing some: A social relations approach to social dominance in toddlers. *Merrill-Palmer Quarterly, 45,* 188–214.

Hay, D. F. (1979). Cooperative interactions and sharing between young children and their parents. *Developmental Psychology, 15,* 647–653.

Hay, D. F. (1994). Prosocial development. *Journal of Child Psychology & Psychiatry & Allied Disciplines, 35,* 29–71.

Hay, D. F., & Rheingold, H. L. (1983). *The early appearance of some valued social behaviors.* Unpublished manuscript, State University of New York at Stony Brook.

Hay, D. F., & Ross, H. S. (1982). The social nature of early conflict. *Child Development, 53,* 105–113.

Hayashi, M. L., Rao, B. S. S., Seo, J.-S., Choi, H.-S., Dolan, B., Choi, S.-Y., et al. (2007). Inhibition of P21-activated kinase rescues symptoms of fragile X symdrome in mice. *PNAS Proceedings of the National Academy of Sciences of the United States of America, 104,* 11489–11494.

Hayden, L., Turulli, D., & Hymel, S. (1988, May). *Children talk about loneliness.* Paper presented at the biennial meeting of the University of Waterloo Conference on Child Development, Waterloo, Ontario, Canada.*

Hayne, H., McDonald, S., & Barr, R. (1997). Developmental changes in the specificity of memory over the second year of life. *Infant Behavior and Development, 20,* 233–245.

Haynie, D. L. (2003). Contexts of risk? explaining the link between girls' pubertal development and their delinquency involvement. *Social Forces, 82,* 355–397.

Health Canada (1996). Joint statement: Prevention of fetal alcohol syndrome (FAS) and fetal alcohol effects (FAE) in Canada. Ottawa, ON: Health Canada.*

Health Canada (1998). *Canada's physical activity guide to healthy active living.* Ottawa: Health Canada.*

Health Canada (1999b). Statistical report on the health of Canadians. *Statistics Canada Catalogue # 82-570-XJE,* Ottawa.*

Health Canada (1999a). Toward a healthy future: Second report on the health of Canadians. Ottawa ON: Health Canada.*

Health Canada (May, 1999). AIDs and ethnicity in Canada. *HIV/AIDS Epi Update.* Division of HIV Epidemiology, Bureau of HIV/AIDS, STD, and TB, LCDC, Health Canada.*

Health Canada (2000a). *Children making a community whole: A review of Aboriginal Head Start in Urban and Northern communities.* Ottawa, Canada: Minister of Health.*

Health Canada (2000d). *HIV and AIDS in Canada: Surveillance report to December 31, 1999.* Division of HIV/AIDS Surveillance, Bureau of HIV/AIDS, STD, and TB, LCDC, Health Canada.*

Health Canada (2002). *Sudden Infant Death Syndrome: Joint statement.* Available: www.hc-sc.gc.ca/dca-dea/prenatal/sids-ss.e.html [2003, October 23, 2003].

Health Canada. (2003). *Canadian Perinatal Health Report 2003.* Ottawa: Minister of Public Works and Government Works Canada.*

Healy, B. (1995). *A new perspective for women's health.* New York: Viking.

Heath, S. B. (1998). Working through language. In S. M. Hoyle & C. Temple Adger (Eds.), *Kids' talk: Strategic language use in later childhood* (pp. 217–240). Oxford: Oxford University Press.

Hebert, T. P. (2000). Gifted males pursuing careers in elementary education: Factors that influence a belief in self. *Journal for the Education of the Gifted, 24,* 7–45.

Heckhausen, J., & Dweck, C. S. (Eds.). (1998). *Motivation and self-regulation across the life-span.* New York: Cambridge University Press.

Hecox, K., & Deegan, D. M. (1985). Methodological issues in the study of auditory development. In G. Gottlieb & N. A. Krasnegor (Eds.), *Measurement of audition and vision in the first year of postnatal life: A methodological overview.* Norwood, NJ: Ablex.

Heintz-Knowles, K. E. (2001). Balancing acts: Work-family issues on prime-time T.V. . In J. Bryant & J. A. Bryant (Eds.), *Television and the American Family* (2nd ed., pp. 177–206). Mahwah, NJ: Erlbaum.

Helm, P., & Grolund, J. (1998). A halt in the secular trend toward earlier menarche in Denmark. *Acta Obstetrics and Gynecology Scandinavia, 77,* 198–200.

Helwig, C. C. (2003). Culture and the construction of concepts of personal autonomy and democratic decision making. In J. E. Jacobs & P. A. Klaczynski (Eds.) *The development of judgment and decision making in children and adolescents* (pp. 181–212). Mahwah, NJ: Erlbaum.

Helwig, C. C. (2006). Rights, civil liberties, and democracy across cultures. In M. Killen & J. G. Smetana (Eds.), *Handbook of moral development* (pp. 185–210). Mahwah, NJ: Erlbaum.*

Helwig, C. C. (2008). Heteronomy re-evaluated: A contemporary look at Piaget's Moral Judgment of the Child. In C. Wainryb, J. G. Smetana & E. Turiel (Eds.), *Social development, social inequalities, and social justice. Mahwah, NJ: Erlbaum.* (pp. 27–51). Mahwah, NJ: Erlbaum.*

Helwig, C., & Turiel, E. (2002). Children's social and moral reasoning. In P. K. Smith & C. H. Hart (Eds.), *Blackwell handbook of childhood social development* (pp. 476–480). Malden, MA: Blackwell Publishers.*

Helwig, C., Zelazo, P. D., & Wilson, M. (2001). Children's judgments of psychological harm in normal and noncanonical situations. *Child Development, 72,* 66–81.*

Hembree, S. E., & Vandell, D. (2000). *Reciprocity in rejection: The mutual role of antipathy and children's adjustment.* Unpublished manuscript, University of Wisconsin, Madison.

Hendrick, J., & Stange, T. (1991). Do actions speak louder than words? An effect of the functional use of language on dominant sex role behavior in boys and girls. *Early Childhood Research Quarterly, 6,* 565–576.

Henggeler, S. W., Melton, G. B., & Smith, L. A. (1992). Family preservation using multisystemic therapy: An effective alternative to incarcerating serious juvenile offenders. *Journal of Consulting and Clinical Psychology, 60,* 953–961.

Henggeler, S. W., Sheidow, A. J., & Lee, T. (2007). Multisystemic treatment of serious clinical problems in youths and their families. In D. W. Springer & A. R. Roberts (Eds.), *Handbook of forensic mental health with victoms and offenders: Assessment, treatment, and research* (pp. 315–345). New York: Springer Publishing Co.

Henig, R. M. (2004). *Pandora's baby: How the first test tube baby sparked the reproductive revolution.* New York: Ecco.

Henker, B., & Whalen, C. K. (1999). The child with attention deficit/hyperactivity disorder in school and peer settings. In H. C. Quay & A. E. Hogan (Eds.). *Handbook of disruptive behavior disorders* (157–178). New York: Plenum Press.

Hepper, P. (July 2004). *Handedness in the womb.* Paper presented at the European Neuroscience, Lisbon, Portugal.

Hepworth, S. L., & Rovet, J. (2000). Visual integration difficulties in a 9-year-old girl with Turner syndrome: Parallel disabilities? *Child Neuropsychology, 6,* 262–273.*

Herbert, J., Gross, J., & Hayne, H. (2006). Age-related changes in deferred imitations between 6 and 9 months of age. *Infant Behavior and Development, 29,* 136–139.

Herbert, J., & Hayne, H. (2000). Memory retrieval by 18- to 30-month olds: Age-related changes in representational flexibility. *Developmental Psychology, 36,* 473–484.

Herbert, J., & Martinez, M. (2001). *Neural mechanisms underlying aggressive behaviour.* New York: Cambridge University Press.

Herman, L. M., & Uyeyama, R. K. (1999). The dolphin's grammatical competency: Comments on Kako. *Animal Learning & Behavior, 27,* 18–23.

Herman-Giddens, M. E., Slora, E. J., Wasserman, A. C., Bourdony, C. J., Bhapkar, M. V., Koch, G. G., & Hasemeie, C. M. (1997). Secondary sexual characteristics and menses in young girls seen in office practice: A study from the pediatric research in office settings network. *Pediatrics, 99,* 505–512.

Herman, L. M., & Uyeyama, R. K. (1999). The dolphin's grammatical competency: Comments on Kako. *Animal Learning and Behavior, 27,* 18–23.

Hermann, E., Call, J., Hernandez-Lloreda, M. V., Hare, B., & Tomasello, M. (2007). Humans have evolved specialized skills of social cognition: The cultural intelligence hypothesis. *Science, 317,* 1360–1366.

Herrera, N. C., Zajonc, R. B., Wieczorkowska, G., & Cichomski, B. (2003). Beliefs about birth rank and their reflection in reality. *Journal of Personality and Social Psychology, 85,* 142–150.

Herrnstein, R. (1971). I. Q. *Atlantic, 228,* 44–64.

Herrnstein, R., & Murray, C. (1994). *The bell curve: Intelligence and class structure in American life.* New York: Basic Books.

Hertzman, C., & Williams, R. (2009). Making early childhood count. *Canadian Medical Association Journal, 180,* 68–71.*

Hespos, S. J., & Baillargeon, R. (2001). Infants' knowledge about occlusion and containment events: A surprising discrepancy. *Psychological Science, 12,* 141–147.

Hess, R. D., & Shipman, V. (1967). Cognitive elements in maternal behavior. In J. Hill (Ed.), *Minnesota symposia on child psychology* (pp. 57–81). Minneapolis: University of Minnesota Press.

Hesse, E. (1999). The adult attachment interview: Historical and current perspectives. In J. Cassidy & P. Shaver (Eds.), *Handbook of attachment* (pp. 395–433). New York: Guilford Press.

Heth, C. D., & Cornell, E. H. (1980). Three experiences affecting spatial discrimination learning by ambulatory children. *Journal of Experimental Child Psychology, 30,* 246–264.*

Heth, C.D., Cornell, E.H., & Alberts, D.M. (1997). Differential use of landmarks by 8- and 12-year-old children during route reversal navigation. *Journal of Environmental Psychology, 17,* 199–213.*

Heth, D., & Cornell, E. H. (2007). A geographic information system for managing search for lost persons. In G. L. Allen (Ed.), *Applied spatial cognition: From research to cognitive technology* (pp. 267–284). Mahwah, NJ: Erlbaum.*

Heth, D. C., Cornell, E. H., & Flood, T. L. (2002). Self-ratings of sense of direction and route reversal performance. *Applied Cognitive Psychology, 16,* 309–324.*

Hetherington, E. M. (1966). Effects of paternal absence on sex-typed behaviors in Negro and white preadolescent males. *Journal of Personality and Social Psychology, 4,* 87–91.

Hetherington, E. M. (1972). Effects of father absence on personality development in adolescent daughters. *Developmental Psychology, 7,* 313–326.

Hetherington, E. M. (1991a). Families, lies and videotapes. *Journal of Adolescent Research, 1* (4), 323–348.

Hetherington, E. M. (2006). The influence of conflict, marital problem solving, and parenting on children's adjustment in non-divorced, divorced, and remarried families. In A. Clarke-Stewart & J. Dunn (Eds.), *Families count* (pp. 203–237). New York: Cambridge University Press.

Hetherington, E. M., Bridges, M., & Insabella, G. M. (1998). Five perspectives on the association between divorce and remarriage and children's adjustment. *American Psychologist, 53,* 167–184.

Hetherington, E. M., & Clingempeel, W. G. (1992).Coping with marital transitions: A family systems perspective. *Monographs of the Society for Research in Child Development, 57,* (2, 3, Serial No. 227).

Hetherington, E. M., & Kelly, J. (2002). *For better or for worse: Divorce reconsidered.* New York: W. W. Norton.

Hetherington, E. M., & Morris, W. N. (1978). The family and primary groups. In W. H. Holtzman (Ed.), *Introductory psychology in depth: Developmental topics.* New York: Harper & Row.

Hetherington, E. M., & Stanley-Hagan, M. (2002). Parenting in divorced, single-parent, and stepfamilies. In M. H. Bornstein (Ed.), *Handbook of parenting* (2nd ed.). Mahwah, NJ: Erlbaum.

Hewlett, B. S. (2004). *Fathers in forager, farmer, and pastoral cultures.* New York: Wiley.

Heyman, G. D., & Giles, J. W. (2006). Gender and psychological essentialism. *Enfance, 58,* 293–310.

Higgins, A. T., & Turnure, J. E. (1984). Distractibility and concentration of attention in children's development. *Child Development, 55,* 1799–1810.

Hillier, L., & Morrongiello, B. A. (1998). Age and gender differences in school-age children's appraisal of injury risk. *Journal of Pediatric Psychology, 23,* 229–238.*

Hinde, R. A. (1994). Developmental psychology in the context of the other behavioral sciences. In R. D. Parke, P. Ornstein, J. Reisen, & C. Zahn-Waxler (Eds.), *A century of developmental psychology* (pp. 617–644). Washington, DC: American Psychological Association.

Hines, M. (2004). *Brain gender.* New York: Oxford University Press.

Hines, M., Golombok, S., Rust, J., Johnson, K. J., Golding, J., & the Avon Longitudinal Study of Parents and Children Study Team. (2002). Testosterone during pregnancy and gender role development of preschool children: A longitudinal, parenting study. *Child Development, 73,* 1678-1687.

Hirsch, J., & Kim, K. (1997). New views of early language. *Nature, 103,* 1141–1143.

Hitch, G. J., & Towse, J. N. (1995). Working memory: What develops? In F. E. Weinert & W. Schneider (Eds.), *Memory performance and competencies: Issues in growth and development* (pp. 3–21). Mahwah, NJ: Erlbaum.

Hiyashi, K. (1990). Correlation between temperature and infants' gross motor development (letter). *Developmental Medicine and Child Neurology, 32,* 833–834.

Hiyashi, K. (1992). The influence of clothes and bedclothes on infants' gross motor development (letter). *Developmental Medicine and Child Neurology, 34,* 557–558.

Ho, C., Bluestein, D. N., & Jenkins, J. M. (2008). Cultural differences in the relationship between parenting and children's behavior. *Developmental Psychology, 44,* 507–522.*

Hodapp, R. (2002). Parenting children with Down syndrome and other types of mental retardation. In M. H. Bornstein (Ed.), *Handbook of parenting (2nd ed.).* Mahwah, NJ: Erlbaum.*

Hodapp, R. M., & Dykens, E. M. (2006). Mental retardation. In W. Damon & R. M. Lerner (Gen. Ed.), & K. A. Renninger & I. E. Siegel (Eds.), *Handbook of child psychology: Vol. 4. Child psychology in practice* (6th ed., pp. 453–496). New York: Wiley.

Hodges, E. V. E., & Perry, D. G. (1999). Personal and interpersonal antecedents and consequences of victimization by peers. *Journal of Personality and Social Policy, 76,* 677–685.

Hoff, E. (2005). *Language development* (3rd ed.). Belmost, CA: Wadsworth/Thomson.

Hoff, T. L. (1992). Psychology in Canada one hundred years ago: James Mark Baldwin at the University of Toronto. *Canadian Psychology, 33,* 683–694.*

Hoff-Ginsberg, E., & Shatz, M. (1982). Linguistic input and the child's acquisition of language. *Psychological Bulletin, 92,* 3–26.

Hoffman, L. W. (1977). Changes in family roles, socialization and sex differences. *American Psychologist, 32,* 644–657.

Hoffman, L. W. (2000). Maternal employment: Effects of social context. In R. D. Taylor & M. C. Wang (Eds.), *Resilience across contexts: Family, work, culture and community* (pp. 147–176). Mahwah, NJ: Erlbaum.

Hoffman, L. W., & Youngblade, L. M. (1999). *Mothers at work: Effects on children's well-being.* New York: Cambridge University Press.

Hoffman, M. L. (1984). Empathy, its limitations, and its role in a comprehensive moral theory. In W. M. Kurtines & J. L. Gewirtz (Eds.), *Morality, moral behavior and moral development.* New York: Wiley.

Hofsten, C. von (1989). Motor development as the development of systems: Comments on the special section. *Developmental Psychology, 25,* 950–953.

Hogan, D., & Msall, M. E. (2002). Family structure and resources and the parenting of children with disabilities and functional limitations. In J. G. Borkowski & S. L. Ramey & M. Bristol-Power (Eds.), *Parenting and the child's world* (pp. 311–328). Mahwah, NJ: Erlbaum.

Hohne, E. A., & Jusczyk, P. W. (1994). Two-month-old infants' sensitivity to allophonic differences. *Perception and Psychophysics, 56,* 613–623.

Holden, G. W. (1988). Adults' thinking about a child-rearing problem: Effects of experience, parental status and gender. *Child Development, 59,* 1623–1632.

Holden, G. W. (1997). *Parents and the dynamics of child rearing.* Boulder, CO: Westview Press.

Holden, G. W. (2002). Perspectives on the effects of corporal punishment: Comment on Gershoff (2002). *Psychological Bulletin, 128,* 590–595.

Holden, G. W., & Hawk, C. K. (2003). Meta-parenting in the journey of child rearing: A cognitive mechanism for change. In L. Kuczynski (Ed.), *Handbook of dynamics of parent-child relations* (pp. 189–210). Thousand Oaks, CA: Sage.

Holditch-Davis, D. (1990). The development of sleeping and waking states in high-risk preterm infants. *Infant Behavior and Development, 13,* 513–531.

Hollich, G., Golinkoff, R. M., & Hirsch-Pasek, K. (2007). Young children associate novel words with complex objects rather than salient parts. *Developmental Psychology, 43,* 1051–1061.

Hollich, G., Hirsch-Pasek, K., Golinkoff, R. M., Brand, R. J., Brown, E., Chung, H., Henlon, E. A., & Rocrui, C. (2000).

Breaking the language barrier: An emergentist coalition model for the origins of word learning. *Monographs of the Society for Research in Child Development, 65* (3).

Holobow, N. E., Genesee, F., & Lambert, W. E. (1991). The effectiveness of a foreign language immersion program for children from different ethnic and social class backgrounds: II. *Applied Psycholinguistics, 12,* 179–188.*

Holobow, N. E., Genesee, F., Lambert, W. E., Gastricht, J., & Met, M. (1987). Effectiveness of partial French immersion for children from different social class and ethnic backgrounds. *Applied Psycholinguistics, 8,* 137–151.*

Holowka, S., Brosseau-Lapre, F., & Pettito, L. A. (2002). Semantic and conceptual knowledge underlying bilingual babies' first signs and words. *Language Learning, 52,* 205–262.*

Holt, S. A., Fogel, A., & Wood, R. W. (1998). Innovation in social games. In M. D. P. deLyra & J. Valsiner (Eds.), *Construction of psychological processes in interpersonal communication* (Vol. 4, pp. 787–823). Norwood, NJ: Ablex.

Holyoak, K. J. (2005). Analogy. In K. J. Holyoak & R. G. Morrison (Eds.), *The Cambridge handbook of thinking and reasoning* (pp. 117–142). New York: Cambridge University Press.

Honzik, M. P. (1976). Value and limitations of infant tests: An overview. In M. Lewis (Ed.), *Origins of intelligence.* New York: Plenum.

Honzik, M. P. (1983). Measuring mental abilities in infancy: The value and limitations. In M. Lewis (Ed.), *Origins of intelligence: Infancy and early childhood* (2nd ed.) (pp. 67–105). New York: Plenum.

Honzik, M. P., Macfarlane, J. W., & Allen, L. (1948). The stability of mental test performance between two and eighteen years. *Journal of Experimental Education, 17,* 309–324.

Hopkins, B., & Westra, T. (1988). Maternal handling and motor development: An intracultural study. *Genetic Psychology Monographs, 14,* 377–420.

Hopkins, B., & Westra, T. (1990). Motor development, maternal expectations, and the role of handling. *Infant Behavior and Development, 13,* 117–122.

Hops, H. (2001). Intergenerational transmission of depressive -symptoms: Gender and developmental considerations. In C. Mundt, M. Goldstein, K. Hahlweg, & P. Fiedler (Eds.), *Proceedings of the symposium of interpersonal factors*

in the origin and course of affective disorders. London: Royal College of Psychiatrists.

Hossain, Z., Field, T., Gonzalez, J., Malphurs, J., De Valle, C., & Pickens, J. (1994). Infants of depressed mothers interact better with their non-depressed fathers. *Infant Mental Health Journal, 15,* 348–357.

Horn, J. L. (2002). Selections of evidence, misleading assumptions, and oversimplifications: The political message of The Bell Curve. In J. M. Fish (Ed.), *Intelligence and success: Separating science from myth* (pp. 297–325). Mahwah, NJ: Erlbaum.

Hotton, T., & Haans, D. (2004). Alcohol and drug use in early adolescence. *Health Reports, 15,* 9–19, Statistics Canada, Catalogue 82-003.*

Hout, M. (2002). Test scores, education, and poverty. In J. M. Fish (Ed.), *Race and intelligence: Separating science from myth* (pp. 329–359). Mahwah, NJ: Erlbaum.

Howe, M. L., Courage, M. L., & Petersen, C. (1994). How can I remember that "I" wasn't there? Long-term retention of traumatic experiences and emergence of the cognitive self. *Consciousness and Cognition, 3,* 327–355.*

Howe, M. L., Courage, M. L., & Peterson, C. (1995). Intrusions in preschoolers' recall of traumatic childhood events. *Psychonomic Bulletin and Review, 2,* 130–134.*

Howe, N., & Ross, H. S. (1990). Socialization perspective taking and the sibling relationship. *Developmental Psychology, 26,* 160–165.*

Howe, P. E., & Schiller, M. (1952). Growth responses of the school child to changes in diet and environment factors. *Journal of Applied Physiology, 5,* 51–61.

Howe, T. R., & Parke, R. D. (2001). Friendship quality and sociometric status: Between-group differences and links to loneliness in severely abused and nonabused children. *Child Abuse and Neglect, 25,* 585–606.

Howell, E. M., & Blondel, B. (1994). International infant mortality rates: Biases from reporting differences. *American Journal of Public Health, 84,* 850–852.

Howes, C. (1987). Social competence with peers in young children. Developmental sequences. *Developmental Review, 7,* 252–272.

Howes, C. (1996). The earliest friendships. In W. M. Bukowski, A. F. Newcomb, & W. W. Hartup (Eds.), *The company they keep: Friendship in childhood and adolescence* (pp. 66–86). New York: Cambridge University Press.

Howes, C. (1999). Attachment relationships in the context of multiple caregivers. In J. Cassidy & P. R. Shaver (Eds.), *Handbook of attachment* (pp. 671–687). New York: Guilford.

Howes, C., & Ritchie, S. (2003). *A matter of trust.* New York: Columbia University Press.

Hser, Y. I., Grella, C. E., Hubbard, R. L., Hsieh, S.-C., Fletcher, B. W., Brown, B. S., et al. (2001). An evaluation of drug treatment for adolescents in four U.S. cities. *Archives of General Psychiatry, 58,* 689–695.

Hsu, H.-C., & Fogel, A. (2001). Infant vowel development in a dynamic mother-infant communication system. *Infancy, 2,* 87–109.

Hsu, H.-C., & Fogel, A. (2003). Stability and transitions in mother-infant face-to-face communication during the first 6 months: A microhistorical approach. *Developmental Psychology, 39,* 1061–1082.

Hsu, H.-C., & Jeng, S.-F. (2008). Two-month-olds' attention and affective response to maternal still face: A comparison between term and preterm infants in Taiwan. *Infant Behavior and Development, 32,* 194–206.

Hsu, L. Y. F. (1998). Prenatal diagnosis of chromosomal abnormalities through amniocentesis. In A. Milunsky (Ed.), *Genetic disorders and the fetus* (4th ed.). Baltimore: Johns Hopkins University Press.

Hubbard, F. O. A., & van IJzendoorn, M. H. (1991). Maternal unresponsiveness and infant crying across the first 9 months: A naturalistic longitudinal study. *Infant Behavior and Development, 14,* 299–312.

Hudley, C., & Graham, S. (1993). An attributional intervention to reduce peer-directed aggression among African-American boys. *Child Development, 64,* 124–138.

Huesmann, L. R., Eron, L. D., Lefkowitz, M. M., & Walder, L. O. (1984). The stability of aggression over time and generations. *Developmental Psychology, 20,* 1120–1134.

Huesmann, L. R., & Guerra, N. G. (1997). Children's normative beliefs about aggression and aggressive behavior. *Journal of Personality and Social Psychology, 72,* 408–419.

Huesmann, L. R., & Miller, L. S. (1994). Long-term effects of repeated exposure to media violence in childhood. In L. R. Huesmann (Ed.), *Aggressive behavior: Current perspectives* (pp. 153–186). New York: Plenum Press.

Humphrey, M. M. (1982). Children's avoidance of environmental, simple task internal, and complex

task internal distracters. *Child Development, 53,* 736–745.

Hunius, S., & Geuze, R. H. (2004). Developmental changes in visual scanning of dynamic faces and abstract stimuli in infants: A longitudinal study. *Infancy, 6,* 231–255.

Hunt, C. E. (2001). Sudden infant death syndrome and other causes of infant mortality: Diagnosis, mechanisms and risk of recurrence for siblings. *American Journal of Respiratory and Critical Care Medicine, 164,* 346–357.

Hurtado, A. M., & Hill, K. R. (1992). Paternal effects of offspring survivorship among Ache and Hiwi hunter-gatherers: Implications for modeling pair-bond stability. In B.S. Hewlett (Ed.), *Father-child relations: Cultural and biosocial contexts* (153–176). New York: Aldine de Gruyter.

Husain, G., Thompson, W. F., & Schellenberg, E. G. (2002). Effects of musical tempo and mode on arousal, mood, and spatial abilities. *Music Perception, 20,* 151–171.*

Huston, A. C., & Wright, J. C. (1998). Mass media and children's development. In W. Damon (Gen. Ed.) & I. E. Sigel & K. A. Renninger (Vol. Eds.) (Eds.), *Handbook of child psychology: Vol 4. Child psychology in practice* (pp. 999–1058). New York: Wiley.

Huston, A. C., McLloyd, V., & Garcia-Coll, C. (1994). Children and poverty: Issues in contemporary research. *Child Development, 65,* 275–282.

Huston, A. C., Wright, J. C., Alvarez, M., Truglio, R., Fitch, M., & Piemyat, S. (1995). Perceived television reality and children's emotional and cognitive responses to its social content. *Journal of Applied Developmental Psychology, 16,* 231–251.

Hutchins, E. (1980). *Culture and inference: A Trobriand case study.* Cambridge, MA: Harvard University Press.

Hutchins, E. (1996). *Cognition in the wild.* Cambridge, MA: MIT Press.

Huttenlocher, J. (1974). The origins of language comprehension. In R. L. Solso (Ed.), *Theories in cognitive psychology.* Hillsdale, NJ: Erlbaum.

Huttenlocher, J., & Lui, F. (1979). The semantic organization of some simple nouns and verbs. *Journal of Verbal Learning and Verbal Behavior, 18,* 141–162.

Huttenlocher, J., & Smiley, P. (1987). Early word meanings: The case of object names. *Cognitive Psychology, 19,* 63–89.

Huttenlocher, J., Smiley, P., & Charney, R. (1987). Emergence of action categories in the child: Evidence from verb meanings. *Psychological Review, 90,* 72–93.

Huttenlocher, J., Vasilyeva, M., Waterfall, H. R., Vevea, J. L., & Hedges, L. V. (2007). The varieties of speech to young children. *Developmental Psychology, 43,* 1062–1083.

Huttenlocher, P. R. (1994). Synaptogenesis, synapse elimination, and neural plasticity in human cerebral cortex. In C. A. Nelson (Ed.), *Threats to optimal development. The Minnesota symposia on child psychology* (Vol. 27, pp. 35–54). Hillsdale, NJ: Erlbaum.

Huttenlocher, P. R. (1999). Dendritic synaptic development in human cerebral cortex: Time course and critical periods. *Developmental Neuropsychology, 16,* 347–349.

Huttenlocher, P. R. (2002). *Neural plasticity: The effects of environment on the development of the cerebral cortex.* Cambridge, MA: Harvard University Press.

Huttenlocher, P. R., & Dabholkar, A. J. (1997). Regional differences in synaptogenesis in the human cerebral cortex. *Journal of Comparative Neurology, 387,* 167–178.

Hwang, C. P. (1986). Behavior of Swedish primary and secondary caretaking fathers in relation to mothers' presence. *Developmental Psychology, 22,* 749–751.

Hyde, J. S. (2005). The gender similarities hypothesis. *American Psychologist, 60,* 581–592.

Hyde, J. S., & Linn, M. C. (1988). Gender differences in verbal ability: A meta-analysis. *Psychological Bulletin, 104,* 53–69.

Hyde, J. S., & Plant, E. A. (1995). Magnitude of psychological gender differences. *American Psychologist, 50,* 159–161.

Hyde, J. S., Fennema, E., & Lamon, S. J. (1990). Gender differences in mathematics performance: A meta-analysis. *Psychological Bulletin, 107,* 139–155.

Hyde, J. S., Krajnik, M., & Skuldt-Neiderberger, K. (1991). Androgyny across the life span: A replication and longitudinal follow-up. *Developmental Psychology, 27,* 516–519.

Hymel, S. (1986). Interpretations of peer behavior: Affective bias in childhood and adolescence. *Child Development, 57,* 431–445.*

Hymel, S., Bowker, A., & Woody, E. (1993). Aggressive versus withdrawn unpopular children: Variations in peer and self-perceptions in multiple domains. *Child Development, 64,* 879–896.*

Hymel, S., Vaillancourt, T., McDougall, P., & Renshaw, P. D.

(2002). Peer acceptance and rejection in childhood. In P. K. Smith & C. H. Hart (Eds.), *Blackwell handbook of childhood social development* (pp. 265–284). Malden, MA: Blackwell Publishers.*

Hymel, S., Wagner, E., & Butler, L. (1990). Reputational bias: View from the peer group. In S. R. Asher & J. D. Coie (Eds.), *Peer rejection in childhood.* New York: Cambridge University Press.*

Hymes, D. H. (1972). Models of the interaction of language and social life. In J. Gumprez & D. Hymes (Eds.), *Directions in sociolinguistics: The ethnography of communication* (pp. 35–71). New York: Holt, Rinehart & Winston.

Hyson, M., Copple, C., & Jones, J. (2006). Early childhood development and education. In W. Damon & R. M. Lerner (Gen. Ed.), & K. A. Renninger & I. E. Siegel (Eds.), *Handbook of child psychology: Vol. 4. Child psychology in practice* (6th ed., pp. 3-47). New York: Wiley.

Iftene, F., & Nasreen, R. (2004). Romanian adolescents: Literature review and psychiatric presentation of Romanian adolescents adopted in Romania and Canada. *Canadian Child and Adolescent Psychiatry Review, 13,* 110–113.*

Ikonomov, O. G., Stoynev, A. G., & Shisheva, A. C. (1998). Integrative coordination of circadian mammalian diversity: Neuronal networks and peripheral clocks. *Progress in Neurobiology, 54,* 87–97.

Ilari, B. S. (2002). Music perception and cognition in the first year of life. *Early Child Development and Care, 172,* 311–322.*

Ingersoll, E. W., & Thoman, E. B. (1999). Sleep/wake states of preterm infants: Stability, developmental change, diurnal variation, and relation with caregiving activity. *Child Development, 70,* 1–10.

Ingram, D. (1989). *First language acquisition.* New York: Cambridge University Press.

Inhelder, B., & Piaget, J. (1958). *The growth of logical thinking from childhood to adolescence.* New York: Basic Books.

Inoff-Germain, G., Arnold, G. S., Nottleman, E. D., Susman, E. J., Cutler, G. B., & Chrousos, G. P. (1988). Relations between hormone levels and observational measures of aggressive behavior of young adolescents in family interactions. *Developmental Psychology, 24,* 129–139.

Institute of Medicine. (2004). *Ethical conduct of clinical research involving children.* Washington, DC: National Academic Press.

Ishikawa, F., & Hay, D. F. (2006). Triadic interaction among newly

acquainted 2-year-olds. *Social Development, 15,* 145–168.

Israel, A. C. (1988). Parental and family influences in the etiology and treatment of childhood obesity. In N. A. Krasnegor, G. D. Grave, & N. Kretchmer (Eds.), *Childhood obesity: A behavioral perspective.* Caldwell, NJ: Telford Press.

Izard, C. E. (1994). Innate and universal facial expressions: Evidence from developmental and cross-cultural research. *Psychological Bulletin, 115,* 288–299.

Izard, C. E., Fantauzzo, C. A., Castle, J. M., Haynes, O. M., & Slomine, B. S. (1995). *The morphological stability and social validity of infants' facial expressions.* Unpublished manuscript, University of Delaware.

Izard, C. E., Hembree, E., & Huebner, R. (1987). Infants' emotional expressions to acute pain: Developmental changes and stability of individual differences. *Developmental Psychology, 23,* 105–113.

Jacob, T., & Johnson, S. L. (1997). Parent-child interaction among depressed fathers and mothers: Impact on child functioning. *Journal of Family Psychology, 11,* 391–409.

Jacobs, B. L. (2004). Depression: The brain finally gets into the act. *Current Directions in Psychological Science, 13,* 103–106.

Jacobsen, T., & Hofmann, V. (1997). Children's attachment representations: Longitudinal relations to school behavior and academic competency in middle childhood and adolescence. *Developmental Psychology, 33,* 703–710.

Jacobson, J. L., & Jacobson, S. W. (1996). Prospective longitudinal assessment of developmental neurotoxicity. *Environmental Health Perspectives, 104,* 275–283.

Jacobson, J. L., & Jacobson, S. W. (2004). Prenatal exposure to polychlorinated biphenyls and attention at school age. *Obstetrical & Gynecological Survey, 59,* 412–413.

Jacques, S., Zelazo, P. D., Kirkham, N. Z., & Semcesen, T. (1999). Rule selection versus rule execution in preschoolers: An error-detection approach. *Developmental Psychology, 35,* 770–780.*

Jaffe, S., & Hyde, J. (2000). Gender differences in moral orientation: A meta-analysis. *Psychological Bulletin, 126,* 703–726.

Jakobson, R. (1968). *Child Language, aphasic, and phonological universals.* The Hague: Mouton.

Jang, K. L., Livesley, W. J., Angleitner, A., Riemann, R., & Vernon, P. A. (2002). Genetic and environmental influences on the covariance of facets defining the domains

of the five-factor model of personality. *Personality and Individual Differences, 33,* 83–101.*

Jang, K. L., Livesley, W. J., & Vernon, P. A. (2000). The etiology of personality function: The University of British Columbia Twin Project. *Twin Research, 5,* 342–346.

Jang, K. L., Taylor, S., & Livesley, W. J. (2006). The University of British Columbia Twin Project: Personlaity is something and personality does something. *Twin Research and Human Genetics, 9,* 739–742.

Janssen, I., Katzmarzyk, P. T., Boyce, W. F., King, M. A., & Pickett, W. (2004). Overweight and obesity in Canadian adolescents and their associations with dietary habits and physical activity patterns. *Journal of Adolescent Health, 35,* 360–367.*

Janus, M., & Offord, D. R. (2007). Development and psychometric properties of theEarly Development Instrument(EDI): A measure of children's school readiness. *Canadian Journal of Behavioural Sciences, 39,* 1–22.*

Jarvin, L., & Sternberg, R. J. (2003). Alfred Binet's contributions to educational psychology. In B. J. Zimmerman (Ed.), *Educational psychology: A century of contributions* (pp. 65–79). Mahwah, NJ: Erlbaum.

Jeffrey, R. W. (2001). Public health strategies for obesity treatment and prevention. *American Journal of Health Behavior, 25,* 252–259.

Jellinek, M. B., & Snyder, J. B. (1998). Depression and suicide in children and adolescents. *Pediatric Review, 19,* 255–264.

Jenkins, J. M., Rasbach, J., & O'Conner, T. G. (2003). The role of shared family context in differential parenting. *Developmental Psychology, 39,* 99–113.*

Jensen, A. R. (1969). How much can we boost IQ and scholastic achievement? *Harvard Educational Review, 39,* 1–123.

Jensen, A. R. (1993). Test validity: "g" versus "tacit knowledge." *Current Directions in Psychological Science, 2,* 9–109.

Jensen, P. S., Arnold, L. E., Swanson, J. M., Vitiello, B., Abikoff, H. B., Greenhill, L. L., et al. (2007). 3-year follow-up of the NIMH MTA study. *Journal of the American Academy of Child and Adolescent Psychiatry, 46,* 989–1002.

Jensen, P. S., Hinshaw, S. P., Swanson, J. M., Greenhill, L. L., Conners, C. K., Arnold, L. E., et al. (2001). Findings from the NIMH multi-modal treatment study of ADHD (MTA): Implications and applications for primary care providers. *Journal of Developmental and Behavioral Pediatrics, 22,* 60–73.

Johnson, E. K., & Jusczyk, P. W. (2001). Word-segmentation by 8-month-olds: When speech cues count more than statistics. *Journal of Memory and Language, 44,* 548–567.

Johnson, E. O., Kamilaris, T. C., Chrousos, G. P., & Gold, P. P. (1992). Mechanisms of stress: A dynamic overview of hormonal and biobehavioral homeostasis. *Neuroscience and Biobehavioral Reviews, 16,* 115–130.

Johnson, J. S., & Newport, E. L. (1989). Critical period effects in second language learning: The influence of maturational state on the acquisition of English as a second language. *Cognitive Psychology, 21,* 60–99.

Johnson, M., Beebe, I., Mortimer, J., & Snyder, M. (1998). Volunteerism in adolescence: A process perspective. *Journal of Research on Adolescence, 8,* 309–330.

Johnson, M. H. (1998). The neural basis of cognitive development. In W. Damon (Ed.), *Handbook of child psychology* (5th ed.). New York: Wiley.

Johnson, M. H. (2000). Functional brain development in infants: Effects of an interactive specialization network. *Child Development, 71,* 75–81.

Johnson, M. H. (2002). The development of visual attention: A cognitive neuroscience perspective. In M. H. Johnson & Y. Munakata (Eds.), *Brain development and cognition: A reader* (2nd ed., pp. 134-150). Malden, MA: Blackwell Publishers.

Johnson, M. H. (2005). *Developmental cognitive neuroscience* (2nd ed.). Malden, MA: Blackwell.

Johnson, M. H., Dziurawiec, S., Ellis, H., & Morton, J. (1991). Newborns' preferential tracking of face-like stimuli and its subsequent decline. *Cognition, 90,* 1–19.

Johnson, S. P. (2004). Development of perceptual completion in infancy. *Psychological Science, 15,* 5-11.

Johnson, S. P., Bremner, J. G., Slater, A. M., Mason, U., Foster, K., & Sheshire, A. (2003). Infants' perception of object trajectories. *Child Development, 74,* 94–108.

Johnson, W., Bouchard, T. J., Krueger, R. F., McGue, M., & Gottesman, I. I. (2004). Just one g: Consistent results from three test batteries. *Intelligence, 32,* 95–107.

Johnson, W., Emde, R. N., Pannabecker, B., Stenberg, C., &

Davis, M. (1982). Maternal perception of infant emotion from birth through 18 months. *Infant Behavior and Development, 5,* 313–322.

Johnston, J., & Ettema, J. S. (1982). *Positive images: Breaking stereotypes with children's television.* Beverly Hills, CA: Sage.

Johnston, L. D., O'Malley, P. M., & Bachman, J. G. (1997). National survey results on drug use from the Monitoring the Future study, 1975–1995. Rockville, MD: National Institutes of Health.

Johnston, L. D., O'Malley, P. M., Bachman, J. G., & Schulenberg, J. E. (April, 2007). *Monitoring the Future National Results on Adolescent Drug Use:Overview of key findings 2006.* Washington, DC: NIDA.

Jones, D. C. (1985). Persuasive appeals and responses to appeals among friends and acquaintances. *Child Development, 56,* 757–763.

Jones, M. C., & Bayley, N. (1950). Physical maturing among boys as related to behavior. *Journal of Educational Psychology, 41,* 129–148.

Jones, T. A., & Greenough, W. T. (1996). Ultrastructural evidence for increased contact between astrocytes and synapses in rats reared in a complex environment. *Neurobiology of Learning and Memory, 65,* 48–56.

Jourdan, C. (1991). Pidgins and creoles: The blurring of categories. *Annual Review of Anthropology, 20,* 187–209.

Joyner, K., & Udry, J. R. (2000). You don't bring me anything but down: Adolescent romance and depression. *Journal of Health and Social Behavior, 41,* 369–391.

Judy, B., & Nelson, E. S. (2000). Relations between parents, peers, morality, and theft in an adolescent sample. *High School Journal, 83,* 31–42.

Jusczyk, P., Houston, D. M., & Newsome, M. (1999). The beginnings of word segmentation in English-learning infants. *Cognitive Psychology, 39*(3–4), 159–207.

Jusczyk, P. W., Friederiec, A. D., Wessels, J., Svenkerud, V. Y., and Jusczyk, A. M. (1993). Infants' sensitivity to the sound patterns of native language words. *Journal of Memory & Language, 32,* 402–420.

Jusczyk, P. W., & Krumhansl, C. L. (1993). Pitch and rhythmic patterns affecting infants' sensitivity to musical phrase structure. *Journal of Experimental Psychology: Human Perception and Performance, 19,* 627–640.

Jutras, S. (2003). Play outside! Contributions of urban environment to

the development and well-being of the child. *Canadian Psychology, 44,* 257–266.*

Juvonen, J., Graham, S., & Schuster, M. A. (2003). Bullying among young adolescents: The strong, the weak, & the troubled. *Pediatrics, 112,* 1231–1237.

Kagan, J. (1998). Biology and the child. In W. Damon (Series Ed.), & N. Eisenberg (Vol. Ed.), *Handbook of child psychology: Vol. 3* (pp. 177–235). New York: Wiley.

Kagan, J., & Fox, N. A. (2006). Biology, culture, and temperamental biases. In W. Damon & R. M. Lerner (Gen. Ed.), & N. Eisenberg (Ed.), *Handbook of child psychology: Vol 3. Social, emotional, and personality development* (6th ed., pp. 167–225). New York: Wiley.

Kagan, J., & Moss, H. A. (1962). *Birth to maturity: A study in psychological development.* New York: Wiley.

Kagan, J., & Snidman, N. (2004). *The long shadow of temperament.* Cambridge, MA: Harvard University Press.

Kagan, J. J., Kearsley, R. B., & Zelazo, P. R. (1978). *Infancy: Its place in human development.* Cambridge, MA: Harvard University Press.

Kagan, J. S. (1969). Inadequate evidence and illogical conclusions. *Harvard Educational Review, 39,* 274–277.

Kail, R. (1995). Processing speed, memory, and cognition. In F. E. Weinert & W. Schneider (Eds.), *Memory performance and competencies: Issues in growth and development* (pp. 71–88). Mahwah, NJ: Erlbaum.

Kail, R. (2000). Speed of information processing: Developmental change and links to intelligence. *Journal of School Psychology, 38,* 51–61.

Kail, R., & Park, Y. (1994). Processing time, articulation time, and memory span. *Journal of Experimental Child Psychology, 57,* 281–291.

Kail, R. V. (2000). Speed of information processing: Developmental change and links to intelligence. *Journal of School Psychology, 38,* 51–61.

Kail, R. V. (2003). Information processing and memory. In M. H. Bornstein & L. Davidson (Eds.), *Well-being: Positive development across the life course. Cross currents in contemporary psychology* (pp. 269–179). Mahwah, NJ: Erlbaum.

Kako, E. (1999). Elements of syntax in the systems of three language-trained animals. *Animal Learning and Behavior, 27,* 1–15.

Kalchman, M., Moss, J., & Case, R. (2001). Psychological models for the development of mathematical understanding: Rational numbers and functions. In S. M. Carver & D. Klahr (Eds.), *Cognition and instruction: Twenty-five years of progress* (pp. 1–38). Mahwah, NJ: Erlbaum.*

Kaltiala-Heino, R., Rimpelä, M., Rissanen, A., & Rantanen, P. (2001). Early puberty and early sexual activity are associated with bulimic-type eating pathology in middle adolescence. *Journal of Adolescent Health, 28,* 346–352.

Kamins, M. L., & Dweck, C. S. (1999). Person-versus-process praise and criticism: Implications for contingent self-worth and coping. *Developmental Psychology, 35,* 835–847.

Kamiya, T. (2002). Paternal cognition of infant crying. *Japanese Journal of Developmental Psychology, 13,* 284–294.

Kanaya, T., Ceci, S. J., & Scullin, M. H. (2005). Age differences within secular IQ trends: An individual growth modeling approach. *Intelligence, 33* (613–621).

Kandel, D. (1973). Adolescent marijuana use: Role of parents and peers. *Science, 181,* 1067–1070.

Kandel, E. R., Schwartz, J. H., & Jessel, T. M. (2000). *Principles of neuroscience* (4th ed.). New York: McGraw-Hill.

Karass, J., & Braungart-Rieker, J. M. (2004). Infant negative emotionality and attachment: Implications for preschool intelligence. *International Journal of Behavioral Development, 28,* 221–229.

Karwautz, A., Nobis, G., Haidvogl, M., Wagner, G., Hafferl-Gattermayer, A., Wober-Bingol, C., et al. (2003). Perceptions of family relationships in adolescents with anorexia nervosa and their unaffected sisters. *European Journal of Adolescent Psychiatry, 12,* 128–135.

Katz, L. F., & Gottman, J. M. (1993). Patterns of marital conflict predict children's internalizing and externalizing behaviors. *Developmental Psychology, 29,* 940–950.

Katz, L. F., & Gottman, J. M. (1996). Spillover effects of marital conflict: In search of parenting and co-parenting mechanisms. In J. P. McHale & P. A. Cowan (Eds.), *Understanding how family-level dynamics affect children's development: Studies of two-parent families* (pp. 57–76). San Francisco: Jossey-Bass.

Katz, L. F., & Gottman, J. M. (1997). Buffering children from marital conflict and dissolution. *Journal of Clinical Child Psychology, 26,* 157–171.

Katz, L. F., Kramer, L., & Gottman, J. M. (1992). Conflict and emotions in marital, sibling, and peer relationships. In C. U. Shantz & W. W. Hartup (Eds.), *Conflict in child and adolescent development* (pp. 122–149). Cambridge, England: Cambridge University Press.

Kass, L. (2002). *Life, liberty, and the defense of dignity.* San Francisco, CA: Encounter Books.

Katzmarzyk, P. T. (2001). Obesity in Canadian children. *CMAJ, 164,* 1563–1564.*

Katzmarzyk, P. T. (2002). The Canadian obesity epidemic, 1985–1998. *CMAJ, 166,* 1039–1040.*

Katzmarzyk, P. T., Gledhill, N., & Shepard, R. J. (2000). The economic burden of physical inactivity in Canada. *CMAJ, 163,* 1435–1440.*

Katzmarzyk, P. T., Pérusse, L., Rao, D. C., & Bouchard, C. (1999). Familial risk of obesity and central adipose tissue distribution in the general Canadian population. *American Journal of Epidemiology, 149,* 933–942.*

Katzmarzyk, P. T., Tremblay, S., Morrison, R., & Tremblay, M. (2007). Effects of physical activity on pediatric reference data for obesity. *International Journal of Pediatric Obesity, 2,* 138–143.*

Kaufman, A. S., & Kaufman, N. L. (1983). *Kaufman assessment battery for children: Interpretive manual.* Circle Pines, MN: American Guidance Service.

Kaufman, A. S., & Kaufman, N. L. (2006). *KBIT: Kaufman Brief Intelligence Test* (2nd ed.). Toronto: Pearson Education.

Kauffman, J. (2001). *Characteristics of emotional and behavioral disorders of children and youth* (7th ed.). Columbus, OH: Merrill/Prentice Hall.

Kayed, N. S., & Van Der Meer, A. (2000). Timing strategies used in defensive blinking to optical collisions in 5- to 7-month-old infants. *Infant Behavior and Development, 23,* 253–270.

Kayed, N. S., & van der Meer, A. L. H. (2007). Infants' timing strategies to optical collisions: A longitudinal study. *Infant Behavior and Development, 30,* 50–59.

Kazdin, A. E., & Benjet, C. (2003). Spanking children: Evidence and issues. *Current Directions in Psychological Science, 12,* 99–103.

Keating, D. P. (1990). Adolescent thinking. In J. Adelson (Ed.), *Handbook of adolescent psychology.* New York: Wiley.*

Kee, D. W. (1994). Developmental differences in associative memory: Strategy use, mental effort, and knowledge-access interaction. In H. W. Reese (Ed.), *Advances in child development and behavior* (Vol. 25, pp. 7–32). New York: Academic Press.

Keefer, C. H., Dixon, S., Tronick, E. Z., & Brazelton, T. B. (1991). Cultural mediation between newborn behavior and later development: Implications for methodology in cross-cultural research. In J. K. Nugent, B. M. Lester, & T. B. Brazelton (Eds.), *The cultural context of infancy: Vol. 2. Multicultural and interdisciplinary approaches to parent-infant relations* (pp. 39–61). Norwood, NJ: Ablex.

Keegan, R. T. (1996, Summer). Creativity from childhood to adulthood: A difference of degree and not of kind. In M. A. Runco (Ed.), *Creativity from childhood through adulthood: The developmental issues* [Special issue]. *New Directions for Child Development,* No. 72, 57–66.

Keen, R. (2003). Representation of objects and events: Why do infants look so smart and toddlers look so dumb? *Current Directions in Psychological Science, 12,* 79–83.

Keenan, K., Loeber, R., Zhang, Q., Stouthamer-Loeber, M., & Van Kammen, W. B. (1995). The influence of deviant peers on the development of boys' disruptive and delinquent behavior: A temporal analysis. *Development and Psychopathology, 7,* 715–726.

Keeney, T. J., Cannizzo, S. R., & Flavell, J. H. (1967). Spontaneous and induced rehearsal in a recall task. *Child Development, 38,* 953–966.

Keil, F. (2006). Cognitive science and cognitive development. In W. Damon & R. M. Lerner (Gen. Ed.), & D. Kuhn & R. S. Siegler (Eds.), *Handbook of child psychology: Vol. 2. Cognition, perception, and language* (6th ed., pp. 609–635). New York: Wiley.

Keiley, M. K., Howe, T. R., Dodge, K. A., Bates, J. E., & Pettit, G. S. (2001). The timing of child physical maltreatment: A cross-domain growth analysis of impact on adolescents' externalizing and internalizing problems. *Development and Psychopathology, 13,* 891–912.

Keller, M. B., Klein, D. N., Hirshfield, R. M., Kocsis, J. H., McCullough, M. (1995). Results of the *DSM-IV* mood disorders field trial. *American Journal of Psychiatry, 152,* 843–849.

Kellman, P. J. (1984). Perception of three-dimensional form by human infants. *Perception & Psychophysics, 36,* 353–358.

Kellman, P. J., & Arterberry, M. E. (2006). Infant visual perception. In W. Damon & R. L. Lerner (Gen. Ed.), & D. Kuhn & R. Siegler (Eds.), *Handbook of child psychology, Vol. 2: Cognition, perception, and language (6th Ed.)* (pp. 109–160). New York: Wiley.

Kelmanson, I. A., Broswasser, J., Franco, P., & Kahn, A. (2003). Sighs during sleep in future victims of sudden infant deaths. *Sleep and Hypnosis, 5,* 83–88.

Kennare, R. (2007). Risks of adverse outcomes in the next birth after a first cesarean delivery. *Obstetrics and Gynecology, 109,* 270–276.

Kennedy, W. A. (1969). A follow-up normative study of Negro intelligence and achievement. *Monographs of the Society for Research in Child Development, 34* (2, Serial No. 126).

Kennell, J., Klaus, M., McGrath, S., Robertson, S., & Hinckley, C. (1991). Continuous emotional support during labor in a U.S. hospital. *Journal of the American Medical Association, 265,* 2197–2201.

Kerig, P. K. (2008). Boundary dissolution in the family context: The search for the ties that bind marriage, parenting, and child development. In M. Schultz, M. K. Pruett, P. K. Kerig & R. D. Parke (Eds.), *Feathering the nest: Couples relationships, couples interventions, and children's development.* Washington, DC: American Psychological Association.

Kermami, H., & Brenner, M. E. (2001). Maternal scaffolding in the child's zone of proximal development: Cross-cultural perspectives. *Journal of Research in Childhood Education, 1,* 30–52.

Kerr, M. (2001). Culture as a context for temperament: Suggestions from the life courses of shy Swedes and Americans. In T. D. Wachs & G. A. Kohnstamm (Eds.), *Temperament in context* (pp. 139–152). Mahwah, NJ: Erlbaum.

Kerr, M., & Stattin, H. (2000). What parents know, how they know it and several forms of adolescent adjustment: Further support for a reinterpretation of monitoring. *Child Development, 36,* 366–380.

Kershaw, P., Irwin, L., Trafford, K., & Hertzman, C. (2005). *The British Columbia Atlas of child development. Human early learning partnership* (Vol. 40): Western Geographical Press.

Kesler, S. R. (2007). Turner syndrome. *Child and Adolescent Psychiatry: Clinics of North America, 16,* 709–722.

Khatri, P., Kupersmidt, J., & Patterson, C. (1994, April). Aggression and peer victimization as predictors of self-report of behavioral and emotional adjustment. Poster presented at the biennial meeting of the Conference in Human Development, Pittsburgh, PA.

Kieling, C., Goncalves, R. R. F., Tannock, R., & Castellanos, F. X. (2008). Neurobiology of attention deficit hyperactivity disorder. *Child and Adolescent Psychiatry Clinics of North America, 72,* 285–307.*

Kilgore, K., Snyder, J., & Lentz, C. (2000). The contribution of parental discipline, parental monitoring and school risk to early-onset conduct problems in African American boys and girls. *Developmental Psychology, 36,* 835–845.

Kim, J. K., Conger, R. D., Elder, G. H., & Lorenz, F. O. (2003). Reciprocal influences between stressful life events and adolescent internalizing and externalizing problems. *Child Development, 74,* 127–143.

Kim, M., & Choi, K. S. (2003). Access to structural similarity in the analogical problem solving of children. *School Psychology International, 24,* 218–231.

Kimball, M. M. (1986). Television and sex role attitudes. In T. M. Williams (Ed.), *The impact of television: A natural experiment in three communities* (pp. 265–301). Orlando, FL: Academic Press.

Kindermann, T. A., McCollam, T. L., & Gibson, E., Jr. (1995). Peer networks and students' classroom engagement during childhood and adolescence. In K. Wentzel & J. Juvonen (Eds.), *Social motivation: Understanding children's school adjustment.* New York: Cambridge University Press.

Kingsnorth, S., & Schmuckler, M. A. (2000). Walking skill versus walking experience as a predictor of barrier crossing in toddlers. *Infant Behavior and Development 23,* 331–350.*

Kirtler, A. F., La Greca, A. M., & Prinstein, M. J. (1999). Friendship qualities and social-emotional functioning of adolescents with close, cross-sex friendships. *Journal of Research on Adolescence, 93,* 339–366.

Kisilevksy, B. S., Hains, S. M. J., Jacquet, A.-Y., Granier-Deferre, C., & Lecanuet, J. P. (2004). Maturnal fetal responses to music. *Developmental Science, 7,* 550–559.*

Kisilevsky, B. S., Hains, S. M. L., Lee, K., Sie, S., Huang, H., Ye, H. H., Zhang, W., & Wang, Z. (2003). Effects of experience on fetal voice recognition. *Psychological Science, 14,* 220–224.*

Klahr, D. (2000). *Exploring science: The cognition and development of discovery processes.* Cambridge, MA: MIT Press.

Klahr, D., & MacWhinney, B. (1998). Information processing. In W. Damon (Ed.), D. Kuhn, & R. Siegler (Vol. Eds.), *Handbook of child psychology, Vol. 2. Cognition, perception and language* (5th ed.). New York: Wiley.

Klahr, D., & Siegler, R. S. (1978). The representation of children's knowledge. In H. W. Reese & L. P. Lipsitt (Eds.), *Advances in child development and behavior* (Vol. 12, pp. 61–116). New York: Academic Press.

Klahr, D., & Wallace, J. G. (1976). Cognitive development: An information processing view. Hillsdale, NJ: Erlbaum.

Klaus, M. H., Kennell, J. H., & Klaus, P. H. (1995). *Bonding: Building the foundations of secure attachment and independence.* Reading, MA: Addison-Wesley.

Klebanov, P. K., Brooks-Gunn, J., & McCormick, M. C. (2001). Maternal coping strategies and emotional distress: Results of an early intervention program for low-birthweight young children. *Developmental Psychology, 37,* 654–667.

Klebonoff, M. A., Levine, R. J., Der Simonian, R., Clemens, J. D., & Wilkins, D. G. (1999). Maternal serum paraxanthine, a caffeine metabolite and the risk of spontaneous abortion. *The New England Journal of Medicine, 341,* 1639–1644.

Klein, D. I., & Wender, P. H. (2005). *Understanding depression: A complete guide to its diagnosis and treatment.* New York: Oxford University Press.

Klein, P. D. (1997). Multiplying the problems of intelligence by eight: A critique of Gardner's theory. *Canadian Journal of Education, 22,* 377–394.*

Klein, P. D. (1998). A response to Howard Gardner: Falsifiability, empirical evidence and pedagogical usefulness in educational psychologies. *Canadian Journal of Education, 23,* 103–112.*

Klesges, R., Malott, J., Boschee, P., & Weber, J. (1986). The effects of parental influences on children's food intake, physical activity and relative weight. *International Journal of Eating Disorders, 5,* 335–345.

Klesner, J. (2002). Depression symptoms on early adolescence: Their relations to classroom problem behavior and peer status. *Journal of Research on Adolescence, 12,* 463–478.

Knox, D. L., Fagley, V. S., & Miller, P. M. (2004). Care and justice moral orientation among African American college students. *Journal of Adult Development, 11,* 41–45.

Kobayashi, Y. (1994). Conceptual acquisition and change through social interaction. *Human Development, 37,* 233–241.

Kochanska, G. (1995). Children's temperament, mother's discipline, and security of attachment: Multiple pathways to emerging internalization. *Child Development, 66,* 597–615.

Kochanska, G. (1997). Multiple pathways to conscience for children with different temperaments: From toddlerhood to age 5. *Developmental Psychology, 33,* 228–240.

Kochanska, G. (2002a). Committed compliance, moral self, and internalization: A mediational model. *Developmental Psychology, 38,* 339–351.

Kochanska, G., Aksan, N., Prisco, T. R., & Adams, E. E. (2008). Mother-child and father-child mutually responsive orientation in the first two years and children's outcomes at preschool age: Mechanisms of influence. *Child Development, 79,* 30–44.

Kochanska, G., & Murray, K. T. (2000). Mother-child mutually responsive orientation and conscience development: From toddler to early school age. *Child Development, 71,* 417–431.

Kochanska, G., Coy, K. C., & Murray, K. T. (2001). The development of self-regulation in the first four years of life. *Child Development, 72,* 1091–1111.

Kochanska, G., Gross, J. N., Mei-Hua, L., & Nichols, K. E. (2002). Guilt in young children: Development, determinants, and relations with a broader system of standards. *Developmental Psychology, 73,* 461–482.

Kochanska, G., & Thompson, R. A. (1997). The emergence and development of conscience in toddlerhood and early childhood. In J. E. Grusec & L. Kuczynski (Eds.), *Parenting and children's internalization of values* (pp. 53–77). New York: Wiley.*

Kochenderfer, B. J., & Ladd, G. W. (1996). Peer victimization: Manifestations and relations to school adjustment. *Journal of School Psychology, 34,* 267–283.

Kochenderfer-Ladd, B., & Wardrop, J. (2001). Chronicity and instability in children's peer victimization experiences as predictors of loneliness and social satisfaction trajectories. *Child Development, 72,* 134–151.

Kohlberg, L. (1969). *Stages in the development of moral thought and action.* New York: Holt.

Kohlberg, L. (1985). *The psychology of moral development.* San Francisco: Harper & Row.

Kohlberg, L., & Candee, D. (1984). The relationship of moral judgment to moral action. In W. M. Kurtines & J. L. Gewirtz (Eds.), *Morality, moral behavior and moral development.* New York: Wiley.

Kohlberg, L. A. (1966). A cognitive-developmental analysis of children's sex-role concepts and attitudes. In E. E. Maccoby (Ed.), *The development of sex differences* (pp. 82–173). Stanford, CA: Stanford University Press.

Kokko, K., & Pulkkinen, L. (2000). Aggression in childhood and long-term unemployment in adulthood: A cycle of maladaptation and some protective factors. *Developmental Psychology, 36,* 463–472.

Kolb, B., Gorny, G., Li, Y., Samaha, A., & Robinson, T. E. (2003). Amphetamine or cocaine limites the ability of later experience to promote structural plasticity in the neocortex and neclues accumbens. *Proceedings of the National Academy of Sciences, 100,* 10523–10528.

Konner, M. (1976). Maternal care, infant behavior and development among the !Kung. In R. B. Lee & I. Devore (Eds.), *Kalahari hunter-gathers: Studies of the !Kung San and their neighbors* (pp. 218–245). Cambridge, MA: Harvard University Press.

Konner, M. (1977). Infancy about the Kalhari Desert San. In P.H. Leiderman, S.R. Tulkin, & A. Rosefeld (Eds.), *Culture and infancy: Variations in the human experience* (pp. 287–328). New York: Academic Press.

Konstantareas, M. M. (2006). Social skills training in high functioning autism and Asperger's disorder. *Hellenic Journal of Psychology, 3,* 39–56.*

Koopmans-van Beinum, F. J., Clement, C. J., & van den Dikkenberg-Pot, I. (2001). Babbling and the lack of auditory speech perception: A matter of coordination? *Developmental Science, 4,* 61–70.

Kopp, C. B. (1982). The antecedents of self-regulation. *Developmental Psychology, 18,* 199–214.

Kopp, C. B. (1994). *Baby steps: The "whys" of your child's behavior in the first two years.* New York: W. H. Freeman.

Kopp, C. B. (2002). Commentary: The co-development of attention and emotional regulation. *Infancy, 3,* 199–208.

Koren, G. (1993). Cocaine and the human fetus: The concept of teratophilia. *Neurotoxicology and Teratology, 15,* 301–304.*

Koren, G., Nulman, I., Rovet, J., Greenbaum, R., Loebstein, M., & Einarson, T. (1998). Long-term neurodevelopmental risks in children exposed in utero to cocaine. The Toronto Adoption study. In J. A. Harvey & B. E. Kosofsky (Eds.), *Cocaine: Effects on the development of the brain. Annals of the New York Academy of Sciences, Vol. 846* (pp. 306–313). New York, NY: New York Academy of Sciences.*

Korner, A. (1974). The effect of the infant's state, level of arousal, sex and ontogenic stage on the caregiver. In M. Lewis & L. Rosenblum (Eds.), *The effect of the infant on its caregiver.* New York: Wiley.

Korner, A. F. (1989). Infant stimulation: The pros and cons in historical perspective. *Bulletin of National Center for Clinical Infant Programs, 10,* 11–17.

Kornhaber, M. L., & Gardner, H. (2006). Multiple intelligences: Developments in implementation and theory. In M. A. Constas & R. J. Sternberg (Eds.), *Translating theory and research into educational practice: Developments in content domains, large-scale reform, and intellectual capacity* (pp. 255–276). Mahwah, NJ: Erlbaum.

Korsten-Reck, U., Kasper, T., Korsten, K., Kromeyer-Hauschild, K., Bos, K., Berg, A., et al. (2007). Motor abilities and aerobic fitness of obese children. *International Journal of Sports Medicine, 28,* 762–767.

Kovacs, D. M., Parker, J. G., & Hoffman, L. W. (1996). Behavioral, affective and social correlates of involvement in cross-sex friendship in elementary school. *Child Development, 67,* 2269–2286.

Kovelman, I., Baker, S. A., & Petitto, L. A. (2008). Bilingual and monolingual brains compare: A functional magnetic resonance imaging investigation of syntactic processing and a possible "neural signature" of bilingualism. *Journal of Cognitive Neuroscience, 20,* 153–169.*

Kowal, A., & Kramer, L. (1997). Children's understanding of differential parental treatment. *Child Development, 68,* 113–126.

Kozulin, A. (1990). *Vygotsky's psychology: A biography of ideas.* Cambridge, MA: Harvard University Press

Krahe, B., & Moller, I. (2004). Playing violent electronic games, hostile attributional style, and aggression-related norms in German adolescents. *Journal of Adolescence, 27*, 53–69.

Kramer, L., & Gottman, J. M. (1992). Becoming a sibling—with a little help from my friends. *Developmental Psychology, 28*, 685–699.

Kramer, L., & Ramsburg, D. (2002). Advice given to parents on welcoming a second child: A critical review. *Family Relations, 51*, 2–14.

Krebs, D., & Janicki, M. (2004). Biological foundations of moral norms. In M. Schaller & C. S. Crandell (Eds.), *The psychological foundations of culture* (pp. 125–148). Mahwah, NJ: Erlbaum.*

Krebs, D. L. (2000). The evolution of moral dispositions in the human species. In D. LeCroy & P. Moller (Eds.), *Evolutionary perspectives on human reproductive behavior. Annals of the New York Academy of Science. V. 907* (pp. 132–148). New York, NY: New York Academy of Sciences.*

Krebs, D. L. (2005). The evolution of morality. In D. M. Buss (Ed.), *The handbook of evolutionary psychology* (pp. 757–771). Hoboken, NJ: John Wiley.*

Krebs, D. L. (2008). Morality: An evolutionary account. *Perspectives on Psychological Science, 3*, 149–172.*

Krebs, D. L., & Denton, K. (2005). Toward a more pragmatic approach to morality: A critical evaluation of Kohlberg's model. *Psychological Review, 112*, 629–649.*

Kreppner, J. M., Rutter, M., Beckett, C., Castle, J., Colvert, C. G., & et al. (2007). Normality and impairment following profound early institutional deprivation: A longitudinal follow-up into early adolescence. *Developmental Psychology, 43*, 931–946.

Kress, J. S., & Elias, M. J. (2006). School based social and emotional learning programs. In W. Damon & R. Lerner (Gen. Ed.), & K. A. Renninger & I. E. Siegel (Eds.), *Handbook of child psychology: Vol. 4. Child psychology and practice* (6th ed., pp. 592–618). New York: Wiley.

Krishnan, V., & Morrison, K. B. (1995). An ecological model of child maltreatment in a Canadian province. *Child Abuse & Neglect. 19*, 101–113.*

Kristjansson, E. A., Fried, P. A., & Watkinson, B. (1989). Maternal smoking during pregnancy affects children's vigilance performance. *Drug and Alcohol Dependence, 24*, 11–19.*

Kruesi, M. J., Hibbs, E. D., Zahn, T. P., & Keysor, C. S. (1992). A 2-year prospective follow-up study of children and adolescents with disruptive behavior disorders: Prediction by cerebrospinal fluid 5-hydroxyindoleacetic acid, homovanillic acid and autonomic measures? *Archives of General Psychiatry, 49*, 429–435.

Krumhansl, C. L., & Jusczyk, P. W. (1990). Infants' perception of phrase structure in music. *Psychological Science, 1*, 70–73.

Kuczynski, L. (1983). Reasoning, prohibitions, and motivations for compliance. *Developmental Psychology, 19*, 126–134.*

Kuczynski, L., Kochanska, G., Radke-Yarrow, M., & Girnius-Brown, O. (1987). A developmental interpretation of young children's noncompliance. *Developmental Psychology, 23*, 799–806.*

Kuczynski, L., Marshall, S., & Schell, K. (1997). Value socialization in a bidirectional context. In J. E. Grusec & L. Kuczynski (Eds.), *Parenting and children's internalization of values: A handbook of contemporary theory* (pp. 23–50). New York: Wiley.*

Kuczynski, L., & Parkin, C. M. (2007). Agency and bidirectionality in socialization. In J. E. Grusec & P. Hastings (Eds.), *Handbook of socialization* (pp. 259–283). New York: Guilford.*

Kuhl, P. K. (2004). Early language acquisition: Cracking the speech code. *Nature, 5*, 831–843.

Kuhl, P. K., et al. (1997). Cross-language analysis of phonetic units in language addressed to infants. *Science, 277*, 685–686.

Kuhl, P. K., & Miller, J. D. (1975). Speech perception by the chinchille: voice-voiceless distinction in alveolar plosive consonants. *Science, 190*, 69–72.

Kuhl, P. K., Andruski, J. E., Christovich, I. A., Christovich, L. A., et al. (1997). Cross-language analysis of phonetic units in language addressed to infants. *Science, 277*, 684–686.

Kuhn, D., & Franklin, S. (2006). The second decade: What develops (and how?). In W. Damon & R. M. Lerner (Gen. Ed.), & D. Kuhn & R. Siegler (Eds.), *ndbook of child psychology: Vol. 2. Cognition, perception, and language* (6th ed., pp. 953–994). New York: Wiley.

Kurtz, B. E., & Borkowski, J. G. (1987). Development of strategic skills in impulsive and reflective children: A longitudinal study of metacognition. *Journal of Experimental Child Psychology, 43*, 129–148.

Kuczynski, L. (Ed.). (2003). *Handbook of dynamics in parent-child relations.* Thousand Oaks, CA: Sage.

Kumanyika, S. (1993). Ethnicity and obesity development in children. In C. L. Williams & S. Y. S. Kimm (Eds.), Prevention and treatment of childhood obesity (pp. 81–92). Annals of the New York Academy of Sciences, Vol. 699. New York: The New York Academy of Sciences.

Kupersmidt, J., & Dodge, K. A. (Eds.). (2004). *Children's peer relations: From development to intervention.* Washington, DC: American Psychological Association.

La Barbera, J. D., Izard, C. E., Vietze, P., & Parisi, S. A. (1976). Four- and six-month-old infants' visual responses to joy, anger, and neutral expressions. *Child Development, 47*, 535–538.

La Freniere, P. J. (2000). *Emotional development: A biosocial perspective.* New York: Wadsworth.

Lacourse, E., Côté, S., Nagin, D. S., Vitaro, R., Brendgen, M., & Tremblay, R. E. (2002). A longitudinal-experimental approach to testing theories of antisocial behavior development. *Development and Psychopathology, 14*, 909–924.*

Ladd, G. W. (1981). Effectiveness of a social learning method for enhancing children's social interaction and peer acceptance. *Child Development, 52*, 171–178.

Ladd, G. W. (2005). *Peer relationships and social competence of children and youth.* New Haven, CT: Yale University Press.

Ladd, G. W., Birch, S. H., & Buhs, E. S. (1999). Children's social and scholastic lives in kindergarten: Related spheres of influence? *Child Development, 70*, 1373–1400.

Ladd, G. W., & Golter, B. S. (1988). Parents' management of preschooler's peer relations: Is it related to children's social competence? *Developmental Psychology, 24*, 109–117.

Ladd, G., & Pettit, G. (2002). Parent's and children's peer relationships. In M. H. Bornstein (Ed.), *Handbook of parenting.* Mahwah, NJ: Erlbaum.

LaFrance, M., Hecht, M. A., & Levy Paluck, E. (2003). The contingent smile: A meta-analysis of sex differences in smiling. *Psychological Bulletin, 129*, 305–334.

Laible, D. J., Carlo, G., & Raffaelli, M. (2000). The differential relations of parent and peer attachment to adolescent adjustment. *Journal of Youth and Adolescence, 29*, 45–59.

Laible, D. J., & Thompson, R. A. (1998). Attachment and emotional understanding in preschool children. *Developmental Psychology, 34*, 1038–1045.

Laird, R. D., Pettit, G. S., Dodge, K. A., & Bates, J. E. (2003). Change in parents' monitoring knowledge: Links with parenting, relationships quality, adolescent beliefs and antisocial behavior. *Social Development, 12*, 401–419.

Lalonde, C. E., & Chandler, M. J. (2003). Children's understanding of interpretation. *New Ideas in Psychology, 20*, 163–198.*

Lamb, M. E. (Ed.). (1987). *The father's role: Cross-cultural perspectives.* New York: Wiley.

Lamb, M. E. (Ed.). (2004). *The role of the father in child development* (4th ed.). New York: Wiley.

Lamb, M. E., & Ahnert, L. (2006). Childcare and youth programs. In W. Damon & R. L. Lerner (Gen. Ed.), & K. A. Renninger & I. E. Sigel (Eds.), *Handbook of child psychology: Vol. 4. Child psychology and practice* (6th ed., pp. 950–1016). New York: Wiley.

Lamb, M. E., & Campos, J. (1982). *Development in infancy.* New York: Random House.

Lamb, M. E., & Roopnarine, J. L. (1979). Peer influences on sex role development in preschoolers. *Child Development, 50*, 1219–1222.

Lamb, M. E., Suomi, S. J., & Stephenson, G. R. (1979). *Social interaction analysis: Methodological issues.* Madison, WI: University of Wisconsin Press.

Lamb, S., & Zakhireh, B. (1997). Toddlers' attention to the distress of peers in a day care setting. *Early Education and Development, 8*, 105–118.

Lambert, M. C., Weisz, J. R., & Knight, F. (1989). Over- and undercontrolled clinic referral problems of Jamaican and American children and adolescents: The culture general and the culture specific. *Journal of Consulting & Clinical Psychology, 57*, 467–472.

Lambert, S. R., & Drack, A. V. (1996). Infantile cataracts. *Survey of Ophthalmology, 40*, 427–458.

Lambert, W. E. (1987). The effects of bilingual and bicultural experiences on children's attitudes and social perspectives. In P. Homel, M. Palij, & D. Aranson (Eds.), *Childhood Bilingualism.* Hillsdale, NJ: Erlbaum.*

Lambert, W. E., & Tucker, G. R. (1972). *The bilingual education of children.* Rowley, MA: Newbury House.*

Lambert, W. E., Genesee, F., Holobow, N. E., & Chartrand, L. (1993). Bilingual education for majority English-speaking children. *European Journal of Psychology of Education, 8,* 3–22.*

Lampl, M., Johnson, M. L., & Frongillo, E. A. (2001). Mixed distribution analysis identifies saltation and statis growth. *Annals of Human Biology, 28,* 403–411.

Landau, B., Gleitman, H., & Spelke, E. (1981). Spatial knowledge and geometric representation in a child blind from birth. *Science, 213,* 1275–1278.

Landau, B., Spelke, E., & Gleitman, H. (1984). Spatial knowledge in a young blind child. *Cognition, 16,* 225–260.

Lander, E. S. (1996). The new genomics: Global views of biology. *Science, 274,* 536–538.

Landy, S., Peters, R. DeV., Arnold, R., Allen, A. B., Brookes, F., & Jewell, S. (1998). Evaluation of "Staying on Track": An early identification, tracking, and referral system. *Infant Mental Health Journal, 19,* 34–58.*

Lane, H. (1976). *The wild boy of Aveyron.* Cambridge, MA: Harvard University Press.

Langlois, J. H. (1985). From the eye of the beholder to behavioural reality: The development of social behaviors and social relations as a function of physical attractiveness. In C. P. Herman (Ed.), *Physical appearance, stigma, and social behavior.* Hillsdale, NJ: Erlbaum.

Langlois, J. H., & Downs, C. A. (1980). Mothers, fathers and peers as socialization agents of sex-typed play behaviors in young children. *Child Development, 51,* 1237–1247.

Langlois, J. H., Kahakanis, L., Rubenstein, A. J., Larson, A., Hallam, N., & Smoot, M. (2000). Maxims or myths of beauty: A meta-analytic and theoretical review. *Psychological Bulletin, 126,* 390–423.

Langlois, J. H., Roggman, L. A., Casey, R. J., Ritter, J. M., Rieser-Danner, L. A., & Jenkins, V. Y. (1987). Infant preferences for attractive faces: Rudiments of a stereotype? *Developmental Psychology, 23,* 363–369.

Laplante, D., Brunet, A., Schmitz, N., Ciampi, A., & King, S. (2008). Project Ice Storm: Prenatal maternal stress affects cognitive and linguistic functioning in 5½-year-old children. *Journal of the American Academy of Child and Adolescent Psychiatry, 47,* 1063–1072.*

Laporte, L., Marcoux, V., & Guttman, H. A. (2001). Characteristics of families of women with restricting anorexia nervosa compared with families of normal probands. *Encaphale, 27,* 109–119.

Larson, R., Monetia, G., Richards, M. H., & Wilson, S. (2002). Continuity, stability, and change in daily emotional experience across adolescence. *Child Development, 73,* 1151–1165.

Larson, R., & Richards, M. H. (1994). *Divergent realities: The emotional lives of mothers, fathers and adolescents.* New York: Basic Books.

Larson, R., & Verma, S. (1999). How children and adolescents around the world spend time: Work, play, and developmental opportunities. *Psychological Bulletin, 125,* 701–736.

Larzelere, R. E. (1996). A review of the outcomes of parents use of nonabusive or customary physical punishment. *Pediatrics, 98,* 824–828.

Larzelere, R. E. (2000). Child outcomes of nonabusive and customary physical punishment by parents: An updated literature review. *Clinical Child and Family Psychology Review, 3,* 199–221.

Lassonde, M., Mottron, L., Peretz, I., Schiavetto, A., Hébert, S., & Décarie, J-C. (1999). Loss of global visual and auditory processing following right temporal lobe lesion. *Brain and Cognition, 40,* 162–166.*

Laursen, B. (1995). Conflict and social interaction in adolescent relationships. *Journal of Research on Adolescence, 5,* 55–70.

Laursen, B., Hartup, W. W., & Koplas, A. L. (1996). Towards understanding peer conflict. *Merrill-Palmer Quarterly, 42,* 76–102.

Laursen, B., & Jensen-Campbell, L. A. (1999). The nature and functions of social exchange in adolescent romantic relationships. In W. Furman, B. Brown, & C. Feiring (Eds.), *The development of romantic relationships in adolescence. Cambridge studies in social and emotional development* (pp. 50–74). New York: Cambridge University Press.

Lavelli, M., & Fogel, A. (2002). Developmental changes in mother-infant face-to-face communications: Birth to three months. *Developmental Psychology, 38,* 288–305.

Law, K., Stroud, L., La Grasse, L., Niaura, R., Lin, J., & Lester, B. (2003). Smoking during pregnancy and newborn neurobehavior. *Pediatrics, 111,* 1318–1323.

Lawlor, D. A., Batty, G. D., Morton, S. M. B., Deary, I. J., Macintyre, S., Ronalds, G., et al. (2005). Early life predictors of childhood intelligence: Evidence from the Aberdeen children of the 1950s study. *Journal of Epidemiology & Community Health, 59,* 656–663.

Lazar, I., & Darlington, R. (1982). Lasting effects of early education: A report from the Consortium of Longitudinal Studies. *Monographs of the Society for Research in Child Development, 47,* 1–151.

Leaper, C. (1994). Exploring the consequences of gender segregation on social relationships. In C. Leaper (Ed.), *Childhood gender segregation: causes & consequences. New Directions for child development.* No. 65 (pp. 67–86). San Francisco, CA: Jossey-Bass.

Leaper, C. (2002). *Parenting girls and boys.* Mahway, NJ: Erlbaum.

Leaper, C., Anderson, K. J., & Sanders, P. (1998). Moderators of gender effects on parents' talk to their children: A meta-analysis. *Developmental Psychology.*

Leaper, C., & Friedman, C. K. (2007). The socialization of gender. In J. E. Grusec & P. D. Hastings (Eds.), *Handbook of socialization* (pp. 561–587). New York: Guilford.

Lederberg, A. R., Prezbindowski, A. K., & Spencer, P. E. (2000). Word-learning skills of deaf preschoolers: The development of novel mapping and rapid word-learning strategies. *Child Development, 71,* 1571–1585.

Ledingham, J. E., & Schwartzman, A. E. (1984). A year follow-up of aggressive and withdrawn behavior in childhood: Preliminary findings. *Journal of Abnormal Child Psychology, 12,* 157–188.*

LeDoux, J. (2002). *Synaptic self: How our brains become who we are.* New York: Viking Press.

Lee, D. N., & Aronson, E. (1974). Visual proprioceptive control of standing in human infants. *Perception & Psychophysics, 15,* 529–432.

Lee, D. N., & Lishman, J. R. (1975). Visual proprioceptive control of stance. *Journal of Human Movement Studies, 1,* 87–95.

Lee, K. (1994). The crying pattern of Korean infants and related factors. *Developmental Medicine and Child Neurology, 36,* 601–607.

Lee, K. (2000). Crying patterns of Korean infants in institutions. *Child: Care, Health, and Development, 26,* 217–228.

Lee, K., Cameron, C. A., Xu, F., Fu, G., & Board, J. (1997). Chinese and Canadian children's evaluations of lying and truth telling: Similarities and differences in the context of pro- and antisocial behaviors. *Child Development, 68,* 924–934.*

Lee, V. E., Brooks-Gunn, J., Schnur, E., & Liaw, F. (1990). Are Head Start effects sustained? A longitudinal follow-up comparison of disadvantaged children attending Head Start, no preschool,

and other preschool programs. *Child Development, 61,* 495–507.

Lefrancois, G. R. (1973). *Of children.* Belmont, CA: Wadsworth.

Legerstee, M. (1991). The role of person and object in eliciting early imitation. *Journal of Experimental Child Psychology, 51,* 423–433.*

Legerstee, M., Barna, J., & DiAdamo, C. (2000). Precursors to the development of intention at 6 months: Understanding people and their actions. *Developmental Psychology, 36,* 622–634.*

Legerstee, M., Bosman, T. G., & Fels, S. (1992). People and objects affect the quality of vocalizations in infants with Down syndrome. *Early Development and Parenting, 1,* 149–156.*

Legerstee, M., Varghese, J., & van Beek, Y. (2002). Effects of maintaining and redirecting infant attention on the production of referential communication in infants with and without Down syndrome. *Journal of Child Language, 29,* 23–48.*

Lehmann, M., & Hasselhorn, M. (2007). Variable memory strategy use in children's adaptive intratask learning behavior: Developmental changes and working memory influences in free recall. *Child Development, 78,* 1068–1082.

Lei, T., & Cheng, S. (1989). A little but special light on the university of moral judgment development. In L. Kohlberg, D. Candee, & A. Colby (Eds.), *Rethinking moral development.* Cambridge, MA: Harvard University Press.

Leiderman, P. H. (1983). Social ecology and childbirth: The newborn nursery as environmental stressor. In N. Garmezy & M. Rutter (Eds.), *Stress, coping and development in children.* New York: McGraw-Hill.

Lejeune, L., Anderson, D. L., Campos, J. J., Witherington, D. C., Uchiyama, I., & Barbu-Roth, M. (2006). Responsiveness to terrestrial optic flow in infancy; Does locomotor experience play a role? *Human Movement Science, 25,* 4–17.

Lemerise, E. A., & Arsenio, W. F. (2000). An integrated model of emotion process and cognition in social information processing. *Child Development, 71,* 107–118.

Lemmon, K., & Moore, C. (2007). The development of prudence in the face of varying future rewards. *Developmental Science, 10,* 502–511.*

Lengua, L. J. (2002). The contribution of emotionality and self-regulation to the understanding of children's response to multiple risk. *Child Development, 73,* 144–161.

Lenneberg, E. H. (1967). *Biological foundations of language.* New York: Wiley.

Lenneberg, E. H., Rebelsky, F. G., & Nichols, I. A. (1965). The vocalizations of infants born to deaf and hearing parents. *Human Development, 8,* 23–37.

Lepper, M. R. (1985). Microcomputers in education: Motivation and social issues. *American Psychologist, 40,* 1–18.

Lepper, M. R., & Gurtner, J. (1989). Children and computers: Approaching the twenty-first century. *American Psychologist, 44,* 170–178.

Leshner, A. (2001, August). Understanding the risks of prescription drugs. NIDA notes. Directors Column. Retrieved from http://www.aida.nih.gov/NIDA_Notes/NNVol16N3/DirRepVol16N3.html.

Lesser, G. S., Fifer, G., & Clark, D. H. (1965). Mental abilities of children from different social class and cultural groups. *Monographs of the Society for Research in Child Development, 30* (4, Serial No. 102), 1–115.

Lester, B. M. (1988). Neurobehavioral assessment of the infant at risk. *Early identification of infants with developmental disabilities.* New York: Grune & Stratton.

Lester, B. M. (2005). *Why is my baby crying? The parent's survival guide for coping with crying problems and colic.* New York: Harper Collins.

Lester, B. M., Als, H., & Brazelton, T. B. (1982). Regional obstetric anesthesia and newborn behavior: A reanalysis toward synergistic effects. *Child Development, 53,* 687–692.

Lester, B. M., Boukydis, C. F. Z., Garcia-Coll, C. T., Hole, W., & Peuker, M. (1992). Infantile colic: Acoustic cry characteristics, maternal perception of cry, and temperament. *Infant Behavior and Development, 15,* 15–26.

Lester, B. M., Boukydis, C. F. Z., & Twomey, J. E. (2000). Maternal substance abuse and child outcome. In C. H. Zeanah (Ed.), *Handbook of infant mental health* (pp. 161–175). New York: Guilford.

Leung, G. M., Lai-Ming, H., Tin, K. Y. K., Schooling, C. M., & Lam, T. (2007). Health consequences of cesarean birth during the first 18 months of life. *Epidemiology, 18,* 479–484.

Leventhal, T., & Brooks-Gunn, J. (2000). The neighborhoods they live in: The effects of neighborhood residence on child and adolescent outcomes. *Psychological Bulletin, 126,* 309–337.

Levine, L., Tuber, S. B., Slade, A., & Ward, M. J. (1991). Mothers' mental representations and their relationship to mother-infant attachment. *Bulletin of the Menninger Clinic, 55,* 454–469.

Levine, L. J. (1995). Young children's understanding of the causes of anger and sadness. *Child Development, 66,* 697–709.

Levitt, C., Hanvey, L., Avard, D., Chance, G., & Kaczorowski, J. (1995). *Survey of routine maternity care and practices in Canadian hospitals.* Ottawa, ON: Health Canada and Canadian Institute of Child Health.*

Levitt, M. J., Weber, R. A., & Clark, M. C. (1986). Social network relationships as sources of maternal support and well-being. *Developmental Psychology, 22,* 310–316.

Levy, G. D. (1994). High and low gender schematic children's release from proactive interference. *Sex roles, 30,* 93–108.

Levy, S., & et al. (2007). The diploid genome sequence of an individual human. *PLoS Biology, 5,* 2113–2144.

Lewinsohn, P. M., & Rohde, P. (1993). The cognitive-behavioral treatment of depression in adolescents: Research and suggestions. *The Clinical Psychologist, 46,* 177–183.

Lewinsohn, P. M., Rohde, P., & Seeley, J. R. (1993). Psychosocial characteristics of adolescents with a history of suicide attempts. *Journal of the American Academy of Child and Adolescent Psychiatry, 32,* 600–668.

Lewis, C., & Lamb, M. E. (2003). Father's influences on children's development: The evidence from two parent families. *European Journal of Psychology of Education, 18,* 211–228.

Lewis, M. (1983). On the nature of intelligence: Science or bias? In M. Lewis (Ed.), *Origins of intelligence: Infancy and early childhood* (2nd ed., pp. 1–24). New York: Plenum.

Lewis, M. (1991). *Shame, the exposed self.* New York: Free Press.

Lewis, M. (1992). *Shame: The exposed self.* New York: Free Press.

Lewis, M. (1995). Embarrassment: The emotion of self-exposure and evaluation. In J. P. Tangney & K. Fischer (Eds.), *Self-conscious emotions* (pp. 198-218). New York: Guildford.

Lewis, M. (1998). Emotional competence and development. In D. Pushkar, W. M. Bukowski, A. E. Schwartzman, D. M. Stack, & D. R. White (Eds.), *Improving competence across the lifespan* (pp. 27–36). New York: Plenum Press.

Lewis, M. (2000). Self-conscious emotions: Embarrassment, pride, shame, and guilt. In M. Lewis & J. Haviland (Eds.), *Handbook of emotions* (2nd ed., pp. 623-636). New York: Guildford Press.*

Lewis, M., Alessandri, S., Sullivan, M. W. (1992). Differences in shame and pride as a function of children's gender and task difficulty. *Child Development, 63,* 630–638.

Lewis, M., & Brooks, J. (1974). Self, other and fear: Infants' reactions to people. In M. Lewis & L. Rosenblum (Eds.), *The origins of fear.* New York: Wiley.

Lewis, M., & Brooks-Gunn, J. (1979). *Social cognition and the acquisition of self.* New York: Plenum Press.

Lewis, M., & Freedle, R. (1973). The mother-infant dyad. In P. Pliner, L. Kranes, & T. Alloway (Eds.), *Communication and affect: Language and thought.* New York: Academic.

Lewis, M., & Michaelson, L. (1985). *Children's emotions and moods.* New York: Plenum.

Lewis, M., & Ramsay, D. (2002). Cortisol response to embarrassment and shame. *Child Development, 73,* 1034–1045.*

Lewis, M. & Wilson, C. D. (1972). Infant development in lower-class American families. *Human Development, 15,* 112–127.

Lewis, M. D. (2000). The promise of dynamic systems approaches for an integrated account of human development. *Child Development, 71,* 36–43.*

Lewkowicz, D. J. (2001). The concept of ecological validity: What are its limitations and is it bad to be invalid? *Infancy, 2,* 437–450.

Liben, L. S. (1991). Adults' performance on horizontality tasks: Conflicting frames of reference. *Developmental Psychology, 27,* 285–294.

Liben, L. S. (1999). Developing an understanding of external spatial representations. In I. E. Sigel (Ed.), *Development of mental representation: Theories and applications* (pp. 297–321). Mahwah, NJ: Erlbaum.

Liben, L. S., & Bigler, R. S. (2002). The developmental course of gender differentiation. *Monographs of the Society for Research in Child Development, 67* (269, Pt. 2).

Liben, L. S., & Golbeck, S. L. (1980). Sex differences in performance on Piagetian spatial tasks: Differences in competence or performance. *Child Development, 51,* 594–597.

Liberman, I. Y., Shankweiler, D., Liberman, A. M., Fowler, C., & Fischer, F. W. (1976). Phonetic segmentation and recoding in the beginning reader. In A. S. Reber & D. Scarborough (Eds.), *Reading: Theory and practice.* Hillsdale, NJ: Erlbaum.

Liddle, H. A., & Rowe, C. L. (Eds.). (2006). *Adolescent substance abuse: Research and clinical issues.* New York: Cambridge.

Liebert, R. M., & Baron, R. A. (1972). Some immediate effects of televised violence on children's behavior. *Developmental Psychology, 6,* 469–475.

Lillard, A. S. (1993). Pretend play skills and the child's theory of mind. *Child Development, 64,* 348–371.

Lillard, A. S. (1998). Ethnopsychologies: Cultural variations in theory of mind. *Psychological Bulletin, 123,* 3–33.

Lillard, A. S. (2005). *Montessori: The science behind the genius.* Oxford: Oxford University Press.

Lillard, A. S. (2006). The socialization of theory of mind: Cultural and social class differences in behavior explanation. In A. Antonietti, O. Liverta-Simpio & A. Marchetti (Eds.), *Theory of mind and language in developmental contexts* (pp. 65–76). New York: Springer.

Lin, C., Verp, M. S., & Sabbagha, R. E. (1993). *The high risk fetus: Pathophysiology, diagnosis, management.* New York: Springer/Verlag.

Lindberg, M. (1980). Is knowledge base development a necessary and sufficient condition for memory development? *Journal of Experimental Child Psychology, 30,* 401–410.

Lindell, S. G. (1988). Education for childbirth: A time for change. *Journal of Obstetrics, Gynecology and Neonatal Nursing, 17,* 108–112.

Linn, S., Lieberman, E., Schoenbaum, S. C., Monson, R. R., Stubblefield, P. G., & Ryand, K. J. (1988). Adverse outcomes of pregnancy in women exposed to diethylstilbestrol in utero. *Journal of Reproductive Medicine, 33,* 3–7.

Lipsitt, L. P. (2003). Crib death: A biobehavioral pehnomenon? *Current Directions in Psychological Science, 12,* 164–170.

Lipton, J. S., & Spelke, E. S. (2003). Origins of number sense: Large-number discrimination in human infants. *Psychological Review, 14,* 396–401.

Liu, M., Chen, X., Rubin, K. H., Zheng, S., Cui, L., Li, D., et al. (2005). Autonomy- vs. connectedness-oriented parenting behaviours in Chinese and Canadian mothers. *International Journal of Behavioral Development, 29,* 489–495.*

Liu, S., Liston, R. M., Joseph, K. S., Heaman, M., Sauve, R., & Kramer, M. S. (2007). Maternal mortality and severe morbidity associated with low-risk planned cesarean delivery versus planned vaginal delivery at term. *CMAJ, 176,* 455–460.*

Loeber, R., & Hay, D. F. (1993). Developmental approaches to aggression and conduct problems. In M. Rutter & D. F. Hay (Eds.), *Development through life: A handbook for clinicians* (pp. 488–516). Oxford: Blackwell Scientific Publications.

Loebstein, R., & Koren, G. (1997). Pregnancy outcome and neurodevelopment of children exposed in utero to psychoactive drugs: The Motherisk experience. *Journal of Psychiatry and Neuroscience, 22,* 192–196.*

Lollis, S., Ross, H., & Leroux, L. (1996). An observational study of parents' socialization or moral orientation during sibling conflicts. *Merrill-Palmer Quarterly, 42,* 475–494.*

Lorenz, K. (1952). *King Solomon's ring.* New York: Crowell.

Losh, M., & Capps, L. (2006). Understanding of emotional experience in autism: Insights from the personal accounts of high functioning children with autism. *Developmental Psychology, 42,* 809–818.

Lovaas, O. I., & Smith, P. (1988). Intensive behavioral treatment for young autistic children. In B. Lahey & A. Kazdin (Eds.), Advances in clinical child psychology (Vol. 2). New York: Plenum.

Lovett, S. B., & Pillow, B. H. (1995). Development of the ability to distinguish between comprehension and memory: Evidence from strategy-selection tasks. *Journal of Educational Psychology, 87,* 523–536.

Lowe, X., Eskenazi, B., Nelson, D. O., Kidd, S., Alme, A., & Wyrobek, A. J. (2001). Frequency of XY sperm increases with age in fathers of boys with Klinefelter syndrome. *American Journal of Human Genetics, 69,* 1046–1054.

Lowes, J., & Triggerman, M. (2003). Weight concerns of young children. *British Journal of Health Psychology, 8,* 135–147.

Lowrance, W. W., & Collins, F. S. (2007). Ethics: Identifiability in genomic research. *Science, 317,* 600–602.

Lozoff, B., Jimenez, E., & Smith, J. B. (2006). Double burden iron deficiency in infancy and low socioeconomic status. *Archives of*

Pediatrics and Adolescent Medicine, 160, 1108–1113.

Luca, P., Laurin, N., Misener, V. L., Wigg, K. G., Anderson, B., Cate-Carter, T., et al. (2007). Association of the dopamine D1 gene, DRD1, with inattention symptoms in families selected for reading problems. *Molecular Psychiatry, 12,* 776–785.*

Luecke-Aleksa, D., Anderson, D. R., Collins, P. A., & Schmitt, K. L. (1995). Gender constancy and television viewing. *Developmental Psychology, 31,* 773–780.

Lummis, M., & Stevenson, H. W. (1990). Gender differences in beliefs and achievement: A cross-cultural study. *Developmental Psychology, 26,* 254–263.

Luria, A. R. (1976). *Cognitive development: Its cultural and social foundation.* Cambridge, MA: Harvard University Press.

Luthar, S. S. (2003). The culture of affluence: Psychological costs of material wealth. *Child Development, 74,* 1581–1593.

Luthar, S. S. (2006a). Overscheduling versus other stressors: Challenges of high socioeconomic status families. *Social Policy Report, Society for Research in Child Development.*

Luthar, S. S. (2006b). Resilience in development: A synthesis of research across five decades. In D. Cicchetti & D. J. Cohen (Eds.), *Developmental Psychopathology: Risk, disorder, and adaptation* (pp. 740–795). New York: Wiley.

Luthar, S. S. (2007). Conceptual issues in studies of resilience: Past, present, and future research. In B. M. Lester, A. S. Masten & B. McEwen (Eds.), *Resilience in children.* New York: Blackwell.

Luthar, S. S., Cicchetti, D., & Becker, B. (2000). The concept of resilience: A critical evaluation and guidelines for future work. *Child Development, 71,* 543–562.

Luthar, S. S., & Latendresse, S. J. (2005). Children of the affluent: Challenges to well-being. *Current Directions in Psychological Science, 14,* 49–53.

Lykken, D. T., McGue, M., Tellegen, A., & Bouchard, T. J., Jr. (1992). Genetic traits that may not run in families. *American Psychologist, 47* (12), 1565–1577.

Lynch, M. P., Eilers, R. E., Oller, D. K., & Urbano, R. C. (1990). Innateness, experience, and music perception. *Psychological Science, 1,* 70–73.

Lyons-Ruth, K., & Jacobvitz, D. (1999). Attachment disorganization. In J. Cassidy & P. R. Shaver (Eds.), *Handbook of attachment* (pp. 520–544). New York: Guilford.

Lyons-Ruth, K., Lyubchik, A., Wolfe, R., & Bronfman, E. (2002). Parental depression and child attachment: Hostile and helpless profiles of parent and child behavior among families and risk. In S. H. Goodman & I. Gotlib (Eds.), *Children of depressed parents* (pp. 89–120). Washington, DC: American Psychological Association.

Lytton, H. (2000). Toward a model of family-environmental and child-biological influences on development. *Developmental Review, 20,* 156–179.*

Lytton, H., & Romney, D. M. (1991). Parents' differential socialization of boys and girls: A meta-analysis. *Psychological Bulletin, 109,* 267–296.*

MacBeth, T. M. (1996). Indirect effects of television: Creativity, persistence, school achievement, and participation in other activities. In T. M. Mac Beth (Ed.), *Tuning in to young viewers: Social science perspectives on television* (pp. 149–219). Thousand Oaks, CA: Sage.

Maccoby, E. E. (1998). *The two sexes.* Cambridge, MA: Harvard University Press.

Maccoby, E. E. (2000). Perspectives on gender development. *International Journal of Behavioral Development, 24,* 398–406.

Maccoby, E. E., & Jacklin, C. (1980). Sex differences in aggression: A rejoinder and reprise. *Child Development, 51,* 964–980.

Maccoby, E. E., & Jacklin, C. N. (1974). *The psychology of sex differences.* Stanford, CA: Stanford University Press.

Maccoby, E. E., & Martin, J. A. (1983). Socialization in the context of the family: Parent-child interaction. In E. M. Hetherington (Ed.), *Socialization, personality, and social development: Vol. 4. Handbook of child psychology* (pp. 1–102). New York: Wiley.

MacDonald, K. (1999). Love and confidence in protection as two independent systems underlying intimate family relationships. *Journal of Family Psychology, 13,* 492–495.

MacDonald, K., & Parke, R. D. (1984). Bridging the gap: The relationship between parent-child play and peer interactive competence. *Child Development, 55,* 1265–1277.

MacDonald, K., & Parke, R. D. (1986). Parent-child physical play: The effects of sex and age of children and parents. *Sex Roles, 15,* 367–378.

Macfarlane, J. A. (1975). Olfaction in the development of social preferences in the human neonate. In

M. A. Hofer (Ed.), *Parent-infant interaction.* Amsterdam: Elsevier.

Mackey, M. C. (1995). Women's evaluation of their childbirth performance. *Maternal-Child Nursing Journal, 23,* 57–72.

MacLean, K. (2003). The impact of institutionalization on child development. *Development and Psychopathology, 15,* 853–884.*

MacWhinney, B. (1996). Lexical connectionism. In P. Broeder & J. M. J. Murre (Eds.), *Models of language acquisition: Inductive and deductive approaches.* Cambridge, MA: MIT Press.

Madigan, M., Moran, G., & Pederson, D. R. (2006). Unresolved states of mind, disorganized attachment relationships, and disrupted interactions of adolescent mothers and their infants. *Developmental Psychology, 42,* 293–304.*

Madigan, M., Moran, G., Scheuengel, C., Pederson, D. R., & Otten, R. (2007). Unresolved maternal attachment representations, disrupted maternal behavior, and disorganized attachment in infancy: Links to toddler behavior problems. *Journal of Child Psychology and Psychiatry, 48,* 1042–1050.*

Magai, C., & McFadden, S. H. (1995). *The role of emotions in social and personality development.* New York: Plenum.

Maggi, S. (2008). Changes in smoking behaviors from late childhood to adolescence: 4 years later. *Drug and Alcohol Dependence, 94,* 251–253.*

Maggi, S., Hertzman, C., & Vaillancourt, T. (2007). Changes in smoking behaviors from late childhood to adolescence: Insights from the Canadian National Longitudinal Survey of Children and Youth. *Health Psychology, 26,* 232–240.*

Magnusson, D. (1988). Individual development from an interactional perspective: A longitudinal study. In D. Magnusson (Ed.), *Paths through life* (Vol. 1). Hillsdale, NJ: Erlbaum.

Magnusson, D. (Ed.). (1996). *The life-span development of individuals: Behavioral, neurobiological and psychosocial perspectives.* Cambridge, England: Cambridge University Press.

Magnusson, D. (1996). Towards a developmental science. In D. Magnusson (Ed.), *The lifespan development of individuals.* Cambridge, England: Cambridge University Press.

Magnusson, D., & Stattin, H. (2006). The person in context: A holistic-interactionistic approach. In W. Damon & R. M. Lerner (Gen. Ed.), & R. M. Lerner (Ed.), *Handbook of child psychology: Vol. 1. Theoretical models of* *human development* (6th ed., pp. 400–464). New York: Wiley.

Main, M. (1973). *Exploration, play and level of cognitive functioning as related to child-mother attachment.* Unpublished doctoral dissertation. Johns Hopkins University, Baltimore, MD.

Main, M., & Cassidy, J. (1988). Categories of response to reunion with the parent at age 6: Predictable from infant attachment classification and stable over a 1-month period. *Developmental Psychology, 24,* 415–426.

Main, M., & Hesse, E. (1990). Parents' unresolved traumatic experiences are related to infant disorganized attachment status: Is frightened and/or frightening parental behavior the linking mechanism? In M. T. Greenberg, D. Cicchetti, & E. M. Cummings (Eds.), *Attachment in the preschool years: Theory, research, and intervention* (pp. 161–182). Chicago, IL: University of Chicago Press.

Main, M., Hesse, H., & Kaplan, N. (2005). Predictability of attachment behavior and representational processes at 1, 6, and 19 years of age: The Berkeley Longituindal Study. In K. E. Grossmann, K. Grossmann & E. Waters (Eds.), *Attachment from infancy to adulthood* (pp. 245–304). New York: Guilford.

Main, M., Kaplan, N., & Cassidy, J. (1985). Security in infancy, childhood, and adulthood: A move to the level of representation. *Monographs of the Society for Research in Child Development, 50,* 66–104.

Main, M., & Weston, D. (1981). The quality of the toddler's relationship to mother and father: Related to conflict behavior and readiness to establish new relationships. *Child Development, 52,* 932–940.

Malatesta, C. Z. (1982). The expression and regulation of emotion: A lifespan perspective. In T. Field & A. Fogel (Eds.), *Emotion and early interaction* (pp. 1–24). Hillsdale, NJ: Erlbaum.

Malatesta, C. Z., Culver, C., Tesman, J., & Shepard, B. (1989). The development of emotional expression during the first two years of life: Normative trends and patterns of individual differences. *Monographs of the Society for Research in Child Development, 54,* 1–2.

Malcolm, L. A. (1970). Growth of the Asai child of the Madang district of New Guinea. *Journal of Biosocial Science, 2,* 213–226.

Mallick, S. K., & McCandless, B. R. (1966). A study of catharsis on aggression. *Journal of Personality and Social Psychology, 4,* 591–596.

Mandler, J. M. (1998). Representation. In W. Damon (Gen. Ed.), D. Kuhn, & R. S. Siegler (Vol. Eds.), *Handbook of child psychology: Vol. 2. Cognition, perception, and language* (pp. 255–308). New York: Wiley.

Mangelsdorf, S. C., Shapiro, J. R., & Marzolf, D. (1995). Developmental and temperamental differences in emotion regulation in infancy. *Child Development, 66,* 1817–1828.

Mangelsdorf, S., Watkins, S., & Lehn, L. (1991, April). *The role of control in the infant's appraisal of strangers.* Paper presented at the biennial meeting of the Society for Research in Child Development, Seattle, Washington.

Maratsos, M. (1983). Some current issues in the study of the acquisition of grammar. In P. H. Mussen (Ed.), *Handbook of child psychology* (Vol. 3, pp. 707–786). New York: Wiley.

Maratsos, M. (1989). Innateness and plasticity in language acquisition. In M. Rice & R. L. Shiefelbusch (Eds.), The teachability of language.
Baltimore, MD: Brooks/Cole.

Maratsos, M. (1993). Discussion in the symposium *Issues in the acquisition of inflectional processes,* presented at the meetings of the Society for Research in Child Development, New Orleans, LA.

Maratsos, M. (1998). The acquisition of grammar. In W. Damon (Series Ed.), & D. Kuhn & R. S. Siegler (Vol. Eds.), *Handbook of child psychology: Vol. 2. Cognition, perception, and language* (5th ed., pp. 421–466). New York: Wiley.

Marcella, S., & McDonald, B. (1990). The infant walker: An unappreciated household hazard. *Connecticut Medicine, 54,* 127–129.

Marche, T. A., & Howe, M. L. (1995). Preschoolers report misinformation despite accurate memory. *Developmental Psychology, 31,* 554–567.*

Marcovitch, S., Cesaroni, L., Roberts, W., & Swanson, C. (1995). Romanian adoption: Parents dreams, nightmares, and realities. *Child Welfare, 74,* 936–1032.*

Marcovitch, S., Goldberg, S., Gold, A., Washington, J., Wasson, C., Krekewich, K., & Handley-Derry, M. (1997). Determinants of behavioral problems in Romanian children adopted in Ontario. *International Journal of Behavioral Development, 20,* 17–31.*

Marcus, G. F. (1995). Children's overregularization of English plurals: A quantitative analysis. *Journal of Child Language, 22,* 447–460.

Marean, G. C., Werner, L. A., & Kuhl, P. K. (1992). Vowel categorization by very young infants. *Developmental Psychology, 28,* 396–405.

Mares, M., & Woodward, E. H. (2001). Prosocial effects on children's interactions. In D. G. Singer & J. Singer (Eds.), *Handbook of children and the media* (pp. 183–203). Thousand Oaks, CA: Sage.

Mares, M. L., & Woodard, E. H. (2007). Positive effects of television on children's social interaction: A meta-analysis. In G. W. Preiss, B. M. Gayle, N. Burrell, M. Allen & J. Bryant (Eds.), *Mass media effects research: Advances through meta-analysis* (pp. 281–300). Mahwah, NJ: Erlbaum.

Mareschal, D., & Shultz, T. (1999). Development of children's seriation: A connectionist approach. *Cognitive Science: Journal of Neural Computing, Artificial Intelligence and Cognitive Research, 11* (149–186).

Marini, Z. A. (1992). Synchrony and asynchrony in the development of children's scientific reasoning. In R. Case (Ed.), *The mind's staircase: Exploring the conceptual underpinnings of children's thought and knowledge* (pp. 55–74). Hillsdale, NJ: Erlbaum.*

Markman, E. M. (1977). Realizing that you don't understand: A preliminary investigation. *Child Development, 48,* 986–992.

Markman, E. M. (1979). Realizing that you don't understand: Elementary school children's awareness of inconsistencies. *Child Development, 50,* 643–655.

Markman, E. M. (1989). *Categorization and naming in children.* Cambridge, MA: MIT Press.

Markman, E. M., & Hutchinson, J. E. (1984). Children's sensitivity to constraints on word meaning: Taxonomic versus thematic relations. *Cognitive Psychology, 16,* 1–27.

Marks, D. J., Miller, S. R., Schulz, K. P., Newcorn, J. H., & Halperin, J. M. (2007). The interaction of psychosocial adversity and biolglical risk in childhood aggression. *Psychiatry Research, 151,* 221–230.

Marleau, J. D., Saucier, J.-F., & Allaire, F.-F. (2006). Birth order, behavioural problems, and the mother-child relationships in siblings aged 4 to 11 years from a two-child family. *The Canadian Journal of Psychiatry, 51,* 855–863.*

Marlier, L., Schaal, B., & Soussignan, R. (1998). Neonatal responsiveness to the odor of amniotic and lacteal fluids: A test of perinatal chemosensory continuity. *Child Development, 69,* 611–623.

Martin, C., & Fabes, R. A. (2001).

The stability and consequences of young children's same-sex peer interactions. *Developmental Psychology, 37,* 431–446.

Martin, C. L., & Halverson, C. F. (1983). The effects of sex-typing schemas on young children's memory. *Child Development, 54,* 563–574.

Martin, C. L., & Little, J. K. (1990). The relation of gender understanding to children's sex-typed preferences and gender stereotypes. *Child Development, 61,* 1427–1439.

Martin, C. L., & Ruble, D. N. (2004). Children's search for gender cues. *Current Directions in Psychological Science, 13,* 67–70.

Martin, J. A., Hamilton, B. E., Sutton, P. D., Ventura, S. I., Menacker, F., & Munson, M. L. (2005). *Births: Find data for 2003* (National Vital Statistics Report, Vol. 54, No. 2). Hyattsville, MD: National Center for Health Statistics.

Martin, L. R., Friedman, H. S., Clark, K. M., & Tucker, J. S. (2005). Longevity following the experience of parental divorce. *Social Science and Medicine, 61,* 2177–2189.

Martin, M. O., Mullis, I. V. S., & Chrostowski, S. J. (2004). *TIMMS 2003 Technical Report.* Chestnut Hill, MA: Boston College. .

Martinez, A. (1992). Scientific knowledge about television violence. Ottawa: Canadian Radio, Television and Telecommunications Commission.

Martinez, F. D., Wright, A. L., & Taussig, L. M. (1994). The effect of paternal smoking on the birth-weight of newborns whose mothers do not smoke. *American Journal of Public Health, 84,* 1489–1491.

Martini, F. H. (1995). *Anatomy and physiology* (3rd ed.). Upper Saddle River, NJ: Prentice Hall.

Martini, M., & Kirkpatrick, J. (1981). Early interactions in the Marquesas Islands. In T. M. Field, A. M. Sostek, P. Vietze, & P. H. Leiderman (Eds.), *Culture and early interactions* (pp. 189–214). Hillsdale, NJ: Erlbaum.

Martinussen, R., Hayden, J., Hogg-Johnson, S., & Tannock, R. (2005). A meta-analysis of working memory impairments in children with attention deficit/hyperactivity disorder. *Journal of the American Academy of Child and Adolescent Psychiatry, 44,* 377–384.*

Martorell, R. (1984). Genetics, environment and growth: Issues in the assessment of nutritional status. In A. Velasquez & H. Bourges (Eds.), *Genetic factors in nutrition.* Orlando, FL: Academic Press.

Masgoret, A.-M., & Gardner, R. C. (2003). Attitudes, motivation, and second language learning: A meta-analysis of studies conducted by Gardner and associates. *Language Learning, 53,* 123–163.*

Mash, E. J., & Johnston, C. (2005). Attention-deficit/Hyperactivity disorder (ADHD) and the family: A developmental psychopathology perspective. In J. F. Hudson & R. M. Rapee (Eds.), *Psychopathology and the family* (pp. 93–124). New York: Elsevier Science.*

Masoni, S., Maio, A., Trimarchi, G., de Punzio, C., & Gioretti, P. (1994). The couvades syndrome. *Journal of Psychosomatic Obstetrical Gynecology, 15,* 125–131.

Massey, C. M., & Gelman, R. (1988). Preschooler's ability to decide whether a photographed unfamiliar object can move itself. *Developmental Psychology, 24,* 307–317.

Masten, A. S., & Obradovic, J. (2007). Competence and resilience in development. In B. M. Lester, A. S. Masten & B. McEwen (Eds.), *Resilience in children.* New York: Blackwell.

Matas, L., Arend, R., & Sroufe, L. A. (1978). Continuity of adaptation in the second year: The relationship between quality of attachment and later competence. *Child Development, 49,* 547–556.

Maticka-Tyndale, E. (2001). Sexual health and Canadian youth: How do we measure up? *The Canadian Journal of Human Sexuality, 10,* 1–12.*

Maticka-Tyndale, E., Barrett, M., & McKay, A. (2000). Adolescent sexual and reproductive health in Canada: A review of national data sources and their limitations. *The Canadian Journal of Human Sexuality, 9,* 41–65.*

Maurer, D., & Maurer, C. (1988). *The world of the newborn.* New York, NY: Basic Books.

Maurer, D., & Salapatek, P. (1976). Developmental changes in the scanning of faces by young infants. *Child Development, 47,* 523–527.*

Maurer, D., Stager, C. L., & Mondloch, C. J. (1999). Cross-modal transfer of shape is difficult to demonstrate in one-month-old infants. *Child Development, 70,* 1047–1057.*

May, P. A. (1995). A multiple-level, comprehensive approach to the prevention of Fetal Alcohol Syndrome (FAS) and other alcohol-related birth defects (ARBD). *International Journal of the Addictions, 30,* 1549–1602.

Maynard, A. E. (2002). Cultural teaching: The development of teaching skills in Maya sibling interactions. *Child Development, 73,* 969–982

Mazzocco, M. M. M., Murphy, M. M., & McCloskey, M. (2007). The contribution of syndrome research to understanding mathematical learning disability: The case of fragile X and Turner syndromes. In D. B. Berch & M. M. M. Mazzocco (Eds.), *Why is math so hard for some children? The nature and origins of mathematical learning difficulties and disabilities* (pp. 173–193). Baltimore, MD: Paul H. Brookes Publishing.

McCall, R., Beach, S. R., & Lan, S. (2000). The nature and correlates of underachievement among elementary school children in Hong Kong. *Child Development, 71,* 785–801.

McCall, R. B., Applebaum, M. I., & Hogarty, P. S. (1973). Developmental changes in mental performance. *Monographs of the Society for Research in Child Development, 38* (3, Serial No. 150), 1–84.

McCall, R. B., Hogarty, P. S., & Hurlburt, N. (1972). Transitions in infant sensorimotor development and the prediction of childhood IQ. *American Psychologist, 27,* 728–748.

McConaghy, N., & Silove, D. (1992). Do sex linked behaviors in children influence relationships with their parents? *Archives of Sexual Behavior, 21,* 409–479.

McDougall, P., & Hymel, S. (2007). Same-gender versus cross-gender friendship conceptions. *Merrill-Palmer Quarterly, 53,* 347–380.*

McDougall, P., Hymel, S., Vaillancourt, T., & Mercer, L. (2001). The consequences of childhood peer rejection. In M. R. Leary (Ed.), *Interpersonal rejection* (pp. 213–247). London: Oxford University Press.*

McDowell, D. J., O'Neil, R., & Parke, R. D. (2000). Display rule application in a disappointing situation and children's emotional reactivity: Relations with social competence. *Merrill-Palmer Quarterly, 46,* 306–324.

McDowell, D. J., & Parke, R. D. (2000). Differential knowledge of display rules for positive and negative emotions: Influences from parents influences on peers. *Social Development, 9,* 415–432.

McEachin, J. J., Smith, T., & Lovaas, O. I. (1993). Long-term outcome for children with autism who receive early intensive behavioral treatment. *American Journal on Mental Retardation, 97,* 359–372.

McGraw, M. (1940). Neuromuscular development of the human infant as exemplified in the achievement of erect locomotion. *Journal of Pediatrics, 17,* 747–771.

McGue, M., & Bouchard, T. J. (1987). Genetic and environmental determinants of information processing and special mental abilities: A twin analysis. In R. J. Sternberg (Ed.), *Advances in the psychology of human intelligence* (Vol. 5). Hillsdale, NJ: Erlbaum.

McHale, J. L., Laurett, A., Talbot, J., & Pouguatte, C. (2001). Retrospect and prospect in the psychological study of coparenting and family group process. In J. L. McHale & W. Grolnick (Eds.), *Restrospect and prospect in the psychological study of families* (pp. 127–165). Mahwah, NJ: Erlbaum.

McHale, J. P. (2008). The construct of co-parenting: Evolution of a key family paradigm. In M. Schultz, M. K. Pruett, P. Kerig & R. D. Parke (Eds.), *Feathering the next: Couples' relationships, couples' interventions, and children's development.* Washington, DC: American Psychological Association.

McHale, J. P., Laurette, A., Talbot, J., & Pouquette, C. (2002). Retrospect and prospect in the psychological study of coparenting and family group process. In J. P. McHale & W. Grolnick (Eds.), *Retrospect and prospect in the psychological study of families* (pp. 127–165). Mahwah, NJ: Erlbaum.

McHale, J. P., & Rasmussen, J. L. (1998). Coparental and family group-level dynamics during infancy: Early family precursors of child and family functioning during preschool. *Development and Psychopathology, 10,* 39–59.

McHale, S. M., Crouter, A. C., & Whiteman, S. D. (2003). Family contexts of gender development in childhood and adolescence. *Social Development, 12,* 125–148.

McHale, S. M., Shanahan, L., Updergraff, K. A., Crouter, A. C., & Booth, A. (2004). Developmental and individual differences in girls' sex-typed activities in middle childhood and adolescence. *Child Development, 75,* 1575–1593.

McIntyre, L., Officer, S., & Simpson, A. C. (1996). Education and training: A Canadian perspective. Paper developed for the Canada–U.S.A. Women's Health Forum, August.

McKay, A. (2006). Trends in teen pregnancy in Canada with comparisons to U.S.A. and England/Wales. *The Canadian Journal of Human Sexuality, 15,* 157–161.*

McKenna, J. J., & Mosko, S. (1990). Evolution and the sudden infant death syndrome (SIDS). *Human Nature, 1,* 291–330.

McKenna, J. J., & Mosko, S. (1993). Evolution and infant sleep: An experimental study of infant-parent co-sleeping and its implications for SIDS. *Acta Paediatrica, 389* (Suppl.), 31–36.

McKown, C., & Weinstein, R. S. (2003). The developmetn and consequences of stereotype consciousness in middle childhood. *Child Development, 74,* 498–515.

McLanahan, S., & Sandefur, G. (1994). *Growing up with a single parent.* Cambridge, MA: Harvard University Press.

McLaughlin, F., Rusen, I. D., & Liu, S. L. (1999). Preterm birth. *Canadian Perinatal Surveillance System Fact Sheet.* Health Canada, Laboratory Centre for Disease Control.*

McLellan, J. A., & Youniss, J. (2003). Two systems of youth service: Determinants of voluntary and required youth community service. *Journal of Youth and Adolescence, 32,* 47–58.

McLoyd, V. C., Aikens, N., & Burton, L. (2006). Childhood poverty, policy, and practice. In W. Damon, R. Lerner, A. Renninger, & I. Sigel (Eds.), *Handbook of child psychology: Vol. 4. Child psychology in practice* (6th ed., pp. 700–775). New York: Wiley.

McLoyd, V. C., Harper, C. I., & Copeland, N. L. (2001). Ethnic minority status, interparental conflict and child adjustment. In J. Grych & F. D. Fincham (Eds.), *Interparental conflict and child development* (pp. 98–125). New York: Cambridge University Press.

McLoyd, V. C., Hill, N., & Dodge, K. (Eds.). (2005). *African American family life: Ecological and cultural diversity.* New York: Guilford Press.

McMurray, B., & Aslin, R. N. (2005). Infants are sensitive to within-category violation in speech perception. *Cognition, 95,* B15–B26.

McMurray, B., Tanenhaus, M., & Aslin, R. N. (2002). Gradient effects of within-category phonetic variation on lexical access. *Cognition, 86,* B33–B42.

McNeill, D. (1970). *The acquisition of language: The study of developmental psycholinguistics.* New York: Harper & Row.

Meador, K. J., Baker, G. A., Finnell, R. H., Kalyjian, L. A., Liporace, J. D., Loring, D. W., et al. (2006). In utero antiepileptic drug exposure: Fetal death and malformations. *Neurology, 67,* 407–412.

Medical Research Council, Natural Sciences and Engineering Research Council, & Social Sciences and Humanities Research Council (1998). *Tri-council policy statement: Ethical conduct for* *research involving Humans.* Ottawa, ON: Author.*

Medrich, E. A. (1981). *The serious business of growing up: A study of children's lives outside the school.* Berkeley: University of California Press.

Mehler, J., Dupoux, E., Nazzi, T., & Dehaene-Lambertz, G. (1996). Coping with linguistic diversity: The infant's viewpoint. In J. L. Morgan & K. Demuth (Eds.), *Signal to syntax: Bootstrapping from speech to grammar in early acquisition* (pp. 101–116). Mahwah, NJ: Erlbaum.

Mehler, J., Jusczyk, P., Lambertz, G., Halsted, N., Bertoncini, J., & Amieltison, C. (1988). A precursor of language acquisition in young infants. *Cognition, 29,* 143–178.

Mehler, P. S. (2003). Bulimia nervosa. *New England Journal of Medicine, 349,* 875–881.

Mehler, P. S., & Crews, C. K. (2001). Refeeding the patient with anorexia nervosa. *Eating Disorders: The Journal of Treatment and Prevention, 9,* 167–171.

Mehta, M. A., Sahakian, B. J., & Robbins, T. (2001). Comparative psychopharmacology of methylphenidate and related drugs in human volunteers, patients with ADHD, and experimental animals. In M. V. Solanto, A. F. T. Arnsten, & F. X. Castellanos (Eds.), *Stimulant drugs and ADHD: Basic and clinical neuroscience* (pp. 303–331). New York: Oxford University Press.

Meier, R. P., & Newport, E. L. (1990). Out of the hands of babes: On a possible sign advantage in language acquisition. *Language, 66* (1), 1–23.

Meisel, J. M. (1995). Parameters in acquisition. In P. Fletcher & B. MacWhinney (Eds.), *The handbook of child language.* Oxford: Blackwell.

Meltzoff, A. N. (1981). Imitation, intermodal coordination and representation in early infancy. In G. Butterworth (Ed.), *Infancy and Epistemology.* Brighton: Harvester Press.

Meltzoff, A. N. (1988a). Infant imitation and memory: Nine-month-old infants in immediate and deferred tests. *Child Development, 59,* 217–225.

Meltzoff, A. N. (1988b). Infant imitation after a 1-week delay: Long-term memory for novel acts and multiple stimuli. *Developmental Psychology, 24,* 470–476.

Meltzoff, A. N. (1990). Towards a developmental cognitive science. *Annals of the New York Academy of Sciences, 608,* 1–37.

Meltzoff, A. N., & Borton, R. W. (1979). Intermodal matching by human neonates. *Nature, 282,* 403–404.

Meltzoff, A. N., & Moore, M. K. (1983). Newborn infants imitate adult facial gestures. *Child Development, 54,* 702–709.

Mendle, J., Turkheimer, E., & Emery, R. E. (2007). Detrimental psychological outcomes associated with early pubertal timing in adolescent girls. *Developmental Review, 27,* 151–171.

Mennella, J. A., & Beauchamp, G. K. (1993). The effects of repeated exposure to garlic-flavored milk on the nursling's behavior. *Pediatric Research, 34,* 805–808.

Mennella, J. A., & Beauchamp, G. K. (1996). The human infants' response to vanilla flavors in mother's milk and formula. *Infant Behavior & Development, 19,* 13–19.

Mennella, J. A., & Beauchamp, G. K. (1999). Experience with a flavor in mother's milk modifies the infant's acceptance of flavored cereal. *Developmental Psychobiology, 35,* 197–203.

Mercer, J. R. (1971). Sociocultural factors in labeling mental retardates. *Peabody Journal of Education, 48,* 188–203.

Mercier, E. M., Barron, B., & O'Conner, K. M. (2006). Images of self and others as computer users: The role of gender and experience. *Journal of Computer Assisted Learning, 22,* 335–348.

Merewood, A. (2000). Sperm under siege. In K. L. Freiberg (Ed.), *Human Development 00/01* (28th ed., pp. 41-45). Guilford, CT: McGraw-Hill.

Merriman, W., & Bowman, L. (1989). The mutual exclusivity bias in children's word learning. *Monographs of the Society for Research in Child Development, 54.*

Merriman, W., Evey-Burke, J. A., Marazita, J. M., & Jarvis, L. H. (1996). Young two-year-olds' tendency to map novel verbs onto novel actions. *Journal of Experimental Child Psychology, 63,* 466–498.

Mervis, C. B., & Klein-Tasman, B. P. (2000). Williams syndrome: Cognition, personality, and adaptive behavior. *Mental Retardation and Developmental Disabilities Research Review, 6,* 148–158.

Mervis, C., & Mervis, J. (1982). Leopards are kitty cats: Object labeling by mothers for their thirteen-month-olds. *Child Development, 53,* 267–273.

Messinger, D., Fogel, A., & Dickson, K. L. (2001). All smiles are positive, but some smiles are more positive than others. *Developmental Psychology, 37,* 642–653.

Messinger, D. S., & Lester, B. M. (2006). Prenatal substance exposure and human development. In A. Fogel, B. J. King & S. Shankar (Eds.), *Human development in the 21st century: Visionary policy ideas from systems scientists.* Bethesda, MD: Council on Human Development.

Methot, S., Berthiaume, C., Aunos, M., & Pidgeon, C. (2001). Fragile X syndrome: A review of the literature./Le syndrome du X fragile: Etat des connaissances. *Revue Francophone de la Deficience Intellectuelle, 12,* 181–194.*

Metz, E., McLellan, J., & Youniss, J. (2003). Types of voluntary service and adolescents' civic development. *Journal of Adolescent Research, 18,* 188–203.

Milan, A. (2000). One Hundred Years of Families. *Canadian Social Trends, 4* (Spring).

Milan, S., Snow, S., & Belay, S. (2007). The context of preschool children's sleep: Racial/ethnic differences in sleep locations, routines, and concerns. *Journal of Family Psychology, 21,* 20–28.

Miller, C. J., Miller, S. R., Newcorn, J. H., & Halperin, J. M. (2008). Personality characteristics associated with persistent ADHD in late adolescents. *Journal of Abnormal Child Psychology, 36,* 165–173.*

Miller, G. A. (1956). The magical number seven, plus or minus two: Some limits on our capacity for processing information. *Psychological Review, 63,* 81–97.

Miller, J. G., & Bersoff, D. M. (1992). Culture and moral judgment: How are conflicts between justice and interpersonal responsibilities resolved? *Journal of Personality and Social Psychology, 62,* 541–554.

Miller, J. G., & Bersoff, D. M. (1999). Development in the context of everyday family relationships: Culture, interpersonal morality, and adaptation. In M. Killen & D. Hart (Eds.), *Morality in everyday life: Developmental perspectives* (pp. 259–282). New York: Cambridge University Press.

Miller, J. L., & Eimas, P. D. (1994). Observations on speech perception, its development, and the search for a mechanism. In J. C. Goodman & H. C. Nusbaum (Eds.), *The development of speech perception: The transition from speech sounds to spoken words* (pp. 37–56). Cambridge, MA: MIT Press.

Miller, K. F., Smith, C. M., Zhu, J., & Zhang, H. (1995). Preschool origins of cross-national differences in mathematical competence: The role of number-naming systems. *Psychological Science, 6,* 56–60.

Miller, L. T., & Vernon, P. A. (1996). Intelligence, reaction time, and working memory in 4- to 6-year-old children. *Intelligence, 22,* 155–190.*

Miller, L. T., & Vernon, P. A. (1997). Developmental changes in speed of information processing in young children. *Developmental Psychology, 33,* 549–554.*

Miller, M. N., & Pumariega, A. J. (2001). Eating disorders: Bulimia and anorexia nervosa. In V. H. Booney & A. J. Pumariega (Eds.), *Clinical assessment of child and adolescent behavior* (pp. 234–268). New York: Wiley. **Miller, P., & Sperry, L. L.** (1987). The socialization of anger and aggression. *Merrill-Palmer Quarterly, 33,* 1–31.

Miller, P. H. (1990). The development of strategies of selective attention. In D. F. Bjorklund (Ed.), *Children's strategies: Contemporary views of cognitive development* (pp. 157–184). Hillsdale, NJ: Erlbaum.

Miller, P. H. (2000). How best to utilize a deficiency. *Child Development, 71,* 1013–1017.

Miller, P. H. (2002). *Theories of developmental psychology* (4th ed.). New York: Worth.

Miller, P. H., & Aloise-Young, P. A. (1995). Preschoolers' strategic behavior and performance on a same-different task. *Journal of Experimental Child Psychology, 60,* 284–303.

Miller, P. H., & Seier, W. L. (1994). Strategy utilization deficiencies in children: When, where, and why. In H. W. Reese (Ed.), *Advances in child development and behavior* (Vol. 25, pp. 107–156). New York: Academic Press.

Miller, P. H., Seier, W. L., Probert, J. S., & Aloise, P. A. (1991). Age differences in the capacity demands of a strategy among spontaneously strategic children. *Journal of Experimental Child Psychology, 52,* 149–165.

Miller, P. H., & Weiss, M. G. (1981). Children's attention allocation, understanding of attention, and performance on the incidental learning task. *Child Development, 52,* 1183–1190.

Mills, J. L. (1999). Cocaine, smoking, and spontaneous abortion. *New England Journal of Medicine, 340,* 380–381.

Milstein, R. M. (1980). Responsiveness in newborn infants of overweight and normal weight parents. *Appetite, 1,* 65–74.

Minami, M., & McCabe, A. (1995). Rice balls and bear hunts: Japanese and North American family narrative patterns. *Journal of Child Language, 22,* 423–446.

Minuchin, P. (2001). Looking toward the horizon: Present and future in the study of family systems. In J. L. McHale & W. Grolnick (Eds.), *Retrospect and prospect in the psychological study of families* (pp. 259–278). Mahwah, NJ: Erlbaum.

Mishra, R. (1997). Cognition and cognitive development. In J. W. Berry, P. R. Dasen, & T. S. Saraswathi (Eds.), Handbook of cross-cultural psychology: Vol. 2, Basic process and human development (2nd ed., pp.143–175). Boston: Allyn & Bacon.

Mistry, J., Rogoff, B., & Herman, H. (2001). What is the meaning of meaningful purpose in children's remembering? Istomina revisited. *Mind, Culture, and Activity, 8,* 28–41.

Mitchell, E. A., Ford, R. P. K., Stewart, A. W., Taylor, B. J., Bescroft, D. M., Thompson, J. M. P., Scragg, R., Hassall, I. B., Barry, D. M. J., Allen, E. M., & Roberts, A. P. (1993). Smoking and the sudden infant death syndrome. *Pediatrics, 91,* 893–896.

Mitchell, J. E., Fletcher, L., Hanson, K., Mussell, M. P., Siem, H., Crosby, R., et al. (2001). The relative efficacy of fluoxetine and manual-based self-help in the treatment of outpatients with bulimia nervosa. *Journal of Clinical Psychopharmacology, 21,* 298–304.

Mitchell, P. (1997). *Introduction to theory of mind.* London: Arnold.

Miyake, K., Chen, S., & Campos, J. J. (1985). Infant temperament, mother's mode of interaction, and attachment in Japan: An interim report. In I. Bretherington & E. Waters (Eds.), *Growing points of attachment theory and research. Monographs of the Society for Research in Child Development, 50* (1–2, Serial No. 209).

Mize, J., & Ladd, G. W. (1990). Toward the development of successful social skills for preschool children. In S. R. Asher & J. D. Coie (Eds.), *Peer rejection in childhood.* New York: Cambridge University Press.

Moeller, T. G. (2001). *Youth aggression and violence.* Mahwah, NJ: Erlbaum.

Moffitt, A. R. (1971). Consonant cue perception by twenty to twenty-four week old infants. *Child Development, 42,* 717–732.

Moffitt, T. E. (2003). Life course persistent and adolescence-limited antisocial behavior: A 10-year research review and a research agenda. In B. B. Lahey, T. E. Moffitt & A. Caspi (Eds.), *Causes of conduct disorders and juvenile delinquency* (pp. 49–75). New York: Guilford.

Moffitt, T. E., & Caspi, A. (2006). Evidence from behavioral genetics for environmental contributions to antisocial conduct. In J. E. Grusec & P. Hastings (Eds.), *Handbook of socialization* (pp. 259–283). New York: Guildford.*

Moffitt, T. E., Caspi, A., Belsky, J., & Silva, P. A. (1992). Childhood experience and the onset of menarche: A test of a sociobiological model. *Child Development, 63,* 47–58.

Moffitt, T. E., Caspi, A., Harkness, A. R., & Silva, P. A. (1993). The natural history of change in intellectual performance: Who changes? How much? Is it meaningful? *Journal of Child Psychology & Psychiatry & Allied Disciplines, 34,* 455–506.

Moffitt, T. E., Caspi, A., Rutter, M., & Silva, P. A. (2001). *Sex differences in antisocial behavior.* Cambridge, UK: Cambridge University Press.

Mohn, G., & van Hof-van Duin (1986). Development of binocular and monocular visual fields of human infants during the first year of life. *Clinical Visual Science, 1,* 51–64.

Molfese, D. L. (1973). Cerebral asymmetry in infants, children, and adults: Auditory evoked responses to speech and musical stimuli. *Journal of the Acoustical Society of America, 53,* 363.

Molfese, D. L., & Betz, J. C. (1988). Electrophysiological indices of the early development of lateralization for language and cognition, and their implications for predicting later development. In D. L. Molfese & S. J. Segalowitz (Eds.), *Brain lateralization in children: Developmental implications* (pp. 171–190). New York: Guilford Press.

Molfese, D. L., & Molfese, V. J. (1985). Electrophysiological indices of auditory discrimination in newborn infants: The bases for predicting later language development? *Infant Behavior and Development, 8,* 197–211.

Molfese, D. L., Morse, P. A., & Peters, C. J. (1990). Auditory evoked responses to names for different objects: Cross-modal processing as a basis for infant language acquisition. *Developmental Psychology, 26,* 780–795.

Molfese, V. J., & Martin, T. B. (2001). Intelligence and achievement: Measurement and prediction of developmental relations. In D. L. Molfese & V. J. Molfese (Eds.), *Developmental variations in learning: Applications to social, executive function, language, and reading skills* (pp. 1–22). Mahwah, NJ: Erlbaum.

Mondloch, C. J., Lewis, T. L., Budreau, D. R., Maurer, D., Dannemiller, J. L., Stephens, B. R., & Kleiner-Gathercoal, K. A. (1999). Face perception during early infancy. *Psychological Science, 10,* 419–422.*

Mondschein, E. R., Adolph, K. E., & Tamis-LeMonda, C. S. (2000). Gender biases in mothers' expectations about infant crawling. *Journal of Experimental Child Psychology, 77,* 304–316.

Money, J. (1987). Propaedeutics of dioecious G-I/R: Theoretical foundations for understanding dimorphic gender-identity/role. In J. M. Reinisch, L. A. Rosenblum, & S. A. Sanders (Eds.), *Masculinity/femininity: Basic perspectives.* New York: Oxford University Press.

Money, J. (1993). Specific neurocognitional impairments associated with Turner (45, X) and Klinefelter (47, XXY) syndromes: A review. *Social Biology, 40,* 147–151.

Money, J., & Annecillo, C. (1987). Crucial period effect in psychoendocrinology: Two syndromes abuse dwarfism and female (CVAH) hermaphroditism. In M. H. Bornstein (Ed.), *Sensitive periods in development: Interdisciplinary perspectives.* Hillsdale, NJ: Erlbaum.

Money, J., & Ehrhardt, A. A. (1972). *Man and woman, boy and girl.* Baltimore, MD: Johns Hopkins University Press.

Monk, C., Fifer, W. P., Myers, M. M., Sloan, R. P., Trien, L., & Hurtado, A. (2000). Maternal stress responses and anxiety during pregnancy: Effects on fetal heart rate. *Developmental Psychology, 36,* 67–77.

Montague, D. P. F., & Walker-Andrews, A. S. (2002). Mothers, fathers, and infants: The role of person familiarity and parental involvement in infants' perception of emotion expressions. *Child Development, 75,* 1339–1352.

Moon, C., Cooper, R. P., & Fifer, W. P. (1993). Two-day-olds prefer their native language. *Infant Behavior & Development, 16,* 495–500.

Moore, C., & Corkum, V. (1994). Social understanding at the end of the first year. *Developmental Review, 14,* 349–372.*

Moore, C., & D'entremont, B. (2001). Developmental changes in pointing as a function of attentional focus. *Journal of Cognition and Development, 2,* 109–129.*

Moore, C., Barresi, J., & Thompson, C. (1998). The cognitive basis of future-oriented prosocial behavior. *Social Development, 7,* 198–218.*

Moore, D. S. (2001). *The dependent gene: The fallacy of "nature vs. nurture."* New York: Freeman

Moore, K. L. (1989). *Before we are born.* Philadelphia: Saunders.

Moore, K. L., & Persaud, T. V. N. (1998). *Before we are born* (5th ed.). Philadelphia, PA: Saunders.

Moore, M., & Russ, S. W. (2006). Pretend play as a resource for children: Implications for pediatricians and health professionals. *Journal of Developmental and Behavioral Pediatrics, 27,* 237–348.

Moore, M. R., & Brooks-Gunn, J. (2002). Adolescent parenthood. In M. H. Bornstein (Ed.), *Handbook of parenting* (2nd ed., pp. 173–214). Mahwah, NJ: Erlbaum.

Moran, G., Forbes, L., Evans, E., Tarabulsy, G. M., & Madigan, M. (2008). Both maternal sensitivity and atypical maternal behavior independently predict attachment security and disorganization in adolescent mother-infant relationships. *Infant Behavior and Development, 31,* 321–325.*

Moran, G., & Pederson, D. R. (1998). Proneness to distress and ambivalent relationships. *Infant Behavior and Development, 21,* 493–503.*

Moran, S., & Gardner, H. (2006). Extraordinary achievements: A developmental and systems analysis. In W. Damon & R. M. Lerner (Gen. Ed.), & D. Kuhn & R. S. Siegler (Eds.), *Handbook of child psychology: Vol. 2. Cognition, perception, and language* (6th ed., pp. 905–949). New York: Wiley.

Morelli, G., Rogoff, B., & Angellio, C. (2003). Cultural variation in young children's access to work or involvement in specialised child-focused activities. *International Journal of Behavioral Development, 27,* 264–274.

Morelli, G. A., Rogoff, B., Oppenheim, D., & Goldsmith, D. (1992). Cultural variation in infants' sleeping arrangements: Questions of independence. *Developmental Psychology, 28,* 604–613.

Morelli, G. A., & Tronick, E. Z. (1992). Male care among Efe foragers and Lese farmers. In B. Hewlett (Ed.), *Father–child relations: Cultural and biosocial contexts* (pp. 231–262). New York: Aldine de Gruyther.

Moreno, M. A. (2006). Eating disorder: Bulimia. Retrieved 28 November, 2007, from http://www.emedicine.com.

Morgan, B. L. (1998). A three-generational study of tomboy behavior. *Sex Roles, 39,* 787–858.

Morgan, G. A., & Ricciuti, H. (1969). Infants' responses to strangers during the first year. In B. M. Foss (Ed.), *Determinants of infant behavior* (Vol. 4, pp. 253–272). London: Methuen.

Morgan, J. L. (1990). Input, innateness, and induction in language acquisition. *Developmental Psychology, 23,* 661–678.

Morgan, J. L. (1994). Converging measures of speech segmentation in preverbal infants. *Infant Behavior and Development, 17,* 387–403.

Morgan, J. L., & Saffran, J. R. (1995). Emerging integration of sequential and suprasegmental information in preverbal speech segmentation. *Child Development, 16,* 911–936.

Moris, P., Meesters, C., & van den Berg, S. (2003). Internalizing and externalizing problems as correlates of self-reported attachment styles and perceived parental rearing in normal adolescents. *Journal of Child and Family Studies, 12,* 171–183.

Morison, S. J., Ames, E. W., & Chisholm, K. (1995). The development of children adopted from Romanian orphanages. *Merrill-Palmer Quarterly, 41,* 411–430.*

Morris, P., Huston, A. C., Duncan, G. J., Crosby, D. A., & Bos, J. M. (2001). *How welfare and work policies affect children: A synthesis of research.* New York: Manpower Demonstration Research Corporation.

Morris, P. A., & Gennetian, L. A. (2003). Identifying the effects of income on children's development using experimental data. *Journal of Marriage and Family, 65,* 716–729.

Morrisette, P., Ricard, M., & Goiun-Decarie, T. (1995). Joint visual attention and pointing in infancy: A longitudinal study. *British Journal of Developmental Psychology, 13,* 163–175.*

Morrison, F. J., Holmes, D. L., & Haith, M. M. (1974). A developmental study of the effect of familiarity on short-term visual memory. *Journal of Experimental Child Psychology, 18,* 412–425.

Morrongiello, B. A. (1996). Unintentional injuries in children: Why do boys have more injuries than girls? *The Canadian Health Psychologist, 3,* 22–26.*

Morrongiello, B. A. (1997). Children's perspectives on injury and close-call experiences: Sex differences in injury-outcome processes. *Journal of Pediatric Psychology, 22,* 499–512.*

Morrongiello, B. A., & Dawber, T. (1999). Parental influences on toddler's injury-risk behaviors: Are sons and daughters socialized differently? *Journal of Applied Developmental Psychology, 20,* 227–251.*

Morrongiello, B. A., & Dawber, T. (2000). Mothers' responses to sons and daughters engaging in injury-risk behaviors on a playground: Implications for sex differences in injury rates. *Journal of Experimental Child Psychology, 76,* 89–103.*

Morrongiello, B. A., Fenwick, K. D., Hillier, L., & Chance, G. (1994). Sound localization in newborn human infants. *Developmental Psychobiology, 27,* 519–538.*

Morrongiello, B. A., Hewitt, K. L., & Gotowiec, A. (1991). Infant discrimination of relative distance in the auditory modality: Approaching versus receding sound sources. *Infant Behavior Development, 14,* 187–208.

Morrongiello, B. A., & Hogg, K. (2004). Mothers' reactions to children's behaving in ways that can lead to injury: Implications for gender differences in children's risk taking and injuries. *Sex Roles, 50,* 103–118.*

Morrongiello, B. A., Klemencic, N., & Corbett, M. (2008). Interactions between child behavior patterns and parent supervision: Implications for children's risk of unintentional injury. *Child Development, 79,* 627–638.*

Morrongiello, B. A., Midgett, C., & Stanton, K. L. (2000). Gender biases in children's appraisals of injury risk and other children's risk taking behaviors. *Journal of Experimental Child Psychology, 77,* 317–336.*

Morrongiello, B. A., & Rennie, H. (1998). Why do boys engage in more risk taking than girls? The role of attributions, beliefs, and risk appraisals. *Journal of Pediatric Psychology, 23,* 33–43.*

Morrongiello, B. A., Timney, B., Humphrey, G. K., Anderson, A., & Skory, C. (1995). Spatial knowledge in blind and sighted children. *Journal of Experimental Child Psychology, 59,* 211–233.*

Moshman, D. (1998). Cognitive development beyond childhood. In W. Damon (Gen. Ed.), D. Kuhn & R. S. Siegler (Vol. Eds.), *Handbook of child psychology: Vol. 2. Cognition, perception, and language* (pp. 947–978). New York: Wiley.

Moskowitz, D. S., Schwartzman, A. E., & Ledingham, J. E. (1985). Stability and change in aggression and withdrawal in middle childhood and early adolescence. *Journal of Abnormal Psychology, 94,* 30–41.*

Moss, E., Cyr, C., Bureau, J.-F., Tarabulsy, G. M., & Dubois-Comtois, K. (2005). Stability of attachment during the preschool period. *Developmental Psychology, 41,* 773–783.*

Moss, E., Gosselin, C., Parent, S., Rousseau, D., & Dumont, M. (1998). Attachment and joint problem-solving experiences during the preschool period. *Social Development, 6,* 1–17.*

Moss, E., & St-Laurent, D. (2001). Attachment at school age and academic performance. *Developmental Psychology, 37,* 863–874.*

Moss, E., St-Laurent, D., Rousseau, D., Parent, S., Gosselin, C., & Saintonge, J. (1999). L'attachment à l'âge scolaire et la développement des troubles de comportement. *Canadian Journal of Behavioural Science, 31,* 107–118.*

Moss, E., Smolla, N., Cyr, C., Dubois-Comtois, K., Mazzarello, T., & Berthiaume, C. (2006). Attachment and behavior problems in middle childhood as reported by adult and child informants. *Development and Psychopathology, 18,* 425–444.*

Moss, H. (1967). Sex, age and state as determinants of mother-infant interaction. *Merrill-Palmer Quarterly, 13,* 19–36.

Mounts, N. S. (2000). Parental management of adolescent peer relationships: What are its effects on friend selection? In K. Kerns & J. M. Contreras & A. M. Neal-Barnett (Eds.), *Family and peers: Linking two social worlds* (pp. 169–194). Westport, CT: Praeger.

Mounts, N. S., & Steinberg, L. (1995). An ecological analysis of peer influences on adolescent grade point average and drug use. *Developmental Psychology, 31,* 915–922.

Muckle, G., Dewailly, E., & Ayotte, P. (1998). Prenatal exposure of Canadian children to polychlorinated biphenyls and mercury. *Canadian Journal of Public Health, 89 (Supp. 1),* S20–S25.*

Mueller, E., & Brenner, J. (1977). The origins of social skills and interaction among playgroup toddlers. *Child Development, 48,* 854–861.

Mueller, E., & Lucas, T. A. (1975). A developmental analysis of peer interaction among toddlers. In M. Lewis & L. A. Rosenblum (Eds.), *Friendship and peer relations.* New York: Wiley.

Mullane, J. C., & Corkum, P. V. (2007). The relationship between working memory, inhibition, and performance on the Wisconsin Card Sorting Test in children with and without ADHD. *Journal of Psychoeducational Assessment, 25,* 211–221.*

Mullen, M. K., & Yi, S. (1995). The cultural context of talk about the past: Implications for the development of autobiographical memory. *Cognitive Development, 10,* 407–419.

Mumme, D. L., Fernald, A., & Herrera, C. (1996). Infants' responses to facial and vocal emotional signals in a social referencing paradigm. *Child Development, 67,* 3219–3237.

Munakata, Y., McClelland, J. L., Johnson, M. J., & Siegler, R. S. (1997). Rethinking infant knowledge: Toward an adaptive process account of successes and failures in object permanence tasks. *Psychological Review, 104,* 686–713.

Munroe, R. H., Munroe, R. L., & Brasher, A. (1985). Precursors of spatial ability: A longitudinal study among the Logoli of Kenya. *The Journal of Social Psychology, 125,* 23–33.

Murata, M. (2000). Secular trends in growth and changes in eating patterns of Japanese children. *American Journal of Clinical Nutrition, 72,* 1379s–1383s.

Murphy, K., & Schneider, B. H. (1994b). Coaching socially rejected early adolescents regarding behaviors used by peers to infer liking: A dyad specific intervention. *Journal of Early Adolescence, 14,* 83–95.*

Murphy, M. M., & Mazzocco, M. M. (2008). Mathematics learning disabilities in girls with fragile X or Turner syndrome during late elementary school. *Journal of Learning Disabilities, 41,* 29–46.

Murray, J. P., Liotti, M., Mayberry, H. S., Pu, Y., Zamarripa, F., Liu, Y., et al. (2006). Children's brain activations while viewing televised violence revealed by fMRI. *Media Psychology, 8,* 25–37.

Murray, K., & Kochanska, G. (2002). Effortful control: Factor structure and relation to externalizing and internalizing behaviors. *Journal of Abnormal Child Psychology, 30,* 503–514.

Murray, T. A. (1996). *The worth of a child.* Berkeley, CA: University of California Press.

Mustard, C. A., & Roos, N. P. (1994). The relationship of prenatal care and pregnancy complication to birthweight in Winnipeg, Canada. *American Journal of Public Health, 84,* 1450–1457.*

Muzzatti, B., & Agnoli, F. (2007). Gender and mathematics: Attitudes and stereotype threat susceptibility in Italian children. *Developmental Psychology, 43,* 747–759.

Myers, D. G. (2000). *The American paradox: Spiritual hunger in an age of plenty.* New Haven, CT: Yale University Press.

Myers, N. A., Clifton, R. K., & Clarkson, M. G. (1987). When they were young: Almost-threes remember two years ago. *Infant Behavior and Development, 10,* 123–132.

Myers, S. M. (2007). The status of pharmacotherapy for autism spectrum disorders. *Expert Opinion of Pharmacotherapy, 8,* 1579–1603.

Myles-Worsley, M., Cromer, C. C., & Dodd, D. H. (1986). Children's preschool script reconstruction: Reliance on general knowledge as memory fades. *Developmental Psychology, 22,* 22–30.

Nader, P. R. (1993). The role of the family in obesity: Prevention and treatment. In C. L. Williams & S. Y. S. Kimm (Eds.), *Prevention and treatment of childhood obesity* (pp. 147–153). Annals of the New York Academy of Sciences, Vol. 699. New York: The New York Academy of Sciences.

Nagin, D., & Tremblay, R. E. (1999). Trajectories of boys' physical aggression, opposition, and hyperactivity on the path to physically violent and nonviolent juvenile delinquency. *Child Development, 70,* 1181–1196.*

Naigles, L. (1990). Children use syntax to learn verb meanings. *Journal of Child Languages, 17,* 357–374.

Nantais, K. M., & Schellenberg, E. G. (1999). The Mozart effect: An artifact of preference. *Psychological Science, 10,* 370–373.*

Nash, J. M. (1997, February 3). Fertile minds. *Time,* pp. 49–62.

National Center for Health Statistics. (1976). *NCHS growth charts.* Washington, DC: U.S. Department of Health and Human Services.

National Center for Health Statistics. (2000). 2000 CDC growth charts: United States. Retrieved 5 August 2008, from http://www.cdc.gov/growthcharts/.

National Center for Health Statistics. (2002). *Overweight prevalence.* Retrieved from www.cdc.gov/nchs/fastats/overwt.htm

National Center for Health Statistics. (2006). Overweight prevalence. Retrieved 8 August, 2008, from www.cdc.gov/nchs/fastats/overwt.htm.

National Institute of Child Health and Human Development, Early Child Care Network. (1997). The effects of infant child care on infant-mother attachment security: Results of the NICHD study of early child care. *Child Development, 68,* 860–879.

National Institutes of Health. (2002). *The National Human Genome Research Institute Website.* www.nhgri.nih.gov/.

National Joint Committee on Learning Disabilities. (1994). Learning disabilities: Issues on definition, a position paper of the National Joint Committee on Learning Disabilities. In *Collective perspectives on issues affecting learning disabilities: Position papers and statements.* Austin, TX: Pro-Ed.

Naus, M. J. (1982). Memory development in the young reader: The combined effects of knowledge base and memory processing. In W. Otto & S. White (Eds.), *Reading expository text.* New York: Academic.

Nazzi, T., & Gopnik, A. (2001). Linguistic and cognitive abilities in infancy: When does language become a tool for categorization? *Cognition, 80,* 30–37.

Neal, M. V. (1968). Vestibular stimulation and developmental behavior of the small premature infant. *Nursing Research Report, 3,* 2–5.

Neisser, U. (Ed.). (1998). *The rising curve: Long-term gains in IQ and related measures.* Washington, DC: American Psychological Association.

Neisser, U., Boodoo, G., Bouchard, T. J., Boykin, A. W., Brody, N., Ceci, S. J., Halpern, D. F., Loehlin, J. C., Perloff, R., Sternberg, R. J., & Urbina, S. (1995). *Intelligence: Knowns and unknowns.* Washington, DC: American Psychological Association.

Nelson, C. A. (1999a). Change and continuity in neurobehavioral development: Lessons from the study of neurobiology and neural plasticity. *Infant Behavior and Development, 22,* 416–429.

Nelson, C. A. (1999b). Neural plasticity and human development. *Current Directions in Psychological Science, 8,* 42–45.

Nelson, C. A. (2001). The development and neural basis of face recognition. *Infant and Child Development, 10,* 3–18.

Nelson, C. A., & Bosquet, M. (2000). Neurobiology of fetal and infant development: Implications for infant mental health. In C. Zeanah (Ed.), *Handbook of infant mental health* (pp. 37–59). New York: Guilford Press.

Nelson, C. A., Thomas, K. M., & De Haan, M. (2006). Neural bases of cognitive development. In W. Damon & R. L. Lerner (Gen. Ed.), & D. Kuhn & R. Siegler (Eds.), *Handbook of child psychology. Vol. 2: Cognition, perception and language* (pp. 3–57). New York: Wiley.

Nelson, G., Pancer, S. M., Hayward, S., & Peters, R. D. (2005). *Partnerships for prevention: The story of the Highfield Community Enrichment Project.* Toronto, ON: University of Toronto Press.

Nelson, K. (1973). Structure and strategy in learning to talk. *Monographs of the Society for Research in Child Development, 38* (1, 2).

Nelson, K. (1988). Constraints on word learning? *Cognitive Development, 3,* 221–246.

Nelson, K. (1989). Strategies for first language teaching. In M. L. Rice & R. L. Schiefelbusch (Eds.), *The teachability of language.* Baltimore, MD: Brooks/Cole.

Nelson, K. (1993). Events, narratives, memory: What develops? In C. A. Nelson (Ed.), *Memory and affect in development. The Minnesota symposia on child psychology* (Vol. 26, pp. 1–24). Hillsdale, NJ: Erlbaum.

Nelson, K. (1996). *Language in cognitive development: The emergence of the mediated mind.* New York: Cambridge University Press.

Nelson, K. (2007). *Young minds in social worlds: Experience, meaning and memory.* Cambride, MA: Harvard University Press.

Nelson, K., & Fivush, R. (2004). The emergence of autobiographical memory: A social cultural developmental theory. *Psychological Review, 111,* 486–511.

Nelson, K. E., Welsh, J., Camarata, S. M., Butkovsky, L., & Camarata, M. (1995). Available input for language-impaired children and younger children of matched language levels. *First Language, 15,* 1–17.

Nelson, L. D., Scheibel, K. E., Ringman, J. M., & Sayre, J. W. (2007). An experimental approach to detecting dementia in Down syndrome: A paradigm for Alzheimer's disease. *Brain and Cognition, 64,* 92–103.

Neumann, C. G., Murphy, S. P., Gewa, C., Grillenberger, M., & Bwibo, N. O. (2007). Mean supplementation improves growth, cognitive, and behavioral outcomes in Kenyan children. *Journal of Nutrition, 137,* 1119–1123.

Neville, B., & Parke, R. D. (1997). Waiting for paternity: Interpersonal and contextual implications of the timing of fatherhood. *Sex Roles, 37,* 45–59.

Neville, H. J. (1991). Neurobiology of cognitive and language processing: Effects of early experience. In K. R. Gibson & A. C. Petersen (Eds.), *Brain maturation and cognitive development: Comparative and cross-cultural perspectives* (pp. 355–380). New York: Aldine de Bruyter.

Neville, H. J., & Bruer, J. T. (2001). Language processing: How experience affects brain organization. In D. B. Bailey, J. T. Bruer, F. J. Simons & J. W. Lichtman (Eds.), *Critical thinking about critical periods* (pp. 151–172). Baltimore: Paul H. Broker.

Nevin, M. M. (1988). Dormant dangers of DES. *The Canadian Nurse, 84,* 17–19.*

Newcomb, A. F., Bukowski, W. M., & Pattee, L. (1993). Children's peer relations: A meta-analytic review of popular, rejected, neglected, controversial, and average sociometric status. *Psychological Bulletin, 113,* 99–128.

Newcomb, M. D., & Bentler, P. M. (1989). Substance use and abuse among children and teenagers. *American Psychologist, 44,* 242–248.

Newcombe, N. S., & Huttenlocher, J. (2003). *Making space: The development of spatial representation and reasoning.* Cambridge, MA: MIT Press.

Newcombe, N. S., Huttenlocher, J., Drummey, A. B., & Wiley, J. (1998). The development of spatial location coding: Place learning and dead reckoning in the second and third years of life. *Cognitive Development, 13,* 185–200.

Newcomer, S., & Udry, J. R. (1987). Parental marital status effects on adolescent sexual behavior. *Journal of Marriage and the Family, 48,* 235–240.

Newell, K., Scully, D. M., McDonald, P. V., & Baillargeon, R. (1989). Task constraints and infant grip configurations. *Developmental Psychobiology, 22,* 817–832.

Newport, E. L. (1990). Maturational constraints on language learning. *Cognitive Science, 14,* 11–28.

NHLBI Growth and Health Study Research Group. (1992). *American Journal of Public Health, 82,* 1613–1620.

NICHD Early Child Care Research Network. (1999). Chronicity of maternal depressive symptoms, maternal sensitivity, and child functioning. *Developmental Psychology, 35,* 1297–1310.

NICHD Early Child Care Research Network. (2000a). The relation of child care to cognitive and language development. *Child Development, 71,* 960–980.

NICHD Early Child Care Research Network. (2000b). Factors associated with fathers' caregiving activities NICHD Early Child Care Research Network. (2003). Does amount of time spent in child care predict socioemotional adjustment during the transition to kindergarten? *Child Development, 74,* 976–1005.

NICHD Early Child Care Research Network. (2003). Frequency and intensity of activity of third grade children in physical education. *Archives of Pediatrics and Adolescent Medicine, 157,* 185–190.

NICHD Early Child Care Research Network. (2004a). Are child developmental outcomes related to before/after school care arrangements. *Child Development, 75,* 280–295.

NICHD Early Child Care Research Network. (2004b). Trajectories of physical aggression from toddlerhood to middle childhood: Predictors, correlates, and outcomes. *Monographs of the Society for Research in Child Development.*

Nigg, J. T., & Goldsmith, H. H. (1994). Genetics of personality disorders: Perspectives from personality and psychopathology research. *Psychological Bulletin, 115,* 346–380.

Nightingale, E. O., & Meister, S. B. (1987). *Prenatal screening, policies, and values: Three examples of neural tube defects.* Cambridge, MA: Harvard University Press.

Ninio, A., & Snow, C. (1996). *Pragmatic development.* Boulder, CO: Westview Press.

Nisan, M., & Kohlberg, L. (1982). Universality and variation in moral judgment: A longitudinal and cross-sectional study in Turkey. *Child Development, 53,* 865–876.

Nisbett, R. E. (1998). Race, genetics, and IQ. In C. Jencks & M. Philips (Eds.), *The black-white test score gap* (pp. 96–102). Washington, DC: Brookings Institute.

Nittrouer, S. (2001). Challenging the notion of innate phonetic boundaries. *Journal of the Acoustical Society of America, 110,* 1598–1605.

Nolan, E. E., Gadow, K., & Sprafkin, J. (2001). Teacher reports of DSM-IV ADHD, ODD, and CD symptoms in schoolchildren. *Journal of the American Academy of Child and Adolescent Psychiatry, 40,* 241–249.

Noll, J. G., Trickett, P. K., Harris, W. W., & Putnam, F. W. (2009). The cumulative burden borne by offspring whose mothers were sexually abused as children: Descriptive results from a multigenerational study. *Journal of Interpersonal Violence. Special Section. Research Methodology, 24,* 424–449.

Noll, J. G., Trickett, P. K., Susman, E. J., & Putnam, F. W. (2006). Sleep disturbances and childhood sexual abuse. *Journal of Pediatric Psychology, 31,* 469–480.

Norlander, T., Erixon, A., & Archer, T. (2000). Psychological androgyny and creativity: Dynamics of gender roles and personality traits. *Social Behavior and Personality, 28,* 423–435.

North, A. S., & Noyes, J. M. (2002). Gender influences on children's computer attitudes and cognition. *Computers in Human Behavior, 18,* 135–150.

Northway, M. L. (1973). Child study in Canada: A causal history. In L. M. Brockman & J. H. Whiteley & J. P. Zubek (Eds.), *Child development: Selected readings* (pp. 10–46). NY: McClelland and Stewart.*

Novak, G. (1996). *Developmental Psychology: Dynamic systems and behavioral analysis.* Reno, NV: Context Press.

Novich, L. R., & Bassok, M. (2005). Problem solving. In K. J. Holyoak & R. G. Morrison (Eds.), *The Cambridge handbook of thinking and reasoning* (pp. 321–349). New York: Cambridge University Press.

Nucci, L. P., & Turiel, E. (1978). Social interactions and the development of social concepts in preschool children. *Child Development, 49,* 400–407.

Nugent, J. K., Lester, B. M., & Brazelton, T. B. (Eds.). (1989). *Biology, culture, and development.* Norwood, NJ: Ablex.

Nugent, J. K., Lester, B. M., & Brazelton, T. B. (1991). *The cultural context of infancy, Vol. 2: Multicultural and interdisciplinary approaches to parent-infant relations.* Westport, CT: Ablex.

Nulman, I., Ickowicz, A., Koren, G., & Knittel-Keren, D. (2007). Fetal alcohol spectrum disorder. In I. Brown & M. Percy (Eds.), *A comprehensive guide to intellectual and developmental disabilities* (pp. 213–227). Baltimore, MD: Paul H. Brookes Publishing.*

Nunes, T., & Bryant, P. (1996). *Children doing mathematics.* Oxford: Blackwell.

Nwokah, E. E., Hsu, H., Dobrowolska, O., & Fogel, A. (1994). The development of laughter in mother-infant communication: Timing parameters and temporal sequences. *Infant Behavior & Development, 17,* 23–35.

O'Brien, M., Huston, A. C., & Risley, T. (1983). Sex-typed play of toddlers in a day care center. *Journal of Applied Developmental Psychology, 4,* 1–9.

O'Conner, N., & Hermelin, B. (1976). Backward and forward recall by deaf and hearing children. *Journal of Experimental Psychology, 28,* 83–92.

O'Neil, R., Parke, R. D., & McDowell, D. J. (2001). Objective and subjective features of children's neighborhoods: Relations to parental regulatory strategies and children's social competence. *Journal of Applied Developmental Psychology, 21,* 135–155.

O'Sullivan, J. T. (1996). Children's metamemory about the influence of conceptual relations on recall. *Journal of Experimental Child Psychology, 62,* 1–29.*

O'Sullivan, J. T., & Pressley, M. (1984). Completeness of instruction and strategy transfer. *Journal of Experimental Child Psychology, 38,* 275–288.*

Ochs, E. (1988). *Culture and language development.* Cambridge: Cambridge University Press.

Oehler, J. M., Eckerman, C. D., & Wilson, W. H. (1988). Social stimulation and the regulation of premature infant's state prior to term age. *Infant Behavior and Development, 12,* 341–356.

Official Languages Act. (1985). *R.S. 1985, C. 31 (4th supp).* Available at: http://laws.justice.gc.ca/e/o-3.01/88156.html [2003, Dec. 9].

Ogbu, J. (1988). Black education: A cultural-ecological perspective. In H. P. McAdoo (Ed.), *Black families* (pp. 169–186). Beverly Hills, CA: Sage.

Ohan, J. L., Cormier, N., Hepp, S. L., Visser, T. A. W., & Strain, M. C. (2008). Does knowledge about attention-deficit/hyperactivity disorder impact teachers' reported behaviors and perceptions? *School Psychology Quarterly, 23,* 436–449.*

Okamoto, Y., & Case, R. (1996). Exploring the microstructure of children's central conceptual structures in the domain of number. In R. Case & Y. Okamoto (Eds.), *The role of central conceptual structures in the development of children's thought. Monographs of the Society for Research in Child Development, 61,* Serial No. 246 Nos. 1 & 2.*

Ollendick, T. H., & King, N. J. (1998). Empirically supported treatments for children with phobic and anxiety disorders: Current status. *Journal of Clinical Child Psychology, 22,* 156–167.

Oller, D. K., Wieman, L. A., Doyle, W. J., & Ross, C. (1976). Infant babbling and speech. *Journal of Child Language, 3,* 1–11.

Olney, D. K., Pollitt, E., Kariger, P. K., Khalfan, S. S., Ali, N. S., Tielsch, J. M., et al. (2006). Combined iron and folic acid supplementation with or without zinc reduces time to walking unassisted among Zanzibari infants 5- to 11-months old. *Journal of Nutrition, 136,* 2427–2434.

Olsen, O. (1997). Meta-analysis of the safety of home birth. *Birth, 24,* 4–13.

Olson, D. R., & Cole, M. (2006). *Technology, literacy, and the evolution of society: Implications of the work of Jack Goody.* Mahwah, NJ: Erlbaum.

Olweus, D. (1993). *Bullying and school: What we know and what we can do.* Oxford: Blackwell.

Olweus, D. (2000). *Bullying.* New York: Oxford University Press.

Olweus, D. (2003). *Social problems in school.* Malden, MA: Blackwell.

Olweus, D., Mattson, A., Schalling, D., & Low, H. (1988). Circulating testosterone levels and aggression in adolescent males: A causal analysis. *Psychosomatic Medicine, 50,* 261–272.

Opie, I., & Opie, P. (1959). *The lore and language of schoolchildren.* Oxford: Clarendon Press.

Organization for Economic Co-operation and Development. (1998). *OECD Health Data 98* (CD-ROM).

Ornstein, P. A., Larus, D. M., & Clubb, P. A. (1992). Understanding children's testimony: Implications of research on the development of memory. In R. Vasta (Ed.), *Annals of Child Development* (Vol. 8). London: Jessica Kingsley Publishers.

Ornstein, P. A., Naus, M. J., & Liberty, C. (1975). Rehearsal and organizational processes in children's memory. *Child Development, 46,* 818–830.

Ostrov, J. M., & Crick, N. R. (2006). How recent developments in the study of relational aggression and close relationships in early childhood advance the field. *Journal of Applied Developmental Psychology, 27,* 189–192.

Ottosson, H., Ekselius, L., Grann, M., and Kullgren, G. (2002). Cross-system concordance of personality disorder diagnoses of DSM-IV and diagnostic criteria for research of ICD-10. *Journal of Personality Disorders, 16,* 283–292.

Overton, W. F., & Byrnes, J. P. (1991). Cognitive development. In R. M. Lerner, A. C. Petersen, & J. Brooks-Gunn (Eds.), *Encyclopedia of adolescence* (Vol. 1). New York: Garland.

Pagini, L., Boulerice, B., Tremblay, R. E., & Vitaro, F. (1997). Behavioral development in children of divorce and remarriage. *Journal of Child Psychology and Psychiatry and Allied Disciplines, 38,* 769–781.*

Pagini, L., Larocque, D., Vitaro, F., & Tremblay, R. E. (2003). Verbal and physical abuse toward mothers: The role of family configuration, environment, and coping strategies. *Journal of Youth and Adolescence, 32,* 215–222.*

Pagini, L., Tremblay, R. E., Vitaro, F., Kerr, M., & McDuff, P. (1998). The impact of family transition on the development of delinquency in adolescent boys: A 9-year longitudinal study. *Journal of Psychology and Psychiatry and Allied Disciplines, 39,* 489–499.*

Paley, B., Cox, M. J., Burchinal, M. R., & Payne, C. C. (1999).

Attachment and family functioning: Comparison of spouses with continuous-secure, earned-secure, dismissing and preoccupied attachment stances. *Journal of Family Psychology, 13,* 580–597.

Palincsar, A. S., & Brown, A. L. (1984). Reciprocal teaching of comprehension fostering and comprehension monitoring activities. *Cognitive and Instruction, 1,* 117–175.

Papageorgiou, A. B. (1982). *"My daddy might have loved me": Student perceptions of differences between being male and female.* Denver: University of Colorado.

Papp, L. M., Cummings, E. M., & Goeke-Morey, M. C. (2002). Marital conflicts in the home when children are present versus absent. *Developmental Psychology, 38,* 774–783.

Paradis, M. (1990). Differential recovery of languages in a bilingual patient following selective amytal injection: A comment Berthier et al. (1990). *Brain and Language, 39,* 469–470.*

Paradis, M. (1996). Selective deficit in one language is not a demonstration of different anatomical representation: Comments on Gomez-Tortosa et al. (1995). *Brain and Language, 54,* 170–173.*

Parke, R. D. (1977). Punishment in children: Effects, side effects and alternative strategies. In H. Hom & P. Robinson (Eds.), *Psychological processes in early education* (pp. 71–97). New York: Academic.

Parke, R. D. (1988). Families in life-span perspective: A multilevel developmental approach. In E. M. Hetherington, R. M. Lerner & M. Perlmutter (Eds.), *Child development in life-span perspective* (pp. 159–190). Hillsdale, NJ: Erlbaum.

Parke, R. D. (1996). *Fatherhood.* Cambridge, MA: Harvard University Press.

Parke, R. D. (2002a). Fatherhood. In M. H. Bornstein (Ed.), *Handbook of parenting* (2nd ed.). Mahwah, NJ: Erlbaum.

Parke, R. D., & Buriel, R. (2006). Socialization in the family: Ethnic and ecological perspectives. In W. Damon & R. M. Lerner (Gen. Ed.), & N. Eisenberg (Ed.), *Handbook of child psychology: Vol. 3. Social, emotional and personality development* (6th ed., pp. 429–504). New York: Wiley.

Parke, R. D., Coltrane, S., Duffy, S., Buriel, R., Dennis, J., Powers, J., et al. (2004). Economic stress, parenting and child adjustment in Mexican-American and European-American families. *Child Development, 75,* 1632–1656.

Parke, R. D., & Clarke-Stewart, K. A. (2002). History of developmental psychology: Theory and themes. In D. K. Freedheim (Ed.), *Handbook of psychology* (Vol. History of Psychology). New York: Wiley.

Parke, R. D., Gailey, C., Coltrane, S., & DiMatteo, R. (2008). The pursuit of perfection: Transforming our construction of parenthood and family in the age of new reproductive technologies. In P. Essed & D. T. Goldberg (Eds.), *Cloning cultures.* Durham, N.C.: Duke University Press.

Parke, R. D., McDowell, D. J., Cladis, M., & Leidy, M. S. (2006). *Family and peer relationships: The role of emotion regulatory processes.* Washington, DC: American Psychological Association.

Parke, R. D., Lio, S., Schofield, T., Tuthill, L., Vega, E., & Coltrane, S. (2008b). Neighborhood environments: A multi-measure, multilevel approach. In L. C. Mayes & M. Lewis (Eds.), *The environment of human development: A handbook of theory and measurement.* New York: Cambridge University Press.

Parke, R. D., McDowell, D. J., Kim, M., & Leidy, M. S. (2005). Family-peer relationships: The role of emotional regulatory processes. In D. K. Snyder, J. A. Simpson & J. N. Hughes (Eds.), *Emotional regulation in families: Pathways to dysfunction and health.* Washington, DC: American Psychological Association.

Parke, R. D., & O'Neil, R. (1997). The influence of significant others on learning about relationships. In S. Duck (Ed.), *Handbook of personal relationships: Theory, research, and interventions* (2nd ed.) (pp. 29–59). Hoboken, NJ: Wiley.

Parke, R. D., & O'Neil, R. (2000). The influence of significant others on learning about relationships: From family to friends. In R. S. L. Mills & S. Duck (Eds.), *The developmental psychology of interpersonal relationships* (pp. 15–47). New York: Wiley.

Parke, R. D., Simpkins, S. D., McDowell, D. J., Kim, M., Killian, C., Dennis, J., et al. (2002). Relative contributions of families and peers to children's social development. In P. K. Smith & C. H. Hart (Eds.), *Handbook of childhood social development* (pp. 156–178). Malden, MA: Blackwell.

Parker, J. G., & Asher, S. R. (1987). Peer acceptance and later personal adjustment: Are low accepted children at risk? *Psychological Bulletin, 102,* 357–389.

Parker, J. G., & Asher, S. R. (1993). Friendship and friendship quality in middle childhood. *Developmental Psychology, 29,* 611–621.

Parker, J. G., & Gamm, B. K. (2003). Describing the dark side of preadolescents' peer experiences: Four questions (and data) on preadolescents' enemies. In E. V. E. Hodges & N. A. Card (Eds.), *Enemies and the darker side of peer relationships* (pp. 55–72). San Francisco: Jossey-Bass.

Parker, J. G., & Gottman, J. M. (1989). Social and emotional development in a relational context: Friendship interaction from early childhood to adolescence. In T. J. Berndt & G. W. Ladd (Eds.), *Peer relationships in child development.* New York: Wiley.

Parker, J. G., & Seal, J. (1996). Forming, losing, renewing and replacing friendships: Applying temporal parameters to the assessment of children's friendship experiences. *Child Development, 67,* 2248–2268.

Parkhurst, J. T., & Asher, S. R. (1992). Peer rejection in middle school: Subgroup differences in behavior, loneliness and interpersonal concerns. *Developmental Psychology, 28,* 231–241.

Parten, M. (1932). Social play among preschool. *Journal of Abnormal and Social Psychology, 28,* 231–241.

Pascalis, O., de Haan, M., & Nelson, C. A. (2002). Is face processing species-specific during the first year of life? *Science, 5,* 427–434.

Pascual-Leone, J. (1980). Constructive problems for constructive theories. In R. H. Kluwe & H. Spada (Eds.), *Developmental models of thinking* (pp. 263–296). New York: Academic Press.

Pascual-Leone, J. A. (1989). Constructive problems for constructive theories: The current relevance of Piaget's work and a critique of information processing simulation psychology. In H. Spada & R. Kluwe (Eds.), *Developmental models of thinking.* New York: Academic Press.

Patrick, E., & Abravanel, E. (2000). The self-regulatory nature of preschool children's private speech in a natural listening setting. *Applied Psycholinguistics, 21,* 45–61.

Patrikakou, E. N., Weissberg, R. P., Redding, S., & Walberg, H. J. (2005). School-family partnerships: Enhancing the academic, social, and emotional learning of children. In E. N. Patrikakou, R. P. Weissberg, S. Redding & H. J. Walberg (Eds.), *School-family partnerships for children's success* (pp. 1–17). New York: Teachers College Press.

Patterson, A., & Rafferty, A. (2001). Making it work: Towards employment for the young adult with autism. *International Journal of Language and Communication Disorders, 36 (Suppl.),* 475–480.

Patterson, C. J. (1995). Families of the lesbian baby boom: Parents' division of labor and children's adjustment. *Developmental Psychology, 31,* 115–123.

Patterson, C. J. (2004). Gay fathers. In M. E. Lamb (Ed.), *The role of the father in child development* (pp. 397–416). New York: Wiley.

Patterson, C. J., & Hastings, P. D. (2007). Socialization in the context of family diversity. In J. E. Grusec & P. D. Hastings (Eds.), *Handbook of socialization* (pp. 328–351). New York: Guilford.*

Patterson, C. J., & Kister, M. C. (1981). Development of listener skills for referential communication. In W. P. Dickerson (Eds.), *Children's oral communication skills.* New York: Academic.

Patterson, D. (2007). Genetic mechanisms involved in the phenotype of Down syndrome. *Mental Retardation and Developmental Disabilities Research Reviews, 13,* 199–206.

Patterson, G. R. (1982). *Coercive family process.* Eugene, OR: Castalia Press.

Patterson, G. R. (1996). Some characteristics of a developmental theory for early-onset delinquency. In M. F. Lenzenweger & J. J. Haugaard (Eds.), *Frontiers of developmental psychopathology* (pp. 81–124). New York: Oxford University Press.

Patterson, G. R. (2002). The early development of coercive family processes. In J. B. Reid, G. R. Patterson, & J. Snyder (Eds.). *Antisocial behavior in children and adolescents* (pp. 25–44). Washington, DC: American Psychological Association.

Patterson, G. R., & Bank, L. (1989). Some amplifying mechanisms for pathologic processes in families. In M. Gunnar & E. Thelen (Eds.), *Systems and development: The Minnesota Symposium on Child Psychology* (Vol. 22, pp. 167–209). Hillsdale, NJ: Erlbaum.

Patterson, G. R., & Capaldi, D. M. (1991). Antisocial parents: Unskilled and vulnerable. In P. A. Cowan & E. M. Hetherington (Eds.), *Family transitions.* Hillsdale, NJ: Erlbaum.

Patterson, G. R., DeBarshyshe, B., & Ramsey, R. (1989). A developmental perspective on antisocial behavior. *American Psychologist, 44,* 329–335.

Pearson, B. Z., Fernandez, S. C., & Oller, D. K. (1993). Lexical development in bilingual infants and toddlers: Comparison to monolingual norms. *Language Learning, 43,* 93–120.

Pedersen, F. A., Zaslow, M., Cain, R., & Anderson, B. (1980). *Cesarean birth: The importance of a family perspective.* Paper presented at the International Conference on Infant Studies, New Haven, CT.

Pederson, D. R., & Moran, G. (1995). A categorical description of infant–mother relationships in the home and its relation to Q-sort measures on infant-mother interaction. In E. Waters, B.E. Vaughn, G. Posada, & K. Kondo-Ikemura (Eds.), *Caregiving, cultural, and cognitive perspectives on secure-base behavior and working models. New grouping points of attachment theory and research. Monographs of the Society for Research in Child Development,* 60 (2–3, Serial No. 244), 111–132.*

Pederson, D. R., & Moran, G. (1996). Expressions of the attachment relationship outside of the Strange Situation. *Child Development, 67,* 915–927.*

Peet, K., Hodges, E., Kikas, E., & Salmivalli, C. (2007). Hostile attributions and behavioral strategies in children: Does relationship matter? *Developmental Psychology, 43,* 889–900.

Pegg, J. E., Werker, J. F., & McLeod, P. J. (1992). Preference for infant-directed over adult-directed speech: Evidence from 7-week-old infants. *Infant Behavior and Development, 15,* 325–345.*

Pell, M. D. (1998). Recognition of prosody following unilateral brain lesion: Influence of functional and structural attributes of prosodic contours. *Neuropsychologia, 36,* 701–715.*

Pell, M. D. (1999a). Fundamental frequency encoding of linguistic and emotional prosody by right-hemisphere-damaged speakers. *Brain and Language, 69,* 161–192.*

Pell, M. D. (1999b). Some acoustic correlates of perceptually "flat affect" in right-hemisphere-damaged speakers. *Brain and Cognition, 40,* 219–223.*

Pell, M. D. (2006). Cerebral mechanisms for understanding emotional prosody in speech. *Brain and Language, 96,* 221–234.*

Pell, M. D. (2007). Reduced sensitivity to prosodic attitudes in adults with focal right hemisphere brain damage. *Brain and Language, 101,* 64–79.*

Pennington, B. F. (2005). *The development of psychopathology: Nature and nurture.* New York: Guilford.

Penny, A. M., Waschbusch, D. A., Klein, R. M., Corkum, P. V., & Eskes, G. (2009). Developing a measure of sluggish cognitive tempo for chidlren: Content validity, factor structure, and reliability. *Psychological Assessments, 21,* 380–389.*

Pepler, D., Corter, C., & Abramovitch, R. (1982). Social relations among children. Comparisons of siblings and peer interaction. In K. Rubin & H. S. Ross (Eds.), *Peer relationships and social skills in childhood* (pp. 209–227). New York: Springer-Verlag.*

Pepler, D. J., & Craig, C. L. (2000). *Making a difference in bullying* (Report # 60): Lamarsh Centre for Research on Violence and Conflict Resolution.*

Pepler, D., Craig, W. M., Connolly, J. A., Yuile, A., McMaster, L., & Jiang, D. (2006). A developmental perspective on bullying. *Aggressive Behavior, 32,* 276–284.*

Pepperberg, I. M. (2000). *The Alex studies: Cognitive and communicative abilities of grey parrots.* Cambridge, MA: Harvard University Press.

Peretz, I. (2001). Brain specialization for music: New evidence from congenital amusia. In R. J. Zatorre & I. Peretz (Eds.), *The biological foundations of music. Annals of the New York Academy of Science* (Vol. 930, pp. 153–165). New York: New York Academy of Science.*

Peretz, I. (2006). The nature of music from a biological perspective. *Cognition, 1000,* 1–32.*

Perner, J., Ruffman, T., & Leekam, S. R. (1994). Theory of mind is contagious: You can catch it from your sibs. *Child Development, 65,* 1228–1238.

Perry, B. D. (1997). Incubated in terror: Neurodevelopmental factors in the "cycle of violence." In J. D. Osofsky (Ed.), *Children in a violent society* (pp. 124–149). New York: The Guilford Press.

Perry, D. G., Perry, L. C., & Weiss, R. J. (1989). Sex differences in the consequences children anticipate for aggression. *Developmental Psychology, 25,* 312–320.

Perry-Jenkins, M., Repetti, R., & Crouter, A. C. (2000). Work and family in the 1990s. *Journal of Marriage and the Family, 62,* 981–998.

Persson, G. E. B. (2005). Young children's prosocial and aggressive behaviors and their expenses of being targeted for similar behaviors by peers. *Social Development, 14,* 206–228.

Peter, T., Roberts, L. W., & Buzdugan, R. (2008). Suicidal ideation among Canadian youth: A multivariate analysis. *Archives of Suicide Research, 12,* 263–275.*

Peters, D. R., Petrunka, K., & Arnold, R. (2003). The Better Beginnings, Better Futures project: A universal, community-based prevention approach for primary school children and their families. *Journal of Clinical Child and Adolescent Psychology, 32,* 215–227.*

Peters, R. D. (2005). A community-based approach to promoting resilience in young children, their families, and their neighborhoods. In R. D. Peters, B. Leadbeater & R. J. McMahon

Peters, R. DeV. (1994). Better Beginnings, Better Futures: A community-based approach to primary prevention. *Canadian Journal of Community Mental Health, 13,* 183–188.*

Petersen, A. C., & Taylor, B. (1980). The biological approach to adolescence. In J. Adelson (Ed.), *Handbook of adolescent psychology.* New York: Wiley.

Peterson, C. (1999). Children's memory for traumatic injury: Two years later. *Developmental Psychology, 35,* 1493–1506.*

Peterson, C. (2002). Children's long-term memory for autobiographical events. *Developmental Review, 22,* 270–402.*

Peterson, C., & Bell, M. (1996). Children's memory for traumatic injury. *Child Development, 67,* 3045–3070.*

Peterson, C., & Biggs, M. (1997). Interviewing children about trauma: Problems with "specific" questions. *Journal of Traumatic Stress, 10,* 279–290.*

Peterson, C., Dowd, C., & Tobin, J. (1999). Interviewing preschoolers: Comparisons of yes/no and wh-questions. *Journal of Law and Human Behavior, 23,* 539–556.*

Peterson, C., & Grant, M. (2001). Forced-choice: Are forensic interviewers asking the right questions? *Canadian Journal of Behavioural Science, 33,* 118–127.*

Peterson, C., & Parsons, B. (2005). Interviewing former 1- and 2-year-olds about medical emergencies 5 years later. *Law and Human Behavior, 29,* 743–754.*

Peterson, C., Parsons, T., & Dean, M. (2004). Providing misleading and reinstatement information a year after it happened: Effects on long-term memory. *Memory, 12,* 1–13.*

Peterson, C., & Rideout, R. (1998). Memory for medical emergencies experienced by 1- and 2-year-olds. *Developmental Psychology, 34,* 1059–1072.*

Peterson, C., Sales, J. M., Rees, M., & Fivush, R. (2007). Parent-child talk and children's memory for stressful events. *Applied Cognitive Psychology, 21,* 1057–1075.*

Peterson, C., & Whalen, N. (2001). Five years later: Children's memory for medical emergencies. *Applied Cognitive Psychology, 15,* s7–s24.*

Petitto, L. (1993). On the ontogenetic requirements for early language acquisition. In B. de Boysson-Bardies, S. de Schonen, P. W. Jusczyk, P. McNeilage, & J. Morton (Eds.), *Developmental neurocognition: Speech and face processing in the first year of life* (pp. 365–383). Dordrecht, Netherlands: Kluwer Academic Press.*

Petitto, L. A., & Marenette, P. (1991). Babbling in the manual mode: Evidence for the ontogeny of language. *Science, 251,* 1493–1496.*

Petitto, L. A. (2000). On the biological foundations of human language. In K. Emmorey and H. Lange (Eds.), *The signs of language revisited: An anthology in honor of Ursula Bellugi and Edware Klima.* Mahwah, NJ: Erlbaum.*

Petitto , L. A., & Holowka, S. (2002). Evaluating attributions of delay and confusion in young bilinguals: Special insights from infants acquiring a signed and spoken language. *Sign Language Studies, 3,* 4–33.*

Petitto , L. A., Katerelos, M., Levy, b. G., Gavna, K., Tetreault, K., & Ferraro, V. (2001). Bilingual signed and spoken language acquisition from birth: Implications for the mechanisms underlying bilingual language acquisition. *Journal of Child Language, 28,* 453–496.*

Petrill, S. A., & Deater-Deckard, K. (2005). Task orientation, parental warmth and SES account for a significant proportion of the shared environmental variance in general cognitive ability in early childhood: Evidence from a twin study. *Developmental Science, 7,* 25–32.

Pettit, G. S., Bakshi, A., Dodge, K. A., & Coie, J. D. (1990). The emergence of social dominance in young boys' play groups: Developmental differences and behavioral correlates. *Developmental Psychology, 26,* 1017–1025.

Pettit, G., Laird, R. D., Dodge, K. A., Bates, J. E., & Criss, M. N. (2001). Antecedents and behavior problem outcomes of parental monitoring and psychological control in early adolescence. *Child Development, 72,* 283–298.

Phillips, J. (1969). *The origin of intellect: Piaget's theory.* San Francisco: Freeman.

Phillips, R. B., Sharma, R., Premachandra, B. R., Vaughn, A. J., & Reyes-Lee, M. (1996). Intrauterine exposure to cocaine: Effect on neurobehavior of neonates. *Infant Behavior and Development, 19,* 71–81.

Physical Activity and Health. (1996). *Physical activity and health:report of the Surgeon General.* Atlanta, GA: National Center for Chronic Disease Prevention and Health Promotion, Centers for Disease Control and Prevention, Department of Health and Human Services.

Piaget, J. (1926). *Language and thought of the child.* London: Kegan Paul, Trench, & Trubner.

Piaget, J. (1929). *The child's conception of the world.* London: Kegan Paul, Trench, & Trubner.

Piaget, J. (1932). *The moral judgment of the child.* New York: Harcourt, Brace.

Piaget, J. (1950). *The psychology of intelligence.* London: Kegan Paul, Trench, & Trubner.

Piaget, J. (1952). Jean Piaget. In E. G. Boring (Ed.), *A history of psychology in autobiography* (Vol. 4). New York: Russell and Russell.

Piaget, J. (1985). *The equilibration of cognitive structures.* Chicago: University of Chicago Press.

Pick, H. L. (1984). Cognition and action in development: A tutorial discussion. In W. Prinz & A.F. Sanders (Eds.), *Cognition and motor processes* (pp. 309–325). Berlin, Germany: Springer-Verlag.

Pickens, J. N. (1994). Perception of auditory-visual distance relations by 5-month-old infants. *Developmental Psychology, 30,* 537–544.

Pierroutsakos, S. L., & DeLoache, J. S. (2003). Infants' manual exploration of pictorial objects varying in realism. *Infancy, 4,* 141–156.

Pinker, S. (1994). *The language instinct: How the mind creates language.* New York: Morrow.

Pinhas, H. O., & Zeitler, P. (2000). "Who is the wise man? — the one who forsees consequences": Childhood, obesity, new associated comorbidity, and prevention. *Preventive Medicine, 31,* 702–705.

Pinto, J. (2006). Developing body representations: A review of infants' responses to biological-motion displays. In G. Knoblich, I. M. Thornton, M. Grosjean & M. Shiffrar (Eds.), *Human body perception from the inside out: Advances in visual cognition* (pp. 305–322). New York: Oxford University Press.

Pisecco, S., Baker, D. B., Silva, P. A., & Brooke, M. (2001). Boys with reading disabilities and/or ADHD: Distinctions in early childhood. *Journal of Learning Disabilities, 43,* 98–106.

Pleck, J. H., & Masciadrelli, B. P. (2004). *Paternal involvement by U.S. residential fathers: Levels, sources, and consequences.* Hoboken, NJ: Wiley.

Plomin, R. (1990a). *Nature & nurture: An introduction to human behavioral genetics.* Pacific Grove, CA: Brooks/Cole.

Plomin, R. (1995). Genetics and children's experiences in the family. *Journal of Child Psychology and Psychiatry, 36,* 33–68.

Plomin, R., DeFries, J. C., Craig, I. W., & McGuffin, P. (2002). *Behavior genetics in the postgenomic era.* Washington, DC: American Psychological Association.

Plomin, R., DeFries, J. C., McClearn, G. E., & McGuffin, P. (2001). *Behavioral genetics* (4th ed). New York: Worth.

Plomin, R., DeFries, J. C., McClearn, G. E., & Rutter, M. (1997). *Behavior genetics* (3rd ed.). New York: W. H. Freeman.

Plomin, R., McClearn, G. E., Pedersen, N. L., Nesselroade, J. R., & Bergeman, C. S. (1988). Genetic influence on childhood family environment perceived retrospectively from the last half of the life span. *Developmental Psychology, 24,* 738–745.

Plomin, R., & Petrill, S. A. (1997). Genetics and intelligence: What's new? *Intelligence, 24,* Special issue, 53–78.

Plomin, R., & Rutter, M. (1998). Child development, molecular genetics and what to do with genes once they are found. *Child Development, 69,* 1223–1242.

Plunkett, K., Karmiloff-Smith, A., Bates, E., Elman, J. L., & Johnson, M. H. (1997). Connectionism and developmental psychology. *Journal of Child Psychology and Psychiatry, 38,* 53–80.

Pollak, S. D., & Sinha, P. (2002). Effects of early experience on children's recognition of facial displays of emotion. *Developmental Psychology, 38,* 784–791.

Pollitt, E. (1994). Poverty and child development: Relevance of research in developing countries to the United States. *Child Development, 65,* 283–295.

Pollitt, E., Gorman, K., & Metallinos-Katsaras, E. (1992). Long-term developmental consequences of intrauterine and postnatal growth retardation in rural Guatemala. In G. J. Suci & S. R. Robertson (Eds.), *Future directions in infant development research* (pp.

43–70). New York: Springer-Verlag.

Pols, H. (2002). Between the laboratory and life: Child development research in Toronto, 1919–1956. *History of Psychology, 5,* 135–162.

Pomerantz, E. M., Grolnick, W. S., & Price, C. E. (2005). The role of parents in how children approach achievement: A dynamic process perspective. In A. J. Elliot & C. S. Dweck (Eds.), *Handbook of competence and motivation* (pp. 229–278). New York: Guilford.

Pomerantz, E. M., & Ruble, D. N. (1998). The multidimensional nature of control: Implications for the development of sex differences in self-evaluation. In J. Heckhansen & C.S. Dweck (Eds.), *Motivation and self-regulation across the life span* (pp. 159–184). New York, NY: Cambridge University Press

Pomerleau, A., Bolduc, D., Malcuit, G., & Cossette, L. (1990). Pink or blue: Environmental gender stereotypes in the first two years of life. *Sex Roles, 22,* 359–367.*

Pomerleau, A., Sabatier, C., & Malcuit, G. (1998). Quebecois, Haitian, and Vietnamese mothers' report of infant temperament. *International Journal of Psychology, 33,* 337–344.*

Pons, F., Harris, P. L., & de Rosnay, M. (2004). Emotion comprehension between 3 and 11 years: Developmental periods and hierarchical organization. *European Journal of Developmental Psychology, 1,* 127–152.

Porges, S. W. (1995). Orienting in a defensive world: Mammalian modifications of our evolutionary heritage. A Polyvagal theory. *Psychophysiology, 32,* 301–318.

Porter, R. H., Makin, J. W., Davis, L. B., & Christensen, K. M. (1992). Breast-fed infants respond to olfactory cues from their own mother and unfamiliar lactating females. *Infant Behavior and Development, 15,* 85–93.

Posada, G., Gao, Y., Wu, F., Posada, R., Tascon, M., Schöelmerich, A., Sagi, A., Kondo-Ikemura, K., Haaland, W., & Synnevaag, B. (1995). The secure-base phenomenon across cultures: Children's behavior, mothers' preferences, and experts' concepts. In E. Waters, B. E. Vaughn, G. Posada, & K. Kondo-Ikemura (Eds.), *Caregiving, cultural, and cognitive perspectives on secure-base behavior and working models: New growing points of attachment theory and research. Monographs of the Society for Research in Child Development, 60* (2–3, Serial No. 244).

Posada, G., Jacobs, A., Richmond, M. K., Carbonell, O. A., Alzate,

G., Bustamante, M. R., et al. (2002). Maternal caregiving and infant security in two cultures. *Developmental Psychology, 38,* 67–78.

Postlethwait, J. H., & Hopson, J. L. (1995). *The nature of life* (3rd ed.). New York: McGraw-Hill.

Poulin, F., & Boivin, M. (2000). The role of proactive and reactive aggression on the formation of boys' friendships. *Developmental Psychology, 36,* 233–240.*

Poulin, F., & Dishion, T. J. (2008). Methodological issues in the use of peersociometric nominations with middle school youth. *Social Development, 17,* 908–921.*

Poulin, F., Dishion, T., & Haas, E. (1999). The peer influences paradox: Friendship quality and deviancy training within male adolescents. *Merrill-Palmer Quarterly, 45,* 42–61.

Poulin-Dubois, D., Frank, I., Graham, S.A., & Elkin, A. (1999). The role of shape and similarity in toddlers' lexical extensions. *British Journal of Developmental Psychology, 17,* 21–36.*

Poulin-Dubois, D., & Goodz, N. (2001). Language differentiation in bilingual infants: Evidence from babbling. In J. Cenoz & F. Genesee (Eds.), *Trends in bilingual acquisition. Trends in language acquisition research* (Vol. 1, pp. 95–106). Amsterdam: John Benjamins Publishing Co.*

Poulin-Dubois, D., & Graham, S. A. (2007). Cognitive processes in early word learning. In E. Hoff & M. Shatz (Eds.), *Blackwell handbook of language development* (pp. 191–211). Malden, MA: Blackwell Publishing.*

Poulin-Dubois, D., Graham, S. A., & Sippola, L. (1995). Early lexical development: The contribution of parental labelling and infants' categorization abilities. *Journal of Child Language, 22,* 325–343.*

Poulin-Dubois, D., Serbin, L. A., & Derbyshire, A. (1998). Toddler's intermodal knowledge about gender. *Merrill-Palmer Quarterly, 44,* 338–354.*

Poulin-Dubois, D., Serbin, L. A., Kenyon, B., & Derbyshire, A. (1994). Infants' intermodal knowledge about gender. *Developmental Psychology, 30,* 436–442.*

Povinelli, D. J., Bering, J., & Giambrone, S. (2000). Toward a science of other minds: Escaping the argument by analogy. *Cognitive Science, 24,* 509–541.

Powell, D. R. (2006). Families and early childhood interventions. In W. Damon & R. M. Lerner (Gen. Ed.), & K. A. Renninger & I. E. Siegel (Eds.), *Handbook of child psychology: Vol. 4. Child psychol-*

ogy in practice (6th ed., pp. 548–591). New York: Wiley.

Powlishta, K. K. (1989). *Salience of group membership: The case of gender.* Unpublished doctoral dissertation. Stanford University, Stanford, CA.

Pratt, M. W., & Fiese, B. H. (Eds.). (2004). *Family stories and the life course.* Mahwah, NJ: Erlbaum.

Pratt, M. W., Hunsberger, B., Prancer, S. M., & Alisat, S. (2003). A longitudinal analysis of personal values socialization: Correlates of a moral self-ideal in late adolescence. *Social Development, 12,* 563–585.

Pratt, M. W., Kerig, P., Cowan, P. A., & Cowan, C. P. (1988). Mothers and fathers teaching 3 year olds: Authoritative parenting and adult scaffolding of young children's learning. *Developmental Psychology, 24,* 832–839.*

Pressley, M., & Hilden, K. (2006). Cognitive strategies. In W. Damon & R. M. Lerner (Gen. Ed.), & D. Kuhn & R. S. Siegler (Eds.), *Handbook of child psychology: Vol. 2. Cognition, perception, and language* (6th ed., pp. 511–556). New York: Wiley.

Preston, S. D., & de Waal, F. B. M. (2002). Empathy: Its ultimate and proximate bases. *Behavioral and Brain Sciences, 25,* 1–72.

Price, J. R., Roberts, J. E., Hennon, E. A., Berni, M. C., Anderson, K. L., & Sideris, J. (2008). Syntactic complexity during conversation of boys with Fragile X syndrome and Down syndrome. *Journal of Speech, Language, and Hearing Research, 51,* 3–15.

Price-Williams, D. R., Gordon, W., & Ramirez, M., III. (1969). Skill and conservation: A study of pottery-making children. *Developmental Psychology, 1,* 769.

Prinstein, M. J., & LaGreca, A. M. (2002). Peer crowd affiliation and internalizing distress in childhood and adolescence: A longitudinal follow-back study. *Journal of Research on Adolescence, 12,* 325–351.

Prochner, L., & Doyon, P. (1997). Researchers and their subjects in the history of child study: William Blatz and the Dionne quintuplets. *Canadian Psychology, 38,* 103–110.*

Proffitt, D. R., & Bertenthal, B. I. (1990). Converging operations revisited: Assessing what infants perceive using discrimination measures. *Perception & Psychophysics, 47,* 1–11.

Provence, S., & Lipton, R.C. (1962). *Infants in institutions.* New York: International Universities Press.

Pryce, C. R. (1993). The regulation of maternal behavior in marmosets and tamarins. *Behavioral Processes, 30,* 201–224.

Pryce, C. R., Doebli, M., & Martin, R. D. (1993). Effects of sex steroids on maternal motivation in the common marmoset (*Callithrix jacchus*): Development and application of an operant system with maternal reinforcement. *Journal of Comparative Psychology, 107,* 99–115.

Pryce, C. R., Abbott, D. H., Hodges, J. K., & Martin, R. D. (1988). Maternal behavior is related to prepartum urinary estradiol levels. *Physiology and Behavior, 44,* 717–726.

Pryce, C. R., Martin, R. D., & Skuse, D. (1995). *Motherhood in human and nonhuman primates: Biosocial determinants.* Basel, Switzerland: Karger.

Purcell, P., & Stewart, L. (1990). Dick and Jane in 1989. *Sex Roles, 22,* 177–185.

Putnam, S. P., Sanson, A. V., & Rothbart, M. K. (2002). Child temperament and parenting. In M. Bornstein (Ed.), *Handbook of parenting* (2nd ed., pp. 255–278). Mahwah, NJ: Erlbaum.

Quinn, P., Slater, A., Brown, E., & Hayes, R. A. (2001). Developmental change in form categorization in early infancy. *British Journal of Developmental Psychology, 19,* 207–218.

Quinn, P. C., Kelly, D. J., Lee, K., Pascalis, O., & Slater, A. M. (2008). Preference for attractive faces in human infants extends beyond conspecifics. *Developmental Science, 11,* 76–83.*

Rabinowitz, F. M., Grant, M. J., Howe, M. L., & Walsh, C. (1994). Reasoning in middle childhood: A dynamic model of performance on transitivity tasks. *Journal of Experimental Child Psychology, 58,* 252–288.

Rabinowitz, F. M., Howe, M. L., & Saunders, K. (2002). Age, memory load, and individual differences in working memory as determinants of class-inclusion reasoning. *Journal of Experimental Child Psychology, 81,* 157–193.*

Radke-Yarrow, M., & Zahn-Waxler, C. (1983). Roots, motives and patterns in children's prosocial behavior. In J. Reykowski, T. Karylowski, D. Bar-Tal, & E. Staub (Eds.), *Origins and maintenance of prosocial behaviors.* New York: Plenum.

Radziszewska, B., & Rogoff, B. (1988). Influence of adult and peer collaborators on the development of children's planning skills. *Developmental Psychology, 24,* 840–848.

Raine, A. (2002). Biosocial studies of antisocial and violent behavior in children and adults: A review. *Journal of Abnormal Child Psychology, 30,* 311–326.

Raine, A., & Liu, J. (1998). Biological predispositions to violence and their implications for biosocial treatment and prevention. *Psychology, Crime & Law, 4,* 107–125.

Rakic, P. (1995). Corticogenesis in human and nonhuman primates. In M. S. Gazzaniga (Ed.), *The cognitive neurosciences* (pp. 127–145). Cambridge, MA: MIT Press.

Rakison, D. H. (2005). Developing knowledge of objects' motion properties in infancy. *Cognition, 96,* 183–214.

Rakison, D. H. (2007). Fast tracking: Infants learn rapidly about object trajectories. *Trends in Cognitive Sciences, 11,* 140–142.

Rakison, D. H. (2007). Inductive categorization: A methodology to examine the basis for categorization and induction in infancy. *Cognition, Brain, Behavior, XI* (773–790).

Rakison, D. H., & Butterworth, G. (1998a). Infants' attention to object structure in early categorization. *Developmental Psychology, 34,* 1310–1325.*

Rakison, D. H., & Butterworth, G. (1998b). Infants' use of object parts in early categorization. *Developmental Psychology, 34,* 49–62.*

Rakison, D. H., & Cohen, L. B. (1999). Infants' use of functional parts in basic-level categorization. *Developmental Science, 2,* 423–431.*

Rakison, D. H., & Oakes, L. M. (Eds.). (2003). *Early category and concept development: Making sense of the blooming, buzzing confusion.* London: Oxford University Press.

Ramey, C. T., & Ramey, S. L. (1992). Early educational intervention with disadvantaged children—to what effect? *Applied and Preventive Psychology, 1,* 130–140.

Ramey, C. T., & Ramey, S. L. (1998). Early intervention and early experience. American Psychologist, 53, 109–130.

Ramey, C. T., & Ramey, S. L. (2006). The malleability of intelligence by early intervention. In D. Teti (Ed.), *Handbook of developmental psychology.* College Park, MD: University of Maryland Press.

Ramey, C. T., Ramey, S. L., Gaines, K. R., & Blair, C. (1995). Two-generation early intervention programs: A child development perspective. In S. Smith (Ed.), *Two-generation programs for families in poverty: A new intervention strategy* (pp. 202–215). Norwood, NJ: Ablex.

Ramirez, J. M. (2003). Hormones and aggression in children and adolescence. *Aggression and Violent Behavior, 8,* 621–644.

Rao, G. (2006). *Child obesity.* New York: Prometheus Books.

Rauscher, F. H., Shaw, G. L., & Ky, K. N. (1993). Music and spatial task performance. *Nature, 365,* 611.

Rauscher, F. H., Shaw, G. L., & Ky, K. N. (1995). Listening to Mozart enhances spatial-temporal reasoning: Towards a neurophysiologicl basis. *Neuroscience Letter, 185,* 44–47.

Ray, J. W., & Klesges, R. C. (1993). Influences on the eating behavior of children. In C. L. Williams & S. Y. S. Kimm (Eds.), *Prevention and treatment of childhood obesity* (pp. 57–69). Annals of the New York Academy of Sciences, Vol. 699. New York: The New York Academy of Sciences.

Reburn, C. J., & Wynne-Edwards, K. E. (1999). Hormonal changes in males of a naturally biparental and an unparental mammal. *Hormones and Behavior, 35,* 163–176.*

Reid, J. B., Patterson, G. R., & Snyder, J. J. (Eds.). (2002). *Antisocial behavior in children and adolescents: A developmental analysis and model for intervention.* Washington, DC: American Psychological Association.

Reiff, M. I., & Tippins, S. (Eds.). (2004). *ADHD: A complete authoritative guide.* Elk Grove Village, IL: American Academy of Pediatrics.

Reilly, T. W., Entwisle, D. R., & Doering, S. G. (1987). Socialization into parenthood: A longitudinal study of the development of self evaluations. *Journal of Marriage and the Family, 49,* 295–308.

Reiner, W. G., & Gearhart, J. P. (2004). Discordant sexual identity in some genetic males with cloacal exstrophy assigned to female sex at birth. *The New England Journal of Medicine, 350,* 333–341.

Reiss, A., & Hall, S. S. (2007). Fragile X syndrome: Assessment and treatment implications. *Child and Adolescent Psychiatry: Clinics of North America, 16,* 663–675.

Reiss, D., Neiderhiser, J. M., Hetherington, E. M., & Plomin, R. (2000). *The relationship core: Deciphering genetic and social influences on adolescent development.* Cambridge, MA: Harvard University Press.

Renninger, K. A., & Sigel, I. E. (Eds.). (2006). *Child psychology in practice (Vol. 4).* New York: Wiley.

Renshaw, P. D., & Brown, P. J. (1993). Loneliness in middle childhood: Concurrent and longitudinal predictors. *Child Development, 64,* 1271–1284.

Repetti, R. (1989). Effects of daily workload on subsequent behavior during marital interaction: The roles of withdrawal and spouse support. *Journal of Personality and Social Psychology, 57,* 651–659.

Repetti, R. (1996). Short-term and long-term linking job stressors to father child interaction. *Social Development, 1,* 1–15.

Repetti, R., & Wood, J. (1997). The effects of stress and work on mothers' interactions with preschoolers. *Journal of Family Psychology, 1,* 90–108.

Rescorla, L. A. (1980). Overextension in early language development. *Journal of Child Language, 7,* 321–335.

Rescorla, L., Achenbach, T. M., Ivanova, M. Y., Dumecni, L., Almqvist, F., Bilenberg, N., et al. (2007). Problems reported by parents of children ages 6 to 16 in 31 cultures. *Journal of Emotional and Behavioral Disroders, 15,* 130–142.

Rescorla, L., Achenbach, T. M., Ivanova, M. Y., Dumenci, L., Almqvist, F., Bilenberg, N., et al. (2007). Epidemiological comparisons of problems and positive qualities reported by adolescents in 24 countries. *Journal of Consulting and Clinical Psychology, 75,* 351–358.

Rest, J. R., Narvaez, D., Bebeau, M., & Thoma, S. J. (2000). *Postconventional moral thinking: A neokohlbergian approach.* Mahwah, NJ: Erlbaum.

Revkin, S. K., Piazza, M., Izard, V., Cohen, L., & Dehaene, S. (2008). Does subitizing reflect numerical estimation. *Psychological Science, 19,* 607–614.

Reynolds, W., Raftis, S., & Michel, D. (1994). Pregnancy and substance abuse: A needs assessment to investigate the development of health promotion materials for high-risk women. Kingston, ON: AWARE Press.*

Rhee, S. H., & Waldman, I. D. (2002). Genetic and environmental influences on antisocial behavior: A meta-analysis of twin and adoption studies. *Psychological Bulletin, 128,* 490–529.

Rheingold, H. L. (1982). Little children's participation in the work of adults, a nascent prosocial behavior. *Child Development, 53,* 114–125.

Rheingold, H. L., & Cook, K. V. (1975). The content of boys' and girls' rooms as an index of parent behavior. *Child Development, 46,* 459–463.

Rheingold, H. L., & Eckerman, C. (1970). The infant separates himself from his mother. *Science, 168,* 78–83.

Rheingold, H. L., & Eckerman, C. O. (1973). The fear of strangers hypothesis: A critical review. In H. Reese (Ed.), *Advances in child development and behavior* (Vol. 8, pp. 185–222). New York: Academic Press.

Rheingold, H. L., Hay, D. F., & West, M. J. (1976). Sharing in the second year of life. *Child Development, 47,* 1148–1158.

Ricard, M., & Gouin-Decarie, T. (1993). Distance-maintaining in infants' reaction to an adult stranger. *Social Development, 2,* 145–164.

Richards, M. H., Crowe, P. A., Larson, R., & Swarr, A. (1998). Developmental patterns and gender differences in the experience of peer companionship during adolescence. *Child Development, 69,* 154–163.

Richland, L. E., Morrison, R. G., & Holyoak, K. J. (2006). Children's development of analogical reasoning: Insights from scene analogy problems. *Journal of Experimental Child Psychology, 94,* 249–273.

Richland, L. E., Zur, O., & Holyoak, K. J. (2007). Cognitive supports for analogies in the mathematics classroom. *Science, 316,* 1128–1129.

Riemann, R., Angleitner, A., & Strelau, J. (1997). Genetic and environmental influences on personality: A study of twins reared together using the self- and peer-report NEO-FFI scales. *Journal of Personality, 65,* 449–475.

Riese, M. L. (1990). Neonatal temperament in monozygotic and dizygotic twin pairs. *Child Development, 61,* 1230–1237.

Rivara, F., Bergman, A., Lo Gerfo, J., & Weiss, T. (1982). Epidemiology of childhood injuries. II. Sex differences in injury rates. *Developmental & Behavioral Pediatrics, 3,* 103–106.

Rivera, S. M., Wakeley, A., & Langer, J. (1999). The drawbridge phenomenon: Representational reasoning or perceptual preference? *Developmental Psychology, 35,* 427–435.

Roberts, G., & Nanson, J. (2000). Best practices: Fetal alcohol syndrome/fetal alcohol effects and the effects of other substance use during pregnancy. Ottawa, ON: Health Canada.*

Roberts, M. W. (1988). Enforcing chair timeouts with room timeouts. *Behavior Modification, 12,* 353–370.

Roberts, M. W., & Powers, S. W. (1990). Adjusting chair timeout enforcement procedures for oppositional children. *Behavior Therapy, 21,* 257–271.

Roberts, W. L. (1999). The socialization of emotional expression: Relations with prosocial behavior and competence in five samples. *Canadian Journal of Behavioral Science, 31,* 72–85.*

Robertson, D., Snarey, J., Ousley, O., Bowman, D., Harenski, K., & Kilts, C. (2007). The neural processing of moral sensitivity to issues of justice and care: An fMRI study. *Neuropsychologia, 45,* 755–766.

Robila, M., & Krishnakumar, A. (2005). Effects of economic pressure on marital conflict in Romania. *Journal of Family Psychology, 19,* 246–251.

Robinson, J. L., Kagan, J., Reznick, J. S., & Corley, R. (1992). The heritability of inhibited and uninhibited behavior. A twin study. *Developmental Psychology, 28,* 1030–1037.

Robinson, T. N., Saphir, M. N., Kraemer, H. C., Varady, A., & Haydel, K. F. (2001). Effects of reducing television viewing on cildren's requests for toys: A randomized controlled trial. *Journal of Developmental Pediatrics, 22,* 179–184.

Rochat, P. (2001). Origins of self-concept. In J. G. Bremner & A. Fogel (Eds.), *Blackwell handbook of infant development. Handbook of development psychology* (pp. 191–212). Malden, MA: Blackwell Publishers.

Rochat, P., & Morgan, R. (1995). Spatial determinants in the perception of self-produced leg movements in 3- to 5-month-old infants. *Developmental Psychology, 31,* 626–636.

Rochat, P., & Striano, T. (2000). Perceived self in infancy. *Infant Behavior and Development, 23,* 513–530.

Roche, A. F. (Ed.). (1979). Secular trends: Human growth, maturation, and development. *Monographs of the Society for Research in Child Development, 44* (Serial No. 179).

Rock, A. M. L., Trainor, L. J., & Addison, T. L. (1999). Distinctive messages in infant-directed lullabies and songs. *Developmental Psychology, 35,* 527–534.*

Rodearmel, S. J., Wyatt, H. R., Stroebele, N., Smith, S. M., Ogden, L. G., & Hill, J. O. (2007). Small changes in dietary sugar and physical activity as an approach to preventing excessive weight gain: The America on the Move family study. *Pediatrics, 120,* 869–879.

Rodgers, J. L. (2001). The confluence models: An academic "tragedy of the commons?" In E. L. Grigorenko & R. J. Sternberg (Eds.), *Family-environment and intellectual functioning: A life-span perspective* (pp. 71–95). Mahwah, NJ: Erlbaum.

Rodkin, P. C., Farmer, T. W., Pearl, R., & Van Acker, R. (2000). Heterogeneity of popular boys: Antisocial and prosocial configurations. *Developmental Psychology, 30,* 14–24.

Rodriguez-Martin, A., Novalbos Ruiz, J. P., Martinez Nieto, J. M., Escobar Jimenez, L., & Castro de Haro, A. L. (2005). Characteristics of eating disorders in a university-based Spanish population. *European Journal of Clinical Nutrition, 59,* 459–462.

Roeser, R. W., Eccles, J. S., & Sameroff, A. (2000). School as a context of early adolescents' academic and social-emotional development: A summary of research findings. *Elementary School Journal, 1000,* 443–471.

Roffwarg, H. P., Muzio, J. N., & Dement, W. C. (1966). Ontogenetic development of the human sleep-dream cycle. *Science, 152,* 604–619.

Rogoff, B. (1990). *Apprenticeship in thinking: Cognitive development in social context.* New York: Oxford University Press.

Rogoff, B. (1998). Cognition as a collaborative process. In D. Kuhn & R. Siegler (Eds.), & W. Damon (Series Ed.), *Handbook of child psychology: Vol. 2. Cognition, perception and language* (5th ed., pp. 679–744). New York: Wiley.

Rogoff, B. (2002). How can we study cultural aspects of human development? *Human Development, 45,* 387–389.

Rogoff, B. (2003). *The cultural nature of human development.* New York: Oxford University Press.

Rogoff, B., & Mistry, J. (1990). The social and functional context of children's remembering. In R. Fivush & J. A. Hudson (Eds.), *Knowing and remembering in young children* (pp. 197–222). New York: Cambridge University Press.

Rogoff, B., & Waddell, K. J. (1982). Memory for information organized in a scene by children from two cultures. *Child Development, 53,* 1224–1228.

Roisman, G. I., Masten, A. S., Coatsworth, J. D., & Tellegen, A. (2004). Salient and emerging development tasks in the transition to adulthood. *Child Development, 75,* 123–133.

Roisman, G. I., Padron, E., Sroufe, L. A., & Egeland, B. (2002). Earned-secure attachment states in retrospect and prospect. *Child Development, 73,* 1204–1219.

Rolls, B. J., Engell, D., & Birch, L. L. (2000). Serving portion size influences 5-year-old but not 3-year-old children's food intake. *Journal of American Dietetic Association, 100,* 232–234.

Romski, M. A., & Sevcik, R. A. (1996). *Breaking the speech barrier: Language development through augmented means.* Baltimore: Brookes.

Roncadin, C., Pascual-Leone, J., Rich, J. B., & Dennis, M. (2007). Developmental relations between working memory and inhibitory control. *Journal of the International Neuropsychological Society, 13,* 59–67.*

Roopnarine, J. (2004). African American and African Caribbean fathers: Level, quality and meaning of involvement. In M. E. Lamb (Ed.), *The role of the father in child development* (4th ed., pp. 58–97). Hoboken: Wiley.

Rosch, E., & Mervis, C. B. (1975). Family resemblances: Studies in the internal structure of categories. *Cognitive Psychology, 7,* 573–605.

Rosch, E., Mervis, C. B., Gray, W. D., Johnson, D. M., & Boyes-Braem, P. (1976). Basic objects in natural categories. *Cognitive Psychology, 8,* 382–439.

Rose, A. J. (2002). Co-rumination in the friendships of girls and boys. *Child Development, 73,* 1830–1843.

Rose, A. J., & Rudolph, K. D. (2006). A review of sex differences in peer relationship processes: Potential trade-offs for the emotional and behavioral development of girls and boys. *Psychological Bulletin, 132,* 98–131

Rose, A. J., Carlson, W., & Waller, E. (2007). Predictive associations of co-rumination with friendship and emotional adjustment: Considering the socioemotional trade offs of co-numeration. *Developmental Psychology, 43,* 1019–1031.

Rose, S. A. (1990). Cross-modal transfer in human infants: What is being transferred? In A. Diamond (Ed.), *The development and neural basis of higher cognitive function. Annals of the New York Academy of Sciences, 608,* 38–47.

Rose, S. A. (1994). Relation between physical growth and information processing in infants born in India. *Child Development, 65,* 889–903.

Rose, S. A., & Feldman, J. F. (1995). Prediction of IQ and specific cognitive abilities at 11 years from infancy measures. *Developmental Psychology, 31,* 685–696.

Rose, S. A., Feldman, J. F., Wallace, I. F., & McCarton, C. (1989). Infant visual attention: Relation to birth status and developmental outcome during the first 5 years. *Developmental Psychology, 25,* 560–576.

Rose, S. A., Gottfried, A. W., & Bridger, W. H. (1981). Cross-modal transfer in 6-month-old infants. *Developmental Psychology, 17,* 661–669.

Rose, S. A., Jankowski, J. J., & Feldman, J. F. (2002). Speed of processing and face recognition at 7 and 12 months. *Infancy, 3,* 435–455.

Rosenblum, L. D., Schmuckler, M. A., & Johnson, J. A. (1997). The McGurk effect in infants. *Perception & Psychophysics, 59,* 347–357.*

Rosenblum, T., & Pinker, S. (1983). Word magic revisited: Monolingual and bilingual children's understanding of the word-object relationships. *Child Development, 54,* 773–780.

Rosenstein, D., & Oster, H. (1988). Differential facial response to four basic tastes in newborns. *Child Development, 59,* 1555–1568.

Rosenzweig, M. R. (2003). Effects of differential experience on brain and behavior. *Developmental Neuropsychology, 24,* 523–540.

Rosenzweig, M. R., Leiman, A. S., & Breedlove, S. M. (1996). *Biological psychology.* Sunderland, MA: Sinauer Associates.

Rosmus, C., Johnson, C.C., Chan. Y., & Yang, F. (2000). Pain response in Chinese and non-Chinese infants: Is there a difference? *Social Sciences and Medicine, 51,* 175–184.*

Ross, H. S., & Conant, C. L. (1992). The social structure of early conflict: Interactions, relationships, and alliances. In C. U. Shantz & W. W. Hartup (Eds.), *Conflict in child and adolescent development.* Cambridge: Cambridge University Press.

Ross, H. S., Conant, C., Cheyne, J. A., & Alevizos, E. (1992). Relationships and alliances in the social interactions of kibbutz toddlers. *Social Development, 1,* 1–17.*

Rotenberg, K. J. (1995a). Development of children's restrictive disclosure to friends. *Journal of Genetic Psychology, 156,* 279–292.*

Rotenberg, K. J. (1995b). Moral development and children's differential disclosure to adults versus peers. In K.J. Rotenberg (Ed.), *Disclosure processes in children and adolescents. Cambridge studies in social and emotional development* (pp. 135–142). New York, NY: Cambridge University Press.*

Rotenberg, K. J., Fox, C., Green, S., Ruderman, L., Slater, K., Stevens, K., et al. (2005). Construction and validation of a children's interpersonal trust belief scale. *British Journal of Developmental Psychology, 23,* 271–292.

Rotenberg, K. J., Michalik, N., Eisenberg, N., & Betts, L. R. (2008). The relations among young children's peer-reported trustworthiness, inhibitory control, and preschool adjustment. *Early Childhood Research Quarterly, 23,* 288–298.

Rotenberg, K. J., & Morgan, C. J. (1995). Development of a scale to measure individual differences in children's trust-value basis of friendship. *Journal of Genetic Psychology, 156,* 489–502.*

Rotenberg, K. J., & Sliz, D. (1988). Children's restrictive disclosure to friends. *Merrill-Palmer Quarterly, 34,* 203–215.

Rothbart, M. (1981). Measurement of temperament in infancy. *Child Development, 52,* 569–578.

Rothbart, M. K., Ahadi, S. A., & Hershey, K. L. (1994). Temperament and social behavior in childhood. *Merrill-Palmer Quarterly, 40,* 21–39.

Rothbart, M. K., & Bates, J. (2006). Temperament. In W. Damon & R. M. Lerner (Gen. Ed.), & N. Eisenberg (Ed.), *Handbook of child psychology: Vol. 3. Social, emotional, and personality development* (6th ed., pp. 99–166). New York: Wiley.

Rothbaum, F., Pott, M., Azuma, H., Miyake, K., & Weisz, J. (2000). The development of close relationships in Japan and the United States: Paths of symbiotic harmony and generative tension. *Child Development, 71,* 1121–1142.

Rothbaum, F., Weise, J., Pott, M., Miyake, K., & Morelli, G. (2000). Attachment and culture: Security in the United States and Japan. *American Psychologist, 35,* 1093–1104.

Rotherman-Borus, M. J., & Langabeer, K. A. (2001). Developmental trajectories of gay, lesbian, & bisexual youths. In A. R. D'Augelli & C. Patterson (Eds.), *Lesbian, gay, and bisexual identities among youth: Psychological perspectives* (pp. 97–128). New York: Oxford University Press.

Rotherman-Borus, M. J., Piacentini, J., Cantwell, C., Belin, T. R., & Song, J. (2000). The 18-month impact of an emergency room intervention for adolescent female suicide attemptees. *Journal of Consulting and Clinical Psychology, 68,* 1081–1093.

Rovee-Collier, C. (1997). Dissociations in infant memory: Rethinking the development of implicit and explicit memory. *Psychological Review, 104,* 467–498.

Rovee-Collier, C. (1999). The development of infant memory. *Current Directions in Psychological Science, 8,* 80–85.

Rovee-Collier, C., & Gerhardstein, P. (1997). The development of infant memory. In C. A. Nelson & C. Hulme (Eds.), *The development of memory in childhood: Studies in developmental psychology.* East Sussex, England: Psychology Press.

Rovee-Collier, C. K. (1986). *Infants and elephants: Do they ever forget?* Paper presented at a Science and Public Policy Seminar, Washington, DC.

Rovee-Collier, C. K. (1987). Learning and memory in infants. In J. D. Osofsky (Ed.), *Handbook of infant development* (pp. 98–148). New York: Wiley.

Rovee-Collier, C. K., & Lipsitt, L. P. (1982). Learning, adaptation and memory in the newborn. In P. Stratton (Ed.), *Psychobiology of the human newborn.* New York: Wiley.

Rovee-Collier, C. K., & Shyi, G. (1992). A functional and cognitive analysis of infant long-term retention. In C. J. Brainard, M. L. Howe, & V. Reyna (Eds.), *Development of long-term retention* (pp. 3–55). New York: Springer-Verlag.

Rovet, J. (2004). Turner syndrome: A review of genetic and hormonal influences on neuropsychological functioning. *Child Neuropsychology, 10,* 262–279.*

Rovet, J., & Buchanan, L. (1999). Turner syndrome: A cognitive neuroscience approach. In H. Tager-Flusberg (Ed.), *Neurodevelopmental disorders. Developmental cognitive neuroscience* (pp. 223–249). Cambridge, MA: The MIT press.*

Rovet, J., & Ireland, L. (1994). Behavioural phenotype in children with Turner syndrome. *Journal of Pediatric Psychology, 19,* 779–790.*

Rovet, J., & Netley, C. (1983). The triple X chromosome syndrome in childhood: Recent empirical findings. *Child Development, 54,* 831–845.*

Rovet, J., Netley, C. Keenan, M., Bailey, J., & Stewart, D. (1996). The psychoeducational profile of boys with Klinefelter syndrome. *Journal of Learning Disabilities, 29,* 180–196.*

Rowland, C. F., & Pine, J. M. (2000). Subject-auxilary inversion errors and wh- acquisition: "What do children know?". *Journal of Child Language, 27,* 157–181.

Rowland, C. F., & Pine, J. M. (2003). The development of inversion in questions: A reply to Van Valen. *Journal of Child Language, 30,* 197–212.

Rozin, P. (1996). Towards a psychology of food and eating: From motivation to module to model to marker, morality, meaning, and metaphor. *Current Directions in Psychological Science, 5,* 18–24.

Rubenstein, A. J., Kalakanis, L., & Langlois, J. H. (1999). Infant preferences for attractive faces: A cognitive explanation. *Developmental Psychology, 35,* 848–855.

Rubenstein, A. J., Langlois, J. H., & Roggman, L. A. (2002). What makes a face attractive and why? The role of averageness in defining facial beauty. In G. Rhodes & L. A. Zebrowitz (Eds.), *Facial attractiveness: Evolutionary, cognitive, and social perspectives. Advances in cognition* (Vol. 1, pp. 1–33). Westport, CT: Ablex Publishing.

Rubin, J. Z., Provenzano, F. J., & Luria, A. (1974). The eye of the beholder: Parents' views on sex of newborns. *American Journal of Orthopsychiatry, 43,* 720–731.

Rubin, K. H. (1982). Non-social play in preschoolers: Necessarily evil? *Child Development, 53,* 651–657.*

Rubin, K. H., Bukowski, W., & Parker, J. G. (1998). Peer interactions, relationships, and groups. In W. Damon (Gen. Ed.) & N. Eisenberg (Vol. Ed.), *Handbook of child psychology: Vol. 3. Social, emotional, and personality development* (5th ed., pp. 619–700). New York: Wiley.*

Rubin, K. H., Bukowski, W. M., & Parker, J. G. (2006). Peer interactions, relationships, and groups. In W. Damon & R. M. Lerner (Gen. Ed.), & N. Eisenberg (Ed.), *Handbook of child psychology: Vol.3. Social, emotional, and personality development* (6th ed., pp. 571–645). New York: Wiley.*

Rubin, K. H., & LeMare, L. (1990). Social withdrawal in childhood: Assessment issues and social commitments. In S. R. Asher & J. D. Coie (Eds.), *Children's status in the peer group.* New York: Cambridge University Press.*

Rubin, Z. (1980). *Children's friendships.* Cambridge, MA: Harvard University Press.*

Rubin, Z., & Sloman, J. (1984). How parents influence their children's friendship. In M. Lewis (Ed.), *Beyond the dyad.* New York: Plenum.*

Ruble, D. N. (1987). The acquisition of self-knowledge: A self-socialization perspective. In N. Eisenberg (Ed.), *Contemporary topics in developmental psychology.* New York: Wiley.

Ruble, D. N., Martin, C. L., & Berenbaum, S. (2006). Gender development. In W. Damon & R. M. Lerner (Gen. Ed.), & N. Eisenberg (Ed.), *Handbook of child psychology: Vol. 3: Social, emotional, and personality development* (6th ed., pp. 858–932). New York: Wiley.

Rudolph, K. D., Lambert, S. F., Clarke, A. G., & Kurlakowsky, K. D. (2001). Negotiating the transition to middle school: The role of self-regulatory processes. *Child Development, 72,* 929–946.

Rudy, D., & Grusec, J. E. (2001). Correlates of authoritarian parenting in individualistic and collectivist cultures and implications for understanding the transmission of values. *Journal of Cross-Cultural Psychology. Special Issue: Perspectives on cultural transmission, 32,* 202–212.*

Rudy, D., & Grusec, J. E. (2006). Authoritarian parenting in individualistic and collectivist groups: Associations with maternal emotion and cognition and children's self-esteem. *Journal of Family Psychology, 20,* 68–78.*

Ruff, H. A., & Capozzoli, M. C. (2003). Development of attention and distractibility in the first 4 years of life. *Developmental Psychology, 39,* 877–890.

Ruff, H. A., & Lawson, K. R. (1990). Development of sustained focused attention in young children during free play. *Developmental Psychology, 26,* 85–93.

Ruff, H. A., & Rothbart, M. K. (1996). *Attention in early development: Themes and variations.* New York: Oxford University Press.

Ruihe, H., & Guoliang, Y. (2006). Children's understanding of emotional display rules and use of strategies. *Psychological Science (China), 29,* 18–21.

Rumelhart, D. E., & McClelland, J. L. (1987). *Parallel distributed processing: Volume 1, Foundations.* Boston, MA: The MIT Press.

Runco, M. A. (1996, Summer). Personal creativity: Definition and developmental issues. In M. A. Runco (Ed.), *Creativity from childhood through adulthood: The developmental issues* [Special issue]. *New Directions for Child Development,* No. 72, 3–30.

Russell, A., & Finnie, V. (1990). Preschool children's social status and maternal instructions to assist group entry. *Developmental Psychology, 26,* 603–611.

Russell, A., Russell, G., & Midwinter, D. (1991). Observer effects on mothers and fathers: Self-reported influence during a home observation. *Merrill-Palmer Quarterly, 38,* 263–283.

Rust, J., Golombok, S., Hines, M., Johnston, K., Golding, J., & The ALSPAC Study Team. (2000). The role of brothers and sisters in the gender development of preschool children. *Journal of Experimental Child Psychology, 77,* 292–303.

Rutter, M. (1992). Nature, nurture and psychopathology. In B. Tizard & V. Varma (Eds.), *Vulnerability and resilience in human development.* London: Jessica Kingsley.

Rutter, M. (1996). Transitions and turning points in developmental psychopathology: As applied to the age span between childhood and mid-adulthood. *International Journal of Behavioral Development, 19,* 603–626.

Rutter, M. (2002). Nature, nurture, and development: From evangelism through science toward policy and practice. *Child Development, 73,* 1–21.

Rutter, M. (Ed.). (2003). *Autism: Neural basis and treatment possibilities.* London: Novartis.

Rutter, M. (2006). *Genes and behavior.* New York: Blackwell.

Rutter, M. (2006). The psychological effects of early institutional rearing. In P. Marshall & N. A. Fox (Eds.), *The development of social engagement: Neurobiological perspectives* (pp. 355–391). Oxford, UK: Oxford University Press.

Rutter, M., Kreppner, J., O'Conner, T., & the English & Romanian Adoptees (ERA) Study Team. (2001). Risk and resilience following profound early global privation. *British Journal of Psychiatry, 179,* 97–103.

Rymer, R. (1993). *Genie: A scientific tragedy.* New York: HarperCollins.

Saadeh, W., Rizzo, C. P., & Roberts, D. G. (2002). Spanking. *Clinical Pediatrics, 41,* 87–88.

Saarni, C. (1999). *The development of emotional competence.* New York: Guilford.

Saarni, C., Campos, J. J., & Camras, L. (2006). Emotional development. In W. Damon & R. M. Lerner (Gen. Ed.), & N. Eisenberg (Ed.), *Handbook of child psychology: Vol. 3. Social, emotional, and personality development* (6th ed., pp. 226–299). New York: Wiley.

Sachs, B. P., Fretts, R. C., Gardner, R., Hellerstein, S., Wampler, N. S., & Wise, P. H. (1995). The impact of extreme prematurity and congenital anomalies on the interpretation of international comparisons of infant mortality. *Obstetrics and Gynaecology, 85,* 941–946.

Sadeh, A. (1996). Stress, trauma, and sleep in children. *Child & Adolescent Psychiatric Clinics of North America, 5,* 685–700.

Saffran, J. R. (2001). Words in a sea of sound: The output of infant statistical learning. *Cognition, 81,* 149-169.

Saffran, J. R. (2002). Constraints on statistical language learning. *Journal of Memory and Language, 47,* 172–196.

Saffran, J. R. (2003). Statistical language learning: Mechanisms and constraints. *Current Directions in Psychological Science, 12,* 110–114.

Saffran, J. R., Aslin, R. N., & Newport, E. L. (1996). Statistical learning by 8-month-old infants. *Science, 274,* 1926–1928.

Saffran, J. R., & Griepentrog, G. J. (2001). Absolute pitch in infant auditory learning: Evidence for developmental reorganization. *Developmental Psychology, 37,* 74–85.

Saffran, J. R., Werker, J., & Werner, L. A. (2006). The infant's auditory world. In W. Damon & R. M. Lerner (Gen. Ed.), & D. Kuhn & R. Siegler (Eds.), *Handbook of Child Psychology: Vol. 2: Cognition, Perception and Language* (pp. 58–108). New York: Wiley.

Sagi, A., Koren-Karie, N., Gini, M., Ziv, Y., & Joels, T. (2002). Shedding further light on the effects of various types and quality of early child care on infant-mother attachment relationship: The Haifa study of early child care. *Child Development, 73,* 1166–1186.

Sagi, A., Lambe, M. E., Lewkowicz, K. S., Shoham, R., Dvir, R., & Estes, D. (1985). Security of infant-mother, -father, and metapelet attachments among kibbutz-reared Israeli children. In I. Bretherington & E. Waters (Eds.), *Growing points of attachment theory and research. Monographs of the Society for Research in Child Development, 50* (1-2, Serial No. 209).

Sagi, A., van IJzendoorn, M. H., Aviezer, O., Donnell, F., & Mayseless, O. (1994). Sleeping out of home in a kibbutz community arrangement: It makes a difference for infant-mother attachment. *Child Development, 65,* 992–1004.

Sagi-Schwartz, A., & Alviezer, O. (2005). Correlates of attachment to multiple caregivers in kibbutz children from birth to emerging adulthood: The Haifa longitudinal study. In K. E. Grossmann, K. Grossmann & E. Waters (Eds.), *Attachment from infancy to adulthood* (pp. 165–197). New York: Guilford.

Saklofske, D. H., Caravan, G., & Schwartz, C. (2000). Concurrent validity of the Wechsler Abbreviated Scale of Intelligence (WASI) with a sample of Canadian children. *Canadian Journal of School Psychology, 16,* 87–94.*

Saklofske, D. H., Hildebrand, D. K., & Gorsuch, R. L. (2000). Replication of the factor structure of the Wechsler Adult Intelligence Scale—Third Edition with a Canadian sample. *Psychological Assessment, 12,* 436–439.*

Saklofske, D. H., Hildebrand, D. K., Reynolds, C. R., & Willson, V. L. (1998). Substituting symbol search for coding on the WISC-III: Canadian normative tables for Performance and Full Scale IQ scores. *Canadian Journal of Behavioural Science, 30,* 57–68.*

Saklofske, D. H., Tulsky, D. S., Wilkins, C., & Weiss, L. G. (2003). Canadian WISC-III directional base rates of score discrepancies by ability level. *Canadian Journal of Behavioural Science, 35,* 210–218.*

Salapatek, P., & Kessen, W. (1966). Visual scanning of triangles by the human newborn. *Journal of Experimental Child Psychology, 3,* 155–167.

Salatas Waters, H. (2000). Memory strategy development: Do we need yet another deficiency. *Child Development, 71,* 1004–1012.

Salmon, C. A., & Daly, M. (1998). Birth-order and familial sentiment: Middleborns are different. *Evolution and Human Behavior, 19,* 299–312.*

Saltaris, C., Serbin, L. A., Stack, D. M., Karp, J. A., & Schwartzman, A. E. (2004). Nurturing cognitive competence in preschoolers: A longitudinal study of intergenerational continuity and risk. *International Journal of Behavioral Development, 28,* 105–115.*

Samela, J. A. (1979). Growth pattern of elite French-Canadian female gymnasts. *Canadian Journal of Applied Sport Sciences, 4,* 218–222.*

Sameroff, A. J. (1989). General systems and the regulation of development. In M. R. Gunnar & E. Thelen (Eds.), *Systems and development.* (Vol. 22, pp. 219–235). Hillsdale, NJ: Erlbaum.

Sameroff, A. J. (1994). Developmental systems and family functioning. In R. D. Parke & S. G. Kellam (Eds.), *Exploring family relationships with other social systems* (pp. 199–214). Hillsdale, NJ: Erlbaum.

Sameroff, A. J. (2007). Biopsychosocial influences on the development of resilience. In B. M. Lester,

A. S. Masten & B. McEwen (Eds.), *Resilience in children.* New York: Blackwell.

Sameroff, A. J., & Chandler, M. J. (1975). Reproductive risk and the continuum of caretaking casualty. In F. Horowitz (Ed.), *Review of child development research* (Vol. 4). Chicago: University of Chicago Press.

Sameroff, A. J., & Fiese, B. H. (2000). Transactional regulation: The developmental ecology of early intervention. In J. P. Shonkoff & S. J. Meisels (Eds.), *Handbook of early childhood intervention* (2nd ed., pp. 135–159). New York: Cambridge University Press. .

Sameroff, A. J., Seifer, R., Barocas, R., Zax, M., & Greenspan, S. (1987). Intelligence quotient scores of 4-year-old children: Social-environmental risk factors. *Pediatrics, 79,* 343–350.

Sameroff, A., Seifer, R., Baldwin, A., & Baldwin, C. (1993). *Continuity of risk from childhood to adolescence.* Unpublished paper. University of Rochester.

Sampaio, R., & Truwit, C. (2001). Myelination in the developing human brain. In C. A. Nelson & M. Luciana (Eds.), *Handbook of developmental cognitive neuroscience* (pp. 35–44). Cambridge, MA: MIT Press.

Samuels, C. A., Butterworth, G., Roberts, T., & Graupner, L. (1994). Babies prefer attractiveness to symmetry. *Perception, 23,* 823–831.

Sanchez-Martin, J. R., Fano, E., Ahero, L., Cardas, J., Brain, P. F., & Azpiraz, A. (2000). Relating testosterone levels and free play social behavior in male and female preschool children. *Psychoneuroendocrinology, 25,* 773–783.

Sanders, L. D., Weber-Fox, C. M., & Neville, H. J. (2007). Varying degrees of plasticity in different subsystems of language. In J. R. Pomerantz & M. Crair (Eds.), *Topis in integrative neuroscience: From cells to cognition.* New York: Cambridge University Press.

Sanderson, J. A., & Siegal, M. (1991). *Loneliness in young children.* Unpublished manuscript. University of Queensland, Brisbane, Australia.

Sann, C., & Streri, A. (2007). Perception of object shape and texture in human newborns: Evidence from cross-modal transfer tasks. *Developmental Science*(10). 399–410

Sann, C., & Streri, A. (2008). Intermanual transfer of object texture and shape in human neonates. *Neuropsychologia, 46,* 698–702.

Sarnthein, J., vonStein, A., Rappelsberger, P., Petsche, H., Rauscher, F. H., & Shaw, G. (1997). Persistent patterns of brain activity: An EEG coherence study of the positive effect of music on spatial-temporal reasoning. *Neurological Research, 19,* 107–116.

Savage-Rumbaugh, S., & Shanker, S. (1998). *Apes, language, and the human mind.* New York: Oxford University Press.

Savig, S. K., Tolbert, P. E., Altshul, L. M., & Korrick, S. A. (2007). Organochlorine exposures during pregnancy and infant size at birth. *Epidemiology, 18,* 120–129.

Savin-Williams, R. (1987). *Adolescence: An ethological perspective.* New York: Springer-Verlag.

Savin-Williams, R. (1998). *"... and then I became gay." Young men's stories.* New York: Routledge.

Savin-Williams, R., & Cohen, K. M. (2004). Homoerotic development during childhood and adolescence. *Child and Adolescent Psychiatry Clinics, 13,* 529–549.

Savin-Williams, R., & Diamond, L. M. (2000). Sexual identity trajectories among sexual minority youths: Gender comparisons. *Archives of Sexual Behavior, 29,* 607–627.

Savin-Williams, R., & Ream, G. (2003). Sex variations in the disclosure to parents of same-sex attractions. *Journal of Family Psychology, 17,* 429–438.

Saxe, G. B. (1991). *Culture and cognitive development: Studies in mathematical understanding.* Hillsdale, NJ: Erlbaum.

Scahill, L., & Schwab-Stone, M. (2000). Epidemiology of ADHD in school-age children. *Child and Adolescent Psychiatry Clinics, 9,* 541–555.

Scaramella, L. V., & Conger, R. D. (2003). Intergenerational continuity of hostile parenting and its consequences: The moderating influence of children's negative emotional reactivity. *Social Development, 12,* 420–439.

Scarr, S. (1996). How people make their own environments: Implications for parents and policy makers. *Psychology, Public Policy & Law, 2,* 204–228.

Scarr, S. (1997). Behavior-genetic and socialization theories of intelligence: Truce and reconciliation. In R. J. Sternberg & E. L. Grigorenko (Eds.), *Intelligence, heredity, and environment* (pp. 3–41). New York: Cambridge University Press.

Scarr, S. (1998). How do families affect intelligence? Social-environmental and behavior-genetic perspectives. In J. J. McArdle & R. W. Woodcock (Eds.), *Human cognitive abilities in theory and practice*

(pp. 113–136). Mahwah, NJ: Erlbaum.

Scarr, S., & McCartney, K. (1983). How people make their own environments: A theory of genotype environment effects. *Child Development, 54,* 424–435.

Scarr, S., & Weinberg, R. A. (1976). IQ test performance of black children adopted by white families. *American Psychologist, 31,* 726–739.

Scarr, S., & Weinberg, R. A. (1983). The Minnesota adoption studies: Genetic differences and malleability. *Child Development, 54,* 260–267.

Schaal, B., Tremblay, R. E., Soussignan, R., & Susman, E. J. (1996). Male testosterone linked to high social dominance but low physical aggression in early adolescence. *Journal of the American Academy of Child & Adolescent Psychiatry, 19,* 1322–1330.*

Schachar, R. J., Sandberg, S., & Rutter, M. (1986). Agreement between teachers' ratings and observations of hyperactivity, inattentiveness and defiance. *Journal of Abnormal Psychology, 114,* 331–345.

Schaffer, H. R. (1971). *The growth of sociability.* London: Penguin.

Schaffer, H. R. (1977). *Mothering.* Cambridge, MA: Harvard University Press.

Schaffer, H. R. (1996). *Social development.* Cambridge, MA: Blackwell.

Schaffer, H. R., & Emerson, P. E. (1964). The development of social attachments in infancy. *Monographs of the Society for Research in Child Development, 29* (3, Serial No. 94).

Schank, R. C., & Abelson, R. P. (1977). *Scripts, plans, goals and understanding.* Hillsdale, NJ: Erlbaum.

Scharf, M. (2001). A "natural experiment" in childrearing ecologies and adolescents' attachment and separation representation. *Child Development, 72,* 236–251.

Schellenberg, E. G. (2006a). Exposure to music: The truth about the consequences. In G. E. McPherson (Ed.), *The child as musician: A handbook of musical development* (pp. 113–134). New York: Oxford University Press.*

Schellenberg, E. G. (2006b). Long-term positive associations between music lessons and IQ. *Journal of Educational Psychology, 98,* 457–468.*

Schellenberg, E. G., Nakata, T., Hunter, P. G., & Tamoto, S. (2007). Exposure to music and cognitive performance: Tests of chidlren and adults. *Psychology of Music, 35,* 5–19.*

Schellenberg, E. G., & Peretz, I. (2008). Music, language and cognition: Unresolved issues. *Trends in cognitive sciences, 12*, 45–46.*

Schellenberg, E. G., & Trehub, S. E. (1996). Natural musical intervals: Evidence from infant listeners. *Psychological Science, 7*, 272–277.*

Schieffelin, B. B., & Ochs, E. (1987). *Language socialization across cultures.* New York: Cambridge University Press.

Schmajuk, M., Liotti, M., Busse, L., & Woldorff, M. G. (2006). Electrophysiological activity underlying inhibitory control processes in normal adults. *Neuropsychologia, 44*, 384–395.*

Schmidt, L. A., & Fox, N. A. (2002). Molecular genetics of temperamental differences in children. In J. Benjamin & R. P. Epstein (Eds.), *Molecular genetics and the human personality* (pp. 245–255). Washington, DC: American Psychological Association.*

Schmuckler, M. A. (1993). Perception-action coupling in infancy. In G.J.P. Savelsbergh (Ed.), *The development of coordination in infancy* (pp. 123-173). Amsterdam: North-Holland/Elsevier Science.*

Schmuckler, M. A. (1997). Children's postural sway in response to low- and high-frequency visual information for oscillation. *Journal of Experimental Psychology: Human Perception and Performance, 23*, 528–545.*

Schmuckler, M. A. (2001). What is ecological validity? A dimensional analysis. *Infancy, 2*, 419–436.*

Schmuckler, M. A., Collimore, L. M., & Dannemiller, J. L. (2007). Infants' reactions to object collision on hit and miss trajectories. *Infancy, 12*, 105–118.*

Schmuckler, M. A., & Fairhall, J. L. (2001). Visual-proprioceptive intermodal perception using point light displays. *Child Development, 72*, 949–962.*

Schmuckler, M. A., & Jewell, D. T. (2007). Infants' visual-proprioceptive intermodal perception with imperfect contingency information. *Developmental Psychobiology, 49*, 387–398.*

Schmuckler, M. A., & Li, N. S. (1998). Looming responses to obstacles and apertures: The role of accretion and deletion of background texture. *Psychological Science, 9*, 49–52.

Schmuckler, M. A., & Proffitt, D. R. (1994). Infants' perception of kinetic depth and stereokinetic displays. *Journal of Experimental Psychology: Human Perception and Performance, 20*, 122–130.*

Schmuckler, M. A., & Tsang-Tong, H. Y. (2000). The role of visual and body movement information in infant search. *Developmental Psychology, 36*, 499–510.*

Schneider, B. H. (1998). Cross-cultural comparison as doorkeeper in research on the social and emotional adjustment of children and adolescents. *Developmental Psychology, 34*, 793–797.*

Schneider, B. H. (2000). *Friends and enemies: Peer relations in childhood.* London: Arnold.*

Schneider, B. H., Atkinson, L., & Tardiff, C. (2001). Child-parent attachment and children's peer relations: A quantitative review. *Developmental Psychology, 37*, 87–100.*

Schneider, B. H., Attili, G., Vermigli, P., & Younger, A. (1997a). A comparison of middle class English-Canadian and Italian Mothers' beliefs about children's peer-directed aggression and social withdrawal. *International Journal of Behavioral Development, 21*, 133–154.*

Schneider, B. H., Fonzi, A., Tani, F., & Tomada, G. (1997). A cross-cultural exploration of the stability of children's friendships and predictors of their continuation. *Social Development, 6*, 32–339.*

Schneider, B. H., Fonzi, A., Tomada, G., & Tani, F. (2000). A cross-national comparison of children's behavior with their friends in situations of potential conflict. *Journal of Cross-Cultural Psychology, 31*, 259–266.*

Schneider, B. H., Woodburn, S., del Toro, M. P. S., & Udvari, S. J. (2005). Cultural and gender differences in the implications of competition for early adolescent friendship. *Merrill-Palmer Quarterly, 51*, 163–191.*

Schneider, W., & Bjorklund, D. F. (1998). Memory. In W. Damon (Gen. Ed.), and D. Kuhn, & R. S. Siegler (Vol. Eds.), *Handbook of child psychology: Vol. 2. Cognition, perception, and language* (pp. 467–521). New York: Wiley.

Scholl, T. O., Heidiger, M. L., & Belsky, D. (1996). Prenatal care and maternal health during adolescent pregnancy: A review and meta-analysis. *Journal of Adolescent Health, 15*, 444–456.

Schoppe-Sullivan, S. J., Brown, G. L., Cannon, E. A., Mangelsdorf, S. C., & Sokolowski, M. S. (2008). Maternal gatekeeping, coparenting quality, and fathering behavior in families with infants. *Journal of Family Psychology, 22*, 289–298.

Schoppe-Sullivan, S. J., Diener, M. L., Magelsdorf, S. C., Brown, G. L., McHale, J. L., & Frosch, C. A. (2006). Attachment and sensitivity in family context: The roles of parent and infant gender. *Infant and Child Development, 15*, 367–385.

Schott, G., & Selwin, N. (2000). Examining the "male, antisocial" stereotype of high computer users. *Journal of Educational Computing Research, 23*, 291–303.

Schwartz, D., Dodge, K., Pettit, G., & Bates, J. (1997). The early socialization of aggressive victims of bullying. *Child Development, 68*, 665–675.

Schwartz, L. L. (2003). A nightmare for King Solomon: The new reproductive technologies. *Journal of Family Psychology, 17*, 229–237.

Schwartzman, A. E., Ledingham, J., & Serbin, L. A. (1985). Identification of children at risk for adult schizophrenia. *International Review of Applied Psychology, 34*, 363–380.*

Scrimsher, S., & Tudge, J. (2003). The teaching/learning relationship in the first years of school: Some revolutionary implications of Vygotsky's theory. *Early Education and Development, 14*, 293–312.

Segalowitz, S. (1994). Developmental psychology and brain development: A historical perspective. In G. Dawson and K.W. Fischer (Eds.), *Human behavior and the developing brain* (pp. 67–92). New York, NY: Guildford Press.*

Selby, J. M., & Bradley, B. S. (2003). Infants in groups: A paradigm for the study of social experience. *Human Development, 46*, 197–221.

Seligman, M. E. P. (1974). Depression and learned helplessness. In R. J. Friedman & M. M. Katz (Eds.), *The psychology of depression: Contemporary theory and research* (pp. 83–113). Washington, DC: Winston-Wiley.

Selman, R. L. (1980). *The growth of interpersonal understanding.* New York: Academic.

Selman, R. L., & Byrne, D. F. (1974). A structural-developmental analysis of levels of role taking in middle childhood. *Child Development, 45*, 803–806.

Selman, R. L., & Dray, A. (2006). Risk and prevention: Building bridges between research and practice. In W. Damon & R. L. Lerner (Gen. Ed.), & K. A. Renninger & I. E. Sigel (Eds.), *Handbook of child psychology: Vol 4, Child Psychology and Practice* (6th ed.). New York: John Wiley.

Selman, R. L., & Jacquette, D. (1978). Stability and oscillation in interpersonal awareness: A clinical-developmental analysis. In C. B. Keasey (Ed.), *The XXV Nebraska symposium on motivation.* Lincoln: Univ. of Nebraska Press.

Semel, E., & Rosner, S. R. (2003). *Understanding Williams syndrome: Behavioral patterns and interventions.* Mahwah, NJ: Erlbaum.

Senghas, A., & Coppola, M. (2001). Children creating languages: How Nicaraguan sign language acquired a spatial grammar. *Psychological Science, 12*, 323–328.

Serbin, L. A. (1997). Research on international adoption: Implications for developmental theory and social policy. *International Journal of Behavioral Development, 20*, 83–92.*

Serbin, L. A., & Stack, D. M. (1998). Introduction to special section: Studying intergenerational continuity and the transfer of risk. *Developmental Psychology, 34*, 1159–1161.*

Serbin, L. A., Cooperman, J. M., Peters, P. L., Lehoux, P. M., Stack, D. M., & Schwartzman, A. E. (1998). Intergenerational transfer of psychosocial risk in women with childhood histories of aggression, withdrawal, or aggression and withdrawal. *Developmental Psychology, 34*, 1246–1262.*

Serbin, L. A., Peters, P. L., McAffer, V. J., & Schwartzman, A. E. (1991). Childhood aggression and withdrawal as predictors of adolescent pregnancy, early parenthood, and environmental risk for the next generation. *Canadian Journal of Behavioural Science, 23*, 318–331.*

Serbin, L. A., Poulin-Dubois, D., Colburne, K. A., Sen, M. G., & Eichstedt, J. A. (2001). Gender stereotyping in infancy: Visual preferences for and knowledge of gender-stereotyped toys in the second year. *International Journal of Behavioral Development, 25*, 7–15.*

Serbin, L. A., Stack, D. M., Schwartzman, A. E., Cooperman, J., Bentley, V., Saltaris, C., & Ledingham, J. E. (2002). A longitudinal study of aggressive and withdrawn children into adulthood: Patterns of parenting and risk to offspring. In R. J. McMahon & R. D. Peters (Eds.), *The effects of parental dysfunction on children* (pp. 43–69). New York: Kluwer Academin.*

Serpell, R., & Haynes, B. P. (2004). The cultural practice of intelligence testing: Problems of international export. In R. J. Sternberg & E. L. Grigorenko (Eds.), *Culture and competence: Contexts of life success* (pp. 163–185). Washington, DC: American Psychological Association.

Serpell, R., & Hatano, G. (1997). Education, schooling, and literacy. In J. W. Berry, P. R. Dasen, & T. S. Saraswathi (Eds.), *Handbook of cross-cultural psychology: Vol. 2. Basic process and human development* (2nd ed., pp. 339–376). Boston: Allyn & Bacon.

Shaffer, R. (1996). *Social development.* New York: Blackwell.

Shakin, M., Shakin, D., & Sternglanz, S. H. (1985). Infant clothing: Sex labeling for strangers. *Sex Roles, 12,* 955–963.

Shanley, M. L. (2001). *Making babies, making families.* Boston: Beacon Press.

Shatz, M. (1983). Communication. In P. H. Mussen (Ed.), *Handbook of child psychology* (Vol. 3, pp. 841–889). New York: Wiley.

Shatz, M. (1994). Theory of mind and the development of socio-linguistic intelligence in early childhood. In C. Lewis & P. Mitchell (Eds.), *Children's early understanding of mind: Origins and development* (pp. 311–329). Hillsdale, NJ: Erlbaum.

Shatz, M., & Gelman, R. (1973). The development of communication skills: Modifications in the speech of young children as a function of listener. *Monographs of the Society for Research in Child Development, 38*(5, Serial No. 152), 1–37.

Shaywitz, B. A., Shaywitz, S. E., Pugh, K. R., & Constable, R. T. (1995). Sex differences in the functional organization of the brain for language. *Nature, 373,* 607–609.

Shea, A. K., & Steiner, M. (2008). Cigarette smoking during pregnancy. *Nicotine & Tobacco Research, 10,* 267–289.*

Shea, D. L., Lubinski, D., & Benbow, C. P. (2001). Importance of assessing spatial ability in intellectually talented young adolescents: A 20-year longitudinal study. *Journal of Educational Psychology, 93,* 604–614.

Shenfield, T., Trehub, S. E., & Nakata, T. (2003). Maternal singing modulates infant arousal. *Psychology of Music, 31,* 365–375.*

Shepardson, D. P., & Pizzini, E. L. (1992). Gender bias in female elementary teachers' perceptions of the scientific ability of students. *Science Education, 76* (2), 147–153.

Sherman, S. L., Allen, E. G., Bean, L. H., & Freeman, S. B. (2007). Epidemiology of Down syndrome. *Mental Retardation and Developmental Disabilities Research Reviews, 13,* 221–227.

Sherry, J. L. (2007). Violent video games and aggression: Why can't we find effects? In R. W. Preiss, B. M. Gayle, N. Burrell, M. Allen & J. Bryant (Eds.), *Mass media effects research: Advances through meta-analysis* (pp. 245–262). Mahwah, NJ: Erlbaum.

Sherwood, N. E., Neumark-Sztainer, D., Story, M., Beuhring, T., & Resnick, M. D. (2002). Weight-related sports involvement in girls: Who is at risk for disordered eating? *American Journal of Health Promotion, 16,* 341–344.

Shields, A., Ryan, R. M., & Cicchetti, D. (2001). Narrative representations of caregivers and emotional dysregulation as predictors of maltreated children's rejection by peers. *Developmental Psychology, 37,* 321–337.

Shields, M. (2005). Measured obesity: Overweight Canadian children and adolescents. *Nutrition: Findings from the Canadian community health survey,* (Catalogue no. 82-620-MWE2005001).*

Shiffman, S. (1993). Smoking cessation treatment: Any progress? *Journal of Consulting and Clinical Psychology, 61,* 718–722.

Shirley, M. M. (1931). *The first two years, a study of twenty-five babies: I Postural & locomotor development.* Minneapolis, MN: University of Minnesota Press.

Shonkoff, J. P., & Phillips, D. (Eds.). (2000). *From neurons to neighborhoods.* Washington: National Academy Press.

Shrum, W., & Cheek, N. H. (1987). Social structure during the school years: Onset of the degrouping process. *American Sociological Review, 52,* 218–223.

Shweder, R. A. (1999). Culture and development in our postcultural age. In A. S. Masten (Ed.), *Cultural processes in child development* (Vol. 29, pp. 137–148). Mahwah, NJ: Erlbaum.

Shweder, R. A., Goodnow, J., Hatano, G., LeVine, R. A., Markus, H., & Miller, P. (1998). The cultural psychology of development: One mind, many mentalities. In W. Damon (Gen. Ed.) & R. M. Lerner (Vol. Ed.), *Handbook of child psychology* (Vol. 1, pp. 865–938). New York: Wiley.

Shweder, R. A., Goodnow, J. J., Hatano, G., LeVine, R. A., Markus, H. R., & Miller, P. J. (2006). The cultural psychology of development: One mind, many mentalities. In W. Damon & R. M. Lerner (Gen. Ed.), & R. M. Lerner (Ed.), *Handbook of child psychology: Vol. 1. Theoretical models of human development* (6th ed., pp. 716–792). New York: Wiley.

Siddiqui, A. (1995). Object size as a determinant of grasping in infancy. *Journal of Genetic Psychology, 156,* 345–358.

Siegel, A. W., & White, S. H. (1975). The development of spatial representatives of large scale environments. In H. W. Reese (Eds.), *Advances in child development and behavior* (Vol. 10). New York: Academic.

Siegler, R. (2000). The rebirth of children's learning. *Child Development, 71,* 26–36.

Siegler, R. S. (1983). Information processing approaches to development. In P. Mussen (Ed.), *Manual of child psychology.* New York: Wiley.

Siegler, R. S. (1987). The perils of averaging data over strategies: An example from children's addition. *Journal of Experimental Psychology: General, 116,* 250–264.

Siegler, R. S. (1992). The other Alfred Binet. *Developmental Psychology, 28,* 179–190.

Siegler, R. S. (1996). *Emerging minds: The process of change in children's thinking.* New York: Oxford University Press.

Siegler, R. S. (1998). *Children's thinking* (3rd ed.). Upper Saddle River, NJ: Prentice-Hall.

Siegler, R. S., & Alibali, M. W. (2005). *Children's thinking* (4th ed.). Upper Saddle River, NJ: Prentice Hall.

Sigman, M. (1995). Nutrition and child development: More food for thought. *Current Directions in Psychological Science, 4,* 52–55.

Signorella, M. L., Bigler, R. S., & Liben, L. S. (1993). Developmental differences in children's gender schemata about others: A meta-analytic review. *Developmental Review, 13,* 147–183.

Signorella, M. L., Bilger, R. S., & Liben, L. S. (1993). A meta-analysis of children's memories for own-sex and other-sex information. Journal of Applied Developmental Psychology, 18, 425–445.

Silberg, J. L., Rutter, M., & Eaves, L. J. (2001). Genetic and environmental influences on the temporal association between early anxiety and later depression in girls. *Biological Psychology, 49,* 1040–1049.

Silverman, I., & Choi, J. (2005). Locating places. In D. Buss (Ed.), *The evolutionary psychology handbook* (pp. 177–199). Hoboken, NJ: Wiley.*

Silverman, I., & Choi, J. (2006). Non-Euclidean navigational strategies of women: Compensatory response or evolved dimorphism? *Evolutionary Psychology, 4,* 75–84.*

Silverman, I., Choi, J., & Peters, M. (2007). The hunter-gatherer theory of sex differences in spatial abilities: Data from 40 countries. *Archives of Sexual Behavior, 36,* 261–268.*

Simion, F., Regolin, L., & Bulf, H. (2008). A predisposition for biological motion in the newborn baby. *PNAS Proceedings of the National Academy of Sciences of the United States of America, 205,* 809–813.

Simmons, R. G., & Blyth, D. A. (1987). *Moving into adolescence: The impact of pubertal change and school context.* Hawthorne, NY: Aldine.

Simmons, R. G., Blyth, D. A., & McKinney, K. L. (1984). The social and psychological effects of puberty on white females. In J. Brookes-Gunn & A. C. Peterson (Eds.), *Girls at puberty: Biological, psychological and social perspectives.* New York: Plenum.

Simmons, R. G., Burgeson, R., Carlson-Ford, S., & Blyth, D. A. (1987). The impact of cumulative change in early adolescence. *Child Development, 58,* 1220–1234.

Simons, R. L., Lin, K., & Gordon, L. C. (1998). Socialization in the family of origin and male dating violence: A prospective study. *Journal of Marriage and the Family, 60,* 467–478.

Simpkins, D., & Parke, R. D. (2001). The relations between parental friendships and children's friendships: Self-report and observational analysis. *Child Development, 72,* 569–582.

Singer, D. G., & Singer, L. T. (Eds.). (2001). *Handbook of children and the media.* Thousand Oaks, CA: Sage Publications.

Skinner, B. F. (1957). *Verbal behavior.* New York: Appleton-Century-Crofts.

Skodak, M., & Skeels, H. (1949). A final follow-up study of one hundred adopted children. *Journal of Genetic Psychology, 75,* 85–125.

Slaby, R. G., & Frey, K. S. (1975). Development of gender constancy and selective attention to same-sex models. *Child Development, 46,* 849–856.

Slater, A. (2000). Visual perception in the young infant: Early organization and rapid learning. In D. Muir & A. Slater (Eds.), *Infant development: The essential readings* (pp. 95–116). Oxford: Blackwell.

Slater, A. M., Bremner, G., Johnson, S. P., Sherwood, P., Hayes, R., & Brown, E. (2000). Newborn preferences for attractive faces: The role of internal and external facial features. *Infancy, 1,* 265–274.

Slater, A., Mattock, A., & Brown, E. (1990). Size constancy at birth: Newborn infants' responses to retinal and real size. *Journal of Experimental Child Psychology, 49,* 314–322.

Slater, A., Quinn, P., Brown, E., & Hayes, R. A. (1999). Intermodal perception at birth? Intersensory redundancy guides newborn infants' learning of arbitrary auditory-visual pairings. *Developmental Science, 2,* 333–338.

Slater, A. M., & Morison, V. (1985). Shape constancy and slant perception at birth. *Perception, 14,* 337–344.

Slaughter-Defoe, D. T., Nakagawa, K., Takanishi, R., & Johnson, D. J. (1990). Toward cultural/ecological perspectives on schooling and achievement in African- and Asian-American children. *Child Development, 61,* 363–383.

Slobin, D. I. (1979). *Psycholinguistics.* Glenview, IL: Scott, Foresman.

Slobin, D. I. (1982). Universal and particular in the acquisition of language. In L. R. Gleitman & H. E. Wanner (Eds.), *Language acquisition: The state of the art.* New York: Cambridge University Press.

Slobin, D. I. (1985). *The cross-linguistic study of language acquisition* (Vols. 1 & 2). Hillsdale, NJ: Erlbaum.

Slobin, D. I. (Ed.). (1992). *The cross-linguistic study of language acquisition: Vol. 3.* Hillsdale, NJ: Erlbaum.

Slomkowski, C., Rende, R., Conger, K. J., Simons, R. L., & Conger, R. D. (2001). Sisters, brothers, and delinquency: Evaluating social influence during early and middle adolescence. *Child Development, 72,* 271–283.

Smetana, J. (2000). Middle-class African American adolescents' and parents' conceptions of parental authority and parenting practices: A longitudinal investigation. *Child Development, 71,* 1672–1683.

Smetana, J., & Daddis, C. (2002). Domain-specific antecedents of parental psychological control and monitoring: The role of parenting beliefs and practices. *Child Development, 73,* 563–580.

Smetana, J., Daddis, C., & Chuang, S. S. (2003). "Clean your room!" Longitudinal investigation of adolescent-parent conflict and conflict-resolution in middle-class African American families. *Journal of Adolescent Research, 18,* 631–650.

Smetana, J. G. (1995). Morality in context: Abstractions, ambiguities, and applications. In R. Vasta (Ed.), *Annals of child development* (Vol. 10, pp. 83–130). London: Jessica Kingsley.

Smetana, J. G. (1997). Parenting and the development of social knowledge reconceptualized: A social domain analysis. In J. E. Grusec & L. Kuczynski (Eds.), *Parenting and children's internalization of values* (pp. 162–192). New York: Wiley.

Smetana, J. G. (Ed.). (2005). *Changing conceptions of parental authority: New directions for child development.* San Francisco, CA: Jossey-Bass.

Smetana, J. G. (2006). Social domain theory: Consistencies and variations in children's moral and social judgments. In M. Killen & J. G. Smetana (Eds.), *Handbook of moral development* (Vol. Erlbaum). 119–154: Mahwah, NJ.

Smetana, J. G., & Asquith, P. (1994). Adolescents' and parents' conceptions of parental authority and adolescent autonomy. *Child Development, 65,* 1147–1162.

Smetana, J. G., & Braeges, J. L. (1990). The development of toddler's moral and conventional judgements. *Merrill-Palmer Quarterly, 36,* 329–346.

Smetana, J. G., & Gaines, C. (1999). Adolescent-parent conflict in middle-class African American families. *Child Development, 70,* 1447–1463.

Smetana, J. G., & Letourneau, K. J. (1984). Development of gender constancy and children's sex-typed free play behavior. *Developmental Psychology, 20,* 691–696.

Smith, A. M., Fried, P. A., Hogan, M. J., & Cameron, I. (2006). Effects of prenatal marijuana on visuospatial working memory: An fMRI study in young adults. *Neurotoxicology and Teratology, 28,* 286–295.*

Smith, B. A., Fillion, T. J., & Blass, E. M. (1990). Orally mediated sources of calming in 1- to 3-day-old human infants. *Developmental Psychology, 26,* 731–737.

Smith, C. L. (1979). Children's understanding of natural language hierarchies. *Journal of Experimental Child Psychology, 27,* 437–458.

Smith, D. (2001). Prevention: Still a young field. *Monitor on Psychology, 3,* 70–72.

Smith, D. E., & Mosby, G. (2003). Jamaican child-rearing practices: The role of corporal punishment. *Adolescence, 38,* 369–381.

Smith, D. J., Stevens, M. E., Sudanagunta, S. P., Bronson, R. T., Makhinson, M., Watabe, A. M., O'Dell, T. J., Fung, J., Weier, H. U., Chang, J. F., & Rubin, E. M. (1997). Functional screening of 2Mb of human chromosome 21q22.2 in transgenic mice implicates minibrain in learning defects associated with Down syndrome. *Nature Genetics, 16,* 28–36.

Smith, P. K., & Drew, L. M. (2002). Grandparenthood. In M. H. Bornstein (Ed.), *Handbook of parenting.* Mahwah, NJ: Erlbaum.

Smith, P. K., Pepler, D., & Craig, W. M. (Eds.). (2004). *Bullying in schools: How successful can interventions be?* New York: Cambridge University Press.*

Smith, S. (Ed.). (1995). *Two-generation programs for families in poverty: A new intervention strategy.*

Norwood, NJ: Ablex.

Smith, T. M. (1994). Adolescent pregnancy. In R. Simeonsson (Ed.), *Risk, resilience, and prevention: Promoting the well-being of all children.* Baltimore: Brooks Publishing.

Smollar, J., & Youniss, J. (1982). Social development through friendship. In K. H. Rubin & H. S. Ross (Eds.), *Peer relationships and social skills in childhood.* New York: Springer-Verlag.

Snarey, J., & Hooker, C. (2006). Lawrence Kohlberg. In *Encyclopedia of spiritual and religious development* (pp. 251–255). Thousand Oaks, CA: Sage.

Snarey, J. R., Reimer, J., & Kohlberg, L. (1985). Development of social-moral reasoning among kibbutz adolescents: A longitudinal cross-cultural study. *Developmental Psychology, 21,* 3–17.

Snow, C. E. (1989). Understanding social interaction and language acquisition: Sentences are not enough. In M. H. Bornstein & J. S. Bruner (Eds.), *Interaction in human development* (pp. 83–104). Hillsdale, NJ: Erlbaum.

Society for Research in Child Development. (1993). Ethical standards of research with children. In *Directory of Members* (pp. 337–339). Ann Arbor, MI: SRCD.

Sokal, M. M. (1992). Origins and early years of the American Psychological Association, 1890–1906. *American Psychologist, 47,* 111–122.

Sokolov, J. L. (1993). A local contingency analysis of the fine-tuning hypothesis. *Developmental Psychology, 29,* 1008–1023.

Solomon, J., & George, C. (1999). The measurement of attachment security in infancy and childhood. In J. Cassidy & P. R. Shaver (Eds.), *Handbook of attachment* (pp. 287–318). New York: Guildford.

Solomon, S. E., Rothbaum, E. D., & Balsam, K. F. (2004). Pioneers in partnership: Lesbian and gay male couples in civil unions and married heterosexual siblings. *Journal of Family Psychology, 18,* 275–286.

Sontag, L. W. (1944). Differences in modifiability of fetal behavior and physiology. *Psychosomatic Medicine, 6,* 151–154.

Sophian, C., & Crosby, M. E. (2008). What eye fixation patterns tell us about subitizing. *Developmental Neuropsychology, 33,* 394–409.

Sosa, R., Kennell, J., Klaus, M., Robertson, S., & Urrutia, J. (1980). The effect of a supportive companion on perinatal problems, length of labor and mother-infant

interaction. *New England Journal of Medicine, 303,* 597–600.

Sostek, A. M., & Anders, T. F. (1981). The biosocial importance and environmental sensitivity of infant sleep-wake behaviors. In K. Bloom (Ed.), *Prospective issues in infancy research.* Hillsdale, NJ: Erlbaum.

Southard, M., & Pasnak, R. (1997). Effects of maturation on preoperational seriation. *Child Study Journal, 27,* 255–268.

Sowell, E. R., Peterson, B. S., Thompson, P. M., Welcome, S. E., Henkenius, A. L., & Toga, A. W. (2003). Mapping cortical change across the human life span. *Nature Neuroscience, 6,* 309–315.

Spearman, C. (1927). *The abilities of man.* New York: Macmillan.

Spelke, E. (2000). Core knowledge. *American Psychologist, 55,* 1233–1243.

Spelke, E. S. (1987). The development of intermodal perception. In P. Salapatek & L. Cohen (Eds.), *Handbook of infant perception: Vol. 2. From perception to cognition* (pp. 233–274). New York: Academic.

Spence, J., & Buckner, C. (2000). Instrumental and expressive traits, trait stereotypes, and sexist attitudes. *Psychology of Women Quarterly, 24,* 44–62.

Spencer, J. P., Clearfield, M., Corbetta, D., Ulrich, B., Buchanan, P., & Schöner, G. (2006). Moving toward a grand *theory* of development: In memory of Esther Thelen. *Child Development, 77,* 1521–1538.

Spencer, J. P., & Thelen, E. (2000). Spatially specific changes in infants' muscle coactivity as they learn to reach. *Infancy, 1,* 275–302.

Spencer, J. P., Vereijken, B., Diedrich, F. J., & Thelen, E. (2000). Posture and the emergence of manual skills. *Developmental Science, 3,* 216–233.

Spencer, M. B. (2006). Phenomenology and ecological systems theory: Development of diverse groups. In W. Damon & R. M. Lerner (Gen. Ed.), & R. M. Lerner (Ed.), *Handbook of child psychology: Vol. 1. Theoretical models of human development* (6th ed., pp. 829–893). New York: Wiley.

Spergel, I. A., Ross, R. E., Curry, G. D., & Chance, R. (1989). *Youth gangs: Problem and response.* Washington, DC: Office of Juvenile Justice and Delinquency Prevention.

Sperling, G. (1960). The information available in brief visual presentations. *Psychological Monographs, 74.*

Spiker, D., & Ricks, M. (1984). Visual self-recognition in autistic children: Developmental variations. *Child Development, 55,* 214–225.

Spoth, R. L., Redmond, C., & Shin, C. (2001). Randomized trial of brief family interventions for general populations: Adolescent substance use outcomes 4 years following baseline. *Journal of Consulting and Clinical Psychology, 69,* 627–642.

Spoth, R. L., Redmond, C., & Shin, C. (2003). Randomized trial of brief family interventions for general populations: Adolescent substance use outcomes four years following baseline. *Journal of Consulting and Clinical Psychology, 69,* 627–642.

Springer, S. P., & Deutsch, G. (1993). *Left brain, right brain.* New York: Freeman.

Sroufe, L. A. (1996). *Emotional development: The organization of emotional life in the early years.* New York: Cambridge University Press.

Sroufe, L. A., Egeland, B., Carlson, E. A., & Collins, W. A. (2005). *The development of the person: The Minnesota study of risk and adaptation from birth to adulthood.* New York: Guilford Press.

Sroufe, L. A., & Wunsch, J. P. (1972). The development of laughter in the first year of life. *Child Development, 43,* 1326–1344.

Sroufe, L. A., Waters, E., & Matas, L. (1974). Contextual determinants of infant affectional response. In M. Lewis & L. Rosenblum (Eds.), *Origins of fear.* New York: Wiley.

Stake, J. E., & Nickens, S. D. (2005). Adolescent girls' and boys' science peer relationships and perceptions of the possible self as a scientist. *Sex Roles, 52,* 1–11.

Stams, G. J. M., Juffer, F., & van IJzendoorn, M. H. (2002). Maternal sensitivity, infant attachment and temperament in early childhood predict adjustment in middle childhood: The case of adopted children and their biologically unrelated parents. *Developmental Psychology, 38,* 806–821.

Starr, A. S. (1923). The diagnostic value of the audio-vocal digit memory span. *Psychological Clinic, 15,* 61–84.

Starr, J. M., Deary, I. J., Lemmon, H., & Whalley, L. J. (2000). Mental ability age 11 years and health status age 77 years. *Age and Ageing, 29,* 253–258.

Statistics Canada. (1998). Births, 1996. *The Daily,* July 8, 1998. (Statistics Canada Cat. No. 11-001-XIE).*

Statistics Canada. (2006a). *Births* (Catalogue no. 84F0210X).

Ottawa: Statistics Canada.*

Statistics Canada. (2006b). *Women in Canada: A gender-based statistical report* (Catalogue no. 89-503-XIE). Ottawa: Statistics Canada.*

Statistics Canada. (2007). Cansim database, Table 106-9002. Retrieved January 14, 2009, from http://cansim2.statcan.gc.ca/cgi-win/cnsmcgi.pgm

Statistics Canada. (2007a). *Table 106-9002—Pregnancy outcomes, by age group, Canada, provinces and territories, annual,* CANSIM (database). Retrieved January 25, 2010, from http://cansim2.statcan.gc.ca/cgi-win/cnsmcgi.exe?Lang=E&CNSM-Fi=CII/CII_1-eng.htm*

Statistics Canada. (2007b). *Families and households highlight tables, 2006 Census* (Catalogue no. 97-553-XWE2006002). Ottawa: Statistics Canada.*

Statistics Canada. (2008). *Deaths: 2005* (Catalogue no. 84F0211X). Ottawa: Statistics Canada.*

Stattin, H., & Magnusson, D. (1990). *Pubertal maturation in female development* (Vol. 2). Hillsdale, NJ: Erlbaum.

Steele, C. M. (1997). A threat in the air: How stereotypes shape intellectual identity and performance. *American Psychologist, 52,* 613–629.

Steele, K. M., Bass, K. E., & Crook, M. D. (1999). The mystery of the Mozart effect: Failure to replicate. *Psychological Science, 10,* 366–373.

Stein, M. B., Jang, K. L., & Livesley, W. J. (2002). Heritability of social anxiety- related concerns and personality characteristics: A twin study. *Journal of Nervous and Mental Disease, 190,* 218-224.*

Steinberg, L. (1987). Impact of puberty on family relations: Effects of pubertal status and pubertal timing. *Developmental Psychology, 23,* 451–460.

Steinberg, L., Darling, N. E., & Fletcher, A. C. (1995). Authoritative parenting and adolescent adjustment: An ecological journal. In P. Moen & G. H. Elder, Jr. & K. Luscher (Eds.), *Examining lives in context: Perspectives on the ecology of human development* (pp. 423–466). Washington, DC: APA.

Steinberg, L., Dornbusch, S. M., & Brown, B. B. (1992). Ethnic differences in adolescent achievement: An ecological perspective. *American Psychologist, 47,* 723–729.

Steinberg, L., Mounts, N. S., Lamborn, S. D., & Dornbusch, S. M. (1991). Authoritative parenting and adolescent adjustment across varied ecological niches. *Journal of Research on Adolescence, 1,* 19–36.

Steiner, J. E. (1979). Human facial expression in response to taste and smell stimulation. In H. W. Reese & L. P. Lipsitt (Eds.), *Advances in child development and behavior* (Vol. 13). New York: Academic.

Stemler, S. E., Grigorenko, E. L., Jarvin, L., & Sternberg, R. J. (2006). Using the theory of successful intelligence as a basis for augmenting AP exams in Psychology and Statistics. *Contemporary Educational Psychology, 31,* 344–376.

Stenberg, C., & Campos, J. (1989). *The development of anger expressions during infancy.* Unpublished manuscript. University of Denver, Denver, Colorado.

Stenberg, C., Campos, J., & Emde, R. N. (1983). The facial expression of anger in seven-month-old infants. *Child Development, 54,* 178–184.

Stephan, K. E., Marshall, J. C., Friston, K. J., Rowe, J. B., Ritzl, A., Zilles, K., et al. (2003). Lateralized cognitive processes and lateralized task control in the human brain. *Science, 301,* 384–386.

Stern, M., & Karraker, K. H. (1989). Sex stereotyping of infants: A review of gender labeling studies. *Sex Roles, 20,* 501–522.

Sternberg, R. J. (1985). *Beyond IQ: A triarchic theory of human intelligence.* Cambridge, England: Cambridge University Press.

Sternberg, R. J. (2001). Successful intelligence: Understanding what Spearman had rather than what he studied. In J. M. Collis & S. Messick (Eds.), *Intelligence and personality* (pp. 347–373). Mahwah, NJ: Erlbaum.

Sternberg, R. J. (2005). The triarchic theory of successful intelligence. In D. P. Flanagan & P. L. Harrison (Eds.), *Contemporary intellectual assessment: Theories, tests, and issues* (pp. 103–119). New York: Guildford.

Sternberg, R. J., & Grigorenko, E. L. (Eds.). (2001). *Environmental effects on cognitive abilities.* Mahwah, NJ: Erlbaum.

Sternberg, R. J., Grigorenko, E. L., & Bridglall, B. L. (2007). Intelligence as a socialized phenomenon. In E. W. Gordon & B. L. Bridglall (Eds.), *Affirmative development: Cultivating academic ability* (pp. 49–72). Lanham, MD: Rowman & Littlefield.

Sternberg, R. J., & Jarvin, L. (2003). Alfred Binet's contributions as a paradigm for impact on psychology. In R. J. Sternberg (Ed.), *The anatomy of impact: What makes the great works of psychology great* (pp. 89–107). Washington, DC: APA.

Sternberg, R. J., Nokes, C., Geisser, P. W., Prince, R., Okatcha, F., Bundy, D. A., & Grigorenko, E. L. (2001). The relationship between academic and practical intelligence: A case study in Kenya. *Intelligence, 29,* 401–418.

Sternberg, R. J., & Preiss, D. D. (2005). *Intelligence and technology: The impact of tools on the nature and development of human abilities.* Mahwah: Erlbaum.

Sternberg, R. J., & Wagner, R. K. (1993). The geocentric view of intelligence and job performance is wrong. *Current Directions in Psychological Science, 2,* 1–6.

Sternberg, R. J., & Wagner, R. K. (1994). *Mind in context.* New York: Cambridge University Press.

Sternberg, R. J., Wagner, R. K., & Okagaki, L. (1993). Practical intelligence: The nature and role of tacit knowledge in work and at school. In H. W. Reese & W. Puckett (Eds.), *Advances in lifespan development* (pp. 205–227). Hillsdale, NJ: Erlbaum.

Stevahn, L., Johnson, D. W., Johnson, R. T., Overle, K., & Wahle, L. (2000). Effects of conflict resolution training integrated into a kindergarten curriculum. *Child Development, 71,* 772–784.

Stevenson, H. W. (2001). Schools, teachers, and parents. In A. Thornton (Ed.), *The well-being of children and families* (pp. 341-355). Ann Arbor: The University of Minnesota Press.

Stevenson, H. W., Chen, C., & Lee, S. Y. (1993). Mathematics achievement of Chinese, Japanese, and American children: Ten years later. *Science, 259,* 53–58.

Stevenson, H. W., Chen, C., & Uttal, D. H. (1990). Beliefs and achievement: A study of black, white, and hispanic children. *Child Development, 61,* 508–523.

Stevenson, H. W., Lee, S., & Mu, X. (2000). Successful achievement in mathematics: China and the United States. In C. F. M. van Lieshout & P. G. Heymans (Eds.), *Developing talent across the life span* (pp. 167–182). Philadelphia, PA: Psychology Press.

Stevenson, H. W., & Stigler, J. W. (1992). *The learning gap.* New York: Summit Books.

Stevenson-Hinde, J. (2005). The interplay between attachment, temperament, and maternal style: A Madingley persepective. In K. E. Grossmann, K. Grossmann & E. Waters (Eds.), *Attachment from infancy to adulthood.* New York: Guilford.

Stice, L., Presnell, K., & Bearman, S. K. (2000). Relation of early menarche to depression, eating disorder, substance abuse and comorbid psychopathology among adolescent girls. *Developmental Psychology, 37*, 608–617.

Stice, E., Presnell, K., & Bearman, S. K. (2001). Relation of early menarche to depression, eating disorders, substance abuse, and comorbid psychopathology among adolescent girls. *Developmental Psychology, 37*, 608–619.

Stiles, J. (2000). Spatial cognitive development following prenatal or perinatal focal brain injury. In H. S. Levin & J. Grafman (Eds.), *Cerebral reorganization of function after brain damage* (pp. 207–217). New York: Oxford University Press.

Stipek, D., & McCroskey, J. (1989). Investing in children: Government and workplace policies for parents. *American Psychologist, 44*, 416–423.

Stoch, M. B., Smyth, P. M., Moodie, A. D., & Bradshaw, D. (1982). Psychosocial outcome and findings after gross undernourishment during infancy: A 20-year developmental study. *Developmental Medicine & Child Neurology, 24*, 419–436.

Stock, S., Miranda, C., Evans, S., Plessis, S., Ridley, J., Yeh, S., et al. (2007). Healthy Buddies: A novel, peer-led health promotion program for the prevention of obesity and eating disorders in children in elementary school. *Pediatrics, 120*, 1059–1068.

Stolley, K. S. (1993). Statistics on adoption in the United States. *The Future of Children, 3*, 26–42.

Stoneman, Z., Brody, G., & MacKinnon, C. E. (1986). Same sex and cross-sex siblings: Activity choices, roles, behavior, and gender stereotypes. *Sex Roles, 15*, 495–511.

Storch, E. A., Milsom, V. A., DeBraganza, N., Lewin, A. B., Geffken, G. R., & Silverstein, J. H. (1007). Peer victimization, psychosocial adjustment and physical activity in overweight and at-risk-for overweight youth. *Journal of Pediatric Psychology, 32*, 80–89.

Storey, A. E., Walsh, C. J., Quinton, R. L., & Wynne-Edwards, K. E. (2000). Hormonal correlates of paternal responsiveness in new and expectant fathers. *Evolution and Human Behavior, 21*, 79–91.*

Straughtan, R. (1986). Why act on Kohlberg's moral judgments? In S. Modgil & C. Modgil (Eds.), *Lawrence Kohlberg: Consensus and controversy*. Philadelphia: Falmer Press.

Straus, M. A. (2008). The special issue on prevention of violence ignores the primordial violence. *Journal of Interpersonal Violence, 23*, 1314–1320.

Strayer, F. F. (1984). Biological approaches to the study of the family. In R. D. Parke, R. Emde, H. Macadoo, & G. P. Sackett (Eds.), *Review of child development research: Vol. 7. The family*. Chicago: University of Chicago Press.*

Strayer, F. F., Verissimo, M., Vaughn, B. E., & Howes, C. (1995). A quantitative approach to the description and classification of primary social relationships. In E. Waters, B.E. Vaughn, G. Posada, & K. Kondo-Ikemura (Eds.), *Caregiving, cultural, and cognitive perspectives on secure-base behavior and working models. New grouping points of attachment theory and research. Monographs of the Society for Research in Child Development* (pp. 49–70), *60* (2-3, Serial No. 244).*

Strayer, J., & Roberts, W. (2004). Empathy and observed anger and aggression in five-year-olds. *Social Development, 13*, 1–13.*

Strayer, J., & Roberts, W. (2004). Children's anger, emotional expressiveness, and empathy: Relations with parents' empathy, emotional expressiveness, and parenting practices. *Social Development, 13*, 229–254.*

Streissguth, A. (2007). Offspring effects of prenatal alcohol exposure from birth to 25 years: The Seattle Prospective Longitudinal Study. *Journal of Clinical Psychology in Medical Settings, 14*, 81–101.

Streissguth, A. P. (1997). *Fetal alcohol syndrome*. New York: Oxford University Press.

Streri, A. (2002). Hand preference in 4-month-old infants: Global or local processing of objects in the haptic mode. *Current Psychological Letters: Behaviour, Brain, and Cognition, No. 7*, 39–50.

Streri, A., Lemoine, C., & Devouche, E. (2008). Development of inter-manual transfer of shape information in infancy. *Developmental Psychobiology, 50*, 70–76.

Streri, A., Lhote, M., & Dutilleul, S. (2000). Haptic perception in newborns. *Developmental Science, 3*, 319–327.

Streri, A., & Molina, M. (1993). Visual-tactual and tactual-visual transfer between objects and pictures in 2-month-old infants. *Perception, 27*, 1299–1318.

Streri, A., & Pêcheux, M. (1986). Tactual habituation and discrimination of form in infancy: A comparison with vision. *Child Development, 57*, 100–104.

Stunkard, A. J., Foch, T. T., & Hrubeck, Z. (1986). A twin study of

human obesity. *Journal of the American Medical Association, 256*, 51–54.

Stunkard, A. J., Sorenson, T. I., Hanis, C., Teasdale, T. W., Chakraborty, R., Schull, W. J., et al. (1986). An adoption study of human obesity. *The New England Journal of Medicine, 314*, 193–198.

Stuss, D. T., & Alexander, M. P. (2000). Affectively burnt in: A proposed role of the right frontal lobe. In E. Tulving (Ed.), *Memory, consciousness, and the brain: The Tallinn conference* (pp. 215–227). Philadelphia, PA: Psychology Press.*

Subrahmanyam, K., Kraut, R. E., Greenfield, P. M., & Gross, E. F. (2001). New forms of electronic media: The impact of interactive electronic games and Internet on cognition, socialization, and behavior. In D. Singer & J. Singer (Eds.), *Handbook of children and media*. Thousand Oaks, CA: Sage.

Sugita, Y. (2004). Experience in early infancy is indispensable for color perception. *Current Biology, 14*, 1267–1271.

Sulloway, F. J. (1995). Birth order and evolutionary psychology: A meta-analytic overview. *Psychological Inquiry, 6*, 75–80.

Sundara, M., Polka, L., & Molnar, M. (2008). Development of coronal stop perception: Bilingual infants keep pace with their monolingual peers. *Cognition, 108*, 232–242.*

Super, C. M., & Harkness, S. (1981). The infant's niche in rural Kenya and metropolitan America. In L. L. Adler (Ed.), *Cross-cultural research at issue* (pp. 47–55). New York: American Press.

Super, C. M., Herrera, M. G., & Mora, J. O. (1990). Long-term effects of food supplementation and psychosocial intervention on the physical growth of Columbian infants at risk of malnutrition. *Child Development, 61*, 29–49.

Sutton, C. (2001). Resurgence of attachment (behaviors) within a cognitive behavioral intervention: Evidence from research. *Behavioural and Cognitive Psychotherapy, 29*, 357–366.

Swain, I. U., Zelazo, P. R., & Clifton, R. K. (1993). Newborn infants' memory for speech sounds retained over 24 hours. *Developmental Psychology, 29*, 312–323.

Swanson, J. M., Arnold, L. E., Kraemer, H. C., Hechtman, L. T., Molina, B. S. G., Hinshaw, S. P., et al. (2008). Evidence, interpretation, and qualification from multiple reports of long-term outcomes in the multimodal treatment study of children with ADHD

(MTA). Part I: Executive summary. *Journal of Attention Disorders, 12*, 4–14.

Symons, D., Clark, S., Isaksen, G., & Marshall, J. (1998). Stability of Q-sort attachment security from age two to five. *Infant Behavior and Development, 21*, 785–791.*

Symons, D. K., and Clark, S. E. (2000). A longitudinal study of mother-child relationships and theory of mind in the preschool period. *Social Development, 9*, 3–23.*

Tager-Flusberg, H. (1985). Putting words together: Morphology and syntax in the preschool years. In J. Berko-Gleason (Ed.), *The development of language*. Columbia: Bell D. Howell.

Tamburrino, M. B., & McGinnis, R. A. (2002). Anorexia nervosa. A review. *Panminerva Medicine, 44*, 301-311.

Tamis-LeMonda, C. S., Bornstein, M. H., & Baumwell, L. (2001). Maternal responsiveness and children's achievement of language milestones. *Child Development, 72*, 748–767.

Tamis-LeMonda, C. S., & McLure, J. (1995). Infant visual expectation in relation to feature learning. *Infant Behavior and Development, 18*, 427–434.

Tangney, J. P. (1998). How does guilt differ from shame? In J. Bybee (Ed.), *Guilt and children* (pp. 1-17). San Diego: Academic Press.

Tangney, J. P. (2003). Self-relevent emotions. In M. R. Leary & J. P. Tangney (Eds.), *Handbook of self and identity* (pp. 384–400). New York: Guildford.

Tangney, J. P., & Dearing, R. L. (2002). *Shame and guilt*. New York: Guildford.

Tanner, J. (1990). *Fetus into man: Physical growth from conception to maturity*. Cambridge, MA: Harvard University Press.

Tanner, J. M. (1970). Physical growth. In P. H. Mussen (Ed.), *Carmichael's manuscript of child psychology* (Vol. 1, pp. 77–155). New York: Wiley.

Tanner, J. M. (1978). *Fetus into man: Physical growth from conception to maturity*. Cambridge, MA: Harvard University Press.

Tanner, J. M. (1998). Sequence, tempo, and individual variation in growth and development of boys and girls aged twelve to sixteen. In R. E. Muuss & H. D. Porton (Eds.), *Adolescent behavior and society: A book of readings* (5th ed., pp. 34–46). New York: McGraw-Hill.

Tardiff, T. (1993). *Audit-to-child speech and language acquisition in Mandarin Chinese*. Unpublished doctoral dissertation. New Haven, CT.

Tardiff, T. (1996). Nouns are not always learned before verbs: Evidence from Mandarin speakers' early vocabularies. *Developmental Psychology, 32,* 492–504.

Tasbihsazan, R., Nettelbeck, T., & Kirby, N. (2003). Predictive validity of the Fagan test of infant intelligence. *British Journal of Developmental Psychology, 21,* 585–597.

Tatsuno, Y., & Sakai, K. L. (2005). Language-related activations in the left prefrontal regions are differentially modulated by age, proficiency, and task demands. *The Journal of Neuroscience, 25,* 1637–1644.

Taube-Schiff, M., & Lau, M. A. (2008). Major depressive disorder. In M. Hersen & J. Rosqvist (Eds.), *Handbook of psychological assessment, case conceptualization, and treatment, Vol 1: Adults* (pp. 319–351). Hoboken, NJ: John Wiley.*

Teller, D. Y. (1997). First glances. The vision of infants. The Friedenwald Lecture. *Investigative Ophthalmology & Visual Science, 38,* 2183–2203.

Teller, D. Y., & Bornstein, M. H. (1984). Infant color vision. In P. Salapatek & L. B. Cohen (Eds.), *Handbook of infant perception.* New York: Academic.

Temple, C. M., & Sanfilippo, P. M. (2003). Executive skills in Klinefelter's syndrome. *Neuropsychologia, 41,* 1547–1559.

Tenenbaum, H. R., & Leaper, C. (2002). Are parents' gender schemas related to their children's gender-related cognitions? A meta-analysis. *Developmental Psychology, 38,* 615–630.

Tennenbaum, H. R., & Leaper, C. (2003). Parent-child conversations about science: The socialization of gender inequalities. *Developmental Psychology, 39,* 34–47.

Tessier, R., et al. (2003). Kangaroo mother care: A method for protecting high-risk low-birth-weight and premature infants against developmental delay. *Infant Behavior and Development, 26,* 384–397.*

Teti, D. M. (2002). Retrospect and prospect in the study of sibling relationships. In J. McHale & W. Grolnick (Eds.), *Retrospect and prospect in the psychological study of families* (pp. 193–224). Mahwah, NJ: Erlbaum.

Tharp, R. G., & Gallimore, R. (1988). *Rousing minds to life: Teaching, learning, and schooling in social context.* New York: Cambridge University Press.

The Daily. (2000, October). Teenage pregnancy. Ottawa, ON: Statistics Canada.*

Thelen, E. (1995). Motor development: A new synthesis. *American Psychologist, 50,* 79–95.

Thelen, E. (2000). Motor development as foundation and future of developmental psychology. *International Journal of Behavioral Development, 24,* 385–397.

Thelen, E. (2002). Self-organization in developmental processes: Can systems approaches work? In M. H. Johnson & Y. Munakata (Eds.), *Brain development and cognition: A reader* (2nd ed., pp. 336–374). Malden, MA: Blackwell Publishing.

Thelen, E., & Bates, E. (2003). Connectionism and dynamic systems: Are they really different? *Developmental Science, 6,* 378–391.

Thelen, E., Corbetta, D., Kamm, K., Spencer, J. P., Schneider, K., & Zernicke, R. F. (1993). The transition to reaching: Mapping intention and intrinsic dynamics. *Child Development, 64,* 1058–1098.

Thelen, E., & Smith, L. B. (1994). *A dynamic systems approach to the development of cognition and action.* Cambridge, MA: MIT Press.

Thelen, E., & Smith, L. B. (2006). Dynamic systems theory. In R. L. Lerner (Ed.), *Handbook of child psychology: Vol. 1: Theoretical models of human development* (6th ed.). New York: Wiley.

Thevenin, D. M., Eilers, R. E., Oller, D. K., & LaVoie, L. (1985). Where's the drift in babbling about? A cross-linguistic study. *Applied Psycholinguistics, 6,* 3–15.

Thiessen, E. D., & Saffran, J. R. (2003). When cues collide: Use of stress and statistical cues to word boundaries by 7- to 9-month-old infants. *Developmental Psychology, 39,* 706–716.

Thomas, A., & Chess, S. (1986). The New York Longitudinal Study: From infancy to early adult life. In R. Plomin & J. Dunn (Eds.), *Changes, continuities and challenges.* Hillsdale, NJ: Erlbaum.

Thomas, M. S. C., & McClelland, J. L. (2008). Connectionist models of cognition. In R. Sun (Ed.), *The Cambridge handbook of computational psychology* (pp. 23–58). New York: Cambridge University Press.

Thomasson, M. A., & Teller, D. Y. (2000). Infant color vision: Sharp chromatic edges are not required for chromatic discrimination in 4-month-olds. *Vision Research, 40,* 1051–1057.

Thompson, C., Barresi, J., & Moore, C. (1997). The development of future-oriented prudence and altruism in preschoolers. *Cognitive Development, 12,* 199–212.*

Thompson, I. (2000). Human gene therapy: Harsh lessons, high hopes. *FDA Consumer, 34,* 19–24.

Thompson, R. (2006). Emotional regulation in children. In J. Gross (Ed.), *Handbook of emotional regulation* (pp. 249-268). New York: Guildford.

Thompson, R. A. (1987). Development of children's inferences of the emotions of others. *Developmental Psychology, 23,* 124–131.

Thompson, R. A. (1989). Causal attributions and children's emotional understanding. In C. Saarni & P. L. Harris (Eds.), *Children's understanding of emotions* (pp. 117–150). New York: Cambridge University Press.

Thompson, R. A. (1994). *Fatherhood and divorce: The future of children.* Los Altos, CA: Center for the Future of Children

Thompson, R. A. (1995). *Preventing child maltreatment through social support: A critical analysis.* Thousand Oaks, CA: Sage.

Thompson, R. A., Lamb, M. E., & Estes, D. (1982). Stability of infant-mother attachment and its relationship to changing life circumstances in an unselected middle-class sample. *Child Development, 53,* 144–148.

Thompson, W. F., Schellenberg, E. G., & Husain, G. (2001). Arousal, mood, and the Mozart effect. *Psychological Science, 12,* 248–251.*

Thornberry, T. P., Krohn, M. D., Lizotte, A. J., Smith, C. A., & Tobin, K. (2003). *Gangs and delinquency in developmental perspective.* New York: Cambridge University Press.

Thorne, B. (1986). Girls and boys together . . . but mostly apart: Gender arrangements in elementary schools. In W. W. Hartup & Z. Rubin (Eds.), *Relations and relationships.* Hillsdale, NJ: Erlbaum.

Thurber, C. A., & Weisz, J. R. (1997). "You can try or you can just give up": The impact of perceived control and coping style on childhood homesickness. *Developmental Psychology, 33,* 508–517.

Thurstone, L. L. (1938). *Primary mental abilities.* Chicago: University of Chicago Press.

Tinsley, B. J. (2003). *How children learn to be healthy.* New York: Cambridge University Press.

Tinsley, B. J., Holtgrave, D. R., Erdley, C. A., & Reise, S. P. (1997). A multi-method analysis of risk perceptions and health behaviors in children. *Educational and Psychological Measurement, 57,* 197–209.

Tinsley, B. J., Lees, N. B., & Sumartojo, E. (2004). Children and adolescent HIV risk: Familial and

cultural perspectives. *Journal of Family Psychology, 18,* 208–224.

Tobin-Richards, M., Boxer, A. O., & Petersen, A. C. (1983). The psychological impact of pubertal change: Sex differences in perceptions of self during early adolescence. In J. Brooks-Gunn & A. C. Petersen (Eds.), *Girls at puberty: Biological, psychological, and social perspectives.* New York: Plenum.

Tolan, P. H., Gorman-Smith, D., & Henry, D. B. (2003). The developmental ecology of urban males' youth violence. *Developmental Psychology, 39,* 274–291.

Tolman, E. C. (1948). Cognitive maps in rats and men. *Psychological Review, 55,* 189–209.

Tomada, G., & Schneider, B. H. (1997). Relational aggression, gender, and peer acceptance: Invariance across culture, stability over time, and concordance among informants. *Developmental Psychology, 33,* 601–609.*

Tomasello, M. (1995). Language is not an instinct. *Cognitive Development, 10,* 131–156.

Tomasello, M. (1999). *The cultural origins of human cognition.* Cambridge, MA: Harvard University Press.

Tomasello, M. (2003). *Constructing a language: A usage-based theory of language acquisition.* Cambridge, MA: Harvard University Press.

Tomasello, M. (2006). Acquiring metalinguistic constructions. In W. Damon & R. M. Lerner (Gen. Ed.), & D. Kuhn & R. Siegler (Eds.), *Handbook of child psychology. Vol. 2. Cognition, perception, and language* (6th ed., pp. 255–298). New York: Wiley.

Tomasello, M., Carpenter, M., Call, J., Behne, T., & Moll, H. (2005). Understanding and sharing intentions: The origins of cultural cognition. *Behavioral and Brain Sciences, 28,* 675–735.

Tomasello, M., Carpenter, M., & Liszkowski, U. (2007). A new look at infant pointing. *Child Development, 78,* 705–722.

Tomasello, M., & Farrar, J. (1986). Joint attention and early language. *Child Development, 57,* 1454–1463.

Tomlinson, M., Cooper, P., & Murray, L. (2005). The mother-infant relationship and infant attachment in a South African peri-urban settlement. *Child Development, 76,* 1044–1054.

Torff, B., & Gardner, H. (1999). The vertical mind—The case for multiple intelligences. In M. Anderson (Ed.), The development of intelligence. East Sussex, England: Psychology Press.

Towers, H., Spotts, E., & Reiss, D. (2003). Unraveling the complexity of genetic and environmental influences on family. In F. Walsh (Ed.), *Normal family processes* (3rd ed., pp. 608–631). New York: Guildford.

Trabasso, T., Issen, A. M., Dolecki, P., McLanahan, A., Riley, C., & Tucker, T. (1978). How do children solve class-inclusion problems? In R. S. Siegler (Ed.), *Children's thinking: What develops?* Hillsdale, NJ: Erlbaum.

Trainor, L. J. (1996). Infant preferences for infant-directed versus non-infant directed playsongs and lullabies. *Infant Behavior and Development, 19,* 83–92.*

Trainor, L. J., Austin, C. M., & Desjardins, R. N. (2000). Is infant-directed speech prosody a result of the vocal expression of emotion? *Psychological Science, 11,* 188–195.*

Trainor, L. J., McDonald, K. L., & Alain, C. (2002). Automatic and controlled processing of melodic contour and interval information measured by brain activity. *Journal of Cognitive Neuroscience, 14,* 430–442.*

Trainor, L. J., & Desjardins, R. N. (2002). Pitch characteristics of infant-directed speech affect infants' ability to discriminate vowels. *Psychological Bulletin and Review, 9,* 335–340.*

Trehub, S. E. (2006). Infants as musical connoisseurs. In G. E. McPherson (Ed.), *The child as musician: A handbook of musical development* (pp. 33–49). New York: Oxford University Press.*

Trehub, S. E., & Hannon, E. E. (2006). Infant music perception: Domain-general or domain-specific mechanisms? *Cognition, 1000,* 73–99.*

Trehub, S. E., & Trainor, L. J. (1993). Listening strategies in infancy: The roots of music and language development. In S. McAdams & E. Bigand (Eds.), *Thinking in sound: The cognitive psychology of human audition* (pp. 278–327). New York: Oxford University Press.*

Trehub, S. E., Schellenberg, E. G., & Kamenetsky, S. B. (1999). Infants' and adults' perception of scale structure. *Journal of Experimental Psychology: Human Perception & Performance, 25,* 965–975.*

Trehub, S. E., Thorpe, L. A., & Trainor, L. J. (1990). Infants' perception of good and bad melodies. *Psychomusicology, 9,* 5–19.*

Trehub, S. E., Unyk, A. M., & Trainor, L. J. (1993). Maternal singing in cross-cultural perspective. *Infant Behavior and Development, 16,* 285–295.*

Tremblay, M. S., & Willms, J. D. (2000). Secular trends in the body mass index of Canadian children. *CMAJ, 163,* 1429–1433.*

Tremblay, H., & Rovira, K. (2007). Joint visual attention and social triangular engagement at 3 and 6 months. *Infant Behavior and Development, 30,* 366–379.

Tremblay, R. E. (2000). The development of aggressive behavior during childhood: What have we learned in the past century? *International Journal of Behavioral Development, 24,* 129–141.*

Tremblay, R. E., Japel, C., Perusse, D., McDuff, P., Boivin, M., Zoccilillo, M., & Montplaisir, J. (1999). The search for the age of "onset" of physical aggression: Rousseau and Bandura revisited. *Criminal Behavior and Mental Health, 9,* 8–23.*

Tremblay, R. E., Pagini-Kurtz, Mâsse, L. C., Vitaro, F., & Pihl, R. O. (1995). A bimodal preventive intervention for disruptive kindergarten boys: Its impact through mid-adolescence. *Journal of Consulting and Clinical Psychology, 63,* 560–568.*

Tremblay, R. E., Schaal, B., Boulerice, B., Arsenault, L., Soussignan, R. G., & Paquette, D. (1998). Testosterone, physical aggression, and dominance, and physical development in adolescence. *International Journal of Behavioral Development, 22,* 753–777.*

Trick, L. M. (2008). More than superstition: Differential effects of featural hergeneity and change on subitizing and counting. *Perception & Psychophysics, 70,* 743–760.*

Trick, L. M., & Pylyshyn, Z. W. (1994). Why are small and large numbers enumerated differently? A limited-capacity preattentive stage in vision. *Psychological Review, 101,* 80–102.*

Trick, L. M., Enns, J. T., & Brodeur, D. A. (1996). Life span changes in visual discrimination: The number discrimination task. *Developmental Psychology, 32,* 925–932.*

Trickett, P. K. (1997). Sexual and physical abuse and the development of social competence. In S. S. Luthar, J. A. Burack, D. Cicchetti, & J. Weiz (Eds.), *Developmental psychopathology perspectives on risk and disorder* (pp. 390–416). New York: Cambridge University Press.

Trickett, P. K., & Putnam, F. W. (1998). The developmental impact of sexual abuse. In P. Trickett & C. Schellenbach (Eds.), *Violence against children in the family and the community.* Washington: APA Books.

Trocmé, N., Fallon, B., MacLaurin, B., Daciuk, J., Felstiner, C., Black, T., et al. (2005). *Canadian incidence study of reported child abuse and neglect—2003: Major findings.* Ottawa: Minister of Public Works and Government Services Canada.*

Tronick, E. Z., Messinger, D. S., Weinberg, M. K., Lester, B. M., LaGasse, L., Seifer, R., et al. (2005). Cocaine exposure is associated with subtle compromises of infants' and mothers' social-emotional behavior and dyadic features of their interaction in the face still face paradigm. *Developmental Psychology, 41,* 711–722.

Tronick, E. Z., Morelli, G. A., & Ivey, P. K. (1992). The Efe forager infant and toddler's pattern of social relationships: Multiple and simultaneous. *Developmental Psychology, 28,* 568–577.

Tronick, E. Z., Thomas, R. B., & Daltabuit, M. (1994). The Quechua manta pouch: A caretaking practice for buffering the Peruvian infant against the multiple stressors of high altitude. *Child Development, 65,* 1005–1013.

Troseth, G. L., Pierroutsakos, S. L., & DeLoache, J. S. (2004). From the innocent to the intelligent eye: The early development of pictorial competence. In R. V. Kail (Ed.), *Advances in child development and behavior* (Vol. 32, pp. 1–35). San Diego, CA: Elsevier.

Trudeau, N., Poulin-Dubois, D., & Joannette, Y. (2000). Language development following brain injury in early childhood: A longitudinal case study. *International Journal of Language and Communicative Disorders, 35,* 227–249.*

True, M. M., Pisani, L., & Oumar, F. (2001). Infant-mother attachment among the Dogan of Mali. *Child Development, 72,* 1451–1466.

Tudge, J., & Scrimsher, S. (2003). Lev S. Vygotsky on education: A cultural-historical, interpersonal, and individual development approch to development. In B. J. Zimmerman & D. J. Schunk (Eds.), *Educational psychology: A century of contributions* (pp. 207–228). Mahwah, NJ: Erlbaum.

Tuladhar, R., Harding, R., Granage, S. M., Adamson, T., & Horne, R. S. C. (2003). Effects of sleep position, sleep state, and age on heart rate responses following provoked arousal in term infants. *Early Human and Development, 71,* 157–169.

Turati, C. (2004). Why faces are not special to newborns: An alternative account of the face preference. *Current Directions in Psychological Science, 13,* 5–8.

Turati, C., Simion, F., Milani, I., & Umilta, C. (2002). Newborns preference for faces: What is cruical? *Developmental Psychology, 38,* 875–882.

Turati, C., Valenza, E., Leo, I., & Simion, F. (2005). Three-month-olds' visual preference for faces and its underlying visual processing mechanisms. *Journal of Experimental Child Psychology, 90,* 255–273.

Turiel, E. (1983). *The development of social knowledge: Morality and convention.* New York: Cambridge University Press.

Turiel, E. (1998). The development of morality. In W. Damon (Ed.) & N. Eisenberg (Vol. Ed.), *Handbook of child psychology: Social, emotional, and personality development.* (pp. 863–932). New York: Wiley.

Turiel, E. (2002). *The culture of morality.* New York: Cambridge University Press.

Turiel, E. (2006). The development of morality. In W. Damon & R. M. Lerner (Gen. Ed.), & N. Eisenberg (Ed.), *Handbook of child psychology: Vol. 3. Social, emotional and personality development* (6th ed., pp. 789–857). New York: Wiley.

Turiel, E., Killen, V., & Helwig, F. C. (1988). Morality: Its structure, functions and vagaries. In J. Kagan and S. Lamb (Eds.), *The emergence of morality in young children.* Chicago: University of Chicago Press.

Turkheimer, E. (2000). Three laws of behavior genetics and what they mean. *Current Directions in Psychological Science, 9,* 160–164.

Turkheimer, E., Haley, A., Waldron, M., D'Onofrio, B., & Gottesman, I. I. (2003). Socioeconomic status modifies heritability of IQ in young children. *Psychological Science, 14,* 623–628.

Turnbull, W., & Carpendale, J. I. M. (1999). A social pragmatic model of talk: Implications for research on the development of children's social understanding. *Human Development, 42,* 328–355.*

Turnbull, W., & Carpendale, J. I. M. (2001). Talk and the development of social understanding. *Early Education and Development, 12,* 455–477.*

Turner, H. A., & Finkelhor, D. (1996). Corporal punishment as a stressor among young. *Journal of Marriage and Family, 58,* 155–166.

Turner, J. S., & Rubinson, L. (1993). *Contemporary human sexuality*. Englewood Cliffs, NJ: Prentice Hall.

Turner-Bowker, D. M. (1996). Gender stereotyped description in children's picture books: Does "Curious Jane" exist in literature? *Sex Roles, 35,* 461–488.

Turnure, J. E. (1970). Children's reactions to distractors in a learning situation. *Developmental Psychology, 2,* 115–122.

UNAIDS. (2006). Overview of the global AIDS epidemic. In *2006 Report on the global AIDS epidemic*. Retrieved June 18, 2008, from http://www.unaids.org/en/KnowledgeCentre/HIVData/GlobalReport

Underwood, M. K. (2003). *Social aggression among girls*. New York: Guilford.

Underwood, M. K. (2004). Gender and peer relations. In J. Kupersmidt & K. A. Dodge (Eds.), *Children's peer relations* (pp. 21-36). Washington, DC: American Psychological Association.

Underwood, M. K., Schockner, A. E., & Hurley, J. C. (2001). Children's response to same- and other-gender peers: An experimental investigation with 8-, 10-, and 12-year-olds. *Developmental Psychology, 37,* 362–372.

Ungerer, J. A., Brody, L. R., & Zelazo, P. R. (1978). Long-term memory for speech in 2- to 4-week-old infants. *Infant Behavior and Development, 7,* 177–186.

UNICEF. (2004). Facts for breastfeeding. Retrieved 21 October, 2004, from http://unicef.org/ffl/04/.

Updegraff, K. A., McHale, S. M., & Crouter, A. C. (1996). Gender roles in marriage: What do they mean for girls' and boys' school achievement? *Journal of Youth and Adolescence, 25,* 73–88.

Urban Institute. (2000). *Child care patterns of school-age children with employed mothers*. Washington, DC: The Urban Institute Press.

U.S. Department of Education, National Center for Educational Statistics. (1997). *Children with special educational needs*. Washington, DC: U.S. Government Printing Office.

U.S. Department of Energy. (2002). *Human genome news*. Washington, DC: Government Printing Office.

U.S. Department of Health and Human Services. (2007). *HIV and its transmission*. Retrieved January 23, 2008, from http://www.cdc.gov/hiv/resources/factsheets/transmission.htm

Uttal, D. (2000). Seeing the big picture: Map use and the development of spatial cognition. *Developmental Science, 3,* 247–286.

Uzgiris, I. C. (1989). Infants in relation: Performers, pupils and partners. In W. Damon (Ed.), *Child development: Today and tomorrow*. San Francisco: Jossey-Bass.

Valencia, R. R., & Suzuki, L. A. (2001). *Racial and ethnic minority psychology*. Thousand Oaks, CA: Sage.

Valiente, C., & Eisenberg, N. (2006). Parenting and children's adjustment: The role of children's emotional regulating. In D. K. Snyder, J. A. Simpson & J. N. Hughes (Eds.), *Emotion regulation in couples and families* (pp. 123–142). Washington, DC: American Psychological Association.

Valsiner, J. (Ed.). (1989). *Child development in cultural context*. Toronto, Canada: Hogrefe and Huber.*

Van Den Bergh, B. R. H. (1992). Maternal emotions during pregnancy and fetal and neonatal behavior. In J. G. Nijhuis (Ed.), *Fetal behavior: Development and perinatal aspects*. New York: Oxford University Press.

Van den Boom, D. (1990). Preventive intervention and the quality of mother infant interaction and infant exploration in irritable infants. In W. Koops, H. J. G. Soppe, J. L. Van der Linden, P. C. M. Molenaar, & J. J. F. Schroots (Eds.), *Developmental psychology behind the dikes: An outline of developmental psychological research in the Netherlands*. Delft, Netherlands: Uitgeverij Eburon.

Van Den Boom, D. C. (1994). The influence of temperament and mothering on attachment and exploration: An experimental manipulation of sensitive responsiveness among lower-class mothers with irritable infants. *Child Development, 65,* 1457–1477.

Van Den Oord, E. J., Boomsma, I., & Verhulst, F. C. (1994). A study of problem behaviors in 10- to 15-year old biologically related and unrelated international adoptees. *Behavior Genetics, 24,* 193–205.

Van Den Oord, E. J., Verhhulst, F. C., & Boomsma, D. I. (1992). *A genetic study of maternal and paternal ratings of problem behaviors in three-year-old twins*. Unpublished manuscript.

van der Mark, I. L., van IJzendoorn, M. H., & Bakermans-Kranenburg, M. J. (2002). Development of empathy in girls during the second year of life: Associations with parenting, attachment, and temperament. *Social Development, 11,* 451–468.

Van Duuren, M., Kendall-Scott, L., & Stark, N. (2003). Early aesthetic choices: Infant preferences for attractive premature infant faces. *International Journal of Behavioral Development, 27,* 212–219.

van IJzendoorn, M. H., & Sagi, A. (1999). Cross-cultural patterns of attachment: Universal and contextual dimensions. In J. Cassidy & P. R. Shaver (Eds.), *Handbook of attachment* (pp. 713–734). New York: Guilford.

van IJzendoorn, M. H., Vereijken, C. M. J. L., Bakermans-Kranenburg, M. J., & Riksen-Walraven, J. M. (2004). Assessing attachment security with the attachment Q sort: Meta-analytic evidence for the validity of the observer AQS. *Child Development, 75,* 1188–1213.

Van Oostrum, N., & Howard, P. (1997). The effects of hostile attribution on adolescents' aggressive response to social situations. *Canadian Journal of School Psychology, 13,* 49–59.

van Rijn, H., van Someran, M., & & van der Maas, H. (2003). Modeling developmental transitions n the balance scale task. *Cognitive Science, 27,* 227–257.

Vandell, D. L. (2000). Parents, peer groups, and other socializing influences. *Developmental Psychology, 36,* 699–710.

Vandell, D. L., Henderson, V. K., & Wilson, K. S. (1988). A longitudinal study of children with varying quality day care experiences. *Child Development, 59,* 1286–1292.

Vandell, D. L., Pierce, K. M., & Dadisman, K. (2005). Out-of-school settings as a developmental context for children and youth. In R. V. Kail (Ed.), *Advances in child development and behavior* (Vol. 33, pp. 43–77). New York: Academic Press.

Vandell, D. L., & Wilson, K. (1987). Infants' interactions with mother, siblings and peer contacts and relations between interaction systems. *Child Development, 58,* 176–186.

Vander, A. J., Sherman, J. H., & Luciano D. S. (1994). *Human physiology*. 6th ed. New York: McGraw-Hill.

Vaughn, B. E., & Bost, K. K. (1999). Attachment and temperament. In J. Cassidy & P. Shaver (Eds.), *Handbook of attachment* (pp. 198–225). New York: Guilford Press.

Vaughn, B. E., Kopp, C. B., & Krakow, J. B. (1984). The emergence and consolidation of self-control from eighteen to thirty months of age: Normative trends and individual differences. *Child Development, 55,* 990–1004.

Vaughn, B. E., Strayer, F. F., Jacques, M., Trudel, M., & Seifer, R. (1991). Maternal descriptions of two- and three-year-old children: A comparison of attachment Q-sorts in two sociocultural communities. *International Journal of Behavioral Development, 14,* 279–291.

Vaughn, K. K., & Fouts, G. T. (2003). Changes in television and magazine exposure and eating disorder symptomology. *Sex Roles, 49,* 313–320.*

Venter, J. C., et al. (2001). The sequence of the human genome. *Science, 291,* 1304–1351.

Verp, M. S. (1993). Environmental causes of pregnancy loss and malformation. In C. Lin, M. S. Verp, & R. E. Sabbagha (Eds.), *The high-risk fetus: Pathophysiology, diagnosis, and management*. New York: Springer-Verlag.

Verschueren, K., & Marcoen, A. (2002). Perceptions of self and relationship with parents in aggressive and nonaggressive rejected children. *Journal of School Psychology, 40,* 501–522.

Vieuillet, E., Magnan, A., Ecalle, J., Thai-Van, H., & Collet, L. (2007). Auditory processing disorder in chidren with reading disability: Effects of audiovisual training. *Brain 130,* 2915–2928.

Vigil, J. M., Geary, D. C., & Byrd-Craven, J. (2005). A life history assessment of early childhood sexual abuse in women. *Developmental Psychology, 41,* 553–561.

Vitaro, F., Brendgen, M., & Tremblay, R.E. (2000). Influence of deviant friends on delinquency: Searching for moderator variables. *Journal of Abnormal Child Psychology, 28,* 313–325.*

Vitaro, F., Brendgen, M., Pagini, L., Tremblay, R. E., & McDuff, P. (1999). Disruptive behavior, peer association, and conduct disorder: Testing the developmental links through early intervention. *Development & Psychopathology, 11,* 287–304.*

Volkmar, F. R., Lord, C., Bailey, A., Schultz, R. T., & Klin, A. (2004). Autism and pervasive developmental disorders. *Journal of Child Psychology and Psychiatry, 45,* 135–170.

Volling, B. L., McElwain, N. L., & Miller, A. L. (2002). Emotional regulation in context: The jealousy complex between young siblings and its relation to child and family characteristics. *Child Development, 73,* 581–600.

Voorhees, C. V., & Mallnow, E. (1987). Behavioral teratogenesis: Long-term influences on behavior from early exposure to environmental agents. In J. D. Osofsky (Ed.), *Handbook of infant development* (2nd ed., pp. 913–971). New York: Wiley.

Voyer, D., Russell, A., & McKenna, J. (2002). On the reliability of laterality effects in a dichotic emotion recognition task. *Journal of Clinical and Experimental Neuropsychology, 24,* 605–614.*

Vurpillot, E. (1968). The development of scanning strategies and their relation to visual differentiation. *Journal of Experimental Child Psychology, 6,* 632–650.

Vygotsky, L. S. (1978). *Thought and language.* Cambridge, MA: MIT Press.

Wachs, T. D. (2000). *Necessary but not sufficient: The respective roles of individual and multiple influences on individual development.* Washington, DC: APA.

Wachs, T. D., & Kohnstamm, G. A. (Eds.). (2001). *Temperament in context.* Mahwah, NJ: Erlbaum.

Waddington, C. H. (1962). *New patterns in genetics and development.* New York: Columbia University Press.

Waddington, C. H. (1966). *Principles of development and differentiation.* New York: Macmillan.

Wade, C., & Tavris, C. (1999). Gender and culture. In L. A. Peplau, S. C. De Bro, R. Veniegas & P. L. Taylor (Eds.), *Gender, culture and ethnicity: Current research about women and men.* Mountain View, CA: Mayfield.

Wadhera, S., & Millar, W. (1997, Winter). Teenage pregnancies, 1974 to 1994. *Health Reports, 9.* Ottawa: Statistics Canada.*

Wahler, R. G. (1967). Infant social attachments: A reinforcement theory interpretation and investigation. *Child Development, 38,* 1079–1088.

Wahler, R. G., & Dumas, J. E. (1987). Family factors in childhood psychology: Toward a coercion-neglect model. In T. Jacob (Ed.), *Family interaction and psychopathology: Theories, methods, and findings* (pp. 581–625). New York: Plenum.

Wahlstein, D. (2002). The theory of biological intelligence: History and a critical appraisal. In R. J. Sternberg & E. L. Grigorenko (Eds.), *The general factor of intelligence: How general is it?* Mahwah, NJ: Erlbaum.*

Wahlsten, D. (1979). A critique of the concepts of heritability and heredity in behavior genetics. In J. R. Royce & L. P. Mos (Eds.), *Theoretical advances in behavior genetics* (pp. 425–470). Alphen aan den Rijn, the Netherlands: Sijthoff & Noordhoff.*

Wahlsten, D. (1990). Insensitivity of the analysis of variance to heredity-environment interaction. *Behavior and Brain Sciences, 13,* 109–161.*

Wahlsten, D. (1994a). The intelligence of heritability. *Canadian Psychology, 35,* 244–260.*

Wahlsten, D. (1994b). Nascent doubts may presage conceptual clarity: Reply to Surbey. *Canadian Psychology, 35,* 265–267.*

Wahlsten, D., & Gottlieb, G. (1997). The invalid separation of effects of nature and nurture: Lessons from animal experimentation. In R. J. Sternberg & E. L. Grigorenko (Eds.), *Intelligence, heredity, and environment* (pp. 163–192). Cambridge, England: Cambridge University Press.*

Wainright, J. L., & Patterson, C. J. (2008). Peer relations among adolescents with female same-sex parents. *Developmental Psychology, 44,* 117–126.

Wainryb, C. (2006). *Moral development in culture: Diversity, tolerance, and justice.* Mahwah, NJ: Erlbaum.

Wainryb, C., Shaw, L. A., Laupa, M., & Smith, K. R. (2001). Children's, adolescents', and young adults' thinking about different types of disagreements. *Developmental Psychology, 37,* 373–386.

Wakschlag, L. S., Gordon, R. A., Lahey, B. B., Loeber, R., Green, S. M., & Leventhal, B. L. (2001). Maternal age at first birth and boys' risk for conduct disorders. *Journal of Research on Adolescence, 10,* 417–441.

Walden, T. (1991). Infant social referencing. In J. Garber & K. Dodge (Eds.), *The development of emotional regulation and dysregulation.* New York: Cambridge University Press.

Walker, H. M. (1995). *The acting out child: Coping with classroom disruption.* Longmont, CO: Sopris West.

Walker, L. J. (1988). The development of moral reasoning. *Annals of Child Development, 5,* 33–78.

Walker, L. J. (1996). Is morality engendered in early parent-child relationships? A commentary on the Lollis, Ross, & Leroux study. *Merrill-Palmer Quarterly, 43,* 148–159.*

Walker, L. J. (2006). Gender and morality. In M. S. Killen, J. G. (Ed.), *Handbook of moral development* (pp. 93–115). Mahwah, NJ: Erlbaum.*

Walker, L. J., Hennig, K. H., & Krettenauer, T. (2000). Parent and peer contexts for children's moral reasoning development. *Child Development, 71,* 1033–1048.

Walker, L. J., Pitts, R. C., Hennig, K. H., & Matsuba, M. K. (1999). Reasoning about morality and real-life moral problems. In M. Killen & D. Hart (Eds.), *Morality in everyday life: Developmental perspectives* (pp. 371–407). New York: Cambridge University Press.*

Walkowiak, J., Weiner, J., Fastabend, A., Heinzow, H., Kramer, U., Schmidt, E., et al. (2001). Environmental exposure to polychlorinated biphenyls and quality of the home environment: Effects on psychodevelopment in early childhood. *The Lancet, 358,* 1602–1607.

Wallace, G., & Corballis, M. C. (1973). Short-term memory and coding strategies in the deal. *Journal of Experimental Psychology, 99,* 344–348.

Wallach, M. A., & Kogan, N. (1965). *Modes of thinking in young children: A study of the creativity-intelligence distinction.* New York: Holt, Rinehart and Winston.

Wallen, K. (1996). Nature needs nurture: The interaction of hormonal and social influences on the development of behavioral sex differences in rhesus monkeys. *Hormones and Behavior, 30,* 364–378.

Walton, G. E., Bower, N. J. A., & Bower, T. G. R. (1992). Recognition of familiar faces by newborns. *Infant Behavior and Development, 15,* 265–269.

Wang, Q. (2004). The emergence of cultural self-constructs: Autobiographical memory and self-description in European American and Chinese children. *Developmental Psychology, 40,* 3–15.

Ward, L. M., & Friedman, K. (2006). Using TV as a guide: Associations between television viewing and adolescents' sexual attitudes and behavior. *Journal of Research on Adoelscence, 16,* 133–156.

Waschbusch, D. A., Andrade, B. F., & King, S. (2006). Attention-deficit/hyperactivity disorder. In C. A. Essau (Ed.), *Child and adolescent psychopathology: Theoretical and clinical implications* (pp. 52-77). New York: Routledge/Taylor & Francis Group.*

Watamura, S. E., Donzella, B., Alwin, J., & Gunnar, M. R. (2003). Morning to afternoon increases in cortisol concentration for infants and toddlers at child care: Age differences and behavioral correlates. *Child Development, 74,* 1006–1020.

Waters, E., & Beauchaine, T. P. (2003). Are there really patterns of attachment? Comment on Fraley and Spieker (2003). *Developmental Psychology, 39,* 417–422.*

Waters, E., Merrick, S., Treboux, D., Crowell, J., & Albersheim, L. (2000). Attachment security in infancy and early adulthood: A twenty-year longitudinal study. *Child Development, 71,* 684–689.

Waters, E., Vaughn, B. E., Posada, G., & Kondo-Ikemura, K. (1995). Caregiving, cultural, and cognitive perspectives on secure-base behavior and working models: New growing points of attachment theory and research. *Monographs of the Society for Research in Child Development, 60* (2–3, Serial No. 244).

Watson, J. B. (1926). What the nursery has to say about instincts. In C. Murcheson (Ed.), *Psychologies of 1925* (pp. 1–35). Worcester, MA: Clark University Press.

Watson, J. B. (1928). *Psychological care of infant and child.* New York: Norton.

Watson-Gegeo, K. A., & Gegeo, D. W. (1986). Calling-out and repeating routines in Kwara'ae children's language socialization. In B. B. Schieffelin & E. Ochs (Eds.), *Language socialization across cultures* (pp. 17–50). Mahwah, NJ: Erlbaum.

Waxman, S., & Gelman, R. (1986). Preschoolers' use of superordinate relations in classification and language. *Cognitive Development, 1,* 139–156.

Waxman, S. R., & Lidz, J. L. (2006). Early word learning. In W. Damon & R. M. Lerner (Gen. Ed.), & D. Kuhn & R. Siegler (Eds.), *Handbook of child psychology: Vol. 2: Cognition, perception, and language* (6th ed.). New York: Wiley.

Waxman, S. R., Shipley, E. F., & Shepperson, B. (1991). Establishing new subcategories: The role of category labels and existing knowledge. *Child Development, 62,* 127–138.

Webb, S. J., Monk, C. S., & Nelson, C. A. (2001). Mechanisms of postnatal neurobiological development: Implications for human development. *Developmental Neuropsychology, 19,* 147–171.

Weber, R., Ritterfield, U., & Mathiak, K. (2006). Does playing violent video games induce aggression? Empirical evidence of a functional magnetic resonance imaging study. *Media Psychology, 8,* 39–60.

Wechsler, D. (1952). *Wechsler Intelligence Scale for Children.* New York: Psychological Corporation.

Wechsler, D. (1958). *The measurement and appraisal of adult intelligence* (4th ed.). Baltimore: Williams & Wilkins.

Wechsler, D. (2003). *Wechsler Intelligence Scale for Children* (4th ed.) New York: Psychological Corporation.

Wegman, M. E. (1994). Annual summary of vital statistics—1993. *Pediatrics, 93,* 771–782

Wegman, M. E. (1995). Annual summary of vital statistics—1994. *Pediatrics, 94,* 792–803.

Weinberg, R. A., Scarr, S., & Waldman, I. D. (1992). The Minnesota Transracial Adoption Study: A followup of IQ test performance at adolescence. *Intelligence, 16,* 117–135.

Weinraub, M., & Lewis, M. (1977). The determinants of children's responses to separation. *Monographs of the Society for Research in Child Development, 42* (Serial No. 172).

Weisner, T., & Gallimore, R. (1977). My brother's keeper: Child and sibling caretaking. *Current Anthropology, 18,* 169–190.

Weiss, L. G., Saklofske, D. H., Prifitera, A., Chen, H.-Y., & Hildebrand, D. K. (1999). The calculation of WISC-III General Ability Index using Canadian norms. *Canadian Journal of School Psychology, 14,* 1–9.*

Weiss, M., Hechtman, L. T., & Weiss, G. (1999). *ADHD in adulthood: A guide to current theory, diagnosis and treatment.* Baltimore: Johns Hopkins University Press.

Weissberg, R., & Greenberg, M. (1998). School and community competence-enhancement and prevention programs. In W. Damon (Gen. Ed.), I. Sigel, & K. A. Renninger (Vol. Eds.), *Handbook of child psychology: Vol. 4. Child psychology in practice.* New York: Wiley.

Weissman, M., Warner, V., Wickramaratne, P., Moreau, D., & Olfson, M. (1997). Offspring of depressed parents: Ten years later. *Archives of General Psychiatry, 54,* 932–940.

Weisz, J. R., Chaiyasit, W., Weiss, B., Eastman, K. L., & Jackson, E. W. (1995). A multimethod study of problem behavior among Thai and American children in school: Teacher reports versus direct observations. *Child Development, 66,* 402–415.

Weisz, J. R., Suwanlert, S., Chaiyasit, W., Weiss, B., Walter, B. R., & Anderson, W. W. (1988). Thai and American perspectives on over- and under-controlled child behavior problems: Exploring the threshold model among parents, teachers, and psychologists. *Journal of Consulting and Clinical Psychology, 56,* 601–609.

Weitzman, N., Birns, B., & Friend, R. (1985). Traditional and nontraditional mothers' communication with their daughters and sons. *Child Development, 56,* 894–898.

Weizman, Z. O., & Snow, C. E. (2001). Lexical output as it relates to children's vocabulary acquisition: Effects of sophisticated expo-

sure as a support for meaning. *Developmental Psychology, 37,* 265–279.

Wellman, H. M. (1977). Preschoolers' understanding of memory relevant variables. *Child Development, 48,* 1720–1723.

Wellman, H. M. (1978). Knowledge of the interaction of memory variables: A developmental study of metamemory. *Developmental Psychology, 14,* 24–29.

Wellman, H. M., & Lempers, J. D. (1977). The naturalistic communicative abilities of two-year-olds. *Child Development, 48,* 1052–1057.

Wellman, H. M., Collins, J., & Glieberman, J. (1981). Understanding the combinations of memory variables: Developing conceptions of memory limitations. *Child Development, 52,* 1313–1317.

Wellman, H. M., Cross, D., & Watson, J. (2001). Meta-analysis of theory-of-mind development: The truth about false-belief. *Child Development, 72,* 655–684.

Wells, K. C. (2001) Comprehensive versus matched psychosocial treatment in the MTA study: Conceptual and empirical issues. *Journal of Clinical Child Psychology, 30,* 131–135.

Wendland-Carro, J., Piccinini, C. A., & Millar, W. S. (1999). The role of an early intervention on enhancing the quality of mother-infant interaction. *Child Development, 70,* 713–721.

Wentworth, H., Haith, M. M., & Hood, R. (2002). Spatiotemporal regularity and interevent contingencies as information for infants' visual expectations. *Infancy, 3,* 303–322.

Wentzel, K. R., Barry, C. M., & Caldwell, K. A. (2004). Friendships in middle school: Influences on motivation and school adjustment. *Journal of Educational Psychology, 96,* 195–203.

Werker, J. F. (1989). Becoming a native listener. *American Scientist, 77,* 54–59.*

Werker, J. F., & McLeod, P. J. (1989). Infant preference for both male and female infant-directed talk: A developmental study of attentional and affective responsiveness. *Canadian Journal of Psychology, 43,* 230–246.*

Werker, J. F., & Polka, L. (1993). Developmental changes in speech perception: New challenges and new directions. *Journal of Phonetics, 21,* 83–101.*

Werker, J. F., & Tees, R. C. (1983). Developmental changes across childhood in the perception of non-native speech sounds. *Canadian Journal of Psychology, 37,* 287–286.*

Werker, J. F., & Tees, R.C. (1984). Cross-language speech perception: Evidence for perceptual reorganization during the first year of life. *Infant Behavior and Development, 7,* 49–63.*

Werker, J. F., Gilbert, J. H. V., Humphrey, K., & Tees, R. C. (1981). Developmental aspects of cross-language speech perception. *Child Development, 52,* 349–355.*

Werker, J. F., Pegg, J. E., & McLeod, P. J. (1994). A cross-language investigation of infant preference for infant-directed communication. *Infant Behavior & Development, 17,* 323–333.*

Werner, E. E. (1984). Resilient children. *Young Children, 40,* 68–72.

Werner, E. E. (1995). Resilience in development. *Current Directions in Psychological Science, 4,* 81–85.

Werner, E. E., Bierman, J. M., & French, F. F. (1971). *The children of Kauai.* Honolulu: University of Hawaii Press.

Werner, J. S., & Siqueland, E. R. (1978). Visual recognition memory in the preterm infant. *Infant Behavior and Development, 1,* 79–84.

Wertsch, J. V., & Tulviste, P. (1992). L. S. Vygotsky and contemporary developmental psychology. *Developmental Psychology, 28,* 543–553.

Westhues, A., & Cohen, J. S. (1994). *Intercountry adoption in Canada.* Ottawa: Human Resources Development Canada*

Westhues, A., & Cohen, J. S. (1997). A comparison of the adjustment of adolescent and young inter-country adoptees and their siblings. *International Journal of Behavioral Development, 20,* 47–65.*

Whalen, C. K. (2001). ADHD treatment in the 21st century: Pushing the envelope. *Journal of Clinical Child Psychology, 30,* 136–140.

Whitall, J., & Clark, J. E. (1994). The development of bipedal interlimb co-ordination. In S. P. Swinnen, J. Massion, & H. Heuer (Eds.), *Interlimb co-ordination: Neural, dynamical and cognitive constraints.* San Diego, CA: Academic Press.

White, B. L. (1967). An experimental approach to the effects of environment on early human behavior. In J. P. Hill (Ed.), *Minnesota symposia on child psychology* (Vol. 1). Minneapolis, MN: University of Minnesota Press.

Whitehurst, G. J., & Lonigan, C. J. (1998). Child development and emergent literacy. *Child Development, 69,* 848–872.

Whiting, B., & Edwards, C. (1988). *Children of different worlds. The formation of social behavior.* Cam-

bridge, MA: Harvard University Press.

Whiting, B. B., & Whiting, J. W. M. (1975). *Children of six cultures: A psychocultural analysis.* Cambridge, MA: Harvard University Press.

Whitlock, J. L., Powers, J. L., & Eckenrode, J. (2006). The virtual cutting edge: The internet and adolescent self-injury. *Developmental Psychology, 42,* 407–417.

Wicks-Nelson, R., & Israel, A. C. (2000). *Behavior disorders in childhood.* Upper Saddle River, NJ: Prentice Hall.

Wierzbicki, M. (1993). Psychological adjustment of adoptees: A meta-analysis. *Journal of Clinical Child Psychology, 22,* 447–454.

Wiesenfeld, A., Malatesta, C., & DeLoach, L. (1981). Differential parental response to familiar and unfamiliar infant distress signals. *Infant Behavior and Development, 4,* 281–295.

Wiesner, T. S. (1993). Overview: Sibling similarity and difference in different cultures. In C. W. Nuckolls (Ed.), *Siblings in South Asia: Brothers and sisters in cultural context.* (pp. 1–17). New York: Guilford Press.

Wigfield, A., Battle, A., Keller, L. B., & Eccles, J. S. (2002). Sex differences in motivation, self-concept, career aspiration, and career choice: Implications for cognitive development. In A. V. McGillicuddy-DeLisa (Ed.), *Biology, society, and behavior: The development of sex differences in cognition.* Westport, CT: Ablex Publishing.

Wigfield, A., Eccles, J., & Schiefele, U. (2006). Motivation. In W. Damon & R. M. Lerner (Gen. Ed.), & N. Eisenberg (Ed.), *Handbook of child psychology: Vol. 3. Social, emotional, and personality development* (6th ed., pp. 933–1002). New York: Wiley.

Wilcox, A., Kobayashi, L., & Murray, I. (1997). Twenty-five years of obstetric patient satisfaction in North America: A review of the literature. *Journal of Perinatal and Neonatal Nursing, 10,* 36–47.

Wilcox, A. J., Baird, D. D., & Weinberg, C. R., et al. (1995). Fertility in men exposed prenatally to diethylstibestrol. *New England Journal of Medicine, 332,* 1411–1416.

Wiley, E. W., Bialystok, E., & Hakuta, K. (2005). New approaches to using census data to test the critical-period hypothesis for second-language learning. *Psychological Science, 16,* 341-343.*

Willatts, P. (1990). Development of problem solving strategies in infants. In D. F. Bjorklund (Ed.), *Children's strategies* (pp. 23–66). Hillsdale, NJ: Erlbaum.

Willford, J. A., Leach, S. H., & Day, N. L. (2006). Moderate alcohol exposure and cognitive status of children at age 10. *Alcoholism: Clinical and Experimental Research, 30,* 1051–1059.

Williams, J. E., & Best, D. L. (1990). *Measuring sex stereotypes: A multinational study* (Rev. ed.). Newbury, CA: Sage.

Williams, R. J., & Gloster, S. P. (1999). Knowledge of fetal alcohol syndrome (FAS) among natives in Northern Manitoba. *Journal of Studies on Alcohol, 60,* 833–836.*

Williams, W. M., Blythe, T., White, N., Li, J., Gardner, H., & Sternberg, R. J. (2002). Practical intelligence for school: Developing metacognitive sources of achievement in adolescence. *Developmental Review, 22,* 162–210.

Williams, W. M., & Ceci, S. J. (1997). Are Americans becoming more or less alike? Trends in race, class, and ability differences in intelligence. *American Psychologist, 52,* 1226–1235.

Willinger, M., Hoffman, H. T., & Hartford, R. B. (1994). Infant sleep position and risk for sudden infant death syndrome. *Pediatrics, 93,* 814–819.

Willis, T. A., & Yaeger, A. M. (2003). Family factors and adolescent substance use: Models and mechanisms. *Current Directions in Psychological Science, 12,* 222–226.

Willoughby, T., Wood, E., & Kraftcheck, E. R. (2003). When can a lack of structure facilitate strategic processing of information? *British Journal of Educational Psychology, 73,* 59–69.*

Wilson, B. J., & Weiss, A. J. (1993). The effects of sibling coviewing on preschooler's reactions to a suspenseful movie scene. *Communication Research, 20,* 214–248.

Wilson, R. S. (1983). The Louisville twin study: Developmental synchronies in behavior. *Child Development, 54,* 298–316.

Wilson, R. S., & Harpring, E. B. (1972). Mental and motor development in infant twins. *Developmental Psychology, 7,* 277–287.

Wimmer, H., & Perner, J. (1983). Beliefs about beliefs: Representation and constraining function of wrong beliefs in young children's understanding of deception. *Cognition, 13,* 103–128.

Winestock, S. L. (1994). *William Emet Blatz: The development of a developmental psychologist.* Unpublished doctoral dissertation, York University, Toronto.*

Winner, E. (2006). Development in the arts: Drawing and music. In W. Damon & R. L. Lerner (Gen. Ed.), & D. Kuhn & R. S. Siegler (Eds.), *Handbook of child psychology. Vol. 2: Cognition, perception, and language* (pp. 859–904). New York: Wiley.

Wintre, M. G., & Vallance, D. D. (1994). A developmental sequence in the comprehension of emotions: Intensity, multiple emotions and valence. *Developmental Psychology, 30,* 509–514.

Witelson, S. F. (1983). Bumps on the brain: Neuroanatomical asymmetries as a basis for functional symmetries. In S. Segalowitz (Ed.), *Language functions and brain organization* (pp. 117–144). New York: Academic.

Witherington, D. C., Campos, J. J., Anderson, D. L., Lejeune, L., & Seah, E. (2005). Avoidance of heights on the visual cliff in newly walking infants. *Infancy, 7,* 285–298.

Wolchik, S. A., Wilcox, K. L., Tein, J-Y., & Sandler, I. N. (2000). Maternal acceptance and consistency of discipline as buffers of divorce stressors on children's psychological adjustment problems. *Journal of Abnormal Child Psychology, 28,* 87–102.

Wolff, P. H. (1987). *The development of behavioral states and the expression of emotions in early infancy: New proposals for investigation.* Chicago: University of Chicago Press.

Wood, D., Bruner, J., & Ross, G. (1976). The role of tutoring in problem solving. *Journal of Child Psychology and Psychiatry, 17,* 89–100.

Wood, E., Willoughby, T., Bolger, A., Younger, J., & Kaspar, V. (1993). Effectiveness of elaboration strategies for grade school children as a function of academic achievement. *Journal of Experimental Child Psychology, 56,* 240–253.*

Wood, E., Willoughby, T., McDermott, C., Motz, M., Kaspar, V., & Ducharme, M. J. (1999). Developmental differences in study behavior. *Journal of Educational Psychology, 91,* 527–536.*

Woodward, J. Z., & Aslin, R. N. (1990, April). *Segmentation cues in maternal speech to infants.* Paper presented at the 7th biennial meeting of the International Conference on Infant Studies, Montreal, Quebec, Canada.*

Woody-Dorning, J., & Miller, P. H. (2001). Children's individual differences in capacity: Effects on strategy production and utilization. *British Journal of Developmental Psychology, 19,* 543–557.

Worchel, F. F., & Allen, M. (1997). Mothers' ability to discriminate cry types in low-birthweight premature and full-term infants. *Children's Health Care, 26,* 183–195.

Wright, M. J. (1996). William Emet Blatz: A Canadian pioneer. In G. A. Kimble, C. A. Boneau & M. Wertheimer (Eds.), *Portraits of pioneers in psychology* (Vol. 2, pp. 199–211). Washington, DC: American Psychological Association.*

Wright, M. J. (2002). Flashbacks in the history of psychology in Canada: Some early "headline" makers. *Canadian Psychology, 43,* 21–34.*

Wright, M. J., & Myers, C. R. (1982). *History of academic psychology in Canada.* Toronto: Hogrefe Publishing.*

Wynn, K. (1992). Addition and subtraction by human infants. *Nature, 358,* 749–750.

Wynne-Edwards, K. E. (2001). Hormonal changes in mammalian fathers. *Hormones and Behavior, 40,* 139–145.*

Wynne-Edwards, K. E., & Lisk, R. D. (1989). Differential effects of paternal presence on pup survival in two species of dwarf hamster (*Phodopus sungorus* and *Phodopsus campbelli*). *Physiology and Behavior, 45,* 465–469.*

Wyrobek, A. J., Eskenazi, B., Young, S., Arnheim, N., Tiemann-Boege, I., Jabs, E. W., et al. (2006). Advancing age has differential effects on DNA damage, chromatin integrity, gene mutations, and aneuploidies in sperm. *Proceedings of the National Academy of Sciences, 103,* 9601-9606.

Wyshak, G., & Frisch, R. E. (1982). Evidence for a secular trend in age of menarche. *New England Journal of Medicine, 306,* 1033–1035.

Xie, H., Cairns, B. D., & Cairns, R. B. (2005). The development of aggressive behavior among girls: Measurement issues, social functions, and differential trajectories. In D. J. Pepler, K. C. Madsen, C. Webster & K. S. Levene (Eds.), *The development and treatment of girlhood aggression* (pp. 105–136). New York: Guilford.

Xue, G., Dong, Q., Jin, Z., Zhang, L., & Wang, Y. (2004). An fMRI study with semantic access in low proficiency second language learners. *Neuroreport, 15,* 791–796.

Yale, M. E., Messinger, D. S., Cobo-Lewis, A. B., & Delgado, C. F. (2003). The temporal coordination of early infant communication. *Developmental Psychology, 39,* 815–824.

Yau, J., & Smetana, J. (2003). Conceptions of moral, social-conventional, and personal events among Chinese preschoolers in Hong Kong. *Child Development, 74,* 647–658.

Yonas, A., Arterberry, M. E., & Granrud, C. E. (1987). Space perception in infancy. *Annals of Child Development* (Vol. 4, pp. 1–34). Greenwich, CT: JAI Press.

Yoshida, H., & Smith, L. B. (2003). Shifting ontological boundaries: How Japanese- and English-speaking children generalize names for animals and artifacts. *Developmental Science, 6,* 1–17.

Young, C., McMahon, J., Bowman, V., & Thompson, D. (1989). Maternal reasons for delayed prenatal care. *Nursing Research, 38* (4).

Young, S. K., Fox, N. A., & Zahn-Waxler, C. (1999). The relations between temperament and empathy in two-year-olds. *Developmental Psychology, 35,* 1189–1197.

Young, W. C., Goy, R. W., & Phoenix, C. H. (1967). Hormones and sexual behavior. *Science, 143,* 212–218.

Youngblade, L. M., & Dunn, J. (1995). Individual differences in young children's pretend play with mother and sibling: Links to relationships and understanding other people's feelings and beliefs. *Child Development, 66,* 1472–1492.

Youniss, J. (1980). *Parents and peers in social development.* Chicago: University of Chicago Press.

Youniss, J., & Yates, M. (1997). *Community service and social responsibility in youth.* Chicago: University of Chicago Press.

Yuill, N., & Pearson, A. (1998). The development of bases for trait attribution: Children's understanding of traits as causal mechanisms. *Developmental Psychology, 34,* 574–586.

Yussen, S. R., & Berman, L. (1981). Memory predictions for recall and recognition in first, third, and fifth grade children. *Developmental Psychology, 17,* 224–229.

Zaff, J. F., Moore, K. A., Papillo, A. R., & Williams, S. (2003). Implications of extracurricular activity participation during adolescence on positive outcomes. *Journal of Adolescent Research, 18,* 599–630.

Zahn-Waxler, C. (2000). The development of empathy, quiet and internalization of distress: Implications for gender differences in internalizing and externalizing problems. In R. Davidson (Ed.), *Anxiety, depression, and emotion: Wisconsin Symposium on Emotion* (Vol. 1, pp. 222–235). New York: Oxford University Press.

Zahn-Waxler, C., Cole, P. M., Welsh, J. D., & Fox N. A. (1995). Psychophysiological correlates of empathy and prosocial behaviors in preschool children with problem behaviors. *Development and Psychopathology, 7,* 27–48.

Zahn-Waxler, C., Radke-Yarrow, M., & King, R. A. (1979). Child rearing and children's prosocial initiations toward victims of distress. *Child Development, 50,* 319–330.

Zahn-Waxler, C., Radke-Yarrow, M., Wagner, E., & Chapman, M. (1992). Development of concern for others. *Developmental Psychology, 28,* 126–136.

Zahn-Waxler, C., Schiro, K., Robinson, J. L., Emde, R. N., & Schmitz, S. (2001). Empathy and prosocial patterns in young MZ and DZ twins: Development and genetic and environmental influences. In R. N. Emde & J. K. Hewitt (Eds.), *Infancy to early childhood* (pp. 141–162). New York: Oxford University Press.

Zajonc, R. B. (2001). The family dynamics of intellectual development. *American Psychologist, 56,* 490-496.

Zajonc, R. B., & Mullally, P. R. (1997). Birth order: Reconciling conflicting effects. *American Psychologist, 52,* 685–699.

Zani, B. (1993). Dating and interpersonal relationships in adolescence. In S. Jackson & H. Rodriguez-Tome (Eds.), *Adolescence and its social worlds* (pp. 95–119). Hillsdale, NJ: Erlbaum.

Zarbatany, L., Hartmann, D. P., & Rankin, D. B. (1990). The psychological functions of preadolescent peer activities. *Child Development, 61,* 1067–1080.*

Zarbatany, L., McDougall, P., & Hymel, S. (2000). Gender-differentiated experience in the peer culture: Links to intimacy in preadolescence. *Social Development, 9,* 62–69.

Zatorre, R. J., & Halpern, A. R. (1993). Effect of unilateral temporal lobe excision on perception and imagery of songs. *Neuropsychologia, 31,* 221–232.*

Zeanah, C. H., Smyke, A. T., & Dumitrescu, A. (2002). Attachment disturbances in young children. II. Indiscriminate behavior and institutional care. *Journal of the American Academy of Child and Adolescent Psychiatry, 41,* 983–989.

Zeifman, D., Delaney, S., & Blass, E. M. (1996). Sweet taste, looking and calm in 2- and 4-week old infants: The eyes have it. *Developmental Psychology, 32,* 1090–1099.

Zelazo, N. A., Zelazo, P. R., Cohen, K. M., & Zelazo, P. D. (1988, April). *Specificity of practice effects on elementary neuromotor patterns.* Paper presented at the International Conference on Infant Studies, Washington, DC.

Zelazo, P. D., & Frye, D. (1998). Cognitive complexity and control: II. The development of executive function in childhood. *Current Directions in Psychological Science, 7,* 121–126.*

Zelazo, P. D., Frye, D., & Rapus, T. (1996). An age-related dissociation between knowing rules and using them. *Cognitive Development, 11,* 37–63.

Zelazo, P. D., Helwig, C. C., & Lau, A. (1996). Intention, act, and outcome in behavioural prediction and moral judgment. *Child Development, 67,* 2478–2492.*

Zelazo, P. D., Müller, U., Frye, D., & Marcovitch, S. (2003). The development of executive function in early childhood. *Monographs of the Society for Research in Child Development, 38,* ii–138.*

Zelazo, P. R. (1983). The development of walking: New findings and old assumptions. *Journal of Motor Behavior, 15,* 99–137.

Zelazo, P. R. (1998). McGraw and the development of unaided walking. *Developmental Review, 18,* 449–471.*

Zelazo, P. R., Zelazo, N. A., & Kolb, S. (1972). "Walking" in the newborn. *Science, 176,* 314–315.

Zemach, I. K., Chang, S., & Teller, D. Y. (2007). Infant color vision: Prediction of infants' spontaneous color preferences. *Vision Research, 47,* 1368–1381.

Zemach, I. K., & Teller, D. Y. (2007). Infant color vision: Infants' spontaneous color preferences are well behaved. *Vision Research, 47,* 1362–1367.

Zerbe, K. J. (1993). *The body betrayed: Women, eating disorders, and treatment.* Washington, D.C.: American Psychiatric Press.

Zhang, W., Ji, L., Gong, X., Zhang, Q., Wang, Y., & Chen, X. (2003). A longitudinal study on the development of 3- to 4-year-old children's aggressive behavior. *Psychological Science (China), 26,* 49–52.

Zigler, E., Abelson, W. D., Trickett, P. K., & Seitz, V. (1982). Is an intervention program necessary in order to improve economically disadvantaged children's IQ scores? *Child Development, 53,* 340–348.

Zill, N. (1986). *Happy, healthy and insecure.* New York: Cambridge University Press.

Zimmer-Gembeck, M. J., Siebenbruner, J., & Collins, W. A. (2001). Diverse aspects of dating: Associations with psychosocial functioning from early to middle adolescence. *Journal of Adolescence, 24,* 313–336.

Zimmerman, F., Christakis, D., & Meltzoff, A. N. (2007). Associations between media viewing and language development in children under age 2 years. *The Journal of Pediatrics, 151,* 364–368.

Zimring, E. (2000). Penal proportionality for the young offender: Notes on immaturity, capacity, and diminished responsibility. In T. Grisso & R. G. Schwartz (Eds.), *Young on trial: A developmental perspective on juvenile justice* (pp. 271–289). Chicago: University of Chicago Press.

Zucker, R. A., Fitzgerald, H. E., & Moses, H. D. (1995). Emergence of alcohol problems and the several alcoholisms: A developmental perspective on etiologic theory and life course trajectory. In D. Cicchetti & D. Cohen (Eds.), *Developmental psychopathology: Vol. 2. Risk, disorder and adaptation* (pp. 677–711). New York: Wiley.

Zukow-Goldring, P. (2002). Sibling caregiving. In M. H. Bornstein (Ed.), *Handbook of parenting* (Vol. 3, pp. 188–208). Mahwah, NJ: Erlbaum.

Credits

Chapter 15

Page 578: © Donald C. Martin/SuperStock; **Page 582:** © David M. Grossman/The Image Works; **Page 598:** © Nancy Acevedo; **Page 603:** © Laura Dwight; **Page 606:** © Paul Conklin/PhotoEdit. **Epilogue: Page 615:** Photo © Michael Escoffery/Art Resource, NY. © Michael Escoffery/Artists Rights Society (ARS), New York.

TEXT AND LINE ART

Statistics Canada information is used with the permission of Statistics Canada. Users are forbidden to copy the data and redisseminate them, in an original or modified form, for commercial purposes, without permission from Statistics Canada. Information on the availability of the wide range of data from Statistics Canada can be obtained from Statistics Canada's Regional Offices, its World Wide Web site at www.statcan.gc.ca, and its toll-free access number 1-800-263-1136.

Figure 1-1 (page 7) from Siegler, *Children's Thinking*, © 1998. Reproduced by permission of Pearson Education Inc.

Figure 1-3 (page 16) from *Child Development in a Social Context* (C. Kopp and J. Krako, eds.). Gararino, J., "Sociocultural risk: Dangers to competence," p. 648. Copyright © 1982 Addison-Wesley Publishing Company, Inc. Reprinted by permission of Pearson Education, Inc., Glenview, IL.

Table 1-6 (page 37) based on American Psychological Association, 1992; Society for Research on Child Development Committee on Ethical Conduct in Child Development Research, 1993.

Figure 2-7 (page 63) from *Handbook of Mental Deficiency: Psychological Theory and Research* (N. Ellis, ed., McGraw-Hill, Inc.) by Gottesman, I. (1963), "Genetic aspects of intelligent behavior." Reprinted by permission of the author.

Figure 2-8 (page 66) from *Individual Development and Evolution: The Genesis of Novel Behavior* by Gottlieb, G. figure 14-3, p. 186. Copyright © 1992 Oxford University Press, Inc. Used by permission of Oxford University Press, Inc.

Figure 2-9 (page 67) from *American Journal of Mental Deficiency*, 71, by Baumeister, A. A. (1967), "The effects of dietary control on intelligence in phenylketonuria," pp. 840–847. Reprinted by permission of the American Association on Mental Retardation.

Table 2-5 (page 72) from *Science*, 212, by Bouchard, T. J. and McGue, M., "Familial Studies of Intelligence: A Review," pp. 1055–1059. Copyright © 1981 American Association for the Advancement of Science. Adapted with permission.

Figure 2-10 (page 72) from *Developmental Psychology*, 7, by Wilson, R. S. and Harpring, E. B., "Mental and motor development in infant twins," pp. 277–287. Copyright © 1972 American Psychological Association. Adapted with permission.

Figure 3-1 (pages 83–84) from *Nature of Life*, 3rd ed., 1995 by Postlethwait, J. and Hopson, J., "Concept Integrator: The Marvel of Human Development," pp. 348–349. Published by The McGraw-Hill Companies. Reprinted by permission of J. Postlethwait and J. Hopson.

Figure 3-3 (page 97) from *Time*, April 15, 2002, p. 53. Copyright © 2002 Time Inc. Reprinted by permission.

Figure 3-5 (page 99) from *Toward a Healthy Future: Second Report on the Health of Canadians,* Health Canada, 1991. © Adapted and reproduced with the permission of the Minister of Public Works and Government Services Canada, 2001.

Figure 3-6 (page 104) from *Human Physiology*, 6th ed., by Vander, A. J., Sherman, J. H., and Luciano, D. S., p. 683. Copyright © 1994 The McGraw-Hill Companies. Adapted by permission.

Table 3-2 (page 108) from *Current Research in Anesthesia and Analgesia*, 32, by Agpar, V. A., "A proposal for a new method of evaluation of the newborn infant," p. 267. Copyright © 1953. Published by John Wiley & Sons, Inc.

Figure 3-7 (page 110) from *Infancy* by Field, T., p. 117. Copyright © 1990 by the President and Fellows of Harvard College. Reprinted by permission of the publisher, Harvard University Press, Cambridge, MA.

Figure 4-1 (page 121) from *Prospective Issues in Infancy Research* (K. Bloom, ed.) by Sostek, A. M. and Anders, T. F., "The biosocial importance and environmental sensitivity of infant sleep-wake behaviors," p. 108. Copyright © 1981 Lawrence Erlbaum Associates, Inc. Reprinted with permission.

Table 4-3 (page 128) adapted from *Handbook of Infant Development*, 2nd ed., (J. Osofsky, ed.). Brazelton, T. B., Nugent, J. K., and Lester, B. M., "Neonatal behavioral assessment scale," pp. 780–817. Copyright © 1987 by John Wiley & Sons, Inc. Reprinted with permission of John Wiley & Sons, Inc.

Figure 4-2 (page 135) from *The World of the Newborn* by Maurer, D. and Maurer, C., "Visual discrimination in infants" (1988). Reprinted with permission.

Figure 4-4 (page 138) from *Journal of Experimental Child Psychology*, 37, by Bertenthal, B. I., Profitt, D. R., and Cutting, J. E., "Infant sensitivity to figural coherence in biochemical motions," pp. 213–230. Copyright © 1984 Academic Press, Inc. Reprinted with permission.

Figure 4-5 (page 138) from *Child Development*, 47 (1976). Maurer, D. and Salapatek, P., "Developmental changes in the scanning of faces by young infants," pp. 523–527. Reprinted with permission of the Society for Research in Child Development.

Figure 4-6 (page 140) from *Child Development*, 59 (1988). Dannemiller, J. L., and Stephens, B. R., "A critical test of infant pattern preference models," pp. 210–216. Reprinted with permission of the Society for Research in Child Development.

Figure 4-9 (page 145) from *Nature*, 181, by Meltzoff, A. N. and Borton, R. W., "Intermodal matching by human neonates," pp. 403–404. Copyright © 1979 Macmillan Magazines Limited. Reprinted with permission.

Figure 4-13 (page 151) from *American Psychologist*, 51 (1996). Bauer, P. J., "What do infants recall of their lives?" pp. 29–41. Copyright © 1996 by the American Psychological Association.

Figure 5-1 (page 157) from *A Child's World*, 4th ed., by Papalia, D. E., and Olds, S. W., p. 172. Copyright © 1996 by The McGraw-Hill Companies, Inc. Reprinted by permission of the publisher.

Figure 5-2 (page 157) from *Biological Psychology* by Rosenzweig, M. R., Leiman, A. L., and Breedlove, S. M., Fig. 4.1, p. 100. Copyright © 1996 by Sinauer Associates, Inc. Reprinted by permission of Sinauer Associates, Inc.

Figure 5-3 (page 158) from *The Nature of Life*, 3rd ed., by Postlethwait, J. H., and Hopson, J. L. New York: McGraw-Hill, 1995, Fig. 32.8A, p. 718. Reprinted by permission of Janet Hopson.

Figure 5-4 (page 158) from *Fundamentals of Anatomy & Physiology*, 3rd ed., by Frederic H. Martini, Fig. 12.7 (b & d), p. 389. Copyright © 1995 by Prentice Hall, Inc. Reprinted by permission of Pearson Education, Inc.

Figure 5-5 (page 159) from *Fundamentals of Anatomy & Physiology*, 3rd ed., by Frederic H. Martini, Fig. 12.7 (b & d), p. 389. Copyright © 1995 by Prentice Hall, Inc. Reprinted by permission of Pearson Education, Inc.

Figure 5-6 (page 162) reprinted by permission of the publisher from *The Postnatal Development of the Human Cerebral Cortex, Vols. I–VIII*, by Jesse LeRoy Conel. Cambridge, Mass.: Harvard University Press. Copyright © 1939, 1975 by the President and Fellows of Harvard College.

Figure 5-7 (page 163) adapted from *American Psychologist*, 46 (1991). Fox, N. A., "If it's not left, it's right: Electroencephalograph asymmetry and the development of emotion," pp. 863–872. Copyright © 1991 by the American Psychological Association.

Table 5-1 (page 167) from Bernstein, Douglas A. and Peggy W. Nash, *Essentials of Psychology*, 3rd ed. Copyright © 2005 by Houghton Mifflin Company. Adapted with the permission of Houghton Mifflin Publishing Company.

Figure 5-9 (page 171) reprinted with permission from *Science*, 176 (1972). Zelazo, P. R., Zelazo, N. A., and Kolb S., "'Walking' in the Newborn," pp. 314–315. Copyright © 1972 AAAS.

Figure 5-10 (page 173) from *Child Development*, 45 (1974). Adelson, E. and Fraiberg, S., "Gross motor development in infants blind from birth," pp. 114–126. Reprinted with permission of the Society for Research in Child Development.

Figure 5-12 (page 178) from "2CCC: The Millennium Notebook." From *Newsweek*, June 2, 1997, p. 10. Copyright © Newsweek, Inc. All rights reserved. Reprinted by permission.

Figure 5-14 (page 183) reprinted from *Journal of the American Dietetic Association*, 100, Rolls, B. J., Engell, D., and Birch, L. L., "Serving portion size influences 5-year-old but not 3-year-old children's food intake," pp. 232–234. Copyright © 2000 with permission from American Dietetic Association.

Figure 5-15 (page 184) from *Health Psychology*, 14 (1995). Epstein, L. H., Valoski, A. M., Vara, L. S., McCurley, J., Wisniewski, L., Kalarchin, M. A., Klein, K. R., and Shrager, L. R., "Effects of decreasing sedentary behavior and increasing activity on weight change in obese children," pp. 109–115. Copyright © 1995 by the American Psychological Association.

Figure 5-16 (page 187) adapted from *The Nature of Life*, 3rd ed., by Postlethwait, J. H. and Hopson, J. L. New York: McGraw-Hill, 1995, Fig. 32.8A, p. 718. Reprinted by permission of Janet Hopson.

Figure 5-17 (page 188) from *Monographs of the Society for Research in Child Development*, 44 (Serial No. 179, 1979). Roche, A. F., "Secular trends in human growth, maturation, and development." Reprinted with permission of the Society for Research in Child Development.

Figure 5-18 (page 190) from *Girls at Puberty: Biological, Psychological, and Social Perspectives* (J. Brooks-Gunn and A. C. Petersen, eds.). Tobin-Richards, M., Boxer, A. O., and Petersen, A. C.,

"The psychological impact of pubertal change: Sex differences in perceptions of self during early adolescence," pp. 127–154. Copyright © 1983 by Plenum Press. With kind permission of Springer Science and Business Media.

Figure 6-1 (page 203) from *Child Development*, 43 (1972). Sroufe, L. A. and Wunsch, J. P., "The development of laughter in the first year of life," pp. 1326–1344. Reprinted with permission of the Society for Research in Child Development.

Figure 6-2 (page 204) reprinted from *Psychological Issues*, Vol. 10. Emde, R. N., Gaensbauer, T. J., and Harmon, R. J., "Emotional expression in infancy: A biobehavioral study." By permission of International Universities Press, Inc. Copyright © 1976 by IUP.

Figure 6-3 (page 206) from *The Origins of Fear* (M. Lewis and L. Rosenblum, eds.). Lewis, M. and Brooks, J., "Self, other, and fear: Infants' reactions to people," pp. 195–227. New York: Wiley, 1974. Reprinted by permission of Michael Lewis.

Figure 6-4 (page 207) reprinted by permission of the publisher from *Infancy: Its Place in Human Development*, by Jerome Kagan, Richard B. Kearsley, and Philip R. Zelazo, p. 107. Cambridge, Mass.: Harvard University Press. Copyright © 1978 by the President and Fellows of Harvard College.

Figure 6-5 (page 209) from *Developmental Psychology*, 33 (1997). Thuber, C. A. and Weisz, J. R., "You can try or you can just give up: The impact of perceived control and coping style on childhood homesickness," pp. 508–517. Copyright © 1997 by the American Psychological Association.

Figure 6-6 (page 210) from *Child Development*, 63 (1992). Lewis, M., Alessandri, S., and Sullivan M. W., "Differences in shame and pride as a function of children's gender and task difficulty," pp. 630–638. Reprinted with permission of the Society for Research in Child Development.

Figure 6-7 (page 217) from *Emotional Development in Young Children*, by Denham, S. A. New York: Guilford, 1998, Fig. 1.2, p. 15. Reprinted by permission of the publisher, via The Copyright Clearance Center.

Table 6-3 (page 222) from *Social Development*, by Schaffer, H. R., Table 15, p. 129 and Table 16, p. 136. Copyright © 1996 by H. Rudolph Schaffer. Reprinted by permission of Blackwell Publishing Ltd.

Table 6-4 (page 224) from *Social Development*, by Schaffer, H. R., Table 15, p. 129 and Table 16, p. 136. Copyright © 1996 by H. Rudolph Schaffer. Reprinted by permission of Blackwell Publishing Ltd.

Table 6-5 (page 226) from *Review of Child Development Research*, Vol. 3, 1973 (B. Caldwell and H. Ricciuti, eds.). Table 1 from Ainsworth, M. D., "The development of infant-mother attachment." Reprinted with permission of the Society for Research in Child Development.

Figure 6-8 (page 240) from *Child Development*, 75 (2004). Carlson, E. A., Sroufe, L. A., and Egeland, B., "The construction of experience: A longitudinal study of representation and behavior," pp. 66–83. Reprinted with permission of the Society of Research in Child Development.

Figure 6-9 (page 241) from *Social Cognition and the Acquisition of Self*, by Lewis M. and Brooks-Gunn, J. New York: Plenum Press. Copyright © 1979 by Michael Lewis and Jeanne Brooks-Gunn. With kind permission of Springer Science and Business Media.

Table 6-9 (page 241) from *Social Development*, by Schaffer, H. R., Table 22, p. 158. Copyright © 1996 by H. Rudolph Schaffer. Reprinted by permission of Blackwell Publishing Ltd.

Figure 7-1 (page 257) reprinted from *Cognitive Psychology*, 21, Johnson, J. S. and Newport, E. L., "Critical period effects in second language learning: The influence of maturational state on the acquisition of English as a second language," pp. 60–99. Copyright © 1989, with permission from Elsevier.

Figure 7-2 (page 269) from *Theories in Cognitive Psychology* (R. L. Solso, ed.). Huttenlocher, J., "The origins of language comprehension." Copyright © 1974 Lawrence Erlbaum Associates, Inc. Reprinted by permission of the publisher.

Figure 7-3 (page 271) from *Breaking the Speech Barrier: Language Development through Augmented Means* by Romski, M. and Sevcik, R. A. Baltimore, MD: Paul H. Brookes Publishing Co., 1996, pp. 28, 56. Reprinted by permission.

Figure 7-4 (page 273) from *Meaningful Differences in the Everyday Experience of Young American Children* by Hart, B. and Risley, T. R. Baltimore, MD: Paul H. Brookes Publishing Co., 1995, pp. 234, 235. Reprinted by permission.

Table 7-3 (page 275) from *Language Development* by Hoff-Ginsberg, E., "Examples of children's overextended word uses," p. 101, Table 3.2. Copyright © 1997 Brooks/Cole Publishing Company, Pacific Grove, CA 93950, a division of International Thomson Publishing Inc. By permission of the publisher. Based on Rescorla, L. A., *Journal of Child Language*, 7, pp. 321–335, and Bowerman, M., *The Development of Communication*, pp. 263–287, Waterson & Show (eds.). Chichester: Wiley.

Table 7-4 (page 276) from *The Acquisition of Language: The Study of Developmental Psycholinguistics* by McNeill, D. Copyright © 1970 Scott Foresman-Addison Wesley. Reprinted with permission.

Table 7-5 (page 277) from *Psycholinguistics*, by Slobin, D. I. Copyright © 1979 Scott Foresman-Addison Wesley. Adapted with permission.

Figure 7-7 (page 285) from *Development Psychology*, 10, by Entwisle, D. R. and Frasure, N. E., "A contradiction resolved: Children's processing of syntactic cues," pp. 852–857. Copyright © 1974 American Psychological Association. Adapted with permission.

Figure 8-1 (page 307) from *Cognition*, 23, by Baillargeon, R., "Representing the existence and the location of hidden objects: Object permanence in 6- and 8-month-old infants," pp. 21–41 (1986). Reprinted with kind permission from Elsevier Science–NL, Sara Burgerhartstraat 25, 1055 KV Amsterdam, The Netherlands.

Figure 8-2 (page 308) from *Psychological Science*, 12 (2001). Hespos, S. J. and Baillargeon, R., "Infants' knowledge about occlusion and containment events: A surprising discrepancy," pp. 140–147. Reprinted by permission of Blackwell Publishing Ltd.

Figure 8-5 (page 311) from *Children's Minds* by Margaret Donaldson. Copyright © 1978 by Margaret Donaldson. Used by permission of W. W. Norton & Company, Inc., and A. P. Watt Ltd.

Figure 8-6 (page 313) from *Of Children* by LeFrancois, G. R., p. 305. Copyright © 1973 Wadsworth Publishing Company. Reprinted with permission.

Figure 8-7 (page 316) from *International Journal of Psychology*, 19, by Dasen (1984), p. 410. Reprinted by permission of International Union of Psychological Science.

Figure 8-8 (page 318) courtesy of Mark Schmuckler.

Table 8-3 (page 319) from *1977 Nebraska Symposium on Motivation in Child Psychology*, 5th ed. (Keasy, C. B., ed.), by Selman, R. and Jaquette, D., "Stability and oscillation in interpersonal awareness: A clinical-developmental analysis," Table 1, p. 266. Adapted by permission of The University of Nebraska Press, Lincoln, NE.

Figure 8-9 (page 320) from *Child Development*, by Selman, R. L. and Byrne, D. L., "A structural developmental analysis of levels of role-taking in middle childhood." Copyright © 1972 Society for Research in Child Development, Inc. Adapted with permission.

Figure 8-10 (page 331) from *Developmental Psychology*, 24, by Radziszewska and Rogoff, "Influence of adult and peer collaborators on the development of children's planning skills," pp. 840–848. Copyright © 1988 American Psychological Association. Adapted with permission.

Figure 9-1 (page 342) from *Advances in the Psychology of Learning and Motivation Research and Theory*, 2, by Atkinson, R. C. and Shiffrin, R. M., "Human memory: A proposed system and its control processes." Reprinted by permission of Academic Press.

Figure 9-2 (page 343) from *Children's Thinking*, 3rd ed., by Siegler, R. Copyright © 1998 Prentice-Hall, Inc., Upper Saddle River, NJ. Reprinted with permission.

Figure 9-3 (page 346) from *Children's Thinking: What Develops?* (Siegler, R. S., ed.), "Knowledge structures and memory development," by Chi, M. T. H. Copyright © 1978 Lawrence Erlbaum Associates, Inc. Reprinted with permission.

Figure 9-4 (page 348) from *Attention in Early Development: Themes and Variations* by Holly Alliger Ruff and Mary Klevjord Rothbart, Figure 7.6, p. 130. Copyright © 1996 by Oxford University Press, Inc. Used by permission of Oxford University Press, Inc.

Figure 9-7 (page 351) reprinted from *Journal of Experimental Child Psychology*, 6, Vurpillot, E., "The development of scanning strategies and their relation to visual differentiation," pp. 632–650. Copyright © 1968, with permission of Elsevier.

Figure 9-8 (page 354) from *Developmental Psychology*, 33 (1997). Coyle, T. R. and Bjorklund, D. F., "Age differences in, and consequences of, multiple- and variable-strategy use on a multitrial sort-recall task," pp. 372–380. Copyright © 1997 by the American Psychological Association.

Figure 9-10 (page 361) from *Psychonomic Bulletin and Review*, 2, Howe, M. L., Courage, M. L., and Peterson, C. (1995), "Intrusions in preschoolers' recall of traumatic childhood events," pp. 130–134. Reprinted with permission.

Figure 9-11 (page 365) from Siegler, Robert S., Alibali, Martha W., *Children's Thinking*, 4th ed., © 2005. Adapted and reprinted by permission of Pearson Education, Inc., Upper Saddle River, NJ.

Figure 9-12 (page 369) reprinted from *Journal of Environmental Psychology*, 21, Cornell, E. H., Hadley, D. C., Sterling, T. M., Chan, M. A., and Boechler, P., "Adventures as a stimulus for cognitive development," pp. 219–231. Copyright © 2001 with permission from Elsevier.

Figure 9-14 (page 375) from *Psychological Science*, 6 (1995). Miller, K. F., Smith, C. M., Zhu, J., and Zhang, H., "Preschool origins of cross-national differences in mathematical competence: The role of number-naming systems," pp. 56–60. Reprinted by permission of Blackwell Publishing Ltd.

Figure 9-15 (page 376) from *Current Direction in Psychological Science*, 7, Zelazo, P. D., and Frye, D., (1998), "Cognitive complexity and control: II. The development of executive function in childhood," pp. 121–126. Reprinted with permission from Blackwell Publishers.

Table 10-1 (page 386) from *Current Directions in Psychological Science*, 2 (1993). Sternberg, R. J. and Wagner, R. K., "The geocentric view of intelligence and job performance is wrong," pp. 1–6. Reprinted by permission of Blackwell Publishing Ltd.

Table 10-2 (page 387) from *Frames of Mind: Theory of Multiple Intelligences* by Howard Gardner. Copyright © 1983 by Howard Gardner. Published by Basic Books and William Heinemann. Reprinted by permission of Basic Books, L. L. C., and the Random House Group Ltd.

Table 10-3 (page 391) items similar to those in *Weschler Intelligence Scale for Children—Fourth Edition* (WISC-IV). Copyright © NCS Pearson, Inc. Reproduced with permission. All rights reserved.

Figure 10-1 (page 394) from *Origins of Intelligence* (M. Lewis, ed.). Honzik, M. P., "Value and limitations of infant tests: An overview," p. 67. Copyright © 1976 Plenum Press. With kind permission of Springer Science and Business Media.

Figure 10-2 (page 404) reprinted from *Advances in Motivation and Achievement: Vol. 9. Culture, Race, Ethnicity, and Motivation* (P. Pintrich and M. Maehr, eds.). Chen, C., Stevenson, H. W., Hayward, C., and Burgess, S., "Culture and academic achievement: Ethnic and cross-national differences," pp. 119–151. Copyright © 1995 with permission of Elsevier.

Figure 10-3 (page 405) from *Advances in Motivation and Achievement*, 9 (Pintrich, P., Maehr, M., eds.). by Chen, C., Stevenson, H. W., Hayward, C., and Burgess, S. (1995) "Culture and academic achievement: Ethnic and cross-national differences," pp. 119–151. Reprinted by permission of JAI Press Inc.

Figure 10-4 (page 406) reprinted with permission from *Science*, 259 (1993). Stevenson, H. W., Chen, C., and Lee, S. Y., "Mathematics Achievement of Chinese, Japanese, and American Children: Ten Years Later," pp. 53–58. Copyright © 1993 AAAS.

Figure 10-6 (page 408) adapted from *American Psychologist* 31 (1976). Scarr, S. and Weinberg, R. A., "IQ test performance of black children adopted by white families," pp. 726–739. Copyright © 1976 by the American Psychological Association.

Figure 10-7 (page 410) from *Child Development* 66 (1995). Chen, C. and Stevenson, H. W., "Motivation and mathematics achievement: A comparative study of Asian-American, Caucasian-American, and east Asian high school students," pp. 1215–1234. Reprinted with permission of the Society for Research in Child Development.

Figure 11-2 (page 433) from *Child Abuse & Neglect*, 23 by J. E. Durrant (1999), "Evaluating the success of Sweden's corporal punishment

ban," p. 438. Reprinted with kind permission from Elsevier Science–NL, Sara Burgerhartstraat 25, 1055 KV Amsterdam, The Netherlands.

Figure 11-3 (page 434) from *Handbook of Child Psychology*, 4 (E. M. Hetherington, ed.), by Maccoby, E. E., and Martin, J. A., "Socialization in the context of family: Parent-child interaction." Copyright © 1983 by John Wiley & Sons, Inc.

Figure 11-4 (page 434) from *Genetic Psychology Monographs*, 75 (1967), pp. 43–88. Baumrind, Diana, "Child care practices anteceding three patterns of preschool behavior." Copyright © 1967, Published by Heldref Publications. Reprinted by permission of the author, Dr. Diana Baumrind, Institute of Human Development.

Table 11-1 (page 435) from *Genetic Psychology Monographs*, 75 (1967), pp. 43–88. Baumrind, Diana, "Child care practices anteceding three patterns of preschool behavior." Copyright © 1967, Published by Heldref Publications. Reprinted by permission of the author, Dr. Diana Baumrind, Institute of Human Development.

Figure 11-5 (page 438) from *Handbook of Personal Relationships*, 2nd ed. (S. Duck, ed.) by Parke, R. D. and O'Neil, R., p. 56. Copyright © 2000 by John Wiley & Sons, Inc. Reprinted with permission of John Wiley & Sons, Inc.

Figure 11-6 (page 439) from *Journal of Personality and Social Psychology*, 85 (2003). Herrera, N. C., Zajonc, R. B., Wieczorkowska, G., and Cichomski, B., "Beliefs about birth rank and their reflection on reality," pp. 142–150. Copyright © 2003 by the American Psychological Association.

Figure 11-7 (page 444) from *Child Development*, 63 (1992). Conger, R. D., Conger, K. J., Elder, G. J., Jr., Lorenz, F. O., Simons, R. L., and Witbeck, L. B., "A family process model of economic hardship and adjustment of early adolescent boys," pp. 526–541. Reprinted with permission of the Society for Research in Child Development.

Figure 11-8 (page 447) adapted from Statistics Canada, *Canadian Social Trends*, catalogue number 11-008, No. 56, Spring 2000, p. 4.

Figure 11-9 (page 447) from *Life-Span Development*, 8th ed., by Santrock, J. W. Copyright © 2002 by The McGraw-Hill Companies, Inc. Reprinted with permission of the publisher.

Figure 11-10 (page 453) from *Growing Up with a Single Parent*, by Sara McLanahan and Gary Sandefur. Cambridge, MA: Harvard University Press, 1994, p. 41.

Figure 11-11 (page 456) adapted from *Developmental Psychology*, 31 (1995). Patterson, C. J., "Families of the lesbian baby boom: Parents' division of labor and children's adjustment," pp. 115–123. Copyright © 1995 by the American Psychological Association.

Figure 11-12 (page 457) adapted from *Facts at a Glance: A fact sheet reporting national, state-level, and city-level trends in teen childbearing*. June 2007, Publications #2007-12. Copyright © 2007 Child Trends.

Figure 12-1 (page 471) from *Developmental Psychology*, 17 (1981). Ellis, S., Rogoff, B., and Cromer, C., "Age segregation in children's social interactions," pp. 399–407. Copyright © 1981 by the American Psychological Association.

Figure 12-2 (page 472) from *Child Development*, 69 (1998). Richards, M. H., Crowe, P. A., Larson, R., and Swarr, A., "Developmental patterns and gender differences in the experience of peer companionship during adolescence," pp. 154–163. Reprinted with permission of the Society for

Research in Child Development.

Figure 12-3 (page 477) adapted from *Psychological Bulletin*, 115 (1994). Crick, N. R., and Dodge, K. A., "A review and reformulation of social information processing mechanisms in children's social adjustment," pp. 74–101. Copyright © 1994 by the American Psychological Association.

Figure 12-4 (page 478) from *Monographs of the Society for Research in Child Development*, 51 (2, Serial No. 213, 1986). Dodge, K. A., Pettit, G. S., McLaskey, C. L., and Brown, M. M., "Social competence in children," p. 40. Reprinted with permission of the Society for Research in Child Development.

Figure 12-6 (page 484) from *Child Development*, 55 (1984). Asher, S. R., Hymel S., and Renshaw, P. D., "Loneliness in children," pp. 1456–1464. Reprinted with permission of the Society for Research in Child Development.

Figure 12-7 (page 485) from *Developmental Psychology*, 24, by Caspi, A., Elder, G., and Bem, D., "Moving against the world: Life course patterns of shy children," pp. 824–831. Copyright © 1988 American Psychological Association. Reprinted with permission.

Figure 12-8 (page 486) from *Child Development*, 72 (2001). Bolger, K. E. and Patterson, C. J., "Developmental pathways from child maltreatment to peer rejection," pp. 549–568. Reprinted with permission of the Society for Research in Child Development.

Table 12-3 (page 491) from *Conversations of Friends: Speculations on Affective Development* (J. M. Gottman and J. G. Parker, eds.). Gottman, J. M. and Mettetal, G., "Speculations on social and affective development: Friendship and acquaintanceship through adolescence." New York: Cambridge University Press, 1986, p. 237. Reprinted with permission of Cambridge University Press.

Figure 13-1 (page 509) reproduced by permission of Sage Publications Ltd. from *International Journal of Behavioral Development*, 25 (2001). Serbin, L. A., Poulin-Dubois, K. A., Colburne, K. A., Sen, M. G., and Eichstedt, J. A., "Gender stereotyping in infancy: Visual preferences for and knowledge of gender-stereotyped toys in the second year," pp. 7–15.

Figure 13-2 (page 512) from *Child Development*, 51 (1980). Liben, L. S. and Golbeck, S. L., "Sex differences in performance on Piagetian spatial tasks: Differences in competence or performance," pp. 594–597. Reprinted with permission of the Society for Research in Child Development.

Figure 13-3 (page 519) adapted from *Developmental Psychology*, 31 (1995). Luecke-Aleksa, D., Anderson, D. R., Collins, P. A., and Schmitt, K. L., "Gender constancy and television viewing," pp. 773–780. Copyright © 1995 by the American Psychological Association.

Figure 13-4 (page 524) from *Child Development*, 74 (2003). Ellis, B. J., Bates, J. E., Dodge, K. A., Fergusson, D. M., Horwood, L. J., Pettit, G. S., and Woodward, L., "Does father absence place daughters at a special risk for early sexual activity and teenage pregnancy?" pp. 801–821. Reprinted with permission of the Society for Research in Child Development.

Figure 14-1 (page 543) adapted from *Vita Humana*, 6 by Kohlberg, L. (1963), "The development of children's orientations towards a moral order. 1. Sequence in the development of moral thought," pp. 11–23. Reprinted by permission of S. Karger AG, Basel, Switzerland.

Table 14-2 (page 559) adapted from *Developmental Psychology*, 19 (1983). Eisenberg, N., Lennon, R., and Roth, K., "Prosocial development: A longitudinal study," pp. 846–855. Copyright © 1983 by the American Psychological Association.

Figure 14-4 (page 562) adapted from *Developmental Psychology*, 20 (1984). Huesmann, L. R., Eron, L. D., Lefkowitz, M. N., and Walder, L. O., "The stability of aggression over time and generations," pp. 1120–1134. Copyright © 1984 by the American Psychological Association.

Figure 14-6 (page 565) from *Handbook of Child Psychology: Vol. 3: Social, Emotional, and Personality Development* (W. Damon and N. Eisenberg, eds.). Coie, J. D. and Dodge, K. A., "Aggression and antisocial behavior," pp. 779–862. Copyright © 1998 by John Wiley & Sons, Inc. Reprinted with permission of John Wiley & Sons, Inc.

Figure 14-8 (page 569) adapted from *American Psychologist*, 44 (1989). Patterson, G. R., DeBaryshe, B. D., and Ramsey, E., "A developmental perspective on antisocial behavior," pp. 329–335. Copyright © 1989 by the American Psychological Association.

Figure 15-1 (page 585) from *Journal of Consulting and Clinical Psychology*, 56 (1988). Weisz, J. R., Suwanlert, S., Chaiyasit, W., Weiss, B., Walter, B. R., and Anderson, W. W., "Thai and American perspectives on over- and under-controlled child behavior problems: Exploring the threshold model among parents, teachers, and psychologists," pp. 601–609. Copyright © 1988 by the American Psychological Association.

Table 15-3 (page 591) from Gelfand and Drew, *Understanding Child Behavior Disorders*, 4th ed. Copyright © 2003 Wadsworth, a part of Cengage Learning, Inc. Reproduced by permission. www. cengage.com/permissions.

Table 15-4 (page 592) from *Diagnostic and Statistical Manual of Mental Disorders*, 4th ed., text revision. Copyright © 2000 by the American Psychological Association.

Table 15-5 (page 594) from *Diagnostic and Statistical Manual of Mental Disorders*, 4th ed., text revision. Copyright © 2000 by the American Psychological Association.

Table 15-8 (page 597) from *Diagnostic and Statistical Manual of Mental Disorders*, 4th ed., text revision. Copyright © 2000 by the American Psychological Association.

Table 15-9 (page 601) from Gelfand and Drew, *Understanding Child Behavior Disorders*, 4th ed. Copyright © 2003 Wadsworth, a part of Cengage Learning, Inc. Reproduced by permission. www. cengage.com/permissions.

Figure 15-4 (page 602) from *Journal of Abnormal Psychology*, 107 (1998). Hankin, B. L., Abramson, L. Y., Moffitt, T. E., Silva, P. A., McGee, R., and Angell, K. E., "Development of depression from pre-adolescence to young adulthood: Emerging gender differences in a 10 year longitudinal study," pp. 128–140. Copyright © 1998 by the American Psychological Association.

Name Index

Subject Index

abnormality, 582–584
  average (deviation from), 583
  ideal (deviation from), 583–584
  medical model, 583
  social judgment, 584–587
Aboriginal Head Start (AHS) program, 412–413
abortion (spontaneous), 85
absolutism, 548
academic achievement. *See* intellectual performance
accommodation, 302
achievement motivation
  cultural context, 409
  defined, 408
  entity theory, 409
  family, 409
  gender differences, 508, 528
  helpless children, 482
  incremental theory, 409
  intellectual performance, 408–411
  learning goals, 409
  mastery-oriented children, 409
  observational learning model, 13
  performance goals, 409
  See also intellectual performance
acquired immune deficiency syndrome (AIDS), 102
acrophobia, 591
active genetic–environmental interaction, 67
activity level (gender differences), 507
adaptation, 12, 302
adolescence and adolescents
  aggression, 563–565
  depressive behaviours, 601
  eating disorders, 184–186
  as Eriksonian stage, 11
  See also delinquency; teenage pregnancy
adoption
  intelligence, 408
  international adoption, 228–229
  parenthood, 444–445
  studies, 69–70, 73
adult partnering (problem-solving), 330, 331
adulthood (as stage), 11
age
  age cohort, 17
  conceptual age, 197–198
  peer acceptance, 480
  of viability, 86
aggression, 560–574
  adolescence, 563, 565
  aggressive rejected children, 475, 477
  biology, 565–567
  bullying, 482–483, 561
  catharsis myth, 570–571
  child care, 245
  cognitive modification strategies, 571–572
  control of, 570–574
  criminal behaviour (adult), 562
  delinquent behaviour, 572–573
  development of, 560–564
  environmental influences, 567
  family, 567–569
  gangs, 570
  gender differences, 562–565
  hormones, 566
  hostile aggression, 561

infancy, 563
instrumental aggression, 561
intervention programs, 571, 572–573
neighbourhoods, 570
neurotransmitters, 566
origins of, 564–570
overt aggression, 564
parenting styles, 568
peers, 570
physical discipline, 567–568
preschool children, 561, 563
proactive aggression, 561
reactive aggression, 561
relational aggression, 564
serious violent crimes, 565
serotonin, 566
siblings, 568
social skills, 571
television, 28–30, 569–570
temperament, 567
testosterone, 566
turning points, 563
verbal aggression, 508, 561
video games, 569–570
young offenders, 567
AIDS (acquired immune deficiency syndrome), 102
alcohol (prenatal development), 90–92
alleles, 48
alphafetoprotein assay (AFP), 51, 61
altruistic behaviour, 552, 554. *See also* prosocial
  behaviour
American Psychological Association (formation of),
  4
American Sign Language (ASL), 283
amniocentesis, 51, 60
amniotic sac, 85
anal stage, 10–11
analogy, 364–366
androgyny, 531–532
anemia, 54
anger, 206–207
animistic thinking, 309
anorexia nervosa, 184–186
anxiety disorders, 507, 591
Apgar scoring system, 108
appearance, 479
approach–avoidance behaviour, 232
assimilation, 302
assisted reproductive techniques, 58
associative learning, 396
associative play, 469
at-risk children
  Aboriginal Head Start (AHS) program, 412–413
  attachment, 228–229
  bullying, 482–483
  Concordia Longitudinal Risk Project, 34
  cumulative risk, 403–408
  delinquency, 572–573
  depression, 604–605
  early deprivation, 167
  infant temperament, 75
  intelligence, 403–408
  language development, 270–271
  longitudinal studies, 34
  poverty, 444–445

resilience of, 111–113
resilience research, 8
street math *vs.* academic math, 332
success factors, 112–113
vulnerability, 111–113
attachment, 219–246
  approach–avoidance behaviour, 232
  assessment methods, 225–229
  Attachment Q-Sort (AQS), 227
  avoidant, 231
  breadth of, 224
  caregiving styles, 232–234
  child care, 242–246
  cognitive development, 237
  consequences of quality of, 237–242
  cultural context, 223, 230–231, 233–234, 235
  defined, 219
  development of, 219–224
  evolution of, 222
  fathers, 222–224
  infant temperament, 235–236
  insecure-avoidant, 225, 235
  insecure-disorganized, 226
  insecure-resistant, 226, 235
  interactive synchrony, 232
  intergenerational continuity, 234–235
  internal working models, 234
  international adoption and, 218–219
  multiple caregivers, 242–246
  nature of, 225–229
  outside of family, 224
  parents (role of), 232–236
  phases in, 222
  primary reinforcer, 220
  quality of, 225–229, 232–236, 236–242
  resistant, 231
  secondary reinforcer, 220
  secure attachment, 225, 230–231, 235
  secure base, 225
  self-awareness, 240–242
  sensitive care, 232
  social development, 238–240
  stability in quality of, 236–242
  Strange Situation, 225–227, 231
  See also attachment theories
attachment theories, 219–221
  cognitive developmental view, 220–221
  ethological theory, 221
  imprinting, 221
  learning theory, 220
  primary reinforcer, 220
  psychoanalytic theory, 220
  secondary reinforcer, 220
attention
  control of, 347–348
  defined, 347
  developmental changes, 347–352
  distractions, 348
  memory, 352–363
  planning, 350–352
  relevance, 348, 350, 351
  selective, 348
attention deficit/hyperactivity disorder (ADHD),
  596–600
  behaviour therapy, 600